CONTEMPORARY AUSTRALIAN CORPORATE LAW

THIRD EDITION

The rules, doctrines and policies governing corporations and financial markets are complex and ever-changing in response to global, social and commercial needs. *Contemporary Australian Corporate Law* is a well-established foundational text that explores these rules and laws in detail, including the history and context in which they are established, how they are developed and how they will continue to evolve in the future.

The third edition has been updated to include recent developments in legislation, case law and corporate governance. Discussion of financial markets and financial services has been modified in response to changes to the *Corporations Act 2001* (Cth), including amendments to the continuous disclosure requirements in ch 6CA. It considers the recently passed *Treasury Laws Amendment (Financial Market Infrastructure and Other Measures) Act 2024* (Cth) which covers climate disclosure obligations. The clear structure and detailed exploration of key concepts encourages students to develop a contextual understanding of corporate law.

Written by a team of experienced corporate law academics, *Contemporary Australian Corporate Law* helps students develop a critically informed understanding of corporate law and the role of corporations in contemporary Australia.

Stephen Bottomley is an Emeritus Professor in the ANU Law School at the Australian National University.

Kath Hall is a governance educator with Women on Boards and an experienced non-executive director.

Peta Spender is an Emeritus Professor in the ANU Law School at the Australian National University and a Senior Member in the Regulatory List at the Administrative Review Tribunal.

Beth Nosworthy is an Associate Professor in the Adelaide Law School at the University of Adelaide.

CONTEMPORARY AUSTRALIAN CORPORATE LAW

THIRD EDITION

Stephen Bottomley
Kath Hall
Peta Spender
Beth Nosworthy

CAMBRIDGE
UNIVERSITY PRESS

CAMBRIDGE
UNIVERSITY PRESS

Shaftesbury Road, Cambridge CB2 8EA, United Kingdom

One Liberty Plaza, 20th Floor, New York, NY 10006, USA

477 Williamstown Road, Port Melbourne, VIC 3207, Australia

314–321, 3rd Floor, Plot 3, Splendor Forum, Jasola District Centre,
New Delhi – 110025, India

103 Penang Road, #05–06/07, Visioncrest Commercial, Singapore 238467

Cambridge University Press is part of Cambridge University Press & Assessment,
a department of the University of Cambridge.

We share the University's mission to contribute to society through the pursuit of education, learning and research at the highest international levels of excellence.

www.cambridge.org
Information on this title: www.cambridge.org/highereducation/isbn/9781009448215

First published 2018
Second edition 2021
Third edition 2026

Cover designed by Shaun Jury
Typeset by Lumina Datamatics Ltd

A catalogue record for this publication is available from the British Library

A catalogue record for this book is available from the National Library of Australia

ISBN 978-1-009-44821-5 Paperback

Additional resources for this publication at www.cambridge.org/highereducation/isbn/9781009448215/resources.

Please be aware that this publication may contain several variations of Aboriginal and Torres Strait Islander terms and spellings; no disrespect is intended. Please note that the terms 'Indigenous Australians', 'Aboriginal and Torres Strait Islander peoples' and 'First Nations peoples' may be used interchangeably in this publication.

CONTENTS

ABOUT THE AUTHORS

Stephen Bottomley has been researching and teaching corporate law for over 35 years. He has taught undergraduate courses in corporate law, takeovers and securities markets law, and postgraduate courses in corporate governance and government corporations. He is a distinguished scholar with the following affiliations: Life Member of the Society of Corporate Law Academics (formerly the Corporate Law Teachers Association of Australia and New Zealand); Life Member of the Australasian Law Academics Association; and Fellow of the Australian Academy of Law. From 2013–17 he was Dean of the Australian National University College of Law. In 2020, he received the Lifetime Achievement Legal Research Medal in the Australian Legal Research Awards.

Kath Hall has been researching and teaching corporate law for nearly 20 years. She has taught undergraduate courses on corporate law, and postgraduate courses on corporate governance, and transnational anti-corruption law. Her research reflects a strong theoretical and practical understanding of the complexities involved in regulating global corporations and transnational corruption. In 2013, she was awarded an Australian National University College of Law Award for Excellence in Teaching and in 2014 a Vice-Chancellors Commendation for Teaching Excellence. In 2012–14 she was a non-residential Fellow at Harvard University's Edmond J Safra Center for Ethics, and between 2016–19 she was a lead researcher on a large empirical project investigating positive organisational responses to whistleblowing. Kath was also the Deputy Director, ANU Transnational Research Institute on Corruption (2016–19) and member, International Bar Association Anti-Corruption Committee (2012–16).

Peta Spender has been researching and teaching corporate law for many decades and has taught courses in corporate law, financial markets law, takeovers, corporate governance and litigation. She is the co-author of a leading Australian casebook on litigation. Peta was a founding Presidential Member of the ACT Civil and Administrative Tribunal and is currently a Senior Member in the Regulatory List of the Administrative Review Tribunal. She is a Life Member of the Society of Corporate Law Academics and a Fellow of the Australian Academy of Law. Over the years, Peta has served as Acting Dean, Deputy Dean and Head of School at the Law School in the ANU College of Law, Governance and Policy at the Australian National University.

Beth Nosworthy has been researching and teaching corporate law for nearly two decades. She worked as an Associate in the Supreme Court of South Australia and as a commercial lawyer with an Adelaide firm before returning to study–first, at the University of Oxford and then the University of Adelaide. She commenced her academic career at the University of Adelaide, and has taught corporate law and equity at the undergraduate and postgraduate level, winning the Executive Dean's Award for Excellence in Teaching in 2017. She established the Entrepreneur and Venture Advice Clinic within the Clinical Legal Education program, and was clinical director from 2018–23. From 2022–5 she was the Deputy Dean at the University of Adelaide Law School. Beth was a major contributor to the program design and curriculum development for the Adelaide University Law degree, including responsibility for the subject Ethics and the Future of Law. She is a member of the Executive Committee of the Society of Corporate Law Academics.

PREFACE

Welcome to the third edition of *Contemporary Australian Corporate Law*. As with the first and second editions, our primary purpose in writing this book is to explain the rules, principles, doctrines and policies that constitute corporate law in Australia. We do this by locating those rules in their legal, social, economic and political context: our purpose is to provide students of corporate law with the capacity to develop a contextual understanding of this important area of law.

This book is written for undergraduate and postgraduate law students who are studying corporate law for the first time, and for those returning to investigate specific aspects of the law. We have made no assumptions about the background that individual students may bring to the reading of this book. We know that corporate law is studied by students with a range of disciplinary interests—from economics and commerce to political science and international relations, and more.

We take the view that corporate law is not just a branch of business or commercial law. It is the law that governs and facilitates one of the most significant legal, social and economic structures in contemporary society: the corporation. In its many different forms and settings, the corporation is integral to the contemporary social fabric—be it business, government, community or personal. This book is published by a corporation; it has been written using technology that is developed, built and supplied by multinational chains of corporations.

It is easy to be critical of corporations and their activities. There are many—too many—examples of corporate misfeasance and misbehaviour that involve environmental damage, financial collapse, personal injury and death, or neglect of human rights. We refer to some of this behaviour in this book. However, as the late US corporate law academic Professor Lynn Stout once emphasised: 'We created corporations; now we share the planet with them'.[1] This underlines the need to understand the parameters of corporate behaviour, and that means understanding the law that governs that behaviour.

Of course, not everyone is sceptical about the role of corporations. Historically, the significance of the corporate form has sometimes been praised in glowing terms. In 1911, for example, one commentator described the limited liability company as 'the greatest single discovery of modern times', adding that 'even steam and electricity are far less important'![2] While we do not share in this hyperbole (and, in any event, the company was not 'discovered'; it was created by law), we recognise that, alongside the harm they can cause, corporations are a mechanism for providing great benefit to society.

And so, to repeat our earlier point, the aim of this book is to assist students to develop a critically informed understanding of corporate law and the role of corporations in contemporary society.

1 Lynn Stout, *The Shareholder Value Myth* (Berrett-Koehler Publishers, 2012) 103.
2 Cited in W Hackney and T Benson, 'Shareholder Liability for Inadequate Capital' (1982) 43 *University of Pittsburgh Law Review* 837, 841.

Each of us has taught and written about corporate law for many years. This book is the product of those years and the many interactions we have had with our students and fellow researchers, and we are grateful to them for their questions, comments and insights. We are also thankful for the feedback provided by anonymous reviewers of this text. We welcome future feedback on the book from teachers, students and practitioners.

Once again, the writing of this edition has been a genuinely collaborative exercise. We have read and commented on each other's chapters and we take collective responsibility for the entirety of the book. Necessarily though, responsibility for individual chapters was allocated as follows:

- Stephen Bottomley: 1, 2, 4, 14, and 16
- Kath Hall: 3, 5, 6, 7, 8 and 15
- Peta Spender: 9, 17, 18 and 19
- Beth Nosworthy: 10, 11, 12, 13, 15 and 16.

The covers of the two previous editions of this book have depicted city structures, symbolising the role of corporations in contemporary human enterprise. The cover image for this new edition is a reminder of the much older cultural and environmental heritage in which Australian corporations operate, with sometimes devastating consequences.

This edition reflects the law as at December 2024.

ACKNOWLEDGEMENTS

We are grateful to the team at Cambridge University Press for supporting this book into its third edition; we particularly thank Emily Baxter and Bonnie de Somer for their advice and support. We also thank Ellie Gleeson for her excellent editorial work.

We also extend thanks to those who provided their time and expertise during the manuscript review: Tim Connor, Peter Dixon, Ross Grantham, Hannah Harris, Bill Hundy, Radha Ivory, Igor Mescher, Juliette Overland, Ashley Pearson, Asanka Perera, Brent Scafidas and Benedict Sheehy.

Finally, and most importantly, we thank our families for their assistance and encouragement during the writing of this book; for Stephen Bottomley (Sheri, Kristen, Sarah, Taryn and Jenna), for Kath Hall (Andrew, Olivia, Sophie and Zac), for Peta Spender (Walter, Grace, Eugene and Gabriel), and for Beth Nosworthy (Craig, Lillian and Oliver).

The authors and Cambridge University Press would like to thank the following for permission to reproduce material in this book:

Extracts from Helen Anderson, 'Piercing the Veil on Corporate Groups in Australia: The Case for Reform' (2009) 33(2) *Melbourne University Law Review* 333; extracts from Commonwealth Law Reports (CLR) and Federal Law Reports (FLR): reproduced with permission of Thomson Reuters (Professional) Australia Limited, legal.thomsonreuters.com.au; extracts from Law Reports, Appeal Cases (AC) (Third Series): reproduced with permission of the Incorporated Council of Law Reporting for England and Wales; extracts from Australian Corporations and Securities Reports (ACSR): originally published by LexisNexis; extracts from Commonwealth legislation: sourced from the Federal Register of Legislation and reproduced under Creative Commons Attribution 4.0 International (CC BY 4.0). For the latest information on Australian Government law, please go to https://www.legislation.gov.au.

Every effort has been made to trace and acknowledge copyright. The publisher apologises for any accidental infringement and welcomes information that would redress this situation.

TABLE OF CASES

AAPT Ltd v Cable & Wireless Optus Ltd (1999) 32 ACSR 63, 292, 686
ABC Developmental Learning Centres Pty Ltd v Wallace (2006) 161 A Crim R 250, 101–2
ABC Developmental Learning Centres Pty Ltd v Wallace (2007) 16 VR 409, 102
Aberdeen Railway Co v Blaikie Brothers (1854) 1 Macq 461, 326, 417–18, 421, 427, 432
ABN AMRO Bank NV v Bathurst Regional Council (2014) 224 FCR 1, 402, 637, 644, 645
Accurate Financial Consultants Pty Ltd v Koko Black Pty Ltd [2007] VSC 40, 164
Acehill Investments Pty Ltd v Incitec Ltd [2002] SASC 344, 488
ACM Gold Ltd and Mt Leyshon Gold Mines Ltd (1992) 7 ACSR 231, 658
Adams v Cape Industries plc [1990] 2 WLR 657, 96
Adler v Australian Securities and Investments Commission (2003) 46 ACSR 504, 443
Adstream Building Industries Pty Ltd v Queensland Cement & Lime Co Ltd (No 4) [1985] 1 Qd R 127, 677
Advance Bank Australia Ltd v Fleetwood Star Pty Ltd (1992) 10 ACLC 703, 183
Advance Housing Pty Ltd (in liq) v Newcastle Classic Developments Pty Ltd (1994) 14 ACSR 230, 544
Afro-West Mining Ltd v Australian Mining Investments Ltd (1988) 14 ACLR 709, 675
AG Coombs Pty Ltd v M & V Consultants Pty Ltd (in liq) (2018) 55 VR 513, 539
AIG Australia Ltd v Jaques (2014) 44 VR 780, 319
Airpeak Pty Ltd v Jetstream Aircraft Ltd (1997) 73 FCR 161, 486
Airservices Australia v Ferrier (1996) 185 CLR 483, 549–50
Aleyn v Belchier (1758) 1 Eden 132, 385
Al-Kateb v Godwin (2004) 219 CLR 562, 386
Allco Funds Management v Trust Company (RE Services) Ltd [2014] NSWSC 1251, 436
Allegiance Mining NL [2008] ATP 3, 696
Allen v Atalay (1994) 12 ACLC 7, 485
Allen v Gold Reefs of West Africa Ltd [1900] 1 Ch 656, 155–6, 385, 449
Allen v Hyatt (1914) 30 TLR 444, 423
Almario v Allianz Australia Workers Compensation (NSW) Insurance Ltd (2005) 62 NSWLR 148, 567
Ampol Petroleum Ltd v RW Miller (Holdings) Pty Ltd [1972] 2 NSWLR 850, 398
Ananda Marga Pracaraka Samgha Ltd v Tomar (No 3) [2012] FCA 184, 478
Andar Transport Ltd v Brambles Ltd (2004) 217 CLR 424, 87–8
Andrews v Queensland Racing Ltd (2009) 74 ACSR 538, 148
Angas Law Services Pty Ltd (in liq) v Carabelas (2005) 226 CLR 507, 339, 434
ANZ Banking Group Ltd v Australian Glass and Mirrors Pty Ltd (1991) 9 ACLC 702, 185
ANZ Executors & Trustee Co Ltd v Qintex Australia Ltd (recs and mgrs apptd) [1991] 2 Qd R 360, 132, 248
Aquisite Pty Ltd v Moss [2023] FCA 410, 497
Asden Developments Pty Ltd (in liq) v Dinoris [2017] FCAFC 117, 544
Ashburton Oil NL v Alpha Minerals NL (1971) 123 CLR 614, 389, 707

Percival v Wright [1902] 2 Ch 421, 422–4
Permanent Building Society (in liq) v Wheeler (1994) 11 WAR 187, 331, 332, 348, 354, 371, 372, 400
Permanent Trustee Australia Ltd v Perpetual Trustee Co Ltd (1995) 13 ACLC 66, 486
Perseverance Corporation Ltd v Butte Mining plc (1990) 3 ACSR 433, 691
Peters' American Delicacy Co Ltd v Heath (1939) 61 CLR 457, 156, 449
Peters v The Queen (1998) 192 CLR 493, 337, 405
Pharmaceutical Society v London and Provincial Supply Association Ltd (1880) 5 App Cas 857, 100
Phosphate Co-operative Co of Australia Ltd v Shears (No 3) [1989] VR 665, 695
Pine Investments v McDonnell & East Ltd (1983) 8 ACLR 199, 708–9
Pine Vale Investments Ltd v McDonnell & East Ltd (1983) 9 ACLR 199, 701
Pinnacle VRB Ltd (No 5) (2001) 39 ACSR 43, 711
Pinnacle VRB Ltd (No 8) (2001) 39 ACSR 55, 711–12
Pinnacle VRB Ltd v Reliable Power Inc (2001) 39 ACSR 8, 696
Pioneer Concrete Services Ltd v Yelnah Pty Ltd (1986) 5 NSWLR 254, 90, 96
Platt v Platt [1999] 2 BCLC 745, 424
Potts v National Australia Bank Ltd (2023) 4156 ALR 384, 355
Powell and Duncan v Fryer, Tonkin and Perry (2000) 18 ACLC 480, 381
PowerTel Ltd (No 2) [2003] ATP 27, 679
Prest v Petrodel Resources Ltd [2013] 2 AC 415, 90–1
Primelife Corporation Ltd v Aevum Ltd (2005) 53 ACSR 283, 696
Programmed Maintenance Services Ltd 02 (2008) 66 ACSR 242, 668
Punt v Symons & Co (1903) 2 Ch 506, 397
Pyneboard Pty Ltd v Trade Practices Commission (1983) 152 CLR 328, 56

Qantas Airways Ltd v Transport Workers Union of Australia (2023) 278 CLR 571, 392
Qintex Australia Finance Ltd v Schroders Australia Ltd (1990) 3 ACSR 267, 97, 132
Queensland Bacon Pty Ltd v Rees (1966) 115 CLR 266, 375
Queensland Mines Ltd v Hudson (1978) 18 ALR 1, 430–2, 440
Queensland North Australia Pty Ltd v Takeovers Panel (2015) 106 ACSR 186, 670, 675
Quin v Vlahos (2021) 64 VR 319, 375

R (on the Application of People & Planet) v HM Tresury [2009] EWHC 3020, 408
R v Board of Trade; Ex parte St Martins Preserving Co Ltd [1965] 1 QB 603, 505
R v Byrnes (1995) 183 CLR 501, 432, 435
R v Evans [1999] VSC 488, 614
R v Farris (2015) 107 ACSR 26, 610, 616
R v Firns (2001) 51 NSWLR 548, 608, 613–14
R v Fodera (2007) 65 ACSR 109, 337
R v Glynatsis (2103) 230 A Crim R 99, 617
R v Hannes (2000) 36 ACSR 72, 615
R v Hughes (2000) 202 CLR 535, 32–3
R v Panel on Takeovers and Mergers; Ex parte Datafin [1987] QB 815, 605
R v Rivkin (2004) 59 NSWLR 284, 614–15

TABLE OF STATUTES

COMMONWEALTH

ACT

NSW

NT

QLD

US

NZ

CANADA

CHAPTER

1

CONTEXT, HISTORY AND REGULATION

1.05 Introduction: the importance of context

Corporate law, like all law, has a context; indeed, it has many contexts. To understand corporate law today, we need to appreciate the forces—social, political, economic, global and local—which shape that law. Modern corporations and contemporary Australian corporate law should be understood as a product of, and a compromise between, various social, economic and legal ideas and philosophies. This is the focus of the first two chapters of this book.

We begin by looking at two contextual settings of contemporary Australian corporate law: its history and its regulatory structure. This chapter will explain the history of the modern corporation and the various approaches to regulating corporate conduct. History is important; it assists in understanding how and why modern corporations and the law that regulates them have developed into their current form. A deeper appreciation of modern corporations and their regulatory framework can be gained by understanding why things have developed as they have.

The corporation and corporate law were not invented in a single session by the work of enlightened lawyers or politicians. Things have evolved in a piecemeal and sometimes inconsistent fashion. They were not developed in harmony. Key steps in the evolution of the corporation as a legal structure often occurred despite the intentions of law-makers. This book will refer to and compare the historical antecedents of the various concepts and ideas which comprise modern corporate law in Australia. Chapter 1 presents an historical overview and framework to assist the reader with subsequent material. Necessarily, this will be a truncated version of corporate history. When reading the chapter, it is important to bear in mind that 'history means interpretation'.[1] Historians take different views and provide different accounts of historical events. This is true of corporate law history, and it is not our intention to canvass the full range of historical arguments. The reader is encouraged to pursue more detailed studies, using the materials referred to in the footnotes.[2]

In this chapter, we ask the reader to temporarily postpone the quest for a more detailed explanation of the legal concepts that are introduced. We will come back to examine these concepts in detail elsewhere in the book.

1.10 Some perennial questions

Corporate lawyers might think that the corporation is a legal structure over which they have a unique claim to expertise. However, many of the features that are integral to modern corporations—such as automatic incorporation on registration, limited liability of members, and the division of functions between managers and members—owe their origins to the efforts of merchants, business people, politicians, and economists, as well as those of lawyers.[3] The basic features of modern corporations developed because of concerns that emerged between the seventeenth and nineteenth centuries. This section identifies some broad themes that have underpinned the rise of the corporation and corporate law. The details of the history are supplied in subsequent sections of the chapter.

It is important to keep in mind that at the time when early corporate law was developed, English law was in the process of laying down its modern liberal foundations. The political philosophy of liberalism emphasises that society is made up of private individuals who possess rights, owe each other duties, and should be personally liable for their actions. How could a legal system built upon such ideas accommodate the growth of group enterprises? The history of corporate law can be interpreted as a series of attempts to address this fundamental question. This question subsumes four points of tension which are central to corporate regulation in a liberal legal system.

First, there is the 'group versus individual' issue. To what extent should the law recognise corporations, rather than individuals or investors, as bearers of rights, obligations and liabilities? In the corporate law context, this question has arisen in a number of ways. For example, should members of a group enterprise be able to minimise the risk of commercial failure by limiting their liability, or should the same principles of legal responsibility apply as for individual traders? Should a group be able to hold title to

1 EH Carr, *What is History?* (Penguin, 2nd ed, 1987) 23.

2 In addition, note Richard Dale, *The First Crash: Lessons from the South Sea Bubble* (Princeton University Press, 2005); R Harris, *Industrialising English Law: Entrepreneurship and Business Organisation 1720–1844* (Cambridge University Press, 2000); P Johnson, *Making the Market: Victorian Origins of Corporate Capitalism* (Cambridge University Press, 2010).

3 See, eg, R Kostal, *Law and English Railway Capitalism* (Clarendon Press, 1994).

property as distinct from the individual members? Should a group be able to pursue or defend legal claims to the exclusion of individual members?

A second tension lies between the roles of management and 'ownership' of the corporation. Liberal philosophy emphasises the freedom of the individual to own property and, within limits, to control its use and disposal. However, the efficient operation of a group enterprise will often require that control of the enterprise and its assets be exercised by a small group of managers on behalf of the larger group of members. Thus, most large corporations are structured in a way that separates the 'ownership' function of members from the management function of directors and company officers.[4] Accordingly, issues of internal responsibility and accountability are important in the development of modern corporations. Equally important is the question of external responsibility and accountability. For example, how should the relationship between the association and outside parties, such as creditors and customers, be addressed? Should this be a matter of contractual negotiation, or should the state set standards or rules?

This takes us to the third tension, which is the debate between facilitation and intervention. What is the role of government regulation in relation to corporations? If, for example, corporations are regarded primarily as private entities, then, arguably, the role of the state should be primarily facilitative rather than interventionist. The law should assist individuals in the private pursuit of profit because this, in turn, will promote economic efficiency. There should be a minimum of mandatory or punitive rules regarding corporate behaviour. The opposing view in this debate stresses the role of corporations as important social and economic actors, justifying a more interventionist role by the state. This perspective points to the impact that corporate operations can have on the environment, people's financial welfare,[5] and the health and safety of workers, among other issues. It also acknowledges the increasing role played by corporations in key aspects of twenty-first century life, including the development of technology to gather, control and use vast amounts of information and data.[6]

The fourth tension is the 'private versus public' issue. This involves a debate about the legal and political status of corporations. For example, to what extent should corporations be regarded simply as associations created by, and operating for the benefit of, private initiative, versus a view that corporations owe their legal existence to the state and therefore have broad public or social responsibilities?

These perennial debates provide the basic elements for a conceptual framework to which the reader can refer and develop throughout this book. We begin this process by examining the historical manifestation of these issues.

4 We qualify the word 'ownership' because, as we will see, it is not strictly accurate to say that the corporation is 'owned' by its members.

5 See, eg, *Royal Commission into Misconduct in the Banking, Superannuation and Financial Services Industry* (Final Report, 4 February 2019).

6 See, eg, A Godwin, PW Lee, and R Teele Langford (eds), *Technology and Corporate Law: How Innovation Shapes Corporate Activity* (Edward Elgar, 2021). This has been described variously as 'platform capitalism': N Srnicek, *Platform Capitalism* (Polity Press, 2017); 'informational capitalism': JE Cohen, *Between Truth and Power: The Legal Constructions of Informational Capitalism* (Oxford University Press, 2019); and 'chokepoint capitalism': R Giblin and C Doctorow, *Chokepoint Capitalism* (Beacon Press, 2022).

1.15 English company law in the seventeenth and eighteenth centuries

The origins of today's corporate structures can be traced back to medieval times.[7] However, a more manageable starting point for present purposes is the developments in England beginning in the seventeenth century. This is a convenient point from which to chart the development of the corporation, as well as the beginnings of legislative and regulatory responses.

As we have noted, the features regarded as intrinsic to the modern corporation did not develop at the same time. Across the seventeenth and eighteenth centuries, we see these various features emerging in different types of joint enterprise. It is only later that they came to be united within a single type of entity.

One of the earliest examples of joint enterprise to bear some resemblance to the business corporations of today were companies incorporated either by the Crown or by Parliament. These were associations, formed for some commercial or ostensibly public purpose, that petitioned for grants of legal status as entities in their own right. The new entities had legal capacities distinct from the individuals involved in the enterprise. These grants of incorporation could be acquired only by Royal Charter from the Crown or by a private Act of Parliament. Such a Charter or Act might define aspects of the legal relationships which would exist between the newly created legal entity and the individuals who participated in the enterprise. Limited liability of members for debts of the business was not necessarily an express part of the grant of incorporation, although it was often assumed that each member was liable only to the extent of his or her capital contribution. Charters often purported to limit the grant of incorporation to a defined number of years, although many companies continued to trade on the basis of outdated charters, as seen below.

These early corporations were based on an idea that lies at the heart of the development of the modern company—the joint stock principle. Each original member of the company contributed to a common fund that was managed by a committee selected from the members. Profits, in the form of dividends, were then distributed to the members in proportion to their shareholding. In this context, the term 'joint stock' referred to the trading or floating capital that was used by the company in the course of the enterprise. It was possible for members to transfer their share in the enterprise to others without seeking the permission of other members. This free transferability meant that membership in a joint stock venture was often shaped more by the expectation of financial gain than by personal involvement in the enterprise. The advantage of the common fund of capital—or joint stock—was that it permitted the risks associated with expensive and long-term ventures (such as foreign trade) to be spread across a large number of investors.

The most prominent examples of these chartered companies were large foreign trading companies, such as the East India Company and the Hudson Bay Company. As their names suggest, the principal advantage of incorporation by charter was that it gave an

7 See J Braithwaite and P Drahos, *Global Business Regulation* (Cambridge University Press, 2000) ch 9; SJ Stoljar, *Groups and Entities—An Inquiry into Corporate Theory* (ANU Press, 1973).

exclusive right to conduct trade in a particular geographical area. These monopoly trading rights and special privileges were the main reason for seeking incorporation, as a recompense for the risks involved in undertaking large-scale foreign trading ventures. The advantage for the state in granting corporate status to the venture, particularly in the case of the foreign trading companies, was that trade could be encouraged and controlled, while revenue in the form of taxes and duties could be raised. Thus, chartered companies played a critical role in Britain's colonial expansion.[8]

Alongside the joint stock principle was the idea that ownership of the capital contributed by investors could be separated from the control of that capital. While investors or financiers bought shares in a company, owning shares in the company did not necessarily give them other rights that are customarily associated with property ownership. Adam Smith, in his book *The Wealth of Nations* (published in 1776), noted that the joint stock principle usually resulted in a division of functions within the company:

> The trade of a joint stock company is always managed by a court of directors. The court, indeed, is frequently subject, in many respects, to the controul [sic] of a general court of proprietors. But the greater part of those proprietors seldom pretend to understand any thing of the business of the company; and when the spirit of faction happens not to prevail among them, give themselves no trouble about it, but receive contentedly such half yearly or yearly dividend, as the directors think proper to make to them. This total exemption from trouble and from risk, beyond a limited sum, encourages many people to become adventurers in joint stock companies, who would upon no account, hazard their fortunes in any private copartnery.[9]

The separation of ownership of shares by members from control of the business by its managers is fundamental to all contemporary large-scale corporate enterprises. This underlies perennial questions about the extent to which minority shareholders should be bound by the decisions of the majority, and whether a company's directors should be regulated by specific contractual obligations created by their company or by statutory rules that apply to all companies. These questions are dealt with later in this book.

The principal disadvantage of petitioning for incorporation was that it imposed considerable costs on merchants, with the added uncertainty of an outcome dependent on the discretion of the Crown or Parliament. For this reason, charters were usually only sought by traders seeking the benefits of a monopoly over an area of trade. Domestic commercial ventures rarely sought incorporation, being content to obtain most of the benefits by careful wording of the agreement by which the association was established.[10]

8 See, eg, W Dalrymple, *The Anarchy: The Relentless Rise of the East India Company* (Bloomsbury, 2019); P Stern, *Empire Incorporated: The Corporations that Built British Colonialism* (Belknap Press, 2023).

9 Adam Smith, *An Inquiry into the Nature and Causes of the Wealth of Nations* (Clarendon Press, 1976) 741.

10 WR Cornish and G de N Clark, *Law and Society in England 1750–1950* (Sweet & Maxwell, 1989) 248. For discussion of the direct and indirect costs of incorporation, see GM Anderson and RD Tollison, 'The Myth of the Corporation as a Creation of the State' (1983) 3(2) *International Review of Law and Economics* 107, 112.

During the seventeenth and eighteenth centuries, the alternative to incorporation was to trade as a commercial partnership. The idea of the partnership preceded the incorporated company. Since the Middle Ages, the most widely used form of partnership in English law was the *societas* (as it was called in Roman law). This form of association had no legal status, although it was usual to trade under a firm name. The individual partners shared the profits and losses as well as bearing the liabilities of the enterprise between them. The direct involvement of all partners in the business imposed practical limits on the size of the partnership and the size of the business. This was less of a problem for the alternative form of partnership, again derived from Roman law, known as the *commenda*. This allowed for a distinction to be made between the active partners, who bore full liability, and the dormant partners, who were liable only for the amount which they undertook to contribute. This form of partnership was not widely used in England, one reason being that English accounting practice was slow to recognise the need to separate the accounts of the firm from the capital accounts of the individual partners.[11] Instead, the *societas* was used more frequently, although over time its structure came increasingly to approximate that of the *commenda*.

When identifying the main forms of business association in common usage during this period, we emphasise the differences between the terms 'company', 'partnership' and 'corporation'.[12] In the eighteenth century, 'company' did not carry the specific legal meaning it has today. The term was used primarily to refer to a commercial association having a particular economic form. Companies were regarded as being comprised of a large number of members, with the business being managed by a smaller committee. The term 'partnership' was used to refer to a relatively small association of individuals, most of whom would have some involvement in managing the enterprise. At common law, both companies and partnerships were regarded as sharing the same legal features. In particular, neither had any separate legal status.[13] A joint stock company was regarded as a company even though it was not incorporated. If a joint stock company was incorporated by charter or special Act, the term 'corporation' would be used to describe its legal status. It is only later that the term 'company' came to have an exclusively legal meaning, denoting a distinct legal entity with its own legal status.

The rapid expansion of trade in the eighteenth century meant that commercial associations often required large accumulations of capital. This led to the gradual transformation of partnerships from the *societas* to larger, more dispersed forms. Like the *commenda*, these large partnerships often consisted of a number of passive investors joining together on the basis of the joint stock principle. In practice, there was little difference between unincorporated joint stock companies and corporations which operated under a grant of incorporation by charter or statute, other than the monopoly rights which were granted in the latter case. In most other respects, incorporation or the lack of

11 CA Cooke, *Corporation, Trust and Company: An Essay in Legal History* (Manchester University Press, 1950) 46. Holdsworth lists other reasons, including legislative hostility to the notion of limited liability: W Holdsworth, *A History of English Law* (Methuen, 2nd ed, 1937) 96–7.

12 The following discussion relies on P Ireland, 'The Rise of the Limited Liability Company' (1984) 12(3) *International Journal of Sociology of Law* 239.

13 The concept of corporate separate legal status is discussed in detail in Chapter 3.

it made little practical difference.[14] Nevertheless, unincorporated firms were classified for legal purposes as 'partnerships' and were treated accordingly.

It was usual for an unincorporated company's constitution to provide that shares in joint stock were freely transferable by members. An organised and sometimes volatile market developed to facilitate the trading of these shares. The periods during which stock prices rose dramatically and subsequently fell had a significant influence on attitudes towards the regulation of the corporate form. There were concerns about the practice whereby entrepreneurs would either form an unincorporated joint stock company or, more frequently, take over a disused charter company. The public would then be invited to invest by purchasing joint stock. These invitations were often associated with inflated or vague promises about the company's prospects and likely returns, and these ventures came to be described as 'bubbles'.[15] The author of a 1923 text on the history of English company law provided the following description of the worst of these practices:

> In some cases only sixpence or a shilling per cent. was demanded upon first subscription, and so gullible had the public become that in many cases some obscure opener of books of subscription, contenting himself with what he had got in the morning, was not to be found in the afternoon, the room he had hired for the day being shut up, and he and his subscription book never heard of again![16]

The most prominent example of this sort of speculation involved the South Sea Company and what became known as the 'South Sea Bubble'. This company was formed in 1711, initially with the object of obtaining a trade monopoly with rich Spanish colonies in South America and the West Indies. The venture was sufficiently successful: in 1719, the company offered to take over almost all the national debt from the British Government. Under this scheme, the company would pay creditors of the Government, mostly holders of annuities,[17] in full. The payment could either be in cash or in the form of shares in the company. In short, creditors of the British Government were being offered the chance to swap their claims against the Government for shares in what looked to be a prosperous company. The Government benefited because, under the scheme, the interest payable on the debt owed to the annuity holders was to be reduced. The benefit to the company lay in holding a loan on which the Government paid interest and the anticipation that this could be used by the company to raise further sums to extend its trading venture. It was hoped that a close association with the Government would be good publicity and a source of investor confidence. The success of the scheme depended upon the market value of the company's shares remaining high so that annuity holders would be tempted to invest. The scheme was a huge success initially, judging by the large numbers of people who invested in the company and the upward surge in the company's

14 W Holdsworth, *A History of English Law* (Methuen, 2nd ed, 1937) 215.

15 Cooke cites examples of joint stock companies which were set up 'To make salt water fresh' and 'For an undertaking which shall in due time be revealed': CA Cooke, *Corporation, Trust and Company: An Essay in Legal History* (Manchester University Press, 1950) 81.

16 R Formoy, *The Historical Foundations of Modern Company Law* (Sweet & Maxwell, 1923) 28.

17 An annuity is a form of investment which gives an investor the right to receive a fixed sum of money on an annual basis for a defined period of years.

share price. Eventually the share price collapsed, and the South Sea Bubble was burst. This speculation boom rapidly spilt into the stocks of other companies, many of which were formed solely to take advantage of the investment frenzy.

Apart from the potential for fraud and wild speculation, there were further implications raised by the joint stock principle and the separation of management functions from membership. Throughout the eighteenth and nineteenth centuries, these were highlighted by writers from diverse political perspectives. Adam Smith, described as the 'father' of classical laissez-faire economics, conceded that grants of monopolies and special privileges by the state might be necessary for the introduction of new types of commerce. However, he argued that, in the long term, this form of government intervention impeded the growth of productivity and free trade.[18] In part, this was because the directors of these companies were managing other people's money. He stated:

> ... it cannot well be expected, that they should watch over it with the same anxious vigilance with which the partners in a copartnery frequently watch over their own. ... Negligence and profusion, therefore, must always prevail, more or less, in the management of the affairs of such a company.[19]

Smith argued that the joint stock company form was only appropriate for certain types of ventures, such as banking, insurance, and the construction of canals and aqueducts. In these essential trades, the operations of the company were so routine or uniform that the risk of managerial abuse was minimal.

The liberal philosopher John Stuart Mill acknowledged the risk that 'hired servant' directors of a joint stock company might not exhibit the same commitment to the job as the owner–managers of private partnerships. Mill also urged that the joint stock company had two advantages: it had the capacity to undertake large-scale enterprise on a continuing basis, and it was possible to hire directors with the skills appropriate to the enterprise in question.[20]

From a different political perspective to that of Smith and Mill, in the nineteenth century Karl Marx saw the rise of the joint stock company as evidence of the inevitable contradictions and instabilities within capitalism. Marx argued that because those who owned the capital—the members—were not directly involved in its management, then the potential for expansion into new risky business ventures would no longer be governed by the knowledge and experience of the owners. Moreover, the economic role of the capitalist was now carried out by a person who was 'a mere manager, administrator of other people's capital'.[21] This 'private production without the control of private property'[22] meant capitalism would be driven by financial speculation rather than the needs of production, leading to its eventual decline.

18 See Adam Smith, *An Inquiry into the Nature and Causes of the Wealth of Nations* (Clarendon Press, 1976) ch 1.

19 Ibid 741.

20 JS Mill, *Principles of Political Economy* (Longmans, 1923) ch IX.

21 Karl Marx, *Capital: A Critique of Political Economy* (vol III) https://www.marxists.org/archive/marx/works/download/pdf/Capital-Volume-III.pdf

22 Ibid 304.

1.20 The *Bubble Act* and its consequences

The unparalleled level of share speculation eventually led to the collapse of many of the 'bubble companies' in 1720. The loss of investor confidence that followed caused a general panic in the stock market which burst the investment bubble. Just prior to these events, the British Parliament passed the first instance of modern company legislation—the *Bubble Act 1720*.[23] The purpose of this Act was an attempt to confine the benefits of the boom market to the South Sea Company. The Act sought to achieve this by making it illegal to form a joint stock company and to create transferable shares without a grant of legal authority, either by Act of Parliament or by Royal Charter. In other words, unincorporated companies with transferable shares were prohibited, and only incorporated companies and common law partnerships were allowed to continue.

While there were only a few immediate prosecutions under the Act, it had a symbolic impact, expressing widespread disapproval and concern at the excesses produced by rampant financial speculation. Although the Act did not result in an increase in the number of petitions to Parliament for incorporation, it influenced the scope of speculative activity. In the face of legal restrictions in the Act, the main alternative to incorporation for commercial enterprises was to operate as a partnership. However, the problem for business people was that the partnership had its own legal restrictions. Under the common law, a partnership could not hold property in its own name. Interests in the partnership could only be transferred with the consent of the other partners, each partner was liable for the debts of the partnership, and the partnership was subject to dissolution on the death or withdrawal of any one partner. Partnerships at common law lacked two features needed for an investment vehicle: free transferability of shares and continuity of existence.

To meet the demands for a commercial entity that would overcome these limitations but not fall foul of the *Bubble Act*, lawyers developed a de facto corporation: an association based on the equitable trust. Investors subscribed funds which were then vested in trustees to be held on trust and managed according to the purposes specified in a deed of settlement. The deed contained a series of mutual promises and undertakings between the investors (members of the company) and the trustees.[24] These 'deed of settlement companies' continued to use the joint stock principle but relied upon equity law to overcome the legislative prohibitions and the common law restrictions. As the English legal historian Maitland described it:

> [I]n truth and in deed we made corporations without troubling King or Parliament, though perhaps we said we were doing nothing of the kind.[25]

These companies had joint stock, which divided ownership into units, but in order to escape the prohibitions of the *Bubble Act* there would be some nominal restriction on the

23 *Bubble Act 1720*, 6 Geo I, c 18, ss 18–21.

24 The deeds of settlement were the forerunners of the modern company constitution.

25 FW Maitland, *Collected Papers* (III) (Cambridge University Press, 1911) 283.

transfer of stock.[26] As with earlier companies based on the joint stock principle, owners of shares in deed of settlement companies had little, if any, involvement in management of the company, which was conducted by a managing committee.

Deed of settlement companies were only recognised in equity, whereas the courts of common law only recognised incorporated companies or partnerships. Deed of settlement companies, as far as the common law was concerned, were classified as partnerships. The position has been summed up as follows:

> The two branches of the law were thus in conflict over the new business unit, and against the common law's attitude that there was no such thing as an unincorporated joint stock company, was the definite development of an institution somewhere between partnership and incorporated company, under Chancery jurisdiction.[27]

The unintended effect of the prohibitions in the *Bubble Act* was to give the courts of equity a prominent role in the development of the joint stock company.

By the end of the eighteenth century, commercial enterprise was increasingly organised on the basis of deed of settlement companies.[28] While these companies became popular, incorporated companies continued to be created. The industrial boom, with its demand for canals and railways, meant that companies formed for such purposes could confidently seek a private Act from Parliament. These Acts conferred a varying range of benefits on the companies. Some Acts granted the power to sue and be sued in the name of a company officer. Others granted special powers relating to the acquisition of land. But obtaining a grant of incorporation to secure these benefits was not guaranteed, remaining within the realm of Royal or Parliamentary prerogative.[29] Incorporation was seen as a privilege conferred by the state. We will see in Chapter 2 that this historical view continues to have implications for the regulation of corporations today.

Another point of distinction between companies established by deed of settlement and those given incorporated status deserves emphasis. We have seen that corporations were created by charter or statute so that people could pursue a joint, profit-making interest for some public purpose. The grant of corporate status, together with the attendant privileges, was clothed with the rhetoric of public responsibility.[30] In contrast, the deed of settlement company developed as a vehicle for organising and promoting private interests. This shift in perspective, from public to private purposes, is important in the development of modern corporate culture. As we noted earlier in this chapter (see Section 1.10), it has implications for arguments about the appropriate degree of state regulation of corporations.

26 This concept has remained in the form of the modern proprietary company.

27 CA Cooke, *Corporation, Trust and Company: An Essay in Legal History* (Manchester University Press, 1950) 96.

28 LCB Gower, *Gower's Principles of Modern Company Law* (Sweet & Maxwell, 5th ed, 1992) 31.

29 See, eg, R Kostal, *Law and English Railway Capitalism* (Clarendon Press, 1994).

30 CA Cooke, *Corporation, Trust and Company: An Essay in Legal History* (Manchester University Press, 1950) 49.

1.25 The nineteenth century

During the late eighteenth and early nineteenth centuries, there was periodic repetition of the speculative fervour that marked the demise of the South Sea Bubble. As one historian describes it:

> Prospectuses routinely contained false or exaggerated claims about a new company's subscribed capital, investors, and managers. Respectable securities brokers were hired, 'on very tempting rates of commission', to trade in bubble company scrip. Company accounts were faked and suppressed. Dividends were declared from capital accounts. Sham directors held lavish entertainments at the sham offices of sham companies. All of this and more was done to create the illusion of the 'bona fide character of the undertaking'.[31]

Early in the nineteenth century, the prohibitions in the *Bubble Act* were enforced sporadically.[32] At the same time, the use of the deed of settlement company was gaining acceptance. Faced with widespread avoidance, the Act was repealed in 1825. At this time, there were three types of association in use: the common law partnership, the unincorporated joint stock company formed by deed of settlement, and the incorporated company formed by charter or special Act of Parliament. Of these, the first two were the most numerous.

In the period between the repeal of the *Bubble Act* and the 1840s, the idea of a company structured around the joint stock principle continued to gain acceptance. There were many factors behind this.[33] Among these were the continued availability of this form of organisation via charter or special Act of Parliament, the extension of certain joint stock privileges to provincial banks (such as the right to sue and be sued in the name of a public officer), and a continuing interest in a form of partnership which would allow for non-active investing partners to limit their liability to the extent of their contribution.[34] According to one legal historian, in this period:

> [T]he economic group, focused through a joint stock fund, had established itself as the most important of developing business forms; its existence was no longer questioned although its powers and immunities were.[35]

At the same time, continuing evidence of fraudulent company promotions led to a growing belief that some form of legal regulation was necessary. During this period, calls for legislative action were catalysed by publicity surrounding widespread business failure and malpractice.[36] This was a time when there was debate about the need for, and policies to be pursued in, the legal regulation of companies and corporations.

31 R Kostal, *Law and English Railway Capitalism* (Clarendon Press, 1994) 23.

32 CA Cooke, *Corporation, Trust and Company: An Essay in Legal History* (Manchester University Press, 1950) 97–9.

33 WR Cornish and G de N Clark, *Law and Society in England 1750–1950* (Sweet & Maxwell, 1989) 252–3.

34 This latter form of partnership, known as the *société en commandite*, was based upon the idea of the *commenda* and was recognised in civil law jurisdictions.

35 CA Cooke, *Corporation, Trust and Company: An Essay in Legal History* (Manchester University Press, 1950) 110.

36 Some of these fraudulent practices are described in Charles Dickens' *Martin Chuzzlewit*, first published in 1843.

One issue which figured prominently in public debate was whether members of a joint stock company should be permitted to limit their liability to creditors of the company. The idea that each member's liability would be limited to the amount which he or she contributed to the joint stock fund was not new. Members of unincorporated joint stock companies could attempt to limit their liability in a number of ways; for example, by inserting a provision to this effect in contracts with third parties. It was also common for deeds of settlement to contain such clauses, although there were doubts whether this statement would be effective unless it was also included within the contract with a creditor.[37] While the main impetus behind the emergence of the corporation continued to be the advantage of the joint stock arrangement, in the early nineteenth century there was discussion about the extent to which the law should sanction limited liability as an intrinsic feature of joint stock enterprise.

On the one hand, the group form of commercial enterprise was necessary for large-scale economic activity. Limited liability was an incentive for investors to risk their money in these group enterprises. On the other hand, because of their scale, group enterprises had greater potential to put the interests of creditors at risk. As recognised by Adam Smith and Karl Marx, non-owning managers could easily be tempted to trade beyond the means of their company. John Stuart Mill's reply was that creditors were capable of taking care of themselves, and that laws which impeded limited liability were unduly protective and paternalistic. Mill argued that, provided limited liability associations were required to publicise their accounts, creditors should be left to make their own judgments about whether to deal with a particular company.[38] This debate about whether the primary concern of company law should be for members and investors or for the interests of creditors has been a continuing theme in corporate law reform.

1.30 Early company legislation

After 1825, we see the beginnings of a distinct legal regime for the unincorporated joint stock company. The *Trading Companies Act 1834*[39] allowed for some of the advantages of incorporation to be granted to such bodies by way of Letters Patent. It appears that this Act, which was administered by the courts of common law, was regarded as too inflexible by comparison with the deed of settlement company.

A Board of Trade report on the law of partnership in 1837 recommended that partnerships should be limited to 15 members.[40] Partnerships with more than this number would need to register a deed of settlement. Presumably, this was to avoid the difficulties of enforcing obligations on a partnership with a large and fluctuating membership.[41] However, the British Parliament decided not to give express recognition to the equitable

37 One such clause was held to be ineffective against a third party in *Re Sea, Fire & Life Insurance Co* (1854) 3 De GM & G 459.

38 JS Mill, *Principles of Political Economy* (Longmans, 1923) ch IX [6].

39 *Trading Companies Act*, 4 & 5 Wm IV, c 94.

40 H Bellenden Ker, *Report on the Law of Partnership* (House of Commons, Parliamentary Papers XLIV, Session 1837–38, 1837) ('the 1837 report').

41 This recommendation lives on in the Australian *Corporations Act 2001* (Cth)'s restriction on outsized partnerships: s 115.

form of joint stock company, preferring to adhere to the common law classifications of incorporated company and partnership. The response to the 1837 report was simply to revise the existing legislation. The *Chartered Companies Act 1837*[42] continued to allow for specific privileges to be granted to companies by way of Letters Patent.

1.30.05 The *Joint Stock Companies Act 1844*

The 1837 report was followed by what has proven to be an enduring feature of corporate law reform—the convening of a Parliamentary Committee to examine and report on the issues.[43] Chaired by William Gladstone (President of the Board of Trade), this Committee's recommendations led to the enactment of the *Joint Stock Companies Act 1844*.[44] This Act 'for the Registration, Incorporation and Regulation of Joint Stock Companies' was the first step towards establishing a system of company law based on legislative regulation, rather than common law doctrine.[45] The Act signalled the merging of the joint stock fund as a form of economic activity with the idea of incorporation. The development of company law became separate from that of partnership, as the legislative branch of government assumed a role alongside the courts of equity.

Drawing on the Gladstone Committee's recommendations, the 1844 Act was based upon two elements that continue to underpin contemporary corporate regulation: public registration of companies and public financial accountability.

First, the Act introduced the process of incorporation by registration. All newly created deed of settlement companies with more than 25 members, or with shares freely transferable without the consent of all the members, were required to be registered with the Board of Trade, a government department. Registration involved the filing of documents, including the deed of settlement, with the Registrar and payment of the appropriate fee. The registration requirement was intended to act as a form of public notification about the creation of the company. This process of incorporation by administrative procedure automatically conferred certain legal privileges on the company. For example, the company could sue and be sued and hold and dispose of property in its own right. This shift from close supervision of each instance of incorporation by tailor-made charter or Act of Parliament to a general system of incorporation by registration marks one of the major steps towards the present system of company regulation.

The second significant element in the Act was a set of requirements concerning the publicity of the company's financial affairs. These were aimed at the growing public concern with corporate fraud. When he introduced the legislation, Gladstone argued that 'publicity is all that is necessary. Show up roguery and it is harmless'.[46] The Act required

42 *Chartered Companies Act 1837*, 7 Wm IV & 1 Vict c 73.

43 Select Committee on Joint Stock Companies, *First Report of the Select Committee on Joint Stock Companies* (House of Commons, Vol VII, 1844) ('the Gladstone Committee').

44 *Joint Stock Companies Act 1844*, 7 & 8 Vict, c 110.

45 CA Cooke, *Corporation, Trust and Company: An Essay in Legal History* (Manchester University Press, 1950) 138.

46 Quoted in R McQueen, *A Social History of Company Law: Great Britain and the Australian Colonies 1854–1920* (Ashgate, 2009) 164.

registered companies to prepare annual balance sheets for audit. Both the balance sheet and the auditor's report were to be filed with the Registrar of Companies.

It is interesting to note that despite the grant of separate legal status to each newly incorporated body, the 1844 Act used the term 'company' as a collective noun; various sections in the Act, when referring to obligations imposed on the company, used the words 'they' and 'them'. This suggests that the company was still regarded essentially as a collection of individuals rather than as an entity in its own right.[47] We will see in the next chapter that this conceptualisation continues to have important implications for corporate regulation.

The 1844 Act did not provide for limited liability of members as a consequence of incorporation. Instead, each shareholder in the company was liable for the company's debts. Because the purpose of the Act was to protect the public rather than to offer inducements to incorporate, limited liability was outside the purview of this legislative change. However, the 1844 Act was amended in 1855 with the consequence that limited liability became an entitlement consequent to incorporation of a company.[48] The liability of a shareholder was limited to the amount, if any, which was owed to the company for his or her shares. As a prerequisite to obtaining this privilege, the Act provided that by various means the company must advertise the fact that its members had the benefit of limited liability. The inclusion of the word 'Limited' after the company's name was made mandatory, and the deed of settlement had to state that the company was formed with limited liability. The 1855 Act was an amendment to the existing legislation and so the benefits of limited liability were restricted to the large deed of settlement companies with which the 1844 Act was concerned. Limited liability had not yet been sanctioned for smaller business operations. Even with this restricted scope, the 1855 legislation met strong opposition. Much of this condemnation was expressed in highly moralistic terms. For example, an article published in the *Law Times* in 1858 argued 'it would appear as if the immunity it provides for dishonesty, by exempting men from liability to pay their debts and perform their contracts and make reparation for their wrongs, taints the moral character of those who adopt it'.[49]

1.30.10 The *Joint Stock Companies Act 1856*

In 1856, the Acts of 1844 and 1855 were consolidated by the *Joint Stock Companies Act 1856*.[50] This Act put in place many of the features that are found in contemporary corporations legislation.

The 1856 Act introduced the process of incorporation by registration of a Memorandum of Association. This document contained basic information about the company, such as its name and the purposes for which it was to be incorporated. Along with this registration document, each company was required to have Articles of Association. The Act supplied a model set of Articles (or regulations) which could be adopted by any

47 See P Ireland, I Grigg-Spall and D Kelly, 'The Conceptual Foundations of Modern Company Law' (1987) 14(1) *Journal of Law and Society* 149.

48 *Limited Liability Act 1855*, 18 & 19 Vict, c 133.

49 Cited in R Formoy, *The Historical Foundations of Modern Company Law* (Sweet & Maxwell, 1923) 120.

50 *Joint Stock Companies Act 1856*, 19 & 20 Vict, c 47.

company. The Articles originated from the deeds of settlement which had been required by the previous legislation, and the model provisions were based upon widely used precedents. Today, the Memorandum and the Articles are reflected in the modern company constitution and in the 'replaceable rules' found in the *Corporations Act*; this is explained in Chapter 5 of this book.

In the 1856 Act, the minimum number of people necessary to incorporate was reduced from 25 to 7. The legislation required that partnerships of more than 20 persons must be incorporated under the Act in order to carry on business. Limited liability was available on terms to be specified in each company's Memorandum and Articles of Association. Interestingly, what was missing from the legislation was the previous emphasis on publicity of company financial affairs. For example, the 1856 Act contained no requirements relating to audited accounts. These provisions were included in the model set of Articles, which did not require that the information be filed with the Registrar.

The 1856 Act continued the idea that there was no separation between the company and its members. Section 3, for example, permitted seven or more persons to 'form themselves into an incorporated company', suggesting that the company was still regarded as co-extensive with the people who formed it.

The philosophy behind this legislation was expressed clearly by Robert Lowe, Vice-President of the Board of Trade and an ardent supporter of the Act:

> The principle is the freedom of contract, and the right of unlimited association—the right of people to make what contracts they please on behalf of themselves, whether those contracts may appear to the Legislature beneficial or not, as long as they do not commit fraud, or otherwise act contrary to the general policy of the law.[51]

In short, the legislation was built upon the liberal philosophy that individuals, not governments, are best placed and motivated to protect their own interests.

1.30.15 The *Companies Act 1862*

Several consolidating Acts followed, culminating in the *Companies Act 1862*[52] which was the model for the first company statutes in Australia. Three aspects of this Act are worth mentioning. First, the wording of the incorporation section revealed a shift in how the idea of the company was understood. Section 6 provided that persons could 'form an incorporated company', indicating that the company was now regarded as something distinct from its members. Second, the Act continued to relegate provisions about accounts and audits to the model Articles of Association. Publicity of financial affairs had not re-emerged as a major public concern. Finally, the Act was considerably longer than previous Acts, with 212 sections compared to 116 in the 1856 Act. Corporate legislation was becoming a more detailed and technical matter.

51 Quoted in WR Cornish and G de N Clark, *Law and Society in England 1750–1950* (Sweet & Maxwell, 1989) 257.

52 *Companies Act 1862*, 25 & 26 Vict, c 89.

In a number of ways, the 1862 legislation continued the laissez-faire philosophy that had underpinned the 1856 Act. There is evidence that despite this philosophy and the reduced minimum membership requirement, this Act was not intended for use by sole traders or the smaller private partnerships. The privileges of corporate status were aimed instead at joint stock enterprises—the nineteenth century equivalent of modern public companies.[53]

There are different interpretations of the rationale behind this policy.[54] One view is that the legislation between 1856 and 1862 was designed to serve the interests of the English investor class to stop the flight of investment and incorporations from England to Europe. Another interpretation is that the legislation embodied a permissive attitude towards the creation and operation of companies and had the effect of shifting the risk of company failure onto creditors, such as banks and large merchants. This worked to the advantage of the 'middling class', providing a device to protect them from the risk of bankruptcy and debtors' prison and encouraging their participation in economic growth.

Historical research[55] shows that even by the mid-1880s, the unincorporated partnership was still the most widely used form of associated commercial activity. This was due in part to the continuing ambivalence towards incorporation and limited liability. By the early 1900s, this picture had changed dramatically. By then, contrary to the intention of the early legislators, the heaviest users of the companies legislation were sole proprietors and small businesses. What may have prompted the dramatic growth in the use of the limited company form by small partnerships was the attraction of limited liability in the context of the economic Long Depression from 1873 to 1896. This factor, combined with the increasing ease of incorporation, meant that incorporations of small firms soon outstripped joint stock company incorporations. Gradually, the term 'private company' came into use to describe what were little more than incorporated partnerships. An event of key importance in the process of recognising private companies was the case of *Salomon v Salomon & Co Ltd*[56] which was litigated between 1895 and 1896, being decided finally by the House of Lords. As will be seen in Chapter 3, this is cited as the case which confirmed and approved the concept of the one-person limited liability company.[57]

1.35 Summarising developments in British corporate history

We now turn our attention to the Australian history of corporate regulation. We start by emphasising two features of the historical developments described earlier. First, the development of company law shifted away from a reliance on judicial decisions towards an increasingly legislated structure. Although the role of the courts remained

53 See P Ireland, 'The Rise of the Limited Liability Company' (1984) 12(3) *International Journal of Sociology of Law* 239, 244.

54 Described in R McQueen, *A Social History of Company Law: Great Britain and the Australian Colonies 1854–1920* (Ashgate, 2009) 96–117.

55 See P Ireland, 'The Rise of the Limited Liability Company' (1984) 12 *International Journal of Sociology of Law* 239.

56 *Salomon v Salomon & Co Ltd* [1897] AC 22.

57 Legislative provision for private companies came in the *Companies Act 1907* (UK). In the Australian colonies, Victoria made similar provision in 1896.

important,[58] by the late nineteenth century the courts were being displaced as the main regulatory focus by an ever-growing regulatory bureaucracy. During the nineteenth century, the practical significance of the companies legislation had changed. Initially, the legislature had offered incorporation as a way of facilitating the large-scale raising of public funds by joint stock companies. By the end of the century, most companies on the register were small affairs hoping to escape the disadvantages of partnership law and gain the benefit of limited liability. Company law had expanded to encompass large commercial investment-based enterprise, small one-person businesses, and non-profit organisations such as clubs and charities.[59]

The second feature to emphasise is that private and public companies, which today are treated as two aspects of the same concept, had different historical origins. Public companies developed from the joint stock companies via the deed of settlement companies. In the process, the basic legal elements of modern corporations were put into place. Private companies joined the process later on, as sole proprietors and partnerships took advantage of incorporation laws and rapidly became the numerically dominant species of corporation.

1.40 The history of Australian corporate law

The history of company law in Britain overlaps with the early decades of the British colonisation of Australia. However, the issues that underpinned developments in British corporate history were not simply echoed in Australia. The picture is more complex than this. Certainly, Australian corporate history continued the trend towards the increased use of the corporate form in all areas of commercial life. But the Australian context, involving the transformation of a penal colony into a pastoral economy and then into a bureaucratised, industrial nation, provided its own set of influences on the development of corporate regulation. It would be misleading to assume that the history of corporate law in Australia simply picked up where British history left off. We also acknowledge that while our focus is on the development of corporate law in its legislative and judicial contexts, there was—and continues to be—a very different understanding of ideas about groups, property and ownership among First Nations people in this country.

In Australia, the rise of liberal political ideas shaped attitudes towards corporate regulation. However, liberalism in Australia demonstrated different emphases to Britain. The ideas of the English jurist and philosopher Jeremy Bentham were particularly influential.[60] Conditions in the first century of white settlement, such as the great distances between population groups and the absence of pre-existing institutional structures, laid the foundations for a system of government that was more interventionist than that in

58 As will be seen throughout this book, the courts have continued to play a significant role in developing key areas of company law and in determining the reach of statutory provisions.

59 Clubs and charities could incorporate as companies limited by guarantee, a form of company introduced in the 1862 Act.

60 ID McNaughton, 'Colonial Liberalism 1851–1892' in G Greenwood (ed), *Australia: A Social and Political History* (Angus & Robertson, 1955) 99.

Britain.[61] A particular consequence was a heavy emphasis on legislation as a source of legal rules and method of economic regulation. These themes became particularly important with regard to an issue that did not trouble business people or law-makers in Britain: the divergences between the corporate legislation passed by the different States, and the resulting drive for unified legislation with national application.

1.40.05 Small beginnings: 1788–1850s

Early corporate activity in the colonies was dominated by the English-based deed of settlement companies, companies with Royal Charters, and companies incorporated by a special Act of Parliament. There were practical commercial reasons for this, since the early colony was closely allied to British needs and to the British supply of labour and capital. The pastoral boom in the 1830s was financed mainly by British capital, and British banking companies established themselves in New South Wales.

The first local company to be established was the Bank of New South Wales, which started as a joint stock company under a charter granted by Governor Macquarie in 1817.[62] Because of doubts over the validity of its original charter, and because of shareholder unrest about the bank's performance, the bank adopted a deed of settlement in 1828, giving it the legal status of a partnership, with the consequence of unlimited liability of members. In 1850, the bank formed a new deed of settlement and took advantage of new legislation which incorporated the company.

1.40.10 Boom and Depression: 1850s–1890s

This was a period in which the colonial economies expanded rapidly, spurred on by the gold rushes of the 1850s. This economic growth culminated in the great boom of the 1880s, closely followed by the depression in the 1890s. The number of company incorporations increased across these four decades, although historical research shows that many companies operating in Australia, especially large financial enterprises, continued to prefer English registration.[63]

The Victorian gold rush in the 1850s prompted the creation of many new public companies concerned with mining, waterworks and other activities associated with the development of the gold fields. However, it was not until the boom period of the 1880s that there was a dramatic increase in the number of new companies. This was due to a growth of investment in speculative land developments which were funded largely by a continuing inflow of capital from Britain.[64] This land boom was especially marked in Victoria, with many leading financial and political figures being involved in company incorporations, particularly building societies and the 'land banks'. The promise of easy

61 By contrast, the species of liberal thought that shaped the development of American political life was based on the philosopher John Locke, who emphasised the importance of protecting the rights of the individual citizen: see Stephen Bottomley and Simon Bronitt, *Law in Context* (Federation Press, 5th ed, 2023) 4–6.

62 The Bank of New South Wales was the forerunner of today's Westpac Banking Corporation.

63 R McQueen, 'Why High Court Judges Make Poor Historians' (1990) 19(3) *Federal Law Review* 245, 250.

64 J Waugh, 'Company Law and the Crash of the 1890s in Victoria' (1992) 15(2) *University of New South Wales Law Journal* 356, 357.

money offered by these companies attracted many small-time investors, spurred on by the belief that 'it was impossible to lose money by "investing" in land'.[65]

The rise in incorporations is demonstrated by company registration figures: in 1875 there were 13 company registrations in New South Wales and 27 in Victoria; by 1888 (the peak year of the boom) these figures had risen to 227 and 342 respectively. The depression in the early 1890s resulted in many companies being wound up, and in 1890, New South Wales saw 122 registrations while there were only 64 in Victoria.[66] Nevertheless, despite the effects of the depression, this was a period during which the corporate form gained increased acceptance in the conduct of economic activity.

The colonies, and subsequently the states, had a strong reliance on British legislation for regulating commercial activity until well into the twentieth century.[67] Prior to the 1900s, the lack of any strong local involvement in large-scale commercial ventures meant that there was little impetus to establish a local set of company laws. In the mid-1800s, each of the colonies passed specific statutes which dealt with a variety of business associations, such as friendly societies, benefit building societies, banking companies, mining companies,[68] and partnerships. South Australia enacted the *Associations Incorporation Act 1858*, the first instance of such legislation in Australia or Britain, which created a unique form of incorporation for non-profit associations.[69] Between 1863 and 1874, each of the colonial legislatures (except Western Australia) enacted their first general companies statutes, each based on the *Companies Act 1862* (UK). Again, there was some practical sense in using this precedent given the importance of British business interests to the developing Australian economy. Moreover, many companies operating in the colony were either registered in Britain or operated with boards in both Britain and the colony. Despite these advantages, there were some difficulties in implementing the English legislation, particularly because of the absence of any established bureaucracy with the facilities to administer the legislation adequately.[70] That said, the legislation required little in the way of enforcement, being concerned mainly with the lodgement of basic corporate and financial information with the relevant colonial authority. The public registers contained little detailed information of use to company outsiders.[71] For example, it was common practice during the land boom of the 1880s for promoters to buy an area of land and then form a company for the purpose of acquiring the property from the promoters (who were now the

65 M Cannon, *The Land Boomers: The Complete Illustrated History* (Lloyd O'Neil, 1986) 18.

66 These figures are taken from R McQueen, 'Limited Liability Company Legislation—The Australian Experience' (1991) 1(1) *Australian Journal of Corporate Law* 22.

67 A Castles, *An Australian Legal History* (Law Book Co, 1982) 453.

68 Victorian legislation to encourage the mining industry is discussed in P Lipton, 'A History of Company Law in Colonial Australia: Economic Development and Legal Evolution' (2007) 31(3) *Melbourne University Law Review* 805.

69 See S Bottomley, 'The Corporate Form and Regulation: Associations Incorporation Legislation in Australia' in R Tomasic and R Lucas (eds), *Power, Regulation and Resistance: Studies in the Sociology of Law* (Canberra College of Advanced Education, 1986) 44.

70 See R McQueen, 'Limited Liability Company Legislation–The Australian Experience' (1991) 1(1) *Australian Journal of Corporate Law* 22, 25.

71 J Waugh, 'Company Law and the Crash of the 1890s in Victoria' (1992) 15(2) *University of New South Wales Law Journal* 356, 368.

company's directors) at a highly inflated price.[72] The legislation provided few mechanisms whereby potential investors might be able to discover the existence of the directors' interests.[73] There were no legislative requirements for companies to have their accounts audited, although it was common practice for audits to be conducted.[74]

The growth of speculative mining ventures led to the first instance in which colonial legislators departed from English precedent in companies legislation.[75] The absence of effective administration of the existing English-model legislation had led to a practice known as 'dummying', whereby investors would obtain partly-paid shares in a mining company under a false name. The aim was to avoid having to pay any further amounts owing on the shares if the company either made a later call on the shareholder or it was wound up. This practice was possible because of the administrative difficulties in maintaining the accuracy of share registers. Hoping to deter this practice and encourage investment in speculative mining ventures, Victoria introduced the *Companies (Mining) Act 1871* which permitted the incorporation of 'no-liability companies'. In effect, this legislation simply accepted the consequences of dummying by providing that shareholders who did not respond to a call from the company forfeited their shares without further liability to the company. Furthermore, if the company became insolvent, shareholders were not liable to the company's creditors for any amounts unpaid on their shares.

1.40.15 Early moves towards uniformity: 1890s–1930s

Following the economic crash in the 1890s, there was growing acceptance of the need for more direct governmental regulation of economic activity. As noted already, the depression involved the collapse of many companies. In 1893, for example, 13 banks were closed within a six-week period. Between 1891 and 1893, 54 banks (including 'land banks') were closed.[76] As is frequently the case, the collapses revealed evidence of fraud and malpractice. In Victoria:

> [t]he falsifying of balance sheets, the payment of dividends from non-existent profits, and the publication of misleadingly optimistic forecasts, were among the shocking features of the crash. Men who were widely known and trusted, who had been knighted by the Queen, who occupied the highest political and business positions, took leading parts in the manipulations.[77]

Although the effects of the crash differed across the country, during the 1890s all states revised their company law statutes.

72 T Sykes, *Two Centuries of Panic: A History of Corporate Collapses in Australia* (Allen & Unwin, 1988) 141.

73 J Waugh, 'Company Law and the Crash of the 1890s in Victoria' (1992) 15(2) *University of New South Wales Law Journal* 356, 371.

74 Ibid 377.

75 See the account in R McQueen, 'Limited Liability Company Legislation—The Australian Experience' (1991) 1(1) *Australian Journal of Corporate Law* 22; P Lipton, 'A History of Company Law in Colonial Australia: Economic Development and Legal Evolution' (2007) 31(3) *Melbourne University Law Review* 805.

76 T Sykes, *Two Centuries of Panic: A History of Corporate Collapses in Australia* (Allen & Unwin, 1988) 176.

77 M Cannon, *The Land Boomers: The Complete Illustrated History* (Lloyd O'Neil, 1986) 28.

In Victoria, where the land boom had been most pronounced, the magnitude of the depression and the associated corporate collapses focused attention on the need for a thorough reform of corporations legislation. The result was the *Companies Act 1896*. The inspiration for this Act came from many sources. Not surprisingly, existing English legislation was referred to, as well as legislation in New Zealand and Canada.[78] A further source was the recommendations of the Davey Committee in England. That Committee's 1895 report on joint stock companies was concerned principally with strengthening the accounting and audit requirements of the existing legislation.[79] Interestingly, although these aspects of the report were adopted immediately in Victoria, the response in England was much slower. It took nearly 25 years before all the recommendations were acted upon.

The new Victorian legislation introduced many features that are now standard in Australian corporate law. Companies were required to maintain proper books of account from which an annual balance sheet was to be prepared. The Act provided for compulsory annual audits of the balance sheet, with the audit to be lodged with the Registrar and provided to shareholders. Statutory duties were prescribed for directors and auditors[80] and there were new provisions dealing with the winding up of companies. The passage of this legislation through the Victorian Parliament was marked by fierce debate between politicians who saw the necessity of controlling fraud and those whose concern was to encourage business activity. On the one hand, the following statement from the Parliamentary Debates expressed a sentiment which continues to be influential:

> The blessings of associated capital are great ... but at the same time we cannot but recognise that in the name of legitimate enterprise are perpetrated most terrible frauds, bringing widespread ruin upon people.[81]

On the other hand, the conservatively controlled Victorian Legislative Council forced many changes to the original Bill. One of the most significant was the creation of a new category of company that was exempt from the new accounting and auditing provisions. This category, the proprietary company, was the equivalent of the English private company, although English legislation made no comparable provision until 1908. As originally defined, a proprietary company was limited to a maximum of 25 members and was required to add the words 'proprietary limited' to its name.[82]

The problems of adequate administration and enforcement continued under the new legislation.[83] The states allocated the task of corporate regulation to different branches

78 J Waugh, 'Company Law and the Crash of the 1890s in Victoria' (1992) 15(2) *University of New South Wales Law Journal* 356, 385–6.

79 Board of Trade, United Kingdom, *Report of the Departmental Committee Appointed by the Board of Trade to Inquire What Amendments Are Necessary in the Acts Relating to Stock Companies Incorporated with Limited Liability under the Companies Acts, 1862 to 1890* (C 779, 1895) ('the Davey Committee').

80 See Chapter 10 for a history of the law on directors' duties.

81 Victoria, *Parliamentary Debates*, Legislative Assembly, 30 June 1896, 123–4 (IA Isaacs).

82 *Companies Act 1896* (Vic) s 2.

83 See R McQueen, 'Limited Liability Company Legislation—The Australian Experience' (1991) 1(1) *Australian Journal of Corporate Law* 22, 37ff.

of their bureaucracies, resulting in noticeable variations in company regulation between the states. According to McQueen's research, the New South Wales Registrar-General's Department was strict in enforcing the provisions of the Act. One consequence of this was that the practice of dummying was not as prevalent in New South Wales, and this State did not follow the Victorian expedient of passing 'no liability' legislation.[84] The disparity in approaches to company law enforcement between the different states not only created confusion for business people, it also created opportunities for fraud. These factors resulted in a growing number of calls from the business community for a uniform scheme of corporations legislation and administration to apply nationally.[85]

The question of uniform legislation was debated during the Constitutional Conventions held between 1891 and 1897. McQueen identifies two competing concerns in this debate.[86] On the one hand, Sir Samuel Griffith supported uniformity between state legislation in order to reduce confusion in dealing with the large number of English-registered companies. On the other hand, the large number of company collapses in the 1890s depression gave added support to calls for national Commonwealth legislation. The significant differences of opinion on this issue are a reason for the resulting ambiguity in the wording of the Commonwealth's power over corporations, found in s 51(xx) of the *Australian Constitution*. Section 51(xx) provides that the Commonwealth Parliament shall have power to make laws with respect to foreign corporations, and trading or financial corporations formed within the limits of the Commonwealth.

This section has two possible interpretations, each having different implications for any attempt to introduce a national scheme of corporations legislation. One interpretation concludes that the Commonwealth is restricted to legislating with respect to corporations that are already incorporated, either overseas or in one of the states. This interpretation means that the Commonwealth Parliament has no power under s 51(xx) to incorporate companies, hampering the possibility of effective national corporations legislation. An alternative reading of the section contrasts the words 'formed within the limits of the Commonwealth' with 'foreign corporations', thereby giving the Commonwealth the capacity to legislate for company incorporations. As we will see later, the High Court has opted for the first of these interpretations.[87]

In the years immediately following Federation, the interest shown by the Commonwealth in achieving national corporations legislation encountered opposition from powerful interest groups. Commercial and professional bodies were suspicious of the Commonwealth's intentions, particularly in a political climate in which support for the new Labor Party and more interventionist economic regulation was growing.[88]

Those interest groups opposed to national legislation found support in the 1909 case of *Huddart, Parker & Co Ltd v Moorehead* ('*Huddart Parker*'),[89] the first occasion on

84 See the description of 'dummying' at Section 1.40.10 above.

85 R McQueen, *A Social History of Company Law: Great Britain and the Australian Colonies 1854–1920* (Ashgate, 2009) 310.

86 R McQueen, 'Why High Court Judges Make Poor Historians' (1990) 19(3) *Federal Law Review* 245, 251–5.

87 See Section 1.40.30 below, discussing *New South Wales v Commonwealth* (1990) 169 CLR 482.

88 R McQueen, 'Why High Court Judges Make Poor Historians' (1990) 19(3) *Federal Law Review* 245, 256–7.

89 *Huddart, Parker & Co Ltd v Moorehead* (1909) 8 CLR 330.

which the High Court examined s 51(xx). The case involved a challenge to provisions of a Commonwealth restrictive trade practices statute. While those provisions were held invalid by a majority of four to one, the Court was unanimous in its view that s 51(xx) confined the Commonwealth's legislative power to corporations that had already come into existence. This inability to legislate for the incorporation of companies proved to be an effective bar to entry by the Commonwealth into the field of corporate regulation for nearly a century.

Into the twentieth century, each state maintained and revised its own corporations legislation, together with its own system of companies administration. During the early 1930s, there was renewed discussion on the need for federal corporations legislation. Not surprisingly, this was thwarted by constitutional considerations and so attention turned towards the possibility of uniform legislation across the states. Even though this failed, the 1930s was a period of considerable activity in company law reform, with New South Wales, South Australia and Queensland each passing new Acts, largely based upon the *Companies Act 1929* (UK). It is worth noting that the category of proprietary company was introduced into New South Wales legislation at this time; Victorian legislation had made similar provision in 1896.[90] Inevitably, the different state Acts and administrative practices continued to diverge.

1.40.20 The first uniform legislation: 1950s–1980

The Australian economy entered a phase of relative prosperity during the 1950s following the Second World War. This economic growth highlighted the differences in state legislation and administration which made corporate activity on a national scale quite cumbersome; for example, there were different registration requirements in each state. Once more, support was expressed for the idea of all state corporations legislation being brought into line. In 1959, the State and the Commonwealth Attorneys-General met to devise a method of bringing uniformity to the legislation. The result was the *Uniform Companies Acts*, which, with various modifications, were adopted by all states and territories between 1961 and 1962. The *Uniform Companies Acts*, which became operative between July 1962 and July 1963, were based largely on the *Companies Act 1958* (Vic). Various other sources were consulted, including the *Model Business Corporation Act* from the United States; the 1945 report of the Cohen Committee on company law amendment in the United Kingdom;[91] and the report of a Commission of Inquiry on company law in Ghana prepared by leading UK company law academic, Professor Gower.[92]

The uniformity produced by this intergovernmental agreement in the early 1960s was tenuous. First, the changes to the legislation were not matched by administrative uniformity. The various uniform Acts continued to be administered by the different state bureaucracies, each of which exhibited different patterns in administrative practice and

90 *Companies Act 1936* (NSW).

91 Board of Trade, United Kingdom, *Report of the Committee on Company Law Amendment* (Report, 1945) ('the Cohen Committee').

92 Summarised in Otto Kahn-Freund, 'Final Report of the Commission of Inquiry into the Working and Administration of the Present Company Law of Ghana' (1962) 25(1) *Modern Law Review* 78.

quality. Second, the legislative uniformity was gradually eroded during the 1960s as different states began to amend their versions of the uniform corporations legislation in response to local developments in the companies and securities field.

The 1960s began with a number of spectacular corporate collapses and ended with a period of intense investment speculation associated with the nickel mining boom between 1968 and 1972. The company collapses occurred mainly in the retail and property development industries.[93] It may be that some of these collapses occurred because business people had not adjusted their management practices and skills to meet the relative prosperity of the 1950s and 1960s.[94] In other cases, the problems were caused by the desire to exploit that prosperity for fraudulent purposes. The Victorian Government appointed special investigators to report on three of the largest collapses involving the two retail groups headed by Reid Murray Holdings Ltd and Cox Brothers (Australia) Ltd, and the Stanley Korman property development and finance empire which operated in New South Wales and Victoria. The reports revealed instances of corporate behaviour and malpractice that have continued to occur in Australian corporate life.[95] Key factors included inactive or incompetent directors; self-interested senior managers who were able to control their boards; inadequate or apathetic supervision by auditors, debenture trustees and regulators; and the growing complexity of company structures.

The dramatic boom and crash in the mining industry at the end of the 1960s resulted in serious attention being paid to securities laws at both state and federal levels. The flurry of speculation in mineral securities attracted a large number of small and first-time investors who were spurred on by the flotation of a great number of public companies, many of them highly suspect. Most prominent in this speculation fever was a mining company called Poseidon NL, which became a household name in Australia for a short time between 1969 and 1970. The market value of shares in this company rose from below $1 in September 1969 to a high of $280 in February 1970. The magnitude of this jump, and the short period over which it occurred, gives some idea of the intensity of market activity at the time. In 1970, New South Wales, Victoria, Queensland and Western Australia each enacted uniform legislation to regulate the securities industry. The legislation provided for the licensing of investment advisers and stockbrokers, as well as prohibiting various improper practices in the share market. From the outset, there were significant differences between the Acts and once again the uniformity was illusory.[96]

In March of the same year, Labor Senator Lionel Murphy, later a judge of the High Court of Australia, succeeded in establishing a Senate Select Committee to examine the

93 A very readable account is found in T Sykes, *Two Centuries of Panic: A History of Corporate Collapses in Australia* (Allen & Unwin, 1988).

94 Ibid 296.

95 See, eg, Parliament of Victoria, *Final Report of an Investigation into the affairs of Reid Murray Holdings Ltd, Reid Murray Acceptance and Certain Other Companies* (Parliamentary Paper No C2, 1966–67); Parliament of Victoria, *Interim Report of an Investigation under Division 4 of Part VI of the Companies Act 1961 into the Affairs of Stanhill Development Finances Ltd and Other Companies* (Votes and Proceedings, 1964–65).

96 See comments in Senate Select Committee on Securities and Exchange, Parliament of Australia, *Australian Securities Markets and their Regulation* (Parliamentary Paper 98, 1974) 15.22 ('the Rae Report).

securities industry and the operations of the stock exchanges in the wake of the excesses of the mining boom. The Committee became known by the name of its chair, Senator Peter Rae, and its major term of reference was to 'inquire into and report upon the desirability and feasibility of establishing a securities and exchange commission by the Commonwealth'.[97] 'The Rae Committee' met between 1970 and 1974, producing three interim reports and a massive four-volume final report in 1974 ('the Rae Report'). In one estimation, the final report was:

> [T]he first (and only) major document in this country which analysed the workings of the securities market, which examined problems encountered by the regulators, both official and unofficial of that market during a time of extreme pressure and which posed solutions to those problems.[98]

The Rae Report recommended the creation of both national securities legislation and a national body to regulate the securities market, similar to the Securities and Exchange Commission in the United States. The Report argued that only a national regulatory body could 'eliminate the variation in administrative practice and standardise the quality of administrative action' in the securities industry.[99]

At the same time as the Rae Committee was conducting its hearings, the High Court and the federal government were each involved in other developments. Towards the end of 1971, in *Strickland v Rocla Concrete Pipes Ltd* ('*Concrete Pipes*')[100], the High Court held that the earlier decision in *Huddart Parker* should be overruled insofar as it relied on the now discredited reserved powers doctrine. Although the *Concrete Pipes* decision did not expressly deal with the power of the Commonwealth to incorporate companies under s 51(xx), the door was nevertheless open again for the federal government to push for national legislation.

Before the Rae Committee's final report was published, the federal Labor Government had prepared its own draft scheme for national legislation to regulate the securities industry and the public issuing of shares. The Corporations and Securities Industry Bill 1974 (Cth) drew on aspects of the existing state securities industry statutes as well as overseas legislation. The narrow focus of the Bill assumed that the states would continue to legislate for the creation of companies and their internal affairs. However, the Bill lapsed when the Whitlam Labor Government was dismissed in November 1975.

Coincidentally, with this attempt at federal securities legislation, the three states which were then controlled by Liberal–Country party coalition governments (New South Wales, Victoria and Queensland) entered into their own agreement to establish the Interstate Corporate Affairs Commission (ICAC) in 1974. Western Australia joined this agreement in 1975. The objectives of the ICAC were to promote greater uniformity in the companies and securities legislation and to establish common standards and coordination in administering the law. The ICAC was set up to achieve this. Each of these states

97 Ibid v.

98 R Baxt, C Maxwell and S Bajada, *Stock Markets and the Securities Industry* (Butterworths, 3rd ed, 1988) 13.

99 Senate Select Committee on Securities and Exchange, Parliament of Australia, *Australian Securities Markets and their Regulation* (Parliamentary Paper 98, 1974) 16.3.

100 *Strickland v Rocla Concrete Pipes Ltd* (1971) 124 CLR 468.

duly amended its 1961 *Uniform Companies Act* to produce uniform legislation. In addition, a uniform *Securities Industry Act* was drafted and passed in 1975 in each of the four ICAC states. The 1975 legislation was similar to the 1970 securities legislation, but this time with greater uniformity.

Meanwhile, in the federal arena, the newly elected Liberal–Country party coalition government was initiating its own attempts to produce uniform national legislation, but met strong opposition from the smaller states. Their concerns focused on their need to attract capital, by way of company registrations, and any federal interference was seen as an undue impediment.[101] Eventually, however, the state resistance was worn down. An agreement on a nationally uniform scheme was reached in 1978.

1.40.25 The co-operative scheme: 1980–90

The objectives of the co-operative scheme were to promote commercial certainty, reduce business costs, achieve greater efficiency in the capital markets, and maintain the confidence of investors through suitable measures for their protection. The goals were to be achieved through uniform legislation that would be administered uniformly by the different state corporate affairs bureaucracies.

Unlike previous attempts at uniformity, the co-operative scheme involved the Commonwealth government as well as the six state governments (and, from 1986, the Northern Territory). The basis of the arrangement between the eight governments was a Formal Agreement, signed in December 1978. Uniformity was achieved by an 'application of laws' mechanism. The Commonwealth passed the initial legislation in a form that was agreed upon by all states and the Northern Territory. Because of doubts about the Commonwealth's constitutional jurisdiction, this legislation was expressed to apply only in the Australian Capital Territory. Each state and the Northern Territory then agreed to pass legislation that applied the Australian Capital Territory legislation as a state or territory law. The scheme attempted a compromise between national legislation enacted by the Commonwealth, and uniform legislation enacted by the states, neither of which had met with success.

The main pieces of legislation in the scheme were the *Companies Act 1981* (Cth), dealing with general matters of incorporation, company affairs, and winding up; the *Companies (Acquisition of Shares) Act 1980* (Cth), dealing with takeovers; the *Securities Industry Act 1980* (Cth), which covered the securities industry and the stock market; the *Companies and Securities (Interpretation and Miscellaneous Provisions) Act 1980* (Cth); and, later, the *Futures Industry Act 1986* (Cth), which regulated the newly developed trading in futures contracts. For convenience, each Act became known as the *Companies Code*, the *Securities Industry Code* etc; while, in each state, the legislation was referred to as the *Companies [name of State] Code*.

The monitoring of the co-operative scheme and the regulation of the legislation involved three levels of administration, each with different responsibilities. At the top was the Ministerial Council for Companies and Securities, established by the Formal

101 A Sutton and R Wild, 'Companies, the Law and the Professions: A Sociological View of Australian Companies Legislation' in R Tomasic (ed), *Legislation and Society in Australia* (Allen & Unwin, 1979) 213.

Agreement. The Council was constituted by one minister (in practice, the Attorney-General) from each of the governments who were parties to the agreement. The Council's function was to review the formulation and operation of the legislation and its administration. Any amendments to the legislation required approval by the Ministerial Council.

At the next level was the National Companies and Securities Commission (NCSC). This was the first national body in Australia established to regulate the companies and securities area, and its creation owed much to the recommendations of the earlier Rae Report. It was established by the *National Companies and Securities Commission Act 1979* (Cth) and was responsible to the Ministerial Council for the general administration and development of policy in the co-operative scheme. The Formal Agreement required the NCSC, as far as possible, to decentralise its functions, via delegation to the already existing state and territory Corporate Affairs Commissions or Offices.

These state bodies formed the third level of administration, and were responsible for the day-to-day operation of the scheme. Under the scheme, these bodies were formally responsible to the NCSC for the way in which delegated power was carried out. The state bodies were bureaucracies funded and staffed by, and therefore subject to the will of, the different state and territory governments.

An important advantage of the co-operative scheme was that a company trading in more than one participating jurisdiction did not have to lodge documents in any place other than its jurisdiction of incorporation. The scheme removed the need for companies to register in jurisdictions outside of the home jurisdiction, and foreign companies needed only to register in one of the participating jurisdictions to enter the ambit of the scheme.

The viability of the scheme depended ultimately upon the willingness of the states to cooperate, and on the capacity of the NCSC to administer the legislation effectively. In 1987, the Senate Standing Committee on Constitutional and Legal Affairs published a report on the co-operative scheme which identified three problems.[102] First, there was no direct ministerial responsibility and accountability to federal parliament. The NCSC was responsible only to the Ministerial Council which was not responsible to any other person or body. Under the Formal Agreement, any legislative reforms were decided by the Ministerial Council and then put to federal parliament for enactment. Although federal parliament retained a right to reject or amend such proposals, this could act as a trigger for any dissenting state to withdraw from the scheme, thereby ending uniformity.

Second, the report criticised the administrative duplication and inefficiency in the co-operative scheme, which was administered by nine different bureaucracies (eight corporate affairs offices in the states and territories, and the NCSC). These bureaucracies were all funded and staffed by different governments. The administrative agencies exercised considerable discretion in policing the scheme, and there was evidence of different administrative and enforcement practices between the agencies. There was criticism of

102 Senate Standing Committee on Constitutional and Legal Affairs, Parliament of Australia, *The Role of Parliament in Relation to the National Companies Scheme* (Parliamentary Paper 113, 1987) ch 3.

chronic under-funding of the NCSC which limited its capacity to investigate and enforce the legislation.

The final problem with the co-operative scheme was that due to the ever-present threat of withdrawal by one of the states and the involvement of two levels of government, the scheme had an in-built tendency to produce 'lowest common denominator' decision-making. Reform proposals could be effectively vetoed by the threat that one state might withdraw from the scheme.

The Committee's report argued there was increasing support for the idea that the Commonwealth should take over responsibility for legislation and administration in the companies and securities field, and the report recommended that accordingly.

In September 1987, the Commonwealth Attorney-General announced that the Labor government would seek to assume full constitutional responsibility for companies and securities legislation in Australia. Apart from the Senate Committee's report, the Commonwealth's resolve was strengthened by public disquiet following the share market crash in October 1987 and the subsequent spate of corporate collapses. Once more, the process of corporate law reform received added impetus from an economic crisis. It is important to note that neither at this stage, nor at any of the preceding intergovernmental meetings, did the substance of the corporations legislation receive any serious review. For the most part, attention was restricted to the processes of creating and administering the law.[103]

The Commonwealth's plans were opposed by all states except New South Wales (then under a Labor government). The states announced that any Commonwealth legislation would be challenged in the High Court. After a period of intense lobbying and political manoeuvring, the Commonwealth passed the *Corporations Act 1989* (Cth) which covered all those areas of companies and securities previously dealt with by the *Companies Code, Companies (Acquisition of Shares) Code, Securities Industry Code,* and the *Futures Industry Code*. The *Corporations Act 1989* (Cth) was the principal component of a legislative package that included the *Australian Securities Commission Act 1989* (Cth), which sought to establish a new national regulatory body in place of the NCSC. Another significant part of the legislative package was the *Close Corporations Act 1989* (Cth), which provided for the incorporation of a wholly new form of corporation intended primarily for small business.

1.40.30 The *Corporations Act 1989* in the High Court

The legislation was passed in May 1989, although it was not proclaimed. One month later, four States—New South Wales (now with a Liberal–National party Government), Western Australia, South Australia and Queensland (which withdrew from the action four months later)—announced a High Court challenge to the legislation. The challenge focused on the constitutional power of the Commonwealth regarding incorporation under s 51(xx) of the *Constitution*. In February 1990, the High Court handed down its decision in *New South Wales v Commonwealth* ('the *Incorporation Case*'),[104] holding that the Commonwealth

103 See R McQueen, 'An Examination of Australian Corporate Law and Regulation 1901–1961' (1992) 15(1) *University of New South Wales Law Journal* 1.

104 *New South Wales v Commonwealth* (1990) 169 CLR 482.

Government had no power to legislate for the incorporation of trading and financial corporations. This decision continues to determine the way in which corporations legislation is structured and administered in Australia.

A majority of six judges (Deane J dissenting) delivered a single judgment which analysed s 51(xx) in terms of its grammatical construction, previous High Court decisions, and the history of the section.[105] As to the wording of the section, the majority view was that the phrase 'formed within the limits of the Commonwealth' refers to corporations that have already been or that shall have been created in Australia. The phrase does not give the Commonwealth the power to incorporate corporations. The majority's conclusion was that 'the power conferred by s 51(xx) to make laws with respect to artificial legal persons is not a power to bring into existence the artificial legal persons upon which the laws made under the power can operate'.[106] According to the majority, this construction is supported by precedent and history. The majority partially resurrected the *Huddart Parker* case, which had otherwise been overruled by the *Concrete Pipes* decision. While the *Concrete Pipes* case had rejected the use of the reserved powers doctrine in interpreting the section, the majority in the *Incorporation case* held that this 'rejection of the decision in *Huddart Parker* did not extend to the views expressed in that case concerning the power of the Commonwealth to provide for the creation of corporations'.[107] Reference was also made to the convention debates that preceded the final drafting of the *Constitution*. According to the majority, 'the history of the paragraph plainly indicates that the draftsmen of the provision did not contemplate that it should confer any power otherwise than in respect of corporations already formed'.[108]

A further factor referred to by the majority (but not used as a basis for its decision) was the complex set of requirements the Commonwealth had introduced in an attempt to secure a firm constitutional basis for the Act.[109] For example, each corporation was required to register an annual statement that it was wholly or substantially engaged in trading or financial activities. Cessation of either of these activities would result in the corporation being wound up.

Deane J, in the minority, analysed the wording, precedents, and history of s 51(xx). His Honour was highly critical of the 'unacceptably narrow and technical construction of those words' that had found favour with the majority.[110] In Deane J's opinion, to distinguish between the power to legislate in respect of corporations formed in Australia and the power to form those corporations makes as much sense as saying that 'a legislative power with respect to locally manufactured motor vehicles would not extend to laws governing the local manufacture of motor vehicles'.[111] His Honour was also critical of the majority's approach to *Huddart Parker*. Deane J argued that 'what was said

105 Recall that s 51(xx) gives the Commonwealth power to make laws with respect to 'Foreign corporations, and trading or financial corporations formed within the limits of the Commonwealth'.

106 *New South Wales v Commonwealth* (1990) 169 CLR 482, 498.

107 Ibid 500.

108 Ibid 502.

109 Ibid 503.

110 Ibid 512.

111 Ibid 505.

about incorporation in the majority judgments in *Huddart Parker* cannot properly be divorced from the reasoning which permeated them. The attempt to restore partial validity to those judgments must be rejected.'[112]

While the High Court's decision was limited to the question of incorporation under the *Corporations Act 1989*, it was recognised that as a result of the decision the entire Act, together with the parallel provisions in the *Close Corporations Act 1989*, had been rendered inoperative. The High Court's decision meant that, once more, a political agreement about corporate regulation had to be negotiated between the Commonwealth and state governments.

1.40.35 The national scheme: 1991–2001

The result of these negotiations was a new agreement reached in Alice Springs in June 1990 whereby the Commonwealth agreed with the states and the Northern Territory on a new national scheme of uniform companies and securities regulation to be based on the *Corporations Act 1989* and the *Australian Securities Commission Act 1989*. This national scheme of legislation and administration operated from January 1991 until June 2001 when it was replaced by the current 'referral of powers' scheme.

The national scheme relied on a more elaborate version of the application of laws mechanism that had underpinned the co-operative scheme in the 1980s. The first component of the national scheme was national uniform legislation. The Commonwealth agreed to amend the *Corporations Act 1989* in order to limit its application to the Australian Capital Territory. The states and the Northern Territory each passed their own legislation. These Acts (for example, the *Corporations (Western Australia) Act 1990* (WA)) applied the substantive and interpretive provisions of the *Corporations Act 1989* as the law of each state and Territory jurisdiction, thereby ensuring that the substantive law on corporations applied Australia-wide. Although the corporations legislation was state legislation, it was applied in each state (and the Northern Territory) as if it were Commonwealth legislation. Each state and Territory Act conferred power on Commonwealth authorities and officers to exercise powers within each state and the Northern Territory under Commonwealth laws relating to matters such as administrative review and criminal law.

The second component of the scheme was the uniform administration of the legislation. The main responsibility for this lay with the Australian Securities and Investments Commission (ASIC), which was the single regulatory body, directly accountable to the Commonwealth Attorney-General.[113]

The third component of the national scheme was a single court system to adjudicate matters arising under the scheme. This was achieved by the cross-vesting of jurisdiction between the state Supreme Courts and the Federal Court.

One of the curiosities of the national scheme was the structure of the corporations legislation. The *Corporations Act 1989* separated the machinery provisions (matters such as cross-vesting of judicial jurisdiction and the power to make regulations) from

112 Ibid 509.

113 The scheme also relied on other Commonwealth authorities, such as the Director of Public Prosecutions.

the substantive provisions of the law. The latter provisions were contained within the Corporations Law, which was located in s 82 of the *Corporations Act 1989*.

Once again, the constitutional validity of the national scheme was called into question by two decisions of the High Court in 1999 and 2000.

In June 1999, the cross-vesting arrangements in the scheme were held to be constitutionally invalid by the High Court in *Re Wakim; Ex parte McNally; Re Wakim; Ex parte Darvall; Re Brown; Ex parte Amann* ('*Re Wakim*').[114] A majority of six judges (Kirby J dissenting) held that those parts of the scheme that purported to vest state judicial power in the Federal Court were invalid because ss 75–7 of the *Constitution* do not permit state jurisdiction to be conferred on the Federal Court. As was noted above, the national scheme of corporate law was based upon state legislation over which, according to *Re Wakim*, the Federal Court could not be given jurisdiction. The majority judges acknowledged the policy behind the cross-vesting scheme but held it to be irrelevant to the interpretation of the *Constitution*. Early in his judgment, Gleeson CJ stated that:

> The cross-vesting legislation has been commended as an example of co-operation between the Parliaments of the Federation. Approval of legislative policy is irrelevant to a judgment as to constitutional validity; just as disapproval of the policy would be irrelevant.[115]

As a result of *Re Wakim*, up until the commencement of the current scheme in 2001, disputes under the corporations legislation had to be heard in the state Supreme Courts, although the Federal Court retained some limited jurisdiction.[116]

In May 2000, the High Court's decision in *R v Hughes* ('*Hughes*')[117] raised significant doubts about the validity of the second component of the national scheme—uniform administration. In a unanimous judgment, the Court held that the Commonwealth cannot authorise its officers or authorities to undertake functions or exercise powers conferred by a state law unless those functions or powers are supported by one or more of the heads of legislative power in the *Constitution*. In *Hughes*, the Court concluded that the Commonwealth Director of Public Prosecutions could exercise prosecutorial powers and functions conferred by the *Corporations (Western Australia) Act 1990* (WA) because the offences could be related to the Commonwealth's powers concerning external affairs and trade and commerce (*Constitution* ss 51(i), (xxix)).

In his judgment, Kirby J commented pointedly on the complex structure of the national scheme legislation:

> So complex is the interlocking legislation, with fiction piled upon fiction, that it must be doubted whether any of those presenting and enacting it were truly aware of precisely what they were doing. It may be hoped that this and other

114 *Re Wakim; Ex parte McNally* (1999) 198 CLR 511.

115 Ibid [2].

116 The Federal Court's jurisdiction applied mainly in relation to companies incorporated in the Australian Capital Territory or in the Northern Territory.

117 *R v Hughes* (2000) 202 CLR 535.

> recent decisions, together with the great national importance of the subject matter of the legislation, will encourage its early reconsideration and the adoption of a simpler constitutional foundation to reduce the perils that are otherwise bound to recur, possibly with serious results.[118]

As a result of *Hughes,* there were doubts about the capacity of ASIC and other Commonwealth authorities to regulate certain areas of state corporations legislation. In particular, given the High Court's earlier decision in the *Incorporation Case,*[119] there were significant doubts about the capacity of ASIC in relation to the incorporation of companies.

The decisions in *Re Wakim* and *Hughes* signalled the need for yet another revision of the structure of Australian corporate law and regulation, resulting in the current scheme.

1.45 The parameters of twenty-first century corporate law

Before we look at the current scheme of corporate law, it is worth pausing to emphasise the two main parameters of this area of law. Corporate law in Australia is only concerned with the legal relations between certain sets of actors. First, corporate law deals with the rights, interests, duties and liabilities of specific corporate 'insiders': the members of the company and its directors. The second parameter concerns relations between the company as a legal actor and certain 'outsiders': primarily creditors and others who enter into contracts with companies. Corporate regulators can also be thought of as significant outsiders. It should be remembered that corporate law is not concerned directly with the role of corporations as employers, taxpayers (or tax avoiders), or as economic or environmental actors. Whether this demarcation is defensible is a question that we raise in the next chapter of this book.

With these parameters in mind, we can now examine the legal scheme of modern Australian corporate law.

1.50 The current scheme

The principal enactments in the current national scheme are the *Corporations Act 2001* (Cth) and the *Australian Securities and Investments Commission Act 2001* (Cth) ('*ASIC Act*'). These Acts commenced operation on 15 July 2001 and were introduced in response to the High Court's decisions in the cases of *Re Wakim* and *Hughes.* As was noted in Section 1.40.35 above, the High Court in *Re Wakim* held that the arrangements in the pre-existing legislation for the cross-vesting of jurisdiction between state and federal courts were invalid. In *Hughes,* the Court called into question the capacity of Commonwealth officers and authorities to exercise certain powers and functions under the legislation. As a consequence, in December 2000, the Commonwealth, New South Wales and Victoria agreed that the states would pass legislation to refer the necessary powers to the Commonwealth to enable the Commonwealth to enact corporations

118 Ibid [60].

119 *New South Wales v Commonwealth* (1990) 169 CLR 482. See the discussion at Section 1.40.30.

legislation which would apply in the territories and in all participating states. The remaining states each introduced the necessary legislation in May and June 2001; this is described at Section 1.50.10, below.

1.50.05 The constitutional basis of the *Corporations Act 2001*

The *Corporations Act 2001* is Commonwealth legislation intended to apply in the territories and in those states that have agreed to refer power to the Commonwealth. The Act relies on three sources of Commonwealth power, set out in s 3:

(1) the Commonwealth's legislative powers in s 51 of the *Constitution*: these powers do not apply to the *Corporations Act* insofar as it deals with the registration of companies;

(2) the Commonwealth's power to legislate with regard to the territories, found in s 122 of the *Constitution*: this, together with the legislative powers in s 51, ensures that the legislation applies in the Australian Capital Territory and the Northern Territory;

(3) the legislative powers that are referred to the Commonwealth by the states under s 51(xxxvii) of the *Constitution*: these referrals are intended to supply the Commonwealth with the constitutional authority that it does not otherwise have because of the High Court's decisions in *New South Wales v Commonwealth* and other cases discussed earlier in this chapter.

The Commonwealth has the power to legislate with respect to matters that are incidental to the matters referred to the Commonwealth by the states (*Constitution* s 51(xxxix)). This means that existing Commonwealth legislation, such as the *Crimes Act 1914* and the *Evidence Act 1995*, applies to matters under the *Corporations Act*. The Commonwealth administrative laws also apply: the *Administrative Review Tribunal Act 2024*; the *Administrative Decisions (Judicial Review) Act 1977*; the *Freedom of Information Act 1982*; the *Ombudsman Act 1976*; and the *Privacy Act 1988*.

1.50.10 The referral of powers

The *Corporations Act* relies, in part, on a referral of power by the states. The referral of powers is effected by a state passing the necessary legislation; for example, the *Corporations (Commonwealth Powers) Act 2001* (NSW). This referral legislation is substantially the same in each referring state.

The basis of the agreement between the Commonwealth and the states was that the Commonwealth would initially restrict itself to enacting an agreed package of legislation based on the pre-existing Corporations Law and the *Australian Securities Commission Act 1989*. Thereafter, the Commonwealth would have power to amend that legislation, subject to agreed limitations.

This cautiously structured agreement requires each referring state to make two referrals of power, identified in ss 4(4)–(5) of the *Corporations Act*. The first is the 'initial reference'. This is a referral by a state of sufficient power to enable the Commonwealth to enact the initial *Corporations Act* and the *ASIC Act* (see s 4(4)). The second is the 'amendment reference'. This is a referral by a state of power to make express amendments to the initial legislation in relation to the formation of corporations, corporate regulation, and the regulation of financial products and services (see s 4(5)). A state that makes both of these referrals is described in the *Corporations Act* as a 'referring State' (s 4(1)).

Note that the amendment reference limits the Commonwealth to making 'express amendments'. This is defined to mean the direct amendment of the *Corporations Act* or the *ASIC Act* but does not include the enactment of a provision that has a substantive effect otherwise than as part of those Acts (s 4(9)). The purpose of this limitation is to prevent the Commonwealth from using the amendment power as an indirect method of legislating on other matters that fall outside the agreed scope of the referral. In particular, the state referral Acts expressly provide that they are not intended to enable the Commonwealth to use the amendment reference for the purpose or object of regulating industrial relations matters even if that would fall within a matter referred to the Commonwealth by the amendment reference.

The first exercise of power under the amendment reference was the enactment of the *Financial Services Reform Act 2001* (Cth) which repealed and replaced chs 7 and 8 of the *Corporations Act*. Under the agreement between the Commonwealth and the states, the initial reference and the amendment reference terminates five years after the commencement date of the *Corporations Act* unless the referring state agrees to fix a later date. Each referring state has since agreed to extend the referral of power for further periods. At the time this chapter was written, the latest agreement of an extension of the referral of power occurred in June 2021, with an expiry in July 2031.[120]

The scheme also contemplates the termination of one or both of a state's referrals before the end of a given five-year period. If a state's initial reference terminates, then that state ceases to be a referring state (s 4(6)). This means that the state no longer falls within the jurisdiction of the *Corporations Act*.

The current legislative scheme establishes a system of corporate legislation that is regulated and adjudicated on a national basis. However, the survival of the scheme depends upon continued political co-operation between the Commonwealth and the states. It is desirable that the scheme be given a more certain legal foundation. This could be achieved through a constitutional amendment pursuant to a referendum to give full responsibility for registering and regulating corporations.

1.50.15 The jurisdiction of the legislation

The *Corporations Act* uses the expression 'this jurisdiction' to define the geographical range of its coverage. That expression is defined in s 9 to mean each referring state plus the Australian Capital Territory and the Northern Territory. If each state makes and continues the relevant referrals, then 'this jurisdiction' consists of the whole of Australia (s 5(2)). The Act does not apply to a non-referring State unless that application is otherwise based upon some legislative power of the Commonwealth. The *ASIC Act* is also expressed to apply in 'this jurisdiction' (*ASIC Act* s 4). A company that is registered under

120 See, eg, in New South Wales, the *Corporations (Commonwealth Powers) Proclamation 2021* (NSW).

the *Corporations Act*[121] is incorporated in the jurisdiction covered by the Act (s 119A(1)). The company is also taken to be registered in the state or territory that is specified in the company's application for registration (s 119A(2)). The latter provision is necessary because of state laws (for example, stamp duties legislation) that impose obligations or rights on a company by reference to the state or territory of registration. If the state in which a company is registered ceases to be a referring State then the company continues to be registered under the Act, and the company can nominate another state or territory as the one in which it is taken to be registered (ss 119A(3)–(4)).

A company that was already in existence when the *Corporations Act* commenced is taken to be registered under the Act with the same attributes (s 1378). The company is taken to be registered in the state or territory in which it was registered immediately before the commencement of the Act.

1.55 Regulations and other delegated legislation under the *Corporations Act*

Many of the detailed regulatory requirements in the contemporary system of Australian corporate law are not found in the *Corporations Act* but in rules and regulations made under the authority of the Act. This includes the *Corporations Regulations 2001* (Cth) that are made under pt 9.12 of the Act (ss 1363–1369A). The main purpose of the *Corporations Regulations* is to give effect to the primary provisions in the Act, such as defining key terms, specifying procedures and forms, and prescribing various amounts, fines and penalties. However, the *Corporations Regulations* are not solely concerned with matters of 'machinery'. Increasingly, they have been used for more significant purposes, such as modifying the operation of sections in the Act or specifying exemptions from the operation of the Act. Such is the reliance on delegated legislation that, in some parts of the Act, the number of sections is greatly exceeded by the number of regulations.[122]

In addition to the *Corporations Regulations*, ASIC has power under the Act to issue legislative instruments (previously known as 'class orders') that omit, modify or vary the application of provisions in the Act generally, or in relation to a class of persons. Such instruments might be made in response to perceived gaps in the Act, or to unintended consequences of the operation of the legislation, or in anticipation of foreshadowed amendments to the Act or Regulations. Consequently, a particular provision in the *Corporations Act* can be comprised of the formal text in the legislation plus a set of modifications and amendments is found in the applicable legislative instruments.[123]

121 The registration of companies under the Act is discussed in Chapter 3 of this book.

122 See, eg, the Australian Law Reform Commission's analysis of Chapter 7 of the *Corporations Act*: Australian Law Reform Commission, *Interim Report B: Financial Services Legislation* (Report 139, September 2022).

123 S Bottomley, 'The Notional Legislator: The Australian Securities and Investments Commission's Role as a Law-Maker' (2011) 39(1) *Federal Law Review* 1. The Australian Law Reform Commission has expressed concern about the reliance on legislative instruments to make notional amendments to the *Corporations Act*; see Australian Law Reform Commission, *Confronting Complexity: Reforming Corporations and Financial Services Legislation* (Report 131, November 2023) [2.13]–[216].

Other sources of constraint that can affect corporate operations are found in:

- the operating rules made by licensed financial market operators (such as the Australian Securities Exchange) that govern the admission of companies and other entities to the official list of the exchange and the trading of securities on that market[124]
- accounting and auditing standards made by the Australian Accounting Standards Board and the Auditing and Assurance Standards Board.[125]

1.60 Administration and enforcement of the *Corporations Act*

A concern of corporate law reformers since the 1960s has been the desire for a uniform set of corporate rules that is applied and regulated nationally. Furthermore, disputes about the application of the legislation should be adjudicated within a single system. We now outline the role of the Australian Securities and Investments Commission (and related regulatory bodies), and the jurisdiction of courts under the *Corporations Act*.

1.60.05 The Australian Securities and Investments Commission

The Australian Securities and Investments Commission (ASIC) is the sole authority responsible for administering the *Corporations Act*.[126] The Commission is a body corporate established under s 8 of the *ASIC Act 2001* (Cth).

Some of the diverse regulatory philosophy which informs the work of ASIC can be found in s 1(2) of the *ASIC Act* which states that in performing its functions and exercising its powers ASIC must strive to:

(a) maintain, facilitate and improve the performance of the financial system and the entities within that system in the interests of commercial certainty, reducing business costs, and the efficiency and development of the economy; and
(b) promote the confident and informed participation of investors and consumers in the financial system; and
(c) [repealed]
(d) administer the laws that confer functions and powers on it effectively and with a minimum of procedural requirements; and
(e) receive, process and store, efficiently and quickly, the information given to ASIC under the laws that confer functions and powers on it; and

124 The content of the operating rules of a licensed market are prescribed by the *Corporations Regulations 2001* (Cth) reg 7.2.07.

125 Accounting standards are made pursuant to the *Corporations Act* s 334; auditing standards are made pursuant to s 336.

126 Alongside ASIC, other government agencies have a role in regulating aspects of corporate activity that lie outside the parameters of the *Corporations Act*, including the Australian Competition and Consumer Commission (regulating market competition, fair trading and consumer protection) and the Australian Prudential Regulation Authority (responsible for licensing of, and setting prudential standards for, banking, superannuation and insurance businesses). ASIC has entered into Memoranda of Understanding with these agencies, see Section 1.60.10.

(f) ensure that information is available as soon as practicable for access by the public; and
(g) take whatever action it can take, and is necessary, in order to enforce and give effect to the laws of the Commonwealth that confer functions and powers on it.

A careful reading of this list reveals a possible tension between the goals of investor protection, publicity and enforcement on the one hand, and facilitating company performance and promoting efficiency and commercial certainty on the other. This is an example of the debate between facilitation and intervention, discussed earlier at Section 1.10.

In relation to the *Corporations Act*, ASIC's functions include:

- the regulation and surveillance of public fundraising and the securities markets (including consideration of licence applications for market licensees)
- investigations under, and enforcement of, the Act (including exercising discretion to grant exemptions or other relief from the legislation)
- the collection and processing of information on companies (including registration of companies, lodgement of disclosure and takeover documents)
- advising the Minister (in practice, the Commonwealth Treasurer) on the practical operation of the Act and on proposals for law reform (*ASIC Act* s 11).

ASIC publishes a variety of regulatory material which has the purpose of publicly indicating ASIC's policies and practices in the exercise of its regulatory discretion. There has been public discussion about whether ASIC's functions under the Act are too broad for a single body to perform effectively. In July 2024, a report by the Senate Standing Committee on Economics recommended that the Commission's functions should be divided between a companies regulator and a financial conduct authority.[127]

ASIC is formally accountable and responsible to the relevant Commonwealth Minister, and to the Commonwealth Parliament. The Minister has the power to give ASIC directions about the policies it should pursue or the priorities it should follow in relation to the corporations legislation, and ASIC is required to comply with any such direction (s 12). The Minister may also direct ASIC to investigate alleged or suspected contraventions of the *Corporations Act*.

ASIC's overall effectiveness and capability is reviewed and assessed on a biennial basis by the Financial Regulator Assessment Authority (FRAA), an independent statutory body established in response to recommendations made by the Royal Commission into Misconduct in the Banking, Superannuation and Financial Services Industry in 2019.[128] The FRAA reports on the results of its assessments to the relevant Commonwealth Minister. The Minister may also request the FRAA to consider (or not consider) particular matters when conducting an assessment.[129]

127 Senate Standing Committee on Economics, Parliament of Australia, *Australian Securities Commission: Investigation and Enforcement* (Report, July 2024) [8.8].

128 The FRAA is established by the *Financial Regulator Assessment Authority Act 2021* (Cth), which also requires the Authority to conduct biennial reviews of the Australian Prudential Regulation Authority. See www.fraa.gov.au for more information.

129 *Financial Regulator Assessment Authority Act 2021* (Cth) s 13(2).

1.60.10 Other bodies under the *ASIC Act*

The *ASIC Act* creates a number of other bodies with specialised functions. These bodies operate in conjunction with, but independently of, ASIC's functions.

The Takeovers Panel

This is an unincorporated body under pt 10 of the *ASIC Act*. The Panel's functions regarding takeovers are specified in pt 6.10 div 2 of the *Corporations Act*. As discussed in Chapter 19, the Panel has the power to conduct hearings and make declarations and orders regarding unacceptable conduct in a takeover. The idea behind the Panel was that it operates as 'a peer review group body which would be able to come to quick decisions on matters relating to takeovers'.[130] The members of the Panel are required to have knowledge of, or experience in, business, company administration, financial markets, law, economics or accounting. Membership of the Panel is on a part-time basis.

The Companies Auditors Disciplinary Board

This Board falls under *ASIC Act* pt 11. Company auditors are required to be registered with ASIC under s 324BA of the *Corporations Act*. The role of the Disciplinary Board—an unincorporated body—is to determine, on an application by ASIC, whether the registration of an auditor should be cancelled or suspended (*Corporations Act* s 1292).

The Financial Reporting Council (FRC) and the Australian Accounting Standards Board (AASB)

Part 12 of the *ASIC Act* establishes three bodies: the Financial Reporting Council (FRC), the Australian Accounting Standards Board (AASB), and the Auditing and Assurance Standards Board (AUASB). The FRC is directly responsible to the Minister, who appoints members of the Council. The FRC was established to provide broad oversight of the process for setting accounting and auditing standards (s 225). The FRC appoints the members of the AASB and AUASB (other than the chairs) and oversees the operations of those Boards.

The Parliamentary Joint Committee on Corporations and Financial Services

Part 14 of the *ASIC Act* establishes the Parliamentary Joint Committee on Corporations and Financial Services. The duties of this Committee are to inquire into activities of the Commission and the Takeovers Panel, as well as the operation of the corporations legislation. The Committee has 10 members with equal representation from the Senate and the House of Representatives. The Committee is required to examine the annual reports produced by each of the bodies mentioned above. Further, either House of Parliament may refer questions to the Committee for inquiry and report.

130 Explanatory Memorandum, Corporations Legislation Amendment Bill 1994 (Cth) [278].

While the Committee does, from time to time, receive references to inquire into broader questions of corporate law reform,[131] much of its work is concerned with inquiries into Bills that are referred by Parliament.

Abolition of Corporations and Markets Advisory Committee

A close reading of the *ASIC Act* shows a gap between pt 8 and pt 10: pt 9 was repealed in 2018. This was due to the unfortunate decision of the federal coalition government in 2014 to defund the Corporations and Markets Advisory Committee (CAMAC), which had been created by pt 9. CAMAC's statutory function was to advise and make recommendations to the Minister on reforms to the corporations legislation and its administration, and on matters connected with companies or a segment of the financial products and financial services industry. Members of the Committee were appointed by the Minister on a part-time basis, based on their knowledge of, or experience in, business, company administration, the financial markets, law, economics or accounting. Throughout this book, reference will be made to the many reports produced by this Committee since its inception in 1989 when it was established under its previous name: the Companies and Securities Advisory Committee (CASAC).[132] The Commonwealth Treasury has now taken over the functions previously performed by CAMAC.

The abolition of CAMAC was unanticipated and widely opposed by legal and industry experts. The apparent rationale for this action was to achieve budgetary savings, even though at the time of its abolition CAMAC's operating budget was 'modest'.[133] In our view, there is a strong argument for the re-establishment of CAMAC, or a similar body, to provide independent and consultation-supported advice to government, drawing on a broad base of expertise, on matters of corporate law and governance, the regulation of financial markets, and insolvency. Such advice would be provided either in response to government request or at the initiative of the body.

In addition to those bodies set up by the *ASIC Act*, ASIC has established co-operative relationships with a number of international and Australian regulatory agencies. Memoranda of Understanding have been entered into with agencies such as the Australian Competition and Consumer Commission, the Australian Prudential Regulation Authority, the United States Securities Exchange Commission, the United Kingdom's Financial Services Authority, the Securities Commission of New Zealand, and the Australian Taxation Office. Responding to the global nature of modern corporate structures and finance, ASIC is also involved in the work of the International Organization of Securities Commissions (IOSCO).

131 See, eg, the 2008 inquiry into shareholder participation and engagement: Parliamentary Joint Committee on Corporations and Financial Services, Parliament of Australia, *Better Shareholders—Better Company: Shareholder Engagement and Participation in Australia* (Report, June 2008).

132 See Ian Ramsay, 'A History of the Corporations and Markets Advisory Committee and its Predecessors' in P Hanrahan and A Black (eds), *Contemporary Issues in Corporate and Competition Law: Essays in Honour of Professor Robert Baxt* (LexisNexis Butterworths, Australia, 2019) 56–72.

133 Law Council of Australia (Business Law Section), *Submission on the Exposure Draft of the Australian Securities and Investments Commission Amendment (Corporations and Markets Advisory Committee Abolition) Bill 2014* (Submission, October 2014).

The prosecution of offences under the corporations legislation is the joint responsibility of ASIC and the Commonwealth Director of Public Prosecutions (DPP). The relationship between these two bodies is governed by a Memorandum of Understanding signed in 2006. Under that agreement, if ASIC has gathered sufficient evidence to form a belief that an offence may have been committed, including indictable matters and offences involving fraud or dishonesty, it refers the matter to the DPP, which then decides whether charges should be laid. However, ASIC can prosecute minor regulatory offences where there is a guilty plea without referring the matter to the DPP.[134]

1.65 Jurisdiction of the courts

Part 9.6A of the *Corporations Act* specifies the scheme for the cross-vesting of civil and criminal jurisdictions regarding corporate law matters between state courts and the Federal and Family Courts. This is based on the cross-vesting scheme that operated before the High Court's decision in *Re Wakim*. The original rationale for the cross-vesting scheme is still relevant. As described by Kirby J, it provides a 'beneficial facility ... for the efficient use of hard-pressed resources and the reduction of inconvenience, delay and cost to litigants'.[135]

In summary, jurisdiction in civil matters arising under the *Corporations Act* and the *ASIC Act* is conferred on the Federal Court of Australia, the Family Court, the Supreme Court of each state and territory, each state Family Court, and (subject to the general jurisdictional limits relating to amounts or value of property) on the lower courts of each state and territory (*Corporations Act* ss 1337B, 1337C, 1337E). For these purposes, a 'civil matter' is defined broadly as any matter other than a criminal matter (s 9). Civil matters range from a simple action for recovery of a debt from a corporation to a complex application for a court order for the winding up of a company. The jurisdiction of the state and territory Supreme Courts also includes matters arising under the *Administrative Decisions (Judicial Review) Act 1977* (Cth) (hereafter '*AD(JR) Act* matters') involving or related to decisions made under the corporations legislation by Commonwealth authorities or officers (s 1337B(3)).

Section 1337G provides that all courts having jurisdiction in civil matters and *AD(JR) Act* matters under the corporations legislation must 'severally act in aid of, and be auxiliary to, each other in all those matters'.

The *Corporations Act* provides for the transfer of a civil matter (or an *AD(JR) Act* matter) commenced in one court to another as follows:

- Federal Court and Supreme Courts: if it appears to a court that, having regard to the interests of justice, it is more appropriate for a proceeding to be determined by another court that has jurisdiction in the matter, then the matter may be transferred to that other court (s 1337H). Limitations apply where the proceedings involve an *AD(JR) Act* matter.

134 Commonwealth Director of Public Prosecutions, *Annual Report 1999–2000* (Report, 2000) 17.
135 *Gould v Brown* (1998) 193 CLR 346, [274].

- Federal and state Family Courts: if a proceeding arises out of, or is related to another proceeding pending in the Federal Court or another state or territory court, then the matter may be transferred if that other court is the most appropriate to determine the proceeding (s 1317J(2)).
- Lower courts: if it is in the interests of justice to do so, a lower court can transfer a matter to another lower court, or to the Supreme Court in the same state as the local court. The transfer may recommend that the proceeding then be transferred to another court. The Supreme Court may decide to deal with the matter itself or to transfer the matter to some other court (this includes transferring the matter back to the lower court (s 1337K).

In addition, s 1317B of the *Corporations Act* gives the Administrative Review Tribunal the jurisdiction to review decisions made by the Minister, ASIC, or the Companies Auditors Disciplinary Board (subject to exclusions listed in s 1317C).

A proceeding or application in a civil matter may be transferred on the application of a party or on the court's own motion (s 1337M). When a court is deciding whether to transfer a proceeding, it must have regard to the principal place of business of any body corporate concerned in the matter, to the place where the events in question took place, and to the other courts that have jurisdiction to deal with the matter (s 1337L).

Jurisdiction in criminal matters can be summarised as follows: the courts of each state and territory that exercise jurisdiction in summary or indictable matters involving offences against state or territory laws have the equivalent jurisdiction with respect to offences under the *Corporations Act* or the *ASIC Act* (s 1338B).

1.65.05 The civil penalty regime

The *Corporations Act* contains an enforcement framework that sits between civil and criminal proceedings. It is known as the civil penalty regime and is found in pt 9.4B of the Act. This Part, which was introduced in 1993, applies to a number of sections throughout the *Corporations Act* that have been designated as civil penalty provisions (listed in s 1317E), including the directors' duty sections in ss 180–183.[136] The civil penalty regime allows ASIC to take enforcement action in response to contraventions of these designated sections. It brings the possibility of public regulation to bear on areas, such as directors' duties, 'that are commonly associated with private law'.[137]

The civil penalty regime was introduced as a consequence of recommendations made in the 1989 Report of the Senate Standing Committee of Legal and Constitutional Affairs. Those recommendations were prompted by a submission made to the Committee by Professor Brent Fisse.[138] Fisse's ideas were set out in his work with Professor John Braithwaite in their

136 Discussed in Chapter 10 of this book.

137 M Welsh 'Realising the Public Potential of Corporate Law: Twenty Years of Civil Penalty Enforcement in Australia' (2014) 42(1) *Federal Law Review* 217.

138 Senate Standing Committee on Legal and Constitutional Affairs, Parliament of Australia, *Company Directors' Duties: Report on the Social and Fiduciary Duties and Obligations of Company Directors* (Report, 1989) [13.11]–[13.15].

Figure 1.1 Example of corporate enforcement pyramid

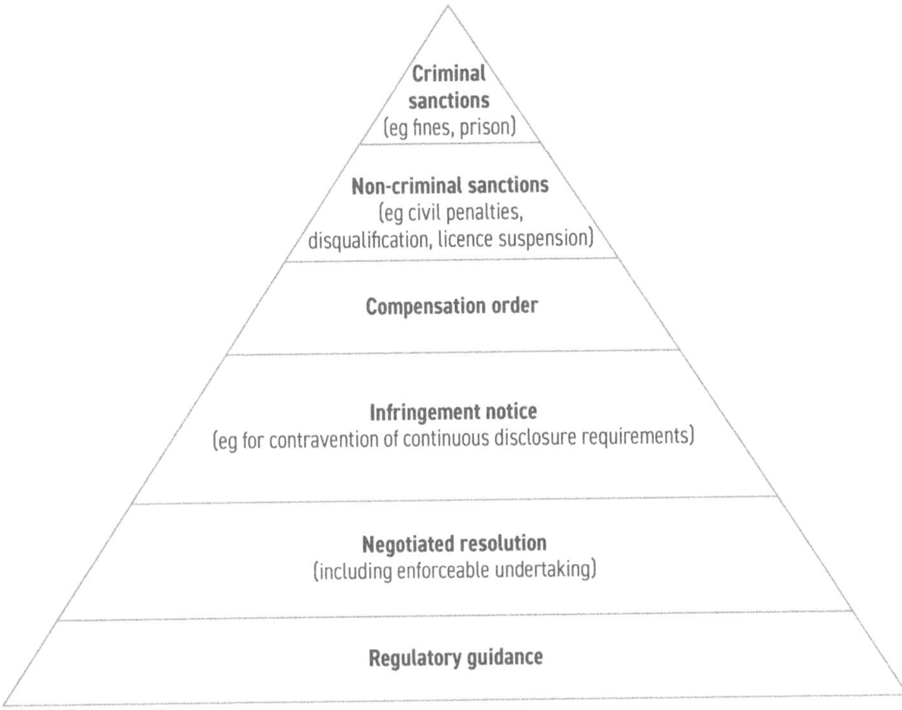

book *Corporations, Crime and Accountability*.[139] The authors argue that to achieve effective compliance with rules, a 'pyramidal enforcement' model is needed. Enforcement of legal rules by agencies such as ASIC should begin at the base of the pyramid with a broad range of informal methods. Only when compliance at this level is not effective does the enforcement escalate progressively up the pyramid. There are many ways of illustrating this idea; Figure 1.1 is one representation of a corporate enforcement pyramid:[140]

In theory, this enforcement strategy begins at the base of the pyramid with advice and warnings before moving up to administrative actions such as infringement notices and enforceable undertakings,[141] followed by civil penalties and criminal sanctions as the last resort. The shape of the pyramid indicates that the enforcement strategies at the apex will be less frequent; those at the base will be more commonly used.

The introduction of these ideas into the *Corporations Act* was prompted by two underlying beliefs. First, a system of corporate law enforced predominantly by criminal penalties had two adverse consequences: directors and other corporate actors could be discouraged

139 B Fisse and J Braithwaite, *Corporations, Crime and Accountability* (Cambridge University Press, 1993) 140–5. See also I Ayres and J Braithwaite, *Responsive Regulation: Transcending the Deregulation Debate* (Oxford University Press, 1992).

140 Note that this diagram does not attempt to include every enforcement action available to ASIC. See generally Senate Economic References Committee, Parliament of Australia, *Performance of the Australian Securities and Investments Commission* (Report, June 2014) ch 4.

141 See s 1317DAC and *ASIC Act 2001* ss 12GX–GXH for the issue of infringement notices; and *ASIC Act 2001* ss 93A and 93AA for enforceable undertakings. See also Sections 17.20.10 and 17.40.05.

from legitimate risk-taking by the threat of criminal sanctions; and the stigma of criminal liability could attach to minor or procedural misbehaviour (for example, a failure to comply with the detail of annual directors' reporting requirements in s 299) rather than being limited to serious criminal behaviour. Second, the enforcement pyramid works on the basis that 'actors, individual or corporate, are most likely to comply if they know that enforcement is backed by sanctions which can be escalated in response to any given level of non-compliance'.[142]

The practical implementation of this regulatory model has drawn some criticism. ASIC's enforcement practices were scrutinised by the Royal Commission into Misconduct in the Banking, Superannuation and Financial Services Industry. In its Final Report, the Commission observed that:

> The regulatory pyramid ... reflects two very practical observations: not all contraventions of law are of equal significance; and regulators do not have unlimited time or resources. But it is wholly consistent with the analyses that are expressed by the metaphor of the regulatory pyramid, that serious breaches of law by large entities call for the highest level of regulatory response. And that is what has been missing. Too often serious breaches of law by large entities have yielded nothing more than a few infringement notices, an enforceable undertaking ... not to offend again (with or without an immaterial 'public benefit payment') or some agreed form of media release.[143]

Having looked at the policy context, we now turn to the details of the civil penalty regime which, in Figure 1.1, sits in the upper part of the enforcement pyramid. Note that in the context of contraventions of the directors' duties provisions, additional sections can also come into operation.[144]

If there is a contravention of a civil penalty provision, there are two possible consequences. The first consequence is that ASIC may apply to the court for a declaration of contravention (s 1317J(1)). The court must make the declaration if it is satisfied there has been a contravention of the relevant section (s 1317E). Once a declaration of contravention has been made ASIC can then apply for a range of orders. These are discussed in detail in Chapter 10 of this book in the context of directors' duties and the reader is directed to that discussion (see Section 10.35.10). In summary, the possible orders are:

(1) A pecuniary penalty order (s 1317G). This is an order to pay a financial penalty, which becomes a debt payable to ASIC (s 1317GAA). The penalty amounts are significant and are part of a broader strategy 'to combat misconduct and improve community confidence in the corporate and financial sector'.[145] For an individual

142 B Fisse and J Braithwaite, *Corporations, Crime and Accountability* (Cambridge University Press, 1993) 140–3.

143 *Royal Commission into Misconduct in the Banking, Superannuation and Financial Services Industry* (Final Report, 2019) vol 1, 433. An enforceable undertaking is an administrative settlement used by ASIC as an alternative to civil court action: *ASIC Act 2001* (Cth) s 93AA.

144 For example, a disqualification order under s 206C. The application of the civil penalties to the directors' duties sections (ss 180–83) is discussed in detail in Chapter 10 at Section 10.35.10.

145 Explanatory Memorandum, Treasury Laws Amendment (Strengthening Corporate and Financial Sector Penalties) Bill 2018 (Cth) 1.12.

the amount is the greater of 5000 penalty units;[146] or if the court can determine the benefit derived and detriment avoided because of the contravention, three times that amount (s 1317G(3)). For a body corporate, the amount is the greater of 50,000 penalty units, or three times the benefit derived and detriment avoided (if that can be determined), or 10 per cent of the annual turnover of the body corporate in the 12 months preceding the contravention, capped at the equivalent of 2.5 million penalty units.

(2) A relinquishment order (s 1317GAB). This is an order to pay to the Commonwealth an amount equal to the benefit derived and detriment avoided because of a contravention of a civil penalty provision. The court can make a relinquishment order even if a pecuniary penalty order has been made (s 1317GAB(3)).
(3) A disqualification order (s 206C). This is an order disqualifying a person from managing corporations for a period that is determined by the court to be appropriate.

The second possible consequence is a compensation order (ss 1317H, HA). This may be sought by ASIC or by the company (ss 1317J(1), (2)). The person who has contravened the Act may be ordered to compensate the company for damage it has suffered if the damage has resulted from the contravention. Note that a compensation order does not require that there has been a declaration of contravention.

Notwithstanding the idea of graduated enforcement that underlies the pyramid model, criminal proceedings can apply. This will occur where a section expressly provides for a criminal offence (see, for example, s 184 regarding directors' duties and s 1043A regarding insider trading)[147]. As explained in *Australian Securities and Investments Commission v Whitebox Trading Pty Ltd*, even though a civil penalty provision does not itself create a criminal offence, a person who contravenes such a provision may be guilty of an offence by virtue of s 1311(1).[148] That section makes it an offence for a person to do something that is forbidden by a provision in the Act, or to fail to do something the person is required to do.[149] If the person is convicted of the offence they cannot then be subject to a declaration of contravention or a pecuniary penalty order for the same conduct (s 1317M).

Further, assuming that there is an applicable offence provision, criminal proceedings may commence for conduct that is substantially the same as conduct constituting the contravention of a civil penalty provision even if a declaration of contravention or a pecuniary penalty order or a compensation order or a disqualification order has been made (s 1317P).

1.70 Interpretation of the *Corporations Act*

The remainder of this book will be primarily concerned with the substantive provisions of the *Corporations Act*, together with relevant case law. This chapter has demonstrated that the current Act is an amalgamation of over a century of ideas about the nature of corporate activity and how it should be regulated. It is necessary, then, to consider the formalities and some practicalities of how the Act is interpreted.

146 The value of a penalty unit is currently set at $210 (*Crimes Act 1914* (Cth) s 4AA).
147 Discussed in Chapter 10 at Section 10.35.15, and Chapter 17 at Section 17.30 respectively.
148 *Australian Securities and Investments Commission v Whitebox Trading Pty Ltd* (2017) 251 FCR 448.
149 Subsection 1311(1A) has the effect of excluding a range of provisions from the operation of s 1311.

1.70.05 The interpretation provisions

Section 7 of the *Corporations Act* notes that the 'dictionary' in s 9 of the Act defines most of the terms used in the Act, but also notes that interpretation provisions that relevant to a single section maybe found in that section.

The *Acts Interpretation Act 1901* (Cth) applies to the *Corporations Act* and the *ASIC Act*. Of particular importance are ss 15AA–AD of the *Acts Interpretation Act*. The intention of these sections is to encourage a purposive and policy- oriented approach to statutory interpretation. In the context of the corporations legislation, these sections emphasise the need to determine the underlying purpose or object of the provisions in the *Corporations Act*. Section 15AA of the *Acts Interpretation Act* states that:

> In interpreting a provision of an Act, the interpretation that would achieve the purpose or object of the Act (whether or not that purpose or object is expressly stated in the Act) is to be preferred to each other interpretation.

By virtue of s 15AB, in determining the meaning of a provision in the *Corporations Act*, material outside the text of the legislation may be relied on to confirm the ordinary meaning of a provision, taking its context and policy into account, or to clarify ambiguities, obscurities or absurdities in drafting. Section 15AB(2) contains a detailed, but non-exhaustive, list of such material. The list includes explanatory memoranda[150] relating to the Bill that introduced the particular provision, and parliamentary second reading speeches. The list in s 15AB(2) also refers to reports of Royal Commissions, Parliamentary Committees and other committees of inquiry. Any such report must have been put before either House of Parliament before the time at which the particular provision was enacted.

1.70.10 Interpretation: issues and debates

The interpretation of complex and ever-changing legislation that has a direct impact on business and society, such as the *Corporations Act*, raises a number of issues. Here we note three of them: the relevance of ASIC statements about the interpretation of the Act, the complexity of the legislation, and the impact of the general law on the interpretation of the legislation.

ASIC's interpretation of the Act

The non-exhaustive list of extra-statutory material in s 15AB(2) of the *Acts Interpretation Act* does not make express reference to the regulatory guides published by ASIC. Regulatory guides are formal statements by the Commission about how it will exercise specific powers under the *Corporations Act* and how it interprets the law it administers. Those who are affected by the legislation should expect that ASIC will publicise its policies about how it intends to apply those rules so that they can appropriately plan their actions.[151]

150 Unfortunately, in many instances, explanatory memoranda merely paraphrase the provisions in the proposed legislation, providing little useful information about government policy.

151 Sir Anthony Mason, 'Corporate Law: The Challenge of Complexity' (1992) 2(1) *Australian Journal of Corporate Law* 1, 4.

Should these statements be taken into account by the courts in interpreting the statute? An answer to this question was indicated in *Bond Corporation Holdings Ltd v Grace Brothers Holdings Ltd*, where Sheppard J stated that while regulatory guides 'are proper to be considered', they cannot bind a judge in the task of interpreting an Act: '[n]othing done by an officer of the executive government can control the construction of an Act of Parliament unless the Parliament itself has said so'.[152] The opinions and interpretations of an administrative agency can provide guidance to a court but, as High Court Chief Justice Gageler has written, s 15AB does 'not result in extrinsic material being substituted for the words of the statute'.[153]

Complexity of the legislation

Partly because of its history, the *Corporations Act* contains a mixture of drafting styles. Some provisions are worded in an open-textured manner that lay down broad principles, allowing courts and regulators the opportunity to exercise interpretative discretion. Other provisions are lengthy, detailed and technical, attempting to deal with a particular issue in precise terms and to minimise the scope for regulatory or judicial discretion. In some instances, this might be because Parliament has attempted to 'cover the field' of a particular problem. Another reason is that the legislation simply reflects the complexity of modern corporate and commercial transactions.[154]

Inevitably, this complexity has attracted criticism. Sir Anthony Mason has remarked that too much legislative detail 'can obscure the identification of policy goals and guidelines, reducing the role of the courts to an application of the statutory language which, on its own, does not always make much economic, social or practical sense'.[155]

One response to this complexity was the Corporations Law Simplification Task Force, established in 1993 by the Commonwealth Attorney-General, an aim of which was to make the *Corporations Act* more 'accessible' to people affected by its provisions but who lack professional skills in the use of legislation. One manifestation of this 'user-friendly' approach was the insertion of a Small Business Guide into the body of the legislation. Found in pt 1.5, the guide summarises the main rules in the Act that apply to proprietary companies limited by share capital. The Task Force was discontinued in March 1997. More recently, the Australian Law Reform Commission recommended sweeping changes to the design and structure of ch 7 of the Act, dealing with financial services and markets, to address the 'legislative maze'.[156] If accepted, those recommendations will have implications for the design of the remainder of the Act.

152 *Bond Corporation Holdings Ltd v Grace Brothers Holdings Ltd* (1983) 1 ACLC 1009, 1030. See also *Commissioner of Taxation v Consolidated Media Holdings Ltd* (2012) 250 CLR 503 holding that extrinsic materials cannot displace the clear meaning of the text.

153 S Gageler, 'Legislative Intention' (2015) 41(1) *Monash Law Review* 1, 7. See also S Gageler, 'Deference' (2015) 22(3) *Australian Journal of Administrative Law* 151.

154 See I Ramsay, 'Corporate Law in the Age of Statutes' (1992) 14(4) *Sydney Law Review* 474.

155 Sir Anthony Mason, 'Corporate Law: The Challenge of Complexity' (1992) 2(1) *Australian Journal of Corporate Law* 1, 1–2. See also Stephen Bottomley, 'The Complexity of Corporate Law' (2022) 44(3) *Sydney Law Review* 415.

156 Australian Law Reform Commission, *Confronting Complexity: Reforming Corporations and Financial Services Legislation* (Report 141, November 2023) 59.

This debate about the form of legislation is long-standing in modern liberal legal systems. The tension arises because liberal political philosophy requires, on the one hand, that laws should be specific and predictable so that individuals can plan their transactions within the framework of the law. This demands precision and detail in legislative drafting. On the other hand, laws should also be capable of general application, in a manner that is consistent with the purpose underlying the rule. This demands that rules be drafted so that they apply equally to all relevant classes of person affected, while allowing for individual exceptions. The *Corporations Act* continues to contain examples of both types of drafting.

The impact of general law

This chapter has focused on the statutory development of corporate law in Australia, but common law and equity ('general law') also continue to play a major role in corporate law and the application of the *Corporations Act*. The relationship between the general law and the Act varies from one corporate law topic to another. Being aware of this variability is an important step in learning about modern Australian corporate law.

The general law and the *Corporations Act* can interact in one of three ways:

1. The Act expressly replaces the pre-existing general law: an example is found in pt 2F.1A, dealing with shareholder derivative actions, where s 236(3) abolishes the right to bring such an action at general law. This is covered in Chapter 14 at Section 14.35.
2. The Act draws on, perhaps with some modification, general law rules: examples are found in ss 128–9, setting out the assumptions that a person who has dealings with a company is entitled to make. This is dealt with in Chapter 6 on corporate contracting. These assumptions can be understood by reference to an established body of case law. The question confronting the courts in this situation is the extent to which the legislators intended to depart from the general law: to what extent should the general law principles constrain the interpretation of the statute?
3. The Act and the general law operate side by side: the prime example of this is found in pt 2D.1, dealing with the duties of company directors and officers. These sections, which are enforceable by ASIC, operate alongside general law doctrines on directors' duties, which (depending on the circumstances) provide a cause of action for a company or its shareholders. The law on directors' duties (statutory and general law) is dealt with in Chapters 10–13. The question here is: to what extent should the general law principles influence the interpretation of the sections?

1.75 Amending the corporations legislation

Amendments to the *Corporations Act* and the *ASIC Act*, as Commonwealth legislation, must pass through the usual processes in both Houses of the federal Parliament. However, the Commonwealth does not have a free hand in deciding amendments. First, the Commonwealth's power to amend is limited by the amendment reference from the states, which is defined in terms of express amendments. Second, the current scheme of corporations legislation is based upon an intergovernmental agreement between the states, territories and Commonwealth. A key part of that agreement deals with the processes by which the legislation may be amended. The agreement contains a mechanism for state involvement in the law reform process, via the Legislative and Governance Forum for Corporations (previously called the Ministerial Council for Corporations). The Forum consists of one Minister from each state, the Northern Territory, and the Commonwealth, and is chaired by the Commonwealth Minister.

The agreement requires the Commonwealth to use its best endeavours to ensure there is consultation and voting on legislative amendments. Further, the Commonwealth is required to refrain from moving amendments that lie outside the scope of the reference from the states. The states are required to obtain a vote from the Forum regarding any amendment to a state/territory law that would significantly override the *Corporations Act*. The Commonwealth must obtain the approval of at least three states before making an amendment to the legislation in areas where approval of the Forum is required.

The prime responsibility for legislative policy in relation to the legislation lies with the Commonwealth Department of the Treasury. Before 1996, the Department of Attorney-General had responsibility for corporate law and policy. The shift to Treasury suggests that corporate law reform is regarded as an aspect of economic policy and corporate regulation is seen as business regulation. A wider view would recognise that corporate activity has long ceased to be exclusively associated with private business activity, and that the corporate form of organisation now permeates all aspects of Australian society including government, welfare and social services, and family financial planning.

1.80 A global model of corporate law?

It is appropriate at the end of this chapter to consider some wider aspects of corporate regulation. Australian corporate law is the product of many influences, including its British antecedents, the history of Australian federalism, and shifting economic and political philosophies about the acceptability of governmental involvement in corporate and business affairs. This reminds us that our contemporary system of corporate law and regulation does not operate in a vacuum. It is shaped and affected by wider legal, political and economic contexts. It increasingly operates in a global context. This has led some legal scholars to reflect on whether there are discernible patterns and developments in global corporate law and regulation. One influential argument in recent years is that, despite some minor differences in patterns of share ownership, capital market structures and business culture, corporate law systems around the world are converging on the Anglo-US (and Australian) model of corporate law and governance that gives priority to the interests of shareholders over other stakeholders.[157] In this view, corporate law has evolved to the point where the shareholder-centered model dominates other contenders, including the stakeholder model that tends to be favoured by proponents of corporate social responsibility and ethical capitalism.

This 'convergence thesis' has been criticised because, while at a distance there are similarities in the corporate law systems of countries such as Australia, the United

157 This argument is usually attributed to H Hansmann and R Kraakman, 'The End of History for Corporate Law' (2001) 89(2) *Georgetown Law Journal* 439.

Kingdom and the United States, on closer inspection the differences are significant. American corporate law scholar Christopher Bruner summarises the position:

> [G]eneralizations regarding the so-called Anglo-American, Anglo-Saxon, or common-law corporate governance model obscure more than they illuminate. Australia, Canada, the United Kingdom, and the United States do exhibit substantial similarities in their business cultures, financial structures, and legal traditions, yet they nevertheless diverge markedly in terms of the degree of governance power granted to shareholders and the degree to which corporate (or company) law in a given country prioritizes the shareholders' interests.[158]

The main problem with the convergence argument is that it disregards the important role played by local legal, regulatory, political, economic and social conditions in shaping corporate practices and the way they are regulated. Another difficulty is the notion that corporate law 'evolves' in a regular or linear series of steps, each improving on what has come before. The historical summary presented in this chapter shows, to the contrary, that Australian corporations legislation has developed in an uneven way, as governments and pressure groups have responded to problems, usually in periods of significant economic crisis.[159] We will discuss the convergence thesis again in the next chapter at Section 2.50.

These debates about the shape and purpose of corporate regulation serve as a prelude to the next chapter of this book in which we consider broader theoretical perspectives on the corporation as a social, economic and political actor.

1.85 Summary

This chapter began by identifying four perennial questions or tensions that permeate the history, and current development, of corporate law: how to balance the rights and obligations of the group with those of the individuals who comprise that group; how to ensure the accountability of those who manage a corporation to those who are notionally its owners; whether the role of the law is simply to facilitate the creation and efficient operation of corporations, or whether it should have a regulatory or interventionist role; and whether corporations are essentially private structures or also have public responsibilities. These questions overlap; the answer to one will be shaped by the answer to another.

By explaining the history and current structure of our corporate law, this chapter has shown that there is no single 'right' or 'permanent' answer to any of these questions. Over time, the answers have oscillated in response to shifting economic, political, social and, more recently, environmental factors. This chapter has charted the historical origins of contemporary Australian corporate legislation, commencing with the situation in England in the seventeenth century. In considering early English history, we saw that the core features of the modern corporation and corporate law—the joint stock idea, limited

158 CM Bruner, *Corporate Governance in the Common-Law World: The Political Foundations of Shareholder Power* (Cambridge University Press, 2014) 287.

159 See M Welsh, P Spender, I Lynch Fannon and K Hall, 'The End of the "End of History for Corporate Law"?' (2014) 29(2) *Australian Journal of Corporate Law* 147.

liability of members, incorporation by registration, public disclosure of company financial information—were developed at different times, rather than in a single legislative package, and arose in response to the demands of the economy and commercial practice at different historical junctures.

This chapter demonstrated how development of corporate law, although based on the English framework, responded to local economic imperatives (the creation of the 'no liability' mining company being a prime example). Australian corporate law has also had to contend with the politics of a federal system of government. This chapter illustrated that there have been several attempts to achieve a uniform system of corporations legislation that is administered and adjudicated on a uniform basis. This chapter explained the structure of the current 'referral of powers' scheme, including the role of the Australian Securities and Investments Commission and the jurisdiction of the courts in dealing with corporate law matters. Issues in the interpretation of the *Corporations Act* were also examined.

Finally, this chapter briefly considered recent arguments about the development of corporate law on a global scale, emphasising the continued importance of local legal, regulatory, political, economic and social conditions.

As a final point, despite many years of legislative reform to different parts of the *Corporations Act,* Australian corporate law reformers have not recently undertaken a thorough review of the models and assumptions that might guide future regulation in the corporations and securities area, as has been done in countries such as New Zealand and the United Kingdom. The processes of Australian corporate law reform have tended to be more piecemeal. Any such review would require consideration of the underlying philosophy of a contemporary corporate law system, and in the next chapter we outline the main theoretical perspectives to be considered.

CHAPTER

2

CORPORATE LAW THEORY AND DEBATES

2.05 Introduction: the importance of corporate theory

We began Chapter 1 by emphasising the need to be aware of the different contexts within which corporations and corporate law are created and operate. We considered the historical and regulatory contexts of contemporary Australian corporate law. This chapter considers the importance of the different theoretical and ideological perspectives that assist in understanding the nature of the corporation, the role and purpose of corporations in contemporary society, and the rationales for and against the regulation of corporate activity.

Corporate lawyers talk frequently about 'the corporation', or 'the company', but often do not pause to think about or explain the meaning of the term.[1] For example, directors owe duties to 'the corporation', but there are competing judicial opinions about who is to be included within this category. The corporation is often referred to as a legal entity which is capable of exercising its own legal rights. This includes the right to own property (for example, real estate, plant and machinery), to create property (for example, shares, debentures and other securities) and to initiate legal actions on its own behalf. On other occasions, the corporation is referred to as though it were an item of property—something that can be owned and controlled, bought and sold (for example, in a takeover bid). This dual role as both owner or creator of property and item of property is one of the distinguishing—and confusing—aspects of corporate law.[2]

Each of these uses of the term 'the corporation' relies on some concept of what the corporation is. The way in which lawyers, judges, regulators, politicians, economists and corporate insiders talk about corporations, corporate law, and corporate activity reflects a wide range of ideas and assumptions about the nature, role and purposes of the corporation and the degree to which, and the manner in which, corporate activity should or should not be regulated. These ideas are drawn from a variety of conceptual frameworks or theories that have had prominence at different times. However, all of these theories continue to exert some degree of influence on modern corporate law. The theories behind legislative changes or judicial decisions in the twenty-first century still have to contend with the theories or ideas that prompted legal developments over a century ago.

One difficulty in discussing corporate theory is that theories are not always expressly acknowledged or explained; they tend to remain submerged beneath the text of the statute or judicial decisions. Nevertheless, lawyers, legislators and judges rely implicitly upon these different theories whenever they prefer one decision over another, argue for one interpretation of a section over another, resolve an ambiguity in legal principle one way rather than another, or urge one type of legal reform rather than another (or opt for no reform at all).

1 In this chapter, we will use the terms 'corporation' and 'company' interchangeably. Note that in strict legal terms, the 'company' is a subset of the broader class of entities called 'corporations'. This is explained in detail in Chapter 4.

2 Jeffrey Nesteruk, 'Legal Persons and Moral Worlds: Ethical Choices within the Corporate Environment' (1991) 29(1) *American Business Law Journal* 75.

In this chapter, we discuss a range of perspectives that fall under the umbrella term 'corporate theory'. Taken together these theories address three questions:

(1) What is the corporation, and from where does it gain its political and social legitimacy?
(2) What is the purpose of the corporation, and whose interests should it serve?
(3) How, if at all, should the exercise of power by—and within—corporations be regulated, and by whom?

These are interrelated questions and some theories help to answer more than one of them. Each theory also says something about one or other of the four perennial issues introduced in Chapter 1: the tensions between group versus individual; management versus ownership; facilitation versus intervention; and public versus private.[3] Thinking about corporations and corporate law, whether it be through one of the approaches described in this chapter or some other perspective, means making a choice about the range of values represented in each of these distinctions. As one writer has emphasised:

> To subscribe to a particular theory of the corporation ... often reflects a particular political attitude about corporate activity and correspondingly implies that corporations should be treated in a certain way.[4]

This chapter surveys the main examples of corporate theory. While each author of this book has their own theoretical preference, we try to put our views on hold and invite the reader to consider their own position.[5]

2.10 Concession theory

Stated simply, concession theory[6] treats the corporation as an artificial entity created by the state: corporations exist 'only because governments say so'.[7] From this perspective, the status of the company as a legal actor, distinct from its members or directors, is regarded as a concession (or privilege) granted by the state. There are different versions of this theory; we can call them the 'strong' and 'mild' versions.

Under the strong version, corporate status is regarded as a government-granted privilege that must be earned on a continuing basis. One expression of this approach is found in a judgment of Cooke J in the New Zealand Court of Appeal:

3 See Chapter 1 at Section 1.10.

4 Susanna Kim Ripken, *Corporate Personhood* (Cambridge University Press, 2019) 21.

5 The following works are of use: Eric W Orts, *Business Persons: A Legal Theory of the Firm* (Oxford University Press, 2013); F Hallis, *Corporate Personality* (Oxford University Press, 1930); S Stoljar, *Groups and Entities: An Inquiry into Corporate Theory* (ANU Press, 1973); LC Webb (ed), *Legal Personality and Political Pluralism* (Melbourne University Press, 1958); M Wolff, 'On the Nature of Legal Persons' (1938) 54(4) *Law Quarterly Review* 494; Lorraine Talbot, *Great Debates in Company Law* (Palgrave, 2014); Susanna Kim Ripken, *Corporate Personhood* (Cambridge University Press, 2019) 21).

6 This is sometimes called 'fiction theory'. For reasons outlined in the text, we think this latter description is misleading. Fiction theory is discussed in S Stoljar, *Groups and Entities: An Inquiry into Legal Theory* (ANU Press, 1973) 183ff; Susan Watson, *The Making of the Modern Company* (Hart Publishing, 2022) 212–21.

7 Eric W Orts, *Business Persons: A Legal Theory of the Firm* (Oxford University Press, 2013) 13.

> [L]imited liability is a privilege. It is a privilege healthy as tending to the expansion of opportunities and commerce, but it is open to abuse. Irresponsible structural engineering–involving the creating, dissolving or transforming of incorporated companies to the prejudice of creditors–is a mischief to which the courts should be alive.[8]

The strong version posits that 'corporations, as creatures of the State, have only those rights granted them by the State'.[9] Those rights include the legal capacity of corporations to enter into contracts, own property, issue shares, and commence and defend legal actions in their own right. Consequently, the government *must* regulate corporations to enable and then control the continued exercise of these rights.

In the mild version, corporate status is presumed to apply once the basic legislative prerequisites for incorporation have been met; for example, minimum membership and directorship requirements. The House of Lords' decision in *Salomon v Salomon & Co Ltd*[10] (discussed in Chapter 3) provides an example of this aspect of concession theory. Lord Halsbury noted that the company is an 'artificial creation of the legislature' but stressed that once it was properly incorporated 'the company has a real existence'.[11] Under this version, there is a presumption in favour of government regulation,[12] but it is not a mandate: governments *may* regulate corporate activity.

Concession theory makes two claims about corporations in the strong and mild versions.

The first claim concerns the metaphysical status of corporations: they are 'artificial' entities. The term 'artificial' does not mean the same thing as 'fictitious'; this theory does not argue that corporations do not exist as organisational or operational entities. Rather, concession theory treats the corporation as a construction that is capable of bearing rights and duties separately from those individuals who populate it. As Gageler J (now Gageler CJ) has explained, '[t]o refer to an "artificial" legal person necessarily implies no more than the existence of a unit or entity, not being merely a natural person, in respect of which legal personality has been conferred or recognised'.[13] The existence of corporations as legal entities is dependent on law, as is the extent to which corporations can enjoy that existence: '[c]orporate personality exists merely for legal and business convenience'.[14]

The second claim concerns the public/private status of the corporation. Concession arguments were particularly prominent in legal writing during the first half of the nineteenth century. Recall from Chapter 1 that this was also the period during which liberal

8 *Nicholson v Permakraft (NZ) Ltd (in liq)* [1985] 1 NZLR 242, 250.

9 S Padfield, 'Rehabilitating Concession Theory' (2014) 66(2) *Oklahoma Law Review* 327, 334 citing argument in *First National Bank of Boston v Bellotti*, 434 US 765, 778 n 14 (1978).

10 *Salomon v Salomon & Co Ltd* [1897] AC 22.

11 Ibid 29, 33–4.

12 S Padfield, 'Rehabilitating Concession Theory' (2014) 66 *Oklahoma Law Review* 327, 329.

13 *Communications, Electrical, Electronic, Energy, Information, Postal, Plumbing and Allied Services Union of Australia v Queensland Rail* (2015) 256 CLR 171 [53].

14 D Bonham and D Soberman, 'The Nature of Corporate Personality' in JS Ziegel (ed), *Studies in Canadian Company Law* (Butterworths, 1967) 5.

political theory was taking root. One problem for liberal thinkers was how to accommodate the growing popularity of the corporation as a form of legal organisation within a political ideology that viewed society as comprised primarily of the state and individual citizens, and in which the interests of the latter should prevail. The philosophical options were either to support the corporate form as a convenient device for the free and voluntary association of individuals, or to regard corporations as a state-sponsored threat to the rights of individuals. These different attitudes are evident in the works of thinkers such as John Stuart Mill and Adam Smith, referred to in Chapter 1. Concession theory seeks to resolve this tension by tying the corporation to the state, and preserving the political status of the individual: 'the theory claims that a group as such has no rights unless the state chooses to grant it legal personality'.[15] By controlling corporate activity, concession theory has the capacity to emphasise the wider public interest over the private interests of individuals involved in the corporation.

Early judicial attitudes in England and the United States reflected this approach.[16] In the mid-nineteenth century, it was established that, once incorporated, a company should only have the power to carry out activities of the type specified in its Memorandum of Association. As Lord Hatherley stated in the 1875 case of *Ashbury Railway Carriage & Iron Co v Riche*:

> [T]he Legislature has said, you may meet altogether, and form yourselves into a company, but in doing that you must tell all who may be disposed to deal with you the objects for which you have been associated.[17]

Transactions outside the scope of the corporation's stated objects were invalid because they were beyond its powers (or 'ultra vires'). As will be seen in Chapter 5, the ultra vires doctrine has been abolished in Australia, but concession theory has continued to find expression in some judicial reasoning. For example, in a High Court decision in 1990, Brennan J stated that a company's 'existence, capacities and activities are only such as the law attributes to it'.[18] Another illustration can be found in *Environment Protection Authority v Caltex Refining Co Pty Ltd*,[19] where the High Court held that corporations are not entitled to claim the privilege against self-incrimination. In part, this decision was based on the view that, to use McHugh J's words, the corporation is an 'artificial entity' and a 'creature of the law'.[20] Coming to the same conclusion, Mason CJ and Toohey J noted the approach in the United States which similarly denies the self-incrimination

15 See D Bonham and D Soberman, 'The Nature of Corporate Personality' in JS Ziegel (ed), *Studies in Canadian Company Law* (Butterworths, 1967) 5; cf R Romano, 'Metapolitics and Corporate Law Reform' (1984) 36(4) *Stanford Law Review* 923, 933 (noting that concession theory could plausibly support arguments for limited state regulation).

16 M Stokes, 'Company Law and Legal Theory' in W Twining (ed), *Legal Theory and Common Law* (Blackwell, 1986) 162; M Horwitz, 'Santa Clara Revisited: The Development of Corporate Theory' (1985) 88(2) *West Virginia Law Review* 173, 186.

17 [1874–80] All ER Rep Ext 2219, 2230.

18 *Northside Developments Pty Ltd v Registrar-General* (1990) 170 CLR 146.

19 *Environment Protection Authority v Caltex Refining Co Pty Ltd* (1993) 178 CLR 477.

20 Ibid 553, 555. See also Murphy J's judgment in *Pyneboard Pty Ltd v Trade Practices Commission* (1983) 152 CLR 328.

privilege to corporations. They cited the United States case of *Hale v Henkel* in which Brown J, relying on the concession theory, stated that:

> [T]he corporation is a creature of the State. It is presumed to be incorporated for the public. It receives certain privileges and franchises, and holds them subject to laws of the State and the limitations of its charter. Its powers are limited by law.[21]

Concession theory has been invoked when courts seek to go behind the separate legal entity of the corporation and impose liability upon corporate officers.

In summary, concession theory argues that incorporated activity is based on a presumption of state-imposed restrictions and regulations. It is a theory that is concerned with the status and role of corporations as legal and social actors. In particular, we can find aspects of concession theory in arguments, discussed later in this chapter, about the need for corporate social responsibility and in the idea that corporations are social enterprises.[22]

There are various criticisms of concession theory. One is that the theory has become irrelevant in a modern legal system that permits the creation of companies by a simple process of registration. Critics say that the theory made more sense at a time when grants of incorporation could be acquired only for specified purposes and only as the result of a Royal Charter from the Crown or a private Act of Parliament.[23] In reply, it can be argued that the demise of the Royal Charter or private Act did not end the state's role in creating corporations Instead, that role shifted from Parliament to the executive arm of government. Other critics argue that the key attributes of incorporation—separate legal status, perpetual succession, limited liability of members—can be achieved by ordinary contractual or trust arrangements and therefore the state does not have a special role in creating or regulating corporations.[24] One response to this criticism is that even if it is possible to contractually mimic some of the features that flow from corporate status,[25] the essential quality of separate corporate status lies beyond the capacity of ordinary contract.[26] A final criticism is that concession theory, especially in its strong form, 'is too authoritarian' with respect to corporate enterprises.[27] The argument here is that, ironically, rather than protecting individual rights such as freedom of association and rights to own property, the full application of concession theory threatens those rights because it makes corporations subject to 'the whims of government'.[28] A more nuanced approach would recognise the important role of self-regulation in the modern corporate sector.

---

21 *Hale v Henkel*, 201 US 43 (1906), cited in *Environment Protection Authority v Caltex Refining Co Pty Ltd* (1993) 178 CLR 477, 491.

22 See, eg, S Padfield, 'Corporate Social Responsibility and Concession Theory' (2015) 6 *William & Mary Business Law Review* 1; J Parkinson, *Corporate Power and Responsibility: Issues in the Theory of Company Law* (Clarendon Press, 1994) 22–3; K Greenfield, 'From Rights to Regulation in Corporate Law' in F MacMillan Patfield (ed), *Perspectives on Company Law 2* (Kluwer, 1997) 1.

23 See Chapter 1.

24 See R Hessen, *In Defense of the Corporation* (Stanford University Press, 1979).

25 Some commentators doubt this is possible. See, eg, Katharina Pistor, *The Code of Capital: How the Law Creates Wealth and Inequality* (Princeton University Press, 2019) 55.

26 See Susan Watson, 'The Corporate Legal Person' (2015) 19(1) *Journal of Corporate Law Studies* 137, 166.

27 Eric Orts, *Business Persons: A Legal Theory of the Firm* (Oxford University Press, 2013) 21.

28 Ibid.

An underlying limitation of concession theory is that it does not have much to say about what goes on inside a corporation. An approach that does address internal corporate relations is aggregate theory.

2.15 Aggregate theory

As we have seen, the advent of general incorporation legislation, and the accompanying rise in the number of incorporations, meant that the relevance of concession theory was questioned. Parliamentary permission for particular grants of incorporation was no longer required. Under the new general companies legislation, instead of the state creating corporations it was easier to think of each corporation as an exercise by individuals of their right of association. Aggregate theory pushes these individual rights to the fore. It begins with the premise that the corporation 'has no existence or identity that is separate and apart from the natural persons in the corporation'.[29]

There are different versions of aggregate theory—some making stronger claims than others. The early foundations for this theory were laid in judicial analyses at the turn of the twentieth century, which applied a contractual framework to questions of internal company management. In *Automatic Self-Cleansing Filter Syndicate Co Ltd v Cuninghame*,[30] for example, the English Court of Appeal affirmed that a company's constitution (then known as its Memorandum and Articles of Association[31]) formed a contract between members that regulates the internal affairs of the company. Internally, the corporation was regarded as an association (or aggregation) of individuals who are joined by mutual agreement. The earlier decision in *Ashbury Railway Carriage & Iron Co v Riche* showed that this contractual view could be accommodated within a mild version of concession theory:

> The memorandum of association is as it were the area beyond which the action of the company cannot go, but inside that area they [the members] may make such regulations for their own government as they think fit.[32]

Most advocates of aggregate theory have taken a stronger line than this, conceding much less scope for the imposition of external legal constraints upon corporations. They ask why corporations should be subject to specialised regulatory regimes that differ from those applying to other contractual forms of association, such as partnerships. In this argument:

> [T]he authority of the sovereign toward the corporation ... is no greater and no less than its authority toward any other private agreement among contracting parties.[33]

29 Susanna K Ripken, 'Corporations Are People Too: A Multi-Dimensional Approach to the Corporate Personhood Puzzle' (2009) 15(1) *Fordham Journal of Corporate & Financial Law* 97, 110.

30 *Automatic Self-Cleansing Filter Syndicate Co Ltd v Cuninghame* [1906] 2 Ch 34.

31 See Chapter 1 at Section 1.30.10.

32 *Ashbury Railway Carriage & Iron Co v Riche* [1874–80] All ER Rep Ext 2219, 2225 (Cairns LC).

33 Note, 'The Constitutional Rights of the Corporate Person' (1982) 91(8) *Yale Law Journal* 1641, 1648.

This stronger version of aggregate theory asserts both the primary status of the individuals who comprise the corporation and the private status of the corporation. In this view, the role of the law should be confined to facilitating the formation of these contractual relationships.

We have seen that the origins of contemporary Australian corporate law can be traced back to early forms of partnership.[34] Today, the process of incorporation still involves the creation or adoption of corporate constitutional documents that specify the rights and powers of members and directors. Jennifer Hill observes that 'company law in Australia has thus always had a strong contractual element to it'.[35] The current legal basis for this approach is discussed in Chapter 5. Contractual arguments continue to influence modern Australian and English judicial and legislative attitudes towards the exercise of managerial power within the corporation. According to one writer:

> By adopting a contractual conception of the company the legal model gives as the reason for the vesting of centralized authority to manage the company in the board of directors the contractual agreement of the owners of the company. Thus by invoking the idea of the freedom of a property owner to make any contract with respect to his property the power accorded to corporate managers appears legitimate, being the outcome of ordinary principles of freedom of contract.[36]

Since the 1970s, the preoccupation with justifying managerial power and autonomy within the corporation has led to the development of even stronger arguments that have their basis in aggregate theory. These arguments have drawn on the law and economics school of theory, and we consider them next.

2.20 Economic theories

There are two principal strands of scholarship in the law and economics analysis of the corporation. One is agency theory, which addresses the problems that arise from the separation of the ownership (or investment) and the control (or management) functions in large corporations.[37] The second strand is transaction-cost economics, which examines why different forms of economic organisation—for example, firms rather than markets—are used to organise and structure production relations in different situations.[38] Although these two strands have different emphases and analytical approaches, they

34 See Chapter 1 at Section 1.15.

35 J Hill, 'Close Corporations in Australia—The Close Corporations Bill 1988' (1989) 15(1) *Canadian Business Law Journal* 43, 48.

36 M Stokes, 'Company Law and Legal Theory' in W Twining (ed), *Legal Theory and Common Law* (Blackwell, 1986) 162.

37 Agency theory is associated principally with the work of Michael Jensen and William Meckling, in particular their influential article 'Theory of the Firm: Managerial Behavior, Agency Costs and Ownership Structure' (1976) 3(4) *Journal of Financial Economics* 305.

38 Transaction-cost economics is associated principally with the work of Oliver Williamson; see, eg, Oliver Williamson, *The Mechanisms of Governance* (Oxford University Press, 1996).

complement each other.[39] We can present an amalgamated description of these two approaches, due to their commonalities.[40]

From an economic perspective, the corporation (a legal concept) is analysed as a type of firm (an economic concept). A firm consists of a series of transactions, or contracts, between individual actors such as investors, managers, employees, creditors and customers; it is, in effect, a version of the broader market. Agency theory describes this arrangement of the firm as 'a nexus of contracts'. As Jensen and Meckling explain it, the firm:

> ... serves as a nexus for contracting relationships and which is also characterized by the existence of divisible residual claims on the assets and cash flows of the organization which can generally be sold without permission of the other contracting individuals.[41]

In this context, the term 'contract' does not necessarily correspond to the strict legal idea of contract.[42] Instead, contract is used to draw attention to the voluntary and adaptive nature of the arrangements made between the participants who comprise the firm.

This economic framework denies the existence of the organisation as an entity that is separate from the individual contractors. As two pre-eminent law and economics theorists, Frank Easterbrook and Daniel Fischel, put it: '[t]he "personhood" of a corporation is a matter of convenience rather than reality'.[43] Furthermore, this perspective insists that the only relevant function of a company is to maximise the returns to individual investors. Thus, corporations should be treated in the same way as sole traders—they are simply different ways of organising business.

Economic theory focuses on the fact that, in large firms, control is exercised by managers who act separately from a dispersed and diffuse group of investors who contribute capital to the business. Separating the management role from the capital contribution function allows management to be performed by specialists. The managers are 'agents' of the investors, although this term is not used in the strict legal sense. Economists also assume that the managers of the firm are rational economic actors who are guided by self-interest. This means there is always a risk they will use their discretionary powers to increase their own gains in ways that will not necessarily coincide with maximising the firm's profits. Investors in the firm want to ensure that managers are operating the firm in a way that maximises profits rather than managerial self-interest. Investors will therefore incur 'monitoring costs', keeping an eye on the managers. For their part, managers

39 Ibid 173. There is an analysis of both strands in W Bratton, 'The "Nexus of Contracts" Corporation: A Critical Appraisal' (1989) 74(3) *Cornell Law Review* 407, 417ff.

40 These are not the only forms of economic analysis: M Whincop, 'A Relational and Doctrinal Critique of Shareholders' Special Contracts' (1997) 19(3) *Sydney Law Review* 314 uses a relational contract perspective.

41 M Jensen and W Meckling, 'Theory of the Firm: Managerial Behavior, Agency Costs and Ownership Structure' (1976) 3(4) *Journal of Financial Economics* 305, 311.

42 For a critique of the contract argument, see V Brudney, 'Corporate Governance, Agency Costs, and the Rhetoric of Contract' (1985) 85 *Columbia Law Review* 1403, 1412.

43 F Easterbrook and D Fischel, *The Economic Structure of Corporate Law* (Harvard University Press, 1991) 12.

want to retain their positions and will seek to assure investors that their interests will not be harmed. Managers will therefore incur 'bonding costs'. The different costs incurred by both parties are referred to jointly as 'agency costs'.[44]

Contracts between managers and investors are meant to minimise these agency costs (or, in the language of transaction-cost economics, reduce managerial opportunism). This is done by including protective provisions in the contract that deal with conflicts of interest, disclosure requirements, and so on. However, for a number of reasons, the process of negotiating and monitoring the performance of these contracts is imperfect. Investors are limited in the amount of time and knowledge they can devote to negotiations, keeping informed about the firm's performance, analysing financial data provided by the firm, and attending general meetings. In firms with widespread ownership, the prospects of collective action amongst investors will be small, so there is little prospect of sharing the burden of monitoring management of the firm. In summary, the transaction costs of negotiating effective contracts are high, and the prospects of effective monitoring are low.

Applying this analysis to companies, the economic framework highlights two mechanisms that reduce transaction costs and act as an efficient substitute for investor monitoring of management behaviour.

The first mechanism is the operation of various market forces, in particular:

(1) The market for corporate securities: in an efficient capital market, the price of a company's shares is assumed to reflect all available information about that company.[45] One piece of information is the terms of the corporate contract and the degree of protection that they offer to shareholders. In effect, the market does the job of monitoring the company that would otherwise be done by the investors, thereby reducing agency costs.
(2) The market for corporate control:[46] in an efficient market, underperforming companies will be taken over by those who place a higher value on the company's assets. This prospect provides an incentive for the company's current directors and managers to aim for performance, lest they be displaced as a result of a takeover.[47]
(3) The market for company managers: economists argue that 'competition for managerial services, both inside and outside the company, encourages managers to act in shareholders' best interests'.[48] This is said to control the risk of abuse of managerial power because directors and managers are aware that if they do not maximise the value of the company they will not be re-elected or re-appointed.

44 M Jensen and W Meckling, 'Theory of the Firm: Managerial Behavior, Agency Costs and Ownership Structure' (1976) 3(4) *Journal of Financial Economics* 305.
45 See the discussion in Chapter 17 at Section 17.10.05. There is considerable debate about the efficiency of capital markets. For a general account, see J Fox, *The Myth of the Rational Market: A History of Risk, Reward and Delusion on Wall Street* (HarperCollins, 2009).
46 H Manne, 'Mergers and the Market of Corporate Control' (1965) 73(2) *Journal of Political Economy* 110.
47 There are many factors that can affect the operation of this market, including the presence of large, or 'block', shareholders in the company, and the complexity of takeover laws.
48 H Butler and L Ribstein, 'Opting Out of Fiduciary Duties: A Response to the Anti-Contractarians' (1990) 65(1) *Washington Law Review* 1, 27.

According to economic theory, the operation of these competitive market forces supplies information about companies and constrains the misuse of corporate power.

The second mechanism is a system of corporate law rules. The key features of modern corporate law, such as separate legal status, limited liability, and mandatory directors' duties of care and loyalty, are said to operate as a set of standard contractual terms that are read into each corporate constitution. As Easterbrook and Fischel describe it:

> [C]orporate law is a set of terms available off-the-rack so that participants in corporate ventures can save the costs of contracting. ... Corporate law—and in particular the fiduciary principle enforced by the courts—fills in the blanks and oversights with the terms that people would have bargained for had they anticipated the problems and been able to contract costlessly in advance. On this view corporate law supplements but never displaces actual bargains.[49]

This passage emphasises the private and voluntary nature of corporate relationships within the economic framework. Corporate law has a facilitating role, providing a set of 'default' rules which allow for tailor-made contracts to be constructed in specific instances. Individuals establishing a corporation should have the freedom to opt out of statutory or judicially created rules and to construct their own contractual arrangements. Some law and economics writers take a less stringent view, suggesting the idea that corporate law ought to prescribe some mandatory rules and impose some duties and responsibilities in order to correct potential problems which arise from the agency relationship.[50]

In summary, this contract-based analysis treats the corporation as a shorthand expression for a multiplicity of private, consensual, contract-based relations between economic actors, each seeking to maximise his or her own benefits. The corporation is regarded not as a creation of the state, but of private initiative and enterprise. In Brudney's cautious estimation, one advantage of this view over other theories is that it 'aids in illuminating the internal operation of the firm ... [D]ecomposing the enterprise advances understanding beyond that offered by the entity concept in law'.[51]

Law and economics analysis has had a lot of support in corporate law scholarship, particularly in the United States. It also has its critics.[52] One criticism points to the reliance on the idea of contract. In law and economic theory, complex relationships within the corporation are reduced to binary exchanges between individual actors, the

49 F Easterbrook and D Fischel, *The Economic Structure of Corporate Law* (Harvard University Press, 1991) 34. For an argument that fiduciary obligations should not be regarded as hypothetical contract terms, see D DeMott, 'Beyond Metaphor: An Analysis of Fiduciary Obligation' (1988) *Duke Law Journal* 879.

50 See, eg, C Riley, 'Contracting Out of Company Law: Section 459 of the Companies Act 1985 and the Role of the Courts' (1992) 55(6) *Modern Law Review* 782. See also (1989) 89(7) *Columbia Law Review*, which contains a number of articles on contractual freedom in corporate law.

51 V Brudney, 'Corporate Governance, Agency Costs, and the Rhetoric of Contract' (1985) 85 *Columbia Law Review* 1403, 1403–4.

52 See generally Shawn Bayern, *The Analytical Failures of Law and Economics* (Cambridge University Press, 2023).

purpose of which is to maximise returns to individual members. The idea of the corporation as an organisation is either downplayed or ignored. The role of key corporate players, such as shareholders, is reduced to a set of 'inputs' into a 'web of voluntary agreements'.[53] Another criticism is that a contractual paradigm regards corporations as private entities, and corporate law as a body of rules that facilitates private, voluntary, individual agreements. Consequently, as Kent Greenfield observes, '[b]ecause corporations are seen as private creations, corporate law is insulated from politics and concerns about the public interest'.[54] This ignores the prominent public and social impact that many corporations exert, and the consequent expectation that they might meet certain wider, social standards; for example, those standards relating to human rights or the environment.[55] This argument is examined later in this chapter in the discussion of corporate social responsibility.

2.25 Team production theory

When productive activity of some sort requires the financial input and effort of multiple people in a team or group, it can be difficult to attribute any particular part of the outputs or benefits of that activity to any particular person's contribution to producing them. This problem applies to corporations, especially if we expand the category of people providing inputs from only shareholders to include employees, managers, creditors and others. The problems that are said to arise include 'shirking', where individual members of the team do not put in as much effort as others to achieve the most profitable outcomes, preferring to 'free ride' on the efforts of others knowing that they will still get a share of the resulting benefits. Another potential problem is 'rent-seeking', where team members spend a lot of effort and group resources arguing with each other about the size of their share of the group's outputs. One way to avoid these problems could be to use individual contracts to lock in each team member's claim in advance. In anything but the smallest group, however, that will likely be an expensive and time-consuming exercise.

Team production theory seeks to address these problems and, at the same time, supply an explanation for why corporations are structured as they are. As it applies to corporations, this theory says that when individual contracts are not feasible, the 'second best' way to address these problems is to rely on the law. As described by Margaret Blair and Lynn Stout (the originators of this theory),[56] corporate law offers a solution to team production problems by requiring team members to hand over certain rights (such as rights over the team's joint output) to the corporation. As a separate entity, the corporation then

53 Stephen Bainbridge, 'In Defence of the Shareholder Wealth Maximization Norm: A Reply to Professor Green' (1993) 50(4) *Washington and Lee Law Review* 1423, 1426.

54 K Greenfield, *The Failure of Corporate Law: Fundamental Flaws and Progressive Possibilities* (University of Chicago Press, 2006) 30.

55 For an argument about the public law dimensions of corporate governance, see S Bottomley, *The Constitutional Corporation: Rethinking Corporate Governance* (Ashgate, 2007).

56 Margaret Blair and Lynn Stout, 'A Team Production Theory of Corporate Law' (1999) 85(2) *Virginia Law Review* 247.

owns the team assets; the use of those assets is determined by an internal hierarchy of authority that is dominated by the board of directors. In this way, as Blair and Stout see it:

> [t]he team production model of the public corporation both highlights and explains the essential economic function served by that otherwise puzzling institution, the board of directors.[57]

Team production theory seeks to address a difficulty that lies at the heart of the 'agency model', described earlier: if directors are said to be the agents of the shareholders, why are the rights and powers of shareholders so limited when it comes to controlling the directors? The answer, according to team production theory, is that instead of being there simply to look after shareholders' interests, the role of directors is to:

> protect the enterprise-specific investments of *all* the members of the corporate 'team', including shareholders, managers, rank and file employees, and possibly other groups, such as creditors.[58]

In this view, the board of directors is a 'mediating hierarchy' that operates independently of all the various constituencies that make up the corporation.

Team production theory shares some common ground with economic theories of the corporation, in so far as it sees the corporation as comprised of a nexus of multiple inputs (in this case, investments), and it uses the criterion of economic efficiency as its benchmark. Ironically, because it argues that shareholders are not the only or primary team members, it also shares some ground with stakeholder theories, which we examine later in this chapter, but with the proviso that directors are not under the control of any particular members of the corporate team.

One critique of the team production model is that it does not address the question of who monitors or provides oversight of the work of the directors. If shareholders are not the primary set of interests to be considered by directors, then their incentive to monitor is decreased. A different criticism is that, because the interests of team members will not necessarily be the same, the board must seek to balance them in some way. That, in turn, provides an incentive for team members to engage in 'rent-seeking' behaviour, to gain favourable outcomes from the board which, in turn, imposes costs on company productivity.[59]

2.30 Natural entity theory

This theory makes two claims. The first claim is that corporations are a natural product of human interaction and initiative. Corporate law does not therefore create corporations; instead, it simply gives formal recognition and public legitimacy to their existence.

57 Ibid 251.

58 Ibid 253.

59 See David Millon, 'New Game Plan or Business as Usual? A Critique of the Team Production Model of Corporate Law' (2000) 86 *Virginia Law Review* 1001.

This theory was popular in the early 1900s.[60] According to one commentator, early writers:

> saw corporations as natural expressions of desires of the corporators. Consequently, corporations obtained their political and thus legal status independently from the state. From this independence was inferred autonomy ... that demanded the respect and consequent restraint of the state.[61]

This line of thought was supported by arguments about the inevitability of economic concentration. The emergence of 'big business' was the result of natural, impersonal market forces.[62]

The second claim made by natural entity theory is that a corporation has an existence separate from its members and managers. This asserts that the corporation is a 'group-person', possessing its own group will and with its own capacity for action. A strong version of this theory was described in the late nineteenth century by the German legal philosopher Otto von Gierke, who argued that '[e]very group has a real and independent communal life, a conscious will, and an ability to act that are distinct from the lives and wills of its individual members'.[63] One legal feature underlying this claim is that corporations can remain in existence, with the same corporate identity, even though membership and management of the entity changes over time.

A less emphatic version of this theory—sometimes called 'organic theory'—uses the human body as an analogy for the corporation, with directors being likened to the mind of the company. This organic version of natural entity theory is frequently referred to in cases dealing with the criminal or civil liability of a corporation.

The idea of a corporate mind allows legal concepts such as mens rea, which are premised on the actions of individual human actors, to be applied to corporations without making significant changes to the substantive criminal law or notions of individual responsibility.[64]

Natural entity theory differs from aggregate and economic theories because it treats the corporation as more than a set of individual contractual relations between shareholders.[65] It agrees with concession theory that there *is* a point in recognising the corporation has a separate existence apart from its members. It differs from concession theory, however, in that it regards the corporation as a real or natural entity, rather than an artificial

60 There are also more recent proponents. See, eg, Eva Micheler, *Company Law: A Real Entity Theory* (Oxford Academic Press, 2021).

61 G Mark, 'The Personification of the Business Corporation in American Law' (1987) 54 *University of Chicago Law Review* 1331, 1470.

62 D Millon, 'The Ambiguous Significance of Corporate Personhood' (2001) 2(1) *Stanford Agora: An Online Journal of Legal Perspectives* 39 https://scholarlycommons.law.wlu.edu/wlufac/648/.

63 O von Gierke, *Associations and Law: The Classical and Early Christian Stages* in SK Ripken, 'Corporations Are People Too: A Multi-Dimensional Approach to the Corporate Personhood Puzzle' (2009) 15(1) *Fordham Journal of Corporate & Financial Law* 97, 114, n 58.

64 This is discussed in Chapter 3 at Section 3.40.

65 Note that aggregate theory and natural entity theory are similar in that each has a difficulty in explaining the idea of the one-person proprietary company permitted by the *Corporations Act 2001* (Cth) ss 114, 221.

construct dependent on the state for recognition. According to natural entity theory, 'the state does not create the corporation, but rather recognises an entity that maintains itself independent of that recognition'.[66]

Natural entity arguments appeared in Anglo-American legal writing partly as a response to a difficulty in early versions of aggregate theory. If corporations were nothing more than contractual arrangements, then how could the grant of legal privileges—such as perpetual succession, limited liability and separate legal status—which were not generally associated with other commercial contractual relationships, such as partnerships, be justified? The natural entity theorist's answer is that these are not privileges. Instead, they simply reflect the 'true' or 'real' nature of the corporation. Corporate law is not a set of default contract terms (as law and economics theory says), nor is it essential to the existence of the corporation (as concession theory insists). This theory is sceptical of the role of corporate law in general. If corporations are the natural product of private initiative,[67] then there is no reason why they should be regulated more closely than ordinary individuals or partnerships. Natural entity theory appears to arrive at a similar conclusion to aggregate theory. Another consequence of this argument is that if corporations are natural entities, they should be entitled to the same rights and privileges, and be held to the same standards and responsibilities, as natural persons.

2.35 An organisational perspective

We now consider another theory or, more accurately, a disciplinary approach that regards corporations from a group perspective.

Judicial and legislative attempts to respond to the problems of corporate misbehaviour are limited by a restricted view about what happens 'inside' the corporation. As discussed later in this book, the basic legal view regards the corporation as a collection of individuals (members and directors) who are bound together by specific legal relations. The difficulty with this view, as one corporate law writer says, is that: 'corporate practitioners and legal academicians tend to view the corporation as a "black box" which need not be understood in its internal workings in order to be operated'.[68] From the perspective of political scientists, sociologists and communications theorists, corporations—especially large corporations—should be understood as complex organisational environments that determine the status of, and shape the decisions made by, the individuals and groups who work in and with them.[69] These organisational environments are made up of formal and informal networks of communications, understandings, and behaviour patterns that link corporate insiders. Organisational theory suggests that the

66 J Coates, 'State Takeover Statutes and Corporate Theory: The Revival of an Old Debate' (1989) 64(4) *New York University Law Review* 806, 818–19.

67 D Millon, 'The Ambiguous Significance of Corporate Personhood' (2001) 2(1) *Stanford Agora: An Online Journal of Legal Perspectives* 39, https://scholarlycommons.law.wlu.edu/wlufac/648/.

68 J Coffee, 'Beyond the Shut-Eyed Sentry: Toward a Theoretical View of Corporate Misconduct and an Effective Legal Response' (1977) 63(7) *Virginia Law Review* 1099, 1110.

69 J Nesteruk, 'Legal Persons and Moral Worlds: Ethical Choices Within the Corporate Environment' (1991) 29(1) *American Business Law Journal* 75, 82.

larger the organisation the more likely it is that the flow of information up and down the organisational hierarchy will be distorted and the exercise of control will become diffuse. Research shows that in such situations the board of directors is likely to have only a limited impact on decision-making in the corporation. Furthermore, corporate decisions will not be the product of routine procedure and rational deliberation. Instead, they will be the result of 'an amalgam of independent decisions, a compromise among the views of several teams, or the relatively unalloyed preference of a certain subset of players'.[70]

The organisational perspective emphasises that corporations are decision-making organisations. This refers to the many informal decisions that are made on a daily basis by corporate managers and employees, as well as the fewer number of formal decisions made at general meetings of members and meetings of the board of directors. Decision-making processes within any one corporation are likely to vary depending on the type of decision. As one writer has noted:

> Explanation of corporate decision making should not be based upon [the] conception of a corporation as an organic, unified entity. ... [D]ifferent aspects of corporations become relevant with respect to particular decision-making contexts. For example, the dimensions of a corporation which are pertinent to decisions about an industrial relations problem may be radically different from those which are pertinent to choice between alternative sources of finance.[71]

Importantly, organisational theories direct our attention to *how* decisions are made, not just to the outcome or effect of those decisions:

> Corporate decisions can be assessed not just by the efficiency or fairness of their results, but also by assessing the quality of all of the formal and informal processes that are involved in reaching those decisions.[72]

According to one argument, corporate decision-making processes can be assessed according to three criteria: accountability, deliberation and contestability.[73] Accountability requires corporate officeholders to explain their use of office and power, paying attention to matters such as conflict of interest. The idea of deliberation is that corporate decision-making should be based on consideration of all relevant arguments. Finally, contestability refers to the realistic possibility that corporate decisions can be contested where they conflict with the corporation's interests.

One set of questions raised by this perspective concerns the ethical responsibility of individuals within the corporation. If internal corporate norms and rules shape and determine decision-making, then is the ethical responsibility of individuals in the corporation enhanced or diminished? Corporate lawyers have not given much attention to the effect of hierarchies within corporations on an individual's capacity to make ethically

70 S Kriesberg, 'Decisionmaking Models and the Control of Corporate Crime' (1976) 85(8) *Yale Law Journal* 1091, 1104.

71 G Lowe, 'Corporations as Objects of Regulation' (1987) 5 *Law in Context* 35, 37.

72 S Bottomley, *The Constitutional Corporation: Rethinking Corporate Governance* (Ashgate, 2007) 15.

73 For a detailed explanation, see Bottomley, ibid.

defensible decisions. Instead, this has been the subject of sociological inquiry. In a study of large American corporations conducted in the 1980s, sociologist Robert Jackall observed that:

> Bureaucracy transforms all moral issues into immediately practical concerns. A moral judgment based on a professional ethic makes little sense in a world where the etiquette of authority relationships and the necessity for protecting and covering for one's boss, one's network, and oneself supersede all other considerations.[74]

Organisational theory invites us to consider how this perspective fits with a body of corporate law based on objective standards of honest behaviour and proper conduct intended to apply to all corporations. An important implication of this work is that there will often be a divergence between the legal designation of improper corporate conduct and the views of business people: 'the law often runs into a widely held business view that the conduct it forbids is not morally reprehensible'.[75] Organisational theory can help us understand why the law may have only a limited impact on internal corporate processes. This is not to say that the law is irrelevant. Law plays a vital part in structuring the behaviour of corporations and corporate actors. But an organisational perspective reminds us that it is only a part of the picture, and at times the legal image of the corporation may appear to be overly simplified when compared with the images produced by sociologists, organisational theorists or economists.

2.40 Feminist perspectives

When one begins to explore the relationship between corporations, corporate law and gender, the immediate impression is that women and their perspectives are invisible. Debates about the role of corporations and their constituents seem to be viewed through masculine perspectives and cultures that emphasise ideas and values such as power, authority and duty.[76] Similarly, much of the language that pervades corporate law discourse has a strongly combative and masculine tone: for example, takeovers are conducted by 'raiders' who engage in a 'battle' with the 'target' company, hoping that there are no 'white knights', 'scorched earth', 'poison pill' or 'crown jewels' defences to defeat their bid.

Nevertheless, there have been important feminist analyses of the many issues embedded in the corporate world, leading some to categorise the corporation as inherently gendered.[77] To some extent, feminist analysis of corporations and corporate law

74 R Jackall, *Moral Mazes: The World of Corporate Managers* (Oxford University Press, 1988) 111.

75 C Stone, *Where the Law Ends: The Social Control of Corporate Behaviour* (Harper and Row, 1975) 228.

76 S Machold, P Ahmed and S Farquhar, 'Corporate Governance and Ethics: A Feminist Perspective' (2008) 81 *Journal of Business Ethics* 665. See also B Sjåfjell and IL Fannon (eds), *Creating Corporate Sustainability: Gender as an Agent for Change?* (Cambridge, 2018).

77 C O'Sullivan, 'The Gendered Corporation: The Role of Masculinities in Shaping Corporate Culture' in B Sjåfjell and IL Fannon (eds), *Creating Corporate Sustainability: Gender as an Agent for Change?* (Cambridge, 2018), 258. See also K Hall, 'Starting from Silence: The Future of Feminist Analysis of Corporate Law' (1994) 7 *Corporate and Business Law Journal* 149; P Spender, 'Women and the Epistemology of Corporations Law' (1995) 6(2) *Legal Education Review* 195; K Hall, 'The Interior

emerged out of a disagreement with law and economics contractual theories and a sympathy towards the view that corporations encompass a wider range of interests and constituencies beyond shareholders.[78]

In an early contribution, Kathleen Lahey and Sarah Salter suggested that feminist critiques of the corporation can be grouped under three headings.[79] The first is liberal feminism, which concentrates on the need for gender equality in society at large, and within corporate organisations in particular. This perspective accepts the organisational structure of the corporation as given and looks for ways in which women can overcome marginalisation and exclusion in the corporate environment. Some liberal feminist writers have studied the effects those structures have on individual behaviour.[80] They conclude that, in a hierarchical corporate structure, each individual is responsible for changing his or her situation. This diverts attention from the responsibility which the organisation has for the unequal treatment of female and male employees. The solution offered is for corporations to recognise and enforce individual rights to equal treatment and equal pay. This solution falls short of trying to create organisational structures that distribute and decentralise power and authority.

Lahey and Salter describe the second category as 'socialist feminism'. Here, the perspective lies outside the corporation. In their words, 'socialist feminist analysis is more concerned with the effect of corporatism on the larger culture, and on the role of women as workers in that culture'.[81] Socialist feminists argue that corporations dominate the capacity for individual action in modern society. Historically, modern business corporations were developed as instruments to be used by the owners of private property. Instead, it is the individual managers and workers that have become the agents and instrumentalities of the corporations. The lives of women, as workers in both the corporation and the home, become doubly devalued in this corporation-determined social order.

The third category is radical feminist literature and 'explores the reasons behind the development of the corporate form in the first place and the role that it plays in serving the needs of liberal and capitalist patriarchy'.[82] Radical feminists argue that modern society is fundamentally shaped by male values, embedded in dichotomies such as public versus private, individual versus group, or self-interest versus cooperation. In business, the emphasis on pursuing individual self-interest and competitive profit-maximisation

---

Design of Corporate Law: Why Theory is Vital to the Development of Corporate Law in Australia' (1996) 7(1) *Australian Journal of Corporate Law* 1.

78 T O'Neill, 'The Patriarchal Meaning of Contract: Feminist Reflections on the Corporate Governance Debate' in F MacMillan Patfield (ed), *Perspectives on Company Law 2* (Kluwer, 1997) 27.

79 K Lahey and S Salter, 'Corporate Law in Legal Theory and Legal Scholarship: From Classicism to Feminism' (1985) 23(4) *Osgoode Hall Law Journal* 543. T Gabaldon, 'The Lemonade Stand: Feminist and Other Reflections on the Limited Liability of Corporate Shareholders' (1992) 45(6) *Vanderbilt Law Review* 1387 adds two more headings to this list. Kellye Testy cautions that 'many writers move quite fluidly between several of the theoretical strands': 'Capitalism and Freedom—For Whom?: Feminist Legal Theory and Progressive Corporate Law' (2004) 67(4) Case Studies in Conservative and Progressive Legal Order 87, 94.

80 Lahey and Salter cite Rosabeth Kanter, *Men and Women of the Corporation* (Basic Books, 1977).

81 K Lahey and S Salter, 'Corporate Law in Legal Theory and Legal Scholarship: From Classicism to Feminism' (1985) 23 *Osgoode Hall Law Journal* 543, 549.

82 Ibid 553. See also P Spender, 'Exploring Corporations Law Using a Gender Analysis' (1996) 3 *Canberra Law Review* 82, 85.

and property acquisition are examples of this.[83] The hierarchical image of the corporation which is promoted by corporate law is cited as further evidence. Large corporations, being bureaucratic organisations, are centrally concerned with maintaining discipline and control. Bureaucratic control is exercised by methods of 'separation, isolation, and depersonalization, as well as depowerment of the individuals, knowledge, and activities that it organizes'.[84] Feminist legal theorists identified these as components of a distinctly male view of the individual's role in society. In contrast, they emphasise the obligations of care, responsibility and responsiveness which corporate participants owe to each other.[85]

There is a body of work that analyses *specific* corporate law issues from feminist perspectives.[86] As summarised by Testy, some of this work criticises the idea that shareholders should be the sole focus of directors' concerns, arguing that a wider constituency of interests should be considered. Instead of the nexus of contracts posited by law and economics theory, some feminist writers view the firm as a 'web of relationships', only some of which are prescribed by law; for example, director–shareholder.[87] Other work argues that 'feminist insights into concepts of care and connection can and should give increased substantive content to director and officer duties'; and there are arguments directed at the effect the exercise of corporate power has on individuals, especially women.[88] Following from this, there is considerable debate about the importance of gender diversity on company boards. There is some evidence that board gender diversity can positively affect a board's monitoring role because 'women on boards ask more questions'.[89] Several countries, especially in Europe, have enacted rules that specify quotas for gender representation. As an example, since 2006, Norway has required all public companies to have a minimum of both genders represented on their boards. The prescribed minimum varies according to the size of the board.[90] The thinking behind these legislative initiatives is summed up by Peta Spender:

> [T]he participation of women on boards is a measure of economic citizenship and democratic leadership, and therefore the percentage of women on boards should reflect their workforce participation.[91]

83 T Gabaldon, 'The Lemonade Stand: Feminist and Other Reflections on the Limited Liability of Corporate Shareholders' (1992) 45 *Vanderbilt Law Review* 1387, 1420.

84 K Lahey and S Salter, 'Corporate Law in Legal Theory and Legal Scholarship: From Classicism to Feminism' (1985) 23 *Osgoode Hall Law Journal* 543, 554; referring to K Ferguson, *The Feminist Case Against Bureaucracy* (Temple University Press, 1984).

85 See T O'Neill, 'The Patriarchal Meaning of Contract: Feminist Reflections on the Corporate Governance Debate' in F MacMillan Patfield (ed), *Perspectives on Company Law 2* (Kluwer, 1997) 7, 29–34.

86 See, eg, P Spender, 'Exploring Corporations Law Using a Gender Analysis' (1996) 3 *Canberra Law Review* 82; K Hall, 'Starting from Silence: The Future of Feminist Analysis of Corporate Law' (1995) 7 *Corporate & Business Law Journal* 149. For a US perspective, see AM Choike, UR Rodrigues and K Alces Williams (eds), *Feminist Judgments: Corporate Law Rewritten* (Cambridge University Press, 2023).

87 See, eg, S Machold, P Ahmed and S Farquhar, 'Corporate Governance and Ethics: A Feminist Perspective' (2008) 81(3) *Journal of Business Ethics* 665, 673–4.

88 K Testy, 'Capitalism and Freedom—For Whom?: Feminist Legal Theory and Progressive Corporate Law (2004) 67 *Law and Contemporary Problems* 87, 98.

89 Akshaya Kamalnath, *The Corporate Diversity Jjgsaw* (Cambridge University Press, 2022) 42.

90 B Sjafjell, 'Gender Diversity in the Boardroom and Its Impacts: Is the Example of Norway a Way Forward?' (2015) 20(1) *Deakin Law Review* 25.

91 P Spender, 'Gender Quotas on Boards—Is it Time for Australia to Lean in?' (2015) 20(1) *Deakin Law Review* 95, 96–7.

Other commentators raise concerns that imposing quotas might lead to token appointments or misperceptions that women board members are merely making up the numbers.[92]

2.45 Corporate purpose

An important question prompted by the theories we have discussed is whether corporations should be confined to the pursuit of profits for the benefit of shareholders or whether they should have regard to wider concerns, including the environmental and social impact of their operations. In short, what is the underlying purpose of the corporation as a legal, economic and social structure?

For example, from a natural entity perspective in which corporations have a status analogous to natural persons, then presumably they should be bound by similar social and ethical expectations and obligations to those of other citizens. This position was elaborated in a famous article by Harvard law professor E Merrick Dodd, published in 1932.[93] He argued that, because corporations are natural entities, they have social responsibilities in addition to their profit-making goals. Dodd was critical of the traditional legal view of corporations as essentially private organisations run for the exclusive benefit of the owner-shareholders. In his view, because the corporate entity is not merely an aggregate of shareholders, and because the shareholders in modern public corporations have become 'absentee owners' who are separated from the processes of corporate management, the directors should not be regarded merely as agents of the shareholders.[94] Directors must make decisions in the interests of the corporation as a separate entity and should expect that the corporation's interests as a 'good citizen' will not always accord with the interests of its shareholders. In Dodd's argument, this means that directors are justified in making decisions which favour interests other than the shareholders', such as those of the company's employees, consumers of its products, the local communities in which the company operates, and the environment. As long as these decisions can be justified in terms of the corporation's obligations as a 'good citizen', then any objections raised by the shareholders can be overridden. To assist corporations in discharging this social function, representatives of interests other than the shareholders, such as employees, could be appointed to the board of directors.

Dodd's argument called for a fundamental reconceptualisation of the corporation, moving away from an exclusive focus on shareholders' rights to include the interests of society. It is an argument that has been raised many times since, under a variety of labels. In earlier editions of this book, we grouped these arguments under the heading

92 Arguments noted in Akshaya Kamalnath, *The Corporate Diversity Jjgsaw* (Cambridge University Press, 2022) 42.

93 EM Dodd, 'For Whom are Corporate Managers Trustees?' (1932) 45(7) *Harvard Law Review* 1145. This was part of a famous debate, conducted in the pages of the *Harvard Law Review*, between Dodd and another leading corporate governance thinker, Adolf Berle.

94 This perspective on corporate management, sometimes labelled 'managerialism', was given great impetus in the pioneering US study by AA Berle and GC Means, *The Modern Corporation and Private Property* (Macmillan, first published 1932).

'corporate social responsibility' (CSR). While CSR concerns continue to be expressed, they have since been subsumed into a broad debate about 'corporate purpose' in which a focal point is the responsibility of corporations for the pursuit of environmental, social and governance (ESG) standards. While there is debate about the scope of the three words in ESG, most commentators agree that 'environmental' includes sustainability and climate-change matters; 'social' includes maintaining ethical standards in company operations; and 'governance' includes an expectation that company boards should behave accountably and transparently.[95]

In the vast literature on the debate about ESG (and CSR),[96] there are arguments, based on the idea of 'shareholder primacy', that corporations should have the maximisation of returns to shareholders as their primary focus. Only if it is consistent with that goal should corporations be altruistic and take into account wider social, welfare or environmental concerns. A variant of this argument is that directors should not focus exclusively on achieving short-term profits for the company but should take a long-term approach in which costly but ethical investments today will yield returns for shareholders in the long term. This perspective has been given the label 'enlightened shareholder value', and we return to it below. At the other end of the spectrum, there are arguments that corporations must be regarded primarily as public actors and that shareholder interests should not take precedence over the concerns of the wider constituency of groups and people who can be affected by the company's activities or who, conversely, can affect the company's ability to carry out its operations. This can include suppliers, creditors, employees, customers, communities in which the company's operations are based, and public interest pressure groups. This is sometimes called 'stakeholder theory', because this wider group of interests has a 'stake' in what the company does. Again, we discuss this in more detail later in this chapter.

Not surprisingly, these arguments have received criticism from a range of perspectives. One critique is that it is not appropriate for directors to take into account interests or concerns other than those of the shareholders to whom they owe their primary and direct legal duties. The renowned economist Milton Friedman was one such critic; his argument was summed up in the title of one of his papers: 'The Social Responsibility of Business is to Increase its Profits'.[97] Related to this is the concern that requiring corporate managers to consider broad social responsibilities when making decisions would expose them to a vague and undefined standard of conduct and impede effective decision-making. Finally, another set of criticisms takes a more cynical view, arguing

95 See Elizabeth Pollman, 'The Making and Meaning of ESG' (Working Paper No 659, European Corporate Governance Institute, October 2022).

96 For an introduction to CSR, see A Crane, A McWilliams, D Matten, J Moon and DS Siegel (eds), *The Oxford Handbook of Corporate Social Responsibility* (Oxford University Press, 2008); Bryan Horrigan, *Corporate Social Responsibility in the 21st Century: Debates, Models and Practices Across Government, Law and Business* (Edward Elgar, 2010). On corporate purpose, see E Pollman and R Thompson (eds), *Research Handbook on Corporate Purpose and Personhood* (Edward Elgar, 2021).

97 *New York Times Magazine*, 13 September 1970, reprinted in W Zimmerli, K Richter and M Holzinger (eds), *Corporate Ethics and Corporate Governance* (Springer, 2007) 173.

that concerns for ESG (or CSR) are an exercise in corporate 'window dressing'[98] or public image protection that deflects critical attention away from deeper concerns about the misuse or exploitation of corporate power.

2.45.05 Enlightened shareholder value

Arguments in favour of a broad corporate purpose have received mixed responses from legislators. In the United Kingdom, the notion of corporate purpose have been given statutory recognition under the label 'enlightened shareholder value'. This idea begins from the orthodox proposition that directors must act in the best interests of the shareholders, but urges this be done by 'striking a balance between the competing interests of different stakeholders in order to benefit the shareholders in the long run'.[99] This is now reflected in s 172(1) of the *Companies Act 2006* (UK), which, under the heading 'Duty to promote the success of the company', provides that:

> (1) A director of a company must act in a way that he [sic] considers, in good faith, would be most likely to promote the success of the company for the benefit of its members as a whole, and in doing so have regard (amongst other matters) to—
>
> (a) the likely consequences of any decision in the long term;
> (b) the interests of the company's employees;
> (c) the need to foster the company's business relationships with suppliers, customers and others;
> (d) the impact of the company's operations on the community and the environment,
> (e) the desirability of the company maintaining a reputation for high standards of business conduct; and
> (f) the need to act fairly between the members of the company.

This section maintains the idea that the company's members are the sole focus for directors, but it 'seeks to provide a broader context for fulfilling that duty'.[100] The section has been criticised on the one hand because '[a]ll it requires is that the director should *think about*' interests beyond those of the members.[101] Courts in the United Kingdom have affirmed that '[i]t is for the directors themselves to determine the weight to be attached to the list of factors referred to in s.172. The weighing of factors is a commercial decision, which the Court is ill-equipped to take, except in a clear case.'[102]

By contrast, and with two exceptions noted below, Australian corporate law does not expressly refer to broader social or other responsibilities. There is no equivalent

98 A term used by Friedman in W Zimmerli, K Richter and M Holzinger (eds), *Corporate Ethics and Corporate Governance* (Springer, 2007) 175. Another example is L Fu, 'Corporate Green Initiatives as Real Circular Economy or Window-dressing?' in G Donleavy and C Noronha (eds), *Comparative CSR and Sustainability: New Accounting for Social Consequences* (Routledge, 2022).

99 J Armour, S Deakin and S Konzelmann, 'Shareholder Primacy and the Trajectory of UK Corporate Governance' (2003) 41(3) *British Journal of Industrial Relations* 531, 537.

100 Corporations and Markets Advisory Committee, *The Social Responsibility of Corporations* (December 2006) 103.

101 LE Talbot, *Critical Company Law* (Routledge-Cavendish, 2008) 183 (emphasis in original).

102 *Lawrence v Cowell* [2023] EWHC 2644 (Ch) [151].

of the UK section in the *Corporations Act 2001* (Cth), although the idea has been considered on a number of occasions. In its 1989 review of the duties and obligations of company directors, the Senate Standing Committee on Legal and Constitutional Affairs concluded that the interests of groups other than shareholders are best covered by specific legislation dealing with industrial relations, trade practices, and consumer and environmental protection. The Committee argued that 'to require directors to take into account the social impact their decisions might have would be an extension of Australian company law fraught with most important consequences'.[103] This argument was repeated by the Corporations and Markets Advisory Committee in its 2006 report on corporate social responsibility, which cautioned that 'a non-exhaustive catalogue of interests to be taken into account serves little useful purpose for directors and affords them no guidance on how various interests are to be weighed, prioritised or reconciled'.[104]

The two exceptions can be found in s 299(1)(f) of the *Corporations Act*, which requires the annual directors' report to give details of the company's performance in relation to any environmental regulation that applies to the company's operations, and in the Treasury Laws Amendment (Financial Market Infrastructure and Other Measures) Act 2024, which requires all companies with financial reporting requirements to publish an annual 'sustainability report' on climate-related matters.[105]

Outside the parameters of the *Corporations Act*, the *Listing Rules* of the Australian Securities Exchange (ASX) require a company listed on ASX to include a 'corporate governance statement' in its annual report to the ASX.[106] That statement must indicate the extent to which the company has followed the ASX's Corporate Governance Council's *Corporate Governance Principles and Recommendations.* If those Principles and Recommendations have not been followed, the company must explain why not. Principle 3 requires a listed entity to act legally, ethically and responsibly, emphasising that:

> Investors and the broader community expect a listed entity to act lawfully, ethically and responsibly and that expectation should be reflected in its statement of values. In formulating its values, a listed entity should consider what behaviours are needed from its officers and employees to build long term sustainable value for its security holders. This includes the need for the entity to preserve and protect its reputation and standing in the community and with

103 Senate Standing Committee on Legal and Constitutional Affairs, Parliament of Australia, *Company Directors' Duties: Report on the Social and Fiduciary Duties and Obligations of Company Directors* (Parliamentary Paper 395, 1989) [2.13].

104 Corporations and Markets Advisory Committee, Parliament of Australia, *The Social Responsibility of Corporations* (December 2006) 111. A similar conclusion was reached by the Parliamentary Joint Committee on Corporations and Financial Services, *Corporate Responsibility: Managing Risk and Creating Value* (Parliamentary Paper 121, June 2006) 54-6.

105 See the discussion in Chapter 7 at Section 7.40. Similar requirements already exist in the UK: see *Companies (Strategic Report) (Climate-related Financial Disclosure) Regulations 2022* (UK) SI 2022/31.

106 See ASX, *Listing Rules* (at 19 December 2016) r 4.10.3. The *Listing Rules* may be enforced by a court order on the application of specified applicants including ASIC, the ASX, or a person aggrieved by any failure to comply with the *Listing Rules: Corporations Act* s 793C.

key stakeholders, such as customers, employees, suppliers, creditors, law makers and regulators.[107]

2.45.10 Stakeholder theory

We noted earlier that there are arguments that corporations should have direct responsibilities to a wider range of interests beyond their members. These arguments are usually grouped under the heading of 'stakeholder theory'.

Stakeholder theory emerged partly as a response to economic contract-based theories about the corporation. Contract-based theorists concentrate on relations between shareholders and directors or managers, placing emphasis on the pursuit of shareholder wealth maximisation. Stakeholder theory regards corporations as comprised of other important constituencies in addition to shareholders. These non-shareholder constituencies include corporate employees, secured and unsecured creditors, customers or clients, and the local communities in which corporations operate.

The proposition is that non-shareholder stakeholders are unlikely or unable to protect their interests by using private contracts with each corporation. Accordingly, in addition to contract law, a system of public corporate regulation is needed because corporations are institutions whose conduct can have significant public ramifications.

Once more, there are many varieties of stakeholder theory, partly because the term 'stakeholder' has no fixed definition. Versions of this theory range from the idea of enlightened shareholder value, which we have discussed above, to communitarian theory, which says that 'all those involved in the corporation are potentially members of one community; while they clearly have significantly divergent interests, needs, and values, they also have some significant shared goals and bonds'.[108] One general feature of stakeholder theory is that it avoids classifying corporations either as exclusively private arrangements (as economic theory does) or as purely public creations (as concession theory sometimes does). As one writer has described it:

> Corporations really are both private and public simultaneously. They are not states; they carry out economic activities for a profit, a profit that justifiably is returned to those who take the risk of investing in what they do. At the same time, corporations are not purely private individuals. They are institutions that sometimes act as quasi-governments and, even when they do not, they take actions that affect every aspect of people's lives, including people who have no formal contractual relationship with them.[109]

Stakeholder theory challenges several aspects of contemporary corporate law structure, such as the nature of directors' duties (should they be owed just to shareholders?), the

107 ASX Corporate Governance Council, *Corporate Governance Principles and Recommendations* (Australian Securities Exchange, 4th ed, February 2019) https://www.asx.com.au/content/dam/asx/about/corporate-governance-council/cgc-principles-and-recommendations-fourth-edn.pdf.

108 A Etzioni, 'The Corporation as a Community: Stakeholder Theory Corporations as Communities' in M Boylan (ed), *Business Ethics* (Wiley-Blackwell, 2nd ed, 2014) 87.

109 A Wolfe, 'The Modern Corporation: Private Agent or Public Actor?' (1993) 50(4) *Washington and Lee Law Review* 1673, 1692.

rights of shareholders (what sort of rights should arise out of share ownership?), and the mechanisms of corporate governance (should non-shareholders be represented on the board? Should general meetings be open to non-shareholders?).

2.45.15 Global developments

At the end of Chapter 1, we noted that Australian corporate law increasingly operates in a global context. This is especially so for arguments about stakeholderism and ESG reporting.

Concern about the global impact of corporate operations has seen the promulgation of a large number of international guidelines, norms, standards, and codes focused on promoting responsible corporate behaviour, particularly with regard to human rights. Some of these initiatives are developed by inter-governmental bodies, some by industry bodies, and some by international non-governmental organisations (NGOs). Three examples illustrate the scope of these international initiatives.

First, the Organisation for Economic Co-operation and Development (OECD)'s *Guidelines for Multinational Enterprises on Responsible Business Conduct.*[110] These voluntary principles and standards, first formulated in 1976 and since revised, are recommendations to multinational enterprises.[111] They are not legally enforceable, although the matters covered by the Guidelines may be regulated by national laws or other international obligations. The Guidelines set out a number of general policies for multinational enterprises. The first two policies state that such enterprises should '[c]ontribute to economic, environmental and social progress with a view to achieving sustainable development', and '[r]espect the internationally recognised human rights of those affected by their activities'.[112]

Second, the United Nations Global Compact. This non-binding initiative, established in 2000, encourages companies to 'do business responsibly' by aligning their operations to 10 principles on human rights, labour, the environment and anti-corruption.[113] The principles are drawn from the *Universal Declaration of Human Rights,* the International Labour Organization's *Declaration on Fundamental Principles and Rights at Work,* the *Rio Declaration on Environment and Development,* and the *United Nations Convention Against Corruption.*One concern of the Global Compact is the extent to which global supply chains are dependent on forms of modern slavery, including forced or compulsory labour, child labour and debt bondage. In Australia, the *Modern Slavery Act 2018* (Cth) requires some corporations to report annually on the risks of modern slavery in their operations and supply chains. A review of the operation of the Act in 2023 found, however, that because of problems with enforceability, '[m]odern slavery reporting is not being taken seriously enough' and that reporting by a number of corporations was 'a

110 Organisation for Economic Co-operation and Development, *OECD Guidelines for Multinational Enterprises on Responsible Business Conduct* (OECD Publishing, 2023).

111 The *OECD Guidelines* expressly decline to define the term 'multinational enterprise' but note that it usually involves linked companies or other entities established in more than one country: Ibid 12.

112 Ibid 14.

113 'The Ten Principles of the UN Global Compact', *United Nations Global Compact* (Web Page) <https://unglobalcompact.org/what-is-gc/mission/principles>.

tick-box exercise'.[114] The Compact has been criticised because it does not specify how companies are to implement the standards: '[t]he concern is that companies may enhance their reputations simply by signing the Compact without making serious commitments to operating in a sustainable fashion'.[115]

Third, the United Nations *Guiding Principles on Business and Human Rights*[116] (adopted by the United Nations Human Rights Council in 2011). The Principles focus on human rights and apply both to states and to corporations within their jurisdictions. Among other things, the Principles provide that States should set out clear expectations about respect for human rights by all business enterprises in their jurisdiction. This responsibility to respect human rights requires business enterprises to 'avoid causing or contributing to adverse human rights impacts through their own activities'.[117] The commentary to the Principles notes that 'the responsibility to respect human rights is a global standard of expected conduct for all business enterprises wherever they operate ... it exists over and above compliance with national laws and regulations protecting human rights'.[118] Importantly, the 'responsibility' outlined in the Principles does not equate to a legal obligation for corporations to observe human rights.[119] Nevertheless, the idea of a corporate responsibility to respect human rights 'poses a challenge for corporate governance theory' because the standard model of corporate law in countries such as the United Kingdom (and Australia), which gives primary attention to the rights and interests of shareholders, 'may be inadequate to deal with the complex changes in governance and regulation that such a responsibility would appear to impose on corporations'.[120]

2.50 Why is corporate theory important?

We began this chapter by emphasising the importance of corporate theory. Corporate law might be thought of solely as an essentially pragmatic discipline—as a set of rules and doctrines designed to facilitate the achievement of collective goals through the medium of the corporate form. But corporate law is not value-free. Each rule and doctrine embodies (or, at least, permits) a choice about the law's position on fundamental questions, such as whether corporations are essentially private entities, how the interests of an individual shareholder should be weighed against those of the majority, or whether corporations should be held to account for their impact on climate change.

Understanding the rules and doctrines of corporate law is essential. By becoming aware of the main theoretical frameworks that influence the development of modern

114 John McMillan, *Report of the Statutory Review of the Modern Slavery Act 2018 (Cth): The First Three Years* (Report, Commonwealth of Australia, 2023).

115 M Regan and K Hall, 'Lawyers in the Shadow of the Regulatory State: Transnational Governance on Business and Human Rights' (2016) 84(5) *Fordham Law Review* 2001, 2020.

116 Office of the United Nations High Commissioner for Human Rights, *Guiding Principles on Business and Human Rights: Implementing the United Nations 'Protect, Respect and Remedy' Framework*, UN Doc HR/PUB/11/04 (2011) 13

117 Ibid 14.

118 Ibid 13.

119 P Muchlinski, 'Implementing the New UN Corporate Human Rights Framework: Implications for Corporate Law, Governance and Regulation' (2012) 22(1) *Business Ethics Quarterly* 145, 147.

120 Ibid 162.

corporate law, and noticing how they take different positions on those fundamental questions, we are in a better position to develop a critical understanding of the legal rules and doctrines that make up corporate law. None of the different theories we have discussed is intrinsically 'better' than the others; each has its strengths and weaknesses. Each theory gives a different position from which to argue for or against a particular legislative initiative or judicial interpretation.

2.55 Summary

We began this chapter by referring back to four sets of issues or debates that underpin corporate law: (1) whether and how to recognise the interests of the corporation as a group entity versus those of the individuals in the company; (2) the extent to which management of the company should operate separately from the members as the notional 'owners' of the company; (3) whether the role of the law should merely be to facilitate the capacity of people to form and operate corporations or to be more interventionist or regulatory; and (4) whether corporations are to be regarded as private economic and social actors or as a significant part of the public dimension of social and economic life. Each of the theories and perspectives we have looked at says something different about these debates. We conclude this chapter by summarising the different positions. Each of the theories or perspectives we have looked at has many different permutations and so we must be cautious about over-generalising.

Concession theory ties the existence of corporations to the will of the state; it regards corporations as public bodies, even though they may act for private purposes. Consequently, concession theory presumes corporate law must have a role, not only in creating corporations but in specifying and regulating the conditions for their continued existence. Concession theory says little about the internal governance of corporations.

In contrast, aggregate theory and the law and economics arguments begin from a strong private and individualistic premise. This is summed up in the idea that a corporation can be regarded as a 'nexus of contracts'. Accordingly, there is a presumption that the law has no greater role to play in regulating corporations than it has for other contract-based forms of enterprise (for example, partnerships). Unlike other theoretical perspectives, law and economics theory pays attention to the relations between the individual players within the corporation:

> When we look at corporations and corporate law through a contractual lens we are able to see some things quite clearly (for example, the different roles played by various participants in the corporate enterprise, and the need to assess the variable impact of market forces and legal rules on them).[121]

Team production theory develops the 'nexus of contracts' idea into a broader idea about the corporation as a privately constructed 'team' in which participants each contribute towards the production of the group's outputs. This theory does not give special status to the shareholders; it recognises a wider range of inputs. It does, however,

121 S Bottomley, *The Constitutional Corporation: Rethinking Corporate Governance* (Ashgate, 2007) 29–30.

prioritise the role of directors in making decisions about the allocation of the benefits produced by the team, and it emphasises the importance of the corporation's separate legal status as the owner of team assets.

Natural entity theory shares with aggregate theory the idea that corporations are the product of private initiative which the law should facilitate rather than regulate. But unlike aggregate (or law and economics) theory it treats the corporate entity—the group—as a social construct, not merely a collection of individuals. The sum, says this theory, is greater than its parts.

Each of these theories has something to say about the status of 'the corporation'. The remaining perspectives described in this chapter focus on the behaviour and impact of corporate operations on people within the corporation and on society.

Organisational theories invite us to think about the ways corporations operate as decision-making structures. This is an internal perspective on the corporation, examining how the organisational setting can affect and shape the actions of individual corporate actors. Organisational theories have less to say about questions of whether corporations are public or private actors, or the role of the law in relation to them.

Feminist theorists shed light on the internal aspects of corporate life, as well as taking an 'external' view. Some writers point to the effect of internal corporate hierarchies on the prospects for gender equality, while others study the role of corporations in society and their role in perpetuating patterns of disempowerment for women.

Next, this chapter considered the perspectives that can be grouped under the idea of 'corporate purpose', including the 'enlightened shareholder value' and 'stakeholder' arguments, with the latter posing a challenge to the standard legal model of the corporation that focuses on shareholder interests. At the risk of generalisation, these arguments recognise that corporations are private entities, but emphasise the public role that they do, or can, play. While some advocates press for ESG and similar concerns to be enshrined in legal requirements, others see more capacity in self-regulation or industry standards.

Finally, we noted that corporate law operates in a wider global context. We described some examples of the international guidelines and principles that can affect the ways in which corporations operate transnationally and, by implication, domestically.

This chapter presented a collection of theories and perspectives that are important to understand corporations and their legal, social, economic and political settings. We should be wary of trying to find a single theory that explains all aspects of corporate law and corporate operations. Notwithstanding the force with which they are expressed, none of these arguments can claim to be 'right'. The range of corporate structures, and the variety of national and international contexts in which they operate, makes it unlikely that one theory or perspective can supply a single overarching explanation of contemporary corporate life. It is possible to find aspects of many of these theoretical perspectives at work in the contemporary corporate law system.

CHAPTER

3

THE COMPANY AS A SEPARATE LEGAL ENTITY

3.05 Introduction

In this chapter, we explore in detail two key corporate law concepts: the separate legal status of the corporation and limited liability. We discuss limitations and inroads into these concepts, as well as how the corporation—separate from the people who invest in or run it—can be liable in tort and criminal law.

This chapter builds on the themes raised in Chapter 2: the relevance of different theoretical and ideological perspectives on the corporation and its role and purpose in contemporary society. To reiterate why these questions are important:

> The broad and basic purpose of examining corporate theory is to develop a framework within which we can assess the values and assumptions that either unite or divide the plethora of cases, reform proposals, legislative amendments, and practices that constitute modern corporate law. This law has not sprung up overnight. We need some way of disentangling the differing philosophical and political perspectives from which it has been constructed. Indeed, the great benefit of theoretical inquiry is to reveal the existence of these differences in the first place.[1]

3.10 The separate legal entity doctrine

One of the most fundamental principles of corporate law is that, once the requirements for incorporation have been met and a company is registered, it is recognised as its own separate legal entity.[2] This means that for legal purposes it exists separate from shareholders, directors and founders and can sue and be sued, enter contracts in its own name, employ staff, borrow money, own property, and engage in most other legal acts that a natural person can do. While companies must clearly act through people (most often directors and managers), the legal obligations that arise from such actions are usually those of the company and not the individuals involved.[3] This is reflected in s124(1) of the *Corporations Act* which states that '[a] company has the legal capacity and powers of an individual both in and outside this jurisdiction. A company also has all the powers of a body corporate.'

As discussed in Chapter 2, this view of the corporation, as a separate legal entity that comes into existence on registration, is consistent with versions of concession theory that see the corporation as having a metaphysical status enabling it to bear rights and duties separately from the individuals who populate it.[4] The doctrine was famously established in the decision of the House of Lords in *Salomon v Salomon & Co Ltd* ('*Salomon's Case*'),

1 Stephen Bottomley, 'Taking Corporations Seriously: Some Considerations for Corporate Regulation' (1990) 19(3) *Federal Law Review* 203, 204.

2 As stated in s 119 of the *Corporations Act*, a company comes into existence at the beginning of the day on which it is registered.

3 This topic is discussed below in the context of a company's liability for torts and crimes, and in Chapter 5 where a company's capacity to enter contracts is discussed.

4 For a discussion of the effects of granting corporations personhood, and whether this privilege should be extended in other contexts, see Michelle Worthington and Peta Spender, 'Constructing Legal personhood: Corporate Law's Legacy' (2021) 30(3) *Griffith Law Review* 348.

referred to in Chapter 1.[5] This case was an important turning point in corporate law. Prior to the decision in 1897, it was generally assumed that the benefits of incorporation were primarily for use by large joint stock enterprises, rather than small 'one-person' companies. By the time of *Salomon's Case*, however, most of the companies being incorporated in England were small private companies. The decision in *Salomon's Case* was therefore important as it affirmed that incorporation had the same effect and benefits for small companies as for large companies.

The case involved a boot manufacturer, Aaron Salomon, who successfully ran his business as a sole trader for over 30 years.[6] In 1892, he set up a company, A Salomon & Co Ltd, under the *Companies Act 1862* (UK) to enable his children to gain an interest in the business and to obtain limited liability. All the requirements of the Act were met, including for there to be seven shareholders: Salomon, his wife, and their five eldest children (each granted one share in the company). Salomon was appointed the managing director of the company, and two of his sons were appointed directors.

The company, A Salomon & Co Ltd, then purchased the boot manufacturing business from Salomon in exchange for £1,000 cash, £10,000 in debentures, 20,000 fully paid shares and the payment of business debts worth £8,000. The effect of this arrangement was that the business was now owned by the company, with Salomon becoming a secured creditor, the controlling shareholder (with 20,001 shares) and the company's managing director.

Not long after incorporation, there was an economic downturn and the boot manufacturing industry suffered severely as a result. To enable the business to survive, Salomon took a personal loan for £5,000 from a man named Mr Broderip. Salomon then granted Broderip an interest (via a mortgage) in his debentures, with the result that Broderip became the legal owner of the debentures and Salomon the beneficial owner.

Despite the loan, the company was unable to pay its debts (including interest on the debentures) and was put into liquidation. At that point, the assets and business of the company were worth about £6,000. It also had a debt of £5,000 that it owed to Broderip, which was repaid. The issue then became how the remaining £1,000 was to be allocated. Salomon, relying upon his interest in the debentures, claimed the amount as a secured creditor. This left the unsecured creditors, who were owed approximately £1,1000, without payment. The liquidators objected to this payment to Salomon on the basis that the company was really a 'one-person company' and therefore Salomon should not be entitled to be paid before genuine trade creditors.

At first instance, Vaughan Williams J found for the liquidator on the basis that the company was Salomon's agent or a 'mere alias' for him.[7] The effect of this decision was, that as principal, Salomon had to indemnify the company for all its business and liabilities. On appeal, the Court of Appeal also held for the liquidator on the basis that the company was acting as a trustee and holding the business on trust for Salomon. This finding also meant that Salomon needed to pay the company the amount owing to the trade creditors.

5 *Salomon v Salomon & Co Ltd* [1897] AC 22.

6 For a detailed discussion of the background to this case, see P Johnson, *Making the Market: Victorian Origins of Corporate Capitalism* (Cambridge, 2010) 153–8.

7 *Broderip v Salomon* [1895] 2 Ch 323, 332.

Both the first instance and the Court of Appeal decisions reflected the concerns of the time that the 'one-person' company was an abuse of the corporate form.[8] In Lindley LJ's opinion, although the company had the required number of shareholders, 'six of them are members simply in order to enable the seventh himself to carry on business with limited liability'.[9] As such, the incorporation of the company was nothing more than 'an instrument for cheating honest creditors'.[10]

Lopes LJ, in the Court of Appeal, was even more direct in his criticism of this practice. He stated:

> It never was intended that the company ... should consist of one substantial person and six mere dummies, the nominees of that person, without any real interest in the company. The Act contemplated the incorporation of seven independent bona fide members, who had a mind and a will of their own, and were not the mere puppets of an individual who, adopting the machinery of the Act, carried on his old business in the same way as before, when he was a sole trader. To legalise such a transaction would be a scandal.[11]

In a decision that changed the course of corporate law history, the House of Lords disagreed with both the first instance and Court of Appeal decisions and found that the company was validly created. In the opinion of all six judges, the central issue was whether the requirements of the *Companies Act 1862* had been complied with. While they acknowledged that a company is an 'artificial creation of the Legislature', they held that a company validly incorporated is a separate legal entity, even where there is little change to who is actually running the business. As Lord McNaughton stated:

> The company is at law a different person altogether from subscribers to the memorandum; and, though it may be that after incorporation the business is precisely the same as it was before, the same persons as managers, and the same hands receive the profits, the company is not in law the agent of the subscribers or trustee for them.[12]

The Court also rejected the idea that a 'one-person' company is different in law to any other company. As noted by Lord McNaughton:

> It has become the fashion to call companies of this class 'one man companies'. This is a taking nickname, but it does not help one much in the way of argument. If it is intended to convey the meaning that a company which is under the absolute control of one person is not a company legally incorporated, although the requirements of the Act of 1862 may have been complied with, it is inaccurate and misleading: if it merely means that there is a predominant partner possessing an overwhelming influence and entitled practically to the whole of the

8 See the discussion in E Manson 'The Reform of Company Law' (1895) 11(3) *Law Quarterly Review* 346.
9 *Broderip v Salomon* [1895] 2 Ch 323, 337.
10 Ibid 340–1.
11 Ibid 341.
12 *Salomon v Salomon & Co Ltd* [1897] AC 22, 51.

> profits, there is nothing in that that I can see contrary to the true intention of the Act of 1862, or against public policy, or detrimental to the interests of creditors.[13]

The Lords criticised the lower courts for focusing on the purpose for which the company was incorporated, stating that the motives of the persons incorporating the company were irrelevant. According to Lord Halsbury LC:

> [The lower courts] have been struck by what they have considered the inexpediency of permitting one man to be in influence and authority the whole company; and, assuming that such a thing could not have been intended by the Legislature, they have sought various grounds upon which they might insert into the Act some prohibition as a result.[14]

Instead, the House of Lords considered that the words of the statute were clear and that it was the intention of Parliament to allow seven or more persons to register a company 'whatever may have been the ideas or schemes of those who brought it into existence'.[15] Salomon's control of the company was completely consistent with what the statute allowed him to do and did not provide evidence of fraud or misconduct that justified making him liable for the debts of the company. As Lord McNaughton clearly stated:

> I cannot understand how a body corporate thus made 'capable' by statute can lose its individuality by issuing the bulk of its capital to one person, whether he be a subscriber to the memorandum or not ... Nor are the subscribers as members liable, in any shape or form, except to the extent and in the manner provided by the Act. That is, I think, the declared intention of the enactment.[16]

The effect of this decision was that any debts owed by the company to the secured creditors (including Salomon) had to be paid first.[17] Once this was done, due to the shortage of funds remaining, none of the unsecured creditors were paid on the company's winding up.

3.10.05 The importance of *Salomon's Case*

As indicated above, the House of Lords in *Salomon's Case* recognised the separate legal status of a company, even in circumstances where it was incorporated to take over the business of a sole trader.[18] Although one of the key drivers for the development of the corporate form was to enable collective or group enterprises (discussed in Section 3.25 below), *Salomon's Case* made it clear that the legal status of the company was equally available to large and small companies. As Lord McNaughton noted, it did not matter

13 Ibid 53.

14 Ibid 34.

15 Ibid 31 (Lord Halsbury LC).

16 Ibid 51.

17 The issue of who gets paid first on insolvency is discussed in detail in Chapter 16 at Section 16.30.

18 It is important to remember that, in this case, Salomon was not a sole trader and that other family members were involved in the enterprise. For a discussion of some of the patriarchal assumptions that underlie the judges' reasons, see Peta Spender, 'Resurrecting Mrs. Salomon' (1999) 27(2) *Federal Law Review* 217, 242.

whether most of the people involved in a company were nominee or 'dummy' shareholders or directors as '[w]hen the memorandum is duly signed and registered ... the subscribers are a body corporate'.[19]

The decision in *Salomon's Case* confirmed that individuals could legitimately minimise their personal risk using the corporate form. The idea that a person's liability could be limited to the amount they had promised or contributed to the capital of a company was not new at the time *Salomon's Case* was decided. As discussed in Chapter 1, members of unincorporated joint stock companies were already limiting their liability for the debts of a company via deeds of settlements and provisions in contracts with third parties. However, there was some debate at the time about whether limited liability should be available to small companies.

Salomon's Case confirmed that the benefits of limited liability could be available to anyone who conducted their business through the corporate form. This meant that Salomon and his family, as the shareholders in the company, could not be called upon to contribute to the debts of the company beyond any amount they owed on their shares. This principle is now reflected in s 516 of the *Corporations Act*, which provides that a member need not contribute to the company more than the amount (if any) unpaid on the shares that they own. For example, if one or more persons buy 100 $1 shares in a company, but at the time they only pay 50 cents towards the cost of each share, the maximum they can later be called upon to contribute to the company is the remaining 50 cents per share ($50). Similarly, in a company limited by guarantee, the liability of members is limited to the amount they promise to contribute via a guarantee to the capital of the company.[20]

Limited liability is now widely accepted as one of the most foundational principles of corporate law.[21] It allows one or more persons to set up a company without incurring personal liability for the legitimate debts of the company beyond the price of their shares.[22] This feature gives the company a significant advantage over other business structures such as the partnership or trust, where the individuals involved can be liable for all the debts of the business. The effect of limited liability is often justified by its economic benefits, including encouraging people to invest in companies, enabling risk-taking by those running the company, decreasing costs to shareholders in monitoring the actions of corporate managers, and encouraging shareholders to diversify their investments. Indeed, it is commonly argued that the challenges created for creditors through the effect of limited liability are less than the difficulties that would be created for shareholders if there was unlimited liability. As Anderson explains:

> With unlimited liability, shareholders would be concerned about the risk of losing their personal assets in the event of nonpayment of a debt by the company.

19 *Salomon v Salomon & Co Ltd* [1897] AC 22, 51.

20 *Corporations Act* s 517.

21 For strong critiques of this position, see P Ireland, 'Limited Liability, Shareholder Rights and the Problem of Corporate Irresponsibility' (2010) 34(5) *Cambridge Journal of Economics* 837; E Sangkuhl, 'Rethinking Limited Liability' (2007) 11(1) *University of Western Sydney Law Review* 124.

22 As discussed in Chapter 11 at Section 11.25, directors can face liability for the debts of the company when they trade while insolvent.

> The risk could be disproportionate to the return; a small investment could render the shareholder liable for a large corporate debt, yet the return, should the company be successful, would remain small. Shareholders would therefore need to monitor the company's behaviour. To reduce their exposure to loss of personal assets through many companies, and because monitoring is time-consuming and costly, shareholders would limit their investments to a small number of companies. This would effectively limit investors' ability to reduce their risk through the diversification of their portfolio of investments, which would in turn drive up their required rate of return.[23]

As Anderson also notes, under the economic theories of the corporation discussed in Chapter 2 at Section 2.20, limited liability is one of the default rules that make up the standard form contract which is corporate law.[24] The aim of such rules is to lower the costs of transacting:

> Default rules save firms the cost of negotiating and inserting terms into each of the contracts they form. Corporate law rules and norms deal with disputes between corporate stake-holders—managers, shareholders, employees, suppliers, customers and the broader community—and aim to achieve a balance between the objective of shareholder wealth maximisation and the protection of those who may be adversely affected by the activities of the corporation.[25]

One consequence of limited liability is that the risk of a company not being able to pay its debts is borne by creditors who are considered to be the 'cheapest cost avoiders' because (at least in theory) 'the contract creditor is able at low cost to determine whether it needs the added assurance of a personal guarantee'.[26] Risk is 'externalised' to creditors who then have recourse to the company's assets for payments of any debts. To protect themselves, creditors can seek security for their debts (in the form of personal guarantees from directors or major shareholders, or mortgages over company property), include provisions in contracts to ensure repayment, or make inquiries into the finances of the company. In reality, such protections can be of limited value as they are usually only available to financiers and other large creditors. As Anderson notes:

> [T]here are many obstacles to the ability of creditors to self-protect under a limited liability regime. The contention that creditors can self-protect is based on the theoretical 'efficient markets' hypothesis, which assumes that all relevant information is available and immediately digested by the market, leading to accurate assessment and pricing of risk. This does not always happen in practice. Frequently, there is a lack of full or timely information about the risk attaching to an investment or to a debtor company's financial position. Small

23 H Anderson, 'Piercing the Veil on Corporate Groups in Australia: The Case for Reform' (2009) 33(2) *Melbourne University Law Review* 333, 338.

24 Ibid 337.

25 Ibid.

26 SM Bainbridge, 'Abolishing Veil Piercing' (2001) 26(3) *Journal of Corporation Law* 479, 502.

> closely held companies are more likely to deprive creditors of vital information about solvency than are larger companies with mandated public disclosure or a board well separated from its shareholders.[27]

This issue, of a corporation's liability for tort and the risks for involuntary creditors, is discussed further at Section 3.50.05 below.

3.15 The adoption of *Salomon's Case*

Since the decision in *Salomon's Case*, courts have consistently upheld and applied its findings on the separate legal entity principle. The effects of treating a company as separate from its participants include that the company:

- can sue and be sued in its own name
- can incur its own obligations in contract, tort, criminal and other law
- has perpetual succession (meaning that it continues to exist in law despite any change in its members or directors until it is deregistered)
- can own property
- can enter contracts with its directors and shareholders.

A case often cited to show the effect of this doctrine is *Lee v Lee's Air Farming Ltd*.[28] Mr Lee ran a crop-dusting business through the company Lee's Air Farming Ltd. Lee was the major shareholder of the company, as well as the governing director. Lee was also the sole employee of the company. The company took out workers compensation insurance in relation to Lee. When Lee was killed in a plane crash, his widow claimed compensation under that insurance policy. The insurance company argued that Lee was not a 'worker' within the meaning of the workers compensation legislation, which defined a worker as a person 'who entered into or works under a contract of service ... with an employer', as he was, in effect, the employer as well.

The Privy Council rejected this argument and held that, as the company was a separate legal entity, it could employ Lee under a contract of service. It recognised that a person can have more than one role in relation to a company, including as a shareholder, a director, and an employee. A person can also enter separate contracts with a company in these different roles. In this case, Lee had validly entered a contract of service with the company, and was employed by it, even though he was also the person who controlled and owned the company.

As demonstrated by the High Court decision of *Andar Transport Pty Ltd v Brambles Ltd*,[29] the issue of applying the separate legal entity doctrine to 'one-person' companies still arises. In this case, the respondent Brambles provided laundry services to hospitals. From 1990 onwards, it was Brambles' practice to contract out its laundry delivery services to companies which then employed drivers to load, deliver and unload linen.

27 H Anderson, 'Piercing the Veil on Corporate Groups in Australia: The Case for Reform' (2009) 33(2) *Melbourne University Law Review* 333, 340.

28 *Lee v Lee's Air Farming Ltd* [1961] AC 12.

29 *Andar Transport Ltd v Brambles Ltd* (2004) 217 CLR 424.

Daryl Wail, who had previously been employed by Brambles, incorporated a company, Andar Transport Pty Ltd, to enter into such a contract with Brambles. Wail was the controlling shareholder, managing director, and nominated 'driver' for Andar.

In 1993, Wail injured his back while unloading laundry and sued Brambles for negligence. He argued that his injury was sustained using Brambles' system for unloading trolleys. Brambles argued that the company (Andar), as Wail's employer, had not taken steps to provide a safe system of work for its driver. On this basis, Brambles argued that Andar should be liable for contributory negligence.

While the case primarily involved questions about the interpretation of the indemnity clauses in the contract between Andar and Brambles, it was also necessary for the Court to determine the extent of Andar's duty to Wail. On this question, the majority of the High Court held that Andar owed Wail a duty of care to provide a safe working environment.[30] This was the case even though Wail was the controlling shareholder and director of the company. Quoting Mason JA in *Shedlezki v Bronte Bakery Pty Ltd*,[31] the majority stated:

> [I]t matters not that the plaintiff had control or the capacity to control the defendant's activities, for the principle that a corporation is a legal entity distinct from the corporators applies with equal force to a company which is 'a one person' company.[32]

Kirby J also emphasised the significance of the separate legal entity doctrine:

> No party to this appeal argued a challenge so fundamental as to the doctrine in *Salomon's* case. It is too late in the day, and inappropriate in this case, to suggest that in law Mr Wail and Andar were the same legal entity. In law, they had different duties and responsibilities.[33]

3.20 Exceptions to the separate legal entity doctrine

The courts have been reluctant to depart from the separate legal entity doctrine due to its fundamental place at the heart of corporate law. The doctrines of separate legal entity and limited liability have been responsible for the corporate form becoming commonplace in all areas of society. In the limited instances where the courts have been willing to disregard or look behind the doctrines (sometimes called 'piercing the corporate veil') to make those in control of the company (whether shareholders or directors) liable for the actions or debts of the company, it has usually been because there was evidence that the corporate structure had been set up to perpetuate fraud or to avoid an existing legal obligation. It must be noted, however, that such cases are rare in Australia and most cases that raise such issues are decided on their facts rather than on the basis of

30 The majority was comprised of Gleeson CJ, McHugh, Gummow, Hayne and Heydon JJ (Kirby J dissenting).

31 *Shedlezki v Bronte Bakery Pty Ltd* (1970) 72 SR(NSW) 378.

32 *Andar Transport Ltd v Brambles Ltd* (2004) 217 CLR 424.

33 Ibid [79].

any established exceptions to the separate legal entity doctrine.[34] As Rogers AJA noted in *Briggs v James Hardie & Co Pty Ltd*, 'there is no common, unifying principle, which underlies the occasional decision of the courts to pierce the corporate veil'.[35] Similarly, Worthington and Spender note that:

> In the main, corporate law treats the separate legal personality of the corporate device as sacred and its disregard as profane ... the law may disregard or reverse the conferral of legal personality upon the corporate device by piercing the corporate veil. However, this is a rare and momentous judicial or legislative act that is carefully delimited, not least as an option of last resort. Further, the case law is regarded as incoherent and fact-driven, and in many respects emphasises the sanctity of corporate legal personality.[36]

It is important to remember that just because a person chooses to use a corporate structure to limit their liability for the debts of the business or sets up a company with limited capital (for example, a $1 company), this is not in itself fraud or a sham. As stated by one judge:

> [T]he great reason why so many people form their businesses into limited liability companies and others invest their money in them is in order that they may be under no personal liability in respect of the transactions of those companies, and that is a perfectly legitimate object.[37]

3.25 Common law contexts in which the separate legal entity doctrine may not apply

3.25.05 Evasion of a legal obligation

In cases where a company is established to avoid an existing legal obligation, or to carry on an illegal activity, the courts have been willing to disregard the separate legal status of the company and find that the participants in the company are liable for its actions. A commonly cited example of this is the case of *Gilford Motor Co Ltd v Horne* ('*Gilford Motor*').[38] In that case, Mr Horne was employed as managing director of Gilford Motor. There was a provision in his contract that stated that if he left the company, he promised not to compete with it or try to solicit its customers (a restraint of trade clause). After resigning, Horne set up his own company to run a business in competition with Gilford Motor. The shareholders in the new company were Horne, his wife, and one of his business associates.

34 John Farrar has described Commonwealth authority on piercing the corporate veil as 'incoherent and unprincipled': see J Farrar, 'Fraud, Fairness and Piercing the Corporate Veil' (1990) 16(4) *Canadian Business Law Journal* 474, 478. For a detailed discussion of where the courts have been willing to pierce the corporate veil before 2000, see I Ramsay and D Noakes, 'Piercing the Corporate Veil in Australia' (2001) 19(4) *Company and Securities Law Journal* 250.

35 *Briggs v James Hardie & Co Pty Ltd* (1989) 16 NSWLR 549, 567.

36 M Worthington and P Spender, 'Constructing Legal Personhood: Corporate Law's Legacy' (2021) 36(3) *Griffith Law Review* 348, 356, footnotes omitted.

37 *Commissioners of Inland Revenue v Sansom* [1921] 2 KB 492, 500 (Lord Sterndale MR).

38 *Gilford Motor Homes Co Ltd v Horne* [1933] Ch 935.

Gilford Motor sued Horne under the restraint of trade clause and argued that the Court should disregard the fact that it was the company that had contacted the customers and find both it and Horne in breach. The Court agreed, finding that the company had been formed for the sole or dominant purpose of avoiding the restraint of trade clause. Therefore, both Horne and the company were in breach and an injunction was issued against both defendants.

In the case of *Pioneer Concrete Services Ltd v Yelnah Pty Ltd*,[39] the Court refused to apply the decision in *Gilford Motor* as there was not enough evidence on the facts that the company had been formed 'for the sole or for the dominant purpose' of evading a legal obligation.

This exception is still relevant today, as evidenced in the 2013 UK case of *Prest v Petrodel Resources Ltd*.[40] However, as that case clarifies, it will only be in rare circumstances that the courts will allow the corporate veil to be pierced. *Prest's Case* arose out of high-profile divorce proceedings between the oil tycoon Michael Prest and his wife Yasmin. It concerned the ownership of a number of residential properties, including the family home, that belonged to companies within the Petrodel Group. This group of companies was wholly owned and controlled by Michael Prest. The question to be decided by the Court was whether the companies could transfer any of the properties to Yasmin Prest, given that in law they belonged to the companies.

In a unanimous decision, the Supreme Court allowed the appeal and ordered that the properties be transferred to Yasmin Prest as part of the £17.5 million divorce settlement. It found that, as Michael Prest had contributed money towards the purchase of the properties, they were held by the company for him on a resulting trust. Although, on the facts, it was not necessary to 'pierce the corporate veil', the Court went on to discuss the circumstances in which the corporate veil could be pierced. In delivering the leading judgment, Lord Sumption stated:

> 'Piercing the corporate veil' is an expression rather indiscriminately used to describe a number of different things. Properly speaking, it means disregarding the separate personality of the company. There is a range of situations in which the law attributes the acts or property of a company to those who control it, without disregarding its separate legal personality. The controller may be personally liable, generally in addition to the company, for something that he has done as its agent or as a joint actor. Property legally vested in a company may belong beneficially to the controller, if the arrangements in relation to the property are such as to make the company its controller's nominee or trustee for that purpose ... But when we speak of piercing the corporate veil, we are not (or should not be) speaking of any of these situations, but only of those cases which are true exceptions to the rule in *Salomon v A Salomon & Co Ltd*, i.e. where a person who owns and controls a company is said in certain circumstances to be identified with it in law by virtue of that ownership and control.[41]

39 *Pioneer Concrete Services Ltd v Yelnah Pty Ltd* (1986) 5 NSWLR 254.

40 [2013] 2 AC 415 ('*Prest's Case*').

41 Ibid [16].

Lord Neuberger noted that, in Commonwealth countries, there was little or no consensus on when exceptions to the separate legal entity doctrine apply. As he continued:

> In Australia, in *Briggs v James Hardie & Co Pty Ltd* (1989) 16 NSWLR 549, 567, Rogers AJA in the New South Wales Court of Appeal observed that, 'there is no common, unifying principle, which underlies the occasional decision of courts to pierce the corporate veil', and that 'there is no principled approach to be derived from the authorities'. In *Constitution Insurance Co of Canada v Kosmopoulos* [1987] 1 SCR 2, 10, Justice Wilson in the Supreme Court of Canada said that '[t]he law on when a court may ... "[lift] the corporate veil" ... follows no consistent principle'. The New Zealand Court of Appeal in *Attorney-General v Equiticorp Industries Group Ltd (In Statutory Management)* [1996] 1 NZLR 528, 541, said that '"to lift the corporate veil" ... is not a principle. It describes the process, but provides no guidance as to when it can be used.' In the South African Supreme Court decision, *Cape Pacific Ltd v Lubner Controlling Investments (Pty) Ltd* 1995 (4) SA 790 (A), 802–803, Smalberger JA observed that '[t]he law is far from settled with regard to the circumstances in which it would be permissible to pierce the corporate veil'.[42]

In Lord Sumption's opinion, at common law, the corporate veil should only be pierced when no other legal remedy is available and then limited to situations when a person has used a company to avoid an existing legal obligation. He called this the 'evasion principle', and stated that it applies where a legal obligation, liability or restriction has been deliberately avoided by interposing a company between a person and their legal obligations.[43] As Lord Sumption noted, this had not occurred on the facts of this case as Michael Prest had vested the properties in the companies a long time before the marriage broke down. There was also no evidence that in doing so he was seeking to avoid any obligations to his wife.

At the same time as recognising 'the evasion principle', Lord Sumption noted there are other cases that have been decided on the basis of concealment. These cases did not involve the court disregarding the separate legal status of the company; rather, they involved situations where the courts were willing to look behind the company to discover facts that were concealed by its use. Lord Sumption labelled this 'the concealment principle', and found that it applied when a legal right exists against a person who owns or controls a company, that right would exist whether or not the company was involved, and the company has deliberately been placed between the parties to conceal important facts such as who is the true owner or controller of the company. Unlike the evasion principle, the courts do not need to pierce the corporate veil for the concealment principle to apply.

The Supreme Court concluded that piercing the corporate veil should only be done as a last resort and that other remedies, particularly those available in equity and

42 Ibid [75].
43 Ibid [28].

tort, should be used when they can achieve the same result. Importantly, the Court stopped short of rejecting the concept of piercing the corporate veil. As Lord Neuberger noted:

> I have reached the conclusion that it would be wrong to discard a doctrine which, while it has been criticised by judges and academics, has been generally assumed to exist in all common law jurisdictions, and represents a potentially valuable judicial tool to undo wrongdoing in some cases, where no other principle is available. Accordingly, provided that it is possible to discern or identify an approach to piercing the corporate veil, which accords with normal legal principles, reflects previous judicial reasoning (so far as it can be discerned and reconciled), and represents a practical solution ... I believe that it would be right to adopt it as a definition of the doctrine.[44]

This decision is important for the detailed discussion it contains on how to approach exceptions to the separate legal entity doctrine and for Lord Sumption's discussion of the evasion and concealment principles. It is likely to guide Australian courts in future cases on the question of when exceptions to the doctrine exist. However, larger questions still remain. As discussed in Section 3.35 below, many of the corporate scandals of the 2000s led to criticism of the separate legal entity doctrine and to arguments that courts should be able to disregard the doctrine, particularly in the context of group debts or where tort victims are involved.[45]

3.25.10 Fraud

It has generally been accepted that there is another exception to the separate legal entity doctrine: where the corporate structure is used to perpetuate a fraud or to conceal a fraudulent operation. This was the case in *Re Darby*,[46] where two individuals, Mr Darby and Mr Gyde, registered a company in the Channel Islands called City of London Investment Corporation Ltd (CILIC). They then used CILIC to register an English company, Welsh Slate Quarries Ltd (WSQ), and sought investments in that company from the public via a prospectus. The money raised through the public sale of shares in WSQ was transferred back to CILIC, and then on to Darby and Gyde.

When WSQ failed, action was taken against Darby and Gyde to recover the profits they had made from the scam. In law, as CILIC had established WSQ, it was the 'promoter' and was liable for any false statements contained in the prospectus. However, the Court was willing to look behind the separate legal nature of CILIC and impose liability for fraud on Darby and Gyde, who it considered were the true promoters of the scheme. This was done on the basis that the corporate structure of CILIC was 'a mere alias' for Darby and Gyde, who had, in reality, committed the fraud.[47]

44 Ibid [80].

45 Ross Grantham, 'The Corporate Veil: An Ingenious Device' (2013) 32(2) *University of Queensland Law Journal* 311, 314.

46 *Re Darby* [1911] 1 KB 95.

47 Ibid 97.

3.25.15 Agency

In *Salomon's Case*, both the first instance judge and the House of Lords recognised that a company can act as an agent for its controller. However, as confirmed by the House of Lords, the mere fact that a particular shareholder owns most of the shares in a company does not create an implied agency relationship. For such an agency relationship to exist, the facts must show that the principal (usually a controlling shareholder) has appointed the company to act on its behalf. In particular, it must be clear that the company is entering into contracts and incurring legal obligations on behalf of the principal and not in its own right.

Such an argument of implied agency was made in the case of *Smith, Stone & Knight Ltd v Birmingham Corporation.*[48] In this case, Smith, Stone & Knight Ltd carried on a manufacturing business. It subsequently purchased a waste business and set up a subsidiary company (Birmingham Waste Co Ltd) to run that business. Smith, Stone & Knight Ltd owned 497 of the 502 shares in Birmingham Waste, with the remaining shares held by each of the 5 directors. The local council sought to compulsorily acquire the land on which Birmingham Waste operated—land that was owned by Smith, Stone & Knight Ltd. The relevant legislation provided that Smith, Stone & Knight Ltd was entitled to compensation as the owner of the land; however, Birmingham Waste was only entitled to compensation as the tenant if it held a lease over the premises for more than one year. Birmingham Waste did not have a formal lease to operate on the land.

Smith, Stone & Knight Ltd argued that it should still be entitled to compensation for the disruption to Birmingham Waste's business on the basis that the waste business was not separate from the manufacturing business. It argued that an agency relationship existed between the companies, with Birmingham Waste acting as the agent of Smith, Stone & Knight Ltd. In contrast, the council argued it did not need to pay compensation to Smith, Stone & Knight Ltd as Birmingham Waste was a separate company carrying on its own business and it did not have the requisite one-year lease.

On the facts, it was shown that the two companies operated with almost identical staff, no independent books or bank accounts, and the income of Birmingham Waste was treated as the income of Smith, Stone & Knight Ltd. On this basis, Atkinson J held that Birmingham Waste was, in law, an agent carrying on Smith, Stone & Knight Ltd's business. He noted that such an outcome could only be reached by positively answering six questions:

(1) Were the profits of the subsidiary treated as the profits of the parent company?
(2) Were the persons conducting the business appointed by the parent company?
(3) Was the parent company the head and brain of the trading venture?
(4) Did the parent company decide what should be done in the venture and how capital should be allocated?
(5) Were the profits of the business due to the parent company's skill and direction?
(6) Was the parent company in effectual and constant control?

48 *Smith, Stone & Knight Ltd v Birmingham Corporation* [1939] 4 All ER 116.

On the basis of these questions, Atkinson J considered there existed an implied agency relationship between Birmingham Waste and Smith, Stone & Knight Ltd. In so deciding, he did not deny the separate legal status of either company; rather, via the law on agency, he found that the actions of the subsidiary were the actions of the principal. Atkinson J stated that, '(i)f either physically or technically the Waste company was in occupation, it was for the purposes of the service it was rendering to the claimant (Smith, Stone & Knight) ... and I think that those facts would make that occupation in law the occupation of the claimants'.[49] He ordered that compensation be paid to Smith, Stone & Knight Ltd for the disruption to its waste business.

Atkinson J's approach to determining if an agency relationship existed has since been criticised on the basis that control by a parent company of a subsidiary should not, on its own, create an agency relationship.[50] As Rogers AJA has noted, if this were the case, 'then that conclusion could apply in relation to just about every holding company and fully owned subsidiary and the principle of limited liability in relation to the activities of subsidiaries would be left in tatters'.[51] As a result, the agency argument has rarely been successful in circumventing the separate legal entity doctrine.

3.30 Statutory inroads into the separate legal entity doctrine

Over time, situations have arisen where Parliament has considered it appropriate to make directors and officers liable for the debts of a company. For example, s 588G of the *Corporations Act* provides that directors are liable for the debts of a company if they continue to trade after the company becomes insolvent. Under s 95A(2) of the *Corporations Act*, a company is insolvent when it cannot pay its debts as and when they fall due for payment. Section 588G of the *Corporations Act* is discussed in detail in the context of directors' duties in Chapter 11 at Section 11.25. The effect of s 588G is to make directors personally liable for a company's debts if, at the time of the debt, there were reasonable grounds for a director suspecting that the company was or would become insolvent, and the director was or should have been aware of these grounds.

3.35 Corporate groups

Corporate groups are a common feature of many business operations and are discussed extensively in Chapter 4 at Section 4.65.05. In the present context, we consider the special challenges that groups create with the separate legal entity doctrine.

Aside from small proprietary companies, most business ventures today are conducted through groups of interrelated corporations. These structures allow businesses

49 Ibid 121.

50 J Harris, 'Lifting the Corporate Veil on the Basis of an Implied Agency: A Re-Evaluation of Smith, Stone & Knight' (2005) 23(1) *Company and Securities Law Journal* 7; A Hargovan and J Harris, 'The Relevance of Control in Establishing an Implied Agency Relationship between a Company and Its Owners' (2005) 23(7) *Company and Securities Law Journal* 459, 459.

51 *Briggs v James Hardie & Co Pty Ltd* (1989) 16 NSWLR 549, 567 (Rogers AJA).

to spread their operations, profits and liabilities between different companies, often with taxation advantages. Corporate groups are common where businesses operate in different jurisdictions or offer a range of different services or products.

When discussing corporate groups, specific terminology is used. The company at the apex of the group is called the 'parent' or 'holding' company. The parent company will own enough shares in the other companies to control their management and operations. These other companies are called 'subsidiaries' of the parent company, and can be partly or fully owned.

It is often argued that, in particular circumstances, corporate groups should be regarded as a single entity in law. These arguments are most strongly advocated where one company within a group becomes insolvent or incurs liability in tort that it cannot meet, or where the same directors manage a number of companies.[52] This is discussed further below at Section 3.50.

At common law, these arguments are rejected. Outside any statutory provisions to the contrary (such as s 588V discussed below), the courts will consider that each company in a group is a separate legal entity possessed of its own rights and liabilities. While, in practice, a group of companies is often regarded as one economic entity, this is not the position in law. As noted by Hadden:

> Businessmen, accountants and investors all think about corporate groups rather than individual companies as the main focus of their activities. Only lawyers and legislators ... cling to the tradition that individual companies are the only proper focus of attention and that corporate groups are no more than simple or complex combinations of individual companies.[53]

This situation is exemplified in the case of *Walker v Wimborne*.[54] The facts involved an action by the liquidator of Asiatic Electric Co Pty Ltd ('Asiatic') against its three directors: Raymond Wimborne, Pearl Wimborne and David Wimborne. These three individuals were the only directors of several other companies, which they administered as a group together with Asiatic. The group of companies encountered financial difficulties after completing work for Chevron Sydney Ltd on a hotel in Kings Cross. By the end of the work, Asiatic was owed over $100,000 which Chevron was unable to pay.

To cover costs within the group, the three directors moved funds between the companies to meet debts as they arose. In particular, they paid three debts owed by other companies from Asiatic funds. When Asiatic became insolvent, the liquidator argued that these payments involved a breach of directors' duties as the payments were not made in Asiatic's best interests. The three directors argued in response that they had acted for

52 S Lo, 'Piercing the corporate veil for evasion of tort obligations' (2017) 46(1) *Common Law World Review* 42; H Anderson, 'Challenging the Limited Liability of Parent Companies: A Reform Agenda for Piercing the Corporate Veil' (2012) 22(2) *Australian Accounting Review* 129; H Hansmann and R Kraakman, 'Toward Unlimited Liability for Corporate Torts' (1991) 100(7) *Yale Law Journal* 1879.

53 T Hadden, 'The Regulation of Corporate Groups in Australia' (1992) 15(1) *University of New South Wales Law Journal* 61, 61.

54 *Walker v Wimbourne* (1976) 137 CLR 1.

the benefit of the group of companies, as the payments had prevented some of the other companies from going into liquidation.

The High Court rejected the idea that a director can act in the interests of a group of companies and confirmed that directors owed duties to each individual corporate entity that they manage.[55] Mason J commented that:

> [T]he emphasis given by the primary judge to the circumstance that the group derived a benefit from the transaction tended to obscure the fundamental principles that each of the companies was a separate and independent legal entity, and that it was the duty of the directors of Asiatic to consult its interests and its interests alone in deciding whether payments should be made to other companies.[56]

While this case establishes the legal position in Australia, different arguments were used in the case of *DHN Food Distributors Ltd v London Borough of Tower Hamlets* to enable companies in a group to be treated as one entity.[57] The facts of that case were similar to *Smith, Stone & Knight* discussed at Section 3.25.15. DHN ran a food distribution business and was the holding company in a group of companies. There were two subsidiary companies that were wholly owned by DHN. One subsidiary company owned the land on which DHN's warehouse was located, and the other owned the vehicles used by DHN. The land owned by the first subsidiary was compulsorily acquired by the London Borough Council, and DHN sought compensation for disturbance to its business.

The Court of Appeal refused to adopt a legalistic approach to the issue and held that the companies within the group were partners of each other. On this basis, DHN was entitled to make the claim. Lord Denning MR explained the reasoning as follows:

> These subsidiaries are bound hand and foot to the parent company and must do just what the parent company says ... This group is virtually the same as a partnership in which all the three companies are partners. They should not be treated separately so as to be defeated on a technical point.[58]

This decision has been subject to extensive criticism, both by other courts and by academic commentators, for its minimisation of the relationship between parent and subsidiary companies.[59] It was not followed in the Australian cases of *Pioneer Concrete Services Ltd v Yelnah Pty Ltd*,[60] *Dennis Willcox Pty Ltd v Federal Commissioner of Taxation*,[61] and *State Bank of Victoria v Parry*[62] and it is now accepted that the fact that a parent company has

55 For a further discussion of the issue of liability within corporate groups, see J Harris and A Hargovan, 'Cutting the Gordian Knot of Corporate Law: Revisiting Veil Piercing in Corporate Groups' (2011) 26(1) *Australian Journal of Corporate Law* 39.

56 *Walker v Wimbourne* (1976) 137 CLR 1, 6–7.

57 *DNH Food Distributors Ltd v London Borough of Tower Hamlets* [1976] 1 WLR 852.

58 Ibid 860.

59 See, eg, *Woolfson v Strathclyde Regional Council* (1978) SLT 159, [96]; *Adams v Cape Industries plc* [1990] 2 WLR 657, [538]; D Powles, 'The "See-through" Corporate Veil' (1977) 40(3) *Modern Law Review* 339.

60 *Pioneer Concrete Services Ltd v Yelnah Pty Ltd* (1986) 5 NSWLR 254.

61 *Dennis Wilcox Pty Ltd v Federal Commissioner of Taxation* (1988) 14 ALD 794 (Jenkinson J).

62 *State Bank of Victoria v Parry* (1990) 2 ACSR 15.

control over a subsidiary is not sufficient reason to justify piercing the corporate veil.[63] As Rogers AJA noted in *Briggs v James Hardie & Co Pty Ltd*,[64] such an argument is 'entirely too simplistic'.[65] He continued:

> The law pays scant regard to the commercial reality that every holding company has the potential and, more often than not, in fact, does, exercise complete control over a subsidiary.[66]

In *Qintex Australia Finance Ltd v Schroders Australia Ltd*,[67] Rogers CJ commented on the challenges created by the operation of the separate legal entity doctrine to corporate groups. He stated:

> It may be desirable for parliament to consider whether the distinction between the law and commercial practice should be maintained. This is especially the case today when the many collapses of conglomerates occasion many disputes. Regularly, liquidators of subsidiaries, or of the holding company, come to court to argue as to which of their charges bears the liability ... As well, creditors of failed companies encounter difficulty when they have to select from among the moving targets the company with which they consider they concluded a contract. The result has been unproductive expenditure on legal costs, a reduction in the amount available to creditors, a windfall for some, and an unfair loss to others. Fairness or equity seems to have little role to play.[68]

Concerns such as these led to amendments to the *Corporations Act* in 1993 to introduce s 588V.[69] This section, while limited to the context of insolvency, is an important inroad into the application of the separate legal entity doctrine as it makes a parent company liable for the debts of a subsidiary where insolvent trading is involved. For liability to attach, there must be reasonable grounds for the parent company to suspect, at the time a debt is incurred by a subsidiary, that the subsidiary company is insolvent. It must also be shown that either the parent company or one or more of its directors were aware, or should have been aware, of those grounds.

Despite such reform, concerns over liability within corporate groups remains. As Harris and Hargovan wrote in 2011:

> The tendency to ignore the separate relationship between each group company, has been a matter of public concern in recent years. Several large corporate

63 See Anthea Nolan, 'The Position of Unsecured Creditors of Corporate Groups: Towards a Group Responsibility Solution which gives Fairness and Equity a Role' (1993) 11(8) *Company and Securities Law Journal* 461, 479–80.

64 *Briggs v James Hardie & Co Pty Ltd* (1989) 16 NSWLR 549.

65 Ibid 577.

66 Ibid.

67 *Qintex Australia Finance Ltd v Schroders Australia Ltd* (1990) 3 ACSR 267.

68 Ibid 269. For another discussion of the separate legal entity doctrine and corporate groups, see Jason Harris and Anil Hargovan, 'Cutting the Gordian Knot of Corporate Law: Revisiting Veil Piercing in Corporate Groups' (2011) 26 *Australian Journal of Corporate Law* 39.

69 For discussion of s 588V, see I Ramsay, 'Holding Company Liability for the Debts of an Insolvent Subsidiary: A Law and Economics Perspective' (1994) 17(2) *University of New South Wales Law Journal* 520.

collapses (including Ansett, Westpoint and Allco Finance Group), as well as the actions of the James Hardie group in seeking to shelter group assets from tort victims and the Patricks group of companies in seeking to minimise employee entitlements through the use of corporate groups, raise an important question about the use of corporate groups in Australia. Specifically, these developments raise a public concern as to what extent should company law ignore the separate entity status of individual members of a corporate group? This is an issue that is frequently before the courts both in Australia and overseas.[70]

3.40 Corporate liability for civil and criminal wrongs

The fact that a company is a separate legal entity means it can commit and be liable for criminal and civil wrongs.[71] Although a corporation acts through people (usually the board of directors, managers or shareholders), as a juristic person it can attract primary liability for these actions. One of the key ways such liability has been understood is through an analogy with human beings.[72] In *HL Bolton (Engineering) Co Ltd v TJ Graham & Sons Ltd*,[73] Lord Denning famously commented:

> A company may in many ways be likened to a human body. It has a brain and a nerve centre which controls what it does. It also has hands which hold the tools and act in accordance with directions from the centre. Some of the people in the company are mere servants and agents who are nothing more than hands to do the work and cannot represent the directing will or mind. Others are directors and managers who represent the directing mind and will of the company, and control what it does.[74]

Using this framework, often called the 'organic theory', the state of mind of directors and managers can create the mental state of mind of the company. As Lord Denning continued:

> [I]n cases where the law requires personal fault as a condition of liability in tort, the fault of the manager will be the personal fault of the company ... So also in the criminal law, in cases where the law requires a guilty mind ... the guilty mind of the directors or managers will render the company itself guilty.[75]

Before discussing this issue in more detail, it is interesting to note that research published in 2016 suggests that the extent of corporate wrongdoing in Australia is significant.[76]

70 J Harris and A Hargovan, 'Cutting the Gordian Knot of Corporate Law: Revisiting Veil Piercing in Corporate Groups' (2011) 26(1) *Australian Journal of Corporate Law* 39.

71 Under most Acts Interpretation Acts, 'person' is defined to include a body corporate: see, eg, s 22 of the *Acts Interpretation Act 1901* (Cth).

72 See discussion at in Chapter 2 at Section 2.30.

73 [1957] 1 QB 159.

74 Ibid 172.

75 Ibid 159.

76 M Grudnoff et al, *Corporate Malfeasance in Australia* (Discussion Paper, Australia Institute, April 2016) <https://australiainstitute.org.au/wp-content/uploads/2020/12/P247-Corporate-malfeasance-

Drawing on government data published by the Australian Securities and Investments Commission (ASIC), the Australian Competition and Consumer Commission (ACCC),[77] the Australian Taxation Office (ATO), the Fair Work Ombudsman, the Fair Work Commission, and the Australian Bureau of Statistics, the Australia Institute found that:

- between 2005–15, the ACCC took action against 669 companies: 167 for competition issues, 489 cases to safeguard consumers and in relation to unfair trade issues, and 13 others
- from mid-2011 to the end of 2015, ASIC concluded 3115 cases against individuals and corporations, of which 2095 (67 per cent) were criminal matters. However, this does not represent the full number of matters resolved by ASIC as it, like most regulators, uses a range of administrative sanctions to resolve cases and reserves litigation for the most serious cases
- during the period studied, the ATO litigated approximately 400 cases a year against corporations, in addition to a large number of out of court settlements. In 2014–15, corporate settlements raised revenue of $3.5 million
- every year, approximately 5,000 cases go to court involving organisations (mainly companies) as defendants, and on average around 4,000 of those defendants are found guilty.

In 2020, the Australian Law Reform Commission released its report on Australia's corporate criminal regime.[78] It noted the challenges it faced in conducting the review based on the fact that 'there is a dearth of data relating to corporate crime in Australia, which effectively obscures the extent and nature of such crime, and renders evidence based regulation of corporate conduct difficult'.[79] It recommended that national policies and principles be developed to enable the collection of information on corporate crime rates, corporate crime victimisation, and corporate enforcement action at both state and federal level.[80]

3.45 Corporate liability in criminal law

As the above discussion indicates, corporate misconduct can take a variety of forms, including tax evasion, market manipulation, consumer protection, unfair trade practices, and breaches of the *Corporations Act*. Corporations can also be liable for other crimes, including environmental damage, failure to provide safe working conditions, manslaughter, breach of employment conditions, and foreign bribery.

The requirement for mens rea, or proof of intent in criminal law, has created problems in the context of the corporation. As a result, many regulatory offences (including

in-Australia.pdf>. See also D Bartlett et al, 'Corporate Crime in Australia: The Extent of the Problem' (2020) 613 *Trends and Issues in Crime and Criminal Justice* 1.

77 The Australian Competition and Consumer Commission (ACCC) is responsible for promoting competition and protecting consumers and small businesses against other businesses.

78 Australian Law Reform Commission Report, *Corporate Criminal Responsibility* (Report 136, April 2020).

79 Ibid [3.112].

80 Ibid 13, Recommendation 1.

many provisions in the *Corporations Act*) operate as strict liability offences; that is, corporate liability exists without proof of fault.[81] Where a corporation is charged with an offence that requires fault, questions arise as to how this can be established. Which directors or managers are the 'mind' of the corporation? What if there are different 'states of mind' between directors and managers, or between some directors and other directors?

These questions have been around for a long time. In *Pharmaceutical Society v London and Provincial Supply Association Ltd*,[82] a case decided before *Salomon's Case*, Lord Blackburn considered that a corporation could be guilty of a crime requiring intent. He commented:

> I do not feel the least difficulty arising from what seems to have troubled some of the learned judges in the court below ... I quite agree that a corporation cannot, in one sense commit a crime—a corporation cannot be imprisoned, if imprisonment be the sentence for the crime; a corporation cannot be hanged or put to death if that be the punishment for the crime; and so, in those senses a corporation cannot commit a crime. But a corporation may be fined, and a corporation may pay damages ... If you could get over the first difficulty of saying that the word 'person' here may be construed to include an artificial person, a corporation, I should not have the least difficulty upon the other grounds that have been suggested.[83]

In *Lennard's Carrying Co Ltd v Asiatic Petroleum Co Ltd*,[84] the House of Lords looked to the state of mind of the individuals in control of the company. In *Northside Developments Pty Ltd v Registrar-General*,[85] Dawson J suggested that this approach was an extension of the law of agency, in that it allows any person with actual or implied authority to 'be regarded not only as the agent of the company, but also as the company itself—an organic part of it'.[86]

In most cases, it will be the directors or managers that are taken to be the mind of the company. For example, in *Tesco Supermarkets Ltd v Nattrass*,[87] the House of Lords noted that corporate managers who had been entrusted with a significant degree of freedom from higher authority could be taken to represent the company's state of mind. In that case, the company owned a chain of supermarkets. At one store, washing powder was advertised on sale. When the reduced price product was sold out, a store employee put out the same washing powder at the normal price. The following day, a customer tried to buy the item at the reduced price but was told there were no more discount items available and that he had to pay the normal price. Tesco was charged under the *Trade*

81 For example, many of the sections of the Act related to the provision of information to the general public and the regulator are strict liability offences. See, eg, ss 142–6 (registered office) and ss 148, 150, 153, 156 (company name).

82 *Pharmaceutical Society v London and Provincial Supply Association Ltd* (1880) 5 App Cas 857.

83 Ibid 869.

84 *Leonard's Carrying Co Ltd v Asiatic Petroleum Co Ltd* [1915] AC 705.

85 *Northside Developments Pty Ltd v Registrar-General* (1990) 170 CLR 146.

86 Ibid.

87 *Tesco Supermarkets Ltd v Natrass* [1972] AC 153.

Descriptions Act 1968 (UK) for falsely advertising the price of the washing powder. In its defence, Tesco argued that the company had taken all reasonable precautions and exercised all due diligence to avoid the commission of the offence, and that the conduct of the store manager was not the conduct of the corporation.

The House of Lords accepted the defence and found that the store manager was not the 'directing mind' of the corporation and therefore his conduct was not attributable to it. The corporation had done all it could to enforce the rules regarding advertising. Lord Reid noted that in order for liability to attach to the actions of an individual, they must be acting as the company. He continued:

> Normally the board of directors, the managing director and perhaps other superior officers of a company carry out the functions of management and speak and act as the company. Their subordinates do not. They carry out orders from above and it can make no difference that they are given some measure of discretion. But the board may delegate some part of their function of management giving to their delegate full discretion to act independently of instructions from them.[88]

In *ABC Developmental Learning Centres Pty Ltd v Wallace,*[89] the Victorian Supreme Court acknowledged there are circumstances where the 'directing will and mind' theory of corporate attribution is not adequate. In this case, ABC Developmental Learning Centres was part of the ABC group of companies which was successfully prosecuted in the Magistrates Court for breach of the *Children's Services Act 1996* (Vic). The prosecution arose out of a situation in 2003 where a child under the age of three escaped from a childcare centre owned by ABC and wandered into the surrounding streets. While the child was returned unharmed, the Acting Magistrate held that these events contravened provisions of the Act which required ABC and its staff to ensure that every reasonable precaution was taken to protect children from any hazard likely to cause injury and that children were adequately supervised. The Acting Magistrate attributed liability to ABC and held that the failure of the two staff to supervise the child (allowing him to climb a playground fence) was ultimately the failure of the company.

On appeal to a single judge of the Victorian Supreme Court, ABC argued that the conduct of junior employees could not be attributed to the company. Bell J dismissed the appeal and held ABC was guilty of the offences. In particular, he relied upon the approach of the Privy Council in *Meridian Global Funds Asia Ltd v Securities Commission*[90] where it was noted that in exceptional circumstances the primary rules of attribution 'will not provide an answer'.[91] In these cases, 'the court must fashion a special rule of attribution' based on the usual rules of statutory interpretation and taking into account the language of the statute, and its content and policy.[92]

88 Ibid.
89 *ABC Developmental Learning Centres Pty Ltd v Wallace* (2006) 161 A Crim R 250.
90 *Meridian Global Funds Asia Ltd v Securities Commission* [1995] 2 AC 500.
91 Ibid 507.
92 Ibid.

Adopting this approach, Bell J held that the actions of the junior employees could be attributed to the company due to the terms of the offence and the policy objectives of the enabling statute. After considering the nature of the charges brought against ABC, and the policy of the Act, Bell J found that the protection, supervision and care of young children were paramount considerations in the legislation. He held that '(a) children's service proprietor that is a company can only protect children from hazards and supervise them through employees'.[93] As a result:

> The terms of the offence and the policy of the legislation are such that the actions of such persons, done within the scope of their work, can be attributed to the company. If their actions do not comply with the standards expressed, it can count as non-compliance for the purposes of a prosecution.[94]

As mentioned previously, in April 2019, the federal government commissioned the Australian Law Reform Commission (ALRC) to undertake a review of the corporate criminal responsibility regime.[95] The review was in response to recommendations made in the final report of the Royal Commission into Misconduct in the Banking, Superannuation and Financial Services Industry and the ASIC Enforcement Review Taskforce on the need to strengthen Australia's corporate criminal liability laws.[96] The terms of reference of the ALRC review were to consider whether, and if so what, reforms are necessary to improve Australia's corporate criminal liability regime.

The ALRC's final report was tabled in Parliament in August 2020.[97] Some of the key findings were that:

- Corporations are most often prosecuted for relatively minor regulatory offences. Smaller corporations are more likely to be prosecuted than larger corporations.
- Prosecutors withdraw a significantly higher number of charges against corporations than they withdraw against individuals for corporate crimes, suggesting that existing laws present real difficulties for prosecuting corporations.
- There is significant complexity in the Commonwealth legislative landscape, with over 3,100 offences across the 25 Commonwealth statutes relevant to corporate misconduct.
- Existing penalty and sentencing options for corporations are inadequate and often disproportionately affect shareholders, employees and third parties who were not connected with the corporation at the time of the offending.[98]

3.45.05 *Criminal Code Act 1995* (Cth)

Several of the ALRC's recommendations related to provisions dealing with corporate liability under pt 2.5 of the Code, located in sch 1 of the *Criminal Code Act 1995* (Cth)

93 *ABC Developmental Learning Centres Pty Ltd v Wallace* (2006) 161 A Crim R 250, [28].

94 Ibid. The finding was affirmed in *ABC Developmental Learning Centres Pty Ltd v Wallace* (2007) 16 VR 409.

95 Australian Law Reform Commission, *Corporate Criminal Responsibility* (Report 136, April 2020).

96 *Royal Commission into Misconduct in the Banking, Superannuation and Financial Services Industry* (Final Report, 4 February 2019); Australian Government, The Treasury, *ASIC Enforcement Review Taskforce Report* (18 December 2017).

97 Australian Law Reform Commission, *Corporate Criminal Responsibility* (Report 136, April 2020).

98 Ibid 7–8.

('*Criminal Code*'). These provisions replace the concept of the directing will and mind in Australia, and apply to offences within Commonwealth legislation, including offences under the *Corporations Act*.[99] Section 12.1(2) of the *Criminal Code* states that a body corporate can be found guilty of an offence, including one punishable by imprisonment. In the case of such an offence, the penalty imposed on a corporation will usually be a fine (s 4B).

Under s 12.2 of the *Criminal Code*, the physical element of a criminal offence can be attributed to a company if it is committed by an employee, agent, or officer of the company acting within the actual or apparent scope of their employment or within their actual or apparent authority.[100] This provision relies on agency principles and is wider than the common law 'directing will and mind' principle, as it allows for liability for employees acting within their employment or authority. The ALRC recommended an amendment be made to s 12.2 to simplify its wording so that liability would apply for acts by any person acting at the direction, or with the agreement or consent (express or implied), of an officer, employee, or agent of the body corporate, acting within actual or apparent authority.[101]

Under s 12.3(1) of the *Criminal Code*, the fault element of an offence can be attributed to a company where it expressly, tacitly or impliedly authorises or permits the commission of the offence. A company is taken to have authorised or permitted the commission of an offence where:

- the board of directors or a high managerial agent intentionally, knowingly or recklessly carried out the relevant conduct or expressly, tacitly or impliedly authorised or permitted the commission of the offence. This ground does not apply where the company can show it exercised due diligence to prevent the conduct, authorisation or permission of the high managerial agent;
- a corporate culture existed within the body corporate that directed, encouraged, tolerated or led to non-compliance with the relevant provision; or
- the body corporate failed to create and maintain a corporate culture that required compliance with the relevant provision (s 12.3(2)).

Under s 12.3(6), a 'high managerial agent' is defined to include an employee, agent, or officer with duties of such responsibility that their conduct may fairly be assumed to represent the body corporate's policy; and 'corporate culture' is defined to mean an attitude, policy, rule, course of conduct or practice existing within the body corporate or that part of it in which the relevant activities took place.

These provisions have been criticised for being hard to prove, particularly in the context of large corporations. As the ALRC noted:

> Traditional methods of attribution that look to the directing mind of the organisation in determining corporate fault are more easily proved against smaller corporations. ... Larger corporations often have a greater degree of devolved authority and are structured around divisions and business units (and in

99 *Corporations Act* s 1308A.
100 The concepts of actual and apparent authority are discussed in detail in Chapter 6.
101 Australian Law Reform Commission, *Corporate Criminal Responsibility* (Report 136, April 2020) 224.

> multinational companies there may be additional layers of management around regions and countries). Thus, there is no one person who can be said to be directing the operations of the corporation. Organisational hierarchies mean that decisions and their implementation are necessarily separated, not always documented, and often opaque.[102]

As a result, the ALRC proposed two options for reform. The first was to replace 'high managerial agent' with 'officer, employee, or agent of the body corporate, acting within actual or apparent authority'.[103] The second was to replace s 12.3 with a provision to the effect that, if it is necessary to establish a state of mind, other than negligence, of a body corporate, it is sufficient to show that:

> (a) one or more officers, employees, or agents of the body corporate, acting within actual or apparent authority, engaged in the relevant conduct, and had the relevant state of mind; or
> (b) one or more officers, employees, or agents of the body corporate, acting within actual or apparent authority, directed, agreed to or consented to the relevant conduct, and had the relevant state of mind.[104]

It would be a defence if the body corporate proved that it took reasonable precautions to prevent the commission of the offence.

3.45.10 Vicarious liability

Whereas the above discussion relates to direct liability of companies in criminal law, companies can be indirectly liable for the criminal acts of their employees. This is called 'vicarious liability' and is based on the similar principle that applies in tort cases that are discussed below. Under vicarious liability, a corporation can be held liable for the acts or omissions of its employees and agents committed within the course of their employment or within the scope of their authority where such liability is clear in the relevant legislation. While the common law does not recognise vicarious liability for criminal offences, such liability can exist under statute in relation to offences of strict or absolute liability, or where the statute demonstrates such an intention. For example, s 769B of the *Corporations Act* provides that in relation to offences in ch 7 of the Act (dealing with financial services and markets), 'conduct engaged in on behalf of a body corporate by a director, employee or agent of the body, within the scope of the person's actual or apparent authority ... is taken ... to have been engaged in also by the body corporate'.

Other statutory examples include:

- s 85 of the *Proceeds of Crime Act 1987* (Cth), which provides that if a director, employee or agent of the company commits an offence under that Act, the company is deemed to be liable

102 Ibid 229.
103 Ibid 14.
104 Ibid 228.

- s 84 of the *Competition and Consumer Act 2010* (Cth), which imputes to the company the conduct and state of mind of every director, employee or agent of the company acting within the scope of his or her actual or apparent authority.

3.50 Corporate liability in tort

A company can be liable in tort, either through the principle of vicarious liability or through direct liability, where it causes or contributes to injury to a person. Vicarious liability makes an employer (including a company) liable for the acts or omissions of its employees where they were acting within the scope of their employment. In contrast, direct liability can arise in common law or under statute in circumstances where a company itself is liable for the wrong. Examples of torts that companies can commit include negligence, passing off, defamation, injurious falsehood, deceit, conspiracy and breach of statutory duty.

3.50.05 Policy considerations with corporate liability in tort

One issue that continues to be the subject of debate is the situation where a company that is part of a group of companies is liable for damages in tort but has limited assets to pay the claim.[105] We know that the separate legal entity doctrine prevents tort victims from making claims against other companies within the group for any shortfall. However, this can create unfair situations where tort victims—who are, in essence, involuntary creditors—are penalised for the fact that the entity that causes them loss has limited funds, while other companies within the group may have adequate funds to pay the claim.

Unlike contract creditors, the involuntary tort creditor has no ability to self-protect against the risk of non-payment by choosing not to deal with that company. If the company is insolvent or unable to compensate the injured person, it is therefore natural for them to look to those behind the company, or to other companies within the group, for payment. This issue arose in Australia in the context of the James Hardie & Co Pty Ltd litigation. James Hardie was one of Australia's largest corporations and was involved in the mining, manufacture and sale of asbestos products from the early 1920s until 2001, when it moved its headquarters overseas. The company had various subsidiaries that operated the asbestos operations from the 1930s onwards.

Throughout the 1970s, it became clear that asbestos was a highly toxic substance. As a result, between 1995 and 2000, the parent company (James Hardie & Co Pty Ltd) began to remove the assets from the subsidiaries, leaving them with most of the asbestos liabilities. A compensation fund was then established to meet the asbestos claims for the next 50 years. In reality, the fund was underfunded and began to run out of money after just

105 See, eg, S Lo, 'Piercing the Corporate Veil for Evasion of Tort Obligations' (2017) 46(1) *Common Law World Review* 42; M Warren, 'Corporate Structures, the Veil and the Role of the Courts' (2016) 40(1) *Melbourne University Law Review* 1; C Witting and J Rankin, 'Tortious Liability of Corporate Groups: From Control to Coordination' (2014) 22(1) *Tort Law Review* 91; H Hansmann and R Kraakman, 'Toward Unlimited Liability for Corporate Torts' (1991) 100(7) *Yale Law Journal* 1879; H Anderson, 'Challenging the Limited Liability of Parent Companies: A Reform Agenda for Piercing the Corporate Veil' (2012) 22(2) *Australian Accounting Review* 129; D Millan, 'Piercing the Corporate Veil, Financial Responsibility and the Limits of Limited Liability' (2007) 56(5) *Emory Law Journal* 1305.

two years of operation. This situation caused substantial public outcry in Australia and criticism of the corporate rules (including the separate legal entity doctrine) that allowed the situation to arise.

The liability of the board of directors of James Hardie for these actions is discussed in detail in Chapter 11. For now, it is sufficient to note that the case raised questions about whether it was permissible for victims to take action against other companies within a group of companies. The main arguments in favour of limiting the operation of the separate legal entity doctrine were that:

- unlike other creditors, involuntary tort claimants do not choose to assume the risk of the subsidiary's insolvency
- leaving tort claimants to bear the risk of uncompensated loss is economically inefficient as they are not in a position to avoid that risk due to their lack of a contractual relationship with the company
- limiting the liability of other companies within a group reduces the deterrence for harmful behaviour in the corporate group context
- there is an ethical question of whether companies should be able to profit from business operations without bearing the costs of injury.[106]

These questions have not been answered by the courts. In the case of *Briggs v James Hardie & Co Pty Ltd*,[107] Rogers AJA suggested that separate considerations should apply when determining the liability of a parent company for the tortious liability of its subsidiary. In this case, Briggs was employed by a subsidiary company of James Hardie & Co Pty Ltd and, as a result of his work, contracted asbestosis. He sued both the subsidiary and the parent company for negligence. The subsidiary was insolvent and to succeed against the parent company it was necessary for the Court to go behind the separate legal entity doctrine to attribute liability.

The New South Wales Court of Appeal was asked to resolve, as a preliminary matter, whether there was sufficient evidence to hold the parent company liable for the acts and omissions of the subsidiary. The Court held that there was and that the question should be determined at trial. Rogers AJA rejected as too simplistic the idea that complete control of the subsidiary by the parent company was on its own sufficient to result in liability being attributed to the parent. However, he did suggest that different considerations might apply where a claim is in tort rather than in contract. He stated:

> Generally speaking, a person suffering injury as a result of the tortious act of a corporation has no choice in the selection of the tortfeasor. The victim of the negligent act has no choice as to the corporation which will do him harm. In contrast, a contracting party may readily choose not to enter into a contract with a subsidiary of a wealthy parent. The contracting entity may inquire as to the amount of paid up capital and, generally speaking, as to the capacity of the

106 'Annexure T' in DF Jackson, *Report of the Special Commission of Inquiry into the Medical Research and Compensation Fund* (Report, September 2004) <https://www.austlii.edu.au/cgi-bin/viewdoc/au/other/nsw/NSWBCPubInq/2014/1.html>.

107 *Briggs v James Hardie & Co Pty Ltd* (1989) 16 NSWLR 549.

other party to pay the proposed contract debt and may guard against the possibility that the subsidiary may be unable to pay.[108]

In May 2000, the Companies and Securities Advisory Committee issued a report on liability within corporate groups, in which it rejected the need for reform to the application of limited liability. The arguments put to the Committee opposing reform were that:

- the interests and profiles of group companies differ significantly
- reform would create different liability in Australia to overseas jurisdictions
- the separate legal entity doctrine is an important legal principle that is entrenched within commercial practice
- allowing companies within groups to operate separately from each other stimulates investment and can aid competition, growth, and development
- the courts can analyse the circumstances of each case and, in specific instances, find exceptions to the doctrine
- making a parent company liable for the torts of a subsidiary company could weaken the economic foundation of all the other companies in the group
- if the tort claims were large or numerous, they could destroy an entire corporate group comprising vastly differing interests
- the imposition of such liability may give rise to increased litigation, particularly against larger corporate groups.[109]

3.55 Summary

This chapter explored two of the most important corporate law concepts: the separate legal entity doctrine and limited liability. It is important to remember that although these two doctrines operate to make the corporation a highly desirable and popular legal structure for conducting business, they are distinct ideas, with limited liability benefiting shareholders and the separate legal entity doctrine applying to the company. Furthermore, these concepts, and in particular the separate legal entity doctrine, have provoked much discussion and criticism from both the judiciary and academia. Exceptions to the separate legal entity doctrine are rare and, after *Prest's Case* are likely to remain so.

A key issue is the operation of the separate legal entity doctrine in the context of corporate groups. Here, the courts have adopted a strict approach, even where it has been argued (as in the context of tort victims) that injustice is caused by maintaining the separate legal status of each entity within the group.

Finally, this chapter discussed how a company can be liable in criminal law and tort. In the former context, the application of the 'directing will and mind' concept still operates under common law, unless it has been replaced by statute as in the case of the *Criminal Code Act 1995* (Cth). In tort, a company can be liable through vicarious liability or directly where the company has committed the wrong.

108 Ibid 578–9. The case did not proceed any further than this decision.
109 Companies and Securities Advisory Committee, *Corporate Groups* (Final Report, May 2000) <https://takeovers.gov.au/sites/takeovers.gov.au/files/2021-04/corporate_groups_final_report_may_2000.pdf>.

CHAPTER

4

FORMATION AND TYPES OF COMPANIES

4.05 Introduction

A company is a legal entity, distinct from its creators, members, directors and managers. Chapter 3 of this book discusses the separate legal status of the company in detail. For the purposes of this chapter, we emphasise that for a company to come into existence there must be a conferral of that status by the state. Unlike some other forms of association, such as a partnership, it is not legally effective for a group of people to simply declare themselves to be a company. A company is a type of corporation. The corporate status of a company is brought into existence through a process of registration under the *Corporations Act 2001* (Cth). Other types of corporate entities are created by different legislative mechanisms, and we briefly describe some of these later in this chapter.

This chapter describes the range of basic company structures available under the *Corporations Act*, focusing on three ways in which companies can be categorised: the proprietary or public status; how the liability of their members is structured; and the relationship to other companies. This chapter examines the role of corporate groups, as well as the difference between closely-held, one-person, and widely-held companies.

4.05.05 Defining 'corporation'

A company is a type of corporation. While the focus of this book is on companies, some sections in the *Corporations Act* refer to 'corporation' and others refer to 'company'. Accordingly, it is useful to focus for a moment on the scope of the term 'corporation'.

Section 57A defines the term 'corporation' for the purposes of the *Corporations Act* (the Act). It does this by specifying, in a non-exhaustive way, four types of entity that fall within the definition, and by excluding others. Once the specific exclusions are noted, the definition of 'corporation' in the Act is open-ended.

The effect of ss 57A(1) and (3) is that the term 'corporation', wherever it is used in the Act, includes (but is not limited to) four types of entities:

(1) a company: this is defined in s 9 to mean a company registered under the Act, and this type of corporation is the focus of this book. For the purposes of the Act, a company is a subset of the broader category of 'corporation'
(2) any body corporate: this term is not defined comprehensively in the Act;[1] under general law, the term 'body corporate' refers to 'any body whatsoever that has corporate personality'[2]
(3) an unincorporated body that may be sue or be sued, or may hold property in the name of its secretary or an office-holder of the body
(4) an Aboriginal and Torres Strait Islander corporation that is registered under the *Corporations (Aboriginal and Torres Strait Islander) Act 2006* (Cth).

There are two specific exclusions from the definition in s 57A(2). First, an 'exempt public authority' is not a corporation for the purposes of the Act. This term is defined in s 9 to mean a body corporate incorporated within Australia (or an external Territory) that is either a 'public authority' or an 'instrumentality or agency of the Crown'. None of these terms are defined in the Act, and so reference must be made to case law. In *Federal Commissioner of Taxation v Bank of Western Australia*, Hill J noted that a private body established for profit cannot be a 'public authority'. Rather, the body must be 'an agency or instrument of government set up to exercise control or execute a function in the public interest' and, further, 'must perform a traditional or inalienable function of government and have government authority for so doing'.[3]

The second exclusion is a 'corporation sole'. This is also not defined in the Act. The term refers to the largely historical circumstance where the occupant of a particular position or office was given corporate status. As described in Blackstone's *Commentaries:*

> Corporations sole consist of one person only and his [sic] successors, in some particular station, who are incorporated by law, in order to give them some legal capacities and advantages, particularly that of perpetuity, which in their natural persons they could not have had. In this sense the king is a sole corporation; so is a bishop ...[4]

4.10 The registration process

In s 9 of the Act, a company is defined as 'a company registered under this Act'. The process whereby a new company is created as a separate legal entity under the Act is relatively straightforward. The main steps are as follows.

1 Section 9 makes two clarifying points about the term 'body corporate' but does not offer a full definition.
2 *Oates v Consolidated Capital Services Ltd* (2009) 76 NSWLR 69.
3 *Federal Commissioner of Taxation v Bank of Western Australia* (1995) 61 FCR 407, 429.
4 Sir William Blackstone, *Commentaries on the Laws of England* (Garland Publishing, 1978) vol 1, 469. See also S Stoljar, *Groups and Entities: An Inquiry into Corporate Theory* (ANU Press, 1973) ch 9.

First, the company's name mut be reserved. An application may be made to the Australian Securities and Investments Commission (ASIC) to reserve a specified name (s 152). Part 2B.6 of the Act deals with the availability and restrictions on the use of company names. This includes requirements, noted later in this chapter, to include the words 'Limited', 'Proprietary', 'No Liability' (as appropriate) or their abbreviations at the end of the company's name. A company may be registered with a name consisting only of the Australian Company Number (ACN) that it receives on registration (s 148(1)). The *Corporations Regulations 2001* (Cth) specify prohibitions or restrictions on the use of certain words and phrases in a company's name. These include 'Trust' and 'Incorporated', as well as words that suggest a connection with the Commonwealth or a state or territory government, the Royal Family, or Sir Donald Bradman.[5] Once a company is registered, it must set out its name (if it has one) and ACN on all public documents and negotiable instruments that the company signs or issues (s 153).

The second step is preparing internal management rules and obtaining consents. Each company has rules that govern its internal management and its capital structure. The company's original incorporators must decide whether the company will rely initially on the replaceable rules in the Act, or whether the company will have a constitution which replaces those rules in whole or in part. If there is to be a constitution, then each person who is to be a member when the company is registered must agree in writing to the terms of the constitution (s 136(1)).

Each person who is to be a member, director or company secretary[6] of the company at the time that it is registered must give their consent to act in that capacity (s 120). A proprietary company must have at least one director, who must ordinarily reside in Australia,[7] and a public company must have a minimum of three directors, two of whom must ordinarily reside in Australia (s 201A). A public company must have at least one secretary (again, ordinarily residing in Australia); a proprietary company is not required to have a secretary (s 204A). If the company is to have a share capital, the members must also consent to take up a specified number of shares, and to pay the amount per share required on registration. After the company is registered, the company must keep these agreements and consents.

The third step is lodgement of the application for registration (and payment of registration fees). The application is made on the prescribed form and must contain the information set out in s 117(2). The required information includes:

- the type of company to be registered (the different types of company are explained later in this chapter)
- the company's proposed name (unless the ACN is to be used)
- the name and address of each person who has consented to become a member
- the present name, former names, place and date of birth of each person who has consented to become a director or company secretary

5 *Corporations Regulations 2001* (Cth) reg 2B.6.01, sch 6.
6 A proprietary company is not required to have a secretary (s 204A(1)).
7 Section 201A(1A) specifies a minimum of two directors for a proprietary company when it has crowd-sourced funding (CSF) shareholders. This is also known as 'equity crowdfunding' and is discussed in Chapter 9.

- the address of the company's proposed registered office
- if the company has a share capital—the number of shares which each member agrees to take up, and the amount which each member agrees to pay
- if the company is limited by guarantee—the amount of the guarantee that each member has agreed to (companies limited by guarantee are explained later in this chapter).

If the company is to be a public company the application must be accompanied by a copy of its constitution (if any). Registration can be done by lodging hard-copy documents with ASIC, or it can be done online.[8]

The final step is registration by ASIC. Following lodgement of the application for registration, ASIC 'may' give the company an ACN, register the company and issue a certificate of registration (s 118). The certificate of registration includes the company's name, ACN, type of company, and date of registration. It states that the company is registered as a company under the Act and names the state or territory in which the company is taken to have been registered. Importantly, the certificate is conclusive evidence that all of the registration requirements have been complied with, and that the company was duly registered on the date specified in the certificate (s 1274(7A)). This section is not binding on the Crown as represented by ASIC. ASIC is not precluded by s 1274(7A) from challenging the validity of a company's registration.[9]

A company comes into existence at the beginning of the day on which it is registered.

In practice, the incorporation process is often shortened by the use of 'shelf companies'. Accountants, lawyers and other professional advisers commonly register a number of inactive companies, which are then kept 'on the shelf' as a ready-made supply for clients who want to commence an enterprise or activity. Rather than incorporating a new company, the client simply purchases a pre-existing shelf company—this is an 'off-the-rack' method of commencing a business via the corporate form. Details such as the company's name, internal management rules, and share structure are then amended to reflect the special requirements of the client.

4.15 The consequences of registration

The relative ease with which a company can be brought into existence might draw attention away from the significance of the legal consequences that flow from registration. From the day of registration, the directors, members and company officers are subject to a complex web of legal rights, duties, regulatory requirements and liabilities. There are also consequences for the newly created company. These consequences stem from the fact that, upon registration, a company comes into existence as a body corporate (s 119).

The key consequences of a company's status as a body corporate are summarised here, and are dealt with more fully in Chapter 3.

8 See Australian Securities and Investments Commission, *Steps to register a company* (Information Sheet 61, 2024) https://asic.gov.au/for-business/registering-a-company/steps-to-register-a-company/.

9 *Australian Securities Commission v SIB Resources NL* (1991) 30 FCR 221 found that, as a result of the Commission's successful challenge to the validity of incorporation, the company should be wound up on the application of the Commission or the Attorney-General.

A company can sue and be sued in its own right. Generally speaking, when a wrong is done to a company, then only the company has standing to bring legal action regarding that wrong. This is known as the 'proper plaintiff principle'. Historically, this principle caused significant difficulties for company members when the wrong to the company was done by those who control the actions of the company. These difficulties and the legislative response to them are discussed in Chapter 14.

A company has perpetual succession. A company continues as the same legal entity regardless of changes in its members or management, or changes in name or type of corporation. This means that control of a company can be passed from one person or group to another without affecting the legal existence of the corporate entity. A company's legal existence is 'perpetual' in that it can only be terminated by the company being dissolved as a consequence of a winding up or, where the company is defunct, by having its registration cancelled (see Chapter 16).

A company has the power to acquire, hold and dispose of property, independently of the owners or managers of the company. The members and directors of a company have no legal or equitable interest in the company's property. In the words of one judge:

> The fact that an individual by himself or his nominees holds practically all the shares in a company may give him control of the company ... but it does not ... make the property or assets of the company his, as distinct from the corporation's. Nor does it make any difference if he acquires not practically the whole, but absolutely the whole, of the shares. The business of the company does not thereby become his business.[10]

Some of the most frequently encountered problems in corporate law, both with small family businesses and large publicly-traded companies, occur when those who run the business ignore, or do not fully appreciate, the position of the company as a separate legal entity. This may result from the fact that, in practice, the registration of a company is regarded only as one step in a longer process of achieving some particular goal; for example, establishing a business, taxation minimisation, or eligibility to receive external funding.

4.20 Types of corporation

In corporate law, the terms 'company' or 'corporation' are often used as though there is a standard type of corporate organisation to which corporate law rules and principles can be applied. A moment's reflection reveals that there is great diversity in corporate forms and their uses. Corporate enterprises range from a single company providing a not-for-profit welfare service, to a complex multi-corporate profit-making conglomerate that operates on a global scale. As the renowned economist JK Galbraith observed, '[T]here is no such thing as *a* corporation. Rather there are several kinds of corporations all deriving from a common but very loose framework.'[11]

10 *Gramophone & Typewriter Ltd v Stanley* [1908] 2 KB 89, 96–7 (Cozens-Hardy MR).
11 JK Galbraith, *The New Industrial State* (Penguin, 1970) 82–3.

Understanding the diversity of different corporate types is an important prerequisite to appreciating the wide impact of corporate law principles. An important question for law reformers is whether the law should pay greater attention to this diversity, so that specific legal principles and regulatory regimes apply to different types of corporation.

This chapter explains the basic types of corporate structures and organisation. The chapter is concerned primarily with companies registered and operating under the *Corporations Act*. However, at the outset, it is useful to be aware of the existence of other corporate forms.

4.25 Some other types of corporate entities

Here we describe three different types of corporate legal entity that exist outside the Act. This discussion emphasises that, in certain circumstances, there are alternative ways to achieve some of the benefits of corporate status.

4.25.05 Incorporated associations

Each Australian state and territory has an *Associations Incorporation Act* that provides a form of incorporation for associations with non-profit objectives.[12] These Acts were originally introduced to offer a relatively simple alternative to the *Corporations Act* for groups, such as community and sporting organisations, who seek the advantages of corporate legal status without the regulatory costs.[13] However, over time some of these Acts have been amended with the introduction of disclosure and liability provisions drafted in terms similar to those found in the *Corporations Act*.

There are differences in detail between these statutes, but the scope and operation can be understood by using the *Associations Incorporation Act 1991* (ACT) as an example. An association with at least five members may seek incorporation. An association is ineligible if it has the object of trading or obtaining pecuniary gain for its members or it has capital divided into shares held by its members. Trading or obtaining pecuniary gain is only a disqualification where the purpose is to return the income earned to members for their gain. It is permissible for a non-profit association to trade in order to raise funds to support its non-profit activities.[14] Once incorporated, an association has all of the legal features of a body corporate, such as perpetual succession and the capacity to acquire, hold and dispose of property in its own name (these features are discussed in Chapter 3). Members and officers have limited liability, subject to the Act and to the rules of the association. The abbreviation 'Inc.' must be included in the name of the association. Annual accounts must be prepared, audited, and presented to the annual general

12 *Associations Incorporation Act 1991* (ACT); *Associations Incorporation Act 2009* (NSW); *Associations Act 2003* (NT); *Associations Incorporation Act 1981* (Qld); *Associations Incorporation Act 1985* (SA); *Associations Incorporation Act 1964* (Tas); *Associations Incorporation Reform Act 2012* (Vic); *Associations Incorporation Act 2015* (WA).

13 A charity can incorporate under this legislation or may instead choose an unincorporated structure (such as a trust) or incorporate under the *Corporations Act* (in which case, certain exemptions from provisions in the *Corporations Act* may apply: see s 111L).

14 In NSW, income and asset thresholds are used to determine whether an association's trading activities continue to meet the legislation's objects.

meeting of the association. The Act also contains provisions analogous to those found in the *Corporations Act* concerning matters such as pre-incorporation contracts, the authentication and execution of documents, and the effect of restrictions in the association's rules concerning its powers.

4.25.10 Co-operatives

A co-operative (or 'co-op') is an incorporated entity that is owned and democratically controlled by its members. Co-operatives range from small, local community concerns to multi-million-dollar trading businesses. States and territories have legislation that either adopts a uniform national legislative template for co-operatives, known as the Co-operatives National Law (CNL), or is consistent with that template. In New South Wales, for example, the National Law is set out as an appendix to the *Co-operatives (Adoption of National Law) Act 2012* (NSW). Under the CNL, a co-operative becomes a corporation once it is registered (s 28). The CNL sets out seven 'co-operative principles' with which incorporated entities must comply (s 10). These include the idea that co-operatives are autonomous, self-help organisations controlled by their members, and that members will usually receive limited compensation, if any, on the capital that they put into the co-operative. The CNL contains provisions that either directly apply specified sections of the *Corporations Act* to co-operatives, or that are worded in similar terms. For example, the provisions in the CNL concerning the duties and liabilities of directors and officers of a co-operative closely resemble the equivalent sections in the *Corporations Act*.

4.25.15 Statutory corporations

It is common practice for governments to create particular corporations by special Acts of Parliament. These statutory corporations fall outside the operation of the *Corporations Act* unless their Act of incorporation provides otherwise. Commonwealth examples range from well-known entities (such as the Australian Human Rights Commission, the Australian Broadcasting Corporation, and Airservices Australia), to the esoteric (such as the Fisheries Research and Development Corporation). Universities such as the Australian National University and the University of Adelaide are statutory corporations. Occasionally, a statutory corporation is later converted into a company incorporated under the *Corporations Act*, as part of a process of privatising governmental instrumentalities. The conversion of the Commonwealth Bank in 1990 and its subsequent public share offer was a prominent example of this process.

Along with statutory corporations, there are a large number of companies created wholly or partly by federal, state or territory governments under the *Corporations Act*. These companies may be used by governments to engage in commercial ventures as government business enterprises, or for the provision of other government services. Significant policy questions are raised when a government has a total, controlling, or substantial membership interest in a corporation created under general incorporation legislation. In particular, should the corporation be regarded as a public institution or is it similar to any other privately incorporated body? The answer to this question will determine the types of accountability mechanisms to be imposed.

Most Australian jurisdictions have enacted legislation to control different aspects of the activities of government owned corporations.[15]

4.30 Companies under the *Corporations Act 2001* (Cth)

The legislation discussed in the previous paragraphs is aimed at specific types of corporate organisations, established for specific purposes or with particular organisational structures. Where the intention is to conduct a profit-making enterprise with the aim of returning those profits to members, then incorporation under the *Corporations Act* will be appropriate. We now turn our attention to the different possibilities under that legislation.

Within the parameters of the *Corporations Act*, companies can be categorised according to three criteria:

(1) Is the company proprietary or public?
(2) How is the liability of the members structured?
(3) What is the relationship of the company to other corporations?

These criteria can overlap; for example, we can categorise a company both by whether it is proprietary or public, and by its relationship to other companies. We look at each of these three criteria and discuss some other ways companies governed by the *Corporations Act* can be classified.

4.35 Proprietary and public companies

All corporations incorporated under the *Corporations Act* are classified either as proprietary or public companies. These two categories have different historical origins: the modern public company developed from the English joint stock companies of the nineteenth century, while the proprietary company was a later legislative creation. Chapter 1 describes this history. A proprietary company is sometimes described as a private company; in the United Kingdom this is the standard legal terminology.[16] However, the labels 'public' and 'private' can cause confusion. Political theorists and sociologists frequently refer to the 'public/ private divide' in their analyses of modern society, where the 'public' is the realm of governments and the 'private' is the realm of individual citizens. The corporate law categories of public company and proprietary/private company have little to do with that distinction. Instead, these labels are used to indicate a company's capacity to raise funds from outside sources, and the extent of its obligations to disclose its financial affairs. To avoid confusion, we will use the terms 'proprietary' and 'public' company.

15 *Public Governance, Performance and Accountability Act 2013* (Cth); *Territory Owned Corporations Act 1990* (ACT); *State Owned Corporations Act 1989* (NSW); *Government Owned Corporations Act 2001* (NT); *Government Owned Corporations Act 1993* (Qld); *Government Business Enterprises (Competition) Act 1996* (SA); *Government Business Enterprises Act 1995* (Tas); *State Trading Concerns Act 1916* (WA); *State Owned Enterprises Act 1992* (Vic).

16 *Companies Act 2006* (UK) s 4.

4.35.05 Proprietary companies

Under the *Corporations Act*, a proprietary company must satisfy the following five requirements:

(1) It must have a share capital (s 112(1)). A person becomes a member of a proprietary company by acquiring ownership of one or more shares in the company. This means that in a proprietary company the terms 'member' and 'shareholder' mean the same thing.

(2) It must have at least one member (s 114) but cannot have any more than 50 non-employee shareholders as members (s 113). An employee shareholder is a shareholder who is also an employee of the company (or was, when they became a shareholder) (s 113(2)(b)). The Act allows for more than 50 employee shareholders because this recognises the beneficial effect that employee share schemes can have on a company's operations. The minimum requirement of one member was discussed in *Re Dungowan Manly Pty Ltd (in liq)*, where Black J noted that although s 114 does not provide a penalty for breach, the requirement should not be disregarded. In that case, the Court disallowed a scheme which would have cancelled all of the shares in the company with the consequence that the company would have had no members.[17] Section 231 describes how 'a person' becomes a member, and the term 'person' is defined in s 2C of the *Acts Interpretation Act 1901* (Cth) to include a body politic or corporate as well as an individual. This means that a company can be a member of another company.

(3) It must have at least one director, who must ordinarily reside in Australia (s 201A(1)).[18] A body corporate cannot be appointed as a director of a company (s 201B(1)), which also specifies the minimum age for an individual to be appointed as a director).[19] As discussed in Chapter 10, a company can be classified as a 'shadow director' (see para (b)(ii) of the definition of director in s 9) for the purposes of incurring directors' liability: see *Standard Chartered Bank of Australia Ltd v Antico*.[20] A company can be a member of another corporation—this can lead to the creation of complex corporate groups.

The minimum membership and minimum director requirements in points (2) and (3) can overlap. A proprietary company may consist of one person occupying both the roles of sole member and sole director. The idea of a 'one-person' company is examined in more detail later in this chapter.

(4) It must not engage in any activity that would activate the operation of the fundraising provisions in ch 6D of the *Corporations Act*. This means that a proprietary

---

17 *Re Dungowan Manly Pty Ltd (In liq)* (2017) 124 ACSR 218.

18 However, s 201A(1A) specifies a minimum of two directors for a proprietary company when it has crowd-sourced funding (CSF) shareholders. This is also known as 'equity crowdfunding' and is discussed in Chapter 9.

19 However, ss 1224 and 1224F specify that the sole director of a company that is a corporate collective investment vehicle (CCIV) must be a public company. See the description of CCIVs at Section 4.60.

20 *Standard Chartered Bank of Australia Ltd v Antico* (1995) 38 NSWLR 290.

company is not able to offer its shares for public subscription nor invite offers for subscription. It can offer its shares to existing company members or employees (s 113(3)).[21]

(5) It must include the words 'Proprietary Limited' or the abbreviation 'Pty Ltd' at the end of its name (ss 148(2), 149). This serves to indicate to persons who deal with, or intend to become members of, the company that it is bound by the above requirements and limitations.

In Chapter 1, we noted that public disclosure by companies of financial information has long been thought of as the necessary quid pro quo for the privilege of limited liability.[22] The historical reason for this is that the publication of such material is presumed to counter the possibilities of fraud and also to provide information to persons who are considering whether to trade with or invest in a company. This rationale can be seen more clearly (although there is continued debate)[23] in relation to large public companies whose main method of raising finances is by public solicitation. But it is less clear that the rationale applies with the same force to smaller proprietary companies. On the one hand, it can be argued that while proprietary companies with a small capital base can pose a risk to outsiders, those outsiders will frequently resort to other mechanisms to protect their interests, such as contractual terms and personal guarantees from the company directors. On the other hand, without a system of mandatory public disclosure, many creditors, such as trade suppliers, would be deprived of information that helps to ascertain the risk and creditworthiness of the companies with which they deal.[24] This debate has been addressed by the recognition in legislation in Australia of a sub-species of proprietary company.

The *Corporations Act* makes a distinction between large and small proprietary companies. The purpose of this distinction is to implement a legislative policy whereby smaller enterprises should not necessarily have to meet the same financial reporting requirements as large business operations.

A large proprietary company is defined as a proprietary company that meets any two of the following three criteria for a financial year (s 45A(3) and reg 1.0.02B):[25]

(1) it has a consolidated revenue of $50 million or more
(2) the value of its consolidated gross assets is $25 million or more
(3) it has at least 100 employees[26]

21 If a proprietary company does engage in activity which requires lodgement of a prospectus, then ASIC may require the company to change to a public company under s 165.

22 See, eg, Companies and Securities Advisory Committee, *Report on an Enhanced Statutory Disclosure System* (Report, September 1991) 30.

23 See Chapter 17 regarding the debate about mandatory disclosure.

24 See Board of Trade, *Report of the Company Law Committee* (Cmnd 1749, 1962) [60].

25 Note that these amounts are those prescribed by the *Corporations Regulations 2001*, as permitted by s 45A(3). Note, too, that the criteria apply to the company and to any entities it controls.

26 According to data from the Australian Small Business and Family Enterprise Ombudsman's office, in June 2023, 97.3 per cent of Australian businesses had between 0–19 employees: see 'Number of Small Businesses in Australia', *Australian Small Business and Family Enterprise Ombudsman* (Web Page) <https://www.asbfeo.gov.au/small-business-data-portal/number-small-businesses-australia>.

A small proprietary company is defined as a proprietary company that, for a financial year, falls below any two of those three criteria (s 45A(2)). The advantages the *Corporations Act* gives to small proprietary companies include the following:

- a small proprietary company does not have to prepare a financial report and directors' report for a financial year unless a direction that this should be done is given either by shareholders with at least 5 per cent of the votes or by ASIC (ss 293–4)
- where a small proprietary company is directed to prepare a financial report, the report does not have to be audited unless shareholders with at least 5 per cent of the votes have directed that the financial report be prepared and audited (ss 293, 301(2)), or ASIC has given a direction under s 294.

Note that the categorisation of a proprietary company as large or small is determined based on factors that may vary from one financial year to the next. This means that over a number of years a company may have to meet different financial reporting requirements as its business expands or contracts and, consequently, as its status as a large or small proprietary company changes.

In historical terms, proprietary companies were a relatively late addition to our corporate law system (see Chapter 1). While many proprietary companies are responsible for large business operations with annual revenue worth hundreds of millions of dollars, most proprietary companies tend to be small-to middle-size trading concerns, or small family companies. This is recognised by the inclusion of a 'Small Business Guide' in pt 1.5 of the *Corporations Act,* which summarises the main provisions in the Act that apply to proprietary companies limited by shares. Many proprietary companies are incorporated for purposes other than the active conduct of a business venture, such as tax minimisation and property planning objectives. This serves as a reminder that modern corporate law is not concerned exclusively with business concerns—a large number of corporations are non-commercial, non-trading concerns that operate more like partnerships or sole-proprietorships.

4.35.10 Public companies

The public company is a residual category and is defined in the *Corporations Act* as any company other than a proprietary company (s 9). The principal legal characteristics of a public company are as follows:

(1) it must have at least one member (s 114); unlike a proprietary company, there is no statutory maximum
(2) it must have a minimum of three directors, at least two of whom must ordinarily reside in Australia (s 201A(2))
(3) it may raise funds by making offers or invitations to the public to purchase or subscribe for securities (see Chapter 9). To enhance the marketability of its securities, a public company may decide to apply for listing on a securities exchange (see Chapter 17).

A public company need not have a share capital, in which case it is classified as a company limited by guarantee. This is discussed later in this chapter.

4.35.15 Other differences between proprietary and public companies

The *Corporations Act* makes other distinctions between proprietary and public companies. One important set of distinctions is found in the provisions of the Act that operate as replaceable rules which may govern a company's internal management (see s 134; the concept of replaceable rules is discussed in Chapter 5). A summary list of these replaceable rules is found in s 141. Some of these rules are only relevant to proprietary companies, while in one instance (s 249X, governing who can appoint a proxy at a general meeting) the rule is replaceable only for proprietary companies and is mandatory for public companies. Examples of replaceable rules that are relevant only to proprietary companies are:

- s 194: dealing with the capacity of directors of proprietary companies to vote on contracts that involve the company and in which they have a declared interest
- s 254D: granting a pre-emption right for existing shareholders in a proprietary company when fresh shares are issued[27]
- s 254W(2): giving directors of a proprietary company the power to pay dividends as they see fit
- s 1072G: giving directors of a proprietary company a discretion to refuse to register a transfer of shares in a company for any reason.[28]

Other differences between proprietary and public companies relate to the directors and administration of the corporation. For example:

- Public companies must appoint each director by a separate resolution unless there is unanimous agreement to a single resolution (s 201E).
- A director of a public company may be removed before the end of his or her term by an ordinary resolution of the members regardless of anything in the company's constitution (s 203D). The removal of directors in a proprietary company is governed by the company's constitution, which might permit removal by a resolution of the board or of the general meeting (see, for example, the replaceable rule in s 203C permitting removal by a members' resolution).
- A director of a public company who has a material interest in a matter being considered by the board must not vote on that matter or be present while it is being discussed unless permitted by other non-affected members of the board (s 195).
- Chapter 2E of the *Corporations Act* closely regulates the giving of financial benefits to related parties of public companies.

There are many other differences regarding matters such as members' and directors' meetings, financial reporting, appointment and resignation of auditors, and takeovers. These are discussed elsewhere in this book.

27 In this context, a pre-emption right means that existing shareholders must be offered the new shares first before they are then offered to potential new shareholders. One aim of these pre-emptive rights is to preserve existing voting and control patterns in the company.

28 Until 1995, it was mandatory for a proprietary company to include a clause in its constitution that restricted the right of members to transfer their shares. The replaceable rule in s 1072G makes this optional.

4.35.20 Changing proprietary/public status

As prescribed by s 162(1), a public company may convert to proprietary status and a proprietary company may convert to public company status by passing a special resolution[29] to that effect and lodging with ASIC the documents required by s 163 (for example, a copy of the special resolution). A change in a company's status does not create a new legal entity (s 166(1)). A proprietary company may be required by ASIC to change its status to a public company if it breaches the proprietary company requirements set out in s 113 regarding the maximum number of non-employee shareholders and the restriction on public fundraising (s 165).

Further discussion about changing company status can be found later in this chapter at Section 4.45.

4.40 Liability of members to the company

The second way in which the *Corporations Act* classifies corporations is by reference to how the liability of members is structured. There are four alternatives listed in s 112.

4.40.05 Company limited by shares

This is a company in which the capital is divided into shares and a member is only liable to pay to the company the amount that is unpaid on their shares (ss 9 and 516). For example, a shareholder may subscribe to 2,000 $1 shares in a company. Assume that the company does not require the full $1 per share to be paid at the time of initial subscription, and the shareholder pays 20 cents per share. The shareholder is now a member of the company and has an outstanding liability to the company for the remaining 80 cents per share ($1,600). Once the shares have been fully paid, the liability to the company of that shareholder (and any future holders of those shares) has been discharged.

A company limited by shares is required to include the word 'Limited' or the abbreviation 'Ltd' at the end of the company's name (s 148(2)). This requirement originates in the idea that creditors will be warned that their loans can only be satisfied out of the company's assets, not those of the member shareholders. Since the majority of companies incorporated today are limited liability companies, it is likely that this warning is simply assumed by creditors.

Companies with a share capital can be either proprietary or public. A public company with a share capital may choose to apply to have its shares listed for trading on a securities exchange, but this is not a requirement of the *Corporations Act* (see Chapter 17). The holding of shares in a proprietary company can be distinguished from a public company in another way. A number of proprietary companies are small organisations where there is a close association between the shareholders, and between the shareholders and the directors. In such a situation, share ownership is primarily a means of allocating liability and of structuring power and control in the company. In contrast, share ownership in public companies is frequently a function of investment rather than

29 A special resolution is one that meets the requirements in s 250MA, including that it must be passed by at least 75 per cent of the votes cast by members who are entitled to vote on the resolution.

a means of apportioning control. Shareholders in public companies may regard themselves primarily as investors, while shareholders in a proprietary company may regard themselves foremost as members. As seen in Chapter 14, these differences in perspective are often ignored by corporate law doctrine.

4.40.10 Company limited by guarantee

A company limited by guarantee does not have a share capital and has no power to issue shares (s 124(1)). In this type of company, the members undertake that, if the company is wound up, they will contribute a specified amount to the property of the company for distribution to the company's creditors (ss 9, 517). The liability of members only arises if the company is wound up and has insufficient assets to meet its liabilities at that time. Members are not required to pay any capital to the company while it is a going concern. Equally, the company is prohibited from paying a dividend to its members (s 254SA).

Without the input of share capital, these companies will rely on outside sources for funds. Trading entities are unlikely to adopt this form of incorporation because of the lack of starting capital. Welfare, social and not-for-profit organisations with small capital needs that can be met by membership subscriptions, donations or government grants are the most common users of this type of incorporation.[30] However, not all guarantee companies are small affairs.

Ironically, one of the largest collapses in Australian corporate history was a company limited by guarantee—the National Safety Council of Australia Victorian Division. This company had 300 full-time employees and, at the time it was wound up, had losses estimated at $65,644,000. The collapse was triggered by large-scale fraud committed by the company's chief executive officer. An action brought by a creditor against the directors resulted in one director being found personally liable to pay approximately $97 million and a significant judicial decision on the duties of care owed by non-executive directors.[31]

Because they do not have a share capital, companies limited by guarantee must be incorporated as public companies and must include the word 'Limited' or the abbreviation 'Ltd' at the end of the company name (s 148(2)). Non-profit or community organisations that operate as companies limited by guarantee might want to avoid any unwanted impression of commercial activity that could be conveyed by this addition to the company name. Accordingly, under s 150, ASIC may permit the registration of a company limited by guarantee without the word 'Limited' in its name if the company is a not-for-profit entity registered under the *Australian Charities and Not-for-profits Commission Act 2012* (Cth) as a charity,[32] and its constitution prohibits the payment of fees to its directors, and requires directors to approve all other payments made by the company to the directors.

30 Many such groups find that incorporation is a prerequisite to the receipt of government funding: see S Bottomley, 'The Corporate Form and Regulation: Associations Incorporation Legislation in Australia' in R Tomasic and R Lucas (eds), *Power, Regulation and Resistance: Studies in the Sociology of Law* (Canberra College of Advanced Education, 1986) 44, 47.

31 *Commonwealth Bank of Australia v Friedrich* (1991) 5 ACSR 115, discussed in Chapter 11.

32 'Charity' is defined extensively in *Charities Act 2013* (Cth) pt 2.

4.40.15 Unlimited liability company

A public or a proprietary company can be registered as an unlimited liability company. This type of incorporation dates back to early English company statutes, which permitted incorporation by registration but did not grant limited liability to the company's members. As its name suggests, the members of such a company are financially liable without any limit for the debts of the company if its assets are insufficient to meet its liabilities (s 9). Unlimited liability companies must be incorporated with a share capital. This means that, on winding up of the company, each member will, first, be liable to pay to the company any unpaid amounts on their shares. If this is insufficient to meet the liabilities of the company, then members will be asked to make further contributions to discharge the company's debts.

There is no requirement that these companies include in their name any indication of their members' unlimited liability, but an unlimited proprietary company must include the word 'Proprietary' at the end of its name (s 148(3)).

The main advantage of this type of incorporation is that an unlimited liability company is not subject to the limitations on share capital reductions that are imposed on a company limited by shares (s 258A). This means that shareholders can have their capital returned to them and be released from further liability to the company while it is still an operating entity. This form of company is sometimes used by professional practices, such as lawyers or accountants.

4.40.20 No liability company

This type of company has no contractual right under its constitution to recover any amounts unpaid on shares from a current shareholder (ss 9, 112(2) and 254M(2)). A shareholder may elect to forfeit the shares rather than pay any unpaid amount which is called by the company. The statutory right of a shareholder to forfeit shares instead of paying some or all of the outstanding amounts can be negated by prior agreement between the shareholder and the company.[33]

This form of incorporation was first introduced by the *Mining Companies Act 1871* (Vic) in response to the problem of 'dummying'—a practice whereby shareholders in speculative mining ventures were registered under fictitious names to avoid having to pay unpaid amounts on their shares. There is debate about whether this legislation was a creative move to encourage investment in speculative mining ventures, or 'a backward looking, short-term expedient to the problems created by the lack of an effective corporate enforcement mechanism in the colonies'.[34] Whatever view is taken of its history, this category of incorporation is now restricted to companies with share capital whose sole object (as stated in the company constitution) is mining purposes (s 112(2)),[35] although many large mining companies

33 *Theseus Exploration NL v Foyster* (1972) 126 CLR 507.

34 R McQueen, 'Limited Liability Company Legislation—The Australian Experience' (1991) 1(1) *Australian Journal of Corporations Law* 22, 36.

35 'Mining purposes' is defined in s 9 to include 'prospecting for ores, metals or minerals', but does not include quarrying operations for the sole purpose of 'obtaining stone for building, roadmaking or similar purposes'.

are incorporated as public companies limited by shares. A no liability company is prohibited from engaging in activities that are outside its mining purposes (s 112(3)).

This type of company is identified by the words 'No Liability' or the abbreviation 'NL', which must be included at the end of the company name (s 148(4)). No liability companies must be incorporated as public companies (s 112(1)). Subject to some exceptions, these companies are bound by the provisions of the *Corporations Act* relating to public companies. If a no liability company is listed on the Australian Securities Exchange, it will also be subject to specific listing rules. Other sections specific to no liability companies are found in ss 254P–254R of the *Corporations Act*, dealing with the process by which shares in a no liability company may be forfeited.

4.45 Change of status

Part 2B.7 (ss 162–7) of the *Corporations Act* permits certain changes of company status. A change of status has the potential to affect the liability of present and past members and creditors, and any conversion is subject to procedural restrictions to protect members and creditors. In *Windsor v National Mutual Life Association of Australasia Ltd*, the Federal Court held that the sections dealing with change of company type are intended to cover the field and that a company cannot change its status by some other method, such as a scheme of arrangement.[36]

For a change of company status to be effective, the members must first pass a special resolution approving the change. That resolution must then accompany an application lodged with ASIC. For certain types of change, other documentation must be submitted with the application. In general, the changes requiring specific documentation are those with the potential to increase the obligations or liabilities of members: a change from limited liability to unlimited liability, or a change from liability limited by guarantee to liability limited by shares (see s 163). In all cases, the change of status is effected when ASIC publishes a notice that the details of the company's registration will be altered to reflect the company's new status (s 164).

The permissible conversions are set out in Table 4.1.

A change in status does not mean that a new legal entity is created, and the change does not affect the company's existing property, rights, obligations, or its role in any legal proceedings (s 166(1)).

4.50 Registration patterns

In 2022–3, there were 3.2 million companies registered in Australia. Although ASIC data does not break down this number into proprietary and public companies, other data from 2013 shows that nearly 99 per cent of all companies registered in Australia are proprietary companies, with 87 per cent of those companies having only one or two shareholders.[37]

36 *Windsor v National Mutual Life Association of Australasia Ltd* (1992) 34 FCR 580 (Black CJ and Beaumont J).

37 Data from P Hanrahan, *The Law of Close Corporations—Australia* (Report, 2014) a report prepared for the International Academy of Comparative Law World Congress.

Table 4.1 Permissible conversions s 162(1)

This type of company may change ...	... to this type of company
Proprietary company limited by shares	• Unlimited proprietary company • Unlimited public company • Public company limited by shares
Unlimited proprietary company	• Proprietary company limited by shares* • Public company limited by shares* • Unlimited public company
Public company limited by shares	• Unlimited public company • Unlimited proprietary company • Proprietary company limited by shares • No liability company
Company limited by guarantee	• Public company limited by shares • Unlimited public company • Proprietary company limited by shares • Unlimited proprietary company
Unlimited public company	• Public company limited by shares* • Proprietary company limited by shares* • Unlimited proprietary company
Public no liability company	• Public company limited by shares** • Proprietary company limited by shares**

* This change is permitted only if, within the last three years, the company was not a limited company that became an unlimited company.
** This change is permitted only if all the issued shares are fully paid up.

Public companies limited by shares account for approximately 1 per cent of all registrations. The next most popular form of incorporation is companies limited by guarantee.

While these figures provide some perspective on the make-up of corporate Australia, they refer only to company registrations. The figures tell us nothing about the economic significance of these different categories, nor are they an indication of the actual number of businesses run via these corporations. According to the Australian Bureau of Statistics, in June 2023, 41 per cent of the 2.5 million active businesses in Australia were structured as companies; the rest are run as partnerships, trusts or sole proprietorships.[38]

Many corporations are grouped together as part of a single business operation. This important feature of corporate organisation is discussed next.

38 Australian Bureau of Statistics, *Counts of Australian Businesses, including Entries and Exits* (27 August 2024) <https://www.abs.gov.au/statistics/economy/business-indicators/counts-australian-businesses-including-entries-and-exits/latest-release>.

4.55 A company's relationship to other companies

The third way in which we can categorise companies under the *Corporations Act* is as holding companies or subsidiary companies. Section 46 deems a company[39] to be a subsidiary of another if:

(1) the first company controls the composition of the subsidiary's board of directors. This includes having the power to appoint or remove all, or a majority, of the directors of the subsidiary. For these purposes, the power to appoint directors includes the situation where appointment to the board of the subsidiary follows necessarily from appointment as a director or officer of the first company (s 47); or
(2) the first company can cast or control the casting of more than half of the maximum votes that might be cast at a general meeting of the subsidiary; or
(3) the first company holds more than half of the subsidiary company's issued share capital.

These criteria do not include cases where the first company holds shares or has power only in a fiduciary capacity (s 48(2)). Section 48 contains further exceptions to the definition.

The standard implied by the reference to 'control' of the composition of the subsidiary's board of directors in s 46 was considered in *Mount Edon Gold Mines (Australia) Ltd v Burmine Ltd*,[40] where the Court was urged by the plaintiff to hold that practical or de facto control was sufficient to satisfy the test. White J disagreed, holding that:

> [E]ach of the three subparagraphs ... is concerned with legal power. It is difficult to see how, in the absence of a legal power, a body corporate could be said to control the composition of the board of another body corporate, by virtue of what it in fact does, when another body holds more than one-half the maximum number of votes that might be cast at a general meeting of the company.[41]

His Honour explained the difficulties inherent in the plaintiff's argument in the following example:

> [S]uppose that the shares of a company are held as to 80 per cent by shareholder A, as to 15 per cent by shareholder B and as to 5 per cent by shareholder C, and that, perhaps as a result of apathy, shareholder A is customarily absent from general meetings of the company. In the result, shareholder B is accustomed to appoint his nominees to the board of directors of the company and to remove directors of the company as it may decide, whether or not shareholder C agrees. In such a case, if the plaintiff is correct, the company is a subsidiary of shareholder B, a situation that is liable to be changed on short notice if shareholder A decides at any time to exercise its rights.[42]

39 The section refers to the wider category of 'body corporate'. For ease of explanation, we refer to 'companies'.
40 *Mount Edon Gold Mines (Australia) Ltd v Burmine Ltd* (1994) 11 WAR 291.
41 Ibid 310.
42 Ibid.

The source of legally enforceable power to control the composition of the subsidiary's board might be found in that company's constitution or in a separate agreement among the subsidiary's shareholders, conferring control on the holding company.

A holding company is defined as a body corporate that has a subsidiary (s 9). The *Corporations Act* permits the creation of a wholly owned subsidiary, which is a company that has no members other than its holding company or a nominee or other wholly owned subsidiary of the ultimate holding company (s 9).

Subsidiary-holding company relationships are not restricted to simple two-company situations. In the case where company C is a subsidiary of company B, and company B is a subsidiary of company A, then company C is also classified as a subsidiary of company A (s 46(b)). This would apply to any further subsidiaries of company C. In this example, company B is also a holding company in relation to company C, and company A is called the 'ultimate holding company' in this chain (s 9).

The *Corporations Act* uses the term 'related body corporate' in various places. This term applies to both a subsidiary and its holding company, and to subsidiaries of the holding company of another subsidiary (s 50).

Although these provisions recognise that corporations can be linked by relations of control and influence, the legislation and the case law continue to take the individual company to be the primary focus of corporate law. This point is elaborated below at Section 4.65.05.

4.60 Registrable Australian bodies and foreign companies

While the primary focus of this chapter, and this book, is on the 'standard' types of corporation described above, it should be noted that the *Corporations Act* also contains sections that deal with specific corporate types. As examples, we briefly mention three of these: registrable Australian bodies, foreign companies, and corporate collective investment vehicles.

The first two types are dealt with in ch 5B of the Act. The category of 'registrable Australian body' permits certain bodies corporate that are created outside the jurisdiction of the *Corporations Act* to carry on business in the jurisdiction. This includes incorporated associations and co-operatives. The definition of registrable Australian body in s 9 refers to either a body corporate or an unincorporated body that can sue or be sued, or hold property in the name of its secretary or an appointed officer. To carry on business within the jurisdiction of the *Corporations Act*, a body must make an application to be registered in the jurisdiction (s 601CA). The concept of carrying on business is defined to include 'administering, managing, or otherwise dealing with, property situated in Australia' (s 21(2)(b)) but it does not include the matters listed in s 21(3), such as merely holding property, maintaining a bank account, or completing an isolated transaction within a 31-day period.

Second, a foreign company is a body corporate incorporated outside Australia or an unincorporated body that does not have its principal place of business in Australia (see the full definition in s 9). Such a company can only carry on business in Australia if it has applied for and been granted registration under pt 5B.2 div 2. The phrase 'carrying on business' has the same meaning as for registrable Australian bodies.

Registration requires, among other things, the appointment of at least one natural person or company as a local agent who is responsible for the company's compliance with the *Corporations Act* and is personally liable for penalties resulting from contraventions of the law (ss 601CF–601CJ).

The third example is found in ch 8B of the *Corporations Act*, which provides for the creation of corporate collective investment vehicles (CCIVs). These sections were added in 2022 in response to a 2009 report that recommended the introduction of a form of collective investment that was more internationally recognised than the existing managed investment schemes in ch 5C of the Act.[43] A CCIV is a company limited by shares that operates as an 'umbrella' investment vehicle, managing distinct investment sub-funds. Chapter 8B modifies the application of other provisions in the Act in relation to CCIVs; for example, a CCIV can have only one director, and that must be a public company (s 1224).

4.65 Further ways of classifying corporations

The different ways of classifying companies discussed above are expressly recognised in the *Corporations Act*. There are other important features of corporate life that are not fully recognised by legislation or common law.

4.65.05 Corporate groups

In the world of commerce and finance, the single, isolated company is not a common occurrence. Small trading concerns run by proprietary companies are likely to operate this way, but medium to large trading, financial or industrial concerns are likely to be run by complex groups of interrelated companies. These corporate groups can transcend national boundaries; '[t]he Transnational Corporation ..., often with diverse and integrated relationships with various national and foreign corporate entities, is typical of the modern corporate group'.[44]

There is no generally accepted definition of what constitutes a corporate group, and there are no comprehensive figures on the number or extent of these structures in Australia. A study of Australian listed companies in 2007 found that nearly 88 per cent of the sample companies were structured as part of a corporate group.[45] The predominance of corporate groups prompts the question as to whether the group should be given some degree of formal recognition in corporate law.

As discussed in Chapter 2, the doctrines and rules of Australian corporate law assume that each company exists and operates as an independent legal actor, with little regard

43 Australian Financial Centre Forum, *Australia as a Financial Centre: Building on Our Strengths* (Report, Department of the Treasury, 17 November 2009) ('the Johnson Report').

44 M Addo, 'Human Rights Perspectives of Corporate Groups' (2005) 37 *Connecticut Law Review* 667.

45 S van der Laan and G Dean, 'Corporate Groups in Australia: State of Play' (2010) 20(2) *Australian Accounting Review* 121: this study defined 'corporate group' in terms of subsidiary/holding company relationships, inter-company guarantees, and tax consolidation arrangements. See also I Ramsay and G Stapledon, 'Corporate Groups in Australia' (2001) 29(1) *Australian Business Law Review* 7.

being given to the social and economic context within which those companies operate. Neither Australian legislators nor the judiciary have taken comprehensive steps to recognise the existence of corporate groups. Professor Tom Hadden has commented that:

> Businessmen, accountants and investors all think about corporate groups rather than individual companies as the main focus of their activities. Only lawyers and legislators ... cling to the tradition that individual companies are the only proper focus of attention and that corporate groups are no more than simple or complex combinations of individual companies.[46]

The standard authority for the Australian position is found in Mason J's judgment in the 1976 High Court case of *Walker v Wimborne*,[47] which involved a number of companies managed by common directors. Mason J referred to 'the fundamental principles that each of the companies [in the case] was a separate and independent legal entity'.[48] This and related cases are discussed in Chapter 3; they rely on an 'entity model' of corporate organisation because they focus on the constituent entities in the group. It is an approach that ignores the 'underlying unity of economic purpose, common personnel, common membership and control' that may be found in a corporate group.[49] As Rogers J remarked in *Briggs v James Hardie & Co Pty Ltd*, the law on corporate groups 'pays scant regard to commercial reality'.[50]

The entity model originated at a time when the economic world could be described as:

> a world of small firms, explored by a single trader or partnerships with few associates, assembling limited financial and labor resources, engaged in a local and one-product market, normally possessing no business relationships with commercial partners and holding no significant market share.[51]

Modern commercial practice is quite different and may be more accurately reflected in the 'enterprise model'.[52] The enterprise model has been influenced by economic perspectives:

> If the owners of an enterprise choose to fragment it into several constituent corporations— and we must assume that they act as rational investors in doing so—then they must believe that such a form of enterprise organization will maximize the return on their investment, given their acceptable level of risk ... [Because of this] the profitability of any one constituent corporation is largely irrelevant to them, except as it contributes to the overall effort.[53]

46 T Hadden, 'The Regulation of Corporate Groups in Australia' (1992) 15(1) *University of New South Wales Law Journal* 61; J Dine, *The Governance of Corporate Groups* (Cambridge University Press, 2000).

47 *Walker v Wimborne* (1976) 137 CLR 1.

48 Ibid 6.

49 *Varangian Pty Ltd v OFM Capital Ltd* [2003] VSC 444 [142].

50 *Briggs v James Hardie & Co Pty Ltd* (1989) 16 NSWLR 549, 577.

51 JE Antunes, *Liability of Corporate Groups* (Kluwer, 1994) 16.

52 See P Blumberg, *The Law of Corporate Groups: Procedural Law* (Little, Brown, 1983) ch 1.

53 JM Landers, 'A Unified Approach to Parent, Subsidiary, and Affiliate Questions in Bankruptcy' (1975) 42(4) *University of Chicago Law Review* 589, 591.

Economists assume that investors and managers in the constituent companies within a group will be more concerned with the financial fortunes of the overall group than with those of the individual corporations. To achieve this goal, it may be necessary to favour the interests of some companies over others in the interests of group prosperity. In the view of one commentator, 'there are no economically compelling reasons why the profit centres within the group should correspond with the centres of legal right and entitlement, namely, the individual companies'.[54]

There are well-recognised economic reasons for structuring a business via a group of companies. A group might be structured to achieve financial savings and managerial efficiencies in a business, or to enable certain business assets to be isolated from the risks entailed in another related business activity. A group of companies might divide responsibility for its operations into various managerial units, or divisions, within the group.

Corporate groups can be organised 'horizontally' (for example, an association between several companies operating at the same level of production in an industry) or 'vertically', where companies operating at different points along the same production process are inter-linked (for example, supplier of raw materials, processor, wholesaler). There are also 'conglomerate' groups formed by companies that are not linked either horizontally or vertically and in which the constituent corporations may have diverse businesses.

The creation of a corporate group may not be the product of deliberate planning. A group may be the result of more gradual processes, such as the growth and diversification of a business, or because of takeover acquisitions. These processes can mean that one company's location and significance within a group might change over time, such as where a holding company finds itself the subject of a successful takeover by one of its previous subsidiaries. Companies within a group can operate as active trading entities, as management vehicles, or lie dormant. Frequently, the holding company that ultimately controls the group will do little more than own shares and not be engaged directly in any productive or operational processes. Finally, a corporate group may be created to take advantage of legal rules (such as tax legislation) or as a device to avoid their application.[55]

As noted, there is no commonly accepted definition of what constitutes a corporate group. This arises because of the nature of the constituent entities and the way in which they are related. Should attention be restricted to groups comprised only of corporate entities, or should it include the use of unincorporated entities and arrangements such as trusts, partnerships, and joint ventures? If attention is limited solely to groups of companies, what criteria should be used in defining the ties that bind those companies into a group? Is the legislative definition of holding–subsidiary company relationships in s 46 sufficient? If this definition is considered to be too limited, should the concept of a corporate group be limited to relationships based on share ownership? According to Mason J in *Walker v Wimborne*, 'the word "group" is generally applied to a number of companies

54 D Prentice, 'Groups of Companies: The English Experience' in K Hopt (ed), *Groups of Companies in European Law* (Walter de Gruyter, 1982) 103, n 17.

55 M Eisenberg, 'Corporate Groups' in M Gillooly (ed), *The Law Relating to Corporate Groups* (Federation Press, 1993) 5.

which are associated by common or interlocking shareholding, allied to unified control or capacity to control'.[56]

In addition to group structures determined by share ownership, we could consider ties created by contract and authority.[57] Contractual agreements between different entities may be used to allow for cooperation between these entities while retaining an 'arms-length' relationship between them. Control by the use of authority may result from share ownership, whether a majority or a minority shareholding which is sufficient to guarantee de facto or working control of a company. Alternatively, a creditor corporation (for example, a bank) may, as a condition of the loan, be in a position to dictate the business policy of a borrowing company, even without formal board representation. Ties of authority may not often be evident to people outside the group or by all of those inside the constituent corporations. Insiders and outsiders may have different perceptions about the boundaries and control of a particular group enterprise.

The entity-based approach favoured by Australian courts has different effects upon the interests of creditors and shareholders of individual companies within a corporate group.

Under the entity model, creditors who establish legal relations with a business run by a corporate group must do so via one of the constituent companies. A creditor may simply wish to do business with that particular company, having no dealings with the wider group at all. Regardless of the creditor's intentions, the fact that the debtor company is part of a larger group can have a significant impact on the risks associated with the credit transaction.[58] Because of the group context, these risks may be more difficult to ascertain than is the case when dealing with an isolated company.

An example of these problems can be found in a case that dealt with the financial affairs of the Qintex group, a diversified conglomerate of approximately 170 companies with interests in media, television, holiday resorts and entertainment.[59] Between 1988 and 1989, Qintex Australia Ltd (Qintex), an intermediate holding company in the group, borrowed sums totaling $185.5 million. In return, the company issued unsecured debentures.[60] These debentures were issued under deeds drawn up by Qintex that also appointed ANZ Executors and Trustees Company Ltd (ANZ) to act as the trustee for the interests of the debenture-holders. In late 1989, Qintex defaulted on the loans, and ANZ

56 *Walker v Wimborne* (1976) 137 CLR 1.

57 H Collins, 'Ascription of Legal Responsibility to Groups in Complex Patterns of Economic Integration' (1990) 53(6) *Modern Law Review* 731. Eisenberg argues that share ownership should be the only concern: M Eisenberg, 'Corporate Groups' in M Gillooly (ed), *The Law Relating to Corporate Groups* (Federation Press, 1993) 1.

58 Here we refer to 'voluntary creditors' who exercise some degree of choice in dealing with the company. This includes financial institutions (eg banks, who are more likely to investigate the financial status of the company before the transaction and seek some security for the loan) and trade creditors (eg suppliers of goods and services who are less likely to make such checks and who, therefore, will generally be unsecured). Similar problems confront so-called 'involuntary creditors' (eg people with personal injuries claims against the company). One such problem is ascertaining which company should be the defendant in any legal action: see, eg, *Briggs v James Hardie & Co Pty Ltd* (1989) 16 NSWLR 549.

59 T Skyes, *The Bold Riders* (Allen & Unwin, 1996) contains a detailed and readable account of the rise and fall of the Qintex group.

60 A debenture is a document which acknowledges a company's indebtedness. The loan may be secured or unsecured.

(acting in the interests of the creditors) successfully obtained a court judgment of $110 million against the company. Qintex was not able to meet that court judgment, with the result that ANZ turned its attention to Qintex's numerous subsidiaries. Relying on a clause in each of the trust deeds, ANZ instructed Qintex to obtain guarantees of the indebtedness to ANZ from about 90 of the Qintex wholly owned subsidiaries. This would then allow ANZ to seek payment from those companies. The Court refused to enforce the clauses in the deeds. The Court agreed with Qintex that to do otherwise would involve the subsidiary company managers in a breach of their duties to their companies:

> Under a different legal system it may be that each company in a group would be jointly and severally liable for the debts of every other company. But that is not the course the law has taken. The decision in *Walker v Wimborne* [citation omitted] is binding authority for considering each company in a group as a separate entity having assets and liabilities of its own that are distinct from those of all the others. The creditor who happens to deal with the only financially viable entity in the group may be exceptionally astute, or simply unusually fortunate; but, in either event, he is not in law liable to have his just claims defeated by arbitrary redistribution of assets or liabilities of his corporate debtor.[61]

While the position enunciated in *Walker v Wimborne* has been confirmed on a number of occasions in Australian courts, there was judicial recognition of the problems it can create; in another case involving the Qintex group, Rogers J observed that:

> It may be desirable for Parliament to consider whether this distinction between the law and commercial practice should be maintained. This is especially the case today when the many collapses of conglomerates occasion many disputes. Regularly, liquidators of subsidiaries, or of the holding company, come to court to argue as to which of their charges bears the liability. ... As well, creditors of failed companies encounter difficulty when they have to select from amongst the moving targets the company with which they consider they concluded a contract. The result has been unproductive expenditure on legal costs, a reduction in the amount available to creditors, a windfall for some, and an unfair loss to others. Fairness or equity seems to have little role to play.[62]

The 'entity' approach can work to the advantage of shareholders in one of the constituent corporations in a group. This was illustrated by the facts of *Re Spargos Mining NL*, which involved an action for oppression brought against the directors of Spargos Mining NL by one of its minority shareholders.[63] As the result of a takeover, the Spargos company had become part of an extensive web of corporations known as the Independent Resources Group. Companies within the group were controlled, directly or indirectly, by Independent Resources Ltd (IRL). This control was exercised through a combination of 'close and common management links, as well as an interlocking web of complex mutual

61 *ANZ Executors & Trustee Co Ltd v Qintex Australia Ltd (recs and mgrs apptd)* [1991] 2 Qd R 360, 365.
62 *Qintex Australia Finance Ltd v Schroders Australia Ltd* (1990) 3 ACSR 267, 269.
63 *Re Spargos Mining NL* (1990) 3 WAR 166. See also *Re Enterprise Gold Mines NL* (1991) 9 ACLC 168.

shareholdings'.[64] Shortly after the takeover, the Spargos board came to be dominated by representatives of the IRL board. At the time of the takeover, Spargos had been a company with considerable prospects; as described by Murray J, 'it was at least on the threshold of becoming a major gold producer, operating its own mine and having other interests of some value'.[65] After being subsumed within the IRL group, the company's situation deteriorated. Primarily, this was due to a policy whereby Spargos was used as a 'cash box' to fund, directly or indirectly, various activities undertaken by other companies in the group. The directors of IRL, who also sat on the boards of many of the subsidiaries in the group, would decide to embark on a particular venture and then select another company within the IRL group to conduct the transaction. Spargos was then tied into the venture: either directly, by lending money to finance the acquisition; or indirectly, by supplying guarantees or security for loans taken out elsewhere. Spargos gained little in return, except, as the judge noted, 'the benefit expressed in the philosophy that the transaction was thought to be of benefit to the IRL group as a whole'.[66] The financial situation of Spargos gradually declined. By the time the case was heard, the judge was able to note that Spargos had lost control of its main asset, the goldmine, in which it had by then been reduced to a 50 per cent interest.[67]

Under the previous equivalent of s 232 of the *Corporations Act*, the Court found this amounted to oppressive or unfair conduct against the members of the company, and ordered (among other things) the appointment of a new board. Murray J expressed his scepticism about the way in which the group had been run:

> One can understand that philosophy [of favouring group interests] within a group of corporate entities where there is a unity of control in the form of major shareholdings and representation upon the various Boards, but it is an approach which tends to take little account of the particular interests of individual companies and therefore of individual small shareholders in those corporate entities. The tendency is always to advance the interest of the majority shareholding which is common to a number of the corporate entities involved.[68]

A different approach was taken in *Equiticorp Finance Ltd (in liq) v Bank of New Zealand*.[69] The Equiticorp Group ('the Group') was comprised of companies located in Australia and New Zealand. Hawkins was a director on the boards of many of the Group's companies and was described as the Group's chief executive with general authority for the conduct of the Group's business. The Bank of New Zealand ('the Bank') had provided a loan to one company within the Group. The loan was to be used to finance a takeover. There were difficulties in the course of the takeover, and the Bank became concerned about the level of its exposure to the Equiticorp Group. Seeking to restore credibility with the Bank, and

64 *Re Enterprise Gold Mines NL* (1991) 9 ACLC 168, 174.
65 *Re Spargos Mining NL* (1990) 3 WAR 166, 179 (Murray J).
66 Ibid 178 (Murray J).
67 Ibid 179.
68 Ibid 178–9.
69 *Equiticorp Finance Ltd (in liq) v Bank of New Zealand* (1993) 32 NSWLR 50.

under some pressure from Bank officers, Hawkins decided to use funds deposited with the Bank towards repaying the debt. Those funds had been deposited by two other corporations in the Group, and Hawkins was a director of one of those two corporations. Soon afterwards, those two corporations went into liquidation, and the liquidators claimed, among other things, that the use of the funds had been in breach of the director's fiduciary duties to those companies. In the New South Wales Court of Appeal, Clarke and Cripps JJA in the majority (Kirby P dissenting) held that there had not been any breach of duty. Their Honours recognised the difficulty that arises when the directors of one corporation in a group enter into a transaction on behalf of that corporation because they believe that the transaction is of benefit to the group as a whole. To reach a decision about such a situation, the majority judges applied a test that had been formulated in the United Kingdom case of *Charterbridge Corporation Ltd v Lloyds Bank Ltd.*[70] There, Pennycuick J had held that the proper test in the corporate group situation is:

> [w]hether an intelligent and honest man in the position of a director of the company concerned, could, in the whole of the existing circumstances, have reasonably believed that the transactions were for the benefit of the company.[71]

While they noted some reservations about this test,[72] Clarke and Cripps JJA held that, in the circumstances, Hawkins and his fellow directors had justification for their belief that 'the welfare of the group was intimately tied up with the welfare of the individual companies'.[73]

The duties of directors in this type of situation is discussed in more detail in Chapter 12. For present purposes, the significance of the decision is that the test in *Charterbridge* allows directors of one company in a group to have regard to the wider interests of the group, rather than being solely and exclusively concerned with the interests of that individual company. Section 187 of the *Corporations* Act now provides that a director of a wholly owned subsidiary may act according to the best interests of the holding company, provided that:

(1) the subsidiary's constitution expressly authorises this
(2) the director acts in good faith in the best interests of the holding company
(3) the subsidiary is not insolvent at the time, and does not become insolvent because of the director's act.

The *Corporations Act* recognises the phenomenon of corporate groups in other areas as well. One of these is found in s 588V, specifying when a holding company may be liable for the insolvent trading of its subsidiary. Another is the area of corporate financial reporting.

70 *Charterbridge Corporation Ltd v Lloyds Bank Ltd* [1970] Ch 62.

71 *Equiticorp Finance Ltd (in liq) v Bank of New Zealand* (1993) 32 NSWLR 50, 97.

72 Their Honours' preferred approach, expressed obiter dictum, was to say that where a director of one company fails to consider the interests of that company then there has been a breach of duty to that company. If the transaction nevertheless proves to be in the company's interests, then no consequences would flow from the breach: *Equiticorp Finance Ltd (in liq) v Bank of New Zealand* (1993) 32 NSWLR 50, 148.

73 Ibid 149.

If financial disclosure is to be meaningful for members, creditors and regulators, it must be recognised that many businesses are run by group structures. To understand properly the financial position of a particular company, it will be necessary to consider the broader financial position of the group by reference to consolidated accounts for the entire group. However, the group will not necessarily be composed of strict holding–subsidiary company relationships. Ideally, the reporting requirements should be capable of producing meaningful financial disclosure for a flexibly constituted set of relationships between a range of business entities. The requirement to produce consolidated financial statements is set by the accounting standards (s 295(2)). The relevant standard (AASB 10 *Consolidated Financial Statements*)[74] is structured around the concept of the control that one entity has over another. The concept of 'control' is defined broadly in terms of having power to direct activities that significantly affect the returns on investment. Where a company is required to prepare consolidated financial statements, then a director or officer of a controlled entity must give all information requested which is necessary to prepare those financial statements (s 323).

A similar approach is taken in ch 2E of the *Corporations Act* which regulates financial transactions between a public company and its related parties. The term 'related party' includes an entity that controls the public company (s 228), and the term 'entity' includes bodies corporate, partnerships and other unincorporated bodies, trustees and individuals (s 9). Control, for this purpose, is defined in s 50AA(1):

> [A]n entity controls a second entity if the first entity has the capacity to determine the outcome of decisions about the second entity's financial and operating policies.

The related-party provisions in ch 2E are discussed further in Chapter 13 of this book.

In its 2000 report on corporate groups, the now-discontinued Companies and Securities Advisory Committee made a number of recommendations to reform the law concerning corporate groups,[75] including that:

- the test of control in s 50AA should replace the holding/subsidiary company test found in s 46
- a wholly owned corporate group (that is, a parent company with its wholly owned subsidiaries) should be able to 'opt-in' to be a consolidated corporate group, thereby treated as a single legal structure (recognising the entity approach discussed above)
- the *Corporations Act* should permit directors of solvent partly-owned group companies to act in good faith and in the interests of the parent company (a parallel provision to s 187)
- wholly owned group companies should be able to merge with each other or with the parent company with the approval of the directors of all the merging companies.

These recommendations have not been adopted.

74 Australian Accounting Standards Board, *Consolidated Financial Statements AASB 10* (at 7 April 2022) <https://aasb.gov.au/admin/file/content105/c9/AASB10_07-15_ACOMPdec21_01-22.pdf>.

75 Companies and Securities Advisory Committee, *Corporate Groups* (Final Report, May 2000).

4.65.10 Closely-held and widely-held companies

An obvious feature that can be used to distinguish between different companies is the size and distribution of shareholdings in a company and the nature of the relationship between the company's members and the directors. The term 'closely-held company' is used to describe a company that has a small membership and in which there is a close association between the members and the directors. It may be that all of the members are involved in managing the company as directors or, in the case of many family companies, there may be other ties that bind the corporate participants. Many incorporated small businesses are closely held. At the other extreme, a 'widely-held company' is one with a diverse and usually large membership, most of whom will have little, if any, direct contact with the directors or managers. In these companies, the directors are practically, as well as legally, separated from members. Many listed public companies fall within this description. There are other possibilities falling between these extremes.[76]

The terms 'closely-held' and 'widely-held' are not necessarily synonymous with 'proprietary' and 'public'. The latter terms indicate certain legal requirements and capacities which apply to different companies. The other terms tell us about the internal organisation of the corporation; however, these are broad descriptions, not precise definitions.

Although Australian corporate law does distinguish between proprietary and public companies, it has been slow to recognise the implications of the closely- and widely-held distinction. Cases on the duties owed by directors have occasionally acknowledged that the size of a company and the proximity of relations between directors and members may be relevant to determining the nature of those duties.[77] There is no clear indication that Australian courts recognise a distinct corporate law jurisprudence for closely-held companies.[78]

On rare occasions, evidence of close or partnership-like relations between incorporators has been acknowledged by the courts in deciding whether to wind up a company. These cases concern the exercise of the courts' discretion to order that a company be wound up on the grounds that this is just and equitable.[79] In *Ebrahimi v Westbourne Galleries Ltd*,[80] the House of Lords ordered that a corporation, which ran a business previously run by a partnership, be wound up on this basis. This was because there was clear evidence that the relations of mutual confidence between the erstwhile partners had broken down. In the course of his judgment, Lord Wilberforce stated that:

76 Hadden distinguishes between participant or partnership companies, extended partnership companies, large unquoted companies, and public quoted companies: Tom Hadden, *Company Law and Capitalism* (Weidenfeld and Nicholson, 1972) 44–6.

77 See, eg, *Glavanics v Brunninghausen* (1996) 19 ACSR 204; *Mesenberg v Cord Industrial Recruiters Pty Ltd* (1996) 39 NSWLR 128.

78 See Chapter 13 at Section 13.10.25 for a discussion of closely-held company case law in relation to fiduciary obligations.

79 The just and equitable ground for winding up is found in s 461(1)(k).

80 *Ebrahim v Westbourne Galleries Ltd* [1973] AC 360.

> [A] limited company is more than a mere legal entity, with a personality in law of its own:
>
> ... there is room in company law for recognition of the fact that behind it, or amongst it, there are individuals, with rights, expectations and obligations inter se which are not necessarily submerged in the company structure.[81]

This approach towards so-called 'quasi-partnership' companies has been followed by some Australian courts.[82] We discuss this area of law in more detail in Chapters 13 and 14.

It is only rarely that Australian corporate law explicitly recognises the particular issues presented by companies with different membership structures. In general, the law applies uniformly to companies of all types. This application of one set of laws to diverse corporate forms has long been questioned. One commentator remarked:

> Many laws, if not most, are appropriate to some types of corporation, but ill-fitting to others. If the laws governing corporations are to be improved, draftsmen must thoughtfully consider the application of each provision to corporations of widely different dimensions and characteristics. This observation applies not only to the statutes known as 'corporation acts', but also to securities transfer laws, tax laws, and accounting rules.[83]

4.65.15 One-person companies

It is possible to incorporate a proprietary company with one person as the sole director and the sole shareholder, creating what might be called the ultimate in closely-held corporations. While the idea of a one-person company seems at odds with the idea of a company as a form of association, there are at least two rationales for allowing one-person incorporations. First, it avoids the artificiality of involving other persons in the company simply to satisfy formal incorporation requirements. This can be of particular benefit to women; when these reforms were introduced in the mid-1990s, the Attorney-General, Michael Lavarch, pointed to research showing that the previous minimum requirement of two people had often led 'to women becoming directors of companies controlled by their spouse in which they do not play any meaningful role. This [could] expose these women to the legal liabilities of a company director, without them having any influence over the operation of the company.'[84] More recent research on family violence and economic abuse indicates, however, that despite these reforms women continue to be coerced into becoming co-directors.[85] The second rationale is that allowing the incorporation of one-person companies offers the protection and benefits of incorporation to sole traders.

81 Ibid 378. Having said this, Lord Wilberforce at 380 went on to stress that: 'A company, however small, however domestic, is a company not a partnership or even a quasi-partnership.'

82 See, eg, *Mopeke Pty Ltd v Airport Fine Foods Pty Ltd* (2007) 25 ACLC 254.

83 AE Conard, 'The Corporate Census: A Preliminary Exploration, (1975) 63(2) *California Law Review* 440, 462. See also G Lowe, 'Corporations as Objects of Regulation' (1987) 5 *Law in Context* 35, 47.

84 Commonwealth, *Parliamentary Debates*, House of Representatives, 8 February 1995, 707–8 (Michael Lavarch).

85 See Vivien Chen, 'Hidden Risks of Economic Abuse Through Company Directorships' (2024) 47(1) *University of New South Wales Law Journal* 105.

This type of company is generally subject to the same general rules and principles that apply to other companies under the *Corporations Act*, although it does receive specialised treatment on some matters.[86] The following points summarise the main specialised provisions:

- if the sole director/shareholder dies, becomes mentally incapacitated or bankrupt, then the person's personal representative or trustee (as appropriate) may appoint another person or themselves as director (ss 201F(2)–(3))
- the director can exercise all powers of the company except those which the *Corporations Act*, or the company's constitution (if there is one) allocate to the general meeting (s 198E)
- a director's resolution or declaration is passed by recording it in the company's minute books and signing the record (s 248B)
- a member's resolution is passed by the member recording the resolution and signing the record in the company's minute books (s 249B). One such resolution concerns the remuneration paid to the person as director (s 202C)
- the director can appoint another director by recording and signing the appointment in the company records (s 201F(1)).

4.70 Choosing the form of incorporation

Many factors can influence the decision to incorporate and the choice of a particular form of incorporation. Some of these factors have been mentioned: does the business or association operate on a profit-making or non-profit basis? From what sources does the business intend to raise finance? What existing relations, if any, does the business or association have with other entities? In some cases, the answers will compel a particular form of incorporation. For example, if the intention is to raise finance from the investing public, then incorporation as a public company will be necessary.

One factor in deciding whether to incorporate in *any* form is the requirement in s 115 of the *Corporations Act*. This section prohibits the formation of a partnership or association that has the object of acquiring gain for itself or its members and consists of more than 20 persons unless it is incorporated in some form. The section permits the *Corporations Regulations* to specify higher maximum memberships for certain professional partnerships and associations. The membership limit for professional partnerships is: accountants 1,000; legal practitioners 400; architects, pharmaceutical chemists or veterinary surgeons 100; and actuaries, medical practitioners, patent or trademark attorneys, sharebrokers or stockbrokers 50.[87] The original rationale for this restriction was the wish 'to prevent the mischief arising from large trading undertakings being carried on by large fluctuating bodies, so that persons dealing with them did not know with whom they were contracting, and so might be put to great difficulty and expense'.[88]

86 Note that a one-person company, registered under the *Corporations Act*, is not the same thing as a 'corporation sole' (see Section 4.05.05).

87 *Corporations Regulations 2001* (Cth) reg 2A.1.01.

88 *Smith v Anderson* (1880) 15 Ch D 247, 273 (James LJ).

Beyond this mandatory requirement, it is not possible to list definitively the factors which should be taken into account in the decision to incorporate or the choice of a particular corporate form. Experience suggests that the following factors may be the more prominent:

- Limited liability of members: this is the most obvious advantage to be gained by incorporation. However, in practice, the advantages may be eroded; it is common for major finance creditors to require the directors of small companies to give personal guarantees for loans to the company. Trade creditors are less likely to use this device, either because they lack bargaining power or because the sums involved are too small. The advantage of limited liability will often be confined in application to claims by trade creditors or so-called involuntary creditors (such as tort victims).
- Capacity to issue certain types of financial security in return for capital or loans: unlike unincorporated forms of business association such as partnerships, a company has the capacity to issue certain types of financial instruments and security charges. These are listed in s 124 of the *Corporations Act* and include shares, debentures, and circulating security interests. This is discussed in more detail in Chapter 8.
- Taxation: given the variety of situations within which a company can operate, it is difficult to be categorical about the taxation advantages of incorporation. There is some evidence that taxation is a major factor in decisions to incorporate small businesses.[89] In comparison with other forms of business association, corporations enjoy beneficial marginal rates of income tax.

There are disadvantages to incorporation, although these will vary depending on the type of company. The principal disadvantage which may be perceived by incorporators is the cost of maintaining the legal structure and complying with the continuing regulatory requirements. This cost can arise from the obligations to maintain registers, prepare accounts, hold annual general meetings, and submit annual returns. Fewer direct costs may also be incurred, particularly in widely-held companies due to the separation between shareholders and managers. Economists argue that shareholders face costs in monitoring the performance of managers, while the managers bear the cost of convincing shareholders that their interests are being catered for. This is discussed in Chapter 2.

4.75 Summary

This chapter explained the formal process by which a company comes into existence through registration under the *Corporations Act*. Against the backdrop of other types of corporate entity, this chapter described the range of company structures available under the *Corporations Act*, focusing on the three ways in which companies can be categorised: in terms of their proprietary or public status; according to how they structure the liability of their members; and by reference to their relationship to other companies.

89 Joint Statutory Committee on Corporations and Securities, Parliament of Australia *Close Corporations Act 1989* (Senate Paper No 54, December 1992) 21.

This chapter examined the important role of corporate groups, as well as the difference between closely-held (and one-person) and widely-held companies.

Corporate structures have proven to be remarkably adaptable to the forces of social and economic change since the nineteenth century. Today, the globalisation of trade, the regionalisation of world markets, restructured political alliances, and acceptance of the involvement of organised business and labour in political governance all provide fertile ground for the diversified application of company forms. Law students and practitioners of corporate law must be aware of the range of situations and contexts within which companies operate. This is necessary to avoid overly simple assumptions about the capacity of corporate law to facilitate and regulate company conduct.

It is appropriate to conclude with a related point. Corporate law tells us only some things about companies. Each company has a number of dimensions:[90] these include the legal dimension (which has been the focus of this chapter), the economic/financial dimension, and the organisational dimension (for example, management structures and industrial relations). A company is 'a conglomeration of different relationships and practices—linked to each other, but in a variety of ways which may be complementary or contradictory'.[91]

90 This is taken from G Lowe, 'Corporations as Objects of Regulation' (1987) 5 *Law in Context* 35, 42–6.
91 Ibid 38.

CHAPTER

5

THE INTERNAL RULES OF A COMPANY

5.05 Introduction

Companies come into existence through registration. As discussed in Chapter 4, for a company to be registered it must have a constitution and/or have adopted all or some of the replaceable rules set out in the *Corporations Act*. The constitution and/or replaceable rules establish the internal rules that govern how the company operates. This chapter discusses the importance of these rules, whom they bind, and how they can be amended. It also discusses the rules that apply when there is a variation of the rights attaching to shares.

5.10 An overview of the internal management of a company

Companies act through people—namely, their directors, officers or members—and there need to be rules to govern how the internal processes of the company operate. These rules govern a wide range of issues including how shares will be allocated, the rights attaching to shares, the rights and responsibility of members and directors, and how meetings will be held. Historically, it was necessary for the persons setting up a company to adopt a Memorandum of Association and Articles of Association to deal with such issues. The Memorandum of Association contained basic information about the company such as: its name; the amount of its share capital; the number of shares issued; that the liability of members was limited; and the names, addresses, occupation and number of shares taken by each member. It also contained an objects clause, which stated the purpose of the company.

The Articles of Association contained the company's internal rules. These rules governed: how members' and directors' meetings were held; how directors were appointed and removed; and how the company would be wound up. The companies legislation at the time included a set of model Articles of Association in Table A annexed to the statute.

In 1998, the requirement for a Memorandum and Articles of Association was removed, and companies must now have a corporate constitution and/or to adopt some or all of the replaceable rules in the *Corporations Act*. The replaceable rules will automatically apply if the company does not adopt its own constitution or use a combination of replaceable rules and a constitution. Companies formed before 1998 that still have Memorandum and Articles are treated as if those documents comprise the company's constitution.[1] In the following discussion, all references to the corporate constitution include a reference to the Memorandum and Articles of Association.

5.15 Objects clauses and ultra vires

Prior to 1984, a company needed to include in the Memorandum of Association a statement of the company's objects or purpose. Companies were only allowed to carry on the type of business for which they were incorporated, and any action beyond that purpose was invalid. For example, a company established to carry on an interior design business might have provided in its Memorandum that the purpose of the company was:

> to carry on in Australia the business of manufacturing, developing, fabricating, finishing and acting as importer, exporter, buyer, seller of interior design items, fabrics or furniture; and to carry on either alone or jointly the business of interior design, interior decorating and consulting and advising on interior design, and to do all incidental things necessary for the attainment of the above objects.

The effect of an objects clause was that acts done by the company outside of the stated purpose were ultra vires and void. Not surprisingly, this doctrine created significant problems for third parties dealing with companies as they would be presumed to have read the Memorandum to ascertain what the full powers of the company were.

This position was changed in 1984 and today all companies are given the powers of a natural person under s 124 of the *Corporations Act*. Only no-liability companies are still required to include an objects clause in their constitution restricting the company's activities to mining (see s 112(2)). Whilst some not-for-profit and charitable companies choose to include an objects clause in their constitution, most commercial companies incorporated today do not.

Further confirming that the doctrine of ultra vires no longer applies to companies, s 125(2) of the *Corporations Act* provides that an act of a company is not invalid merely because it is contrary to or beyond any objects or purpose stated in the company's constitution. The effect of this provision is to ensure that third parties dealing with a company are protected if there is a limitation on the purpose or power of a company contained in the constitution. However, any directors that authorise an act beyond a company's purpose may be liable for breach of directors' duties, and a member may take an action for oppression or winding up the company on just and equitable grounds. These types of actions are discussed in Chapters 11 and 14.

1 *Company Law Review Act 1998* (Cth) s 1414.

5.20 The corporate constitution

Under s 134 of the *Corporations Act*, a company's internal management may be governed by the replaceable rules set out in the Act, by a constitution, or by a combination of both. The persons setting up a company can adopt a constitution either on registration—if each person named as a member agrees in writing to the terms of a constitution—or after registration, if the members pass a special resolution in the general meeting adopting the constitution.[2] If a constitution is adopted, it needs to be lodged with ASIC.

By allowing companies to write their own constitution, the law recognises the private nature of corporate arrangements. Persons setting up a company can choose the rules that will govern them. In large public companies, this choice is limited as shareholders are bound by the constitution in operation at the time they purchase shares.[3] In smaller companies, new members are also bound by any existing constitution, but may be able to propose changes to it in general meeting.

5.25 The replaceable rules

When setting up a company, individuals can choose to adopt either a constitution or the replaceable rules outlined in the *Corporations Act*, or both. If they do not formally adopt a constitution or the replaceable rules, the replaceable rules will automatically apply by default. Many of the provisions previously contained in the Articles of Association are now included in the Act as replaceable rules. A replaceable rule is a section of the Act that only applies if a company has not adopted a rule dealing with the same matter in its constitution (s 135(2)). There is a list of replaceable rules in s 141 of the Act and in Table 5.1 below. A company's constitution can displace or modify any of these sections or subsections. Some sections (such as ss 194, 203C, 249X, 254D, 254W(2), 1072G) only apply to proprietary companies.

5.30 Internal rules for one director/shareholder companies

As discussed in Chapter 4, a proprietary company must have at least one shareholder and one director, who can be the same people. Section 135 of the *Corporations Act* provides that the replaceable rules do not apply to a one-person proprietary company.

Instead, ss 198E, 201F, 202C and 249B contain provisions that govern the internal workings of these companies. For example, s 198E(1) provides that a single director may exercise all of the powers of the company except any powers that the *Corporations Act* or the company's constitution (if any) requires the company to exercise in the general meeting. Section 249B provides that a company that has only one member may pass a resolution in circumstances where the member records the resolution in writing and signs it. The resolution must also be recorded in the company's minute book: s 251A.

---

2 *Corporations Act 2001* (Cth) s 136(1).

3 See, eg, *Constitution*, Qantas Airways Limited (at 5 November 2021) <https://www.qantas.com/content/dam/qantas/pdfs/about-us/corporate-governance/qantas-constitution.pdf>.

Table 5.1 Sections of the *Corporations Act* that operate as replaceable rules

Subject matter	Section number
Officers and employees	
Voting and completion of transactions—directors of proprietary companies	Section 194
Power of directors	Section 198A
Negotiable instruments	Section 198B
Managing director	Section 198C
Company may appoint a director	Section 201G
Directors may appoint other directors	Section 201H
Appointment of managing directors	Section 201J
Alternate directors	Section 201K
Remuneration of directors	Section 202A
Director may resign by giving written notice to company	Section 203A
Removal by members in proprietary company	Section 203C
Termination of appointment of managing director	Section 203F
Terms and conditions of office for secretaries	Section 204F
Inspection of books	
Company or directors may allow member to inspect books	Section 247D
Circulating resolutions of companies with more than 1 director	Section 248A
Calling directors' meetings	Section 248C
Chairing directors' meetings	Section 248E
Quorum at directors' meetings	Section 248F
Passing of directors' resolutions	Section 248G
Meetings of members	
Calling of meetings of members by a director	Section 249C
Notice to joint members	Section 249J(2)
When notice by post or fax is given	Section 249J(4)
Notice of adjourned meetings	Section 249M
Quorum	Section 249T
Chairing meetings of members	Section 249U
Business at adjourned meetings	Section 249W(2)
Who can appoint a proxy in proprietary companies only	Section 249X
Proxy vote valid even if member dies, revokes appointment etc	Section 250C(2)

Table 5.1 (cont.)

Subject matter	Section number
How many votes a member has	Section 250E
Jointly held shares	Section 250F
Objections to right to vote	Section 250G
How voting is carried out	Section 250J
When and how polls must be taken	Section 250M
Shares	
Pre-emption for existing shareholders on issue of shares in proprietary company	Section 254D
Other provisions about paying dividends	Section 254U
Dividend rights for shares in proprietary companies	Section 254W(2)
Transfer of shares	
Transmission of shares on death	Section 1072A
Transmission of shares on bankruptcy	Section 1072B
Transmission of shares on mental incapacity	Section 1072D
Registration of transfers	Section 1072F
Additional general discretion for directors of proprietary companies to refuse to register transfers	Section 1072G

These provisions are not replaceable rules and apply regardless of anything in a company's constitution to the contrary.

5.35 The statutory contract

A company's constitution and any replaceable rules operate as a unique type of contract called a statutory contract. Section 140(1) of the *Corporations Act* provides that the constitution and any replaceable rules have the effect of a contract between:

(1) the company and each member;
(2) the company and each director and secretary; and
(3) between each member and each other member.

This creates a different form of contract to what we normally encounter in contract law. For example, new members in a company are bound by and have rights under the constitution and/or any replaceable rules as soon as their shares are issued or transferred, and their names included in the members register. Members' express consent to these rules is not necessary for them to be bound. Similarly, any directors and/or secretaries appointed by the company become subject to the constitution and/or any replaceable rules when they are appointed to that role, regardless of whether they are aware of the rules or not.

Another difference between the statutory contract and a normal contract is how it can be varied. If a company has a constitution, it can only be added to or varied by special resolution of the members in the general meeting.[4] A special resolution requires the consent of 75 per cent of members present and voting at the meeting (ss 9, 250MA). For normal contracts to be varied, all parties must agree to the variation. The right of members to vary the constitution by special resolution is subject to several legal constraints, including the equitable rules on majority powers and the statutory rules on the variation of class rights (both discussed below).

Where a company has adopted some or all of the replaceable rules, these rules operate as terms of the statutory contract between the company and each member, the company and each director and secretary, and between a member and each other member. As these rules exist as sections of the *Corporations Act*, they can only be varied by Parliament.

The replaceable rules are unlikely to suit every company. The persons setting up a company need to carefully consider the rules they adopt and whether any additional provisions are necessary. For example, if the members want particular rules to govern how disputes will be resolved (such as, using arbitration or mediation before litigation) or what will happen if the company is wound up, these rules need to be included in the constitution.

Certain companies cannot use the replaceable rules. These include public companies limited by guarantee that have omitted the word 'Limited' from their name (s 150), no liability public companies (s 112), and companies listed on the Australian Securities Exchange (ASX).[5] These companies must have their own constitution.

5.35.05 The effect of the statutory contract

As the constitution and/or any replaceable rules operate as a statutory contract between the key participants in a company, these parties gain both rights and obligations under them. As indicated above, s 140(1) provides that a statutory contract exists between the company and each member; the company and each director and company secretary; and a member and each other member.

The effect of s 140 is not to give these parties a right to enforce every provision of the constitution or replaceable rules. Instead, s 140 confers rights and obligations on each party in their particular corporate capacity. In other words, a member has the right to enforce provisions relevant to them as a member; a director has the right to enforce provisions relevant to them as a director; and members can enforce relevant provisions against other members.[6] As the Court noted in *Smolarek v Liwszyc*:[7]

> It is accordingly plain from [section 140], that it imposes a duty upon each of the parties to that deemed contract to comply with the replaceable rules so far as they apply to that person ... Of course, a provision of the statutory contract

4 *Corporations Act* s 136(2).
5 See ASX, *Listing Rules* (at 19 December 2016) r 1.1.
6 *Hickman v Kent or Romney Marsh Sheepbreeders' Association* [1915] 1 Ch 881.
7 *Smolarek v Liwszyc* (2006) 32 WAR 101.

> cannot be enforced unless it affects the member in his or her capacity as a member ... If the act or omission complained of is a wrong to the company alone, the members' standing to sue becomes doubtful.[8]

To explain this further, once a person becomes a member of a company, they are bound by and gain rights under the provisions of the company's constitution and/or replaceable rules that are relevant to them as a member. This means they can only enforce those provisions or rules that deal with matters personal to them in that capacity (see *Eley v Positive Government Security Life Assurance Co Ltd*,[9] discussed below). For example, provisions dealing with how general meetings will be held, how voting rights can be exercised, or how dividends will be declared confer membership rights that can be enforced by any member against the company. In the same way, a provision stipulating that if members want to sell their shares, they must first offer them to other members (called a 'right of pre-emption') can be enforced between members.[10] A similar provision exists for proprietary companies in the replaceable rule in s 254D, which gives pre-emptive rights to existing shareholders when new shares are issued. Finally, members have a personal right to ensure the appointment and removal of directors is done in accordance with any relevant provisions contained in the constitution.[11]

Directors often enter a separate contract of service with a company through which they gain additional rights and obligations over and above those that apply via the constitution or replaceable rules. These contracts cannot override provisions in the corporate constitution; rather, they exist alongside them. For example, if the constitution provides for the appointment of a director for a specified period, this provision will be enforceable in contract despite anything different that may be contained in the contract for service. However, as provisions in the constitution can be altered by special resolution of the members in general meeting, the rules relevant to directors can be changed without their consent. In *Shuttleworth v Cox Brothers & Co (Maidenhead) Ltd*,[12] the Court held the constitution could be amended to provide that a director could be removed on the written request of all the other directors. The directors signed such a request and the director, who was appointed for life under the constitution, was removed. The Court rejected the argument that the statutory contract could only be altered with the director's consent and found that the removal was valid.

The list of contractual relationships set out in s 140 is exhaustive and other relationships between participants in a company—such as between a director and a member—are not governed in contract by provisions of the constitution. Similarly, there is no contractual relationship created under s 140 between the company, a director or member, and a third party. Any provision in the constitution that seeks to create rights or impose

8 Ibid [39].

9 *Eley v Positive Government Security Life Assurance Co Ltd* (1875) 1 Ex D 20.

10 See, eg, *Gibbins Investments Pty Ltd v Savage* (2011) 84 ACSR 1.

11 See *Links Agricultural Pty Ltd v Shanahan* [1999] 1 VR 466; *Andrews v Queensland Racing Ltd* (2009) 74 ACSR 538. However, other provisions dealing with matters such as directors' remuneration would not be able to be enforced by a member.

12 *Shuttleworth v Cox Brothers & Co (Maidenhead) Ltd* [1927] 2 KB 9.

obligations on a third party is not enforceable in contract.[13] This was stated by the Court in *Hickman v Kent or Romney Marsh Sheepbreeders' Association* as follows:

> [A]n outsider to whom rights purport to be given by the articles in his [sic] capacity as an outsider, whether he is or subsequently becomes a member, cannot sue on those articles.[14]

This situation was demonstrated in *Eley v Positive Government Security Life Assurance Co Ltd* ('*Eley's Case*').[15] Here, one party, Mr Baylis, approached Mr Eley (a solicitor) requesting his assistance in setting up a company. Eley agreed to contribute money to the company on the basis that he would be employed as the company's solicitor. A provision confirming Eley's appointment was included in the Articles of Association. After a number of years, the company changed its solicitors. Eley sought to enforce the provision appointing him as the company's solicitor under the predecessor of s 140. The Court rejected his claim on the basis that a statutory contract only exists between the parties listed in the section, and as such Eley had no contractual right to enforce the provision under the Articles. This was the case even though Eley owned shares in the company, as the provision in question related to an issue that was separate from his rights as a member.[16]

Under s 140(2) of the *Corporations Act*, any change to the constitution made after a person becomes a member that requires them to take up additional shares, increases their liability to the company, or imposes restrictions on their rights to transfer shares is not binding unless that person agrees to the change in writing.

5.40 Remedies for breach of the statutory contract

A contravention of a replaceable rule is not a breach of the *Corporations Act* (s 135(3)). While the replaceable rules appear in the legislation, they are only binding on the parties listed in s 140 in contract law and do not attract statutory remedies under the Act.

5.40.05 Seeking a declaration or injunction

The most common remedies sought for breach of the constitution or the replaceable rules are an injunction to restrain the breach and/or a declaration as to the validity of any action. A member, director or secretary commencing an action for breach of the statutory contract must first show that the breach adversely affects them in their specific capacity as a member, director or secretary. Once this is established, they may seek a declaration or injunction under the common law requiring the other party (usually the company) to comply with or refrain from breaching the terms of the statutory contract. These remedies are discretionary and are not granted unless some important interest needs protecting.[17]

13 *Hickman v Kent or Romney Marsh Sheepbreeders' Association* [1915] 1 Ch 881.
14 Ibid 897.
15 *Eley v Positive Government Security Life Assurance Co Ltd* (1875) 1 Ex D 20.
16 The principle established in *Eley's Case* was supported in *Morris v Hanley* (2003) 173 FLR 83.
17 See *Shaw Stockbroking Ltd v Australian Stock Exchange Ltd* (1998) 26 ACSR 702, 716, affd *McLachlan v Australian Stock Exchange* (1998) 30 ACSR 26.

It is key to remember that the *Corporations Act* provisions dealing with breach of that Act and providing for consequences on breach (such as s 1324 that deals with statutory injunctions) do not apply to breaches of the constitution or replaceable rules. Examples of declarations that members have sought under the ordinary jurisdiction of the court include:

- that a meeting is invalid if the requirement for a quorum is not met[18]
- that a meeting is invalid if the required notice under the company's constitution is not given[19]
- that a meeting is invalid if there is no chairperson appointed as required by the company's constitution[20]
- that a share transfer done without compliance with the pre-emption provisions contained in the company's constitution is voidable and entitles a member to have the register of members rectified[21]
- that a variation of class rights done without complying with a constitutional provision requiring consent from the party affected results in the variation being invalid.[22]

The provisions of the constitution are enforced strictly. In the case of *Inspector James v Ryan (No 3)*,[23] the Full Bench of the Industrial Court of New South Wales had to determine if an appointment of a director was invalid where the provisions of the company's constitution were not observed. Clause 3.2 of Dekorform Pty Ltd's constitution provided that its parent company, Alesco Corporation Limited, could appoint a person to be a director by notice to Dekorform. Clause 13.6 provided that Alesco could exercise a power by notice in writing executed by the company, or on behalf of the company by a director, secretary or executive officer of Alesco. The notice needed to be delivered or sent by facsimile or other electronic means to Dekorform. Under the constitution, the replaceable rules were expressly displaced by clause 13.5.

The case involved charges under s 8(1) of the *Occupational Health and Safety Act 2000* (NSW) ('*OHS Act*'). This section imposed a duty on employers to ensure the health, safety and welfare of its employees. In July 2006, an employee of Dekorform was fatally injured in the course of their employment. Under s 26 of the *OHS Act*, 'if a company contravenes any provision of the Act, each director of a company is also taken to have contravened the Act (subject to limited defences)'.

It was alleged that Ryan was liable as a director of Dekorform under the *OHS Act*. However, one of the key issues was whether Ryan was validly appointed as a director, as Alesco had not given written notice to Dekorform of his appointment. Adopting a strict interpretation of the provisions in the company's constitution, Marks J, at first instance,

18 *Re Chinese Cultural Club Ltd* (2004) 49 ACSR 568.

19 *Myer Queenstown Garden Plaza Pty Ltd v Port Adelaide City Corporation* (1975) 11 SASR 504.

20 *Colorado Constructions Pty Ltd v Platus* (1966) 2 NSWLR 598.

21 *Grant v John Grant & Sons Pty Ltd* (1950) 82 CLR 1; *Carew-Reid v Public Trustee* (1996) 20 ACSR 443; *Homestake Gold of Australia Ltd v Peninsula Gold Pty Ltd* (1996) 20 ACSR 67.

22 *Wilson v Meudon Pty Ltd* [2006] ANZ ConvR 93.

23 *Inspector James v Ryal* [2010] NSWIRComm 127.

found that Ryan was not a director of Dekorform.[24] Alesco had failed to deliver notice of Ryan's appointment to Dekorform and therefore Ryan had not been appointed by valid means. The effect of this finding was that Ryan was not personally liable for the company's offences under the *OHS Act*.

The Full Bench of the Industrial Court of New South Wales agreed with Marks J's conclusion. It noted that clause 13.5 excluded the operation of the replaceable rules and therefore the giving of notice in accordance with clause 13.6 was 'the only means under Dekorform's constitution by which [a director's] appointment could be made'.[25] It considered that the appointment of a director is a fundamental exercise of power within a corporation and any provisions in the constitution dealing with the matter had to be complied with if the appointment was to be valid.

The Full Bench came to this conclusion notwithstanding the fact that Ryan and all the other directors in both Dekorform and Alesco believed Ryan was a director and that he was named in the documents filed with ASIC. The Court found that 'it cannot be right that a practice relating to the important function of appointing directors developed inconsistently with the company's constitution could supplant the requirements of the constitution'.[26] It also rejected the argument that Ryan was a de facto director, as defined in s 9 of the *Corporations Act*. This was on the basis that Ryan had not acted in the position on an ongoing basis (his involvement was confined to the signing of three documents: a circulating resolution of directors, a power of attorney and a deed of cross guarantee) and he was not performing top-level management functions at Dekorform.[27]

5.40.10 Rectification and damages

The contractual remedy of rectification is not available if there has been a mistake in the wording of the corporate constitution, or the wording does not represent the actual intentions of the members.[28] If a provision in the constitution is inaccurate, the appropriate remedy is for the members to pass a special resolution altering the constitution under s 136(2).

The limitation on the availability of rectification as a remedy is due to the special nature of the statutory contract, and the problem of determining the actual intention (or the consensus ad idem) of the members. This is because the consent of only 75 per cent of the members needs to be given to alter the constitution.[29] As Hodgson J notes, it is also due to the nature of the constitution:

> In my view, it is clear that the remedy of rectification is not confined to documents which are strictly contractual documents ... [R]ectification can be

24 *Inspector James v Ryan* [2009] NSWIRComm 215.
25 *Inspector James v Ryan (No 3)* [2010] NSWRIRComm 127, [170].
26 Ibid [158].
27 Ibid [178].
28 *Lion Nathan Australia Pty Ltd v Coopers Brewery Ltd* (2006) 156 FCR 1; *Simon v HPM Industries Pty Ltd* (1989) 7 ACLC 770.
29 *Simon v HPM Industries Pty Ltd* (1989) 7 ACLC 770, 778.

> applied to such documents as conveyances of land, settlements, policies of life insurance, disentailing deeds, bills of exchange and leases. However, even if these documents are not strictly contractual documents, they do appear to have the function of giving effect to private agreements or intentions. Although some of such documents, such as conveyances or transfers of land, are placed upon a public register, this is essentially to inform interested persons of private transactions between the parties to the document ...
>
> The original articles of association of a company do, in one sense, give effect to private agreements or intentions of the corporators. However, registration of the articles is required, so that persons dealing with the company can ascertain what are the provisions regulating the affairs of the company. Furthermore, the statutory contract established by the Companies legislation is a contract binding the company, which was not a party to the original agreements or intentions. In those circumstances, it seems that as a matter of principle, a distinction can be drawn between articles of association and the kinds of documents in relation to which the remedy of rectification is granted.[30]

There is ongoing debate on whether the remedy of damages should be available for breach of the statutory contract. Traditionally, damages have not been available where a claim is brought by a member against a company for breach of the statutory contract.[31] However, in *McLaughlin v Dungowan Manly Pty Ltd*,[32] the Supreme Court of New South Wales granted damages to the holders of shares in a home unit company which was redeveloped in a way that constituted a variation of their class rights, a topic which is discussed below. On appeal to the New South Wales Court of Appeal, Bathurst CJ noted that '(t)here is some doubt as to whether the statutory contract formed by section 140 of the Act gives rise to a claim for damages for breach'.[33]

5.40.15 Additional members' remedies under a shareholders' agreement

Members in a company may enter into a shareholders' agreement, giving them additional rights in contract against each other. A shareholders' agreement is a contract between some or all of the company's members. The agreement will generally deal with issues specific to their investment that are not covered in the constitution. The benefits of a shareholders' agreement are that it can be created any time after incorporation, it can deal with issues particular to the members in question, and it is private as it does not need to be lodged with ASIC. Shareholders' agreements often contain provisions dealing with issues such as transfers of shares between members, share buy outs, dividend payments, dispute resolution, additional contribution of funds, confidentiality

30 Ibid 779.
31 *Houldsworth v City of Glasgow Bank* (1880) 5 App Cas 317.
32 [2010] NSWSC 89.
33 *Dungowan Manly Pty Ltd v McLaughlin* (2012) 90 ACSR 62.

and restraint of trade (or non-compete clauses). Neither the company's constitution nor the provisions of the *Corporations Act* can be overridden by a shareholders' agreement, although such agreements may supplement and clarify the parties' rights.[34] The situation may also be less clear where all shareholders are party to an agreement that seeks to vary constitutional rights.

5.40.20 Additional members' remedies under statute

As discussed in Chapter 14, members have a number of other remedies available to them under the *Corporations Act* that can prevent or compel actions by directors or a majority of shareholders. These include:

- an action under s 232 in relation to oppressive conduct
- an order under s 461 to have the company wound up where it is just and equitable to do so or where the directors have acted in their own interest
- an order seeking to prevent a variation of the rights attached to shares where the procedure (if any) set out in the company's constitution is not followed or, where there is not such procedure, the requirements set out in ss 246B–G are not followed.

5.45 Interpretation of provisions in the statutory contract

There are conceptual challenges involved in characterising the constitution and/or replaceable rules as a contract. Despite this, Australian courts apply the ordinary principles for interpreting and enforcing contracts when determining the meaning of these provisions. This means that the provisions of the constitution and the replaceable rules are interpreted as if they form part of a commercial contract.

The leading case confirming this approach is *Lion Nathan Australia Pty Ltd v Coopers Brewery Ltd*.[35] This case involved a hostile takeover bid by Lion Nathan Ltd, Australia's second largest brewer, of Coopers Brewery Limited in 2005. One of the key issues was the interpretation of key provisions in Coopers' Articles of Association. The Articles had originally been prepared in the 1920s, when Coopers was converted from a family partnership to a company limited by shares. The Articles had been altered several times since then. In 2003, Coopers had bought back shares in the company from its shareholders. This was a share buy-back scheme in accordance with div 2 pt 2J.1 of the *Corporations Act*. Lion Nathan owned a type of shares in the company that granted it pre-emptive rights (meaning a first right of refusal) over shares in Coopers. These rights were set out in the Articles of Association of Coopers.

34 *Cordiant Communication (Australia) Pty Ltd v Communications Group Holdings Pty Ltd* (2005) 55 ACSR 185, [131]. See also Michael Duffy, 'Shareholders Agreements and Shareholders' Remedies Contract versus Statute?' (2008) 20(2) *Bond Law Review* 1.

35 (2006) 156 FCR 1. See also JPG Lessing and R Johns, 'Resisting a hostile takeover: the Lion Nathan bid for Coopers Brewery' (Conference Paper, 61st ALTA Conference, 4–7 July 2006) <https://web.archive.org/web/20080727091943/http://epublications.bond.edu.au/cgi/viewcontent.cgi?article=1104&context=law_pubs>.

In 2005, Lion Nathan issued proceedings against Coopers arguing that Lion Nathan should have been offered the right to purchase any of the shares bought back by Coopers. To resolve this issue, the Court had to determine whether the article giving pre-emptive rights to Lion Nathan applied to a share buy-back.

Finn J of the Federal Court, at first instance, held that the expression 'any transfer of shares' in the Articles of Association did not encompass a share buy-back. This meant that Lion Nathan's pre-emptive right did not apply where a buy-back was involved. Finn J had regard to Coopers' previous Articles of Association in determining the underlying purpose of the pre-emptive rights scheme. On appeal, the Full Court of the Federal Court held that Finn J was justified in considering extrinsic materials when interpreting the pre-emptive rights scheme in the Articles of Association. The Court noted that:

- a company constitution is similar to a commercial contract, and should be construed to promote business efficacy
- company constitutions, like other commercial documents, must be read as a whole
- the constitution should be interpreted in light of the broader commercial context in which it is created
- extrinsic evidence may be used to assist in interpreting the constitution
- the principles applicable to the implication of terms into contracts apply to constitutions, although courts have been slow to imply terms into constitutions.

In 2014, the members of Coopers changed the company's constitution to make it harder for any other hostile takeover bid to be made. The amendment changed the way shares would be priced in the context of a takeover bid as opposed to when existing members buy shares off each other. According to a newspaper report:

> [I]t is reported that at a closed-door meeting of [Coopers'] tight-knit 143 shareholders, held at the Coopers' brewery in Adelaide, a tiny amendment was made to its constitution, which governs the way fair value of Coopers' shares is calculated ... The Coopers constitution ... has been strengthened even more to what is referred to inside the Adelaide brewer as 'belt and braces' protection that should keep it independent.[36]

5.50 Altering the constitution

As indicated above, under s 136(2) of the *Corporations Act*, a corporate constitution can only be altered if the members pass a special resolution approving the alteration. There may be additional requirements stated in a company's constitution that must be complied with before an alteration is passed—such as unanimous consent of all members to any alteration—but a constitution cannot be made unalterable (s 136(3)). Where the constitution of a public company is amended, notice must be given to ASIC of the change (s 136(5)).

36 E Greenbalt, 'Coopers puts up "not for sale" sign', *The Australian* (online, 8 October 2014).

5.50.05 Restrictions on the majority's power to alter the constitution

While s 136(2) of thc *Corporations Act* clearly allows an alteration to the corporate constitution via a special resolution of members passed at a general meeting, this power is subject to certain restrictions. These restrictions exist because, in making such a decision, the majority of members are acting as one of the two organs of the company, the other being the board of directors.[37] As a result, the majority members' power to vote on an alteration to the constitution must be exercised in good faith and for a proper purpose. As the High Court noted in *Ngurli Ltd v McCann*:[38]

> Shareholders ... *as individuals* in general meeting can usually exercise their votes for their own benefit. But there is a limit even in general meetings to the extent to which *the majority* may exercise their votes for their own benefit ... It must be exercised, not only in the manner required by law, but also bona fide for the benefit of the company as a whole.[39]

To understand this limitation, it is necessary to appreciate what is meant by a 'majority' and a 'minority' of members. A majority of members will be able to control the decisions of a company in general meeting. How votes are cast in members' meetings is discussed further in Chapter 7. Voting can be on a show of hands or a poll can be requested so that members vote based on the number of shares they hold. In a small company, there may be one or two shareholders who together own enough shares to pass a general resolution and/or a special resolution. In this case, these members are generally called a majority. In a large public company, there will often be many shareholders who own small numbers of shares; a majority will exist where one or more shareholders hold as little as 20 per cent of the issued shares. This is because the members owning small parcels of shares may not attend general meetings and, even if they do, may not be able to assemble themselves together to block or pass an ordinary or special resolution. In this instance, even though these shareholders might own over 50 per cent of the shares in the company, they are still defined as minority shareholders if individually their shareholdings are small.

Determining which members control the general meeting is important. There are limits on what a majority of members can do in general meeting, particularly in the context of altering the corporate constitution. Until 1995, when the case of *Gambotto v WCP Ltd*[40] (*'Gambotto's Case'*) was decided, the position in Australia was that the majority members' power to alter the constitution had to be exercised bona fide in the interests of the company as a whole.[41]

As Lindley MR stated in *Allen v Gold Reefs of West Africa Ltd*:

37 Confirmed in *Australasian Centre for Corporate Responsibility v Commonwealth Bank of Australia* (2016) 248 FCR 280.

38 *Ngurli v McCann* (1953) 90 CLR 425.

39 Ibid 439 (emphasis added).

40 *Gambotto v WCP Ltd* (1995) 182 CLR 432.

41 *Allen v Gold Reefs of West Africa Ltd* [1900] 1 Ch 656.

> The power [to amend the constitution] must ... be exercised subject to those general principles of law and equity which are applicable to all powers conferred on majorities and enabling them to bind minorities. It must be exercised, not only in the manner required by law, but also bona fide for the benefit of the company as a whole, and it must not be exceeded.[42]

This test was based on an equitable principle known as 'fraud on the minority' that required that any powers that could be exercised by a majority of shareholders in the general meeting had to be exercised for a proper purpose.[43] Failure by the majority to exercise a power for a proper purpose could result in equitable remedies being available to minority members, including rescission of a contract, an injunction, or an account of profits. The onus of proof in establishing an improper purpose lay with the minority shareholders. However, this situation changed after *Gambotto's Case,* which is examined in detail later in this chapter.

The *Allen* test was discussed in *Peters' American Delicacy Co Ltd v Heath,*[44] where the High Court noted the challenges involved in determining what is in the best interests of the company as a whole where members have differing interests. In this case, the Articles of Association contained conflicting provisions on how dividends and bonus shares would be distributed. One set of Articles stated that dividends would be paid to members in proportion to the amount paid up on their shares.[45] This meant members with fully paid shares would receive more bonus shares than members with partly paid shares. However, another Article provided that bonus shares would be distributed on the basis of how many shares a member owned. A majority of shareholders in general meeting passed a special resolution to alter the later Article, so that bonus shares would be issued on the basis of the amount paid up on shares. The holders of partly paid shares opposed this resolution and sought a declaration that the alteration was invalid as it only benefitted the fully paid shareholders not the company as a whole.

The High Court held that the amendment did not constitute a fraud on the minority. However, the judges expressed differing views on the suitability of the *Allen* test. Latham CJ considered that the alteration was valid unless the minority members could establish that the resolution was passed fraudulently or oppressively or was 'so extravagant that no reasonable person could believe that it was for the benefit of the company'.[46] Dixon J expressed concern about the test 'for the benefit of the company as a whole' and considered it was 'inappropriate, if not meaningless' where an amendment adjusted the rights of conflicting members.[47] Dixon J considered the test was 'a very general expression negativing purposes foreign to the company's operations, affairs and organizations'.[48]

42 Ibid 671.

43 *Vatcher v Paull* [1915] AC 372; *Houghton v Immer (No 155) Pty Ltd* (1997) 44 NSWLR 46.

44 (1939) 61 CLR 457.

45 See Chapter 8 at Section 8.15 for a discussion of partly- and fully-paid shares.

46 *Peters' American Delicacy Co Ltd v Heath* (1939) 61 CLR 457, 482.

47 Ibid.

48 Ibid.

5.50.10 The decision in *Gambotto's Case*

The *Allen* test came under review in *Gambotto v WCP Ltd.*[49] In this case, the majority members of WCP Ltd wanted to expropriate (or acquire) the shares of the minority shareholders. The majority shareholders, who owned 99.7 per cent of the shares in WCP, were subsidiaries of a major corporate entity, Industrial Equity Group. The remaining 0.3 per cent of the shares were held by 71 individual shareholders, including Mr Gambotto and Ms Sandri. A shareholders' meeting was convened to consider adding a new article that would allow a majority shareholder with 90 per cent of the issued shares in WCP to acquire all the remaining shares in the company. The price offered for the shares ($1.80 per share) was higher than an accountant's valuation of the shares ($1.365 per share). The effect of this change would be that WCP became a wholly owned subsidiary of Industrial Equity, and this would enable certain taxation and accounting advantages to be claimed by WCP. Gambotto and Sandri instituted proceedings prior to the meeting being held to prevent the resolution being passed. They also did not attend the meeting. However, the special resolution was passed by three of the remaining minority shareholders, with the majority shareholders not voting on the resolution.

At first instance, McLelland J in the New South Wales Supreme Court held that an amendment that permits minority shares to be expropriated by majority shareholders is an unjust oppression of the dissenting minority shareholders.[50] The New South Wales Court of Appeal reversed this decision, finding in favour of the majority shareholders on the basis that expropriating the minority's shares was not of itself oppressive, and on the facts there were considerable financial benefits for WCP if the expropriation was permitted.[51]

The High Court rejected this conclusion and overturned the Court of Appeal's decision on the basis that the amendment was not done for a proper purpose.[52] It held that the test set out in *Allen's* case was not appropriate where there was a conflict of interests between the shareholders, and proposed a new test for assessing the validity of changes to the constitution in this context. The language used by the Court in proposing this new test is important to understanding how and when it applies. An extended quote from the majority judgment of Mason CJ, Brennan, Deane and Dawson JJ is provided below:

> [T]he courts have struggled to strike a balance between the interests of the majority and the minority. On the one hand, the courts have recognised that the proprietary rights attaching to shares are subject to modification, even destruction, by a special resolution altering the articles and that the power to vote is exercisable by a shareholder to his or her own advantage. On the other hand, the courts have acknowledged that the power to alter the articles should

49 *Gambotto v WCP Ltd* (1995) 182 CLR 432.

50 *Gambotto v WCP Ltd* (1992) 8 ACSR 141.

51 *WCP Ltd v Gambotto* (1993) 30 NSWLR 385.

52 *Gambotto v WCP Ltd* (1995) 182 CLR 432.

not be exercised simply for the purpose of securing some personal gain which does not arise out of the contemplated objects of the power ...

In the context of a special resolution altering the articles and giving rise to a conflict of interests and advantages, whether or not it involves an expropriation of shares, we would reject as inappropriate the 'bona fide for the benefit of the company as a whole' test of Lindley MR in *Allen v Gold Reefs of West Africa Ltd* ... It seems to us that, in such a case not involving an actual or effective expropriation of shares or of valuable proprietary rights attaching to shares, an alteration of the articles by special resolution regularly passed *will be valid unless it is ultra vires, beyond any purpose contemplated by the articles or oppressive* as that expression is understood in the law relating to corporations. Somewhat different considerations apply, however, in a case such as the present where what is involved is an alteration of the articles to allow an expropriation by the majority of the shares, or of valuable proprietary rights attaching to the shares, of a minority. In such a case, the immediate purpose of the resolution is to confer upon the majority shareholder or shareholders power to acquire compulsorily the property of a minority shareholder or shareholders ...

Such a power could not be taken or exercised simply for the purpose of aggrandizing the majority. In our view, such a power can be taken only if (i) it is exercisable for a proper purpose and (ii) its exercise will not operate oppressively in relation to minority shareholders. In other words, an expropriation may be justified where it is reasonably apprehended that the continued shareholding of the minority is detrimental to the company, its undertaking or the conduct of its affairs – resulting in detriment to the interests of the existing shareholders generally – and expropriation is a reasonable means of eliminating or mitigating that detriment.

Accordingly, if it appears that the substantial purpose of the alteration is to secure the company from significant detriment or harm, the alteration would be valid if it is not oppressive to the minority shareholders. So, expropriation would be justified in the case of the shareholder who is competing with the company ... [or] if it were necessary in order to ensure that the company could continue to comply with the regulatory regime governing the principle business which it carries on ....

Notwithstanding that a shareholder's membership of a company is subject to alterations of the articles which may affect the rights attaching to the shareholder's shares and the value of those shares, we do not consider that, in the case of an alteration to the articles authorising the expropriation of shares, it is a sufficient justification of an expropriation that the expropriation, being fair, will advance the interests of the company as a legal and commercial entity or those of the majority ... of corporators. This approach does not attach sufficient weight to the proprietary nature of a share ... It is only right that exceptional circumstances should be required to justify an amendment

> to the articles authorizing the compulsory expropriation by the majority of the minority's interest in a company. To allow expropriation where it would advance the interests of the company as a legal and commercial entity or those of the general body of corporators would, in our view, be tantamount to permitting expropriation by the majority for the purpose of some personal gain and thus be made for an improper purpose ...
>
> As noted in the preceding paragraphs, an alteration to the company's articles permitting the expropriation of shares ... must also be fair in the circumstances. Fairness in this context has both procedural and substantive elements. The first element, that the process used to expropriate must be fair, requires the majority shareholders to disclose all relevant information leading up to the alteration and it presumably requires the shares to be valued by an independent expert. Whether it also requires the majority shareholders to refrain from voting on the proposed amendment is a question that is best left open at this stage.
>
> The second element, that the terms of the expropriation itself must be fair, is largely concerned with the price offered for the shares. Thus, an expropriation at less than market value is prime facie unfair, and it would be unusual for a court to be satisfied that a price substantially above market value was not a fair value ...
>
> It is for the majority to prove that the alteration is valid because it was made for a proper purpose and is fair in all the circumstances.[53]

In making its decision, the High Court sought to strike a balance between the interests of the majority and minority shareholders. A key issue for the Court when balancing these interests was the proprietary nature of shares. A share is personal property, as are the rights attaching to shares. As the High Court stated, a share 'is more than a "capitalized dividend stream": it is a form of investment that confers proprietary rights on the investor'.[54] By giving themselves the right to acquire the minority members' shares, the majority were taking away the minority's property and the Court considered this could only be done where due regard was had to the legitimate proprietary interests of the minority. Competing with this position was the established principle that a majority of members in general meeting have power to pass a special resolution, provided the resolution is in the best interests of the company.[55] On the face of it, this resolution complied with that rule.

The Court distinguished between two situations: where there is an alteration to the constitution that involves an expropriation of shares or the valuable rights attached to shares; and where the alteration does not involve such expropriation. These two situations are discussed separately below.

53 Ibid 443–7 (emphasis added).

54 Ibid 447.

55 See *Ngurli Ltd v McCann* (1953) 90 CLR 425.

The test to be applied where an alteration involves a conflict of members' interests and an expropriation of shares or the valuable rights attaching to shares

The majority judgment held that a different test applies to alterations of the constitution that involve the expropriation of shares or the valuable proprietary rights attached to shares. Where an alteration seeks to take away shares or property rights attached to shares, a two-stage test applies:

(1) Was the exercise of the power done for a proper purpose?
(2) Was it fair in all the circumstances?

First, as indicated in the extract from the High Court majority judgment above, an alteration that seeks to expropriate members' shares or the rights attaching to shares must be for a proper purpose; it must be necessary to prevent the company from suffering significant detriment or harm. Examples of such alterations given by the High Court include where an expropriation involves removing a shareholder that is competing with the company,[56] or where it is necessary to meet legislative requirements (such as laws requiring 100 per cent ownership for a television licence).[57] As these examples indicate, the test for a proper purpose is strict and the circumstances where it will be met are rare. The majority judgment made it clear that an expropriation to secure tax, administrative or commercial advantages for the majority shareholders is not a proper purpose in relation to the expropriation of shares.[58]

Second, the alteration must be fair in all the circumstances. Fairness in this context requires two elements:

(1) The process for the expropriation must be fair. This requires that all relevant information surrounding the alteration must be provided to members and the shares must be valued by an independent expert; and
(2) The price offered for the shares must be fair. This means that the price must at least be equal to the market price for the shares and must also take account of other relevant factors such as the assets of the company, any dividend payments, the nature of the company and its likely future activities.

This two-part test was applied in *Bundaberg Sugar Ltd v Isis Central Sugar Mill Co Ltd*.[59] In this case, the constitution of Bundaberg Sugar was altered (a number of years before legal action was taken) to provide that the shares of any member who ceased to be a sugar supplier to the company would be forfeited to the company. The main purpose for this provision was to ensure that Bundaberg Sugar could retain its status as a co-operative, which enabled it to claim considerable taxation benefits. The Supreme

56 A case involving a shareholder competing with the company is *Sidebottom v Kershaw Leese and Co Ltd* [1920] 1 Ch 154.

57 *Gambotto v WCP Ltd* (1995) 182 CLR 432, 445.

58 McHugh J differed in opinion on this issue and considered that an expropriation that allowed the company to reduce its potential tax liability could be for a proper purpose.

59 *Bundaberg Sugar Ltd v Isis Central Sugar Mill Co Ltd* [2007] 2 Qd R 214.

Court of Queensland held that a forfeiture of shares under the provision was the same as an expropriation of shares. As a result, the Court considered whether there was a proper purpose for the expropriation by forfeiture of the members' shares and concluded there was as it was detrimental to the company to lose its co-operative status:

> The continued shareholding by persons who do not supply sugar to the defendant would be detrimental to the company and the conduct of its affairs (the loss of the valuable tax deductions) if it were to lose its co-operative status. It is reasonable for it to preserve that status by doing business only with its members.[60]

However, as compensation had not been paid to the members whose shares were forfeited, the action failed to satisfy the second limb of the test established in *Gambotto's case*: that the expropriation was fair in all the circumstances.

In *Gray Eisdell Timms Pty Ltd v Combined Auctions Pty Ltd*,[61] Young J held that an amendment to a company's constitution providing that the company could sell the shares of any member who was not actively engaged in a pawnbroking business, or acting as a nominee of such a person, was invalid. In that case, the company, Combined Auctions Pty Ltd, had been established as an auction house for pawnbrokers. It claimed that it had adopted the provision due to the perceived threat of a takeover. However, Young J held that the amendment was invalid under the first test in *Gambotto's Case* as it was not necessary to protect the company from harm. This was because at least one-third of the members of the company were not pawnbrokers at the time the provision was introduced and the amendment did not come into effect for five years, suggesting that the threat to the company was not immediate.[62]

While the High Court did not define what was meant by 'valuable proprietary rights attaching to shares', in *Shears v Phosphate Co-operative Co of Australia Ltd*,[63] an alteration that attempted to remove or restrict voting rights was held by the Full Court of the Supreme Court of Victoria to attract the *Gambotto* test. Yet, as discussed below, it is not always clear if the rights attaching to shares have been varied. For example, in the older decision of *Greenhalgh v Arderne Cinemas Ltd*,[64] a company's share capital was divided into 10-shilling and 2-shilling shares. After a disagreement, the company decided at a general meeting to subdivide the 10-shilling shares into 2-shilling shares. This had the effect of decreasing Greenhalgh's voting power within the company. Greenhalgh argued it was an unauthorised variation of rights attaching to his shares. However, the Court held that the voting rights attaching to the shares had not been varied and it was only Greenhalgh's level of control within the general meeting that had been affected.

60 Ibid [91].

61 *Gray Eisdell Timms Pty Ltd v Combined Auctions Pty Ltd* (1995) 17 ACSR 303.

62 This decision was overturned on appeal on other grounds: see *Combined Auctions Pty Ltd v Gray Eisdell Timms Pty Ltd* (1997) 16 ACLR 252.

63 *Shears v Phosphate Co-operative Co of Australia Ltd* (1989) 7 ACLC 812.

64 *Greenhalgh v Arderne Cinemas Ltd* [1946] 1 All ER 512.

The test to be applied where an alteration involves a conflict of members' interests but there is no expropriation of shares or the valuable rights attaching to shares

The High Court has referred to situations where there is an alteration of the constitution giving rise to a conflict of interests and advantages between shareholders that does not involve an expropriation of shares or the rights attaching to shares. The Court considered that such an amendment would be valid unless it is 'ultra vires, beyond any purpose contemplated by the articles or oppressive as that expression is understood in the law relating to corporations'.[65] The Court did not elaborate further on the test or when it would apply:

> Although the decision of the majority of the High Court can be expressed relatively simply, it becomes less straightforward if one attempts to fit previously decided cases within this framework. For example, the *Peters' American Delicacy* case involved a resolution to alter the articles so that bonus shares would be distributed in proportion to the amount paid up on shares rather than in proportion to the number of shares held. The alteration therefore disadvantaged partly-paid shareholders. The case clearly gave rise to a conflict of interests between majority and minority shareholders. But did it involve an expropriation of proprietary rights attaching to shares? If it did not, then the resolution would be valid provided it was not ultra vires, passed for an improper purpose or oppressive.[66]

5.50.15 Onus of proof

One other important change made by the High Court in *Gambotto's Case* was to clarify which party bears the onus of proof in cases involving an expropriation of shares or the valuable proprietary rights attaching to shares. Previously, alterations to the constitution were prima facie valid, and the onus of proof was on the minority to prove otherwise.[67] In *Gambotto's Case*, the Court held that it is for the majority, rather than the minority, to prove the validity of any alteration. This was based on the need to alleviate 'the sting of practical difficulties, such as poor access to information, that would otherwise confront minority shareholders'.[68]

5.50.20 The reaction to *Gambotto's Case*

The High Court's decision in *Gambotto's Case* provoked a lot of discussion and criticism.[69] There was concern that the High Court had gone too far in favouring minority

65 *Gambotto v WCP Ltd* (1995) 182 CLR 432, 444.

66 E Boros, 'The Implications of Gambotto for Minority Shareholders' in IM Ramsay (ed), *Gambotto v WCP Ltd: Its Implications for Corporate Regulation* (Centre for Corporate Law and Securities Regulation, 1996) 79.

67 See *Winthrop Investments Ltd v Winns Ltd* [1975] 2 NSWLR 666.

68 *Gambotto v WCP Ltd* (1995) 182 CLR 432, 444.

69 See, eg, I Ramsay (ed), *Gambotto v WCP Ltd: Its Implications for Corporate Regulation* (Centre for Corporate Law and Securities Regulation, 1996).

members' rights.[70] There was also concern that the decision imposed unnecessary burdens on corporate restructures and buy-outs involving the purchase of minority members' shares, and that it could allow small shareholders to become obstructionist in their actions. Similarly, there was concern that the decision could be extended by subsequent court decisions. However, as Ramsay and Saunders noted in 2011 (16 years after the decision was handed down) whilst many subsequent judicial decisions were critical of *Gambotto*, none have sought to extend the principles to other situations.[71] As a result, the tests established by the High Court relating to alterations to the corporate constitution are now largely confined to the factual situations expressly discussed in *Gambotto*. It is also interesting to note that the approach adopted by the High Court has not been adopted in the United Kingdom. There, the Privy Council has held that the appropriate test should be whether an alteration to the constitution provides a reasonable benefit to the company.[72]

5.50.25 When do the tests established in *Gambotto's Case* not apply?

As was made clear by the High Court in *Gambotto*, there must be an alteration of the constitution giving rise to a conflict of interests and advantages for the tests in that case to apply. In other words, the alteration must apply differently (in words or effect) to some members than to others. If an alteration applies equally to all members, the test in *Allen's* case will still apply and to be valid the alteration must be 'bona fide for the benefit of the company as a whole'.[73] In *Bundaberg Sugar*, the Supreme Court of Queensland considered what it meant for a resolution to give rise to a conflict of interests and advantages. This was because the company argued that the resolution (providing that the shares of any member who ceased to be a sugar supplier to the company would be forfeited to the company) created 'a regime which treats all members of the company equally in the sense that any member who ceases to be a supplier of sugar to the mill is liable to have its shares forfeited'.[74] However, as the Court stated:

> This is not a case where the articles affect all shareholders equally. They operate differentially, or allow the directors to act differentially, with respect to different classes of members: those who supply sugar and those who do not. The shares of members in the second class may be taken from them, compulsorily, and either destroyed by cancellation or sold or re-allotted to an existing member or members who will, by definition, be one of the majority class of shareholders; those who supply sugar.[75]

70 For a thorough discussion of the subsequent research and comment on *Gambotto's Case*, see I Ramsay and B Saunders, 'What Do You Do With a High Court Decision You Don't Like? Legislative, Judicial and Academic Responses to *Gambotto v WCP Ltd*' (2011) 25(2) *Australian Journal of Corporate Law* 112.

71 Ibid 135–40.

72 See *Citco Banking Corporation v Pusser's Ltd* [2007] 2 BCLC 483.

73 See *Heydon v NRMA Ltd* (2000) 51 NSWLR 1.

74 *Bundaberg Sugar Ltd v Isis Central Sugar Mill Co Ltd* [2007] 2 Qd R 214 [76].

75 Ibid [81].

One other restriction on the application of *Gambotto's Case* is that it only applies to alterations of the constitution after it has been adopted. It does not apply where the constitution registered on incorporation provides for the expropriation of a member's shares. If that exists, and the power is exercised reasonably, the provision in the constitution will prevail and a minority shareholder will not have a right to complain if their shares are expropriated in accordance with the provision.[76]

5.50.30 Reform of the compulsory acquisition provisions

Parts 6A.1 and 6A.2 of the *Corporations Act*, dealing with compulsory acquisitions in the context of a corporate takeover, were amended after the decision in *Gambotto's Case*. Under s 664A, any person who owns 90 per cent of the shares in a class or has 90 per cent of the voting power in a company may compulsorily acquire the remainder of the shares in the class. The power must, however, be exercised within six months of the member acquiring 90 per cent of the shares or voting rights.

5.55 Protection of class rights

For various reasons, the directors or shareholders may want to alter the rights attaching to shares. Generally, ordinary shares carry the right to vote at general meetings, participate in the company's profits via the payment of dividends, and receive any surplus profits on winding up. Class rights are discussed further at Section 8.15.10.

As discussed above, where the rights attaching to shares are stated in the constitution, and an alteration to those rights involves an alteration to the constitution, the requirements of s 136 and *Gambotto's Case* must be complied with. However, not all variations of the rights attaching to shares involve an alteration to the constitution. Only the rights attaching to some types or classes of shares (such as preference shares) need to be stated in the constitution, although it is common for a constitution to state whether shares with different rights can be issued.[77]

Sections 246B–246G of the *Corporations Act* set out the process to be followed if a variation to the rights attaching to shares is proposed. While these provisions apply to both companies limited by shares and by guarantee, we will discuss them by reference to the rights of shareholders.

There are three questions to be answered before provisions dealing with how an alteration must be done apply:

(1) Is the company's share capital divided into classes?
(2) Are the rights in question 'class rights'?
(3) Does the proposed change amount to a 'variation or cancellation' of those class rights?

These questions address whether there has been an alteration of class rights.

76 See *Associated World Investments Pty Ltd v Aristocrat Leisure Ltd* (1998) 16 ACLC 455; *Accurate Financial Consultants Pty Ltd v Koko Black Pty Ltd* [2007] VSC 40 [106].

77 Section 254A(2) requires that before a corporation allots preference shares it must set out in its constitution, or in a special resolution, the rights of the holders of those shares.

In answering the first question, whether or not the company's share capital is divided into classes, Australian courts have applied a commonsense approach. In *Crumpton v Morrine Hall Pty Ltd*, there was no express reference in the company's constitution to different classes of shares. There was a provision that prescribed how class rights could be altered if the company did have classes of shares, and the question in that case was whether this procedure should be followed. Jacobs J addressed this issue quite simply. If shares of the company could be meaningfully differentiated by reference to the different rights they carried, then they can be described as different classes of shares:

> [W]hen you have a ... company and the shares are divided into different groups so that one group has quite different rights from another group it makes no difference that the [constitution] avoid[s] the use of the word 'class'. In fact the groups of shares are different, the rights attaching to them are different, with the result that the capital is divided into different classes.[78]

This approach was reinforced in *Clements Marshall Consolidated Ltd v ENT Ltd*:

> [T]he expression 'class of shares' has no special meaning ... It refers to a category of shares which differs sufficiently in respect of rights, benefits, disabilities, or other incidents, as to make it distinguishable from any other category of shares ... in the capital structure of the company.[79]

The second question involves considering whether the rights in question are the type of rights which attract legal protection. Using the language of s 246B, the precise question is whether the rights in question are 'attached to shares' that form a class of shares. A useful discussion of this issue is found in *Cumbrian Newspapers Group Ltd v Cumberland and Westmorland Herald Newspaper and Printing Co Ltd*.[80] Scott J identified three different categories of rights. First, there are rights or benefits which attach to particular shares. Dividend and voting rights are common examples. These are legal rights that form part of the shares. Second, there are rights or benefits conferred by the constitution on a person in his or her capacity as a shareholder. Pre-emption rights and the right to appoint a director once a member's shareholding reaches a specified amount are examples. These rights are conferred on a person once they become a member. Third, there are rights that are given to a person in some capacity other than as a member. A provision that confers the right to act as the corporation's solicitor is an example.[81] Of these three types of rights, only the first and second are class rights for the purposes of the variation of class rights provisions in the legislation.

The third question is whether the proposed change amounts to a 'variation or cancellation' of class rights, which is the expression used in s 246B. There is no legislative definition of this expression. There is a pre-existing body of case law that has considered what constitutes a variation of class rights. An illustration is provided by *Greenhalgh v*

78 *Crumpton v Morrine Hall Pty Ltd* [1965] NSWR 240, 245–6.

79 *Clements Marshall Consolidated Ltd v ENT Ltd* (1988) 13 ACLR 90.

80 *Cumbrian Newspapers Group Ltd v Cumberland and Westmorland Herald Newspaper and Printing Co Ltd* [1987] Ch 1.

81 Scott J refers to *Eley v Positive Government Security Life Assurance Co Ltd* (1875) 1 Ex D 20 as an example.

Arderne Cinemas Ltd. Here, the company's share capital was divided into 10-shilling and 2-shilling shares and each share had one vote. Greenhalgh held a sufficient number of 2-shilling shares in the company that allowed him to block any special resolution. At a general meeting, the majority of shareholders passed an ordinary resolution whereby all 10-shilling shares were subdivided into five 2-shilling shares, each with one vote per share. As a result, Greenhalgh's proportional voting power in the company was diminished and he could no longer block a special resolution.

Greenhalgh brought an action, arguing that the subdivision had varied the right attaching to his shares. The Court disagreed. As Lord Greene MR stated:

> Instead of Greenhalgh finding himself in a position of control, he finds himself in a position where control has gone, and to that extent ... [his rights] are affected as a matter of business. As a matter of law, I am quite unable to hold that, as a result of the transaction, the rights are varied; they remain what they always were – a right to have one vote per share pari passu with the ordinary shares for the time being issued which include the new 2s. ordinary shares resulting from the subdivision.[82]

The Court held that Greenhalgh's rights had not been varied; instead, his enjoyment of those rights had been lessened. The same approach was taken in *White v Bristol Aeroplane Co Ltd* where Lord Evershed MR held that 'there is to my mind a distinction, and a sensible distinction, between an affecting of the rights and an affecting of the enjoyment of the rights'.[83]

In addition to the three broad questions on whether there has been an alteration of class rights, s 246C of the *Corporations Act* deems four situations to involve variations:

(1) If shares in one class are divided into further classes with the result that the rights attached to all of those shares are not the same, there is a variation of the rights of every share that was in the class before the division (s 246C(1)).[84]
(2) If the rights attaching to some of the shares in a class are varied, there is a variation of the rights of every other share that was in the class before the variation (s 246C(2)).[85]
(3) If a company with only one class of shares issues new shares, there is a variation of the rights of the existing shares if the new shares have different rights and those rights are allowed or not provided for in the company's constitution or in a notice, document or resolution that is lodged with ASIC (s 246C(5)).
(4) If a company issues new preference shares that rank equally with existing preference shares, there is a variation of the rights of the existing preference shares unless the new issue is authorised by the terms of issue of the existing preference shares, or by the company's constitution as it was at the time the existing shares were issued (s 246C(6)).

82 *Greenhalgh v Arderne Cinemas Ltd* [1946] 1 All ER 512, 518.
83 *White v Bristol Aeroplane Co Ltd* [1953] Ch 65, 74.
84 Section 246C(3) applies in a similar way to a company without share capital.
85 Section 246C(4) applies in a similar way to a company without share capital.

Once it has been established that a variation (or cancellation) of class rights is involved, s 246B outlines the procedure to be followed. This procedure is in addition to the requirements for altering the constitution if such a change is also required. First, s 246B(1) provides that if the company's constitution specifies a procedure for the variation or cancellation of rights attached to shares, then that procedure must be followed. That procedure can only be changed if the procedure itself is complied with.

Second, and alternatively, if the company has no constitution, or has a constitution that does not specify a variation or cancellation procedure, then the rights can only be varied or cancelled by a special resolution of the company and either a special resolution passed at a meeting of the class of shareholders or with the written consent of members with at least 75 per cent of the votes in the class (s 246B(2)). If the resolution or consent of the class is unanimous, then the variation or cancellation takes effect on the date of the resolution or consent, unless a later time is specified (s 246E). If the resolution or consent is not unanimous, then it takes effect one month later, unless there is a court challenge (s 246D(3)).

The words used in s 246B(2) are not clear in relation to which class of members must approve the variation or cancellation. Arguably, it is only those members whose rights have been negatively affected and not the members of the class proposing the change. Section 246B(2)(c) simply states the resolution must be passed at a meeting 'of the class of members holding shares in the class'. A narrow interpretation is consistent with the general purpose of the section; namely, to protect shareholders from having the rights attached to their shares varied or cancelled in a way that is inconsistent with the procedure (if any) set out in the constitution or done without their permission. It is at least arguable that only a separate meeting of members negatively affected by the variation or cancellation needs to be held.

Under s 246D, any non-consenting shareholders in a class have a right of appeal to the court to have the variation or cancellation set aside. The application must be made by members who have at least 10 per cent of the votes in that class, and the question to be decided by the court is whether the shareholders in the class have been unfairly prejudiced by the variation, cancellation or modification. If so, the court may set aside the change to the class rights.

5.60 Summary

This chapter focused on how the internal workings of a company are regulated. It discussed the replaceable rules and the corporate constitution.

A key theme in this discussion was that, within certain limits, the persons who set up a company can write their own rules for how that company will operate. There is considerable flexibility to select rules that suit the particular business involved. As a result, the constitution of a large publicly listed company will be quite different from the constitution of a small company. This chapter discussed changes to the law in this area. In particular, the corporate constitution has replaced the former Articles of Association and Memorandum of Association and the ultra vires doctrine has been abolished.

Other important issues discussed in this chapter were the statutory contract, members' right to approve changes to the constitution, and restrictions on the power to vary the rights attaching to shares. These areas of law result in key rights being preserved for members in a company. The nature of the statutory contract means that members can take action in contract to ensure any provisions in the constitution that apply to them are complied with. The statutory and judicial rules that regulate how the constitution can be altered ensure that a special resolution is required, and that any change does not significantly prejudice minority members' interests. Finally, the common law and statute ensure that members' approval is required before there is any alteration of class rights. Together, these rules ensure that significant power is given to members in areas of relevance to them.

CHAPTER

6

CORPORATE CONTRACTING

6.05 Introduction

So far, we have established what a company is (Chapter 3), how a company is created (Chapter 4), and what rules govern a company's internal operations (Chapter 5).

This chapter discusses the legal capacity of a company to enter contracts. We discuss how companies enter contracts through agents and the statutory assumptions that protect third parties when dealing with companies. We also discuss pre-incorporation contracts.

There are several competing policy issues in this area of law. It is important that companies can enter contracts easily and be bound by their obligations. It is also important that third parties are not prejudiced if the internal requirements of a company, in terms of capacity or authority to act as the company, are not complied with. Both the law of contract and the *Corporations Act* seek to balance these issues, sometimes in interesting ways. It is useful to keep these policy perspectives in mind when studying this area of law.

6.10 Companies entering contracts directly

Under s 124 of the *Corporations Act*, a company has the legal capacity and powers of an individual. This means that, from the time the company is registered, it can enter contracts in its own right. There are two ways in which a company can enter a contract: directly or through an agent.

To enter a contract directly, the common seal of a company must be used on the contract and the contract signed in accordance with the requirements of s 127(2), or the contract must be signed by two directors or by a director and company secretary in accordance with s 127(1). A common seal is a rubber stamp with the company's name and Australian Company Number (ACN) on it. Prior to 1998, companies were required to have a common seal. Now, under s 123, a company may choose whether to have a seal or not.[1] If a common seal is used on a document, s 127(2) requires that it must be signed by two directors or by one director and the company secretary. In a proprietary company with a single director, where that person is also the company secretary, that director can witness the use of the common seal.[2]

The advantage of a contract being entered into using the common seal is that this counts as a direct act of the company, with the common seal acting like the company's signature. As stated by Mason CJ in *Northside Developments Pty Ltd v Registrar-General*:[3]

> The affixing of the seal to an instrument makes the instrument that of the company itself; the affixing of the seal is in that sense a corporate act, having effect similar to a signature by an individual ... Thus, it may be said that a contract executed under the common seal evidences the assent of the corporation itself and such a contract is to be distinguished from one made by a director or officer on behalf of the company, being a contract made by an agent on behalf of the company as principal.[4]

1 *Corporations Act* s 123.

2 In a sole director company, where that person is also the only shareholder, the director can sign a contract to bind the company: s 198E.

3 *Northside Developments Pty Ltd v Registrar-General* (1990) 170 CLR 146.

4 Ibid 160.

The disadvantage is that many companies today do not have a common seal, or if they do it is not often used. In these instances, the only way a company can directly enter a contract is by complying with s 127(1).

As stated above, s 127(1) provides that a company can execute a document directly without using a common seal if the document is signed by two directors or by a director and a company secretary. Under s 204A(1), a public company is required to have a company secretary but a proprietary company does not have this requirement. In a single director company, where that person is also the company secretary, or the only shareholder, that director can sign contracts alone.[5] In all of these instances, the company is taken to have entered the contract directly, provided that the requirements of s 127 are complied with.

In 2022, the *Corporations Act* was amended to allow for electronic execution of documents.[6] Section 110A(2) permits the execution of documents (including contracts and deeds) by a person signing an electronic form of the document provided that:

(a) the method used to sign identifies the person and indicates the person's intention in respect of the information recorded in the document; and
(b) the method is either:
  (i) as reliable as appropriate for the purpose for which the information was recorded, in light of all the circumstances, including any relevant agreement; or
  (ii) proven in fact to have fulfilled the functions described in paragraph (a), by itself or together with further evidence.

Section 110A(4) allows for 'split executions' of documents, meaning that a person is not required to sign the same form, sign the same page or use the same method as another person. Under s 127(2A), where a company executes a document with a common seal, remote witnessing of the fixing of the seal is permitted where:

(a) the person observes, by electronic means, the fixing of the seal;
(b) the person signs the document (or a copy of the document); and
(c) the document includes a statement that the person observed the fixing of the seal by electronic means.

Sometimes, situations can arise when a document appears to have been validly executed by a company under s 127, but in reality:

- one of the parties who signed the document was not validly appointed,
- there was an internal error of company procedure in signing the document, or
- a person who signed was committing fraud or forgery.

These situations raise the question of whether a third party should be affected by such irregularities and whether the contract is still enforceable against the company. Sections 128–9 of the *Corporations Act*, discussed at Section 6.25.05 deal with these issues.

5 *Corporations Act* ss 127(1), 198E.
6 See *Corporations Amendment (Meetings and Documents) Act 2022* (Cth).

These sections of the Act were introduced in 1984 to protect third parties where internal requirements were not followed, or a person signs a document did not have authority or was acting fraudulently. Prior to these sections being enacted, companies and third parties had to rely on the common law 'indoor management rule', discussed at Section 6.25, to determine liability under the contract. While this common law rule still exists, its application has been substantially reduced by the introduction of ss 128–9.

6.15 Companies entering contracts via agents

In practice, many company contracts are entered into by persons who work for or manage a company. These contracts can still be binding on the company under the general law of agency[7] which recognises that one party—a principal—can enter a contract with a third party, where the contract is negotiated and concluded by an agent acting on behalf of the principal. In the corporate context, the principal is the company, and the agent is usually a manager or employee acting with authority on the company's behalf. Provided that an agent acts within their authority, any contract entered into for the company will be binding on the company and the third party.

The key issue in this context is the source and extent of the agent's authority. A contract is only binding on a company if it is entered into by an agent with actual or implied authority to act for the company and to enter the particular contract, or if there has been a representation or holding out by the company that the agent has authority to enter the contract (apparent or 'ostensible' authority). To determine if an agent has authority to act for a company, the common law rules of agency apply. Before discussing these rules, it is important to remember that the principal in these cases is the company, represented either by the board of directors or by a person acting with delegated power to manage the company. A single director generally does not have authority to act as the company unless they are given authority to do so; for example, in a sole director company or with a managing director.[8]

The fact that companies commonly enter contracts through agents can create problems for both companies and third parties, particularly where an agent enters a contract on behalf of a company without the appropriate authority to do so. For example, a manager may be given authority to enter contracts up to a particular monetary amount. If they enter a contract over that amount, the company may not wish to be bound by the contract. This situation raises two competing positions. On the one hand, companies should not be allowed to avoid contracts by arguing that their agent lacked authority. On the other hand, where an agent acts beyond their authority, the company and its shareholders may be prejudiced if the company is held to the contract. While agency law may find the agent liable for acting outside their authority, in practice the key issue before the courts will be which of the two parties (the company or the third party) should bear

7 For a detailed discussion of the law of agency, see G Dal Pont, *Law of Agency* (Lexis Nexis, 4th ed, 2020).

8 *Northside Developments Pty Ltd v Registrar-General* (1990) 170 CLR 146; *J Wright Enterprises Pty Ltd (in liq) v Port Ballidu Pty Ltd* [2010] QSC 213.

the cost of the contract.[9] As discussed below, a central issue in these cases will usually be deciding exactly what is covered by the agent's authority.

6.15.05 Actual and implied actual authority

The clearest situation for determining an agent's authority is where it is expressly granted. This is called 'actual authority'. Under s 126, a company is bound by a contract entered into by an agent with actual authority to bind the company. For example, an employee may be given express authority to negotiate a contract with a supplier to purchase a new computer. In this case, the existence and extent of the agent's actual authority is determined by looking at the terms of the agreement between the company and the agent. The agreement may be written or verbal, or implied from the circumstances, and the ordinary principles of contract will apply to determine the scope of such an agreement.

Examples of written agreements conferring actual authority can include provisions in the constitution authorising a manager to enter contracts up to a specified amount, or an employment contract conferring specific powers on an employee. In large companies, the systems of delegating authority can be complex, as recognised by Barrett J in *Vero Insurance Ltd v Kassem*:[10]

> Most large companies have in place well documented systems of delegations to officers of different ranks. Internal delegations are often accompanied by powers of attorney executed under common seal embodying, by way of safeguard, limitations and requirements for multiple signatures and sometimes allowing sub-delegations. Arrangements of that kind give those companies a ready and convenient means of proving the authority of officers on any occasion on which it becomes necessary or desirable to do so, particularly in a legal context.[11]

While actual authority arises from express agreement, implied actual authority arises by implication from the circumstances. For example, under the replaceable rules in ss 201J and 198C, the board may appoint a managing director and grant that person such powers and authority as it sees fit. In such a situation, the granting of actual authority to the managing director also gives them implied actual authority to do all things incidental to their express powers. Similarly, under s 198D, the directors may delegate any of their powers to a committee of directors, a single director, an employee or any other person (unless the constitution provides otherwise). In delegating power directly, the board is also taken to have granted implied actual authority to do all actions necessary to give effect to the actual authority.

9 If an agent has made a representation that they have authority to enter a contract and they do not, with the result that the company is not bound by the contract, then the third party may be able to sue the agent for breach of warranty of authority. Similarly, if an agent acts without authority and the contract is found to be binding on the company, it may be able to sue the agent for breach of their duties to the company or breach of contract. However, neither action is likely to recover the true 'damage' to the company; namely, either the failure to obtain a binding contract, or the actual damage caused by being bound.

10 *Vero Insurance Ltd v Kassem* (2010) 79 ACSR 330.

11 Ibid.

Implied actual authority of a managing director

Being appointed to a role can also give rise to implied actual authority. As explained by Lord Denning in *Hely-Hutchinson v Brayhead Ltd*, it is implied that a person appointed to a role (such as manager) has the authority necessary to enter contracts that are common or customary in such a role:[12]

> [Actual authority] is *express* when it is given by express words, such as when a board of directors pass a resolution which authorises two of their number to sign cheques. It is *implied* when it is inferred from the conduct of the parties and the circumstances of the case, such as when the board of directors appoint one of their number to be managing director. They thereby impliedly authorise him [sic] to do all such things as fall within the usual scope of that office.[13]

A managing director is generally taken to have implied authority to enter contracts necessary for the day-to-day running of the company. In *Entwells Pty Ltd v National and General Insurance Co Ltd*, Ipp JA noted that a managing director's usual task is to 'deal with every day matters, to supervise the daily running of the company, to supervise the other managers, and indeed, generally, be in charge of the business of the company'.[14] Subject to the particular type and size of the company involved, a managing director is not impliedly authorised to give security or guarantees, or borrow money to finance the company outside of the ordinary course of business.[15] Further, it will usually be implied that a managing director can authorise agents to make all the contracts that the managing director can make.[16]

Implied authority of a company secretary

The role of a company secretary varies depending upon the size and nature of a company. Although, under s 204A(1), a proprietary company does not need to have a company secretary, if it does that person will be an officer of the company.[17]

The general function of a company secretary is to ensure the company complies with its statutory obligations, including maintaining the company registers, lodging company returns with ASIC, and organising director and member meetings as required by the *Corporations Act*. In many organisations, a company secretary also plays a role in supporting the effectiveness of the board and its committees.[18]

---

12 *Hely-Hutchinson v Brayhead Ltd* [1968] 1 QB 549.

13 Ibid 583 (emphasis added).

14 *Entwells Pty Ltd v National and General Insurance Co Ltd* (1991) 6 WAR 68.

15 *Re Tummon Investments Pty Ltd (in liq)* (1993) 11 ACSR 637.

16 See *Crabtree-Vickers Pty Ltd v Australian Direct Mail Advertising and Addressing Co Pty Ltd* (1975) 133 CLR 72.

17 Section 9 defines an officer as including a director and company secretary. This makes the company secretary subject to any duties or obligations that apply to company officers.

18 Robyn McKenzie et al, *Responsibilities within the Governance Space: A Study of the Role of the Company Secretary on Contemporary Boards* (13 April 2019) <https://ssrn.com/abstract=3338309>. See also RL Trubshaw, 'Responsibilities within the governance space: A study of the role of the company secretary on contemporary boards' (Master of Philosophy-Accountancy Thesis, Queensland University of Technology, 2018) <https://eprints.qut.edu.au/122924/1/Robyn_Trubshaw_Thesis.pdf>.

This can include:

- advising the board and its committees on governance matters
- monitoring that board and committee policy and procedures are followed
- coordinating the timely completion and dispatch of board and committee papers
- ensuring that the business at board and committee meetings is accurately captured in the minutes, and
- helping to organise and facilitate the induction and professional development of directors.[19]

The role of the company secretary carries implied authority to enter into contracts related to the administration of the company but does not generally include managerial authority unless this has been conferred.[20] The courts have taken a wide view of what administrative matters a company secretary has authority over. For example, in *Panorama Developments (Guildford) Ltd v Fidelis Furnishing Fabrics Ltd*,[21] the Court held that a company secretary had implied authority to enter contracts to hire cars. The company secretary of Fidelis had, without authority, hired luxury cars from Panorama on the basis that the cars were needed to carry the company's important customers. Instead, the company secretary used the cars for his own private purposes. The Court held that hiring cars was within the general authority of a company secretary. Lord Denning MR noted that the company secretary:

> is an officer of the company with extensive duties and responsibilities ... He [sic] is no longer a mere clerk. He regularly makes representations on behalf of the company and enters into contacts on its behalf which come within the day-to-day running of the company's business ... He is certainly entitled to sign contracts connected with the administrative side of a company's affairs, such as employing staff, and ordering cars, and so forth.[22]

In *Club Flotilla (Pacific Palms) Ltd v Isherwood*,[23] the Court held that a company secretary's role did not include substantive matters such as conducting litigation.

Implied actual authority of a single director

The role of a director does not include implied authority to bind the company. As stated by Dawson J in *Northside Developments Pty Ltd v Registrar-General*:[24]

> The position of director does not carry with it an ostensible authority to act on behalf of the company. Directors can act only collectively as a board and the function of an individual director is to participate in decisions of the board.[25]

19 ASX Corporate Governance Council, *Corporate Governance Principles and Recommendations* (Australian Securities Exchange, 4th ed, February 2019) recommendation 1.4.
20 *Holpitt Pty Ltd v Swaab* (1992) 33 FCR 474.
21 [1971] 2 QB 711.
22 Ibid 716–17.
23 *Club Flotilla (Pacific Palms) Ltd v Isherwood* (1987) 12 ACLR 387.
24 *Northside Developments Pty Ltd v Registrar-General* (1990) 170 CLR 146.
25 Ibid 146 [31]. Note: ostensible authority is the same as apparent authority.

As most people dealing with companies will not be aware of the extent of an agent's authority, the law on 'apparent authority' has developed to protect third parties who reply upon a representation made by a company that an agent has authority.

6.20 Apparent authority

The rules on apparent authority derive from estoppel. Unlike actual authority, which involves looking for an agreement between the parties that gives rise to an actual or implied grant of authority, apparent authority arises where there has been a representation or holding out by the company that a person is its agent or has authority to enter into a particular contract. Where a company allows (by act or omission) a person to appear as if they are an agent, it will later be estopped from arguing otherwise. Apparent authority relies on a representation of authority being made to a third party, and the third party depends upon that representation in entering the contract.

As discussed below, sometimes an argument of implied actual authority and apparent authority will both be available on the facts. However, it is important to remember that the nature of the inquiry into an agent's authority is different. This is because actual authority arises from an agreement between the parties (company and agent) and apparent authority arises from an appearance of authority, or a representation made to a third party. As Lord Diplock stated in *Freeman & Lockyer v Buckhurst Park Properties (Mangal) Ltd*:

> Actual authority and apparent authority are quite independent of one another. Generally they co-exist and coincide, but either may exist without the other and their respective scopes are different ... An 'actual' authority is a legal relationship between principal and agent created by a consensual agreement to which they alone are parties. Its scope is to be ascertained by applying ordinary principles of construction of contracts ...
>
> An 'apparent' or 'ostensible' authority, on the other hand, is a legal relationship between the principal and the contractor created by a representation, made by the principal to the contractor, intended to be and in fact acted upon by the contractor, that the agent has authority to enter on behalf of the principal into a contract of a kind within the scope of the 'apparent' authority, so as to render the principal liable to perform any obligations imposed ... by such contract.[26]

Freeman & Lockyer demonstrates the challenges the courts can face when deciding if a company should be bound by the acts of an agent acting without authority. The facts in this case involved one party, Kapoor, entering a contract to purchase a property (Buckhurst Park Estates) and then joining with another party, Hoon, to establish a company (Buckhurst Park Properties) ('Buckhurst') to complete the purchase and on-sell the property. Kapoor, Hoon and their nominees were the directors of the company. Kapoor was responsible for paying the expenses of the company and was entitled to repayment

26 *Freeman & Lockyer v Buckhurst Park Properties (Mangal) Ltd* [1964] 2 QB 480.

from the funds of the sale. Kapoor engaged a firm of architects, Freeman & Lockyer, to assist in preparing a planning application for the property, which was proving hard to sell. No board resolution was passed to approve the contract with Freeman & Lockyer. When Kapoor disappeared, Freeman & Lockyer sought payment of their fees from the company. In response, the company argued that Kapoor was not authorised to enter the transaction on behalf of the company.

The trial judge held that Kapoor had apparent authority to bind the company. Buckhurst appealed and Lord Diplock discussed the conditions under which apparent authority is taken to exist. These are that:

(1) there has been a representation that the agent had authority to enter into a contract of the kind sought to be enforced against the company
(2) the representation was made by a person or persons who have actual authority to manage the business of the company either generally or in relation to the matter to which the contract relates
(3) the contractor was induced by the representation to enter the contract.

A fourth condition was included in Lord Diplock's list: that the contract must not be ultra vires, meaning that it must not be outside the purpose or powers of the company as stated in its constitution. As discussed in Chapter 5, the doctrine of ultra vires has now been abolished in Australia, and, under s 124, companies have the powers of a natural person.

On the facts in this case, all three conditions were met. The first and second conditions were established as the board knew that Kapoor was acting as managing director in employing agents and taking other steps to find a purchaser, although he had not been officially appointed to the position:

> They permitted him to do so, and by such conduct represented that he had authority to enter into contracts of a kind which a managing director or an executive director responsible for finding a purchaser would in the normal course be authorised to enter into on behalf of the company.[27]

As this case shows, the representation (or 'holding out') that establishes apparent authority can take a variety of forms, including a representation by conduct; that is, permitting or acquiescing in an agent acting in a particular role or manner in the conduct of the company's business. In *Flexirent Capital Pty Ltd v EBS Consulting Pty Ltd*, Whelan J noted that:

> [A] holding out may be of a general character, arising for example out of an office or position in which the principal places the agent, or it may be specific to a particular transaction. The holding out may take the form of the setting up of an organisation or structure which presents to outsiders an appearance of authority in the agent.[28]

27 [1964] 2 QB 480, 485.
28 *Flexirent Capital Pty Ltd v EBS Consulting Pty Ltd* [2007] VSC 158 [203].

In *Pacific Carriers Ltd v BNP Paribas,*[29] the High Court explained this concept in more detail. The Court noted that a holding out 'might result from permitting a person to act in a certain manner without taking proper safeguards against misrepresentation'.[30] It continued:

> [T]he representational conduct commonly takes the form of the setting up of an organizational structure consistent with the company's constitution. That structure represents to outsiders a complex of appearances as to authority. The assurance with which outsiders deal with a company is more often than not based, not upon inquiry, or positive statement, but upon an assumption that company officers have the authority that people in their respective positions would ordinarily be expected to have ...
>
> A kind of representation that often arises in business dealings is one which flows from equipping an officer of a company with certain title, status and facilities.[31]

Returning to the second requirement in *Freeman & Lockyer,* the representation must be made by the board or a person with actual authority to manage the company or to enter the contract in question. In *Freeman & Lockyer,* this requirement was satisfied as the board had allowed Kapoor to act as if he had power to manage the company. However, this requirement is not always easy to satisfy. For example, it is not met if an agent holds another person out as having authority to bind the company or if a single director holds someone out as an agent, unless it is a single director company.

The issue of holding out was discussed in *Crabtree-Vickers Pty Ltd v Australian Direct Mail Advertising and Addressing Co Pty Ltd.*[32] The facts of this case involved the purchase of a printing machine by Australian Direct Mail Advertising and Addressing Co Pty Ltd ('the Company'). The Company was a family company with four directors: Bruce McWilliam Snr, Bruce McWilliam Jr and both of their wives. Bruce McWilliam Snr was the chairman of the board and, although he no longer worked full-time for the company, he remained fully involved in management decisions. Bruce McWilliam Jr was called the 'managing director'; however, he was never formally appointed, and his actual authority was limited. Also involved in the company was Peter McWilliam, the other son of Bruce McWilliam Snr. Peter had resigned as a director when he became a bankrupt but had continued to be employed by the company in relation to sales and technical matters. A committee consisting of Bruce Snr, Bruce Jr and Peter collectively managed the Company's affairs.

The committee tasked Peter with getting information and quotes for a new printing machine. He was not authorised to buy a machine. Despite this, Peter placed an order for a machine and related equipment with Crabtree-Vickers on behalf of the Company. He used a blank company order form he had obtained from Bruce Jnr and signed the document on Bruce Jr's behalf.

---

29 *Pacific Carriers Ltd v BNP Paribas* (2004) 218 CLR 451.

30 Ibid.

31 Ibid [36]. [38].

32 *Crabtree Vickers Pty Ltd v Australian Direct Mail Advertising and Addressing Co Pty Ltd* (1975) 133 CLR 72.

A dispute arose as to whether the Company was bound under the contract. The Company argued that Peter had no actual authority to enter the contract, and that his only authority was to obtain information and quotes. The High Court agreed and proceeded to consider whether Peter had apparent authority to bind the Company. The Court noted that both Peter and Bruce Jr made verbal representations that Peter had authority to enter the contract, with Bruce Jr also allowing Peter to appear to have authority by providing him with a blank company order form. Supplying Peter with a blank order amounted to a representation as it was 'arming him with a document which, when he signed it, would bear the hallmark of authenticity'.[33]

The Court held that, under the second requirement of *Freeman & Lockyer*, these representations did not create apparent authority as Bruce Jr had not been validly appointed as the managing director or been given authority to enter the specific contract. As such, he could not hold Peter out as having any more authority than he had. As Whelan J noted in *Flexirent Capital Pty Ltd v EBS Consulting Pty Ltd*:[34]

> The holding out must be conducted by the principal, not the agent. A third party cannot rely upon the agent's own representation as to authority. But this does not mean that the agent's conduct is to be ignored. The principal may hold out the agent as having authority by permitting the agent to act in a certain way or to make representations about himself or herself, or the principal may hold the agent out by equipping or arming the agent with a document or thing which enables the agent to assert authority with the hallmark of authenticity.[35]

The result in *Crabtree-Vickers* can be criticised on the basis that it imposes an unreasonable expectation on third parties to inquire into an agent's authority. The contract in *Crabtree-Vickers* was not binding because Bruce Jr did not have actual authority to enter the contract and could not make a representation through words or conduct that Peter had authority. While it is highly unlikely that a third party would know this, the High Court considered that it was this limitation on Bruce Jr's authority, plus the readiness of Crabtree-Vickers to enter a large contract after only dealing with one person from the company, that influenced the result. The case was followed in *Perkins v National Australia Bank Ltd*,[36] and has since been ameliorated by the introduction of the statutory assumptions, discussed below.

The final requirement for estoppel is that the representation must be relied upon by the third party. This is easy to satisfy unless it can be shown that the third party knew or ought to have known that the agent lacked authority. In *Northside Developments Pty Ltd v Registrar-General*[37] (discussed further below), the Court held that, if any third parties have some reason to doubt an agent's authority, they are taken to be 'put on inquiry' and

33 (1975) 133 CLR 72.
34 *Flexirent Capital Pty Ltd v EBS Consulting Pty Ltd* [2007] VSC 158.
35 Ibid [203].
36 [1999] SASC 280.
37 *Northside Developments Pty Ltd v Registrar-General* (1990) 170 CLR 146.

must ask questions to determine if authority actually exists. Failure to ask such questions denies them the right to enforce the contract via estoppel.

6.20.05 Acquiescence

On occasions, an argument for implied actual authority and apparent authority can be made on the same facts where an agent has been allowed to act in a particular role or way. This overlap most often arises due to acquiescence (failure to object) by the board or by a person with actual authority to a person acting as an agent. For example, in *Junker v Hepburn*,[38] there were two directors of a company: Scott Hepburn and Veronica Roller. Roller allowed Hepburn to negotiate a loan, including providing bank account details for where the money was to be paid, and securing a later extension to the loan. The bank details provided by Hepburn were for a personal, rather than the company's, bank account. When the loan was not repaid, the plaintiffs sought to enforce a guarantee provided by Roller under the loan. Roller argued that Hepburn was not authorised to provide the bank details.

The Court found that Roller had acquiesced to Hepburn providing the bank details. This gave rise to implied authority for Hepburn to act. As the Court noted:

> An implied grant of actual authority can result from acquiescence in the course of behaviour by persons who have actual authority to delegate. For example, if directors as a board stand by whilst a single director enters into transactions outside his or her authority, the board's acquiescence in that course of dealing can constitute the grant, by implication, of actual authority to enter into those transactions.[39]

Similarly, in *Brick & Pipe Industries Ltd v Occidental Life Nominee Pty Ltd*,[40] the Court held that the board of Brick & Pipe had acquiesced to a director having effective control over the company. This case arose in the context of a guarantee being granted to Occidental Life by Abraham Goldberg, using the common seal of Brick & Pipe. Brick & Pipe was one company within a group of companies referred to by the Court as the 'Goldberg Group'. When the Goldberg Group collapsed, the validity of the guarantee was challenged by the new board of Brick & Pipe, who argued that Goldberg did not have authority to enter the guarantee on behalf of Brick & Pipe.[41]

The guarantee had been granted as security for a loan to another company within the Goldberg Group, and Brick & Pipe did not derive any benefit from the transaction. The guarantee was also executed without the knowledge of the Brick & Pipe board, which consisted of a chairperson and a number of other directors who had remained on the board after the Goldberg Group took over the company, plus Goldberg, his wife, and son in-law, Mr Furst. Brick & Pipe's Articles of Association required that use of the company seal had to be authorised by the board, and co-signed by a director and

38 *Junker v Hepburn* [2010] NSWSC 88.

39 Ibid [43].

40 *Brick & Pipe Industries Ltd v Occidental Life Nominee Pty Ltd* [1992] 2 VR 279.

41 Brick & Pipe was sold as part of a receivership, which is discussed in detail in Chapter 15.

secretary. Goldberg had executed the guarantee without such authorisation, using Brick & Pipe's common seal, and had signed as director, with Furst signing as company secretary. At the time, Furst was only a director of Brick & Pipe, not a company secretary. Although some attempt was made by Goldberg to appoint Furst as company secretary, no formal board meeting was held to approve this appointment or the guarantee.

In deciding whether Brick & Pipe was bound by the guarantee, all three judges of the Appeal Division of the Victorian Supreme Court held that, under *Companies (Victoria) Code* s 68A (a similar section to s 129 of the *Companies Act 1981* (Cth)), the fact that there was no board meeting authorising the use of the common seal did not affect the validity of the contract as Occidental Life was entitled to assume that the company's constitution had been complied with. On the question of whether it was entitled to assume that Furst was company secretary, the Court found Goldberg had implied actual authority to hold Furst out in this manner. Ormiston J noted that the board had acquiesced in Goldberg's control of Brick & Pipe, that it had never attempted to interfere with his actions, and that Goldberg had on occasions even obtained board approval to transactions after he had entered them. Ormiston J continued:

> Throughout the dealings with the Occidental Group, Mr. Goldberg had been known as the alter ego of each of the Goldberg Group of companies ... Nothing had occurred to indicate that he found it necessary to refer to any board, nor had any board attempted to interfere ... [even though] in the case of Brick and Pipe there was still a considerable number of outside directors ... In the circumstances it would be remarkable if that company could now say that Mr. Goldberg was not a person who could hold out on its behalf that a particular person held a position [of secretary] in that company.[42]

The Court concluded that Goldberg had sufficient authority through the board's acquiescence to represent Furst as the company secretary, and the contract was binding on Brick & Pipe.

6.25 The effect of non-compliance with internal matters on the validity of a contract

It can be argued that a contract is not valid if an internal rule of the company has not been complied with when entering the contract. This is dealt with by the common law 'indoor management rule', which provides that a person dealing with a company is entitled to assume that the company's constitution and internal rules have been complied with.[43] An expanded version of the indoor management rule is now contained in ss 128–129 of the *Corporations Act* (discussed below). While the common law rule continues to exist, in practice it is not often relevant as the statutory provisions are wide enough to cover most circumstances.

42 *Brick & Pipe Industries Ltd v Occidental Life Nominee Pty Ltd* [1992] 2 VR 279, 311.

43 See *Royal British Bank v Turquand* (1856) 119 ER 886; *Northside Developments Pty Ltd v Registrar-General* (1990) 170 CLR 146, 154–5 (Mason CJ).

In *Morris v Kanssen*,[44] the House of Lords approved the following statement of the indoor management rule taken from Halsbury's Laws of England:

> [P]ersons contracting with a company and dealing with a company in good faith may assume that acts within its constitution and powers have been properly and duly performed and are not bound to inquire whether acts of internal management have been regular.[45]

This rule evolved from the judgments of the Exchequer Chamber in *Royal British Bank v Turquand*.[46] This case involved a loan to a company, Cameron's Coalbrook Steam, Coal and Swansea and Loughor Railway Company ('the Company'), with the Bank taking as security for the loan a bond signed by two of the Company's directors. The Company seal had been used on the bond document. However, the Company's Deed of Settlement (equivalent to its constitution) provided that the directors were only authorised to borrow money in this way if their actions had been approved by an ordinary resolution of the general meeting. The Company argued that, as no valid resolution had been passed, it was not bound by the bond document.

The Exchequer Chamber disagreed and held that the bond was valid and the Company was bound. It found there was no requirement for the Bank to look into whether the internal workings of the Company had been complied with and was therefore entitled to assume the approval had been obtained. The Court held that the doctrine of constructive notice only operated to attribute to the Bank knowledge of the provisions of the constitution, not whether those provisions had been complied with. As a result, the Bank did not need to inquire into such internal matters and was entitled to assume that proper approval for the loan had been given.

The rule in *Turquand's Case* was applied in Australia by the High Court in *Northside Developments Pty Ltd v Registrar-General*.[47] *Northside Developments* was decided before ss 128 and 129 were introduced into the *Corporations Act*. The application of the rule in *Turquand's Case* raises similar policy issues to those in the agency case; namely, how to balance the interests of those dealing with a company (who need contracts that appear to be validly entered into by the company to be enforceable) and the shareholders of a company (who are adversely affected when a company is liable on a contract that was entered into without authority or approval).

As Mason CJ noted in *Northside Developments Pty Ltd v Registrar-General*:

> The precise formulation and application of [indoor management] rule call for a fine balance between competing interests. On the one hand, the rule has been developed to protect and promote business convenience which would be at hazard if persons dealing with companies were under the necessity of investigating their internal proceedings in order to satisfy themselves about the

44 *Morris v Kanssen* [1946] AC 459, 474.

45 LexisNexis, *Halsbury's Laws of England*, vol 5 (1932) 423.

46 *Royal British Bank v Turquand* (1856) 119 ER 886 ('*Turquand's Case*').

47 *Northside Developments Pty Ltd v Registrar-General* (1990) 170 CLR 146.

actual authority of officers and the validity of instruments. On the other hand, an over-extensive application of the rule may facilitate the commission of fraud and unjustly favour those who deal with companies at the expense of innocent creditors and shareholders who are the victims of unscrupulous persons acting or purporting to act on behalf of companies.[48]

6.25.05 The statutory assumptions

Sections 128 and 129 of the *Corporations Act* were introduced between 1983 and 1985 to protect third parties dealing with a company in good faith; for example, s 129 includes a wider version of the indoor management rule and the common law rule on apparent authority. It includes other assumptions and protections that a third party can rely upon. In *Bank of New Zealand v Fiberi Pty Ltd*,[49] Kirby J noted the policy behind the sections was commercial convenience, which prioritised 'efficacy of business transactions ... above the financial and other interests of the innocent officers, members and creditors of a particular corporation'.[50]

Section 128(1) provides that a person who has dealings with a company is entitled to make the assumptions set out in s 129 about the validity of those dealings, and the company is unable to assert that the assumptions are incorrect. It has been held that 'dealings with a company' include a single transaction (*Advance Bank Australia Ltd v Fleetwood Star Pty Ltd*)[51] and negotiations or other steps in relation to a contemplated transaction (*Soyfer v Earlmaze Pty Ltd*)[52]. The meaning of the words was considered in the case of *Australia and New Zealand Banking Group Ltd v Frenmast Pty Ltd*.[53] On the facts, Frenmast was one of three companies set up to run a licorice manufacturing business. Frenmast owned land that it leased to the second company, which manufactured the licorice and sold it to the third company.

ANZ provided loans facilities to Frenmast that were guaranteed by the two other companies and some of the individuals involved in the business (the Tiricovski brothers). ANZ then sought a guarantee from Frenmast in relation to loans to one of the other companies and to Robert Tiricovski. The document appeared to bear the signatures of two directors but one of the signatures was forged.

ANZ sued to enforce the guarantee against Frenmast and relied on the assumption in s 129(5) of the Act that the document had been duly executed. The trial judge, Adams J, held that ANZ was not entitled to rely upon this assumption as there was no evidence of dealings between ANZ and Frenmast in respect of the guarantee. Of particular importance was the fact that ANZ had not dealt with anyone within Frenmast who had actual or apparent authority to enter the guarantee on behalf of the company.

On appeal, the New South Wales Court of Appeal found Adams J's reasoning to be incorrect and overturned the decision. The Court found that for the requirement of

48 Ibid 164–5.

49 *Bank of New Zealand v Fiberi Pty ltd* (1994) 12 ACLC 48.

50 Ibid 52.

51 *Advance Bank Australia Ltd v Fleetwood Star Pty Ltd* (1992) 10 ACLC 703.

52 *Soyfer v Earlmaze Pty Ltd* [2000] NSWSC 1068.

53 *New Zealand Banking Group Ltd v Frenmast Pty Ltd* (2013) 282 FLR 351.

'dealings with the company' to be met, it was not necessary for ANZ to deal with a person who had authority to bind the company. All that was required was that ANZ had dealings with a person with authority to negotiate the transaction. On the facts, Robert Tiricovski had such authority as he had been the main contact point for ANZ for a number of years and the other director was aware of that fact. ANZ was entitled to assume that the director had authority to negotiate the guarantee with bank.

Section 128(3) provides that the assumptions can be made even when fraud by the person acting on behalf of a company is involved. It is also not necessary that a third party actually makes the assumptions set out in s 128(3) as these automatically apply regardless of whether the third party considered the issues or not (subject to s 128(4)). However, under s 128(4), a person is not entitled to make the assumptions if they knew or suspected that the assumptions were incorrect.

Section 129 contains seven assumptions that operate to the benefit of third parties. Each of the assumptions is separate and discrete, such that more than one assumption may apply.[54] The assumptions operate to prevent a company asserting in proceedings that any of the issues dealt with in the section are incorrect. The assumptions also move the burden of proof from the third party to the company in relation to those issues. The assumptions do not 'validate an instrument to which they are directed but, in a practical sense, they prevent the invalidity of it being successfully asserted (by the company)'.[55]

The main issues covered by s 129 include:

- non-compliance with the company's constitution and any replaceable rules that apply
- the authority of a director or company secretary who appears to be such from ASIC records available to the public and based on information from the company
- the authority of a person held out by the company to be an officer or agent of the company
- the proper performance of duties by officers and agents of the company
- the due execution of documents by the company
- the authority of an officer or agent of a company authorised to issue a document to warrant that it is genuine.

Section 129(1)

Section 129(1) provides that a person can assume that a company's constitution (if it has one) and any of the replaceable rules that apply have been complied with. This section reflects the indoor management rule and its predecessor (*Companies Act 1981* s 68A). For example, if a company's constitution requires that a board meeting be held to approve the use of the company seal, a person having dealings with the company may, in relation to those dealings, assume that such a meeting has been held if the seal is used.

In *Brick & Pipe*, discussed above, the Court held that the fact that there was no board meeting authorising the use of the common seal did not affect the validity of the

54 Section 129(8). See *Bank of New Zealand v Fiberi Pty Ltd* (1994) 12 ACLC 48.

55 *Story v Advance Bank Australia Ltd* (1993) 31 NSWLR 722, 742.

guarantee granted to Occidental Life.[56] The effect of s 129(1) was to allow Occidental Life to assume that the company's constitution had been complied with. While a person does not need to have knowledge of the constitution or the replaceable rules to benefit from the assumptions,[57] they do need to refer to them in legal proceedings if they wish to claim that benefit.[58]

Section 129(2)

Section 129(2) provides that a third party may assume that a person who appears on the information provided to ASIC to be a director or secretary of a company has been duly appointed and is authorised to exercise the powers and perform the duties customarily exercised or performed by a director or secretary of a similar company. This assumption is available to third parties regardless of whether they know about the information and operates to protect them where such a person has not been properly appointed.[59]

Companies are required to provide information to ASIC on its directors and company secretaries under s 205B, which requires a company to lodge with ASIC, within 28 days, the personal details of any director or secretary appointed by the company and, under pt 2N.1, dealing with the company's annual return. This information is available to the public and operates as a form of holding out by the company that the persons named on the ASIC register are appointed to the positions indicated and have the customary authority that goes with such a role. The information must be available to the public at the time of the dealing with the company. In *ANZ Banking Group Ltd v Australian Glass and Mirrors Pty Ltd*,[60] the Court found that a company held out a person as a company director and another as the company secretary by lodging documents with ASIC that named them as such.

Section 129(3)

This section overlaps with the law of apparent authority and the relevant cases discussed above at Section 6.20. Section 129(3) provides that 'a person is entitled to assume that someone who is *held out by the company* to be an officer or agent has been duly appointed and has *the authority* to exercise the powers and perform the duties customarily performed by such an officer or agent of a similar company'.[61] Section 9AD defines a company officer as including a director, company secretary, and senior executive. It follows that for a third person to rely upon the assumption in s 129(3) they must not only show that there was a holding out that a particular person was an officer or agent, but also that they exercised a power that is customarily within the scope of powers exercised by such an officer or agent. It is not necessary, however, that the third party show that the holding out was made to them directly.

56 *Brick & Pipe Industries Ltd v Occidental Life Nominee Pty Ltd* [1992] 2 VR 279.
57 *Oris Funds Management Ltd v National Australia Bank Ltd* [2003] VSC 315.
58 *Bell Resources Holdings Pty Ltd v Commissioner for Australian Capital Territory Revenue Collections* (1990) 93 ALR 354, 370.
59 *Re Madi Pty Ltd* (1987) 5 ACLC 847.
60 *ANZ Banking Group Ltd v Australian Glass and Mirrors Pty Ltd* (1991) 9 ACLC 702.
61 Emphasis added.

To determine if there has been a holding out, the common law rules of apparent authority apply as set out in *Freeman & Lockyer* (discussed at Section 6.20 above). There must be a representation (by words or conduct) that the person is an officer or agent of the company, and the representation must be made 'by the company'; that is, by a group or person with authority to manage the company, such as the board or a managing director. The third party does not need to rely upon the representation. Under s 128(4), if the third party knew or suspected that the officer or agent had not been duly appointed, they are not entitled to make any of the assumptions set out in s 129.

Section 129(4)

Section 129(4) provides that any person who has dealings with a company can assume that its officers and agents properly perform the duties they owe to the company. This is particularly relevant to the duties of officers and directors discussed in Chapter 10. This subsection can overlap with ss 129(2)–(3), so that a person having dealings with a company can assume that anyone who appears on the information provided to ASIC to be a director or secretary of a company, or who is held out by the company to be a director, secretary or officer, is properly performing their duties in those dealings.[62]

Sections 129(5) and 129(6)

Under s 127(1), a company can enter a contract directly where the document is signed by two directors or by a director and a company secretary. If a common seal is used on a document, s 127(2) requires that it must be witnessed by two directors or by one director and the company secretary. In a proprietary company with a single director, where that person is also the company secretary the director can witness the use of the common seal or can sign the document under ss 127(1) and (2).

Sections 129(5) and (6) then allow a third party to assume that a document that appears to have been signed in accordance with ss 127(1) or (2) has been duly executed. The key requirement is that the document must *appear* to have been executed correctly; for example, a document just bearing the signature of one director does not attract the protection offered by s 129(5). This is different to the position under the section's predecessor (*Companies Act 1981* s 68A), which required not only that a document appear to have been executed properly but also that the persons who signed had been held out to be a director and secretary, either on public documents or by the company.

The case of *Caratti v Mammoth Investments Pty Ltd*[63] confirmed that this requirement no longer applies. This case involved the Caratti family, who were divided over the application of the family's wealth after the death of Sergio Caratti. On the one side was Allen Caratti, and on the other his mother Maddeleine and his brother John.[64] One of the Caratti companies, Navarac Pty Ltd, owned Young River Cattle Station in Western Australia. Allen, purporting to still be a director of Mammoth Investments Pty Ltd, which

62 See *Commonwealth Bank of Australia v Ridout Nominees Pty Ltd* [2000] WASC 37.

63 *Caratti v Mammoth Investments Pty Ltd* (2016) 50 WAR 84.

64 See J Barrett, 'WA property tycoon involved in "corrupt and dishonest" schemes', *Australian Financial Review* (online, 8 September 2014) <http://www.afr.com/real-estate/commercial/wa-property-tycoon-involved-in-corrupt-and-dishonest-schemes-20140908-jeqat>.

held a lease over Young River granted by Navarac, tried to grant a sublease over the land to Granite Hill Pty Ltd. At the time, Allen was no longer a director of Mammoth, having been removed by his mother. He was also not named as a director on any documents lodged with ASIC. However, Allen signed the lease as a director and forged his mother's signature on the lease document. Later, another lease was granted by Navarac over Young River to Esperance Cattle Company Pty Ltd, with Navarac's directors Aaron Caratti (John's son) and Maddeleine Caratti signing the document.

In legal proceedings, the question was whether the sublease granted by Mammoth to Granite Hill was binding upon Mammoth. At first instance, Martin CJ found that, although Granite Hill was entitled to make an assumption under s 129(5) that the document had been duly executed, this assumption did not preclude Esperance Cattle (as a bona fide third party granted valid title in the land) from then establishing that the sublease was not valid. As a result, the Court held that the document was not binding on Mammoth and Esperance Cattle was entitled to possession of Young River Station.

On appeal, the Western Australian Court of Appeal found that under s 128(3), the operation of s 129 was such that, once it applied, the sublease could be treated as if it validly conferred title. The fact that another third party had subsequently been granted the same interest under a validly executed contract did not change this fact. Furthermore, the fact that Allen had not been held out as a director of the company (either on documents lodged with ASIC or by the board), or that he had forged Maddeleine Caratti's signature did not preclude the operation of s 129(5). On the face of it, the lease appeared to have been executed according to the requirements of s 127(1) and therefore it was binding on Mammoth.

Section 129(7)

The final assumption available under s 129(7) allows a person who has dealings with a company to assume that any officer or agent who has authority to issue a document or a certified copy of a document on the company's behalf also has authority to warrant that the document is genuine or that it is a true copy.

6.25.10 Limitations on the application of the statutory assumptions: s 128(4)

The benefit of s 129 is limited by the requirement in s 128(4) that the third party neither knew nor suspected that the assumptions were incorrect. This section has given rise to considerable speculation due to the inclusion of the word 'suspected'. A third party with actual knowledge that any of the assumptions are incorrect is not entitled to rely upon them. However, under the common law, a person is prohibited from relying upon a representation of apparent authority or the indoor management rule if they were 'put on inquiry' in the circumstances that the agent did not have authority or the internal rules of the company had not been complied with. This rule was applied in *Northside Developments Pty Ltd v Registrar-General* ('*Northside*').[65] Northside Developments' ('Northside') main business related to a piece of land that it owned. There were three directors in the

65 *Northside Developments Pty Ltd v Registrar-General* (1990) 170 CLR 146.

company, including Robert Sturgess, and a company secretary, Gerard Sturgess, who was Robert's son. Gerard had not been properly appointed as the company secretary, but his consent to act as the company secretary had been filed with the corporate regulator.

Robert and Gerard entered into a mortgage over the land owned by Northside with Barclays Credit Union. The mortgage secured a loan to another company controlled by Robert, and Northside derived no benefit from the loan. The mortgage was executed on behalf of Northside using the company's seal and signed by Robert and Gerard as director and secretary respectively. Northside's Articles of Association (the predecessor document to a constitution) required that the company seal could only be used with the authority of all the directors.

When the company to whom the loan had been made defaulted, Barclays sold the land owned by Northside to a third party pursuant to its rights under the mortgage. Northside then sought to dispute the transfer of the land.[66] The issue to be decided was whether the mortgage was binding on Northside despite it not having been executed in accordance with the company's Articles of Association. Barclays argued it was entitled to rely upon the indoor management rule and that it was not affected by any failure of Sturgess and his son to comply with the Articles. In contrast, Northside argued that Barclays was 'put on inquiry' in the circumstances of the case and needed to ask further questions about Robert and Gerard's authority, as it was clear that Northside was not benefiting from the loan that was securing the mortgage. As Mason CJ noted:

> [T]o hold that a person dealing with a company is put upon inquiry when that company enters into a transaction which appears to be unrelated to the purposes of its business and from which it appears to gain no benefit is, in my opinion, to strike a fair balance between the competing interests [in this case].[67]

As the case was decided before the introduction of the predecessor sections to ss 128 and 129, the High Court had to decide the issue based on the indoor management rule. All five judges of the High Court differed in their opinions as to the foundations of the indoor management rule. However, all agreed that the mortgage was invalid, and that Barclays should have been put on inquiry by the circumstances of the case. As Mason CJ noted, '[a] person, even one who has no special relationship with the company concerned, may be put upon inquiry by the very nature of the transaction'.[68] On the facts, it was clear to Barclays that the loan was being made to companies unrelated to Northside, and that Northside was gaining no benefit from it. These facts should have led Barclays' officers to make inquiries of Robert and Gerard that they had the necessary authority to execute the mortgage on behalf of the company using the company's seal.

It is likely that this case would have been decided differently under ss 128 and 129. Under s 129(1), Barclays would have been entitled to assume that the company's

66 Under the *Real Property Act 1900* (NSW), Northside could sue the Registrar-General as a nominal defendant to recover nominal damages where another person had wrongly been registered as the proprietor of land.

67 (1990) 170 CLR 146, 187.

68 Ibid 155.

constitution had been complied with, and this would have prevented Northside arguing there was no board approval to use the company seal. In addition, under ss 129(2) and (6), Barclays would have been entitled to assume that Gerard was validly appointed as company secretary, and that the mortgage had been validly executed, as it appeared to comply with the requirements of s 127(2).[69] In addition, it is unlikely that s 128(4) would have applied to limit these assumptions.

In *Eden Energy Ltd v Drivetrain USA Inc*,[70] the Court noted that a person dealing with a company is not required to make any inquiry in order to rely on the assumptions in s 129. Corboy J, referring to other relevant cases on this issue, stated:

> [A] person does not lose the benefit of the assumptions in s 129 merely because, in the circumstances, their suspicions *ought* to have been aroused: *Sunburst Properties Pty Ltd (in liq) v Agwater Pty Ltd* [2005] SASC 335 [178] (Gray J). Section 128(4) does not incorporate the concept of being 'put upon enquiry': *Errichetti Holdings Pty Ltd v Western Plaza Hotel Corporation Pty Ltd* [2006] WASC 113 [74] (Master Newnes (as his Honour then was)); *Sunburst Properties* [178].
>
> ... The expression 'knew or suspected' in s 128(4) does not encompass the knowledge that a person is deemed to possess in equity through a failure to make usual enquiries or a failure to enquire when put on notice of the need to enquire ... In short, actual knowledge is required and constructive knowledge is not actual knowledge.

Returning to the case of *Northside*, the effect of the assumption in s 129(1) would be that, in the absence of actual knowledge or actual suspicion that the constitution has not been complied with (or that Gerard was not validly appointed), the bank would be entitled to make the assumption set out in the section. The relevant time to consider whether actual knowledge or suspicion existed was when the transaction was made: *Barclays Finance Holdings Ltd v Sturgess*.[71] Furthermore, the onus of proof would be on the company to prove that there was actual knowledge or suspicion by the bank. In *Sunburst Properties Pty Ltd (in liq) v Agwater Pty Ltd*,[72] Justice Gray of the Supreme Court of South Australia considered that the test in s 128(4) is subjective, and requires proof that the third party actually knew or actually suspected that the assumption was incorrect. This is in contrast to the common law test discussed in *Northside*, which considers what a reasonable person in the third party's position would have asked in relation to the agent's authority.[73] The inconsistency between these two tests leaves it open to future courts to add new insight into the operation of s 129(4).

69 The doctrine of constructive notice does not apply in the context of ss 128 and 129, so a person dealing with a company is not taken to have knowledge of any documents publicly available or any information a reasonable person would have known that would affect their ability to rely upon the assumptions: see *Oris Funds Management Ltd v National Australia Bank Ltd* [2003] VSC 315.

70 *Eden Energy Ltd v Drivetrain USA Inc* (2012) 90 ACSR 191, 211 [83].

71 *Barclay's Finance Holdings Ltd v Sturgess* (1985) 3 ACLC 662.

72 *Sunburst Properties Pty Ltd (in liq) v Agwater Pty Ltd* [2005] SASC 335 [178].

73 *Bank of New Zealand v Fiberi Pty Ltd* (1994) 12 ACLC 48.

6.30 Authority by ratification

Authority by ratification deals with a situation where the person who purports to act for the company has neither actual nor apparent authority, but their actions are later ratified by the company as principal. For this to occur, the agent's actions must be ratified, or approved, by a majority of members in general meeting. If this occurs, it operates as a retrospective grant of actual authority to the agent, such that their actions are binding on the company. For the ratification to be effective, the contract must have been entered into on behalf of the company, not by the agent acting in their own name; the company must have had authority to enter the contract at the time it was made; and ratification must relate to the entire contract.

6.35 Pre-incorporation contracts

An issue can arise as to the validity of contracts entered into on behalf of a company before it is registered. It is not uncommon for the founders of a company (called 'promoters') to execute contracts before or at the same time as a company is being registered, such as contracts for leasing premises, buying stock, building websites and so on. Promoters are also generally involved in the preliminary matters required to set up a company, including negotiating shareholder agreements, preparing the company's constitution, contacting directors and shareholders, and arranging fundraising. In all of these actions, promoters act as fiduciaries in relation to the company. Fiduciary duties are discussed extensively in Chapters 10–12.

When a promoter enters a contract on behalf of a company that has not yet been registered, ss 131–3 apply to determine the rights and liabilities of the parties under the contract. Prior to these sections being introduced, the common law position was that a company could not enter a contract before incorporation as it had no legal existence. The law of agency did not apply as there was no principal to appoint an agent or later to ratify the agent's conduct. This meant that any contract entered into before a company was registered was not binding on the company and was not binding on the person purporting to act as agent, unless it could be shown the agent intended to contract as the principal.[74] This created problems for the other parties to the contract.

The difficulties with pre-incorporation contracts have been overcome by ss 131–3, which replace the common law. Under s 131(1), a company becomes bound by, and is entitled to the benefit of, a pre-incorporation contract entered into on its behalf or for its benefit if the company is registered and ratifies the contract within an agreed time or within a reasonable time after the contract is entered into. Once the contract is ratified, it is binding on the company and can be enforced against it by the third party. The concept of 'a reasonable time' is not defined in the Act and must be decided on the facts of each case. In *Classic International Pty Ltd v Lagos*,[75] it was held that a period of one month to ratify a commercial lease was reasonable.

74 *Newborne v Sensolid (Great Britain) Ltd* [1954] 1 QB 45; *Black v Smallwood* (1966) 117 CLR 52.
75 *Classic International Pty Ltd v Lagos* (2002) 60 NSWLR 241.

The *Corporations Act* does not specify how ratification should occur. In practice, pre-incorporation contracts are ratified by the board of directors passing a resolution approving the contract, or where the company signs a document to that effect. The partial performance of a contract may also result in implied ratification. The power to ratify a contract on behalf of a company can also be delegated to an individual under s 126(1). A pre-incorporation contract is formed on the date it is ratified, rather than on the date it was initially entered into.[76]

If a contract is not ratified or is not ratified within the specified time or a reasonable time, the person who entered the contract can be liable to pay damages to the other party to the contract (s 131(2)). The amount of damages is the amount the company would have been liable to pay if the contract had been ratified and then breached by the company. This includes loss of profit by the other party and amounts spent in reliance upon the contract. Under s 131(3)(c), the company may have to repay some or all of the damages to the person who entered the contract on its behalf. The court may order the company to transfer to the other contracting party property that the company received under the contract or pay an amount to that party to the contract.

Promoters need to ensure any contracts entered into before a company is registered are ratified. Alternatively, promoters can wait until after registration to contract on the company's behalf. The later approach is best as, even if a company ratifies a contract, a promoter may be liable to pay damages if the company breaches the contract. Under s 131(4), a promoter may be ordered to pay the whole or part of any damages the ratifying company is ordered to pay upon breach. This provision is aimed at deterring promoters who set up companies to get the benefit of limited liability, but the company is under-capitalised and unable to pay its debts on registration.

Sections 131 and 132 provide ways promoters can protect themselves from liability under pre-incorporation contracts. One is to obtain a signed release of liability from the other party to the contract (s 132(1)). Another is to have the company and the third party enter into a new contract on the same terms and conditions once the company is registered (ss 131(1)–(3)).

6.40 Summary

This chapter addressed the question of how companies enter contracts. This issue can cause problems for companies and the third parties dealing with them.

In law, the most effective way for a company to enter a contract is directly via the use of the common seal or where two directors or a director and a secretary sign a document as the company. In reality, these requirements are not often complied with and the question becomes whether an individual can act as an agent for the company. This depends on whether that person had actual, implied actual or apparent authority.

This chapter discussed the indoor management rule and ss 128 and 129 of the *Corporations Act*, which were introduced to clarify the protections available to third parties. Some of these provisions overlap with the law of agency. The operation of s 129 is

76 *Keswick Developments Ptd Ltd v Kevroy Pty Ltd* [2009] QSC 176.

broad and includes other assumptions that can protect a third party. As discussed, in Australia the question of whether actual knowledge is needed under s 128(4) for these assumptions not to apply is still unsettled.

Finally, the chapter discussed pre-registration contracts. This area of law has been substantially clarified with the introduction of ss 131–3, which allows for ratification of contracts entered into before a company is incorporated.

CHAPTER

7

DECISION-MAKING, MEETINGS AND REPORTING

7.05 Introduction

As discussed in earlier chapters, a company has the legal powers and capacity of an individual, in addition to any specific powers conferred by law (s 124). The two key decision-making organs that can act as the company in exercising these powers are the board of directors and the members in general meeting. The general law and the *Corporations Act 2001* (Cth) divide the company's powers and responsibilities between these two groups. This chapter discusses this division of powers. It also discusses how meetings of members and directors are held, and the requirements on companies to prepare and disclose key information, including financial reports.

7.10 Decision-making

There are many long- and short-term decisions that need to be made within companies. The responsibility for making these decisions is divided between the board of directors and the members in general meeting. The exception to this is when a company is in financial difficulty and must appoint a receiver or liquidator. In reality, many day-to-day decisions will be made by managers and other employees within a company acting under delegation from the board. Provided a decision is properly made, the board and shareholders in general meeting act as the company when making decisions.[1]

The division of power between the board and the members in general meeting is determined by looking at the company's constitution and at the relevant sections of the *Corporations Act*. As discussed in Chapter 4, the constitution contains the rules on the internal workings of a company. Under the replaceable rule contained in s 198A, or a similar provision contained in the company's constitution, the power to manage the business of a company is vested in the board of directors or their delegate.[2] This power

1 See *Australasian Centre for Corporate Responsibility v Commonwealth Bank of Australia* (2016) 248 FCR 280, where the Court held that a resolution passed by the members in general meeting is an act of the company.

2 One point of interest is that the *Corporations Act* assumes, rather than requires, directors to act as a board, with the Act only referring to the board in ss 46 and 47 (definition of subsidiary company) and in s 200B (dealing with termination payments). Section 198A does not specify that directors must act as a board (even though it does refer to the general meeting). This does not change the result that directors must act collectively; rather, it is a point to note.

is broad and includes all areas of decision-making not reserved specifically for members in general meeting. Section 198A(2) provides that 'the directors may exercise all of the powers of the company except any powers that [the Corporations Act] or the company's constitution (if any) requires the company to exercise in general meeting'. It is possible for companies to alter this balance of power by including different provisions in the corporate constitution; however, most companies adopt similar provisions to s 198A.

7.10.05 Application of the division of powers

In reality, this model is an oversimplification of how decisions are made. For example, the size and complexity of the operations of large public companies means that the board is rarely able to exercise its full power to manage the company. Instead, it must delegate much of this power to senior managers.[3] The board's role then becomes one of monitoring those managers who have delegated authority to run the business or parts of it. As noted by Rogers CJ in *AWA Ltd v Daniels*,[4] 'many companies today are too big to be supervised and administered by a Board of Directors except in relation to matters of high policy'.[5] His Honour continued:

> The board of a large public corporation cannot manage the corporation's day to day business. That function must by business necessity be left to the corporation's executives.
>
> If the director of a large public corporation were to be immersed in the details of the day to day operations the director would be incapable of taking more abstract, important decisions at board level.[6]

The position in small proprietary companies is also not as neat in practice as suggested by the legal division of powers. Where the shareholders and directors of a company are the same people, it can be impractical and artificial to hold separate board and members' meetings. However, in the absence of a provision in the constitution altering the balance of power, the law maintains this formal separation of powers. Not surprisingly, this can result in confusion for the individuals involved in a small company.

Added to this is the fact that each decision-making organ within a company is sovereign within their area of power. In other words, neither group can interfere with or direct the other as to how to exercise their powers. Members cannot order or seek to influence directors in their decisions, and the directors cannot interfere with the decision-making of members. This can lead to tensions between shareholders and directors, particularly where there are different views as to how a company should be managed.[7] While shareholders have a financial interest in a company, in law their ability to influence management is limited. In large public companies this can result

3 For a detailed discussion of the law on delegation, see Chapter 11 at Section 11.20.05.
4 *AWA Ltd v Daniels* (1992) 7 ACSR 759.
5 Ibid 832.
6 Ibid 866 (citations omitted).
7 See, eg, the discussion of *Automatic Self-Cleansing Filter Syndicate Co Ltd v Cuninghame* [1906] 2 Ch 34 at Section 7.25.

in shareholders taking action to express their views through 'shareholder activism': defined as any 'action taken by shareholders to bring about change in a company or influence its behaviour'.[8] Before considering these issues, we must first discuss the powers allocated to the members and the board.

7.15 Members' rights

The term 'members' includes shareholders in a company limited by shares, members of a company limited by guarantee, and members of an unlimited company. As discussed below, members hold important rights in a company. Chapter 5 discussed members' rights to enforce the corporate constitution via contract. The rights granted to members through the constitution are called 'personal rights'. In this chapter, we discuss the rights members have to act collectively in the general meeting and to make decisions as the company. We discuss how members' meetings are held. In Chapter 14, we discuss members' statutory rights, including the right to take legal action on behalf of the company (called 'derivative rights'); to take legal action for oppressive, unfairly discriminatory and unfairly prejudicial conduct; and to apply to have the company wound up.

There are often different types of members in companies, particularly large companies. Some are small- to medium-sized investors looking to achieve a return on their investment in the form of dividends and/or an increase in the value of the shares on sale. These investors generally rely on general meetings and information made public throughout the year to stay up to date on the company's activities. Other members include institutional investors such as fund managers, superannuation/pension funds (industry, government or corporate), life companies, universities, and banks. These investors may have sufficiently large shareholdings to be able to meet with executives of a company to discuss its performance outside of members' meetings.[9] This can offer large investors an opportunity to inform the board of their views on the company's performance and receive information on its future progress and direction.

7.15.05 Members' powers in the general meeting

As indicated above, directors are usually granted the broad power to manage a company under the *Corporations Act* (s 198A) or the company's constitution. In contrast, members are given specific decision-making powers under the *Corporations Act*, the constitution, and the general law. Shareholders in companies listed on the Australian Securities Exchange (ASX) must be given additional rights via the company constitution to vote on

8 S Gillan and L Starks, 'The Evolution of Shareholder Activism in the United States' (2007) 19(1) *Journal of Applied Corporate Finance* 55, 55.

9 C Cuffe, 'How institutional investors influence listed companies' *Firstlinks* (Web Page, 29 August 2013) <https://cuffelinks.com.au/institutional-investors-influence-listed-companies/>. For a detailed discussion of institutional investors' role in corporate governance, see L Griggs, 'Institutional Investors and Corporate Governance' (1996) 3 *James Cook University Law Review* 44; Joseph McCahery, Zacharias Sautner and Laura Starks, 'Behind the Scenes: The Corporate Governance Preferences of Institutional Investors' (2016) 71 *Journal of Finance* 2905.

a range of issues including when the company makes a significant change to its activities or its main undertaking is sold.[10] An example of a provision from a public company's constitution conferring such power on the board might be as follows:

> The Directors are responsible for managing the business of the company and may exercise to the exclusion of the members in general meeting all the powers which are not required by the *Corporations Act*, by the *Listing Rules* or by this Constitution to be exercised by the members in general meeting.

As this mock provision demonstrates, the board of directors is the most powerful decision-making body in a company as it is able to exercise all the powers not expressly granted to the members (see replaceable rule s 198A(2)). Although members are given rights in general meeting, including the right to appoint the directors, these rights are limited to the areas specifically allocated to them in law. Indeed, many of the rights relate to structural or procedural issues, such as adopting or amending the corporate constitution; changing the company from one type to another; varying the rights attached to the company's shares; appointing and removing the directors and auditor; approving related party transactions; and commencing a members' voluntary winding up.

7.15.10 Members' powers to make decisions under the *Corporations Act 2001* (Cth)

Adopting or amending the constitution

As discussed in Chapter 5, any changes to the company's constitution must be approved by a special resolution of the members in a general meeting (s 136(2)). A constitution may stipulate additional conditions to be met for an amendment to the constitution but cannot take this power away from members (s 136(4)).

The members must agree if a company wants to adopt a constitution on or after registration. If the constitution is adopted on registration, all the initial members must consent. If a company wants to adopt a constitution after registration, this must be approved by a special resolution of the members in a general meeting (s 136(1)).

Either the directors or the members can propose the adoption of, or changes to, the constitution.

Changing the company's name or type

If a company wishes to change its name, this must be approved by a special resolution of the members in a general meeting (s 157). Similarly, if the type of company changes (for example, a proprietary company is to change to a public company), this must be approved by a special resolution of the members in a general meeting (s 162). The requirements of s 163 (applying to ASIC for a change of type) and s 164 (ASIC's role in relation to a change of type) must also be complied with. Although a company may change its type, this change does not create a new company.

10 ASX, *Listing Rules* (at 19 December 2016) rr 11.1–2.

Appointing the directors

Whether members, the board, or both have the power to appoint directors depends on the terms of the company's constitution. The replaceable rule in s 201G provides that the members may appoint a director via an ordinary resolution. Section 201H(1) (a replaceable rule) provides that, in a proprietary company, the directors may appoint a director, but that appointment must be confirmed by an ordinary resolution of the members in a general meeting passed within two months of the director's appointment (s 201H(2)). In a public company, the directors may appoint an additional director, and that appointment must also be confirmed by an ordinary resolution passed by the members at the company's next annual general meeting (s 201H(3)). If an appointment is not confirmed as required in either a proprietary or a public company, the person ceases to be a director. Sometimes, the constitution of a proprietary company will vary the replaceable rules and provide that only the board or a governing director has the power to appoint a director.

On the face of it, s 201G (and any similar provision in a constitution) grants a powerful right to members to determine who will manage and run the company. In practice, the power of directors to appoint an additional director under s 201H may increase the likelihood that the members will approve that appointment. This can lead to a situation where the board has indirect control over the appointment of new directors. As Berle and Means recognised over 90 years ago, where the shareholding in a company is dispersed and attendance at meetings is limited, it is unlikely that any shareholder or group of shareholders will control the general meeting.[11] This, in combination with the rules on proxy voting (discussed below), can result in members' approval of the appointment of a director being 'almost automatic'.[12] Section 201E reduces the risk of members in a public company being asked to vote on or approve the appointment of two more directors in one resolution. It provides that such a resolution cannot be passed unless the form of the resolution has previously been agreed to by the meeting without any vote being cast against it. Any non-conforming resolution appointing directors is void.

Removing the directors

The constitution will often contain provisions on the retirement of directors and the circumstances in which they will cease to hold office. In a proprietary company, the replaceable rule in s 203C gives the power to remove a director to the members in a general meeting. In some proprietary companies, this provision is varied and the constitution allocates the power to the board or to a governing director, or requires a unanimous decision of a general meeting to remove a director.

In a public company, any resolution or request or notice that seeks to remove a director from office or requires them to vacate their office is void to the extent it contains such a request (s 203E). Under s 203D, the power to remove a director is given to

11 A Berle and G Means, *The Modern Corporation and Private Property* (Transactions Publishers, 1932).
12 Ibid 53.

the members in general meeting. This section is not a replaceable rule and operates despite anything to the contrary in the company's constitution, any agreement between the company and the director, or any agreement between all or any of the members and the director. Notice of a proposed resolution by the members to remove a director must be given to the company at least two months before the meeting is held (s 203D(2)). The company must give the relevant director a copy of the notice as soon as practicable after it is received (s 203D(3)). The director is then entitled to put their case to the members via a written statement which the company must circulate and by speaking to the resolution at the meeting (s 203D(4)). It is possible to remove more than one director in a single resolution.[13]

As directors will often be appointed via contract, their removal by the members may amount to a breach of contract. This may give a director the right to sue for damages.[14]

Varying the rights attached to shares

As discussed in Chapter 8, the directors may seek to vary or cancel the rights attaching to shares. These rights include the right to vote, the right to receive a dividend, and rights on winding up. If such a variation is proposed, it will need to be approved by the members before it is effective. Whether such approval is required will depend on whether the constitution contains a provision setting out a procedure for varying class rights. If it does, then this procedure must be followed. If it does not, then under s 246B(2) the variation must be approved by a special resolution of the general meeting and a special resolution, or the consent in writing, of at least 75 per cent of the votes of the members whose rights are being affected.

Decisions related to share capital

Members' approval is required for a number of issues related to share capital. These are discussed further in Chapter 8 and include:

- an issue of shares that amounts to a variation of class rights of the existing shareholders[15]
- consolidating or subdividing the company's shares[16]
- a share issue by a publicly listed company that involves increasing the company's issued capital by more than 15 per cent in a year, or a share issue to a director or senior executive[17]
- a share buy-back under an employee share scheme, an on-market offer, an equal access scheme that involves the purchase of more than 10 per cent of the company's issued capital in a 12-month period and a selective buy-back[18]

13 See *NRMA Ltd v Scandrett* (2002) 43 ACSR 401.

14 Robert Austin and Ian Ramsay, *Ford, Austin and Ramsay's Principles of Corporations Law* (Lexis Nexis, 16th ed, 2014) [7.250].

15 *Corporations Act* s 257D.

16 Ibid s 254H.

17 ASX, *Listing Rules* (at 19 December 2016) r 7.1

18 *Corporations Act* ss 257B(4)–(5).

- a reduction of share capital provided it is fair and reasonable to the members as a whole and does not materially prejudice the company's ability to pay its creditors[19]
- the provision of financial assistance to a person or entity to purchase shares in the company or its holding company where assistance materially prejudices the interests of the company, its shareholders or the company's ability to pay its creditors.[20]

Disclosure and voting on directors' remuneration

Public pressure for disclosure and accountability of directors in relation to their remuneration packages has led to various amendments to the *Corporations Act*. In 1998, the *Company Law Review Act 1998* (Cth) introduced a requirement for directors of listed companies to include a remuneration report in their annual directors' report. The remuneration report must include a discussion of the board's policy on the nature and amount of remuneration paid to key management personnel, the relationship of such policy to the company's performance, and the nature and amount of each element of the remuneration package (s 300A). Section 300A was further amended in 2004 to require disclosure on any part of a remuneration package that is dependent on a director or manager satisfying performance criteria, and of any options forming part of a remuneration package.[21] At the same time, ss 250S and 250R were introduced. Section 250S requires the person chairing the annual general meeting of a listed company to allow a reasonable opportunity for the members to ask questions about or make comments upon the directors' remuneration report. Section 250R gives members a right to vote on the adoption of the remuneration report. While this vote is advisory only, and does not bind the company or the directors (ss 250R(2), (3)), it is designed to 'facilitate more active involvement by shareholders and improve the accountability of directors for decisions regarding remuneration'.[22] Any key management personnel whose remuneration is dealt with in the report, or any closely related party of such a person, is not able to vote on the resolution (s 250R(4)).

In 2011, the 'two strikes rule' was introduced.[23] Under this rule, if the advisory vote on the remuneration report in a publicly listed company receives a 'no' vote from 25 per cent or more of the votes cast, the next remuneration report must include an explanation of the directors' proposed action in response to that result, or an explanation of why the directors have not taken any action.[24] If this subsequent remuneration report receives a similar negative vote of 25 per cent or more, the members must vote at the same meeting on whether there should be a resolution requiring all the directors of the company to stand for re-election. If this resolution then receives more than 50 per cent

19 Ibid ss 256B–D.

20 Ibid s 260A.

21 *Corporations Amendment Regulations (2004) (No 7)* (Cth) pt 2M.3.

22 Explanatory Memorandum, Corporate Law Economic Reform Program (Audit Reform and Corporate Disclosure) Bill [5.435].

23 *Corporations Amendment (Improving Accountability on Director and Executive Remuneration) Act 2011* (Cth).

24 *Corporations Act* s 300A(1)(g).

of the votes cast, the company must, within 90 days, hold a special meeting for members to elect new directors.[25]

7.15.15 Additional rights under the *Corporations Act 2001* (Cth)

In addition to the rights set out above, individual members or groups of members are granted further rights under the *Corporations Act*, including:

- ss 249D and 249N: the power to convene meetings and to request resolutions (discussed further below)
- s 249P the right to require the company to distribute a statement to all members prior to a general meeting
- s 250S: the right to ask questions or make comments at the annual general meeting
- s 314: the right to receive a copy of the company's financial report (discussed further below)
- s 173(2): the right to inspect the company's registers free of charge (discussed in Chapter 14)
- s 461: the right to apply to wind up the company (discussed in Chapters 14 and 16)
- ss 236 and 237: the right to bring an action for oppression or a statutory derivative action (discussed in Chapter 14)
- s 1324: the right to apply for an injunction in situations to restrain breaches of the *Corporations Act* (discussed in Chapter 14).

7.15.20 Members' reserve powers

In limited circumstances, where the board cannot act on a matter within its powers the members in general meeting can intervene under their reserve powers. The circumstances in which this can be done are rare, and there are few cases discussing this power. One example of this power is where the board is in deadlock and is incapable of making a decision. This situation arose in *Barron v Potter*,[26] where the Court held that 'if directors having certain powers are unable or unwilling to exercise them ... there must be some power in a company to do itself that which under other circumstances would otherwise be done'.[27] Section 195(4) provides that members of a public company may, in general meeting, deal with an issue where the board of directors lack a quorum.

In *Massey v Wales*,[28] the facts involved two directors of a company who had fallen out with each other. One director convened a board meeting to appoint an additional director

25 Ibid ss 250V(1), 250W(2). For further discussion on the efficacy and policy behind this rule, see J Borthwick, A Jun and S Ma, 'Changing board behaviour: The role of the "Two Strikes" rule in improving the efficacy of Australian Say-on-Pay' (2020) 60(S1) *Accounting and Finance* 827; L Chapple and T Hubner, 'The 'Two Strikes' Rule on the Remuneration Report: Threats and Opportunities for Boards' (2013) 28(2) *Australian Journal of Corporate Law* 166; P Clarkson, J Walker and S Nicholls, 'Disclosure, Shareholder Oversight and the Pay-Performance Link' (2011) 7(2) *Journal of Contemporary Accounting and Economics* 47.

26 *Barron v Potter* [1914] 1 Ch 895.

27 Ibid 903.

28 *Massy v Wales* (2003) 57 NSWLR 718.

without telling the other director. That director then joined with the new director to institute legal proceedings in the name of the company—a decision that was later ratified at a shareholders' meeting.

The issue before the Court was whether the decision at the shareholders' meeting was valid. Hodgson JA in the Supreme Court of New South Wales held that the ratification was not valid as it involved an exercise of management power and the shareholders could not exercise such powers. He rejected the view that shareholders have unlimited reserve powers when the board is deadlocked. Instead, he found that in such circumstances the board is only permitted to appoint new directors in order to resolve the deadlock and ensure that the board can function again.

A different issue arises where the members in general meeting ratify a breach of duty by the directors. The power to ratify a breach arises because members are the beneficiaries of these duties. This issue is discussed further in Chapters 10 and 13.[29]

7.20 The board of directors

The board of directors is the more powerful of the two groups that can act as the company, as they have the widest decision-making authority. Unless the board has delegated power or authority to an individual or a group (such as a managing director or committee), directors must make decisions collectively. As noted by Dawson J in *Northside Developments Pty Ltd v Registrar-General,*[30] '[d]irectors can act only collectively as a board and the function of an individual director is to participate in decisions of the board'.[31] This means that board meetings are an important part of the life of a company.

As discussed in Chapter 4, a proprietary company must have at least one director who must ordinarily reside in Australia (ss 201A, 201BB). A public company must have at least three directors, two of whom ordinarily reside in Australia (s 201A). Only a natural person (not a company or other legal entity) can be a director and the person must be over 18 years of age. A public company must have at least one secretary, while a proprietary company is not required to have a secretary (s 204A). A director can be appointed at the time a company is registered or later according to ss 117, 201G and 201H. The term of office is normally stated in the constitution. For a company listed on the ASX, no director, except the managing director, can hold office for more than three years without standing for re-election.[32]

7.20.05 Types of directors

There are two types of directors: executive and non-executive. Executive directors are employees of the company. They also have a seat on the board. Non-executive directors are appointed from outside the company. The category of non-executive director includes independent directors (discussed further below). All directors have the same responsibilities and duties regardless of their title, unless something different is provided for in the constitution.

29 See Sections 10.40.05 and 13.10.10–13.25.15.

30 *Northside Developments Pty Ltd v Registrar-General* (1990) 170 CLR 146.

31 Ibid 205.

32 ASX, *Listing Rules* (at 19 December 2016) r 14.4.

Executive directors

Executive directors are employees of the company. They bring to the board knowledge of the workings of the company. For example, in large public companies, members of the senior management team such as the Chief Executive Officer ('CEO'), Chief Financial Officer ('CFO') and Chief Operations Officer ('COO') will often be directors and on the board. Executive directors have a dual legal relationship with the company: one as a director that carries fiduciary obligations (discussed further in Chapter 13) and the other as an employee under a contract of service. Precisely how these different relationships affect the duties they owe as directors is considered in Chapters 11–13.

Managing director or Chief Executive Officer

A managing director is responsible for the company's day-to-day business. In a large public company, they oversee the senior management of the company. The replaceable rules in ss 201J and 198C provide that directors may appoint one or more directors to be a managing director, and then confer on that person any powers that can be exercised by the board. In a large company, the managing director is often called the CEO. They serve the vital function of supervising the management team in the company and reporting to the board on the business of the company.

Chief Financial Officer

The CFO is responsible for managing the financial position of the company. This includes managing financial risks, undertaking financial planning, keeping all necessary financial records up to date and in order, and reporting to the CEO and the board. CFOs are often appointed to the board as executive directors and are covered by the definition of an 'officer' in s 9 of the *Corporations Act*. It is increasingly common for CFOs in large public companies to be involved in shaping the overall strategy and direction of the company.

Chief Operations Officer

The COO oversees the business operations of the company. The COO reports to the CEO and often to the board. They will often be the 'second-in-command' after the CEO. Bennett and Miles note that the role of the COO is hard to define:[33]

> When you start to examine COOs as a class, one thing immediately becomes clear: there are almost no constants. People with very different backgrounds ascend to the role and succeed in it. ... [T]here is no single agreed-upon description of what the job entails or even what it's called. Often, companies turn responsibility for all areas of operations over to the COO ... [including] production, marketing and sales, and research and development.[34]

33 N Bennett and S Miles, 'Second in Command: The Misunderstood Role of the Chief Operating Officer' (2006) 84(5) *Harvard Business Review* 70.

34 Ibid.

Company secretary

Only a public company is required to have at least one company secretary (s 204A(2)). The role of the company secretary includes keeping the company's registers and public information up to date, arranging members' and directors' meetings (including sending out notices, preparing the agenda, and attending all meetings), and keeping minutes. Under s 188, the company secretary is responsible for lodging notices and reports with ASIC. The company secretary comes within the definition of 'officer' in s 9 of the *Corporations Act*.

In many large public companies, the role of the company secretary includes a strong compliance and governance component. This can include overseeing the company's compliance program and ensuring all company obligations are met; maintaining, implementing and communicating company policies and procedures; providing advice on corporate governance principles and director responsibilities; maintaining the register of conflict of interests and related party transactions; and maintaining a complete list of company delegations.[35]

As discussed in Chapter 6, a company secretary is taken to have implied authority to enter contracts within their area of responsibility, subject to any express agreement to the contrary. In *Panorama Developments (Guildford) Ltd v Fidelis Furnishing Fabrics Ltd*,[36] it was held that the role of company secretary did not just include acting as a clerk, but also included the authority to sign contracts connected to the administration of the company's affairs, such as employing staff and ordering cars. The extent of a company secretary's authority to enter contracts will depend on the circumstances and practices of the company in question.

Chairperson

The chairperson is a director appointed to chair the meetings of directors. Often, they also chair the meetings of members. The replaceable rules in ss 248E and 249U of the *Corporations Act* require a chairperson for both directors' and members' meetings. For example, s 248E provides that the directors may elect a director to chair their meetings. If the directors have not elected a chairperson prior to a meeting, or if the person elected to act as chair is not available, the directors must elect another director to act as the chairperson at the meeting. A common practice is for the directors to annually appoint a chairperson at the first board meeting after the members' annual general meeting. As it is the directors who appoint the chairperson, if that person loses the confidence of the board, the directors can appoint another chairperson.

Under s 249U, the directors can elect a person to chair the members' meetings. If no chairperson is elected, or the person elected as chair is unable or unwilling to act for all or part of a meeting, the directors must elect another person present at the meeting to act as the chairperson. If the directors do not appoint a chairperson, then the members must do so (s 249U(3)).

35 'The Role of the Company Secretary', *Get on Board Australia* (Web Page, 21 October 2016) <http://getonboardaustralia.com.au/the-role-of-the-company-secretary/>.

36 *Panorama Developments (Guildford) Ltd v Fidelis Furnishing Fabrics Ltd* [1971] 2 QB 711.

The role of the chairperson is to run the meeting and ensure appropriate procedures are followed. This includes finalising the agenda; arranging for management to provide the necessary information to the board; ensuring the board addresses each item on the agenda; assisting the board to reach consensus on matters under discussion; putting questions to the meeting; declaring resolutions to be carried or defeated; asking for general business; and closing the meeting.[37] In large public companies, the chairperson commonly communicates between the board and the CEO between meetings, and is the public face of the company in terms of external communications.[38] With listed companies, the ASX Corporate Governance Council recommends that the roles of chairperson and CEO are not exercised by the same person.[39]

In *Colorado Constructions Pty Ltd v Platus*, Street J noted it was 'an indispensable part of any meeting that a chairman [sic] should be appointed and should occupy the chair. In the absence of some person ... the meeting is unable to proceed to business'.[40]

In large public companies, it has become increasingly common for the chairperson to be an independent director.[41] This is because the chairperson carries heightened governance responsibilities as noted by Rogers CJ in *AWA Ltd v Daniels*:[42]

> The chairman [sic] is responsible to a greater extent than any other director for the performance of the board as a whole and each member of it. The chairman has the primary responsibility for selecting matters and documents to be brought to the board's attention, for formulating the policy of the board and promoting the position of the company.

Non-executive directors

Non-executive directors are directors who are not involved in the daily management of the company and are not employed by the company. They are sometimes referred to as 'outside directors'. A non-executive director may be characterised as an independent director depending upon the extent of their connections with the company. Some of the advantages of non-executive directors are that they bring outside knowledge to the board and can play an oversight role in respect of executive directors. However, a risk for non-executive directors is they must rely on the information provided to them by management in making their decisions.

---

37 See Australian Institute of Company Directors, *Types of Directors: Board Composition* (1 January 2020) http://aicd.companydirectors.com.au/~/media/cd2/resources/director-resources/director-tools/pdf/05446-1-10-mem-director-t-bc-types-of-directors_a4_web.ashx; *Kelly v Wolstemholme* (1991) 9 ACLC 785.

38 See Australian Institute of Company Directors, *Types of Directors: Board Composition* (1 January 2020) http://aicd.companydirectors.com.au/~/media/cd2/resources/director-resources/director-tools/pdf/05446-1-10-mem-director-t-bc-types-of-directors_a4_web.ashx.

39 ASX Corporate Governance Council, *Corporate Governance Principles and Recommendations* (Australian Securities Exchange, 4th ed, 2019) Recommendation 2.5.

40 *Colorado Constructions Pty Ltd v Platus* (1966) 2 NSWR 598, 600.

41 Many industry governance codes recommend that the chairperson is independent: see, eg, ASX Corporate Governance Council, *Corporate Governance Principles and Recommendations* (Australian Securities Exchange, 4th ed, 2019) Recommendation 2.5.

42 *AWA Ltd v Daniels* (1992) 7 ACSR 759, 867.

Independent directors

Independent directors have become increasingly important to companies in Australia. A sign of good corporate governance is for large boards to have a majority of independent directors. Recommendation 2.1 of the ASX Corporate Governance Council's *Corporate Governance Principles and Recommendations* suggests a majority of the board of a listed company should be comprised of independent directors, being non-executive directors who are not a member of management and who are free from 'any business or other relationship that could materially interfere (or could reasonably be perceived to materially interfere) with the independent exercise of that director's judgment'.[43]

The *Recommendations* provide guidance on factors relevant to assessing the independence of a director. These include whether the person:

- is or has been employed in an executive capacity by the company or any of its related entities within the last three years
- is or has been a partner, director or senior employee of a provider of material professional services to the company or any of its subsidiaries within the last three years
- is or has been in a material business relationship (for example, as a supplier or customer) with the company or any of its subsidiaries, or an officer of, or otherwise associated with, someone with such a relationship, within the last three years
- is, represents, or is or has been within the last three years an officer or employee of, or professional adviser to, a substantial holder
- has close personal ties with any person who falls within any of the categories described above.[44]

In each case, the materiality of the interest, position or relationship will need to be assessed by the board to determine whether it might interfere, or be seen to interfere, with the director's capacity to bring an independent judgment to bear on issues before the board and to act in the company's best interests.[45] It is suggested in the *Recommendations* that each listed company identify in its annual report which directors are independent and why.[46] It is also suggested that the board regularly assess whether the non-executive directors remain independent.[47]

The term 'independent director' is used interchangeably with 'non-executive director', although this is not correct. A director can be a non-executive director, but not be independent due to the factors listed above. An executive director can, clearly, never be independent.

Nominee directors

Nominee directors are appointed to the board to represent a specific set of interests, such as those of a major shareholder, a holding company, a major creditor or employees.

43 ASX Corporate Governance Council, *Corporate Governance Principles and Recommendations* (4th ed, February 2019) 12.

44 ASX Corporate Governance Council, *Corporate Governance Principles and Recommendations* (4th ed, February 2019) 14.

45 Ibid.

46 Ibid 13.

47 Ibid 14.

In *Levin v Clark*,[48] the plaintiff purchased a majority interest in a company. The vendor of the shares took a mortgage from the plaintiff in the context of assisting the purchaser with payment monies. The Articles of Association of the company provided for the appointment of two governing directors. It was agreed that the two people occupying these positions would remain in office after the company was sold but were only to exercise their powers if the purchaser defaulted under their mortgage to the vendor. When the plaintiff did default, the two directors attempted to exercise their powers in the vendor's interest. The plaintiff argued that they had breached their fiduciary duty by acting in the interests of the mortgagee rather than the company as a whole. Jacobs J rejected this argument:

> It is of course correct to state as a general principle that directors must act in the interests of the company. There is no necessity to refer to the large body of authority which supports this as a general proposition. However, that leaves open the question in each case—what is the interest of the company? It is not uncommon for a director to be appointed to a board of directors in order to represent an interest outside the company—a mortgagee or other trader or a particular shareholder. It may be in the interests of the company that there be upon its board of directors one who will represent these other interests and who will be acting solely in the interests of such a third party and who may in that way be properly regarded as acting in the interests of the company as a whole. To argue that a director particularly appointed for the purpose of representing the interests of a third party cannot lawfully act solely in the interests of that third party, is in my view to apply the broad principle, governing the fiduciary duty of directors, to a particular situation, where the breadth of the fiduciary duty has been narrowed by agreement amongst the body of shareholders.[49]

As this case indicates, the appointment of a nominee director can result in conflicts of interest. While their appointment is done to provide representation for a particular interest group at the board level, legally the nominee directors are required to act in the best interests of the company. As Jacobs J indicated above, this involves balancing the expectations of the person or entity that has appointed them with their legal obligation to act in the best interests of the company on whose board they sit. In the absence of agreement to the contrary, as existed in *Levin's* case, if an actual conflict of interest occurs, the nominee must comply with their duty to the company or resign from the company's board.[50]

Under s 187, directors appointed to the board of a wholly owned subsidiary may take the interests of the holding company into consideration if: the constitution allows the director to do so; the director acts in good faith in the best interests of the holding

48 *Levin v Clark* [1962] NSWR 686. For further discussion of these issues, see RP Austin, 'Representatives and Fiduciary Responsibilities—Notes on Nominee Directorships and Life Arrangements' (1995) 7(1) *Bond Law Review* 19.

49 *Levin v Clark* [1962] NSWR 686, 700.

50 *Scottish Co-operative Wholesale Society Ltd v Meyer* [1959] AC 324.

company; and the subsidiary is not insolvent at the time the director acts and does not become insolvent because of the director's act.

Alternate director

An alternate director who is appointed to act in the place of another director can participate in one or more board meetings. The replaceable rule in s 201K allows for a director, with the other directors' approval, to appoint an alternate director who can use all or any of the directors' powers.

7.20.10 The role of the board

As indicated, the role of the board differs significantly between large and small companies. In large public companies, the board must delegate its power to manage the company to senior managers, and the directors then monitor the work of these managers. Monitoring management is at the heart of the role of the corporate board. In *AWA v Daniels,* Rogers J noted the significant powers that senior management has in a large corporation in the context of discussing the directors' duty to act with care and diligence (discussed further in Chapter 11 at Section 11.10.10):

> The board of a large public corporation cannot manage the corporation's day to day business. That function must by business necessity be left to the corporation's executives. If the director of a large public corporation were to be immersed in the details of day to day operations the director would be incapable of taking more abstract, important decisions at board level ...
>
> In the context of the present case directors rely on management to:
>
> **(a)** carry out the day to day control of the corporation's business affairs
> **(b)** establish proper internal controls, management information systems and accounting records
> **(c)** reduce to writing if appropriate and communicate policies and strategies adopted by the board
> **(d)** implement the policies and strategies adopted by the board
> **(e)** have a knowledge of and review detailed figures, contracts and other information about the corporation's affairs and financial position and summarise such information for the board where appropriate
> **(f)** prepare proposals and submissions for consideration by the board
> **(g)** prepare a budget
> **(h)** attend to personnel matters including hiring and firing of staff and their terms of employment.[51]

In addition to monitoring the activities of senior management, the board in a large company will be responsible for setting and overseeing the implementation of the company's strategic goals and business plan; appointing the CEO and chairperson; approving the financial statements, major capital expenditures and annual budget; overseeing the

51 *AWA Ltd v Daniels* (1992) 7 ACSR 759, 866–7.

accounting and reporting systems; and ensuring the company has in place an appropriate risk management strategy.[52]

In a small company, the board will have a more extensive role in managing the company. For example, the same people may run the business on a day-to-day basis, be directors of the company, and also be shareholders. Despite the lack of separation between those managing a company and its shareholders, in law, the division between the decision-making powers of these groups is maintained.

7.25 Where members disagree with a decision of the directors

The specific powers granted to members do not include the power to make management decisions unless this is granted under the constitution. Members who disagree with this allocation of power can alter the constitution to provide that key management matters need to be decided by the members in general meeting.[53] These provisions are not uncommon in small companies where the directors and members are the same or similar people.

The question of the exact division of power between members and directors has been addressed by case law. The answer was provided in the 1906 case of *Automatic Self-Cleansing Filter Syndicate Co Ltd v Cuninghame*:[54] if the board is granted the power to manage the company, the general meeting has no power to intervene in or influence the exercise of that power unless the members vote to change the constitution. In this case, a small group of shareholders owned enough votes in the company to pass an ordinary resolution. They proposed a resolution at a members' meeting directing the board to sell some of the company's assets. Under the company's Articles of Association, the board had the power to manage the company, except for a provision stating that the board's powers were subject to any resolution passed by special resolution at the general meeting. Another provision in the constitution expressly authorised the board to sell the company's property on such terms as the board thought fit. The general meeting passed the resolution; however, the board refused to act on it.

The English Court of Appeal held that, under the constitution, the board was the only organ within the company authorised to sell the company's assets. This meant that the board did not need to act on the members' direction. Cozens-Hardy LJ stated:

> [T]he shareholders have by their express contract mutually stipulated that their common affairs should be managed by certain directors to be appointed by the shareholders in the manner described by [the constitution] ... If you once get

52 See the similar responsibilities listed for publicly listed companies: ASX Corporate Governance Council, *Corporate Principles and Recommendations* (Australian Securities Exchange, 4th ed, 2019). For a study of the top 20 listed companies and their statements on board responsibility, see R Grayson-Morison and I Ramsay, 'Responsibilities of the Board of Directors: A research note' (2014) 32(1) *Company and Securities Law Journal* 69.

53 For a discussion of the practicality of this option, see E Boros, 'How Does the Division of Power Between the Board and the General Meeting Operate?' (2010) 31(2) *Adelaide Law Review* 169.

54 [1906] 2 Ch 34.

> a stipulation of that kind in a contract made between the parties, what right is there to interfere with the contract, apart, of course, from any misconduct on the part of the directors?[55]

This approach was adopted in *John Shaw & Sons (Salford) Ltd v Shaw*,[56] where Greer LJ stated the position in even stricter terms:

> If powers of management are vested in the directors, they and they alone can exercise those powers. The only way in which the general body of shareholders can control the exercise of the powers vested by [the constitution] in the directors is by altering the articles, or if the opportunity arises under [the constitution], by refusing to re-elect the directors of whose actions they disapprove. They cannot themselves usurp the powers which by the articles are vested in the directors any more than the directors can usurp the powers vested by [the constitution] in the general body of shareholders.[57]

In *Howard Smith Ltd v Ampol Petroleum Ltd*,[58] the Privy Council noted that 'directors, within their management powers, may take decisions against the wishes of the majority of shareholders, and indeed the majority of shareholders cannot control them in the exercise of these powers while they remain in office'.[59]

In Australia, this position was adopted in *NRMA v Parker*.[60] In this case, members in NRMA tried to use their statutory powers under s 249D of the *Corporations Act* (discussed below) to requisition a special members' meeting to consider a motion advising the directors how to act in relation to employment issues. The board instituted legal proceedings challenging the validity of the resolution. McLelland J held that it was not within the members' powers to seek to express an opinion by resolution on how a power vested in the directors should be exercised. As a result, the board were not required to convene the special meeting.

In the subsequent case of *NRMA Ltd v Snodgrass*,[61] the New South Wales Court of Appeal distinguished the *Parker* decision. In the *Snodgrass* case, the resolution proposed an alteration to the constitution. The members requisitioned the board to convene a special members' meeting to consider an alteration to the constitution to require newly appointed directors to publish full details of their election campaign funding. The proposed provision required any director who did not publish their details to be disqualified from acting as a director. At both first instance and on appeal the Court held that proposing such a resolution was a proper purpose for convening a meeting.[62] The NRMA constitution provided that 'subject to the law and other provisions of the constitution'

55 Ibid 44.
56 *John Shaw & Sons (Salford) Ltd v Shaw* [1935] 2 KB 113.
57 Ibid 134.
58 *Howard Smith Ltd v Ampol Petroleum Ltd* [1974] AC 821.
59 Ibid 837.
60 *NRMA v Parker* (1986) 6 NSWLR 517.
61 *NRMA Ltd v Snodgrass* (2001) 52 NSWLR 383.
62 Under s 249Q, discussed at Section 7.30.05, a meeting of the company's members must be held for a proper purpose.

management of the company was vested in the directors. It was held that these particular words allowed the constitution to be amended to stipulate how a particular management issues would be addressed.

These cases were considered in the decision of *Australasian Centre for Corporate Responsibility v Commonwealth Bank of Australia.*[63] This case involved the Australasian Centre for Corporate Responsibility (ACCR) proposing, on behalf of over 100 members, three resolutions for consideration at the Commonwealth Bank's (CBA) 2014 annual general meeting. The first proposed resolution expressed that CBA's directors should report to the members on the amount of greenhouse gas emissions the company financed. The second proposed resolution expressed that such a report was not included in the directors' annual report. The third proposed resolution was a special resolution to amend CBA's constitution to require that the directors' annual report disclose the amount of greenhouse gas emissions the company financed.

CBA provided its notice of the 2014 annual general meeting. Only the third proposed resolution was included in the notice. The company stated in its notice of meeting that it did not consider this resolution to be in the best interest of shareholders or the company and recommended that members vote against it. The resolution was not successful at the annual general meeting. In correspondence with the ACCR, CBA stated that it considered the first and second resolutions dealt with management matters and were not capable of being legally binding even if passed.

The ACCR brought proceedings against CBA, seeking an injunction to compel CBA to put the first and second resolutions to the meeting and a declaration that the board had acted outside its powers in recommending members vote against the third resolution. ACCR argued the first and second resolutions were intended to be non-binding as they were expressions of opinion and not an interference with the board's management power. The ACCR also criticised the decision in *NRMA v Parker*.

At first instance, Davies J of the Federal Court found that, as the constitution of CBA included a provision stating that the business of the company was to be managed by or under the direction of the directors, the members could not usurp that power by trying to assert a supervisory function at general meetings. Her Honour did not accept ACCR's criticism of the decision in *Parker* and upheld the principle that members could not propose resolutions that expressed an opinion on management decisions, even non-binding advisory resolutions.

The Full Federal Court (Allsop CJ, Foster and Gleeson JJ) rejected an appeal by ACCR where it had argued that:

- the members did not need to have a specific power to allow them to propose advisory resolutions or,
- in the alternative, that if such a power was required, it was either part of the inherent power of members to propose resolutions or was a power to be implied in CBA's constitution.

63 (2016) 248 FCR 280. For discussion of this case, see M Hey, '*ACCR v CBA* [2015] FCA 785: Nonbinding shareholder resolutions and the implications for shareholder activism' (2015) 40(1) *University of Western Australia Law Review* 399.

In rejecting these arguments, their Honours confirmed that, unless the members are given a specific power in the constitution or under statute, they could not 'control, usurp or exercise the powers of the directors'.[64] It noted that members do not have an inherent power to propose resolutions that are not otherwise within their power.[65] As an example of a statutory power giving members the right to express an opinion, their Honours referred to s 250R which allows the members to vote on an advisory resolution regarding the adoption of the remuneration report.

The Full Court also rejected ACCR's argument that the members had a legitimate interest in the subject matter of the resolutions, and that this made the resolutions effective. Their Honours considered that this 'misunderstands the nature of the company as an entity distinct from its shareholders and directors' and that an 'act of the company (of which a resolution of its members is an example) must necessarily be an act which the company has the capacity or power to undertake'.[66] The Court rejected the submission that the resolutions had to be put to the meeting by the board as the general meeting lacked the power to pass the resolution as an act of the company.[67] While ACCR was not successful in this case, its actions are still considered important in encouraging Australian corporations to pay greater attention to investor concerns, particularly over environmental issues.[68]

7.30 Meetings

Directors' and members' meetings serve an important function in corporate law. Company meetings are either ordinary meetings or special (or extraordinary) meetings. Ordinary meetings are regular meetings held according to an annual meeting schedule; for example, the annual general meeting of members is an ordinary meeting held once a year. Special or extraordinary meetings are unscheduled meetings that are convened to consider urgent or new matters that cannot wait until the next ordinary meeting. Matters upon which a decision is required are framed as resolutions, which are then voted upon at the meeting.

The procedures for holding meetings are set out in the constitution (if there is one) and/or in the *Corporations Act*. As will be seen in the discussion below, most of the provisions

64 *Australasian Centre for Corporate Responsibility v Commonwealth Bank of Australia* (2016) 248 FCR 280, citing *Commissioner of Taxation (Cth) v Commonwealth Aluminium Corporation Ltd* (1980) 143 CLR 646, 660–1 and *Automatic Self-Cleansing Filter Syndicate Co Ltd v Cuninghame* [1906] 2 Ch 34.

65 *Australasian Centre for Corporate Responsibility v Commonwealth Bank of Australia* (2016) 248 FCR 280 [50], [56].

66 Ibid [47].

67 Ibid [45].

68 For further discussion on this issue, see S Bottomley, 'Rethinking the Law on Shareholder-Initiated Resolutions at Company General Meetings' (2019) 43(1) *Melbourne University Law Review* 93; B Sheehy, H Pender and B Jacobsen 'Corporate social responsibility/ESG shareholder activism in Australia: A case study of the Australasian Centre for Corporate Responsibility' (2021) 36(2) *Australian Journal of Corporate Law* 156; B Jacobson and H Pender, 'The Case for Regulatory Reform on Members' Resolutions in Australia' (2016) 34(2) *Company and Securities Law Journal* 292, 296–302; S Milne and N Wakefield-Evans, 'Shareholder Requisitions—The 5%/100 Member Provision' (2003) 31(4) *Australian Business Law Review* 285, 285–91; P Darvas, 'Section 249D and the "Activist" Shareholder' (2002) 20(7) *Company and Securities Law Journal* 390, 403–8; HX Xian Chia and I Ramsay, 'An Analysis of Shareholder Resolutions Involving Australian Listed Companies from 2004–2013' (2016) 34(8) *Company and Securities Law Journal* 618.

in the *Corporations Act* dealing with company meetings are replaceable rules that can be altered by a provision in the constitution. Ensuring that the correct procedures for meetings are followed provides verification that a valid decision has been made. The rules for meetings are detailed and technical but are necessary for the proper functioning of a company.

The rules for directors' and members' meetings cover a number of standard matters. These include who can convene a meeting, who can propose a resolution, what the notice requirements are, what the quorum is, how the meeting must be conducted, and how the decisions of the meeting need to be recorded. The *Corporations Act* provides that, in a proprietary company, an actual meeting does not need to be held where there is a circulating resolution of the members. A circulating resolution is one signed by all eligible participants (ss 248A and 249A). These resolutions are a convenient way to make a decision in a small company.

In 2022, important changes were made to the *Corporations Act*, allowing for technology to be used in arranging and holding company meetings.[69] These reforms were the result of temporary measures put in place to help companies deal with the challenges presented by the COVID-19 pandemic.[70] Section 249R now provides that a company can hold a meeting of its members physically and/or virtually. A key condition, however, is that holding a meeting using technology must be permitted in the company's constitution. This means that companies need to amend their constitution via a special resolution passed at a general meeting before virtual meetings can be held.[71]

Under s 249S, members must be given a reasonable opportunity to participate in a virtual meeting, meaning the meetings must be held at a reasonable time and place, using reasonable technology to connect more than one physical venue, and allowing members to ask questions and make comments orally or in writing. Section 1322(3A) gives members the right to apply to court to have the meeting invalidated on the basis that they did not have a reasonable opportunity to participate in the meeting. The court will only make an order where it considers there has been a substantial injustice which cannot be remedied any other way.

Companies can also circulate meeting materials by electronic means. This is provided for in a new div 2 pt 1.2AA of the *Corporations Act* that deals with sending documents using technology. Under ss 110C and 110D, companies can send the following documents using electronic means:

- a document that relates to a meeting of the members
- a document that relates to a resolution to be considered by the members without a meeting, and
- a report mentioned in s 314, including a financial report, directors' report and auditor's report.

69 *Corporations Amendment (Meetings and Documents) Act 2022* (Cth).

70 *Corporations (Coronavirus Economic Response) Determination (No 3) 2020* (Cth); *Treasury Laws Amendment (2021 Measures No 1) Act 2021* (Cth).

71 For a discussion on the effectiveness of the provisions and whether they increase shareholder accessibility and engagement or reduce the accountability of directors and management, see L Freeburn and I Ramsay, 'Virtual Shareholder Meetings in Australia' (2021) 32(2) *International Company and Commercial Law Review* 53.

Members retain the right to elect to receive documents in physical form (s 110E) and can also elect not to receive documents at all or to receive only some documents (ss 110E(4), (5)).

Under s 248D, directors' meetings can also be called and held using technology consented to by all the directors.

7.30.05 Members' meetings

Annual general meeting

A public company (other than a public company that has only one member) must hold an annual general meeting (AGM) once a year (s 250N). The meeting must be held within five months of the end of the company's financial year. A proprietary company has the option to hold an AGM, unless it is required to do so by its constitution.

The purpose of the AGM is to provide key financial and business information to the members. Section 250R(1) lists matters that can be part of a public company AGM, including consideration of the annual financial report, directors' report and auditor's report of the company, election of the directors, appointment of the auditor, and voting on the directors' remuneration.

Convening an extraordinary members' meeting

Members holding at least 5 per cent of the votes that may be cast at a general meeting can convene an extraordinary meeting (s 249F). In smaller companies, there can be a provision in the constitution allowing members to convene a meeting. Under the replaceable rule in s 249C, a director can convene a meeting. In publicly listed companies, the power of directors to call a members' meeting cannot be displaced by the constitution (s 249CA). Where a director calls a meeting, the company secretary will be responsible for organising the meeting and the company will be liable to pay the costs. Where members with 5 per cent of the votes convene a meeting, they are responsible for organising the meeting and paying the costs. This can be a significant hurdle for members in large companies.

One way around the issue of cost is for members to requisition the directors to convene a meeting at the expense of the company. Under s 249D, members with at least 5 per cent of the votes may request the company to call a meeting. The requisition must be in writing and include details on any resolution to be proposed at the meeting (s 249D(2)). The directors are obliged to call the meeting and the company must pay the costs. Under s 249D(5), the directors must call the members' meeting within 21 days of receiving the notice, and the meeting must be held within two months of the company receiving the request.[72] If the directors do not call the meeting within 21 days, then members who hold at least 50 per cent of the votes from those requesting the meeting may call the meeting themselves and the company must reimburse them for their reasonable costs (s 249E(4)).

The court also has the power to call a members' meeting if there is no other practical way to do so (s 249G).

72 To 'call' a meeting, the directors must notify the other members of the details of when and where the meeting will be held and what is on the agenda of the meeting.

Proposing a resolution

Members with at least 5 per cent of the votes in the company, or at least 100 members entitled to vote at the meeting, may request a proposed resolution be included in the agenda of an AGM or an extraordinary members' meeting (s 249N). This power was used by the members in *Australasian Centre for Corporate Responsibility v Commonwealth Bank of Australia*,[73] considered above.

Members with at least 5 per cent of the votes, or at least 100 members entitled to vote at the meeting, may request that the company send information to all members prior to the meeting (s 249P). This information may be a statement about a proposed resolution or any other matter to be considered at the general meeting. Provided the statement is no more than 1000 words and is not defamatory, the company is required to distribute this statement to all members at the same time (or as soon as practicable thereafter) and in the same way as the notice of the meeting (s 249P(6)). If the statement is received in time to include it with the notice of the meeting, the company pays the cost. If the statement is not included in time to send it with the notice of the meeting, the shareholders are jointly and individually liable for the cost of distributing the statement; however, the members can decide in general meeting that the company pay the costs.

Notice of a meeting

Section 249L requires that the notice of a general meeting must include:

- details on the place, date and time of the meeting if there is only one location for the meeting
- if there are two or more locations at which the members can attend the meeting: the date and time for the meeting at each location, and the main location for the meeting
- if virtual meeting technology is being used to hold the meeting: sufficient information to allow the members to participate in the meeting by means of the technology
- the general nature of the business to be conducted
- any special resolutions to be proposed, and
- where members are entitled to appoint a proxy, the details of that proxy.

The meeting must be held at a time that is reasonable and this timing must be reasonable at the physical location of the meeting or the virtual meeting (s 249S(3)). In *Howard v Mechtler*,[74] Austin J held that convening a meeting at 6 p.m. on 30 December was not an unreasonable time to hold a meeting.

Members who attend a physical meeting or by using virtual meeting technology are taken for all purposes to be 'present' at the meeting while so attending (s 249RA(3)).

All companies, other than listed companies, must give their members and directors at least 21 days' notice of a general meeting or a period as provided for in the constitution

73 *Australasian Centre for Corporate Responsibility v Commonwealth Bank of Australia* (2016) 248 FCR 280. For discussion of this case, see M Hey, '*ACCR v CBA* [2015]: Nonbinding Shareholder Resolutions and the Implications for Shareholder Activism' (2015) 40(1) *University of Western Australia Law Review* 399.

74 *Howard v Mechtler* (1999) 30 ACSR 434.

(s 249H(1)). A meeting may be called with shorter notice if: (1) the meeting is an AGM and all of the members entitled to vote at the meeting agree to the shorter notice before the meeting is held; or (2) the meeting is a general meeting and members with at least 95 per cent of the votes that may be cast at the meeting agree before notice is given (s 249H(2)). However, at least 21 days' notice of a general meeting in a public company must be given where a resolution is proposed to remove a director under s 203D or to appoint another director in place of a director removed under that section, or to remove an auditor under s 329 (ss 249H(3)–(4)). With a listed company, s 249HA(1) requires at least 28 days' notice of a general meeting, even if a shorter period is provided for in the constitution.

Under s 249J, notice of a general meeting must be given individually to each director and to each member entitled to vote. If a company has an auditor, it is entitled to receive notice of a general meeting in the same way as members (s 249K).

Quorum

A quorum is the minimum number of people that must be in attendance for a valid meeting to be held. Under the replaceable rule in s 249T, the quorum for a general meeting of the members is two members, who must be present throughout the meeting. If a quorum is not present within 30 minutes of the start time specified for the meeting, the directors must adjourn the meeting to a later time (s 249T(3)). Under the replaceable rule in s 249W, only the unfinished business from the previous meeting can be dealt with at the subsequent meeting. The requirement that the quorum must be present throughout the meeting has a possible exception: in *Ball v Pearsall*,[75] Young J held that if a member leaves a meeting with the purpose of removing the quorum, the meeting may nevertheless continue.

Voting

Not all shares carry the right to vote and it is important to consult the constitution to determine if there are limits or enhancements on the voting rights attached to shares. Under the replaceable rule in s 250E, and subject to any rights or restrictions attaching to the shares, each shareholder with a share capital has one vote on a show of hands (s 250E(1)(a)), and one vote per share if there is a poll (s 250E(1)(b)).[76] Decisions in the general meeting are passed by majority vote, unless a special resolution is required, when there must be the approval of three-quarters of the members who are present at the meeting or who vote by proxy.[77] In a company without share capital, each member has one vote per resolution, irrespective of whether the vote is taken on a show of hands or a poll (s 250E(2)). In all companies, unless otherwise provided for in the constitution, the chairperson of the general meeting has a casting vote in addition to any votes they may have as a member of the company (s 250E(3)).

Under the replaceable rule in s 250J, a vote in the general meeting will be decided on a show of hands, unless a poll is demanded. Proxy votes can be counted for a decision

75 *Ball v Pearsall* (1987) 10 NSWLR 700.

76 See also ASX, *Listing Rules* (at 19 December 2016) rr 6.8, 6.9.

77 See the definition of a 'special resolution' in s 9.

on a show of hands. A poll is a vote entitling each shareholder to one vote per share, or such other arrangement as set out in the constitution. However, under s 250H, any shareholder with the right to cast two or more votes may refrain from casting all their votes or may cast their votes in different ways. This power to split votes can be useful when a nominee holds votes on behalf of more than one principal and wants to vote differently in their interests. Section 250G provides that any challenge to a person's right to vote must be made at the meeting and determined by the chairperson, whose decision is final.

Under s 250JA(1), a listed company must conduct a poll if:

- the notice of meeting sets out an intention to propose a resolution
- the company has given notice of a members' resolution under s 249Q, or
- a poll is demanded.

This requirement cannot be overridden by a company's constitution (s 250JA(2)).[78]

Companies can choose to use electronic devices for poll voting at face-to-face meetings. To enable such voting, shareholders are handed a mobile device containing details of their shareholding when they register at the meeting. If a poll is requested, the shareholder presses the relevant voting button. The chairperson then accesses the results on a screen visible to the members. The two benefits of this form of voting are that it is quicker to determine the results of a poll and there is an electronic audit trail of all the votes cast at the meeting. Technology has developed so that mobile devices can now deal with split votes (where one proportion of a shareholding is voting in favour of a resolution and another proportion is voting against) which are common with nominee holdings.

Under s 253UB, a right is now granted to members with at least five per cent of the votes that may be cast at a meeting to request an independent person to observe and prepare a report on a poll. The request must be in writing and made at least five days before the meeting date.[79]

Under the replaceable rule in s 250K, a poll may be taken on any resolution and a demand for a poll may be withdrawn. Under s 250L, a poll needs to be supported by at least five members entitled to vote on the resolution, by members with at least five per cent of the votes that may be cast on the resolution, or by the chairperson, unless the constitution provides for a lower number. Proxy votes can be used to support a poll (s 249Y(1)).

Proxy voting

Section 249X is a replaceable rule for proprietary companies and a mandatory rule for public companies. It provides that any member of a company entitled to vote at the general meeting may appoint a proxy to attend the meeting and vote on their behalf (s 249X(1)). A proxy may be an individual or a body corporate (s 249X(1A)). Where a body corporate is appointed as a proxy, it may then appoint an individual to act as its representative (s 250D(1)(d)). The appointment may state the percentage or total number of votes available to the proxy to vote at the meeting (s 249X(2)). A member who is entitled

78 *Corporations Amendment (Meetings and Documents) Act 2022* (Cth).

79 Ibid.

to cast two or more votes at a meeting may appoint up to two proxies to attend and vote at the meeting (s 249X(3)). Where the appointment of two proxies does not specify the percentage or number of votes to be cast by the proxy, the proxy may exercise half of the member's votes.

A proxy has the same rights as the member to speak at the meeting, to vote (subject to any limitations in their appointment), and to demand a poll (s 249Y(1)). The member appointing the proxy need not specify how they want the proxy to vote. Even if they do specify how the proxy should vote, unless the proxy is the chairperson of the meeting (discussed below), there is no obligation upon the proxy to vote, either on a show of hands or on a poll. However, if they do vote, they must do so in accordance with the member's instructions (s 250BB).

The notice of a meeting where members are entitled to appoint a proxy (which is compulsory in a public company) must include a statement indicating: that the member has the right to appoint a proxy; whether the proxy has to be a member of the company; and, where the member can cast two or more votes, that they can appoint two proxies and indicate what portion of votes each proxy can exercise (s 249L(1)). In a listed company, details must be provided of an address and fax number for sending in the proxy and may include an electronic address or other electronic means by which the company will receive notice of a proxy (s 250BA). Unless the constitution provides otherwise, for a proxy to be valid it must be signed by the member making the appointment,[80] and include details on the member's name and address, the company's name, the proxy's name or the name of the office held by the proxy, and the meeting at which the appointment is to be used (s 250A).

To be valid, the form appointing a proxy must be received by the company no less than 48 hours before the meeting, unless the constitution specifies a shorter period (s 250B).[81] The proxy notification is taken to have been received by the company when the letter, fax or email (if allowed) arrives at the company's registered office.

It is common for proxy forms to allow the member to appoint the chairperson of the meeting as their proxy. In such cases, according to s 250BB, the chairperson is obligated to cast the votes for any proxies they possess during a poll. This rule was introduced into the *Corporations Act* in 2011 in response to concerns that chairpersons could 'cherrypick' which proxies they would vote, according to which resolutions were in the best interests of the board.[82] Section 250BC creates a more difficult situation where proxies can be transferred to the chairperson if a member appoints a proxy and specifies how the proxy is to vote, but the proxy does not vote on a poll as directed. In these circumstances, provided the company has notice of the directed proxies, then if the proxies are not voted they fall to the chairperson to vote. Under the replaceable rule in s 250J(1A), the number

80 *Corporations Regulations 2001* (Cth) reg 2G.2.01 allows for electronic authentication of the appointment of a proxy.

81 Ibid reg 5.6.36: this provides, in relation to court-ordered members meetings, that it is not possible for the company to specify a longer period than 48 hours for the receipt of proxy forms.

82 See the discussion in Explanatory Memorandum to s 250BC as introduced by the Corporations Amendment (Improving Accountability on Director and Executive Remuneration) Bill 2011 (Cth) [8.87], [8.88].

and instructions contained in any proxies must be disclosed by the chairperson before a vote is taken. As noted by Wooton J in *Re Marra Developments Ltd*,[83] this makes these proxies 'far more important in determining the outcome of the dispute ... than anything that happens at the meeting'. For a listed company, the details of any proxies are disclosed in the minutes of the meeting.

Validation of incorrect procedure

Under s 1322(2), a procedural irregularity does not cause a meeting or resolution to be invalid unless a court is of the opinion that the irregularity has caused or may cause substantial injustice that cannot be remedied by a court order. Section 1322(1)(b) provides that a procedural irregularity includes a failure to have the required quorum at a members', directors' or creditors' meeting, or a defect, irregularity or deficiency of notice or time. If the court is of the opinion that such an irregularity has or may cause substantial injustice, then the court will declare the proceeding to be invalid (s 1322(2)).

Section 1322(3) provides that a meeting, notice of a meeting, or any proceeding at a meeting is not invalidated just because of an accidental omission to give notice or the failure of a person to receive notice. However, a court may declare a meeting void in such cases upon the application of the person who failed to receive notice, any person entitled to vote at the meeting, or ASIC (s 1322(3)). Section 1322(3A) provides that, even where a member has not had a reasonable opportunity to participate in a meeting, the meeting will only be invalid if the court is of the opinion that substantial injustice has been caused or may be caused, and the injustice cannot be remedied by a court order (s 1322(3A)(a)). Where the court is of that opinion, it will declare the meeting void or a part of the meeting or a proceeding at the meeting void (s 1322(3A)(b)).

The purpose of s 1322 was discussed in *Beck v Weinstock*,[84] and French CJ has additionally noted that:

> Corporations, in contemporary Australian society, serve the purposes of enterprises, large and small, owned and operated by men and women, some of whom are sophisticated, knowledgeable and well advised on matters of corporate governance and some, perhaps many, of whom are not. Section 1322(4) and related provisions reflect a long-standing legislative recognition that mistakes will happen in corporate governance and that it is not in the public interest that the validity of decisions made in relation to corporations be unduly vulnerable to innocent errors which may be corrected without substantial injustice to third parties. In accordance with its evident purpose, s 1322(4)(a) is to be construed broadly and applied pragmatically, principally by reference to considerations of substance rather than those of form.[85]

Section 1322(4) covers the orders that a court may give, and s 1322(6) requires a court to be satisfied of certain matters before it grants an order.

83 *Re Marra Developments* (1976) 1 ACLR 470, 472.
84 *Beck v Weinstock* (2013) 251 CLR 425.
85 *Weinstock v Beck* (2013) 251 CLR 396 [39].

7.30.10 Directors' meetings

It is usual for the rules on the conduct of directors' meetings to be contained in the constitution. These rules are often more flexible than the rules for members' meetings and may provide that:

- directors can regulate their meetings as they think fit
- any director may convene a meeting, and
- decisions at a meeting are to be made on a majority vote.

Sections 248A–G of the *Corporations Act* deal with the conduct of directors' meetings, although most of these provisions are replaceable rules. For example, s 248A provides that the directors can pass a resolution without a meeting if all the directors entitled to vote sign a document containing a statement that they are in favour of the resolution, and the document also contains the resolution. Such a provision, requiring the written consent of all the directors to pass a resolution, is commonly included in the constitution of smaller companies. Large companies may allow a resolution to be passed outside of a meeting with a majority of directors voting in support of it.[86]

Directors' meetings may be called or held using any technology consented to by all the directors and a consent may be a standing one (s 248D). It is common for ordinary directors' meetings to be held on a regular basis; for example, on the same day and at the same time each month. A standing notice can be issued for such meetings or notice of the next meeting may be included in the company minutes of the previous meeting.

Under the replaceable rule in s 248F, the quorum for a directors' meeting is two directors. In larger companies, this number is often higher. It is usual for each director to have one vote, with the chairperson holding a casting vote (s 248G).

7.35 Decision-making in single director/shareholder companies

Section 198E provides that a single director may exercise all the powers of the company except any that the constitution requires to be exercised in general meeting. Under s 201E, a director in a single director/single shareholder proprietary company can appoint an additional director by recording that appointment and signing the record. Similarly, under s 249D, resolutions can be passed by a single member making a record of the resolution and signing that record. The resolution must also be recorded in the company's minute book (s 251A(1)(e)).

7.40 Reporting and disclosure

Over the last few decades, there has been increasing focus in corporate regulation on companies disclosing key information for the benefit of members, creditors, employees, consumers and the public. Most of these disclosure obligations have focused on

86 See, eg, *Constitution*, Qantas (at 24 October 2014) cl 16.8 <https://www.qantas.com.au/infodetail/about/corporateGovernance/Constitution.pdf>.

improving the financial information disclosed by companies. For example, the *Corporate Law Economic Reform Program (Audit Reform and Corporate Disclosure) Act 2004* (Cth) increased the roles and responsibilities of auditors; the amount of information that must be disclosed by listed companies; the responsibilities of the CEO and CFO of listed companies in relation to financial statements; and the way in which accounting and auditing standards are set and operate.

More recently, the focus has shifted to companies disclosing information in relation to environmental, social and governance issues (ESG). While there has been longstanding debate on whether large companies should voluntarily disclose such information, steps are now being taken in Australia and around the world to make such reporting mandatory. As noted by Treasury:

> The Government has legislated Australia's commitment to reduce emissions by 43% by 2030 and achieve net zero emissions by 2050. Financial markets will be critical in financing the substantial investment required to meet these targets.
>
> To appropriately price climate-related risks and opportunities, value assets and allocate capital efficiently, investors need information on climate risks and opportunities and the actions being taken by individual companies to meet their climate change targets. Climate-related financial disclosures are an important mechanism through which companies can communicate this information to investors. Effective disclosures will ensure the financial effects of climate change are routinely considered in business and investment decisions.[87]

In September 2024, the government passed the *Treasury Laws Amendment (Financial Market Infrastructure and Other Measures) Act 2024* (Cth). This legislation sets out a three-phased approach where the requirements first apply to a relatively limited group of very large companies and financial institutions and then expand to apply progressively to smaller entities over a three-year period. The information that companies must disclose includes:

- governance processes, controls and procedures used to monitor and manage climate-related financial risks and opportunities
- material climate-related risks and opportunities to their business, and how the entity identifies, assesses, and manages risk and opportunities
- where risks and opportunities are concentrated in the entity's supply chain, the anticipated time horizon and metrics that help investors understand the scale and impact of risks and opportunities.

The climate-related financial disclosures are to be incorporated into a new annual sustainability report, which is added to the existing obligations to prepare annual financial reports under ch 2M of the *Corporations Act*.[88]

87 Australian Government, Treasury, *Policy Impact Analysis: Climate-related Financial Disclosures* (September 2023) 2.

88 Explanatory Memorandum, Treasury Laws Amendment (Financial Market Infrastructure and Other Measures) Bill 2024 (Cth), 140.

> In general, the amendments aim to replicate existing reporting obligations for annual financial reporting, including who must prepare annual financial reports, recordkeeping, presentation of reports at AGMs, provision of financial reports to members and the public, role of the regulator, legal liability and audit and assurance.[89]

These reforms aim to enhance transparency and enable shareholders and investors to have consistent and comparable information regarding how companies are managing climate-related risks and opportunities. They align with global trends towards standardised sustainability reporting and supporting the transition to a net-zero economy and are aimed at 'not only prompting companies to recognise their impact on people and the planet but also provide a means to proactively address them by blending finance and the broader impact of the business'.[90]

As these reforms recognise, parties other than shareholders benefit from increased corporate disclosure including employees, investors and consumers. A disadvantage includes greater costs of compliance for companies and potential information overload for shareholders.[91]

As discussed in Chapter 17, companies listed on the Australian Securities Exchange are subject to additional disclosure regulation, including requirements for periodic disclosure (annual, half-yearly or quarterly reporting, usually via audited accounts); continuous disclosure (a continuing obligation to report events as they occur); and special occasion disclosure (the obligation to disclose information during special events such as takeovers and fundraising by initial public offers). The discussion in the remainder of this chapter does not cover the continuous disclosure requirements for listed companies as these are discussed in Chapter 17.

7.40.05 Members' information

Minute books

Section 251A(1) requires every company to keep minute books and obliges the company to record, within one month, proceedings and resolutions of any meetings of members, directors and committees of directors, and any resolutions passed by the members or directors without a meeting.

The minutes must be signed within a reasonable time either by the chairperson of the meeting or the chairperson of the next meeting (s 251A(2)). If a resolution is passed without a meeting, the minutes of that resolution must be signed within a reasonable time after the resolution is passed (s 251A(3)).

A minute that is signed in accordance with s 251A is taken to be evidence of the meeting or resolution to which it relates (s 251A(6)). The company must keep its minute books

89 Ibid.

90 P Andon, 'ESG standards are changing: What's the impact on business?' *BusinessThink, University of New South Wales*, (Web Page, 13 November 2023) <https://www.businessthink.unsw.edu.au/articles/esg-standards-changing-impact-business>.

91 See generally R Elliott and P Jacobson, 'Costs and Benefits of Business Information Disclosure' (1994) 8(4) *Accounting Horizons* 80.

at its registered office, its principal place of business, or at another place approved by ASIC (s 251A(5)). It must also ensure that the minute books for members' meetings and resolutions are open for inspection by members free of charge (s 251B).

The importance of ensuring that accurate minutes are kept in accordance with s 251A was highlighted in the High Court decision of *Australian Securities and Investments Commission v Hellicar*.[92] This case is discussed in Chapter 11 (at Section 11.15.05) in the context of directors' duty of care and diligence. A key issue in the case was whether the directors of James Hardie, at board meetings in February 2001, had discussed and approved a media release stating that a foundation, which had been set up to compensate asbestos victims, was fully funded. The minutes of the February meetings recorded that the directors had tabled and approved the media release; however, the minutes were not prepared within one month as required under s 251A(1). The non-executive directors of the board argued that the February minutes were false, even though the minutes for February were subsequently adopted at the April board meeting.

In a combined judgment, French CJ, Gummow, Hayne, Crennan, Kiefel and Bell JJ held that insufficient weight had been given to these board minutes in the lower court decisions.[93] They considered that, even though the evidentiary presumption contained in s 251A(6) did not apply on the facts, the board minutes were still relevant as business records of the company. As such, the February minutes were evidence that a draft ASX announcement had been tabled and approved at that meeting. The April board minutes were evidence that the board had approved the minutes of the February meeting as an accurate record. According to the High Court, the minutes were a relatively contemporaneous record of events.[94] Heydon J, in a separate judgment, noted that, although there were some errors in the minutes, these were small and qualitatively different from the mistake that would have been made if the minutes had included a resolution that was never passed.[95]

As a result of this decision, companies are now encouraged to pay greater attention to their record-keeping and to ensure their minutes are accurate. This is particularly important as the High Court noted the criminal sanctions that can apply to non-compliance with s 251A and emphasised the significant evidentiary value accorded to the minutes.[96]

Financial records

All companies are required to keep key financial records. 'Financial records' are defined in s 9 to include invoices, receipts, payment orders, documents of prime entry, and working papers. Under s 286, a company must have records that correctly record and explain its transactions and financial position and performance, and enable true and fair financial statements to be prepared and audited. A company that does not keep or retain

92 *Australian Securities and Investments Commission v Hellicar* (2012) 247 CLR 345.
93 Ibid 345.
94 Ibid 354.
95 Ibid 456.
96 Ibid 357.

financial records as required under s 286 is presumed to be insolvent during that period (s 588E(4)), and directors may be liable for contravention of s 344(1), which is a civil penalty provision.

Members have limited access to the company's books and financial records. Under s 247D (a replaceable rule), the directors may authorise a member to inspect the company's books. Members may be authorised to have access by a resolution passed at the general meeting. Finally, a member may apply for a court order under s 247A to inspect the financial records.

The court will only grant such an order if it is satisfied the member is acting in good faith and the inspection is for a proper purpose.

Financial reports

Preparing accurate financial reports is a key responsibility of those running a company. The *Corporations Act* contains requirements aimed at making companies disclose relevant information about their business and financial position. For example, s 341(1) requires companies, other than small proprietary companies, to report to members via an annual financial report, an annual directors' report, and an auditor's report on the financial report.

Company registers

Companies are required to maintain registers, a task that is often outsourced in large public companies. These include a register of members (s 169), option-holders (s 170), and debenture-holders (s 171). Only companies that have issued options or debentures are required to maintain these registers, while every company must maintain a register of members. The register of members must include the member's name and address, the number and class of shares held, and whether those shares are partly or fully paid up (s 169). The register must also contain the name and address of any member who has sold or transferred their shares in the previous seven years (s 169(7)). Under s 170, the register of debenture-holders must include details of the debenture-holder's name and address, and the number of debentures held. This information is required for the option-holders' register, plus additional information including when an option can be exercised and any consideration for the grant of the options (s 170). Under s 172, the registers must be kept at the company's registered office, its principal place of business, a place in Australia where the work involved in maintaining the registers is done, or another place in Australia approved by ASIC. Section 176 provides that, in the absence of evidence to the contrary, these registers are proof of the matters shown within them.

Any person is allowed to inspect the register kept by a company (s 173(1)). Any person whose name appears on a register can inspect that register free of charge. Under s 173(3), the company may charge other people to inspect the register for a fee up to the prescribed amount, and must provide a copy of the register, or part thereof, within seven days of such a request and the payment of any fee required by the company. In *AXA Asia Pacific Holdings Ltd v Direct Share Purchasing Corporation Pty Ltd*,[97] the Federal Court

97 *AXA Asia Pacific Holdings Ltd v Direct Share Purchasing Corporation Pty Ltd* (2009) 173 FCR 434.

was asked to review the fee that Direct Share Purchasing Corporation was charged by AXA for a copy of its members' share register. AXA had charged Direct Share $17,195.39 for providing it with a CD-ROM containing a PDF copy of the members' register. The *Corporations Regulations 2001* (Cth) reg 1.1.01 and sch 4 item 3(b) provide that the fee for a copy of a register kept on a computer is to be a 'reasonable amount that does not exceed the marginal cost to the company of providing a copy'. The Court held that a reasonable fee was $250 and ordered AXA to refund the difference.

Sections 177(1) and (1A) provide that information in the register cannot be used to contact or send material to members unless that information is relevant to their shareholding or the company agrees to the information being sent. Under s 173(3A), a person applying for a copy of the register must specify the purposes for which it will be used.

Auditor's report

As discussed below, some companies are required to prepare an auditor's report. If such a report is required, the auditor is under a statutory duty to report to the members whether, in their opinion, the annual financial report is in accordance with the *Corporations Act*, complies with the relevant accounting standards, and provides a true and fair view (s 308(1)). The nature and content of an auditor's report is discussed further at Section 7.45.10.

7.40.10 Information provided to ASIC

Registered office

A company must advise ASIC of the address of its registered office (s 121). This address cannot be a post office box, and the company must notify ASIC of any changes. A registered office is important to the functioning of a company as it provides a location where registers and records of the company are kept, and where notices and other communications can be sent. For example, s 109X provides that a document may be served on a company by leaving it at, or posting it to, the company's registered office.

It is common for small companies to use the address of their lawyer or accountant as the company's registered address. The registered office of a public company must be open to the public for at least three hours each business day, between 9 a.m. and 5 p.m.

Extract of particulars

Prior to 2003, all companies were required to lodge an annual return with ASIC. Currently, each company is sent an extract of particulars once a year and must notify ASIC if there are any changes or if there is any incorrect information (s 346C). This process is much simpler than the previous requirement of an annual return. The extract is sent to companies on their review date, which is either the anniversary of the company's registration if the company was registered after 2001, the date of the company's incorporation or registration as recorded on the ASIC register, or such other date as determined by ASIC and notified to the company (s 346A). Under s 347A, the directors are required to pass a solvency resolution within two months of the company's review date. The company must notify ASIC if the directors pass a negative solvency resolution or if they do not pass a solvency resolution within two months of the review date (s 347B).

7.45 Financial reporting

As indicated above, the *Corporations Act* contains requirements aimed at making companies disclose relevant information about the business and financial position of the company. This information is increasingly important to members, creditors, investors, employees and the public.

7.45.05 Financial records

Under s 286(1), a company must keep written financial records that correctly record and explain its transactions and financial position and performance and enable true and fair financial statements to be prepared and audited. The minimum books of account required under this section are a general ledger and general journal. ASIC's advice to the owners of small proprietary companies is that, in addition to the above requirements, they also keep financial statements, computer backup disks, cash records, bank account statements, a sales journal and debtors' ledger, work in progress records, invoices and statements received and paid, a creditors' ledger, unpaid invoices, and tax returns.[98] Under s 288, if financial records are kept in electronic form, they must be convertible into hard copy, which must be made available within a reasonable time to any person entitled to inspect the records. Financial records must be retained by a company for at least seven years after the transaction covered in the records (s 286(2)).

Directors must have reasonable access to the financial records of the company at all times (s 290(1)). However, a director may be refused access if it is shown that they intend to misuse the information or that inspection could materially harm the company.[99]

7.45.10 Financial reports

Chapter 2M of the *Corporations Act* contains rules on the preparation and disclosure of financial information and the auditing of the financial accounts.[100] Not all companies are required to prepare audited annual financial accounts, with public and listed companies subject to the greatest disclosure requirements. Generally, small proprietary companies do not need to prepare annual financial statements, have their accounts audited, or lodge their financial statements with ASIC. A proprietary company is classified as a small company if it satisfies any two or more of the following criteria:

- the consolidated revenue for the financial year of the company and any entities it controls is $50 million or less
- the value of the consolidated gross assets at the end of the financial year of the company and any entities it controls is $25 million or less
- the company and any entities it controls has 100 or fewer employees at the end of the financial year (ss 45A(2), 45A(3), reg 1.0.02B).

98 Australian Securities and Investments Commission, *What Books and Records Should my Company Keep?* (January 2012) <http://asic.gov.au/for-business/running-a-company/company-officeholder-duties/what-books-and-records-should-my-company-keep/>.

99 *Deluge Holdings Pty Ltd v Bowlay* (1991) 9 ACLC 1486.

100 *Corporations Act* s 285 provides a list of financial reporting requirements.

Annual financial report

Section 292(1) requires public companies and large proprietary companies to prepare a financial report and a directors' report every year. A small proprietary company can be requested to prepare a financial report by shareholders holding at least five per cent of the votes in the company (ss 292(2), 293(1)). If such a request is made, it can provide that only some (including none) of the accounting standards must be complied with, a directors' report or part of such a report need not be prepared, and the financial report must be audited (s 293(3)). A small proprietary company can also be directed by ASIC to prepare a financial report or it may specify the particular requirements that the company is to comply with (ss 292(2), 294(1)). The *Corporations Act* does not specify a timeline for the preparation of a financial report.

The deadline for a public company to send its financial report to members is either 21 days before the annual general meeting or four months after the end of the financial year. A proprietary company must send the reports to members within four months from the end of the financial year (s 315) and the financial report must be lodged with ASIC within four months from the end of the financial year (s 319(3)).

The requirements for an annual financial report are set out in s 295. They include the financial statements for the year, notes to the financial statements, and the directors' declaration about the statements and notes. Under s 295(2), the financial statements for the year are those required by the accounting standards, being the standards made by the Australian Accounting Standards Board. Under the accounting standards, the basic components of the financial statements are the balance sheet, the profit and loss statement, and the cash flow statement. Where a parent company controls other entities, the parent company is required to prepare consolidated financial statements.[101]

Directors' declaration on the financial reports

A directors' declaration needs to be included in the financial reports. This is a statement made in accordance with a board resolution, which states whether:

- in the directors' opinion, there are reasonable grounds to believe that the company will be able to pay its debts as and when they become due and payable
- in the directors' opinion, the financial statements and notes are in accordance with the *Corporations Act*, including compliance with the accounting standards, and provide a true and fair view of the company
- if the company has adopted international financial reporting standards, that the notes to the financial statements contain an explicit and unreserved statement of compliance with those reporting standards
- if the company is listed, that the directors have been given the declarations required by s 295A. This requires the CEO and CFO of a listed company to provide a declaration stating whether the financial records have been properly maintained in

101 Australian Accounting Standards Board, *Consolidated Financial Statements* AASB 10 (at 7 April 2022) <https://aasb.gov.au/admin/file/content105/c9/AASB10_07-15_ACOMPdec21_01-22.pdf>.

accordance with s 286, the financial statements and notes comply with the accounting standards, and the financial statements and notes give a true and fair view of the company.

The declaration must be dated. Although the declaration is made by all the directors, via a joint resolution, it will usually be signed by one director on behalf of all the other directors.

Directors' report

A directors' report must be prepared each financial year by all public companies and all large proprietary companies (s 292). The directors' report must be adopted by a resolution of directors and dated and signed by the directors. The directors' report must include:

- general information required by ss 299 and 299A for listed companies
- specific information required by ss 300 and 300A for listed companies
- a copy of the auditor's independence declaration under s 307C.

Section 299(1) provides that the directors' report must include: a review of the company's operations; details of significant changes in the company's affairs; a statement of the company's principal activities and any significant changes in the activities; a reference to likely developments in the company's future operations and expected results of those operations; and, if the company's operations are subject to any particular and significant environmental regulation, details of the company's performance in relation to those regulations. For a listed company, the directors' report must also contain an operating and financial review to enable shareholders to make an informed assessment of its operations, financial position, business strategies and future prospects (s 299A).

Under s 300(1), the directors' report must set out a range of specific information including: details of dividends or distributions to members; the directors' and officers' names, and the names of the partners, directors and/or other officers of the corporation's auditor; options over an issue of shares; and indemnities given or insurance premiums paid to officers or auditors. Public companies must include additional information on the directors' qualifications, experience and special responsibilities, the directors' attendance at board meetings, and the directors' attendance at committee meetings (s 300(10)). Listed companies must also include information on the directors' relevant interests in shares, the directors' contract or options over shares, and the directors' contracts to call shares (s 300(11)).

Auditor's report

An auditor is a person or organisation employed to carry out an audit and present a reliable and independent report to the company on the accounts and financial position of the company. As noted in the Explanatory Memorandum to the 2004 amendments to the *Corporations Act*:

> Audited financial statements are an important part of the financial information that is available to the capital markets and an essential element of effective

> corporate governance ... This sound operation of Australia's financial markets is dependent upon parties such as auditors providing information or services to investors free from any bias, undue influence or conflict of interest.[102]

The requirement for auditor independence is found in s 324CA, which provides that an individual or audit company is not independent if they conduct an audit when there is a conflict of interest in relation to the company being audited and the individual or audit company does not, as soon as possible once becoming aware of the conflict, take all reasonable steps to ensure that the conflict of interest situation ceases to exist. Section 324CD defines 'conflict of interest situations'. Individual auditors must lodge an independence declaration with the directors, and this declaration must be included in the annual directors' report (ss 307(3), 298(1)(c)). The declaration must state that, to the best of the auditor's knowledge or belief, there has been no contravention of the auditor independence requirements in any applicable codes of professional conduct in preparing their report (s 307C(5B)).

Not all companies need to appoint an auditor. A public company must appoint an auditor within one month of the company being registered, unless the members have appointed an auditor at a general meeting (s 327A(1)). However, a proprietary company may choose to appoint an auditor (s 325). Small proprietary companies are not required to appoint an auditor unless ASIC or members holding at least five per cent of the votes in the company direct it to prepare an audited financial report (ss 293(3)(c), 294).

To enable an auditor to prepare a report, s 310(a) provides that they have a right of access at all reasonable times to the company's books. An auditor must carry out an audit of the company's annual financial report, and, if appropriate, its half-yearly financial report (ss 308, 309). The auditor must provide a report to members stating whether, in the auditor's opinion, the financial reports are in accordance with the *Corporations Act*, in compliance with accounting standards, and are a true and fair view of the company (ss 308(1), 309(1)). If the report does not comply with the accounting standards, the auditor's report must quantify the effect of non-compliance (to the extent that it is practicable to do so) and provide a description of any defects or irregularities (ss 308(2), 308(3)(a), 309(2), 309(3)(a)). In addition, the auditor must state whether they were given all information, explanation and assistance necessary for the conduct of the audit, whether sufficient financial records have been kept, and whether other required records and registers have been kept (ss 308(3)(b), 309(3)(b)). Finally, if the financial statements include any additional information, the auditor's report must state whether that additional information was necessary to give a true and fair view, and if the directors' report includes a remuneration report the auditor must provide their opinion on whether that remuneration report complies with s 300A.

7.50 Failure to comply

Failure to comply with the requirements for keeping financial records (s 286) is a strict liability offence, and directors who fail to take all reasonable steps to comply with

102 Explanatory Memorandum, Corporate Law Economic Reform Program (Audit Reform and Corporate Disclosure) Bill 2003 (Cth) [4.8], [4.9].

pts 2M.2 (financial records) and 2M.3 (financial reporting) contravene s 344(1), which is a civil penalty provision. Civil penalties are discussed in Chapter 1. A director will have taken all reasonable steps to comply with the financial records provisions if they employ competent staff and have appropriate procedures in place that define what staff are required to do.[103] Section 588E(4) provides that a company that fails to keep and retain financial records as required by s 286 is presumed to be insolvent for the purposes of the directors' duty to prevent insolvent trading contained in s 588G and any transactions covered by ss 588FA–G.

7.55 Summary

This chapter discussed some of the 'nuts and bolts' issues of corporate law. Understanding which groups can make decisions as the company, and how meetings are held, is fundamental to the workings of a company and those involved. This chapter also considered the role of increased shareholder activism, and of reforms designed to increase corporate reporting on environmental issues. Understanding the rules and requirements on the provision of information to members and the public is important in the context of both good corporate governance and increased corporate accountability. They are also some of the most practical issues involved in the everyday running of companies.

103 *Australian Securities Commission v Fairlie* (1993) 11 ACLC 669.

CHAPTER

8

CORPORATE FINANCE

8.05 Introduction

In this chapter, we examine the law relating to corporate finance, focusing on how companies raise capital by issues shares or taking on debt. We examine the nature of share finance (including different types of shares), the different forms of debt finance (including debentures), and the nature of security interests. We consider share capital transactions including dividends, alterations and reduction of capital, share buy-backs and financial assistance transactions. This area of corporate law uses specific terminology. We define these terms in the text, noting that other sources, such as legal and business glossaries, may also assist.

8.10 The concept of capital

In this and subsequent chapters, frequent reference is made to the concept of a company's capital. The meaning of 'capital' varies depending upon the context:

> According to the context the word may mean wealth, a factor or means of production, the value of those means of production, the net worth of a business enterprise, the present value of a future sequence of receipts, money, the money value of assets and possibly other things as well. Capital is thus thought of in physical terms, in value terms and in money terms.[1]

The main aspect of capital to understand here is the distinction between share capital (also known as 'equity') and debt capital. Share capital is raised by a company issuing shares. Under s 124(1), a company has the legal capacity and powers of an individual including the power to issue and cancel shares. This includes the power to issue bonus shares, preference shares and partly-paid shares (s245A(1)). Under the replaceable rule s 198A, it is the board that has the power to decide on issuing shares.

Except for bonus shares, shares are issued by a company in return for an issue price that is paid by the person purchasing the shares. Shares provide shareholders with

1 J Farrar, N Furey and B Hannigan, *Farrar's Company Law* (Butterworths, 3rd ed, 1991) 149.

benefits such as dividends and the right to vote in company meetings. A company can issue shares on terms that provide that the shareholder does not have to pay the full issue price at the time the shares are issued. If shares in a company are partly-paid, the shareholder is liable to pay the remaining amount owed on the shares if called upon by the company to do so up to the amount of the issue price and in accordance with the terms of the offer (s 254M(1)).[2]

The legal relationship between the company and its shareholders is complex. It is often said that shareholders 'own' the company, although this is not legally correct. Shareholders do not have rights to any part of a company or its property. Rather, a share is a 'chose in action' with certain features including the right to:

- be bought and sold, used as security and passed on via a will
- vote at the company's general meeting
- participate in dividends, and
- participate in the distribution of surplus assets when the company is wound up.[3]

Ultimately, however, the rights and liabilities of shareholders are determined by the terms of the share issue, the company's constitution and the provisions of the *Corporations Act*. The legal nature of a share is discussed further at Section 8.15.15.

By comparison, 'debt capital' refers to borrowings by the company. The legal relationship between the company and a lender is that of debtor and creditor and is largely regulated by contract law. Importantly, lenders do not become members of the company that they provide finance to and usually do not have voting rights in the company. Their claims are *against*, not *in*, the company.[4] However, the relationship between a company and its creditors may be subject to statutory regulation. For example, when the company raises debt through issuing debentures, the *Corporations Act* requires that certain disclosures be made. Likewise, when a loan is secured, the *Personal Property Securities Act 2009* (Cth) may apply. This is dealt with at Section 8.20.15.

8.10.05 Sources of corporate finance and the consequences

Different types and sizes of company will have different needs for finance and different ways of raising it. Small companies may need small amounts of capital borrowed from financial institutions, such as banks, on short-or medium-term loans. For some companies, capital raising will be a once-off process, while others will have a continuing demand. The company must also decide whether it needs short, medium-or long-term finance.

There are many different sources of finance available to companies. This chapter focuses on the most common forms of finance within the categories of share and debt capital.

2 If shares are subsequently transferred to another person, that person becomes liable for any call on the shares by the company up to the amount unpaid on the shares.

3 A chose in action is personal property that cannot be enjoyed by physical possession but is enforceable by legal action. See further discussion at Section 8.15.15 and *Re BCCI (No 8)* [1998] AC 214.

4 Fady Aoun, Olivia Dixon, Emma Armson, Marina Nehme, *Corporations and Financial Markets* (Thomson Reuters, 8th ed, 2022) 812.

The main consequence of a company raising finance by issuing shares is that the suppliers of the finance—the shareholders—become members of the company. For this reason, equity funding is used for longer-term financing. As discussed in Chapter 3, shareholders bear the risk that they will lose their investment if a company fails. Correspondingly, it is appropriate for shareholders to have some control within the company through the exercise of voting rights or, in small companies, by direct involvement in management, as a means of monitoring that risk.

8.15 Share finance

8.15.05 The legal nature of a share

The share is one of the basic elements of corporate law. However, there is some uncertainty about the legal nature of shares. In ordinary usage, a 'share' is taken to give each shareholder a recognised proprietary interest in a company. However, in law this is not strictly correct as share ownership does not create any legal interest in the assets of the company.

Instead, shares give shareholders particular rights in the company as well as representing an amount of the company's capital. As stated by Lord Wrenbury in 1923, shares represent 'a fractional part of the capital'.[5] But a share does not give the shareholder any proprietary interest in the company's property, nor does it give proportionate ownership of the company itself.[6] The company is the owner of its property.

Under s 1070A(1), a share is personal property that can be transferred and is capable of devolution via a will or by operation of law. As an item of property, the share is distinct from the company's property. This means that, subject to any limitations imposed by a constitution, a shareholder can sell their shares without transferring any property interest in the company's assets. Under English law, a share is a 'chose in action'.[7] A chose in action is personal property that cannot be enjoyed by physical possession but is enforceable by legal action. Debts, patents, and copyright are included in this category. Similarly, shares are regarded as an intangible form of personal property. This allows shares to be transferred (bought and sold), used as security, and devolved by a will.[8] The general law developed these characteristics of a share and they are now expressed in s 1070A.

The juridical nature of a share was debated by commentators after the High Court's judgment in *Gambotto v WCP Ltd*.[9] As discussed in Chapter 5, this case involved the compulsory acquisition of shares pursuant to amendments to the company's constitution. The case provoked considerable controversy and led to a debate in the literature about the legal and normative elements of shares and shareholding.[10]

5 *Bradbury v English Sewing Cotton Co Ltd* [1923] AC 744, 767.

6 See *Macaura v Northern Assurance Co Ltd* [1925] AC 619; *Short v Treasury Commissioners* [1948] 1 KB 116, 122 (Evershed LJ).

7 *Colonial Bank v Whinney* (1886) 11 App Cas 426.

8 *Corporations Act* s 1070A; *Sydney Futures Exchange Ltd v Australian Stock Exchange* (1995) 56 FCR 236, 254–6; *White v Shortall* (2006) 68 NSWLR 650.

9 *Gambotto v WCP Ltd* (1995) 182 CLR 432.

10 H Bird, 'A Critique of the Proprietary Nature of Share Rights in Australian Publicly Listed Corporations' (1998) 22(1) *Melbourne University Law Review* 131, 138–41; P Spender, 'Guns and

8.15.10 Types of share finance

The *Corporations Act* does not prescribe a minimum amount of share capital as a prerequisite for registration or operation of a company. A company can be incorporated with only one share. The Act also does not prescribe a minimum issue price for the shares issued. A company can issue shares on such terms, and with such rights and restrictions, as it determines (s 254B(1)). When we refer to 'a company issuing shares', it is usually the board of directors who exercise this power. However, there are important instances when members' approval is required for decisions about share capital, as discussed further below.

The word 'shares' is not defined in the *Corporations Act*, but it falls within the broader category of 'securities' which is defined in s 92 as including 'shares in a body'. The concept of 'securities' is discussed further in Chapters 17 and 19.

Prior to 1998, the *Corporations Act* required a company limited by shares to state in its constitution the amount of share capital with which the company was to be registered (the company's authorised share capital) and to divide this into shares of a fixed amount (the share's par value). This requirement no longer exists (see s 254C),[11] although it is open for a company to include in its constitution a limitation on the number of shares to be issued. This might be appropriate where the company's initial shareholders want to limit the further issue of shares and guard against later dilution of their interests in the company.[12]

When a company issues shares, it can determine the issue price and whether the shares are to be fully or partly paid at the time of issue. Relevant factors in determining the price of shares include the need to make the shares attractive to initial investors, having regard to the company's current and future market value and the rights attached to the shares. One consequence of this is that a company may issue shares at one time for a certain price and with certain rights, and later, as a result of profitable trading, issue shares with the same rights but at a higher price. A key point to understand here is that the *issue price* of a share will not necessarily be the same as the *market price*. The issue price is the amount the company receives as consideration for the share. The market price is the price at which the current owner of the shares can sell those shares. The market price will be affected by many factors, only one of which is the original issue price of the share. Where a company is not performing well, it is possible that the value of its shares will fall below the issue price of those shares—equally, the reverse may happen.

The total value of the shares issued to shareholders is known as the company's 'issued or subscribed capital'. In theory, this figure is of interest to creditors. Corporate law

---

Greenmail: Fear and Loathing after *Gambotto*' (1998) 22(1) *Melbourne University Law Review* 96, 110–18; I Ramsay and B Saunders, 'What Do You Do With a High Court Decision You Don't Like? Legislative, Judicial and Academic Responses to *Gambotto v WCP Ltd*' (2011) 25(2) *Australian Journal of Corporate Law* 112, 130–2.

11 The 1998 reforms were prompted, among other things, by Companies and Securities Law Review Committee, *Shares of No Par Value and Partly-Paid Shares* (Report No 11, 1990) and Corporations Law Simplification Program, *Share Capital Rules: Proposal for Simplification* (Australian Government, November 1994).

12 See generally J Mannolini, 'The Brave New World of No Par Value Shares' (1999) 17(1) *Company and Securities Law Journal* 30.

operates on a simplified model of corporate finance that assumes that the amount of capital raised via shares is then converted into fixed and circulating assets, which the company uses to conduct its business. If the company were to be wound up, the subscribed capital represents the maximum amount available to creditors from shareholder funds. This is discussed further in Section 8.25 below.

When a company issues shares, it will not always seek the full price at the time of issue. A shareholder may purchase partly paid shares (s 254A(1)(c)) and will remain liable to pay the company for some or all of the balance owing on the shares (s 254M). As discussed in Chapter 3, the issue price of the share represents the limit of the shareholder's liability to the company under the principle of limited liability (s 516). At any given time, a company's paid-up capital represents the total of all amounts paid for shares issued by the company. That part of the issued share capital which has not yet been paid up by shareholders is the 'uncalled or reserve capital'. Because the uncalled capital is an enforceable debt owing to the company, it can be used as security for loans. Section 124(1)(e) gives a company the legal capacity to grant a security interest over its uncalled capital.

A company may grant options over unissued shares[13] and must maintain a register of options over unissued shares.[14] An option is a contractual agreement in which the company promises to issue a stated number of shares to the option-holder at some time in the future. The terms of the option will address the number of shares to be issued, the time (or times) at which the option may be exercised, and the price to be paid for the shares on the exercise of the option. The option-holder seeks the advantage that, when the shares are actually purchased, their market value has risen. Until the option is exercised, the option-holder is not a member of the company and has no rights of membership.[15]

Public companies may issue options which can be traded on licensed financial markets. These options have standardised terms and contracts. An option that allows the holder to buy shares is known as a 'call option', while an option that allows the holder to sell shares is known as a 'put option'. Share options are commonly given to corporate executives in larger companies as part of their remuneration package. The expectation here is that the executives will be incentivised to improve the company's performance which will increase the value of the company shares. The trading of shares and options (which may also be classified as derivatives) in the financial markets is discussed in Chapter 17.

8.15.15 Classifying shares

Shares in a company can be divided into classes of shares with different rights attached. This might be done for organisational reasons, so that voting rights are concentrated in the hands of one group of shareholders who then have control of decision-making in the general meeting. Different classes may also be created for investment reasons: offering shares with high dividend entitlements to attract new investors to the company.

13 *Corporations Act* s 124(1)(c).

14 Ibid s 170.

15 *Re Compania de Electricidad de la Provinicia de Buenos Aires* [1980] Ch 146.

The power to issue shares with different rights is derived from s 254B(1). A company must notify the Australian Securities and Investments Commission (ASIC) when it divides shares into different classes if the shares were not previously so divided (s 246).

While the *Corporations Act* uses the expression 'class of shares', it offers little assistance in defining the term. Section 57 states that where shares in a company are not divided into two or more classes then all of the shares are taken to constitute one class.

The question of whether share capital is divided into different classes often arises when the rights attached to one group of shares are varied. This is discussed in Chapter 5. From the cases discussed in Chapter 5, we can learn more about defining classes of shares. In *Crumpton v Morrine Hall Pty Ltd,*[16] for example, there was no express reference in the company's constitution to different classes of shares. There was, however, a provision which prescribed how rights could be altered if the company did have classes of shares. The issue was whether this procedure should have been followed. Jacobs J held that if some shares can meaningfully be differentiated from other shares by reference to the rights they offer, then they are different classes of shares. In *Clements Marshall Consolidated Ltd v ENT Ltd,* Neasey J confirmed this approach by saying that the expression 'class of shares' refers to 'a category of shares which differs sufficiently in respect of rights, benefits, disabilities, or other incidents, as to make it distinguishable from any other category of shares, if there are any, in the capital structure of the company'.[17]

Even if only one shareholder has shares with different rights, they can still be a class of shares.[18] ASIC has provided guidance on when shares are regarded as being in the same class:

> —that is, where:
>
> **(a)** precisely the same rights, obligations and other incidents are attached to each of them; or
>
> **(b)** any difference in rights, obligations or other incidents is temporary and can be compensated for by a simple and certain adjustment in cash.[19]

In the same Regulatory Guide, ASIC states that:

> Classes in this context are distinguished only by differences in the rights and obligations attached to the [shares] rather than by differences in how particular persons can use the rights when the [shares] come into their hands. Differences in the rights exercisable by particular shareholders are not differences between classes of [shares], even if, for some purposes, they distinguish classes of shareholders.[20]

16 *Crumpton v Morrine Hall Pty Ltd* [1965] NSWR 240.

17 *Clements Marshall Consolidated Ltd v ENT Ltd* (1988) 13 ACLR 90, 93.

18 *Crumpton v Morrine Hall Pty Ltd* [1965] NSWR 240; *Cumbrian Newspapers Group Ltd v Cumberland and Westmorland Herald Newspaper and Printing Co Ltd* [1987] Ch 1. See Chapter 5 for further details.

19 Australian Securities and Investments Commission, *Takeover Bids* (Regulatory Guide 9, June 2013) reg 9.46.

20 Ibid reg 9.47.

There is no legal restriction on the type or number of classes of shares that may be created by a company, nor the rights attached to them. In structuring share capital, companies are free to respond to investment trends, taxation incentives and other factors. We next look at some recognised classes of shares.

Ordinary shares

Ordinary shares are the standard reference point when discussing corporate share capital. Where all shares in a company are of one type, they are classified as ordinary shares. This is a residual category, covering those shares that are not classifiable in another category of shares. However, ordinary shares may be divided into different classes, according to differences in voting and other rights attaching to those shares.

Preference shares

The word 'preference' is a descriptor term, meaning that these shares generally have rights to priority, or preference, over ordinary shares on matters such as repayment of capital, participation in surplus assets and profits, and dividend entitlements (s 254A(2)). However, the *Corporations Act* does not define the term 'preference share' and it is not possible to identify a standard form of preference share.

The best way to think about preference shares is as a hybrid security with characteristics of both a share and debt. A hybrid security has the characteristics of an interest-bearing security (debt) and an equity. As such, they are useful instruments of corporate finance.[21] The principal appeal of hybrids is they 'allow issuers to "cherry pick" the aspects of debt and equity financing that satisfy their particular objectives'.[22] For example, while preference shareholders often get priority in the payment of any dividends or surplus assets, they usually have restricted voting rights. Section 254A(2) requires that before a company allots preference shares it must set out in its constitution, or in a special resolution, the rights of the holders of those shares regarding repayment of capital, participation in surplus assets or profits, dividends, voting, and priority in relation to other shares.

In *Re Capel Finance Ltd*, the shares in a new share scheme were described as 'redeemable preference shares' (discussed further below).[23] This meant that the holders of the shares could 'redeem' them by notice in writing to the company. However, the preference shares did not carry any priority or preference (as against the holders of existing or future classes of shares) in the repayment of capital; on winding up; in the profits of the company; or in voting or attending the general meetings of the company. Barrett J held that these shares, if issued, would not be preference shares.

> A preference share is a share with some preference or priority over ordinary or common shares. It is not possible for 'preference shares' to exist except as a result of a process of differentiation from shares which are not 'preference

21 K Tomasic, '*Beck v Weinstock*: Preference in Name but not in Nature?' (2013) 31(7) *Company and Securities Law Journal* 457, 457.

22 C Marston, 'The Accounting and Taxation Regulation of Hybrid Securities' (2006) 24(3) *Company and Securities Law Journal* 186, 186.

23 *Re Capel Finance Ltd* (2005) 52 ACSR 601.

> shares'. These shares did not carry any priority in respect of the matters identified in CA s 254A(2) or any other matters.[24]

In *Beck v Weinstock*,[25] the High Court held that the question of what is a 'preference share' is to be answered by reference to the rights set out in the constitution. The majority stated:

> If a company's [constitution] provided that shares of an identified class carried some right with respect to repayment of capital, participation in surplus assets or profits, cumulative or non-cumulative dividends, voting, or priority of payment of capital or dividend which *preferred the holder of a share of that class over the holder of some other class of share for which the [constitution] provided*, those shares were preference shares.[26]

In that case, the company had a provision in its constitution which allowed it to issue 14 classes of shares. Classes 'A' to 'D' were described as 'preference shares'. Classes 'E' to 'N' were described as 'ordinary shares'. Certain shares that fell within the description of preference shares were issued but no ordinary shares were ever issued. The question for the High Court was whether preference shares could be issued when no ordinary shares had ever been issued. The High Court ruled that the disputed shares had rights which preferred the holder of those shares over the holder of any ordinary share in the company. The fact that no ordinary shares were ever issued did not deny the shares from being preference shares.

While preference shares are legally regarded as part of a company's share capital, when the rights of preference shareholders are compared with those of ordinary shareholders the position of preference shareholders is more like that of creditors.[27] In cases where the interests of ordinary and preference shareholders conflict, the courts have tended towards a strict approach in interpreting the rights of the preferential shareholders.[28]

A company may convert an ordinary share into a preference share, or a preference share into an ordinary share (s 254G). In doing so, there must be compliance with the *Corporations Act* dealing with the variation of class rights. The conversion of ordinary shares to preference shares requires that the rights of the shareholders regarding repayment of capital, participation in surplus assets and profits, dividends, voting, and priority over other shares be set out in the constitution, or be approved by a special resolution of the company (s 254G(2)).

Redeemable preference shares

Some preference shares are issued on the basis that they may be redeemed by the company before winding up. This means that the company may repay the holders of those

---

24 Ibid 602.

25 *Beck v Weinstock* (2013) 251 CLR 425.

26 Ibid (Hayne, Crennan and Kiefel JJ) (emphasis added).

27 J Hill, 'Preference Shares' in RP Austin and R Vann (eds), *The Law of Public Company Finance* (Lawbook, 1986) 139.

28 *Re Isle of Thanet Electricity Supply Co Ltd* [1950] Ch 161; *Webb v Earle* (1875) LR 20 Eq 556; *Dimbula Valley (Ceylon) Tea Co Ltd v Laurie* [1961] 1 Ch 353.

shares the amount they paid for them. This repayment may happen at a fixed time, on the happening of a particular event, at the company's option, or at the shareholder's option (s 254A(3)). The effect of this is that redeemable preference shares are like quasi-loans of capital to the company, with the shareholders still benefitting from any dividend entitlements prior to their shares being redeemed. Despite the similarity with debt capital, redeemable preference shares are regarded as part of a company's share capital. However, Hill observed that the 'modern' redeemable preference share 'is designed to give greater protection to the investor/shareholder, thereby further assimilating [their] position with that of the secured creditor'.[29]

Redeemable preference shares represent an exception to the principle that a company must preserve its share capital. The main concern here is that because capital is being handed back to shareholders, the interests of creditors may be adversely affected. For this reason, the *Corporations Act* sets constraints on the issue of redeemable preference shares. First, a preference share is only redeemable if it is issued on that basis. A non-redeemable share cannot subsequently be converted into a redeemable share (s 254G(3)). Second, the shares can only be redeemed on the terms on which they have been issued. Once redeemed, the shares are then cancelled (s 254J(1)). Third, the moneys used for redemption must come from the profits of the company or from the proceeds of a fresh issue of shares made for that purpose, and the redeemable preference shares must be fully paid up at the time (s 254K). A failure to comply with the preconditions for redemption attracts the operation of the civil penalty provisions (s 254L).

Employee shares

Employee shares are a way to achieve greater levels of employee participation in the company's business. The employer company offers shares to its employees (usually at less than the market price) to provide an incentive to increase the company's profits and reinforce a link between the success of the business and the work of the employees. As a result, there may be restrictions on the employees' capacity to dispose of shares. ASIC supports the operation of such schemes where the terms are designed to achieve interdependence between the employer and its employees for their long-term mutual benefit.[30]

Bonus shares

A company has the power to issue bonus shares (s 254A(1)). The *Corporations Act* describes these as shares where no consideration is payable to the issuing company (s 254A(1)(a)).

29 Jennifer Hill, 'Preference Shares' in RP Austin and R Vann (eds), *The Law of Public Company Finance* (Lawbook Co, 1986) 143.

30 Australian Securities and Investments Commission, *Employee Incentive Schemes* (Regulatory Guide 49, November 2015) reg 49.6. See generally A O'Connell, 'Employee Share Ownership in Unlisted Entities: Objectives, Current Practices and Regulatory Reform' (2009) 37(4) *Australian Business Law Review* 211.

It has been held that:

> The essential characteristic of a bonus share is that it is paid for, not by the shareholder, but by the capitalisation of an amount standing to the credit of one of the company's accounts or reserves.[31]

Bonus shares are often given to shareholders instead of (or as well as) dividends and are given in amounts which are proportionate to the member's existing shareholding. They need not be issued to all shareholders—this will depend upon the constitution.

8.20 Debt finance

If a company raises debt finance by borrowing funds, the creditors do not become members of the company. As discussed in Chapter 4, a distinction is drawn between voluntary creditors (usually those with a contractual relationship to the company) and involuntary creditors (for example, tort victims who have damages claims against the company). In this chapter, the focus is on voluntary creditors. There are different types of voluntary creditors, such as trade creditors who supply goods and services to the company and secured or unsecured finance creditors who supply finance to the company.

8.20.05 Sources of debt finance

The sources to which a company may look for debt finance, and the form which that takes, depends upon a variety of factors. Four significant factors are:

1. the size and nature of the business conducted by the company
2. the prevailing commercial and financial environment
3. the anticipated duration of the debt arrangement: is it to be a short-, medium-, or long-term?, and
4. the prevailing system of tax regulation.

Debt finance: context

A study published in 2012 by the Reserve Bank of Australia[32] provided interesting observations about the use of debt finance. The focus of the study was on financing for small business, but this type of business constitutes the highest percentage of companies in Australia. The following discussion draws on this study.

The study found that incorporated businesses are more likely to use debt than unincorporated business, although smaller businesses are less likely than larger businesses to have any debt. Survey data shows that the smaller businesses tend to raise more of their debt from financial intermediaries (mainly from banks). Only the largest businesses can access debt funding directly from capital markets because the fixed costs of organising direct debt raising—for example, by debentures—are large.[33]

Smaller businesses pay more, on average, for debt than both households and larger businesses. The key reason for the difference in borrowing costs is that smaller businesses

31 *BTR Nylex Ltd v Churchill International Inc* (1992) 9 ACSR 361, 371 (Brooking J).

32 M Matic, A Gorajek and C Stewart, *Small Business Finance Roundtable* (Reserve Bank of Australia, May 2012).

33 Ibid 16.

are typically viewed as having more volatile revenue streams and carry more risk. Smaller businesses can make greater use of unsecured debt products and riskier forms of loan collateral, such as inventory, vehicles, equipment and accounts receivable.[34]

The higher cost of small business debt facilities leads many small business-owners to use household debt products to fund their business; for example, a significant percentage of small business-owners use personal credit cards to manage the business's cash flow or use residential property as loan collateral. Smaller businesses also utilise alternative sources of debt; for example, equipment and vehicle leasing.[35] Another important form of alternative debt finance for smaller businesses is debtor finance, which is short-term funding in exchange for selling its accounts receivables.[36]

The average small business obtains up to half of its debt funding from its trade suppliers when it obtains inventory, equipment and services without immediate payment. Payment terms for trade credit agreements vary considerably between businesses and are usually determined by the relative bargaining positions of businesses and the perceived creditworthiness of the borrower.[37]

Debt finance: instruments

The following section focuses upon the legal aspects of one form of debt finance—debentures—and the creation of security interests or charges in relation to a debt. When a company borrows money, it may be asked to acknowledge the debt in a formal document and to give security to protect the lender against the possibility of non-repayment. Where these two features are incorporated into one document, this may be described as a 'debenture'. The obligation to give security arises in many contexts. Of particular significance for companies is the creation of charges that are a form of security over the property of the company. This is discussed below.

8.20.10 Debentures

Definition of debentures

At common law, debenture may be broadly defined as a written acknowledgement of a debt owed by a company. Debentures are now regulated by ch 2L of the *Corporations Act*. Section 9 defines a 'debenture' as a chose in action that includes an undertaking by a body to repay money deposited with or lent to the body. It may, but need not, include a charge. As a chose in action, a debenture is an intangible personal property right that may be transferred from one owner to another.

The debenture trust deed

Debentures may also be issued as a series where a company wishes to raise a large sum of money by borrowing small amounts from several different lenders. Each lender (or debenture-holder) will be treated equally as regards repayments, interest and security.

34 Ibid 17–18.
35 Ibid 18–19.
36 Ibid 20.
37 Ibid.

As the debenture-holders within a series may be a diverse group—and unable, either individually or collectively, to monitor the loan, the company's performance or to protect their interests —a trustee is appointed to act for them (s 283AA). The trustee holds the rights under the debentures on trust for the beneficial holders. This allows the borrowing company to deal directly with the trustee rather than a large and diverse group of lenders.

8.20.15 Security interests and charges

When a company defaults on its obligations under a loan contract, the creditor can seek to enforce the repayment of the debt by taking legal action based upon the contract. There is a risk, however, that the creditor's claim will have to compete with, and be postponed to, the interests of other creditors. This is important when the company is approaching insolvency or has become insolvent, as discussed in Chapters 15 and 16. To avoid this situation, many large creditors protect their position by obtaining a security over the company's assets. Sykes and Walker provide the following definition of a security:

> [A] security can be defined as an interest vested in a person called 'the creditor' in certain property owned by another called 'the debtor', whereby certain rights are made available to the creditor over such property in order to satisfy an obligation personally owed or recognised as being owed to the creditor by the debtor or some other person.

Sykes and Walker note that this definition covers most, but not all, situations in which a security is granted.[38]

Because a company has the legal capacity and powers of an individual (s 124), it can give the same types of security over its borrowings as a natural person. Section 124 also recognises that companies can give security over uncalled capital. Where a company grants security over its property, it is subject to the general registration regime that applies under the *Personal Property Securities Act 2009* (Cth) ('*PPSA*') as corporate property is personal property for the purposes of this Act.

It is worth noting here that creditors can seek to protect their interests by other means than seeking a grant of security. It is common practice for finance creditors of small companies to require personal guarantees from the directors either in addition to or substitution for a security on a loan. In this way, a director of the company agrees to accept personal liability for the company's loan so that, if the company defaults on the loan, the creditor can look to the guarantor/director for satisfaction of the debt.

While an unsecured creditor takes the risk that the company will not be able to pay its debts, a secured creditor takes a *security interest* from the borrower that allows the creditor to have access to the company's property that is the subject of the security interest in the event of the company being unable to repay its debts. The company's property that is subject to the security interest is referred to as 'collateral'.

38 E Sykes and S Walker, *The Law of Securities* (Law Book, 5th ed, 1993) 12. It is important to note that, in the corporate law context, the word 'security' is also used to describe a particular class of property created by a corporation, which includes debentures, shares, and interests in a managed investment scheme: see *Corporations Act* s 92 and Section 17.20.10.

A 'security interest' is defined in s 9 of the *Corporations Act* to include a 'PPSA security interest' and a charge, lien or pledge. 'Charge' is defined in s 9 and includes a charge within the general law meaning of a charge. 'PPSA security interest' is defined in s 12 of the *PPSA* as a 'an interest in personal property provided for by a transaction that, in substance, secures the payment or performance of an obligation'.

An important distinction in this context is between a *non-circulating* and *circulating* security interest. Prior to the *PPSA* reforms, these were referred to as 'fixed' and 'floating' charges. A fixed charge would attach to particular company assets—such as plant and equipment—which prevented the company from dealing with the property without the consent of the secured party. In contrast, a floating charge would float above the charged property; for example, cash, book debts, inventory, or sometimes all of the debtor's current and future property. This arrangement made it possible for the company to deal with charged property without asking permission of the secured party. A floating charge would become fixed if the company defaulted on the loan or dealt with the property in ways that were contrary to the contract creating the security. This was known as 'crystallisation' of the charge. Depending on the terms of the contract creating the charge, crystallisation could occur automatically without notice being given by the secured party.[39]

Under the *PPSA*, similar types of interests are created in the form of 'non-circulating security interests' or 'circulating security interests'. A circulating security is a right against the company's property that initially 'circulates' above a class or category of property, as opposed to 'fixing' to particular property.[40] A 'non-circulating security interest' is a security interest in a non-circulating asset. It attaches to specific property—identified in the security agreement—owned by the company. Where a non-circulating security interest has been created, the company is not entitled to sell or otherwise dispose of the collateral free of the security interest without the secured party's consent.

Registration of security interests

The *PPSA* establishes a publicly accessible online register of personal (including corporate) property securities ('PPS Register'). The data in the PPS Register includes details of the registered security interests in personal property, details of the grantor in the secured party, and a description of the collateral. While registration is not compulsory, it is in the secured party's interest to register the security interest as registration is the most common method of perfecting the security interest.[41] By perfecting the security interest, the secured party may gain priority over competing security interests of third parties in the same collateral.

Priority rules

Where two or more security interests are attached to the same property, the priority rules in the *PPSA* or the parties' agreement become important. These rules determine

39 *Fire Nymph Products Pty Ltd v Heating Centre Pty Ltd (in liq)* (1992) 7 ACSR 365.

40 *PPSA* s 30.

41 The act of perfection will usually involve the registration of the security interest on the PPS Register but may also involve perfection by possession of the collateral or control: see *PPSA* ss 19–21.

the order in which the proceeds of sale of the collateral (or secured property) are to be distributed among the parties in enforcement proceedings. The *PPSA* has default priority rules, plus specific rules that apply to particular types of security interests. Priority rules may be displaced by an agreement to the contrary between the grantor and secured parties.

The default priority rules are as follows:

(1) The priority between unperfected security interests in the same collateral is determined according to the order of attachment of the security interest (s 55(2)).
(2) A perfected security interest has priority over an unperfected security interest in the same collateral (s 55(3)).
(3) Where two or more security interests are perfected, priority is determined by the 'priority time' for each security interest (s 55(4)). Pursuant to s 55(5) the priority time for a security interest is the earliest of the following times:
    (a) the registration time for the collateral
    (b) the time the secured party first perfects a security interest by taking possession or control of the collateral
    (c) the time the security interests is temporarily perfected, or otherwise perfected, due to the operation of the *PPSA*.
(4) A security interest that is perfected by control has priority over a security interest perfected by other means (s 57(1)).[42]

The priority rules in the *PPSA* intersect with the rules that apply when a company is approaching insolvency or has become insolvent. These rules are discussed in Chapters 15 and 16.[43]

8.25 Maintenance of capital

For the remainder of this chapter, we return to share or equity finance to discuss the rules regarding the maintenance of share capital.

As mentioned above, corporate law operates from a simplified model of corporate finance. This model assumes that a company raises its initial capital by issuing shares and the amount of capital raised is reflected in the number of shares issued. That capital is then converted into non-circulating and circulating assets, which the company uses to conduct its business. If the company conducts its business successfully, it will earn an amount in excess of the initial capital sum—otherwise known as profits. If the company needs further capital later, it can either use its profits, make a call on existing uncalled share capital, issue more of its shares, or borrow the money. While corporate law recognises departures from this model, it forms the basis for most legal principles regarding corporate finance.

42 See generally *PPSA* pt 2.6.
43 For a comprehensive discussion of the *PPSA*, see A Duggan and D Brown, *Australian Personal Property Securities Law* (LexisNexis, 2nd ed, 2015).

Under this simple model, the main concern of a company's creditors[44] is assumed to be ensuring the company's issued share capital is only used in the legitimate course of business and is available to repay their loans. It is these funds that should, in theory, still be available to pay the creditors if the company was wound up.

The effect of this simple model is that once a company has raised capital it is in the interests of shareholders and creditors (subject to fluctuations in the company's performance) for the company to maintain the value of that capital. This is the principle of capital maintenance and this principle underpins the discussion in the remainder of this chapter.

The case usually cited as authority for this principle of capital maintenance is *Trevor v Whitworth*,[45] decided in 1887. The case involved a company incorporated under the *Companies Act 1862* (UK). The company's objects, as stated in its Memorandum of Association, were to acquire and then carry on the business of flannel manufacturers. The company's Articles of Association permitted the company to repurchase its shares from members and, at the board's discretion, to sell or extinguish those shares. There was no such power stated in the Memorandum.[46] Whitworth was a deceased shareholder. His shares had been sold back to the company by his executors, but the full purchase price had not been paid. When the company was later wound up, the executors brought a claim against the liquidators for the unpaid amount. The main question before the House of Lords was whether the company had the power to purchase its own shares, as authorised in the Articles. The House of Lords held that such actions were contrary to the idea that a company should maintain its share capital in the interests of creditors. In Lord Watson's words:

> Paid up capital may be diminished or lost in the course of the company's trading; that is a result which no legislation can prevent; but persons who deal with, and give credit to a limited company, naturally rely upon the fact that the company is trading with a certain amount of capital already paid, as well as upon the responsibility of its members for the capital remaining at call; and they are entitled to assume that no part of the capital which has been paid into the coffers of the company has been subsequently paid out, except in the legitimate course of its business.[47]

The rule in *Trevor v Whitworth* provides that, subject to normal commercial activity, a company must maintain its share capital. What is the rationale for this decision? Although Lord Watson portrayed the paid-up capital as something equivalent to a physical asset which must be preserved, a more convincing explanation is that the rule is tied to the boundaries of limited liability. Recall from Chapter 1 that, in the mid-nineteenth century, there was intense debate about the virtues of granting limited liability by statute. Judicial attitudes about limited liability were still cautious by the time *Trevor v Whitworth*

44 See the discussion above at Section 8.20 and Chapter 4.

45 *Trevor v Whitworth* (1887) 12 App Cas 409. This was not the first case to enunciate and apply this principle.

46 It was then common for companies to include share repurchase powers in their memoranda: see E Magner, '"Repurchase", Redemption, and the Maintenance of Share Capital' in R Austin and R Vann (eds), *The Law of Public Company Finance* (Law Book Co, 1986) 170.

47 *Trevor v Whitworth* (1887) 12 App Cas 409, 423–4.

was decided. The House of Lords emphasised that limited liability gives protection to shareholders by placing a limit on the amount that creditors can seek from them. In return, the Court reasoned, the interests of creditors should be protected by restricting the company's use of the share capital to the purposes stated in the objects clause: a 'company cannot employ its funds for the purpose of any transactions which do not come within the objects specified in the memorandum'.[48] The Court felt this restriction was reinforced by what was then a statutory requirement that the Memorandum should state the company's nominal share capital. Creditors 'have a right to rely, and were intended by the Legislature to have a right to rely, on the capital remaining undiminished by any expenditure outside these limits, or by the return of any part of it to the shareholders'.[49] If the company was permitted to purchase its own shares, this would reduce the pool of capital available for creditors in the event of a winding up.[50] Lord Macnaghten summarised this argument, stating that:

> [T]he notion of a limited company taking power to buy up its own shares is contrary to the plain intention of the [Companies] Act of 1862, and inconsistent with the conditions upon which, and upon which alone, Parliament has granted to individuals who are desirous of trading in partnership the privilege of limiting their liability.[51]

In *Trevor v Whitworth* and earlier cases,[52] the courts sought to balance the 'privilege' of limited liability with the interests of company creditors. This reasoning was adopted in subsequent cases. For example, Lord Macnaghten commented in *Ooregum Gold Mining Co of India Ltd v Roper*, that 'the dominant and cardinal principle ... is that the investors shall purchase immunity from liability beyond a certain limit, on the terms that there shall be and remain a liability up to that limit'.[53] Although the idea of capital maintenance delineating limited liability is laudable, the capital maintenance rule is a clumsy tool for creditor protection in modern corporate dealings. As stated by Ford, Austin and Ramsay:

> As a measure of creditor protection, the law of maintenance of capital is defective. For one thing, there are no significant minimum capital requirements to be met by those who wish to obtain the privilege of limited liability, and thus companies can and frequently are formed with capital of only $2. Moreover the doctrine of maintenance of capital does not provide a guarantee that the subscribed capital will remain; subscribed capital may be reduced or eliminated in the course of trading.[54]

48 (1887) 12 App Cas 409, 414 (Lord Herschell).
49 Ibid 415 (Lord Herschell).
50 It would also place unpaid shareholders, such as Whitworth, in competition with creditors when the company was wound up.
51 *Trevor v Whitworth* (1887) 12 App Cas 409, 433.
52 A discussion of the significance of *Trevor v Whitworth* within the context of contemporary decisions is in E Magner, '"Repurchase", Redemption, and the Maintenance of Share Capital' in R Austin and R Vann (eds), *The Law of Public Company Finance* (Law Book, 1986) 170–5.
53 *Ooregum Gold Mining Co of India Ltd v Roper* [1892] AC 125, 145.
54 R Austin and I Ramsay, *Ford's Principles of Corporations Law* (LexisNexis, 17th ed, 2018) [24.360].

It could be argued that the value of share capital is largely irrelevant to most creditors of modern companies who are more concerned with cash flow and asset valuations.[55]

For these reasons, it is common for creditors to seek protection through contractual means where they can. This might include imposing borrowing limits on a company, obtaining security over corporate assets (discussed above), or obtaining personal guarantees from directors. Few providers of finance (such as banks) would be content to use a company's issued share capital as the sole indicator of the company's creditworthiness.[56]

While the commercial context within which companies and creditors operate has become more complex since *Trevor v Whitworth*, the rule still forms the basis of many aspects of the modern law of corporate finance in Australia.[57] Moreover, the capital maintenance rule has been surprisingly resilient, as demonstrated by comments made in 2014 by the Victorian Court of Appeal regarding the payment of dividends out of capital:

> The prohibition was a vestigial remnant of the 19th century doctrine of the maintenance of capital whereby shareholders were entitled to assume that no part of the capital would be paid out by the company except in the legitimate course of business. Despite changes made by the *Corporations Law Review Act 1998* (which included the abolition of par value and the facilitation of a reduction in share capital without court approval), transactions which affected a company's share capital remained closely regulated.[58]

The rule in *Trevor v Whitworth* forms the historical basis of laws relating to the following:

- the determination and payment of dividends
- self-acquisition and control of shares
- share capital reductions
- share buy-backs
- financial assistance in the acquisition of shares.

These topics are discussed in the remainder of this chapter. However, as we go through these topics it will become apparent that they also raise important questions about corporate control and the appropriate mechanisms for changes in that control.[59] In many ways, the material in the remainder of this chapter is an important adjunct to the material on corporate governance which is considered in Chapters 10–13.

55 J Harris, A Hargovan and M Adams, *Australian Corporate Law* (LexisNexis, 8th ed, 2023) [11.7].

56 For a critique of the capital maintenance rule, see J Armour, 'Legal Capital: An Outdated Concept?' (2006) 7(1) *European Business Organization Law Review* 5; see also W Schön, 'The Future of Legal Capital' (2004) 5(3) *European Business Organization Law Review* 429.

57 See, eg, *ANZ Executors & Trustee Co Ltd v Qintex Australia Ltd (recs and mgrs apptd)* [1991] 2 Qd R 360 (McPherson J) citing *Australasian Oil Exploration Ltd v Lachberg* (1958) 101 CLR 119.

58 *ICM Investments Pty Ltd v San Miguel Corporation* (2014) 48 VR 503, 535–6.

59 See, eg, B McLaughlin and J Balazs, 'Corporate Privatisations by Selective Capital Reductions: The Third Way' (2005) 23(6) *Company and Securities Law Journal* 347; S Webber, 'Weight Loss Without Dieting: Selective Capital Reduction to Gain Control of a Company Without Launching a Takeover' (1996) 6(1) *Australian Journal of Corporate Law* 125.

8.30 Dividends

As investors, shareholders expect to make money either from the increase in the price of their shares or from returns in the form of dividend payments. The company may choose to pay all or part of its profits to members in the form of a dividend. In public companies, the payment of dividends attracts investors to purchase shares in the company which assists in maintaining or increasing the company's share price. However, the market for shares in proprietary companies is usually limited, therefore dividend payments are the way that shareholders obtain financial returns on their investment. While shareholders may also be employed by small proprietary companies to derive wages or salaries, this income arises from their status as an employee, not a shareholder.

Traditionally, the general meeting was required to 'declare' that dividends be paid under provisions in company constitutions.[60] There is a distinction between a *determination* to pay a dividend, which is a revocable decision to fix the amount or time for payment of a dividend (s 254V(1)), and the *declaration* of a dividend, which immediately creates a debt (s 254V(2)). It is common for dividends to simply be determined by the company, rather than declared, because the declaration of a dividend would create a debt under s 254V(2). This is discussed further below.

Modern corporate law leaves matters such as the rate of dividend payment, the form in which it may be paid, the method of payment, and related matters to be decided by the company. The replaceable rule in s 254U provides that the directors may determine that a dividend is payable and may fix the amount to be paid and the time and method of payment. Under this replaceable rule, dividends may be paid in cash, by the issue of shares, the grant of options, the transfer of assets, or some other method. In the case of proprietary companies, a wider discretion is granted by the replaceable rule in s 254W(2), which states that, subject to the terms on which shares have been issued, the directors may pay dividends as they see fit. It is important to remember that ss 254U and 254W may be replaced by a different provision in a company's constitution. Indeed, these provisions are commonly replaced in closely-held proprietary companies, such as family companies, where the constitution may state that the consent of a particular party is required before a dividend is determined or that a dividend may only be paid if it is declared by shareholders at a general meeting on the recommendation of directors. A distinction must also be drawn between final and interim dividends. A final dividend is one which is determined to be payable (or declared) by reference to profits revealed in the company's end-of-year financial statements. An interim dividend is one which is determined to be payable (or declared) during the company's financial year, based upon an anticipation of profits to be shown at the end of the year.

Dividend rights may vary between different classes of shares. The *Corporations Act* provides that, in a public company, each share in a class has the same dividend rights unless the constitution or a special resolution provides for different dividend rights

60 *Bond v Barrow Haematite Steel Co* [1902] 1 Ch 353.

(s 254W(1)). In the case of a special resolution, this would have to be passed before the issue of the shares, otherwise the variation of class rights provisions in the *Corporations Act* would be activated.

8.30.05 When can a company pay a dividend?

Traditionally, dividends could only be paid out of profit. The common law tests used to determine what constituted 'profit' were complex. In 2010, the profit test was replaced with a test that measures assets over liabilities, so that a dividend may only be paid if the company's assets exceed its liabilities. Section 254T states as follows:

> **(1)** A company must not pay a dividend unless:
> > **(a)** the company's assets exceed its liabilities immediately before the dividend is declared and the excess is sufficient for the payment of the dividend; and
> > **(b)** the payment of the dividend is fair and reasonable to the company's shareholders as a whole; and
> > **(c)** the payment of the dividend does not materially prejudice the company's ability to pay its creditors.
>
> **(2)** Assets and liabilities are to be calculated for the purposes of this section in accordance with accounting standards in force at the relevant time (even if the standard does not otherwise apply to the financial year of some or all of the companies concerned).

As stated above, the first limb of the test in s 254T refers to 'balance sheet' solvency; that is, the company's ability to pay a dividend depends on whether its assets exceed its liabilities by an amount sufficient to cover the payment of the dividend. Sections 254T(1)(b) and (c), which relate to the requirement that the payment of the dividend must be fair and reasonable and must not materially prejudice creditors, mirror similar conditions for a reduction of capital and financial assistance, which are discussed at Sections 8.45 and 8.55, respectively, below.

There are considerable uncertainties about the operation of s 254T. The most recent provision is negatively drafted and prohibits the payment of a dividend unless the three requirements in the legislation are satisfied. However, it is not clear that a dividend is lawful just because these conditions are met. For example, it is not clear whether a payment that satisfied the test would still be valid if the company did not record a profit in the year the dividend was paid.[61]

8.30.10 Payment of dividends

Once a dividend is declared, it represents a debt owed by the company to entitled shareholders. Unless there is a provision in the constitution requiring that a dividend be

61 See generally S Alevras and J du Plessis, 'The Payment of Dividends: Legal Confusion, Complexities and the Need for Comprehensive Reform in Australia' (2014) 32(5) *Company and Securities Law Journal* 312.

'declared', the time at which the debt arises under s 254U is when the time fixed for payment arrives. The company does not incur a debt to shareholders merely by deciding it will pay a dividend and determining the amount or time for payment. Before the time fixed for payment arrives, the decision to pay the dividend may be revoked at any time (s 254V(1)).[62]

The situation is different if a company has a constitution which provides for the formal 'declaration' of dividends. In this case, the company incurs a debt at the time the dividend is declared (s 254V(2)) and this declaration cannot subsequently be revoked.[63] In this circumstance, each shareholder who is entitled to receive a dividend becomes a creditor of the company, ranking behind other non-member creditors.[64] However, the rule in s 254T still applies: a dividend may only be paid if the requirements of that section are satisfied. If there is a downturn in the company's financial position between the date of declaration and the date of payment, a company could find itself in a position where it could not lawfully discharge its debt to the shareholders without breaching that section.

From a director's point of view, the time at which the liability arises is important because incurring a debt by way of a dividend may give rise to liability for insolvent trading under s 588G, where the company is either insolvent or becomes insolvent through payment of the dividend. Section 588G is discussed further in Chapter 11 in the context of directors' duties. Further, payment of a dividend where liabilities exceed assets may amount to an unauthorised reduction of capital, creating liability for the directors under s 256D(3). Reductions of capital are discussed below.

The insolvency provisions of the *Corporations Act* contain other provisions relevant to the declaration of dividends by an insolvent company. For example, s 563A has the effect that any dividends that constitute a debt and are unpaid when a winding up commences will be postponed until all debts to non-member creditors have been satisfied. Winding up for insolvency is discussed in Chapter 16 and s 563A is discussed at Section 16.30.

Different provisions apply when a company has paid a dividend before winding up. Where the company was insolvent at the time the dividend was paid, the *Corporations Act* gives the liquidator power to apply for a court order to undo the payment if it amounts to a 'voidable transaction'.[65] Voidable transactions are discussed in Chapter 16. The purpose of this power is to prevent the company's controllers from disposing of assets in favour of certain creditors to the disadvantage of the general body of unsecured creditors. These provisions attempt to balance the interests of unsecured creditors of the company with those of persons who have engaged in fair transactions with the company before winding up.[66]

62 *Bluebottle UK Ltd v Deputy Commissioner of Taxation* (2007) 232 CLR 598.

63 Ibid.

64 *Corporations Act* s 563A.

65 This term is defined in a number of ways by s 588FE. The various definitions apply to different types of transactions, and each sets a different period of time before winding up during which the transaction must fall in order to be voidable.

66 Explanatory Memorandum, Corporate Law Reform Bill 1992 (Cth) [1034].

It is worth noting how the law deals with payment of dividends within corporate groups. The profits of a subsidiary company, even a wholly owned subsidiary, cannot be used by a holding company as a source for the payment of dividends by the holding company. Only where a subsidiary declares and pays a dividend in favour of the holding company may the latter then use those funds.[67] On the other hand, where a subsidiary company incurs a debt by way of a dividend and the subsidiary is, or thereby becomes insolvent, then the holding company may be liable to pay the subsidiary's debt under s 588V. Section 588V imposes liability upon holding companies for insolvent trading by their subsidiaries in certain circumstances. For further details, see Chapter 3 at Section 3.35.

8.35 Alteration of share capital

As discussed above, the rule in *Trevor v Whitworth* requires that a company maintain its share capital. However, there are occasions when a company may wish to alter aspects of its share capital by ordinary resolution passed in the general meeting. Some of the ways in which a company may seek to do this include:

(1) consolidating existing shares into a smaller number of new shares or dividing existing shares into a larger number of new shares (s 254H).[68] A share division might be done to increase the proportion of a member's shareholding, so as to guarantee continued control of the company.[69] Any unpaid amounts on shares prior to a conversion are divided equally among the replacement shares
(2) cancelling shares that have been forfeited, usually for non-payment of a call (s 258D).[70]

Neither of these types of capital alteration has implications for the rule in *Trevor v Whitworth*. In the case of (1), there is no change to the company's issued share capital. Under the simple model on which *Trevor v Whitworth* is based, the pool of capital to which creditors can look is unaffected. In the case of a cancellation of shares, Lord Herschell stated in *Trevor v Whitworth* that the forfeiture of shares 'does not involve any payment by the company, and it presumably exonerates from future liability those who have shewn themselves unable to contribute what is due from them to the capital of the company'.[71] In the case of fully paid shares, a forfeiture which does not operate to reduce the capital of the company may be valid because a forfeiture of fully-paid shares cannot reduce a company's nominal or issued capital.[72]

Other types of capital alteration do compromise the rule in *Trevor v Whitworth* and are closely regulated by the *Corporations Act*. These are discussed below.

67 *Industrial Equity Ltd v Blackburn* (1977) 137 CLR 567.
68 Where the company is listed on the ASX, *Listing Rule* r 7.25 prohibits reorganisations of capital that would result in a decrease in the trading price of securities to less than 20 cents.
69 See, eg, *Greenhalgh v Arderne Cinemas Ltd* [1946] 1 All ER 512.
70 *Bundaberg Sugar Ltd v Isis Central Sugar Mill Co Ltd* [2007] 2 Qd R 214.
71 *Trevor v Whitworth* (1887) 12 App Cas 409, 417.
72 *Bundaberg Sugar Ltd v Isis Central Sugar Mill Co Ltd* [2007] 2 Qd R 214 (Chesterman J).

8.40 Self-acquisition and control of shares

Part 2J.2 of the *Corporations Act* restricts a company acquiring shares in itself or a company that controls it. Except in certain limited circumstances, the *Corporations Act* prohibits:

- a company directly acquiring its own shares or any right or interest in its own shares (s 259A)
- a company taking security over shares in itself or in a company that controls it (s 259B)
- the issue or transfer of shares or interests in shares of the company to an entity that it controls (s 259C).[73]

Section 259A was interpreted in *U & D Coal Ltd v Australian Kunqian International Energy Co Pty Ltd*:[74] see the discussion at Section 8.50.10.

8.45 Reduction of share capital

8.45.05 Reasons for reducing share capital

A reduction of share capital occurs when money paid to a company for a share is returned to the member. Despite the rule in *Trevor v Whitworth*, a reduction of share capital can assist a company in maintaining a profitable business and can be beneficial to creditors. Accordingly, the *Corporations Act* regulates, rather than prohibits, reductions of share capital.

There are situations where it will be commercially desirable or economically necessary for a company to reduce its share capital. An example this is when a company decides to discontinue or reduce part of its business. The company may have surplus assets it no longer uses. This is called an 'excess reduction'. The company pays the cash equivalent of that unneeded capital back to the shareholders in return for their shares.

Alternatively, a company may have accumulated large and permanent trading losses and decided to reduce its issued share capital to a level which more accurately represents the asset-backing of the company.[75] This involves cancelling issued shares without a return of capital to shareholders and is called a 'loss reduction'. An advantage of a loss reduction is that it enhances the company's capacity to pay dividends on the remaining shares. A failure to pay adequate dividends can depress the market value of the shares, making the company vulnerable to a takeover offer.

Another way a company can reduce its share capital is by cancelling some or all of its uncalled share capital. This type of reduction is mentioned in Note 1 to s 256B(1) and is discussed below.

73 For the purposes of pt 2J.2, 'control' is defined in the *Corporations Act*: ss 50AA, 259E.

74 *U & D Coal Ltd v Australian Kunqian International Energy Co Pty Ltd* (2014) 32 ACLC ¶14-047.

75 The courts require that the loss be permanent, otherwise a reduction may adversely affect the interests of creditors: *Re Jupiter House Investments (Cambridge) Ltd* [1985] 1 WLR 975.

A reduction of share capital is one of several ways in which a company can remove minority shareholders from a company's share register. A reduction of share capital can be used to alter the balance of control within a company.[76]

8.45.10 Regulating reductions of capital

The legislation aims to balance the interests of shareholders with the harm that might be caused to creditors when there is a reduction of capital. This intention is stated in s 256A:

> ... The rules are designed to protect the interests of shareholders and creditors by:
>
> **(a)** addressing the risk of these transactions leading to the company's insolvency
> **(b)** seeking to ensure fairness between the company's shareholders
> **(c)** requiring the company to disclose all material information.

The *Corporations Act* regulates share capital reductions by authorising certain types of reduction, and by specifying conditions and procedures for other reductions.

Authorised reductions

Some capital reductions that are specifically authorised are listed in pt 2J.1 div3 of the Act. The list covers share capital reductions which do not adversely affect the interests of creditors or shareholders, or which are sufficiently regulated by other provisions in the *Corporations Act*:

(1) Section 258A: An unlimited company may reduce its capital in any way.
(2) Section 258B: Where the holding of shares in a home unit company gives the shareholder a right to occupy or use property owned by the company without separate consideration, this is an authorised reduction provided it is permitted by the company's constitution (s 258B(1)). Before the introduction of strata or unit title systems, the right to occupy real property was sometimes based on holding shares in a company. A person had a right to occupy an apartment in a block of units because they held shares in a company. Similarly, the transfer of an interest in land to a person in exchange for a right of occupancy or use is an authorised reduction of capital (s 258B(2)). This commonly occurs as part of a conversion of a block of units to strata or unit title. The person surrenders the shares in return for a transfer of strata title of the apartment. The capital reduction involved in the transfer is authorised under s 258B.
(3) Section 258C: A company may pay a brokerage or commission to a person in respect of that person or another person agreeing to take up shares in the company.
(4) Section 258D: A company may pass an ordinary resolution to cancel forfeited shares. This is discussed above at Section 8.35.

76 *Winpar Holdings Ltd v Goldfields Kalgoorlie Ltd* (2001) 40 ACSR 221; *Nicron Resources Ltd v Catto* (1992) 8 ACSR 219.

(5) Section 258E: A company may reduce its shares by buying back any redeemable preference shares out of the proceeds of a fresh issue of shares (s 254K), or by buying back its own shares out of its own share capital. Each of these reductions is authorised by s 258E. Section 254K is discussed above at Section 8.15.10.

(6) Section 258F: A company may reduce its share capital by cancelling any paid-up capital that is lost or not represented by available assets; however, this does not apply if the company also cancels shares. This section is not intended to apply to short-term trading losses which are incurred in the ordinary course of business, but to cases where company assets are lost; for example, by theft or fire.[77]

Equal and selective reductions

Section 256B governs share capital reductions which are not otherwise authorised by law. This section covers two types of share reduction: equal reductions and selective reductions.

An equal reduction relates only to ordinary shares, applies to each holder of those shares in proportion to the number of shares they hold, and is made on the same terms for each of those shareholders (s 256B(2)). If any of these conditions are not met, then the reduction is classified as a selective reduction. The terms of an equal reduction can differ between shareholders, provided that the differences relate only to accrued dividend entitlements, or to unpaid amounts on shares, or that they ensure each shareholder is left with a whole number of shares (s 256B(3)).

Section 256B(1) sets three requirements for a reduction of share capital (either equal or selective). These requirements are not crucial to the validity of the transaction because a reduction which contravenes one or more of these requirements is not invalid (s 256D(2)). Instead, the three requirements can be used to determine liability of persons for contravening s 256B, and in hearing an application for an injunction under s 1324.

THE FIRST REQUIREMENT: FAIR AND REASONABLE TO SHAREHOLDERS

The first requirement is that the reduction must be fair and reasonable to the company's shareholders as a whole. The 'fair and reasonable' requirement is read as a composite requirement or a single concept. In *Re Rancoo Ltd*, Hayne J held that 'the expression "fair and reasonable" is but a single expression intended to convey a single overall meaning which is not to be identified by reference to particular constituent elements'.[78] The *Rancoo* approach was followed in *Elkington v CostaExchange Ltd.*[79]

In that case, CostaExchange Ltd ('Costa') was an unlisted public company that was 92 per cent owned by two companies and their related entities. Costa was heavily indebted and needed to refinance its banking facilities. Costa entered into a transaction with a private equity firm to raise capital and reduce debt under which:

- the private equity firm would acquire a 50 per cent interest in Costa
- a banking syndicate would agree to refinance the remaining debt

77 Explanatory Memorandum, Company Law Review Bill 1997 (Cth) [12.39].

78 *Re Rancoo Ltd* (1995) 13 ACLC 880, 882.

79 *Elkington v CostaExchange Ltd* (2011) 29 ACLC ¶11-079.

- an 8 per cent interest in the company held by minority shareholders would be cancelled via a selective reduction of capital.

The cancellation of the shares held by the minority was approved by special resolutions passed at a general meeting and at a special meeting of shareholders whose shares were to be cancelled. The explanatory notes accompanying the notice of meeting included an independent expert's report, which valued the shares in the company differently depending on whether they were owned by majority or minority shareholders. The expert considered that the price offered for the minority shares was less than the value of the shares measured on a control basis, but more than the value of the shares measured on a minority basis. The expert concluded that minority shareholders would be better off if the proposed transactions were completed and concluded that the lower price (which assessed the value of the shares on a minority basis) was fair and reasonable. The expert justified the lower price for the minority members' shares on the basis that those members were unable to influence the operations of the company, there was a low likelihood of the minority shareholders receiving an alternative offer, and, in the absence of the proposed transactions proceeding, the company was unlikely to have capacity to undertake programs required to enhance the profitability of the company. On this basis, the expert formed the opinion that the selective capital reduction was fair and reasonable to shareholders as a whole. Mr Elkington was a minority shareholder in Costa who claimed that the price offered for the shares was unfair and applied for an injunction under s 1324 to restrain Costa from making the capital reduction.

Ferguson J dismissed the application. He held that in assessing what is fair and reasonable to the shareholders as a whole, many factors will be relevant, with the price to be paid being only one consideration. Factors that were relevant in the present case included the company's indebtedness and inability to grow the business in the absence of the proposed transactions, the non-payment of dividends for several years, and the limited ability of the minority shareholders to otherwise sell their shares.[80] Taking into account these factors, there was no reason why the shares should be valued on a control rather than a minority basis. The interests of all shareholders, not just the minority, are to be considered in determining whether the selective capital reduction is fair and reasonable.[81]

The Explanatory Memorandum to the Bill (which introduced the current s 256B) states that the factors which could be relevant to determining whether a reduction is fair and reasonable include the adequacy of any consideration paid to shareholders, whether the reduction has the practical effect of depriving some shareholders of their rights (although the test directs attention to the shareholders as a whole), whether the reduction is being used to bring about a takeover while avoiding the takeover provisions, or whether the reduction should more properly proceed as a scheme of arrangement.[82]

The Explanatory Memorandum states that the fair and reasonable test directs attention to the effect of the reduction rather than its purpose, and that this avoids the application

80 Ibid [49].

81 Ibid [4].

82 Explanatory Memorandum, Company Law Review Bill 1997 (Cth) [12.24].

of the High Court's decision in *Gambotto v WCP Ltd* ('*Gambotto's Case*')[83] to a reduction of share capital under s 256B. The application of *Gambotto's Case* is raised by the similarity between the effect of a cancellation of shares in a reduction of capital and the expropriation of shares which occurred in that case. In *Winpar Holdings Ltd v Goldfields Kalgoorlie Ltd* ('*Winpar*'), the New South Wales Court of Appeal held that the principles in *Gambotto's Case* have no application to a reduction of share capital under the *Corporations Act*.[84] Giles JA (Beazley JA and Davies AJA agreeing) found that the approach in pt 2J.1 was comprehensive, adding the *Gambotto* principles would be conflicting and confusing.[85]

In *Winpar*, Goldfields Kalgoorlie Ltd ('GK') called a shareholders' meeting to approve a selective reduction of share capital via the cancellation of shares held by a minority shareholder with a payment of 55 cents per share. This was 8 cents above the value determined by an independent valuer. The effect of the capital reduction was to give the majority shareholder in GK 100 per cent ownership. Winpar was a minority shareholder and argued that the special benefits that accrued to the majority shareholder from their 100 per cent ownership should be allocated to the minority shareholders. The New South Wales Court of Appeal rejected Winpar's argument and found there was a fair and reasonable allocation of benefits to all shareholders. The majority shareholder received the benefit of 100 per cent ownership. The minority shareholders obtained a higher price. There was no necessary unfairness or unreasonableness if the advantage was shared.

THE SECOND REQUIREMENT: NO MATERIAL PREJUDICE TO CREDITORS

The second requirement is that the reduction does not materially prejudice the company's ability to repay its creditors. This expresses the key concern underlying the rule in *Trevor v Whitworth*. In *Re CSR Ltd*,[86] the Full Federal Court held that in order to prove a 'material prejudice' to a company's ability to pay its creditors, the proponent must establish 'the creation of a material as opposed to theoretical increase, in the likelihood that the reduction in capital will result in a reduced ability to pay creditors'.[87] In that case, CSR Ltd ('CSR') commenced proceedings seeking orders pursuant to s 411(1) of the *Corporations Act* for the convening of a meeting of its shareholders to consider a scheme of arrangement. The scheme involved the demerger of CSR's sugar and renewable energy business to facilitate the creation of two listed companies (Sucrogen and New CSR), which was to be implemented by way of a reduction in the capital of CSR and a scheme of arrangement between CSR and its existing shareholders. Interveners in the proceedings (including ASIC and James Hardie Industries) opposed the scheme on the basis that the demerger could prejudice the prospects of recovery of damages from New CSR by persons injured as a result of their exposure to asbestos by CSR. CSR's application was granted because the interveners had only established that CSR would be unable to pay its creditors in a 'worst case' scenario, where there was less than 5 per cent chance

83 *Gambotto v WCP Ltd* (1995) 182 CLR 432.

84 *Winpar Holdings Ltd v Goldfields Kalgoorlie Ltd* (2001) 40 ACSR 221.

85 Ibid [94]–[96].

86 *Re CSR Ltd* (2010) 183 FCR 358.

87 Ibid [45] (Keane CJ and Jacobson J).

of the liabilities occurring.[88] It was not appropriate to refuse the scheme merely on a theoretical fear of adverse consequences.[89] Section 256B requires that the prejudice be material rather than theoretical.[90]

THE THIRD REQUIREMENT: APPROVAL BY SHAREHOLDERS

Third, the reduction must be approved by the company's shareholders as set out in s 256C. The method of approval depends on whether an equal or a selective reduction is proposed. An equal reduction must be approved by an ordinary resolution passed at a general meeting of the company.[91] A selective reduction can be approved in one of two ways. One method is to pass a special resolution at a general meeting, with no votes cast in favour of the resolution by any person (or their associates) who is to receive consideration from the reduction or whose liability for unpaid capital is to be reduced. The second method is where an ordinary resolution can be agreed to at a general meeting by all of the ordinary shareholders in the company. This may be suitable for companies with a small number of shareholders. In either case, where the selective reduction involves the cancellation of shares, the reduction must be approved by a special resolution of a meeting of the shareholders whose shares are to be cancelled.

The directors exercise the company's power to reduce its share capital. The shareholders in a general meeting only have the function of approving a proposed resolution. They cannot effectuate it. Therefore, the shareholders must vote on a proposal to approve a capital reduction put forward by the directors on behalf of the company. The shareholders cannot act on behalf of the company in proposing a reduction of capital themselves.[92]

THE FOURTH REQUIREMENT: NOTICES AND LODGEMENT WITH ASIC

One further requirement for a selective reduction is that a copy of any of these resolutions must be lodged with ASIC, and the reduction cannot proceed until 14 days after that lodgment.

For equal and selective reductions, ASIC must be sent a copy of the notice of the meeting, and any document relating to the reduction be sent to shareholders before the general meeting. Documentation sent to shareholders must include a statement that contains all the information that is material to the shareholders' decision on how to vote. The statement does not have to include information which has previously been disclosed to shareholders (s 256C(4)).

88 Ibid [89] (Finkelstein J).

89 Ibid.

90 Ibid [46] (Keane CJ), [68] (Jacobson J); L Floyd, '"Commercial morality" as a Legal Concept: The Full Federal Court Decision in *Re CSR Ltd*' (2010) 28(6) *Company and Securities Law Journal* 411, 415; D Nguyen, 'The Relevance of Scientific Uncertainty and Commercial Morality to Schemes of Arrangement: *Re CSR Ltd*' (2010) 38(6) *Australian Business Law Review* 351, 355–7.

91 In a proprietary company, the resolution may be passed without actually holding a meeting: see s 249A, allowing circulating resolutions and discussed in Chapter 7.

92 *Re Molopo Energy Ltd* (2014) 104 ACSR 46, [77]: see E Boros, 'Shareholders' Remedies: Altering the Division of Power Between the Board and the General Meeting' (2015) 33(2) *Company and Securities Law Journal* 129, 131; J Harris, 'Barbarians at the Gate? Activist Investors and s 249N of the *Corporations Act 2001* (Cth)' (2016) 34(2) *Company and Securities Law Journal* 151, 154–5.

If any shares are cancelled in a reduction of capital, the company must lodge a notice with ASIC within one month of the cancellation. That notice must set out the number of shares cancelled, the amount paid by the company on cancellation, and the class to which the cancelled shares belong (s 254Y).[93]

A failure to comply with the procedures set out in s 256B may result in a civil penalty being imposed.[94] However, the contravention of s 256B does not affect the validity of the reduction or of any related contracts or transactions, and the company itself is not guilty of an offence (s 256D).[95] Under s 256D, a person involved in the contravention is liable under the civil penalty provisions in pt 9.4B. Section 79 explains how a person may be involved in a contravention. See below at Section 8.55.10 for a further discussion of this accessorial liability.

8.45.15 Protecting interests affected by a reduction

The *Corporations Act* contains a number of mechanisms to protect the interests of shareholders and creditors affected by a reduction of capital. This is aimed at addressing the risk of corporate insolvency, ensuring fairness between shareholders, and requiring disclosure of all material information of the company as stated in s 256A.

The interests of shareholders are protected by the notice, meeting, and resolution requirements. These procedures seek to ensure a reduction is supported by the informed consent of the shareholders. For example, in *Re Allgas Energy Ltd*, the Court declined to confirm a reduction of capital because new information about the reduction presented at the shareholders' meeting had not been made available to the proxy voters.[96] The statutory and general law rules regarding directors' duties apply to a reduction of capital. This is confirmed by s 260E which states that:

> A director is not relieved from any of their duties under this Act (including sections 180, 181, 182, 183 and 184), or their fiduciary duties, in connection with a transaction merely because the transaction is authorised by a provision of this Chapter or is approved by a resolution of members made under a provision of this Chapter.

Section 260E applies to all transactions affecting share capital that are dealt with in ch 2J of the *Corporations Act*.

The *Corporations Act* deals with the protection of creditors' interests in a reduction in a different way. The reduction process does not specifically require the approval of the company's creditors. To some extent, the risk to creditors may be met by the combined effect of s 588G (the insolvent trading provision) and s 1317H which, as noted in s 256E, makes directors personally liable if the company became insolvent because of a debt incurred by a reduction of share capital (s 588G(1A)). This would not be relevant where the reduction involves a cancellation of shares.

93 Note that s 254Y applies in any situation where a company cancels its shares.

94 See *Corporations Act* pt 9.4B discussed in Chapter 1 at Section 1.65.05.

95 See *Winpar Holdings Ltd v Goldfields Kalgoorlie Ltd* (2001) 40 ACSR 221.

96 *Re Allgas Energy Ltd* [1998] 1 Qd R 472. This case was decided under the old section that required court approval prior to a reduction of capital.

Another protection for creditors is provided by the notice and lodgement requirements described above. As explained in the Explanatory Memorandum, the requirement to lodge notice of the meeting and accompanying documents with ASIC before the meeting, coupled with the mandatory 14-day waiting period after lodgement, means creditors and other interested persons will have at least 35 days' notice of a proposed reduction.[97]

Members and creditors are given further protection by seeking an injunction and/or damages under s 1324. A person whose interests have been, are, or would be affected by a contravention of the reduction of share capital provisions may apply for an injunction. Section 1324(1A) states that the interests of a member or creditor are affected if a company contravenes the requirement that the reduction should not prejudice the ability to pay creditors. In *Re Molopo Energy Ltd*, it was held that if it appeared that a reduction of capital might materially prejudice the company's ability to pay its creditors and it could not be affirmatively shown that the reduction would not have that effect, then the reduction is prohibited.[98] In other words, the onus is on the company to ensure that the reduction does not prejudice its ability to pay creditors.

Further, the interests of a member are affected if the company contravenes the requirement that the reduction should be fair and reasonable. The company bears the onus of proving its conduct does not constitute a contravention. For further discussion of s 1324, see Chapter 14.

8.45.20 Reductions of share capital and class rights

A reduction of capital can be problematic where a company's share capital is divided into different classes. One question that arises when a reduction involves a particular class of shares is whether the reduction amounts to a variation of class rights and, if so, whether ss 246B–G should apply. Certainly, the *Corporations Act* envisages these sections may be relevant: s 256E includes the class rights sections in its list of other provisions in the *Corporations Act* that may be relevant to a reduction of share capital. For a further discussion of variation of class rights, see Chapter 5.

8.50 Share buy-backs

A buy-back is a repurchase of shares by the company. It involves a company making an offer to shareholders to buy back their shares. The shareholder can choose whether to sell their shares or not, taking into account the circumstances; for example, the tax treatment of the buy-back relative to dividends.

8.50.05 Problems and advantages of buy-backs

During a buy-back, a company can diminish its financial resources by acquiring its own shares. Recall that the rule in *Trevor v Whitworth* arose from a company repurchasing its own shares. The judgment noted that the questions raised by share repurchases are similar to questions raised by reductions of share capital. As Lord Herschell observed,

97 Explanatory Memorandum, Company Law Review Bill 1997 (Cth) [12.28].
98 *Re Molopo Energy Ltd* (2014) 104 ACSR 46 [87]–[89].

'the stringent precautions to prevent the reduction of the capital of a limited company, without due notice and judicial sanction, would be idle if the company might purchase its own shares wholesale, and so effect the desired result'.[99] However, a key difference between a reduction of shares and a buy-back is that a buy-back is optional.

There are problems that can arise with share buy-backs, some of which are covered by the *Corporations Act*; for example:[100]

(1) share buy-backs could be used to discriminate unfairly between shareholders, with some members being bought out at prices in excess of the market value of the shares. This practice could result in a breach of the fiduciary duties imposed on directors, particularly the requirement that directors exercise their powers for a proper purpose.[101]
(2) directors might use the buy-back power improperly to maintain or improve their control of the company, or to eliminate opposing interests from the company. This conduct would involve a breach of directors' common law and statutory duties, although those rules have not always been consistently applied in Australian courts.
(3) a share repurchase power might open the door to 'greenmail',[102] whereby a dissident shareholder could threaten either a hostile takeover or disruption of the company's affairs unless their shares were bought by the company at a premium on the market price.[103]
(4) there is a risk that a public company may manipulate or distort the market price of its shares by purchasing its own shares. The potential for insider trading might also increase.[104]

Should each problem be dealt with by existing specific rules; for example, laws relating to fiduciary duties, or rules prohibiting market manipulation and insider trading? Or should these rules be supplemented by a general regulation of buy-backs? Australian company legislation has taken the latter course.

There are many advantages for a company to repurchase its shares.[105] These advantages are particularly relevant to small or closely-held companies. In this type of company, it is important to retain the control in one or two shareholders. Where a shareholder dies or leaves the company and the remaining members are not able to purchase those shares, a buy-back power provides an efficient mechanism whereby the existing

99 *Trevor v Whitworth* (1887) 12 App Cas 409, 416.
100 These examples are taken from Companies and Securities Law Review Committee, *A Company's Purchase of its Own Shares* (Discussion Paper No 5, 1986) ch 4.
101 See the discussion in Chapter 12.
102 'Greenmail' refers to the payment of a high price by a company or a majority shareholder to acquire shares from a greenmailer (usually a minority shareholder) who owns a strategic stake in the company. The high price is paid so that the acquirer can achieve control of the company.
103 See I Udechuku and K Smith, 'Greenmail: Appropriate Regulation' (1989) 7(5) *Company and Securities Law Journal* 313, 315.
104 For further discussion of market manipulation and insider trading, see Chapter 17.
105 Companies and Securities Law Review Committee, *A Company's Purchase of its Own Shares* (Discussion Paper No 5, 1986) ch 3.

power balance can be preserved. Even in large companies, it may be desirable to buy out a dissident shareholder. A share buy-back may be a defensive tactic in the face of an unwanted takeover bid. Buy-backs can be a mechanism for an efficient allocation of investment funds. For example, one benefit of a company repurchasing its own shares is that the number of outstanding shares on the market is reduced. When this happens, the relative ownership stake of each investor increases because there are fewer shares, the earnings per share increases, and this is generally followed by a spike in the share price. Therefore '[i]f a company has surplus funds, shareholders are given an opportunity to invest funds elsewhere to maximise return or to increase their relative holding by not accepting the repurchase offer'.[106]

Given that there is no clear policy reason for either a blanket prohibition or the deregulation of buy-backs, the *Corporations Act* attempts to balance the capital maintenance principle with concerns for commercial practice. Until 1989, buy-backs were strictly prohibited in Australia. Amendments that commenced in 1990 were, in part, a response to a recommendation of the Companies and Securities Advisory Committee that corporations should be able to repurchase their own shares, subject to strict procedural controls. The current buy-back provisions are the product of amendments introduced by the *First Corporate Law Simplification Act 1995* (Cth) which changed the 1990 rules because they were said to be too expensive and procedurally complicated. The purpose of the present regulations governing buy-backs is the same as that for the rules relating to reductions in share capital: to address the risk of corporate insolvency, to ensure fairness between shareholders, and to require disclosure of all material information (s 256A).

8.50.10 Regulation of share buy-backs

Under s 257A of the *Corporations Act*, a company may buy back[107] its own shares on two conditions: the buy-back must not materially prejudice the company's ability to pay its creditors, and the procedures in pt 2J.1 div 2 must be followed. The first of these conditions duplicates one of the requirements for a reduction of share capital in s 256B. It is possible for a company's constitution to impose further restrictions or a complete prohibition on the company buying back its own shares. A buy-back may comply with s 257A but nevertheless amount to unacceptable circumstances for the purposes of ch 6 of the *Corporations Act* (s 657A) and the buy-back may be subject to the jurisdiction of the Takeovers Panel.[108]

In *Re George Raymond Pty Ltd*, Byrne J noted that a buy-back is a contractual agreement for the sale and purchase of shares, in which the shareholder agrees to transfer the

106 D Partlett and G Burton, 'The Share Repurchase Albatross and Corporation Law Theory' (1988) 62(2) *Australian Law Journal* 139, 142–3. For a further discussion of reasons why companies engage in buy-backs, see A Lamba and I Ramsay, 'Share Buy-Backs: An Empirical Investigation' (Report, Centre for Corporate Law and Securities Regulation, May 2000) 3.

107 For these purposes, a 'buy-back' is defined as the acquisition by the company of shares in itself: *Corporations Act* s 9.

108 See *Re Village Roadshow Ltd (No 3)* (2005) 23 ACLC 10; see also Chapter 19.

shares to the company and the company agrees to pay for them.[109] The company incurs a debt in the amount agreed to be paid for the shares.[110]

The procedures in pt 2J.1 div 2 recognise four types of buy-back. Each type has its own procedures (some of which are common to all buy-backs) and these are summarised in the table in s 257B. The four types of buy-back are:

- equal access scheme
- selective buy-back
- employee share scheme
- on-market buy-back.

Equal access scheme

An equal access scheme (defined in s 257B(2)) is a buy-back that satisfies all of the following conditions:

(a) the offers under the scheme relate only to ordinary shares (that is, preference shares cannot be bought back under an equal access scheme);
(b) the offers are to be made to every person who holds ordinary shares to buy back the same percentage of their ordinary shares;
(c) all of those persons have a reasonable opportunity to accept the offers made to them;
(d) buy-back agreements are not entered into until a specified time for acceptances of offers has closed; and
(e) the terms of the offers are all the same.

Section 257B(3) states that in applying s 257B(2), the following should be ignored:

(a) differences that relate to shares having different accrued dividend entitlements;
(b) differences in consideration attributable to the fact that the offers relate to shares on which different amounts remain unpaid; or
(c) differences in the offers introduced solely to ensure that each shareholder is left with a whole number of shares.

Additional approval and lodgement requirements may also apply to equal access schemes, as set out below.

Approval at a general meeting

Generally speaking, a company's power to buy back its shares is exercised by the company's directors. Any exercise of this power will be subject to the fiduciary and statutory duties which govern the actions of directors. In certain situations, however, the *Corporations Act* requires shareholders in general meeting to have the opportunity to scrutinise and approve a proposed buy-back scheme. This occurs when the proposed buy-back will have the result that the company will exceed the '10/12 limit'.

109 (2001) 19 ACLC 553.

110 Ibid. Some care must be taken to ensure that a company does not become a transferee of its own shares if nominated as a substitute purchaser by a transferee shareholder. This would require compliance with pt 2J.1 divs 1 or 2 to be effective: *Salter v Gilbertson* (2003) 6 VR 466.

The 10/12 limit is reached when a company buys back 10 per cent of the smallest number, at any time in the last 12 months, of votes attaching to voting shares in the company.

The calculation of the 10 per cent figure is cumulative across the last 12 months; that is, the company must count the number of voting shares that have been bought back during the last 12 months, together with the voting shares that will be bought back in the proposed buy-back (ss 257B(4), (5)). In such a situation, the equal access scheme must be approved by an ordinary resolution (s 257C(1)).

Lodgement requirements

If the scheme dooes not require approval by a resolution of a general meeting—that is, if the 10/12 limit is not exceeded—then, 14 days before the buy-back agreement is entered into, the company must lodge with ASIC the terms of the offer and any accompanying documents (ss 257F, 257E). If the scheme does require the passing of a resolution, then, 14 days before the resolution is passed, the company must lodge with ASIC a notice of the meeting and any accompanying documents (ss 257F, 257C(3)), and also lodge the terms of the offer and accompanying documents (s 257E).[111] In either case, if the company wants to act earlier than 14 days after making the required lodgements, it must also lodge a notice of intention to carry out the buy-back (s 257F).

Shares cancelled

Once the buy-back agreement has been entered into, all rights attaching to the shares are suspended and the shares are transferred back to the company and cancelled. A company must not dispose of shares that have been bought back (s 257H). ASIC must be notified of the cancellation under s 254Y.

Selective buy-back

A company may engage in a selective buy-back. This type of buy-back must be approved by one of two methods (s 257D). Either a special resolution can be passed at a general meeting, in which no votes are cast in favour by any person (or their associates) whose shares are proposed to be bought back, or an ordinary resolution can be passed at a general meeting by all the ordinary shareholders in the company. For an example of the voting procedures required by ss 257B and 257D, see *Re CIC Australia Ltd (No 2)*.[112] For the purposes of s 257D, the word 'associates' is defined in ss 10, 11 and 15 of the *Corporations Act*.[113]

The reason for these tighter requirements is that selective buy-backs have the potential to prompt greenmail claims, or result in other inequities between shareholders.[114] A related reason is that the selective buy-back power may be useful in allowing the company to buy out a dissident shareholder. In other words, selective buy-backs may be useful

111 The offer must be accompanied by a statement that sets out all information known to the company that is material to the decision of whether to accept the offer: *Corporations Act* s 257G.

112 *Re CIC Australia Ltd (No 2)* [2015] NSWSC 1314 [10].

113 For a discussion of voting by associates in a selective buy-back, see *Bateman v Newhaven Park Stud Ltd* (2004) 49 ACSR 454, [33]–[47].

114 Companies and Securities Law Review Committee, *A Company's Purchase of its Own Shares* (Discussion Paper No 5, 1986).

as a form of takeover defence. As discussed in Chapter 19, takeover defences are subject to scrutiny by legislation and common law principles in order to protect the interests of shareholders.

The notice of the general meeting must be accompanied by a statement that sets out all information known to the company that is material to a shareholder's decision on how to vote. The statement does not have to include information that has previously been disclosed to shareholders (s 257D(2)). The notice and accompanying documentation must be lodged with ASIC before it is sent to any shareholder.[115] A notice under s 257D will often include an independent expert's report as to whether the consideration offered is fair and reasonable but such a report is not mandatory, provided it can be established that shareholders have received sufficient information on the proposed buy-back to make informed decisions on the buy-back resolution.[116]

In *BPESAM IV M Ltd v DRA Global Ltd*, the Federal Court granted an urgent injunction preventing a company from acting upon shareholder approval for a selective share buy-back agreement after it was discovered that there were significant errors in the company's financial information.[117] The Court held that the directors needed to keep shareholders informed of any material changes to the financial position of the company and that, if the company wished to proceed with the buy back, it should have gone back to the shareholders with the correct financial information.

A selective buy-back must comply with lodgement, disclosure, and cancellation requirements that are similar to those that apply to an equal access scheme (s 257D(3)).

Employee share scheme buy-back

Some companies aim to encourage employee participation by allowing employees, including executive directors, to acquire shares in the company. An employee share scheme buy-back is one where the company buys shares held by, or on behalf of, employees, and this is approved at a general meeting (s 9). The requirement for approval at a general meeting is less onerous than a requirement for a resolution, because s 257B only requires a resolution (as per s 257C) if the employee share scheme buy-back will exceed the 10/12 limit.

Fourteen days before the buy-back is entered into, the company must lodge with ASIC a notice of intention to carry out the buy-back (s 257F), and the same rules regarding cancellation of the shares apply as for equal access and selective buy-backs.

On-market buy-back

The *Corporations Act* permits a listed company to buy back its shares during the ordinary course of trading on a prescribed financial market (s 257B(6)). This type of buy-back must meet the same requirements regarding the 10/12 limit, notice, and cancellation of shares as an employee share scheme buy-back (s 257B(1)).

115 ASIC has discretion to waive the need for a resolution: *Corporations Act* s 257D(4).
116 *Re Village Roadshow Ltd (No 3)* (2005) 23 ACLC 10 [25]–[28].
117 *BPESAM IV M Ltd v DRA Global Ltd* (2020) 381 ALR 252.

On-market buy-backs are also regulated by the Listing Rules of licensed markets; for example, the ASX *Listing Rules* ('*LRs*'). In summary, the *LRs* require that the purchase price must not be more than five per cent above the average market price for that class of shares over the last five days on which sales in those shares were recorded.[118]

The use of the *LRs* to regulate on-market buy-backs has the advantage of greater flexibility in enforcement, but it carries with it uncertainties surrounding the status of the *LRs* and the role of the bodies such as ASX. This is discussed in Chapter 17.

Protecting interests affected by a buy-back

As with reductions of capital, the use of the buy-back provisions may bring the operation of other sections of the *Corporations Act* into play, which can protect the interests of shareholders and creditors. Section 257J lists these provisions, only some of which are mentioned here.

A failure to follow the mandatory buy-back procedures is a contravention of the requirement in s 259A that a company can only acquire shares in itself through the buy-back provisions. By virtue of s 259F, that contravention does not affect the validity of the acquisition, and the company is not guilty of an offence, but a person who is involved in the contravention (for example, a director) is liable under the civil penalty provisions in pt 9.4B. Section 79 explains what it means for a person to be involved in a contravention. This is discussed in further detail below at Section 8.55.10.

Section 259A was interpreted in *U & D Coal Ltd v Australian Kunqian International Energy Co Pty Ltd.*[119] In that case, Australian Kunqian International Energy Co Pty Ltd ('KQ') acquired shares in U & D Coal Ltd ('UDC') following an initial public offering (IPO). Subsequently, KQ issued a notice under s 737 of the *Corporations Act* alleging that the prospectus for the IPO contravened s 724 of the *Corporations Act* and that KQ was entitled to repayment of the subscription price for the shares. UDC contested the validity of the s 737 notice. Sections 724 and 737 are discussed in Chapter 9.

The parties reached an agreement under which UDC would acquire and cancel the IPO shares from KQ. It then applied to the Court for an order under s 259A permitting UDC to acquire shares in itself under the terms set out in the settlement, including provisions that required a proposed meeting of shareholders to consider extending the same buy-back terms to other shareholders who had acquired their shares under the IPO.

Sifris J held that s 259A(c) allowed a company to acquire shares in itself under a court order and there was no reason why s 259A(c) should not apply to the terms of the parties' settlement. Although there was a possibility that other parties might be treated differently from KQ (particularly the 480 minority shareholders who had also obtained their shares under the IPO), this was not a compelling reason to withhold approval of the compromise reached between UDC and KQ. In the circumstances, there was no requirement to treat everyone the same.

If the company is or becomes insolvent when the buy-back takes place, directors may be liable under the insolvent trading provision in s 588G. That section notes that entering

118 See ASX, *Listing Rules* (at 19 December 2016) rr 7.29, 7.33.
119 (2014) 32 ACLC ¶14-047.

into a buy-back agreement constitutes the incurring of a debt by the company, activating the section in situations of insolvency (s 588G(1A)). Section 588G is a civil penalty provision (see pt 9.4B).

If a company contravenes the buy-back provisions by prejudicing its ability to pay its creditors (one of the requirements in s 257A), this is deemed to affect the interests of creditors who may seek an order for injunction or damages under s 1324 (s 1324(1A)). Again, the company bears the onus of establishing that its conduct did not contravene s 257A.

A proposed buy-back of shares may involve a reduction of capital where the shares are paid for out of share capital. In that case, the effect of s 258E is that the company does not have to comply with the reduction of share capital provisions provided that the buy-back complies with ss 257A–J. Where a company wants to remove a select group of shareholders from its register, the result of a selective buy-back will be the same as a selective reduction of capital. A company has a choice as to which method it will use. The disadvantage of a buy-back is that its success depends upon the shareholders' willingness to accept the buy-back offer.

A proposed buy-back may involve a variation of class rights, which require attention to the provisions set out in ss 246B–G. Similarly, the takeover provisions and the related party provisions may also apply. In addition, a company contemplating a buy-back will need to ensure it will not be in breach of the prohibitions against market manipulation in ss 1041A–C. These prohibitions are discussed in Chapter 17.

Finally, the statutory and general law rules regarding directors' duties will be applicable in a buy-back, as emphasised in s 260E.[120]

8.55 Financial assistance transactions

8.55.05 The problems and benefits of financial assistance transactions

Where a company gives financial assistance to a person who is about to, or has already, purchased shares in the company, this is known as a 'financial assistance transaction'. These transactions raise similar concerns to buy-backs. Both types of activity can adversely affect the interests of creditors, either by producing an imbalance between a company's issued share capital and the available asset backing, or by diminishing the pool of capital available to creditors.[121]

A financial assistance transaction may have advantages for a company. In the simplest case, if a company lends money to a person to enable them to buy shares in the company and the loan is well secured and has a good rate of interest, then the company, and the creditors, can benefit.

120 For a further discussion of share buy-backs with examples, see Australian Securities and Investments Commission, *Share Buy-backs* (Regulatory Guide 110, July 2007).

121 See, eg, the report of the Greene Committee from which the statutory prohibition of financial assistance originates: Company Law Amendment Committee, *Report of the Company Law Amendment Committee* (Cmnd 2657, 1926) ('the Greene Committee').

On the other hand, financial assistance transactions can harm the interests of creditors and minority shareholders, particularly in the context of a takeover or change in control of a company. A situation which provokes the concern of regulators arises where person B borrows money from an independent source to fund a takeover of company X. Once in control of the company, B then repays the loan with funds borrowed from the company. The company has provided the funds for the purchase of its own shares. But even this scenario may not be objectionable in all cases. In its 1962 report on the reform of the companies' legislation in the United Kingdom, the Jenkins Committee argued that it would be proper if B, having gained control of company X, caused the company to validly pay a dividend, which B then used to repay the original loan. 'Such a payment [of the dividend] cannot prejudice the rights of creditors, while minority shareholders will directly benefit from it.'[122]

8.55.10 The regulation of financial assistance transactions

Historically, financial assistance transactions were prohibited unless detailed procedural requirements for shareholder approval by special resolution were satisfied, and creditors were given the opportunity to challenge the procedure. The current provisions in pt 2J.3 are more permissive and are intended to minimise difficulties for ordinary commercial transactions.[123]

In general terms, the financial assistance provisions in the *Corporations Act* follow a similar pattern to those governing reductions of share capital and buy-backs concerning the preconditions, the shareholder approval requirements, the notice and lodgement requirements, and the consequences of contravention.

Permitted financial assistance transactions

Section 260A sets out the circumstances in which a company can financially assist a person to acquire shares or units of shares in that company or its holding company. The basic requirement is that financial assistance can only be given if it does not materially prejudice the interests of the company or its shareholders, or the company's ability to pay its creditors. If that is the case, the next requirement is that the assistance must be approved by a special or a unanimous resolution of shareholders, as described below. Alternatively, it may be that financial assistance is specifically exempted from s 260A; the exemptions are also described below.

Before examining the requirements in more detail, some specific features of s 260A should be noted:

(1) The section refers to acquiring shares or 'units of shares' in the company. The term 'unit' is defined in s 9. In relation to shares, a unit means a right or interest in a share, whether legal or equitable, and includes an option to acquire such a right or interest. Thus, the scope of these sections extends beyond simple, direct legal ownership of shares. For the sake of simplicity, the following discussion

122 United Kingdom Board of Trade, *Report of the Company Law Committee* (Cmnd 1749, 1962) [175] ('the Jenkins Committee).

123 Explanatory Memorandum, Company Law Review Bill 1997 (Cth) [12.76].

refers only to an acquisition of shares, but the reader should bear in mind this extended application.

(2) An 'acquisition of shares' may occur by way of a fresh issue of shares, a transfer of shares, or by any other means (s 260A(3)).

(3) The section applies whether the financial assistance is given before or after the acquisition of the shares. In *Law Society of New South Wales v Milios*, Austin J confirmed that s 260A applies if the financial assistance comes after the completion of the acquisition of shares, provided that there is a link between the assistance and the acquisition 'which draws the transaction within the policy concerns which the section addresses'.[124]

What is financial assistance?

The *Corporations Act* does not define 'financial assistance', other than to suggest it can take the form of the payment of a dividend by a company (s 260A(2)(b)). The court will look at the commercial realities and consider the transaction as a whole before deciding whether it constitutes the giving of financial assistance as prohibited by s 260A.[125] Clearly, financial assistance could include a gift of shares by a company.[126] It could also include a loan by the company in the same circumstances.[127] The term can encompass less direct forms of assistance, such as a guarantee given by a company. For example, the financial assistance provision could cover the situation where B wishes to purchase shares in company X from C. B borrows the money from D, with company X acting as guarantor of the loan. It also covers the payment of costs related to the purchase of shares, such as stamp duty, valuation or due diligence costs.[128]

Another instance of indirect financial assistance could be the provision of security.[129] In *Heald v O'Connor*,[130] Mr Heald agreed to sell to Mr O'Connor all the shares in a particular company. To enable payment for the shares, Heald agreed to lend a sum of money to O'Connor which was to be secured by a charge over the company's assets. The company subsequently granted that security. The Court held that, by giving the security, the company had given financial assistance to O'Connor as purchaser of the shares, since without the security Heald would not have been willing to make the loan. Other examples of indirect assistance are the release by a company of an obligation or the forgiving of a debt.

In the absence of specific legislative guidance, courts have had to determine what constitutes financial assistance on the particular facts of a case. The underlying principle in this process was set out by Hoffmann J in *Charterhouse Investment Trust Ltd v Tempest Diesels Ltd*, opining that:

124 *Law Society of New South Wales v Milios* (1999) 48 NSWLR 409, 414 [25].

125 *Connective Services Pty Ltd v Slea Pty Ltd* (2019) 267 CLR 461; *Charterhouse Investment Trust Ltd v Tempest Diesels Ltd* (1985) 1 BCC 99544, 99551.

126 *Re VGM Holdings Ltd* [1942] Ch 235.

127 *Australian Securities and Investments Commission v Adler* (2002) 41 ACSR 72; *DJE Constructions Pty Ltd v Maddocks* [1982] 1 NSWLR 5.

128 *Connective Services Pty Ltd v Slea Pty Ltd* (2019) 267 CLR 461 [33].

129 *Firmin v Gray & Co Pty Ltd* [1985] 1 Qd R 160.

130 *Heald v O'Connor* [1971] 1 WLR 497.

> [T]he words [financial assistance] have no technical meaning and their frame of reference is ... the language of ordinary commerce. One must examine the commercial realities of the transaction and decide whether it can properly be described as the giving of financial assistance by the company.[131]

To assist in this determination, different approaches have emerged. These approaches have generally resolved in favour of the 'impoverishment' test which asks whether the transaction involves the conversion of the company's assets into something of lesser value; for example, where cash is converted into an unsecured loan without interest to the purchaser of the shares.[132] In 2019, in *Connective Services Pty Ltd v Slea Pty Ltd*, the High Court rejected the application of such tests to determine whether financial assistance existed, holding instead that the term should be given a broad commercial meaning. The case involved a pre-emptive rights clause in the two appellant companies' constitutions ('the Connective companies'). These clauses provided that before a shareholder could transfer their shares in the company, they had to offer them to existing shareholders in proportion to the number of shares already held by that shareholder. Slea Pty Ltd held 33.3 per cent of the shares in the Connective companies, along with two other shareholders: Millsave Holdings Pty Ltd ('Millsave') and Haron.

It was alleged that the sole director and shareholder of Slea Pty Ltd, Mr Tsialtas, had entered into an agreement to sell Slea's shares in the Connective companies to Minerva Financial Group Pty Ltd. In response to this, the Connective companies commenced legal proceedings against Slea Pty Ltd, seeking to compel Slea Pty Ltd to offer its shares to the other shareholders under the pre-emptive clauses. Slea Pty Ltd countered these proceedings by seeking an injunction restraining the legal action on the basis that they constituted financial assistance by the Connective companies.

The High Court considered that the three elements necessary to establish a contravention of s 260A(1) of the *Corporations Act* are:

- financial assistance given by the company
- to acquire shares or units of shares in the company, and
- which materially prejudices the interests of the company or its shareholders or its ability to pay its creditors.

The High Court held that financial assistance did not need to involve the diminution or depletion of assets; rather, 'any action by the company can be financial assistance if it eases the financial burden that would be involved in the process of acquisition or if it improves the person's "net balance of financial advantage" in relation to the acquisition'.[133]

---

131 (1985) 1 BCC 99544, 99546 cited in *Dempster v National Companies and Securities Commission* (1993) 9 WAR 215; *Milburn v Pivot Ltd* (1997) 78 FCR 472; *Tallglen Pty Ltd v Optus Communications Pty Ltd* (1998) 16 ACLC 1526, 1530; *Wambo Mining Corporation Pty Ltd v Wall Street (Holding) Pty Ltd* (1998) 16 ACLC 1601, 1607; *Re HIH Insurance Ltd and HIH Casualty and General Insurance Ltd; Australian Securities and Investments Commission v Adler* (2002) 41 ACSR 72 [342]; *Kinarra Pty Ltd v On Q Group Ltd* (2008) 26 ACLC 193 [26].

132 *Australian Securities and Investments Commission v Adler* (2002) 41 ACSR 72 [344] (Santow J).

133 *Connective Services Pty Ltd v Slea Pty Ltd* (2019) 267 CLR 461 [22] quoting *Victor Battery Co Ltd v Curry's Ltd* [1946] Ch 242.

On the facts, the action by the Connective companies in commencing and funding the legal proceedings against Slea Pty Ltd was financial assistance, as it eased the financial burden on the other shareholders in relation to acquiring the shares. The pre-emptive rights proceedings would normally have been brought by Millsave and Haron in their own right.[134]

An additional issue that arises with s 260A is whether the payment of a dividend amounts to financial assistance. While s 260A(2)(b) states expressly that financial assistance may take the form of paying a dividend, payment of a dividend may be quite proper, as was the case in *Re Wellington Publishing Co Ltd*.[135] Wellington acquired the entire share capital of another company that possessed large undistributed profits. It was then proposed that those reserves should be used to declare a dividend which would be applied by Wellington to pay for the shares it had acquired. In the New Zealand Supreme Court, Quilliam J held that no financial assistance had been given:

> The expression 'financial assistance' is an indefinite one and it is beyond normal experience to regard that expression as applying to the payment of a dividend. The payment of a dividend is part of the normal functions of a company, and indeed, in the final analysis, is probably as much the reason for the company's existence as is the earning of profits the reason for an individual trader being in business. To be more precise, a dividend must be regarded as first and foremost a return on investment. In the customary usage of words the payment by a company of a dividend to a shareholder is not to be regarded as giving financial assistance to that shareholder.[136]

The capital maintenance principle is not breached by the proper determination or declaration and payment of dividends where the company's assets exceed its liabilities.[137] This same principle is at stake in ss 260A–C.

Another issue with the notion of financial assistance is whether the transaction in question needs to assist the person to acquire shares. In *Burton v Palmer*, Mahoney JA held that 'the mere agreement of the company to pay its present indebtedness' does not amount to financial assistance.[138] He considered that term 'assistance' in this context meant 'the furnishing of something which is needed or, at the least which is wanted, in order that the transaction be carried out. ... [The term] has a meaning which is closer to need or want; it does not mean something which is merely co-operation'.[139] However, in *Independent Steels Pty Ltd v Ryan*, Fullagar J suggested that the words 'need or want' are not to be interpreted too narrowly.[140] His Honour stated that financial assistance might occur even in the case where 'the purchaser did not mind whether or not it was given the assistance'.[141]

134 *Connective Services Pty Ltd v Slea Pty Ltd* (2019) 267 CLR 461 [37] ('*Connective Services*').

135 [1973] 1 NZLR 133.

136 Ibid 136. Cited with approval in *Rossfield Group Operations Pty Ltd v Austral Group Ltd* [1981] Qd R 279, 286 (Connolly J).

137 See Section 8.30.05.

138 *Burton v Palmer* (1980) 2 NSWLR 878, 885 [36].

139 Ibid [39].

140 *Independent Steels Pty Ltd v Ryan* (1989) 15 ACLR 518, 524–5.

141 Ibid 525.

Finally, in order to establish that financial assistance is caught by s 260A, it is necessary to show that the assistance is linked to the acquisition of shares.[142] Although the section does not require the company to have knowledge that the financial assistance is being used to aid the acquisition of shares, this issue can still arise in litigation. An example is found in the English case of *Belmont Finance Corporation v Williams Furniture Ltd (No 2)*.[143] The facts were a complex version of a relatively simple situation: B, although lacking the necessary funds, wished to purchase shares in A Ltd as part of an agreed takeover. It was arranged that A Ltd would purchase certain assets from B. After the price had been paid for the assets, B then made the takeover by purchasing shares in A Ltd. The question for the Court was whether the purpose of the asset purchase was really to provide B with the funds necessary to acquire the shares in A Ltd.

Buckley LJ identified three factors relevant to deciding what the purpose of the asset purchase was: whether the asset purchase was in the company's commercial interests; whether the price paid for the assets by A Ltd was fair; and whether the sole or a part purpose of the purchase was to provide funds for the share acquisition. His Honour noted that the legislation would not be breached merely because an asset purchase was followed by an acquisition of shares. In Australia, under s 260A, these issues would be assessed in determining whether the asset purchase overcomes the criterion of material prejudice.

Material prejudice

The preceding comment reminds us that characterising a transaction as financial assistance is only half the task. Section 260A(1)(a) also requires that the financial assistance does not involve material prejudice to the interests of shareholders, the company, or the company's capacity to pay its creditors. What constitutes material prejudice is a question of fact to be answered in each case. The onus is on the company to show that the financial assistance does not materially prejudice the company, its shareholders, and its creditors.[144]

An example of a transaction where material prejudice was established is *Australian Securities and Investments Commission v Adler*.[145] In that case, Mr Adler was a director of HIH, a listed insurance company. Adler caused HIHC, a subsidiary of HIH, to make an unsecured loan of $10 million to a company, PEE, which he controlled as trustee under a trust ('AEUT') for HIH. The loan was made with the knowledge of only Mr Williams and Mr Fodera, the Chief Executive Officer and the Chief Financial Officer of HIH respectively, and was in breach of the company's investment guidelines. Part of the loan funds were used to purchase HIH shares with the purpose of signalling Adler's confidence in the company and stabilising its falling share price.

Santow J held as follows:

> HIHC suffered material prejudice as a result of its financial assistance, so contravening s 260A of the Corporations Act. It did so by exchanging cash for either

142 Section 260A(1).

143 *Belmont Finance Corporation v Williams Furniture Ltd (No 2)* [1980] 1 All ER 393.

144 *Kinarra Pty Ltd v On Q Group Ltd* (2008) 26 ACLC 193.

145 *Australian Securities and Investments Commission v Adler* (2002) 41 ACSR 72. This case is discussed further in Chapter 13 at Section 13.25.10.

> unsecured indebtedness owed to it, or alternatively in the first instance equitable rights by way of resulting or other trust in respect of the HIH shares. ... Such rights against PEE were from the start of materially lesser value than the cash handed over. This is because such equitable rights would be likely to be contentious and to require expensive litigation to enforce in Court. Thereafter material prejudice also resulted from the other elements of the transaction, that is, the lack of safeguards in, and disadvantageous terms of, the AEUT trust documentation and the circumstances which, from its inception, rendered the investment in HIH shares inherently likely to give rise to the loss that in fact occurred. These included Mr Adler's intention, not to make a quick profit, but to support the HIH share price. A loss was inherently likely from the inception, and did in fact eventuate ...[146]

This analysis looks at the whole of the transaction and the commercial realities to see whether it materially prejudices the interests of the company, shareholders or creditors. It follows the approach adopted by Hoffmann J in *Charterhouse Investment Trust Ltd v Tempest Diesels Ltd* that it is:

> necessary to look at all interlocking elements in a commercial transaction as a whole, and to determine where the net balance of financial advantage lay.[147]

However, there are some uncertainties about the interpretation of s 260A. As Young J has observed, there are 'considerable problems in the s 260A(1) definition of what are the interests of the company or its shareholders which are not to be materially prejudiced'.[148] While the example given in the Explanatory Memorandum (where a company lends money to another company that is bordering on insolvency) is relatively clear, other situations are harder to determine. The following questions, among others, are not answered by the section:

- The section treats the interests of the company and its shareholders as being aligned. What happens where this is not the case? The section does not refer to the interests of the shareholders 'as a whole', an expression used elsewhere in the *Corporations Act* (for example, s 232). Does this mean that material prejudice to any member will suffice?
- The section does not indicate the timeframe within which the prejudice is to be assessed; for example, will the risk of material prejudice to shareholders' interests in the short term satisfy the test, even where there are good prospects for long-term improvements in their position?
- It is not clear, despite the examples given in the Explanatory Memorandum, that prejudice is to be determined solely in financial terms. Financial assistance transactions may be used to alter the balance of control in a company, thereby prejudicing the corporate governance interests of existing shareholders.

146 Ibid 162 [355].
147 *Charterhouse Investment Trust Ltd v Tempest Diesels Ltd* (1985) 1 BCC 99544, 99547.
148 *Re Bidvest Australia Ltd* (1998) 16 ACLC 1553, 1554.

Some of these questions were answered by the High Court in *Connective Services* (discussed above). It noted the purpose of the section is to be protective, particularly to minority shareholders, and that the reference to the interests of shareholders 'must mean both the shareholders collectively and each shareholder individually'.[149]

One consequence of the indeterminate nature of material prejudice is that it might lead directors to use the shareholder approval mechanism out of a sense of caution. This is underlined by the fact that, where an application for an injunction or damages is sought under s 1324 in relation to a contravention of s 260A(1)(a), the court must assume that the conduct constitutes a contravention unless the company or person proves otherwise (s 1324(1B)).

If the financial assistance does entail material prejudice, then it will require shareholder approval. The approval can be given in one of two ways: either by a special resolution with no votes being cast in favour by the person (or their associates) who is acquiring the shares; or by a resolution agreed to by all ordinary shareholders (that is, unanimous approval) (s 260B(1)). If a special resolution is passed, a copy must be lodged with ASIC within 14 days. For an example of the disclosures that are required to be given to shareholders under s 260B, see *Milburn v Pivot Ltd.*[150] In that case, the documentation sent to shareholders who approved the transaction under s 260B was 'evasive, inadequate and incomplete'.[151]

Exempted transactions

A number of transactions are exempted from the operation of s 260A and are listed in s 260C. They cover situations that are commercially unobjectionable and do not give rise to the concerns about financial assistance identified above. Section 260C specifies that to be exempted the assistance must be given in the ordinary course of commercial dealing. The exclusions in s 260C are as follows:

(1) Acquisition or creation by a company of a lien on its partly paid shares for an amount payable to the company on those shares (sub-s (1)(a)): it is common for a constitution to give it a right of lien over partly paid shares for any outstanding calls on those shares and for other moneys owing to the company. The effect is to make the member's shares a security for the amounts owed.

(2) Agreement between a company and subscriber for payment of shares by instalments (sub-s (1)(b)): this exempts such an agreement provided, once again, that it is made in the ordinary course of commercial dealing.

(3) Provision of finance as company's ordinary business (sub-s (2)): this exclusion is aimed at companies, such as banks and finance companies, whose business includes 'providing finance'. This is defined in s 9 as lending money, giving guarantees, providing security for loans made by someone else, or drawing, accepting, indorsing, negotiating or discounting bills of exchange, cheques,

149 *Connective Services Pty Ltd v Slea Pty Ltd* (2019) 267 CLR 461 [25].
150 *Milburn v Pivot Ltd* (1997) 78 FCR 472.
151 Ibid 521.

payment orders or promissory notes so that someone else can obtain funds. The financial assistance must be given in the ordinary course of that business and be on ordinary commercial terms. A loan made by a finance company for the direct purpose of financing the purchase of its shares would most likely fall outside this exclusion.[152] In *Ex parte D*, Pidgeon J indicated that the type of transaction that would fall within this exemption would be the case of a customer who is given a loan by a bank to enable him to increase his share portfolio when the bank knows that the customer may well acquire shares in the bank: 'the advance would be on a small scale and the purpose of acquiring shares is a similar purpose to which the bank normally lends money'.[153] His Honour also noted that the onus is on the defendant to establish that the exemption applies.

(4) Guarantee or security provided by a subsidiary company of a borrower (sub-s (3)): this exclusion will apply where a company is under a liability to repay money it has received in response to a public invitation or offer for debentures. It is common practice for the liability of the borrowing company to be guaranteed by one of its subsidiary companies, or for the subsidiary to guarantee the repayment of the debt. This excludes the guarantee or security from the financial assistance rules, provided that the guarantee or security is given in the ordinary course of commercial dealing.

(5) Financial assistance given under an employee share scheme (sub-s (4)): this requires that financial assistance be approved by ordinary resolution at a general meeting of the company. If the company is a subsidiary of another domestic company, then the parent company must also pass a resolution. An employee share scheme is defined in s 9 (see the discussion of employee share scheme buy-backs above at Section 8.50.10).

(6) Reductions of share capital and buy-backs (sub-s (5)(a)): this excludes reductions of share capital carried out under pt 2J.1 div 1 from the financial assistance rules. In *Re Bidvest Australia Ltd*, Young J expressed his inclination towards the view that this exemption applies only to a discrete reduction of capital, and not to a reduction that is caught up in a scheme of arrangement.[154] Similarly, sub-s (5)(b) excludes share buy-backs carried out in accordance with pt 2J.1 div 2.

(7) Purchase by a company of its shares pursuant to a court order (sub-s (5)(c)): this exclusion is a necessary adjunct to other provisions; for example, ss 232–5, giving the court power to make orders in cases of oppression or unfair discrimination or prejudice against a member.

(8) Discharge of an ordinary company liability (sub-s (5)(d)): this excludes cases where a company discharges an existing liability on ordinary commercial terms that was incurred as a result of a transaction entered on ordinary commercial terms.

152 *Steen v Law* [1964] AC 287.

153 *Ex parte D* (1995) 13 ACLC 1348, 1360.

154 *Re Bidvest Australia Ltd* (1998) 16 ACLC 1553, 1554. Schemes of arrangement are discussed in Chapter 15.

Consequences for contravening s 260A

The consequences for contravening s 260A follow the same pattern as for contraventions of the reduction of capital and the buy-back provisions. This includes the application of directors' duties in s 260E.

A company can contravene s 260A by giving financial assistance that materially prejudices the interests of shareholders or its ability to pay its creditors, or by failing to obtain the approval of shareholders. Pursuant to s 260D, where there is a contravention, the financial assistance transaction, and any transaction or contract that is connected with it, is still valid and the company is not guilty of an offence. However, any person who is involved in the contravention (as defined in s 79) is liable under the civil penalty provisions in pt 9.4B (s 260A(2)). While the requirements set out in s 260A are not crucial to the validity of the transaction, they are relevant in determining liability of persons for contraventions of the financial assistance provisions. In *Australian Securities and Investments Commission v Adler*, Williams and Adler were found to be involved in the contravention of s 260A. Santow J applied the test of the High Court in *Yorke v Lucas*,[155] finding that Williams and Adler (but not Fodera) had intentionally participated in the contravention because they each had the necessary knowledge of the essential facts.[156]

A contravention (or threatened contravention) of s 260A may be used to support an application for an injunction or damages under s 1324. The defendant will bear the onus of establishing that there has not been a contravention.

Directors may be liable under s 588G if the debt which is incurred by the financial assistance agreement is entered into when the company is insolvent or causes the company to become insolvent.[157]

8.60 Summary

This chapter examined the law relating to corporate finance. We explored the nature of shares and the types of shares issued by companies. We considered the nature of debt finance used by companies and the types of instruments and obligations it creates. We discussed share capital transactions including dividends, reduction of capital, share buy-backs and financial assistance transactions.

155 *Yorke v Lucas* (1985) 158 CLR 661.

156 *Australian Securities and Investments Commission v Adler* (2002) 41 ACSR 72, [357]–[359].

157 For a critique and commentary on the financial assistance provisions, see K Wellington, 'Regulating Financial Assistance: An Obsolete Regime' (2008) 26(1) *Company and Securities Law Journal* 7; Y-Y Cho and V Kishore, 'The "material prejudice" Test and the Financial Assistance Prohibition' (2004) 78(11) *Australian Law Journal* 194; P Cornwell, 'Material Prejudice and Financial Assistance: The Financier's Viewpoint' (2004) 78 *Australian Law Journal* 746.

CHAPTER

9

CORPORATE FUNDRAISING

9.05 Introduction

There are three ways of becoming a shareholder: by subscribing to a new issue of shares in a company; by purchasing shares from an existing shareholder; or by transmission of ownership in shares due to the operation of law (for example, where shares are transferred to the beneficiary under a will). In this chapter, we focus on the first method: the issuing of shares and securities as a means of fundraising, commonly referred to as 'raising capital' or 'equity raising'. The term 'subscription' describes the relationship where a company issues shares directly to a shareholder. The legal relationship between the company that issues and the shareholder who subscribes for new shares can be analysed using the contractual rules of offer and acceptance.

A company's power to issue shares is provided by s 124(1)(a) of the *Corporations Act*. This power is usually exercised by the directors. The power to issue shares is subject to the fiduciary duties governing directors. Many of the significant cases on directors' duties arise from the exercise of a power to issue shares.[1]

The corporate constitution can impose limitations on the issue of new shares. For example, the replaceable rule in s 254D requires that all unissued shares in a proprietary company should, before being issued, be offered to existing members pro rata according to their existing shareholdings. This is to ensure that the power of existing members is not diluted by a fresh issue of shares.

However, our primary focus in this chapter is the issue of securities by public companies. Generally speaking, only public companies are permitted to raise capital by issuing securities to a broad cross-section of the public.[2] This is regulated by ch 6D of the *Corporations Act*.

9.10 Raising share capital under ch 6D

9.10.05 Introduction

Underpinning the regulation of companies is a significant policy that requires them to disclose certain types of information about their business and financial structure to the public. This disclosure enables investors and others who deal with the company to protect their interests and promotes the efficient allocation of resources on the basis of adequate and relevant information.

This chapter addresses one of the key legislative expressions of that policy: the fundraising provisions in ch 6D of the *Corporations Act*.[3] The aim of the fundraising provisions is to ensure investors are provided with sufficient information via the publication of a prospectus or other disclosure document that enables them to make informed decisions regarding their initial investment in a company. Australian companies' legislation inherited this philosophy of mandatory prospectus disclosure from the United Kingdom. The 1895 report of the Davey Committee in the United Kingdom[4] described the purpose and scope of this policy as follows:

> It may be a counsel of perfection and impossible of attainment to say that a prospectus shall disclose everything which could reasonably influence the

1 See, eg, *Harlowe's Nominees Pty Ltd v Woodside (Lakes Entrance) Oil Co NL* (1968) 121 CLR 483; *Hogg v Cramphorn Ltd* [1967] Ch 254; *Howard Smith Ltd v Ampol Petroleum Ltd* [1974] AC 821.

2 Proprietary companies are permitted to raise capital by making offers to a broad cross-section of the public under the equity crowdfunding regime in pt 6D.3A of the *Corporations Act*. This is discussed below at Section 9.75ff.

3 Other instances of this policy can be found in the takeover provisions of the *Corporations Act* discussed in Chapter 19.

4 Board of Trade, United Kingdom, *Report of the Departmental Committee Appointed by the Board of Trade to Inquire What Amendments Are Necessary in the Acts Relating to Stock Companies Incorporated with Limited Liability under the Companies Acts, 1862 to 1890* (Command Paper 7779, 1895).

> mind of an investor of average prudence. But this ... is the ideal to be aimed at. ... [I]f people will not avail themselves of the means of information, or even use the information when given, it is not the law which is in fault.[5]

The arguments for and against mandatory disclosure by companies in the financial markets are discussed at Section 17.10.05. In relation to fundraising, two arguments are used to justify mandatory disclosure requirements. The 'investor protection' argument is that disclosure is necessary to protect investors from fraudulent corporate practices, and from making uninformed investment decisions. By contrast, the 'investor confidence' argument is that mandatory disclosure is necessary to ensure investors, particularly individual and unsophisticated investors, retain confidence in the financial markets. A drop in confidence can lead to 'capital flight' where investors find alternative investment options to those offered in financial markets.

Putting these two claims together, mandatory disclosure has three benefits:

- It acts as a 'disinfectant'.[6] By requiring the publication of information, the legislation reduces the possibility that companies will deliberately set out to mislead investors.
- It aims to ensure that investment decisions are efficient. This aspiration is premised on the belief that, when given the necessary information, investors are more likely to direct their resources towards the most productive use.
- It aims to provide a level playing field by ensuring all investors begin from the same information base.

Recently, it has been recognised that disclosure may be a necessary but not sufficient tool for investor protection, particularly for retail investors,[7] and that disclosure of relevant information does not necessarily translate to good decision-making.[8]

9.10.10 Terminology and context

In general terms, 'fundraising' involves a company seeking capital by way of entering into a direct relationship with investors through offering them the opportunity to buy (subscribe for) the company's securities. This is called a 'primary offering of securities'.

The concept of 'securities' is broader than 'shares', although shares fall within this definition. The definition of the word 'securities' for the purposes of ch 6D is discussed

5 Quoted in PL Cottrell, *Industrial Finance 1830–1914: The Finance and Organization of the English Manufacturing Industry* (Routledge, 1980) 69.

6 This is derived from the famous quote attributed to Brandeis J: 'Sunlight is said to be the best of disinfectants; electric light the most efficient policeman' in LD Brandeis, *Other People's Money, and How the Bankers Use It* (FA Stokes, 1914) 92.

7 For an explanation of this term, see Sections 18.05.05 and 18.05.10.

8 Australian Securities and Investments Commission and Dutch Authority for the Financial Markets, *Disclosure: Why it Shouldn't be the Default* (Report 632, October 2019). See also P Tapley and A Godwin, 'Disclosure (Dis)Content: Regulating Disclosure in Prospectuses and Product Disclosure Statements' (2021) 38(5) *Company & Securities Law Journal* 315. Tapley and Godwin argue (at 315) that the reason for the limited correlation between disclosure and informed decision-making include variations in financial literacy levels among investors and the inherent complexity of decisions about financial products. See the discussion about the financial literacy of retail investors at Section 18.05.05.

below at Section 9.20. 'Securities' will generally be used in preference to 'shares' for the remainder of this chapter.

As stated above, generally speaking, only public companies are permitted to raise share capital under ch 6D. Proprietary companies[9] are prohibited from engaging in activity that may require disclosure to investors under ch 6D, except for an offer to existing shareholders or to employees of the company or its subsidiary or an equity crowdfunding (ECF) offer (s 113(3)). Equity crowdfunding is discussed below at Section 9.75ff. Proprietary companies must have no more than 50 non-employee shareholders (s 113(1)) and this often acts as an impediment to large-scale fundraising.[10] Securities must not be offered in a body that has not been formed or does not exist if the offer would need disclosure to investors under ch 6D (s 726). Therefore, a public company must be formed prior to an offer of securities.

Fundraising regulated by ch 6D of the *Corporations Act* often takes place on a financial market, also known as a stock market or securities exchange, such as the ASX. The *Corporations Act* uses the term 'licensed financial market', as these markets often trade financial instruments not included in the definition of securities, such as derivatives. This terminology is explained in more detail in Chapter 17. Where a disclosure document states or implies that securities are to be listed on a financial market, the issue or transfer of those securities will be void if the company fails to quote the securities on the relevant market within the requisite time period (s 723(3)(c)).[11]

There are many forms of primary offers of securities; for example, in an Initial Public Offering (IPO) the securities offered are new securities, which are not yet listed. Therefore, the securities of the company are offered to the public for the first time. Other primary offers may involve the issue of securities of a class that are already traded on a stock market; for example, rights issues.[12]

There are two characteristics of IPOs that are relevant to the way IPOs are regulated. First, the issuing body offers its securities for subscription to investors outside of the operation of established markets. This means that investors are directly exposed to the risk associated with these securities before those securities are subject to pricing in the stock market. Second, these securities are offered to investors in circumstances where the issuer has the relevant information about the securities and the investor is dependent on the issuer to disclose that information; that is, there are asymmetries of information between the issuer and the investors.

These two characteristics have formed the basis of a specialised regulatory regime for capital raising. The effect of this regime is that public companies can only offer their securities directly to investors where the offer to subscribe to those securities is attached to or accompanied by a disclosure document (s 727(2)); that is, a document in which the issuing company is required to disclose material information to investors. An example of such a disclosure document is a 'prospectus'.

9 The differences between public and proprietary companies are discussed at Section 4.35.

10 For a discussion of the interaction between s 113 and ch 6D, see *Re Capilano Honey Ltd* (2018) 131 ACSR 9.

11 *Re G8 Communications Ltd* (2016) 112 ACSR 22.

12 See *Corporations Act* s 9A.

A prospectus is the most common type of disclosure document that must be provided to investors prior to fundraising under ch 6D. However, ch 6D pt 6D.2 div 3 allows other types of disclosure documents to be prepared, which are discussed below at Section 9.30. For ease of reference, the term 'disclosure document' will be used throughout this section to describe a general disclosure document required by ch 6D; whereas a reference to 'prospectus' generally refers to the meaning of that word in the *Corporations* Act.[13]

How do people use disclosure documents?

The Australian Securities and Investments Commission (ASIC) conducted a study of the use of prospectuses in IPOs in 2017. The study found that institutional investors valued the prospectus because it was the main source of information on an IPO, and it is a regulated document which means that directors and others involved in the offer potentially have liability. These investors felt this liability added weight to the credibility and reliability of the document.[14] Conversely, retail investors gleaned information from a variety of sources such as financial intermediaries (for example, brokers) and social media.[15] ASIC stated:

> In general, retail investors valued information that they perceived to be independent and easy to understand, and that had been prepared by someone they perceived as having a high level of expertise. ... The prospectus was seen as a key source of information, although many retail investors said the document was hard to read and could not be relied on to tell the whole truth about an IPO (given that it was perceived to be a marketing document).[16]

9.10.15 When must a disclosure document be issued by a company seeking to raise share capital?

Previously, the test to determine if a disclosure document was required was whether the issue of securities was an offer to the public or to a section of the public. Now, there is a general prohibition on making an offer for securities unless it is accompanied by a relevant disclosure document. For example, in relation to IPOs, ch 6D states the rule in s 706: an offer of securities for issue needs disclosure to investors, with exemptions allowed in ss 708 and 708AA.

Overview of the disclosure requirements in ch 6D

The fundraising provisions in the *Corporations Act* are contained in ch 6D. The main features of these provisions are as follows:

(1) *Detailed regulation of the circumstances in which a disclosure document must be lodged with ASIC.* Unless an offer for securities is excluded, a disclosure document must

13 See, eg, *Corporations Act* s 710.

14 Australian Securities and Investments Commission, *Investors in Initial Public Offerings* (Report 540, August 2017) [6].

15 Ibid [12].

16 Ibid [12]–[13].

be lodged with ASIC (s 718(1)). This makes the document available to ASIC and the general public. ASIC will not pre-vet the document, but may use its power under s 739 to issue a stop order so that no securities are allotted or issued by the company.

(2) *Broadly worded, market-oriented standards governing the contents of a disclosure document.* Previously, the provisions required a detailed list of matters for inclusion in a disclosure document. Now, there is a requirement under s 710 that the disclosure document (in this provision called a prospectus) contains all such information as investors and their professional advisers would reasonably require for the purpose of making an informed assessment of the particular investment offered. This is accompanied by an obligation to supplement the disclosure document with material developments occurring during its currency and by a more extensive liability regime applying to misstatements in, or omissions from, a disclosure document.

(3) *Abolition of pre-vetting of disclosure documents by ASIC, and an increased responsibility by those who frame the disclosure document.* The model of regulation has changed from a paternalistic prior intervention by ASIC to a liability model, where the issuers of the disclosure document are criminally or civilly liable to the investor who suffers damage as a result of relying upon false information contained in the disclosure document.

9.15 The basic framework of ch 6D

The basic disclosure requirements are set out in ss 706 and 707.

Section 706 is concerned with issue offers (primary trading). It states that disclosure to investors is required unless s 708 or 708AA says otherwise. There is a policy presumption in favour of formal disclosure for an issue of securities.

Section 707 is concerned with sale offers: an offer of securities for sale by an existing holder (secondary trading). It states that disclosure is required in certain situations in ss 707(2), (3) or (5). Each of these situations applies unless s 708 says otherwise. This is a policy presumption against formal disclosure for a sale of securities.[17]

If an offer of securities needs disclosure to investors, s 709 states a prospectus must be prepared unless a different type of disclosure document—for example, an offer information statement—is permitted to be used (see s 709(4)). Section 721 imposes a requirement that the offer be made in or accompanied by a prospectus or other disclosure document as appropriate.

Section 9 defines the term ‘disclosure document’ for an offer of securities to mean a prospectus, a profile statement, or an offer information statement. These terms are explained below. Each of these documents is required to be lodged with ASIC. As defined in s 9, a disclosure document does not qualify as a prospectus, profile statement or offer information statement unless it is lodged with ASIC.

17 See Australian Securities and Investments Commission, *Disclosure for on-sale of securities and other financial products* (Regulatory Guide 173, March 2016).

Section 727(1) states that a person must not make an offer of securities or distribute an application form for an offer of securities, that needs disclosure to investors, unless a disclosure document for the offer has been lodged with ASIC. In *Australian Securities and Investments Commission v ActiveSuper Pty Ltd (in liq)*[18] ('*ActiveSuper*'), White J identified three elements necessary to establish a contravention of s 727:

> ... first, the principal made, or distributed, an application form for an offer of securities, secondly, the offer needed disclosure to investors under Pt 6D.2 and, thirdly, a disclosure document for the offer had not been lodged with ASIC.[19]

In *ActiveSuper*, numerous Australian investors with relatively modest amounts of superannuation were induced to use their superannuation funds for investment in property in the United States and in companies incorporated in the British Virgin Islands. 'Most of the invested moneys were not used for the purposes contemplated by the investors and were substantially, if not wholly, lost'.[20] The Court found that the offer engaged the requirements of ch 6D and the defendants had failed to give a disclosure document to the investors or lodge it with ASIC, resulting in a breach of ss 726 and 727.

Significant consequences may flow when offers are made without lodging the requisite disclosure document. For example, the securities purchase may be voidable, the directors of the offeror may be disqualified, and the offerees may have a claim in damages.[21]

9.15.05 Which offers will require a disclosure document to be lodged with ASIC?

The answer to the question of which offers need a disclosure document to be lodged with ASIC is found by going through a series of steps:

(1) Analyse the term 'offer of securities' as used in ss 706, 721 and 727.
(2) Decide whether the offer needs disclosure or is excluded under s 708.
(3) Decide whether a prospectus must be prepared or a shorter document may be used; for example, a short-form prospectus, profile statement or offer information statement.

We now address each of these steps in more detail.

9.20 Step 1: 'Offer of securities'

Section 700 defines the word 'securities'. This section states that, in ch 6D, 'security' has the same meaning as it has in ch 7, so one must look to the definition in ss 92(4) and (5)

18 *Australian Securities and Investments Commission v Activesuper Pty Ltd (in liq)* (2015) 235 FCR 181.

19 (2015) 235 FCR 181 [254]. These elements of White J's reasoning are set out in *Gore v Australian Securities and Investments Commission* (2017) 249 FCR 167, [133] (Rares J) ('*Gore*'). Note that *Gore* was overruled on other grounds in *Australian Securities and Investments Commission v Whitebox Trading Pty Ltd* (2017) 251 FCR 448.

20 *Australian Securities and Investments Commission v Activesuper Pty Ltd* (in liq) (2015) 235 FCR 181, 190.

21 *Australian Securities and Investments Commission v Astra Resources Ltd (No 2)* (2016) 113 ACSR 162.

which defines securities for ch 7 (except for paragraphs (e) and (f) of s 92(5)).[22] The relevant provisions of s 92(5) are as follows:

> **(a)** a share in a body; or
> **(b)** a debenture of a body; or
> **(c)** a legal or equitable right or interest in a security covered by paragraph (a) or (b); or
> **(d)** an option to acquire, by way of issue, a security covered by paragraph (a) (b) or (c); or
> ...[23]

At the time of writing, the general definition of 'offer a security' in s 9 does not cover securities offered under ch 6D.[24] Therefore, general contract law on offers and invitations to treat applies with some adaptation.[25]

9.25 Step 2: Offers that do not need disclosure

To reiterate, s 706 states that an offer for securities for issue needs disclosure unless ss 708 or 708AA applies. Section 708AA is discussed below at Section 9.25.35. There are some offers for securities for sale that need disclosure, but at this stage the focus is on the issue of shares for subscription (primary issues), therefore s 708 applies. The heading of s 708 states 'Offers that do not need disclosure'.

9.25.05 Small-scale offerings

This exemption is available under s 708(1) when three conditions are satisfied:

- the offers are personal offers for issue or sale of a body's securities
- none of the offers result in a breach of the 20 investors ceiling
- none of the offers result in a breach of the $2 million ceiling.

The rationale of this exemption is that it assists small–medium enterprises (SMEs) who wish to raise funds by issuing shares but do not have access to a broad base of public investors. The exemption was intended to cover SME fundraising by allowing SMEs access to a certain number of investors but not requiring them to bear the costs of preparing and publishing a disclosure document. The exemption is based on a policy assumption about the costs involved in producing a disclosure document relative to the small number of potential future investors who might take up the offer.

To comprehend the scope of this exemption, three further concepts must be considered: personal offers, 20 investors ceiling, and sophisticated investors.

22 Paragraphs (e) and (f) are excluded from the definition of securities in ch 6D due to the wording of s 700 which indicates that those subsections are not included in the ch 6D definition.

23 In this chapter, we focus on the financial products referred to in the relevant provisions of s 92(5). Note that s 700 also excludes certain interests in simple corporate bonds from the definition of securities.

24 This is due to the combination of this definition and s 764A, which creates a legislative gap.

25 *Australian Securities and Investments Commission v Australian Investors Forum Pty Ltd (No 2)* (2005) 53 ACSR 305 [97] (Palmer J).

9.25.10 Personal offers

A 'personal offer' is defined by s 708(2) as one that:

(a) may only be accepted by the person to whom it is made; and

(b) is made to a person who is likely to be interested in the offer, having regard to:

  (i) previous contact between the person making the offer and that person; or

  (ii) some professional or other connection between the person making the offer and that person; or

  (iii) statements or actions by that person that indicate that they are interested in offers of that kind.

The concept underlying sub-para (b) is that there must be some pre-existing basis for the offer to be made to the offeree. Then, it does not matter how many offers are made, as long as no more than 20 applications are accepted (and the $2 million ceiling is not breached).

9.25.15 Twenty investors ceiling

The 20 investors ceiling is breached if the offer results in securities in the body being issued to more than 20 people in any 12-month period (s 708(3)(a)) or if more than $2 million is raised from investors (s 708(3)(b)).[26]

Section 727 will be breached if a person who has relied on the small-scale offerings exemption offers to issue or transfer securities without disclosure to investors where the issue or transfer would result in a breach of the 20 investors ceiling or the $2 million ceiling (s 727(4)). It is also a breach to advertise an offer of securities which relies on the small-scale offerings exemption (s 734(1)).

9.25.20 Sophisticated investors

A sophisticated investor may be described as a person who is well-advised or informed and therefore does not need the information contained in the disclosure document as they are able to assess for themselves the benefit of the investment. The obligation to give disclosure to sophisticated investors is exempted in the following circumstances:

(1) Section 708(8)(a): an offer of securities for issue or sale does not need disclosure if the minimum amount payable for the securities on acceptance of the offer is at least $500,000.

(2) Section 708(8)(c): an offer of securities for issue or sale does not need disclosure if it 'appears' from a certificate, given by a qualified accountant no more than six months before the offer is made, that the offeree has net assets of at least $2.5 million or a gross income for each of the last two financial years of at least $250,000 a year (as stated in reg 6D.2.03). The asset and income criteria are alternatives.

26 *Australian Securities and Investments Commission v Pegasus Leveraged Options Group Pty Ltd* (2002) 41 ACSR 561.

9.25.25 Offers made through an Australian Financial Services Licensee

Section 708(10) states that an offer of securities for issue or sale does not need disclosure where the offer is made through a financial services licensee. The licensee must be satisfied on reasonable grounds that the person to whom the offer is made has previous experience in investing in securities. The previous experience must allow the investor to assess the merits of the offer, the value of the securities, the risks of the investment, their own information needs and the adequacy of the information given by the person making the offer. The licensee is required to provide a written statement of their reasons for being satisfied as to those matters before or at the time when the offer is made.

The written statement must be directed to the investor. The person making the offer will need to obtain and rely on it to be sure the exemption is available. It is not clear whether a written statement applying to securities generally, or to a class of securities, would satisfy the requirement for the exemption. However, the statement addresses the investor's experience—rather than anything particular to the offer—so a general statement may suffice. The investor must sign a written acknowledgement before or at the time when the offer is made, stating that the licensee has not given them a disclosure document in relation to the offer (s 708(10)(d)).

In *Australian Securities and Investments Commission v Maxwell*,[27] Brereton J held that the licensee's satisfaction on reasonable grounds of the matters in the exemption is a condition of the availability of the exemption and requires the licensee to significantly investigate the experience of the investor to form the relevant opinion. Similarly, Barrett J in *Australian Securities and Investments Commission v Elm Financial Services Pty Ltd*[28] commented that proof of the matters stated in s 708(10)(b) must be approached diligently and carefully. His Honour stated that the 'licensee has a statutory duty to make inquiry about all matters relevant to the opinion it must form and then, of course, consider whether, in the factual circumstances, there exist the reasonable grounds for it to be satisfied as to the matters stated'.[29] His Honour found that the 'most cursory attention to the statutory criteria would have made it immediately clear [to the licensee in that case] that there were no reasonable grounds for forming the relevant opinions about the relevant investors'.[30]

9.25.30 Professional investors

An offer of securities does not need disclosure to investors if it is made to a 'professional investor' (s 708(11)(a)), or a person who has or controls gross assets of at least $10 million (s 708(11)(b)). The term 'professional investor' is defined in s 9 to cover investors such as financial services licensees, institutional investors regulated by the Australian Prudential Regulation Authority, trustees of a superannuation fund or an approved deposit fund with net assets of at least $10 million, listed entities and their related companies, and exempt public authorities.

27 *Australian Securities and Investments Commission v Maxwell* (2006) 59 ACSR 373, 386 [50].
28 *Australian Securities and Investments Commission v Elm Financial Services Pty Ltd* (2005) 55 ACSR 544 [10].
29 Ibid.
30 Ibid [11].

This contemplates an investor with a high level of expertise or assets. In *MIS Funding No 1 Pty Ltd v Buckley*,[31] Elliott J held that 'control' as used in the definition of 'professional investor' meant that if a person held and controlled the majority of shares in a company, and commensurate voting rights, that person would be considered to be in control of a company and its assets. Finally, note that the $10 million figure in s 708(11)(b) refers to gross rather than net assets.

9.25.35 Rights issues

Companies can raise funds from existing shareholders by undertaking a rights issue. The term 'rights issue' is defined in s 9A as an offer of securities where the offer is made to existing shareholders in the same percentage as the securities they hold; that is, the offer is made in the same proportion to their existing shareholdings. The terms of the offer made to each shareholder must be identical (s 9A(1)(c)). Pursuant to s 708AA, disclosure to investors is not required for a rights issue of quoted securities—for example, on the ASX—if certain conditions are met. To qualify for this exemption from the disclosure requirements, a listed company must give the market operator, such as the ASX, a notice ('a cleansing notice') that includes the following statements:

- the company has complied with its financial reporting obligations under ch 2M[32] and its continuous disclosure obligations under ss 674 and 674A[33]
- the potential effect the issue of shares will have on the control of the company and the consequences of that effect (s 708AA(7)).[34]

9.25.40 Proving an exemption under pt 6D.2

An offeror bears the onus of establishing that one or other of the exemptions in pt 6D.2 of the *Corporations Act* is applicable in a particular case.[35] For an example of the application of the exemptions in s 708 to particular facts (albeit unsuccessful), see *Australian Securities and Investments Commission v Astra Resources plc*.[36]

9.30 Step 3: Deciding whether a prospectus is required or a shorter document may be prepared

Section 705 contains a useful table which clearly sets out the requirements of this step. The types of disclosure documents can be classified into three categories:

(1) Prospectus and short-form prospectus: a prospectus is the standard full-disclosure document. A short-form prospectus can save costs: if the issuer has lodged information with ASIC for other reasons (for example, annual reporting requirements),

---

31 *MIS Funding No 1 Pty Ltd v Buckley* (2013) 96 ACSR 691 [57].
32 See Chapter 7.
33 See Chapter 17.
34 See *Re Golden Gate Petroleum* (2010) 77 ACSR 17 [26].
35 *Australian Securities and Investments Commission v Cycclone Magnetic Engines Inc* (2009) 71 ACSR 1 [40].
36 *Australian Securities and Investments Commission v Astra Resources plc* (2015) 107 ACSR 232 [223]–[246].

it may issue a shorter prospectus that refers to that other material. This is referred to as 'incorporation by reference' (ss 709(1), 712).

(2) Profile statement: with approval by ASIC, certain types of securities may be offered via a profile statement. This is prepared in addition to a prospectus and contains basic information. Anyone who is given a profile statement must be given a copy of the full prospectus free of charge, if requested (ss 709(2), 721(3)).
(3) Offer information statement: if the amount to be raised via the issue of securities is $10 million or less, an offer information statement may be used instead of a full prospectus. This document has fewer disclosure requirements than a prospectus and must contain a warning to that effect (ss 709(4), 715).

9.35 Lodgement of a disclosure document

Section 718 requires that a disclosure document, duly signed and with all appropriate consents (ss 351, 720), must be lodged with ASIC if it is to be used for an offer of securities. The consents needed for a primary offer of securities include the consent of each director of the company (s 720).

9.35.05 Exposure period

Section 727(3) prohibits a person from accepting an application for non-quoted securities offered under a disclosure document or issuing or transferring those securities until seven days after lodgement of the disclosure document. This seven-day period is referred to as the 'exposure period'. ASIC may extend the exposure period for a further seven days. The 7- to 14-day period gives ASIC and the market an opportunity to consider the disclosure document before the commencement of fundraising, so that if disclosure is defective the market can draw the defect to ASIC's attention or the aggrieved parties can seek injunctions to prevent the fundraising.[37]

During this period, ASIC may examine the disclosure document to determine if disclosure is inadequate or if false or misleading statements have been made. ASIC states that:

> The primary objectives of the post-lodgement review program are to ensure adequate protection for investors and maintain investor confidence. In reviewing, we are only concerned with disclosure deficiencies and contraventions of the *Corporations Act*. Our review of the document does not consider whether the securities offered are desirable investments.[38]

If ASIC becomes aware of a problem, it may use its stop order power under s 739 to prevent the company from issuing the securities.[39] The stop order power may be exercised where the document is not worded and presented in a clear, concise and effective manner (s 715A) or if the offer contravenes s 728 (s 739(1A)).[40]

37 Explanatory Memorandum, Corporate Law Economic Reform Program Bill 1998 (Cth) 65 [8.19].

38 Australian Securities and Investments Commission, *Offering Securities under a Disclosure Document* (Regulatory Guide 254, August 2020) reg 254.315.

39 See Ibid Part L; *Thompson v Australian Securities and Investments Commission* (2002) 117 FCR 159.

40 Australian Securities and Investments Commission, *Prospectuses: Effective Disclosure for Retail Investors* (Regulatory Guide 228, August 2019).

The stop order power in s 739 allows ASIC to make an order that no offers, issues, sales or transfers of securities be made while the order is in force or to restrain conduct that breaches s 734; for example, prohibited advertising (s 739(1A)). Under s 739(2), ASIC must hold a hearing and give a reasonable opportunity to any interested person to make oral or written submissions on whether an order should be made. However, if ASIC considers that any delay in making an order under s 739(1A) would be prejudicial to the public interest, ASIC may make an interim order (s 739(3)). The interim order may be made without holding a hearing and can last for up to 21 days.

The stop order power in s 739 was considered in *Thompson v Australian Securities and Investments Commission*.[41] In that case, the applicant, WAC Pty Ltd ('WAC'), was a commercial radio station. WAC agreed to sell its issued share capital to IMM Ltd. The WAC sale was conditional upon IMM raising $6.5 million through the issue of ordinary shares. On 1 March 2002, IMM prepared a prospectus and lodged it with ASIC. On 2 April 2002, IMM advised the market that the share offer had been oversubscribed and the directors had resolved to close the offer. ASIC subsequently advised the IMM directors that it believed a third party had a prior claim to a broadcasting licence used by WAC. The IMM directors investigated but disagreed and notified ASIC accordingly. On 8 April 2002, ASIC issued an interim order under s 739(3) that no offers, issues, sales or transfers of securities be made in relation to the IMM offer. On 16 April 2002, WAC applied for a review of ASIC's decision to make the interim order, claiming that WAC would suffer a financial detriment if the sale agreement could not be completed. The applicants argued that ASIC had no power to make the order because, at the date of the order, IMM had ceased offering securities.

Branson J found that ASIC had the power to issue the interim order at the relevant time and therefore dismissed WAC's application. Her Honour stated as follows:

> In considering the proper interpretation of s 739, it is appropriate to start from the premise that the section is a provision designed for the protection of potential investors. ... [I]ts inclusion in the Act reflects an appreciation by the legislature that s 724 may provide ineffective protection to an applicant for securities where the relevant disclosure document contains a material misstatement or omission. It would therefore seem logical for the ambit of s 739 to be at least co-extensive with that of s 724. Further, ... the terms of s 739(1) indicate that the power given by s 739 to ASIC in respect of an offer of securities under a disclosure statement lodged with it is not intended to come to an end until it becomes impossible for any stop order made by ASIC to operate according to its terms. That is, until it is no longer possible for any relevant offers, issues, sales or transfers of the relevant securities to be made. ... It would not ... promote the purpose underlying the Act to adopt a construction of s 739 which left what could be a critical aspect of a fundraising process (that is, the issue of securities after the close of the offer) beyond the power of ASIC to issue a stop order. Nor ... would it promote the purpose underlying the Act if s 739 were construed

41 *Thompson v Australian Securities and Investments Commission* (2002) 117 FCR 159.

> in a way which would allow a person who has offered securities under a suitably worded disclosure document to close an offer during the life of an interim order under s 739(3) thus preventing the making of an order under s 739(1).[42]

9.40 The content of a disclosure document

The policy objective of promoting informed markets in securities requires that offerors disclose all information relating to securities that is relevant to an offeree's decision to take up the offer. A disclosure document is the principal vehicle for doing this, supplemented as required by the continuous and periodic disclosure regimes discussed in Chapter 17.

Fundraising and IPOs often generate 'blue sky' statements. These statements are bold strategies for the future which may or may not materialise and, in the context of fundraising, may not result in a profit for the investor. The problem of blue sky statements preceded the creation of company law. Legislative attempts to curb blue sky statements date from the *Bubble Act* of 1720, as discussed in Chapter 1 at Section 1.20. Historically, at common law, stringent disclosure obligations were imposed on companies that issued prospectuses inviting people to take up shares. Such obligations were laid down as early as 1860. In *New Brunswick and Canada Railway and Land Co v Muggeridge*,[43] Kindersley VC stated:

> ... [T]hose who issue a prospectus holding out to the public the great advantages which will accrue to persons who will take shares in a proposed undertaking, and inviting them to take shares on the faith of the representations therein contained, are bound to state everything with strict and scrupulous accuracy.[44]

The former company legislation contained detailed provisions relating to the form and content of prospectuses. However, they were ineffective in implementing the policy which requires disclosure of all material information. Now, the *Corporations Act* relies on general disclosure principles. Its provisions place the onus on the person making an offer to ensure that appropriate disclosures are made, rather than allowing the offeror to rely on the regulator's judgment about what is required for effective disclosure in the circumstances.

9.40.05 General disclosure requirements

The general purpose of the disclosure regime in ch 6D was described by Tamberlin J in *Pancontinental Mining Ltd v Goldfields Ltd*[45] as follows:

> The object of disclosure is to put shareholders in possession of the information required to enable them to make an informed and critical assessment of the offer and an informed decision whether to accept it.[46]

42 *Thompson v Australian Securities and Investments Commission* (2002) 117 FCR 159, 166 [29].
43 *New Brunswick and Canada Railway and Land Co v Muggeridge* (1860) 62 ER 418.
44 Ibid 425.
45 *Pancontinental Mining Ltd v Goldfields Ltd* (1995) 16 ACSR 463.
46 Ibid 467.

Section 710 specifies the information a person offering securities must include in a prospectus:

> A prospectus for a body's securities must contain all the information that investors and their professional advisers would reasonably require to make an informed assessment of the matters set out in the table below.

Section 710 contains a table that outlines the information that a prospectus must contain. In relation to issued securities under an IPO, the information includes:

- the rights and liabilities attaching to the securities offered
- the assets and liabilities, financial position and performance, profits and losses and prospects of the body whose securities are offered.

Typically, a prospectus for an IPO would contain:

- a description of the securities
- a description of the issuing body, particularly who is on the board, the management structure, dividend policy, and risk factors
- details of the offer and what the funds will be used for, the timetable for the fundraising, whether the IPO is underwritten, and whether quotation of the securities will be sought
- expert reports
- historical financial information and profit forecasts with supporting assumptions.

9.40.10 Forecasts

Section 710 requires disclosure of the 'prospects' of the offeror of the shares. This is a statement about the future. The most common type of forecast in a disclosure document is a profit forecast. Section 728(2) states that a person is taken to make a misleading statement about a future matter if they do not have reasonable grounds for making the statement. As stated by Emmett J in *GIO Australia Holdings Ltd v AMP Insurance Investment Holdings Pty Ltd*:

> Forecasting, by its very nature, is prone to error. On the other hand, so long as a forecast is accompanied by appropriate caveats and details of underlying assumptions, a forecast will be of greater assistance than no forecast at all. If an offeror has a reasonable basis for giving ... a forecast, such a forecast ought to be given'.[47]

A forecast must contain reliable or material information[48] which is not merely 'speculative or based on mere matters of opinion or judgement'.[49] It may be necessary to disclose

47 *GIO Australian Holdings Ltd v AMP Insurance Investment Holdings Pty Ltd* (1998) 29 ACSR 584, 621.

48 See generally Australian Securities and Investments Commission, *Prospective financial information* (Regulatory Guide 170, April 2011) that presents ASIC's views about when prospective financial information can or should be disclosed.

49 *AAPT Ltd v Cable & Wireless Optus Ltd* (1999) 32 ACSR 63 [137].

the methodology adopted when making a forecast in a disclosure document, particularly if there is disagreement about the appropriate methodology adopted by the offeror.[50]

The broad interpretive scope of the s 710 requirement is narrowed in three ways.

First, the first sentence in s 710(1) requiring 'all the information that investors and their professional advisers would reasonably require' is qualified by the second sentence (in sub-s (1)(a)) so it applies only to the extent it is reasonable for investors and their professional advisers to expect to find that information in the prospectus.

Second, in s 710(1)(b), the prospectus shall contain this information only if a person whose knowledge is relevant:

(i) actually knows the information; or
(ii) in the circumstances ought reasonably to have obtained the information by making enquiries.

Section 710(3) lists the people whose knowledge is relevant, for example:

- the issuing company
- a director or proposed director of the issuer
- an underwriter or financial services licensee to the issue
- a person named in the prospectus as having made a statement included in the statement or upon which the prospectus is based
- a person named in the prospectus as having performed a particular professional or advisory function.

In *Australian Securities Commission v MacLeod*,[51] an expert geologist, Mr MacLeod, made statements about the potential profitability of a company based on the samples of diamonds taken during exploration. It was held that the statement was misleading because the sample was not of sufficient size from which it could be assessed whether the diamonds were present in commercial quantities.[52] Section 710(3)(f) may apply to such statements and it may be relevant to establish the liability of experts such as MacLeod for misstatements, possibly as an alternative to other persons who may be liable under that provision.

Section 710(3) is an important provision because it creates a linkage between the general obligation to give proper disclosure under s 710 and liability for misstatements and omissions in ss 728 and 729. These provisions are discussed below. Section 710(3) states the ambit of liability (the relevant knowledge) and who is potentially liable for defects in the prospectus.

Third, s 710(2) explains the factors to be considered in determining what information to include in a prospectus, including:

- the nature of securities
- the nature of the issuing body

50 *Reiffel v ACN 075 839 226 Ltd* (2003) 132 FCR 437 [48].

51 *Australian Securities Commission v MacLeod* (2000) 22 WAR 255. On appeal to the High Court, MacLeod's conviction was set aside on other grounds: *MacLeod v Australian Securities and Investments Commission* (2002) 211 CLR 287.

52 *Australian Securities Commission v MacLeod* (2000) WAR 255 265 [41].

- the matters that likely investors may reasonably be expected to know
- the fact that certain matters may reasonably be expected to be known to their professional advisers.

Section 710(2) requires the issuer to consider the audience to whom the offer is directed and the context of the offering. For example, the audience for shares in a demutualised company that was formerly a government-owned enterprise will be different to the audience of a start-up company for experimental technology.

9.40.15 Illustrations of s 710(2)

'The nature of the securities'

Section 710(2) explains the method of determining what information to include in a prospectus. Section 710(2)(a) states that the nature of the securities and of the body providing the securities should be considered. Here, we provide an example of how 'the nature of the securities' can affect the level of disclosure. Consider the distinction between prospectuses where the securities are offered as part of an IPO, and where the securities are part of a class of securities already listed on a licensed financial market and have been quoted for 12 months. The latter are called 'transaction specific' prospectuses. These could be more aptly described as 'continuous disclosure' prospectuses because the offeror is subject to a rigorous regime involving continuous and periodic disclosure. The disclosure regime for listed companies is discussed in Chapter 17. The following explains the way in which this difference affects the level of disclosure in a prospectus:

> An IPO prospectus must fully introduce the company to the market and inevitably becomes a 'cornerstone' document from which subsequent reports (eg annual reports, continuous disclosure requirements etc.) build a progressive updating of the original statement. 'Transaction Specific' prospectuses deal with companies that are already known to the market and accordingly do not have to duplicate background and financial information already previously disclosed.[53]

Continuous disclosure prospectuses are governed by s 713. This provision will be discussed below. At this point, it should be noted that the differing nature of the securities involved gives rise to differing disclosure levels.

'The matters that likely investors may reasonably be expected to know'

Section 710(2)(c) lists 'the matters that likely investors may reasonably be expected to know'. This section asks the issuer to have regard to the kinds of persons likely to consider subscribing for the securities. This intended audience will affect the level and nature of the disclosure required in a prospectus.

53 Securities Institute of Australia, *A Guide to Prospectus Disclosure and Best Practice Guidelines* (1996) 23. See also Australian Securities and Investments Commission, *Offering Securities Under a Disclosure Document* (Regulatory Guide 254, August 2020) pt C.

An example of considering the intended audience is in *Fraser v NRMA Holdings Ltd*.[54] In that case, NRMA at the time of the proceedings consisted of three entities:

(1) NRMA Ltd ('the Association'): a company limited by guarantee formed to promote the interests of motorists and road users and to provide an emergency breakdown service
(2) NRMA Insurance Ltd ('the Insurance Company'): a company limited by guarantee and carrying on a successful insurance and financial services business
(3) NRMA Holdings Ltd ('Holdings'): a public company limited by shares and incorporated under the *Corporations Act*.

Holdings was established by the boards of both the Association and the Insurance Company as part of an overall plan to demutualise those two entities. The plan was to turn both entities into companies limited by shares, with the object of making profits and distributing them to shareholders. In exchange for giving up their interest in the companies, members of the Association and the Insurance Company would be issued with shares in Holdings or cash.

Holdings issued a prospectus to members of both the Association and the Insurance Company. Two dissident directors of the Association brought proceedings in the Federal Court for a declaration that the prospectus was misleading and deceptive and contravened s 52 of the *Trade Practices Act 1974* (Cth) (now s 18 of the *Australian Consumer Law*).[55] For various reasons, s 710 did not apply. However, the case illustrates who constitutes the audience or likely investors in Holdings for the purposes of s 710 and a factual application of the misleading and deceptive test in s 728.

On appeal, the Full Federal Court (Black CJ, von Doussa and Cooper JJ) held that the prospectus was false or misleading and granted the orders sought. The prospectus characterised the shares that the members of both the Association and the Insurance Company would receive as part of the demutualisation process as 'free shares'. The Full Court held that that expression, appearing as often as it did in the prospectus (230 times), would reasonably be expected to lead a reader to assume that such shares could be acquired without outlay, or without significant outlay. The clear impression was that members of the Association or the Insurance Company would not have to give up anything to acquire those shares. In fact, the members of the Association and the Insurance Company would have to give up their rights as members of those companies. Those rights were capable of being significant rights. For example, the demutualisation could mean the removal of the road services for Association members and removal of the insurance rebate for members of the Insurance Company. The characterisation of the shares in Holdings as free shares was therefore misleading and deceptive.

The audience was described by the Full Court as follows:

> [T]he membership of the Association to whom the prospectus ... [was] addressed comprised some 1.8 million people, a large proportion of the adult

54 *Fraser v NRMA Holdings Ltd* (1995) 52 FCR 1; on appeal (1995) 55 FCR 452.
55 *Competition and Consumer Act 2010* (Cth) sch 2 ('Australian Consumer Law').

> population of NSW and the ACT. The common bond between them is that they are motorists. It is difficult to envisage a wider cross section of the community and in determining the alleged effect of conduct that is alleged to be misleading or deceptive it is of course relevant to consider the class of persons likely to be exposed to that conduct. As the learned trial judge observed, the addressees of the prospectus may be expected to include significant numbers of people who, whilst quite astute in dealing with their day-to-day financial affairs, have no experience in dealing with shares, with corporate reorganisation, or with a prospectus. Moreover, 'demutualisation' is an unusual form of corporate reorganisation, even to many experienced investors.[56]

Another useful application of s 710 is in *Exeter Group Ltd v Australian Securities Commission*.[57] This case was an appeal to the former Administrative Appeals Tribunal[58] (AAT) from a refusal of ASIC to register a prospectus because it did not comply with the disclosure requirements under the predecessor to s 710. This case involved an invitation to subscribe for up to a total of 10 million shares of 20 cents each fully paid in the capital of the company. The prospectus stated that an objective of the company was to offer an opportunity to investors of small amounts ($2,000 each) to 'get in on the ground floor'[59] of emerging businesses.

The company was an unlisted public company formed for the purpose of raising funds from at least 300 members of the public under the prospectus. At the time of lodging the prospectus, the company had an issued capital of $1 consisting of five shares held by a private company (the manager) and its nominees. The company had not traded or carried on business prior to the date of the prospectus.

The reason for the share issue was to fund the company so it could search for a takeover target. No target had been identified, nor had any inquiries been made in the 12 months leading up to the court hearing. The prospectus made the following statement: 'The shares offered by this prospectus are considered to be speculative in nature'.[60]

However, almost nothing of a factual nature was disclosed in the prospectus. The company argued that it knew nothing about its future investments and was not obliged to disclose anything.[61]

In interpreting s 710, the AAT stated that:

> The material to be included must fulfil the reasonable expectation of the investor—that is to say an expectation based on reason or a process of ratiocination [thinking or reasoning logically]—and must be such as will enable a proposed investor to make an informed assessment of the matters set out in the subsection. An informed assessment is one based upon awareness, alertness, enlightenment and knowledge rather than upon presentiments, intuition,

56 *Fraser v NRMA Holdings Ltd* (1995) 55 FCR 452, 467.

57 *Exeter Group Ltd v Australian Securities Commission* (1998) 16 ACLC 1382.

58 This body was abolished in 2024. The Administrative Review Tribunal was established in its place on 14 October 2024.

59 *Exeter Group Ltd v Australian Securities Commission* (1998) 16 ACLC 1382 [37].

60 Ibid [8].

61 Ibid [31].

> feelings or blind chance ... Therefore the subsection compelled the disclosure of sufficient basic facts to allow these rational assessments to take place.[62]

In this case, the company had not complied with s 710 because there was no basis upon which any intending investor could make a rational assessment of the prospects of the company.

9.40.20 Specific disclosure requirements

The *Corporations Act* requires a prospectus to contain a number of specific disclosures. These disclosures are clearly stated in s 711. These disclosures are only relevant to prospectuses. The *Corporations Act* also makes provision for the content of short-form prospectuses (s 712), profile statements (s 714) and information statements (s 715).

Disclosure of interests: ss 711(2) and (3)

The prospectus must set out the amount that any person (as listed in s 711(4)) has been paid in the last two years or will be paid and any benefits which will be given to directors or prospective directors or promoters. The final sentence in s 711(3) should be noted: '... it is not sufficient merely to state in the prospectus that a person has been paid or will be paid normal, usual or standard fees'—the specific amount must be stipulated.

Disclosure of persons: s 711(4)

The prospectus must identify individuals by name in relation to the disclosure of interests in ss 711(2) and (3); that is, the prospectus must include the identities of directors, professional advisers, stockbrokers, underwriters and promoters.

Quotation of securities: s 711(5)

If the prospectus implies or states that the securities are to be quoted on a licensed financial market, then the prospectus must state details of the application for admission to the financial market, including details of an application for admission that is yet to be made.

Expiry date: s 711(6)

The prospectus must nominate an expiry date beyond which no securities may be issued. This expiry date must be no later than 13 months after the date of the prospectus.

9.40.25 Content of disclosure documents for listed securities

The disclosure requirements for an offer of listed securities are less onerous than those relating to unlisted securities. A prospectus for an offer of continuously quoted securities is required to contain information about the transaction and other material information that is not available to the market. The rationale is that all material information concerning the activities and financial standing of the entity should have been provided to the market under the continuous and periodic disclosure regimes. Potential investors will have access to that information. The continuous and periodic disclosure regimes are explained in Chapter 17.

62 Ibid [5].

Section 713 sets out an alternative general disclosure test which requires a lower level of disclosure but is deemed to satisfy s 710 if all the elements are satisfied. Section 713(2) provides that a continuous disclosure prospectus must contain 'all the information investors and their professional advisers would reasonably require to make an informed assessment of':

- the effect of the offer on the body; and
- the rights and liabilities attaching to the securities offered; and
- if options are involved—the rights and liabilities attached to the options and underlying securities.

Therefore, this section applies the same 'informed investor' test with respect to a narrower range of matters.

ASIC has the power to exclude a company that has securities quoted on an exchange from issuing a prospectus with reduced content where ASIC believes the company failed to comply with its continuous disclosure obligations.[63] These obligations are discussed in Chapter 17.

9.45 Updating and correcting disclosure

Prospectuses have a maximum life of 13 months after issue (s 711(6)). During this time, the information in the prospectus may need updating or correction; for example, because of concerns raised by ASIC or new developments in the issuing company.

9.45.05 Supplementary and replacement disclosure documents

Under s 719(1), the duty to issue a supplementary or replacement disclosure document is triggered when the person making the offer becomes aware of any of the following which is materially adverse to an investor:

> **(a)** a misleading or deceptive statement in the disclosure document; or
> **(b)** an omission from the disclosure document of information required by [the statutory content rules]
> **(c)** a new circumstance that:
> **(i)** has arisen since the disclosure document was lodged; and
> **(ii)** would have been required [by the statutory content rules] to be included in the disclosure document if it had arisen before the disclosure document was lodged.

Those individuals liable for a disclosure document under s 729 have a duty to inform the person making the offer about deficiencies in the disclosure document (s 730). Continuation of the offer where these matters have arisen is prohibited under s 728(1). Supplementary disclosure documents are used to ensure that the document retains continuing compliance with ch 6D throughout its life (s 719(2)). Replacement disclosure documents stand in substitution of the original disclosure document (s 719(3)).

63 See generally I Ramsay, 'Enforcement of Continuous Disclosure Laws by the Australian Securities and Investments Commission' (2015) 33(3) *Company and Securities Law Journal* 196.

In these circumstances, the offeror is under an obligation to repay the money received under the offer or to make further disclosure and allow the offeree the opportunity to withdraw from the offer (s 724). The documents required to be given by way of further disclosure are set out in a table in s 724(3). If the offeror issues securities in breach of s 724, the offeree may return the securities and have their money repaid (s 737).

9.50 Regulating other sources of information

The purpose of the disclosure document provisions in the *Corporations Act* is to ensure that investors have access to all important information about a securities offer before they make an investment decision. The achievement of that aim could be compromised by promotional campaigns which rely on selective publicity rather than a balanced presentation of facts. The *Corporations Act* contains prohibitions on advertising (subject to exceptions) that are designed to protect inexperienced investors from the subtle powers of advertising and public comment and to ensure that investment decisions are made on the basis of a prospectus.

The key prohibition is in s 734(2), which states that if an offer or intended offer of securities needs a disclosure document, a person must not 'advertise the offer ... or publish a statement that directly or indirectly refers to the offer or intended offer, or is reasonably likely to induce people to apply for the securities'. Section 734(2A) states that advertising or publication may be authorised by other subsections. For example, s 734(6) allows 'tombstone' advertising, and s 734(7) allows certain notices and news reports. Section 734 applies different standards to the advertising of quoted and unquoted securities.[64]

9.50.05 Image advertising: s 734(3)

Image advertising praises the nature or value of a prospective issuer without expressly referring to its impending public offer. Before a company produces a disclosure document, it might run an awareness campaign that pitches the company to the public. This could breach s 734(2) because it might indirectly refer to the offer or induce people to apply for securities.

In deciding whether a statement indirectly refers to an offer or is reasonably likely to induce applications, regard must be had to whether the statement forms part of normal product advertising that is genuinely directed to maintaining or attracting customers for the company's products, whether the statement communicates information which materially deals with the affairs of the company, and whether the statement is likely to encourage investment decisions being made on the basis of the statement, rather than the disclosure document (s 734(3)).

9.50.10 Pathfinders: s 734(9)

A pathfinder is a draft disclosure document designed to assist the company to consult with the market before setting a price for a proposed issue or sale of securities. It is permitted under s 734(9). The company sends the draft to underwriters, brokers and other

64 *Australian Securities and Investments Commission v Maxwell* (2006) 59 ACSR 373 [55].

sophisticated investors to enable it to set a price for the securities to be issued or to finalise the content of a disclosure document. The recipient of the pathfinder must be a 'sophisticated investor' (ss 708(8), 708(10)) or a 'professional investor' (s 708(11)).

9.55 Liability for defective disclosure under ch 6D

9.55.05 General liability

There are several provisions that impose liability where the fundraising activity breaches a requirement of ch 6D. Section 726 prohibits the offering of securities in a body that does not exist. Section 727 prohibits making offers without a current disclosure document; that is, without lodging a disclosure statement; making offers which are not included in or accompanied by a disclosure document; accepting applications within the 'exposure period'; and issuing securities that breach the 20 investors ceiling or $2 million ceiling.[65]

Section 728(1) states, in summary, that a person must not offer securities under a disclosure statement if there is:

(a) a misleading or deceptive statement in the disclosure document, application form or offer document
(b) an omission from the disclosure document of material required by various sections (including the content requirements of s 710)
(c) a new circumstance that has arisen since the disclosure document was lodged, and would have been required by various sections (including s 710) to be included in the disclosure document if it had arisen before lodgement.

9.55.10 Criminal and civil penalty liability

Where a person makes a misleading or deceptive statement or there is omission or new circumstance that has not been disclosed (thereby contravening s 728(1)), and that contravention is materially adverse from the point of view of an investor, the person will commit an offence (s 728(3))—that is, they will be criminally liable—and exposed to a civil penalty under s 728(4).[66]

9.55.15 Civil liability to pay compensation

In addition to any other consequences that might flow from the *Corporations Act*[67] and the general law,[68] a contravention of s 728(1) may lead to liability to compensate investors under s 729. To recover under s 729, investors must prove that:

- they suffered loss or damage
- the loss or damage was 'because' of a contravention of s 728(1)

65 *Australian Securities and Investments Commission v Australian Investors Forum Pty Ltd (No 2)* (2005) 53 ACSR 305; *Australian Securities and Investments Commission v Cycclone Magnetic Engines Inc* (2009) 71 ACSR 1.

66 *R v Williams* (2005) 23 ACLC 601.

67 See, eg, s 1324.

68 The general law is retained pursuant to s 729(4).

- the defendant is a person referred to in the table to s 729(1), regardless of whether the defendant committed or was involved in the contravention
- the loss or damage claimed is a loss or damage for which the table makes the defendant liable.

The table in s 729 establishes a form of strict civil liability, regardless of the degree of involvement (but subject to defences) for the person making the offer, its directors, the proposed directors of the body whose securities are being offered, and the underwriter to the issue. These people are liable for loss or damage caused by any contravention of s 728(1).

In contrast, the expert who consents to the inclusion of a statement in the disclosure document is liable only if the loss or damage is caused by that statement, and others such as professional advisers are liable only if they are involved in the contravention.

Note that the fundraising activity contemplated by s 728 is excluded from other provisions of the *Corporations Act* and the *Australian Securities and Investments Commission Act 2001* (Cth)) ('*ASIC Act*') which create wide-ranging liability for misleading and deceptive conduct in relation to financial products or financial services (*Corporations Act* s 1041H(3)) or a financial service only (*ASIC Act* s 12DA(1A)).

9.60 Defences

Certain people can rely on the defences set out in ss 731–3 to absolve them from liability for a contravention of the disclosure requirements in ch 6D.

9.60.05 Due diligence

To establish the due diligence defence in s 731, the defendant must prove that they 'made all inquiries (if any) that were reasonable in the circumstances and that after doing so, believed on reasonable grounds that there was no misleading or deceptive statement' or no omission, as the case may be. On its wording, the due diligence defence is available to the person who makes the offer. In the case of an offer to issue securities, that person is the issuing body; that is, the company that offers its shares. The company will rely on the implementation of a due diligence and prospectus verification program for the purpose of proving it made all reasonable inquiries were in the circumstances, even though a mistake may have occurred.[69]

To act 'diligently' is to be attentive to one's task or duties. The term is derived from s 11(b)(3) of the United States' *Securities Act 1933* which provides a defence of due diligence to those who have made reasonable investigations into matters contained in a prospectus. The standard of care is specified in the US legislation under s 11(c) which states that the standard is 'that required of a prudent man [sic] in the management of his own property'.

It is now standard practice for issuing companies to form a due diligence committee to supervise the preparation of the disclosure document, to identify all necessary information that must be disclosed, and to verify that information. A disclosure document committee usually consists of those who have knowledge of the content under s 710 or

69 See generally Australian Securities and Investments Commission, *Due Diligence Practices in Initial Public Offerings* (Report 484, July 2016).

who may be liable under s 729 of the *Corporations Act*. The committee must be properly established and instructed by the board to enable the issuing company and its directors to take advantage of the defence in s 731.

9.60.10 Lack of knowledge

The due diligence defence under s 731 applies to prospectuses only. Section 732 sets out a 'lack of knowledge' defence where the disclosure defect relates to an offer information statement or a profile statement.

9.60.15 Reasonable reliance

The 'reasonable reliance' defence is in s 733(1). The defendant must prove that they placed reasonable reliance on information given to them by:

- **(a)** if the defendant is a body—someone other than a director, employee or agent of the body
- **(b)** if the defendant is an individual—someone other than an employee or agent of the individual.

A person is not an agent of a body or individual merely because that person performs a particular professional or advisory function for the body or individual (s 733(2)).

In the typical process adopted for the preparation of a prospectus for an IPO, the directors and officers of the company (who are not members of the due diligence and prospectus verification committees), and experts and advisers (who, again, are not members of those committees) will seek to rely on the work of those committees and their reports to the board. Additionally, each member of the committees will seek to rely on the separate work of other members of the committees. The issuing company may also take advantage of the same 'reasonable reliance' argument, but it will need to ensure the proper establishment and conduct of the due diligence process because of the narrow parameters of the reasonable reliance test. Persons seeking to rely on the defence need to ensure that the due diligence and verification processes are structured in accordance with best practice in order to argue that their reliance on others was reasonable.

9.60.20 Withdrawal of consent defence

A person named in a disclosure statement as a proposed director or underwriter or as the maker of a statement in the disclosure document has a defence if that person can show that they publicly withdrew consent to being named (s 733(3)).[70]

9.65 ASIC relief from the application of ch 6D

ASIC may exercise discretion to exempt persons from compliance with the requirements of ch 6D of the *Corporations Act*. In some circumstances, it will be possible to seek

70 For a discussion of personal liability for defective disclosure generally, see J Harris and S Webbey, 'Personal Liability for Corporate Disclosure Problems' (2011) 29(8) *Company and Securities Law Journal* 463.

relief from the obligation to prepare and lodge a disclosure document pursuant to s 741. Section 741 gives ASIC the power to exempt persons, individually or collectively, from the operation of ch 6D. The section also gives ASIC the power to modify the terms of ch 6D. These powers have been used extensively to issue a range of class orders either exempting certain offers of securities from compliance with ch 6D or by modifying the operation of ch 6D for other offers.

Overall, ASIC may provide relief from the law where doing so produces a 'net regulatory benefit, or any regulatory detriment is minimal and is outweighed by the resulting commercial benefit';[71] for example, film investment schemes. ASIC may also grant relief on a case-by-case basis.[72]

9.70 The hawking prohibition

The original prohibition on hawking focused upon the activity of canvassers who were paid by commission and who personally hawked securities from house to house, offering them in many cases to people who lacked business experience.

Section 992A prohibits 'cold-calling': this bars a person from offering financial products for issue or sale in the course of an unsolicited contact with a retail client.[73] In 2019, the life insurance division of the Commonwealth Bank of Australia pleaded guilty to 87 counts of offering to sell insurance products during unsolicited telephone calls which did not comply with the hawking provisions set out in s 992A.[74] The Bank was fined $700,000.[75] This case followed a recommendation made by the Hayne Royal Commission for a wider prohibition on the unsolicited sales of insurance and superannuation products. The Hayne Royal Commission[76] is discussed in Chapters 1 and 17.

9.75 Equity crowdfunding

9.75.05 Crowdfunding and its different types explained

Crowd-sourced funding—or simply 'crowdfunding'—uses technology to form connections between an entity seeking to raise funds, potential contributors and an intermediary facilitating the fundraising projects.[77] These connections enable substantial sums

71 Australian Securities and Investments Commission, *Offering Securities under a Disclosure Document* (Regulatory Guide 254, August 2020) reg 254.16. See also Australian Securities and Investments Commission, *Applications for Relief* (Regulatory Guide 51, July 2020).

72 See Australian Securities and Investments Commission, *Applications for Relief* (Regulatory Guide 51, July 2020) reg 51.74.

73 See Australian Securities and Investments Commission, *The Hawking Prohibition* (Regulatory Guide 38, September 2021).

74 Australian Securities and Investments Commission, 'CommInsure Pleads Guilty to Hawking Offences' (Media Release 19-313MR, 19 November 2019).

75 *R v The Colonial Mutual Life Assurance Society Ltd* (Downing Centre Local Court, Magistrate Atkinson, 28 November 2019); Australian Securities and Investments Commission, 'CommInsure Sentenced for Hawking Offences' (Media Release 19-32MR, 28 November 2019).

76 *Royal Commission into Misconduct in the Banking, Superannuation and Financial Services Industry* (Final Report, February 2019) Recommendations 3.4, 4.1.

77 A Matthew, 'Crowd-Sourced Equity Funding: The Regulatory Challenges of Innovative Fintech and Fundraising' (2017) 36(1) *University of Queensland Law Journal* 41, 44.

to be raised from large numbers of contributors, each making a small contribution towards the fundraising goal. There are two main types of crowdfunding: reward-based and equity crowdfunding. In the case of reward-based crowdfunding, the contributor obtains a product, an altruistic reward or a charitable goal.[78] The second type of crowdfunding is equity crowdfunding (ECF). In this circumstance, the contributor becomes an investor in the equity of a company and may receive a share of the profits if the project is successful.

ECF allows a company to offer equity in exchange for cash from a large number of investors where the offer (ECF offer) is published through an online funding platform.[79] The following discussion is limited to ECF.

9.75.10 The regulation of equity crowdfunding

ECF challenges financial regulators because contributors are likely to be ordinary members of the general public, who are unsophisticated but enthusiastic 'novel investors' but who nevertheless represent a viable potential capital market for small-medium enterprises (SMEs).[80] SMEs commonly find it difficult to raise equity funding.[81] Therefore, in large numbers, even modest contributions from willing investors can create a sizeable capital injection in a low-cost accessible framework.[82] However, there are well-recognised problems that often arise in fundraising by SMEs, such as the high rate of failure and the risk of fraudulent activity.

Some commentators have criticised the ECF regulatory framework, arguing it treats ECF as merely another form of corporate fundraising which ignores its distinctive and innovative nature as 'a new form of social interaction based on mutuality, cooperation and inclusiveness'.[83]

The *Corporations Amendment (Crowd-sourced Funding) Act 2017* (Cth) created a separate regime in pt 6D.3A of the *Corporations Act* for the making of ECF offers. Part 6D.3A (and its associated regulations) use a series of devices such as modified mandatory disclosure, limiting the products to vanilla financial products (fully paid ordinary shares) (s 738G and reg 6D.3A.01), limiting the offer to a $5 million issue (s 738G), and requiring a risk statement be displayed by the platform (s 738ZA) and in the offer document (s 738J and regs 6D.3A.02, 6D.3A.03) which warns potential investors as follows (in part):

78 Ibid 47.

79 A Levine, B Tam and A Beatty, 'Crowd-sourced Funding Bill 2015: Towards Establishing an Australian Regulatory Framework for Crowd-sourced Equity Funding' (2016) 35(3) *Brief* 43, 43.

80 L Valanciene and S Jegeleviciute, 'Valuation of Crowdfunding: Benefits and Drawbacks' (2013) 18(1) *Economics & Management* 39, 41.

81 R Oakey, 'A Commentary on Gaps in Funding for Moderate "Non-Stellar" Growth Small Businesses in the United Kingdom' (2007) 9(4) *Venture Capital* 223.

82 A Matthew, 'Crowd-Sourced Equity Funding: The Regulatory Challenges of Innovative Fintech and Fundraising' (2017) 36(1) *University of Queensland Law Journal* 41, 45.

83 S Kourabas, 'Shareholder (Dis)Empowerment through Crowd-Sourced Equity Funding' (2023) 46(1) *University of New South Wales Law Journal* 143, 180.

> Crowd-sourced funding is risky. Issuers using this facility include new or rapidly growing ventures. Investment in these types of ventures is speculative and carries high risks.
>
> You may lose your entire investment, and you should be in a position to bear this risk without undue hardship.
>
> Even if the company is successful, the value of your investment and any return on the investment could be reduced if the company issues more shares.
>
> Your investment is unlikely to be liquid. This means you are unlikely to be able to sell your shares quickly or at all if you need the money or decide that this investment is not right for you. ...[84]

The ECF intermediary (also referred to as the 'responsible intermediary' (s 738L(5)) plays a central role because it is the conduit through which all ECF offers are made and through which all funds are received and dispersed (s 738L). ECF intermediaries must hold an Australian Financial Services Licence (AFSL)[85] expressly authorising the provision of ECF services (s 738C) and must conduct prescribed checks on the identity of the company making the offer, its eligibility to engage in crowdfunding, and information about the directors and others named in the offer document. The ECF intermediary must conduct these checks to a reasonable standard (s 738Q).

Under the regime, companies with less than $25 million in assets and annual turnover will be eligible to raise funds (s 738H). Companies may raise up to $5 million via ECF (s 738G) in any 12-month period.[86] An ECF offer must be made by publishing it with an ECF offer document on the platform of the ECF intermediary (s 738L(1)).

Certain protections are given to retail clients[87] under the ECF regime such as only being permitted to pay up to $10,000 per annum for ECF funding via the same ECF intermediary (s 738ZC). The ECF intermediary must reject an application made by the retail client in excess of this cap (s 738ZC(1)). Further, retail clients may take advantage of cooling-off rights. These investors may withdraw an application for securities made pursuant to an ECF offer within five business days of making the application and their application money will be returned (s 738ZD).

9.75.15 Liability for and defences following defective ECF disclosure

The ECF regime provides for civil and criminal liability for defective ECF disclosure which are analogous to the general provisions in ch 6D regulating defective disclosure, such as misleading or deceptive statements or omissions (s 738U), stipulating who is liable for loss or damage (s 738Y), specifying defences (s 738Z) and placing restrictions on advertising (s 738Z).[88]

84 Regulation 6D.3A.03.
85 The AFSL regime is discussed in Chapter 18.
86 Note that s 738E permits offers under s 708 for the same class of securities as those made under the ECF offer: see Section 9.25.
87 'Retail client' as defined in s 738D.
88 See generally Sections 9.50–9.60.

9.80 Summary

This chapter examined the requirements under ch 6D of the *Corporations Act* that apply when a public company offers its securities to a cross-section of the public; for example, under an IPO. Chapter 6D requires that the offer be accompanied by a disclosure document. The most common form of disclosure document is a prospectus. Chapter 6D contains detailed regulation of the offer, the type of disclosure required, and whether exemptions from disclosure apply. The provisions of ch 6D also create a liability regime for breach and certain defences that may be relied upon by participants in the fundraising. Finally, this chapter discussed the provisions of ch 6D that regulate equity crowdfunding in Australia.

CHAPTER

10

AN OVERVIEW OF DIRECTORS' DUTIES

10.05 Introduction[1]

> Did you ever expect a corporation to have a conscience, when it has no soul to be damned, and no body to be kicked?
>
> Edward, First Baron Thurlow 1731–1806[2]

This chapter begins by introducing the concept of corporate governance, and the regulatory role of directors' duties. An appreciation of corporate governance methodologies gives context to the 'hard law' of directors' duties. This chapter then considers who falls within the definition of director, the role of the director within the company, and how that role attracts legal and non-legal regulation. It also identifies who, beyond directors, can also be subject to directors' duties. This chapter revisits the history of directors' duties within Australian corporate law, building on the historical context provided by Chapter 1, and exploring the interrelationship between the duties applicable at common law, in equity, and according to statute. It concludes with the consequences of breach of the civil penalty provisions and options for exoneration and relief under the *Corporations Act*.

10.10 Corporate governance

Lord Chancellor Thurlow's observation at the start of this chapter highlights the difficulties of managing corporate behaviour and effectively punishing misbehaviour.

1 The authors acknowledge that an earlier version of material contained in this chapter appeared in B Nosworthy, 'Finding the Fiduciary: Recognition of the Director-Shareholder Relationship in Closely Held Companies' (PhD Thesis, The University of Adelaide, 2013) <https://digital.library.adelaide.edu.au/server/api/core/bitstreams/4fa38eb1-6a5f-4ef2-901f-e247e58b057b/content>.

2 MA King, *Public Policy and the Corporation* (Chapman and Hall, 1977) 1 as cited in JC Coffee Jr, '"No Soul to Damn: No Body to Kick": An Unscandalized Inquiry into the Problem of Corporate Punishment' (1981) 79(3) *Michigan Law Review* 386; P Redmond, *Companies and Securities Law: Commentary and Materials* (Lawbook, 5th ed, 2009) 146.

It is relevant when considering the legal obligations owed by, to, and within a company. These difficulties have been the subject of significant public scrutiny in Australia in the wake of the Royal Commission into Misconduct in the Banking, Superannuation and Financial Services Industry conducted in 2018, with the Final Report handed down in 2019.[3]

The corporate form suffers from a fundamental deficiency: while it is a distinct legal person, in addition to having no physical form to punish, there is no obligation for it to have an independent mind or will, like a natural person. Only the natural entity theory recognises the potential for a company to have a conscious will separate from that of its members and managers.[4] Other theories consider the company as an artificial entity and emphasise wider public interest only because that existence is conceded by the legislature,[5] or do not recognise the company as having an existence separate from the natural persons in the company.[6]

A solvent company formed under the *Corporations Act* has two decision-making organs—the board of directors and the members in general meeting—that generally operate independently from one another. Further complicating matters are that these decision-making organs are populated by natural persons, with varied interests, values, ideals and goals, such that the organs vary in the projection of these interests, values, ideals and goals depending upon who constitutes that organ at the time.

Thurlow's identification of the phenomenon that a company does not have a single physical or mental existence is not a lament unique in the history of corporate law. There are a number of theoretical debates about the nature of the corporation, which have spawned various theories, such as the concession, law and economic, natural entity, organisational and stakeholder theories set out in Chapter 2. Rather than ascribe wholly to one theory, Australian corporate law operates with a level of pragmatism, drawing from the most convenient or appropriate theory to deal with the current issue at hand. An extension of this pragmatic approach is the differing legislative measures applied to the types of company permitted under the *Corporations Act* discussed in Chapter 3.[7] Another complexity is the diverse sources of regulation imposed upon all companies (commonly called 'hard' and 'soft' law[8]), both within the field of corporate governance and beyond it, including instances where various sources impose the same (or slight variations on the same) duty contemporaneously.

3 *Royal Commission into Misconduct in the Banking, Superannuation and Financial Services Industry* (Final Report, 4 February 2019).

4 See the discussion of natural entity theory in Chapter 2 at Section 2.30.

5 See the discussion of concession theory in Chapter 2 at Section 2.10.

6 See the discussion of aggregate theory in Chapter 2 at Section 2.15.

7 See, eg, s 45A (distinguishing small and large proprietary companies); s 135 (the replaceable rules, which can operate as a default position in relation to company management unless displaced by a company constitution, dealing on occasion quite differently with public and proprietary companies); ss 194–5 (replaceable rules for proprietary companies in relation to director disclosure and voting, in contrast to the provision affecting public company directors in the same circumstances).

8 Soft law, such as recommendations or guidelines, may be widely adopted or industry norm, but can be distinguished from regulation with more traditional legally binding force, such as legislative provisions. See, eg, K Jackson, 'Global Corporate Governance: Soft Law and Reputational Accountability' (2010) 35(1) *Brooklyn Journal of International Law* 41, 44.

10.10.05 Australian corporate governance

> [G]overnance refers to all of the structures and processes by which an entity is run. It embraces not only by whom, and how, decisions are made, but also the values or norms to which the processes of governance are intended to give effect. Notions of accountability lie at the heart of governance. Who is to be held accountable for what is done or not done? How are those who are accountable held to account?[9]

Corporate governance is defined by the Australian Securities Exchange (ASX) as 'the framework of rules, relationships, systems and processes within and by which authority is exercised and controlled in corporations'.[10] This definition is drawn from the comments of the HIH Royal Commission,[11] which stated:

> [a]t its broadest, the governance of corporate entities comprehends the framework of rules, relationships, systems and processes within and by which authority is exercised and controlled in corporations. It includes the practices by which that exercise and control of authority is in fact effected.
>
> The relevant rules include applicable laws of the land as well as the internal rules of a corporation. The relationships include those between the shareholders or owners and the directors who oversee the affairs of the corporation on their behalf, between the directors and those who manage the affairs of the corporation and carry out its business, and within the ranks of management, as well as between the corporation and others to whom it must account, such as regulators. The systems and processes may be formal or informal and may deal with such matters as delegations of authority, performance measures, assurance mechanisms, reporting requirements and accountabilities.
>
> The term corporate governance has a descriptive content, in the sense of denoting a simple statement of a governance model that is in place. It is also commonly used in an aspirational sense, by way of holding out a model which practice should seek to emulate. Reference can be made in this regard to various statements of corporate governance principles or guidelines on good corporate governance practice, some purely hortatory, others more prescriptive, that have been published or promulgated in recent years.[12]

This broad statement raises formal and non-formal systems of control, legal regulation and self-regulation that govern companies. At the heart of these systems are the

9 *Royal Commission into Misconduct in the Banking, Superannuation and Financial Services Industry* (Final Report, 4 February 2019) 394.

10 ASX Corporate Governance Council, *Corporate Governance Principles and Recommendations* (Australian Securities Exchange, 4th ed, 2019) 1 <https://www.asx.com.au/content/dam/asx/about/corporate-governance-council/cgc-principles-and-recommendations-fourth-edn.pdf>.

11 *Royal Commission into HIH Insurance* (Report, May 2003) ('the HIH Royal Commission').

12 Ibid 101–2.

primary relationships between the members, directors and management. Members pool their assets to provide the capital investment in the company and elect the board of directors to direct and manage the company and its assets on their behalf.[13] Generally, in a large company, the board only acts when it meets[14] and delegates power for the day-to-day oversight of the company to management. Consequently, management is accountable to the board, and the board is accountable to the members. By contrast, in small, closely-held companies, this abstraction of accountability may not have as significant an impact. Bosch believes that it 'is because these accountabilities are not well-understood, and even less well-observed, that failures in governance occur'.[15]

Companies and corporate governance are influenced not only by legal thinkers, but also by sociologists, philosophers, economists and other theorists. Each field of study conceptualises the corporate body and corporate regulation slightly differently. In most theoretical views of the corporate body, the board of directors plays a pivotal role, but the interrelationship between the board of directors and other corporate actors is described in various ways depending on the background of the theorist. In one sociologist's description of a company, the board of directors is placed at the apex of a triangle, with a top-down view of the organisation from the perspective of a sustained and fixed identity. In the strata below the board are the members, with management at the base of the triangle.[16] An alternative, dynamic, 'business brain' view of the company by a managerial theorist places the board in the central circle of three concentric rings, surrounded in the closest ring by all stakeholders, who are then surrounded by management in the outermost ring.[17] These views emphasise the important role the board plays within a company, and demonstrates why much corporate governance is directed towards the board and its behaviour.

From a legal perspective, these descriptions do not accurately reflect either the flow of obligations within the corporate structure or the delegation of responsibility, as the descriptions place the members and other stakeholders between the management and the board. This does not fit with the legal understanding of directors' duties, where, for example, the duties under the *Corporations Act* are generally phrased to apply to directors and officers. Consequently, consideration of 'the board' will also involve consideration of senior management in the modern corporation. This will be discussed in detail at Section 10.20.15.

13 Corporations and Markets Advisory Committee, *The Social Responsibility of Corporations* (Report, December 2006) [3.1].

14 Some mechanisms provide exception to this generality, such as circulating resolutions, which permit non-contentious or routine resolutions to be passed in between board meeting dates in proprietary companies with more than one member: *Corporations Act* s 249A.

15 H Bosch, 'The Changing Face of Corporate Governance' (2002) 25(2) *University of New South Wales Law Journal* 270, 270.

16 J Elkington, *Cannibals with Forks: The Triple Bottom Line of 21st Century Business* (Capstone, 1997) 286–7, drawing on the concepts of using metaphor to describe organisation discussed by G Morgan, *Images of Organization* (Sage, 2nd ed, 1997) 18–19.

17 J Elkington, *Cannibals with Forks: The Triple Bottom Line of 21st Century Business* (Capstone, 1997) 286–7; Bob Garratt, *The Fish Rots from the Head: The Crisis in our Boardrooms* (Profile Books, rev ed, 2003) 4.

Regardless of how the decision-making organs within the company are defined,[18] through the combination of *Corporations Act* ss 117, 119 and 124 the company itself is recognised at law as a distinct legal person. As discussed in Chapter 3, there is a perception that punishment of the company is difficult, given its legal status as an individual but lack of a physical form or mind which represents that person.[19] The dichotomy between the 'nexus of contracts' approach to the company[20] and the natural entity theory of the company[21] has been avoided in Australian law, by regulating both the individuals and the company for whom they act.[22] In relation to corporate punishment, a 'dual focus on the firm and the individual is necessary. Neither can safely be ignored.'[23] As Le Mire explains, maintaining this dual regulatory focus provides significant personal disincentives to the individual decision-makers within a company.[24] It also provides a response against the company, as the law acknowledges that the company may have a personality or culture of its own which impacts on the decision-making process of the individuals within it.[25]

The decision-making power is divided between the board of directors and the members in general meeting. Because corporate governance is 'the framework of rules, relationships, systems and processes within and by which authority is exercised and controlled in corporations',[26] it is primarily focused on the behaviour of those organs. This is an oversimplification of how decisions are made in practice in many companies, given the differing nature and structure of companies which exist under Australian law. For example, in most large companies, levels of management exist with significant day-to-day decision-making powers; and, at the other end of the scale, sole-director/shareholder companies exist wherein the board of directors and the members in general meeting comprise the same, single individual. Consequently, the full picture of the corporate governance framework is a complex mixture of legal, quasi-legal, managerial, market-based and commercial factors.

18 See Chapter 7 for a discussion of the organs of the company—being the board of directors and the members in the general meeting.

19 See generally MA King, *Public Policy and the Corporation* (Chapman and Hall, 1977); JC Coffee Jr, '"No Soul to Damn: No Body to Kick": An Unscandalized Inquiry into the Problem of Corporate Punishment' (1980) 79(3) *Michigan Law Review* 386. See especially Section 3.45 in relation to corporate liability in criminal law.

20 As favoured by law and economics scholars: see, eg, FH Easterbrook and DR Fischel, *The Economic Structure of Corporate Law* (Harvard University Press, 1991); A Shleifer and RW Vishny, 'A Survey of Corporate Governance' (1997) 52(2) *Journal of Finance* 737, discussed in Chapter 2 at Section 2.20.

21 See, eg, M Stokes, 'Company Law and Legal Theory' in W Twining (ed), *Legal Theory and Common Law* (Basil Blackwell, 1986); D Millon, 'Theories of the Corporation' (1990) (2) *Duke Law Journal* 201.

22 Laws imposing corporate liability are discussed further in Chapter 3.

23 John C Coffee Jr, '"No Soul to Damn: No Body to Kick": An Unscandalised Inquiry Into the Problem of Corporate Punishment' (1980) 79(3) *Michigan Law Review* 386, 410, discussed in Chapter 2 at Section 2.25.

24 See Sections 10.35.10–10.35.15, where the significant fines (pecuniary penalty orders), disgorgement orders, disqualification orders and criminal penalties for individuals in breach of the *Corporations Act* civil penalty provisions are discussed.

25 S LeMire, 'Document Destruction and Corporate Culture: A Victorian Initiative' (2006) 19(3) *Australian Journal of Corporate Law* 304, 311.

26 *Royal Commission into HIH Insurance* (Report, May 2003) 101.

It includes:

- statutory directors' duties found in the *Corporations Act*,[27] and the underlying duties deriving from the common law and equity (see Section 10.30 and in more detail in Chapters 11–13)
- other statutory obligations in the *Corporations Act* including insider trading provisions (see Chapter 17), members' rights and remedies (see Chapter 14), and the winding up provisions (see Chapter 16)
- the provisions of the *Australian Consumer Law*[28] and the *Australian Securities and Investments Commission Act 2001* (Cth)
- the ASX *Listing Rules* and the ASX *Corporate Governance Principles and Recommendations* (see below and Chapter 17)
- business community expectations and norms.

In the chapters that follow, we consider in greater depth the statutory and general law directors' duties, which form a central part of the legal regulation of Australian corporate governance. These duties require a minimum level of competence and involvement in the task of independently monitoring the running of the company. Conflicts of interest, and the conferral of related party benefits in public companies, are prohibited. These legal duties reflect the authority granted to directors and their role in counterbalancing the powers of management and the members in general meeting. These duties may extend to include not only directors and officers, but senior management employees in certain circumstances. On the other side of the equation, members' rights are created by the statutory contract between the members and the company (among others) according to s 140.

The members have a significant financial interest in the company but their ability to influence management is limited. They do have access to a broad range of members' remedies under the *Corporations Act*, which provide them with power to respond to the behaviour of directors or management. Members also have primary responsibility for certain decisions under the *Corporations Act*, which must be made by the members in general meeting, such as the decision to voluntarily wind up the company. This will be discussed in Chapters 14 and 16. The division of powers and rights between the board of directors and the members in general meeting, protected in law by these various provisions, creates a system of checks and balances on the exercise of authority within the company.

This legal regulation (hard law) is supplemented by a variety of non-legal regulation (soft law). One important feature of the non-legal regulation of corporate governance is

27 In relation to companies limited by guarantee, which remain a common legal structure for charities in Australia, the duties of volunteer directors are regulated by the Australian Charities and Not-for-profits Commission Governance Standards. These standards are thematically similar to the directors' duties under the *Corporations Act* but are articulated as principles that the charity should take reasonable steps to comply with, rather than legal duties on the responsible persons involved. For critical analysis of this approach, see R Teele Langford and M Webster, 'Misuse of Power in the Australian Charities Sector' (2022) 45(1) *University of New South Wales Law Journal* 70.

28 As this book is concerned primarily with corporate law, the detail of these legislative provisions will not be directly addressed. See generally S Corones, *The Australian Consumer Law* (Lawbook, 2nd ed, 2013).

the ASX *Corporate Governance Principles and Recommendations* ('the ASX Principles').[29] Since the 1990s, corporate governance has been a feature of global discussion and concern, and resulted in the creation of private sector codes of practice and guidelines for corporate governance.[30] These codes focus on the behaviour of the board and management, with little consideration for the role of the members. This may reflect the belief that members have little ability to influence the exercise of power in the modern company. More recently, shareholder activism has received more attention, as discussed in Chapter 7.

The ASX Principles apply to entities listed on the ASX on an 'if not, why not' basis—that is, should an entity choose not to apply a Council recommendation to its practice, it must explain the reasons for that refusal—and are a useful tool for directing corporate governance. The fourth edition of the Principles, which takes effect for the full financial year commencing on or after 1 January 2020, contains eight principles and a further 38 recommendations[31] with associated commentary. The Principles are phrased as requiring a listed entity to:

(1) lay solid foundations for management and oversight
(2) structure the board to be effective and add value
(3) instil a culture of acting lawfully, ethically and responsibly
(4) safeguard the integrity of corporate reports
(5) make timely and balanced disclosure
(6) respect the rights of security holders
(7) recognise and manage risk
(8) remunerate fairly and responsibly.[32]

The changes between the third and fourth editions of the ASX Principles reflect the increased focus on good governance. In particular, the amendments to Principle 3 to expressly include the words 'culture' and 'lawfully', and the accompanying Recommendation 3.3 that listed entities should have and disclose a whistleblower policy, reflect the circumstances which led to the Royal Commission into Misconduct in the Banking, Superannuation and Financial Services Industry. One of the key questions identified by Treasury from the Interim Report[33] was 'What more can be done to

29 ASX Corporate Governance Council, *Corporate Governance Principles and Recommendations* (Australian Securities Exchange, 4th ed, 2019) <https://www.asx.com.au/content/dam/asx/about/corporate-governance-council/cgc-principles-and-recommendations-fourth-edn.pdf>. The G20/OECD *Principles of Corporate Governance* provide similar guidance from an international perspective, again with a focus on listed companies: OECD, *G20/OECD Principles of Corporate Governance* (OECD Publishing, 2023) <https://doi.org/10.1787/ed750b30-en>. The ASX and the ASX Principles are discussed in further detail in Chapter 17.

30 The European Corporate Governance Institute maintains an 'Index of Codes', which can be viewed at https://www.ecgi.global/publications/codes.

31 There are 35 specific recommendations said to be of 'general application', and another three recommendations that apply only in certain limited cases: ASX Corporate Governance Council, *Corporate Governance Principles and Recommendations* (Australian Securities Exchange, 4th ed, 2019) 3 <https://www.asx.com.au/content/dam/asx/about/corporate-governance-council/cgc-principles-and-recommendations-fourth-edn.pdf>.

32 Ibid 4.

33 *Royal Commission into Misconduct in the Banking, Superannuation and Financial Services Industry* (Interim Report, 2018).

achieve effective leadership, good governance and appropriate culture within financial services firms so that firms "obey the law, do not mislead or deceive, are fair, provide fit for purpose service with care and skill, and act in the best interests of their clients"?'[34] Whistleblowers were directly responsible for calls for this royal commission in the Senate as early as 2014,[35] and the Final Report also references the earlier work of whistleblowers in highlighting previous misconduct in the financial services sector.[36] A consultation process for the fifth edition of the Principles took place in 2024, with the updated Principles expected to be published in early 2025. However, on 20 February 2025, the ASX Corporate Governance Council closed the consultation on the draft fifth edition, when it became 'clear that a broad consensus has not been reached in support of the proposed changes'[37]. Despite the decision not to move forward with the proposed fifth edition, it is interesting to note some of the key amendment proposals from the consultation draft[38]:

- Inclusion of direct reference to 'long-term sustainable value' in the definition of good corporate governance;
- An acknowledgment that key stakeholders are important to governance, with references throughout the recommendations to 'reflecting on' and 'engaging with' key stakeholders, including Indigenous peoples and local community (but not the environment, although environmental groups are identified in the commentary to Recommendation 3.3);
- Principle 2 (Structure the board to be effective and add value) was to be amended to include setting a timeframe for achieving gender diversity in the composition of their board, as well as disclosing other diversity characteristics beyond gender (such as age, race and background); and
- Inclusion of materiality and environmental, social and governance risks in Recommendation 7.4 where it was proposed that listed entities disclose 'material risks (including material environmental, social and governance risks)', and how it manages or intends to manage those risks.

Despite their 'if not, why not' application, the Principles are a code of recommended good governance practices that are in line with similar codes in most industrialised countries.[39] These codes are private sector mechanisms, drafted by interest groups or committees, with a narrow range of concerns and rely on self-regulation.

34 *Royal Commission into Misconduct in the Banking, Superannuation and Financial Services Industry* (Final Report, 4 February 2019) 5.

35 See, eg, S Letts, 'The Whistleblower, Politician and Journo who Hauled the Banks Before a Royal Commission' *ABC News*, (Web Page, 1 February 2019) <https://www.abc.net.au/news/2019–02-01/how-the-banking-royal-commission-was-born/10758404>.

36 *Royal Commission into Misconduct in the Banking, Superannuation and Financial Services Industry* (Final Report, 4 February 2019) 129.

37 ASX Corporate Governance Council, 'ASX Corporate Governance Council Closes Consultation on Draft Fifth Edition Corporate Governance Principles and Recommendations' (Communique, 20 February 2025) 1 https://www.asx.com.au/content/dam/asx/about/corporate-governance-council/20-feb-asx-corporate-governance-council-closes-consultation.pdf.

38 ASX Corporate Governance Council, Corporate Governance Principles and Recommendations Draft (5th ed, 2024) https://www.asx.com.au/content/dam/asx/about/corporate-governance-council/corporate-governance-principles-and-recommendations-consultation-draft.pdf

39 For further discussion of the Principles, see Chapter 17 at Section 17.20.35.

Questions have been raised about their effectiveness and potential in the context of corporate governance.[40] This is a complex matter and depends on many variables that are often specific to the exercise of power within the individual company, and this discussion, within the context of this chapter, provides an overview of the factors involved in corporate governance within Australia.

10.10.10 Comparative corporate governance

Current corporate governance regimes across the globe are not consistent, as corporate form and corporate practice differ between jurisdictions, and consequently so do the methods of governing them. According to the proponents of the 'law matters' thesis,[41] the history, tradition and role of law within the community is responsible for the majority of the differences.[42]

Corporate governance structures in common law countries, such as Australia, the United Kingdom and the United States of America, are generally based on the shareholder primacy or outsider model of corporate control.[43] This approach has been stated as follows:

> the achievement of corporate goals and profit maximisation is monitored by the owners of the corporation, its shareholders, to whom the corporate management is accountable. The focus of the shareholder approach is profit maximisation for the owners of the corporation.[44]

The corporate governance structures of civil law countries are said to be based on a stakeholder approach, or insider model of corporate control. The corporate governance model adopted in these countries seeks to align the interests of multiple stakeholders, such as employees, managers, creditors, suppliers, customers and other members of the community. However, La Porta et al claim that, in general, civil law countries give investors and creditors weaker legal rights than common law countries.[45]

40 See, eg, I Ramsay and R Hoad, 'Disclosure of Corporate Governance Practices by Australian Companies' (1997) 15(8) *Company and Securities Law Journal* 454; J Segal, 'Corporate Governance: Substance over Form' (2002) 25(2) *University of New South Wales Law Journal* 320; A Klettner, T Clarke and M Adams, 'Corporate Governance Reform: An Empirical Study of the Changing Roles and Responsibilities of Australian Boards and Directors' (2010) 24(2) *Australian Journal of Corporate Law* 148.

41 See Chapter 2 at Section 2.45 for more detail on the 'law matters' thesis.

42 See, eg, R La Porta et al, 'Law and Finance' (1998) 106(6) *Journal of Political Economy* 1113.

43 CLERP, 'Directors' Duties and Corporate Governance: Facilitating Innovations and Protecting Investors' (Corporate Law Economic Reform Program Paper No 3, The Treasury, 1997) <https://treasury.gov.au/sites/default/files/2019-03/full-13.pdf>. [7.2.1]. The acronym 'CLERP' comes from the *Corporate Law Economic Reform Program Act 1999* (Cth). Both before and after 1999, the Commonwealth Government published its proposals for reform in the corporate field as the 'CLERP papers': see, eg, Takeovers Panel, *Corporate Law Economic Reform Program (CLERP) (1997)* (Report, 1997) https://takeovers.gov.au/resources/historical-materials/leg-review/CLERP.

44 'Directors' Duties and Corporate Governance: Facilitating Innovations and Protecting Investors' (Corporate Law Economic Reform Program Paper No 3, The Treasury, 1997) <https://treasury.gov.au/sites/default/files/2019-03/full-13.pdf>. Not all statements within this quotation are accepted: as discussed in Chapter 2 at Section 2.45, 'ownership' of a share may not always be equated with 'ownership' of the company.

45 R La Porta et al, 'Law and Finance' (1998) 106(6) *Journal of Political Economy* 1113, 1116.

Both civil and common law jurisdictions have suffered corporate governance failures in the past, suggesting that neither model is working perfectly.[46] While *CLERP Paper No 3* does not decide which of these two models should be preferred, it highlights the benefits of the shareholder primacy model, such as external accountability in light of the rising dependence on external finance;[47] companies being more flexible and responsive to the market;[48] and that there may be a global shift towards the shareholder primacy model. *CLERP Paper No 3* does not offer any evidence to support this conclusion. As noted in Chapter 1, this 'convergence thesis' is subject to significant criticism.[49]

10.15 Why do we regulate directors' behaviour?

Australian companies must have at least one member[50] and at least one director[51] responsible for managing the company's business. Most proprietary companies and all public companies have a company secretary, responsible for administrative duties.[52] Once registered under the *Corporations Act*, a company has the legal capacity and powers of an individual both within Australia and extra-territorially.[53] Chapter 3 detailed the separate legal personality of registered companies. Creditors seeking recompense for a liability incurred by a company limited by shares may only look to the company and its assets, unless a court decides to 'lift the corporate veil', exposing the shareholders or others to liability for the debt.[54] The key organs of a company are the board of directors and the members in general meeting. Acts of these organs within their respective powers are deemed to be acts of the company, and not merely acts taken by the organs on its behalf. The organs of the company derive their power and authority from the company constitution as outlined in Chapter 5,[55] the statutory replaceable rules as discussed in Chapter 3[56] and the *Corporations Act*.

Although both organs of the company are capable of making decisions which affect the company's interests, the management of the company is primarily vested in a board

46 Given that the ideal corporation as expounded by Berle and Means in their revised edition of their 1932 book can also hardly be said to exist in reality, the use of the description 'perfectly' is ironically intended: AA Berle and GC Means, *The Modern Corporation and Private Property* (Transaction Publishers, rev ed, 1968).

47 'Directors' Duties and Corporate Governance: Facilitating Innovations and Protecting Investors' (Corporate Law Economic Reform Program Paper No 3, The Treasury, 1997) <https://treasury.gov.au/sites/default/files/2019-03/full-13.pdf>: Australian companies are generally very highly leveraged.

48 Ibid.

49 Chapter 1 at Section 1.80.

50 *Corporations Act* ss 113–14.

51 Ibid s 201A. Public companies must have a minimum of three directors.

52 Ibid s 204A(2). Appointment of a secretary in proprietary companies has been optional since March 2000: s 204A(1).

53 Ibid s 124(1).

54 *Briggs v James Hardie & Co Pty Ltd* (1989) 16 NSWLR 549.

55 Public companies that wish to be listed on the Australian Securities Exchange must have a constitution: ASX, *Listing Rules* (at 19 December 2016) r 1.1, Condition 2. ASIC may request the constitution of a proprietary company under *Corporations Act* s 138.

56 See the table listed at *Corporations Act* s 141. The replaceable rules can be displaced or modified by the company's constitution: *Corporations Act* s 135(2).

of directors.[57] Svehla argues that because the powers of management and control of the company's affairs and its assets are vested in its directors the law imposes statutory, common law and equitable duties upon them.[58] Finn suggests that '[t]he freedom which [directors] enjoy in their decision-making, the lack of direct control by their respective beneficiaries, has attracted equity's supervision'.[59] Spigelman CJ suggests that the ability of the directors to dispose of company property is justification to apply the same stringent test with respect to the exercise of power to dispose of property as is applied to trustees of a traditional trust.[60] It is this autonomy and access to company property which attracts the law's regulatory attention to the director.

10.20 Who is a director?

The term 'director' is defined in s 9AC of the *Corporations Act*,[61] and, unless contrary intention appears,[62] includes persons validly appointed as a director, those acting in the position of director (de facto directors), and those in accordance with whose wishes or instructions the directors of the company are accustomed to act (shadow directors). The subjective intention of the individual or others within the corporation is not the relevant consideration—the courts will apply an objective test when determining whether a person should be considered a 'director'.[63] In Australia, it may not be possible to maintain a strict division between the categories of shadow and de facto directors,[64] and it is possible for a person to be both a shadow and de facto director.[65] By contrast, in the United Kingdom, the terms have been held to be mutually exclusive.[66]

57 *Corporations Act* ss 198A–E. Section 198E is not a replaceable rule.

58 J Svehla, 'Director's Fiduciary Duties' (2006) 27(2) *Australian Bar Review* 192, 192.

59 PD Finn, *Fiduciary Obligations* (The Law Book Company Ltd, 1977) 3.

60 *O'Halloran v RT Thomas & Family Pty Ltd* (1998) 45 NSWLR 262, 277; also discussed as the foundation for a category of fiduciary obligations in LS Sealy, 'Fiduciary Relationships' (1962) 20(1) *Cambridge Law Journal* 69, 74-5. Analogies are often made between directors and trustees, but this has been criticised as a distraction: see, eg, R Flannigan, 'Fiduciary Duties of Shareholders and Directors' (2004) *Journal of Business Law* 277, 284; R Flannigan, 'The Adulteration of Fiduciary Doctrine in Corporate Law' (2006) 122(3) *Law Quarterly Review* 449, 450–1.

61 Prior to 2024, the definitions contained in ss 9AB-D were contained in s 9, rather than as separate sections of the *Corporations Act*. Between 2020 and 2024, the Australian Law Reform Commission (ALRC) undertook a 'Review of the Legislative Framework for Corporations and Financial Services regulation': Australian Law Reform Commission, *Confronting Complexity: Reforming Corporations and Financial Services Legislation* (Report No 141, November 2023). One recommendation was to simplify and improve the navigability of the *Corporations Act*: this change was one of the amendments undertaken to achieve that recommendation. There was no change to the substance of the definition of 'director' or 'officer', and so the older case law references to the sub-definitions within s 9 remain valid for interpretation of ss 9AC-D.

62 The notes to s 9AC give examples of provisions that demonstrate contrary intention, including: s 249C (the power to call a meeting of a company's members); s 205B (notice to ASIC of a change of address); and s 251A(3) (signing minutes of meetings).

63 *BCEG International (Australia) Pty Ltd v Xiao* (2022) 162 ACSR 601 [330]; *BCI Finances Pty Ltd (in liq) v Binetter (No 4)* (2016) 348 ALR 227.

64 *Grimaldi v Chameleon Mining NL (No 2)* (2012) 200 FCR 296 [61], [69].

65 *Buzzle Operations Pty Ltd (in liq) v Apple Computer Australia Pty Ltd* (2011) 81 NSWLR 47.

66 *Re Hydrodam (Corby) Ltd* [1994] 2 BCLC 180, 182–3. Note: the definition of a shadow director in that jurisdiction is not identical to the provision in s 9, nor is it qualified in the way discussed at Section 10.20.10: *Buzzle Operations Ptd Ltd (in liq) v Apple Computer Australia Pty Ltd* (2010) 238 FLR 384.

In addition to the labels of de facto and shadow director, directors are often referred to by labels that reflect their particular status in relation to the company itself: executive, non-executive, and independent. Executive directors are full-time employees of the company and will have significant management and administrative duties delegated to them by the board.[67] Non-executive directors will not be involved in the day-to-day management of the company's business, and their engagement with the company will not be through a full-time employment contract. Whether a director is an executive or non-executive director will be a question of fact in each company's circumstances, and will be primarily determined by the executive powers conferred upon the particular director.[68] Non-executive directors may also be labelled as independent if they have no affiliation with the management of the company, or other business or personal relationship that could be seen as materially interfering with their independent judgment. The ASX *Corporate Governance Principles and Recommendations* recommend that the majority of the board should be made up of independent non-executive directors.[69] The commentary attached to the ASX Principles provide examples of interests, positions and associations that might cast doubt on a director's independence, including: previous employment in an executive capacity by the company; having material business relationships with the company, or being involved in entities which have such relationships; holding substantial security in the company;[70] close family ties with anyone who falls into such examples; or length of service as a director of the company.[71]

10.20.05 De facto directors

A person who acts as a director will be considered a de facto director, even if they are not validly appointed as a director. In *Deputy Commissioner of Taxation v Austin*,[72] Austin had resigned as a director but continued to play an active role in the company, including negotiating agreements with the Commissioner on behalf of the company and with the company's creditors for more time to make payments. These are responsibilities typically expected of a director, and Austin was therefore held to be a de facto director. Although stating that it is not practicable to establish a general statement as to what constitutes 'acting in the position of a director', Madgwick J set out two factors as relevant to a decision as to whether a person was a de facto director. The first is the size of the company, as it may impact on the discretion given to individual employees to deal with significant matters. What may demonstrate 'acting as a director' in a small company may not

67 The topics of delegation and reliance are dealt with in detail in Chapter 11 at Sections 11.20.05 and 11.20.10.

68 *AIG Australia Ltd v Jaques* (2014) 44 VR 780.

69 ASX Corporate Governance Council, *Corporate Governance Principles and Recommendations* (Australian Securities Exchange, 4th ed, February 2019) Principle 2, Recommendation 2.4, 15 <https://www.asx.com.au/content/dam/asx/about/corporate-governance-council/cgc-principles-and-recommendations-fourth-edn.pdf>.

70 'Substantial holding' as defined in s 9 of the *Corporations Act*.

71 ASX Corporate Governance Council, *Corporate Governance Principles and Recommendations* (Australian Securities Exchange, 4th ed, February 2019) Recommendation 2.3, box 2.3 <https://www.asx.com.au/content/dam/asx/about/corporate-governance-council/cgc-principles-and-recommendations-fourth-edn.pdf>.

72 *Deputy Commissioner of Taxation v Austin* (1998) 28 ACSR 565.

qualify within a large company, and this may vary depending on the internal practices of the company. The second is how the person claiming to be a director is reasonably perceived by outsiders in their dealings with the company.[73]

In addition to these factors, a necessary condition for a person to be held to be a director is that the person must be exercising top-level management functions.

The courts will not permit a person describing their role as something other than a director to escape being held to be a de facto director if their behaviour fits with the factors listed above, even where they have not been properly appointed.[74] In *Mistmorn Pty Ltd (in liq) v Yasseen*,[75] a person described as a consultant undertaking tasks typically expected of a director was held to be a de facto director.

Although s 201B requires directors to be 'individuals', it does not permit a consultant company to be 'used as a screen'[76] to avoid an individual being found to be a de facto director. In *Grimaldi v Chameleon Mining NL (No 2)*,[77] the Full Federal Court noted that it is possible that, if a consultant to a company is a company itself, and, through the action of its directors or officers, it acts as a director, then it will be a question of fact as to which director or officer within the consultant company will be held to be the de facto director of the company.

10.20.10 Shadow directors

A person in accordance with whose wishes or instructions the directors of the company are accustomed to act is a shadow director. Section 9AC specifically states that a person is not a shadow director merely because 'the directors act on the advice given by the person in the proper performance of functions attaching to the person's professional capacity, or the person's business relationship with the directors or the company'. For example, in *Re Akron Roads Pty Ltd (in liq) (No 3)*,[78] a management consulting company Crewe Sharp Pty Ltd ('Crewe Sharp') was engaged by Akron for Mr Crewe to provide services as director and for Crewe Sharp to provide advice on financial and management matters. When Akron became insolvent and was placed into liquidation, the liquidator argued that Crewe Sharp was a director due to their role invoicing Akron for Crewe's work as a director of Akron, and their provision of other employees of Crewe Sharp to give advice and provide financial and administrative services to Akron.[79] Robson J found that, although Crewe was clearly a director of Akron, Crewe Sharp was not: 'an adviser does not become a shadow director merely because the directors follow his or her advice, particularly when the adviser has been retained to give advice'.[80]

Although a company is not capable of formal appointment as a director under s 201B, a company can be found to be a shadow director.[81] This was considered in

73 Ibid 570.
74 *Stuart v Mordialloc Sporting Club Inc* [2021] VSC 244 [98].
75 *Mistmorn Pty Ltd (in liq) v Yasseen* (1996) 21 ACSR 173.
76 *Grimaldi v Chameleon Mining NL (No 2)* (2012) 200 FCR 296, 339.
77 Ibid [68], [103], [136]–[140].
78 *Re Akron Roads Pty Ltd (In liq) (No 3)* (2016) 117 ACSR 513.
79 Ibid 516.
80 Ibid 565.
81 *Standard Chartered Bank of Australia Ltd v Antico* (1995) 38 NSWLR 290.

Buzzle Operations Pty Ltd (in liq) v Apple Computer Australia Pty Ltd.[82] In that case, it was alleged that Apple Computer Australia Pty Ltd ('Apple') and Mr Likidis, its finance director, were shadow directors of Buzzle Operations Pty Ltd ('Buzzle'). Buzzle was the product of the merger of six retailers of Apple products. The merger occurred under the advice of Apple as to the structure of the merger, the financial accounting system to be used, the due diligence reports required, the transfer of stock from the retailers to Buzzle, and future cash flow. As Apple was the major creditor of all six retailers, and also of Buzzle when it was formed, the liquidator argued that Apple was in effect a shadow director, as the retailers and Buzzle felt they had no choice but to agree with the requirements set by Apple. The question was whether Apple, as a creditor, was able to satisfy the definition of shadow director of Buzzle? White J at first instance stated that for the definition to be satisfied: first, 'the directors of the company must be accustomed to act *as directors of the company* in accordance with the person's instructions or wishes as to *how they should so act*'.[83] Second, 'a person or company is not within the definition [of a shadow director] merely because [they impose] conditions on [their] commercial dealings with the company with which the directors feel obliged to comply'.[84] His Honour continued:

> Unless something more intrudes, the directors are free and would be expected to exercise their own judgment as to whether it is in the interests of the company to comply with the terms upon which the third party insists, or to reject those terms. If, in the exercise of their own judgment, they habitually comply with the third party's terms, it does not follow that the third party has given instructions or expressed a wish as to how they should exercise their functions as directors.[85]

Further, there should be 'a causal connection between the putative shadow director giving the instruction or expressing the wish and the directors acting on it'.[86] Performing an act that the directors would have done in any event is not sufficient to satisfy the requirement of acting 'in accordance with' the instruction. Equally, White J found that this phrase requires 'habitual compliance over a period of time'.[87] Further, a shadow director will not be liable in liquidation for debts incurred prior to such a time that they could be considered a shadow director; that is, the point in time where the board could be said to now be accustomed to acting in accordance with their instructions.[88] Although the directors must collectively be accustomed to act on that person's instructions, a 'governing majority'[89] of the directors acting in that way is sufficient.

82 *Buzzle Operations Pty Ltd (in liq) v Apple Computer Australia Pty Ltd* (2010) 238 FLR 384; affirmed *Buzzle Operations Pty Ltd (in liq) v Apple Computer Australia Pty Ltd* (2011) 81 NSWLR 47.

83 *Buzzle Operations Pty Ltd (in liq) v Apple Computer Australia Pty Ltd* (2010) 238 FLR 384, 439 (emphasis in original).

84 Ibid.

85 Ibid.

86 Ibid 440–41.

87 Ibid 441.

88 Ibid.

89 Ibid 437.

Therefore, despite the *Corporations Act* expressly limiting directorships to natural persons,[90] a company can be held to be a shadow director[91] as can a creditor.[92] The Court of Appeal in *Buzzle Operations Pty Ltd (in liq) v Apple Computer Australia Pty Ltd* agreed in separate judgments with the propositions put forward by White J at first instance as to the definition of a shadow director (see the paragraph above), but were careful to note that a mortgagee will not be held to be a shadow director merely because the directors tended to take the advice provided by that mortgagee.[93]

10.20.15 Officers

Many of the obligations that the *Corporations Act* place upon directors also apply to officers, and sometimes to secretaries and employees. The s 9AD(1) definition of officer[94] encompasses those acting in 'director-like' capacity, receivers, administrators, liquidators and trustees. It provides that an officer includes:

(a) a director or secretary of the corporation; or

(b) a person:

   (i) who makes, or participates in making, decisions that affect the whole, or a substantial part, of the business of the corporation; or

   (ii) who has the capacity to affect significantly the corporation's financial standing; or

   (iii) in accordance with whose instructions or wishes the directors of the corporation are accustomed to act (excluding advice given by the person in the proper performance of functions attaching to the person's professional capacity or their business relationship with the directors or the corporation); or

(c) a receiver, or receiver and manager, of the property of the corporation; or

(d) an administrator of the corporation; or

(e) an administrator of a deed of company arrangement executed by the corporation; or

(f) a restructuring practitioner for the corporation; or

(g) a restructuring practitioner for a restructuring plan made by the corporation; or

(h) a liquidator of the corporation; or

(i) a trustee or other person administering a compromise or arrangement made between the corporation and someone else.

---

90 *Corporations Act* s 201B.

91 *Re Akron Roads Pty Ltd (in liq) (No 3)* (2016) 117 ACSR 513.

92 *Buzzle Operations Pty Ltd (in liq) v Apple Computer Australia Pty Ltd* (2011) 81 NSWLR 47.

93 Ibid 51 [9]-]10] (Hodgson JA), 76-7 [229] (Young JA). Whealy JA agreed with Young JA in respect of this part of the judgment: 81 [287].

94 The definition of 'officer' was introduced by the *Corporate Law Economic Reform Program Act 1999* (Cth) discussed in Section 10.10.10. As with the definition of 'director', this definition was moved from within s 9 to a stand-alone section, s 9AD, in the reforms following the ALRC's *Review of the Legislative Framework for Corporations and Financial Services regulation* concluded in 2024.

This definition catches shadow directors (as defined in Section 10.20.10), shadow officers, and senior managers.[95] Indeed, in *Dwyer v Lippiatt*,[96] White J needed to determine whether Mr Kirk could be considered an officer of a company of which he was described as a 'consultant', when he could not be found to be either a director (due to his status as a bankrupt) or an employee. In finding him an officer under either ss 9AD(1)(b)(ii) or (iii), White J noted that 'there can be no doubt about Kirk's importance to the drive and direction of the company'.[97] White J considered that Kirk may also have fallen within the definition of 'shadow director' discussed above. In *Australian Securities and Investments Commission v Citigroup Global Markets Australia Pty Ltd (No 4)*,[98] Jacobsen J of the Federal Court considered whether a share trader employed by Citigroup with a daily trading limit of $10 million could be considered an officer of Citigroup under the definition in s 9AD, particularly sub-ss (1)(b)(i) and (ii). Jacobsen J stated that 'those categories are concerned with identifying persons who are involved in the management of the corporation'[99] and reflected the history within the various iterations of corporate legislation of separation and distinction between employees and officers.[100] The trader, Mr Manchee, had no involvement in policy-making or in decisions that affected the whole or a substantial part of the business of Citigroup[101] and did not satisfy the definition under s 9AD(1)(b)(i). Despite Manchee's large daily trading limit, which arguably could have resulted in the 'capacity to affect significantly' the financial standing of the company, Jacobsen J compared him to a loans officers of a large bank, who could, 'in general terms, have the capacity to affect the bank's standing if he or she lends recklessly, but the loans officer is an employee, not an officer of the corporation'.[102] Equally, the Court held that ASIC had not proven that $10 million was a 'significant' figure in terms of the business conducted by Citigroup and, as such, Manchee did not satisfy the definition under s 9AD(1)(b)(ii).[103] The Full Federal Court in *Morley v Australian Securities and Investments Commission*[104] held the joint company secretary and general counsel of James Hardie Industries Ltd ('JHIL'), Mr Shafron, to be an officer on the basis that he participated in decisions which affected the whole or a substantial part of the business of JHIL.[105]

95 The definition of 'senior manager' was introduced in the *Corporate Law Economic Reform Program (Audit Reform and Corporate Disclosure) Act 2004* (Cth) to replace the broader definition of 'executive officer', which included a person 'who is concerned, or takes part, in the management of the corporation'. This had unintended consequences within the Act and resulted in ASIC issuing a Class Order (CO 04/899, July 2004) to modify the definition of senior manager for the purposes of ch 6D and pt 7.9 of the *Corporations Act* to recognise this broader definition. CAMAC recommended that the wider definition be generally reinstated, but this has not occurred: Corporations and Markets Advisory Committee, *Corporate Duties Below Board Level* (CAMAC, April 2006) [1.5.1].

96 *Dwyer v Lippiatt* (2004) 50 ACSR 333.

97 Ibid 351.

98 *Australian Securities and Investments Commission v Citigroup Global Markets Australia Pty Ltd (No 4)* (2007) 160 FCR 35.

99 Ibid 99.

100 Ibid 99–100.

101 Ibid 101.

102 Ibid.

103 Ibid.

104 *Morley v Australian Securities and Investments Commission* (2010) 81 ACSR 285.

105 This case was a part of the James Hardie litigation, discussed in detail in Chapter 11 at Section 11.15.05.

On appeal to the High Court in *Shafron v Australian Securities and Investments Commission*,[106] Shafron argued that the conduct which was held to be in breach of his duty of care was undertaken in his role as general counsel, and not in his role as company secretary, and that his responsibilities as general counsel did not satisfy the definition of officer in s 9AD. The High Court rejected both of these arguments. The Court held that:

> regardless of whether any other element of the definition of 'officer' applied to Mr Shafron, s 180(1) of the Corporations Law (and thus the Corporations Act) applied to him because he was a company secretary of JHIL. Because this is so, the relevant statutory inquiry was what were the responsibilities he had within JHIL, not an inquiry which sought to divide the capacities in which those responsibilities were undertaken: whether between a role of company secretary and some other role, or otherwise.[107]

The Court, in relation to s 9AD(1)(b)(i), said 'the inquiry required by this paragraph of the definition must be directed to what role the person in question plays in the corporation. It is not an inquiry that is confined to the role that the person played in relation to the particular issue in respect of which it is alleged that there was a breach of duty.'[108] Further, this definition distinguishes between making decisions of a particular character, and participating in the making of such decisions.[109] The Court also noted that the definition within s 9AD(1)(b) is clearly different from and wider than the persons identified in the other paragraphs of the definition of officer in s 9AD, as they all hold named offices in or in relation to the company. '[T]hose identified in para (b) are identified by what they do (sub-para (i)), what capacity they have (sub-para (ii)) or what influence on the directors they have had and continue to have (sub-para (iii)).'[110] As such, a person satisfying the definition in s 9AD(1)(b)(i) may not necessarily be in substantially the same position as a director.

In contrast, in the decision of *King v Australian Securities and Investments Commission*,[111] the Queensland Court of Appeal declined to find Mr King to be an officer of MFS Investment Management Ltd (MFSIM), which was the responsible entity for a managed investment scheme, Premium Income Fund (PIF). MFS Ltd, the parent company of the group, which included MFSIM, became financially distressed, and MFSIM and senior individuals within the group arranged to draw down $150 million from a bank facility arranged for PIF. The money was to pay debts for MFS group debts, for which PIF was not actually or contingently liable,[112] with no agreement about consideration or repayment.[113] At first instance, ASIC was successful in arguing that this misuse of PIF's funds by MFSIM was a contravention of the *Corporations Act*, and that King and Mr White

106 *Shafron v Australian Securities and Investments Commission* (2012) 247 CLR 465 ('*Shafron*').
107 Ibid 472.
108 Ibid 478.
109 Ibid 479.
110 Ibid 478.
111 *King v Australian Securities and Investments Commission* (2018) 134 ACSR 105.
112 Ibid [9].
113 Ibid [13].

were persons involved in that contravention.[114] Additionally, King and White were found to be officers of MFSIM as the responsible entity for PIF.

On appeal, the Queensland Court of Appeal focused on the case pleaded by ASIC, which alleged that King was an officer as he had capacity to affect significantly the financial standing of MFSIM,[115] reflecting the s 9AD(1)(b)(ii) definition of 'officer'. The particulars and some of the findings of the trial judge reflected facts that fell more obviously into s 9AD(1)(b)(iii): that the relationship between White and King meant that White customarily acted in accordance with King's instructions or wishes.[116] Further, the trial judge also found that King participated in the making of decisions which affected the whole or a substantial part of MFSIM's business—reflecting s 9AD(1)(b)(i) of the definition of 'officer'—which the Court of Appeal criticised as not part of ASIC's pleaded case.[117]

On appeal, King was successful in arguing that he did not have a capacity to affect MFSIM's financial standing, as he did not act in an office or position within that company.[118] As ASIC had not proven that King acted in an office of MFSIM, King was successful in challenging the conclusion that he was an officer.[119] This narrow reading of 'officer' in s 9AD(1)(b)(ii) was overturned by the High Court, with five judges concurring via two separate judgments, delivered by Kiefel CJ, Gageler and Keane JJ, and separately Nettle and Gordon JJ.[120] In contrast to the Queensland Court of Appeal, the High Court held that s 9AD(1)(b)(ii) should not be limited to those who hold or occupy a named office, or a 'recognised position with rights and duties attached to it'.[121]

Textual differences between ss 9AD(1)(a) and (b) of the definition make it clear that sub-s (b) of the definition extends the scope of the term 'officer' beyond its ordinary meaning of 'office holder'. The contrasting language is a powerful textual indication that Parliament did not intend to confine the class of persons described in s 9AD(1)(b), including sub-s (i), by an unexpressed requirement that the relationship between individual and a corporation be identified by reference to a recognised position with rights and duties attached to it.[122]

The case of *King v Australian Securities and Investment Commission* was lengthy and complex, dealing with transactions that took place in 2007; a trial spanning from November 2013 to September 2014 that generated over 5000 pages of transcript; a first instance decision delivered in 2016 and supplemented in 2017; and a Court of Appeal decision in 2018 culminating in a High Court decision in 2020.[123] Devotion of resources to such large, complex litigation must be juxtaposed against the recommendations in the Final Report of the Royal Commission into Misconduct in the Banking, Superannuation

114 Ibid [14].
115 Ibid [230].
116 Ibid [232].
117 Ibid [235].
118 Ibid [238].
119 (2018) 134 ACSR 105 [286]–[288].
120 *Australian Securities and Investments Commission v King* (2020) 270 CLR 1.
121 Ibid [24], [87], [125].
122 Ibid [24].
123 Ibid [9], [17].

and Financial Services Industry. Of particular relevance is Recommendation 6.2, which suggests on the one hand that ASIC should take, 'as its starting point, the question of whether a court should determine the consequences of a contravention'; but on the other, directly recognises that lesser sanctions, such as infringement notices, 'will rarely be an appropriate enforcement tool where the infringing party is a large corporation'.[124]

10.20.20 Conclusion

Those persons with the powers of management and control of the company's affairs and assets are subject to statutory, common law and equitable duties to regulate their behaviour. The chapters that follow deal in detail with individual directors' duties. The answer to the question 'Who owes directors' duties?' is broader than those who are identified on the ASIC register as a director. It includes de facto and shadow directors, and application of those duties extends beyond directors to officers, senior management and, in some instances, employees. The duty varies for each individual and will be discussed within the following chapters. The question 'To whom are directors' duties owed?' is also not as simple as it may first seem and will be answered within the following chapters.

10.25 Historical development of directors' duties

Chapter 1 provided the history of the corporate form and corporations legislation tracing the development from Britain in the seventeenth century to the current *Corporations Act*. The current position regarding obligations owed by directors equally finds its basis in the historical development of the corporate form.

10.25.05 Company law and directors' duties prior to 1900

To overcome the difficulties inherent in achieving incorporation following the *Bubble Act*, Chancery lawyers fashioned a remedy in the form of the deed of settlement company. The deed was the basis for legal protest by the members if the management departed from its provisions.

The eventual introduction of the *Joint Stock Companies Act 1844*[125] enabled these deed of settlement companies to secure corporate status through formal registration (see Section 1.30.05 for more detail). That Act adopted the constitutional structure of the deed of settlement company, vesting management powers in directors, and other powers and functions in the assembly of shareholders in general meeting. However, it did not provide explicit directors' duties, although some accountability mechanisms, including obligations to hold company meetings, to audit and to publish company accounts, were included.[126] As such, directors' duties remained the purview of the common law and equity.[127] Several consolidating acts followed, culminating in the *Companies Act 1862*[128]

124 *Royal Commission into Misconduct in the Banking, Superannuation and Financial Services Industry* (Final Report, 4 February 2019) 37.

125 *Joint Stock Companies Act 1844*, 7 & 8 Vict, c 110.

126 Ibid ss 20, 33, 36.

127 See, eg, *Aberdeen Railway Co v Blaikie Brothers* (1854) 1 Macq 461. The development of common law and equitable directors' duties will be considered in Chapters 11–13.

128 *Companies Act 1862*, 25 & 26 Vict, c 89.

that was the model for the first companies' statutes in Australia. As discussed in Sections 1.40.10–15, English reforms were applied by the Australian colonies, although Victoria implemented its own measures to manage fraudulent practices arising out of its mining boom.[129] The *Companies Act 1896* (Vic) contained the first statutory directors' duty in s 116(2), which placed directors under 'an obligation to the company to use reasonable care and prudence in the exercise of his [sic] powers and duties'. This duty appears to have been prompted by a series of 'sensational collapses of land companies', commencing in New South Wales and following in Victoria in the early 1890s.[130] Its inclusion was vigorously debated, with various iterations of the duty appearing in the draft Bill during the legislative process. Langford, Ramsay and Welsh examined the Parliamentary Debates surrounding the introduction of this duty into statute, and found that its proponents believed that public protection was necessary in light of the earlier corporate collapses and subsequent economic depression.[131] They summarise the opposition to the statutory duty in four general propositions: that including such a duty in legislation would deter people from becoming directors; that the duty was too uncertain; that it related to a moral rather than a legal duty; and that the actions of directors would be subject to judgment with the benefit of hindsight.[132] These grounds of opposition held sway in other jurisdictions at that time,[133] and can still be seen in objections to the regulation of directors' behaviour today. This duty was short-lived, with no reported cases interpreting it, and it was omitted from the Act that replaced it—the *Companies Act 1910* (Vic).[134] Its exclusion from the later Act appears from the Parliamentary Debates to be due to concern that the Victorian law was different from that of England, which had also undertaken revision of its corporate law during that time but did not contain any statutory directors' duties. Further, it was considered that capital investment from England into the Victorian economy through Victorian companies would be eased if the laws were uniform.[135] Although there was no parliamentary discussion directly on the removal of s 116(2) from the 1910 Act, it was omitted and not reintroduced until some 50 years later.

10.25.10 Company law and directors' duties from the 1900s to today

Despite previous praise from the courts for Parliament's abstention from formulating precise legislative rules for the conduct of business affairs,[136] the early twentieth

129 The no-liability company form: *Mining Companies Act 1871* (Vic).

130 J Waugh, 'Company Law and the Crash of the 1890s in Victoria' (1992) 15(2) *University of New South Wales Law Journal* 356, 363–4.

131 R Langford, I Ramsay and M Welsh, 'The Origins of Company Directors' Statutory Duty of Care' (2015) 37(4) *Sydney Law Review* 489, 493.

132 Ibid 493–4.

133 Rob McQueen, *A Social History of Company Law: Great Britain and the Australian Colonies 1854–1920* (Ashgate, 2009) 266–7.

134 R Langford, I Ramsay and M Welsh, 'The Origins of Company Directors' Statutory Duty of Care' (2015) 37(4) *Sydney Law Review* 489, 490, 497.

135 Ibid 497.

136 *Dovey v Cory* [1901] AC 477, 488 (Lord Macnaughten), cited with approval in *Re City Equitable Fire Insurance Co Ltd* [1925] Ch 407, 427 (Romer J).

century saw the gradual introduction of obligations of directors in legislation. Section 149 of the *Companies Act 1929* (UK) required directors to declare any interest they had which might create a direct or indirect conflict with their position as a director. Repeating the existing position under the general law[137] in statute was intended to highlight the responsibilities of directors and provide some protection to shareholders.[138] The section was reproduced in Australia,[139] as was much of the remainder of the Act. The Victorian Act introduced further statutory duties in 1958 with a system resembling the duties in place in the *Corporations Act* beginning to emerge. In particular, s 107(1) required directors to act honestly at all times, and to use reasonable diligence in the discharge of their duties; s 107(2) prohibited all officers of the company from gaining an improper advantage from the misuse of information; s 107(3) created a penalty for breach; and s 107(4) expressly retained the operation of the common law duties.

Despite the major reforms that occurred in company law from the enactment of the *Uniform Companies Acts* (see Section 1.40.20), the substantive provisions relating to directors' duties remained mostly unaltered, as the focus of the reforms was on uniformity of administration and regulation. One alteration included the extension of the provision relating to directors gaining an improper advantage to include misuse of information by employees and former officers,[140] and misuse of position.[141] At this time, it was uncommon to see significant litigation in relation to directors' duties, as the power to institute proceedings in the name of the company was generally reposed in the board of directors who were unlikely to bring such an action. Cases generally arose at the behest of the liquidator, or after a new board had been installed after a change in control.[142] Unless it could be argued to consist of fraud on the minority,[143] shareholders had no ability to overcome the rule that the company, and not the shareholders, was the proper plaintiff for wrongs done to the company, according to *Foss v Harbottle*,[144] to bring an action against the directors. As such, case law was scarce until a number of reforms, including to the duties themselves, granted greater access to this area. One influential reform was the amendment to shareholder remedies permitting greater access to the oppression remedy.[145]

137 The phrase 'the general law' is used extensively in the corporate law field: see, eg, *Corporations Act* s 193. It is intended to refer to both the common law and equity but can be confusing for those unfamiliar with this term.

138 United Kingdom, *Parliamentary Debates*, House of Commons, 25 July 1928 Vol 220 Col 1306–1308; J Kirby, 'The History and Development of the Conflict and Profit Rules in Corporate Law—a Review' (2004) 22(4) *Company and Securities Law Journal* 259, 264.

139 *Companies Act 1936* (NSW) s 129; *Companies Act 1938* (Vic) s 149.

140 *Companies Code* s 229(3).

141 Ibid s 229(4).

142 See, eg, two well-known examples: *Re City Equitable Fire Insurance Co Ltd* [1925] Ch 407, discussed in Chapter 11 at Section 11.10.05; *Regal (Hastings) Ltd v Gulliver* [1967] 2 AC 134, discussed in Chapter 13 at Section 13.10.30.

143 Discussed in detail in Chapter 14 at Section 14.15.20.

144 *Foss v Harbottle* (1843) 67 ER 189.

145 *Companies and Securities Legislation (Miscellaneous Amendments) Act 1983* (Cth) s 89.

During the 1990s, due to a series of high-profile corporate collapses in the late 1980s,[146] directors' duties began receiving more attention from the legislature[147] and reforms were drafted, particularly in relation to directors who had either a personal interest or another duty that was in conflict with the duties they owed to the company.[148] The reforms limited disclosure of conflicts to directors of proprietary companies.[149] A new provision was introduced that prevented directors of public companies from voting, or being present for discussion, at board meetings on matters where they had a material personal interest.[150] Further provisions were introduced to deal with related party transactions in public companies[151] as a response to the corporate collapses of the 1980s where dishonest related party transactions were considered responsible for these collapses. The obligations were placed on the company in relation to transactions with related parties, including directors, but did not include any duties on directors in relation to their personal interests or profits.

The next major review of statutory directors' duties occurred in the lead up to the *CLERP Act*,[152] which sought, among other issues, to address concerns that regulation and uncertainty about directors' duties was adversely distracting directors from risk-taking and wealth creation.[153] The amendments were ultimately enacted by the Commonwealth after the states referred their powers with respect to corporations, corporate regulation and the regulation of financial products and services to the Commonwealth.[154] This allowed for the new national corporations legislation, which reflected the law proposed in CLERP, to be passed in the form of the *Corporations Act* and the *Australian Securities and Investments Commission Act 2001* (Cth).

In 2017, further reforms intended to encourage reasonable risk-taking by directors of companies in financial distress were made.[155] The Explanatory Memorandum to the Bill suggested that Australia's 'current insolvent trading laws put too much focus on stigmatising and penalising failure'.[156] One of these reforms created a limited 'safe harbour' provision to accompany the duty to prevent trading while insolvent which exists in s 588G. The purpose of this provision was to encourage directors to remain in control of their company during financial distress, to engage early and take reasonable risks to

146 See generally T Sykes, *The Bold Riders* (Allen & Unwin, 1996) for an account of collapses such as Rothwells, Bond Corporation and Qintex.

147 See, eg, Senate Standing Committee of Legal and Constitutional Affairs, Parliament of Australia, *Company Directors' Duties* (Report, 1989).

148 Corporate Law Reform Bill 1992 (Cth).

149 Ibid s 231.

150 Ibid s 232A.

151 Ibid pt 3.2A.

152 *Corporate Law Economic Reform Program Act 1999* (Cth), as discussed at Section 10.10.10.

153 'Directors' Duties and Corporate Governance: Facilitating Innovations and Protecting Investors' (Corporate Law Economic Reform Program Paper No 3, The Treasury, 1997) <https://treasury.gov.au/sites/default/files/2019-03/full-13.pdf>.

154 For more detail on the constitutional uncertainties prior to this referral of power, see Sections 1.40.35–1.50.

155 *Treasury Laws Amendment (2017 Enterprise Incentives No 2) Act 2017* (Cth).

156 Explanatory Memorandum, Treasury Laws Amendment (2017 Enterprise Incentives No 2) Bill 2017 (Cth) 3.

assist recovery or restructure, rather than placing the company prematurely into voluntary administration or liquidation.[157]

The Interim and Final Reports of the Royal Commission into Misconduct in the Banking, Superannuation and Financial Services Industry led to the bipartisan political support for the Treasury Laws Amendment (Strengthening Corporate and Financial Sector Penalties) Bill 2018 (Cth), expanding the scope of the civil penalty scheme, increasing the severity of penalties for criminal offences and breaches of the civil penalty scheme, and lowering the threshold for 'dishonesty' under the *Corporations Act*. Following this royal commission, the ALRC conducted a *Review of the Legislative Framework for Corporations and Financial Services Regulation* from 2020–2024, leading to three interim and one final report. The *Treasury Laws Amendment (2023 Law Improvement Package No 1) Act 2023* (Cth) enacted significant amendments to the numbering and structure of the *Corporations Act*, implementing the recommendations of Interim Reports A and B[158] to improve navigability.[159]

10.30 Directors' duties: a summary

Directors are subject to a number of duties under the general law and the *Corporations Act* which can be broken into two themes: duties which relate to care and diligence, and duties which relate to loyalty and good faith. These themes will be discussed in detail in Chapters 11, 12 and 13. The duties in the general law maintain their relevance and operation due to s 185 of the *Corporations Act*, which provides that 'sections 180 to 184 have effect in addition to, and not in derogation of, any rule of law relating to the duty or liability of a person because of their office or employment in relation to a corporation'. The following discussion provides a summary detailing which duties exist at common law, equity and statute, noting where they are significantly similar and explaining where their expression in the statute differs from their development as principles in case law. The relationship between the obligations in the underlying law and their reflection in statute will be considered in later chapters. The impact of the choice of law in relation to remedies sought will be discussed at Section 10.35.05, and the varied pathways for exoneration and relief under the distinct sources of law will be identified in Section 10.40.

10.30.05 The duties of care and diligence

The duties which reflect the theme of care and diligence are contained in ss 180 and 588G of the *Corporations Act*, and at the common law via contract and tort, and in equity. Section 180(1) states:

> A director or other officer of a corporation must exercise their powers and discharge their duties with the degree of care and diligence that a reasonable person would exercise if they:

157 Ibid 7.

158 Australian Law Reform Commission, *Review of the Corporations and Financial Services Legislation* (Interim Report A, Report 137, November 2021) <https://www.alrc.gov.au/publication/fsl-report-137/>; Australian Law Reform Commission, *Review of the Corporations and Financial Services Legislation* (Interim Report B, Report 139, September 2022) <https://www.alrc.gov.au/publication/fsl-report-139/>.

159 Explanatory Memorandum, Treasury Laws Amendment (2023 Law Improvement Package No 1) Bill 2023 (Cth) 30–33.

(a) were a director or officer of a corporation the corporation's circumstances; and

(b) occupied the office held by, and had the same responsibilities within the corporation as, the director or officer.[160]

The requirement for care and diligence is tempered by s 180(2), the business judgment rule, which creates a 'safe harbour' for directors. It can operate as a defence to exculpate a director who has made a well-informed business decision. This business judgment rule does not have a counterpart in common law or equity, but s 180(2) also applies to those duties.

The duty of care in contract is likely to be similar in nature to the duty under s 180(1) of the *Corporations Act*: that the director exercises the care and skill expected of a person who occupies the position in question. This will be examined in Chapter 11.

A director also owes a tortious duty to exercise care and skill in performance of their functions and the discharge of the duties of their office.[161] A director is under a common law duty of care and can be liable as a tortfeasor for negligence.[162] If there is negligence in performing a contract, alternative claims may exist in both contract and tort.[163] However, it is possible to contract out of a tortious duty.

A director's duty of care and skill to the company is further recognised as an equitable duty,[164] and the nature and scope of that duty will be examined in Chapter 11.

Where the company is in financial difficulty, two further statutory duties arise: the director's duty to prevent insolvent trading[165] and the officer's duty to prevent creditor-defeating dispositions.[166] Section 588G of the *Corporations Act* obliges a director to prevent the company from incurring debts if there are reasonable grounds for suspecting that it is insolvent. Section 588GAB prohibits officers from engaging in 'conduct that results in the company making a creditor-defeating disposition' of company property, as part of the anti-phoenixing measures introduced into the Act in 2020. These concepts and the relevant provisions will be addressed in full in Chapter 11.

10.30.10 The duties of loyalty and good faith

The duties which reflect the theme of loyalty and good faith are contained in ss 181, 191–6 and ch 2E of the *Corporations Act*. Chapter 12 will deal with s 181, and the remaining provisions will be detailed in Chapter 13 along with the fiduciary obligation.

Section 181(1) requires directors and officers to exercise their powers and discharge their duties in good faith in the best interests of the company, and for a proper purpose.

160 *Corporations Act* s 180(1).

161 *Daniels v Anderson* (1995) 37 NSWLR 438, 502–5; *Permanent Building Society (in liq) v Wheeler* (1994) 11 WAR 187, 235–7; JD Heydon, 'Are the Duties of Company Directors to Exercise Care and Skill Fiduciary?' in S Degeling and J Edelman (eds), *Equity in Commercial Law* (Lawbook, 2005) 197. Heydon J challenges the finding of this objective duty by the Court in *Daniels v Anderson* but accepts that it exists for the purposes of his argument.

162 *Daniels v Anderson* (1995) 37 NSWLR 438.

163 Following the line of cases that commenced with *Hedley Byrne v Heller & Partners Ltd* [1964] AC 465.

164 *Permanent Building Society (in liq) v Wheeler* (1994) 11 WAR 187, 235–7.

165 *Corporations Act* s 588G.

166 Ibid s 588GAB.

This duty involves two limbs: first, a duty to act in good faith in the best interests of the company; and second, to exercise their powers for a proper purpose. The legal tests attached to each limb are distinct.

Satisfying the first limb of the duty involves both subjective and objective elements. Honest or altruistic behaviour will not prevent a finding of improper conduct if that conduct was carried out for an improper or collateral purpose.[167] Acting in the best interests of the company has been taken to mean, on the one hand, that the directors are acting in the best interests of the members as a collective group,[168] and alternatively that the directors must have regard to the interests of present and future members, as well as the company as a commercial entity, even if this is not in the short-term best interests of the members.[169] The second limb of the duty of loyalty—the requirement that directors exercise their powers for a proper purpose—involves the consideration of two separate issues: the objective purpose for which the power was granted, and the purpose for which the power was actually exercised.

10.30.15 Conflicts of interest

Sections 182–3 deal in part with one of the separate elements that comprise the fiduciary obligation owed by directors to the company in equity.[170] The fiduciary obligation is comprised of two parts: a duty that the directors not place themselves in a position where their duty to the company and their own personal interests or other duties conflict, and a duty not to secretly profit from the relationship with the company.[171] These duties are more generally known as the 'no conflict' and 'no profit' duties.[172] A breach of these duties can be remedied by the receipt of fully informed consent from the company. The statutory treatment of the 'no profit' rule is divided into improper use of position and improper use of information,[173] with criminal liability for breaches of these rules.[174] By contrast, the provision that details elements of the 'no conflict' rule exists separately in s 191, and requires disclosure by directors in all companies, except for single director proprietary companies.[175] The underlying fiduciary obligation is expressly preserved.[176]

167 *Permanent Building Society (in liq) v Wheeler* (1994) 11 WAR 187, 218.
168 *Greenhalgh v Arderne Cinemas Ltd* [1951] Ch 286.
169 *Darvall v North Sydney Brick & Tile Co Ltd* (1988) 6 ACLC 154.
170 *Hospital Products Ltd v United States Surgical Corporation* (1984) 156 CLR 41.
171 First appearing in Australia in *Moss v Moss (No 2)* (1900) 21 LR (NSW) Eq 253, 258 and confirmed by the High Court of Australia in numerous cases from *Hospital Products Ltd v United States Surgical Corporation* (1984) 156 CLR 41 to *Friend v Booker* (2009) 239 CLR 129.
172 The High Court adopted the use of this terminology in the decision of *Chan v Zacharia* (1984) 154 CLR 178.
173 *Corporations Act* ss 182–3. The use of position and use of information sections may be seen as general expressions of the 'business opportunity rule' as discussed in J Glover, *Commercial Equity—Fiduciary Relationships* (Butterworths, 1995) 131.
174 *Corporations Act* s 184.
175 *Corporations Act* s 191; *Digital Pulse Pty Ltd v Harris* (2002) 166 FLR 421, 426. Although the decision on exemplary damages for fiduciary breach was reversed by the New South Wales Court of Appeal in *Harris v Digital Pulse Pty Ltd* (2003) 56 NSWLR 298, the position on this point was not amended. Section 191(2) provides exceptions to the duty to disclose.
176 *Corporations Act* ss 185, 193.

Chapter 2 of the *Corporations Act* reflects elements of the 'no conflict' rule and the defence of fully informed consent, as it is 'designed to protect the interests of a public company's members as a whole, by requiring member approval for giving financial benefits to related parties that could endanger those interests'.[177] The provisions establish the procedure by which members may approve benefits to 'related parties',[178] the information which must be provided,[179] specific exemptions,[180] and the consequences of breach.[181]

10.35 Consequences of breach

This section considers the consequences of breaching directors' duties under private and public law.

10.35.05 Common law and equitable consequences

The remedies available under the common law and equity for breaches of the non-statutory duties owed by directors depend primarily upon the source of the obligation in law. These duties are preserved by s 185 of the *Corporations Act*, and the proper plaintiff will be the company.[182] According to s 198A of the *Corporations Act*, or a similar provision replacing it in the constitution, the board of directors is the appropriate body to institute such proceedings on behalf of the company. If the company is in liquidation, that decision will be made by the liquidator. In certain circumstances (as detailed in Chapter 14), the members may bring an action on behalf of the company where it has failed to do so.

The duty of care, skill, and diligence exists in equity, contract and tort, as discussed at Section 10.30.05. A breach of the common law duty of care will result in damages.[183] The main remedy available for breach of the equitable duty is equitable compensation.[184] Both of these remedies compensate the company for the loss caused by the breach of the duty, but equitable compensation is less constrained by the notions of causation and remoteness which create strict limits upon common law damages.[185] Equitable remedies will only be available where common law remedies are inadequate,[186] and, as such, although an equitable duty may have been breached alongside a common law or statutory duty, if the damages from the breach of those other duties are sufficient, then

177 Ibid s 207.

178 'Related parties' as defined by *Corporations Act* s 228; procedure per *Corporations Act* s 217.

179 Ibid s 219.

180 Ibid ss 210–16.

181 Ibid s 209.

182 *Foss v Harbottle* (1843) 67 ER 189.

183 *Daniels v Anderson* (1995) 37 NSWLR 438.

184 *Tavistock Holdings Pty Ltd v Saulsman* (1990) 3 ACSR 502. Equitable remedies are generally considered at the election of the plaintiff but ordered at the discretion of the court in light of the entire circumstances of a case and so may vary widely: see generally GE Dal Pont, *Equity and Trusts in Australia* (Thomson Reuters, 6th ed, 2015) pt VII.

185 *Hill v Rose* [1990] VR 129.

186 See generally M Tilbury, *Civil Remedies* (Butterworths, 1990) vol 1 [1021]; B Kercher and M Noone, *Remedies* (Lawbook, 2nd ed, 1990) 3; *National Australia Bank Ltd v Bond Brewing Holdings Ltd* (1990) 1 ACSR 405, as discussed in D Wright, 'Discretion with Common Law Remedies' (2002) 23(2) *Adelaide Law Review* 243.

equitable remedies will not be enlivened. Further, equitable remedies can be subject to the discretion of the court.[187] The same analysis is true of the equitable duty of loyalty and good faith as discussed in Section 10.30.10.

By contrast, the fiduciary obligation owed by directors as discussed in Section 10.30.15 may lead to a far broader range of remedies depending on the nature of the breach of duty. If the breach relates to a conflict without a corresponding profit to the fiduciary, then the company may be more interested in restraining the behaviour of the fiduciary through an injunction, rescission of contracts entered into,[188] or equitable compensation for loss caused.[189] If the breach has resulted in a profit to the fiduciary, then the company may seek an account of profits,[190] equitable compensation, or, depending on the circumstances, a constructive trust over property or profits obtained.

In *Timber Engineering Co Pty Ltd v Anderson*,[191] where a fiduciary diverted business away from the plaintiff company to their own competing business, the whole of the competing business was held on constructive trust as a result of the breach, with an allowance for skill and consideration of assets contributed by the fiduciary which were not related to the breach. However, constructive trusts are only ordered where the court finds them appropriate in all the circumstances of the case and in equity generally, and as such another equitable remedy may be more appropriate.[192] Where the benefit has been earned by a third party—that is, not the fiduciary themselves—equity may still order a constructive trust over the benefit obtained.[193]

10.35.10 Regulatory consequences: the civil penalty provisions

Sections 180–3 of the *Corporations Act* are civil penalty provisions.[194] This follows the recommendations of the 1989 Senate Standing Committee on Legal and Constitutional Affairs report, *Social and Fiduciary Duties and Obligations of Company Directors*.[195] The Committee recommended the recasting of these provisions as 'civil penalty provisions', as it was inappropriate to treat all contraventions of the *Corporations Act* as criminal offences. As such, the civil burden of proof now applies to these sections, with civil penalties for misconduct falling short of criminal offences. Section 1317DA defines a

187 See generally D Wright, 'Discretion with Common Law Remedies' (2002) 23(2) *Adelaide Law Review* 243.

188 *Kinsela v Russell Kinsela Pty Ltd (in liq)* (1986) 4 NSWLR 722; *Woolworths Ltd v Kelly* (1991) 22 NSWLR 189; *Camelot Resources Ltd v MacDonald* (1994) 14 ACSR 437.

189 *Tavistock Holdings Pty Ltd v Saulsman* (1990) 3 ACSR 502.

190 *Xiao v BCEG International (Australia) Pty Ltd* (2023) 111 NSWLR 132; *Regal (Hastings) Ltd v Gulliver* [1967] 2 AC 134; *Furs Ltd v Tomkies* (1936) 54 CLR 583.

191 *Timber Engineering Co Pty Ltd v Anderson* [1980] 2 NSWLR 488, 499.

192 This is consistent with discussion in the High Court in both *Hospital Products Ltd v United States Surgical Corporation* (1984) 156 CLR 41, 110 and *Warman International Ltd v Dwyer* (1995) 182 CLR 544 [26]– [29], [33]–[35].

193 *Barnes v Addy* (1874) LR 9 Ch App 244; *Consul Development Pty Ltd v DPC Estates Pty Ltd* (1975) 132 CLR 373.

194 The history of the civil penalty scheme is discussed at Section 1.65.05, including the need to balance the seriousness of penalties inappropriately stifling legitimate risk-taking against the significant risk of harm to the wider community from director misconduct.

195 Senate Standing Committee on Legal and Constitutional Affairs, Parliament of Australia, *Directors' Duties: Social and Fiduciary Duties and Obligations of Company Directors* (Report, November 1989).

'corporations/scheme civil penalty provision' to be a provision specified in the table set out in s 1317E. The consequences for criminal breach remain within the Act and are addressed at Section 10.35.15 below.

ASIC may apply for a declaration of contravention (s 1317J). If, on the balance of probabilities (s 1317L), the court is satisfied that a person has contravened a civil penalty provision, then it must order a declaration of contravention (s 1317E(1)). A declaration of contravention is necessary before ASIC can seek a pecuniary penalty order (s 1317G), a relinquishment order (s 1317GAB) or a disqualification order (s 206C).[196] Unlike the common law and equitable consequences mentioned above, the pecuniary penalty orders and relinquishment orders create a debt payable to ASIC on behalf of the Commonwealth—they do not provide compensation to the company or other injured parties. ASIC or a company damaged by the contravention of a civil penalty provision can apply for a compensation order (ss 1317H–HA), whether or not there has been a declaration of contravention made (s 1317J).

Section 1317G permits ASIC, after successfully obtaining a declaration of contravention, to apply for a pecuniary penalty if 'the contravention materially prejudices the interests of the [company], or its members; or materially prejudices the [company]'s ability to pay its creditors; or is serious'.[197] The maximum penalty to an individual will be the greater of 5000 penalty units[198] ($1.65 million) or, if the court can determine the benefit derived and the detriment avoided because of the contravention, then that amount multiplied by 3.[199] If the contravention was committed by a body corporate, then the maximum pecuniary penalty will be the greater of 50,000 penalty units ($16.5 million), or triple the benefit derived and detriment avoided, if that can be determined, or 10 per cent of the annual turnover of the body corporate in the 12 months preceding the contravention, capped at the equivalent of 2.5 million penalty units ($825 million). These amounts were the result of the consolidation of the penalty frameworks in the *Corporations Act, ASIC Act,*[200] *National Credit Act*[201] and *Insurance Contracts Act*[202] in the wake of the Royal Commission into Misconduct in the Banking, Superannuation and Financial Services Industry,[203] and represent a significant increase over the previous pecuniary penalty amounts.

Similarly, following a declaration of contravention, s 1317GAB permits ASIC to apply for a relinquishment order. This order disgorges the profits made or detriments avoided by a wrongdoer. This remedial mechanism, introduced into the Act by the Treasury

196 ASIC may also issue an infringement notice if it has reasonable grounds to believe that a person has contravened a provision that is subject to such a notice (ss 1317DAC(1), 1317DAM(1)) (eg continuous disclosure obligations and other behaviour in the financial services sector). This is addressed in more detail in Chapters 17 and 18.

197 *Corporations Act* s 1317G(1)(b).

198 Penalty units are valued at $330 as of 7 November 2024.

199 Section 1317GAD defines 'benefit derived' and 'detriment avoided' as the total values 'reasonably attributable' to the contravention.

200 *Australian Securities and Investments Commission Act 2001* (Cth).

201 *National Consumer Credit Protection Act 2009* (Cth).

202 *Insurance Contracts Act 1984* (Cth).

203 *Treasury Laws Amendment (Strengthening Corporate and Financial Sector Penalties) Act 2019* (Cth).

Laws Amendment (Strengthening Corporate and Financial Penalties) Bill 2018, 'prevents wrongdoers from treating civil penalties as a cost associated with gaining unjust financial benefits. [The order] aims to neutralise any financial benefit that might have been gained from misconduct.'[204] Importantly, the court may make a relinquishment order even where a pecuniary penalty order has been made in relation to a breach of a civil penalty provision (s 1317GAB(3)).[205]

Where a declaration of contravention has been obtained, s 206C permits ASIC to apply to the court to disqualify a person from managing companies for a period that the court considers appropriate. ASIC maintains a register of disqualified persons (s 1274AA), which includes a person automatically disqualified due to conviction of certain types of offences (s 206B(1)) or bankruptcy (s 206B(3)) but also those disqualified by the court. When discussing the precursor to s 206C, Merkel J in *Australian Securities Commission v Nandan*,[206] stated that the object of the section 'is to protect the public by preventing a corporate structure from being able to be mis-used to the detriment of the company, its shareholders, creditors, investors and others dealing with the company'. Section 206C(2) permits the court, in determining whether disqualification is justified, to have regard to the person's conduct in relation to the management, business or property of any company, and any other matter the court thinks appropriate. As such, the court is not limited to viewing the conduct that may have been the subject of a declaration of contravention that has led to the disqualification proceedings.

ASIC and the director may agree to a disqualification, but the court still has a duty to consider the appropriateness of the period of disqualification and may order a higher penalty than that agreed by the parties.[207] Disqualification can range from short-term to permanent disqualification. A permanent disqualification order was imposed in *Australian Securities and Investments Commission v Elm Financial Services Pty Ltd*[208] for conduct described as 'flagrant and systematic disregard for fundamental investor protection laws'.[209] Santow J undertook a detailed examination of the provisions relating to court-ordered disqualification in *Australian Securities and Investments Co v Adler*.[210] In assessing the length of disqualification that will be appropriate, courts undertake a balancing act between the objective of public protection and the personal hardship of the defendant, and that longer periods of disqualification should be reserved for cases involving dishonesty.[211]

204 Explanatory Memorandum, Treasury Laws Amendment (Strengthening Corporate and Financial Sector Penalties) Bill 2018 (Cth), [1.180]–[1.190].

205 These orders are subject to the same ordering effect as the civil penalties, in that they are stayed if a criminal proceeding is commenced for similar conduct to that of the civil penalty provision under examination by the court (ss 1317N(1)–(2)).

206 *Australian Securities Commission v Nandan* (1997) 23 ACSR 743, 751.

207 *Australian Securities and Investments Commission v Vizard* (2005) 145 FCR 57; *Australian Securities and Investments Commission v Elm Financial Services Pty Ltd* (2005) 55 ACSR 544.

208 *Australian Securities and Investments Commission v Elm Financial Services Pty Ltd* (2005) 55 ACSR 544.

209 Ibid.

210 (2002) 41 ACSR 72.

211 Ibid.

According to s 181(2), any person 'involved' in a contravention by a director or other officer of s 181(1) also breaches s 181(1) themselves. Sections 182(2) and 183(2) also contain the same wording. Section 79 defines a person as being 'involved' if they have aided, abetted, counselled, procured or induced the contravention, been in any way by act or omission knowingly concerned in or party to the contravention, or conspired with others to effect the contravention. The knowledge requirement is actual knowledge of the essential, material facts of the contravention, but can be inferred where a person has willfully remained ignorant and failed to make an appropriate inquiry.[212] Solicitors providing advice will not usually be 'involved' in a contravention, but this is not always the case. In *Australian Securities and Investments Commission v Somerville*,[213] Windeyer AJ found a solicitor had aided and abetted a number of directors in breaching their duty of care by carrying out the necessary work to procure the transaction, such as advising and recommending the transaction, preparing and obtaining the documents, and then executing the documents—all with knowledge of the relevant facts.[214]

Section 1317K sets a limitation period of six years after the contravention for bringing an action for a declaration of contravention, pecuniary penalty order or a compensation order. The same limitation period is established for relinquishment orders (s 1317GAB(2)(b)). The courts are also provided with guidance by s 1317QF(1) to give preference to compensation or refunds to victims of corporate misconduct when considering whether to order pecuniary penalties, relinquishment orders or imposing fines. Compensation proceedings do not need to have been commenced for the court to make this consideration.[215]

10.35.15 Criminal consequences

Where directors 'are reckless or are dishonest and fail to exercise their powers and discharge their duties in good faith in the best interests of the corporation or for a proper purpose'[216] they can be prosecuted for a criminal offence. It is also a criminal offence if a director, officer or employee uses their position or information obtained through their positions dishonestly 'with the intention of directly or indirectly gaining an advantage for themselves, or someone else, or causing detriment' to the company,[217] or 'recklessly as to whether the use may result in themselves or someone else directly or indirectly gaining an advantage or causing detriment' to the company.[218] According to *R v Fodera*, '[d]ishonesty is judged objectively by the standard of ordinary decent people'.[219] This single-limb test

212 Ibid

213 *Australian Securities and Investments Commission v Somerville* (2009) 77 NSWLR 110.

214 Ibid 126.

215 Explanatory Memorandum, Treasury Laws Amendment (Strengthening Corporate and Financial Penalties) Bill 2018 (Cth), [1.202].

216 *Corporations Act* s 184(1).

217 Ibid ss 184(2)(a), 184(3)(a).

218 Ibid ss 184(2)(b), 184(3)(b).

219 *R v Fodera* (2007) 65 ACSR 109 [22], citing *Peters v The Queen* (1998) 192 CLR 493.

of 'dishonest' is included in the *Corporations Act* in the s 9 definition.[220] The amendment introducing that definition to the *Corporations Act* also clarifies that it is not a defence to a charge of dishonestly using a position or information that the person charged did so with the intention, directly or indirectly, to gain an advantage for the corporation, or that an advantage was the result of the behaviour.[221]

A director or other officer who breaches these provisions may be fined the greater of 4500 penalty units ($1,408,500) or three times the benefit derived and detriment avoided, if that can be determined, or imprisoned for up to 15 years or both (*Corporations Act* sch 3). A body corporate can be subject to the greater of 45,000 penalty units ($14,850,000), three times the benefit derived and the detriment avoided by the contravention or 10 per cent of its annual turnover ending at the end of the month in which the offence was committed, or began being committed. Proceedings for an offence may be commenced within five years after the act or omission alleged to constitute the offence or, with the consent of the Minister, at a later time (s 1316).

10.35.20 Election between regulatory proceedings

Prior to the *CLERP Act*, pt 9.4B of the *Corporations Act* contained both the civil and criminal consequences of contravening a civil penalty provision. Prosecution of a criminal offence was barred where proceedings for a civil penalty order had been commenced. In addition to moving the criminal consequences of breaching the statutory directors' duties into s 184, the *CLERP Act* removed the bar on criminal prosecution while civil penalty proceedings were underway. Now, if a criminal prosecution is commenced while civil proceedings are on foot for a declaration of contravention or pecuniary penalty order in relation to substantially the same conduct, the criminal proceeding will be stayed,[222] but can be resumed if the person is not convicted. The civil proceedings will be dismissed if a criminal prosecution is successful.[223] By contrast, a criminal prosecution can be commenced even where a civil proceeding has already been successfully completed.[224] Evidence obtained in the course of proceedings for a pecuniary penalty order or a relinquishment order against an individual for breach of a civil penalty provision is not admissible in criminal proceedings for substantially the same conduct, regardless of whether the order is made.[225]

10.40 Exoneration and relief for directors

This section considers the circumstances in which directors may be relieved from the consequences of a breach of duties. There are a number of possible methods for relief. The members in general meeting may have authority to ratify some behaviour which

220 Inserted by the *Treasury Laws Amendment (Strengthening Corporate and Financial Sector Penalties) Act 2019* (Cth).

221 *Corporations Act* ss 184(2A), 184(4).

222 Ibid s 1317N.

223 Ibid s 1317M.

224 Ibid s 1317P.

225 Ibid s 1317Q.

would otherwise constitute a breach. Relief may be sought from the court under ss 1317S and 1318. The company may provide indemnification for directors, or they may be insured, although statutory limits have been placed upon both of these options.

10.40.05 Ratification by the members

A defence to a claim of breach of fiduciary obligation is that the beneficiary of the obligation provided fully informed consent to the fiduciary. This consent can be granted prior to the conduct in order to authorise behaviour that would otherwise breach the obligation, or it can be provided after the conduct in the form of ratification. The company acts primarily through two organs: the board of directors and the members in general meeting. As the behaviour usually involves directors, officers or senior management, the members in general meeting can make the decision for the company to consent to the conduct which would otherwise be in breach. This will be done by passing a resolution in general meeting providing fully informed consent to excuse the directors or others from liability for conduct which would otherwise constitute a breach of the obligation. That resolution should be unanimous, unless the constitution allows approval by less than all of the members, in which case a majority could consent.[226] As the defence requires 'fully informed' consent, the general meeting must be provided with all appropriate information in making their decision to authorise or ratify behaviour;[227] otherwise, the ratifying resolution will be ineffective against a claim for breach.

There are limits on the general meeting's ability to ratify behaviour. It is generally accepted that breaches of the statutory directors' duties cannot be ratified.[228] The basis for this outcome is that the civil penalty proceedings involve public rights, as discussed in Section 10.35.10, and the members are not able to ratify acts that may have implications for stakeholders beyond themselves.[229] A resolution of the general meeting ratifying or authorising conduct can still be of use to a director in regard to seeking relief from the court under s 1317S, and to the court in regard to what orders should be made under the civil penalty provisions.[230]

Further, ratification is not available where:

- it would constitute fraud on the minority
- it involved misappropriation of company resources
- the company is nearing insolvency and the rights of the creditors intrude
- it defeated a member's personal right
- it was oppressive or where the majority of the members acted for the same improper purpose as the directors.[231]

226 *Regal (Hastings) Ltd v Gulliver* [1967] 2 AC 134; *Furs Ltd v Tomkies* (1936) 54 CLR 583, 592.

227 *Winthrop Investments Ltd v Winns Ltd* [1975] 2 NSWLR 666.

228 *Angas Law Services Pty Ltd (in liq) v Carabelas* (2005) 226 CLR 507, per Gleeson CJ and Heydon J in relation to the duties under the *Companies Code* that have become ss 180(1) and 182(1) and the criminal counterpart in s 184(2).

229 *Forge v Australian Securities and Investments Commission* (2004) 52 ACSR 1.

230 This issue was left open in *Forge v Australian Securities and Investments Commission* (2004) 52 ACSR 1 as it was not raised on the facts in the first instance.

231 *Miller v Miller & Miller* (1995) 16 ACSR 73, 83.

Fraud on the minority will be considered within Chapter 14, but for the purposes of ratification, the majority in general meeting cannot ratify an action, affirm a voidable contract, or give up a cause of action where that would constitute fraud on the minority.

Ratification will not be effective if the breach involves misappropriation of company property.[232] Misappropriation of company resources can include indirect dealings, such as the creation and disposal of security interests over assets of the company in breach of fiduciary obligation, as discussed by Owen J in *Bell Group Ltd (in liq) v Westpac Banking Corporation (No 9)*.[233]

As the company approaches insolvency, the directors' duty to act bona fide in the interests of the company may require the directors to consider the interests of the creditors, and may extend to positively requiring them not to act so as to prejudice the interests of the creditors.[234] As such, once this duty is enlivened, the members in general meeting, even acting unanimously, do not have the power or authority to ratify behaviour of the directors.[235]

The ratification by the members in general meeting will only correct a wrong done to the company and cannot affect individual member's rights. However, some behaviour by directors involves a wrong to the company and to the members, such as an allotment of shares for an improper purpose.[236] Consideration of this question overlaps with consideration of ratification where the members act for the same collateral purpose as the directors' improper purpose. There is conflicting authority as to whether the members in general meeting are bound to the limitation that their power must be exercised in good faith in the best interest of the company. The directors have been held to be so bound, on the basis that they are fiduciaries.[237] There is disagreement in Australia as to whether the duty to act bona fide in the best interest of the company can be classified as a fiduciary obligation. The English position has accepted a link between being a fiduciary and owing a duty of loyalty, including a duty to act in good faith.[238] The English Court of Appeal decision in *Bamford v Bamford* could be explicable on those grounds. If the only basis of this obligation is the fiduciary position of the directors, then the duty could not apply to the members as they are not fiduciaries. The High Court decision in *Ngurli Ltd v McCann*[239] did subject the majority to a limitation that their power must be exercised for the benefit of the company as a whole, suggesting that the doctrine of abuse of power when concerning actions of the majority in general meeting rests upon the implied limitations of power created by the contract between the members.[240] After *Ngurli Ltd v McCann*, in *Winthrop Investments Ltd v Winns Ltd*,[241]

232 *Cook v Deeks* [1916] 1 AC 554; *Regal (Hastings) Ltd v Gulliver* [1967] 2 AC 134; *Furs Ltd v Tomkies* (1936) 54 CLR 583.

233 *Bell Group Ltd (in liq) v Westpac Banking Corporation (No 9)* (2009) 39 WAR 1.

234 *Walker v Wimborne* (1976) 137 CLR 1.

235 *Kinsela v Russell Kinsela Pty Ltd (in liq)* (1986) 4 NSWLR 722.

236 *Residues Treatment & Trading Co Ltd v Southern Resources Ltd* (1988) 51 SASR 177.

237 *Bamford v Bamford* [1970] Ch 212.

238 See, eg, *Bristol and West Building Society v Mothew* [1998] Ch 1, 16; RT Langford, 'The Duty of Directors to Act Bona Fide in the Interests of the Company: A Positive Fiduciary Duty? Australia and the UK Compares' (2011) 11(1) *Journal of Corporate Law Studies* 215, 220.

239 *Ngurli Ltd v McCann* (1953) 90 CLR 425.

240 Ibid 438.

241 *Winthrop Investments Ltd v Winns Ltd* [1975] 2 NSWLR 666.

the Court of Appeal of New South Wales held that a general meeting could ratify an exercise of the powers of directors to allot shares which had been made for an improper purpose.

According to the Court in *Residues Treatment & Trading Co Ltd v Southern Resources Ltd*, '[a]n important factor in that decision, however, was that the court felt constrained to follow a decision to the same effect of the English Court of Appeal in *Bamford v Bamford*,[242] a constraint which is now recognised not to apply to the Supreme Courts of the Australian States'.[243] King CJ noted the comment of Mahoney JA from *Winthrop Investments Ltd v Winns Ltd*:

> The question remains, therefore, whether it is open to the shareholders in general meeting to elect to affirm a transaction which is voidable because of the directors' collateral purpose, notwithstanding that, for example, the shareholders have the same collateral purpose; or whether a shareholders' resolution that such a transaction be affirmed is, if passed with the purpose of defeating the takeover, ineffective as not being 'for the benefit of the company as a whole' within the principles in *Ngurli Ltd v McCann*.[244]

King CJ continued in obiter:

> If it is correct that a shareholder has a personal right to have the voting power of his shares undiminished by an allotment of shares made for an improper purpose, there is to my mind a substantial argument that an exercise of the voting power of the majority to ratify such an allotment would be beyond the scope of the purpose for which that power exists.[245]

Although this issue did not arise for decision on the facts in *Residues Treatment* given the limitation of the Court's reasoning in *Winthrop Investments Ltd v Winns Ltd* as identified in *Residues Treatment*, the position of the High Court in *Ngurli Ltd v McCann*[246] that the majority shareholders are subject to a limitation that their power must be exercised for the benefit of the company as a whole[247] is preferred.

10.40.10 Relief by the court

Under s 1318, the court may relieve a person for negligence, default, breach of trust or breach of duty if the applicant has acted honestly and that, in the circumstances of the case, the applicant ought fairly be excused for such behaviour. This requires the court to consider whether the applicant has acted honestly, whether in the circumstances of this case that person ought fairly be excused, and finally whether that relief should be in whole or only in part.

242 *Bamford v Bamford* [1970] Ch 212.

243 *Residues Treatment & Trading Co Ltd v Southern Resources Ltd (No 4)* (1988) 51 SASR 177, 204 (King CJ, Matheson and Bollen JJ agreeing on this point).

244 *Winthrop Investments Ltd v Winns Ltd* [1975] 2 NSWLR 666, 702.

245 *Residues Treatment & Trading Co Ltd v Southern Resources Ltd* (1988) 51 SASR 177, 204–5.

246 *Ngurli Ltd v McCann* (1953) 90 CLR 425.

247 Ibid 438.

In 2004, the *Corporations Act* was amended to insert s 1317S, in substantially the same terms as s 1318, which applies to the civil penalty provisions. Application can be made to the court prior to proceedings being commenced against the person (ss 1317S(4), 1318(2)) but the power of the court to provide relief does not extend to future acts.[248] As the terms of s 1317S are substantially the same as s 1318, the following discussion applies to both provisions.

Unlike ratification, relief under s 1318 does not remove the breach; the court excuses the applicant, and some or all of the liability for the breach is removed.[249] The court's power to grant relief applies to both claims brought by the company, and claims brought by third parties.[250]

Although the test for honesty is considered the narrow sense of the word—that is, without moral turpitude[251]—it has proven to be difficult. Awareness that an action lacked sufficient authority[252] or concealment of behaviour[253] has been sufficient to deny relief under ss 1317S and 1318. Even if the court finds the applicant has acted honestly, the court must still consider whether in the circumstances of the case, the applicant should be excused.[254]

For example, in *Vines v Australian Securities and Investments Commission*,[255] the Court of Appeal confirmed the first instance decision denying relief,[256] despite a finding that Mr Vines had acted honestly with no personal gain or benefit from the contraventions. Granting relief is an exercise of discretion, but involves a value judgment as to whether, in the circumstances of the case, the applicant ought fairly be excused.[257] As this matter involved serious contraventions and the impact on public policy both in terms of an informed market and good corporate governance practices, the Court of Appeal was not inclined to upset either the value judgment or exercise of discretion of the trial judge in denying the appeal.[258] In dissent, Santow JA was prepared to find the contraventions to be errors of judgment involving no dishonesty, and grant relief.[259] Courts have similarly discussed that it is relevant whether the contravention was deliberate or occurred due to inadvertence,[260] and identified that where the conduct had a detrimental effect on the company or other shareholders, that was a 'compelling and sufficient reason for concluding that the directors ought not fairly be excused'.[261]

248 *Edwards v Attorney-General (NSW)* (2004) 60 NSWLR 667.

249 *Australian Securities and Investments Commission v Healey (No 2)* (2011) 196 FCR 430 [86]–[87].

250 *Edwards v Attorney-General (NSW)* (2004) 60 NSWLR 667.

251 Ibid [88].

252 *Australian Securities Commission v Nandan* (1997) 23 ACSR 743.

253 *Australian Securities and Investments Commission v Adler* (2002) 42 ACSR 72.

254 *Morley v Australian Securities and Investments Commission (No 2)* (2011) 83 ACSR 620, [49].

255 *Vines v Australian Securities and Investments Commission* (2007) 73 NSWLR 451.

256 *Australian Securities and Investments Commission v Vines* (2005) 65 NSWLR 281.

257 *Vines v Australian Securities and Investments Commission* (2007) 73 NSWLR 451, 549–51, 602.

258 Ibid 550–2, 602.

259 Ibid 601–2.

260 *Duke Group Ltd (in liq) v Pilmer* (1998) 144 FLR 1.

261 *Re Cummings Engineering Holdings Pty Ltd* [2014] NSWSC 250, [88]; *Re ZH International Pty Ltd (in liq)* (2022) 160 ACSR 473, [252].

Relief may be in whole or in part. In *Hall v Poolman*,[262] a director who had breached the insolvent trading provision in s 588G, was relieved in part from liability which was incurred during a period of time when he was engaged in negotiations with the Australian Taxation Office (ATO). If the negotiations had been successful, then the company would likely not have been insolvent. The Court was prepared to relieve the director of liability during the initial period of negotiation with the ATO, but once it became clear during a particular meeting that the dispute would not be resolved in the short term, and there was no reliable prediction of a favourable outcome, relief was denied.[263]

As discussed above, relief under these provisions extends to the insolvent trading provisions. In *Re McLellan*,[264] Goldberg J exercised the discretion in s 1317S to excuse entirely the sole director of The Stake Man Pty Ltd, Mr Carroll, for insolvent trading in breach of s 588G despite finding that the defences in ss 588H(2) and (3) were not made out. The company, which had been a successful business processing and wholesaling raw timber, had expanded into the dry timber field, purchasing a kiln and equipment to process the dried timber. The kiln proved to be problematic, with large periods of time out of operation and expensive repairs, and the company entered financial distress.[265] In 2005, Carroll obtained advice from an accountant, and was told that the company was close to being insolvent. Then, in early 2006, an insolvency practitioner advised Carroll in early 2006 that the company could survive, albeit with further investment.[266] The accountant continued to advise Carroll into 2006 that the company had cash flow issues but was not yet insolvent. When the ATO levied a tax bill beyond the company's cash reserves in May 2006, Carroll met with a business restructure specialist, who advised Carroll to place the company into voluntary administration. Two days later, that course of action was undertaken by Carroll and within a month the creditors had resolved that the company would be wound up.[267] The liquidator alleged breaches of s 588G against Carroll, who relied on ss 588H(2) and (3) in his defence, and applied for relief under ss 1317S and 1318. The application of the law under ss 588G–H will be considered in Chapter 11. Goldberg J was satisfied that Carroll had acted honestly, adopting the criteria set out in *Hall v Poolman*[268] by Palmer J as follows:

> [T]he court should be concerned only with the question of whether the person has acted honestly in the ordinary meaning of that term, that is, whether the person has acted without deceit or conscious impropriety, without intent to gain improper benefit or advantage for himself, herself or for another, and without carelessness or imprudence to such a degree as to demonstrate that no genuine attempt at all has been to carry out the duties and obligations of his or her office imposed by the Corporations Act or the general law.

262 (2007) 65 ACSR 123.
263 Ibid 195–6.
264 *Re McLellan* (2009) 76 ACSR 67.
265 Ibid 70–3.
266 Ibid 78.
267 Ibid 80–1.
268 *Hall v Poolman* (2007) 65 ACSR 123, 193.

Although Carroll permitted the company to incur debts it could not pay, he had taken active steps to obtain advice, monitored stock levels and daily production, and when advised to act to move the company into voluntary administration, had done so without delay.[269]

10.40.15 Indemnification and insurance

Indemnification in this context would mean the company taking responsibility for any compensation due for loss or damage caused by a director. Under s 199A of the *Corporations Act*, a company or related company is prohibited from directly or indirectly exempting or indemnifying its officers or auditors against liabilities to the company. This includes indemnity for pecuniary penalty orders made under s 1317G or compensation orders under ss 1317H–HA. The introduction of these blanket prohibitions into the *Corporations Act*[270] reversed the position at common law, where it was customary for the constitution to exempt officers from liability except for loss caused by 'wilful neglect or default', such as in *Re City Equitable Fire Insurance Co Ltd*,[271] or more generously, up to cases of fraud. The notes to s 199A(3) identify that the prohibition on indemnification for legal costs includes proceedings by ASIC for orders under ss 206C–EAA, 232, 1317E, 1317G–HA or 1324. There are no exceptions to the prohibition in s 199A(1), but two exceptions exist under ss 199A(2)-199A(3) to allow indemnification:

- where the liability is to a third party, not the company or a related company, unless that liability arises out of conduct involving a lack of good faith
- against liability in successfully defending a civil or criminal proceeding, or for judicial relief under ss 1317S or 1318.

The courts have distinguished between the legal impact of ratification and indemnification as follows. Ratification 'requires specific release after full disclosure of the particular cause for claim' or 'specific absolution, ... afforded necessarily for specific and properly disclosed infractions of the director's duties ... [T]he release so given obviates the liability, so far as any right of action to enforce it by existing shareholders is concerned.'[272] Ratification involves the release of rights which give rise to the obligation; whereas, indemnification responds to the consequences of the breach of an obligation owed to the company.[273]

Section 199B prohibits a company or related company from paying or agreeing to pay for insurance that covers officers, past or present, for liability incurred in that position,

269 *Re McLellan* (2009) 76 ACSR 67, 111.

270 The history of the provision is set out in *Whitlam v National Roads and Motorists' Association Ltd* (2006) 58 ACSR 370.

271 *Re City Equitable Fire Insurance Co Ltd* [1925] Ch 407.

272 *Miller v Miller & Miller* (1995) 16 ACSR 73, 87, although this case dealt with the predecessor to s 199A: *Companies Code* s 241.

273 Companies and Securities Law Review Committee, *Company Directors and Officers: Indemnification, Relief and Insurance* (Report No 10, 1990) <https://treasury.gov.au/publication/company-directors-and-officers-indemnification-relief-and-insurance>; I Ramsay, 'Liability of Directors for Breach of Duty and the Scope of Indemnification and Insurance' (1987) 5(3) *Company and Securities Law Journal* 129.

arising out of conduct involving willful breach of duty in relation to the company, or a contravention of ss 182–3. A contract entered into contrary to this provision is void according to s 199C(2). Insurance with respect to costs of defending proceedings is not prohibited, regardless of their outcome.

Indemnities and insurance must be disclosed in the directors' report under s 300(8) but are excluded from the disclosure requirements in s 191. The exceptions to the prohibition on indemnification, insurance premiums and payments for legal costs do not require shareholder approval under the related-party transaction provisions (which are discussed in Chapter 13) according to s 212.

10.45 Summary

This chapter began by highlighting the difficulties surrounding management and control of company behaviour in light of the differing internal structures and approaches to those structures taken by various areas of study. From a legal perspective, the board of directors and the members in general meeting are the legal organs of the company, in addition to the company itself having status as a separate legal entity from its constituent parts. This raises the question of corporate governance, a vast area of work encompassing legal, quasi-legal, formal, non-formal and self-enforced regulation, directed at the ways in which power is exercised and controlled within the corporate form. Directors' duties have a significant role to play within the broader scheme of corporate governance, as the powers of management and control of company affairs vests in the board of directors. This chapter then considered who is regulated under the field of 'directors' duties', as these duties extend beyond those who are formally appointed as directors to include shadow and de facto directors and officers, and, on occasion, senior management employees.

We briefly revisited the historical context of corporate law provided by Chapter 1 and focused on how the directors' duties developed within that landscape of evolving law. This chapter then provided a brief overview of the duties in preparation for their detailed discussion in Chapters 11, 12 and 13. These duties include a duty of care, skill and diligence, a duty to act bona fide in the interests of the company and for proper purposes, and a duty to avoid conflicts of interest and unauthorised profits.

This chapter then considered the consequence of breach for the company, the members, those accused of breaching directors' duties and those otherwise involved in the contravention. The remedies available for breach of the general law duties under s 185 include damages, injunction, rescission, equitable compensation, account of profits, or a constructive trust. The regulatory consequences set out in the *Corporations Act* are primarily the responsibility of ASIC, who can make an application for a declaration of contravention of a civil penalty provision. This then opens the pathways for remedies under the Act, including pecuniary penalty orders, relinquishment orders, disqualification orders, and orders for compensation to the company. The criminal alternatives are established, as is the process of election available to ASIC and the criminal consequences, which include fines and imprisonment. We also considered the ability of directors to seek ratification or authorisation of their behaviour from a unanimous resolution of the members in general meeting under the general law. The *Corporations Act* also provides a method under s 1317S for directors to seek relief if they have acted honestly and ought, in all the circumstances of the case, be fairly excused. This chapter closes with the provisions for indemnification and insurance under the Act, which prevent the directors from re-allocating the risk of their behaviour onto the company.

The next three chapters undertake a detailed analysis of the directors' duties, divided across two distinct themes: duties of care, skill and diligence, and duties of loyalty and good faith. Chapter 11 discusses duties of care, skill and diligence, and Chapters 12 and 13 will be devoted to the various duties of loyalty and good faith. In these three chapters, we draw attention to those points which differ from the general position stated in this chapter, particularly in relation to who owes the duties, and to whom the duties are owed. Reference back to this overview will be useful to understand the role the particular duty plays in the broader scheme of corporate governance, the consequences of breach in either the general law or the civil penalty scheme, and the potential for directors to receive exoneration or relief from the consequences of their breach of duty.

CHAPTER

11

DUTY OF CARE, SKILL AND DILIGENCE

11.05 Introduction

This is the first of three chapters providing an in-depth discussion of directors' duties. The duties are divided into two themes: duties of care, skill and diligence, and duties of loyalty and good faith. The focus in this chapter is on the duties of care, skill and diligence. These duties are imposed by the common law, equity and ss 180(1) and 588G of the *Corporations Act*. This chapter commences with the common law and equitable foundations of the duty of care, skill and diligence, and considers their adoption into statute and the current law within s 180(1). It examines the safe harbour provided by the business judgment rule in s 180(2), and recent discussion on the scope and application of that rule. This chapter examines the ability of directors to delegate their duties and to reasonably rely on the information or advice provided by certain types of persons. Finally, the chapter considers the requirements imposed on directors and officers as a company approaches insolvency in ss 588G and 588GAB. The chapters that follow then consider the duties of loyalty and good faith: Chapter 12 discusses the various duties of good faith, and Chapter 13 canvasses the loyalty element through the duties relating to conflicts of interest.

Although these three chapters refer to 'directors', the duties may be owed by others including de facto directors (Section 10.20.05), shadow directors (Section 10.20.10), officers, shadow officers and senior management employees (Section 10.20.15).

11.10 Common law and equitable foundations

11.10.05 The early case law

Before directors' duties were enacted in legislation, they arose through the common law and equity. These duties still arise in negligence, in equity,[1] and can also be established in contract under the terms of service between an executive director and company.[2] As noted in Section 10.30, unlike other aspects of corporate law, it is not appropriate to simply focus on what is set out in the *Corporations Act*. The scope and content of the general law duties, which has developed significantly over the past century, remains operational and impacts on the court's interpretation of the statutory provisions.

The duty of care, skill and diligence was established in cases from the nineteenth century, initially as a subjective standard of care, dependent on the characteristics of the director in question. This mirrored the role and expectations of directors, when companies appointed large boards and where directorships were an office of status, with little regard to the appointed person's interest or skill in the position.

1 Historically, the duty of care, skill and diligence has been considered a necessary incident to the director's fiduciary position. It is more appropriate in light of the development of fiduciary law within Australia to recognise this duty as equitable in nature, rather than strictly fiduciary: *Permanent Building Society (in liq) v Wheeler* (1994) 11 WAR 187. Detailed consideration of the director's fiduciary obligation can be found in Chapter 13. For further consideration of *Permanent Building Society (in liq) v Wheeler*, see JD Heydon, MJ Leeming and PG Turner, *Meagher, Gummow and Lehane's Equity: Doctrines and Remedies* (LexisNexis Butterworths, 5th ed, 2015) 200–10, [5–325]–[5–375].

2 Non-executive directors may also have a contract of service with the company which imposes this same duty of care. It will be implied if it does not expressly exist.

These elements are present in a well-known example from that period, *Re Cardiff Savings Bank*,[3] which involved the Marquis of Bute, who was installed on the board of directors of the Cardiff Savings Bank as an infant of six months old. Nearly 40 years later, when the bank became insolvent, his behaviour as a director was examined. The liquidator contended that the Marquis was liable for neglect or omission in not complying with the regulations in relation to examinations of the accounts. At the time of liquidation, there were 55 'trustees and managers', including the Marquis, and Stirling J held that it 'could not be expected that each member of the body should take a very active part in the management, or attend every meeting'.[4] The threshold for 'very active' appears to have been almost non-existent in the 1800s, as the Marquis had attended one meeting of the trustees and managers in 1869, signed the minutes on that occasion, but had never attended again nor taken part in the business of the bank.[5] His Honour stated the duty on directors at that time to be 'to use fair and reasonable diligence in the management of their company's affairs'.[6] When considering the standard of duty to be imposed on the Marquis, Stirling J held:[7]

> It may be that he neglected, as he certainly omitted, to attend the meetings to which he was summoned. But neglect or omission to attend meetings is not, in my opinion, the same thing as neglect or omission of a duty which ought to be performed at those meetings ... To hold that the Marquis was guilty of neglect or omission in respect of this duty, in the absence of any knowledge or notice that it was not duly performed, would, in my opinion be to fix him with liability for the neglect and omission of others rather than his own.

This was, clearly, a very low standard of care, and within a few decades the common law began to shift towards a more objective position.

Evidence of this shift can be seen in the case of *Re City Equitable Fire Insurance Co Ltd*.[8] In that case, Romer J made statements with respect to the three elements of care, skill and diligence, which demonstrate this shift and are the genesis of the more objective modern duty of care. In relation to care, Romer J held that 'reasonable care must be, I think, measured by the care an ordinary man [sic] might be expected to take in the same circumstances on his own behalf'.[9] This introduced some objectivity into the duty, without entirely removing the subjectivity evident in earlier years. After that statement, Romer J added two general propositions in relation to skill and diligence. In relation to skill, his Honour also retained some subjectivity:[10]

> A director need not exhibit in the performance of his [sic] duties a greater degree of skill than may reasonably be expected from a person of his knowledge

3 *Re Cardiff Savings Bank* [1892] 2 Ch 100.
4 Ibid 108.
5 Ibid 102.
6 Ibid 108.
7 Ibid 109.
8 *Re City Equitable Fire Insurance Co Ltd* [1925] Ch 407.
9 Ibid 428.
10 Ibid.

> and experience. A director of a life insurance company, for instance, does not guarantee that he has the skill of an actuary or of a physician.

In relation to diligence, his Honour stated that:[11]

> A director is not bound to give continuous attention to the affairs of his [sic] company. His duties are of an intermittent nature. In respect of all duties that ... may properly be left to some other official, a director is, in the absence of grounds for suspicion, justified in trusting that official to perform such duties honestly.

This mix of objectivity and subjectivity, retaining an emphasis on the circumstances of the particular director concerned, remained the test for the standard of care in Australia until the 1980s. In response to the high-profile corporate collapses in the late 1980s, a number of reforms amended the statutory directors' duties and enabled greater access to remedies against directors, leading to a significant increase in cases on directors' duties and development in the law. The *Corporate Law Reform Act 1992* (Cth) introduced an objective standard of care for directors in s 232, which has been refined and now exists as s 180 of the *Corporations Act*, discussed at Section 11.15.

11.10.10 The modern development of the duty of care in the 1980s and 1990s

In the late 1980s and early 1990s, several insolvent trading cases prompted another shift towards a minimum objective standard of competence for directors.[12] In *Commonwealth Bank of Australia v Friedrich*, the Court held that directors were obliged to gain at least a general understanding of the business of the company and the effect that a changing economy might have on that business.[13] Although this case was decided within the context of insolvency, the importance of a director's role in monitoring the company's financial performance was extrapolated beyond those circumstances into the life of a healthy company. Subsequent courts relied upon the authority of this case to introduce further levels of objectivity into the duty of care.

Parliament was also considering reforms to these duties. The 1991 report, *Corporate Practices and Conduct*, issued by the Working Group chaired by Henry Bosch AO[14] and the 1992 report issued by the Committee on the Financial Aspects of Corporate Governance in the United Kingdom[15] set out recommendations reinforcing

11 Ibid 429.

12 *Statewide Tobacco Services Ltd v Morley* (1990) 2 ACSR 405; *Morley v Statewide Tobacco Services Ltd* [1993] 1 VR 423; *Commonwealth Bank of Australia v Friedrich* (1991) 5 ACSR 115.

13 *Commonwealth Bank of Australia v Friedrich* (1991) 5 ACSR 115, 187.

14 Working Group, Australian Merchant Bankers Association, *Corporate Practices and Conduct* (Report, 1991) ('the Bosch Report'). Two further reports from the same Working Group were issued in 1993 and 1995—also referred to as 'the Bosch Reports'—which can lead to some confusion as all deal with corporate governance: Working Group, Australian Institute of Company Directors, *Corporate Practices and Conduct* (Report, 2nd ed, 1993); Working Group, Australian Institute of Company Directors, *Corporate Practices and Conduct* (Report, 3rd ed, 1995).

15 Committee on the Financial Aspects of Corporate Governance, Financial Aspects of Corporate Governance (Report, 1 December 1992) ('the Cadbury Report').

the court's emphasis on a higher, more objective standard of care from directors. At the same time these reports were published, a landmark series of cases were decided, which would ultimately confirm an objective standard of care for the duty under the general law.

One of the most significant cases occurred in the AWA litigation. AWA Ltd was a publicly listed electronics equipment company that was deriving nearly 25 per cent of its profit from foreign exchange currency trading, a relatively new concept in corporate Australia in the 1980s. AWA had initially engaged in currency exchange trading due to the volatility of currency values at the time. This had a particular impact on their business due to the delay between entering an import contract with a foreign manufacturer and the eventual delivery and time for payment under the contract. Approximately three years later, AWA appointed Mr Koval as foreign exchange manager and expanded their managed foreign exchange trading.

Within two years, AWA incurred large losses on the foreign currency market. Koval operated with no effective supervision within the company. Koval concealed foreign exchange trading losses amounting to nearly $50 million by making unauthorised loans to cover those losses. Some of the deficiencies in AWA's internal controls, particularly in relation to Koval's conduct, were uncovered by Mr Daniels, who worked for the accounting firm that has now become Deloitte. Daniels had been engaged by AWA to audit the company's accounts and internal processes. This information was conveyed to the managing director of AWA, Mr Hooke. However, Hooke and Daniels did not pass that information up to the board of AWA. When AWA became aware of the losses, it brought proceedings against Daniels and the accounting firm for negligence in failing to report these findings to the board; in particular, in relation to the activities and lack of control surrounding the foreign currency trading activities. Daniels counterclaimed against the directors of AWA, alleging a breach of their duty of care, skill and diligence. Two important decisions followed: *AWA Ltd v Daniels*,[16] the first instance decision of Rogers CJ in the Commercial Division of the New South Wales Supreme Court; and *Daniels v Anderson*,[17] the appellate decision in that court, in particular the majority judgment of Sheller and Clarke JJA.

At first instance, Rogers CJ confirmed that the duty of care, skill and diligence is an equitable and statutory obligation.[18] However, contrary to the older case law, his Honour held that this duty was objective and required the directors to take reasonable steps to place themselves in a position to guide and monitor the company.[19] That required a general understanding of the business of the company and the effect of the changing economy on that business. Directors needed to 'bring an informed and independent judgment to bear on the various matters that come to the Board for decision'.[20] This was a significant shift from the previous threshold in relation to the skill of directors. No longer

16 *AWA Ltd v Daniels* (1992) 7 ACSR 759.

17 *Daniels v Anderson* (1995) 37 NSWLR 438.

18 *AWA Ltd v Daniels* (1992) 7 ACSR 759, 864, 870. The statutory provision at the time was *Companies Code* s 299(2).

19 Ibid 864, citing *Commonwealth Bank of Australia v Friedrich* (1991) 5 ACSR 115, 187.

20 Ibid 864–5.

would a director be judged against their own personal knowledge or experience. Now, each director was expected to attain a minimum level of understanding of the business and business practice.

Referring back to *Re City Equitable Fire Insurance Co Ltd*,[21] Rogers CJ did recognise that the board of a large public company cannot manage the day-to-day business of the company, and must by necessity rely on the executives of the company to perform that role.[22] Further, his Honour was prepared to draw a distinction between executive and non-executive directors, finding a lesser standard of care for non-executive directors.[23] This had an impact upon his Honour's findings as to the element of diligence:

> A non-executive director does not have to turn him or herself into an auditor, managing director, chairman or other officer ... In relation to auditors, if directors appoint a person of good repute and competence to audit the accounts, absent real grounds for suspecting that the auditor is wrong, the directors have discharged their duty.[24]

On appeal in *Daniels v Anderson*,[25] the majority of Sheller and Clarke JJA (Powell JA dissenting on the question of the directors' duty of care) largely upheld the judgment of Rogers CJ at first instance. The majority agreed with Rogers CJ that directors are required to inform themselves about the affairs of the company.[26] An objective standard of care was firmly established:

> There is no doubt reason for establishing a board which enjoys the varied wisdom of persons drawn from different commercial backgrounds. Even so a director, whatever his or her background, has a duty greater than that of simply representing a particular field of experience. That duty involves becoming familiar with the business of the company and how it is run and ensuring that the board has available means to audit the management of the company so that it can satisfy itself that the company is being properly run. ... In our opinion the responsibilities of directors require that they take reasonable steps to place themselves in a position to guide and monitor the management of the company.[27]

The Court of Appeal agreed that the non-executive directors of AWA were not negligent, but unlike Rogers CJ at first instance, their Honours were less inclined to draw a strict differentiation between the standard of care of executive and non-executive directors. Commenting directly on the extract quoted above, Sheller and Clarke JJA stated that 'it does not accurately state the extent of the duty of directors whether non-executive or

21 *Re City Equitable Fire Insurance Co Ltd* [1925] Ch 407.

22 *AWA Ltd v Daniels* (1992) 7 ACSR 759, 866, 868.

23 The definitions of executive and non-executive director are considered in Chapter 10 at Section 10.20.15.

24 *AWA Ltd v Daniels* (1992) 7 ACSR 759, 868.

25 (1995) 37 NSWLR 438.

26 Ibid 500.

27 Ibid 500–1.

not in modern company law'.[28] Their Honours concluded that there should not be any differentiation between executive and non-executive directors and stated 'the director's duty of care is not merely subjective, limited by the director's knowledge and experience or ignorance or inaction'.[29] As these and other similar cases were progressing through the courts,[30] the statutory duty of care was being reformulated to clarify the objective nature of the duty. Beyond objectivity, the redrafting was designed to take into account the particular circumstances of the company, the manner in which it internally distributes roles and responsibilities, and the particular expertise a director may possess.[31] There was some debate, following the decision in *Daniels v Anderson* and the rejection of a distinction between executive and non-executive directors, as to whether the statutory duty should be amended to reintroduce recognition of the differences in qualifications and experience of the individual director.[32] Ultimately, the amended provision, which remains as the current s 180(1) of the *Corporations Act*, did not include that particular element.

11.10.15 The current common law position

The duty of care, skill and diligence in the common law is recognised to be generally the same as the duty expressed in s 180(1) of the *Corporations Act*. However, the statutory duty continues to be informed by the duty at common law. Both the common law and statutory formulations are concerned with reviewing the actions of a director in terms of the performance of a 'reasonable person', being a director of a company in the same circumstances, in the same position as that director, and having the same responsibilities.

Since the *AWA* decisions, it is accepted that directors are required to take reasonable steps to place themselves in a position to guide and monitor the management of the company.[33] This means that:

(1) a director should become familiar with the fundamentals of the business in which the corporation is engaged
(2) a director is under a continuing obligation to keep informed about the activities of the corporation
(3) directorial management requires a general monitoring of corporate affairs and policies, by way of regular attendance at board meetings
(4) a director should maintain familiarity with the financial status of the corporation by a regular review of financial statements. Indeed, he or she will be unable to avoid liability for insolvent trading by claiming that they had never learned to read financial statements.[34]

28 Ibid 502.
29 Ibid 503.
30 See, eg, *Vrisakis v Australian Securities Commission* (1993) 9 WAR 395.
31 Explanatory Memorandum, Corporate Law Reform Bill 1992 (Cth) [84]–[85].
32 'Directors' Duties and Corporate Governance: Facilitating Innovations and Protecting Investors' (Corporate Law Economic Reform Program Paper No 3, The Treasury, 1997) [6.2] <https://treasury.gov.au/sites/default/files/2019-03/full-13.pdf>.
33 *Daniels v Anderson* (1995) 37 NSWLR 438, 501.
34 *Australian Securities and Investments Commission v Adler* (2002) 41 ACSR 72, 167 citing *Daniels v Anderson* (1995) 37 NSWLR 438, 502–504 and *Commonwealth Bank of Australia v Friedrich* (1991) 5 ACSR 115, 125.

Directors, whether executive or non-executive, are engaged by the company through a contract. For executive directors, this will be a contract of service or employment; whereas, for non-executive directors, it will be a letter of engagement or appointment.[35] 'The scope of any additional contractual duties and obligations owed by a director to the company will depend on the terms of the contract between the parties, although there will generally be an implied duty of skill and care imposed where professional services are proffered.'[36] The High Court considered this in *Astley v Austrust Ltd* in relation to solicitors advising a trustee company, with the majority finding that '[t]he implied term of reasonable care in a contract of professional services arises by operation of law. It is one of those terms that the law attaches as an incident of contracts of that class.'[37] The duty of care in contract is similar in nature to the duty under s 180(1) of the *Corporations Act*: that the director exercises the care and skill expected of a person who occupies the position in question.

A director also owes a tortious duty to exercise care and skill in the performance of their functions and the discharge of the duties of their office.[38] A director is under a common law duty of care and can be liable as a tortfeasor for negligence.[39] If there is negligence in performing a contract, alternative claims may exist in both contract and tort.[40] However, it is possible to contract out of a tortious duty. A director's duty of care and skill to the company is further recognised as an equitable duty.[41]

The standard of care at common law and in equity is that of an objective reasonable person in a similar position to the director in question. All formulations of the duty are concerned with reviewing the actions of a director in terms of the performance of a reasonable person, being a director of a company in the same circumstances, in the same position as that director and having the same responsibilities. However, purely personal circumstances are not considered relevant, such as the standard of education or business experience. *Daniels v Anderson*[42] remains authority for the position that there is a minimum standard of care and diligence that applies to both executive and non-executive directors, but *Australian Securities and Investments Commission v Healey*,[43] discussed below,

35 See, eg, ASX Corporate Governance Council, *Corporate Governance Principles and Recommendations* (Australian Securities Exchange, 4th ed, February 2019) <https://www.asx.com.au/content/dam/asx/about/corporate-governance-council/cgc-principles-and-recommendations-fourth-edn.pdf> Recommendation 1.3.

36 *Astley v Austrust Ltd* (1999) 197 CLR 1.

37 Ibid 22 (Gleeson CJ, McHugh, Gummow and Hayne JJ).

38 *Daniels v Anderson* (1995) 37 NSWLR 438, 502–5; *Permanent Building Society (in liq) v Wheeler* (1994) 11 WAR 187, 235–7.

39 *Daniels v Anderson* (1995) 37 NSWLR 438.

40 Following the line of cases that commenced with *Hedley Byrne v Heller & Partners Ltd* [1964] AC 465.

41 *Permanent Building Society (in liq) v Wheeler* (1994) 11 WAR 187, 235–7. See especially the detailed discussion of this point in JD Heydon, MJ Leeming and PG Turner, *Meagher, Gummow and Lehane's Equity: Doctrines and Remedies* (LexisNexis Butterworths, 5th ed, 2015) 201 [5–325] that accepts there is much (although not universal) support for the proposition that, so far as the duties of directors to exercise reasonable care and skill are equitable, they are not fiduciary. The practical importance of this distinction lies in remedies, and particularly the third-party accessorial liability found through *Barnes v Addy* (1874) LR 9 Ch App 244. For details of this rule, see JD Heydon, MJ Leeming and PG Turner, *Meagher, Gummow and Lehane's Equity: Doctrines and Remedies* (LexisNexis Butterworths, 5th ed, 2015) 219 [5–405].

42 *Daniels v Anderson* (1995) 37 NSWLR 438.

43 *Australian Securities and Investments Commission v Healey* (2011) 196 FCR 291.

indicates that the penalties will be different for an executive or non-executive director. There is a core of non-reducible skills, but if the director holds themselves out as having a particular skill on appointment they will be expected to utilise that skill in performance of their duties. Courts have cautioned, repeatedly,[44] that the context of each case will be key to analysing whether the objective standard of care and diligence has been met, and that general statements as to the standard must be 'viewed with a degree of circumspection having regard to the fact-specific nature of the inquiry'.[45]

Section 185 of the *Corporations Act* preserves the power of the company to enforce these duties in the general law. The distinction between a breach of these duties and a breach of the Act is twofold. First, there is a distinction as to who may bring an action for breach, as the company can bring an action for a breach of the general law duties, but only ASIC may seek a declaration of contravention under s 1317E for a breach of the civil penalty provisions.[46] If a breach can be demonstrated, then the court must order a declaration of contravention.

Second, there is a distinction as to what remedies can be sought, as discussed in detail in Chapter 10 at Section 10.35. We now consider the duty of care, skill and diligence imposed by the *Corporations Act*.

11.15 The *Corporations Act* duty of care and diligence

Section 185 of the *Corporations Act* preserves the operation of the duty of care, skill and diligence alongside the legislative duties. As such, breaches of the general law often occur concurrently with breaches of the *Corporations Act*. ASIC is the only party who can seek a declaration of contravention, or the disqualification of a director, or a pecuniary penalty order.[47] This does not prevent a company from claiming that directors have breached the provisions of the Act. It only prevents the company from seeking those penalties available exclusively to ASIC following a declaration of contravention. The company can seek a compensation order under s 1317H, to compensate for damage[48] caused to the corporation by a breach of a civil penalty provision, including s 180(1), regardless of whether a declaration of contravention has been ordered.[49] Equally, should ASIC take

44 See, eg, *Australian Securities and Investments Commission v Rich* (2009) 75 ACSR 1; *Australian Securities and Investments Commission v Cassimatis (No 8)* (2016) 336 ALR 209; *Boros v Pages Property Investments Pty Ltd* (2021) 395 ALR 756; *Sapphire Holdings Group Ltd v Medina* [2023] VSC 714.

45 *Boros v Pages Property Investments Pty Ltd* (2021) 395 ALR 756 [27].

46 As discussed in Chapter 1 at Section 1.65.05 in general, and Chapter 10 at Section 10.35.10 in relation to directors' duties.

47 *Corporations Act* ss 1317J(1), (4).

48 For example, payment of dividends can constitute damage to a company, despite its benefit to the members, if the payment would not have been made but for the breach of s 180(1): *DSHE Holdings Ltd (recs and mgrs. apptd) (in liq) v Potts* (2022) 405 ALR 70. Special leave to appeal to the High Court on limited grounds was granted, but then later revoked: *Potts v National Australia Bank Ltd* (2023) 4156 ALR 384. In *Hakea Holdings Pty Ltd v McGrath (No 2)* (2022) 162 FCR 316, failure by Mr McGrath to disclose the financial difficulties facing the company (of which he was the sole director and member) that had contracted with Hakea (of which he was also a director) caused damage to Hakea as it did not exercise its right to terminate the contractual relationship earlier.

49 This is made clear in s 1317J, which notes that 'an application for a compensation order may be made whether or not a declaration of contravention has been made under section 1317E'.

action, the company may seek compensation by intervening in an application by ASIC under s 1317J(3), or may apply on its own behalf under s 1317J(2).

The legislative duties that reflect the duties of care and diligence are contained in ss 180(1) and 588G. We start our discussion with the duty of care and diligence under s 180(1).

11.15.05 *Corporations Act* s 180(1): the duty of care and diligence

Section 180(1) states:

> A director or other officer of a corporation must exercise their powers and discharge their duties with the degree of care and diligence that a reasonable person would exercise if they:
>
> **(a)** were a director or officer of a corporation in the corporation's circumstances; and
>
> **(b)** occupied the office held by, and had the same responsibilities within the corporation as, the director or officer.[50]

The influence of the general law on the duty of care, skill and diligence is clear from the format of the duty in the *Corporations Act*. As discussed at Sections 11.10.05–10, the test is objective but is tempered by the subjective circumstances of the particular company and the director's role and functions. Directors must exercise a reasonable degree of care and diligence. Determining whether this has been the case will involve an examination of the context of the particular company and directors[51] and 'by balancing the foreseeable risk of harm against the potential benefits that could reasonably have been expected to accrue to the company from the conduct in question'.[52] The company does not need to suffer actual loss or damage in order for s 180(1) to have been breached—what is required is a foreseeable risk of harm, which can include the risk of suffering penalties for breaching the law or harm to reputation.[53] The requirement for care and diligence is subject to s 180(2), known as the 'business judgment rule', which creates a 'safe harbour' for directors. The business judgment rule does not have a counterpart in common law or equity, but s 180(2) is stated to apply to those duties as well.

The trend in the general law over the past two centuries towards higher standards of behaviour expected from directors has continued in relation to cases dealing with the statutory provisions. As under the general law, the difficulty with applying the objective s 180(1) duty to the behaviour of a director is the requirement to assess the position of the director in question. The office of the director, the role that they perform, and the distribution of responsibilities within that company must be closely considered. This was evident in the cases that followed ASIC's investigation into the collapse of One.Tel, which were some of the first decisions to consider the newly enacted *Corporations Act*.

50 *Corporations Act* s 180(1).

51 *Sapphire Holdings Group Ltd v Medina* [2023] VSC 714, [124].

52 *Australian Securities and Investments Commission v Drake (No 2)* (2016) 340 ALR 75 [395], citing Mason J in *Wyong Shire Council v Shirt* (1980) 146 CLR 40, 47–8.

53 *Australian Securities and Investments Commission v Wilson (No 3)* (2023) 171 ACSR 1.

Prior to its collapse in 2001, One.Tel was the fourth largest telecommunications company in Australia, with operations in seven countries, 1.9 million customers and valued at $3.5 billion. *Australian Securities and Investments Commission v Rich*[54] was a preliminary decision as to ASIC's cause of action against a number of directors and officers involved in the collapse, where Austin J considered the duties of the non-executive chairman of One.Tel, Mr Greaves. Greaves held qualifications as a chartered accountant and was also the chair of One.Tel's finance and audit committee. Greaves argued that a non-executive chair had no special duties over and above the other directors, and that the reference in s 180(1)(b) to 'responsibilities' limited the application of the s 180(1) duty to specific tasks delegated through the articles of the company or by resolution or otherwise.[55] The Court rejected these propositions, finding that a non-executive chairman did owe duties to the company to act with due care, and that Greaves' failure to remain informed as to the company's financial position gave rise to a breach of s 180(1).[56] Further, Greaves' particular background, expertise and appointment to the finance and audit committees contributed to the standard of care owed to the company.[57]

Following this, the Court ordered a declaration of contravention under s 1317E for a breach of s 180(1), and a period of disqualification for four years under ss 206C and 206E for Greaves, based on an agreed set of facts.[58]

The statutory duty has continued to be scrutinised by the courts through a number of large, influential decisions in the past decade. One of the most contentious set of corporate circumstances in Australia's recent past involved the James Hardie group of companies and their liability for disease caused by exposure to asbestos products. The James Hardie group is discussed in Chapter 3, in the context of involuntary tort creditors and the separate legal entity at Section 3.50.05.

To recap: in 2001, the James Hardie group sought to restructure James Hardie Industries Ltd ('JHIL'), the parent of the two subsidiary companies which manufactured and sold asbestos-related products. To deal with potential liability in tort, JHIL established the Medical Research and Compensation Foundation ('MRCF') and claimed, publicly and to the ASX, that it had sufficient funding to satisfy the compensation claims against the subsidiaries. Ostensibly in the pursuit of taxation benefits, JHIL then relocated from Australia to the Netherlands and transferred its assets to a Netherlands-based company, James Hardie Industries NV ('JHINV'). It later became apparent that the MRCF had only been provided with $293 million to satisfy the tort claims, when the claims against the group at that time were in excess of $2.2 billion. The public backlash against this restructuring, and the perception that the company had deliberately quarantined

54 *Australian Securities and Investments Commission v Rich* (2003) 44 ACSR 341.

55 Ibid 348.

56 Ibid 352.

57 Ibid 351–2.

58 *Australian Securities and Investments Commission v Rich* (2004) 50 ACSR 500. ASIC's proceedings against the other One.Tel directors in *Australian Securities and Investments Commission v Rich* (2009) 75 ACSR 1 was not successful but involved significant consideration of the business judgment rule and will be discussed at Section 11.15.10. See also *Australian Securities and Investments Commission v Vines* (2004) 55 ACSR 617, as discussed in B Nosworthy, 'The Corporations Act and Climate Change—Appetite for Change?' (2020) 94(6) *Australian Law Journal* 411, 414.

its assets against the claims of involuntary tort creditors, led to an inquiry examining the relationship between the funding shortfall and the JHIL restructure, led by David Jackson QC.

In 2004, the Jackson Inquiry[59] determined that, although the JHIL restructure was not in breach of the *Corporations Act*, there was a serious question as to whether that indicated a deficiency in the law. There were further questions posed as to the role of corporate governance, and of director and officer liability for statements made on the funding of MRCF during the restructuring process. Subsequent to the report, ASIC commenced civil penalty proceedings against a number of former executives and former and current directors of JHIL. This led to a complex set of cases, including *Australian Securities and Investments Commission v Macdonald (No 11)*;[60] the appeal by all defendants (excluding the CEO, Mr Macdonald) in *Morley v Australian Securities and Investments Commission*;[61] two High Court appeals in relation to that appeal: *Australian Securities and Investments Commission v Hellicar*[62] and *Shafron v Australian Securities and Investments Commission*;[63] a separate trial judgment on the question of relief under s 1317S, *Australian Securities and Investments Commission v Macdonald (No 12)*;[64] and its appeal in *Gillfillan v Australian Securities and Investments Commission*.[65]

In *Australian Securities and Investments Commission v Macdonald (No 11)*, ASIC brought 52 allegations of contraventions of the *Corporations Act* against JHIL, the Netherlands-based JHINV, 7 non-executive directors and 3 executive officers. Ultimately, Gzell J found that 33 of the contraventions were proven, including breaches of the s 180(1) duty of care and diligence by all directors and officers charged. These breaches were associated with misleading and deceptive conduct, making false statements in relation to securities and breaches of the continuous disclosure rules, which centred on the press release regarding the sufficiency of the funding provided to the MRCF. Gzell J focused on what had been discussed at a board meeting held on 15 February 2001, prior to the final ASX announcement on 16 February 2001. The announcement stated:

> James Hardie Industries Limited (JHIL) announced today that it had established a foundation to compensate sufferers of asbestos-related diseases with claims against two former James Hardie subsidiaries and fund medical research aimed at finding cures for these diseases.
>
> The Medical Research and Compensation Foundation (MRCF), to be chaired by Sir Llewellyn Edwards, will be completely independent of JHIL and will commence operation with assets of $293 million.

59 DF Jackson, *Report of the Special Commission of Inquiry into the Medical and Research Compensation Fund* (Final Report, 27 January 2004) ('the Jackson Inquiry').

60 *Australian Securities and Investments Commission v Macdonald (No 11)* (2009) 230 FLR 1.

61 *Morley v Australian Securities and Investments Commission* (2010) 81 ACSR 285. There was also a separate appeal on behalf of the company in *James Hardie Industries NV v Australian Securities and Investments Commission* (2010) 81 ACSR 1.

62 *Australian Securities and Investments Commission v Hellicar* (2012) 247 CLR 345.

63 *Shafron v Australian Securities and Investments Commission* (2012) 247 CLR 465.

64 *Australian Securities and Investments Commission v Macdonald (No 12)* (2009) 73 ACSR 638.

65 *Gillfillan v Australian Securities and Investments Commission* (2012) 92 ACSR 460.

> The Foundation has sufficient funds to meet all legitimate compensation claims anticipated from people injured by asbestos products that were manufactured in the past by two former subsidiaries of JHIL.
>
> JHIL CEO, Mr Peter Macdonald said that the establishment of a fully-funded Foundation provided certainty for both claimants and shareholders. ...
>
> 'James Hardie is satisfied that the Foundation has sufficient funds to meet anticipated future claims,' Mr Macdonald said.[66]

At trial, evidence from JHIL's expert financial advisors indicated that the funding provided was only sufficient if a complex set of assumptions as to the future rate of claims, investment returns across a period of 50 years, and longevity of the fund proved to be correct. The Court held that the directors and officers would have known that these were unrealistic assumptions, which led to the conclusion that the directors and officers should have known that the announcement claiming that the MCRF was fully funded was misleading.

All of the non-executive directors who gave evidence in the trial claimed that the draft ASX announcement was either not before the meeting of 15 February 2001, not discussed, or not approved. Gzell J found that the directors were mistaken, and that the announcement must have been considered or approved at that meeting.[67] The Court then considered whether the approval of that draft announcement was in breach of s 180(1).

The non-executive directors who gave evidence also stated that, had the announcement been considered, they would not have approved it. Gzell J considered that this evidence accorded with the fact that the non-executive directors knew it contained false or misleading or deceptive statements, being 'unequivocal and unqualified' statements as to the sufficiency of funding.[68] Approving the announcement was consequently a breach of their duties under s 180(1). The executive officers were equally found to be in breach of their duties for failing to properly advise the board as to the limitations of the restructuring plan and the misleading nature of the announcement.[69] The question as to whether the non-executive directors were entitled to delegate this matter or rely on the advice of others in relation to the drafting of the announcement is discussed at Section 11.20.10.

All defendants except the CEO, Mr Macdonald, appealed in *Morley v Australian Securities and Investments Commission*.[70] On appeal, Gzell J's finding of fact that the announcement had been approved at the meeting of 15 February 2001 was overturned, and ASIC's case against the non-executive directors failed. However, the Court of Appeal upheld the findings against the executive directors, Morley and Shafron, in relation to their failure to properly brief the board and company in relation to the actuarial model.

ASIC appealed the decision on the question of approval of the announcement and the liability of the non-executive directors in *Australian Securities and Investments Commission v Hellicar*[71] and of the liability of the company secretary and general counsel in *Shafron v*

66 (2009) 230 FLR 1, 34 [121].

67 Ibid 50 [228], [230].

68 Ibid 56–7 [262].

69 Ibid 70 [358] (Macdonald), 77–8 [413] (Shafron), 82–3 [456] (Morley).

70 *Morley v Australian Securities and Investments Commission* (2010) 81 ACSR 285.

71 *Australian Securities and Investments Commission v Hellicar* (2012) 247 CLR 345.

Australian Securities and Investments Commission.[72] The High Court in *Australian Securities and Investments Commission v Hellicar* was satisfied that there was sufficient evidence that the board had approved the announcement; with the result that Gzell J's original findings of contravention against the non-executive directors were reinstated. The matter was then remitted to the New South Wales Court of Appeal for appeals against penalties.[73] The arguments raised in *Shafron v Australian Securities and Investments Commission* were discussed in detail in Chapter 10 at Section 10.20.15.

A final point of interest from the High Court judgment in *Australian Securities and Investments Commission v Hellicar* is the discussion by Heydon J in relation to the overseas directors, who attended the meeting of 15 February by telephone from the United States. Heydon J, in a separate but concurring judgment, agreed with Gzell J at first instance that, by their silence, those directors voted in favour of the resolution approving the draft ASX announcement.[74] The overseas directors contended they were not supplied with the draft, and that consequently they were not in breach of their duty of care and diligence because they had given careful consideration to what was before them. The overseas directors argued they had no duty to attend to anything more unless the chair ensured that they had access to the relevant information. Heydon J rejected that argument, finding that 'the onus was on [the overseas directors] to be cautious when voting on the making of the announcement—either by seeking further information or by explicitly abstaining'.[75] This provides greater context to the duty of care, skill and diligence as it applies to overseas directors, with the onus on them to ensure that they have the appropriate material to make an informed decision or to abstain from voting.

The choices made by ASIC in pursuing this litigation were subject to criticism. In the Court of Appeal, it was argued that ASIC was subject to a duty of fairness in relation to prosecuting civil penalty proceedings. The Court held ASIC had failed to discharge this duty due to the decision not to call the company's solicitor, Mr Robb, who had prepared the draft minutes before the 15 February meeting and was present at the meeting.[76] The High Court was critical of the Court of Appeal's discussion of the source of such a duty,[77] but agreed that ASIC must be subject to a duty that can be described as a duty to conduct litigation fairly.[78]

---

72 *Shafron v Australian Securities and Investments Commission* (2012) 247 CLR 465.

73 *Australian Securities and Investments Commission v Gillfillan* (2012) 92 ACSR 460. The disqualifications imposed by Gzell J on each of the seven non-executive directors were reduced from five to two years and three months with even shorter bans for the overseas directors. The pecuniary penalties payable were also reduced from $30,000 to $25,000 and $20,000 for the overseas directors. The original penalty of $75,000 and seven years was reimposed on Shafron, the company secretary and general counsel. In *Morley v Australian Securities and Investments Commission (No 2)* (2011) 83 ACSR 620, the penalty against Morley, the CFO, was reduced from $35,000 to $20,000 and disqualification from five to two years.

74 *Australian Securities and Investments Commission v Hellicar* (2012) 247 CLR 345, 460 [307]. The Court of Appeal agreed that silence would be considered as voting in favour; however, the Court found contrary to Gzell J and the High Court that such approval had not taken place at the 15 February meeting.

75 Ibid 461 [310]–[311].

76 *Morley v Australian Securities and Investments Commission* (2010) 81 ACSR 285 [701], [794]–[796].

77 *Australian Securities and Investments Commission v Hellicar* (2012) 247 CLR 345, 406–7 [147], [149]–[151], 430 [225], 434–5 [239]–[240].

78 Ibid 407 [152].

The JHIL litigation, particularly against the non-executive directors, raises questions as to director liability under s 180(1) for permitting a company to breach the law. Finding a director personally responsible for any breach of the law by the company has been described as the 'stepping stones' approach to director liability[79] and has been subject to criticism.[80] However, ASIC has been successful in the past decade at using this mechanism to enforce the statutory duty of care against directors for the company's breach of the law.[81] Brereton J, in *Australian Securities and Investments Commission v Maxwell*,[82] considered that a director who causes or allows a company to breach the law is in breach of s 180(1) if they failed to balance the potential benefits to the company with the risk associated with the breach. This basis for liability is instead of any 'general obligation owed by directors at large to conduct the affairs of the company in accordance with the law generally or the *Corporations Act* in particular'.[83] In *Australian Securities and Investments Commission v Cassimatis*,[84] Reeves J raised concern that using this test could encourage law-breaking, as long as the rewards for the company in breach were high enough to outweigh the costs. In *Australian Securities Investments Commission v Mariner Corporation*,[85] Beach J suggested that a relevant distinction could be made between cases where a director deliberately causes a company to breach the law, in contrast to a decision that inadvertently causes non-compliance. Given ASIC's successes in relation to action for false or misleading representations of the environmental or sustainability credentials ('green-washing') of investment fund products,[86] the potential impact of a stepping stones argument for director liability is significant. This question will be further considered at Section 11.15.10 in relation to the application of the business judgment rule to circumstances where the company has breached the law.

While the James Hardie litigation was working its way through the courts, the Centro Property Group was the focus of an ASIC investigation, following the discovery there had been significant errors in the company's 2007 annual report provided to the ASX. In July 2007, shortly before the annual report was filed with the ASX, the board reviewed submissions from the CFO in relation to a refinancing proposal to obtain significant bridging

---

79 See, eg, A Herzberg and H Anderson, 'Stepping Stones—From Corporate Fault to Directors' Personal Civil Liability' (2012) 40(2) *Federal Law Review* 181.

80 See, eg, R Teele Langford, 'Corporate Culpability, Stepping Stones and Mariner: Contention Surrounding Director's Duties where the Company Breaches the Law' (2016) 34(1) *Company and Securities Law Journal* 75; A Zhou, 'A Step Too Far? Rethinking the Stepping Stone Approach to Officers' Liability' (2019) 47(1) *Federal Law Review* 151; C Carr and R Cunningham, 'A Step Too Far? The 'Stepping Stone' Approach and s 180(1) of the *Corporations Act 2001* (Cth)' (2019) 34(1) *Australian Journal of Corporate Law* 58.

81 I Ramsay and B Saunders, 'An Analysis of the Enforcement of Statutory Duty of Care by ASIC' (2019) 36(6) *Company and Securities Law Journal* 497.

82 *Australian Securities and Investments Commission v Maxwell* (2006) 59 ACSR 373.

83 Ibid [104].

84 *Australian Securities and Investments Commission v Cassimatis* (2013) 220 FCR 256.

85 *Australian Securities and Investments Commission v Mariner Corporation* (2015) 241 FCR 502.

86 *Australian Securities and Investments Commission v Vanguard Investments Australia Ltd* [2024] FCA 308, and the settlement reached in relation to similar litigation against Mercer Financial Advice (Australia) Pty Ltd in 2023, which led to a $12 million penalty: Australian Securities and Investments Commission, 'Mercer to Pay $12 Million Penalty for Misleading Representations and Fee Disclosure Failures' (Media Release 23-314MR, 23 November 2023).

loans from major creditors in exchange for guarantees from the Group. When the annual report was filed with the ASX, it failed to disclose this refinancing, the approximately $1.5 billion of short-term liabilities in relation to the financing (instead, classifying them as 'non-current liabilities'), and the four guarantees of short-term liabilities of approximately US$1.75 billion given after the balance date of 30 June 2007. Although the Group had notified the ASX in December 2007 of a halt in trading in its securities, and made a series of announcements across the next three months concerning the corrections, ASIC alleged[87] that the CFO and directors of the relevant companies within the Group had breached ss 180(1), 344[88] and 601FD(1)(b).[89]

Given that the directors' errors in this case related to complex financial documentation, questions arose as to the level of financial literacy required of directors and the ability of the directors to rely on the information provided to them by management and external advisors, such as auditors. The question of reliance will be considered at Section 11.20.10. On the question of the duty of care and diligence, Middleton J found that the errors in the annual report were so obvious that the conclusion that the directors had been negligent was inescapable.[90] Under a heading within the judgment titled 'Reality Check', Middleton J considered the directors' argument that ASIC was trying to extend their responsibility 'beyond reasonable financial literacy and a proper degree of engagement in the affairs of a company'.[91] In refuting the directors' argument, his Honour held:

> Each director relied completely on the processes in place and their advisors. All the directors failed to see the 'obvious errors' because they all took the same approach in relying exclusively upon those processes and advisors. No director stood back, armed with [their] own knowledge, and looked at and considered for [themselves] the financial statements. ... [A]ll that was required of the directors in this proceeding was the financial literacy to understand basic accounting conventions and proper diligence in reading the financial statements. The directors had the required accumulated knowledge of the affairs of Centro, based upon the documents placed before them and discussion at board meetings. Each director then needed to formulate [their] own opinion, and apply that opinion to the task of approving the financial statements.[92]

There was concern in the wake of the Centro decision as to the level of knowledge of complex and detailed accounting standards expected of directors. The statement from Middleton J makes it clear that the primary concern was the failure by the directors to turn their minds to the question of the accuracy of the financial statements.

87 *Australian Securities and Investments Commission v Healey* (2011) 196 FCR 291.

88 Section 344 states that 'A director of a company, registered scheme or disclosing entity contravenes this section if they fail to take all reasonable steps to comply with, or to secure compliance with' the Parts of the Act which set out a company's financial records and financial reporting obligations.

89 This section outlines the duties of officers of responsible entities, which mirror those of directors under ss 180–4.

90 *Australian Securities and Investments Commission v Healey* (2011) 196 FCR 291, 351 [251].

91 Ibid 425–6 [564].

92 Ibid 426 [569], [573].

Additionally, the notes attached to the annual report stated that '[b]orrowings are classified as current liabilities unless the Group has an unconditional right to defer settlement of the liability for at least 12 months after the balance sheet date', which is consistent with the applicable accounting standard (AASB 101).[93] As the directors knew that the Group was negotiating with its creditors, they must have known there could be no unconditional right to defer settlement. As such, no complex accounting knowledge was required in this instance—reading the reports and the definitions should have alerted the directors to the error.

Although Middleton J was not prepared to differentiate between the executive and non-executives in regard to their duty of care and diligence, his Honour did impose significantly different penalties on the basis of that distinction. In *Australian Securities and Investments Commission v Healey (No 2)*,[94] no penalties or disqualifications were ordered against the non-executive directors. His Honour discussed the need for penalties to act as a general deterrent, and noted that the denial of access to ss 1317S and 1318 relief[95] and the declarations of contravention could be considered punitive.[96] This is in addition to the 'reputational damage to the defendants, including the directors, and the effect it has and will have on them, [which] cannot be underestimated in the case of these particular directors'.[97] By contrast, the CEO was subject to a $30,000 civil penalty and the CFO was disqualified from managing corporations for two years.

The effect of this line of cases is that the duty of care and diligence under s 180(1) imposes the same standard of care as the common law and equity.[98] Directors have a core, irreducible requirement of involvement in monitoring the performance of the company. There is no distinction made between the duty imposed upon an executive and a non-executive director,[99] and non-executive directors are expected to engage with the task of directing the company and not simply rely on the opinion of the executive directors or management. Further, a director's duty of care may be increased in circumstances where their appointment was on the basis of a special set of skills or knowledge, or where they have accepted appointment to a specialist committee of the directors. The duty of care and diligence is a key component in the balancing act undertaken by the law, to ensure appropriate corporate conduct through regulation of director behaviour. The duty requires directors to be positively engaged in the task of 'directing' the company, taking care and responsibility for their decisions, employing appropriate skills on behalf

93 Australian Accounting Standards Board, *Presentation of Financial Statements* (AASB 101, July 2015).

94 *Australian Securities and Investments Commission v Healey (No 2)* (2011) 196 FCR 430.

95 See generally Chapter 10 at Section 10.40.10.

96 *Australian Securities and Investments Commission v Healey (No 2)* (2011) 196 FCR 430, 448 [109].

97 *Australian Securities and Investments Commission v Healey (No 2)* (2011) 196 FCR 430; however, Middleton J's remarks following [132] from the heading 'Seriousness of the Contraventions' are not reported in the Federal Court Report but can be found in the original judgment *Australian Securities and Investments Commission v Healey (No 2)* [2011] FCA 1003, [188].

98 *Australian Securities and Investments Commission v Bettles* (2023) 169 ACSR 244 [439].

99 There may be different expectations of conduct for the chair of the board, in relation to their separate responsibilities, such as overseeing the deliberations of the board, ensuring the directors have access to materials needed in reasonable time so as to discharge their own duties to the company: *United Petroleum Australia Pty Ltd v Hudson* [2020] VSCA 14 [124]-[125]; and for setting the agenda for the board: *Australian Securities and Investments Commission v Mitchell (No 2)* (2020) 382 ALR 425.

of the company, and being diligent and conscientious in their attendance and engagement with their role via board meetings. However, it is important that the duty does not inappropriately restrict the degree of discretion that should be afforded to those in senior corporate roles in order to conduct business successfully. As part of that balance, we now turn to consider the application of the business judgment rule in s 180(2) to a claim of breach of s 180(1) and the underlying common law and equitable alternatives.

11.15.10 *Corporations Act* s 180(2): the business judgment rule

Historically, there has been reluctance by the courts to review the business merits of decisions of the directors and management.

> Directors in whom are vested the right and the duty of deciding where the company's interests lie and how they are to be served may be concerned with a wide range of practical considerations, and their judgment, if exercised in good faith and not for irrelevant purposes, is not open to review in the courts.[100]

However, as the duty of care, skill and diligence has become more objective, the business community has voiced concerns that this would constrain appropriate business risk-taking.[101] From 1989 to 1991, a series of recommendations were made to introduce a statutory business judgment rule along the lines of the common law doctrine that existed in the United States.[102] In 1999, the business judgment rule was introduced together with the redrafted s 180(1).[103] The Explanatory Memorandum to the Bill introducing these amendments stated that:

> The fundamental purpose of the business judgment rule is to protect the authority of directors in the exercise of their duties, not to insulate directors from liability. While it is accepted that directors should be subject to a high level of accountability, a failure to expressly acknowledge that directors should not be liable for decisions made in good faith and with due care, may lead to failure by the company and its directors to take advantage of opportunities that involve responsible risk taking.
>
> The statutory formulation of the business judgment rule will clarify and confirm the common law position that the Courts will rarely review bona fide

100 *Harlowe's Nominees Pty Ltd v Woodside (Lakes Entrance) Oil Co NL* (1968) 121 CLR 483, 493. See also *Howard Smith Ltd v Ampol Petroleum Ltd* [1974] AC 821, 832.

101 A number of commentators at the time argued that the courts' traditionally non-interventionist stance would provide sufficient protection: see especially P Redmond, 'Safe Harbours or Sleepy Hollows: Does Australia Need a Statutory Business Judgment Rule?' in I Ramsay (ed), *Corporate Governance and the Duties of Company Directors* (Centre for Corporate Law and Securities Regulation, The University of Melbourne, 1997).

102 Senate Standing Committee on Legal and Constitutional Affairs, Parliament of Australia, *Company Directors' Duties* (Report, November 1989) [3.35]; Companies and Securities Advisory Committee, *Company Directors and officers: Indemnification, Relief and Insurance* (Report No 10, May 1990) Recommendation 13; House of Representatives Standing Committee on Legal and Constitutional Affairs, Parliament of Australia, *Corporate Practices and the Rights of Shareholders* (Report, November 1991) Recommendation 20.

103 *Corporate Law Economic Reform Program Act 1999* (Cth).

> business decisions. However the statutory formulation will provide a clear presumption in favour of a director's judgment.[104]

The business judgment rule, contained in s 180(2) of the *Corporations Act*, operates to exculpate a director who has made a well-informed business decision:

> A director or other officer of a corporation who makes a business judgment is taken to meet the requirements of subsection (1), and their equivalent duties at common law and in equity, in respect of the judgment if they:
>
> **(a)** make the judgment in good faith for a proper purpose; and
>
> **(b)** do not have a material personal interest in the subject matter of the judgment; and
>
> **(c)** inform themselves about the subject matter of the judgment to the extent they reasonably believe to be appropriate; and
>
> **(d)** rationally believe that the judgment is in the best interests of the corporation.

The director's or officer's belief that the judgment is in the best interests of the corporation is a rational one unless the belief is one that no reasonable person in their position would hold.

Section 180(3) defines a 'business judgment' to be any 'decision to take or not take action in respect of a matter relevant to the business operations of the corporation'. *Australian Securities and Investments Commission v Adler* confirmed that a business judgment does not extend to a failure to consider the matter at all.[105] A decision not to comply with the requirements of the *Corporations Act* will also not be a 'business judgment'. The Full Federal Court considered the application of s 180(2) in such circumstances in *Australian Securities and Investments Commission v Fortescue Metals Group Ltd,* although that decision was consequently overturned by the High Court.[106] Fortescue Metals Group Ltd released a series of ASX announcements in 2004, stating that it had entered into legally binding framework agreements with certain Chinese companies to finance and build mining infrastructure in Western Australia. When the media questioned the binding nature of these agreements, Fortescue's share price fell significantly. ASIC commenced an investigation, and ultimately proceedings against Fortescue, for misleading statements under s 1041H of the *Corporations Act* and the continuous disclosure provision in s 674 for failing to correct the earlier announcement.[107]

ASIC argued that Fortescue's director, Mr Forrest, was involved in Fortescue's contravention and had breached s 180(1). Although ASIC was unsuccessful at first instance,[108] on

104 Explanatory Memorandum, Corporate Law Economic Reform Program Bill 1999 (Cth) [6.3]–[6.4].

105 *Australian Securities and Investments Commission v Adler* (2002) 41 ACSR 72. See also *Australian Securities and Investments Commission v Rich* (2009) 75 ACSR 1 [7277].

106 *Australian Securities and Investments Commission v Fortescue Metals Group Ltd* (2011) 190 FCR 364; *Forrest v Australian Securities and Investments Commission* (2012) 247 CLR 486.

107 The continuous disclosure argument within this case is discussed in detail in Chapter 17 at Section 17.20.45.

108 *Australian Securities and Investments Commission v Fortescue Metals Group Ltd (No 5)* (2009) 264 ALR 201 (Gilmour J).

appeal the Full Federal Court found that the ASX release was misleading and deceptive, and considered Forrest's breach of s 180. Keane CJ cited the Explanatory Memorandum to the Act, which provided that 'compliance (or otherwise) with the prospectus requirements imposed by the Law would not be a decision' under s 180(2).[109] This accords with the position in United States that the business judgment rule is not available for a decision by directors to knowingly cause or permit the company to break the law.[110] This point of law was not discussed in the High Court appeal, which ultimately reversed the Full Federal Court's finding on liability.[111] By contrast, in *Australian Securities and Investments Commission v Vocation Ltd (in liq)*, Nicholas J held that a decision to permit the publication of an ASX announcement that was likely to mislead its readers was not a 'decision to take action in respect of a matter relevant to the business operations of Vocation' and consequently was not a business judgment.[112]

Section 180(2) was considered in depth in the decision of *Australian Securities and Investments Commission v Rich*,[113] mentioned previously at Section 11.15.05. ASIC argued that Mr Rich and Mr Silbermann, joint CEO and Finance Director respectively, breached s 180(1) by failing to advise the board of One.Tel Ltd that the company was insolvent. However, Austin J found that ASIC failed to prove the company was insolvent at the relevant time, and so ASIC's argument on the duty of care and diligence also failed.

During the judgment, his Honour gave detailed consideration to a number of elements of the business judgment rule.[114] In particular, the definition of 'business judgment' in s 180(3) was interpreted to include decisions in preparation of making a business judgment, such as planning, budgeting and forecasting, setting of policy goals or division of responsibilities within the board and management.[115] However, his Honour was not prepared to extend the s 180(2) rule to directors' monitoring and oversight duties, including monitoring of the company's financial position, as these did not involve decision-making.[116]

Another important question is whether the business judgment rule operates as a presumption in favour of the directors or as a defence, which has ramifications as to who bears the onus of proof. Austin J in *Australian Securities and Investments Commission v Rich* considered that this question needed to be resolved at an appellate level, although as yet there has been no binding appellate consideration of this issue.[117]

109 *Australian Securities and Investments Commission v Fortescue Metals Group Ltd* (2011) 190 FCR 364 [197]–[198].

110 See generally C Hansen, 'The Duty of Care, the Business Judgment Rule, and The American Law Institute Corporate Governance Project' (1993) 48(4) *The Business Lawyer* 1355, 1367–8, 1373.

111 *Fortescue Metals Group Ltd v Australian Securities and Investments Commission* (2012) 247 CLR 486.

112 *Australian Securities and Investments Commission v Vocation Ltd (in liq)* (2019) 371 ALR 155 [739]–[740]. See also *Australian Securities and Investments Commission v Big Star Energy Ltd (No 3)* (2020) 389 ALR 17 [531], regarding non-disclosure of information to the market under the continuous disclosure obligations.

113 *Australian Securities and Investments Commission v Rich* (2009) 75 ACSR 1.

114 Ibid 626 [7248].

115 Ibid 632–3 [7274]–[7276].

116 Ibid 633 [7278].

117 The Full Federal Court did consider the defence in *Australian Securities and Investments Commission v Fortescue Metals Group Ltd* (2011) 190 FCR 364, but this decision was overturned on appeal to the

The Explanatory Memorandum stated that the '[p]roposed subsection 180(2) acts as a rebuttable presumption in favour of directors which, if rebutted by a plaintiff, would mean the plaintiff would then still have to establish that the officer had breached their duty of care and diligence'.[118] However, without reference to that paragraph and with 'some hesitation in light of the US approach', Austin J in *Australian Securities and Investments Commission v Rich* concluded that s 180(2) operates as a defence, and consequently that the burden of proof falls on the defendant.[119] The question of whether this provision operates as a defence and not a presumption has been considered academically.[120] First, a presumption may be more consistent with the policy underlying the introduction to s 180(2) to encourage 'directors to take advantage of opportunities that involve responsible risk taking' and the mention of 'rebuttable presumption' in the Explanatory Memorandum.[121] Second, a presumption operating in favour of directors exercising a business judgment is consistent with the common law doctrine. Finally, it is consistent with the drafting of s 180(2), in that a plaintiff may rebut the presumption by disproving one element only. For it to function as a defence, a director must establish all elements. However, where it has been considered by the courts, it has been applied as a defence,[122] with the onus of proof falling on the director who relies on the various sub-sections to establish the requirements.[123]

These cases demonstrate that, although it has been over two decades since the business judgment rule in s 180(2) was introduced, it has not been successfully applied to exculpate a director.[124] Had Austin J found that ASIC had made out its case in *Australian Securities and Investments Commission v Rich*, then his Honour was prepared to allow Rich and Silbermann's use of s 180(2).[125] In *Australian Securities and Investments Commission v Mariner Corporation*, Beach J was prepared to allow each of the directors access to the business judgment rule, but dismissed ASIC's case that their decision to announce an

High Court. Unfortunately, the High Court judgment makes no reference to s 180(2), as the Court did not find any misleading or deceptive conduct had occurred in that case, with the consequence that s 180(1) had not been breached. Lee AJA in the Western Australian Court of Appeal decision in *Westpac Banking Corporation v Bell Group Ltd (in liq) (No 3)* (2012) 44 WAR 1 discussed s 180(2) at [866], but consideration of s 180(1) was not central to the issues before the Court, and as such that discussion was also obiter. The matter settled before an appeal to the High Court was heard.

118 Explanatory Memorandum, Corporate Law Economic Reform Program Bill 1999 (Cth) [6.10].

119 (2009) 75 ACSR 1, 631 [7269].

120 See, eg, W Bainbridge and T Connor, 'Another Way Forward? The Scope for an Appellate Court to Reinterpret the Statutory Business Judgment Rule' (2016) 34(6) *Company and Securities Law Journal* 415.

121 See also JJ du Plessis, 'Open Sea or Safe Harbor? American, Australian and South African Business Judgment Rules Compared (Part 2)' (2011) 32(12) *Company Lawyer* 377, 379–80.

122 See the review contained in J Varzaly, 'Protecting the Authority of Directors: An Empirical Analysis of the Statutory Business Judgment Rule' (2012) 12(2) *Journal of Corporate Law Studies* 429, 453.

123 *Great Southern Finance Pty Ltd (in liq) v Rhodes* (2014) 103 ACSR 137, [46].

124 When refusing an injunction under the *Family Law Act 1975* (Cth) in *Hancock v Hancock* [2023] FedCFamC1F 429, Wilson J gave weight to the general caution against a court intruding on the business judgment of directors as provided by s 180(2), and accepted that the expertise of various advisors and directors in relation to the transaction in question should not be disrupted, but as this case did not involve an argument about a breach of the duty of care and diligence, it went no further: [132]–[133].

125 *Australian Securities and Investments Commission v Rich* (2009) 75 ACSR 1 [3766].

off-market bid for another entity without first securing finance was a breach of s 180(1).[126] A receiver has also been allowed access to the business judgment rule, but was held not to have breached the duty of care in the exercise of their power of sale.[127]

11.15.15 Current and future issues for the duty of care and diligence

There is an ever-evolving risk matrix facing companies and their directors and management. Since at least 2016, the impact of climate change on director decision-making has been a growing concern, with the perception that it was only a matter of time before an action for a breach of the duty of care and diligence in relation to failure to consider climate change risks occurred.[128] There has been recent activism in this space: approximately 75 per cent of the 341 climate change disputes identified between 1986 and 2023 were commenced after 2015,[129] and Australia represents the second largest jurisdiction for such disputes after the United States of America),[130] targeted litigation against directors or management in relation to their duty of care and diligence on climate risk has not yet taken place.

Submissions to the fourth edition of the ASX's *Corporate Governance Principles and Recommendations* ('the ASX Principles') in 2019 acknowledged the relationship between the impact of an entity on the environment and other elements of environmental risk,[131] leading to the definition of 'environmental risk' in the published Principles and Recommendations being broadened to include risks associated with 'the entity polluting or degrading the environment, adding to the carbon levels in the atmosphere, or threatening a region's biodiversity or cultural heritage... [and] risks for the entity associated with climate change, reduced air quality and water scarcity'.[132] The consultation

126 *Australian Securities and Investments Commission v Mariner Corporation* (2015) 241 FCR 502.

127 *Deangrove Pty Ltd (recs and mgrs apptd) v Buckby* (2006) 56 ACSR 630.

128 N Hutley and S Hartford Davis, *Climate Change and Directors' Duties—Supplementary Memorandum of Opinion* (Centre for Policy Development, 26 March 2019) <https://cpd.org.au/wp-content/uploads/2019/03/Noel-Hutley-SC-and-Sebastian-Hartford-Davis-Opinion-2019-and-2016_pdf.pdf>.

129 J Setzer and C Higham, *Global Trends in Climate Change Litigation: 2023 Snapshot* (Policy Report, 30 June 2022) 11. In particular, in Australia, see, eg, *Australasian Centre for Corporate Responsibility v Commonwealth Bank of Australia* (2015) 325 ALR 736; the settled matter of *Abrahams v Commonwealth Bank of Australia* (2017) VID879/2017 (Federal Court of Australia); the settled matter of *McVeigh v Retail Employees Superannuation Pty Ltd* (2019) NSD1333/2018 (Federal Court of Australia); *Abrahams v Commonwealth Bank of Australia* (2021) NSD864/2021 (Federal Court of Australia).

130 J Setzer and C Higham, *Global Trends in Climate Change Litigation: 2023 Snapshot* (Policy Report, 30 June 2022) 12. See generally T Gray, B Nosworthy and A Gillam, 'National and International Perspectives on Climate Change Litigation' (2024) 54(1) *Australian Bar Review* 16.

131 ASX Corporate Governance Council, *Fourth edition of the Corporate Governance Principles and Recommendations: Consultation Response* (Australian Securities Exchange, 4th ed, 2019) 11 <https://www.asx.com.au/content/dam/asx/about/corporate-governance-council/cgc-principles-and-recommendations-fourth-edn.pdf>.

132 ASX Corporate Governance Council, *Corporate Governance Principles and Recommendations* (4th ed, February 2019) 35. Water scarcity may become of more importance with the growth in generative artificial intelligence, as research suggests that large language models such as ChatGPT consume 500mL of water per 10–50 responses generated: P Li et al, 'Making AI Less "Thirsty": Uncovering and Addressing the Secret Water Footprint of AI Models' *arXiv* (26 March 2025) 3 <https://arxiv.org/pdf/2304.03271>; see generally J Gupta, H Bosch and L van Vliet, 'AI's excessive water consumption threatens to drown out its environmental contributions', *The Conversation* (online, 22 March 2024) <https://theconversation.com/ais-excessive-water-consumption-threatens-to-drown-out-its-environmental-contributions-225854>.

draft for the fifth edition of the Principles and Recommendations, released in February 2024 but not adopted, had proposed amending this definition to expand it from 'negative' environmental consequences and 'adverse' affects, to any consequence or affect of corporate activity. Although the draft amendments to the Commentary following Recommendation 7.4 identify that companies 'may find it useful to consider their reasonably foreseeable risks, as well as their key stakeholders, when developing their reporting', it concludes that '[t]his Recommendation does not require climate-related financial disclosures.'[133] The draft amendments also identify the potential impact of sustainability reports, discussed in Chapter 7.40 in relation to reporting and disclosure obligations, which were introduced in 2024. These reports impose the Australian Sustainability Reporting Standards[134] on certain corporations.[135] As discussed in Chapter 10, it was announced in February 2025 that the fourth edition of the ASX Principles would remain in effect.

Similarly, following the decision of *Australian Securities and Investment Commission v RI Advice Group Pty Ltd*,[136] scrutiny has grown over corporate responsibilities in relation to cybersecurity.[137] *RI Advice* involved duties under s 912A of the *Corporations Act*—a subset of specialist duties requiring financial services licensees to 'do all things necessary to ensure that the [services] are provided efficiently, honestly and fairly' and to 'have adequate risk management systems' discussed in detail in Chapter 18. This decision highlights expanding judicial expectations of how a reasonable director of a company that provides a service where cyber risk is heightened should mitigate such risks. Rofe J commented:

> Cybersecurity risk forms a significant risk connected with the conduct of the business and provision of financial services. It is not possible to reduce cybersecurity risk to zero, but it is possible to materially reduce cybersecurity risk through adequate cybersecurity documentation and controls to an acceptable level.[138]

It is not difficult to see how an argument could be made, under the general duty of care and diligence in s 180(1), that directors who do not engage in careful consideration of their company's risk assessment and response in relation to both cyber and climate risk, could be held in breach.[139]

133 ASX Corporate Governance Council, 'Corporate Governance Principles and Recommendations Consultation Draft 5th Edition' (Australian Securities Exchange, 2024) <https://www.asx.com.au/content/dam/asx/about/corporate-governance-council/corporate-governance-principles-and-recommendations-consultation-draft.pdf>.

134 *Corporations Act 2001* (Cth) ss 296A–D.

135 Those with ch 2M reporting obligations and, in the final phase from 1 July 2027, capturing any company that meets the thresholds for a large proprietary company: *Corporations Act 2001* (Cth) s 292A.

136 *Australian Securities and Investments Commission v RI Advice Group Pty Ltd* (2022) 160 ACSR 204.

137 ASIC has identified cyber risk as a significant concern since at least 2015: Australian Securities and Investments Commission, 'Cyber Resilience: Health Check' (Report 429, 19 March 2015) <https://download.asic.gov.au/media/3062900/rep429-published-19-march-2015-1.pdf>.

138 *Australian Securities and Investments Commission v RI Advice Group Pty Ltd* (2022) 160 ACSR 204, [58].

139 See generally B Nosworthy, 'The Corporations Act and Climate Change—Appetite for Change?' (2020) 94(6) *Australian Law Journal* 411; B Nosworthy, 'Directors Duties and Cyber Resilience' in D Stephens, M Stubbs and S White (eds), *Digital Resilience* (Springer, 2025).

11.20 Delegation and reliance

In many companies, directors make decisions based upon information provided to them by other officers and employees, such as the CFO or internal auditor, in relation to the financial position of the company. This raises questions: In what circumstances may a director delegate certain responsibilities or rely on an expert opinion provided to them? When would that be considered conflicting with the core, irreducible requirement of involvement in monitoring the performance of the company under s 180(1) and the general law?

The issue of delegation and reliance add complexity to the operation of the duty of care, skill and diligence. Prior to the enactment of the current provisions of the *Corporations Act*, the case law dealt with delegation and reliance as related, if not conjoined, principles and there was a degree of discordance as to directors' ability to delegate and rely. A director's ability to reasonably rely on information provided to them by others was discussed in the *AWA Ltd v Daniels* litigation, and on appeal in *Daniels v Anderson*.[140] At first instance, Rogers CJ held that '[a] director is justified in trusting officers of the corporation to perform all duties that, having regard to the exigencies of business, the intelligent devotion of labour and the articles of association, may properly be left to such officers'.[141] Further, his Honour recognised a degree of business efficacy must be incorporated into the relationship between the directors and the company as 'the business of the corporation could not go on if directors could not trust those who are put into a position of trust for the express purpose of attending to details of management'.[142] On appeal, Clarke and Sheller JJA cited the United States Court of Appeals with approval where it stated that 'when an investment poses an obvious risk, a director cannot rely blindly on the judgment of others'.[143] As a result, they rejected the CEO's argument that he had delegated the responsibility of monitoring Koval and his foreign exchange transactions to others, and was entitled to rely upon them without providing further supervision. In *Statewide Tobacco Services Ltd v Morley*, Ormiston J stated that directors are entitled to delegate certain tasks but are expected to 'take a diligent and intelligent interest in the information either available to [them], or which they might with fairness demand from the executives or other employees and agents of the company'.[144]

Within the *Corporations Act*, separate provisions exist to enable delegation of some responsibilities by directors—and not officers or others—and reasonable reliance by directors on information provided to them by others. These provisions are discussed below but must be considered in light of the current stance in relation to s 180(1): that there is a core, non-delegable requirement of involvement in monitoring the performance of the company. As exemplified in *Australian Securities and Investments Commission v Healey*, any attempt to delegate or rely which would encroach on that core involvement in monitoring will be a breach of s 180(1).[145]

140 These cases are discussed at Section 11.10.05.

141 *AWA Ltd v Daniels* (1992) 7 ACSR 759, 868.

142 Ibid.

143 *Daniels v Anderson* (1995) 37 NSWLR 438, 502 (citing *Federal Deposit Insurance Corporation v Bierman*, 2 F 3d 1424 (7th Cir F 1993) 1432–3).

144 *Statewide Tobacco Services Ltd v Morley* (1990) 2 ACSR 405, 431.

145 *Australian Securities and Investments Commission v Healey* (2011) 196 FCR 291, 426 [567]. This case is discussed in full at Section 11.15.05.

11.20.05 Delegation

Many company constitutions allow the board to delegate responsibilities to a director appointed to be the managing director. This is also provided for in replaceable rule in s 198C of the *Corporations Act*, and the replaceable rule in s 198D that permits delegation by the directors to a committee of directors, a single director, an employee of the company, or any other person. Not only is the exercise of power by a delegate as effective as if it had been exercised by the directors,[146] but under s 190(1) the directors remain responsible for the exercise of the power by the delegate, as if the power had been exercised by the directors. *Daniels v Anderson* confirms that the right to delegate exists, but there remains an obligation to supervise the delegate.[147] However, there are limitations placed on that responsibility by s 190(2) so that the director will not be held responsible if:

> **(a)** the directors believed on reasonable grounds at all times that the delegate would exercise the power in conformity with the duties imposed on directors of the company by [the Corporations Act] and the company's constitution (if any); and
>
> **(b)** the director believed:
>
> **(i)** on reasonable grounds; and
>
> **(ii)** in good faith; and
>
> **(iii)** after making proper inquiry if the circumstances indicated the need for inquiry
>
> that the delegate was reliable and competent in relation to the power delegated.

The term 'reasonable grounds' and whether 'the circumstances indicated the need for inquiry' are not defined within the Act, and so the courts have turned to the test applied in relation to the reasonableness of delegation. In *Australian Securities and Investments Commission v Adler*,[148] Santow J distilled the principles from the general law into the following factors to determine the reasonableness of the delegation:

(1) the function that has been delegated is such that 'it may properly be left to such officers'[149]

(2) the extent to which the director is put on inquiry or, given the facts of the case, should have been put on inquiry[150]

(3) the relationship between the director and delegate must be such that the director honestly holds the belief that the delegate is trustworthy, competent and someone on whom reliance can be placed. Knowledge that the delegate is dishonest or incompetent will make reliance unreasonable[151]

(4) the risk involved in the transaction and the nature of the transaction[152]

146 *Corporations Act* s 198D(3) (a replaceable rule).

147 *Daniels v Anderson* (1995) 37 NSWLR 438, 679–85.

148 *Australian Securities and Investments Commission v Adler* (2002) 41 ACSR 72. This case is discussed in detail in Chapter 13 at Section 13.25.20.

149 *Re City Equitable Fire Insurance Co Ltd* [1925] Ch 407.

150 *Re Property Force Consultants Pty Ltd* [1997] 1 Qd R 300.

151 *Dempster & Biala Pty Ltd v Mallina Holdings Ltd* (1994) 13 WAR 124.

152 *Permanent Building Society (in liq) v Wheeler* (1994) 11 WAR 187.

(5) the extent of steps taken by the director; for example, inquiries made or other circumstances engendering 'trust'
(6) whether the position of the director is executive or non-executive.[153]

Logically, a director who continues to be significantly engaged in the task or function that they purport to have delegated may not be able to rely on a claim of delegation to avoid liability.[154]

11.20.10 Reliance

Under s 189 of the *Corporations Act*, there is a presumption that a director's reliance on information provided by employees, professional advisers or experts, other directors and officers and committees of directors is reasonable, as long as it is made in good faith and after the director has made their own independent assessment of the information or advice.

The limitations to this presumption set out in s 189 are similar but not identical to the limitations in s 190(2) in relation to directors' responsibility for the behaviour of delegates. First, the advice or information must be given by a person within the roles noted above acting within their area of expertise. The director must believe on reasonable grounds that the employee or adviser providing the information or advice is competent in that area, or that the matter is within the area of authority of the director, officer or committee. Second, the director's reliance must be made in good faith. Finally, the director must make their own independent assessment of the information or advice. This condition is qualified by an element of subjectivity, 'having regard to the director's knowledge of the corporation and the complexity of the structure and operations of the corporation'. When proposed in 1998, the draft s 189 included the same 'proper inquiry' test as set out in s 190(2).[155] However, when s 189 was enacted, the requirement had changed to an 'independent assessment', subject to the director's own knowledge and the complexity of the company. This is a more subjective position than provided for in s 190(2) or the Court of Appeal in *Daniels v Anderson.*[156]

Australian Securities and Investments Commission v Macdonald (No 11)[157] discussed whether the directors could delegate the drafting and settlement of the ASX announcement to another director or rely on the advice of management and outside experts. Gzell J held that this was not a question of reliance or delegation, as:

> [a]ll of the non-executive directors ... knew or should have known that if JHIL made the statements as to the sufficiency of funding of the foundation in the draft ASX announcement there was a danger that JHIL would face legal action for publishing false or misleading or deceptive statements ...
>
> This was not a matter in which a director was entitled to rely upon those ... co-directors more concerned with communications strategy to consider the draft ASX announcement.

153 Ibid (Ipp J), although in *Daniels v Anderson* (1995) 37 NSWLR 438 the majority moved away from this distinction.

154 *Twigg v Twigg* (2022) 402 ALR 119, 132–3.

155 Corporate Law Economic Reform Program Bill 1998 (Cth).

156 *Daniels v Anderson* (1995) 37 NSWLR 438.

157 *Australian Securities and Investments Commission v Macdonald (No 11)* (2009) 230 FLR 1.

> This was a key statement in relation to a highly significant restructure of the James Hardie group. Management having brought the matter to the board, none of them was entitled to abdicate responsibility by delegating his or her duty to a fellow director.
>
> Nor was this a case of reliance upon management, a co-director or expert adviser. Management had sought the board's approval and the task of approving the draft ASX announcement involved no more than an understanding of the English language used in the document.[158]

Although the Court of Appeal overturned Gzell J's finding of fact that the announcement had been approved at the meeting of 15 February 2001, their Honours expressed a similar view as Gzell J that this particular announcement was not appropriate for delegation or reliance on others: '[t]hese were not circumstances in which a non-executive director, exercising due care and diligence, could accept without application of his or her mind to the draft news release before the board for its approval. ... We do not think this was an occasion of reasonable reliance on management or others.'[159] Equally, where professional advice is provided on the basis of assumptions that an external advisor is asked to make, which that external advisor may not be in a position to challenge, assess or verify, this may affect the validity of the directors' reliance that advice.[160]

11.25 Duties arising during insolvency

In addition to the duty of care and diligence, there are two insolvency-specific duties imposed by the *Corporations Act*. The first is the director's duty to prevent insolvent trading in s 588G, discussed in Section 11.25.05. Section 588G creates a duty on directors not to continue trading if the company is insolvent and provides that a director who fails to do so can be personally liable for the debts incurred if, at the time, there were reasonable grounds for suspecting that the company was or would become insolvent, and the director was or should have been aware of those grounds. The imposition of personal liability on directors in limited companies is an example of piercing the corporate veil.[161] A similar duty is imposed on a holding company to prevent insolvent trading in a subsidiary under s 588V. The second duty is one of the anti-phoenixing provisions introduced in 2020.[162] Phoenixing is an illegal practice where 'a new company, for little or no value, continues the business of an existing company that has been liquidated or otherwise abandoned to avoid paying outstanding debts',[163] including taxes and employee entitlements.

158 Ibid 56 [259]–[261].

159 *Morley v Australian Securities and Investments Commission* (2010) 81 ACSR 285, [809], [817]. Gzell J's decision was restored on appeal to the High Court in *Australian Securities and Investments Commission v Hellicar* (2012) 247 CLR 345.

160 See *Australian Securities and Investments Commission v Vocation Ltd (in liq)* (2019) 371 ALR 155 [492] (on the role of the external advisor) and [505] (on the impact of the assumptions on which their advice is predicated).

161 See Chapter 3 at Section 3.20.

162 *Treasury Laws Amendment (Combatting Illegal Phoenixing) Act 2020* (Cth). The concept of 'phoenixing' is discussed further in Chapter 16 at Section 16.25.35 in the context of voidable transactions.

163 Australian Securities and Investments Commission, 'Concerns about Illegal Phoenix Activity' (Information Sheet 212, 12 November 2004) <https://asic.gov.au/about-asic/contact-us/reporting-misconduct-to-asic/concerns-about-illegal-phoenix-activity/>.

A common step within the phoenixing process is for assets of the old company to be transferred to the new company at less than true or market value—meaning that once the old company enters liquidation, there are no assets from which to pay the remaining creditors. Sections 588GAA–GAC create offences in relation to such 'creditor-defeating disposition' of company property, which will be discussed further below.

11.25.05 Section 588G

Section 588G of the *Corporation Act* obliges a director to prevent the company from incurring debts if there are reasonable grounds for suspecting that it is insolvent. This provision narrowed the focus of previous provisions,[164] which applied more widely to persons taking part in the management of the company. By contrast, s 588G applies only to directors. Claims for breach of this obligation can be prompted by a liquidator's report (s 533), or following investigation by a new board, from a creditor, or from ASIC taking legal action where it can be shown that a company failed to keep adequate financial records.[165]

There are five elements to be satisfied before insolvent trading has occurred:

(1) the defendant was a director at the time when the company incurred the debt
(2) the company was insolvent at that time
(3) there were reasonable grounds for suspecting insolvency
(4) the debt must have been incurred on or after the commencement of this Act[166]
(5) the director failed to prevent the company incurring the debt.

The first four conditions form part of s 588G(1), and the final condition is contained in s 588G(2), which is a civil penalty provision.[167] If the failure to prevent the company from incurring the debt is dishonest, then that is a criminal offence.[168]

The first condition is that the defendant must be a director at the time the company incurred the debt. Unlike other directors' duties, liability under s 588G is limited to directors. This includes de facto and shadow directors as defined in s 9 of the *Corporations Act* and discussed in Chapter 10 at Sections 10.20.05–10 but excludes other officers and employees.

The second condition is that the company must be insolvent at the time the debt is incurred or become insolvent due to incurring that debt. This is the first of three references to insolvency within s 588G. Discussed in more detail in Section 15.10, solvency is defined in s 95A as the ability to pay all of the company's debts as and when they become due and payable. A company that is not solvent is insolvent under s 95A(2).

According to Owen J in *Bell Group Ltd (in liq) v Westpac Banking Corporation (No 9)*:[169]

---

164 *Corporations Act 1989* (Cth) s 592; *Companies Act 1981* (Cth) s 556.
165 See, eg, *Copeland v Murace* [2023] FCA 14.
166 *Corporations Act* s 2 states that the Act commences on a date set by Proclamation. On 12 July 2001, a Proclamation was issued declaring 15 July 2001 as the commencement date.
167 See the discussion of the Civil Penalty Scheme in Chapter 10 at Section 10.35.10.
168 *Corporations Act* s 588G(3).
169 *Bell Group Ltd (in liq) v Westpac Banking Corporation (No 9)* (2009) 39 WAR 1 [1090].

> [c]ommercial reality dictates that the assessment of available funds is not confined to the company's cash resources. It is legitimate to take into account funds the company can, on a real and reasoned view, realise by sale of assets, borrowing against the security of its assets, or by other reasonable means.

It is more appropriate to consider a cash flow test for determining insolvency under s 95A, rather than a balance sheet test. Solvency or insolvency is 'a question of fact, which falls to be decided as a matter of commercial reality in light of all the circumstances'.[170]

The third condition—that there are 'reasonable grounds for suspecting that the company is insolvent'—was introduced on the basis of recommendations made in the 1988 Harmer Report.[171] This change from 'expect' in the previous Act to 'suspect' in s 588G did not flow on to the defence under s 588H, which will be discussed below. Einfeld J considered the interpretation of the threshold for 'suspecting insolvency' in *Metropolitan Fire Systems Pty Ltd v Miller*, and noted that regardless of the language used, it was an objective test, to be 'judged by the standard appropriate to a director of ordinary competence'[172] and not 'the particular director whose conduct is under scrutiny'.[173] The element of 'suspicion' requires more than 'a mere idle wondering ... it is a positive feeling of actual apprehension or mistrust, amounting to "a slight opinion, but without sufficient evidence" ... Consequently, a reason to suspect that a fact exists is more than a reason to consider or look into the possibility of its existence.'[174]

The fourth condition is that the company incurs a debt at a time after the commencement of this provision and relates to the second condition requiring the company to be insolvent at the time the debt is incurred or become insolvent by incurring that debt. Section 588G(1A) lists a number of actions and provides a specific time for the incurring of a debt for each particular action, including paying a dividend, making a reduction of share capital, buying back shares, redeeming redeemable preference shares at its own option, issuing redeemable preference shares redeemed other than at its own option, providing financial assistance to purchase its shares, and entering into an uncommercial transaction under s 588FB. Section 588F provides that deductions made by a company that must be passed on to the Commissioner of Taxation under the *Income Tax Assessment Act 1936* (Cth) are incurred at the time when the deduction is made.

Outside of those specific examples, the meaning of 'incurring a debt' must be determined in case law. In considering debts under s 588G, the courts have taken a narrow construction excluding; for example, liquidated damages that a company is liable for in relation to providing misleading information.[175] Liability under a guarantee may be a debt, despite being contingent in nature until a demand for payment is made. If the guarantee relates to performance by another, then a failure by that party to perform

170 *Brooks v Heritage Hotel Adelaide Pty Ltd* (1996) 20 ACSR 61, 65.

171 Australian Law Reform Commission, *General Insolvency Inquiry* (Report 45, 1988) ('the Harmer Report').

172 *Metropolitan Fire Systems Pty Ltd v Miller* (1997) 23 ACSR 699, 704.

173 *Quin v Vlahos* (2021) 64 VR 319 [216].

174 *Queensland Bacon Pty Ltd v Rees* (1966) 115 CLR 266, 303; cited by *Quin v Vlahos* (2021) 64 VR 319, [216].

175 *Jelin Pty Ltd v Johnson* (1987) 5 ACLC 463.

will lead to a claim for damages, rather than a debt. However, if the guarantee is for payment of a debt by another, then that is still considered a debt.[176] Early instances of liability were determined by the courts on the basis of voluntariness, with sales tax excluded from consideration as a debt as the company did not create that liability voluntarily,[177] but payroll tax being included as a debt voluntarily incurred from the company's decision to employ.[178] However, more recent cases have held that the provision does not require an element of choice into the incurring of the liability for it to be considered a debt.[179]

In addition to the earlier references to insolvency, the final condition contained in s 588G(2) relates to insolvency. A director will contravene s 588G(2) by failing to prevent the company from incurring a debt if they knew at the time the debt was incurred that there were grounds for suspecting that the company was insolvent, or would become insolvent by incurring that debt, or if a reasonable director, in a 'like position in a company in the company's circumstances', would be so aware. This objective standard of a reasonable director has been held to be a director of ordinary competence with the ability to have a basic understanding of the company's financial status.[180]

As such, if a director is aware of grounds to suspect insolvency, or a reasonable director in their position would be so aware, and they do not 'take all reasonable steps to prevent the company from incurring the debt',[181] then they will have breached s 588G(2).

11.25.10 Section 588GA

Similar to the business judgment rule in s 180(2), which exculpates directors who have made informed business decisions from being found in breach of the duty of care, skill and diligence, s 588GA provides a 'safe harbour' for directors from personal liability for debts incurred while developing 'courses of action that are reasonably likely to lead to a better outcome for the company'.

Section 588GA(1) states that the duty in s 588G(2) does not apply to a director in relation to a debt, if:

> **(a)** at a particular time after the person starts to suspect the company may become or be insolvent, the person starts developing one or more courses of action that are reasonably likely to lead to a better outcome for the company; and
>
> **(b)** the debt is incurred directly or indirectly in connection with any such course of action
>
> ...

176 See, eg, *Metropolitan Fire Systems Pty Ltd v Miller* (1997) 23 ACSR 699; *Hawkins v Bank of China* (1992) 26 NSWLR 562.

177 *Castrisios v McManus* (1990) 4 ACSR 1.

178 *Commissioner of State Taxation v Pollock* (1993) 11 WAR 64; *Standard Chartered Bank of Australia Ltd v Antico* (1995) 38 NSWLR 290.

179 *Australian Securities and Investments Commission v Plymin (No 1)* (2003) 175 FLR 124; *Re Salfa Pty Ltd (in liq)* [2014] NSWSC 1493.

180 *Metropolitan Fire Systems Pty Ltd v Miller* (1997) 23 ACSR 699.

181 *Australian Securities and Investments Commission v Plymin (No 1)* (2003) 175 FLR 124 [325].

There are time limits on the safe harbour to prevent it from extending unreasonably.[182]

When determining whether or not a course of action is likely to lead to a better outcome for the company, s 588G(2) provides that regard may be had to whether the director is: properly informing themselves of the company's financial position; taking appropriate steps to prevent misconduct by officers or employees; ensuring that the company keeps appropriate financial records; obtaining advice from appropriate qualified sources who have been given sufficient information; or developing or implementing a plan for restructure to improve the financial position.

Section 588GA(3) confirms that the burden of proving that the debts incurred fall within the safe harbour falls upon the director seeking to rely on s 588GA(1).

Only those debts incurred in relation to the 'courses of action' will fall within the safe harbour. The safe harbour will not be available to a director of a company that has failed to pay the entitlements of its employees by the time they fall due, or has not complied with its taxation reporting obligations.[183]

Under s 588WA, a similar safe harbour will protect a holding company against a claim of insolvent trading under s 588V, provided that the holding company takes reasonable steps to ensure that the safe harbour applies to the directors and the debt of the subsidiary. However, it will be important for directors of subsidiary companies to take care that the course of action developed will benefit the insolvent subsidiary in order for the debts incurred to be protected under the safe harbour, rather than benefitting the holding company or the company group.

Section 588GA was introduced to encourage 'cultural change', providing an incentive for directors to remain in control of a struggling company and to take reasonable risks to facilitate restructure and rescue, rather than placing the company 'prematurely' into voluntary administration or liquidation.[184] Whether this provision will be sufficient to effect that change is as yet unclear, and at the time of writing there are yet to be any significant decisions on the substance of s 588GA.[185] Interestingly, under s 588HA, an independent review of the impact of this provision on the conduct of directors, and the interests of creditors and employees, must be undertaken to determine whether the safe harbour is achieving its aims. The review concluded that greater education and guidance to support the operation of these provisions was necessary, to promote awareness of them, but that the provisions themselves 'offer considerable assistance in encouraging an active turnaround market'.[186]

182 Ibid s 588GA(1)(b).

183 Ibid s 588GA(4).

184 Explanatory Memorandum, Treasury Laws Amendment (2017 Enterprise Incentives No 2) Bill 2017 (Cth) 3–4.

185 The provision was mentioned in *Copeland v Murace* [2023] FCA 14, but that decision involved a successful striking out application for a statement of claim by the liquidator which did not adequately identify dates associated with the company, including some 40 debts for which no date was provided. Mr Murace successfully argued that the failure to plead specific dates for the debts denied him the possibility of pleading defences under ss 588H and 588GA.

186 The Treasury Review Panel, 'Review of the Insolvent Trading Safe Harbour' (Final Report, 23 November 2021) 5.

11.25.15 Section 588H

There are four defences under s 588H available to directors who have contravened s 588G(2):[187]

(1) that there were reasonable grounds to expect solvency
(2) that the director placed reasonable reliance on information as to solvency provided by others
(3) that the director was ill or had other good reasons not to participate in management at the time when the debt was incurred
(4) that the director took all reasonable steps to prevent the company from incurring the debt.

Although s 588G requires reasonable grounds for suspecting insolvency, ss 588H(2)–(3) retains the former language of 'expecting' solvency. The distinction between reasonable grounds to 'suspect' and 'expect' insolvency was discussed in *Metropolitan Fire Systems Pty Ltd v Miller*, with Einfeld J considering that the threshold of knowledge or awareness to 'suspect' was lower than to 'expect': '[t]he expectation must be differentiated from mere hope in order to satisfy this defence. It implies a measure of confidence that the company is solvent.'[188] The interaction between these defences and the prior proof in s 588G that there were reasonable grounds to suspect insolvency is fraught, as an expectation of solvency is arguably the higher threshold.

These two defences were unsuccessfully argued in *Re McLellan*,[189] the facts of which are set out in Chapter 10 at Section 10.40.10. Mr Carroll was a director, who had taken active steps to obtain advice and monitored stock levels and daily production. Carroll obtained advice from an accountant, Mr Bright, and was told that the company was close to being insolvent. An insolvency practitioner also advised Carroll that the company could survive with further investment. The continued advice to Carroll from Bright was that the company had cash flow issues but was not yet insolvent. Goldberg J was not satisfied that this amounted to the requirements in ss 588H(2) or (3). In relation to s 588H(2), Goldberg J noted that 'the fact that Mr Carroll may have had a "suspicion" of insolvency does not answer the question whether he had an "expectation" that the Company was solvent throughout the relevant period'.[190] His Honour then turned to a staged inquiry, as set out in *Hall v Poolman*,[191] where Palmer J asked:

> How sure are we that this asset can be turned into cash to pay all our debts, present and to be incurred, within 3 months? Is that outcome certain, probable, more likely than not, possible, possible with a bit of luck, possible with a lot of luck, remote, or is there no way of knowing?[192]

187 In addition to these defences, the general provisions of relief under ss 1317S and 1318 are applicable to s 588G: see Chapter 10 at Section 10.40.10.
188 *Metropolitan Fire Systems Pty Ltd v Miller* (1997) 23 ACSR 699, 711.
189 *Re McLellan* (2009) 76 ACSR 67.
190 Ibid 105 [169].
191 *Hall v Poolman* (2007) 65 ACSR 123.
192 Ibid 182 [269].

Goldberg J in *McLellan* held that a director can have a reasonable expectation of solvency only if their honest and reasonable answer is that the asset can certainly or probably be turned into cash to pay all the company's debts present and to be incurred within three months.[193] His Honour was prepared to find that, although Carroll knew throughout the relevant period that the company was not paying its debts as and when they fell due, the full answer on 'reasonable grounds to suspect solvency' depended on both a reliance on the inventory of stock and communications with Bright.[194] In terms of the stock, although there was substantial stock on hand which was saleable, the extent of outstanding and accruing debts was such that Goldberg J was not prepared to find it reasonable for Carroll to expect the stock to be sold within a sufficiently short timeframe to satisfy the *Hall v Poolman* inquiry, and as such s 588H(2) was not satisfied.[195]

In relation to Carroll's argument under s 588H(3), Goldberg J found that, although the advice had been provided by an accountant and Carroll had relied on it, it was not provided within the terms of s 588H(3)(a)(i); namely, a competent and reliable person responsible for providing adequate advice as to the solvency of the company. Bright (the accountant) was engaged by the company for the purpose of giving business advice regarding cashflows, costs and expenses, and an analysis of the business model profits and losses. Although Bright was a competent and reliable person, the Court found that the retainer was not specifically for the provision of advice as to solvency in the relevant period.[196] On this point, in *Newman v Hartwig*, Matthews J articulated clearly a distinction between the role of the external accountant, who is not responsible for the company's bookkeeping, management accounts or monthly reports, and an advisor retained for the purposes of providing advice about solvency. 'It cannot be the case that an external accountant's responsibility for preparing the annual financial statement after the end of the financial year equates to that accountant being responsible for providing adequate information about whether the company was solvent at any point during the course of that financial year.'[197] It may be necessary, then, for the directors or company to retain a qualified and competent person specifically for the purpose of obtaining advice as to solvency, and that requesting that information from their usual financial advisor may not be sufficient.

If a director has breached their common law, equitable or statutory directors' duties, they will not be able to utilise the defences under s 588H, in particular s 588H(4). The policy behind s 588H(4) has been influenced by the statement in the Harmer Report that: 'it is not appropriate for a provision designed to establish a proper standard of conduct by directors to impose liability on a director who was not in a position to influence

193 Ibid 182 [270]–[275].

194 Similarly, in *Newman v Hartwig* (2024) 73 VR 326, Matthews J held that the defendant must establish both an objective and a subjective test—that there were reasonable grounds to expect solvency (objective) and that the director concerned did expect (subjective) the company was and would remain solvent, despite incurring the debt: [360]. In that case, although the subjective element was evident from the defendant's evidence, the objective aspect could not be satisfied: [361]–[362].

195 *Hall v Poolman* (2007) 65 ACSR 123 [175]–[178].

196 Ibid [183]–[186].

197 (2024) 73 VR 326 [369].

the management of the financial affairs of the company at the relevant time'.[198] Only those directors who are unable to participate and influence management at the relevant time for proper reasons will be able to utilise this defence. For example, in *Tourprint International Pty Ltd (in liq) v Bott*, a director who had joined the board of the insolvent company less than a year before it entered into voluntary administration was not permitted to utilise either ss 588H(2) or (4) as he had failed to engage in an active role within the financial management of the company.[199] Mr Bott's argument for non-participation centred on him being excluded from management and deceived by the other directors of the company. Although the Court accepted that Bott had been deceived by one of the other directors,[200] 'failure to have a more active role in management is not referrable to any reason which is a "good reason" for the purposes of s 588H(4)'.[201]

Finally, in relation to the defence that a director took all reasonable steps to prevent the company from incurring a debt, according to s 588H(6), regard will be had to steps taken to appoint an administrator and the timing and result of such actions.

11.25.20 Section 588GAB

Section 588GAB prohibits officers from engaging in conduct that would result in the company making a creditor-defeating disposition if the company is insolvent, would become insolvent because of that disposition or other dispositions at that time, or less than 12 months after the disposition the company either enters into external administration or ceases to carry on business altogether as a direct or indirect result of the disposition.[202] This provision is designed to respond to circumstances where company property is transferred out of company control, either for under-value or for no value, which commonly occurs during illegal phoenixing. The prohibition is both a criminal offence in s 588GAB(1), where recklessness is the fault element; and a civil penalty offence in s 588GAB(2), where the officer knew, or a reasonable person in the position of the officer would know, that the disposition is a creditor-defeating disposition.

A 'creditor-defeating disposition' is defined in s 588FDB as having two elements. The first relates to value: the consideration for the property disposition must be less than the lower of either the market value of the property, or the best price that was reasonably obtainable for the property in the circumstances. The second relates to the effect on a subsequent external administration of the original company: the disposition must have the effect of either preventing the property from being available for the benefit of the creditors during an external administration or hindering or significantly delaying the process of making that property available for the benefit of the creditors via external administration. Section 588FDA(3) specifically extends the concept of 'disposition' to

198 Australian Law Reform Commission, *General Insolvency Inquiry* (Report 45, 1988) [312].

199 *Tourprint International Pty Ltd (in liq) v Bott* (1999) 32 ACSR 201.

200 Ibid [71].

201 Ibid [72]. A potential amendment to s 588H(4), identifying family violence as a valid ground for absence from management, is advocated for in V Chen, 'Hidden Risks of Economic Abuse through Company Directorships' (2024) 47(1) *University of New South Wales Law Journal* 105, 135.

202 Phoenixing and creditor-defeating dispositions are also discussed in Chapter 16 at Section 16.25.35 in the context of voidable transactions.

include a third party, who is not the recipient of the property, but receives some or all of the consideration for the disposition from that recipient.

In addition to this prohibition on officers in s 588GAB, s 588GAC(1) makes it an offence for a person to procure, incite, or encourage a company to make a creditor-defeating disposition when the company is insolvent, becomes insolvent due to that disposition or dispositions made at the time, or the company either is placed into external administration or ceases to do business altogether due to the disposition, within 12 months of the disposition being made. Recklessness is again the fault element for this offence. As is the case with s 588GAB, s 588GAC(2) creates a civil penalty provision mirroring the offence in s 588GAC(1), where the person knows, or a reasonable person in the position of that person would know, that the disposition is a creditor-defeating disposition.

Exceptions are provided in both provisions for external administration processes, or court-ordered compromises and arrangements.[203]

11.25.25 Consequences for breach

Section 588G is a civil penalty provision.[204] Should the director be found to have acted dishonestly during the incurring of the debt, they are guilty of an offence under s 588G(3), with a maximum penalty of 2,000 penalty units ($626,000) and/or five years imprisonment.[205] Additionally, where an application for a civil penalty has been made, a director may be liable to compensate the company for loss or damage (s 588J(1)) or where criminal proceedings are brought (s 588K). This compensation is paid to the company, although the extent of the compensation is determined by the loss of damage to the creditor. A liquidator is also permitted to recover for loss or damage caused to the company under s 588M, which is generally the value of the unsecured debts incurred through the insolvent trading.[206] A creditor may also apply under ss 588R–U, with the permission of the liquidator or through leave of the court, to recover loss or damage in relation to a wholly or partly unsecured debt incurred in breach of s 588G (s 588M(3)). There is a six-year limitation on such actions.[207]

11.30 Summary

This chapter began by considering the history behind the common law and equitable directors' duties of care, skill and diligence, before considering how those duties were translated into statute. It is clear from that discussion that there has been significant movement in the duty of care, skill and diligence over the past 100 years—from a subjective duty, requiring very little from directors who were not actively engaged with their company, to the modern, more objective standard. At common law and in equity, there is a core of non-reducible skills, requiring the director to place themselves in a position

203 *Corporations Act 2001* (Cth) ss 588GAB(3), 588GAC(3).

204 The policy reasons for and definition of the civil penalty provisions are discussed in Chapter 10 at Section 10.35.10.

205 *Corporations Act* sch 3 item 138. The penalty for a body corporate is 20,000 units.

206 *Powell and Duncan v Fryer, Tonkin and Perry* (2000) 18 ACLC 480.

207 *Corporations Act* s 588M(4).

to guide and monitor the company. Further, if the director holds themselves out as having some particular skill on appointment, they will be expected to employ that skill in performance of their duties. However, the duty is not entirely objective, as the director's behaviour will be considered against that of a reasonable director, in the director's position, in a company of the same kind as this particular director.

This development, from purely subjective to mostly objective, is visible in the modern enactment of the duty in s 180(1). The duty under s 180(1) is objective but is tempered by the subjective circumstances of the particular director and company concerned. Further, consideration of the necessities of corporate risk-taking and entrepreneurialism resulted in the business judgment rule in s 180(2). Although it has been more than two decades since enactment of this provision, it remains unclear whether the business judgment rule should be operating as a presumption or a defence.

This chapter concludes with consideration of the specific duties arising in insolvency: the director's duty to prevent insolvent trading in s 588G, and the officer's duty to prevent creditor-defeating dispositions. Recent reforms to this part of the *Corporations Act* aim to incentivise directors to remain in control of companies at risk of insolvency by providing a safe harbour for particular debts, but the practical impact of these provisions cannot yet be determined.

The next chapter will consider the first duty aligned with the theme of loyalty and good faith: the duty to act in good faith in the best interests of the company and for proper purposes.

CHAPTER

12

DUTIES OF GOOD FAITH

12.05 Introduction

Directors' duties can be classified into two themes: duties in relation to care and skill, and duties in relation to loyalty and good faith. Chapter 10 provided an overview of the duties as a whole, and Chapter 11 provided the history and current law in relation to the duties of care and skill. This chapter is the first of two chapters addressing the duties of loyalty and good faith. These duties fall into two categories: those concerned with the way in which directors exercise the powers and discretions vested in them, and those concerned with the standard of conduct expected from directors. This chapter will focus on the first category, which includes the duty to act bona fide in the best interests of the company and for proper purposes, its counterpart in s 181 of the *Corporations Act*, and the limitations on directors not to fetter the future exercise of their discretions. Chapter 13 will deal with the duties of loyalty and good faith that are concerned with the standard of conduct expected from directors, such as the fiduciary obligation of directors, officers and senior employees, the corresponding duties in ss 182–3, and the other *Corporations Act* duties around disclosure and management of conflicts.

This chapter starts with a discussion of the general law in relation to the duty to act bona fide in the best interests of the company and for proper purposes. The discussion examines how the law developed historically and how it exists today. It then considers s 181 of the *Corporations Act*, before moving to consider alternative approaches to this area of law, which demonstrate a development of the stakeholder approach to corporate theory.

12.10 The duty to act bona fide in the best interests of the company and for proper purposes under the general law

12.10.05 Introduction

Within equity,[1] there are relationships in which fiduciary obligations are owed, including the director–company relationship.[2] Fiduciary obligations impose higher standards of behaviour upon the parties than those imposed in arms-length relationships. The precise content of the fiduciary obligations[3] will be considered in Chapter 13, but for now, they can be summarised as the 'no conflict' and 'no profit' rules.[4] The duty to act bona fide in the best interests of the company has a source in equity as a 'duty of good faith'.[5] Although historically, this duty has been characterised as fiduciary, it is unclear whether it can accurately be described as fiduciary in modern Australian law. This is important for the purposes of determining remedies and the liability of any third party who assists in a breach or receives company property as a result of the breach.

1 This jurisdiction is explained in more detail at Section 13.10.05.

2 *Hospital Products Ltd v United States Surgical Corporation* (1984) 156 CLR 41.

3 First appearing in Australia in *Moss v Moss (No 2)* (1900) 21 LR (NSW) Eq 253, 258, and confirmed by the High Court of Australia in numerous cases from *Hospital Products Ltd v United States Surgical Corporation* (1984) 156 CLR 41 to *Friend v Booker* (2009) 239 CLR 129.

4 As adopted by the High Court in *Chan v Zacharia* (1984) 154 CLR 178, 198–9 (Deane J).

5 *Richard Brady Franks Ltd v Price* (1937) 58 CLR 112, 135.

12.10.10 The development of the duty

The duty to act bona fide and for proper purposes in relation to a power or discretion has a long history in equity. A precursor to the duty can be seen as far back as the sixteenth century, where the Lord Chancellor stated, in relation to a power granted in a will, that 'a person having a power, must execute it bona fide for the end designed, otherwise it is corrupt and void'.[6]

The language of the duty underwent a variety of formulations before settling into its current form. When applied to the director–company relationship, it is described as the duty to act bona fide in the interests of the company and for proper purposes. The terms 'acting in good faith' and 'for proper purposes' have been treated as one compound expression,[7] as a duty containing two separate limbs,[8] or without great distinction between the two.[9] This approach is not followed in all jurisdictions. For example, in the United Kingdom and New Zealand, these terms could be considered as two separate duties.[10] However, in this discussion we describe it as a single duty containing two limbs: to act bona fide in the best interest of the company, and to act for proper purposes. Both of these limbs must be satisfied in order for a director to comply with the duty under the general law. Although there is undoubtedly a close connection between the two concepts,[11] they can be considered as distinct limbs.

12.10.15 The first limb: meaning of 'bona fide'

In its early formulations, the first limb was described as a duty to act bona fide for the benefit of the company, or in the interests of the company as a whole.[12] It was also described as a duty to act honestly.[13] Occasionally, the phrase 'bona fide *and* for the benefit of the company' was employed.[14] By the mid-twentieth century, the courts settled on the description of the first limb of the duty as a duty to act 'bona fide in the interests of the company'. This remains today.

We consider below what 'the interests of the company as a whole' means. Before that, we must consider how to approach the term 'bona fide'. It could be interpreted as requiring the director to act honestly, in a subjective sense, or as imposing an objective requirement that the acts of the director are not distorted by some irregularity or impropriety. A wholly subjective test was applied in *Re Smith & Fawcett Ltd*, where the Court considered the application of the duty to a director's refusal to register a transfer of shares. The

6 *Aleyn v Belchier* (1758) 1 Eden 132, 138.

7 *Re Smith & Fawcett Ltd* [1942] Ch 304.

8 *Hogg v Cramphorn Ltd* [1967] Ch 254.

9 *Harlowe's Nominees Pty Ltd v Woodside (Lakes Entrance) Oil Co NL* (1968) 121 CLR 483.

10 See, eg, the separation of the duties as reflected in statute as separate provisions: *Companies Act 2006* (UK) ss 171–2; *Companies Act 1993* (NZ) ss 131, 133. Other texts would include Australia within this category, outlining two separate duties in the general law: see, eg, R Austin and I Ramsay, *Ford, Austin and Ramsay's Principles of Corporations Law* (LexisNexis, 17th ed, 2018) ch 8. As noted above, Australian case law has not been uniform on this division in the general law.

11 *Bell Group Ltd (in liq) v Westpac Banking Corporation (No 9)* (2009) 39 WAR 1 [76].

12 *Allen v Gold Reefs of West Africa Ltd* [1900] 1 Ch 656, 671; although Lord Lindley MR was discussing the use of voting power by a shareholder majority, this case was relied upon by the High Court for applying this duty to directors in *Richard Brady Franks Ltd v Price* (1937) 58 CLR 112, 135.

13 *Richard Brady Franks Ltd v Price* (1937) 58 CLR 112, 138; *Mills v Mills* (1938) 60 CLR 150, 188.

14 *Mills v Mills* (1938) 60 CLR 150, 175.

articles of the company, Smith & Fawcett Ltd, granted the directors an 'absolute and uncontrolled discretion [to] refuse to register any transfer of shares'.[15] Mr Smith and Mr Fawcett each held 4,001 ordinary shares. Fawcett died, and bequeathed those shares to family members. When the family members applied to Smith to be registered as members of the company, Smith refused to register the transfer. Smith also made an offer to purchase some of the shares from Fawcett's family. At first instance, an application to the Court to rectify the register of members was unsuccessful.

On appeal, Lord Green MR for the Court of Appeal, held that the principles to be applied to the discretion conferred upon directors in cases such as these were clear: '[t]hey must exercise their discretion bona fide in what they consider—not what a Court may consider—is in the interests of the company, and not for any collateral purpose'.[16] In much the same way as statutory interpretation insists on express words if the legislature intends to infringe upon common law rights,[17] the Court held that a shareholder has 'a prima facie right [to freely transfer their shares], and that right is not to be cut down by uncertain language or doubtful implications'.[18] Lord Green continued:

> The question, therefore, simply is whether on the true construction of the particular article the directors are limited by anything except their bona fide view as to the interests of the company ... It is said that on the evidence before us we ought to infer that the directors here were purporting to exercise their power to refuse a transfer not bona fide in the interests of the company but for some collateral purpose, namely, the desire of the leading director to acquire part of the shares for himself at an under-value.[19]

However, as the discretion conferred on the directors by these articles was clear and was not framed with limitations, the Court declined to imply any limitation other than that the power must be exercised bona fide in the interests of the company. As the evidence had proceeded by way of sworn affidavits only, and Smith had sworn that the directors had undertaken a bona fide consideration of the interests of the company, the Court was reluctant to draw inferences against the bona fides of the directors without providing the director with the opportunity to be cross-examined and refused the appeal.[20]

The test for 'bona fide' is subjective.[21] However, reference is frequently made to the dictum of Bowen LJ in *Hutton v West Cork Railway Co*[22]—coined the 'amiable lunatic' test—to justify the position that the first limb must contain a broader notion of reasonableness.[23]

15 *Re Smith & Fawcett Ltd* [1942] Ch 304, 304–5, 308.

16 Ibid 306.

17 *Coco v The Queen* (1994) 179 CLR 427; *Al-Kateb v Godwin* (2004) 219 CLR 562.

18 *Re Smith & Fawcett Ltd* [1942] Ch 304, 306.

19 Ibid 308.

20 Ibid 308–9.

21 *Bell Group Ltd (in liq) v Westpac Banking Corporation (No 9)* (2009) 39 WAR 1 [4619].

22 *Hutton v West Cork Railway Co* (1883) 23 Ch D 654, 671.

23 See, eg, *Bell Group Ltd (in liq) v Westpac Banking Corporation (No 9)* (2009) 39 WAR 1 [4602]–[4608]. Owen J's findings were largely upheld, although the appeal judges each accounted for the outcome slightly differently: *Westpac Banking Corporation v Bell Group Ltd (in liq) (No 3)* (2012) 44 WAR 1 [923] (Lee AJA), [1988], [2021] (Drummond AJA), [2795]–[2797] (Carr AJA).

This case dealt with the validity of a resolution of the members in a general meeting to authorise a lump sum payment to the directors after the company entered a scheme of arrangement which would divest its business to another company. The effect of the scheme was that directors and other officials would lose their positions once the divestment had occurred, and the resolution was packaged as compensation. The majority of the members passed a resolution authorising payment to the directors, but one of the dissenting minority members applied to the Court for an injunction restraining the payment. The plaintiff was granted the injunction at first instance because no meeting of the members had been properly called, but the primary judge indicated it was possible that if the meeting was duly called, the shareholders would have had the power to pass the proposed resolution.[24] The plaintiff appealed, seeking to have that position clarified. While discussing the powers of the members, Bowen LJ said:

> [i]t is the money of the company, and the majority want to spend it. What would be the natural limit of their power to do so? They can only spend money which is not theirs but the company's, if they are spending it for the purposes which are reasonably incidental to the carrying on of the business of the company. That is the general doctrine. Bona fides cannot be the sole test, otherwise you might have a lunatic conducting the affairs of the company, and paying away its money with both hands in a manner perfectly bona fide yet perfectly irrational. The test must be what is reasonably incidental to, and within the reasonable scope of carrying on, the business of the company.[25]

In our view, it is better to rely on the other element of this first limb of the duty (the need to act in the interests of the company) and the second limb of the duty (the requirement to act for proper purposes) to catch behaviour described by Bowen LJ above.[26] This was the pathway taken on appeal in the Bell Group litigation, so that 'it matters not whether the director honestly believed that in exercising the power as he did he was acting in the interests of the company; the power having been exercised for an improper purpose, its exercise will be liable to be set aside'.[27] These requirements will be considered next.

12.10.20 The first limb: meaning of 'in the interests of the company'

Although the company as an incorporated entity is a legal person in its own right, the 'interests of the company' have historically been equated with the interests of the members collectively. However, this does not preclude directors taking account of their own interests where they are also members. This issue was considered by the High Court in *Mills v Mills*,[28] where the directors passed a resolution allocating the whole of the company's reserve account to the ordinary shareholders by way of bonus shares; five bonus

24 *Hutton v West Cork Railway Co* (1883) 23 Ch D 654, 662.

25 Ibid 671.

26 *Regentcrest plc (in liq) v Cohen* [2001] 2 BCLC 80 [120]–[123].

27 Ibid [123], as cited by Drummond AJA in *Westpac Banking Corporation v Bell Group Ltd (in liq) (No 3)* (2012) 44 WAR 1 [1988]. See also *Westpac Banking Corporation v Bell Group Ltd (in liq) (No 3)* (2012) 44 WAR 1 [933] (Lee AJA).

28 *Mills v Mills* (1938) 60 CLR 150.

shares for every two ordinary shares held.[29] The company had, prior to this resolution, 34,500 ordinary shares on issue, each carrying the right to one vote, and 11,500 preference shares, each carrying the right to three votes. One of the effects of this resolution, issuing 86,250 new ordinary shares, was that it increased the voting power of the managing director, Neilson Mills, who held predominantly ordinary shares. Neilson's nephew, Ainslie, was a director and shareholder who held predominantly preference shares, a class to which bonus shares were not issued. Ainslie challenged the resolution as a breach of the director's duty to act bona fide in the best interest of the company. Ainslie voted against the resolution. A third director, who did not hold shares, voted with Neilson in favour of the share issue. The resolution took place immediately after Neilson had been pressured to resign as trustee of two trusts, which both held ordinary shares in the company, and through which Neilson had exercised a dominant voting position. This share issue had the effect of restoring the voting power that Neilson had lost through those resignations.

At first instance, Lowe J in the Supreme Court of Victoria held that the scheme of distribution was arrived at honestly and voted for in the best interests of the company, and that the two directors supporting it were aware of the effect that the resolution would have in altering the voting power.[30] On appeal, the High Court considered whether directors must act solely in the interests of the company to satisfy this duty. Latham CJ recognised that it is fairly common for directors to also be members of a company, and that this is considered desirable 'so that their interests may be identified with those of the shareholders of the company'.[31] Latham CJ then observed:

> I do not read the general phrases which are to be found in the authorities with reference to the obligations of directors to act solely in the interests of the company as meaning that they are prohibited from acting in any matter where their own interests are affected by what they do in their capacity as directors. Very many actions of directors who are shareholders, perhaps all of them, have a direct or indirect relation to their own interests. It would be ignoring realities and creating impossibilities in the administration of companies to require that directors should not advert to or consider in any way the effect of a particular decision upon their own interests as shareholders. A rule which laid down such a principle would paralyse the management of companies in many directions. Accordingly, the judicial observations which suggest that directors should only consider the interests of the company and never their own interests should not be pressed to a limit which would create quite an impossible position.[32]

Latham CJ considered that, in a situation where there was a disagreement between the members as to what was in the interests of the company, the question would not be 'a question of the interests of the company at all, but a question of what is fair as between

29 Bonus shares, issued for no consideration and generally out of the company's funds, are discussed in Chapter 8 at Section 8.15.15.

30 *Mills v Mills* (1938) 60 CLR 150, 162.

31 Ibid 163.

32 Ibid 163–4.

different classes of shareholders'.[33] His Honour concluded that the duty to act bona fide in the interests of the company had not been breached in this case.[34]

More recently, Owen J at first instance in the Bell Group litigation held that:

> there is no material difference, for present purposes, between the phrases 'benefit of the company', 'best interests of the company' and 'interests of the company'. In the authorities they are often used interchangeably and, in my view, are all to the same broad effect.[35]

Further, his Honour stressed that the interests of the shareholders will be regarded as those of the company, particularly when questions as to directors' duties arise in a solvent company, not because the shareholders are the company but because their interests intersect with the interests of the company in those circumstances.[36]

The idea that the interests of members correlate with the interests of the company has been confirmed in further High Court decisions.[37] Acting in the best interests of the company has been taken to mean, on the one hand, that the directors are acting in the best interests of the members as a collective group;[38] and, on the other hand, that the directors must have regard to the interests of present and future members, as well as the company as a commercial entity, even if this is not in the short-term best interests of the members.[39] In light of more recent developments in relation to considerations of shareholder primacy, stakeholder theory and 'enlightened shareholder value' (to be discussed further at Section 12.15.20),[40] in our view, the more inclusive and future-focused interpretation is to be preferred.

12.10.25 The first limb: application to corporate groups

Significant difficulties are faced by directors in complying with this duty where the company to whom the duty is owed is part of a larger corporate group.[41] Questions arise as to whether or not a decision which is made with the interests of the group in mind can satisfy the requirement under this duty to act in the interests of the company. The general

33 Ibid 164.

34 Ibid 164–5. Starke J appears to agree with Latham CJ: (1938) 60 CLR 150, 179. Dixon J focused more on the purpose for which the power was exercised than the question of 'the best interests of the company', as did Rich J (Evatt J concurring): (1938) 60 CLR 150, 186–8.

35 *Bell Group Ltd (in liq) v Westpac Banking Corporation (No 9)* (2009) 39 WAR 1 [4384].

36 Ibid [4393].

37 *Ngurli Ltd v McCann* (1953) 90 CLR 425, 438–40; *Ashburton Oil NL v Alpha Minerals NL* (1971) 123 CLR 614, 620; in the NSW Court of Appeal in an insolvent company: *Kinsela v Russell Kinsela Pty Ltd (in liq)* (1986) 4 NSWLR 722, 730.

38 *Greenhalgh v Arderne Cinemas Ltd* [1951] Ch 286 is often cited as authority on this point, but that case concerned the voting rights of shareholders and how those rights must be exercised for the benefit of the company as a whole, rather than the directors' duty to act bona fide in the interests of the company. However, *Greenhalgh* was the authority relied upon by Plowman J in *Parke v Daily News Ltd* [1962] Ch 927 to find that 'the benefit of the company was the benefit of the shareholders as a general body' in the context of this directors' duty (at 963).

39 *Darvall v North Sydney Brick & Tile Co Ltd* (1989) 16 NSWLR 260.

40 As discussed in the context of corporate theory in Chapter 2 at Section 2.45.

41 Corporate groups are also discussed in Chapter 4 at Section 4.65.05.

position is that directors must have primary regard to the interests of the particular company on whose board they sit, and not the wider group as a whole, even in instances of wholly owned subsidiaries. The High Court considered the application of duties to corporate groups in *Walker v Wimborne*[42] and confirmed that, because each company enjoys status as a separate legal entity, it is the duty of the directors to consider the interests of the individual company alone in deciding how to behave, even in circumstances of intra-group loans or financial decisions.[43] Equally, apart from the legal status as separate entities, the ownership structure of the holding company and its subsidiaries may be vastly different, and so regard to the individual company must be a priority.

The practical difficulties of the rule in *Walker v Wimborne* are evident when considering the decision of *Equiticorp Finance Ltd (in liq) v Bank of New Zealand*.[44] The Equiticorp group included companies in both Australia and New Zealand, and Mr Hawkins was a director of a number of the companies within the group. Hawkins was also described as Chairman or Chief Executive of the Equiticorp group. One company within the group had borrowed $200 million from the Bank of New Zealand to finance a takeover. When the Bank became concerned as to the size of its exposure, it placed pressure on Hawkins, who, in an effort to maintain good relations with this major creditor, used liquidity reserves from two other companies within the group, Equiticorp Financial Services Ltd (Aust) ('Financial Services') and Equiticorp Finance Ltd ('Finance'), towards the debt owed to the Bank. When those companies went into liquidation, the liquidators challenged these payments to the Bank as having been made in breach of duty to Financial Services and Finance.

At first instance, instead of relying solely on *Walker v Wimborne*, the Court applied the *Charterbridge Corporation v Lloyds Bank*[45] test, which provides that, in a group situation, when it is clear that the directors have not had regard to the interests of the aggrieved company, the proper test is whether an 'intelligent and honest' person in the position of a director of that company could, in the whole of the circumstances, reasonably have believed that the transactions were for the benefit of the company.[46] On appeal, the parties submitted that this test should also be applied by the Court. The majority, Clarke and Cripps JJA, were unconvinced, stating '[t]he directors are bound

42 *Walker v Wimborne* (1976) 137 CLR 1. Here, the three respondents were found liable for payments they made as directors of a corporate group (there was no interlocking shareholdings, and so the term 'corporate group' can only loosely be applied), where a practice had been for funds to be moved between companies within that group to meet financial needs as they arose. The Court upheld the argument of the liquidator of Asiatic Electric Co Pty Ltd, one of the companies within that group, who asserted that the payments were not made bona fide in the interests of Asiatic, and constituted a misapplication of its funds as the payments gave Asiatic as an individual entity no benefit or advantage.

43 Ibid 7.

44 *Equiticorp Finance Ltd (in liq) v Bank of New Zealand* (1993) 32 NSWLR 50.

45 *Charterbridge Corporation Ltd v Lloyds Bank Ltd* [1970] Ch 62. Here, Pomeroy Developments (Castleford) Ltd was one of a large group of property development companies, with common shareholding, directorate and offices. It executed a charge over land in favour of a bank, to whom another company in the group owed substantial debts. Mr Pomeroy, the officer of Castleford who approved the charge, admitted that he did not consider the interests of Castleford separately from that of the group. Rather, he considered it in the interests of the group that Castleford should enter into these transactions.

46 Ibid 74; cited in *Equiticorp Financial Services Ltd (NSW) v Equiticorp Financial Services Ltd (NZ)* (1992) 29 NSWLR 260, 301–2.

to exercise their powers, bona fide, in what they consider is in the interests of the company and not for any collateral purpose. Whether they did so or not is a question of fact.'[47] The majority noted the difficulties of aligning this factual question with the objective 'intelligent and honest' test set out in *Charterbridge,* confining that test to extremely limited circumstances, such as where 'a director bluntly states that [they] did not consider the interests of the particular company at all and solely had regard to the interests of the group'.[48] In the appeal decision in *Westpac Banking Corporation v Bell Group Ltd (in liq) (No 3),*[49] which will be discussed below, Lee AJA agreed with this reservation expressed by the majority, stating that a '[b]reach of a duty not to act other than in the best interests of the company arises if the failure to consider the separate interests of the company produces a result that fails to meet the best interests of that company... At that point there can be no requirement to consider what an intelligent and honest person would have done'.[50]

There is also guidance to be found for directors under s 187 of the *Corporations Act,* which will be discussed below, in relation to wholly owned subsidiaries.

12.10.30 The first limb: application to other stakeholders

> The impacts of corporate decision-making on a wider range of interests than shareholders are now being given more recognition. The need to ensure protection of those interests also I think serves to explain why modern company courts have become more interventionist, in reviewing the activities of directors than was traditionally the case.[51]

The question of whose interests should be included in 'the interests of the company' is a long-standing one,[52] which has become more complex in light of modern theories justifying corporate behavior and regulation. One variant within the approaches to corporate purpose[53] suggests that directors should not focus exclusively on achieving short-term profits for current members but should take a long-term approach to include ethical investments to yield returns for shareholders. In line with this argument is the notion that, in order to consider the interests of the company, directors must take a more broad view than the immediate interests of the current members, and should consider other stakeholders including creditors, employees, the environment, the community, and others. However, only in the limited circumstances that follow have the courts been willing to consider the 'best interests of the company' as extending beyond the traditional understanding of the interests of the members.

47 *Equiticorp Finance Ltd (in liq) v Bank of New Zealand* (1993) 32 NSWLR 50, 147. The dissenting judgment of Kirby P also preferred the application of the test in *Walker v Wimborne*: (1993) 32 NSWLR 50, 97–9.

48 Ibid 148.

49 *Westpac Banking Corporation v Bell Group Ltd (in liq) (No 3)* (2012) 44 WAR 1.

50 Ibid 182 [1012].

51 *Westpac Banking Corporation v Bell Group Ltd (in liq) (No 3)* (2012) 44 WAR 1, 367 [2051] (Drummond AJA).

52 See, eg, E Merrick Dodd, 'For Whom are Corporate Managers Trustees' (1932) 45(7) *Harvard Law Review* 1145.

53 Discussed in Chapter 2 at Section 2.45.

Despite employees being significant stakeholders, directors do not have any specific positive duty to consider employees' interests when making decisions for the company and, in fact, in cases where the employees' interest conflict with those of the members, should not consider them. A famous quotation from Lord Bowen in *Hutton v West Cork Railway Co*, when considering the resolution to compensate employees who would lose their positions when the company was dissolved, states '[t]he law does not say that there are to be no cakes and ale, but there are to be no cakes and ale except such as are required for the benefit of the company'.[54] This traditional approach was considered by the Senate Standing Committee on Legal and Constitutional Affairs in 1989, which recommended that the Act be amended to provide that the interests of the employees may be taken into account by the directors.[55] This recommendation was never implemented. Given the suggested phrasing of 'may be taken into account', it is arguable that such an amendment would not, in any event, have been of significant use to an aggrieved employee. Similar criticisms have been levelled at the introduction of enlightened shareholder value into the *Companies Act 2006* (UK), which is discussed in detail below.[56]

However, there is judicial variation in the approach to employee interests across jurisdictions. While discussing the operation of the *Fair Work Act 2009* (Cth) in relation to a decision to outsource ground handling operations during the COVID-19 pandemic in *Qantas v Transport Workers Union of Australia*,[57] Gordon and Edelman JJ provide an example that failing to take into account the existence and terms of an enterprise agreement when making decisions about a company's future might constitute a breach of s 181.[58] A more active interpretation was taken in Canada in *Teck Corporation Ltd v Millar*,[59] where the Court held that if a director was to 'observe decent respect for other interests lying beyond those of the company's shareholders in the strict sense'[60]—such as, for example, the interests of the company's employees—no one would argue that in doing so they were not acting bona fide in the interests of the company itself. Conversely, in the UK, it was held that a director who disregards the interests of the members in order to confer a benefit on employees or another stakeholder would be in breach of their duty.[61]

It would also be a breach of duty to disregard interests of the members in order to confer a benefit on a creditor if the company is considered to be solvent. Where the company is insolvent or nearing insolvency, there is a line of authority following *Walker v Wimborne*[62] that suggests that, in discharging their duty to act in good faith in the interests of the company, the directors must have regard to the interests of creditors. This is due to the understanding that, near insolvency, the company's focus shifts from maximising

54 *Hutton v West Cork Railway Co* (1883) 23 Ch D 654, 671.

55 Senate Standing Committee on Legal and Constitutional Affairs, Parliament of Australia, *Company Directors' Duties* (Report, 1989) 89 [6.21]-[6.22].

56 Enlightened shareholder value is also discussed and critiqued in Chapter 2 at Section 2.45.05.

57 *Qantas Airways Ltd v Transport Workers Union of Australia* (2023) 278 CLR 571.

58 Ibid [88].

59 *Teck Corporation Ltd v Millar* (1972) 33 DLR (3d) 288.

60 Ibid 314.

61 *Parke v Daily News Ltd* [1962] Ch 927.

62 *Walker v Wimborne* (1976) 137 CLR 1.

wealth for the members to seeking to prevent any further loss to the creditors. This is reflected in the ranking of creditors in insolvency, which will be considered in Chapter 16, and in the placement of members' claims according to s 563A of the *Corporations Act* beneath all other creditor claimants. Members will not receive any return in a company when its creditors cannot be paid in full.

However, it is clear that outside of situations involving trading whilst insolvent (where creditors have a statutory power to pursue directors personally for the payment of debts),[63] creditors have no standing to enforce the duty to act bona fide in the interests of the company and for proper purposes, as this duty is owed to the company.[64] The company can enforce the duty itself or via a liquidator.[65] The key consequence is that the members cannot ratify or release the directors from a breach of this duty in an insolvency context.[66]

Although this is not as significant as suggesting that the duty is owed to the creditors, it means that in decision-making when the company's financial position is precarious, the interests of the company expand to encompass the interests of the creditors.[67] As the solvency of a company may be difficult to determine, this is an issue to which directors must remain alert, particularly if it alters the legal understanding of 'the interests of the company'. This was considered by the Court in *Kinsela v Russell Kinsela Pty Ltd (in liq)*.[68] The Kinsela family operated a funeral home through the company Russell Kinsela Pty Ltd ('the company'), which offered contributory insurance to cover the cost of a client's funeral services. Through this insurance, the company had built up a substantial commitment for the future provision of funeral services.[69] When the *Funeral Funds Act 1979* (NSW) was passed, which had as its purpose to control and regulate such arrangements in the interests of the contributors, the Kinsela family became concerned due to the company's significant exposure. The financial viability of the company was in doubt, as it had been running at a loss for a number of years with a substantial excess of liabilities over assets, in addition to these significant future obligations. The company was, eventually, put into liquidation.

The primary judge had to consider a challenge by the liquidator in relation to a three-year lease entered into by the company as landlord, with Mr and Mrs Kinsela as tenants, at substantially below the market rental value, with no provision for escalation, with an option to purchase part of the premises at any time also at undervalue. The lease had been ratified by the members at a shareholder meeting, which was relied upon by the Kinselas as indicating 'there could be no question of it not being in the best interests of the company or of it being a breach of fiduciary duty'.[70] Powell J at first instance felt

63 *Corporations Act* s 588G, as discussed in Chapter 11 at Section 11.25.

64 *Spies v The Queen* (2000) 201 CLR 603.

65 *Bell Group Ltd (in liq) v Westpac Banking Corporation (No 9)* (2009) 39 WAR 1.

66 See, eg, *Kinsela v Russell Kinsela Pty Ltd (in liq)* (1986) 4 NSWLR 722 and the discussion in Chapter 10 at Section 10.40.05.

67 In *Re Bryve Resources Pty Ltd* (2022) 163 ACSR 310 [73], Williams J held that the interests of the company are not to be equated to the interests of a creditor, even where that creditor is a substantial one, especially where the decisions made would prejudice the company's financial position further.

68 *Kinsela v Russell Kinsela Pty Ltd (in liq)* (1986) 4 NSWLR 722.

69 Ibid 724.

70 Ibid 726.

'constrained by authority' to agree that, if the lease had been authorised by all of the shareholders after receiving full disclosure, then the directors could not be found to be in breach of this duty. However, as one of the shareholders had not been fully informed, the consent of the shareholders was not complete and the lease was declared voidable.[71] The Kinselas challenged that finding on appeal.

Street CJ, with whom Hope and McHugh JJA concurred, first considered whether the transaction was within the power of the company, and then, if it was, whether the power been validly exercised so as to bind the company. The Articles and Memorandum of this company were not drafted in such a way as to provide explicit powers to the directors. Indeed, it seemed to Street CJ that they had 'the hallmarks of a "shelf" company'.[72] But, there did appear to be a power to enter into a lease, which led Street CJ to undertake a survey of the case law as to whether this power had been validly exercised, and whether it had been exercised in the interests of the company. His Honour held that the principles across the case law:

> were not intended to, and do not, apply in the situation in which the interests of the company as a whole involve the rights of creditors as distinct from the rights of shareholders. In a solvent company the proprietary interests of the shareholders entitle them as a general body to be regarded as the company when questions of the duty of directors arise. If, as a general body, they authorise or ratify a particular action of the directors, there can be no challenge to the validity of what the directors have done. But where a company is insolvent the interests of the creditors intrude. They become prospectively entitled, through the mechanism of liquidation, to displace the power of the shareholders and directors to deal with the company's assets. It is in a practical sense their assets and not the shareholders' assets that, through the medium of the company, are under the management of the directors pending either liquidation, return to solvency, or the imposition of some alternative administration.[73]

When considering the question of ratification, his Honour said that:

> [w]here ... the interests at risk are those of creditors I see no reason in law or in logic to recognise that the shareholders can authorise the breach. Once it is accepted, as in my view it must be, that the directors' duty to a company as a whole extends in an insolvency context to not prejudicing the interests of creditors the shareholders do not have the power or authority to absolve the directors from that breach.[74]

As the company was 'plainly insolvent at the date of the lease', the prejudice to the creditor was a direct and calculated result of the company entering into the lease. The lease

71 For further information on the fully informed consent of the members, see Chapter 13 at Section 13.10.30.

72 *Kinsela v Russell Kinsela Pty Ltd (in liq)* (1986) 4 NSWLR 722, 728.

73 Ibid 730.

74 Ibid, citations to *Nicholson v Permakraft (NZ) Ltd (in liq)* [1985] 1 NZLR 242 and *Walker v Wimborne* (1976) 137 CLR 1 omitted.

was entered into in breach of the directors' duty to the company, in that it directly prejudiced the creditors of the company. The liquidator was entitled to seek it undone as a voidable transaction.[75]

The application of this duty to an insolvent company was also considered in the *Bell Group* decisions. It was pleaded on behalf of the banks that the directors' duty to act bona fide in the best interests of the companies included an obligation to act in the interests of creditors, present or future, of an insolvent company. Lee AJA addressed that pleading directly by reading it down 'to be a pleading of a duty to act in the interests of an insolvent company by not causing the company to act to the prejudice of the interests of its creditors'.[76]

The test becomes more complex where it is unclear whether or not the company is insolvent. In *Kalls Enterprises Pty Ltd (in liq) v Baloglow,* Giles JA said that 'the company need not be insolvent at [the time when the particular decision under challenge is made] and the directors must consider [the creditors'] interests if there is a real and not remote risk that they will be prejudiced by the dealing in question'.[77] This was considered in the United Kingdom by the Supreme Court in *BTI 2014 LLC v Sequana SA,*[78] which discounted the 'real risk' of insolvency test,[79] preferring that the directors know, or ought to know, that the company is insolvent or bordering on insolvency, or that insolvent external administration is probable.[80] Once that is the case, Lady Ardern was prepared to extend the 'creditor duty' beyond mere consideration of the creditors' interests, to a duty 'not to materially harm them either'.[81] Although *BTI 2014 LLC v Sequana SA* rejects the 'real risk' of insolvency trigger, which Keay notes has been accepted in a number of superior courts in Australia, the requirement to consider the interests of the creditors is now similar between the two jurisdictions, following that decision.[82]

12.10.35 The second limb: meaning of 'for proper purposes'

The second limb of the duty—the requirement that directors exercise their powers for proper purposes—involves the consideration of two separate issues: the objective purpose for which a power was granted, and then the purpose for which a power was actually exercised.

This limb has arisen for consideration by the courts, predominantly in the context of share issues. In public companies, this occurs where the company is the target of a hostile takeover.[83] In proprietary companies, it is in the context of dilution of voting power

75 The abilities of the liquidator in relation to such transactions will be considered in Chapter 16.

76 *Westpac Banking Corporation v Bell Group Ltd (in liq) (No 3)* (2012) 44 WAR 1, 168 [910] (Lee AJA).

77 *Kalls Enterprises Pty Ltd (in liq) v Baloglow* (2007) 63 ACSR 557. For further reading, see H Anderson, 'Directors' Personal Liability to Creditors: Theory versus Tradition' (2003) 8(2) *Deakin Law Review* 209.

78 *BTI 2014 LLC v Sequana SA* [2023] 2 All ER 303 ('*BTI v Sequana*').

79 Lord Briggs described the 'real risk of insolvency' test as resting on 'an unsound principle' by assuming that creditors of a limited company will always be among its stakeholders: Ibid [191].

80 Ibid 361 (Lord Briggs, Lord Kitchin agreeing); 368, 369–70 (Lord Hodge); 386–7 (Lady Arden). Lord Reed preferred 'insolvent or bordering on insolvent' (330–1), and was less certain than Lord Briggs and Lord Hodge of the importance of the knowledge of the directors (331).

81 Ibid 372.

82 A Keay, 'The Impact of Sequana on the Directors' Obligation to Consider Creditor Interests In Financially Distressed Companies: Was it Worth the Wait?" (2024) 45(1) *Adelaide Law Review* 156, 178–9.

83 This tends to occur as a defensive move to try to defeat the takeover bid, either by authorising a share issue to a 'white knight' who will not vote in favour of the bid when it is offered to the

of certain shareholders. Although these factual scenarios are dominant in the case law, the requirement to act for proper purposes does not only apply to the issue of shares but to all exercises of directors' discretions and powers.

The requirement that directors exercise their powers and discretions for proper purposes originates in the idea of 'fraud on the power'—a legal principle extending beyond corporate law into any instrument which grants a power. *Vatcher v Paull*[84] was a case considering a power of appointment contained in a marriage settlement rather than the power reposed in a director either by the constitution or the relevant legislation. However, Lord Parker of Waddington (delivering the judgment for the Privy Council) stated that:

> [t]he term fraud in connection with frauds on a power does not necessarily denote any conduct on the part of the appointor amounting to fraud in the common law meaning of the term or any conduct which could be properly termed dishonest or immoral. It merely means that the power has been exercised for a purpose, or with an intention, beyond the scope of or not justified by the instrument creating the power.[85]

There has been some movement over time on the question of whether 'proper purposes' should be considered a separate limb to 'bona fide in the interests of the company', due to the close connection between the two.[86] In *Re Smith & Fawcett Ltd,* the duty was expressed as being that directors 'exercise their discretion bona fide in what they consider—not what a court may consider—is in the interests of the company, and not for any collateral purpose'.[87]

In *Harlowe's Nominees Pty Ltd v Woodside (Lakes Entrance) Oil Co NL* (*'Harlowe's Case'*),[88] Harlowe sought a declaration that the issue by the directors of nine million shares in Woodside to another company (Burmah) was void. Woodside and Burmah worked in collaboration in their explorations for oil and natural gas in south eastern Victoria prior to the allotment, which took place following Harlowe making significant on-market purchases of shares in Woodside. The High Court acknowledged that if the share purchasing by Harlowe 'was to effect changes in the control of Woodside its hopes were seriously prejudiced, if not destroyed, by the allotment to Burmah'.[89] Harlowe argued that Woodside had no immediate need for the additional share capital introduced via the share issue, and that the directors engaged in the share issue for the irrelevant and inadmissible purpose of preventing Harlowe from obtaining the voting power it had expected to obtain or, at least, without duly considering whether or not the making of the issue was truly in the interests of their company as a whole.[90]

---

shareholders, or generally to dilute the present shareholding of the takeover bidder. These issues are considered in detail in Chapter 19 at Sections 19.55.05–10.

84 *Vatcher v Paull* [1915] AC 372.

85 Ibid 378.

86 See, eg, *Australian Metropolitan Life Assurance Co Ltd v Ure* (1923) 33 CLR 199, 217.

87 *Re Smith & Fawcett Ltd* [1942] Ch 304, 306.

88 *Harlowe's Nominees Pty Ltd v Woodside (Lakes Entrance) Oil Co NL* (1968) 121 CLR 483.

89 Ibid 492.

90 Ibid.

The Court did not clearly distinguish between the two limbs. It commenced with a consideration of the impermissible purpose but concludes with considerations of the interests of the company. However, the weight of Harlowe's argument was based primarily on the question of the purpose for which the shares were issued, with an argument in the alternative that the issue was not in the interests of the company as a whole. As there were a variety of benefits to the company readily perceived by the share issue, such as an increase in capital and strengthening their ties with Burmah, this argument was not likely to succeed.

The Court considered that if the directors exercised their judgment in good faith and not for irrelevant purposes, then their decision was not open for review,[91] even if it had the practical consequence of frustrating Harlowe's ambitions, and even if the directors realised that would be the result and found it agreeable.[92] The purpose would become improper if,

> in making the allotment, the directors had an actual purpose of thereby creating an advantage for themselves otherwise than as members of the general body of shareholders, as for instance by buttressing their directorships against an apprehended attack from such as Harlowe, the allotment would plainly be voidable.[93]

This raises the additional question of the test for determining the purpose for which a power or discretion has *actually been exercised*. The majority of cases concerning the exercise of power 'for a proper purpose' are in relation to the issue of shares, and there is significant authority from the courts as to the objective purpose for which the power to issue shares is granted.

The typical purpose behind the power to issue shares is to raise capital.[94] However, the courts have also considered other purposes. As discussed in *Harlowe's Case*, the capital raised through the share allotment was not immediately required by Woodside,[95] but 'the purpose of putting Woodside in a position of vastly greater freedom to plan for increasing participation with its "partner", Burmah, in the activities for which hopes in many quarters were running high' was perceived as a proper purpose by the courts.[96]

Other cases suggest that issuing shares to ensure a sufficient minimum number of shareholders to comply with statutory requirements would be a proper purpose.[97] In contrast, attempting to defeat a hostile takeover,[98] facilitating a takeover through the reduction of an existing majority or creation of a new majority,[99] and entrenching control in one group of shareholders at the expense of another[100] have been held to be

91 *Bell IXL Investments Ltd v Life Therapeutics Ltd* (2008) 68 ACSR 154; *United Petroleum Australia Pty Ltd v Herbert Smith Freehills* (2018) 128 ACSR 324.

92 *Harlowe's Nominees Pty Ltd v Woodside (Lakes Entrance) Oil Co NL* (1968) 121 CLR 483, 493.

93 Ibid 493–4.

94 Ibid 493.

95 Ibid 496.

96 Ibid.

97 *Punt v Symons & Co* (1903) 2 Ch 506, 516; *Whitehouse v Carlton Hotel Pty Ltd* (1987) 162 CLR 285, 292.

98 *Hogg v Cramphorn Ltd* [1967] Ch 254.

99 *Howard Smith Ltd v Ampol Petroleum Ltd* [1974] 1 NSWLR 68.

100 *Whitehouse v Carlton Hotel Pty Ltd* (1987) 162 CLR 285; *Millsave Holdings Pty Ltd v Connective Group Pty Ltd* (2023) 75 VR 239.

improper purposes. It is possible that a company's constitution may expressly state permissible purposes for the use of a power, as discussed in *Whitehouse v Carlton*[101] below. However, a broad conferral of 'all the powers of the directors' onto one director while he remains permanent governing director was not sufficient to demonstrate intention for the director to be free of any restraint upon the exercise of the powers.[102]

These cases demonstrate it is possible to have multiple purposes for the exercise of a power. The courts have put forward different legal tests for determining the situation where directors' actions are motivated by a combination of proper and improper purposes. Does the mere presence of an improper purpose invalidate the exercise of power? We consider two different approaches below, before turning to *Darvall v North Sydney Brick & Tile Co Ltd*,[103] which provides a method for reconciling the tests.

Howard Smith Ltd v Ampol Petroleum Ltd[104] concerned an allotment of shares by the directors of a company, RW Miller Holdings Ltd ('Millers'), to Howard Smith during a takeover contest for Millers between Ampol and Howard Smith.[105] Ampol made a formal offer for the issued shares in Millers, which the board of Millers recommended be rejected by shareholders as being too low. When Howard Smith announced an intention to make a higher offer, Ampol and another company, Bulkships, who between them held just under 55 per cent of Millers' shares, released a press statement indicating that they would act jointly to reject any offer for their shares by Howard Smith or any other source.[106] At the same time, Millers required finance of $10 million in relation to an ongoing project and to secure its financial position. Phrasing the action as protection of the interests of minority members of Howard Smith, who could not accept any offer for their shares on the basis that Ampol and Bulkships would reject it, Millers allotted 4.5 million $1 ordinary shares to Howard Smith in exchange for $2.30 per share, totalling $10.35 million. After the allotment, Ampol and Bulkships no longer held more than 50 per cent of the shareholding in Millers.

Street CJ found that the directors had 'issued the shares so as to reduce the interest of these two shareholders to something significantly less than that of a majority', despite evidence given by some of the directors that capital raising had been the motivator for the share issue. While capital raising 'was the immediate purpose', 'the ultimate purpose was to procure the continuation by Howard Smith of the takeover offer made by that company'.[107] The Privy Council agreed with this finding that the sole purpose of the share issue was to 'destroy an existing majority, or create a new majority which did not previously exist', and, as such, was invalid.[108] Their Lordships discussed the test to be applied if the proper purpose of capital raising existed alongside the improper purpose. After ascertaining the nature of the power to issue shares, the Court indicated in obiter that, 'it is then necessary for the court ... to examine the substantial purpose for which it was

101 *Whitehouse v Carlton Hotel Pty Ltd* (1987) 162 CLR 285.
102 Ibid 291.
103 *Darvall v North Sydney Brick & Tile Co Ltd* (1989) 16 NSWLR 260.
104 *Howard Smith Ltd v Ampol Petroleum Ltd* [1974] 1 NSWLR 68 (on appeal to the Privy Council from Street CJ (in equity)).
105 Takeover disputes are now predominantly dealt with by the Takeovers Panel, discussed in Chapter 19.
106 *Howard Smith Ltd v Ampol Petroleum Ltd* [1974] 1 NSWLR 68, 71–2.
107 *Ampol Petroleum Ltd v RW Miller (Holdings) Pty Ltd* [1972] 2 NSWLR 850, 879.
108 *Howard Smith Ltd v Ampol Petroleum Ltd* [1974] 1 NSWLR 68, 79.

exercised, and to reach a conclusion whether that purpose was proper or not'.[109] This is now recognised as the 'substantial purpose' test.

In contrast, the Court in *Whitehouse v Carlton Hotel Pty Ltd*[110] preferred a 'but for' test, which can be seen in the reasoning of Dixon J in the High Court in *Mills v Mills* discussed above.[111] Charles Whitehouse was the permanent governing director of Carlton Hotel Pty Ltd, holding two A-class shares in the company, which carried unrestricted voting rights. His ex-wife held two B-class shares, which carried full voting rights after the death of Charles, but only if still held by his ex-wife. In addition, there were 6,400 C-class shares held by their children, which carried no voting rights at all, but rights to share in profits and surplus capital.

Due to familial discord during the dissolution of the Whitehouse's marriage, Charles issued two B-class shares to his sons, to prevent his ex-wife from gaining control over the voting power in the general meeting after his death. The shares were issued by Charles, but without a meeting of the directors or a resolution of the board to allot the B-class shares.[112] Charles later fell out with his sons, and at a directors' meeting only attended by himself and a Mrs J Whitehouse,[113] resolved that the B-class shares had not been allotted to the sons and directed that the share register be amended. The sons sued to seek correction of the share register, reinstating their names as B-class shareholders. They were successful at first instance, but overturned on appeal, and were granted leave to appeal to the High Court.

As with *Howard Smith Ltd v Ampol Petroleum Ltd*, the Court found that the allotment was made solely for the purpose of manipulating the voting power of the shareholders but discussed in obiter the relevant test to be applied when more than one purpose exists. The majority acknowledged that 'the preponderant view' of the legal test was whether the impermissible purpose was the dominant or substantial object of the exercise of the power.[114] Their Honours then stated that:

> As a matter of logic and principle, the preferable view would seem to be that, regardless of whether the impermissible purpose was the dominant one or but one of a number of significantly contributing causes, the allotment will be invalidated if the impermissible purpose was causative in the sense that, but for its presence, 'the power would not have been exercised'.[115]

These two approaches have similar themes. Even under the 'but for' test, the impermissible purpose must have been a 'significantly contributing' cause for the directors' actions to be rendered impermissible. The two tests were reconciled in *Darvall v North Sydney*

109 Ibid 77.

110 *Whitehouse v Carlton Hotel Pty Ltd* (1987) 162 CLR 285.

111 *Mills v Mills* (1938) 60 CLR 150, 186. See also the discussion of whether the 'but for' test is appropriate under the *Companies Act 2006* (UK): *Eclairs Group Ltd v JKX Oil & Gas plc* [2016] 3 All ER 641 [17]-[24].

112 The directors at that time were his ex-wife, his sons Alexander and Wilson, and a solicitor, Mr Jones: *Whitehouse v Carlton Hotel Pty Ltd* (1987) 162 CLR 285, 296.

113 Ibid 308. It is not apparent whether this is Charles' wife, or the wife of one of his sons. It is also not apparent whether she was a director at this point in time. In effect, this was an action by Charles.

114 Ibid 294.

115 Ibid (excluding a citation to *Mills v Mills* (1938) 60 CLR 150, 186).

Brick & Tile Co Ltd,[116] where, although entry into a joint venture agreement was prompted by concerns about a takeover offer, the directors had other reasons for contemplating the joint venture, including providing shareholders with an alternative to the takeover offer and advancing the commercial position of the company.[117] Clarke JA noted that 'the bald proposition that it is improper to take action to defeat a take-over offer is too widely stated to constitute a legal principle'.[118] It could not be correct to say that any action taken which may lead to the defeat of a takeover is necessarily improper, as any commercial decision reached where a takeover has been mooted might fall foul of the proper purposes limb of the duty.[119]

12.10.40 The duty: a summary

To summarise, it is accepted that satisfying the duty to act bona fide in the best interests of the company and for proper purposes involves subjective and objective elements. More recent cases have focused on whether the directors believe they are acting in the best interests of the company, rather than deliberately engaging in conduct knowing it is not in the best interests of the company.[120] The better view is that the test as to whether the director was acting bona fide in the best interests of the company is subjective. It may be tempered with questions of reasonableness, but as an objective threshold is applied to the second limb, it may not be necessary within the first limb.

Acting in the best interests of the company has been taken to mean, on the one hand, that the directors are acting in the best interests of the members as a collective group;[121] and on the other hand, that the directors must have regard to the interests of present and future members, as well as the company as a commercial entity, even if this is not in the short-term best interests of the members.[122]

The second limb of the duty—the requirement that directors exercise their powers for proper purposes—involves the consideration of two separate issues: the objective purpose for which the power was granted, and the purpose for which the power was actually exercised.[123]

Honest or altruistic behaviour will not prevent a finding of improper conduct if that conduct was carried out for an improper or collateral purpose.[124] As directors may be motivated by a number of purposes, the court will consider whether the motivating purpose is improper. Two tests have been proposed: the 'but for' test from *Whitehouse v Carlton Hotel Pty Ltd*,[125] and the substantial or dominant purpose test from *Mills v Mills*.[126]

116 *Darvall v North Sydney Brick & Tile Co Ltd* (1989) 16 NSWLR 260.
117 Ibid 283, 330.
118 Ibid 335.
119 Ibid 336.
120 *Australian Securities and Investments Commission v Maxwell* (2006) 59 ACSR 373.
121 *Greenhalgh v Arderne Cinemas Ltd* [1951] Ch 286.
122 *Darvall v North Sydney Brick & Tile Co Ltd* (1989) 16 NSWLR 260.
123 *Howard Smith Ltd v Ampol Petroleum Ltd* [1974] 1 NSWLR 68, 77.
124 *Permanent Building Society (in liq) v Wheeler* (1994) 11 WAR 187, 218.
125 *Whitehouse v Carlton Hotel Pty Ltd* (1987) 162 CLR 285.
126 *Mills v Mills* (1938) 60 CLR 150.

The following test appears to satisfy both requirements. It asks whether the improper purpose was a significant contributing cause to the exercise of the power, and, but for its presence, the power would not have been exercised. If so, then the duty will have been breached.

12.10.45 Is the duty equitable or fiduciary?

For the purposes of determining the available remedies in the general law, it is important to understand whether the duty to act bona fide in the best interests of the company can be correctly described as 'fiduciary' in nature. If it is fiduciary, then a breach could potentially entitle the company to seek compensation from any third party who knowingly received fiduciary property or knowingly assisted the director to breach their duty.[127] Following the decision of the High Court in *Breen v Williams*, there is doubt whether this duty can be accurately described as fiduciary, as the duty requires a director to take positive action, which falls outside the High Court's contemplation of the fiduciary obligation.[128] Fiduciary obligations were, in that decision, confined to proscriptive duties only; that is, the Court held that the fiduciary obligation contained prohibitive or negative duties, which require the fiduciary not to act in a certain way, rather than prescriptive or positive duties, which require positive action from the fiduciary. This question, and the ability to access remedies against third parties, was at the heart of the litigation in the *Bell Group* cases.[129]

The Bell Group of companies had a high profile in Australia in the 1970s and 1980s and was the subject of a takeover by Bond Corporation in 1988. At that time, the Bell Group was highly geared, owing significant unsecured debt borrowings to a number of banks. In 1989, it became apparent to the directors and the major bank creditors that the Group was potentially insolvent. A refinancing arrangement was negotiated, with the banks providing no further finance but requiring the Bell Group to provide security and guarantees and subordinate intra-group debt. The key company within the group, Bell Group Ltd, went into liquidation in April 1991, and the banks recovered $283 million by realising the securities they had gained under the refinancing arrangement.

In 1995, the liquidator and various creditors took action against the banks on the basis that the refinancing arrangement involved a breach of duties by the Bell Group Ltd directors, including the duty to act bona fide in the best interests of the company and for proper purposes. In particular, the liquidator argued that the banks knew that the directors' approval of the refinancing arrangement was a breach of their fiduciary obligations, and as such, the banks were liable for knowing assistance and knowing receipt under *Barnes v Addy*.[130] At first instance, Owen J found that the directors did not

127 *Barnes v Addy* (1874) LR 9 Ch App 244 in relation to breach of trust and trust property. It has been 'assumed, but rarely if at all decided' that this remedial action extends to fiduciary breach and fiduciary property: *Farah Constructions Pty Ltd v Say-Dee Pty Ltd* (2007) 230 CLR 89, 141 [113].

128 *Breen v Williams* (1996) 186 CLR 71, 113 (Gaudron and McHugh JJ), 137–8 (Gummow J).

129 *Bell Group Ltd (in liq) v Westpac Banking Corporation (No 9)* (2009) 39 WAR 1; *Westpac Banking Corporation v Bell Group Ltd (in liq) (No 3)* (2012) 44 WAR 1. For further detailed information on accessorial liability, see generally J Dietrich and P Ridge, *Accessories in Private Law* (Cambridge University Press, 2015).

130 *Barnes v Addy* (1874) LR 9 Ch App 244. See also *Farah Constructions Pty Ltd v Say-Dee Pty Ltd* (2007) 230 CLR 89.

believe that the refinancing arrangements were in the best interests of each company in the Bell Group as a whole, taking into account the creditors, future creditors and members, and that they had entered into the transactions for improper purposes.[131] Further, Owen J held that the banks had notice of the directors' breaches, that these duties were fiduciary, and that the banks were liable as third parties who had knowingly received property as a result of a breach of fiduciary obligations.[132] When discussing the question of whether or not a positive obligation could be classified as fiduciary, Owen J commenced by stating that:[133]

> Where a person has undertaken to act in the interests of another and where the nature of that relationship, its surrounding circumstances and the obligations attaching to it so require, it will be held to be fiduciary. But the fact that it is categorised as fiduciary does not mean that all of the obligations arising from it are themselves fiduciary. Unless there are some special circumstances in the relationship, the duties that equity demands from the fiduciary will be limited to what I have described as the core obligations: not to obtain any unauthorised benefit from the relationship and not to be in a position of conflict. They stem from the fundamental obligation of loyalty.

His Honour then undertook a history of the duty and found on the basis of obiter discussion that the duty to act bona fide in the best interests of the company and for proper purposes is a fiduciary obligation.[134] His Honour did not consider that *Breen v Williams* overruled these authorities, because it did not apply generally or it did not hold that only proscriptive duties could be fiduciary.[135] On appeal, the majority upheld Owen J's conclusions as to a breach of directors' fiduciary duties and third-party liability via *Barnes v Addy*,[136] although their Honours' reasoning in relation to the duty was different to that of Owen J.[137]

The Bell Group litigation was settled by the parties in the same month that the scheduled appeal was to be heard in the High Court,[138] leaving the position in *Breen v Williams*[139] unchanged at the highest level of Australian authority.[140]

The requirements of the duty to act bona fide in the best interests of the company and for proper purposes are relevant to the prohibition on a fiduciary placing themselves

131 *Bell Group Ltd (in liq) v Westpac Banking Corporation (No 9)* (2009) 39 WAR 1 [4295]–[6127].

132 Ibid [4376].

133 Ibid [4552].

134 Ibid [4553]–[4568]

135 Ibid [4569]–[4572].

136 *Westpac Banking Corporation v Bell Group Ltd (in liq) (No 3)* (2012) 44 WAR 1 [1011], [1099], [1113]–[1123], [2079], [2104]–[2126], [2127]–[2173].

137 Ibid [834]–[941] (Lee AJA), [1947]–[2078] (Drummond AJA), [2716]–[2736], [2795]–[2797] (Carr AJA).

138 R Gluyas, 'Banks in Bell Group Settlement', *The Australian* (online, 18 September 2013).

139 *Breen v Williams* (1996) 186 CLR 71.

140 See the discussion in Chapter 17 at Section 17.40.10 in relation to cases such as *Grimaldi v Chameleon Mining NL (No 2)* (2012) 200 FCR 296; *Wingecarribee Shire Council v Lehman Brothers Ltd (in liq)* (2012) 301 ALR 1; and *ABN AMRO Bank NV v Bathurst Regional Council* (2014) 224 FCR 1 as to the flexibility and experimentation undertaken by the intermediate courts in this area, particularly in the non-nominate categories. See Chapter 13 for discussion of the development of the fiduciary obligation and the categories more generally.

in a position of conflict. This is not enough to classify the duty itself as fiduciary. Debate continues as to whether the particular intention of the Court in *Breen v Williams* was to confine fiduciary obligations to proscriptive duties only.[141] The matter has not been considered at the highest appellate levels since the 1980s. In the Explanatory Memorandum which accompanied the Corporate Law Economic Reform Program Bill 1998 (Cth), s 181 was stated 'to mirror the fiduciary duty of a director to act in what they believe to be in the best interests of the corporation and for proper purposes'.[142] The more recent decisions of the intermediate courts suggest that the duty to act bona fide in the interests of the company requires positive steps. This could either indicate a departure from the position that this duty can be classified as fiduciary, or demonstrate that, when applied within corporate law, this duty has diverged from the mainstream of fiduciary law. A number of intermediate court decisions have recognised the duty as being fiduciary in nature,[143] which is the position taken now in the United Kingdom, but until the High Court clarifies or overrules the position established in *Breen v Williams,* this remains unsettled in Australia.[144]

12.15 The statutory duty

12.15.05 The coexistence of equity and statute

Section 185 of the *Corporations Act* preserves the operation of the general law duties, including the duty to act bona fide in the interests of the company and for proper purposes, alongside the legislative duties. This is important for a company whose directors have breached their duties, but where ASIC is not in a position to investigate or take action under the civil penalty provisions. ASIC is the only party who can seek a declaration of contravention, or the disqualification of a director, or a pecuniary penalty order.[145] This does not prevent a company from claiming that directors have breached the provisions of the Act; it only prevents them from seeking those penalties available exclusively to ASIC under the civil penalty provisions, such as disqualification or pecuniary penalty orders.

The company is entitled to seek a compensation order under s 1317H.[146] This is made clear in s 1317J, which notes that 'an application for a compensation order may be made whether or not a declaration of contravention has been made under section 1317E'. The company may seek compensation by intervening in an application by ASIC, under s 1317J(3), or in an action on its own behalf under s 1317J(2). Although the scope for compensation under s 1317H appears quite generous, seeming to mirror the equitable

141 See generally J Heydon, M Leeming and P Turner, *Meagher Gummow and Lehane's Equity* (LexisNexis Butterworths, 5th ed, 2015) [5–380]–[5–425]. See also *Breen v Williams* (1996) 186 CLR 71.

142 Explanatory Memorandum, Corporate Law Economic Reform Program Bill 1998 (Cth) [6.7].

143 See, eg, the decision of Flick J in *Motor Trades Association of Australia Superannuation Fund Pty Ltd v Rickus (No 3)* (2008) 69 ACSR 264 [52].

144 *Breen v Williams* (1996) 186 CLR 71.

145 *Corporations Act* ss 1317(1), (4).

146 Section 1317K provides a time limit for declarations of contravention, pecuniary penalty orders and compensation orders of six years after the contravention. In *OLI 1 Pty Ltd (in liq) v OLG 1 Pty Ltd (No 2)* (2022) 164 ACSR 171, this limited the compensation order made against a company which was a knowing participant in a breach of s 181 by a director.

remedy of account of profits in s 1317H(2), a company may still wish to bring an action for breach of the equitable duty and the statutory duty in the alternative. The company would not be allowed to be compensated twice, and so would need to elect their preferred remedial alternative.

12.15.10 The statutory duty: a brief history

A statutory version of the duty to act bona fide in the interests of the company and for proper purposes was first enacted in s 107 of the *Companies Act 1958* (Vic)[147] to this effect:

> A director shall at all times act honestly and use reasonable diligence in the discharge of the duties of his office.

The duty includes an element from the duty of care, skill and diligence, discussed in Chapter 11. In *Marchesi v Barnes* ('*Marchesi*'),[148] Gowans J suggested that the language used in the statutory enactment originated in *Re Smith & Fawcett Ltd*: '[t]hey must exercise their discretion bona fide in what they consider—not what a Court may consider—is in the interests of the company, and not for any collateral purpose'.[149] Gowans J stated that, under the language of that provision,

> to 'act honestly' refers to acting bona fide in the interests of the company in the performance of the functions attaching to the office of director. A breach of the obligation to act bona fide in the interests of the company involves a consciousness that what is being done is not in the interests of the company, and deliberate conduct in disregard of that knowledge.[150]

The duty in the *Corporations Act* was the result of the *Corporate Law Economic Reform Program Act 1999* (Cth) ('*CLERP Act*'). When the *Corporations Act* was introduced, the relevant section mirrored s 181(1) of the *CLERP Act* and this remains so in the current version of the legislation.

12.15.15 Section 181 of the *Corporations Act*

The duty to act bona fide in the interests of the company and for proper purposes under s 181 of the *Corporations Act* bears striking resemblance to the language discussed above in relation to the duty in equity. Section 181(1) states that:

A director or other officer of a corporation must exercise their powers and discharge their duties:

(a) in good faith in the best interests of the corporation; and
(b) for a proper purpose.

The only visible alterations in the section from the preceding discussion are the use of the phrase 'good faith' instead of bona fide, the insertion of the word 'best' in relation to

147 This was later repeated in *Uniform Companies Acts 1961* (Cth) s 124.
148 *Marchesi v Barnes* [1970] VR 434, 437–8.
149 *Re Smith & Fawcett Ltd* [1942] Ch 304, 306.
150 *Marchesi v Barnes* [1970] VR 434, 437.

the interests of the company, and the overt application to officers in addition to directors. In practice, none of these three alterations result in any difference in application of the duties. The drafting of this provision appears to confirm the discussion above that there are two separate limbs to this duty, as evidenced by the separate paragraphs for each limb.

The main point of contention between the general law and the statutory enactment has been whether the statutory drafting of s 181(1)(a) imports a more objective test than the general law position, due to the change from 'honestly' to 'good faith', and the removal of the words 'in what they believe to be', which had existed in the Bill within cl 181(1)(a).[151] However, case law suggests the tests at general law and in statute are the same.[152]

CLERP separated the civil and criminal consequences of a breach of the provision with a new s 184(1) dealing with the latter. It is an offence under s 184(1) if the directors are reckless or dishonest in the discharge of their duty under s 181(1).[153] Dishonest is defined in s 9 of the Act to mean 'dishonest according to the standards of ordinary people'.[154]

Section 187 provides that a director of a company that is a wholly owned subsidiary of a body corporate is taken to act in good faith in the best interests of the subsidiary if there is a provision within the subsidiary's constitution expressly authorising the director to act in the best interests of the holding company, and the director acts in good faith in the best interests of the holding company, and the subsidiary is not insolvent and does not become insolvent due to the director's act.

Although s 187 was modelled on s 131(2) of the *Companies Act 1993* (NZ), the latter provision is broader, applying to partly-owned subsidiaries. The Australian provision was drafted to apply to wholly owned subsidiaries, as a review of corporate groups was underway at the time.[155] The report from that review recommended the legislation be extended to partly owned subsidiaries if the minority members of the subsidiary passed an ordinary resolution approving the directors' actions.[156] However, that recommendation has not been implemented.

12.15.20 Corporate purpose and directors' duties: an international comparison with enlightened shareholder value

As identified at Section 10.10.10, Australia is generally considered to be a 'shareholder primacy' jurisdiction. This phrase has a narrow and broad interpretation. Narrowly, this can mean that the monitoring obligation of the shareholders, and the corollary

151 Corporate Law Economic Reform Program Bill 1998 (Cth) cl 5 and Explanatory Memorandum cl 6.82. See also *Australian Securities and Investments Commission v Sydney Investment House Equities Pty Ltd* (2008) 69 ACSR 1 [34].

152 *Australian Securities and Investments Commission v Maxwell* (2006) 59 ACSR 373 [109]; *Australian Securities and Investments Commission v Macdonald (No 11)* (2009) 230 FLR 1 [661]–[663].

153 The section previously read 'intentionally dishonest', but 'intentionally' was removed by the Treasury Laws Amendment (Strengthening Corporate and Financial Sector Penalties) Bill 2018, as the definition in s 9 of dishonest is wholly objective.

154 Based on the preference in the High Court in *Peters v The Queen* (1998) 192 CLR 493 for a single-limbed objective test: Explanatory Memorandum, Treasury Laws Amendment (Strengthening Corporate and Financial Sector Penalties) Bill 2018 (Cth) [1.171]–[1.178].

155 Companies and Securities Advisory Committee, *Corporate Groups: Final Report* (CAMAC, May 2000).

156 Ibid Recommendation 3.

accountability of management to the shareholders, prioritise profit maximisation for the shareholders as the primary corporate concern. Broadly, it can mean that the focus of the 'best interests of the company' should be on the shareholders, as a general body, which could encompass both current and future shareholders. Theories about corporate purpose, as discussed in Chapter 2, include recognition of corporate social responsibility, and its more recent iteration particularly in relation to corporate investing as 'environmental, social and governance' matters.[157]

The impact of these theories in relation to directors' duties, particularly the role of corporate purpose and the influence of stakeholders, was considered in the 2006 report of the Parliamentary Joint Committee on Corporations and Financial Services, *Corporate Responsibility: Managing Risk and Creating Value*.[158] The report found that the current duty 'permits directors to have regard to the interests of stakeholders other than shareholders'.[159] It recommended that no further alteration to the statutory duty was required. In support of this recommendation, the report gave examples of behaviour classified as responsible corporate behaviour already taking place under the current provisions, such as maintaining and improving company reputation or good will, and attracting investment from ethical investment funds.[160] However, as discussed at Section 2.45.05, the UK has taken a different approach to encourage directors to engage with wider stakeholder interests under their duty to act in good faith in the best interests of the company and for a proper purpose.

In the UK, corporate social responsibility arguments have been given some statutory recognition under the label of 'enlightened shareholder value' ('ESV').[161] Section 172 of the *Companies Act 2006* (UK) provides that:

> **(1)** A director of a company must act in a way that he considers, in good faith, would be most likely to promote the success of the company for the benefit of its members as a whole, and in doing so have regard (amongst other matters) to—
>
> **(a)** the likely consequences of any decision in the long term,
>
> **(b)** the interests of the company's employees,
>
> **(c)** the need to foster the company's business relationships with suppliers, customers and others,
>
> **(d)** the impact of the company's operations on the community and the environment,
>
> **(e)** the desirability of the company maintaining a reputation for high standards of business conduct, and
>
> **(f)** the need to act fairly between the members of the company.

157 See also S Glazebrook, 'Meeting the Challenge of Corporate Governance in the 21st Century' (2019) 34(2) *Australian Journal of Corporate Law* 106; J Baker, 'Australia is Burning: Aligning Corporate Social Responsibility and Community Expectations Following the Black Summer' (2021) 36 *Australian Journal of Corporate Law* 113.

158 Parliamentary Joint Committee on Corporations and Financial Services, Parliament of Australia, *Corporate Responsibility: Managing Risk and Creating Value* (Report, 21 June 2006).

159 Ibid Recommendation 1, [4.78].

160 Ibid Executive Summary, 'Directors' Duties'.

161 Stakeholder theory is discussed in Chapter 2 at Section 2.45.10.

The phrasing of the statute retains the interests of the company's shareholders as paramount but explicitly permits the directors to consider other interests. The inclusion of ESV in s 172 creates a duty to mirror the discretion alluded to by Lord Bowen in *Hutton v West Cork Railway Co* that 'there are to be no cakes and ale except such as are required for the benefit of the company'.[162] In Australia, it has been accepted that s 181(1) of the *Corporations Act* implicitly permits consideration of other interests, as long as they align with the 'interests of the company'. When s 172 was considered by the Corporations and Markets Advisory Committee in 2006, the provision was described as exemplifying the 'elaborated shareholder benefit approach' by providing a broader context for directors in fulfilling the primary duty to the company.[163]

The ESV approach was put forward by the UK Company Law Review Steering Group in 1999.[164] In line with the reform objectives of the review, the Group sought reforms to 'achieve competitiveness and efficient creation of wealth and other benefits for all participants in the enterprise', as well as 'minimise the negative impacts of corporate activity on participants and to maximise welfare more widely'.[165] In relation to directors and companies, the Group perceived ESV as a remedy to the exclusive focus on the short-term financial bottom line, in the erroneous belief that this equates to shareholder value, which will often be incompatible with the cultivation of co-operative relationships, which are likely to involve short-term costs but to bring greater benefits in the longer term.[166]

The Group sought comments on whether the present law requiring directors to have regard to the interests of the shareholders as a whole should be amended to insert 'additional declaratory clarification' that directors could take account of other external factors.[167]

The reform in s 172 has been subject to criticism. On the one hand, '[a]ll it requires is that the director should *think about*' interests beyond those of the members;[168] and, on the other hand, 'the vague nature of ESV principles and uncertainty surrounding the ability to recover substantial sums for breach of ESV principles make it unlikely that the statutory statement will represent any substantive advance on the common law position'.[169]

However, s 172's role as an incremental step towards a broader understanding of the 'interests of the company' was acknowledged by a member of the Group, who stated that:

162 *Hutton v West Cork Railway Co* (1883) 23 Ch D 654. See above at Sections 12.10.15 and 12.10.30. See also PL Davies, 'Enlightened Shareholder Value and the New Responsibilities of Directors' (WE Hearn Lecture, University of Melbourne, 4 October 2005) <https://law.unimelb.edu.au/__data/assets/pdf_file/0014/1710014/94-Enlightened_Shareholder_Value_and_the_New_Responsibilities_of_Directors1.pdf>.

163 Corporations and Markets Advisory Committee, *The Social Responsibility of Corporations* (Report, December 2006) 102–3.

164 United Kingdom Company Law Review Steering Group, *Modern Company Law for a Competitive Environment: The Strategic Framework* (Consultation Document, February 1999).

165 Ibid [5.1.8].

166 Ibid [5.1.12].

167 Ibid [5.1.50], Question 1.

168 LE Talbot, *Critical Company Law* (Routledge-Cavendish, 2008) 183.

169 R Williams, 'Enlightened Shareholder Value in UK Company Law' (2012) 35(1) *University of New South Wales Law Journal* 360, 362; A Keay, 'Moving Towards Stakeholderism? Constituency Statutes, Enlighted Shareholder Value, and More: Much Ado about Little?' (2011) 22(1) *European Business Law Review* 1.

> The interests of non-shareholder groups thus need to be considered by the directors, but, of course, in this shareholder-centred approach, only to the extent that the protection of those other interests promotes the interest of the shareholders.[170]

The incorporation of stakeholder interests has been considered within Australian corporate law reform on a number of occasions. The Senate Standing Committee on Legal and Constitutional Affairs concluded in 1989 that stakeholder interests were best covered by specific legislation dealing with industrial relations, trade practices, and consumer and environmental protection.[171] The Corporations and Markets Advisory Committee in 2006 considered s 172 and set forward a number of positions:

> On one view, adopting the directors' duties provision in the UK Act in the Corporations Act may be unnecessary if it is designed merely to codify the current common law, as reflected in s 181 of the Corporations Act. Alternatively, this provision could result in a radical change from traditional company law, if interpreted in the Australian context as some form of general departure from the current obligations of directors in s 181 to act in the best interests of the shareholders generally. Arguably, it could also entrench in legislation particular stakeholder and other criteria that, while possibly reflecting current concerns, may not necessarily be appropriate for corporate decision-making in the future.[172]

The first is a valid criticism on the drafting of s 172(1). The current Australian law permits consideration of creditors, employees and wider concerns while they are consistent with the interests of the company.[173] The second criticism does not seem well-founded in light of what has occurred in the years following the enactment of s 172. For example, in *R (on the Application of People & Planet) v HM Treasury*,[174] the Court refused an application for judicial review of a policy adopted by HM Treasury in relation to its investment in the Royal Bank of Scotland ('RBS'). The applicant argued that HM Treasury failed to properly consider under s 172 the environmental and human rights implications of the policy. The Court refused the application on the basis that, although social and environmental considerations may be taken into account by the directors of RBS in the context of s 172, HM Treasury seeking to impose its own policy on climate change or human rights would conflict with the duties of the RBS board under s 172(1).[175] The duty to the shareholders remained paramount, and the other stakeholder interests mentioned in s 172 needed only to be considered.

170 PL Davies, 'Enlightened Shareholder Value and the New Responsibilities of Directors' (WE Hearn Lecture, University of Melbourne, 4 October 2005) <https://law.unimelb.edu.au/__data/assets/pdf_file/0014/1710014/94-Enlightened_Shareholder_Value_and_the_New_Responsibilities_of_Directors1.pdf>.

171 Senate Standing Committee on Legal and Constitutional Affairs, Parliament of Australia, *Company Directors' Duties* (Report, November 1989) [2.13].

172 Corporations and Markets Advisory Committee, *The Social Responsibility of Corporations* (Report, December 2006) 106–7.

173 See Section 12.10.30.

174 *(on the Application of People & Planet) v HM Treasury* [2009] EWHC 3020.

175 Ibid [33]–[34].

The third criticism is hardly unique to corporate law, as any legislation will be reflective of the interests of the time when it is enacted and may require amendment in the future as society develops. The criticism that 'a non-exhaustive catalogue of interests to be taken into account serves little useful purpose for directors and affords them no guidance on how various interests are to be weighed, prioritised or reconciled'[176] is most valid, and remains a hurdle to similar provisions being implemented under Australian law.[177]

12.20 The duty not to fetter discretion

Another aspect of the duty to act bona fide in the best interests of the company and for proper purposes is that a director must retain their independent discretion in order to satisfy the duty. For example, agreeing to vote at board meetings according to the directions of another person would be an inappropriate fettering of discretion.[178] Although this duty can be traced back to cases in the 1800s,[179] it has been judicially lamented that there are not many cases expressing the principle.[180] The duty prohibits directors from inappropriately binding the future exercise of their discretionary powers, or from delegating them, except as permitted by the constitution or the *Corporations Act*. The question as to when it may be appropriate to bind a future exercise of discretion was considered by the High Court in *Thorby v Goldberg*, although primarily through the lens of contract law.[181] A company, Medical-Dental Building Pty Ltd, was to be formed by a number of shareholders, described as the 'O Group', some of whom would go on to be the initial directors, in order to develop a block of land into a multi-storey building of professional suites, shops and offices. The O Group entered into a contract with the plaintiffs, who were described in the contract as the 'G Group', to inject capital into the project, in exchange for a number of future conditions, including occupancy of part of the new building. The contract was later challenged on the grounds of illegality, due to two clauses which required the O Group to cause a meeting of the directors to allot shares to the G Group (which presupposed an alteration to the company's articles had occurred) and then, at that meeting, for three directors to resign and two members of the G Group to be appointed as directors. There was also a variety of other contractual arguments raised, but the argument as to illegality was that as every exercise of the directors'

176 Corporations and Markets Advisory Committee, *The Social Responsibility of Corporations* (Report, December 2006) 111. A similar conclusion was reached by the Parliamentary Joint Committee on Corporations Financial Services, Parliament of Australia, *Corporate Responsibility: Managing Risk and Creating Value* (Report, 21 June 2006).

177 For further discussion, see also R Grantham, 'People, Planet and Profits: Re-Purposing the Company' (2021) 38(4) *Company and Securities Law Journal* 250; J Dreosti, B De Silva and K Walsh, 'A Civil Law Solution to the Social Licence to Operate and Directors' Duties Conundrum in Australia' (2021) 38(6) *Company and Securities Law Journal* 404; V Brand and R Teele Langford, '"Doing the Job That's Required"?: Social Licence to Operate and Directors' Duties' (2022) 44(1) *Sydney Law Review* 111.

178 *Kregor v Hollins* (1913) 109 LT 225; *Boulting v Association of Cinematograph, Television and Allied Technicians* [1963] 2 QB 606.

179 *Harris v North Devon Railway Co* (1855) 20 Beav 284.

180 *Davidson v Smith* (1989) 15 ACLR 732, 734 (Ipp J).

181 *Thorby v Goldberg* (1964) 112 CLR 597.

discretionary powers is required to be in good faith for the benefit of the company as a whole, an agreement that the directors purport to fetter their discretions in advance is contrary to the policy of the law and void.[182]

Kitto J continued:

> There are many kinds of transactions in which the proper time for the exercise of the directors' discretion is the time of the negotiation of a contract, and not the time at which the contract is to be performed. A sale of land is a familiar example. Where all the members of a company desire to enter as a group into a transaction such as that in the present case, the transaction being one which requires action by the board of directors for its effectuation, it seems to me that the proper time for the directors to decide whether their proposed action would in the interests of the company as a whole is the time when the transaction is being entered into, and not the time when their action under it is required. If at the former time they are bona fide of the opinion that it is in the interests of the company that the transaction should be entered into and carried into effect, I see no reason in law why they should not bind themselves to do whatever under the transaction is to be done by the board. In my opinion the defendants' contention that the agreement is void for illegality should be rejected.[183]

As such, as long as the directors considered at the appropriate time—which, in that case, was the time of entering into the contract—that the undertakings were bona fide in the best interests of the company and for proper purposes, this future fettering of their discretions would not be inappropriate. The context of the undertakings is also relevant. *Thorby* involved a limited arrangement, where the directors had given consideration as to whether it was in the best interests of the company prior to entry into the transaction. By contrast, a more expansive fettering of discretion, where directors were required to limit their discretion as to 'all activities of the company' and 'control of the company', remitting another party to be 'the sole decisions maker for all business associated with the company', without any qualification or proviso, consequently prevented directors from giving consideration to, or exercising their discretion, in the interest of the company.[184]

Nominee directors, who are appointed by a special interest group such as a class of shareholders, a major creditor or the company's employees, may be most at risk under this duty.[185] These directors must take particular care in relation to how they represent the interests of their appointor group, while performing their role as a director, in order not to inappropriately fetter their discretion.

182 Ibid 605, 601 (Kitto J, McTiernan J concurring), 616 (Kitto J, Windeyer J), 616 (Menzies J), 617–18 (Menzies J, Owen J concurring).

183 Ibid 605–6.

184 *Australian Securities and Investments Commission v Macro Realty Developments Pty Ltd* (2016) 111 ACSR 638 [19]–[20].

185 See, eg, *Scottish Co-operative Wholesale Society Ltd v Meyer* [1959] AC 324.

12.25 Summary

This chapter is the first of two chapters addressing the duties of loyalty and good faith. It focuses on the duty to act bona fide in the interests of the company and for proper purposes, and its counterpart under s 181(1) of the *Corporations Act*. We traced the development of the duty from its equitable roots, in doctrines relating to the exercise of a power bona fide for the reason for which it was granted, to considerations of the structure of the duty under the general law and in s 181(1), before settling into its current form with two limbs, both of which must be satisfied for the director to be compliant.

The first limb—the duty to act bona fide in the interests of the company—contains two elements. The first, the bona fides of the director, is accepted as a subjective test, considering the behaviour of the director in question. Some decisions have included an objective understanding of the circumstances in which the director exercised their power; it is better to consider objective considerations in the second limb of the duty. The second element—the interests of the company—is traditionally equated with the interests of the members collectively. This raises significant difficulties for directors, faced with complex, interlocking corporate groups, where the directors may also validly consider the benefit to the group. Other stakeholders may be considered, but only as long as their interests align with the interests of the company. This applies to companies approaching insolvency, where the directors must have regard to the interests of the creditors.

The second limb of the duty—the requirement to exercise their powers and discharge their duties for a proper purpose—requires consideration of two questions: What is the objective purpose for which the power was granted? What is the purpose for which the power was actually exercised? If the power is exercised for an improper purpose, then the duty will have been breached. Where there is more than one purpose, the test will be whether or not the improper purpose was a significant contributing cause to the exercise of the power, and, but for its presence, the power would not have been exercised.

This chapter then considered the potential for law reform, discussing the recognition within the *Companies Act 2006* (UK) of ESV in s 172. We agreed that the current s 172 is validly criticised for the lack of utility in providing that directors 'have regard to' other stakeholder considerations when they must retain as their primary consideration the benefit to the members as a whole.

This chapter concluded with the duty not to fetter discretion, which requires directors to retain their independence at the time of decision-making in order to comply with the duty to act bona fide in the interests of the company and for proper purposes.

Chapter 13 addresses the duties of loyalty and good faith through the standard of conduct expected from directors, such as those dealing with conflicts of interest, including the fiduciary duty of directors and senior employees, the corresponding duties in ss 182–3 of the *Corporations Act*, and the other *Corporations Act* duties relating to disclosure of conflicts.

CHAPTER

13

CONFLICTS OF INTEREST

13.05 Introduction

Directors' duties can be classified into two themes: duties in relation to care and skill, and duties in relation to loyalty and good faith. Chapter 10 provided an overview of the duties as a whole, and Chapter 11 provided the history and current law for those duties which are related to care and skill. Chapter 12 was the first of two chapters addressing the duties of loyalty and good faith and discussed the duty to act bona fide in the interests of the company and for proper purposes, and the duty not to fetter discretions. This chapter deals with the standard of conduct expected from directors by the fiduciary obligation, the duties in the *Corporations Act* in ss 182–3, and the duties on disclosure of material personal interest of directors in ss 191–5 and ch 2E. All of these duties raise the issue of conflict of interests, which informs the title of this chapter.

First, this chapter canvasses the history of the fiduciary obligation as it applies to the director–company relationship. The fiduciary obligation includes two duties: a duty of loyalty and a duty to account for benefits gained—more informally termed the 'no conflict' and 'no profit' rules. This chapter then discusses examples of the 'no conflict' and 'no profit' rules from case law, and the modern exceptions to this general principle on the basis of commercial realities, such as the business opportunity rule. It then considers ss 182–3 of the *Corporations Act* that deal with a director's misuse of information or position to gain an advantage for themselves or others, or to cause detriment to the company. While there is a clear relationship between these sections and the 'no profit' rule, they have developed differently since enactment as legislative provisions.

This chapter then considers the requirements for directors to disclose their material personal interests under ss 191–5 of the *Corporations Act*, and the inconsistent treatment of the disclosure requirements with the ability of a fiduciary to seek the fully informed consent of the company in general meeting. Finally, this chapter considers the protection afforded to members of a public company under ch 2E of the *Corporations Act* for related party transactions.

13.10 The fiduciary obligation[1]

The fiduciary obligation involves two duties: a duty of loyalty and a duty to account for benefits gained. These are more informally termed the 'no conflict' and 'no profit'

1 The authors acknowledge that an earlier version of material contained in this chapter appeared in Beth Nosworthy, 'Finding the Fiduciary: Recognition of the Director-Shareholder Relationship in Closely Held Companies' (PhD Thesis, The University of Adelaide, 2013) http://hdl.handle .net/2440/80723.

rules.[2] The 'no conflict' rule is designed to prevent a director 'enter[ing] into engagements in which [they have], or can have, a personal interest conflicting, or which possibly may conflict, with the interests of those whom [they are] bound to protect'.[3] The 'no profit' rule prevents a director from taking 'any secret remuneration or any financial benefit not authorised by the law, or by his contract, or by the trust deed under which he acts, as the case may be',[4] but is not so broad as to imply that directors are not entitled to be paid for their work.

Under the 'no conflict' rule, a director, officer or senior company employee must not permit themselves to be placed in a position where their duty to the company is in conflict with a duty to any other (a conflict of duty and duty), or with their own interests (a conflict of duty and interest). Unlike those provisions that were the subject of such criticism in the Royal Commission into Misconduct in the Banking, Superannuation and Financial Services Industry, (as discussed below), the fiduciary obligation does not attempt to manage conflicts—it prohibits the fiduciary from permitting a conflict to arise. Further, under the 'no profit' rule, a director, officer or senior company employee may not secretly profit from their position within the company. A person who profits from their position is likely to be in a position of conflict, although the two rules do operate independently. The fiduciary must account for any profit obtained to the company and may be subject to other equitable remedies for permitting themselves to be in a position of conflict.

The rationale underlying the strict application of the rule against conflicts is that the potential for a fiduciary to engage in self-interested behaviour at the expense of their beneficiary is so great it must be prohibited.

In the Final Report of the Royal Commission into Misconduct in the Banking, Superannuation and Financial Services Industry, conflicts were a substantial component of the discussion and the recommended reforms. When discussing the conflicts provisions of various statutory instruments, which attempt to provide rules to manage such conflicts rather than banning them outright, Justice Hayne commented:

> [E]xperience shows that conflicts between duty and interest can seldom be managed; self-interest will almost always trump duty.[5]

The recommendations of the Final Report state that:

> Where possible, conflicts of interest and conflicts between duty and interest should be removed. There must be recognition that conflicts of interest and conflicts between duty and interest should be eliminated rather than 'managed'.[6]

As we will see shortly, elements of the fiduciary obligation are reflected in provisions in the *Corporations Act*. However, unlike other duties—such as the duty of care, skill and diligence which is equivalent in the common law, equity and legislation—significant

2 See, eg, *Moss v Moss (No 2)* (1900) 21 LR (NSW) Eq 253; *Chan v Zacharia* (1984) 154 CLR 178.
3 *Aberdeen Railway Co v Blaikie Brothers* (1854) 1 Macq 461, 471.
4 *Dale v Inland Revenue Commissioners* [1954] AC 11, 27.
5 *Royal Commission into Misconduct in the Banking, Superannuation and Financial Services Industry* (Final Report, 4 February 2019) 3 ('the Hayne Report').
6 Ibid 45.

differences remain in the application of the fiduciary obligation and the legislative provisions. Section 185 of the *Corporations Act* confirms that the provisions apply 'in addition to, and not in derogation' of the duties which exist in the general law, and a detailed analysis of the fiduciary obligation remains fundamental to directors' duties in Australian corporate law.

13.10.05 Introduction: a brief history of equity and the fiduciary obligation

Chapter 12 mentioned the relationship between equity and fiduciary obligations when considering the source of the underlying law for the duty to act bona fide in the interests of the company and for proper purposes. In order to discuss the fiduciary obligation as it applies to directors, we must take a short detour through history to the genesis of equity. This is necessarily a brief treatment of the topic, and more detailed information should be sought from specialist texts on the field.[7]

The fiduciary obligation is a principle of 'equity', which is the title used to describe the body of law that was first administered in England by the Court of Chancery. The Court of Chancery evolved in the thirteenth century in response to perceived flaws with the common law system, which centred on the strict 'forms of action' required for a party to bring a dispute to court. For people unable to use one of those forms of action, or those who were disappointed or frustrated by the outcome available in the common law, an avenue of relief was available through petitioning the King for justice. After a time, these petitions came to be addressed to the Chancellor as head of the Chancery, the King's secretariat and the office responsible for issuing royal writs. Initially, when dealing with these applications, the Chancellor was not performing a judicial function, but was acting with executive authority on behalf of the King. It was not until some time later that the title the Court of Chancery came into use.[8] By the seventeenth century, the Chancellors had established a body of equitable principles, built on the individual opinions of the Chancellor at the time, but developing into broader theories of law based on fairness and conscience. Some of these principles survive as 'equitable maxims'. Further, equity developed legal doctrines relating to trusts, unconscionable transactions, and fiduciaries, along with a substantial body of law relating to remedies. Much later, due to frustrations arising from the administration of the common law and equity through two separate court systems, the enactment of the *Judicature Act 1873*[9] brought the administration of these two bodies of law under the control of the one court, although the principles of law remained distinct. Eventually, a similar judicature system was introduced in each state jurisdiction in Australia.

7 See further for equity: PG Turner, JD Heydon and MJ Leeming, *Meagher, Gummow and Lehane's Equity: Doctrines and Remedies* (Butterworths LexisNexis, 5th ed, 2014); S Worthington, *Equity* (Oxford University Press, 2nd ed, 2006); for fiduciary obligations: PD Finn, *Fiduciary Obligations* (Law Book, 1977); LI Rotman, *Fiduciary Law* (Thomson Carswell, 2005); M Conaglen, *Fiduciary Loyalty* (Hart, 2010).

8 According to S Chesterman, 'Beyond Fusion Fallacy: The Transformation of Equity and Derrida's "The Force of the Law"' (1997) 24(3) *Journal of Law and Society* 350, 352, the first mention was in the *Statute of 1340*.

9 *Judicature Act 1873* 36 & 37 Vict, c 66.

The term 'fiduciary' is a relative newcomer in equity—it only achieved recognition in the law reports towards the middle of the nineteenth century. Relationships now referred to as 'fiduciary' were previously termed matters of 'confidence' or 'trust'. However, as equity developed rules and a technical vocabulary, the meaning of the word 'trust' formalised and it became inaccurate to apply it too broadly.[10] Use of words such as 'confidence' also fell out of favour. The word 'fiduciary' has its etymological origins in the Latin noun *fiducia*, meaning confidence, trust or reliance, and the adjective *fiduciarius*, something entrusted or given in trust, both of which are derived from the verb *fido*, meaning 'to trust'.[11] Although the actual word 'fiduciary' can be found as early as 1717,[12] it failed to find favour with the judiciary at that time. Although the label was infrequently applied by the courts, it was adopted in many of the published works on equity available from the 1820s.

Before moving to consider the modern fiduciary obligation and its application to directors, officers and senior company employees, it is necessary to briefly consider its development. Without that context, it can appear to be a restrictive, uncommercial doctrine, ill-suited to the corporate world. From its earliest applications, the key feature of the fiduciary obligation—the prevention of the fiduciary from self-interested dealing when at the expense of their beneficiary—is evident, and it clearly has a role to play where appropriate in curtailing such behaviour in commercial undertakings.

Keech v Sandford[13] is recognised as being 'the progenitor of the modern fiduciary concept'.[14] *Keech* concerned a trust established in favour of an infant over the lease of rights to a market in the town of Romford. Prior to the expiration of the lease, the trustee sought to renew the lease in favour of the infant, but the lessor declined. When the lease expired, the lessor offered the lease to the trustee personally, which the trustee accepted. When the infant came of age, he brought an action against the trustee for an assignment of the lease to himself, and an account of any profits obtained under the lease. Lord Chancellor King found that the trustee held the lease for the infant, and that any profits must be disgorged. In his brief judgment, Lord Chancellor King said:

> This may seem hard, that the trustee is the only person of all mankind [sic] who might not have the lease: but it is very proper that rule should be strictly pursued, and not in the least relaxed; for it is obvious what would be the consequence of letting trustees have the lease, on refusal to renew to the *cestui que* use.[15]

This quote highlights the strict nature of fiduciary obligations: the court looks not only to actual harm to the beneficiary's interests, but also to the potential harm to those interests.

10 PD Finn, *Fiduciary Obligations* (Law Book, 1977) 1; LS Sealy, 'Fiduciary Relationships' (1962) 20(1) *Cambridge Law Journal* 69, 70.

11 LI Rotman, *Fiduciary Law* (Thomson Carswell, 2005) 81.

12 *Bishop of Winchester v Knight* (1717) 1 PWms 406, 407 (Cowper LC).

13 *Keech v Sandford* (1726) Sel Cas Ch 61 ('*Keech*').

14 LI Rotman, *Fiduciary Law* (Thomson Carswell, 2005) 58, although Rotman then proceeds to discuss *Walley v Walley* (1687) 1 Vern 484 as potentially the first example of the application of the fiduciary principle.

15 *Keech v Sanford* (1726) Sel Cas Ch 61. This extract, in fact, amounts to the majority of the judgment. Only the first and final sentences have been excluded.

There was no suggestion of fraudulent activity in *Keech*, but it was considered 'proper' that the rule against conflicts be strict in its application. This theme was continued in the case law which followed, including one case where it was described as 'dangerous' to permit a trustee to deal with shares which had previously been part of the estate over which he was an executor.[16] The courts initially referred to the potential evidentiary difficulties of establishing whether a fiduciary had 'made advantage' as motivation for the strict application of the fiduciary obligation.[17] But as Rotman points out, the real rationale underlying the strict application of the rule against conflicts is that the potential for fiduciaries' self-interested behaviour at the expense of their beneficiary is so great that it must be prohibited.[18] Rotman compares the strict application of the conflicts rule to taking away the fruit of temptation, rather than simply moving it to a higher shelf,[19] which would be the case if the rule required *mala fides* or the existence of actual harm.

13.10.10 The origin of the 'no conflict' rule

The 'no conflict' rule was clearly described in *Aberdeen Railway Co v Blaikie Brothers*,[20] which considered the behaviour of a company director. Blaikie Bros contracted with the Aberdeen Railway Co to supply iron chairs for the railways. When the contract was partially complete, the Railway Co refused to accept or pay for the remaining chairs. Blaikie Bros sought a decree that the Railway Co was obliged to complete the contract or to pay damages. In response, the Railway Co sought to have the contract set aside on the basis that a director of the Railway Co, Thomas Blaikie, was the managing partner of Blaikie Bros, and as such could not contract with Blaikie Bros on behalf of the Railway Co due to this interest. Lord Cranworth LC discussed whether the law precluded a director from dealing on behalf of a company with themselves, or with another firm in which they hold an interest:

> The Directors are a body to whom is delegated the duty of managing the general affairs of the Company.
>
> A corporate body can only act by agents, and it is of course the duty of those agents so to act as best to promote the interests of the corporation whose affairs they are conducting. Such agents have duties to discharge of a fiduciary nature towards their principal. *And it is a rule of universal application, that no one, having such duties to discharge, shall be allowed to enter into engagements in which he has, or can have, a personal interest conflicting, or which possibly may conflict, with the interests of those whom he is bound to protect.*
>
> So strictly is this principle adhered to, that no question is allowed to be raised as to the fairness or unfairness of a contract so entered into.[21]

16 *Blewett v Millett* (1774) 7 Bro PC 367, 373.

17 *Ex parte Lacey* (1802) Ves Jun 625, 627; *Re James* (1803) 8 Ves Jun 337, 345.

18 LI Rotman, *Fiduciary Law* (Thomson Carswell, 2005) 63–4.

19 Ibid 64. The 'fruit of temptation' analogy has been used by a number of authors, including Conaglen, who cites *Harris v Digital Pulse Pty Ltd* (2003) 56 NSWLR 298, 406–7 as authority: M Conaglen, 'The Nature and Function of Fiduciary Loyalty' (2005) 121(3) *Law Quarterly Review* 452, 463.

20 *Aberdeen Railway Co v Blaikie Brothers* (1854) 1 Macq 461.

21 Ibid 471 (emphasis added).

As this extract makes clear, the 'no conflict' rule is concerned with any possibility of conflict which may arise from a director's personal interests, and the rule is strictly applied against directors. Mr Blaikie, as a director of the Railway Co, was obliged to make the best bargain possible for the company in relation to the purchase of the chairs, but, as a member of the partnership Blaikie Bros, would also be seeking the best price to be obtained for selling the chairs. This was a clear conflict, and consequently Railway Co succeeded, as the contract was considered voidable at the company's option. We will return to the question of whether a director is prevented from engaging in any business opportunities which come to their attention by virtue of their position later, as well as the issue of the ratification by the members who can provide fully informed consent.[22]

13.10.15 The origin of the 'no profit' rule

Expression of the 'no profit' rule took place after the pronouncement in *Keech*, towards the latter half of the nineteenth century. It is a hard rule to analyse on its own, as most of the cases where a profit was made in breach of fiduciary obligations involved the breach of the 'no conflict' rule.[23] As such, judicial discussion of the 'no profit' rule is often either couched in terms of, or dealt with as a sub-rule of, the 'no conflict' rule. For example, in *Boardman v Phipps*, Lord Upjohn stated that it was a 'fundamental rule of equity that a person in a fiduciary capacity must not make a profit out of [their] trust which is part of the wider rule that a trustee must not place [themselves] in a position' of conflict.[24]

However, it was settled that the concept of 'no profit' is not so broad as to imply that the fiduciary is not entitled to be paid for his or her work. It was put best by Lord Normand in *Dale v Inland Revenue Commissioners*:

> it is not that reward for services is repugnant to the fiduciary duty, but that he [sic] who has the duty shall not take any secret remuneration or any financial benefit not authorised by the law, or by his contract, or by the trust deed under which he acts, as the case may be.[25]

13.10.20 The current position in Australia

Both the 'no profit' and 'no conflict' rules were adopted into Australian jurisdictions as settled principles applicable to those occupying a 'fiduciary position'[26] and the High Court ultimately clarified that the two rules, 'while overlapping, are distinct'.[27] The late 1800s and early 1900s saw equity dealing with cases associated with public company floats,[28] enabling further refinement of the fiduciary principle through cases such as *Gluckstein v*

22 See Section 13.10.30.

23 M Conaglen, 'The Nature and Function of Fiduciary Loyalty' (2005) 121(3) *Law Quarterly Review* 452, 465–6.

24 *Boardman v Phipps* [1967] 2 AC 46, 123.

25 *Dale v Inland Revenue Commissioners* [1954] AC 11, 27.

26 *Moss v Moss (No 2)* (1900) 21 LR (NSW) Eq 253, 258 (Simpson CJ in Equity).

27 *Chan v Zacharia* (1984) 154 CLR 178, 199.

28 LS Sealy, 'Fiduciary Obligations, Forty Years On' (1995) 9(1) *Journal of Contract Law* 37, 40–2.

Barnes,[29] *Re Coomber*[30] and *Nocton v Lord Ashburton*.[31] These cases began to address issues such as whether members' fully informed consent could counter a claim of breach[32] and the remedies available for a breach of the fiduciary obligation.[33]

The current 'accepted mainstream' of the fiduciary obligation revolves around the duties of good faith imposed to exact standards of good conduct from persons unable to deal with each other at an arms-length due to their relationship.[34] Unfortunately, there is no universally accepted definition of a relationship where one party will owe fiduciary obligations to the other. Instead, the courts rely on a list of relationships where it is presumed there is a fiduciary obligation, which can be rebutted by sufficient contrary intention (usually in the form of an explicit contractual term), known as the 'nominate categories'.

13.10.25 Who owes fiduciary obligations: the nominate categories

Any director, company secretary, officer or other senior management employee will be presumed to owe fiduciary obligations, either through the nominate categories or via an ad hoc analogy to one of those nominate categories, which will both be discussed next. As such, any reference to 'a director' in the discussion which follows within this chapter should be read as including the other categories listed here.

Australian courts have firmly established that certain nominate categories of relationships are fiduciary in nature. Demonstrating that a relationship falls within one of the nominate categories will be sufficient to attach a presumption of fiduciary obligations. Since the decision of *Hospital Products Ltd v United States Surgical Corporation*,[35] the following non-exhaustive list of relationships are recognised as founding a presumption of fiduciary obligations: trustee–beneficiary, solicitor–client, director–company, promoter–company, agent–principal, partner–partner, and employee–employer.[36] Parties to relationships which are considered to be analogous to those contained within the list, or new relationships entirely, can still include fiduciary obligations on an ad hoc basis, such as financial adviser-client.

There are a number of general bases for the nominate categories. A favoured judicial description comes from Mason J's judgment in *Hospital Products*:

29 *Gluckstein v Barnes* [1900] AC 240.
30 *Coomber v Coomber* [1911] 1 Ch 723.
31 *Nocton v Lord Ashburton* [1914] AC 932.
32 See Section 13.10.30 below.
33 With the exception of third-party liability under *Barnes v Addy* (1874) LR 9 Ch App 244, which is discussed in Chapter 12 at Section 12.10.45; see Chapter 10 at Section 10.35.05 for further information on remedies.
34 PD Finn, *Fiduciary Obligations* (Law Book, 1977) 78.
35 *Hospital Products Ltd v United States Surgical Corporation* (1984) 156 CLR 41 ('*Hospital Products*').
36 Ibid 68 (Gibbs J), 96 (Mason J). 'Employee–employer' does on occasion cause controversy, as not all employees will be sufficiently senior to attract the interest of equity. However, the majority of commentators and the High Court in both *Hospital Products Ltd v United States Surgical Corporation* (1984) 156 CLR 41 and *John Alexander's Clubs Pty Ltd v White City Tennis Club Ltd* (2010) 241 CLR 1 included that relationship on the status-based list. More controversial categories of relationship are the priest–penitent, doctor–patient, Crown–Indigenous person, and parent–child relationships, which have been found to be the basis for fiduciary obligations in only limited cases.

> the fiduciary undertakes or agrees to act for or on behalf of or in the interest of another person in the exercise of a power or discretion which will affect the interests of that other person in a legal or practical sense ... The relationship between the parties is therefore one which gives the fiduciary a special opportunity to exercise the power or discretion to the detriment of that other person who is accordingly vulnerable to abuse by the fiduciary of his position.[37]

This promotes two bases for the fiduciary obligation: one of 'undertaking' or 'voluntary assumption' by the fiduciary, and the other of the vulnerability of the beneficiary.

Other judicial pronouncements have included the basis of trust and confidence, such as 'where the facts show the relationship was based on mutual confidence',[38] or '[t]he [fiduciary] duty arises when a relationship or confidence exists between the parties'.[39] These bases are subject to criticism, but can be useful in understanding why the fiduciary obligation exists, why it is applied to directors and others, and what kind of behaviour it is trying to control. There are clear analogies between these bases and the themes underpinning the concept of corporate governance, as discussed in Chapter 10, and why it targets those in authority within companies. Finn considers that equity's supervision of directors is rationalised by their autonomy: '[t]he freedom which they enjoy in their decision-making, the lack of direct control by their respective beneficiaries, has attracted equity's supervision'.[40]

The most pertinent nominate categories for our discussion are director–company, promoter–company, agent–principal, and employee–employer.[41] Any person formally appointed to the role of director of a company (a director de jure) will be caught by the first category,[42] which would extend to de facto and shadow directors, under the maxim 'equity looks to substance rather than form'.[43] Promoter–company will extend the reach of the fiduciary obligation to the time when a company is not yet registered.[44] Agent–principal will catch those purporting or appointed to act as an agent for the company, which would include the majority of officers and some senior management, dependent on their particular roles.[45] The category of employee–employer will see senior employees, such as officers and others involved in the management of the company (for instance, executive directors) owe fiduciary obligations to the company.[46]

37 *Hospital Products Ltd v United States Surgical Corporation* (1984) 156 CLR 41, 96–7.

38 *Fraser Edmiston Pty Ltd v AGT (Qld) Pty Ltd* [1988] 2 Qd R 1, 11.

39 *Daly v Sydney Stock Exchange Ltd* (1986) 160 CLR 371, 377.

40 PD Finn, *Fiduciary Obligations* (Law Book, 1977) 3.

41 As will be discussed in Chapter 15, receivers (court-appointed or private) may also owe fiduciary obligations, as may liquidators (Chapter 16), stockbrokers (Chapter 17) and financial advisers (Chapter 18).

42 See, eg, *Furs Ltd v Tomkies* (1936) 54 CLR 583.

43 *Digital Pulse Pty Ltd v Harris* (2002) 166 FLR 421, 425–6. This point of law was not overturned, although the outcome at first instance was reversed on appeal: *Harris v Digital Pulse Pty Ltd* (2003) 56 NSWLR 298.

44 *Tracy v Mandalay Pty Ltd* (1953) 88 CLR 215. Promoters are also discussed in Chapter 6.

45 *Walden Properties Ltd v Beaver Properties Pty Ltd* [1973] 2 NSWLR 815, 835–6. Agency, and the express and implied authority of agents, are also discussed in Chapter 6.

46 *Green and Clara Pty Ltd v Bestobell Industries Pty Ltd* [1982] WAR 1; *Timber Engineering Co Pty Ltd v Anderson* [1980] 2 NSWLR 488; *Directed Electronics OE Pty Ltd v OE Solutions Pty Ltd (No 8)* [2022] FCA 1404.

Some of these relationships are governed by the law of contract, and any fiduciary obligations must accommodate the terms of that contract.[47] One consequence of this is a conservative approach taken by Australian courts, reflecting a concern that areas of contract and tort are not encroached by this obligation. For example, employment contracts include an implied duty of loyalty, which is not the same as the fiduciary obligation, in addition to contractual duties of good faith or confidentiality.[48] The more senior the employee and the higher the standard of loyalty expected from them, the more relevant this is to determining whether or not the employee owes a fiduciary obligation.[49] For example, in *Blackmagic Design v Overliese*,[50] Mr Overliese was a computer engineer and the Director of Hardware Engineering. Overliese was held to owe fiduciary obligations to Blackmagic, the employer. The facts demonstrating seniority included that Overliese had built up and managed a large team of hardware engineers, had significant responsibilities in relation to defining product specifications, had oversight of new product development alongside the CEO and Product Managers, and held other management responsibilities, including the ability to hire and fire staff.[51]

Due to the various nominate categories applying to a range of people in positions of authority within companies, a starting position will be that any director, company secretary, officer or other senior management employee will be presumed to owe fiduciary obligations.

13.10.30 Who is the beneficiary of the fiduciary obligation?

Directors owe fiduciary obligations. The question then becomes: who is the beneficiary of that obligation?[52]

Directors owe their obligations, including the fiduciary obligation, to the company, rather than to the members. This has been conventional wisdom both academically and in case law for more than a century.[53] However, in his 1977 book on fiduciary obligations, Finn considered this position 'remarkable',[54] suggesting that a more appropriate beneficiary might be the members. Without at least one member, there can be no company, as there is no capital investment to employ for the company's use at the direction of the directors. On that view, the members are entitled to the protected position as the beneficiary of directors' fiduciary obligations, rather than the company.

47 *John Alexander's Clubs Pty Ltd v White City Tennis Club Ltd* (2010) 241 CLR 1, 35–6 citing *Hospital Products Ltd v United States Surgical Corporation* (1984) 156 CLR 41, 97.

48 *Blackmagic Design Pty Ltd v Overliese* (2011) 191 FCR 1.

49 *Smart EV Solutions Pty Ltd v Guy* [2023] FCA 1580; *Woolworths Ltd v Olson* (2004) 184 FLR 121 [212]; *Flanagan Sailmakers v Walker* [2002] NSWSC 1125 [44]–[49].

50 *Blackmagic Design Pty Ltd v Overliese* (2011) 191 FCR 1.

51 Ibid [27].

52 Confusingly, some texts adopt the language of agent–principal and describe this person as the principal.

53 *Carpenter v Danforth*, 52 Barb 582 (NY, 1868) is cited by a Canadian academic as one of the earliest examples (Leonard I Rotman, *Fiduciary Law* (Thomson Carswell, 2005) 412) but the principle is clear in *Aberdeen Railway Co v Blaikie Brothers* (1854) 1 Macq 461. It can certainly be said to exist since the advent of separate legal personality in *Salomon v Salomon & Co Ltd* [1897] AC 22, and has only been strengthened by *Percival v Wright* [1902] 2 Ch 421.

54 PD Finn, *Fiduciary Obligations* (Law Book, 1977) 11.

Around that time, similar arguments were made in relation to other directors' duties and corporate governance. Scholarly works in law and economics, which gained prominence in the 1960s,[55] refer to the relationship between directors and members (as the ultimate recipients of the company's wealth according to this theoretical approach), more than the relationship between directors and companies. These works are concerned with the behaviour of the actors, not the legal forms.[56] From an economist's perspective, the company is a legal fiction interposed between the directors and the real stakeholders who are the collective body of members.[57] But even Berle and Means' classic formulation of the separation of ownership and control is predicated on an assumption that '[a]ny fair statement of the law would have to be based on the theory that the fiduciary duties of directors were limited to the corporation'.[58] Members do not own the assets of the company; they own a 'bundle of rights associated with the corporate enterprise'.[59] However, Rotman notes that, given the various corporate forms which exist and the various parties which hold an interest in them at different times, the proposition that directors owe their fiduciary obligations to 'the company' only narrows slightly the question of 'who' is the beneficiary of the obligation.[60]

The case of *Percival v Wright*[61] is often cited as the commencement of the judicial position that directors owe their fiduciary obligations to the company, and not to individual shareholders. In that case, shareholders of an unlisted, closely-held company contacted the company secretary seeking to sell the shares they held at a price previously determined by an independent valuer. The chair and two directors offered to purchase the shares, and the shareholders accepted. They subsequently discovered that the board had been approached by a potential purchaser of the entire company, and that the price offered for the company during the negotiation prior to and at the time of the share purchase was considerably higher than what was paid by the directors for the members' shares. The shareholders argued that the transfers should be set aside because the directors held a fiduciary position as trustees for the individual shareholders because of

55 See, eg, work involving the 'prisoner dilemma' or 'free rider' problems: R Posner, 'An Economic Approach to the Law' (1975) 53(4) *Texas Law Review* 757 discusses this ascendancy. See generally R Posner, *Economic Analysis of Law* (Aspen, 7th ed, 2007); and for its application to corporate law FH Easterbrook and Daniel R Fischel, *The Economic Structure of Corporate Law* (Harvard University Press, 1991).

56 See, eg, HG Manne, 'Our Two Corporation Systems: Law and Economics' (1967) 53(2) *Virginia Law Review* 259. This is not to suggest that only this field recognises the shareholder as holding such a position: see, eg, Corporations and Markets Advisory Committee, *The Social Responsibility of Corporations* (Report, December 2006) 81 [3.1].

57 It is not only economists who recognise the 'legal fiction' that is the corporation: see, eg, the discussion of Diplock LJ in *Freeman & Lockyer v Buckhurst Park Properties (Mangal) Ltd* [1964] 2 QB 480, 504. See also the discussion in Chapter 2 at Section 2.20.

58 Adolf A Berle and Gardiner C Means, *The Modern Corporation and Private Property* (Macmillan, 1933) 226, as cited in Leonard I Rotman, *Fiduciary Law* (Thomson Carswell, 2005) 412.

59 Leonard I Rotman, *Fiduciary Law* (Thomson Carswell, 2005) 463 (footnote 218); see also R Goddard, '*Percival v. Wright*: the end of a remarkable career?' (2000) 116 *Law Quarterly Review* 197.

60 Leonard I Rotman, *Fiduciary Law* (Thomson Carswell, 2005) 412–3. Rotman cites John C Coffee Jr, 'The Mandatory/Enabling Balance in Corporate Law: An Essay on the Judicial Role' (1989) 89 *Columbia Law Review* 1618, 1664 in support of this position.

61 *Percival v Wright* [1902] 2 Ch 421.

the negotiations for the sale of the undertaking. This argument was rejected by Swinfen Eady J,[62] in a judgment which has been the subject of a great deal of academic criticism[63] and led to attempts by many courts to confine it to its facts.[64] Interestingly, the case itself contains no reference to directors' fiduciary obligations being owed solely to the company—a statement that the directors 'are not trustees for individual shareholders' appears in the headnote to the case, rather than in the body of the text.[65] However, this interpretation of the decision, when taken in combination with the 'proper plaintiff' principle from *Foss v Harbottle*,[66] has been followed by other cases which confirm that the beneficiary of a fiduciary obligation owed by directors will be the company.[67]

Next, we will discuss the circumstances currently recognised by the courts where a director may also owe a fiduciary obligation to a beneficiary other than the company, including when a director purchases shares from a member; when a company is about to be wound up; and in closely-held companies.

When a director purchases shares from a member

The New Zealand decision of *Coleman v Myers*[68] was one of the first to discuss a situation in which directors owe fiduciary obligations to shareholders. Until then, *Percival v Wright* had been instrumental in denying the possibility of a fiduciary obligation within this relationship.[69] Two directors of a company were aware that the company's assets were far more valuable than the company accounts revealed. The directors set up a new company, which made a takeover bid for the shares in the original company at a substantial undervalue. At first instance, Mahon J held that 'in any transaction involving the sale of shares between director and shareholder, the director is the repository of confidence and trust' and so 'there is inherent in the process of negotiation for sale a fiduciary duty owing by the director'.[70] Mahon J criticised the decision of *Percival v Wright* as being contrary to contemporary commercial morality, and concluded that it was wrongly decided.

On appeal, the Court held that the question of whether fiduciary obligations arose depended on the nature of the relationship between the parties,[71] and that in this case the

62 Ibid 426.

63 See, eg, L Loss, 'The Fiduciary Concept as Applied to Trading by Corporate "Insiders" in the United States' (1970) 33(1) *Modern Law Review* 34, 40–1; PD Finn, *Fiduciary Obligations* (Law Book, 1977) 11; R Valentine, 'The Director-Shareholder Fiduciary Relationship: Issues and Implications' (2001) 19(2) *Company and Securities Law Journal* 92, 97.

64 For example, in Canada, New Zealand and Australia, respectively: *Farnham v Fingold* [1971] 3 OR 688; *Coleman v Myers* [1977] 2 NZLR 225, particularly Woodhouse J at 324; *Brunninghausen v Glavanics* (1999) 46 NSWLR 538, 555, where the decision is called 'anomalous' by Handley JA.

65 As noted in *Re Chez Nico (Restaurants) Ltd* [1992] BCLC 192, 208.

66 *Foss v Harbottle* (1843) 67 ER 189.

67 See, eg, *Hospital Products Ltd v United States Surgical Corporation* (1984) 156 CLR 41.

68 *Coleman v Myers* [1977] 2 NZLR 225, referred to with implied approval in *Hurley v BGH Nominees Pty Ltd (No 2)* (1984) 37 SASR 499, 509–11 (Walters J).

69 This is despite findings to the contrary, such as the Privy Council decision in *Allen v Hyatt* (1914) 30 TLR 444, and the development of the special facts doctrine in the US, such as *Strong v Repide*, 213 US 419 (1909).

70 *Coleman v Myers* [1977] 2 NZLR 225, 277–8.

71 Ibid 325 (Woodhouse J), 330 (Cooke J) and 370 (Casey J).

directors owed the shareholders fiduciary obligations. The Court of Appeal commented that although *Percival v Wright* was correctly decided on its own facts, the idea that 'anybody holding the office of director of a limited liability company is for that reason alone released from what otherwise would be regarded as a fiduciary responsibility owed to those in the position of shareholders of the same company' was not the law,[72] and on that point, *Percival v Wright* must be overruled. This approach was confirmed in New Zealand in *Thexton v Thexton*[73], and in England in *Re Chez Nico*[74] and *Platt v Platt.*[75]

In Australia, *Coleman v Myers* was relied upon by Handley JA in his judgment on appeal in *Brunninghausen v Glavanics.*[76] Here, his Honour explicitly declined to follow *Percival*, despite very similar facts.[77] Brunninghausen ('B') and Glavanics ('G') were brothers-in-law. They were both directors and the only shareholders in an importing company. G was rewarded with one-sixth of the shares, at no cost to himself, upon the formation of the company and being a director in name only. Following a falling out, G's separate company began competing with the joint company. G agreed to sell his shares to B, at the prompting of one of their mothers-in-law, to restore family harmony. Prior to the execution of the documents, but after an oral agreement in relation to the purchase of the shares had been made, a potential purchaser made an offer for the joint business which would have significantly increased the value of G's shares. The sale of G's shares was progressed with haste, without alteration to the agreement. G was thereby deprived of the increased value of his share in light of the offer.

At first instance, Bryson J found that the facts gave rise to a fiduciary duty owed by B to G,[78] although his Honour rejected the contention that the director–shareholder relationship 'as such and without more' gave rise to a fiduciary relationship where the director purchases shares from a shareholder.[79] His Honour did find a fiduciary obligation was owed, on the basis that B's conduct fell outside 'the range of honest dealing according to ordinary community standards'[80] and that G was dependent on B for advice and information concerning the negotiations, despite being a co-director. Bryson J also suggested that B owed fiduciary obligations to G in part because the shareholding structure of the joint importing company was more indicative of a 'trading equity with co-owners' artificially contrived into the form of a company.[81] The validity of this line of argument will be considered below, when considering the case of *Ebrahimi v Westbourne Galleries Ltd.*[82]

On appeal, this decision was affirmed in the judgment of Handley JA, with whom Priestley and Stein JJA concurred.[83] Although Handley JA agreed that directors owe their

72 Ibid 324 (Woodhouse J).
73 *Thexton v Thexton* [2001] 1 NZLR 237.
74 *Re Chez Nico (Restaurants) Ltd* [1992] BCLC 192, 208.
75 *Platt v Platt* [1999] 2 BCLC 745, 755.
76 *Brunninghausen v Glavanics* (1999) 46 NSWLR 538 ('*Brunninghausen*').
77 Ibid 559.
78 *Glavanics v Brunninghausen* (1996) 19 ACSR 204, 217 ('*Glavanics*').
79 Ibid 215.
80 Ibid 224.
81 Ibid 222.
82 *Ebrahimi v Westbourne Galleries Ltd* [1973] AC 360 ('*Ebrahimi*').
83 *Brunninghausen v Glavanics* (1999) 46 NSWLR 538.

fiduciary obligations to the company, he held that this principle should not be permitted to preclude recognition of a fiduciary duty to shareholders in relation to dealings in their shares, where this would not compete with any duty owed to the company.[84]

When a company is about to be wound up

In *Mesenberg v Cord Industrial Recruiters Pty Ltd*,[85] it was held that directors in a two-person company may owe fiduciary duties to shareholders when a company is about to be wound up.

Through a 'quasi-partnership' analysis, Young J held that

> where a two person company is in its death throes, but has not yet been wound up, the fiduciary duty imposed on its director is not only owed to the company, but also to the other quasi-partner, and produces what is so akin to a personal right of a shareholder that it is proper for the shareholder to sue to enforce the right.[86]

As such, a director can owe the members a fiduciary obligation through the use of an agency or partnership analogy. However, the use of the 'quasi-partnership' analogy should be approached with caution, as discussed by Lord Wilberforce in *Ebrahimi v Westbourne Galleries*.[87] This decision will be considered in depth in Chapter 14 in relation to the ability of members to seek the winding up of a company on just and equitable grounds.[88] In that case, Lord Wilberforce, with whom Viscount Dilhorne and Lord Pearson agreed,[89] considered that the partnership analogy had limitations. His Lordship reiterated the overarching impact of the *Companies Act 1948* (UK) on the relationship, but felt that equity entitled the Court to subject the exercise of legal rights to equitable considerations such as the personal relationship arising between the individuals within a company 'which might make it unjust or inequitable, to insist on legal rights, or to exercise them in a particular way'.[90] He added that 'there is room in company law for the recognition of the fact that behind it, or amongst it, there are individuals, with rights, expectations and obligations *inter se* which are not necessarily submerged in the company structure'.[91]

While Lord Wilberforce recognised the potential for obligations outside of the company structure to exist, he disliked the tendency to call these directors 'in substance partners' or 'quasi-partners', as it tended to obscure the different legal relationships chosen by the parties, and the obligations flowing from that relationship.[92] This admonition is justified, and care should be taken before using such descriptions as a basis for finding a fiduciary obligation owed to a beneficiary other than the company.

84 Ibid 549–50.
85 *Mesenberg v Cord Industrial Recruiters Pty Ltd* (1996) 39 NSWLR 128.
86 Ibid 139.
87 *Ebrahimi v Westbourne Galleries Ltd* [1973] AC 260.
88 See Chapter 14 at Section 14.40.
89 Lord Cross of Chelsea offered separate reasons, but also found for the appellant.
90 *Ebrahimi v Westbourne Galleries Ltd* [1973] AC 260 379.
91 Ibid.
92 Ibid 380.

Closely-held companies

Many of the case examples raised so far occur within corporate structures which can be described as 'closely-held'. The common features found in closely-held companies are that they have few directors, few shareholders (with the shareholders also often being directors), and are family or private companies.

As discussed above, Bryson J held in *Glavanics* that a director owed fiduciary obligations to a shareholder on the basis of the limited shareholding in that company.[93] Bryson J stated that:

> [f]or the purposes of granting or withholding equitable remedies the importance of the corporate personality and structure is in my opinion, greatly diminished in circumstances of two kinds, one of which is where there are very few members, very few directors and their relationships are not impersonal but close.[94]

This may be open to criticism for either inappropriately redefining types of corporate structure in a way which the *Corporations Act* does not,[95] or for suggesting that there is a 'sliding scale' of corporate personality, and the resulting duties owed by officers of the corporation, depending on the number of directors and shareholders. His Honour emphasised that relationships in larger companies are 'impersonal', which prevents the attachment of fiduciary obligations,[96] but on that basis, the information disequilibrium which was present and pivotal in *Glavanics* is more likely to exist.

According to Young JA in *Crawley v Short*, with whom Allsop P and Macfarlan JA concurred, a fiduciary obligation will be owed where:

> one shareholder undertakes to act on behalf of another shareholder; where one shareholder is in a position to have special knowledge and knows that another shareholder is relying on her to use that knowledge for the advantage of another shareholder as well as herself; and where the company is in reality a partnership in corporate guise, nowadays termed a quasi partnership [sic].[97]

As discussed previously, the use of the phrase quasi-partnership can be criticised. However, Young JA went on to note that:

> there may be closely held corporations where the interests of the shareholders are diverse so that no such duty can be implied. The prime illustration is a home unit company where each shareholder is only interested in his or her own home unit.[98]

93 *Glavanics v Brunninghausen* (1996) 19 ACSR 204, 222.

94 Ibid 216–17.

95 *Corporations Act* ss 114, 201A(1), respectively. Section 219(1) of the *Companies Act 1981* (Cth), which would have been the relevant Act at the time of the transactions (although in force in each state as the *Companies Code*), provided that 'a public company shall have at least 3 directors and a proprietary company shall have at least 2 directors'.

96 *Glavanics v Brunninghausen* (1996) 19 ACSR 204, 217.

97 *Crawley v Short* (2009) 262 ALR 654, 672. His Honour was careful to note that this is not an exhaustive list.

98 Ibid, citing *Woods v Cann* (1963) 80 WN (NSW) 1583.

This highlights a difficulty with a fiduciary obligation owed to a class, such as the members of a company, as not all constituents of that class may have the same interests, placing the fiduciary in an impossible position.

In closely-held companies, directors have been found to owe fiduciary obligations to shareholders on an ad hoc rather than nominate basis.

13.10.35 The fiduciary obligation in the commercial context

The content of the two duties which form the fiduciary obligation—a duty of loyalty and a duty to account for benefits gained (the 'no conflict' and 'no profit' rules)[99]—is now well established in equity in Australian law. The 'no conflict' rule is designed to prevent a director 'enter[ing] into engagements in which [they have], or can have, a personal interest conflicting, or which possibly may conflict, with the interests of those whom [they are] bound to protect'.[100] The threshold for the test of conflict will be whether it causes 'a real, sensible possibility of conflict'.[101] The 'no profit' rule is not so broad as to imply that directors are not entitled to be paid for their work, but the director 'shall not take any secret remuneration or any financial benefit not authorised by the law, or by his contract, or by the trust deed under which he acts, as the case may be'.[102] In circumstances where the company has made no loss, or has even made a profit, the fiduciary will still be required to disgorge any benefit obtained as a result of a breach.[103] Acting *mala fide* is not necessary to breach the 'no conflict' or 'no profit' rules, maintaining the strict nature of the obligations from its early sources.[104] As the obligations are formulated to protect the beneficiary, the fiduciary may be excused by obtaining fully informed consent from the members, either prior to a potential breach or via retrospective absolution.[105] This is often described as the defence of fully informed consent, although it has been described as an obligation in its own right.[106] A director who does not wish to breach their fiduciary obligation must make full disclosure to the members, as to the conflicts or profits arising in the course of the relationship, as fully informed consent cannot be obtained without full disclosure.[107] The onus of proving the members' fully informed consent rests on the fiduciary.[108]

One issue that has arisen in the context of the no conflicts and no profits rules is whether a director can take up a corporate or business opportunity and, if they do, who should provide fully informed consent to absolve the director of a breach. Other issues of

99 See, eg, *Moss v Moss (No 2)* (1900) 21 LR (NSW) Eq 253; *Chan v Zacharia* (1984) 154 CLR 178.

100 *Aberdeen Railway Co v Blaikie Brothers* (1854) 1 Macq 461, 471.

101 *Boardman v Phipps* [1967] 2 AC 46; *Chan v Zacharia* (1984) 154 CLR 178.

102 *Dale v Inland Revenue Commissioners* [1954] AC 11, 27.

103 *Krupace Holdings Pty Ltd v China Hotel Investments Pty Ltd* [2018] NSWSC 862 [64].

104 As discussed above, removing the fruit of temptation rather than moving it to a higher shelf: LI Rotman, *Fiduciary Law* (Thomson Carswell, 2005) 64.

105 *Winthrop Investments Ltd v Winns Ltd* [1975] 2 NSWLR 666; cf *Residues Treatment & Trading Co Ltd v Southern Resources Ltd* (1988) 51 SASR 177, 204 suggesting this could constitute fraud on the minority. In relation to timing of consent and commercial knowledge, see also *Farah Constructions Pty Ltd v Say-Dee Pty Ltd* (2007) 230 CLR 89.

106 See, eg, *Blackmagic Design Pty Ltd v Overliese* (2011) 191 FCR 1 [105]–[108].

107 See, eg, *Boardman v Phipps* [1967] 2 AC 46.

108 *Maguire v Makaronis* (1997) 188 CLR 449, 466–7 (Brennan CJ, Gaudron, McHugh and Gummow JJ).

relevance are whether directors can hold multiple directorships, and whether directors can have an interest in or transact with the company. These issues are all discussed below.

Can directors take up corporate opportunities?

In the course of doing business, companies may consider a wide range of business opportunities. A common concern for directors is whether or not they, or their associates, are able to pursue a business opportunity that has come to their attention due to their position as a director of the company.[109] Directors' duties, and in particular the fiduciary obligation, make it clear that directors must not place themselves in a position where their interests are in conflict with the interests of the company: but what will qualify as a conflict in regard to corporate opportunities? A related question is whether directors are permitted to pursue an opportunity the company has declared it will not pursue, or is unable to pursue, and whether or not this concern continues after the resignation of the director.

The strict nature of the fiduciary obligation is demonstrated in the following cases, which almost universally deny a director the ability to pursue a corporate opportunity that has come to their attention due to their position as a director and in the absence of fully informed consent. In *Industrial Development Consultants Ltd v Cooley*,[110] Mr Cooley, in his capacity as the director of Industrial Development Consultants Ltd ('IDC'), presented a project to design a depot in Letchworth to the Eastern Gas Board, the local body in charge of distribution of gas to consumers in the Cambridgeshire area of England. The Gas Board had a policy in place not to employ development companies, which included IDC, and so the project was rejected. Cooley was also a distinguished architect in his own right, and so the Gas Board offered him the project personally. He accepted the offer, and in order to do so obtained a release from his position as director on the (false) grounds that he was ill. When it was discovered that he was personally undertaking the project, the plaintiff company sued for breach of fiduciary obligation.

Roskill J found in favour of the company on the basis that the opportunity to design the depot had come to Cooley in his capacity as director of the company and, regardless of the fact that the contract was ultimately only offered to him personally, he was duty-bound to pass that opportunity on to the plaintiff.[111] It was precisely the type of contract that the plaintiff had appointed Cooley to seek for them, and he was liable to account for the profits he had obtained personally from the contract.[112] The policy of the Gas Board not to employ development companies did not ameliorate Cooley's breach in personally undertaking the opportunity which had arisen from his position as a fiduciary.

A similarly strict application of the fiduciary obligation regarding corporate opportunities can be seen in *Regal (Hastings) Ltd v Gulliver*.[113] The company (Regal) owned a cinema

109 Similarly, as senior employees may be held to owe fiduciary obligations to their employer, they may be in breach of this duty should they divert work away from their employer to themselves or another associated company, or by misusing confidential information, even where they are not sufficiently senior to be considered an officer of the company: *Chaffey Services Pty Ltd v Doble (No 4)* [2023] WASC 361.

110 *Industrial Development Consultants Ltd v Cooley* [1972] 1 WLR 443.

111 Ibid 451.

112 Ibid 453.

113 *Regal (Hastings) Ltd v Gulliver* [1967] 2 AC 134 ('*Regal (Hastings)*').

in Hastings. Through a subsidiary, the company wished to lease two more cinemas in order to make the business a more attractive package for sale. The landlord requested personal guarantees from the directors of Regal in relation to the rent, which they were unwilling to give. The landlord indicated that the leases would be granted if the subsidiary could demonstrate an issued share capital of £5,000.[114] In exchange for shares, Regal (as directed by the board of directors) contributed £2,000, but rather than seek a loan for the remainder, Regal's four directors put in a further £500 each, the chairman of the board found outside subscribers for another £500, and the company solicitor was asked to and contributed the final £500. After the leases had been established, Regal was sold,[115] with a reasonable profit per share obtained for both Regal and its subsidiary.[116] The new owners of Regal sued the directors and solicitor who had been in place at the time of the share issue, claiming that the directors and solicitor had breached their fiduciary obligations to Regal, as they had personally profited from their investment in the subsidiary.[117] In what has been perceived as a particularly strict application of the fiduciary obligation against a fiduciary, the directors were held to account for the profit they had personally received on the shares which they had purchased in the subsidiary, with an exception for the chairman, who had not subscribed for shares himself, but had found investors for those shares. As he had not profited personally, an account of profits was not ordered against him.[118] Further exception was made for the solicitor, who had only subscribed at the request of his client, Regal.[119]

In *Regal (Hastings)*, in contrast to *Cooley*,[120] the directors at all times acted bona fide, and the opportunity was one which the plaintiff company could not have pursued. Additionally, although Regal was the plaintiff, control of that company had changed hands between the breach and the lawsuit. At all times, the company was the beneficiary of the duty, but those who stood to actually benefit from the lawsuit were not involved in the company at the time of the breach and obtained what was, in essence, a windfall.[121] This issue was directly addressed by Lord Porter in *Regal (Hastings)*:

> [I]t is to my mind immaterial that the directors saw no way of raising the money save from amongst themselves and from the solicitor to the company, or, indeed, that the money could in fact have been raised in no other way.[122]

The opportunity may have been impossible for the company to pursue without the intervention of the directors, but their Lordships declined to perceive impossibility as having an impact on the strict nature of the underlying fiduciary obligation.

114 Ibid 140.
115 Although not to the original purchaser for whom the 'attractive' offer of three cinemas together had been built: ibid 142–3.
116 Ibid 143.
117 Ibid 149–50.
118 Ibid 150–1.
119 Ibid 152.
120 *Industrial Development Consultants Ltd v Cooley* [1972] 1 WLR 443.
121 This strictness has been the subject of academic criticism. See, eg, M Evans, *Equity and Trusts* (LexisNexis Butterworths, 3rd ed, 2012) 143; GE Dal Pont, *Equity and Trusts in Australia* (Lawbook, 5th ed, 2011) 114–15.
122 *Regal (Hastings)* [1967] 2 AC 134, 158.

Questions can arise as to the capacity in which the opportunity comes to the notice of the director, which could impact on whether or not it is considered under the fiduciary obligation owed to the company. In *SEA Food International Pty Ltd v Lam*,[123] the Court was prepared to relax the position first imposed in *Regal (Hastings)*, although the opportunity was one which was within the scope of the company's operation and was taken up by its director. Similarly, in *Regal (Hastings)*, the company had discounted the opportunity because it was perceived as too expensive, although in this instance it was not impossible. Unlike in *Regal (Hastings)*, the opportunity came to the attention of the director prior to his appointment. The Court held that continuing to pursue the opportunity after appointment was not a breach of the director's fiduciary obligation.

A similar question was considered by the Privy Council on appeal from the Supreme Court of New South Wales in *Queensland Mines Ltd v Hudson*[124] with the opposite result to *Regal (Hastings)*. In *Queensland Mines*, the plaintiff company alleged a breach of fiduciary obligations from its former managing director, Mr Hudson, in relation to the exploitation of iron ore opportunities in Tasmania.[125] Hudson had negotiated with the Tasmanian Government in relation to exploration licences for iron and coal, using the name and backing of Queensland Mines throughout much of the negotiation process.[126] The licences were, however, issued in his personal name, and when Queensland Mines was unable due to the financial circumstance of its key backer[127] to contribute financially, Hudson resigned as managing director of Queensland Mines and informed the Tasmanian Government that he would be personally responsible for the obligations owed under the licences.[128]

At first instance, Hudson was called to account for profits made from these licences, as they had arisen directly from his involvement with Queensland Mines and use of the company's name in the negotiating period.[129] The Privy Council disagreed, finding that Hudson had been left 'on his own, for better or for worse, with the Tasmanian licences'.[130] He was not obliged to account.

These two outcomes appear hard to reconcile but are easily distinguished on the facts. In *Regal (Hastings)*, the company was only able to pursue the lease opportunity due to the capital contributed by the directors in the subsidiary company. The directors then profited when the parent company was sold due to their holding in the subsidiary. Lord Russell held that the shares were obtained only by reason of the fact that they were directors of the parent company, and that the (by then) ex-directors were therefore liable to account for the profit made from the shares.[131] In *Queensland Mines*, the company was unable to

123 *SEA Food International Pty Ltd v Lam* (1998) 16 ACLC 552.

124 *Queensland Mines Ltd v Hudson* (1978) 18 ALR 1 ('*Queensland Mines*').

125 Ibid 6–7.

126 Due to the limitations on Queensland Mines (having been formed to exploit uranium deposits in Queensland), it had always been in mind that a new company would be formed to exploit the Tasmanian licence opportunities: *Queensland Mines* (1978) 18 ALR 1, 6–7.

127 Mr Korman, whose family holding company, Stanhill Consolidated Ltd, controlled 51 per cent of the shares in Queensland Mines via another company called Factors Ltd.

128 *Queensland Mines v Hudson* (1978) 18 ALR 1, 7–8. Hudson eventually found an American company to back the exploitation.

129 Ibid 8.

130 Ibid 10.

131 *Regal (Hastings)* [1967] 2 AC 134, 149.

pursue the opportunity due to liquidity problems.[132] The managing director, Hudson, then resigned and, with the full knowledge of the company board, successfully pursued the opportunity. The Privy Council held that once the company had rejected the opportunity, there was no conflict of interest between the director and the company.[133] After the board meeting where the opportunity was rejected, the venture was either 'outside of the scope of the trust and outside the scope of the agency'[134] created by the relationship between director and company, or proceeded with the fully informed consent of the company.

The reference by the Privy Council to trust or agency is open to the same criticisms as quasi-partnership analogies, as it obscures the fact that the director owes a fiduciary obligation without first being found to be an agent or trustee, but the broader point remains valid. It can be seen on the facts of the case that 'Hudson was left on his own, for better or for worse',[135] and was entitled to pursue the opportunity in his own right. Consequently, *Queensland Mines* has been interpreted by some courts as indicating that a fiduciary is not bound to account for a benefit or gain derived by virtue of their position, if they can show that the company rejected the opportunity or gave 'fully informed consent' to the benefit or gain.[136]

Who can provide fully informed consent?

Queensland Mines raises a further question in relation to the available defence for breach of fiduciary obligations: who consents for the company? On an initial reading, the outcome of *Queensland Mines* suggests that the board of directors can consent, and that seeking the consent of the shareholders in general meeting is an unnecessary step. This is in direct contrast to the statements of the High Court in *Furs Ltd v Tomkies* that a director can only make effective disclosure to and obtain consent from the company in general meeting.[137]

It appears throughout much of the Privy Council judgment in *Queensland Mines* that the Court accepted the fully informed consent of the board of Queensland Mines as sufficient to excuse Hudson from breach of his fiduciary obligations. For example, their Lordships stated: 'the board of the company knew the facts, decided to renounce the company's interest, ... and assented to Mr Hudson doing what he could with the licences at his own risk and for his own benefit'.[138] As calling meetings of shareholders is often considered an onerous task, assent being granted by the board might be seen as beneficial by directors.

However, closer inspection of the facts of *Queensland Mines* reveals that this case turned on a narrow scenario where all shareholders had some form of significant representation on the board. There were two shareholders in the company of Queensland Mines. The first, AOE Ltd, holding 49 per cent of the shares, was a company almost wholly owned and controlled by Hudson. The other shareholder, Factors Ltd, holding 51

132 And also possibly limitations as to its original purpose—being exploitation of uranium in Queensland, rather than iron ore in Tasmania. Hudson and Korman had originally intended to incorporate a new entity to exploit the iron ore opportunity in Tasmania, rather than using Queensland Mines: *Queensland Mines v Hudson* (1978) 18 ALR 1, 6.

133 Ibid 9–10.

134 Ibid 10.

135 Ibid.

136 *Hurley v BGH Nominees Pty Ltd (No 2)* (1984) 37 SASR 499, 506 (Walters J).

137 *Furs Ltd v Tomkies* (1936) 54 CLR 583, 590, 592.

138 *Queensland Mines v Hudson* (1978) 18 ALR 1, 9–10.

per cent of the shares, was a subsidiary of a holding company controlled by Mr Korman and his family.[139] The three members of the board of directors of Queensland Mines at the relevant times were Hudson (as managing director), Korman's son, and a director of Factors.[140]

The information held by the board led to the decision to pass up the relevant opportunity, and the same outcome would have been achieved from the shareholders. The consent of the board of directors in this case can be considered as equivalent to the consent of the shareholders, rather than as an exception to the position that fully informed consent must be sought from the company in general meeting. Read in this way, the case seems to be consistent with the accepted approach to the defence of fully informed consent, which is confirmed by the final comment by the Privy Council before advising the appeal be dismissed: 'The shareholders were Factors and AOE, both of whom were represented on the board.'[141] By the board granting consent, the shareholders had, in effect, granted their fully informed consent.

Multiple directorships and directors with interests in and transacting with the company

It is an accepted commercial reality that directors may hold multiple directorships. This conflicts with the strict nature and application of the fiduciary obligation to directors, which suggests a director cannot hold a position on a board of a competitor or personally compete with the company.[142] That position has been relaxed, according to what is now known as the *London and Mashonaland* rule, from the case of the same name.[143] That rule says that a non-executive director[144] may be able to be a director of two competing companies, as long as there is no direct conflict—such as through the divulging of confidential information—or such an appointment is prohibited by express terms of the constitution, or express or implied terms of any other agreement. Once a conflict arises, then

> [a] company is entitled to the unbiased and independent judgment of each of its directors. A director of a company who is also a director of another company may owe conflicting fiduciary duties. Being a fiduciary, a director of the first company must not exercise his or her powers for the benefit or gain of the second company without clearly disclosing the second company's interests to the first company and obtaining the first company's consent. Nor, of course, can the director exercise those powers for the director's own benefit or gain without clearly disclosing his or her interest and obtaining the company's consent.[145]

139 Ibid 5.
140 Ibid 8.
141 Ibid 11.
142 *Aberdeen Railway Co v Blaikie Brothers* (1854) 1 Macq 461.
143 *London and Mashonaland Exploration Co Ltd v New Mashonaland Exploration Co Ltd* [1891] WN 165.
144 Non-executive directors are defined in Chapter 10 at Section 10.20.
145 *R v Byrnes* (1995) 183 CLR 501, 516–17.

Further, where a director breaches their fiduciary obligations with the knowing assistance or knowing participation of another company, that company will also be liable where it benefits from the breaching conduct.[146]

Clearly, it may be impossible for the director to maintain both appointments without breaching their fiduciary obligations.[147] This will be a particular concern for nominee directors, who are appointed by a special interest group such as a class of shareholders, a major creditor, or the company's employees. Their appointment on behalf of these special interest groups is seen as being made in order to provide representation for those interests at the board level. This can be a conflict from the moment of appointment. However, legally, the director will owe their duties to the company, and will be required to act according to s 181(1) of the *Corporations Act* in the best interest of the company, and not their appointor. The director will need to balance the expectations of the appointor that their nominee will act in their interests with the director's legal obligation to act in the interests of the company.

It is also common for directors to own shares in the company, which requires a degree of compartmentalisation of the position of the director. Some companies, via the constitution, make it a requirement of office for a director to hold a nominal parcel of shares. This may be due to a longstanding recognition that owning shares in the company permits the interests of the director to be more closely aligned with the interests of the company,[148] even if some doubt has been drawn on the efficiency of this argument.[149]

The risk associated with multiple directorships is the potential for directors to use company property or information for the benefit of themselves or someone else or divert corporate opportunities to themselves or someone else. This is not a risk limited to directors who hold multiple posts, and general instances of this risk are considered above, but it is heightened in these circumstances.

13.15 Use of position and information: ss 182–3

13.15.05 The relationship between the statute and fiduciary obligation

Sections 182–3 raise legal concepts that have thematic consistency with the fiduciary obligation owed by directors to the company in equity. The statutory treatment of the no conflict and no profit rules is divided into separate consideration of improper use of position and improper use of information,[150] with criminal liability for breaches of these rules.[151] Separately, other provisions deal directly with conflicts of interest, including s 191 and related provisions, which will be dealt with below. Section 185 confirms that these sections

146 *Bluemine Pty Ltd (in liq) v AKA (Civil) Pty ltd* [2022] NSWCA 160.

147 *Fitzsimmons v The Queen* (1997) 23 ACSR 355.

148 *Mills v Mills* (1938) 60 CLR 150, 163–4.

149 P Ali and G Stapledon, 'Extracting Value from Executive Share Options', *Australian Institute of Company Directors* (Web Page, 1 October 2000) <https://www.aicd.com.au/board-of-directors/duties/liabilities-of-directors/extracting-value-from-executive-share-options.html; A Sarhan and B Al-Najjar, 'The Influence of Corporate Governance and Shareholding Structure on Corporate Social Responsibility: The Key Role of Executive Compensation' (2023) 28(4) *International Journal of Finance and Economics* 4532.

150 *Corporations Act* ss 182–3.

151 Ibid s 184.

apply 'in addition to, and not in derogation' of the duties which exist in the general law, such as the fiduciary obligation described above.

A description of the duties in ss 182–3 as the 'statutory fiduciary duties'[152] is not entirely accurate.[153] The Australian jurisdiction is not alone in perpetuating this 'linguistic confusion',[154] as the equivalent sections of the Canadian legislation have also been similarly labelled.[155] Although the equitable fiduciary obligations may have been the original source of the duties expressed in the *Corporations Act*, these statutory duties do not subsume the equitable fiduciary obligations.[156]

While the statutory duties and fiduciary obligations operate in a similar way, there are important distinctions, which reinforce the point that labelling ss 182–183 as the 'statutory fiduciary obligations' is not correct. For example, the statutory duties introduce an element requiring the director not to 'improperly use' their position or information;[157] this is not considered under the equitable concept of the fiduciary obligation, which prohibits secret remuneration or other profits. The statutory provisions may be broader than the fiduciary obligation, which is limited to senior employees—language not present in the statute.[158] The statutory provisions expressly include the gaining of 'an advantage for ... someone else', bypassing the need to engage in a third-party liability argument under *Barnes v Addy*.[159] The provisions also expressly encompass use of position or information to 'cause detriment to the corporation', without requiring there to be a corresponding profit; whereas for the fiduciary obligation the focus is on prohibiting a profit flowing to the fiduciary, and the existence of a loss or otherwise is quite irrelevant.[160] Finally, it is possible to see s 183 as encompassing the equitable duty of confidentiality,[161] which is not a fiduciary duty.

There are other procedural and substantive differences, such as the approach to proving causation, which is higher under the statute than the 'but for' test used in the equitable duty. The defence of fully informed consent that can be obtained under the fiduciary obligation is dealt with differently under the statutory scheme, as the ability to ratify a breach of the equitable duties may not cure a breach of the statutory duties.[162] It may, however, go towards enabling the relevant director or officer to avail themselves of the broader defences contained in the *Corporations Act*, which are discussed at Section 10.40.10.[163]

152 See, eg, Companies and Securities Advisory Committee, *Company Directors and Officers: Indemnification, Relief and Insurance* (Parliament of Australia, 1992) 4.

153 In *Australian Securities and Investments Commission v Bettles* (2023) 169 ACSR 244 [442], s 182(1) was described as being 'similar to, but not the same as' the 'no profit' rule.

154 R Flannigan, 'The Core Nature of Fiduciary Accountability' (2009) (3) *New Zealand Law Review* 375, 387.

155 See, eg, *Peoples Department Stores Inc v Wise* [2004] 3 SCR 461 [32].

156 *Corporations Act* s 185.

157 Ibid ss 182(1), 183(1).

158 *Gunasegaram v Blue Visions Management Pty Ltd* (2018) 129 ACSR 265 [20]; *Chaffey Services Pty Ltd v Doble (No 4)* [2023] WASC 361.

159 *Barnes v Addy* (1874) LR 9 Ch App 244. See further discussion in Chapter 12 at Section 12.10.45.

160 *Regal (Hastings)* [1967] 2 AC 134; *Furs Ltd v Tomkies* (1936) 54 CLR 583; *Krupace Holdings Pty Ltd v China Hotel Investments Pty Ltd* [2018] NSWSC 862.

161 *Vanguard Financial Planners Pty Ltd v Ale* (2018) 354 ALR 711, [217].

162 See, eg, *Angas Law Services Pty Ltd (in liq) v Carabelas* (2005) 226 CLR 507, 523 (Gleeson CJ, Heydon J); *Forge v Australian Securities and Investments Commission* (2004) 52 ACSR 1.

163 *Corporations Act* ss 1317S, 1318.

13.15.10 Sections 182 and 183

Section 182(1) prohibits directors, other officers, and employees from improperly using their position; and s 183(1) prohibits these persons from improperly using information obtained by virtue of holding, or having held, such a position. Both sections prohibit the persons from 'improperly using' their position or information to gain advantage for themselves or someone else, or to cause detriment to the company. As mentioned above, this drafting appears to catch a wider range of persons than the fiduciary obligation, which would be limited to senior employees. Further, the High Court in *Chew v The Queen*[164] confirmed that seeking to gain an advantage for themselves or another is sufficient to breach the provision, whether or not that advantage is actually gained, or detriment caused to the company.[165] The requirement of 'improper' use is considered objectively, to the 'standard of conduct that would be expected of a person in the position of the alleged offender by reasonable persons with knowledge of the duties, powers and authority of the position and the circumstances of the case',[166] so that the actual intent of the director is not a necessary consideration for breach. It is clear that 'use' encompasses positive acts of directors, and it is also possible that mere omissions or failures to act are also captured.[167]

In both ss 182(2) and 183(2), a person who is involved in a contravention according to s 79 breaches the section, bringing an involved person within the ambit of the civil penalty provisions.

It is common to see a breach of either or both of ss 182–183 alongside a breach of another duty, such as ss 180–1. In *Australian Securities and Investments Commission v Adler*,[168] Mr Adler was found to have improperly used his position as a director of HIH Insurance Ltd ('HIH') and Pacific Eagle Equity Pty Ltd ('PEE') and officer of HIH Casualty & General Insurance Co Ltd ('HIHC') and information obtained in those positions to gain an advantage personally, in relation to large, undocumented and unsecured loans.[169] Mr Williams, who was a director and CEO of HIH and director of HIHC, was found to have improperly used his position to gain an advantage for Adler and cause detriment to HIH, HIHC and PEE, in authorising the payments and bypassing the company's investment committee approval process.[170] In addition to those breaches, Adler and Williams were found to be in breach of s 180(1),[171] and Adler also in breach of s 181(1).[172]

These are civil penalty provisions and subject to the civil consequences set out in response to that scheme. In addition, s 184(2) provides that a director, officer or employee commits an offence if they use their position dishonestly, with the intention of gaining an advantage for themselves or someone else, causing detriment to the company, or recklessly as to whether the use may result in such an advantage or detriment. Section 184(3)

164 *Chew v The Queen* (1992) 173 CLR 626.
165 Ibid 633.
166 *R v Byrnes* (1995) 183 CLR 501, 515.
167 *Hakea Holdings Pty Ltd v Neon Underwriting Ltd* (2023) 296 FCR 611, [123].
168 *Australian Securities and Investments Commission v Adler* (2002) 41 ACSR 71 ('*ASIC v Adler*').
169 Ibid [577].
170 Ibid [461].
171 Ibid [453].
172 Ibid [387].

provides similarly in relation to the use of information obtained by virtue of holding, or having held, such an appointment. Sections 184(2A) and (4) provide that dishonest use of position or information with the intention of gaining an advantage for the company, or with the result of an advantage to the company, is not a defence in a proceeding for an offence against sub-ss (2) and (3) respectively. The Explanatory Memorandum suggests that this 'ensures that those who use their position or information dishonestly or recklessly, but gain an advantage for the corporation, still commit the offence'.[173] Additionally, a transaction brought about by behaviour of persons in breach of ss 181–182 will, if the other party entered into the agreement with knowledge of the breach, be voidable at the company's choice and rescission is available.[174]

13.20 Disclosure

Unlike the obligations in equity, the *Corporations Act* does not directly prohibit a director from placing themselves in a position of conflict. The provisions of the *Corporations Act* are concerned with care and diligence, acting in good faith in the best interests of the company, and not improperly using their position or information to gain an advantage or cause detriment.[175] Instead, the *Corporations Act* requires directors to make appropriate disclosure of 'material personal interests' in relation to the 'affairs of the company'. Further, the disclosure requirements are minimum requirements, which cannot be displaced by the constitution. The procedure following the mandated disclosure of these material personal interests differs slightly for proprietary and public companies and is a replaceable rule for proprietary companies but a mandatory rule for public companies. Disclosure of material personal interests must be made under either ss 191 or 192. Under s 194, a director of a proprietary company may remain and vote despite their interest; but, according to s 195, a director of a public company must not be present for discussion of, nor vote in relation to, the topic in which they hold a material personal interest. The provisions require disclosure by directors in all companies, except for single director proprietary companies.[176] The underlying fiduciary obligation is expressly preserved.[177]

When these provisions were introduced into the current *Corporations Act*, they replaced s 231 of the Corporations Law,[178] which required directors of proprietary

173 Explanatory Memorandum, Treasury Laws Amendment (Strengthening Corporate and Financial Sector Penalties) Bill 2018 (Cth) [1.206].

174 *Allco Funds Management v Trust Company (RE Services) Ltd* [2014] NSWSC 1251, [124].

175 *Corporations Act* ss 180–3.

176 *Corporations Act* s 191; *Digital Pulse Pty Ltd v Harris* (2002) 166 FLR 421, 426. Although the decision on exemplary damages for fiduciary breach was reversed by the New South Wales Court of Appeal in *Harris v Digital Pulse Pty Ltd* (2003) 56 NSWLR 298, the position on this point was not amended. Section 191(2) provides exceptions to the duty to disclose.

177 *Corporations Act* ss 185, 193.

178 The 'Corporations Law' refers to the legislative scheme in place prior to the current Act. The Corporations Law was a federal Act (*Corporations Act 1989* (Cth)), but due to issues to do with the head of power in s 51 of the *Constitution*, it was amended to only operate in the ACT. Each State then passed mirror legislation. The scheme separated out the substantive provisions (known as the Corporations Law) from all the other provisions about how the law would function practically. For further information, see Chapter 1 at Section 1.40.35.

companies to disclose any direct or indirect interest in a contract or proposed contract with the company, and any office held or property possessed, directly or indirectly, which might cause duties or interests in conflict with their duties or interests as director.[179] Although the new provisions do not define a number of key terms, the Explanatory Memorandum indicated they were intended to widen the director's obligation to disclose,[180] which provides a general understanding of the breadth of instances where disclosure is required. The choice of expression 'material personal interest' may have been influenced by the appearance of that expression in other Commonwealth legislation.[181]

Section 191(1) of the *Corporations Act* requires that a director 'who has a material personal interest in a matter that relates to the affairs of the company must give the other directors notice of the interest' unless one of the exceptions set out in sub-s (2) applies. The only company type excluded from this section is the sole-director proprietary company under s 191(5). Section 191(1A) provides that this is a strict liability offence, but s 191(4) preserves the validity of the 'act, transaction, agreement, instrument, resolution or other thing' affected by the failure of a director to make disclosure as required.

13.20.05 Material personal interests

Unlike the previously applicable Corporations Law, which used clear drafting, the expression 'material personal interest' is not defined within the Act. In many cases, it is self-evident where a director has a material personal interest. For example, in *Tri-Force Enterprise Ltd v Infinite Water Holdings Ltd*,[182] a director was held to have a material personal interest in a resolution to be considered by the board to convert debt owed by one company ('IWH') to another ('TFE') into shares in IWH to be held by TFE. The director held a majority shareholding of 92 per cent in TFE and this conversion had the effect of reducing the debt owed by IWH from $9 million to $2 million. 'It was an interest involving a substantial relationship to the matters under consideration as part of the ratification motion and as such one which should be regarded as having the capacity to influence [the director's] vote on that motion.'[183]

In other cases, it is less clear what should be considered a 'material personal interest'. In *Grand Enterprises Pty Ltd v Aurium Resources Ltd*,[184] Aurium Resources Ltd and Greater Pacific Gold Limited were renegotiating a joint venture agreement, including an issue of 35 million shares in Aurium to Greater Pacific, which required Aurium shareholder approval under ASX Listing Rule 7.1 due to the size of the issue.

179 Section 232A of the Corporations Law, which applied to public companies, did not require disclosure of material personal interests as such, but instead required the interested directors not to vote or be present during discussion of the issue in which they held an interest. This is similar to the operation of the current s 195 in the *Corporations Act 2001* (Cth).

180 Explanatory Memorandum, Corporate Law Economic Reform Program Bill 1998 (Cth) [6.112].

181 See, eg, *Commonwealth Authorities and Companies Act 1997* (Cth) s 21; *Public Service Act 1999* (Cth) s 13(7); *Parliamentary Service Act 1999* (Cth) s 13(7); *Public Governance, Performance and Accountability Act 2013* (Cth) s 29(1).

182 *Tri-Force Enterprise Ltd v Infinite Water Holdings Ltd* [2024] FCA 78.

183 Ibid [71].

184 *Grand Enterprises Pty ltd v Aurium Resources Ltd* (2009) 256 ALR 1.

At the board meeting where a variation to the joint venture was to be discussed, three of the five directors of Aurium—Mr Remta, Mr Quinn and Mr Benson—declared they had material personal interests and ceased their participation in the discussion. Remta declared an interest as he was a director and chairman of both Aurium and Greater Pacific. Quinn and Benson declared an interest due to direct and indirect shareholdings in Aurium and Greater Pacific.[185] Ultimately, the meeting continued through the two directors without personal interests, who resolved that a variation to the joint venture should be made. Remta settled the explanatory memorandum in his capacity as chairman, and the terms of the notice were drafted by the company secretary and settled by Remta.[186] Although Remta's interest and abstention was disclosed in the explanatory memorandum provided to the shareholders along with notice of the meeting, Quinn and Benson's declarations of interest and abstention were not. The resolution to issue the shares passed.

Grand Enterprises Pty Ltd, an Aurium shareholder, objected to the share issue on the basis that the shareholders had not received full information on the declarations of interest, which were material matters relevant to the resolution.[187] Barker J did not regard Remta's potentially conflicting duties as a common chairman of both Aurium and Greater Pacific as amounting to a 'personal' interest,[188] as Remta did not receive any benefits or other incentives from the proposed transaction, as he was not a shareholder of either entity. His Honour reasoned that the expression 'material personal interest' was, due to the inclusion of the word 'personal', not intended to catch conflicts of duty and duty, as contemplated within the fiduciary obligation, but only conflicts of duty and personal interest.[189] This is an anomalous outcome, as such an interest would have been caught under the former s 231 requirements, and the current provisions were supposed to be broader than that provision. However, as s 193 maintains the application of the general law in addition to the legislation, this means that directors must consider whether an interest which they are not required to disclose under this narrow interpretation of the statutory provisions would still place them in breach of the fiduciary obligation.

Barker J also reached the view that, even if the small holdings of Quinn and Benson in Aurium and Greater Pacific amounted to a 'personal interest', they were not of sufficient size to be regarded as 'material'.[190] Direct holdings of less than 1 per cent of the issued capital of Greater Pacific, in the case of Benson, might be considered a personal interest, but could not be considered an interest in the matter which has a capacity or propensity to influence the director's decision in the administration of the company's affairs. In short, it is insubstantial and cannot be considered a 'material' personal interest.[191]

Although the finding in relation to the personal aspect of the interest may be problematic, it may be a question of confining this case on its facts. Remta held no shares in either company and so, on paper, there might be a possibility of conflict, but on the facts there

185 Ibid [11].
186 Ibid [5]–[7].
187 Ibid [15].
188 Ibid [93].
189 Ibid [69].
190 Ibid [81], [89].
191 Ibid [72].

was no such conflict. As Barker J noted, Benson's direct holdings in Greater Pacific were less than 1 per cent of the issued share capital, and his indirect holdings were around the same amount. Quinn only had indirect shareholding through other companies, which held shares representing 4.2 per cent of Greater Pacific and 6.78 per cent of Aurium.

When the question was raised in the Bell Group litigation, it was considered that the interest in question under these provisions need not be pecuniary.[192]

13.20.10 Exceptions to s 191

Under s 191(2), a director need not give notice under s 191(1) if the interest:

- is one held in common with the other members of the company
- relates to the director's remuneration
- relates to a contract which is subject to approval by the members, and imposes no obligations unless so approved
- arises because 'the director is a guarantor or has given an indemnity or security' for a loan to the company, or because of a right of subrogation under such a guarantee or indemnity
- relates to insurance for the director against liabilities incurred as an officer of the company
- relates to payment of an indemnity under s 199A
- is in a contract with a related body corporate, and merely because the director is also a director of that company.

Under s 191(2)(b), in a proprietary company, no disclosure needs to be made under s 191 if the other directors are aware of the nature and extent of the director's material personal interest. Under s 191(2)(c), disclosure does not need to be repeated once it has been given, as long as the extent of the interest has not materially increased, and, if any new directors have joined the board, that notice is given to that person.

Finally, under s 191(2)(d), a director who utilises the standing notice option under s 192 need not make disclosure under s 191 as long as that notice is still effective to disclose the interest. The notice must be given at a directors' meeting as soon as practicable after the director becomes aware of the interest, and the details of the notice must be recorded in the minutes of the meeting.[193]

The detail of the disclosure required was considered in *Camelot Resources Ltd v MacDonald*,[194] under the former Corporations Law. The disclosure needed to be in sufficient detail that the board could understand the benefit and potential profit to the interested director and needed to be made by that director personally.[195] Although the breach in that case was innocent, Santow J declined to relieve the director from the consequences of the breach, due to the strict nature of the disclosure obligations. This could also be seen as drawing thematic influence from the requirement to seek fully informed

192 *Bell Group Ltd (in liq) v Westpac Banking Corporation (No 9)* (2009) 39 WAR 1.
193 *Corporations Act 2001* (Cth) s 191(3).
194 *Camelot Resources Ltd v MacDonald* (1994) 14 ACSR 437.
195 Ibid 443.

consent in order not to be held in breach of the fiduciary obligation, which was also discussed by Santow J.[196]

13.20.15 The operation of ss 191–2 and the general law

Section 193 preserves the operation of the general law in addition to the requirements set out in ss 191–2 described above. As was considered in *Camelot Resources Ltd v MacDonald*, a contract made in breach of directors' fiduciary obligations will be voidable at the option of the company, unless the director makes full disclosure to the company in the general meeting and the contract is then approved in an ordinary resolution.[197] In order for the disclosure to be meaningful, it must include the nature of and the extent of the interest.[198] The constitution of the company may also vary this position, operating as a contractual alteration to the equitable obligation.[199]

In contrast, the disclosure of material personal interests under the *Corporations Act* is made to the board, not the members. As such, even proper disclosure under these provisions will not excuse a director who has breached their fiduciary obligation, unless it can be argued that disclosure to the board was the equivalent of disclosure to the members, such as it was in *Queensland Mines*.[200] Further, failure to comply with these provisions will not affect the validity of any contract or dealing engaged with by the breaching director according to s 191(4). It will, instead, be considered an offence and the director may be liable for a fine or subject to imprisonment as a result.

13.20.20 Directors of public companies and s 195

Under s 195, directors of public companies who have a material personal interest may not be present for the discussion of or vote on matters in relation to that interest. There are three exceptions set out in s 195:

- disclosure of the interest is not required under s 191, due to the exceptions such as the ability to provide standing notice under s 192
- where the directors who do not have a material personal interest in the matter pass a resolution under s 195(2) setting out the director and their material personal interest and stating 'that those directors are satisfied that the interest should not disqualify the director from voting or being present'
- where the director is entitled to be present and vote due to a declaration or order made by ASIC under s 196.

This provision does not override the constitution, which may deny an interested director from voting on the transaction, even if the disinterested directors pass a resolution under s 195(2).

196 Ibid 442.
197 (1994) 14 ACSR 437.
198 *Krupace Holdings Pty Ltd v China Hotel Investments Pty Ltd* [2018] NSWSC 862, [79].
199 As discussed in *Woolworths Ltd v Kelly* (1991) 22 NSWLR 189, 209.
200 *Queensland Mines Ltd v Hudson* (1978) 18 ALR 1. It is also unlikely that the other party will be able to rely on the statutory assumptions under ss 128–9 of the *Corporations Act*, as they will likely have knowledge of the wrongdoing on the part of the director and be unable to satisfy s 128(4) as discussed in Chapter 6 at Section 6.20.10.

Should there be too many interested directors for the meeting to meet the quorum requirements[201] then, under s 195(4), one or more of the directors, including the interested directors, may call a general meeting and the general meeting may pass a resolution to deal with the matter. Alternatively, ASIC has the power under s 196 to make an order or declaration to enable the interested directors to be present and vote.

Failure to comply with these provisions will not affect the validity of any resolution passed either in the presence of or including a vote by an interested director, or which exceeds the permission of a s 196 order, according to s 195(5). It is, however, an offence and the director may be liable for a fine as a result.

13.25 Chapter 2E: related party transactions

Chapter 2E of the *Corporations Act* also reflects elements of the no conflict rule and the requirement to obtain fully informed consent to be excused for breach. Chapter 2E is 'designed to protect the interests of a public company's members as a whole, by requiring member approval for giving financial benefits to related parties that could endanger those interests'.[202] The provisions establish the procedure by which members may approve benefits to 'related parties',[203] the information which must be provided,[204] specific exemptions,[205] and the consequences of breach.[206]

If a public company (or an entity controlled by a public company) wishes to transact in a way which gives a financial benefit to a related party then, according to s 208(1), if the transaction is not exempt under ss 210–16, it must be approved by the members in general meeting under ss 217–27. These provisions cannot be excluded by the constitution and, under s 230, compliance with these provisions does not relieve a person of any other duty imposed by the general law, the *Corporations Act*, or the constitution.

These provisions rely on the s 50AA definition of 'control' rather than the definitions of holding and subsidiary company,[207] and are not limited to bodies corporate, but include trusts, partnerships and individuals.

13.25.05 Related parties and giving a financial benefit

Two key concepts for ch 2E of the *Corporations Act* are defined in ss 228 and 229. Section 228 defines 'related parties', and s 229 defines 'giving a financial benefit'. Under ss 228(1)–(3), related parties of a public company include:

- an entity that controls a public company
- directors of the public company, and of any entity which controls the public company, and any persons who make up the controlling entity, if it is not a body corporate

201 See s 248F (replaceable rule) and Chapter 5.
202 *Corporations Act* s 207.
203 'Related parties' as defined by ibid s 228; procedure per s 217.
204 Ibid s 219.
205 Ibid ss 210–16.
206 Ibid s 209.
207 Ibid ss 46, 50. For more detail, see Chapter 3 at Section 3.25.

- spouses of any such directors or persons
- parents or children of any of the above.

An entity controlled by any of these related parties is also a related party, unless it is also controlled by the public company under s 228(4). An entity will be a related party if it would satisfy these conditions at any time in the six months prior to the transaction (s 228(5)), or if the entity believes or has reasonable grounds to believe that it will become a related party under the provisions above in the future (s 228(6)).

Entities which act in concert with a related party 'on the understanding that the related party will receive a financial benefit if the public company gives the entity a financial benefit' are also considered related parties under s 228(7).

It is clear that subsidiaries are not considered 'related parties'. Directors of subsidiaries (or sibling companies) may be caught directly through the definitions above but will not be a related party merely by being a director of a subsidiary of the public company.

Section 229(1) identifies that '[i]n determining whether a financial benefit is given for the purposes of this Chapter,' we should 'give a broad interpretation to financial benefits being given, even if criminal or civil penalties may be involved; [that] the economic and commercial substance of conduct is to prevail over its legal form; and [that we should] disregard any consideration that is or may be given for the benefit, even if the consideration is adequate'. The consideration becomes relevant under the exceptions which are discussed below.

Section 229(2) includes within the definition 'giving a financial benefit indirectly, for example, through 1 or more interposed entities; giving a financial benefit by making an informal agreement, oral agreement or an agreement that has no binding force; giving a financial benefit that does not involve paying money (for example by conferring a financial advantage)'. Then, in s 229(3), the following examples are included in the statute:

(a) giving or providing the related party finance or property;
(b) buying an asset from or selling an asset to the related party;
(c) leasing an asset from or to the related party;
(d) supplying services to or receiving services from the related party;
(e) issuing securities or granting an option to the related party;
(f) taking up or releasing an obligation of the related party.

13.25.10 Exceptions

Sections 210–16 set out exceptions to the requirement of member approval. They appear to be designed to exclude financial benefits where the related party is, for example, receiving at arms-length (or less favourable) terms, or is fully informed due to co-incidence of share ownership. Other exceptions include reasonable remuneration or indemnification issues for officers; small transactions that are unlikely to have the kind of effect which s 207 indicates that the ch 2E provisions are concerned with; benefits to members in that capacity which do not discriminate unfairly; and benefits ordered by the court.

13.25.15 The procedure

Should none of these exceptions apply, then a meeting must be called so that a vote of the members can occur. Under s 218, at least 14 days before the notice convening the meeting, the proposed notice of the meeting must be lodged with ASIC by the public company, along with the explanatory statement and any other document that will either accompany the notice of meeting or be given to the members before or at the meeting by the company, the related party or their associates, if that document could reasonably influence the member's vote. Section 219 requires the explanatory statement to set out the nature of the financial benefit to be given, each director's recommendation to the members and their reasons for it, or a reason why no recommendation is given. This naturally includes disclosure of any interest the directors may have in the outcome of the resolution. ASIC may then give the company written comments on the documents within 14 days under s 220, with the exception of commenting on whether the proposed resolution is in the best interests of the company. Should ASIC provide such comments, they must also be distributed to the members with the notice convening the meeting under s 221.

Under s 208(1), member approval must be obtained and the benefit must be given within 15 months of passing the resolution. Subject to a declaration by ASIC, related parties are prohibited from voting on the resolution under s 224. This is in contrast to ratification under the common law where no restriction on voting for the ratification exists. Should the related parties vote in contravention of s 224(1), the resolution remains valid unless it would not have passed without the prohibited votes, but the related party contravenes s 224(6).

Failure to comply with these requirements will be a contravention of s 208 but will not affect the validity of the transaction under s 209 and does not cause the company to be guilty of an offence. Those involved in the contravention will be in breach of s 209(2), which is a civil penalty provision.[208] Further, if the involved person was dishonest, then they commit an offence. If the benefit has not yet been conferred, then the court may order an injunction under s 1324 to prevent the company or entity conferring the benefit.

13.25.20 Application of the law in the HIH collapse

These provisions were considered by the court in the litigation against three senior officers of the HIH group—Mr Adler, Mr Williams and Mr Fodera—and associated entities of Adler, following suspect transactions prior to the group's collapse in 2000.[209] In *Australian Securities and Investments Commission v Adler*, Santow J considered a $10 million transfer from HIHC, a subsidiary of HIH, to Pacific Eagle Equities Pty Ltd ('PEE'), which then purchased nearly $4 million of HIH shares on the market. Adler, at that time, was a director of HIH, an officer of HIHC, and controller of Adler Corporation Pty Ltd ('Adler Corp'). Adler Corp, in addition to holding significant shares in HIH, owned the sole share of PEE, an entity incorporated on 15 June 2000, which managed a unit trust (AEUT). The $10 million transfer from HIHC, which also took place on 15 June 2000, was in exchange for one unit in AEUT, but was inadequately documented and fully unsecured. Williams, the CEO of HIH and a director of HIHC, was aware of the transfer and the use to which the money

208 As discussed in Chapter 10 at Section 10.35.10.

209 *Australian Securities and Investments Commission v Adler* (2002) 41 ACSR 72. Although there was an appeal from this decision in *Adler v Australian Securities and Investments Commission* (2003) 46 ACSR 504, it was largely dismissed.

would be put. Fodera, an executive director and finance director of HIH and director of HIHC, although not fully aware of the details, implemented the transfer and bypassing the relevant responsible officer in HIHC. The other members of HIH's board and investment committee were not informed of, did not approve of, or did not later ratify the transaction. PEE used part of the $10 million it received from HIHC in exchange for the unit in AEUT to purchase just under $4 million shares in HIH on market. ASIC contended that the market was misled into believing that this purchase was financed by Adler himself, or his family interests. The rest of the loan was used to purchase various technology stocks held by Adler Corp, and as loans to other entities associated with Adler.

The net result of the transaction was that HIHC transferred money to PEE, which gave a financial benefit to PEE, Adler and Adler Corp according to s 229. This transaction was not able to satisfy any of the exceptions, such as being at arms-length according to s 210, and as such was a breach of s 208 by HIH and HIHC. As set out in s 209, this does not cause the companies to commit an offence; instead, Adler, Williams, Fodera and Adler Corp were all involved in the contravention of s 208 by HIH and HIHC under s 209(2).[210] PEE's use of the money from HIHC to purchase shares in its parent company HIH on market was also a breach of the financial assistance provisions of the *Corporations Act*.[211]

13.30 Summary

This chapter canvassed the standard of conduct expected from directors by the fiduciary obligation, the duties in ss 182–3, the duties on disclosure of material personal interest of directors in ss 191–5, and ch 2E of the *Corporations Act*. All of these duties relate to the issue of conflict of interests.

This chapter opened with a brief consideration of the history of the fiduciary obligation as it applies to the director–company relationship. Understanding the roots of this obligation in equity assists in positioning it within the broader field of duties owed by directors. The fiduciary obligation places negative prohibitions on those in positions of authority—such as directors, officers and senior company employees—not to place themselves in a position where their personal interests or other duties will conflict with the duty they owe to the company, and a duty not to secretly profit from their position in the company. The beneficiary of this obligation is usually the company, but a number of exceptions to this position exist, including when a director purchases shares from a member, when a company is about to be wound up, and in closely-held companies.

This chapter then addressed modern considerations such as the business opportunity rule, multiple directorships, and directors owning shares in the company. Directors will generally not be permitted to compete with the company by taking up business opportunities that come to their notice due to their appointment, unless they have received the fully informed consent of the members in the general meeting. However, the courts recognise the commercial reality that directors, particularly non-executive directors, can

210 'Involved' is defined in *Corporations Act* s 79.
211 See Chapter 9.

hold multiple directorships, and as long as there is no direct conflict and the appointment is not prohibited by the constitution of the company or any other agreement.

The chapter then moved to ss 182–3 of the *Corporations Act*, which deal with a director's misuse of position or information to gain an advantage for themselves or others, or to cause detriment to the company. These sections have a thematic relationship to the fiduciary obligation but have developed differently since enactment as legislative provisions. The difference between the ability to seek the fully informed consent for ratification of a breach of the fiduciary obligation and the requirements for directors to disclosure their material personal interests under ss 191–5 was also considered. Fully informed consent must be sought from the members in general meeting for any behaviour that is considered a breach of the fiduciary obligation, such as a director being in a position of conflict due to multiple directorships or their own personal interests.

By contrast, the disclosure required under the Act is made to the board of directors, and is of any 'material personal interest', which is not defined in the Act. Failure to seek fully informed consent of the members in general meeting will see any agreement entered into in breach voidable at the option of the company; whereas a failure to comply with the disclosure provisions will not affect the validity of any dealing engaged in by the breaching director, but will be an offence. Finally, this chapter discussed the protection afforded to members of a public company under ch 2E of the *Corporations Act* in relation to related party transactions. If a public company, or an entity controlled by a public company, wishes to transact in a way which gives a financial benefit to a related party that is not exempt under the Act, then the financial benefit must be approved by the members in general meeting. Related parties is defined using the 'controlled' definition, and financial benefit is to be given a broad interpretation, according to the drafting of the Act.

These legal principles and statutory provisions, although quite different in scope and application, are all concerned with the issue of managing the conflicts of interest that may arise in relation to directors. They have different emphasis—from the strictly prophylactic fiduciary obligation and ch 2E prohibitions, to the more directed and discrete provisions in ss 182–3 and the legislative provisions on disclosure. They are all aimed at regulating self-interest and self-interested dealings as they arise in the director–company relationship.

CHAPTER

14

MEMBERS' RIGHTS AND REMEDIES

14.05 Introduction

This chapter addresses the rights of company members to protect their own interests or those of the company. This chapter focuses on the rights of shareholders in a company limited by share capital,[1] but the principles and rules discussed here apply equally to members of companies limited by guarantee. The legal protections and remedies discussed here can arise in a number of situations.[2]

A typical situation is a contest of interests between shareholders and those who control the management of the company. The matters that can give rise to a dispute include: disregard by management of a shareholder's rights (including rights to participate in meetings); dilution of a shareholder's voting power by the issue of new voting shares; ongoing mismanagement of the company; few or no dividends being paid to shareholders; involuntary expropriation of shares; alterations to the constitution that disadvantage minority shareholders; and inadequate provision of information about the company's affairs.

These contests can be subdivided, depending upon who is purporting to speak for the company. On the one hand, there may be a contest between shareholders and directors, where the directors are exercising their powers of company management in ways that adversely affect the shareholders' interests. On the other hand, there may be a contest among shareholders themselves where, for example, a minority group of shareholders

1 In corporate law, the term 'member' includes the term 'shareholder'. In a company without share capital, we refer to 'the members'. In a company with share capital, the terms 'member' and 'shareholder' can be used interchangeably.

2 Note that in this chapter we do not consider the situation where there is a contest between the interests of shareholders and those of the company's creditors, which can arise most clearly when a company is on the brink of insolvency. We deal with these issues in Chapters 15 and 16.

disagrees with a decision made at a general meeting by a majority vote. Here the question is whether the law should give recognition to the position of minority shareholders. This highlights the tension between two competing views of the corporation.

On one view, we might respond to these situations from a contractual perspective, as outlined in Chapter 2. We could argue that shareholders have come together through a process of voluntary agreement embodied in the corporate constitution and the *Corporations Act*. Those documents spell out the rights of members, allowing the possibility that individual members may find themselves out-voted in meetings. These contractual arrangements are reinforced by the law relating to directors' duties (discussed in Chapters 10 to 13) which is intended to protect members from self-serving managerial conduct.

An alternative argument is that because of differences in voting power there is a risk that not all members in a company will be treated fairly, and so the state should provide mechanisms whereby minority members can seek to protect their interests. A related reason why minority shareholders should be given legal avenues to pursue their claims was suggested by Kirby P in the New South Wales Court of Appeal, who argued that minority voices are important to the maintenance of accountability within a corporate governance structure:

> People who pursue a path of integrity, disturbing settled practices long established, generally accepted and widely regarded by those involved to be perfectly reasonable, tend—almost without exception—to invoke at first amusement, bemusement and then extreme irritation on the part of those whose conduct is questioned. ... [Judges] should support corporate gadflies when their cause is the correction of apparently unlawful and self-interested action by directors, defended by oppressive conduct.[3]

This book has addressed some of the legal doctrines and assumptions that can result in conflicts between majority and minority members' interests in a company. Chapter 7 (at Section 7.30.05) examined the legal assumption that decisions in a general meeting are made on the basis of majority rule. From the discussion in Chapter 5, we know it is legally permissible for a three-quarters majority of voting shareholders to amend the constitution (s 136(2)). There is potential for a majority group of shareholders who command a sufficient proportion of the voting power to alter the constitution to achieve a result that favours their own interests; for example, by increasing their dividend entitlements or their voting power.[4] Taking another example, a general meeting might be asked to ratify actions of the directors where those actions would otherwise amount to a breach of the directors' fiduciary duties.

But what if the majority of shareholders have the same personal interests as the directors and they vote to ratify the directors' actions despite evidence this is not in the best interests of the company? What is the legal position of the minority shareholders in these

3 *Parker v NRMA* (1993) 11 ACSR 370, 383, 384.

4 In strict terms, this need not be a majority of shareholders. Remember that voting rights attach to shares and, as a consequence, a single shareholder with sufficient voting rights can out-vote a numerical majority of shareholders who, in total, hold a lesser number of votes.

situations? If neither the directors nor the general meeting are willing to act in the company's interests, can a minority shareholder bring an action on behalf of the company against the wrongdoers? What if the action by the directors or the majority affects the personal rights of the minority shareholder(s)?

The answers to these questions are not straightforward. There is a tension between two principles. One principle, enunciated in 1887 in *North-West Transportation v Beatty*, states that each shareholder is free to exercise their voting power according to their own self-interest.[5] This follows from the fact that a share is an item of personal property, as are the rights that attach to that share. The concept of private property is deeply rooted in our legal culture and carries with it normative ideas of personal autonomy and freedom of choice. This was particularly evident in the decision in *Gambotto v WCP Ltd*, which we examined in Chapter 5 in the context of alterations to the constitution. The High Court, in rejecting the argument that a share was merely a 'capitalized dividend stream', attached great weight to the proprietary nature of the share.[6]

The second principle is that a resolution properly passed by a majority vote in a general meeting is a decision of the company[7] and so those members in the majority should exercise their joint voting power in the best interests of the company as a whole. An example of this principle is found in the High Court's judgment in *Ngurli Ltd v McCann*: 'Voting powers conferred on shareholders and powers conferred on directors by the [corporate constitution] must be used bona fide for the benefit of the company has a whole'.[8] In Chapter 5, we discussed the application of this principle in relation to the alteration of the constitution.

Finally, before moving on to examine the law in detail, we note that in practice a minority shareholder has other options in responding to problems within a company besides activating their legal rights. These other options may often be more appropriate or attractive, because they do not involve the same levels of risk, cost and delay that accompany legal proceedings.

First, there is the 'exit' option: a disgruntled minority member can sell their shares and transfer their investment dollars elsewhere. This assumes that there is a ready market for those shares in which the shareholder can receive full value. This will not often be the case for small proprietary corporations. In a larger public company, if there is a ready market, the threat that disgruntled shareholders might transfer their shares could be a source of discipline over the corporate managers who might fear that too much share activity could attract the attention of takeover bidders. In practice, however, the availability of this exit option to large institutional shareholders may be limited, depending on whether their investment strategy is active or passive, or because the size of their

5 *North-West Transportation v Beatty* (1887) 12 App Cas 589. See also *Peters' American Delicacy Co Ltd v Heath* (1939) 61 CLR 457, 504 (Dixon J).

6 *Gambotto v WCP Ltd* (1995) 182 CLR 432, [28], [31] (Mason CJ, Brennan, Deane and Dawson JJ) ('*Gambotto's Case*').

7 Confirmed in *Australasian Centre for Corporate Responsibility v Commonwealth Bank of Australia* (2016) 248 FCR 280.

8 *Ngurli Ltd v McCann* (1953) 90 CLR 425, 438 (Williams ACJ, Fullagar and Kitto JJ). The case usually cited as the original authority is *Allen v Gold Reefs of West Africa Ltd* [1900] 1 Ch 656.

shareholding may make it difficult to find a buyer, or due to the impact that the sale would have on the market and their other shareholdings.[9]

Second, there is the 'voice' option. Shareholder litigation is an obvious example of this,[10] but there are other ways a disagreement can be voiced. As seen in Chapter 7, a sufficient number of minority members can requisition an extraordinary general meeting to persuade other members about the issue at hand. This option may be limited to situations where there is no permanent block of majority votes in the corporation. However, even where control of the company has become entrenched, a vocal minority shareholder could possibly cause a reconsideration of an issue.

Third, a minority shareholder might rationally decide to do nothing. Shareholders can face considerable obstacles in monitoring, understanding, and correcting the actions of corporate managers. These obstacles include the complexity of the transactions involved, difficulties in obtaining accurate evidence, and problems in mobilising other shareholders. Often, putting up with it, at least for the short-term, may be the most rational option.[11]

Having noted these options, this chapter is concerned principally with the legal remedies that can be sought by minority shareholders. We will see that these are mainly found in the *Corporations Act*, but we begin by looking at the common law history behind the statutory provisions (at Sections 14.10–20). Then we turn to the statute, the three main remedies being actions for oppression and unfairness (at Section 14.30), the statutory derivative action (at Section 14.35), and the winding up remedy (at Section 14.40). This chapter then looks at three other forms of legislative action: injunctive relief (at Section 14.45), access to company information (at Section 14.50), and the use of civil proceedings by the Australian Securities and Investments Commission (ASIC) (at Section 14.55).

14.10 Members' rights and the common law: the rule in *Foss v Harbottle*

Today, the rights of minority members are governed mainly by sections in the *Corporations Act* and by judicial interpretation of those sections. Nevertheless, we begin by examining the historical impact of the decision in *Foss v Harbottle*[12] on the present-day position of minority shareholders and on the development of modern legal principles. This case was decided in 1843. The impact of this case has been substantially diminished by subsequent judicial decisions and legislative provisions. However, in order to understand the thinking behind the present law, it is necessary to understand the scope and impact of this decision.

In *Foss v Harbottle*, two shareholders in the Victoria Park Company brought an action against the five directors of the company. The action was brought on behalf of all the

9 See, eg, P Jahnke, 'Ownership Concentration and Institutional Investors' Governance Through Voice and Exit' (2019) 21(3) *Business and Politics* 327.

10 For example, as of mid-2024, a shareholder class action was proceeding in the Victorian Supreme Court against the casino operator Crown Resorts Ltd, alleging that the company had made misleading or deceptive statements in relation to its compliance with the *Anti-Money Laundering and Counter-Terrorism Financing Act 2006* (Cth).

11 The ideas of 'exit' and 'voice' are taken from A Hirschman, *Exit, Voice and Loyalty: Responses to Decline in Firms, Organizations and States* (Harvard University Press, 1970).

12 *Foss v Harbottle* (1843) 67 ER 189.

shareholders in the company, other than the shareholders who were also directors. The plaintiffs claimed the directors had fraudulently misappropriated the company's assets. The Court held that the two shareholders could not bring the action. The argument on which this decision was based became known as 'the rule in *Foss v Harbottle*', although the rule as it is understood today emerged only in cases subsequent to the decision.[13]

The rule in *Foss v Harbottle* is comprised of two interlocking principles. The first is described as the 'proper plaintiff principle'. This principle was later restated in *Burland v Earle* as follows: 'in order to redress a wrong done to the company, or to recover moneys or damages alleged to be due to the company, the action should prima facie be brought by the company itself'.[14] In *Christianos v Aloridge Pty Ltd*, the Federal Court supplied a more recent statement of this rule:

> It is well established that in an action to redress a wrong done to a company, or to recover money or damages alleged to be due to it, the company is the only proper plaintiff; and that the company's name should only be used as a plaintiff by the direction of the company or its directors or, where the company has been placed in liquidation, by the liquidator.[15]

It is easy to understand the application of this principle when the company incurs loss or damage due to the actions of outsiders. However, the principle also applies when the wrong is committed by company insiders. When the case concerns an alleged breach of duty by the directors, it is the company, as a separate legal entity, that is owed the duty and has suffered the harm, and so it is the company that should bring the action against those directors.

The second proposition in the rule in *Foss v Harbottle* is the 'internal management principle'. Even if the directors in that case had acted as was alleged, the company's constitution provided that the matter was one which could lawfully be put before a general meeting so that the shareholders could decide on the appropriate course of action. The case emphasised it was not the role of the court to take over the job of the general meeting. In the later case of *Edwards v Halliwell*, this principle was summarised as follows: 'where the alleged wrong is a transaction which might be made binding on the company or association and on all its members by a simple majority of the members, no individual member of the company is allowed to maintain an action in respect of that matter'.[16]

Combining these two principles, the rule in *Foss v Harbottle* is based upon the view that the majority wishes should prevail. It assumes all shareholders should be bound by this view because, either expressly or by implication, it forms part of the corporate contract that is now embodied in s 140(1) of the *Corporations Act*. The rule supports a limited role for the courts in intervening in corporate affairs. In *Foss v Harbottle*, Wigram V-C

13 See especially *Mozley v Alston* (1847) 1 Ph 790.

14 *Burland v Earle* [1902] AC 83, 93 (Lord Davey). See *Foss v Harbottle* (1843) 67 ER 189, 202; see also *Edwards v Halliwell* [1950] 2 All ER 1064, 1066.

15 *Christianos v Aloridge Pty Ltd* (1995) 58 FCR 273, 281 (Beaumont, Whitlam and Tamberlin JJ).

16 *Edwards v Halliwell* [1950] 2 All ER 1064, 1066 (Jenkins LJ). See also *Burland v Earle* [1902] AC 83, 93.

made a point of stressing the private nature of the company.[17] The importance of majority rule and judicial non-intervention was justified in 1875 by Mellish LJ in *MacDougall v Gardiner* in the following terms:

> [I]f the thing complained of is a thing which in substance the majority of the company are entitled to do, or if something has been done irregularly which the majority of the company are entitled to do regularly, or if something has been done illegally which the majority of the company are entitled to do legally, there can be no use in having litigation about it, the ultimate end of which is only that a meeting has to be called, and then ultimately the majority gets its wishes. Is it not better that the rule should be adhered to that if it is a thing which the majority are the masters of, the majority in substance shall be entitled to have their will followed? If it is a matter of that nature, it only comes to this, that the majority are the only persons who can complain that a thing which they are entitled to do has been done irregularly.[18]

The rule in *Foss v Harbottle* had some advantages. It promoted certainty and predictability in corporate decision-making by preventing shareholders from pursuing legal action simply whenever they disagreed with a company decision. The rule avoided the prospect of multiple suits being brought by several shareholders in respect of a single complaint. Furthermore, the rule reinforced the view that court resources should not be spent on resolving minor internal corporate irregularities, such as lack of quorum or insufficient notice for a meeting.

However, the rule also resulted in significant problems. One problem is that, in a general meeting, the idea of majority rule must be understood in the context of votes attaching to shares rather than to shareholders. When a vote is taken it will be decided on a show of hands, with each member having one vote, unless a member demands that a poll be taken. On a poll, the vote is decided by counting the number of votes per share that each member holds (see the replaceable rules in ss 250E and 250J). It is therefore possible that on a poll one shareholder who controls many voting shares in a company can outvote many shareholders who, cumulatively, control fewer voting shares. The operation of proxy voting systems can also affect voting outcomes. It cannot be assumed, then, that a majority vote at a general meeting is an indication of the will of the majority of the individual members. Another problem is that the joint operation of the internal management and proper plaintiff principles restricts the capacity of minority shareholders to bring actions to remedy wrongs done to the company. Yet this restriction was not always justified. Lord Denning MR provided a good summation of the problem. Suppose, he says, that directors who hold a majority of its shares defraud a corporation:

> Those directors are themselves the wrongdoers. If a board meeting is held, they will not authorise the proceedings to be taken by the company against themselves. If a general meeting is called, they will vote down any suggestion that the company should sue themselves. Yet the company is the one person who

17 *Foss v Harbottle* (1843) 67 ER 189, 202.
18 *MacDougall v Gardiner* (1875) 1 Ch D 13, 25.

> is damnified. It is the one person who should sue. In one way or another some means must be found for the company to sue. Otherwise the law would fail in its purpose. Injustice would be done without redress.[19]

For this reason, the courts occasionally declined to apply the rule in *Foss v Harbottle*.

14.15 Common law exceptions to *Foss v Harbottle*

The exceptions to the rule in *Foss v Harbottle* developed in a case-by-case manner. The cases reveal no clear policy direction, and they are sometimes difficult to rationalise with each other. Nevertheless, judges, academics and commentators tended to organise the cases under five headings that were recognised as the exceptions to the rule in *Foss v Harbottle*.[20]

14.15.05 Ultra vires actions

It was established early on that when the action about which the shareholder complained was beyond the company's power—that is, it was ultra vires—it could not be ratified by a majority. An individual member could bring an action to restrain an ultra vires transaction.[21] Note, however, that this exception is no longer relevant because of the statutory abolition of the ultra vires doctrine (see Chapter 5 at Section 5.15).

14.15.10 Special majority

The courts have long accepted that a member may challenge the actions of the majority in general meeting when the rules require a special majority of votes be obtained as a prerequisite to a decision but only a bare majority has been obtained. The special majority requirement may be imposed either by statute or by the constitution. This exception recognises that the principle of majority rule has its limitations. There are some actions—such as altering the constitution—which are so important to the rights of shareholders that any special procedures provided for them ought to be followed in all cases. A majority should not be able to circumvent these procedures by ignoring them and then arguing that the capacity to remedy the defect resides in the general meeting, which the majority controls.[22] This type of action is still relevant today.

14.15.15 Infringement of a member's personal rights

If rights are conferred on a member in their capacity as an individual member—for example, by the constitution[23] or by the *Corporations Act*[24]—then the member has a

19 *Wallersteiner v Moir (No 2)* [1975] QB 373, 390.

20 There is debate about whether these are best regarded as exceptions to the rule, or situations in which the rule has no application. An influential analysis is found in K Wedderburn, 'Shareholders' Rights and the Rule in Foss v Harbottle (1957) 15(2) *Cambridge Law Journal* 194.

21 See *Russell v Wakefield Waterworks Co* (1875) 20 LR Eq 474 and the cases cited therein.

22 See *Edwards* v *Halliwell* [1950] 2 All ER 1064 for an example of this exception.

23 For example, rights in relation to voting, dividend entitlements, pre-emption clauses, and participation in any surplus on winding up.

24 For example, rights in relation to the register of members (s 175; see *Grant v John Grant & Sons Pty Ltd* (1950) 82 CLR 1), rights to requisition meetings (s 249D), rights to demand a poll (ss 250K, 250L),

personal right of action to enforce those rights or prevent them from being infringed. These rights are discussed further at Section 14.20.10 below. The rule in *Foss v Harbottle* is concerned with wrongs done to the company, but here our concern is with wrongs done to a member. Such rights are enforceable against the company by a single member either in a personal action or, where the rights are also personal to other members, in a representative action. The personal rights 'exception' is not really an exception to *Foss v Harbottle* at all.[25] As a result, the right of a member to bring an action to protect personal rights has not been affected by the legislative responses to the rule in *Foss v Harbottle* (see Section 14.20.10 above).

14.15.20 Fraud on the minority

This was the most litigated exception to *Foss v Harbottle*. Its relevance is now historical, because of the operation of the statutory remedy for oppression (*Corporations Act* pt 2F.1) and the statutory derivative action (pt 2F.1A)—both of which are discussed later in this chapter.

This exception permitted a shareholder to bring an action against the persons who control a company where those persons exercised their power in a fraudulent manner. 'Controllers' could mean the board of directors together with a majority block of shareholders, or simply the majority shareholders. This exception is usually described as the 'fraud on the minority' or 'fraud on the power' exception, but the real concern was that there had been a 'fraud on the corporation'.[26] The minority member was permitted to bring an action to protect the interests of the company against the actions of its controllers. The term 'fraud' in this context is an equitable concept, with a wider scope than common law notions of deceit or dishonesty. It refers to situations where a power has been exercised for a purpose that is at odds with the reasons for creating that power.[27]

The fraud on the minority exception applied to an undefined range of situations where directors or majority shareholders 'use their powers, intentionally or unintentionally, fraudulently or negligently, in a manner which benefits themselves at the expense of the company'.[28] It is clear, for example, that fraud could be established where the directors appropriated corporate property at the expense of the company.[29]

There was uncertainty beyond these relatively straightforward examples. Some of the difficulties centred on the argument that, according to the internal management principle, if a majority of shareholders in a general meeting is capable of ratifying directors' conduct, then a minority member has no right of derivative action. A number of cases dealt with the capacity of the general meeting to ratify an improper exercise of

---

and the right to receive a copy of the company's annual financial report (s 314). There are many other examples throughout the *Corporations Act*.

25 *Edwards v Halliwell* [1950] 2 All ER 1064, 1067.

26 K Wedderburn, 'Shareholders' Rights and the Rule in Foss v Harbottle' (1958) 16(1) *Cambridge Law Journal* 93, 93.

27 *Vatcher v Paull* [1915] AC 372, 378 (Parker LJ).

28 *Daniels v Daniels* [1978] Ch 406, 414 (Templeman J).

29 A classic example is found in *Cook v Deeks* [1916] 1 AC 554, 564 (Lord Buckmaster LC).

power by directors. Most of these cases concerned the directors' power to issue shares. In 1953, the High Court in *Ngurli Ltd v McCann* held that a general meeting could not ratify a share issue made for improper purposes.[30] Later English decisions took a different view, holding that a bona fide exercise of power by the directors, albeit for an improper purpose, is ratifiable.[31] On this view, there would be no exception to *Foss v Harbottle*. In *Winthrop Investments Ltd v Winns Ltd*, Samuels J in the New South Wales Court of Appeal assumed that the general meeting could ratify an improper share issue by the directors. Mahoney JA agreed but left open the question whether the ratification would be effective if the majority members were motivated by the same improper purpose as the directors.[32] The suggestion was that a 'tainted' ratification would constitute a fraud on the minority.

An important procedural point concerns the form in which the member's action was brought. Under the personal rights exception, a member has capacity to bring either a personal or a representative action to protect their personal rights in situations where a wrong is said to have been done to them by the company. By contrast, cases brought under the fraud on the minority exception took the form of a derivative action. The minority member brought the action on behalf of the company against the wrongdoers in the company. As the allegation was that a wrong has been done to the company, the member's capacity to bring the action derived from the company's right of action. The member sued on behalf of the company, with all other members being bound by the result of the action.[33]

Derivative actions are now dealt with in pt 2F.1A of the *Corporations Act*. Section 236(3) abolishes the right of a person at general law to bring a derivative action and creates a statutory right in its place.

14.15.25 The interests of justice

Some courts were prepared to allow a minority shareholder to bring a derivative action where this was in the interests of justice. The origins of this argument can be traced to *Foss v Harbottle*, where the Court recognised that 'the claims of justice' might override 'any difficulties arising out of technical rules respecting the mode in which corporations are required to sue'.[34] Despite this, there was argument about whether 'the requirements of justice' was a stand-alone exception, or whether it was part of the fraud on the minority exception.

Debate about the fifth exception has now been settled by pt 2F.1A (ss 236–42) which establishes a statutory right of derivative action to the exclusion of the right of action at general law.

30 *Ngurli Ltd v McCann* (1953) 90 CLR 425.

31 *Hogg v Cramphorn Ltd* [1967] Ch 254; *Bamford v Bamford* [1970] Ch 212.

32 *Winthrop Investments Ltd v Winns Ltd* [1975] 2 NSWLR 666.

33 As a matter of procedure, these cases were argued as though the company was the defendant. This is because the minority shareholder, by definition, did not have the capacity to cause the company to bring the action. However, because the company had to be a party to the suit in order to be bound by the result it was joined as a defendant: see *Spokes v Grosvenor Hotel Co* [1897] 2 QB 124.

34 *Foss v Harbottle* (1843) 67 ER 189, 202–3.

14.20 General law remedies still available to minority shareholders

The common law provided a limited and uncertain scope for minority members to voice concerns about the actions of majority shareholders or corporate management. In response to this, statutory remedies and procedures have developed. We examine these legislative provisions later in this chapter. Before doing so, it is necessary to stress that outside the parameters of the statute some general law remedies still exist, for the benefit of members.

14.20.05 *Gambotto's Case* and expropriation of shares

Chapter 5 (at Section 5.50.10) examined one aspect of these general law rights when we looked at the High Court's decision in *Gambotto v WCP Ltd*, concerning alterations to the constitution and the expropriation of minority shares.[35] Here, we note how that decision has been applied in subsequent cases. For example, in *Winpar Holdings Ltd v Goldfields Kalgoorlie Ltd*, it was held that the *Gambotto* principles do not apply where the *Corporations Act* provides a protective mechanism for minority shareholders in a share acquisition.[36] Nor does *Gambotto* apply where a minority member loses shares as part of a selective capital reduction or a takeover offer.[37] In *Heydon v NRMA Ltd*, the New South Wales Court of Appeal considered a demutualisation proposal whereby a company limited by guarantee that operated for the mutual benefit of its members would be converted into a company limited by shares that distributed profits to its shareholders. As a part of this proposal, members of the company limited by guarantee would give up their rights in exchange for shares. Malcolm and Ormiston AJJA held that this did not involve an expropriation of minority shares or of valuable property rights attaching to shares, since all members were affected by the demutualisation. Therefore, the *Gambotto* principles did not apply. In dissent, McPherson AJA argued that *Gambotto's Case* was not confined to expropriations of minority shares by a majority—it extended to any expropriatory amendment.[38]

Another remedy at general law is that a member may have a right of action to complain about the infringement of personal rights which are granted either by statute or by the constitution. We now examine this right of personal action in more detail.

14.20.10 Infringement of a member's personal rights

A member has a right to sue to protect a personal right that is granted either by statute, case law, or by the constitution. In the case of the constitution, this action is based upon s 140(1) which gives the constitution contractual status. We discussed this in Chapter 5 and the reader is referred to that discussion.

As noted earlier (at Section 14.15.15), the courts recognised that the protection of personal rights fell outside the rule in *Foss v Harbottle*. But while this right of action had

35 *Gambotto v WCP Ltd* (1995) 182 CLR 432.

36 *Winpar Holdings Ltd v Goldfields Kalgoorlie Ltd* (2001) 166 FLR 144 (Santow J).

37 Selective reductions are deal with in Chapter 8 at Section 8.45 and takeovers in Chapter 19.

38 *Heydon v NRMA Ltd* (2000) 51 NSWLR 1.

the potential to allow the courts to avoid the strict consequences of the rule in *Foss v Harbottle*, that potential was not always fulfilled. This is because the distinction between what constitutes a personal right and a corporate right is not always clear. Professor Sealy has made the following observation:

> A judge has only to assert that he [sic] regards the case as raising a matter of individual rights to give himself jurisdiction; alternatively he has the choice of declaring that the wrong was one done to the company and he can show the plaintiff the door. ... Characteristically, this vital pre-judgment of the situation is supported by only the barest of reasoning and authority, if any at all; and, of course, the longer that judges go on doing this, the wider the range of potentially contradictory dicta there will be in the reports to confuse future generations.[39]

As Sealy indicates, this flexibility has led to inconsistent decisions. In some cases, the courts adhered to the internal management rule in response to an infringement of a personal right. In other words, the infringement has been categorised as an irregularity that can be remedied or ratified by a general meeting. In *MacDougall v Gardiner*, a general meeting was held during which five shareholders demanded that the vote on a particular issue should be taken by a poll, rather than a show of hands.[40] This demand was made in accordance with provisions in the constitution. The demand was refused, and the shareholders sought an order that the refusal was invalid and an infringement of their personal rights. The Court disagreed, holding that the refusal was simply an internal irregularity that was capable of ratification by the general meeting. The Court justified this by arguing that the category of personal rights should not be allowed to override the interests of the majority in the company.[41]

This decision can be contrasted with *Pender v Lushington*, which was decided only two years later. The constitution of the company stated each member had one vote for every 10 shares held, with a maximum of 100 votes per member. A shareholder sought to avoid this restriction by distributing his shareholding amongst some nominee shareholders. At a general meeting, the chair refused to count the votes held by the nominees. The Court held that a shareholder has an enforceable personal right to have their votes counted and recorded at a general meeting.[42] The judgments in these two cases do not make it clear why the right to have votes counted is personally enforceable while the right to demand a poll is not.

In Australia, the use of the personal rights argument received expansive treatment from King CJ in the 1988 case of *Residues Treatment & Trading Co Ltd v Southern Resources Ltd (No 4)*.[43] The facts of the case involve a takeover offer made to the shareholders in the Southern Resources company, and an attempt by the directors to defend the company against that offer by making an allotment of new shares to a friendly third party.

39 L Sealy, 'The Rule in *Foss v Harbottle*: The Australian Experience' (1989) 10(3) *Company Lawyer* 52, 54.
40 See the explanation at Section 14.10 for the difference between a show of hands and a poll.
41 *MacDougall v Gardiner* (1875) 1 Ch D 13.
42 *Pender v Lushington* (1877) 6 Ch D 70, 81 (Jessel MR).
43 *Residues Treatment & Trading Co Ltd v Southern Resources Ltd (No 4)* (1988) 6 ACLC 1160.

The takeover offeror was the holding company of two minority shareholders in Southern Resources. The effect of the fresh allotment would be to dilute the shareholding of the takeover offeror. The two minority shareholders brought an action against the directors, alleging a breach of fiduciary duty in making the share allotment and seeking to have the allotment set aside. The directors argued the plaintiff had no standing to bring the action because the wrong (if there was one) had been done to the company and the proper plaintiff principle should apply. They argued that a majority of members at a general meeting could approve the share allotment, and the Court should not hear the action. Here, the directors relied on the internal management principle.

The Supreme Court of South Australia unanimously rejected both of these arguments. On the first argument, King CJ reviewed a number of cases in which individual shareholders challenged share allotments by the directors, via a personal action.[44] His Honour found that the issue of the plaintiff's standing had either not been raised or had not been specifically discussed by the courts. Despite the absence of clear authority, in King CJ's opinion there were 'strong indications' that a shareholder has a personal right to be protected against the dilution of his or her voting rights by the improper action of the directors:

> A member's voting rights and the rights of participation which they provide in the decision making of the company are a fundamental attribute of membership and are rights which the member should be able to protect by legal action against improper diminution. The rule in *Foss* v *Harbottle* has no application where individual membership rights as opposed to corporate rights are involved. ... [T]here is a clear trend in cases of the highest authority tending to indicate the existence of a personal right in a shareholder, grounded upon equitable principles, to have the voting power of his shares undiminished by improper actions on the part of the directors and of his [sic] locus standi to institute and prosecute proceedings to protect that right.[45]

King CJ based this personal right of shareholders on equitable principles rather than on the statutory contract created by s 140(1). This is because the directors had not breached the contract in seeking to make the share allotment; they exercised a power given to them by the constitution. However, the directors had not exercised that power for the purpose for which it was conferred, and hence they breached their fiduciary duty.[46]

Turning to the internal management argument, King CJ doubted (without deciding the matter) that a majority vote could ratify a share allotment that was made for an improper purpose. At any rate, his Honour held that where there has not been any ratification by the general meeting, the potential for ratification cannot deprive a member of these personal rights.[47]

44 These include *Ngurli Ltd v McCann* (1953) 90 CLR 425; *Howard Smith Ltd v Ampol Petroleum Ltd* [1974] AC 821; *Whitehouse v Carlton Hotel Pty Ltd* (1987) 162 CLR 285.

45 *Residues Treatment & Trading Co Ltd v Southern Resources Ltd (No 4)* (1988) 6 ACLC 1160, 1165. Cf *Hogg v Cramphorn Ltd* [1967] Ch 254; *Bamford v Bamford* [1970] Ch 212.

46 For an elaboration of this argument, see A Diethelm, 'Impugned Share Allotments and the Rule in *Foss v Harbottle*' (1989) 5(3) *Australian Bar Review* 262, 265.

47 Ratification is discussed in Chapter 10 at Section 10.40.05.

Despite the continued availability of these general law remedies, company members who wished to take legal action against the company or its directors faced considerable uncertainty. For this reason, statutory remedies were gradually made available to address the shortcomings of the common law.

14.25 Statutory remedies available to members

The *Corporations Act* contains several provisions intended to overcome the limitations of the pre-existing case law. It might appear these sections constitute a cohesive 'charter of rights' for company shareholders, but that would be misleading. These sections have been added to the legislation, amended, and interpreted in a piecemeal fashion. In some respects, these sections are a response to the limitations in the common law; in other ways, those limitations have continued to affect the interpretation of the sections.

The remainder of this chapter examines the following sections of the *Corporations Act*:

- ss 232–5 (pt 2F.1): allowing for various types of court-ordered relief on the grounds of oppression or unfairness
- ss 236–42 (pt 2F.1A): the statutory derivative action, which replaces the derivative action at general law
- s 461: the winding-up provision, under which, on certain grounds, the court may order the winding up of the corporation
- s 1324: the injunction provision, which also includes the possibility of an award of compensation, and is linked to breaches of the *Corporations Act*
- s 247A: governing the right of members to have access to corporate information.

We also examine s 50 of the *ASIC Act* that empowers ASIC to commence civil proceedings.

14.30 The remedy for oppression or unfairness: pt 2F.1

Since the mid-1950s, Australian companies legislation has contained provisions that allow a member to seek a court-ordered remedy where the member is being oppressed.[48] The origins of the oppression remedy can be traced to the recommendations of a United Kingdom Board of Trade Committee in 1945. The 'Cohen Committee', as it was called, argued that minority shareholders in proprietary companies faced considerable difficulties in obtaining appropriate remedies at common law. The Cohen Committee recommended the courts be given broad discretionary powers to make orders where 'a minority of the shareholders is being oppressed'.[49] An oppression provision was included in the United Kingdom companies legislation in 1948.[50] It is clear that the oppression remedy was designed to overcome the shortcomings of the common law in relation to minority members.

48 The original Australian provisions were enacted in Queensland (*Companies Act 1931* s 379A), Tasmania (*Companies Act 1959* s 128) and Victoria (*Companies Act 1958* s 94).

49 Board of Trade (UK), *Report of the Committee on Company Law Amendment* (Cmd 6659, 1945) 30, 95 ('the Cohen Committee').

50 *Companies Act 1948* (UK) s 210.

Initially, the courts were cautious in interpreting the term 'oppression'. The legacy of *Foss v Harbottle*, with its underpinnings of judicial non-intervention and majority rule, remained strong. In 1962, the Jenkins Committee in the United Kingdom noted these limitations and recommended the section be amended so that, beyond oppression, a member could complain that the affairs of a corporation were being conducted in a manner that was unfairly prejudicial to that member's interests.[51] It was not until 1983 that similar amendments[52] were made to the legislation in Australia, when the grounds for application were extended to the present formulation whereby a member can complain of conduct that is 'oppressive or unfairly prejudicial to, or unfairly discriminatory against' that member or other members.

The remedy for oppression or unfairness is now found in *Corporations Act* pt 2F.1. The key provision is s 232. This section specifies the types of conduct about which an application can be made under s 233 for a court order, and defines the criteria used in deciding the application. A member can seek an order concerning the conduct of the company's affairs, an actual or proposed act or omission by or on behalf of the corporation, or a resolution (proposed or actual) of members or a class of members.[53] The applicant must show that what has occurred or been proposed is either contrary to the interests of the members as a whole, or that it is oppressive to, unfairly prejudicial to, or unfairly discriminatory against, a member or members. As we discuss below, this remedy is available whether the conduct affects a member in their capacity as a member or in some other capacity.

In the following analysis, keep in mind that pt 2F.1 applies to all types of company, whether with or without share capital.[54] We examine the issues raised by s 232 under four headings: the question of standing, the type of conduct about which an application can be made, the grounds for complaint, and the range of orders the court may make.

14.30.05 Standing

Section 234 gives standing to three categories of applicant: a member of a company, a former member of a company (in limited cases), and a person who is considered appropriate by ASIC. We deal with these in turn.

A member of the company may apply for an order under s 233. Being a member means being registered as a member on the company's register of members at the time the application is made (s 231). A person who has purchased shares but has not been entered on the register at the time the proceedings are commenced is not regarded as a member for these purposes. In *Niord Pty Ltd v Adelaide Petroleum NL*, the Court held that 'an equitable interest as a transferee under an unregistered transfer' is not sufficient to

51 Board of Trade (UK), *Report of the Company Law Committee* (Cmnd 1749, 1962) 73–8 ('the Jenkins Committee').

52 The Explanatory Memorandum, Companies and Securities Legislation (Miscellaneous Amendments) Bill 1983 (Cth) [475] makes it clear that the Jenkins Committee report was the basis for these amendments.

53 The concept of a 'class' of members is discussed in Chapter 8 at Section 8.15.10.

54 This includes companies limited by guarantee: *Australian Securities Commission v Multiple Sclerosis Society of Tasmania* (1993) 10 ACSR 489.

enable a shareholder to bring an action.[55] But what if the failure to register the shareholder forms part of the alleged oppressive conduct? In *Re Independent Quarries Pty Ltd*, the plaintiff held a properly sealed share certificate which had been issued by the company on the basis of a valid share transfer. However, the transfer had not been registered because the register was in the control of a rival shareholder. The Court held the plaintiff should be regarded as a member for the purposes of the application even though they had not been registered.[56] A person to whom a share in a corporation is transmitted by will or by operation of law is a member for the purposes of the section (s 234(d)).

The applicant's status as a member at the time of the application confers standing to bring proceedings. The courts have held a member can make an application in relation to conduct that occurred prior to becoming a member.[57] A member may make an application whether the conduct which they complain of affects them in their capacity as a member, or in some other capacity, or affects some other member (ss 234(a)(i), (ii)).

Part 2F.1 applies to members not only in their capacity as members but also in other capacities in which they may have dealings with the company, such as being a director or employee. This is relevant for shareholders in small companies. Consider a proprietary company with a small number of members who are also the directors. As a result of a dispute, one person is unfairly removed as a director, thereby losing remuneration entitlements and being left to rely on the discretion of the remaining directors for dividend payments. As a shareholder, that person could be trapped in the company either because there is no market for their shares or because of a share transfer restriction clause in the constitution. The member could be left without any way of deriving a benefit from participating in the company. However, not every relationship a member has with a company will provide grounds for relief; we explore this later in this chapter.

The oppression or unfairness remedy is not confined to applications by minority members. The courts recognise that it may be possible for a majority shareholder to be oppressed by a minority. In *Watson v James*, Bergin J stated:

> I do not agree that the section is only available for the protection of minorities. In my opinion this interpretation would impose an unwarranted and restrictive gloss on the language ... of Pt 2F.1 ... Although one would not expect that a controlling shareholder would need recourse to the section the complexities of shareholders' and/or directors' relationships within corporate structures are such that I am not willing to rule out the possibility of such an event.[58]

There is no requirement that the applicant member should have 'clean hands' in order to have standing. Of course, the fact the applicant has participated or acquiesced in the oppressive conduct will be relevant to the court's decision to make an order under the section.[59]

55 *Niord Pty Ltd v Adelaide Petroleum NL* (1990) 54 SASR 87.
56 *Re Independent Quarries pty Ltd* (1994) 12 ACSR 188.
57 *Re Spargos Mining NL* (1990) 3 WAR 166.
58 *Watson v James* [1999] NSWSC 600 [72].
59 *Morgan v 45 Flers Avenue Pty Ltd* (1986) 10 ACLR 692, 706.

Former members of the company have standing in limited situations. Sections 234(b) and (c) state that an application may be made by 'a person who has been removed from the register of members because of a selective reduction, or by a person who has ceased to be a member if the application relates to the circumstances in which they ceased to be a member'.

Finally, s 234(e) provides that an application may be made by 'a person whom ASIC thinks is appropriate having regard to investigations it is conducting or has conducted into the company's affairs or matters connected with the company's affairs'.

14.30.10 Type of conduct

It is important to be clear about the scope or nature of conduct to which s 232 applies, and whose conduct is relevant when considering the application of the section. The application of pt 2F.1 is premised on the fact that the applicant's complaint may relate to the way in which the company's 'affairs' are being conducted (s 232(a)). This term is defined, in a non-exhaustive way, by s 53 of the *Corporations Act*, and includes conduct that relates to membership, control, business, trading, transactions and dealings of the company, as well as its internal management and proceedings, the ownership of shares in the company, the power over voting rights and disposal rights of shares, and the audit of the company. In *Raymond v Cook*, the Queensland Court of Appeal noted that whether particular conduct falls within the ambit of the 'affairs of a company' will depend upon an examination of the facts in each case.[60] The Court added:

> Relevant conduct is not limited to external corporate activity. This jurisdiction [pt 2F.1] is intimately concerned with internal management and abuses thereof by individuals which tend to oppress others in the obtaining of their due entitlements from a properly run company. Section 53 ... expressly includes internal management and proceedings of the company, and many other matters of familiar company dealings and transactions as expressly within the affairs of a company ...[61]

Five further features of s 232 should be noted. First, the section can apply to acts or omissions (s 232(b)). This means that a refusal by the directors to declare a dividend could be the subject of an application,[62] as could a refusal to register a transfer of shares in a proprietary company. Second, the section makes it clear that a resolution of a class of members falls within the range of conduct about which an order may be sought (s 232(c)). Third, the section applies regardless of whether the act, omission, or resolution has already occurred or is proposed for the future. The section can be used by a member to prevent conduct which damages their interests before it actually occurs, or to seek remedies after the conduct has occurred.

Fourth, the section directs attention to the 'conduct' of the company's affairs. In *Fexuto Pty Ltd v Bosnjak Holdings Pty Ltd*, Priestley JA stated that this requires the court to look at

60 *Raymond v Cook* [2000] 1 Qd R 65.

61 Ibid 77.

62 See, eg, *Sanford v Sanford Courier Service Pty Ltd* (1986) 10 ACLR 549.

'the actual conduct of the affairs of the company ... [at] what was being done rather than why it was being done'.[63] Furthermore, the conduct can consist of a single isolated act.[64]

Fifth, the section does not require that the conduct must have been carried out by any particular category of people, such as directors or majority shareholders. In *Re HR Harmer Ltd*, Jenkins LJ held that the section is 'wide enough to cover oppression by anyone who is taking part in the conduct of the affairs of the company whether de facto or de jure'.[65] The section extends to cover the actions of directors, a controlling shareholder,[66] persons with de facto control of the corporation, a class of shareholders or conduct of a related company.

The last-mentioned example deserves emphasis because it raises the question of applications for oppressive or unfair conduct in the context of corporate groups. Early case law had little difficulty in finding that nominee directors had acted oppressively in preferring the interests of the nominating body to that of the company on whose board they sat. In *Scottish Co-operative Wholesale Society Ltd v Meyer*, the Co-operative Society had formed a subsidiary company. The Society held the majority of the shares in that company. The company's board of directors comprised the two remaining shareholders (Mr Meyer and Mr Lucas) and three nominee directors of the Society. The business of the company was dependent on goods supplied by the Society, which decided that the company's business should be brought to an end. It did this by raising the price of its goods and diverting business to one of its own departments. The three nominee directors knew of this and acquiesced to the plan. Meyer and Lucas made an application under the oppression provision in the *Companies Act 1948* (UK). One of the arguments in reply was that the activities of the nominee directors did not constitute conduct in affairs of the company, but instead in the affairs of the Society. The House of Lords disagreed. Viscount Simonds held that the affairs of the Society and the company were so intertwined that actions in the affairs of one were also those of the other.[67] In *Re Norvabron Pty Ltd (No 2)*, an order was made against the nominee directors of a subsidiary in a case where the subsidiary was wholly owned and controlled by a board identical to that of the holding company.[68] It appears that a unified structure between parent and subsidiary is important in these decisions.[69]

14.30.15 The grounds for complaint

Section 232 specifies two grounds for complaint. The applicant can argue the conduct in question is 'contrary to the interests of the members as a whole' (s 232(d)), and/or that it is 'oppressive to, unfairly prejudicial to, or unfairly discriminatory against' a member or members (s 232(e)). We first deal with the second of these two grounds.

63 *Fexuto Pty Ltd v Bosnjak Holdings Pty Ltd* (2001) 37 ACSR 672, [504].
64 *Re Norvabron Pty Ltd (No 2)* (1986) 11 ACLR 279, 289.
65 *Re HR Harmer Ltd* [1959] 1 WLR 62, 75.
66 *Re Great Outdoors Co Ltd* (1985) 3 ACLC 465.
67 *Scottish Co-operative Wholesale Society Ltd v Meyer* [1959] AC 324.
68 *Re Novabron Pty Ltd (No 2)* (1986) 11 ACLR 279; see also *Re Cumberland Holdings Ltd* (1976) 1 ACLR 361.
69 See P Redmond, 'Problems for Insiders' in M Gillooly (ed), *The Law Relating to Corporate Groups* (Federation Press, 1993) 225–6, citing *Morgan v 45 Flers Avenue Pty Ltd* (1986) 10 ACLR 692 as an example of where there was insufficient identity between the two companies.

When considering the ground of oppression, unfair prejudice or unfair discrimination, the immediate question is whether these terms should be read as three alternative tests or as a composite expression. The words 'unfairly prejudicial to, or unfairly discriminatory against' were added to the section in 1983 with the intention of freeing the section from the restrictive interpretation it received from the courts by reference to the term 'oppressive'.[70] The judicial consensus is that the expanded expression prescribes a single or compound test rather than three alternative tests. In *Thomas v HW Thomas Ltd*, the Court of Appeal of New Zealand considered s 209 of the *Companies Act 1955* (NZ), which referred to conduct that is 'oppressive, unfairly discriminatory, or unfairly prejudicial'. The Court held that these words are not distinct alternatives: 'the three expressions overlap, each in a sense helps to explain the other'.[71] The decision in *Thomas* was adopted by the New South Wales Court of Appeal in *New South Wales Rugby League Ltd v Wayde*.[72] This compound interpretation was affirmed more recently by the New South Wales Court of Appeal in *Tzavaras v Tzavaras & Sons Pty Ltd*.[73] Despite this composite reading of these expressions, the courts frequently hear argument on just one element. For example, in *Fexuto Pty Ltd v Bosnjak Holdings Pty Ltd*, Priestley JA observed the trend in so-called 'oppression' cases that '"[u]nfairly prejudicial" conduct has been easier to make out than "oppressive" conduct and is these days the more frequent basis for oppression proceedings'.[74]

We noted earlier that s 232 specifies two grounds for complaint. In earlier versions of this provision, the two grounds were included within the same paragraph. This invited judicial debate about whether the phrase 'contrary to interests of members' should be read as part of the composite expression.[75] The current structure of s 232 resolves this debate; the section is drafted so that the 'contrary to the interests of the members as a whole' ground occurs in a separate paragraph from, and as an alternative to, the 'oppressive or unfair' ground (ss 232(d)–(e)).[76] Nevertheless, the same set of facts may raise issues for each paragraph.[77]

In *Campbell v Backoffice Investments Pty Ltd*, Basten JA noted that the wording of these two paragraphs gives rise to two points of distinction. One is that paragraph (e), unlike paragraph (d), could cover conduct that 'operates prejudicially with respect to a member or class of members, as opposed to members as a whole'. The other is that the phrase 'contrary to the interests of', found in paragraph (d), 'would appear to extend not only beyond disparate treatment of members, but also beyond conduct oppressive to the members as a whole'.[78]

70 Explanatory Memorandum, Companies and Securities Legislation (Miscellaneous Amendments) Bill 1983 (Cth) 171.

71 *Thomas v HW Thomas Ltd* (1984) 2 ACLC 610, 617 (Richardson J).

72 *New South Wales Rugby League Ltd v Wayde* (1985) 1 NSWLR 86, affirmed by the High Court in *Wayde v New South Wales Rugby League Ltd* (1985) 180 CLR 459 without substantive discussion on this point.

73 *Yzavaras v Tzavaras & Sons Pty Ltd* [2023] NSWCA 168 [75]. See also *Hillam v Ample Source International Ltd (No 2)* (2012) 202 FCR 336.

74 *Fexuto Pty Ltd v Bosnjak Holdings Pty Ltd* (2001) 37 ACSR 672 [300].

75 *Morgan v 45 Flers Avenue Pty Ltd* (1986) 10 ACLR 692, 704; *Re Spargos Mining NL* (1990) 3 WAR 166; *Re Polyresins Pty Ltd* [1999] 1 Qd R 599.

76 Confirmed in *Turnbull v NRMA Ltd* (2004) 50 ACSR 44 [32].

77 *Exton v Extons Pty Ltd* (2017) VR 520 [20].

78 *Campbell v Backoffice Investments Pty Ltd* (2008) 66 ACSR 359 [183].

The next question is how the courts have interpreted the joint expression 'oppressive to, unfairly prejudicial to, or unfairly discriminatory against'. To answer this, we first consider interpretations of the single term 'oppressive' as it occurred before 1983 and then turn to examine the subsequent judicial treatment of the joint expression. A note of caution is needed. As indicated, the 1983 amendments were made in response to a narrow interpretation of the oppression remedy. While these earlier decisions are relevant, they must be read in light of more recent interpretations of the wider expression.

The first major case under the original oppression provision in England—*Scottish Co-operative Wholesale Society Ltd v Meyer*—exerted a strong influence on judicial attitudes about the scope of word 'oppressive'.[79] In the *Scottish Co-operative* case, Viscount Simonds resorted to the dictionary, holding that the idea of oppression denoted behaviour that is 'burdensome, harsh and wrongful' to one or more members of the company.[80] The requirement that the behaviour complained of must 'lack probity and fair dealing' was added to this in the same case.[81] In *Re Jermyn Street Turkish Baths Ltd*, Buckley LJ said '[o]ppression must, we think, import that the oppressed are being constrained to submit to something which is unfair to them as the result of some overbearing act or attitude on the part of the oppressor'.[82] In Australia, a review of the existing case law was conducted in *Re Tivoli Freeholds Ltd*.[83] This case referred to, and accepted, the interpretations made in both the cases mentioned.

There was strong similarity between the early decisions on the oppression provision and the pre-existing *Foss v Harbottle* cases in their reliance on the internal management principle. The courts were not keen on reading the statutory provision too broadly in an attempt to reform the unsatisfactory common law situation. For example, in *Re Bright Pine Mills Pty Ltd*, the Court took the view that 'it was not intended by [the legislature] to give jurisdiction to the court (a jurisdiction the courts have always been loathe to assume) to interfere with the internal management of a company by directors'.[84] As Hill notes in her review of the section, the case law under the pre-1983 oppression section was notorious for the limitations that were judicially imposed.[85] It was against this background that the section was amended in 1983.

Cases decided by reference to the amended section indicate a slowly developing trend towards a more flexible approach. In *Fexuto Pty Ltd v Bosnjak Holdings Pty Ltd*, the New South Wales Court of Appeal noted that:

> The addition of the words 'unfairly prejudicial to' and 'unfairly discriminate against', to the original statutory reference to 'oppressive', indicates an intention that the jurisdiction should not be confined by technical distinctions.[86]

79 *Scottish Co-operative Wholesale Society Ltd v Meyer* [1959] AC 324.
80 Ibid 342.
81 Ibid 364 (Lord Keith of Avonholm).
82 *Re Jermyn St Turkish Baths Ltd* [1971] 1 WLR 1042, 1060.
83 *Re Tivoli Freeholds Ltd* [1972] VR 445.
84 *Re Bright Pine Mills Pty Ltd* [1969] VR 1002, 1011.
85 J Hill, 'Protecting Minority Shareholders and Reasonable Expectations' (1992) 10(2) *Company and Securities Law Journal* 86, 92–3.
86 *Fexuto Pty Ltd v Bosnjak Holdings Pty Ltd* (2001) 37 ACSR 672 [4] (Spigelman CJ).

In one of the first cases to consider the new provision, *Re G Jeffrey (Mens Store) Pty Ltd*, Crockett J began by stating that 'the term "oppressive" must be given the same interpretation as it was given prior to the amendment of the subsection', but he went on to acknowledge that 'the newly introduced expressions ... clearly ... [make] the task of the applicant ... less onerous in respect of the conduct about which he is entitled to complain'.[87] On the facts of the case, a shareholder argued he had been locked into a company because no other shareholders would buy him out. The judge declined to apply the section, holding there was nothing inherently unfair in being required to abide by the decisions of the majority of the shareholders or directors. One year later, in *Wayde v New South Wales Rugby League Ltd*, the High Court of Australia had occasion to consider the oppression section. The board of New South Wales Rugby League decided that the Western Suburbs Rugby League club ('Wests') would be refused entry into the 1985 rugby league competition. New South Wales Rugby League was incorporated as a company limited by guarantee, and its membership was comprised of representatives of the different football clubs playing in the competition. The Wests representatives, as members of the company, brought an action under a predecessor of s 232: s 320 of the *Companies Code*.

Four judges of the five-member Court delivered a joint judgment, which stressed that Wests' task was to show that the decisions in question were 'oppressive or *unfairly* prejudicial or discriminatory' to their interests.[88] The joint judgment noted that, in making its decision to exclude Wests from the competition, the board had exercised a discretion that was expressly given to it by the constitution. As long as the discretionary power to discriminate between different members was exercised bona fide and for a proper purpose, then the board's decision was not actionable under the section.

The joint judgment stated that a different approach might be appropriate where the directors were exercising general powers of management rather than a specific grant of discretion. In that type of case, the court 'may be required ... to undertake a balancing exercise between the competing considerations',[89] and would examine the policy that the directors have pursued, to determine its fairness or unfairness. This follows the approach suggested by Richardson J in *Thomas v HW Thomas Ltd*:

> Fairness cannot be assessed in a vacuum or simply from one member's point of view. It will often depend on weighing conflicting interests of different groups within the company.[90]

In his separate concurring judgment, Brennan J noted that the legislative intention behind the amended section was to establish broader grounds for judicial intervention than had existed previously. The earlier judicial definitions of oppression were no longer determinative: '[a]t a minimum, oppression imports unfairness and that is the critical question'.[91] As with the joint judgment, Brennan J stressed that mere prejudice or discrimination is

87 *Re G Jeffrey (Mens Store) Pty Ltd* (1984) 9 ACLR 193, 198.
88 *Wayde v New South Wales Rugby League Ltd* (1985) 180 CLR 459, 468.
89 Ibid 466.
90 *Thomas v HW Thomas* (1984) 2 ACLC 610, 618.
91 *Wayde v New South Wales Rugby League Ltd* (1985) 180 CLR 459, 472.

not enough; there must be proof of oppression or unfairness. But Brennan J differed from the other judges in not making the distinction between a specifically conferred discretion and a general grant of managerial power. His Honour held that unfairness was a question of fact and degree in each case, and the need for judicial intervention should be established on an objective basis by reference to 'ordinary standards of reasonableness and fair dealing'. In the circumstances of *Wayde's* case, this meant that:

> The Court must determine whether reasonable directors, possessing any special skill, knowledge or acumen possessed by the directors and having in mind the importance of furthering the corporate object on the one hand and the disadvantage, disability or burden which their decision will impose on a member on the other, would have decided that it was unfair to make that decision.[92]

The High Court's reasoning in *Wayde's* case was adopted in *Re Spargos Mining NL*, where Murray J characterised the section as being concerned with questions of fairness. According to his Honour:

> [T]he opinion required of the Court is that objectively viewed, the conduct of those in control of the company is in all the circumstances to be regarded as unfair to a particular member, a group of members, perhaps a minority group, or the members as a whole and ... unfairness may lie in the harm suffered as a result of the conduct of management, the prejudice caused, the lack of reasonable commercial justification for the course taken, or simply in the decision making processes within the company.[93]

This passage emphasises that oppression or unfairness can be found in either the effect the conduct has on members (substantive unfairness) or in the procedures used by those who control the company (procedural unfairness). The passage also makes it clear that pt 2F.1 includes, but is not limited to, actions for breach of fiduciary duty by directors.[94] Equally, bona fide actions by directors can be classified as unfair. As Brennan J noted in *Wayde's* case:

> [I]f directors exercise a power—albeit in good faith and for a purpose within the power—so as to impose a disadvantage, disability or burden on a member that, according to ordinary standards of reasonableness and fair dealing is unfair, the court may intervene.[95]

Similarly, unlawfulness, in the sense of a breach of the *Corporations Act*, the constitution, or other unlawful conduct will more readily lead to court intervention under pt 2F.1, although unlawfulness is not necessary to the operation of the section; the conduct of a company's affairs may be oppressive even if it lawful.[96]

92 Ibid 473.
93 *Re Spargos Mining NL* (1990) 3 WAR 166, 189.
94 See, eg, *Re George Raymond Pty Ltd; Salter v Gilbertson* (2000) 18 ACLC 85.
95 *Wayde v New South Wales Rugby League Ltd* (1985) 180 CLR 459, 472.
96 *Australian Securities Commission v Multiple Sclerosis Society of Tasmania* (1993) 10 ACSR 489; *Campbell v Backoffice Investments Pty Ltd* (2009) 238 CLR 304 [176] (Gummow, Hayne, Heydon and Kiefel JJ).

The application of the unfairness test to the conduct of directors was discussed in a subsequent case involving the same plaintiff and group of corporations as in the *Spargos* case. *Jenkins v Enterprise Gold Mines NL* involved an action by a shareholder against directors of a company brought under a predecessor to pt 2F.1. The Court stated that:

> It is for the court to decide whether in balancing the interests of the company as a whole against minority interests the directors have acted so as to unfairly prejudice the interests of the minority. The court decides this 'according to ordinary standards of reasonableness and fair dealing'. Whether the conduct is unfairly discriminatory will be judged on standards which reasonable directors with such skills as directors should have, acting bona fide, would think to be fair.[97]

It is clear from these dicta that we should be cautious in generalising from judgments based upon particular sets of facts. As was noted in *Shamsallah Holdings Pty Ltd v CBD Refrigeration and Airconditioning Services Pty Ltd*, 'the impugned conduct is not to be assessed in a vacuum. It is necessary to look at the history of the company, the extent of its financial needs and the reasonable expectation of its members, among other factors.'[98] Similarly, in *Australian Institute of Fitness Pty Ltd v Australian Institute of Fitness (Vic/Tas) Pty Ltd (No 3)*, Sackar J emphasised that 'the court should be informed by the context in determining whether a decision is unfair'.[99] Furthermore, the courts continue to express caution about intervening in the exercise of corporate powers. In deciding whether to exercise power under s 232, the courts emphasise the need to 'respect the traditional roles of directors and shareholders in relation to corporate management',[100] and not interfere 'unless appropriate cause is shown'.[101] In *Sandy v Yindjibarndi Aboriginal Corporation RNTBC (No 4)*, Pritchard J emphasised that:

> In determining whether conduct is oppressive within the meaning of the section, the courts are not concerned with reviewing the underlying merits of the decisions of the directors. ... Actions for oppressive conduct are not the vehicle for de facto appeals on the merits of management decisions.[102]

With the caution about generalising from specific cases in mind, the following matters are examples of conduct that are *not* likely to constitute oppression or unfairness under s 232:

- being unable to dispose of one's shares as minority shareholder where there is no attempt by the majority to frustrate the disposal[103]

97 *Jenkins v Enterprise Gold Mines NL* (1992) 6 ACSR 539, 550.

98 *Shamsallah Holdings Pty Ltd v CBD Refrigeration and Airconditioning Services Pty Ltd* (2001) 19 ACLC 517 [52] (Owen J).

99 *Australian Institute of Fitness Pty Ltd v Australian Institute of Fitness (Vic/Tas) Pty Ltd (No 3)* (2015) 109 ACSR 369 [90].

100 *McCausland v Surfing Hardware International Holdings Pty Ltd* [2013] NSWSC 902 [651].

101 *HNA Irish Nominee Ltd v Kinghorn (No 2)* (2012) 290 ALR 372 [507].

102 *Sandy v Yindjibarndi Aboriginal Corporation RNTBC (No 4)* (2018) 126 ACSR 370 [115]. This case dealt with an equivalent section in the *Corporations (Aboriginal and Torres Strait Islander) Act 2006* (Cth).

103 *McWilliam v LJR McWilliam Estates Pty Ltd* (1990) 20 NSWLR 703.

- managing the company in an overbearing or conservative but otherwise proper manner to the dissatisfaction of a minority shareholder.[104] Similarly, 'oppression will not be found where a company has merely been mismanaged or managed poorly'[105]
- 'it will not be oppressive for the controllers of a company to insist on the adoption of policies on matters of business judgment concerning matters on which there may be legitimate differences of opinion'[106]
- paying low levels of dividend at the same time as the directors of a small proprietary corporation are paid high but commercially reasonable levels of fees and bonuses[107]
- similarly, 'a mere failure to pay dividends, even where they are able to be paid, does not constitute oppression or unfairness but is capable of being oppressive in some circumstances'. Those circumstances include the history of the company, the extent of its financial needs and the reasonable expectations of its members[108]
- failure by directors to give members access to information that directors are not obliged to give, especially where the members are associated with a competitor[109]
- irreconcilable differences among persons involved in a 'quasi-partnership' company do not of themselves constitute oppression or unfair prejudice (although, as we discuss later in this chapter, they may be grounds for winding up).[110]

With the same caution, the following matters are examples of conduct which may be characterised as oppressive or unfair:

- diversion of the company's business by directors or majority shareholders to another company in which they have an interest, or conducting the company's affairs to advance their own interests at the expense of a minority shareholder[111]
- an alteration of the company's constitution to restrict or extinguish the voting power of a takeover offeror[112]
- management of the company by reference to other interests in a corporate group, to the detriment of the first company[113]

---

104 Regarding overbearing conduct, see *Re G Jeffrey (Mens Store) Pty Ltd* (1984) 9 ACLR 193; cf *Re Bagot Well Pastoral Co Pty Ltd* (1993) 11 ACLC 1. As for conservative conduct, see *Thomas v HW Thomas Ltd* (1984) 2 ACLC 610.

105 *Australian Institute of Fitness Pty Ltd v Australian Institute of Fitness (Vic/Tas) Pty Ltd (No 3)* (2015) 109 ACSR 369 [95].

106 Ibid.

107 *Morgan v 45 Flers Avenue Pty Ltd* (1986) 10 ACLR 692; cf *Sanford v Sanford Courier Service Pty Ltd* (1986) 10 ACLR 549. See also *Shamsallah Holdings Pty Ltd v CBD Refrigeration and Airconditioning Services Pty Ltd* (2001) 19 ACLC 517.

108 *Roberts v Walter Developments Pty Ltd* (1997) 15 ACLC 882.

109 *Shamsallah Holdings Pty Ltd v CBD Refrigeration and Airconditioning Services Pty Ltd* (2001) 19 ACLC 517.

110 *Fexuto Pty Ltd v Bosnjak Holdings Pty Ltd* (2001) 37 ACSR 672 [89] (Spigelman J).

111 *Re Bright Pine Mills Pty Ltd* [1969] VR 1002; *Catalano v Managing Australia Destinations Pty Ltd* (2014) 314 ALR 62.

112 *Shears v Phosphate Co-operative Co of Australia Ltd* (1989) 7 ACLC 812 but compare the finding at first instance: (1986) 6 ACLC 124.

113 *Re Spargos Mining NL* (1990) 3 WAR 166; *Jenkins v Enterprise Gold Mines NL* (1992) 6 ACSR 539. Note that s 187 now permits the director of a wholly owned subsidiary to act in the best interests of the holding company if the subsidiary's constitution permits this, the director acts in good faith, and the subsidiary is not insolvent.

- repeated use of commercial tactics at board and general meetings which have the effect of depriving minority members of the right to fully participate in those meetings[114]
- the issue of shares by directors for the purpose of reducing another shareholder's stake in the company[115]
- a breach of fiduciary duty by a director in a small proprietary company, involving mixing personal and company financial affairs, failure to disclose, failure to call meetings, and obstructing the access of other shareholders/directors to company records[116]
- low dividend payments resulting from a failure by the directors to review the company's dividend policy in the context of the company's improving cash position.[117]

The separate ground for complaint under s 232 is that the conduct is 'contrary to the interests of the members as a whole' (s 232(d)). This ground has not received the same degree of judicial analysis as the oppression or unfairness ground. The decision of the New South Wales Court of Appeal in *Wayde's* case was based on this phrase, with the Court holding that it reflects the broad equitable limitation imposed on the actions of a majority voting block of shareholders by reference to 'the benefit of the corporation as a whole'.[118] The Court went on to argue that '[t]he only legitimate interests of the members would be their interests as corporators. As corporators, considered as a whole, their legitimate interests must be circumscribed by, and found within, the constituting documents of the company'.[119] In *Goozee v Graphic World Group Holdings Pty Ltd*, it was noted that the phrase 'members as a whole' directs the court's attention to the interests of 'an individual hypothetical member'; the test is objective.[120] In *Sandy v Yindjibarndi Aboriginal Corporation RNTBC (No 4)*, Pritchard J reviewed the earlier case authority and noted that the phrase 'contrary to the interests of the members as a whole' has been equated with 'the benefit of the company as a whole', adding that those interests are 'circumscribed by, and found within, the constituting documents of the company'.[121]

Two examples of conduct that could be found to be contrary to the interests of members as a whole are breaches of statutory or fiduciary duty by directors and officers,[122] and the diversion of funds by a company director to another company controlled by that director.[123]

114 *John J Starr (Real Estate) Pty Ltd v Robert R Andrew (Australasia) Pty Ltd* (1991) 9 ACLC 1372.

115 *Kokotovich Constructions Pty Ltd v Wallington* (1995) 13 ACLC 1113.

116 *Martin v Australian Squash Club Pty Ltd* (1996) 14 ACLC 452.

117 *Shamsallah Holdings Pty Ltd v CBD Refrigeration and Airconditioning Services Pty Ltd* (2001) 19 ACLC 517.

118 *New South Wales Rugby League Ltd v Wayde* (1985) 1 NSWLR 86.

119 Ibid 186. This issue was not addressed by the High Court, which upheld the Court of Appeal's decision.

120 *Goozee v Graphic World Group Holdings Pty ltd* (2002) 42 ACSR 534.

121 *Sandy v Yindjibarndi Aboriginal Corporation RNTBC (No 4)* (2018) 126 ACSR 370 [99]–[100], citing the New South Wales Supreme Court of Appeal's decision in *Wayde's* case.

122 *Exton v Extons Pty Ltd* (2017) VR 520 [39].

123 *Bilsborough v Bilsborough* [2016] VSC 211.

14.30.20 Orders

If the court is satisfied that the applicant has established one or more of the grounds in s 232, the court has two decisions to make. The first decision is whether to make any order at all.

Section 232 states that the court 'may' make an order, giving the court discretion to exercise judicial caution about intervening in a company's internal affairs. This point was made by Brooking J in *Zephyr Holdings Pty Ltd v Jack Chia (Australia) Ltd*.[124] His Honour noted that the section requires the court to decide two things: whether the relevant ground for complaint is established and whether the court should exercise its discretion to make an order. He continued:

> If, in a striking case, the court has a very clear view that serious detriment will result from a proposed act to the members as a whole, it may be induced to make an order without hesitation, even though bad faith is not established. Other cases may be much closer to the line. All sorts of gradations are possible. If in a doubtful case, the court decides to refuse relief, it may be difficult to say whether the refusal is based on a failure to establish the 'ground' under [s 232] or on the exercise of a discretion. The two matters must overlap. For the clearer and stronger the 'ground', the greater the prospect of a favourable exercise of discretion.[125]

If the court decides to make an order, the second decision is what order or orders to make. The power to make orders is given by s 233, and the courts have stressed that the powers under that section only arise for consideration after the conditions in s 232 have been met.[126] Section 233 lists several examples but makes it clear that the court can make 'any order ... that it considers appropriate in relation to the company'. The examples listed in s 233 include an order that the company be wound up (although courts have expressed the view that this should be avoided if there is a viable alternative);[127] an order for the purchase of shares by another member or by the corporation;[128] an order directing the company or authorising a member to institute, prosecute, defend or discontinue specified proceedings;[129] or an order requiring a person to do a specified act or thing. For example, the court may order that an issue of shares be set aside, and that the company's register of members be rectified.[130]

In deciding on which remedy to order, the courts have emphasised two points: it must be the least intrusive remedy available in the circumstances, and the aim of the order must be 'to put an end to the oppression'.[131]

124 *Zephyr Holdings Pty Ltd v Jack Chia (Australia) Ltd* (1989) 7 ACLC 239.

125 Ibid 246.

126 See, eg, *CIP Group Pty Ltd v So* (2022) 164 ACSR 566 [68].

127 *John J Starr (Real Estate) Pty Ltd v Robert R Andrew (Australasia) Pty Ltd* (1991) 9 ACLC 1372.

128 Such orders raise the often difficult question of how to value the shares: see *Smith Martis Cork & Rajan Pty Ltd v Benjamin Corporation Pty Ltd* (2004) 207 ALR 136 [70]–[79] for a summary of the relevant principles to be applied.

129 See, eg, *Re Overton Holdings Ltd* [1985] WAR 224 (member authorised to initiate proceedings on behalf of company). The statutory derivative action, described later in this chapter, provides an alternative to this.

130 *Corbett v Corbett Court Pty Ltd* (2015) 109 ACSR 296.

131 *Munstermann v Rayward* [2017] NSWSC 133 [22] (Stevenson J).

The indicative list of orders in s 233 includes an order that the company's existing constitution be modified or repealed. It is equally open to the court to order that the company should adopt a constitution, as implied by s 233(3). Where an order is made about the repeal, modification or adoption of a constitution, sub-s (3) states that the company does not have the power under s 136 to change or repeal the constitution inconsistently with the order unless this is permitted by the court.

Orders for the purchase of the minority members' shares are one of the more frequent forms of relief sought and granted. However, this requires the court to exercise its discretion, having found sufficient evidence of oppression or unfairness. By comparison, in some overseas jurisdictions, minority shareholders have a statutory remedy whereby, in defined instances, a shareholder can require the company to purchase their shares.[132] This 'buy out' or 'appraisal' remedy applies in certain situations where a dissenting shareholder is affected by a fundamental change (as defined in the legislation) to the company, even though there may be no oppression or unfairness. One of the advantages claimed for this type of remedy is that it 'recognises not only that there is a level of change to which it is unreasonable to require shareholders to submit but also that in many cases the presence of a disgruntled minority shareholder will be of little benefit to the company itself'.[133]

In *Jenkins v Enterprise Gold Mines NL*, the Court indicated that s 233 should be interpreted broadly:

> Once the relevant oppression or unfairness is found, it is the obligation of the court to grant whatever relief is best suited to deal with that conduct. ... There is nothing in the language of [pt 2F.1] which suggests that the court should be reluctant to interfere where that is necessary or desirable to give effective relief.[134]

The Court added that if the desired result can be achieved by a general meeting of the corporation, then that might be the preferable approach.

An example of the wide discretion exercisable by the courts is found in *Re Spargos Mining NL* where Murray J ordered that the existing directors of the corporation cease to hold office and appointed an independent board for 12 months with instructions to investigate the affairs of the corporation and report back to the court.[135]

Another example is *Hannes v MJH Pty Ltd*.[136] Mr Hannes was the governing director of a family company. Under the constitution, he had the right to the whole management, government and control of the company, as well as control over the majority of votes at general meetings. Hannes and the other director passed resolutions that allotted ordinary shares to another company controlled by Hannes, and caused the family company to enter into a service agreement with him. That agreement contained terms that were

132 See, eg, *Companies Act 1993* (NZ) ss 110–15; *Business Corporations Act 1982* (Ontario) s 185.
133 New Zealand Law Commission, *Company Law Reform and Restatement* (Report No 9, 1989) 50.
134 *Jenkins v Enterprise Gold Mines NL* (1992) 6 ACSR 539, 561, 562.
135 *Re Spargos Mining NL* (1990) 3 WAR 166.
136 *Hannes v MJH Pty Ltd* (1992) 10 ACLC 400.

favourable to Hannes, including a salary of $90,000, a luxury motor vehicle and provision for a termination payment of $500,000. At first instance, the judge found that Hannes' conduct was oppressive and made orders that restricted his powers and amended the constitution. On appeal, the Court agreed that Hannes' actions had been oppressive, unfairly prejudicial, and unfairly discriminatory. However, the Court held that the trial judge's orders relating to the constitutional amendments had gone too far. As Sheller JA put it: 'I do not think the circumstances permitted the Court, in the exercise of its discretion under the section, to amend the [corporate constitution] so radically to alter the balance of power in the company.'[137]

14.35 The statutory derivative action: pt 2F.1A

Part 2F.1A gives a person a right to bring an action on behalf of a company, in the company's name, against persons who have caused loss to the company. This right of action is known as the 'statutory derivative action'.

The statutory derivative action was added to the *Corporations Act* in 1999. According to the Explanatory Memorandum accompanying those reforms, the intention was to address three shortcomings in the common law derivative action. First, the common law right to bring a derivative action could be removed by a ratification of the impugned conduct by the general meeting of shareholders. Second, a shareholder who sought to enforce a right on behalf of a company faced the risk of having costs awarded against them in a case which was intended to benefit the entire company. Third, the courts had set strict criteria as a prerequisite to granting leave to bring such an action.[138]

The statutory derivative action abolishes the right at common law to bring a derivative action under the fourth (and fifth) exceptions to the rule in *Foss v Harbottle* (s 236(3)).[139] The statutory derivative action does not affect a member's right to bring an action against the company to protect a personal right.

14.35.05 Who may apply for a derivative action?

The derivative action provisions in pt 2F.1A deal with how a person obtains standing to bring such an action. These sections are procedural; they are not concerned with the substantive issues raised in a particular action, although substantive issues are likely to influence the decision about standing.[140] The legislation does not define or delimit the type of matter which can be the subject of a derivative action.

A derivative action is defined in s 236(1) as an action in which a person either brings proceedings on behalf of and in the name of a company or intervenes in any proceedings to which the company is a party for the purpose of taking responsibility for those proceedings on behalf of, and in the name of, the company. There are two broad categories of

137 Ibid 418.

138 Explanatory Memorandum, Corporate Law Economic Reform Program Bill 1998 (Cth) 19.

139 *Karam v Australia and New Zealand Banking Group Ltd* (2000) 34 ACSR 545; *Chapman v E-Sports Club Worldwide Ltd* (2000) 35 ACSR 462.

140 The procedural nature of the provisions was discussed by Santow J in *Karam v Australia and New Zealand Banking Group Ltd* (2000) 34 ACSR 545; affirmed in *Virgtel Ltd v Zabusky* [2006] 2 Qd R 81.

person who can bring a derivative action: members and company officers. To be a 'member' for these purposes, a person must be a current or former member, or be entitled to be registered as a member, of the company or of a related body corporate. The reference to related bodies corporate means that the statutory derivative action is relevant to those corporate groups that are defined by holding/subsidiary company relationships (s 50). To be a 'company officer', a person must be a current or former officer of the company.[141]

The inclusion of company officers as eligible applicants gives the statutory derivative action wider scope than the previous common law action, which was restricted to actions by members. The inclusion of former members also gives these sections wider scope than the oppression provisions which can only be used by a former member in limited circumstances.

The section does not include ASIC as an eligible applicant. Prior to the introduction of pt 2F.1A, there had been a recommendation that the Commission should be listed, on the grounds that this would 'assist in the recognition of the Commission as a protector of the broader public interest in the orderly administration of the affairs of companies'.[142] In contrast, when the statutory derivative action was introduced, the Explanatory Memorandum stated that 'the statutory action is not intended to be regulatory in nature, but to facilitate private parties to enforce existing rights attaching to the company—effectively, the action is designed to be a self-help measure'.[143] As we explain later in this chapter, ASIC has standing under other provisions: notably s 461 of the *Corporations Act* (winding up) and s 50 of the *ASIC Act* (power to commence civil proceedings).

14.35.10 Grounds for granting leave

To commence a derivative action, leave from the court must first be obtained (s 236(1)(b)). The court *must* grant leave if all five criteria set out in s 237(2) are satisfied; if any of the criteria are not proven then the court will refuse leave.[144] The five criteria are as follows.

First, it is probable that the company will not bring the proceedings itself or take responsibility for them (s 237(2)(a)). One way of determining this will be to look at how the board of directors has responded to the notice of intention to apply for leave that the applicant has served on the company (see the discussion of the fifth criteria, below). Another factor will be the extent to which any board decision regarding corporate inaction has been influenced by directors whose actions are the subject of the potential derivative suit.[145]

Second, the applicant is acting in good faith (s 237(2)(b)). The purpose of this requirement is to rule out suits in which the applicant's real goal is pursuit of a personal, rather than a corporate, remedy. The court will be required to review the motives of the applicant—a review which is likely to involve some judgment about the merits of the action.

141 It is not sufficient to be an officer of a related body corporate: *Oates v Consolidated Capital Services Ltd* (2009) 76 NSWLR 69.

142 Companies and Securities Law Review Committee, *Enforcement of the Duties of Directors and Officers of a Company by Means of a Statutory Derivative Action* (Report No 12, 1990) [63].

143 Explanatory Memorandum, Corporate Law Economic Reform Program Bill 1998 (Cth) 21.

144 *Huang v Wang* (2016) 114 ACSR 586 [57].

145 See, eg, *Cassegrain v Gerard Cassegrain Pty Ltd* (2008) 68 ACSR 132 [70].

In *Swansson v RA Pratt Properties Pty Ltd*, Palmer J analysed the good faith requirement as being comprised of two interrelated factors:

> The first is whether the applicant honestly believes that a good cause of action exists and has a reasonable prospect of success. Clearly, whether the applicant honestly holds such a belief would not simply be a matter of bald assertion: the applicant may be disbelieved if no reasonable person in the circumstances could hold that belief. The second factor is whether the applicant is seeking to bring the derivative suit for such a collateral purpose as would amount to an abuse of process.[146]

His Honour went to explain that:

> These two factors will, in most but not all, cases entirely overlap: if the court is not satisfied that the applicant actually holds the requisite belief, that fact alone would be sufficient to lead to the conclusion that the application must be made for a collateral purpose, so as to be an abuse of process. The applicant may, however, believe that the company has a good cause of action with a reasonable prospect of success but nevertheless may be intent on bringing the derivative action, not to prosecute it to a conclusion, but to use it as a means for obtaining some advantage for which the action is not designed or for some collateral advantage beyond what the law offers. If that is shown, the application and the derivative suit itself would be an abuse of the court's process. The applicant would fail the requirement of s 237(2)(b).[147]

In *Chapman v E-Sports Club Worldwide Ltd*, for example, the Court refused to grant an application because, among other things, it appeared that the plaintiff was attempting to use the proceedings to put pressure on other parties in the company to buy him out.[148]

Third, it is in the company's best interests for the court to grant leave (s 237(2)(c)). This criterion lies at the heart of the derivative action because it is the company's interests, rather than those of the applicant or any group of directors or shareholders, that are at stake. However, it is not left to the company alone—through either the board of directors or the general meeting of shareholders—to decide what is in the company's best interests. While the views of these two groups are clearly relevant, the company's interests are a matter for judicial determination. In *Huang v Wang*, Bathurst CJ, citing *Swansson v RA Pratt Properties Pty Ltd*, held that 'that the requirement of best interests requires the applicant to establish on the balance of probabilities that the action is in the best interests of the company, a fact which can only be determined by taking into account all relevant circumstances'.[149] In *Blakeney v Blakeney*, the Court listed the following relevant circumstances:

> First, the character and scale of the company. Second, the nature of the company's business, so that the effects of the proposed litigation on that business

146 *Swansson v RA Pratt Properties Pty Ltd* (2002) 42 ACSR 313 [36]. This analysis was affirmed in *Chahwan v Euphoric Pty Ltd* (2008) 245 ALR 780.

147 *Swansson v RA Pratt Properties Pty Ltd* (2002) 42 ACSR 313 [37].

148 *Chapman v E-Sports Club Worldwide Ltd* (2000) 35 ACSR 462.

149 *Huang v Wang* (2016) 114 ACSR 586 [57], citing *Swansson v RA Pratt Properties Pty Ltd* (2002) 42 ACSR 313.

> may be considered. Third, whether the substance of what the applicant seeks to achieve can be achieved by means other than a derivative action and without the involvement of the company in any litigation. Fourth, evidence as to the ability of the defendant to meet the judgment, or at least a substantial part of it, so as to assess whether the action will be of practical benefit to the company.[150]

In *Re Gladstone Pacific Nickel Ltd*, Ball J noted that this criterion raises two questions: 'One is whether it is in the best interests of the company that the action be brought. The other is whether it is in the best interests of the company that it be brought by the applicant.'[151]

There is one limitation on the court's discretion. The legislation contains a rebuttable presumption (in s 237(3)) that granting leave will *not* be in the company's best interests if the derivative action involves a suit between the company and a third party[152] and the directors have decided that the company will not bring, defend or continue with those proceedings. Importantly, s 237(3)(c) requires that in making that decision the directors must:

- act in good faith for a proper purpose
- not have a material personal interest in the decision
- inform themselves about the subject matter of the decision to the extent they reasonably believe to be appropriate
- rationally believe that the decision is in the best interests of the company.[153]

There is a further implication of the 'best interests' criterion. Even if the company has suffered a wrong that could, in theory, be the subject of a derivative suit, it may not be in the company's interests for action to be taken. For example, the benefit to the company of the potential remedy may be significantly outweighed by the financial or reputational costs of the action.

Fourth, there is a serious question to be tried (s 237(2)(d)). This criterion imports the test that is used by Australian courts in determining interlocutory injunction applications.[154] Under that test, the court must determine that the applicant's claim is not frivolous or vexatious, that it has a real prospect of succeeding, and that the balance of convenience favours granting leave.[155] Put another way, 'the applicant ... must make out a prima facie case in the sense that if the evidence remains as it is there is a probability that at the trial of the proposed action the company will be entitled to relief'.[156] The court may be faced with the prospect of engaging in a 'mini-trial' on the substantive issues of the case. As Bathurst CJ observed in *Huang v Wang*:

> It must be remembered that an application under the section does not involve a consideration of the underlying merits of the proposed litigation,

150 *Blakeney v Blakeney* (2016) 113 ACSR 398 [54].

151 *Re Gladstone Pacific Nickel Pty Ltd* (2011) 86 ACSR 432 [57].

152 The term 'third party' is defined, for these purposes, in s 237(4).

153 Note that s 237(3)(c) follows the wording of the business judgment rule in s 180(2).

154 Confirmed, for example, in *The App Shop Pty Ltd v Jalal Brothers Pty Ltd* [2019] NSWSC 490 [28].

155 *Nicholas John Holdings Pty Ltd v Australia and New Zealand Banking Group Ltd* [1992] 2 VR 715, 722–3 (Hedigan J).

156 *Tydeman v Asgard Group Pty Ltd* [2023] FCA 486 [47] (Stewart J).

except to the extent it is necessary to determine if there is a serious question to be tried.[157]

Fifth, the applicant has notified the company of the application (s 237(2)(e)). Although this is the last criterion in the list, procedurally it precedes the others. Before applying for leave, the applicant must give the company 14 days' written notice of the intention to apply, together with the reasons for the application. This notice will give the board of directors the opportunity to decide whether the company should commence the action in its own right, thereby avoiding the need for a derivative suit. Alternatively, receipt of the notice might lead to the settlement of the dispute out of court, thereby avoiding the need for any litigation at all. However, giving notice is not crucial to the leave application in all cases; the court may grant leave in the absence of such notice provided that it is appropriate to do so (s 237(2)(e)), and provided that the other four criteria have been satisfied. Some guidance about when it will be appropriate to forego the notice can be found in the Explanatory Memorandum to the Bill that introduced these provisions: '[t]he applicant does not need to meet the requirement of 14 days' notice where it is not practical or expedient, thus allowing for an ex parte hearing where there is a need for urgent litigation'.[158]

Neither the right to apply for leave to commence a derivative action nor the right to bring the action once leave has been granted will be negated by the fact that a majority of shareholders in the company has voted to ratify or approve the conduct in question. The court may take that ratification into account in deciding what order to make in the leave application or in the actual proceedings, but it must be satisfied that the act of ratification or approval was well-informed and that the members were acting for proper purposes (s 239). This reverses the common law position in which ratification by members had the effect of negating the possibility of derivative suit.

14.35.15 Other court orders

If the court grants leave to an applicant to commence or intervene in proceedings, then those proceedings cannot later be discontinued, compromised or settled without the leave of the court (s 240). The court has a wide discretion about the types of orders it can make, in hearing either the application for leave or the derivative proceedings. The indicative list in s 241 includes directions requiring mediation between the parties; an order directing the company or a company officer to do, or not to do, any act; and an order appointing an independent person to investigate and report to the court on the company's financial affairs, or the facts or circumstances which gave rise to the proceedings, or the costs incurred by the parties.

Section 242 deals with costs orders in proceedings that are brought after leave has been granted under s 237, and in relation to an application for leave. The section gives the court broad discretion 'at any time' to make 'any orders it considers appropriate'. There has been some difference in how courts have exercised this discretion.[159]

157 *Huang v Wang* (2016) 114 ACSR 586 [60].

158 Explanatory Memorandum, Corporate Law Economic Reform Program Bill 1998 (Cth) 24.

159 For a discussion, see A Monichino, 'Costs in Statutory Derivative Actions: The Lingering Ghost of Wallersteiner' (2015) 33(2) *Company and Securities Law Journal* 104.

In *Sub Rosa Holdings Pty Ltd v Salsa Sudada Production Pty Ltd,* Barrett J described it as 'common place for a person given permission to pursue a claim on behalf of a company to be required, in the first instance, to bear the burden of costs'.[160] This approach was queried by Finkelstein J in *Wood v Links Golf Tasmania Pty Ltd,* who argued that:

> [t]he purpose of permitting a person to bring an action in the name of the company is to prevent conduct which involves some element of harm. In most cases the wrongdoer will be in control of the company. That will be the reason the company itself is not bringing the action. The purpose of ... Part 2F.1A is to increase the likelihood that someone brings a claim which the company ought to have commenced. In those circumstances, I can think of no good reason why the company should not bear the costs.[161]

In *Ananda Marga Pracaraka Samgha Ltd v Tomar (No 3),*[162] Dodds-Streeton J distinguished the decision in *Wood,* partly on the grounds that, in that case, the applicants had already been granted leave to commence a derivative action under s 237. In contrast, in the *Ananda Marga* case, the question of costs was considered at the time of the leave application as part of the 'best interests of the company' criterion. Dodds-Streeton J took into account the 'extremely deleterious' impact that a costs order would have on the company and its operations. Leave was not granted because this would not be in the company's best interests.

One of the major disincentives to shareholder actions is the high cost involved. ASIC has noted that:

> [T]he high cost of litigation means that either members' rights can only be vindicated by shareholders with sufficient resources to bear the cost, at least on an initial basis or that some element of funding must be provided.[163]

A study of all statutory derivative action applications brought in Australia between 2000–19 (168 applications in total), found that while just over half (55 per cent) were successful in obtaining leave, the majority (85 per cent) of those applicants were required to pay all costs at that stage, with no certainty regarding the recovery of costs after the derivative action.[164] The study also found that the main reason for unsuccessful applications was a failure to establish the 'good faith' and/or 'the best interests of the company' criteria in ss 237(2)(b) and (c).[165]

14.35.20 Derivative actions and the remedy for oppression

Before moving on to consider the winding up remedy, it is useful to compare the statutory derivative action with the statutory remedy for oppression or unfairness. There is

160 *Sub Rosa Holdings Pty Ltd v Salsa Sudada Production Pty Ltd* [2006] NSWSC 916 [49].

161 *Wood v Links Golf Tasmania Pty Ltd* [2010] FCA 570 [9].

162 *Ananda Marga Pracaraka Samgha Ltd v Tomar (No 3)* [2012] FCA 184.

163 House of Representatives Standing Committee on Legal and Constitutional Affairs, Parliament of Australia, *Corporate Practices and the Rights of Shareholders* (Australian Government Publishing Service, 1991) 190.

164 L Thai, *Corporate Governance and Statutory Derivative Actions: Comparative Approach to Shareholder Litigation* (Routledge, 2024) 164.

165 Ibid 76.

an overlap between the two remedies in that, under the oppression remedy, s 233(1)(g) permits the court to make and order authorising a member to initiate or continue proceedings in the name and on behalf of the company. In *McMillan v Coolah Home Base Pty Ltd (No 4)*, Parker J noted that '[t]he power to make orders of this type in cases of oppression pre-dates the statutory derivative action regime ... and must now be exercised with an eye to the restrictions on the court's power to authorize such derivative actions'.[166]

While the facts of a case might give rise to claims under both of these remedies, in strict terms, these two actions have different purposes. The oppression or unfairness action is aimed primarily at providing a remedy for the member who brings the action; the derivative action is aimed at seeking a remedy for the company. However, even though a member's statutory right to bring an action for oppression is not derived from the company, the substance of many oppression actions has a strong derivative quality.[167] The language of the oppression refers to actions that are 'contrary to the interests of members as a whole', and a significant number of oppression cases concern the enforcement of corporate rights and duties.[168]

Another point of comparison concerns the outcomes of the two actions. In practice, the oppression remedy 'has largely become an exit remedy'.[169] This is because the remedy is used primarily by minority shareholders in proprietary companies who seek an order for the buy out of their shares in the company.[170] By contrast, the statutory derivative action is oriented towards the plaintiff's wish to remain in the company and to remedy or improve the way in which it operates. The derivative action is more effective in permitting members to give voice to their concerns.[171]

14.40 Winding up: s 461

Another provision of use to a minority shareholder is s 461, which defines the general grounds on which a court may order the winding up of a company. Section 462(2) lists the persons who have standing to apply under s 461 and includes 'a contributory' (s 462(2)(c)). That term is defined in s 9 to include a person who is liable as a member or past member to contribute to the property of the company if it is wound up, and a holder of fully paid shares in the company.

Recall from the earlier discussion at Section 14.30.20 that one possible outcome of an application under s 232 (concerning conduct that is oppressive or unfair, or contrary to interests of members as a whole) is that the court may make an order that the company

166 [2022] NSWC 584 [458], cited *in CIP Group Pty Ltd v So* (2022) 164 ACSR 566 [85].

167 P Hanrahan, 'Distinguishing Corporate and Personal Claims in Australian Company Litigation' (1997) 15(1) *Company and Securities Law Journal* 21, 38.

168 I Ramsay, 'An Empirical Study of the Use of the Oppression Remedy' (1999) 27(1) *Australian Business Law Review* 23.

169 United Kingdom Law Commission, *Shareholder Remedies* (Cm 246, 1997) [6.11].

170 A study in the late 1990s showed that nearly three-quarters of plaintiffs are minority shareholders in proprietary companies: I Ramsay, 'An Empirical Study of the Use of the Oppression Remedy' (1999) 27(1) *Australian Business Law Review* 23, 31.

171 See S Bottomley, 'The Relative Importance of the Statutory Derivative Action in Australia' in F Macmillan (ed), *International Corporate Law Volume 2* (Hart, 2002).

be wound up (s 233(1)(a)). To that extent, there is an overlap between the operation of pt 2F.1 and s 461.

As we saw in relation to winding up orders under pt 2F.1, the courts are cautious about making winding up orders in circumstances where the complaint is one of oppression. Similar reservations apply in the context of s 461 applications. In an often-cited judgment, McPherson J in *Re Dalkeith Investments Pty Ltd* emphasised that 'winding up is to be regarded as a remedy of last resort ... which ought not to be granted if some other less drastic form of relief is available and appropriate'.[172] In *Kokotovich Constructions Pty Ltd v Wallington*, the New South Wales Court of Appeal noted that 'the winding-up of a successful and prosperous company is an extreme step, and one which must require a strong case'.[173] Equally, there is no principle or presumption that it is inappropriate to order the winding up of a solvent company.[174] One concern that a court may have is the effect that a winding up order will have on the interests of employees and other third parties.[175] Certainly, winding up a troubled company can be viewed as a drastic step for the corporation as a legal entity. Yet it may be the only way in which the business can continue to function: by being transferred to a new owner and operator.[176] It is true that winding up applications are often strategic ploys, made in an attempt to induce some other outcome that is more favourable to the applicant.

Of the nine grounds for winding up which are specified in s 461(1), four are of particular relevance to minority shareholders. These overlap with the grounds in pt 2F.1 and it is common for actions to be brought arguing both sections.[177]

First, under s 461(1)(e) a winding up application can be made on the basis that the directors are either acting in the affairs of the corporation in their own interests rather than in the interests of the members as a whole, or in any manner that appears to be unfair or unjust to other members. This paragraph has two alternative limbs. In *Re Cumberland Holdings Ltd*, the New South Wales Supreme Court held that the first limb may be argued in any situation where the directors prefer their own interests (widely defined) to those of one or more members. The judgment pointed out that a minority shareholder could seek the winding up order on this basis, even though the interests of a majority shareholder may have been catered for. Similarly, the unfairness or unjustness of directors' conduct, specified in the second limb, is considered by looking at its effect on 'any significant body of other members'.[178]

The second and third grounds of relevance are found in ss 461(1)(f), (g), which refer to situations where the affairs of the company—or single acts, omissions or resolutions—are oppressive, or unfairly prejudicial to, or unfairly discriminatory against, or are contrary

172 *Re Dalkeith Investments Pty Ltd* (1984) 9 ACLR 47, 252.

173 *Kokotovich Constructions Pty Ltd v Wallington* (1995) 13 ACLC 1113, 1126.

174 *Hillam v Ample Source International Ltd (No 2)* (2012) 202 FCR 336.

175 See, eg, *Roberts v Walter Developments Pty Ltd* (1997) 15 ACLC 882, 905; *Asia Pacific Joint Mining Pty Ltd v Allways Resources Holdings Pty Ltd* [2018] 3 Qd R 520 [46].

176 This and the following point are made by J Hill, 'Protecting Minority Shareholders and Reasonable Expectations' (1992) 10(1) *Company and Securities Law Journal* 86, 97.

177 See, eg, *Wallington v Kokotovich Constructions Pty Ltd* (1993) 11 ACLC 1207, upheld on appeal at *Kokotovich Constructions Pty Ltd v Wallington* (1995) 13 ACLC 1113.

178 *Re Cumberland Holdings Ltd* (1976) 1 ACLR 361, 375.

to the interests of the members as a whole. These paragraphs duplicate the grounds specified in s 232 and the earlier analysis of those grounds applies here.[179]

Fourth, s 461(1)(k) permits the court to order the winding up of a company on the grounds that it would be 'just and equitable' to do so. This is the most frequently used ground for winding up orders under s 461 and so we examine it in more detail.

In the case of application made by a member, an order for winding up on the just and equitable ground requires the court to be satisfied there is no other remedy available, and the applicant is not acting unreasonably in seeking winding up instead of pursuing that other remedy (s 467(4)). The reference to 'no other remedy available' raises an issue when a member seeks remedies under s 461 (winding up) or, in the alternative, ss 232–3 (oppression). In *Asia Pacific Joint Mining Pty Ltd v Allways Resources Holdings Pty Ltd*, the Queensland Court of Appeal confirmed that in such cases the requirement in s 467(4) applies to confine the court's discretion under s 233;[180] that is, 'the requirements of s 467(4) cannot be avoided by a court declaring that it is exercising only the discretion under s 233'.[181]

Below, we discuss some of the more common situations in which the just and equitable ground for winding up has been invoked. It is important to bear in mind that these are only examples, drawn from the case law. The phrase 'just and equitable' is broad and the courts have emphasised repeatedly that:

> [t]he classes of conduct which justify the winding up of a company on the just and equitable ground are not closed, and each application will depend upon the circumstances of the particular case.[182]

14.40.05 The just and equitable ground: breakdown of mutual trust

Much of the case law on the just and equitable ground has involved companies that operate on the basis of close relationships between those who run the company. One example is closely-held companies that are more like incorporated partnerships (sometimes called 'quasi-partnerships').[183] Note, however, that companies that operate in this way can range from small businesses to multi-million dollar commercial ventures.[184] The classic decision which outlines the approach taken in these cases is in *Ebrahimi*

179 It is a rule of statutory construction that when the same words appear in different parts of a statute, they should generally be given the same meaning: *Registrar of Titles (WA) v Franzon* (1975) 132 CLR 611, 618 (Mason J).

180 [2018] 3 Qd R 520.

181 Ibid [62].

182 *Australian Securities and Investments Commission v CME Capital Australia Pty Ltd (No 2)* [2016] FCA 544 [14].

183 We discuss closely-held companies in Chapter 4 at Section 4.65.10. In *Ebrahimi v Westbourne Galleries Ltd* [1973] AC 360, Lord Wilberforce expressed reservations about terms such as 'incorporated partnership' or 'quasi-partnership', saying 'the expressions may be confusing if they obscure, or deny, the fact that the parties ... are now co-members in a company, who have accepted, in law, new obligations' (at 380).

184 For an example of the latter, see *Asia Pacific Joint Mining Pty Ltd v Allways Resources Holdings Pty Ltd* [2018] 3 Qd R 520, concerning a coal-mining venture that involved large Chinese state-owned corporations.

v Westbourne Galleries Ltd,[185] where the House of Lords stated the general principles that should be applied. The just and equitable ground permitted the Court to subject the exercise of legal rights (which might be defined in a constitution) to equitable considerations, including considerations of a personal nature arising between one individual and another. The Court indicated that one or more of the following elements would be required to justify the winding up of the company on this ground:

(1) evidence that the company was an association formed or continued on the basis of personal relationships of mutual confidence. This would be most likely to occur where a pre-existing partnership has been converted into a limited company
(2) evidence of an agreement, or understanding, that some or all of the shareholders will participate in the conduct of the company's business
(3) the existence of a restriction upon the right of members to transfer their interest in the company, so that if confidence is lost, or one member is removed from management, they cannot then readily remove their interest from the company.

More generally, the courts have emphasised that a breakdown of confidence between directors and shareholders in a company does not automatically provide the basis for winding up on the just and equitable ground. As explained in *Re L&B Seafoods Pty Ltd*:

> it is generally necessary to show that the breakdown is of such a nature and degree that it materially frustrates the commercially viable and sensible operations of the company in accordance with the shareholders' expectations, that the loss of confidence is justified and that there is a restriction on the transferability of the shares of the party seeking to wind up the company.[186]

14.40.10 The just and equitable ground: failure of substratum

One situation where the just and equitable ground for winding up has been invoked is where there is a 'failure of substratum'. This describes the situation where the underlying purposes for which a company was originally formed are no longer being realised because of the actions of the company's controllers. As described by Owen J in *Thomas v Mackay Investments Pty Ltd*:

> A company may be wound up where it has become impossible for it to achieve its main objects. If the company engages in conduct which is outside the scope of that which was within the general intention or common understanding of the members when they became members then the company can be wound up.[187]

The rationale for winding up a company in this situation is that it is not fair for shareholders, who invested money in the company on the basis it will pursue a particular business or endeavour, to see their capital used for a different purpose. The case of *Re Tivoli Freeholds Ltd* is an example of this. There, the controllers of the company caused it to stop

185 *Ebrahimi v Westbourne Galleries Ltd* [1973] AC 360.
186 [2022] NSWSC 100 [148] (Henry J).
187 *Thomas v Mackay Investments Pty Ltd* (1996) 22 ACSR 294, 300.

carrying on the business for which it was originally formed (theatre management) and to embark instead on a new type of activity (financing corporate takeovers).[188]

There can be difficulties in applying this argument. First, it is more appropriate in the case of companies with relatively few members, where there is often a strong connection between the members and the purpose for which the capital has been provided. Second, it can be difficult establishing the general intention and 'common understanding' of the members, noting that this will be an objective inquiry.[189] In the *Tivoli Case* Menhennitt J stated that the prime, but not the sole, source for determining this question is the company's constitution, memorandum and its objects clause. This case was decided in 1972, when the constitution was comprised, in part, of a document called the Memorandum of Association which was required to include a statement of the objects for which the company had been incorporated. Section 125 now makes the inclusion of an objects clause optional, and because s 124 gives each company the capacity and powers of an individual, it may be difficult to determine the main objects of the company. Third, it must be shown that the 'failure of substratum' is not merely a short-term discontinuance of that business but a 'final and conclusive abandonment of the business'.[190]

14.40.15 The just and equitable ground: deadlocks

Another situation in which the just and equitable ground for winding up can arise is where the company's operations are deadlocked. In *Re Amazon Pest Control Pty Ltd*, 'a breakdown of relations or loss of confidence between a company's members may ... support a winding up on the just and equitable ground where it frustrates the commercially sensible operations of the company'.[191] Situations of this type will be more likely to arise in a small, closely-held company. Again, the courts have been cautious, preferring to see an apparent deadlock resolved through the procedures in the constitution.

A court will need to be convinced that the deadlock has not been manufactured with the aim of causing the company to be wound up. An example of this occurred in *Morgan v 45 Flers Avenue Pty Ltd*.[192] The plaintiff and the second defendant were brothers who decided to acquire an interest in a scrap metal business run by Metal Recyclers (NSW) Pty Ltd ('Metal'). They did this by forming 45 Flers Avenue Pty Ltd ('Flers') which then acquired shares in Metal. Both brothers were appointed as directors of Metal (there were two other directors). As for the Flers company, the plaintiff and his wife held one share each, as did the second defendant and his wife. Each brother held a further 100 shares as trustee for a family trust. The business of Metal was carried on in a way which recognised that the second defendant was senior in decision-making to the plaintiff. The plaintiff gradually became dissatisfied with this arrangement. It was eventually agreed that he would resign his directorship in Metal, which in turn would lease him a scrap metal yard

188 *Re Tivoli Freeholds Ltd* [1972] VR 445.

189 *International Hospitality Concepts Pty Ltd v National Marketing Concepts Inc (No 2)* (1994) 13 ACSR 368, 370.

190 *Galbraith v Merito Shipping Co* [1947] SC 446, 456 (Moncrieff LJC).

191 *Re Amazon Pest Control Pty Ltd* [2012] NSWSC 1568, [19].

192 *Morgan v 45 Flers Avenue Pty Ltd* (1986) 10 ACLR 692.

at which he could run his own business. It was also agreed that the plaintiff would sell his scrap metal to Metal.

A dispute arose concerning the price for which the plaintiff would sell scrap metal to Metal. The plaintiff began to trade in competition with Metal. At about the same time, the board of Metal resolved to increase the level of directors' remuneration and to pay large bonuses to the directors and to declare low dividends at the expense of the plaintiff. The plaintiff also refused to attend Flers meetings. The plaintiff sought an order under both the oppression and the winding up provisions in relation to Flers. As has already been noted, the oppression action was unsuccessful. In relation to s 461(1)(k), the plaintiff argued it was just and equitable to wind up Flers since its affairs were deadlocked. Young J rejected this argument, saying that 'a person cannot merely refuse to attend meetings of the company and then say that there is a deadlock. ... [T]he principle does not apply where the party who wishes to end the company has also been responsible for the situation which has arisen'.[193] There was no evidence, said Young J, that the other shareholders in the Flers company could not continue to operate the corporation.

14.40.20 Winding up and the public interest

Section 462(2) is not restricted to applications by shareholders—the section includes the possibility of an application for winding up being made by ASIC. This is in contrast to the statutory derivative action sections, which do not give standing to ASIC.

In relation to winding up, ASIC may make an application where it is, or has been, investigating a company (ss 462(2)(e), 464). In *Australian Securities and Investments Commission v ABC Fund Managers Ltd*, the Commission sought winding up of a company on the just and equitable ground. Warren J noted three factors that apply in such an application:

> First, there needs to be a lack of confidence in the conduct and management of the affairs of the company. Second, in these types of circumstances it needs to be demonstrated that there is a risk to the public interest that warrants protection. Third, there is a reluctance on the part of the courts to wind up a solvent company.[194]

While the first and third factors have application even when ASIC is not the applicant, the second factor is of particular relevance in a case brought by the Commission. As was noted in *Australian Securities and Investments Commission v CME Capital Australia Pty Ltd (No 2)*, '[t]here are important public interest considerations when ASIC applies for a winding up order'.[195] In *Australian Securities and Investments Commission v ActiveSuper Pty Ltd (No 2)*, Gordon J explained that:

> [A] risk to the public interest may take several forms. For example, a winding up order may be necessary to ensure investor protection or where a company

193 Ibid 708.

194 *Australian Securities and Investments Commission v ABC Fund Managers Ltd* (2001) 39 ACSR 443 [119].

195 *Australian Securities and Investments Commission v CME Australia Pty Ltd (No 2)* [2016] FCA 544 [23].

has not carried on its business candidly and in a straightforward manner with the public. Alternatively, it might be justified in order to prevent and condemn repeated breaches of the law.[196]

14.45 The injunction remedy: s 1324

This section allows the court to hear an application for an injunction in situations where a person has, is, or will be engaged in conduct that is in contravention of the *Corporations Act* (s 1324(1)).[197] The section covers attempted contraventions; aiding, abetting, counselling or procuring a person to contravene the Act; (attempted) inducements by threats or promises to contravene the Act; being in any way, directly or indirectly, knowingly concerned in or party to a contravention; or conspiring with others to contravene the Act. The scope of the section is made even wider by sub-s (2), under which an application can be made where a person refuses or fails to do an act or thing that the person is required to do by the *Corporations Act*. There is considerable diversity in the judicial interpretation and application of this section, with many aspects still awaiting definitive authority. With that in mind, the potential for the section to operate as a remedy for company members can be explained as follows.

An application can be made either by ASIC or by 'a person whose interests have been, are or would be affected' by the conduct, failure or refusal. In *Broken Hill Proprietary Co Ltd v Bell Resources Ltd*, the Victorian Supreme Court held that a broad interpretation should be given to the question of standing under s 1324, consistent with the objects of the legislation in protecting the public in respect of the commercial activities of corporations.[198] Hampel J decided that applicants who seek to show that their interests have been, are, or would be affected need not show that personal rights of a proprietary or similar nature are or may be affected by the conduct. Moreover, they need not prove that they suffered any special injury arising from the contravention of the *Corporations Act*. However, applicants must establish that their interests go beyond the mere interests of members of the public. This reasoning would include shareholders as persons with standing under s 1324. In *Allen v Atalay* (an interlocutory proceeding), Hayne J stated it was arguable that the *Broken Hill* test would also give standing to 'a creditor having a right to prove in the liquidation of a company'.[199]

In *Australian Securities and Investments Commission v Mauer-Swisse Securities Ltd*, Palmer J noted that where the application is made by ASIC rather than by a private litigant the court will be more likely to give weight to the question whether the injunction 'would have some utility or would serve some purpose within the contemplation of the Corporations Act'.[200]

196 *Australian Securities and Investments Commission v ActiveSuper Pty Ltd (No 2)* (2013) 93 ACSR 189 [23].

197 The court may also grant an interim injunction pending its determination of an application under sub-s (1): s 1324(4).

198 *Broken Hill Proprietary Co Ltd v Bell Resources Ltd* (1984) 2 ACLC 157 (note that the case was decided with reference to s 574 of the *Companies Code*, the predecessor to s 1324).

199 *Allen v Atalay* (1994) 12 ACLC 7, 10.

200 *Australian Securities and Investments Commission v Mauer-Swisse Securities Ltd* (2002) 42 ACSR 605 [36].

For some contraventions of the *Corporations Act*, sub-s (1A) deems that the interests of a person as a member or creditor of a company are affected by the conduct in question. This applies to share capital reductions, share buy-backs, and financial assistance transactions. These provisions are referred to in Chapter 8 of this book.

The grounds for an application under this section relate either to a contravention of the *Corporations Act*, or to a refusal or failure to comply with the *Corporations Act*. Several sections in the legislation, such as the share transaction provisions in ch 2J, deem that breach of the relevant section, while not an offence, is a contravention of the Act, thereby inviting the application of s 1324. Furthermore, despite the decision of Young J in *Mesenberg v Cord Industrial Recruiters Pty Ltd*, the better view is that s 1324 is applicable to breaches by corporate officers of their statutory duty under ss 180–4.[201]

In *Australian Securities and Investments Commission v ActiveSuper Pty Ltd (in liq)*, it was emphasised that 'an injunction under s 1324 is intended to be remedial in character'.[202] Under s 1324, the court may make an order restraining the person from engaging in the conduct and, if the court considers it desirable to do so, an order requiring the person to do some act or thing. Moreover, s 1324(10) permits the court to order that damages be paid by the person who is contravening the Act to the applicant or 'any other person' (in addition to or in substitution for the injunction).

There has been judicial disagreement about whether a court can order damages under s 1324(10) in the absence of an application for an injunction. In *Permanent Trustee Australia Ltd v Perpetual Trustee Co Ltd*, Cohen J held that the Commission could seek an order for damages simply on the basis that it would have been entitled to seek an injunction.[203] By contrast, in *Executor Trustee Australia Ltd v Deloitte Haskins and Sells*, Perry J expressed the view that an order for damages under s 1324(10) could not be made unless there was an application for an injunction.[204] Subsequently, in *Dungowan Manly Pty Ltd v McLaughlin*, Bathurst CJ noted that the 'predominant view' is that 'damages can only be awarded in proceedings where an injunction is actually sought'.[205]

14.50 Access to company information

Part 2F.3 of the *Corporations Act* specifies a procedure whereby a company member may gain access to information in the company's books. Under s 247A, a member may apply to the court for an order authorising the member, or some other person acting on the member's behalf, to inspect—and if authorised, to copy—the company's books. The word 'books' is defined in s 9 to include a register, any other record of information, financial reports or financial records however they are compiled, recorded or stored, and a document.

The court may only make the order if it is satisfied that the applicant has demonstrated they are acting in good faith and that the inspection is to be made for a proper

201 Young J's decision at *Mesenberg v Cord Industrial Recruiters Pty Ltd* (1996) 39 NSWLR 128 was considered and not followed by Einfeld J (Federal Court) in *Airpeak Pty Ltd v Jetstream Aircraft Ltd* (1997) 73 FCR 161; and was doubted by Wheeler J in *Emlen Pty Ltd v St Barbara Mines Ltd* (1997) 24 ACSR 303.

202 *Australian Securities and Investments Commission v ActiveSuper Pty Ltd (in liq)* (2015) 235 FCR 181 [74].

203 *Permanent Trustee Australia Ltd v Perpetual Trustee Co Ltd* (1995) 13 ACLC 66.

204 *Executor Trustee Australia Ltd v Deloitte, Haskins and Sells* (1996) 14 ACLC 1789.

205 *Dungowan Manly Pty Ltd v McLaughlin* (2012) 90 ACSR 62 [5].

purpose. The court can also make other orders relating to the use which may be made of the information gained as a result of the inspection (s 247B). A person who inspects books on behalf of a member (such as an auditor or legal practitioner) can disclose the information only to the member who made the application or to ASIC (s 247C).

The need for a court application and order may be avoided if the company adopts the replaceable rule in s 247D, under which the directors or the general meeting may authorise a member to inspect books of the company.

In *Mesa Minerals Ltd v Mighty River International Ltd*,[206] the Full Court of the Federal Court reviewed the case law and summarised the principles to be applied in considering an application under s 247A. The Court's summary helps to frame our explanation of the operation of pt 2F.3.

An order permitting inspection will only be granted if the court is satisfied the member is acting in good faith and the inspection is to be made for a proper purpose. In the past, there has been debate about whether this refers to two separate requirements or to a single test. The Court in *Mesa Minerals Ltd* confirmed the accepted view that the requirement for good faith and a proper purpose is a composite expression rather than two distinct requirements. In support of this, the Federal Court quoted the judgment of Brooking J in *Knightswood Nominees Pty Ltd v Sherwin Pastoral Co Ltd*: '[a]cting in good faith and inspecting for a proper purpose means acting and inspecting for a bona fide proper purpose'.[207] This composite standard is to be assessed on an objective, not subjective, basis,[208] and the onus of proof lies with the member making the application.[209]

Much of the case law concerning s 247A involves consideration about the meaning of 'a proper purpose'. In *Mesa Minerals Ltd*, the Court noted that a proper purpose is one that is 'connected with the proper exercise of the rights of a shareholder as shareholder'.[210] An example would be seeking to inspect books to ascertain whether there has been a breach of directors' duties, or whether there has been oppressive conduct.[211] The Court in *Mesa Minerals* observed that '[a]n applicant who has a significant holding and who has been a shareholder for "some considerable time" will more easily discharge the onus than one who has recently acquired a token holding'.[212] The applicant must show that the purpose behind the request is 'substantive and not fanciful', and not 'artificial, specious or contrived'.[213] Similarly, the courts have demonstrated a disinclination to allow inspection where the applicant is on a 'fishing expedition' or where the member seeking inspection 'is motivated by idle curiosity, or has in mind harassment, or even

206 *Mesa Minerals Ltd v Mighty River International Ltd* (2016) 241 FCR 241, [22].

207 *Knightswood Nominees Pty Ltd v Sherwin Pastoral Co Ltd* (1989) 7 ACLC 536, 541.

208 *Mesa Minerals Ltd v Mighty River International Ltd* (2016) 241 FCR 241 [22] referring to *Barrack Mines Ltd v Grants Patch Mining Ltd* [1988] 1 Qd R 606.

209 *Mesa Minerals Ltd v Mighty River International Ltd* (2016) 241 FCR 241 [22] citing *Quinlan v Vital Technology Australia Ltd* (1987) 5 ACLC 389, 393.

210 *Mesa Minerals Ltd v Mighty River International Ltd* (2016) 241 FCR 241, [22]. See also *Knightswood Nominees Pty Ltd v Sherwin Pastoral Co Ltd* (1989) 15 ACLR 151, 156–7.

211 *Enares Pty Ltd v Nimble Money Ltd* [2022] FCAFC 126 [42].

212 *Mesa Minerals Ltd v Mighty River International Ltd* (2016) 241 FCR 241, [22] citing *Quinlan v Vital Technology Australia Ltd* (1987) 5 ACLC 389, 393.

213 *Mesa Minerals Ltd v Mighty River International Ltd* (2016) 241 FCR 241, [22] citing *Re Style Ltd; Merim Pty Ltd v Style Ltd* (2009) 255 ALR 63.

blackmail, or wishes to obtain confidential information for the benefit of one of the company's competitors'.[214] It is, however, a proper purpose for an applicant to be pursuing 'a reasonable suspicion of breach of duty'.[215] Furthermore, '[a]pplicants do not necessarily lack a proper purpose merely because they are hostile to other directors'.[216] If the applicant has been granted, or is applying for, leave to commence a statutory derivative action then the court must also be satisfied that the application for inspection is for a purpose connected with the statutory derivative action or the application for leave (s 247A(5)). Finally, the court has a discretion not to grant an order even though it may find that the application is made in good faith and for a proper purpose.[217]

If the applicant has mixed purposes in making the application, it is sufficient if the 'primary or dominant purpose is a proper one'.[218] As an example, in *Humes Ltd v Unity APA Ltd (No 1)*,[219] Unity wanted to inspect the books of Humes in order to determine whether Humes' directors had breached their duty to the company. It was also apparent that access to the information in the books would assist Unity in a takeover bid it was making for Humes. Beach J held that the dominant purpose was to ascertain whether the directors had breached their duties, and that this was a proper purpose. The fact that there was also a secondary purpose was irrelevant.[220]

As noted earlier, the definition of 'books' is potentially broad, and the court has a discretion regarding the scope of access that the member is to be granted. In *Acehill Investments Pty Ltd v Incitec Ltd*, Debelle J noted that '[t]he procedure under s 247A is not intended to be a process as wide-ranging as the process of discovery of documents so that, as a general rule, inspection will be confined to, say, the results of decisions of directors rather than all the documents such as board papers leading to decisions', adding that '[t]here may be occasions where it is proper to admit inspection of board papers'.[221] A member's application is not automatically ruled out by the fact that they may have alternative means of obtaining the information they seek.[222]

The wording of s 247A indicates that the application must relate to books of the company of which the applicant is a member. The section cannot be used to inspect the books of a related company, meaning that s 247A has limited use in a corporate group. Gillooly gives the following example:

> Consider the common situation where a holding company conducts various businesses through wholly owned subsidiaries. Decisions that are crucial to

214 *Knightswood Nominees Pty Ltd v Sherwin Pastoral Co Ltd* (1989) 15 ACLR 151, 156.

215 *Mesa Minerals Ltd v Mighty River International Ltd* (2016) 241 FCR 241 [22] citing *McNeill v Hearing & Balance Centre Pty Ltd* [2007] NSWSC 942 [17].

216 *Mesa Minerals Ltd v Mighty River International Ltd* (2016) 241 FCR 241 [22] citing *Humes Ltd v Unity APA Ltd (No 1)* [1987] VR 467.

217 *Barrack Mines Ltd v Grants Patch Mining Ltd* [1988] 1 Qd R 606; *Humes Ltd v Unity APA Ltd (No 1)* [1987] VR 467.

218 *Mesa Minerals Ltd v Mighty River International Ltd* (2016) 241 FCR 241 [22].

219 *Humes Ltd v Unity APA Ltd (No 1)* [1987] VR 467.

220 See also *Barrack Mines Ltd v Grants Patch Mining Ltd* [1988] 1 Qd R 606.

221 *Acehill Investments Pty Ltd v Incitec Ltd* [2002] SASC 344, [29] citing *Re Claremont Petroleum NL (No 2)* [1990] 2 Qd R 310.

222 *Mesa Minerals Ltd v Mighty River International Ltd* (2016) 241 FCR 241 [22] citing *McNeill v Hearing & Balance Centre Pty Ltd* [2007] NSWSC 942 [23]–[25].

> the interests of members of the holding company will often be made at subsidiary level. Yet even if there are substantial grounds for suspecting that the subsidiary's directors have breached their duties and irreparably damaged both the subsidiary and the holding company, members of the holding company will not be able to gain access to the records of the subsidiary through [s 247A]. The only eligible person to apply to the court is the holding company itself, with the decision to apply normally being made by the Board. If, as is usual within groups, the directors of the holding company and the subsidiary are common or associated, it is extremely unlikely that [s 247A] will be activated.[223]

One rationale for restricting the right of inspection in pt 2F.3 is to protect the confidentiality of corporate information. Members, unlike directors of the corporation, owe no fiduciary duties of confidentiality to the company. Another reason is that the section reinforces the separation of powers between the general meeting and the board of directors. In *Re Augold NL*, Williams J stated that:

> The creation of a statutory right to inspect company documents with the leave of the court should not, in my view, be regarded as affecting the basic rule of company law which has stood for many years that a shareholder would not ordinarily have recourse to the courts to challenge a managerial decision made by or with the approval of its directors.[224]

In addition to an application under s 247A, the *Corporations Act* contains other sections that provide access to corporate information. In particular:

- a member (indeed, any person) may inspect and copy any register which a company is required to keep under *Corporations Act* ch 2C (s 173). This includes the register of members, of option-holders and of debenture-holders
- a person may inspect and obtain a copy or extract of documents which are lodged with ASIC (s 1274; see also s 1274A). Certain documents are exempted from this right of inspection—these are listed in s 1274(2).

14.55 Civil proceedings brought by ASIC: *ASIC Act* s 50

Individual shareholders face considerable obstacles in utilising their legislative rights to protect their interests and enforce their claims. They must contend with the financial costs of litigation, including court fees, professional fees and the potential of paying the other side's costs if the case is lost. There are problems in obtaining information on which to build a case (notwithstanding s 247A). There may be great difficulties in mobilising other shareholders to join or take an interest in the action, especially in companies with widely dispersed shareholdings. Furthermore, many shareholders are likely to be

223 M Gillooly, 'Outside Shareholders in Corporate Groups' in M Gillooly (ed), *The Law Relating to Corporate Groups* (Federation Press, 1993) 174.

224 *Re Augold NL* [1987] 2 Qd R 297.

inexperienced or reluctant litigators; they are, in Marc Galanter's well-known typology, 'one-shotters' in the litigation process.[225]

One solution to these obstacles is to use the class action procedure that is available under pt IVA of the *Federal Court of Australia Act 1976* (Cth).[226] This is discussed in more detail in Chapter 17 at Section 17.40.10. However, where shareholders are unable or unlikely to act, an alternative possibility is for ASIC to begin a civil action against wrongdoers in a company using the power under s 50 of the *ASIC Act*. As Ramsay notes, ASIC is often 'in a superior position to shareholders to enforce corporate rights and duties'.[227] ASIC is, in Galanter's terminology, a repeat player. In theory, this means that it has developed the necessary expertise and has access to specialist knowledge.[228] It can enjoy economies of scale and lower start-up costs than an individual shareholder litigant. ASIC may also 'play for the rules' as well as for the outcome in a particular case. As Galanter explains, repeat players are able to take a longer-term, strategic view of litigation, looking for outcomes that will be favourable in future cases. Finally, ASIC's involvement as a litigant may 'even up' the contest, since many of the companies against which actions may be brought will also be repeat players.

Under s 50 of the *ASIC Act*, where, as a result of an investigation or an examination, it appears to be in the public interest for a person to begin and carry on a proceeding, then ASIC may cause the proceeding to be begun and carried on in the person's name. The words 'it appears to ASIC' have been interpreted by the Federal Court as conferring 'an extremely wide discretion'.[229] However, as emphasised in *Somerville v Australian Securities Commission*, '[t]here must be a causative link between the investigation and the formation by the Commission of its view that it appears to be in the public interest for the proceeding to be begun and carried on'.[230] Note that s 50 only gives power to ASIC to commence proceedings; it does not permit ASIC to take over and continue proceedings that have already been commenced by a private litigant.[231]

The proceedings must either be aimed at recovering damages for fraud, negligence, default, breach of duty; or other misconduct committed in connection with the matter that was under investigation or examination; or at recovering property of the person in whose name the action is being carried. In *Somerville v Australian Securities Commission*, it was noted that the '[f]ruits of the litigation, if any, will benefit the person in whose name the proceeding has been brought, not the Commission'.[232]

---

225 M Galanter, 'Why the "Haves" Come Out Ahead: Speculations on the Limits of Social Change' (1974) 9(1) *Law and Society Review* 95. This description is more likely to apply to individual members rather than to institutional or corporate members.

226 See P Spender, 'Securities Class Actions: A View from the Land of the Great White Shareholder' (2002) 31(2) *Common Law World Review* 123.

227 I Ramsay, 'Enforcement of Corporate Rights and Duties by Shareholders and the Australian Securities Commission: Evidence and Analysis' (1995) 23(3) *Australian Business Law Review* 174, 179.

228 There are many factors to take into account here, particularly the level of funding and resources that is made available to the Commission.

229 *Australian Securities Commission v Deloitte Touche Tohmatsu* (1996) 70 FCR 93, 121, referring to the predecessor to ASIC.

230 *Somerville v Australian Securities Commission* (1995) 60 FCR 319, 325.

231 *Carey v Australian Securities and Investments Commission* (2008) 169 FCR 311.

232 *Somerville v Australian Securities Commission* (1995) 60 FCR 319, 325.

The Commission has explained its approach when deciding to exercise this power, noting the need to 'direct finite resources appropriately' and to be sure that 'commencing and carrying on an action is in the broader public interest, beyond the private interests of the particular plaintiffs on whose behalf we commence the proceedings'.[233] In 2007, ASIC relied on its power under s 50 to bring actions seeking compensation for investors who lost over $300 million in the collapse of the Westpoint Group of property development companies in 2006.[234] Overall, there have been very few cases where ASIC has exercised this power. Recall too that ASIC or a company damaged by the contravention of a civil penalty provision can apply for a compensation order under ss 1317H–HA (discussed in Chapter 10 at Section 10.35.10).

14.60 Summary

This chapter examined various mechanisms available to members to protect their rights or those of the company. This area of corporate law has come to be dominated by the statutory remedies, either because general law principles have been expressly overridden (as with the statutory derivative action), or because the available general law remedies are limited in scope. Nevertheless, it is important to bear in mind that the principles and practices upon which modern statutory provisions have been built have their history in case law. This chapter examined the rule in *Foss v Harbottle* and its exceptions. It then moved on to examine six different sets of provisions in the *Corporations Act* and the *ASIC Act* that, in different ways, offer mechanisms for the protection of members' rights: the remedy for oppressive or unfair conduct, the statutory derivative action, actions for winding up of a company, injunctions, opportunities for access to corporate information, and civil proceedings being commenced by ASIC.

There are two points to note on the issue of the range of legal protections available to members and shareholders.

First, the operation of these rules will be affected by the particular context in which they are raised. In this chapter, we have referred simply to 'members' or 'shareholders'. A moment's reflection reminds us there is no standard type of member or shareholder. Consider, for example, the difference between individual versus corporate or institutional shareholders, or between shareholders pursuing short-term investment gains versus long-term participation in a company's business. Similarly, the company context plays a role in whether and when these legal protections come into play. This refers to differences between small proprietary companies and large publicly listed companies, and to companies whose shares are closely-held, or dominated by a single block shareholder, or that are widely-held by a diversity of shareholders.

233 Australian Securities and Investments Commission, *ASIC's Approach to Involvement in Private Court Proceedings* (Information Sheet 180, June 2013).

234 Australian Securities and Investments Commission, 'Westpoint Compensation Proceedings: Additional FAQs for Investors with FICS Claims' (Media Release, 21 December 2007) <https://download.asic.gov.au/media/1348538/Westpoint%20compensation%20proceedings_%20Additional%20FAQs%20for%20investors%20with%20FICS%20claims.pdf>.

The second point is comparative. At a broad level, the Australian system of corporate law shares many features with other common law legal systems, especially the United Kingdom and the United States. Considered in more detail, differences emerge. Comparative study shows that the levels of shareholder protection, when judged by reference to the rules and remedies that are available, are stronger in Australia and the United Kingdom than in the United States. There are complex historical, economic and socio-political reasons that explain this, and they fall outside the scope of this book.[235]

235 Detailed analyses can be found in CM Bruner, *Corporate Governance in the Common-Law World: The Political Foundations of Shareholder Power* (Cambridge University Press, 2013); M Siems, *Convergence in Shareholder Law* (Cambridge University Press, 2008); R Mitchell et al, 'Shareholder Protection in Australia: Institutional Configurations and Regulatory Evolution' (2014) 38(1) *Melbourne University Law Review* 68.

CHAPTER

15

RECEIVERSHIP, SCHEMES OF ARRANGEMENT, SMALL BUSINESS RESTRUCTURING AND VOLUNTARY ADMINISTRATION

15.05 Introduction

This chapter is the first of two chapters that examine what can happen when a company cannot pay its debts. It discusses the types of action that can be taken (other than winding a company up), focusing upon receivership, schemes of arrangement, small business restructuring and voluntary administration. This chapter commences with a discussion on insolvency, and how it may be determined. This is a complex question, relying on an array of information specific to each company, beyond a company's demonstrated assets and liabilities according to a balance sheet. Each of the actions this chapter considers are demonstrative of different aspects of insolvency law, with different motivations and outcomes. Receiverships differ from other types of arrangements discussed in this chapter because they usually involve a receiver being appointed to look after the interests of one secured creditor. Consequently, the receiver's main responsibility is to protect and enforce a security interest that has been granted by the company to that creditor over particular company property. The duties and powers of receivers vary accordingly from those of administrators and liquidators. In contrast, schemes of arrangement, small business restructuring and voluntary administration usually involve an impartial evaluation of a company's financial position, followed by a binding agreement between the company and its creditors, or a group of creditors. The policy behind these processes is corporate rescue as it can result in the whole or part of the business of the company being saved. Small business restructuring is a new process introduced in January 2021 for the benefit of companies with liabilities of $1 million or less and which are insolvent or likely to become insolvent.

These various methods of addressing the future of a company in financial difficulty can interact, overlap or occur one after the other. Although we will cover each method of external administration individually within this chapter and the next, it is also valuable to consider them together as part of a broader landscape. This can be described visually as shown in Figure 15.1.

Figure 15.1 Potential methods of restructure or winding up available for solvent and insolvent companies

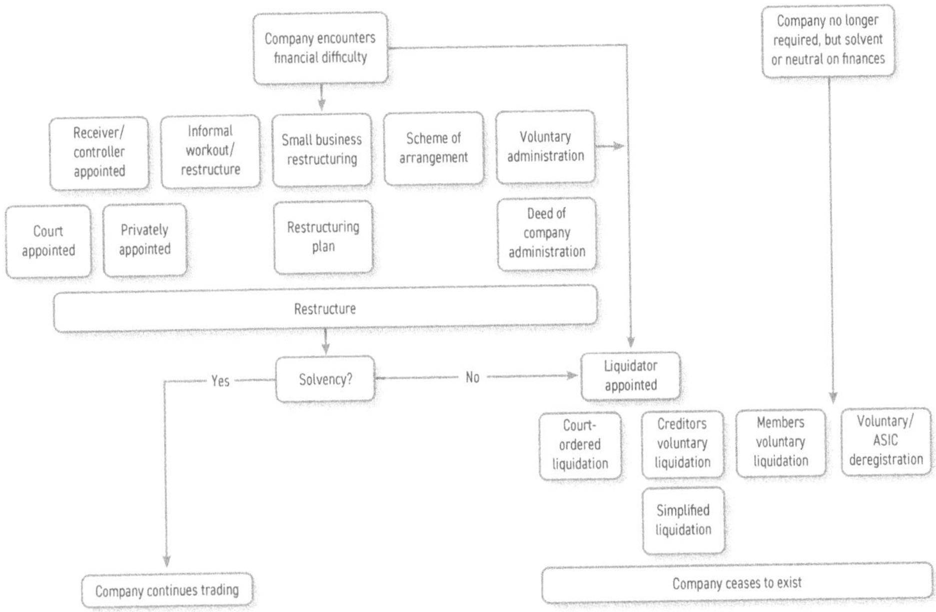

There may be further reform to Australia's insolvency regime. In 2023, the Parliamentary Joint Committee on Corporations and Financial Services released a report into corporate insolvency in Australia.[1] This report is the first major review of the corporate insolvency regime since the Harmer Report in 1988.[2] The 2023 report concluded that there is a need for an independent and comprehensive review of the corporate and personal insolvency system as a whole. This report is discussed at Section 15.55 below.

15.10 Insolvency

External administration refers to the administration of the company by an external party. The processes that form part of external administration are receivership, schemes of arrangement, voluntary administration and liquidation. Liquidation or winding up is the final step in external administration and is discussed in Chapter 16.

Before discussing these processes, it is necessary to consider what it means for a company to be insolvent. Insolvency is a pre-condition to most external administrations.[3] For example, voluntary administration cannot occur unless it can be shown that, as a question of fact, the company is or is nearing insolvency.[4] Insolvency is defined by s 95A of the

1 Parliamentary Joint Committee on Corporations and Financial Services, Parliament of Australia, *Corporate Insolvency in Australia* (Report, 12 July 2023).

2 Australian Law Reform Commission, *General Insolvency Inquiry* (Report 45, 1988) ('the Harmer Report').

3 A member's voluntary liquidation, discussed in Chapter 16 at Section 16.40.05, can only take place when a company is solvent, and is the exception to this position.

4 See, eg, *Corporations Act* s 436A.

Corporations Act 2001 (Cth). The effect of sub-ss (1) and (2) of s 95A is that a company is insolvent if it is not able to pay all of its debts as and when they become due and payable. An important feature of this definition is that insolvency is not measured simply by determining whether the company's debts exceed its assets, known as the 'balance sheet' test of insolvency. This section takes a different approach. This is necessary because a company might, for example, have a balance sheet that shows an excess of assets over debts, but is unable to pay debts at the time they are due because its assets are locked up in investments that cannot readily be released. The definition in s 95A directs attention to the company's cash flow position, known as the 'commercial' or 'cash flow' test of solvency.

The definition in s 95A comprises of two questions. First, is the company 'able to pay' all its debts? Second, are the debts 'due and payable'? We look at these questions in turn.

In determining a company's ability to pay its creditors, it is necessary to look at the overall situation of the company, having regard to 'commercial realities'. As noted in *Re Kerisbeck Pty Ltd*, '[t]he Court must ... assess the overall trading and financial position of the company in question and ascertain whether, in the light of all the facts, that company is able to meet its obligations'.[5]

Accordingly, ability to pay is not decided solely by reference to assets currently held by the company. In *Bell Group Ltd (in liq) v Westpac Banking Corporation (No 9)*,[6] Owen J emphasised that:

> Commercial reality dictates that the assessment of available funds is not confined to the company's cash resources. It is legitimate to take into account funds the company can, on a real and reasoned view, realise by sale of assets, borrowing against the security of its assets, or by other reasonable means. It is a question of fact to be determined in accordance with the evidence.[7]

This confirms the classic statement in *Sandell v Porter*[8] that insolvency is:

> an inability to pay debts as they fall due out of the debtor's own money. But the debtors' own moneys are not limited to [their] cash resources immediately available. They extend to moneys which [they] can procure by realisation, by sale, by mortgage or pledge of [their] assets within a relatively short time—relative to the nature and amount of the debts and to the circumstances, including the nature of the business, of the debtor. The conclusion of insolvency ought to be clear from a consideration of the debtor's financial position in its entirety and generally speaking ought not to be drawn simply from evidence of a temporary lack of liquidity. It is the debtor's inability, utilising such cash resources as [they have] or can command through the use of [their] assets, to meet [their] debts as they fall due which indicates insolvency.[9]

5 *Re Kerisbeck Pty Ltd* (1992) 10 ACLC 619, 621.

6 *Bell Group Ltd (in liq) v Westpac Banking Corporation (No 9)* (2009) 39 WAR 1. The *Bell Group* litigation is discussed in detail in Chapters 12 and 13.

7 Ibid [1090].

8 *Sandell v Porter* (1966) 115 CLR 660.

9 Ibid 670.

In *Lewis v Doran*,[10] the New South Wales Court of Appeal stated that:

> there is no compelling reason to exclude from consideration funds which can be gained from borrowings secured on assets of third parties, or even unsecured borrowings. If the company can borrow without security, it will have funds to pay its debts as they fall due and will be solvent, provided of course that the borrowing is on deferred payment terms or otherwise such that the lender itself is not a creditor whose debt cannot be repaid as and when it becomes due and payable. It comes down to a question of fact, in which the key concept is *ability* to pay the company's debts as and when they become due and payable.[11]

These extracts demonstrate that answering the question as to whether a company is 'able to pay' involves more than simply a consideration of the balance sheet. Any deficiency in assets disclosed by the balance sheet can, of course, be taken into consideration[12]—but the final determination of solvency requires taking a wider view.

The second question in determining insolvency is whether the debts are 'due and payable'. Referring to this phrase in *Southern Cross Interiors Pty Ltd v Deputy Commissioner of Taxation*, Palmer J noted that 'unfortunately' the drafter of s 95A has used two words 'when one would have sufficed', adding that 'the words "due" and "payable" are clearly synonymous in this context'.[13] The case went on to consider the common situation that arises where the due date for payment of a debt as stipulated in the contract has arrived, but the creditor has given the company further time to pay. Is the debt 'due and payable' on the contractually stipulated date, or can the courts take into account 'normal or likely indulgences granted to the company by its creditors'?[14] In *Southern Cross*, Palmer J reviewed the conflicting case law on this question and concluded that:

> [A] contract debt is payable at the time stipulated for payment in the contract unless there is evidence, proving to the Court's satisfaction, that:
>
> - there has been an express or implied agreement between the company and the creditor for an extension of the time stipulated for payment; or
> - there is a course of conduct between the company and the creditor sufficient to give rise to an estoppel preventing the creditor from relying upon the stipulated time for payment; or
> - there has been a well-established and recognised course of conduct in the industry in which the company operates, or as between the company and its creditors as a body, whereby debts are payable at a time other than that stipulated in the creditors' terms of trade or are payable only on demand.[15]

10 *Lewis v Doran* (2005) 219 ALR 555.
11 Ibid.
12 *Aquisite Pty Ltd v Moss* [2023] FCA 410 [203].
13 *Southern Cross Interiors Pty Ltd v Deputy Commissioner of Taxation* (2001) 53 NSWLR 213 [30], [31].
14 Ibid [34].
15 Ibid [54].

As noted, the court's inquiry is factual. This means that the court does not engage in hypothetical analyses. This was explained in *Re Kerisbeck Pty Ltd*:

> If the company is not obliged to repay a debt now or in the immediate future, it should not be subject of a winding up order made on the basis that, if it were obliged, it would not be able to meet that obligation.[16]

The court's task is to ascertain, as a question of fact, from the company's financial position taken as a whole and having regard to commercial realities,[17] whether the company is suffering from a temporary lack of liquidity,[18] or an 'endemic shortage of working capital'.[19]

Finally, there are several instances where insolvency is *presumed* under the *Corporations Act*. For example, where the company is being wound up and it is proven that the company was insolvent at a particular time during the 12 months ending on the relation-back day, then the company is presumed to be insolvent throughout those 12 months.[20] Further, failing to keep appropriate financial records which would at least enable true and fair financial statements to be prepared and audited,[21] or failing to keep financial records for the previous seven years[22] will result in a presumption that the company was insolvent.

15.15 Insolvency law within corporate regulation

Insolvency law is an important part of corporate regulation. It is inevitable that not all companies will succeed, and those that fail will leave behind unpaid debts.[23] The consequences of insolvency can be wide-ranging, regardless of the size of the company concerned. Most failed companies have employees, suppliers, and customers who may be left without full payment of debts owed to them. The larger the company—or the more specific its business—the greater the degree of harm to the community. For example, when HIH Insurance Ltd collapsed in 2001, it was one of Australia's largest insurers, with thousands of employees, tens of thousands of shareholders and over one million policy-holders, particularly in niche insurance markets, such as professional indemnity and public liability insurance.

The Australian Law Reform Commission's *General Insolvency Inquiry*,[24] also known as the Harmer Report, provides a useful summary of the purposes of insolvency law

16 *Re Kerisbeck Pty Ltd* (1992) 10 ACLC 619, 621.

17 *Southern Cross Interiors Pty Ltd v Deputy Commissioner of Taxation* (2001) 53 NSWLR 213, 224–5.

18 As discussed in *Bank of Australasia v Hall* (1907) 4 CLR 1514; *Sandell v Porter* (1966) 115 CLR 666, 670.

19 *Hymix Concrete Pty Ltd v Garritty* (1977) 13 ALR 321, 328.

20 *Corporations Act 2001* (Cth) s 588E(3).

21 Ibid ss 286(1), 588E(4)(a).

22 Ibid ss 286(2), 588E(4)(b).

23 Chapter 16 also discusses winding up of solvent companies, and this chapter acknowledges that it is possible for receivership and voluntary administration to result in something other than the total failure of the company and its business. For the majority of insolvent companies engaging in external administration, however, this is not the case.

24 Australian Law Reform Commission, *General Insolvency Inquiry* (Report No 45, 1988) ('the Harmer Report').

and its role within broader corporate regulation. These purposes assist in understanding the policy behind the methods of external administration examined in this chapter and Chapter 16. The fundamental purpose of insolvency law is to 'provide a fair and orderly process for dealing with the financial affairs'[25] of insolvent companies. In line with that fundamental purpose, insolvency law should also:

- provide mechanisms that enable the insolvent and creditor to participate with the least possible delay and expense
- be impartial, efficient and expeditious
- provide convenient means of collecting or recovering property of the insolvent to be applied to the payment of debts and liabilities
- retain and in some areas reinforce the principle of equal sharing (pari passu) between creditors
- provide as an end result the effective relief or release from financial liabilities and obligation of the insolvent
- as far as convenient and practical, support the commercial and economic processes of the community
- as far as possible and practical, harmonise with the general law
- enable ancillary assistance in the administration of an insolvency originating in a foreign jurisdiction.[26]

Spender summarises these principles and other commercial behaviour into 'four essential tenets' of insolvency law: collective action, harmony with non-insolvency law, strategic behaviour, and rehabilitation.[27] These tenets are visible within the external administration processes discussed in this chapter and Chapter 16. Receivership, which we consider next, demonstrates harmony with non-insolvency laws and strategic behaviour. As will be discussed shortly, receivership developed as an equitable remedy, and the duties and powers of receivers are analysed on the basis of the agency relationship established in the security agreement. The secured creditor may enforce the rights granted to it under the security agreement, or may decide—after a strategic analysis of their position and the position of the company—that an alternative method of external administration would best suit their interests.

By contrast, voluntary administration demonstrates collective action, strategic behaviour, and rehabilitation through engagement by the administrator with the creditors as part of the meeting and reporting processes. Also in line with these tenets is the potential for voluntary administration to result in the company's survival according with the aim in s 435A of maximising the chances of the company or its businesses remaining in existence and, if that is not possible, achieving a better outcome for the creditors than would result from an immediate winding up. The external administration process depends on the course of action taken by the creditors, members and directors of the company.

25 Ibid [33].
26 Ibid.
27 P Spender, 'Scenes from a Wharf: Containing the Morality of Corporate Law' in F Macmillan (ed), *International Corporate Law Annual* (Hart, 2000) vol 1, 65.

15.20 Secured creditors in insolvency

A secured creditor is one who has provided something—usually finance—to the company in exchange for a security interest over company assets. This may be by way of a mortgage over company property or a charge over company assets and will be set out in a security agreement that establishes the proprietary interests of the creditor in that asset. If a question of insolvency in the debtor company arises, a secured creditor will have a number of courses of action open to them. These actions depend on the rights associated with the security under the security agreement and others which are recognised in the *Corporations Act* or by the nature of security arrangements. A secured creditor may choose to allow the insolvency processes—such as voluntary administration or liquidation—to take its course with or without becoming directly involved. As we discuss below, a secured creditor is afforded a degree of protection through the voting mechanisms which occur at the end of a voluntary administration, and, as discussed in Chapter 16, may have the assets over which their security extends excluded from the pool of assets from which the liquidator makes their distribution. If the property secured by the interest will adequately compensate the secured creditor regardless of the process, a secured creditor may be prepared for the company to engage in the voluntary administration process. If their security does not entirely compensate them for the debt—for example, if some aspect of the debt is unsecured—then the creditor may commence a receivership to ensure they get the best return for their debt. The path the creditor chooses depends on their individual circumstances, the secured assets, the debtor company, and its other creditors.

The type of asset and the security over which it is taken plays a part in the creditor's decision. There are two descriptions used for security interests: circulating and non-circulating security interests.[28] These were previously called 'floating' and 'fixed' charges, respectively.[29] For a non-circulating security interest, the creditor's interest in the asset over which the security interest is granted is set and ascertainable as established from the date of entering into the security agreement. The company cannot deal with the asset in any way which would interfere with the creditor's proprietary right in the asset without seeking the creditor's permission. A mortgage over real property is an example of a non-circulating security interest. In contrast, with a circulating security interest, the asset over which the interest is taken may be in flux, such as stock on hand. In this case, although the security is still taken over the asset, the company can deal with it in the normal course of business without seeking the consent of the creditor. The security does not directly attach to the asset until an intervening event specified in the security agreement. After that event, the security attaches directly to the relevant assets, and from that point the company cannot deal with them without the permission of the creditor.[30] The *Corporations Act* treats circulating and non-circulating security interests differently in external administration, and this is discussed below.

28 See Chapter 8 for detailed information on debt capital and Section 8.20.15 for a discussion of charges.

29 *Corporations Act* s 51C.

30 Automatic crystallisation based on a predetermined event, requiring no further intervention by the creditor, has been subject to some mixed reactions in the courts: see, eg, *Stein v Saywell* (1969) 121 CLR 529; *Fire Nymph Products Pty Ltd v Heating Centre Pty Ltd* (1988) 14 NSWLR 460.

If the security agreement is breached by the company—usually for non-compliance with the repayment schedule or by entering into one of the other external administration processes—then the creditor may 'realise the security'. This means they can sell the property or asset over which they have security to seek repayment of their debt. The creditor can choose to do this personally or through an agent to become a mortgagee in possession, or they appoint a receiver to do so on their behalf. The right to private appointment can arise under the *Corporations Act*.[31] Until the 1990s, there were tax advantages to becoming a mortgagee in possession, but with the removal of these benefits,[32] receivership is preferred by secured creditors. The definition in s 9 of the term 'controller' includes both receivers and mortgagees in possession, and the duties and liabilities imposed in pt 5.2 of the *Corporations Act* apply to both a mortgagee in possession and to an appointed receiver.

15.25 Receivership

When taking security in exchange for providing finance to the company, creditors usually request that authority to appoint a receiver be included as a term of the security agreement. This authorises the secured party, in the event of default as defined by the agreement, to appoint a receiver to enforce the security interest by taking control of the secured property. Security may be granted over a range of types of property and over varying proportions of the company's assets and may be a mix of circulating and non-circulating security interests. Consequently, the scope of the receiver's operations will depend on the circumstances of the company and the secured creditor, and the scope of the security agreement entered into between them. For example, if a creditor takes security over all of the company's assets and undertakings, then a receiver appointed under that security will take control over the entire company until the debt is recovered and will be called a 'receiver and manager'.[33] This is the most common method by which creditors such as banks will take security. Management powers must be expressly conferred.[34] By contrast, if security is only taken over a single asset of the company that is not required for the company's business to function, then the receiver will only take control of that asset and will have no further effect on the conduct of the company's business. This chapter refers to controllers of this type as 'receivers'.

15.25.05 Private appointment

A receiver can be appointed in one of two ways: the first, as mentioned above, occurs under the terms of a security agreement. This is a private appointment, deriving from

31 See, eg, *Corporations Act* ss 441A, 441C.

32 The *Insolvency (Tax Priorities) Legislation Amendment Act 1993* (Cth) removed the Commissioner of Taxation's priorities in relation to a number of taxes that a receiver was obliged to pass on but a mortgagee in possession was not.

33 According to s 90 of the *Corporations Act*, a receiver is also a manager if they manage or, under the terms of their appointment, have the power to manage. This definition is extended to all 'controllers' under s 9.

34 *Re Manchester & Milford Railway Co; Ex parte Cambrian Railway Co* (1880) 14 Ch D 645, 653.

the rights of the creditor in the security agreement.[35] Private appointment can occur in limited circumstances under the *Corporations Act*.[36] The second, although far less commonplace, is where the court appoints a receiver, as discussed below. Due to the fact that private appointments are more common, much of the law surrounding the appointment of receivers is managed through the law of contract.[37] The security agreement sets out the circumstances in which a receiver may be appointed. This can include default in payment; the business ceasing, or threatening to cease; the company being insolvent; default of some other obligation specified; or another creditor taking possession of property or appointing a receiver. In the instance of a circulating security interest, the right to appoint a receiver will be linked to the events that cause default.

The purpose of a receivership derives from the nature of the appointment: the receiver is in place to realise the secured asset to satisfy the debt owed to the creditor who appoints them. Receivers have different motivations to other external administrators, such as administrators or liquidators. As noted above, receivership is concerned with recovering the debt for the appointing creditor, with a secondary obligation to the company and other creditors as discussed below. By contrast, as Chapter 16 examines, liquidation is concerned with ensuring the unsecured creditors share equally and fairly in the distribution of an insolvent company's inadequate assets, preventing further harm to the community from insolvent companies and encouraging the investigation of the company's affairs prior to liquidation.

In order to be validly appointed as a receiver, the appointee must be a registered liquidator under s 418(1)(d).[38] They must not be a mortgagee of the company's property, an auditor, director, secretary, senior manager or employee of that company, or a related company,[39] or of the company's mortgagee. The Australian Securities and Investments Commission (ASIC) has the ability under s 418(1)(f) to direct that this section does not apply.

Should there be concern about the validity of the appointment of the receiver, the company or one of the company's creditors can apply to the court under s 418A to make an order declaring that the appointment of the receiver (or their entering into the possession of the company's property) was valid or not.

15.25.10 Powers, duties and liabilities at law and in the *Corporations Act*

A receiver's powers are established by the security agreement, supplemented by the *Corporations Act*. Appointment of a receiver by a creditor creates legal relationships

35 Receivers were originally the realm of the courts of equity; however, modern appointments in relation to company debtors typically occur through the security agreement entered into between the parties. For further background information on receivers, see J O'Donovan, *Company Receivers and Administrators* (Thomson Reuters, 2012).

36 See, eg, *Corporations Act* ss 441A, 441C.

37 By contrast, as receivers were originally a device employed by equity to protect against inappropriate outcomes in the common law, much of receivers' behaviour is governed by equitable principles.

38 An exception to this requirement occurs when the appointment is authorised by a Commonwealth, State or Territory law: s 418(3). Section 1279 establishes that natural persons compliant with the qualifications set out in the regulations are able to be registered as liquidators. The different types of liquidators are discussed in Chapter 16 at Section 16.20.05.

39 As discussed in Chapter 3, related companies are defined in *Corporations Act* ss 46–50AA.

between the creditor and the receiver, the receiver and the company, and the creditor and the company. These relationships grant the receiver certain powers, but also impose duties and liabilities upon them which have the potential to come into conflict.

Powers

Beyond the security agreement, the *Corporations Act* provides in s 420(1) that the receiver 'has power to do, in Australia and elsewhere, all things necessary or convenient to be done for or in connection with, or as incidental to, the attainment of the objectives for which the receiver was appointed'. Without limiting the generality of this provision, s 420(2) then specifies a long list of powers which receivers are presumed to have unless the document under which they are appointed specifically excludes them. These powers include the power to take possession of the relevant property, to convert the property into money, to lease it, to carry on the business of the company and to make or defend an application for winding up.

The private nature of a receiver's appointment is often in conflict with the interests of the company and, if the company is insolvent, the interests of other creditors. This can be seen in the power of sale of a receiver, which was subject to judicial criticism when receivers sold the asset for sufficient value to ensure that their costs and the debt to the creditor appointing them would be satisfied, but did not seek the best price which would benefit the company and the other creditors.[40] To address these criticisms, s 420A was introduced into the *Corporations Act*, which requires a receiver, when exercising the power of sale, to take all reasonable care to sell the property for:

(a) if when it is sold, it has a market value—not less than that market value; or
(b) otherwise—the best price that is reasonably obtainable, having regard to the circumstances existing when the property is sold.

This ameliorates the position in the general law, which only prohibited fraudulent, dishonest or reckless sales, as long as the receiver had regard to the interests of the company and did not sell at gross undervalue.[41] In exercising the power of sale, if the property has a market value, the receiver must sell the property for no less than the market value. If the property does not have a market value, then the best price that is reasonably obtainable must be sought. This situation was considered in detail by the Court in *Jeogla v Australia and New Zealand Banking Group Ltd*[42] in relation to the sale of a large herd of breeding cattle for their equivalent meat value. The difference between the two valuations of the cattle, as breeding stock per head or as meat value per kilogram, was significant. Einstein J considered that the exercise of the power of sale under s 420A, when combined with the duty of care, skill and diligence as set out in s 180(1), required a receiver to take reasonable care to sell and obtain either the market value or the best price.[43] The Court

40 See, eg, *Expo International Pty Ltd v Chant* [1979] 2 NSWLR 820; *Jeogla v Australia and New Zealand Banking Group Ltd* (1999) 150 FLR 359.
41 *Jeogla v Australia and New Zealand Banking Group Ltd* (1999) 150 FLR 359, 442.
42 (1999) 150 FLR 359.
43 Ibid 444.

accepted that under s 420A the power of sale is subject to an objective standard, which requires 'independent valuations of the property and advice as to the most appropriate method of sale in order that the market value or best price be realised'.[44]

Einstein J noted that when first drafted, s 420A did not include the phrase 'market value', which accorded with the recommendation of the Harmer Report that 'obtaining a true market value is costly and difficult for partly manufactured goods or products with a limited market'.[45] However, the Corporate Law Reform Bill 1992, when introduced to Parliament, included that phrase, as did the final enacted section. Although s 420A made no requirement that the property be sold at any particular time, and that it is not necessary to postpone a sale until a more favourable purchase price can be obtained,[46] Einstein J concluded that 'market value' is intended to protect the sale of goods which have an ascertainable value.[47] Only if the property does not have a market value at the date of sale will s 420A(1)(b) apply, requiring all reasonable care to sell the property for the best price obtainable in the circumstances. The cattle did have a market value, and that the first limb of the section applied. The receiver's incorrect choice of valuation for the cattle at meat value rather than breeding stock, the failure to take reasonable care to ensure that the cattle had specialist advertising, promotion and marketing in accordance with the sale of such particular property, and the failure to give sufficiently early notice concerning the cattle to attract prospective buyers for such specialist property were all relevant to a breach of s 420A(1)(a).[48]

A similar consideration was made by the Court in *Florgale Uniforms Pty Ltd v Orders*,[49] where the property in question was customised uniforms. Dodds-Streeton J discussed the fact that for such specialist goods there was no real 'market', and a 'market value' was hard to ascertain. There, the criticisms of the receiver turned less to the price obtained and more to the method of sale, as the receiver sold the goods at auction. The company plaintiff argued, unsuccessfully, that a better price would have been achieved if the receiver had conducted a large-scale 'closing down' sale, targeting the existing customer base of Florgale's uniforms. Dodds-Streeton J concluded on factual grounds that s 420A had not been breached in this case. Both limbs of s 420A(1) require the receiver to take care in selecting the best method of sale for the market for the property.

Receivers are required to exercise their powers bona fide in the interests of the appointing creditor, and in accordance with the purpose for which they were given.[50] If the secured creditor appoints a receiver to take control of and exercise their rights in regard to the secured property, at equity they will be deemed an agent of the creditor.[51]

44 Ibid 445.

45 Australian Law Reform Commission, *General Insolvency Inquiry* (Report 45, 1988) [235].

46 *Jeogla v Australia and New Zealand Banking Group Ltd* (1999) 150 FLR 359, 446. *Downsview Nominees Ltd v First City Corporation Ltd* [1993] AC 295 may support the position that a receiver should accept a short delay in order to achieve a better price on equitable principles. A rushed sale and a lengthy delay are both detrimental to stakeholders.

47 This finding was approved on appeal in *Skinner v Jeogla* (2001) 37 ACSR 106 [36]–[42].

48 *Jeogla v Australia and New Zealand Banking Group Ltd* (1999) 150 FLR 359, 458–9.

49 *Florgale Uniforms Pty Ltd v Orders* (2004) 11 VR 54.

50 *Downsview Nominees Ltd v First City Corporation Ltd* [1993] AC 295, 316; *Expo International Pty Ltd v Chant* [1979] 2 NSWLR 820.

51 *Deyes v Wood* [1911] 1 KB 806.

This exposes the creditor to liability for the acts of their agent—the receiver—in the process of realising the security. The security agreement will set out that the creditor appoints the receiver as an agent of the company, and not as an agent of themselves. This relationship is recognised as a 'special and limited' agency relationship,[52] and does not attract the full force of equity, such as the fiduciary obligations typically owed by an agent.[53] The limited nature of the agency relationship is attributed to the fact that the asset which the receiver is dealing with is, from a proprietary perspective, the asset of the creditor and not the company. The receiver's obligation to account to the company is limited.

Duties

A receiver is listed within the definition of 'officer' in s 9AD(c) of the *Corporations Act*. Consequently, directors' duties as discussed in Chapters 11–13 apply to receivers, with the exception of the duty to prevent insolvent trading under s 588G, which does not extend to officers. As discussed above, receivers are considered agents of the company, and not of the appointing creditor, although they do owe a primary duty to the creditor. Receivers are not subject to the full scope of fiduciary obligations, but may not purchase the secured property, nor may an agent, trustee or company controlled by the receiver.[54] The receiver has possession of the assets subject to the security agreement for the limited purpose of accounting to the creditor, and is obliged to hold the remaining funds for the company and its other unpaid creditors.[55] Should there be surplus funds, the receiver becomes subject to a fiduciary obligation when dealing with those funds.[56]

Under the Act, receivers are subject to a number of specific statutory obligations, such as the requirement to lodge notice of their appointment[57] and six-monthly and final accounts with ASIC,[58] and to report to ASIC.[59] Their reporting obligations include reporting any offences that may have been committed by officers or members of the company, past and present; any misapplication of the company's money or property, or any liability to account for such property; and any negligence, default, breach of duty or breach of trust in relation to the company by any person involved in the formation, promotion, administration, management or winding up of the company.[60]

Liabilities and indemnities

Once appointed, s 419 imposes personal liability on the receiver 'for debts incurred by the person during the course of the receivership, possession or control for services

52 *R v Board of Trade; Ex parte St Martins Preserving Co Ltd* [1965] 1 QB 603, 617; cited with approval in *Expo International Pty Ltd v Chant* [1979] 2 NSWLR 820.

53 *Expo International Pty Ltd v Chant* [1979] 2 NSWLR 820, 829–30. For more information on the fiduciary obligation, see Chapter 13.

54 *Australia and New Zealand Banking Group Ltd v Bangadilly Pastoral Co Pty Ltd* (1978) 139 CLR 195.

55 *Expo International Pty Ltd v Chant* [1979] 2 NSWLR 820.

56 Ibid.

57 *Corporations Act* ss 427–48.

58 Ibid s 432.

59 Ibid s 422.

60 Ibid.

rendered, goods purchased or property hired, leased, used or occupied'. An invalid appointment could lead to the appointee being personally liable for trespass and conversion[61] if they dealt with the company's assets without authority. However, s 419(3) permits the court to impose this liability onto the secured creditor instead of the appointee. The court may also order under s 1322 that any action taken by an improperly appointed receiver is valid and may relieve a person of civil liability incurred as a result of the appointment.[62]

Under s 419A if, after a receiver has been appointed, the company continues to use or occupy property owned by a third party for more than seven days, the receiver will become personally liable for the rent and other amounts payable under any agreement with the third party. To avoid this liability, the receiver must give the third party notice.[63] This provision was inserted in line with a Harmer Report recommendation to that effect, as it is not equitable for a receiver to permit the company—and therefore indirectly the creditor—to continue to obtain benefits under a lease agreement without being liable for the payments that the company would otherwise be liable to make.[64]

As the security documentation will usually provide that the receiver is an agent of the company, they will be entitled to an indemnity from the company, which covers expenses incurred by the receiver. They may also seek one from the appointing creditor. The receiver is entitled to a lien over the secured assets to enforce this indemnity, which results in their costs being recovered prior to the secured creditor's debt. However, this indemnity will be lost in the event of a breach of duty by the receiver.[65] As a receiver is recognised in s 9 as an officer of the company, the limits on indemnity provided by the company imposed by ss 199A–AC of the *Corporations Act* will also apply.[66] These limits do not apply to an indemnity provided by the secured creditor.

15.25.15 The court-appointed receiver

Under the *Corporations Act*, the court has the power to appoint a receiver in circumstances which may not necessitate consideration of the company's solvency.[67] These powers will be exercised 'only after great scrutiny and in extraordinary circumstances'.[68] Further powers exist in all jurisdictions for the Supreme or Federal Court to appoint a receiver where it is 'just and convenient' or 'just or convenient' to do so.[69] That has been interpreted as being circumstances where 'it is practicable and the interests of justice require it'.[70] Such appointments are relatively rare.

61 *Wrights Hardware Pty Ltd v Evans* (1988) 13 ACLR 631, 633–4.
62 Procedural irregularities and s 1322 are discussed in depth in Chapter 7 at Section 7.30.05.
63 *Corporations Act* ss 419A(3)–(8).
64 Australian Law Reform Commission, *General Insolvency Inquiry* (Report 45, 1988) [218]–[220].
65 *James v Commonwealth Bank of Australia* (1992) 37 FCR 445.
66 For further discussion of the limits on indemnity, see Chapter 10 at Section 10.40.15.
67 *Corporations Act* ss 233, 1323, as discussed in relation to members' remedies in Chapter 14.
68 *Bond Brewing Holdings Ltd v National Australia Bank Ltd* (1990) 8 ACLC 330, 342.
69 *Judiciary Act 1903* (Cth) s 77R; *Federal Court of Australia Act 1976* (Cth) s 57; *Supreme Court Act 1970* (NSW) s 67; *Supreme Court Act 1935* (SA) s 29; *Supreme Court Act 1935* (WA) s 25; *Supreme Court Act 1986* (Vic) s 37.
70 *Edwards & Co v Picard* [1909] 2 KB 903, 907.

Standing to apply for such an appointment will be given to any party to a cause or matter before the court, under the court rules in each jurisdiction. There is no obligation to demonstrate a proprietary interest in the asset over which the appointment is sought, and these powers have been used to appoint receivers on the application of both secured and unsecured creditors.[71] Appointment of a receiver may be interlocutory or final; for example, a receiver may be sought to be appointed by a creditor concerned that assets will be dissipated in the course of other legal proceedings. This was the case in *National Australia Bank Ltd v Bond Brewing Holdings Ltd*,[72] where a receiver and manager was appointed until a further order could be made, and was then ordered to continue in place until the trial of a separate action could be completed. That order was overturned on appeal, where the Court noted that a receiver will not be appointed to an insolvent company where the application is opposed by the company.[73]

When a receiver is appointed by the court, the court must provide them with sufficient powers to undertake their tasks. A court-appointed receiver is also an officer of the court, and it is considered contempt of court to interfere with the possession of such a receiver without the leave of the court. Court-appointed receivers are entitled to an indemnity for their remuneration[74] and any liabilities incurred over the course of the receivership, which is also forfeited should they act improperly.

15.25.20 Order of payment

The sum realised by the receiver will be distributed according to a number of legislative provisions. Land tax and customs duty are given first priority for payment on any funds recovered by the receiver.[75] If the security interest was a circulating security interest or a floating charge, s 433 requires that certain creditors, particularly employees, are granted priority to the secured creditor if the company is not being wound up. This is because a circulating security interest allows the company to continue to trade. Employees may have increased the value of the asset which is the subject of the security interest and as such their rights should be given priority.[76] These priorities are set out in s 433.[77] First, s 433(3)(a) stipulates payment to any insured third party under s 562, if moneys from that insurance policy are received. Then, according to s 433(3)(b), any auditor's fees and expenses if the auditor was refused consent to resign by ASIC under s 329(6) are to

71 *Re New York Taxicab Co* [1913] 1 Ch 1; *Re South Australian Barytes Ltd (No 2)* (1977) 19 SASR 91; *Bond Brewing Holdings Ltd v National Australia Bank Ltd* (1990) 8 ACLC 330, 460.

72 *National Australia Bank Ltd v Bond Brewing Holdings Ltd* (1990) 1 ACSR 405.

73 *Bond Brewing Holdings Ltd v National Australia Bank Ltd* (1990) 8 ACLC 330, 467.

74 *Re Deppeler, Moulamein Grain Co-Operative Ltd (in liq) (No 3)* (2023) 168 ACSR 244 confirmed that s 425 does not apply to court-appointed receivers, as they are not appointed under an 'instrument'. Equally, the *Federal Court Rules 1979* (Cth) provide the power to fix remuneration of court-appointed receivers for work done subsequent to their appointment only.

75 *Customs Act 1901* (Cth); *Land Tax Management Act 1956* (NSW) s 47; *Land Tax Act 1915* (Qld) s 37; *Land Tax Act 1936* (SA) s 66; *Land Tax Act 1958* (Vic) s 66; *Land Tax Assessment Act 1976* (WA) ss 14–15.

76 *Stein v Saywell* (1969) 121 CLR 529, 556.

77 These provisions were subject to recent High Court consideration in *Carter Holt Harvey Woodproducts Australia Pty Ltd v Commonwealth* (2019) 268 CLR 524, in the context of a trading trust. The Court confirmed that creditors who would be priority creditors of an insolvent company will also be priority creditors when the company concerned is a trading trust.

be paid. Employee wages and superannuation contributions as set out in ss 556(1)(e), (g), (h) or 560 are next according to s 433(3)(c), but this priority payment is subject to any other auditor's fees as set out in ss 433(6) and (7). These provisions are discussed in Chapter 16. After wages and superannuation contributions, other employee entitlements and retrenchments must be paid before the secured creditor. If the company is being wound up, then s 556 will apply, as discussed in Chapter 16.

15.25.25 Effects of appointment of receiver

The appointment of a receiver has no effect on the company as a separate legal entity, beyond the requirement in s 428 that the words 'receiver appointed' be attached after the name of the company where it first appears in any public document or negotiable instrument. This serves to alert new creditors or those intending to enter into agreements with the company that there is a receiver appointed, and to make further inquiries to ascertain the position of the company. Company officers' powers of management are superseded by the receiver's powers, but they remain subject to the statutory and general law duties which apply to officers and directors. This includes the power to bring an action in the name of the company, such as to challenge the validity of the receiver's appointment or to argue a breach by the secured creditor.[78]

The appointment of a receiver does not automatically terminate employee contracts with the company, but the circumstances of the appointment may lead to such a termination. If the company's business is sold, the receiver negotiates a new contract with employees that is inconsistent with the previous contract, or the role of the receiver is inconsistent with ongoing employment, then the contracts will be terminated. When a receiver is appointed as an agent of the company, rather than the creditor, then employee contracts generally continue.[79] By contrast, the appointment of a receiver by the court will almost invariably terminate existing employee contracts.[80]

15.30 Relationship between receivership and other external administration

A receiver can be appointed alongside other methods of external administration, including schemes of arrangement and voluntary administration. In particular, it is common for the same company to be subject to both receivership and winding up. The fact that a company is being wound up does not prevent a secured creditor from realising their security, either personally or through the appointment of a receiver. The reverse is also true, and the court may adjourn a winding up application if it would be beneficial to the unsecured creditors to allow the receiver to complete their realisation of the asset. Once the company has been wound up, then a receiver's management powers cease, as will their role as agent of the company, unless approval of the court or the liquidator

78 *Newhart Developments Ltd v Co-operative Commercial Bank Ltd* [1978] QB 814.
79 *Re Mack Trucks (Britain) Ltd* [1967] 1 WLR 125.
80 *Reid v Explosives Co Ltd* (1887) 19 QBD 468.

is obtained.[81] Multiple receivers may be appointed over different assets within the one company.[82] It is also possible for receivership and voluntary administration to occur together, but as voluntary administration has a policy objective of corporate rescue, it is more intrusive into the rights of the secured creditor.[83] As will be seen below, only a secured creditor who has commenced appointing a receiver or who holds security over the whole or substantially the whole of the company's assets will be permitted to appoint a receiver during the voluntary administration process.[84]

15.35 Schemes of arrangement

Schemes of arrangement are one of the two main processes available when a company, or part of it, may be able to continue to trade, or where creditors think that they can achieve more return on their debts from an arrangement with the company than on liquidation. The other process is voluntary administration. A new process of restructuring, introduced in 2021 and located in pt 5.3B of the *Corporations Act*, is available to small companies with liabilities of $1 million or less and are insolvent or likely to become insolvent. Both voluntary administration and small business restructuring are discussed below.

A scheme of arrangement involves a rearrangement or compromise of the rights and obligations of a company's creditors and/or its members. Schemes are not only available when a company is insolvent; they can also be undertaken as part of a takeover scheme.[85] In this chapter, we only discuss schemes of arrangement entered into as part of dealing with a company's indebtedness. This type of scheme involves a binding plan between the company and its creditors, or a class of creditors, in which the creditors' rights are deferred, rearranged or extinguished. Such schemes may also affect the rights of members. Registered company liquidators can act as scheme administrators on behalf of a company. The scheme administrator's role and powers are set out in the scheme proposal.

Schemes of arrangement are particularly useful when a company has many creditors, making individual negotiations about the repayment of debt difficult, or where there are different types of creditors. Schemes are also suited to larger companies, where insolvencies are complex, and can be included as part of a liquidation. This was demonstrated in the case of *Re Lehman Brothers Australia Ltd (in liq) (No 2)*,[86] where the liquidators of Lehman Brothers Australia ('LBA') sought court approval to convene a meeting of creditors involved in a class action against the company. LBA was a subsidiary of Lehman Brothers Holdings Inc ('Lehman Brothers'), which had filed for Chapter 11 bankruptcy protection in the United States. After LBA's collapse, several former clients commenced a class action against LBA and sought compensation for losses they suffered as a result of

81 *Corporations Act* s 420C.
82 Ibid ss 434D–G.
83 See, eg, ibid s 440B.
84 Ibid ss 441A–B. An exception also exists for perishables: s 441C.
85 See the discussion of schemes of arrangement and takeovers in Chapter 19 at Section 19.10.05.
86 *Re Lehman Brothers of Australia Ltd (in liq) (No 2)* (2013) 95 ACSR 685. This case is discussed further in J Harris, 'Charting the Limits of Insolvency Reorganisations: *Lehman Brothers Holdings Inc v City of Swan*' (2010) 32(1) *Sydney Law Review* 141.

advice and products recommended by LBA. Prior to the liquidator applying to the court to convene the creditors' meeting, a judgment had been obtained in the class action, and the creditors had tried to enforce this judgment directly against some of the insurers of Lehman Brothers in the United States. The insurers disputed their liability both to LBA and to the creditors.

The Court agreed to make an order convening a meeting of the creditors involved in the class action, and a scheme was subsequently approved by the creditors at a final court hearing. Some of the key elements of the scheme were that the overseas insurers would pay $50 million to LBA for distribution to this group of creditors and, in return, the creditors would release all claims against the insurers. However, the creditors retained the right to prove any outstanding claims not met by this payment in the winding up of LBA.

Despite the usefulness of the scheme of arrangement in this case, the use of schemes for insolvency has become less common since the introduction of voluntary administration in 1992. This is largely because schemes require court involvement and approval; whereas deeds of company arrangement entered into as part of a voluntary administration do not. As a result, voluntary administration can be quicker and cheaper than schemes of arrangement.

15.35.05 A scheme must involve an arrangement or compromise

Under s 411, a scheme of arrangement must include 'a compromise or arrangement' between a company and its creditors, or any class of them. These words have been construed broadly, with the courts increasingly adopting a flexible approach as to what they can cover.[87] This was demonstrated in the case of *Re Fowler v Lindholm; Opes Prime Stockbroking Ltd*,[88] where a stockbroking company became insolvent. The facts involved in this case are complex, and once the company became insolvent, different processes of receivership, voluntary administration, schemes of arrangement, and liquidation were involved. This particular judgment focused on the scheme of arrangement.

Opes Prime was involved in margin lending and lent money to its clients to invest in relatively small stocks traded on the Australian Securities Exchange (ASX). Opes Prime then entered into call loans, where it borrowed money from large commercial banks, using the clients' shares as security for the loans. With the onset of the global financial crisis in late 2007 and early 2008, the commercial banks made calls (that is, demanded repayment) on the loans to Opes Prime. When it became apparent that Opes Prime could not meet these calls, the banks (including ANZ and Merrill Lynch) appointed receivers, who then sold the shares secured by the loans to repay the moneys owing to ANZ and Merrill Lynch. The resulting claims against Opes Prime's by investors who had lost their shares were estimated at over $600 million.[89]

87 See *Re Fowler v Lindholm; Opes Prime Stockbroking Ltd* (2009) 178 FCR 563 [55]; *Australian Securities Commission v Marlborough Gold Mines Pty Ltd* (1993) 177 CLR 485, 501.

88 (2009) 178 FCR 563. For further discussion of the circumstances preceding this case, see S Steele, 'Lessons (to be) Learnt from the Opes Prime Insolvency' (2008) 32(3) *Melbourne University Law Review* 1127.

89 J Harris, 'Before the High Court: Charting the Limits of Insolvency Reorganisations: *Lehman Brothers Holdings Inc v City of Swan*' (2010) 32(1) *Sydney Law Review* 141, 147.

The liquidator, and some of Opes Prime's clients, made claims against the banks in relation to the security they had taken over the clients' shares. A creditors' scheme of arrangement was negotiated between these parties, under which the banks paid $240 million to the liquidator, and the clients accepted 37 cents in the dollar as repayment for their losses and released their claims against the banks and the receivers. Finkelstein J, at first instance, noted the wide purpose that schemes of arrangement can have:

> When first enacted in England as ss 159–161 of the Companies Act 1862, 25 & 26 Vic c 89, the provisions were intended to facilitate compromises and arrangements between insolvent companies and their members and creditors as an alternative to liquidation. Now, they have a much wider purpose, including allowing businesses to restructure and reorganise their affairs to enable them to go forward in a better condition, or to amalgamate their businesses so as to reduce expenses and compete with greater effect.[90]

Finkelstein J then considered whether it was acceptable under s 411 for a scheme to incorporate a release by the creditors of claims against both the company and the receivers (as third parties). He held that, provided there was a sufficient nexus between the release, the creditors, and the company, such an agreement came within the words 'compromise or arrangement' between the creditors and the company. This flexible approach was affirmed by the Full Federal Court, which noted that:

> A scheme of arrangement between a company and its creditors or a class of creditors is no more than a proposal to vary or modify the company's obligations in relation to its debts and liabilities owed to the creditors or class of creditors. There is nothing to prevent the company from proposing, as part of the arrangement, a term to the effect that, in consideration of what the company has provided under the scheme, the creditors will discharge not only the debts and liabilities of the company, but also the liabilities of [third parties].[91]

This approach does not apply to deeds of company arrangement entered into as part of a voluntary administration. In *City of Swan v Lehman Bros Australia Ltd*,[92] the Full Federal Court considered that the provisions in the *Corporations Act* dealing with voluntary administrations did not allow a deed of company arrangement to take away a creditor's right to pursue claims against third parties.[93] The Court's reasoning was based on the differences in the wording of pt 5.1 (dealing with schemes of arrangement) and pt 5.3A (dealing with voluntary administration). This approach was confirmed on appeal, in a joint judgment by French CJ, Gummow, Hayne and Kiefel JJ who held that a deed can

90 *Re Opes Prime Stockbroking Ltd* (2009) 179 FCR 20 [48].
91 *Re Fowler v Lindholm; Opes Prime Stockbroking Ltd* (2009) 178 FCR 563 (68).
92 *City of Swan v Lehman Brothers Australia Ltd* (2009) 179 FCR 243. Discussed further in J Harris, 'Before the High Court: Charting the Limits of Insolvency Reorganisations: *Lehman Brothers Holdings Inc v City of Swan*' (2010) 32(1) *Sydney Law Review* 141.
93 *City of Swan v Lehman Brothers Australia Ltd* (2009) 179 FCR 243 [29].

only bind the creditors of the company and not any third parties. This view was based on a literal reading of sections in pt 5.3A the *Corporations Act*.[94]

15.35.10 The process of approval of a scheme of arrangement

Under ss 411(1) and 412, an application to the court to approve a scheme of arrangement can be made by the company, a creditor or class of creditors, a member or a liquidator, and must include details of the proposed scheme and an explanatory statement detailing the nature of the scheme. It is for the court to decide whether to order a meeting of the affected creditors or members. Factors that a court may consider in deciding whether to order a meeting include whether the explanatory statement complies with the law, whether ultimate approval of the scheme by the court is likely, and whether the proposed scheme is commercially fair and reasonable. Substantive discussion about the fairness of the scheme is, however, usually reserved for the creditors' meeting. In ordering that a creditors' or shareholders' meeting be convened, the court may direct that it be held in a particular manner and at a particular place (s 411(1)). If a court grants leave for a meeting to be convened, this does not mean the court has given its approval to the contents of the scheme.[95]

If an order for a meeting is granted, and the creditors or members approve the scheme by a special majority (defined in s 411(4)), they can then apply back to the court to have the scheme approved. The court is likely to approve the scheme if the procedure for convening the creditors' meeting and distributing the explanatory memorandum were complied with.[96] If an order approving the scheme is made, a copy of the order must be lodged with ASIC.

The role of the court in reviewing a scheme at the first hearing was discussed in *Re CSR Ltd*.[97] In this case, CSR Ltd wanted to separate its two main businesses into two companies: one involved in building products and aluminium production, and the other in sugar and renewable energy. The building products business was facing significant present and future liabilities in relation to claims for asbestos-related diseases. CSR applied to the Court for approval to hold a members' meeting to consider a scheme setting up the new company to take over the debts and liabilities of the building products, and a related capital reduction. At the first hearing, objectors to the proposal, including ASIC and the Attorney-General of New South Wales, spoke against the scheme. The Court was also presented with 11 reports from financial and actuarial experts in relation to the extent of possible future asbestos liabilities faced by CSR.

Stone J declined to make the orders convening the members' meeting on the basis that there was significant uncertainty surrounding the likely amount of future asbestos liabilities. After reviewing the proposed scheme, she held that she could not be satisfied that the provisions of the scheme were consistent with commercial reality, and that, if approved, the scheme would not involve an unfair or oppressive result.[98]

94 *Lehman Brothers Holdings Inc v City of Swan* (2010) 240 CLR 509, [54].
95 *Australian Securities Commission v Marlborough Gold Mines Pty Ltd* (1993) 177 CLR 485.
96 *Re Alabama, New Orleans, Texas and Pacific Junction Railway Co* [1891] Ch 13.
97 *Re CSR Ltd* (2010) 183 FCR 358.
98 Ibid [36].

On appeal, Stone J's decision was reversed. CSR argued, among other things, that it was inappropriate for Stone J to use the discretion given to the Court under s 411(1) to decide preliminary matters related to the proposed scheme. Keane CJ, Jacobson and Finkelstein JJ agreed. Instead, Keane CJ and Jacobson J considered it was appropriate for the Court to refuse to convene a meeting under s 411(1) when 'the making of the order would be futile because the scheme as proposed is unlikely to be finally approved'. However, their Honours continued:

> The hearing before the learned primary judge was an interlocutory hearing ill-suited to the kind of in depth investigation which both sides sought to press on this Court. We are respectfully of the opinion that the key to the determination of the appeal lies in understanding that whether or not the scheme should ultimately be approved by the court is a question not amenable to resolution in the negative on an application for an order concerning a meeting of shareholders.[99]

Finkelstein J made similar comments, suggesting that the function of the Court at the first hearing is 'emphatically not' to consider the merits or fairness of the proposed scheme.[100] In the absence of clear evidence that the scheme is unlikely to be approved, the role of the Court is to allow the meeting to be convened and to consider any objections if and when the scheme is approved and brought back to the court.

The creditors' meeting

At the court-convened meeting, the scheme must be approved by a special majority of creditors or members as defined in s 411(4). In the case of a meeting of creditors, or a class of creditors, this means approval by a majority of creditors present and voting either in person or by proxy who are owed at least 75 per cent of the total amount of debts or claims of all the creditors present at the meeting in person or by proxy. In other words, the scheme must be approved by a simple majority of creditors that are owed at least three-quarters of the total debts of those present or voting by proxy at the meeting.

Where separate meetings of different classes of creditors need to be held, s 411(5) deems these meetings to be a single meeting for the purposes of the Act. This means that the votes cast at each meeting are aggregated to ascertain the overall position taken by the creditors. To determine if there are different classes of creditors, it is necessary to consider the varying rights of the creditors. For example, it is common to hold separate meetings of secured and unsecured creditors, and between different classes of unsecured creditors. The need to adopt a practical approach to this question was noted by Finkelstein J in the *Opes Prime Case*[101] as follows:

> The application of the relevant test involves a comparison of the rights creditors have in the absence of the scheme and any new rights that are established under the scheme ... [P]ractical considerations are relevant. If the charge is

99 *Re CSR Ltd* (2010) 183 FCR 358.
100 Ibid.
101 *Re Opes Prime Stockbroking Ltd* (2009) 179 FCR 20 ('*Opes Prime Case*').

> too insidious in identifying classes, it is possible to end up with any number of classes. In the end schemes of arrangement are propounded in a business context. The judge should adopt a practical businesslike approach to the issue as with the creditors if they were to decide the matter.[102]

The notice to creditors about the meeting must be accompanied by an explanatory statement (s 412(1)). The court approves the explanatory statement at the first hearing, when it orders the convening of the meeting. It must explain the effect of the scheme and compromise or arrangement of creditors' rights; state any material interests of the directors or creditors of the company, and the effect of these interests on the compromise or arrangement; and set out any other material relevant to creditors making a decision.

The second hearing

At the second hearing, the scheme approved by the creditors is put to the court for approval. The court has discretion to refuse to approve the scheme even where a majority of the creditors has approved the scheme.[103] A key focus of the court in determining this issue will be whether the scheme is commercially appropriate. In other words, a court is not likely to approve a scheme that does not return the company to solvency. The court can also impose conditions or make alterations to the scheme of arrangement (s 411(6)).

Termination of a scheme

In most cases, the time for termination of the scheme will be stipulated in the scheme document. For example, a scheme might terminate after a set period of time, after distribution of the payments to creditors, at the discretion of the administrator, or if the creditors of the company resolve that the scheme has attained its purpose.

15.40 Voluntary administration

Voluntary administration was introduced in 1992 as a process that can be used by creditors where they consider they can achieve more return on their debts if the company, or part of it, continues to trade, or if its assets are sold in a process that does not involve immediate liquidation.[104] It was introduced following recommendations by the Australian Law Reform Commission in the Harmer Report.[105] The Report noted the key benefits of voluntary administration as being that it is capable of swift implementation; is generally uncomplicated, inexpensive and flexible; and that it provides an alternative form of dealing with the financial affairs of the company'.[106]

---

102 Ibid [66].

103 *Re Stockbridge Ltd* (1993) 9 ACSR 637.

104 For a discussion of voluntary administration and schemes of arrangement, see J Harris, 'Charting the Limits of Insolvency Reorganisations: *Lehman Brothers Holdings Inc v City of Swan*' (2010) 32(1) *Sydney Law Review* 141.

105 Australian Law Reform Commission, *General Insolvency Inquiry* (Report No 45, 1988).

106 Ibid [54].

Since its introduction, the process has been subject to criticism, largely on the basis it is too costly and complicated for small business.[107] Data indicated that its use declined significantly after 2007, when creditors' voluntary liquidations became easier to achieve. For example, in 2006, voluntary administrations made up 35 per cent of all external administrations commenced in that year; whereas, in 2018, they made up 17.5 per cent.[108]

In March 2020, the Federal Government made temporary changes to the voluntary administration scheme to support businesses affected by the COVID-19 pandemic.[109] These measures had a positive impact for many small businesses, with a 46 per cent decrease in the number of companies that went into administration in March to July 2020 compared to the same period in 2020.[110] As a result, the small business restructuring process was introduced, discussed below.

Even with this reform, there are still calls for the process of voluntary administration to be improved.[111] As Harris writes:

> Part 5.3A has operated without major structural amendments for over 25 years. During that time, it has been used to address the financial distress of thousands of MSMEs [micro, small and medium businesses], as well as restructure some of the largest and most complex businesses in Australia. The procedure can work well, and is working well in many instances, but that appears largely to be due to the ingenuity of practitioners and the flexibility of the courts.
>
> Voluntary administration requires a range of tasks to be undertaken and imposes various obligations and potential liability risks for administrators that contribute to a cost structure that makes it unworkable for many (mostly smaller) businesses. These measures can hinder commercial restructuring efforts, but it is also clear that many businesses in financial distress are simply not viable candidates for corporate rescue.[112]

15.40.05 Commencing a voluntary administration

The role of an administrator is to investigate the financial affairs of a company to decide what is the best course of action for its creditors. If the administrator considers a better

107 See, eg, K Lightman, 'Voluntary Administration: The New Wave or the New Waif in Insolvency Law?' (1994) 2(1) *Insolvency Law Journal* 59; Parliamentary Joint Committee on Corporations and Financial Services Report, Parliament of Australia, *Corporate Insolvency Laws: A Stocktake* (Report, June 2004) [5.21]; K Lindgren, 'Voluntary Administration: Current Issues and Proposals for Reform' (2006) *Federal Judicial Scholarship* 4 <http://www.austlii.edu.au/au/journals/FedJSchol/2006/4.html>.

108 Australian Securities and Investments Commission, *Insolvency Statistics—Summary Analysis of Series 1 and 2* <https://asic.gov.au/regulatory-resources/find-a-document/statistics/insolvency-statistics/insolvency-statistics-up-to-31-july-2022/>.

109 *Coronavirus Economic Response Package Omnibus Act 2020* (Cth) sch 12.

110 Australian Government, The Treasury, 'Fact Sheet: Insolvency Reforms to Support Small Business' (2020) 1 <https://ministers.treasury.gov.au/sites/ministers.treasury.gov.au/files/2020-09/Insolvency-Reforms-fact-sheet.pdf>.

111 Parliamentary Joint Committee on Corporations and Financial Services, Parliament of Australia, *Corporate insolvency in Australia* (Report, July 2023) [7.66]–[7.78].

112 J Harris, 'Promoting an Optimal Corporate Rescue Culture in Australia: The Role and Efficiency of the Voluntary Administration Regime' (PhD Thesis, The University of Adelaide, 2022) 239, cited in Parliamentary Joint Committee on Corporations and Financial Services, Parliament of Australia, *Corporate Insolvency in Australia* (Report, July 2023) [7.72].

financial return can be achieved for creditors by not proceeding directly to liquidation, they can recommend a deed of company arrangement (DOCA) be approved and entered into. In 2023, in evidence provided to the Parliamentary Joint Committee on Corporations and Financial Services, ASIC reported that, of the 700–1,200 voluntary administrations undertaken each year, approximately 35 per cent progress to a DOCA.[113] Some of the common provisions included in a DOCA are that there is a moratorium on creditors enforcing their debts to allow the company more time to pay; that a compromise is entered into where the creditors agree to accept a lesser amount in final settlement of their debts; and/or that there is longer time allowed for the sale of the company's property.

Voluntary administration is commenced in one of three ways. First, a company may appoint an administrator via a board resolution stating that, in the opinion of the directors, the company is insolvent, or is likely to become insolvent at some future time, and that an administrator should be appointed (s 436A(1)). Second, under s 436B(1), a liquidator or provisional liquidator of a company may, by writing, appoint an administrator if they think that the company is insolvent, or is likely to become insolvent at a future time. The liquidator can only appoint themselves, or someone else from their firm, as the administrator with the approval of the company's creditors and the leave of the court (s 436B(2)). Third, a secured creditor with enforceable security over all, or substantially the whole, of the company's property may by writing appoint an administrator if the security interest has become, and is still, enforceable (s 436C(1)).

In practice, the decision to put a company into voluntary administration is usually made by the company's directors. In making this decision, the directors do not need to seek the approval of shareholders, creditors, or the court. However, they do need to believe the company is insolvent or is likely to become insolvent at some future time. In the 2019 case of *Bryan Kevin Hughes as joint and several liquidators of Traditional Therapy Clinics Ltd (In liq)*, the Supreme Court of Western Australia held that not all directors need to have such an opinion for the resolution to be valid.[114] The case involved the company (Traditional Therapy Clinics Ltd), which had five directors. While all the directors voted in favour of a resolution that the company was insolvent or likely to become insolvent, and that an administrator should be appointed, two of the directors were new to the board and did not have enough knowledge to make an informed opinion on the issue of solvency.

The Court held that the words 'in the opinion of directors voting for the resolution' referred to the opinion of the majority of directors. It noted that the alternate approach would leave open the possibility of sabotage by a director after the appointment of an administrator by arguing that they had never formed an opinion regarding the solvency of the company.[115] It also noted that '[t]here is nothing in pt 5.3A which compels a court to take a rigorous and technical view of the appointment process. The whole exercise must necessarily be a matter of commercial judgment.'[116]

113 Ibid [7.6].

114 *Bryan Kevin Hughes as joint and several liquidators of Traditional Therapy Clinics (in liq)* [2019] WASC 139.

115 Ibid [14].

116 Ibid.

A voluntary administration begins as soon as an administrator is appointed (s 435C(1)).

The effect of an administrator being appointed is that, while the normal operations of the company continue:

(a) the directors cannot use their powers[117] and they must help the administrator, including providing the company's books and records, and a report about the company's business, property, affairs and financial circumstances, as well as any further information about these that the voluntary administrator reasonably require[118]
(b) unsecured creditors cannot begin, continue or enforce their claims against the company without the administrator's consent or the court's permission[119]
(c) owners of property used or occupied by the company, or people who lease such property to the company, cannot recover their property[120]
(d) except in limited circumstances, secured creditors cannot enforce their security interest in the company's assets[121]
(e) a court application to put the company in liquidation cannot be commenced;[122] and
(f) a creditor holding a personal guarantee from the company's director or other person cannot act under the personal guarantee without the court's consent.[123]

These restrictions are designed to give the administrator time to conduct their investigation into the financial state of the company, without interference.

There are benefits for directors in voluntary administration. One of the most important is that, once an administrator is appointed, directors may have a defence to any liability under the insolvent trading provisions of the *Corporations Act* (s 588H(5), discussed further in Chapter 11 at Section 11.25). Even if the company is subsequently wound up, the court will have regard to any action the directors took to appoint an administrator, when that decision was taken, and the results of that process in determining whether the directors are personally liable under the insolvent trading provisions (s 588H(6)). In addition, a guarantee provided by a director to cover the debts of the company cannot be enforced after an administrator is appointed without court approval (s 440J(1)).

It has been held that s 440J(1) does not apply to halt an action to enforce a guarantee commenced before the company went into administration. This interpretation was applied in *Mizuho Bank Ltd v Mark Anthony Ackroyd*.[124] In this case, the plaintiff bank lent a company over $44 million and took a guarantee for approximately half of that amount from the defendant director, Mr Ackroyd. In June 2016, the bank commenced proceedings against Ackroyd to enforce the guarantee. In July 2016, the company appointed administrators under s 436A of the *Corporations Act*. Ackroyd brought an application

117 *Corporations Act* s 198G.
118 Ibid s 438B.
119 Ibid s 440D.
120 Ibid ss 440B, 440F.
121 Ibid ss 441A–D.
122 Ibid s 440A.
123 Ibid s 440J. See also Australian Securities and Investments Commission, *Voluntary Administration: A Guide for Creditors* (Information Sheet 74, June 2003).
124 *Mizuho Bank Ltd v Mark Anthony Ackroyd* (2016) 116 ACSR 225.

seeking a stay of the proceedings related to the guarantee on the basis the administrators were precluded from continuing without leave of the court under s 440J.

The New South Wales Supreme Court held that s 440J did not prevent a creditor from proceeding to enforce a guarantee commenced before the voluntary administration. The Court's decision was based on a finding that the words in s 440J did not cover a continuation of proceedings, and there was a relevant distinction between the appointment of an administrator that could trigger liability under a guarantee, and continuing proceedings that had already commenced to enforce a guarantee.

Only a registered company liquidator can be appointed as an administrator (s 448B). Since 2017, the requirements for approval by ASIC are set out in sch 2 of the *Corporations Act*: (*Insolvency Practice Schedule (Corporations)* (*IPSC*)), s 20–5 onwards. These requirements are discussed further in Chapter 16. There is a restriction on creditors, auditors, or officers of the company becoming the administrator, even if they are registered liquidators, without leave of the court (s 448C). The administrator must lodge a notice of their appointment with ASIC by the end of the business day following their appointment and publish a notice of appointment in a national newspaper or daily newspaper that circulates in the jurisdictions in which the company carries on its business within three days. Once appointed, an administrator is required to act in the best interests of the creditors and be independent. They are also defined in s 9 of the Act as officers of the company, and subject to the duties under ss 180–84, discussed in Chapters 10 to 13.

15.40.10 The administrator's role

An administrator is an officer of the company (s 9AD(d)).[125] The central function of an administrator is to investigate and report to creditors on the company's business, property, affairs and financial circumstances. As a result of this investigation, they can recommend one of three options to the creditors. These are: to end the administration and return the company to the directors' control; to approve a DOCA under which the company will pay all or part of its debts and then be released from those debts; or wind up the company and appoint a liquidator (s 438A). Under s 437A, the administrator is provided with wide-ranging powers including the power to perform any function and exercise any power that the company or its officers previously performed or exercised. The administrator can remove a director from office and appoint new directors; execute documents, bring or defend legal proceedings on behalf of the company; and terminate employment contracts (s 442A).

In undertaking its investigations, the administrator must determine whether the company, or any part of its business, is viable or whether it should be liquidated. If the administrator considers that part of the business should be saved, they can start to negotiate a recapitalisation plan, including the sale of all or some of the company's assets.

To enable the administrator to carry out their role, there is a moratorium or stay on any claims being taken against the company and its assets. This includes a stay of all legal proceedings against the company and the guarantors of its debts (ss 440A–AJ). However, the court or the administrator can consent to claims by secured creditors continuing (s 440B(2)).

125 Or under s 9AD(e) if the DOCA is executed.

Further, any secured creditor with a security interest over all, or substantially the whole, of the property of the company can still enforce the security interest within 13 days of the administration beginning, or within 13 days of the secured creditor having been given notice of the administrator's appointment (s 441A).[126] The reason for this exception to the rule that claims against the company are stayed is that there is little point in a secured creditor with such a large interest in the company's property having to wait until the administration ends to enforce their security interest. It also avoids unnecessary delay and costs if a secured creditor has already decided they are going to enforce their security at the end of the administration process, rather than engage in the process and potentially enter into the DOCA.

Under s 443A(1), the administrator is personally liable for all debts incurred in the course of the administration, including for services rendered to the company, goods bought by the company, and property leased by the company. However, under s 443D, the administrator has a right of indemnity against the company's assets for debts incurred in exercising their powers during the administration, including payment of their own remuneration. This indemnity takes priority over all the company's other unsecured debts. As a matter of practice, administrators will ensure a company has sufficient assets to discharge this debt before commencing the administration.

15.40.15 Creditors' meetings

The first creditors' meeting

There are two mandatory creditors' meetings involved in an administration. The first creditors' meeting must be held within eight business days of the appointment of the administrator and provides an opportunity for creditors to decide on two key issues, the first of which is whether to pass a resolution removing the administrator and appointing someone else to act in their place (s 436E(4)). Creditors might choose to remove an administrator if they consider the administrator is too sympathetic to the company's management or lacks independence for some other reason. However, ascertaining such issues can be difficult due to the short time period between calling the meeting and the meeting itself.

The second issue that can be decided at the first creditors' meeting is whether to appoint a committee of inspection and, if so, who are to be the committee's members (s 436E(1)). The purpose of a committee of inspection is to advise and assist the administrator (*Insolvency Practice Schedule (Corporations)* s 80–35).[127] The committee may obtain specialist advice or assistance and the external administrator is required to have regard to any directions given to them by the committee but is not required to follow those directions (*IPSC* ss 80–50, 80–35(2)). If the administrator decides not to comply with a direction of the committee, they must keep a written record of that fact and their reasons for not complying (*IPSC* s 80–35(3)).

Only creditors can vote at creditors' meetings (*Insolvency Practice Rules (Corporations)* r 75–85).[128] To be entitled to vote as a creditor, the person's debt or claim has to have

126 The 'decisions period' referred to in s 441A(1) is defined in s 9 of the *Corporations Act*.

127 The *Insolvency Practice Schedule (Corporations)* (*IPSC*) are contained in sch 2 of the *Corporations Act*.

128 The *Insolvency Practice Rules (Corporations)* (*IPRC*) are contained in section 105-1 of the Insolvency Practice Schedule (Corporations).

been admitted wholly or in part by the administrator; or the person has to have lodged particulars of their debt or claim with the person presiding at the meeting or named as having authority to receive particulars; or, if required, the person has to have lodged a formal proof of debt or claim (*IPRC* r 75–85(3)). At creditors' meetings, if the number of persons entitled to vote exceeds two, a quorum consists of at least two persons present in person or by proxy or attorney (*IPRC* r 75–105(2)(a)). If only one person is entitled to vote, or if only two persons are entitled to vote, a quorum consists of that person or those persons present in person or by proxy or attorney (*IPRC* r 75–105(2)(b)).

Unless a poll is demanded, voting is done verbally. *IPRC* r 75–110 allows a poll to be requested by the chairperson of the meeting or by a creditor participating and entitled to vote at the meeting. Unless a poll is requested, the chairperson must declare that the resolution has been passed, or passed unanimously, or passed by a particular majority, or lost 'on the voices' (*IPRC* r 75–110(3)).

On a poll, a resolution is passed if a majority of the creditors who are voting vote in favour of the resolution and a majority value of the creditors who are voting vote in favour of the resolution (*IPRC* r 75–115(1)). It is necessary that both of these requirements are satisfied for a resolution to be passed; however, the chairperson has a casting vote. The votes counted on a poll include votes cast by a creditor personally, by proxy or by attorney.

Notice for creditors' meetings must be given to in writing to as many creditors as practicably possible. Such notice must include a proxy form (*IPRC* r 75–25) and detail the particulars of any electronic means of participation that will be available to creditors (*IPRC* r 75–35). The time and place of the meeting must be convenient to the majority of creditors (*IPRC* r 75–30) and notice of the meeting must be lodged with ASIC.

The second creditors' meeting

The second creditors' meeting must be held within five business days before or after the end of the 'convening period', which is defined as 20 business days from the day after the administrator is appointed (s 439A). The court is given power under s 439A(6) to extend the convening period. These extensions are common in complex administrations; however, the administrator must make out a proper case for an extension. For example, in *Re Harrisons Pharmacy Pty Ltd (admins apptd) (recs and mgrs apptd),*[129] an extension of six months was sought by an administrator of a group of companies involved in pharmacy and medical businesses. Receivers and managers had been appointed by the secured creditors and were in support of the extension. In granting the extension, Farrell J noted that six months was a long time for an extension, and that 'the court must consider the appropriateness of the time sought'.[130] Farrell J summarised the relevant considerations when granting the extension, including that the extension should be for no longer than is required, that it can result in employees being unsettled or looking for other employment, and that it can expose the assets of the company to market risk.[131] Her Honour

129 [2013] FCA 458.
130 Ibid [7].
131 Ibid.

noted that '[i]t was the intention of the legislature that the Administrations be conducted expeditiously'.[132]

In *Re Autodom Ltd (admins appt) (recs and mgrs apptd)*,[133] an application was made for an extension for four months on the basis that the administrators were experiencing difficulties in formulating a suitable recommendation for the creditors. The employees and a landlord (Mr Hajosa) opposed the application for the extension. Hajosa argued that, due to the s 440B moratorium, it could not take possession of property it had leased to the company. Hajosa argued that the extra cost of prolonging the administration (estimated by Hajosa to be around $200,000) should be taken into account by the Court when deciding whether or not to extend the convening period.

McKerracher J agreed and considered an extension would result in a lower return overall to creditors and cause real prejudice to the employees and Hajosa. Instead, the Court granted an extension of seven days to enable the administrators to convene the second creditors' meeting in accordance with their statutory obligations.

A notice of the second creditors' meeting must be published in a national newspaper or a daily newspaper that circulates in each jurisdiction in which the company has its registered office or carries on business. This notice must be published at least five business days before the creditors' meeting. A written notice must also be sent to as many creditors as possible. The failure to notify a person who might have been a creditor does not invalidate the meeting.[134]

Prior to the second creditors' meeting, the administrator must provide the creditors with a report that complies with the requirements of the *IPRC*. It must include:

(a) a report on the company's business, property, affairs and financial circumstances
(b) a statement setting out whether, in the administrator's opinion, it would be in the creditors' interests for the company to execute a deed of company arrangement, for the administration to end, or for the company to be wound up
(c) reasons for that opinion
(d) any other information known to the administrator that will enable the creditors to make an informed decision about each of the three options
(e) whether there are any voidable transactions in respect of which money, property or other benefits may be recoverable by a liquidator under pt 5.7B of the *Corporations Act*
(f) if a deed of company arrangement is proposed—details of the proposed deed.[135]

The creditors are not bound to accept the administrator's recommendation. At the heart of their decision will be the question of whether liquidation or administration is likely to produce a better outcome for them. Once a decision is made, the company transitions from voluntary administration to either liquidation or a deed of company arrangement. The administration will cease if the creditors decide the company should be wound up.

132 Ibid.
133 [2012] FCA 1393.
134 See *Khoury v Zambena Pty Ltd* (1997) 23 ACSR 344.
135 *IPRC* r 75–225(3).

15.45 A deed of company arrangement

A DOCA will only be chosen as an option by creditors when it appears the company, or part of its business, can be saved, or creditors believe they can achieve a better return from this process than from having the company wound up. A DOCA may be proposed by any person for consideration at the creditors' final meeting, but is usually proposed by the administrator, the directors, or a major shareholder. The DOCA can cover any issues the proposer considers appropriate. This flexibility allows the deed to be drafted to suit the needs and circumstances of the company and its creditors. For example, a deed may propose an extension of the moratorium on the debts of the company, and/or a reorganisation of the company's business with part of the business being sold. A DOCA can include a variation of the secured and/or unsecured creditors' rights to enforce their debts. A common provision in a deed is that creditors will accept less than full payment for their debt and that such payment can be made in instalments.

Under s 444A(4), a deed must contain:

- the name of the administrator
- what property of the company is to be available to pay creditors' claims
- the nature and duration of any moratorium on the company's debts
- the extent to which the company is to be released from its debts
- the conditions (if any) for the deed to come into or continue in operation
- the circumstances that cause the deed to terminate
- the order in which any money available to creditors will be distributed among creditors bound by the deed
- the day on or before claims must have arisen if they are to be admissible under the deed.

The full deed does not need to be presented to the creditors at the second meeting, but the main details of the proposal must be outlined.[136] If a deed is approved, then the administrator and the company have 15 days to execute the deed. This time can be extended by the court.

The administrator responsible for the voluntary administration becomes the administrator of the deed, unless the creditors choose to appoint someone else (s 444A(2)). If a deed is not executed within the required time, the administration terminates according to s 446A, and transitions to a creditors' voluntary winding up (see Chapter 16).

15.45.05 The administration

Under the administration, the DOCA 'is binding on all unsecured creditors for claims arising on or before the day specified in the deed, which must not be later than the date when the administration began' (s 444D). Creditors will be bound by the terms of the DOCA, even if they vote against it, with the exception of secured creditors (s 444D(2)), owners and lessors (s 444D(3)), who may vote against the DOCA and will not be bound by it, unless the court orders that they should be bound (s 444F). Such an order may be made

136 *Re Eastmark Holdings Pty Ltd (recs and mgrs apptd)* (2016) 109 ACSR 116 [37].

in relation to a secured creditor when allowing them to deal with the security would have a material adverse effect on achieving the purposes of the deed, having regard to whether the DOCA will protect their security adequately (s 444F(3)). The DOCA is binding on the company, its officers and members, and the administrator. Under s 447A, 'any person who is bound by the DOCA cannot, without court permission, apply to have the company wound up; start legal proceedings against the company; or prosecute any enforcement process against the company's property'.

Generally, only creditors with claims against the company which would be provable on winding up are entitled to be part of a DOCA.[137] This includes claims that are 'present or future, certain or contingent, ascertained or sounding only in damages'[138] and claims in tort and for damages based on statutory provisions.[139] They do not include costs orders which are made after the administration begins, or future personal injury claims.[140]

A company subject to a DOCA must include in every public document and negotiable instrument where the company's name appears that the company is 'subject to deed of company arrangement' (s 450E(2)). Failure to comply with this requirement can attract a fine or imprisonment. However, a contravention of this section does not render invalid anything done or omitted to be done under pt 5.3A (ss 450E(4)–(5)).

Meetings of creditors may be convened by the deed administrator throughout the time that the DOCA is in operation (*IPRC* r 75–10). A deed administrator may be obliged to convene a meeting in particular circumstances; for example, where a committee of inspection directs the deed administrator to convene a meeting, or creditors with at least 25 per cent in value direct the deed administrator in writing to convene a meeting (*IPRC* r 75–15). ASIC may also require the deed administrator to convene a meeting of creditors (*IPRC* r 75–20). The rules governing these meetings are the same as the rules for the first and second creditors meeting discussed above.

15.45.10 Setting aside a DOCA

Under s 445G, the court has the power to declare either a DOCA or a provision of a DOCA void where there is doubt, based on specific grounds, whether the deed was entered into in accordance with pt 5.3A of the *Corporations Act*. Such an order can be applied for by the deed administrator, a member of the company, a creditor, or ASIC. The court can declare the DOCA valid, despite any contravention of the *Corporations Act*, provided it is satisfied that the Act was substantially complied with and no injustice will result from a person being bound by the deed.

The court has a discretion under s 445G in deciding whether to set aside a deed. In *Deputy Commissioner of Taxation v PDDAM Pty Ltd*,[141] the Court, in deciding not to set aside a deed, took into account the fact that such action would likely result in costly litigation;

137 *Brash Holdings Ltd (admin apptd) v Katile Pty Ltd* [1996] 1 VR 24.

138 *Corporations Act* s 553.

139 *Selim v McGrath* (2003) 47 ACSR 537.

140 *Larkden Pty Ltd v Lloyd Energy Systems Pty Ltd* [2011] NSWSC 1567; *Edwards v Attorney-General (NSW)* (2004) 60 NSWLR 667.

141 *Deputy Commission of Taxation v PDDAM Pty Ltd* (1996) 14 ACLC 659.

would not confer any practical benefit on any of the creditors (including the Tax Office); would impose hardship on employees who would lose their benefits under the deed; and that the deed was not opposed by any other creditor than the Tax Office.[142] The Court confirmed that, even where a deed is not entered into in accordance with the *Corporations Act*, a court can still refuse to declare the deed void where no injustice flows from the breach.

A similar power exists under s 445D, which allows a court to terminate a DOCA on a number of grounds including:

- where false or misleading information about the company's business, property, affairs or financial circumstances was given to the deed administrator or to the creditors and this information can reasonably be expected to have been material in the creditors' decision whether to support the DOCA (s 445D(1)(a))
- where false or misleading information was contained in the report that accompanied the notice of the second meeting of creditors (s 445D(1)(b))
- where there was an omission in the report sent to the creditors and it can reasonably be expected that this omission would have been material to the creditors in deciding whether to support the DOCA (s 445D(1)(c))
- where a person bound by the deed has engaged in a material contravention of the deed (s 445D(1)(d))
- effect cannot be given to the deed without causing injustice or undue delay (s 445D(1)(e))
- the deed or a provision in it, or an act or omission done in relation to it, would be oppressive or unfairly prejudicial to, or unfairly discriminatory against, one or more creditors; or contrary to the interests of the creditors as a whole (s 445D(1)(f))
- the deed should be terminated for some other reason (s 445D(1)(g)).

An order under s 445D can be applied for by a creditor, the company, ASIC or any other interested person including the administrator of the deed (s 445D(2)). If an order to terminate a deed is made under s 445D, the company is deemed to have passed a special resolution to have the company wound up.

The court has a discretion under s 445D whether to make an order terminating a DOCA even where one of the grounds listed in the section applies. In *Deputy Commissioner of Taxation v Comcorp Australia Ltd*,[143] it was argued that important information had been omitted from the deed administrator's report. The information concerned the role of directors in litigation taking place in the Supreme Court. Sundberg J held that failure to set out these details was a contravention of s 439A(4)(c) and a material omission within the meaning of s 445D(1)(c). However, in determining whether the deed should be set aside, Sundberg J considered that the relevant question was whether the creditors would have voted differently had the omitted information been included. He concluded that the creditors would not have voted differently, and that there was nothing to show that it was in the interests of the creditors to terminate the deed.[144]

142 Ibid 670.

143 *Deputy Commissioner of Taxation v Comcorp Australia Ltd* (1995) 13 ACLC 1671.

144 Ibid.

An appeal against this decision by the Deputy Federal Commissioner of Taxation was refused.[145] In commenting on the argument that the information omitted from the administrator's report was important, Carr J noted:

> The Commissioner's submissions do not pay sufficient regard to commercial practicality. Part of his submission is that those who seek deeds of company administration (in this case the directors) have ample opportunity to prepare the information before entering into the administration. Sometimes that may be so, but the submission assumes that insolvency rarely occurs suddenly. The Commissioner's argument that the law provides a mechanism for an administrator to obtain extensions of time is, in my view, not persuasive. The Courts do not grant such extensions of time as a matter of course. Good reason must be shown, otherwise Parliament's intention, [to provide a more expeditious and less expensive way of assisting those creditors and members than under the greater formality of a winding up], might be thwarted.[146]

One of the grounds for terminating a DOCA is where its effect, or the effect of 'any act or omission done or proposed to be done under it, would be oppressive or unfairly prejudicial to, or unfairly discriminatory against, one or more of the creditors; or contrary to the interests of the creditors as a whole' (s 445D(1)(f)). This provision allows the court to consider any unfairness imposed by a DOCA on a particular creditor or creditors and allows the court to set aside a DOCA where such unfairness exists. It follows that this provision can be used by minority creditors against DOCAs that operate to the benefit of majority creditors.

Sydney Land Corporation Pty Ltd v Kalon Pty Ltd[147] involved an application under s 445D by Sydney Land Corporation, as one of eight creditors of the defendant company that had voted against entering a DOCA. Pursuant to the deed, the Sydney Land Corporation, which was owed $2.1 million by Kalon Pty Ltd, was entitled to a payment of $440,000, or 40 million shares in a New Zealand corporation, whose shares appeared to be worthless. The plaintiff argued that the deed was oppressive and unfairly prejudicial to it and sought to terminate the deed pursuant to s 445D(1)(f). The evidence presented to the Court indicated that the amount likely to be received by the creditor under the DOCA was less than if the company was liquidated.

Young J held it was necessary to examine the whole effect of the DOCA and assess its unfairness, if any, to the Sydney Land Corporation. It was also necessary to consider the interests of other creditors, the company, and the public. He noted that:

> [W]hen one is looking at what is oppressive or unfairly prejudicial under s 445D, one looks at it in the background of the general right of a creditor to be paid or to wind the company up, or to have the company administered by the administrator under the deed in a way which keeps the company's business

145 *Deputy Commissioner of Taxation v Comcorp Australia Ltd* (1996) 70 FCR 356.
146 Ibid 376–7.
147 *Sydney Land Corporation Pty Ltd v Kalon Pty Ltd* (1997) 26 ACSR 427.

> going and will see the creditor paid something out of the property of the company. If a scheme in a deed deviates from that, then the creditor is more easily able to say that it is operating oppressively, than otherwise.[148]

On the basis of these considerations, Young J found that the deed was oppressive. In particular, he noted that the Sydney Land Corporation and the other creditors were not likely to be better off under the DOCA than under liquidation; the deed required the Sydney Land Corporation to continue to have a commercial relationship with people in whom it had no confidence; the deed administrator would not have control over the assets or the entities which would make the payment to the plaintiff; and under the DOCA, the claim of creditor was not against the deed administrator but was against a foreign corporation over which the deed administrator did not have any control.[149]

In *Lam Soon Australia Pty Ltd (admin apptd) v Molit (No 55) Pty Ltd*,[150] the Federal Court considered whether a DOCA was unfairly prejudicial to, or unfairly discriminatory against, one of Lam Soon's creditors. Molit (No 55) Pty Ltd ('Molit') had leased the Central Market Plaza supermarket in Adelaide from Lam Soon Australia Pty Ltd ('Lam Soon') on 1 July 1990. The premises were not returning a profit for Lam Soon, but another property in North Adelaide was. By 31 December 1994, Lam Soon's liabilities exceeded its assets by over $4 million. Lam Soon was advised to appoint an administrator and enter a deed of company arrangement. The deed administrator recommended that the Central Market Plaza supermarket be closed, with the result that the lease to Molit was cancelled. The deed administrator also recommended that all of Lam Soon's other creditors continue to be involved with the company through its other supermarket in North Adelaide.

At a meeting of creditors, Molit was the only creditor to vote against the resolution. At first instance, Branson J made an order under s 445D(1)(f) terminating the DOCA on the ground that it was unfairly prejudicial to or unfairly discriminatory to Molit.[151] She noted that a DOCA may still be valid notwithstanding that there is different treatment of classes of creditors;[152] however, such differentiation must be justified on reasonable grounds.

Lam Soon appealed to the Full Federal Court and argued that the DOCA was not oppressive or unfairly prejudicial to Molit as it would receive at least as much under the arrangement as it would receive on winding up the company. It further argued that Molit was in a better position under the DOCA, as it would be paid promptly and would not have to compete with secured creditors. It argued that different treatment of the creditors was justified on the grounds that the debts to Molit were incurred after those of the other creditors, and the other creditors were either statutory bodies or suppliers with whom the company could have ongoing dealings.

The Full Federal Court allowed the appeal and remitted the case to Branson J. In making its decision, the Court noted that, where a business comprises two parts—one that is profitable and one that is not—it would be surprising if a DOCA did not discriminate

148 Ibid 430.
149 Ibid.
150 *Law Soon Australia Pty Ltd (admin apptd) v Molit (No 55) Pty Ltd* (1996) 70 FCR 34.
151 *Molit (No 55) Pty Ltd v Lam Soon Australia Pty Ltd (admin apptd)* (1996) 63 FCR 391.
152 Ibid [77].

between creditors that could have an ongoing relationship with the profitable part of the business, and those that could not.[153] The Court stated:

> Where the basis of a deed of company arrangement is a proposal that an unprofitable part of a company's business be closed and a profitable part continued it is inevitable that there will be a degree of discrimination between those creditors who will have a continuing relationship with the company and those whose relationship with the company will be terminated. The fact that there will be some degree of discrimination in such circumstances is not necessarily unfair and does not necessarily mean that the deed is not for a purpose authorised by s 435A.[154]

The crucial issue in this case was whether the DOCA was unfairly prejudicial to Molit. Determining this issue involved considering whether the other creditors were likely to be paid more under the DOCA than they would receive on a winding up, or whether Molit was likely to receive less under the DOCA than it would on winding up. These issues had not been fully reported by the administrator, and the effect of that issue needed to be decided by the first instance judge.[155]

In *Helenic Pty Ltd (as trustee of the Mastrantonis Family Trust) v Retail Adventures Pty Ltd (admins apptd),*[156] the New South Wales Supreme Court set aside a DOCA on the basis it was prejudicial to creditors who had voted against it. The DOCA involved Retail Adventures Pty Ltd ('RAPL'), which had operated over 260 retail discount stores including Crazy Clarks, Sam's Warehouse, Go-Lo Discount Stores and Chickenfeed. The company also employed nearly 500 staff. Administrators were appointed in October 2012, and between the first and second creditors' meetings the administrators entered an agreement to sell the business as a going concern to DSG Holdings Pty Ltd ('DSG'). DSG was a company related to RAPL. A condition of the sales agreement was that a court order would be obtained to extend the convening period for the second creditors' meeting for a period of not less than 180 days. The Federal Court granted this extension.

When the second meeting of creditors of RAPL was convened, Bicheno Pty Limited, the ultimate holding company of RAPL, proposed in a DOCA that the unsecured creditors accept payment from a deed fund of $5.5 million, and that claims against the directors and third parties be released. The effect of this agreement was that creditors would receive repayments of their debt at 6 cents in the dollar. In the administrator's opinion, the likely return to creditors in a liquidation would be between 20.7 and 45.1 cents in the dollar.

The administrators recommended liquidation. However, the DOCA was approved at the creditors' meeting, mainly due to the votes of a large number of creditors related to RAPL, including some of the company's directors. Some of the unsecured creditors then applied to the Court for an order that the DOCA be set aside and that RAPL be wound up.

153 *Lam Soon Australia Pty Ltd (admin apptd) v Molit (No 55) Pty Ltd* (1996) 70 FCR 34, 48.

154 Ibid.

155 Ibid 50.

156 *Helenic Pty Ltd (as trustee of Mastrantonis Family Trust) v Retail Adventures Pty Ltd (admins apptd)* [2013] NSWSC 1973.

Robb J found that the resolution approving the DOCA was prejudicial to the interests of the unsecured creditors who had voted against it. He noted that it was highly probable that these creditors would receive less under the DOCA than on liquidation, and that the DOCA's uncertainty increased the likelihood of further litigation.[157] In determining whether the prejudice to the creditors was unreasonable, Robb J considered the possible benefits to the related creditors under the DOCA, which included releasing them from possible liability for insolvent trading and voidable transaction claims.[158] His Honour concluded that:

> The plaintiffs, and the other unsecured creditors who might receive 6 cents in the dollar from the deed of company arrangement, if the $5.5 million is paid into the Deed Fund, have been consciously discriminated against by the defendants on the basis of a commercial judgment as to whether their ongoing supply of products to DSG is necessary or desirable for its future operations. Accordingly, the creditors whose debts were acquired by the defendants were paid all, or substantially all, of the amounts that RAPL owed to them, while the remaining creditors were left to their fate under the proposed deed of company arrangement, which may give the 6 cents in the dollar return.[159]

On appeal, the Court of Appeal considered that determining whether there was prejudice to particular creditors should not be limited just to a comparison of the expected returns, but should also include considering whether a trading outcome may be preferable for the creditors as a whole.[160] However, the Court held that expected returns from the DOCA were so much lower than the expected return on liquidation that there clearly was prejudice to the interests of the unrelated creditors.[161]

15.50 Small business restructuring

As mentioned above, a new restructuring process was introduced in 2021 to allow businesses with total liabilities not exceeding $1 million on the day the company enters the process (excluding employee entitlements) to access a single, streamlined process to restructure their debts. Under a new pt 5.3B of the *Corporations Act*, the object of the restructuring process is to allow small companies to retain control of the business, property and affairs while developing a plan to restructure with the assistance of a small business restructuring practitioner, and to enter into a restructuring plan with creditors (s 452A). In *Deputy Commissioner of Taxation v Pope John Hospitality Pty Ltd (restructuring practitioner apptd)*, Derrington J observed that the purpose of pt 5.3B was 'significantly

157 Ibid [182].
158 Ibid [38].
159 Ibid [196].
160 *DSG Holdings Australia Pty Ltd v Helenic Pty Ltd* (2014) 86 NSWLR 293, 134 (Leeming J).
161 For an early discussion of judicial discretion in this context, see K Bennetts, 'Voluntary Administration: Shaping the Process Through the Exercise of Judicial Discretion' (1995) 3(3) *Insolvency Law Journal* 135; A Keay, 'Court Involvement in Voluntary Administration and Deeds of Company Arrangement' (1995) 15(3) *Company and Securities Law Journal* 157.

more modest' than that of pt 5.3A (dealing with voluntary administration), as the former is 'concerned with providing the opportunity for a restructuring plan to be put to the creditors' and the latter 'is concerned with attempting to save the company'.[162]

A restructuring commences when the board passes a resolution stating that, in its opinion, the company is insolvent or is likely to become insolvent at some future time, and a restructuring practitioner[163] should be appointed (s 453B(1)). Under s 453B(2), company is not entitled to appoint a restructuring practitioner if:

> **(a)** the company is already under restructuring; or
>
> ...
>
> **(c)** the company is under administration; or
>
> **(d)** the company has executed a deed of company arrangement that has not yet terminated; or
>
> **(e)** a person holds an appointment as liquidator, provisional liquidator or administrator of the company.

There are three phases to the restructuring process:

(1) the initial phase, when the restructuring plan is formulated by the debtor company in conjunction with a restructuring practitioner. The company has 20 business days to send its restructuring proposal to creditors after the date the restructuring practitioner is appointed (although this can be extended by the restructuring practitioner);

(2) the interim phase, when creditors are asked to vote in writing on the restructuring plan. All unsecured debts which were incurred prior to the company entering restructuring are included in the restructuring plan. A plan is accepted if more than 50 percent of the creditors by value vote to accept the plan;

(3) the final phase, when the plan has been approved and the company is operating under it.[164]

The restructuring plan sets out how the company's creditors will be repaid if the plan is approved. For example, the plan might state how creditors will be repaid as a proportion of the debt owing to them, or as the cents in the dollar they will receive. The plan must be accompanied by a restructuring proposal statement, which includes a schedule setting out the company's creditors, and the amount they are owed by the company.[165] If the plan is not accepted, the restructuring of the company under the *Corporations Act* ends. The company may seek to use an alternative formal insolvency process (such as liquidation or voluntary administration).

162 *Deputy Commissioner of Taxation v Pope Joan Hospitality Pty Ltd (restructuring practitioner apptd)* (2023) 169 ACSR 487 [52]. For further discussion on the new process see J Harris and C Symes, 'The Chimera of Restructuring Reform: An Opportunity Missed for MSMEs in Pt 5.3B' (2021) 36(1) *Australian Journal of Corporate Law* 1; *Re Dessco Pty Ltd* [2021] VSC 94; *Re DST Project Management and Construction Pty Ltd (ACN 623 076 031)* [2021] VSC 108; *Re ENA Development Pty Ltd* [2022] NSWSC 54.

163 For definition of 'officer' see *Corporations Act* ss 9AD(f)–(g).

164 *Corporations Regulations 2001* (Cth) regs 5.3B.02, 5.3B.17, 5.3B.25.

165 Ibid reg 5.3B.16.

Once the restructuring process is underway, the company stays in control of the process, and may undertake transactions that are in the ordinary course of business (s 453K). Payments are made to the company's creditors in accordance with the terms set out in the plan. A moratorium is also applied on unsecured creditor claims and some secured creditor claims. This means:

(a) unsecured creditors cannot begin, continue or enforce their claims (s 454C);
(b) owners of property (other than perishable property) used or occupied by the company, or people who lease such property to the company, cannot recover their property (s 454L; reg 5.3B.30);
(c) there are limits on the circumstances when secured creditors can enforce their security interest in the company's assets (s 453K);
(d) a creditor holding a personal guarantee from the company's directors or their relatives cannot act under the personal guarantee without the court's consent (s 453W); and
(e) ipso facto clauses (which are triggered during insolvency-related events) are stayed for some contracts (s 454C).

When a company has paid off its obligations under the restructuring plan, it is released from all debts or claims that were admissible under the plan.[166] If a company leaves the plan before it has made all the payments under the plan, it remains liable for the original debt owed prior to the plan commencing, minus any repayments that occurred under the plan.[167]

While the new restructuring procedures is simpler that voluntary administration, with fewer reporting obligations and no requirement for creditor meetings, there are questions whether it is sufficiently simple or streamlined to achieve its goals. As Harris and Symes note, the process may still be 'costly for companies, risky for practitioners and potentially unrewarding for creditors'.[168]

15.55 Review of the insolvency regime

As mentioned at the start of this chapter, in July 2023, the Parliamentary Joint Committee on Corporations and Financial Services released its report into corporate insolvency in Australia. The overriding conclusion of the Committee was that Australia's corporate insolvency system is too complex, hard to access and unnecessarily costly.[169] It noted that:

> While reforms introduced following the 1988 ALRC Report 45 (Harmer Report) were cutting-edge at the time, the committee is concerned that Australia's insolvency system may not reflect modern business practice and needs. This is

166 Ibid reg 5.3B.31.

167 Ibid.

168 J Harris and C Symes, 'The Chimera of Restructuring Reform: An Opportunity Missed for MSMEs in Pt 5.3B' (2021) 36(1) *Australian Journal of Corporate Law* 1, 5.

169 Parliamentary Joint Committee on Corporations and Financial Services, Parliament of Australia, *Corporate Insolvency in Australia* (Report, July 2023) [1.2].

> particularly the case for smaller and medium-sized businesses. It also appears that the insolvency system has not kept pace with changes in the Australian and global economy since the Harmer Report, including but not limited to the shift from fixed assets to intangibles and increasing levels of secured debt. The committee also notes evidence suggesting Australia may have also fallen off the international pace in terms of insolvency reform.[170]

The Committee noted that the most common causes of company failure include under capitalisation, cash flow, financial controls and record-keeping, trading losses, strategic management, and economic conditions.[171] It also noted that, typically, when an insolvent company in Australia is liquidated, unsecured creditors receive minimal returns.[172]

The main recommendation of the Committee was that there should be a comprehensive review focused on the harmonisation and simplification of Australia's corporate and personal insolvency laws.

15.60 Summary

This chapter focused on the formal processes of external administration provided for under pts 5.2, 5.1 and 5.3A of the *Corporations Act*. It explained the processes of receivership, schemes of arrangement, voluntary administration and restructuring. Receivership involves a secured creditor who has security over some or all of the company's assets appointing a receiver. The main role of the receiver is to collect and sell the company's charged assets to repay the debt owed to the secured creditor. Schemes of arrangement and voluntary administration can allow a business, or part of it, to continue trading or to secure a better return for creditors than on winding up. The restructuring process allows the directors of a small company to retain control of the company's business while developing a plan to restructure the debts owed to creditors.

170 Ibid [1.3].
171 Ibid [2.39].
172 Ibid [3.52].

CHAPTER

16

WINDING UP AND LIQUIDATION

16.05 Introduction

Winding up and liquidation describe the process by which the business and affairs of a company are brought to an end. Davies et al describe it as follows:

> Where a company no longer has the funds to function, or its members no longer wish it to function, the first thought is that there needs to be a process for bringing the existence of the legal entity to an end. If the death of the company is the desired objective, this is achieved by winding up the company, or liquidating it (the two terms can be used interchangeably). The process of winding up, or liquidation, is designed to ensure that, before the company ceases to exist, all its outstanding obligations are met (so far as they can be) and any surplus assets (if there are any) are distributed to the members according to their agreed entitlement. For reasons which might be obvious, especially given the competing interests which may need to be balanced, this process is not undertaken by the company's own directors but by independent appointees who are qualified insolvency practitioners and who act professionally as company liquidators. ... When this process is completed, the company is removed from the register: it is 'dissolved'.[1]

1 PL Davies, S Worthington and C Hare, *Gower's Principles of Modern Company Law* (Sweet & Maxwell, 11th ed, 2021) 1151.

During the winding up process, the business of the company is brought to an end, its assets are collected and sold, and the proceeds applied in accordance with the priorities set out in the *Corporations Act*. First, the proceeds are applied to creditors and any balance is paid to shareholders. Thereafter, the company is deregistered and ceases to exist. Winding up may be either compulsory (court-ordered) or voluntary. The most common reason for winding up or liquidation is the company's insolvency.

A note on terminology: as the above quote from Davies et al suggests, the terms 'winding up' and 'liquidation' are sometimes used interchangeably and at other times they are differentiated. For the purposes of explanation in this chapter we separate these terms. 'Winding up' is used to refer to the whole process as just described; this accords with the language of the *Corporations Act* pts 5.4 to 5.7. 'Liquidation' refers to the particular task of realising (or selling) the company's assets so that the proceeds are available to be distributed to creditors (and possibly shareholders). Note, however, that the term 'liquidator' is used in the Act, and in practice, to refer to the person appointed to conduct the whole winding up process.

16.10 Policy: winding up and liquidation

Chapter 15 discussed the policies that inform insolvency law, and provided a flow chart that identifies the various forms of external administration which can be involved for both solvent and insolvent companies. At Section 15.10, the principles of insolvency law were distilled into four essential tenets: collective action, harmony with non-insolvency law, strategic behaviour and rehabilitation. Three of the four policy tenets are relevant to this chapter. At the point of winding up and liquidation, the company is beyond rehabilitation but the remaining tenets of insolvency law continue to operate. For example, the law promotes collective action and is designed to keep individual actions against the insolvent company from interfering with the best use of assets for the creditors and members. Under this tenet, the rules ensure that no creditor or member has the ability to exploit the insolvency by individual action and receive more than their entitlement. The pari passu principle applies, which ensures the pooling of the company's assets by the liquidator and the fair and equitable ranking of creditors.[2] The pari passu principle is discussed below at Section 16.30.

Another tenet of insolvency law is harmony with non-insolvency law. This is demonstrated by the ranking of creditors, which is informed by social and corporate law norms. For example, it allows employees to be given priority over other creditors for certain debts. It also requires the deferral of shareholder interests upon liquidation. Finally, the law of liquidation attempts to minimise opportunities for strategic behaviour. This is exemplified by the power of the liquidator to have certain transactions declared void because they are uncommercial or give an unfair preference to a creditor or involve those who control the company putting assets out of the reach of creditors. The concern

2 See also R Langton and L Trotman, 'Sharing the Proceeds of Business Failure—Competition between Feudal and Democratic Principles in Liquidation of Australian Companies' (1999) 11 *Corporate and Business Law Journal* 263; H Anderson, 'The Theory and Reality in Insolvency Law: Some Contradictions in Australia' (2009) 27(8) *Company and Securities Law Journal* 506.

about strategic behaviour continues until deregistration when the company ceases to exist. Unfortunately, the law does not adequately control strategic behaviour. This lack of control is demonstrated by the continuing existence of phoenix companies, where the company ceases to exist but the business is resurrected by another company controlled by the same people, sometimes with the purpose of trying to defeat creditors' claims.[3]

Although most companies are wound up for insolvency, this chapter also discusses voluntary winding up. The policy and law for voluntary winding up includes safeguards to protect the interests of creditors.

16.15 Winding up

16.15.05 What is winding up?

Winding up is either:

- compulsory: by a court due to insolvency or other reason under pt 5.4A of the *Corporations Act*;[4] or
- voluntary: by the members (if the company is solvent) or by creditors.

Within the broader concept of winding up, liquidation is the process by which the company's assets are realised and distributed. A liquidator is the person appointed to manage this process. This ultimately results in the dissolution of the company, at which point the company's existence as a separate legal entity ceases. Liquidation involves a liquidator conducting the affairs of the company to discharge its liabilities in preparation for its dissolution. It may take months, even years, before the company is finally removed from the company register by ASIC.

Liquidation has the following objectives:

(1) to gather and realise the available assets (to convert the company's property into proceeds)
(2) to provide for a fair and equitable distribution of the proceeds among its creditors and, if available, to distribute the surplus among the company's shareholders
(3) where the company is insolvent, to allow for the investigation and examination of the company's transactions and officers' behaviour. This may result in potential recoveries and actions against officers who have breached the *Corporations Act*.

16.15.10 Compulsory winding up in insolvency

Companies may be compulsorily wound up for insolvency under pt 5.4 of the *Corporations Act*.

Sections 459A and 459B provide that a court can make an order requiring that an insolvent company be wound up. A person can apply to the court for the company to be

3 Phoenix companies are discussed at Section 16.25.35. For a general discussion, see H Anderson, 'Corporate Law and the Phoenix Company' in R Tomasic (ed), *Routledge Handbook of Corporate Law* (Taylor & Francis, 2016); H Anderson et al, 'Illegal Phoenix Activity: Is a Phoenix Prohibition the Solution?' (2017) 35(3) *Company and Securities Law Journal* 184.

4 For example, where it is just and equitable to do so under s 461 (see the discussion at Section 14.40).

wound up on the grounds of insolvency, or the court can make an when dealing with an application on some other ground (such as oppression[5]) and the court is satisfied that the company is insolvent. The definition of insolvency is discussed below at Section 16.15.15 and in Chapter 15 at Section 15.10.

An application that the company be wound up in insolvency may be brought by the persons listed in s 459P, including:

- the company
- a creditor, including secured, contingent (a person to whom payment is only due on the occurrence of some future event which may or may not occur), or prospective (a person to whom a debt is due but not immediately payable) creditors
- a contributory, defined in s 9 to include a member (as discussed below)
- a director
- a liquidator or provisional liquidator of the company
- ASIC.

A contingent or prospective creditor, a director, contributory, and ASIC must seek the leave of the court prior to making an application and the court may only grant leave if satisfied that there is a prima facie case that the company is insolvent (ss 459P(2)–(3)).

A 'contributory' is defined in s 9 to mean a person who is liable as a member or past member to contribute to the property of the company if it is wound up. Section 9 also states that the holder of fully paid shares is a contributory. Under s 515, every past and present member of a company is liable to contribute to the property of the company on a winding up. The general rule is that a contributory is only required to pay the amount unpaid on shares in respect of which they are liable. Sometimes (for example, with preference shares) there may be a contractual obligation between the company and a contributory which creates a liability to pay the amount of a premium on shares issued to that contributory.[6]

16.15.15 Proving insolvency

A court cannot make a winding up order pursuant to s 459A unless it is satisfied that, as a question of fact, the company is insolvent. Insolvency is defined by reference to s 95A.[7] The need for the court to inquire into whether a company is insolvent will be circumvented in certain situations. This is because the court must presume that the company is insolvent if any of the six circumstances set out in s 459C(2) has occurred during or after the three-month period ending on the date of the winding up application. This statutory presumption applies unless the contrary is proved. The six circumstances are:

(1) the company's failure to comply with a statutory demand (discussed below)
(2) execution or other process issued on a judgment, decree or order of an Australian court in favour of a creditor has been returned wholly or partly unsatisfied

5 For example, an application for orders under s 233 regarding oppressive conduct under s 232 (see discussion at Section 14.30.20).

6 *DJE Constructions Pty Ltd v Maddocks* [1982] 1 NSWLR 5.

7 This is discussed in Chapter 15 at Section 15.10.

(3) a receiver, or receiver and manager, of company property has been appointed pursuant to an instrument relating to a circulating security interest in that property
(4) an order has been made for the appointment of a receiver or receiver and manager for the purpose of enforcing a security interest in that property
(5) a person has entered into possession or control of that property for the purpose of enforcing such a security interest
(6) a person has been appointed to enter into possession or assume control of that property.

The most common way that creditors prove a company is insolvent is by showing it has failed to comply with a statutory demand.

16.15.20 Statutory demands

The statutory demand procedure provides creditors with an inexpensive method of establishing a company's insolvency.[8] The provisions of pt 5.4 that regulate statutory demands have been interpreted strictly by the High Court in *David Grant & Co Pty Ltd v Westpac Banking Corporation*[9] where Gummow J stated that they 'constitute a legislative scheme for quick resolution of the issue of solvency and the determination of whether the company should be wound up without the interposition of disputes about debts, unless they are raised promptly'.[10] Pursuant to s 459E, a creditor may serve on a company a written demand (using the prescribed form) for repayment of one or more debts that are due and payable. In the usual course of events, the value of the debt (or the combined value of multiple debts) must be a minimum of $4,000 and the company then has 21 days from the date of service to respond.[11] If the company fails to comply, the creditor can rely on this failure as the basis for a winding up application under s 459P.

The statutory demand must comply with s 459E(2) and form 509H[12] is provided for this purpose. Despite many of the forms required by ASIC in relation to companies now being electronic or web-based, this form continues to be required in hard copy and with formal service of the notice to the company.[13] It must be accompanied by an affidavit that verifies that the debt is due and payable by the company.[14] The claim must be for a debt—a liquidated sum. The nature of a 'liquidated sum' was explained by Knox CJ and Starke J in *Spain v Union Steamship Co of New Zealand Ltd* as follows:

> Whenever the amount to which the plaintiff is entitled ... can be ascertained by calculation or fixed by any scale of charges or positive data it is ... liquidated.[15]

8 For a critique of the statutory demand procedure, see C Anderson and C Brown, 'Demanding a Change: Time to Act on Statutory Demands' (2013) 21(2) *Insolvency Law Journal* 97.
9 *David Grant & Co Pty Ltd v Westpac Banking Corporation* (1995) 184 CLR 265.
10 Ibid 270.
11 *Corporations Act* s 9 ('statutory minimum') and reg 5.4.01AAA.
12 *Corporations Regulations 2001* (Cth) sch 2 form 509H.
13 *Corporations Act* s 459E(1). Defects in service may be raised under s 459G.
14 *Corporations Act* s 459E(3).
15 *Spain v Union Steamship Co of New Zealand Ltd* (1923) 32 CLR 138, 142 quoting W Blake Odgers, *The Principles of Procedure Pleading and Practice in Civil Actions in the High Court of Justice* (Stevens and Sons, 5th ed, 1903) 41. See also *Vimblue Pty Ltd v Toweel* [2009] NSWSC 494.

The claim cannot be an unliquidated claim; that is, one requiring a 'process of valuation'[16] or a contingent or prospective claim. An example of an unliquidated claim is an estimate of damages; for example, for breach of contract or negligence.

The company can apply to the court to set aside a statutory demand[17] and the court can make an order setting aside the demand.[18] Examples where the court may set aside a demand include when there is a defect in the statutory demand and substantial injustice will be caused unless the demand is set aside (s 459J(1)(a)) or there is a genuine dispute as to the debt claimed (s 459H). 'Defect' is defined in s 9. A statutory demand will be held to be defective if it:

> is so vague or ambiguous that it fails to identify, to a reasonable person in the shoes of a director of the debtor company, the general nature of the debt to a sufficient degree that the director can assess whether there is a genuine dispute as to the existence or amount of the debt or an offsetting claim.[19]

The courts are strict in their interpretation of statutory demands because of the potentially draconian effect of the presumption of insolvency that flows from them. For example, in *B & M Quality Constructions Pty Ltd v WG Brady Pty Ltd*,[20] the statutory demand referred to the creditor as 'WG Brady Pty Ltd', known to the plaintiff to be a non-existent company, instead of 'W & J Brady Pty Ltd'. The statutory demand was set aside. However, s 459J(2) makes it clear that the court must not set aside a statutory demand merely because of a defect. The court may only order that the demand be set aside if it is satisfied that a substantial injustice will be caused because of the defect.[21] Assaf concludes that where a statutory demand 'is likely to mislead, confuse or fail to properly inform the debtor of the substantive requirements of s 459E [it is] likely [to] cause substantial injustice within the meaning of s 459J(1)(a)'.[22] Examples of defects which have been held to cause substantial injustice include where multiple debts were claimed in a demand and the amounts owing for the individual debts were not specified as required by s 459E(2)[23] and where there was inadequate explanation of the conversion of a foreign debt into Australian currency.[24]

A company may also apply to set aside a statutory demand under s 459G where there is genuine dispute between the company and the creditor about the existence or the amount of a debt to which the demand relates and/or the company has an offsetting claim (s 459H).

16 *Vimblue Pty Ltd v Toweel* [2009] NSWSC 494 [16] (Barrett J).

17 *Corporations Act* s 459G.

18 Ibid s 459J.

19 *LSI Australia Pty Ltd v LSI Consulting Pty Ltd* (2007) 25 ACLC 1602 [54].

20 *B & M Quality Constructions Pty Ltd v WG Brady Pty Ltd* (1994) 116 FLR 218. At 218, the judge described the case as 'an Alice in Wonderland Mad Hatter piece of litigation'.

21 *Spencer Constructions Pty Ltd v G & M Aldridge Pty Ltd* (1997) 76 FCR 452, 457–8. Overall, the courts are very strict about compliance with the form of the statutory demand (as per form 509H); however, a formal defect may not result in the statutory demand being declared invalid if no substantial injustice was caused. See the discussion of Dart J in *SP Hay Pty Ltd v David Gray and Co Pty Ltd* (2019) 133 ACSR 504 [19]–[26] regarding the failure of the creditor to nominate an address for service in the relevant state; see also *Slap Corporation Pty Ltd v Civil, Infrastructure & Logistics Pty Ltd* (2017) 50 VR 542.

22 F Assaf, *Winding Up in Insolvency* (LexisNexis, 3rd ed, 2021) [8.19].

23 *Delta Beta Pty Ltd v Everhard Vissers* (1996) 20 ACSR 583.

24 *MEC Import Sales Pty Ltd v Iozzelli SRL* (1998) 29 ACSR 229.

In *Thomson v Australia and New Zealand Banking Group Ltd*,[25] the Queensland Court of Appeal usefully reviewed the case law on the meaning of 'genuine dispute' and the court's role in deciding such applications, noting that 'a genuine dispute means there must be a plausible contention requiring investigation', adding that '[t]the court is not called on to determine the merits of, or to resolve, the dispute'.

Section 459H sets out a formula the court must apply in calculating the substantiated amount of the demand: an offsetting claim must be subtracted from the total. An offsetting claim is a genuine claim that the company has against the creditor by way of counterclaim, set-off or cross-demand. For example, in *Elm Financial Services Pty Ltd v MacDougal*,[26] Mr MacDougal had been retained by Mr Elm as a financial adviser and securities dealer. He served a statutory demand on Elm for the commissions due to him under this arrangement. The company argued that the demand should be set aside because MacDougal had received secret profits in breach of his duties to the company as its agent. Barrett J held that this constituted an offsetting claim that justified the setting aside of the statutory demand. The arrangements that are made between securities dealers and financial advisers and their principals are discussed in Chapters 17 and 18, respectively.

Statutory demands are commonly used as a debt recovery strategy even though the statutory demand process should not be used to recover debts from companies that are plainly solvent.[27] Solvency does not of itself constitute a reason to set aside a statutory demand although proof of the company's solvency may be a ground to set aside the statutory demand due to substantial injustice under s 459J(1)(a)[28] and may result in the court refusing to make a winding up order under s 459A.[29]

If the statutory demand is not set aside, once the period of time for compliance with the statutory demand has elapsed, the creditor may rely upon the failure of the company to comply with the statutory demand to apply to wind up the company. In accordance with s 459Q, the creditor must file an application that sets out particulars of the service of the demand, a copy of the demand, and an affidavit of debt. If the company is seeking to avoid the winding up, it must have any statutory demand set aside before it is relied upon by the creditor in the winding up application. Leave of the court is required to oppose an application for a winding up in insolvency based on a failure to comply with a statutory demand. The debtor company cannot rely on matters at the winding up hearing that could have been raised beforehand.[30]

The procedure for lodging an application to wind up a company is dealt with under the *Court Rules*.[31] After the filing of an application, the court may appoint a provisional

---

25 *Thompson v Australia and New Zealand Banking Group Ltd* [2024] QCA 73 [37] citing *SGR Pastoral Pty Ltd v Christensen* [2019] QSC 229.

26 *Elm Financial Services Pty Ltd v MacDougall* [2004] NSWSC 560.

27 *Owners Corporation SP66609 v Perpetual Trustee Co Ltd* [2010] NSWSC 497.

28 *Chippendale Printing Co Pty Ltd v Deputy Commissioner of Taxation* (1995) 55 FCR 562.

29 Note, however, that 'where a company raises a defence of solvency, against the background of the statutory presumption of insolvency having been enlivened, the company is required to adduce the "fullest and best" evidence of its financial position in order to discharge its onus': *AG Coombs Pty Ltd v M & V Consultants Pty Ltd (in liq)* (2018) 55 VR 513, 539 [81] (Sloss J).

30 *Corporations Act* s 459S.

31 *High Court Rules 2004* (Cth); *Federal Court Rules 2011* (Cth); *Court Procedures Rules 2006* (ACT); *Uniform Civil Procedure Rules 2005* (NSW); *Supreme Court Rules* (NT); *Uniform Civil Procedure Rules 1999* (Qld); *Supreme Court Civil Rules 2006* (SA); *Supreme Court Civil Supplementary Rules 2014* (SA); *Supreme Court*

liquidator to protect the company's assets and to maintain the status quo pending the hearing of the application. Provisional liquidations are discussed below.

16.15.25 Court order to wind up the company: introduction

The court has discretion to make a winding up order under s 459A. Generally, where the company is insolvent, a person with standing—a person listed in s 459P (as discussed above at Section 16.15.10)—may obtain an order unless the application is an abuse of process[32] (for example, where the defendant company was the 'alter ego' of the plaintiff and her former husband and the alleged debt was the subject of proceedings before the Family Court[33]) or the company is solvent.[34]

An order by the court that an insolvent company be wound up in insolvency under s 459A is made in favour of all creditors and contributories. The applicant acts in the proceedings in a representative capacity. Occasionally, the court will refuse the order because other creditors oppose it on the grounds that their interests would be better served by the company being under another form of external administration—such as a scheme of arrangement or voluntary administration—rather than liquidation.[35]

Upon making a winding up order, the court appoints a liquidator to the company.[36] This terminology is explained below.

16.15.30 Court order to wind up the company: procedure

There is a strict procedure when a creditor applies for a court order to wind up a company where the order is based on an unsatisfied statutory demand. As stated above, this is the most common type of winding up order for insolvency, and due to potentially draconian effects of a winding up order, compliance with the requirements is closely monitored by the court. Applications can be made in the state and territory Supreme Courts as well as the Federal Court (referred to as 'the Court' below). Harmonised court rules (for example, the *Federal Court (Corporations) Rules 2000*)[37] apply to these proceedings across these jurisdictions.

The procedure is set out in Corporations Information Sheet 1 issued by the Federal Court.[38] In summary, it involves the following steps:

(1). The creditor makes an application under s 459P within three months of the company's failure to comply with the statutory demand. As discussed above at Section 16.15.15, there is a presumption of insolvency if a company fails to comply with a statutory demand within the time provided.

Rules 2000 (Tas); *Supreme Court (General Civil Procedure) Rules 2015* (Vic); *Rules of the Supreme Court 1971* (WA).

32 See *Re Kolback Group Ltd* (1991) 4 ACSR 165 where the application was intended to defeat other proceedings against the company.

33 *Roberts v Wayne Roberts Concrete Constructions Pty Ltd* (2004) 50 ACSR 204.

34 *Chippendale Printing Co Pty Ltd v Deputy Commissioner of Taxation* (1995) 55 FCR 562.

35 *Deputy Commissioner of Taxation (Vic) v Avram Investments Pty Ltd* (1992) 9 ACSR 580; see generally *Laucke Flour Mills (Stockwell) Pty Ltd v Fresjac Pty Ltd* (1992) 58 SASR 110.

36 *Corporations Act* ss 472, 532(8).

37 These are known as the *Corporations Rules* and are made under the *Federal Court of Australia Act 1976* (Cth).

38 Federal Court of Australia, *Corporations Information Sheet 1: Winding Up Proceedings Based on an Unsatisfied Statutory Demand* (February 2023) <https://www.fedcourt.gov.au/law-and-practice/guides/corporations-guides/information-sheet-1>.

(2). The necessary affidavits are filed with the court, confirming that the statutory demand process was complied with.
(3). The originating process (the documents by which the civil proceedings are commenced) and the supporting affidavits are served on the defendant company.
(4). ASIC is notified by the plaintiff of the application for winding up orders.
(5). The plaintiff obtains the consent of a registered liquidator, should the order be made, and filing the Consent to Act form. The registration of liquidators is discussed below at Section 16.20.05.
(6). Notice of the application is published by the plaintiff on the ASIC website.
(7). The court hears the application. Generally, a winding up order will be made if the court is satisfied that the formal requirements under the *Corporations Act* and *Corporations Rules* have been met.
(8). If the application is granted, and the winding up order made, the liquidator is notified, notice of the order is lodged with ASIC, and a copy of the order is served on the company.

16.15.35 Effect of a winding up in insolvency

A court-ordered winding up is taken to commence on the day on which the order is made.[39] There may be variations to this commencement date. For example, where the company was previously under a voluntary administration, or has entered into a deed of company arrangement (DOCA), the winding up will commence when the administration began.[40] A separate date that delimits the period within which the liquidator may claw back transactions is called the 'relation-back' day. The relation-back day is defined as the day on which the winding up application was filed[41] or another date if, before the order was made, the company was under administration or subject to a deed of company arrangement or a voluntary winding up.[42] The relation-back day is referred to in multiple provisions which deal with voidable transactions. The voidable transaction provisions are discussed below at Section 16.25.

The immediate effect of the winding up order is that the company ceases to carry on business except to the extent necessary to enable the liquidator to perform their functions. The directors and secretary of the company are obliged to submit a report to the liquidator regarding the affairs of the company.[43] If the liquidator's inquiries reveal that officers or employees of the company have committed offences, been negligent, have otherwise breached their duties, misappropriated money or property, or if the company is unable to pay creditors more than 50 cents in the dollar, the liquidator must lodge a report with ASIC.[44] Finally, after the liquidator has realised the company's property by converting the property into proceeds and distributed any payments to

39 *Corporations Act* s 513A(e).
40 Ibid ss 513A(a)–(d).
41 Ibid s 91 item 14.
42 Ibid s 91.
43 Ibid s 475.
44 Ibid s 533. See generally Australian Securities and Investments Commission, *External administrators: Reporting and lodging* (Regulatory Guide 16, July 2008).

creditors—called, somewhat confusingly, 'dividends'—and made a final return to contributories, the liquidator applies to the court to be released and for ASIC to deregister the company.[45]

There are significant limitations on what the company and its officers can do after the commencement of a winding up in insolvency by the court. Although the directors remain in office, the liquidator takes custody and control of the company's property.[46] Further, the company cannot dispose of any of its property without a court order. Any purported disposition without such an order is void.[47] The word 'disposition' is given a wide interpretation by the courts and includes sale, encumbrance, mortgage, and payments of money.[48] This prohibition does not apply to dispositions by the liquidator or administrator or a disposition made pursuant to a deed of company arrangement.[49] With the commencement of the winding up, members lose their rights to transfer their shares unless the liquidator consents, and their rights cannot be varied without such consent.[50]

A winding up order by the court operates in favour of all creditors and contributories even though they have not been a party to the application.[51] The general policy of liquidation requires that the assets be fairly distributed in accordance with the process set out in s 553 and the priorities nominated in ss 555 and 556. Individual efforts by creditors to obtain payment of their debts is discouraged.

All debts of the company are automatically frozen at the date of liquidation. A person cannot, without the leave of the court, begin or proceed with:

- a court proceeding against the company or in relation to its property; or
- any enforcement process in relation to its property.[52]

The object of these restrictions is to prevent the assets of the company being dissipated in litigation and to oblige creditors to prove their claims or debts in the winding up.[53]

The process by which creditors prove their debts is discussed below at Section 16.20.15. The restrictions also prevent a particular creditor from gaining an advantage over the general body of creditors by proceeding to judgment and execution against the property of an insolvent company.[54]

Employees who remain with the company are discharged at the relevant date. The meaning of 'relevant date' in this context is discussed below. However, such employees have a right to payment for arrears of wages or other entitlements in priority to certain other creditors.[55] This is discussed below at Section 16.30.

45 *Corporations Act* s 480.
46 Ibid s 474.
47 Ibid s 468.
48 *Re Mal Bower's Macquarie Electrical Centre Pty Ltd (in liq)* [1974] 1 NSWLR 254; *Re Loteka Pty Ltd* [1990] 1 Qd R 322.
49 *Corporations Act* s 468.
50 Ibid ss 468A(1), (8).
51 Ibid s 471.
52 Ibid s 471B.
53 See, eg, *Re Gordon Grant and Grant Pty Ltd* [1983] 2 Qd R 314, 317 (McPherson J).
54 *Re Sydney Formworks Pty Ltd (in liq)* [1965] NSWR 646 (McLelland J).
55 *Corporations Act* s 558.

16.20 Liquidators: appointment, powers, duties

The primary task of the liquidator is to gather the company's assets, sell them to realise some proceeds, and then distribute the proceeds among those entitled to them. In undertaking these tasks, liquidators are subject to extensive duties. If the company is solvent, the proceeds are distributed among creditors and shareholders. If the company is insolvent, the proceeds must be distributed among the creditors according to the priority principles that are discussed below at Section 16.30.

16.20.05 Registration and appointment of liquidators

An individual can apply to ASIC for registration as a liquidator.[56]

Liquidators are placed on a rotating list for appointment upon the making of a winding up order by the court, although a plaintiff will often nominate a liquidator.[57] The plaintiff is required to file the liquidator's consent to the appointment with the court.[58]

Liquidators must be independent of the company and its management. There may be a problem of conflict of interest if there has been a past or present association between the liquidator and the company. As discussed below at Section 16.20.15, the liquidator is an officer of the company.[59] Where a liquidation is ordered by the court, liquidators have duties to the court as well as obligations to protect the interests of the company. If a conflict arises between the two sets of responsibilities, the liquidator may apply to the court for directions on how to proceed.[60] ASIC or the court may also appoint a reviewing liquidator to carry out a review of a particular aspect of the liquidation.[61]

The liquidator owes responsibilities to a wide range of interests in a liquidation: the creditors, the company, the shareholders, the regulators, the courts, and the community. As noted by Murray and Harris, the liquidator has no 'client'—rather, a number of stakeholders—and this unique position confers considerable powers upon the liquidator.[62] However, the powers of the liquidator are counterbalanced by fiduciary duties which are discussed below.

It is important to note the difference between a liquidator and a *provisional liquidator*. The court may appoint a provisional liquidator after the filing of an application to wind

56 *Insolvency Practice Schedule (Corporations)* in *Corporations Act* sch 2 s 20–25. For further discussion about the regulation of insolvency practitioners in Australia, see Australian Financial Security Authority, *Regulation and Compliance*, <https://www.afsa.gov.au/about-us/corporate-information/regulation-and-compliance/regulatory-framework>.

57 See, eg, Supreme Court of New South Wales, *Practice Note SC Eq 4—Supreme Court Equity Division—Corporations List*, 10 October 2024, sch 2.

58 *Corporations Act* s 532(9); *Federal Court (Corporations) Rules 2000* r 5.5 form 8.

59 See the definition of 'officer' in *Corporations Act* s 9AD(1)(h).

60 *Insolvency Practice Schedule (Corporations)* 2016 ss 90–10 to 90–20, especially s 90–15. See generally T Porter and C Symes, 'Section 90–15 of the IPS (Corporations)—The New Power for Courts to Exercise When Applications for Directions Are Made from Voluntary Administrators, Liquidators and Others' (2018) 33(2) *Australian Journal of Corporate Law* 275.

61 *Insolvency Practice Schedule (Corporations)* 2016 s 90–23.

62 M Murray and J Harris, *Keay's Insolvency: Personal and Corporate Law and Practice* (Lawbook Co, 11th ed, 2022) [10.195].

up a company and before the making of a winding up order.[63] When a provisional liquidation is ordered, a provisional liquidator takes control of the company on an interim basis to maintain the status quo while the winding up application is being determined. This appointment may alleviate the liability of directors for insolvent trading during the term of the appointment.

16.20.10 Powers of liquidators

The powers of the liquidator in a compulsory winding up are listed in s 477 and divided into two categories: general and specific.

- The general powers in s 477(1) include the power to carry on the company's business for the purpose of winding up the company, pay any class of creditors in full, and to make arrangements or compromises with creditors.[64]
- The specific powers in s 477(2) include the power to bring or defend any legal proceedings in the name of and on behalf of the company (for example, to sue to recover debts owed to the company); to appoint a solicitor; to sign documents on the company's behalf and use its common seal for that purpose; to sell or dispose of any property of the company; to make calls on contributories; and—as a catch-all—to do all things necessary for winding up the affairs of the company and distributing its property.

In a voluntary winding up, s 506 authorises the liquidator to exercise any of the powers conferred upon a liquidator in a compulsory winding up.

16.20.15 Duties of the liquidator

Liquidators owe significant responsibilities to the company, which have been described by Nosworthy and Symes as a hybrid of agency, statutory and fiduciary duties.[65] The characterisation of the relationship as 'fiduciary'[66] means that the liquidator must avoid conflicts of interest[67] and is prohibited from making secret profits.[68] As an agent, the liquidator will be required to perform their duties with skill and care, and failure to do so may render the liquidator liable for negligence at common law.[69] The liquidator is also an officer of the company[70] and owes the company the duties under ss 180–184 of the *Corporations Act*.[71] As

63 *Corporations Act* s 472(2).

64 Where the debt is over $100,000 (as stated in reg 5.4.02), the liquidator may not compromise the debt without first obtaining the consent of the creditors or the court: see *Corporations Act* s 477(2A).

65 B Nosworthy and C Symes, 'The Liquidator: A Hybrid of Agent, Fiduciary and Officer' (2016) 31(1) *Australian Journal of Corporate Law* 65.

66 *Corporate Affairs Commission v Harvey (liquidator of Timberlands Ltd (in liq))* [1980] VR 669; *Australian Securities and Investments Commission v Edge* (2007) 211 FLR 137.

67 *Advance Housing Pty Ltd (in liq) v Newcastle Classic Developments Pty Ltd* (1994) 14 ACSR 230.

68 See generally Chapter 13, particularly the discussion at Sections 13.10.10–30.

69 *Sydlow Pty Ltd (in liq) v TG Kotselas Pty Ltd* (1996) 65 FCR 234.

70 See the definition of 'officer' in *Corporations Act* s 9AD.

71 *Asden Developments Pty Ltd (in liq) v Dinoris* [2017] FCAFC 117. For a discussion of the Asden litigation, see N Saady, 'Lessons for Liquidators: The Asden Litigation and Liquidators' Duties under the Corporations Act' (2017) 25(4) *Insolvency Law Journal* 199.

stated above, a liquidator appointed in a compulsory winding up order is an officer of the court, and has responsibilities to the court.[72]

Other duties of the liquidator are as follows:

- to collect company assets[73]
- to consider if it is necessary to draw up a list of contributories[74]
- to realise company assets[75]
- to report on and investigate the company's affairs[76]
- to repay the company's debts[77]
- to distribute surplus assets[78]
- to bring about dissolution of the company.[79]

When exercising these powers, liquidators must use their commercial and professional judgment in determining any course of action.[80]

Prior to the distribution of the proceeds from the sale of assets, creditors must 'prove' their debt to the liquidator to be entitled to receive a portion of the proceeds on winding up. This follows from the obligation of the liquidator under s 478 to 'cause the company's property to be collected and applied in discharging the company's liabilities' and 'to settle a list of contributories'. As discussed above, the word 'contributories' includes both shareholders and creditors. A creditor who wishes to participate in a liquidation must lodge a proof of debt with the liquidator and the liquidator must decide whether to accept or reject the proof of debt. Unpaid dividends are regarded as debts due to shareholders, but in order to prove the debt the shares must be fully paid (s 553A).

If the liquidator accepts the proof of debt, the creditor will be entitled to repayment of some or all of their debt. If the company is insolvent, creditors are paid a proportion of the debts that are owed to them. Debts are repaid equally, so that if there are insufficient funds to repay all debts in full creditors are to be paid in proportion to their debts (s 555).

Section 553 states that debts and claims are provable in a winding up. The meaning of 'debt' is discussed in Chapter 15 at Section 15.10 and above at Section 16.15.20. However, a 'claim' is wider, and claims that are admissible to proof of debt against the company may be present or future, certain or contingent, ascertained or sounding only in damages (s 553).

A complex area is the projected compensation for claims in tort—for example, for personal injuries—both present and future. Prior to 1992, claims for damages in tort were not provable in a winding up; however, the *Corporations Act* was amended following the

72 *Corporate Affairs Commission v Harvey (liquidator of Timberlands Ltd (in liq))* [1980] VR 669, 695–6.
73 *Corporations Act* s 474.
74 Ibid s 478(1A). For a discussion of the meaning of 'contributory', see Section 16.15.10.
75 *Corporations Act* s 477(2)(c).
76 Ibid s 533.
77 Ibid s 478(1).
78 Ibid s 488(2), noting that this requires special leave from the court.
79 Ibid ss 480–1.
80 *Gray v Bridgestone Australia Ltd; Ewing v Fiandri Pty Ltd* (1986) 10 ACLR 677.

recommendations of the Harmer Report.[81] Section 554A sets out a methodology for the liquidator to determine the amount of debts and claims that are of 'uncertain value'. However, the treatment of product liability claims is an ongoing challenge particularly for latent injuries such as asbestos-related diseases. In these cases, the injuries may manifest a long time after the company has been wound up and there may have been no provisioning for the claims. It has been suggested that a trust be created for future claimants when certain companies are wound up to address this issue.[82]

16.25 Recovery of assets: voidable transactions

16.25.05 Introduction

The liquidator collects the company's property or assets during the liquidation. This includes property that belongs to the company at the commencement of the winding up together with property retrieved by the liquidator taking action on behalf of the company under pt 5.7B div 2 of the *Corporations Act*. This Part is titled 'Recovering property or compensation for the benefit of creditors of insolvent compan[ies]'. These provisions enable creditors to have full access to the company's property so that, as far as possible, their debts can be repaid.

The purpose of pt 5.7B div 2 is to ensure that the liquidator can recover property disposed of by the company prior to the winding up. Creditors' rights can be defeated by transfers of property prior to the appointment of a liquidator. The most prominent examples are transfers to creditors in preference to the general body of creditors and transfers of company property for an amount less than its true value. The provisions discussed below allow the liquidator in certain circumstances to 'clawback' property disposed of prior to the winding up. The liquidator will apply to the court to have the relevant transaction set aside. If the transaction is voided by the court the creditor may lodge its proof of debt and, if the liquidator accepts the debt, the creditor will receive its proportionate share of the debt with all other creditors.[83]

The liquidator's power to clawback property depends upon the nature of the transaction and its timing.[84] By way of overview, there are several types of transactions that are voidable:

(1) unfair preferences (s 588FA)
(2) uncommercial transactions (s 588FB)
(3) unfair loans (s 588FD)

81 Australian Law Reform Commission, *General Insolvency Inquiry* (Report No 45, 1988) ('the Harmer Report').

82 Corporations and Markets Advisory Committee, Parliament of Australia, *Long-tail Liabilities: The Treatment of Unascertained Future Personal Injuries Claims* (Report, 2008).

83 *Corporations Act* s 588FI. Section 588FI is discussed below at Section 16.25.40.

84 For a general discussion of the Australian and UK laws dealing with 'transactional avoidance' in bankruptcy and liquidation, see A Keay, 'Transactional avoidance: critical aspects of English and Australian law' (2000) 9(1) *International Insolvency Review* 5. For an international perspective, see H Rajak, 'Determining the Insolvent Estate—A Comparative Analysis' (2011) 20(1) *International Insolvency Review* 1.

(4) unreasonable director-related transactions (s 588FDA)
(5) creditor-defeating disposition (s 588FDB)
(6) invalid circulating security interest (s 588FJ).

Categories 1–2 are only voidable if they are also 'insolvent transactions', as defined in s 588FC. Therefore, the insolvency of the company must be proved for the transaction to be set aside. Categories 3–5 usually involve companies being wound up in insolvency but the relevant provisions independently stipulate the elements that need to be proved by the person who is seeking to set the transaction aside. Categories 1–6 are discussed below. In addition, there are composite provisions which require proof of an insolvency transaction but have an aggravated element such as a related party dealing (s 588FE(4)) or an obstruction of creditors' rights (s 558FE(5)). Note that some transactions may fall within several of the categories; for example, it may constitute an unfair preference and an uncommercial transaction.[85] This overlap has been judicially recognised[86] and the liquidator may argue that a transaction falls within several alternative categories in pt 5.7B div 2 when seeking relief to avoid the transaction.

As regards timing, creditors are entitled to the company's property for a period backdated from the relevant relation-back day. The relation-back day is discussed above at Section 16.15.35.

As a rule of thumb, the period of backdating from the relation-back day reflects the gravity of the moral hazard associated with different types of transaction. Therefore, the liquidator has different timeframes within which he or she can clawback property according to the moral turpitude of the transaction; for example, there will be a longer timeframe allotted to the liquidator to query transactions involving directors or transactions that obstruct creditors. The clawback period for an insolvent transaction that is an undue preference is six months;[87] whereas an unreasonable director-related transaction is four years[88] and an insolvent transaction made for the purpose of prejudicing or obstructing creditors rights is 10 years.[89] Some of the relevant clawback periods are set out in Table 16.1.

16.25.10 Unfair preferences

The essence of an unfair preference is that a creditor has received more from a company *before* it goes into liquidation than it would otherwise receive *in* the liquidation. Sections 588FA–FI allow the liquidator to seek an order that a payment by a company to a creditor which amounts to that creditor obtaining an unfair advantage over other creditors be declared void. These provisions promote the policy of equal ranking of creditors upon insolvency and discourage transfers to creditors in preference to the general body of creditors.

85 *Re Ashington Bayswater Pty Ltd (in liq)* [2013] NSWSC 1008.
86 *Featherstone v Ashala Model Agency Pty Ltd (in liq)* [2018] 3 Qd R 147; *Re Ashington Bayswater Pty Ltd (in liq)* [2013] NSWSC 1008.
87 *Corporations Act* s 588FE(2).
88 Ibid s 588FE(4).
89 Ibid s 588FE(5).

Table 16.1 Transactions

Transaction	Clawback period (prior to relation-back day)
Insolvent and unfair preference[90]	6 months
Creditor-defeating disposition[91]	12 months
Insolvent and uncommercial transaction[92]	2 years
Insolvent, with a related entity;[93] unreasonable director-related transactions[94]	4 years
Insolvent, purpose of obstructing creditors on winding up[95]	10 years
Unfair loan[96]	Any time

An unfair preference is defined in s 588FA(1) as having been given where:

(a) the company and the creditor are parties to the transaction (even if someone else is also a party); and

(b) the transaction results in the creditor receiving from the company, in respect of an unsecured debt that the company owes to the creditor, more than the creditor would receive from the company in respect of the debt if the transaction were set aside and the creditor were to prove for the debt in a winding up of the company.

The purpose of s 588FA was examined by the Victorian Court of Appeal in *Commonwealth v Byrnes*.[97] The Court stated:

> It has consistently been a primary objective of both individual and corporate insolvency legislation to promote the equitable treatment of unsecured creditors. The statutory regimes for achieving that goal have, throughout successive enactments, comprised a number of essential features. In general terms, the insolvent's property is to be made available for the equal satisfaction of the creditors' claims. ...

One manifestation of the general policy of insolvency law to treat all unsecured creditors equally is the statutory provisions which enable payments validly made to creditors

90 Ibid s 588FE(2).

91 Ibid s 588FE(6B).

92 Ibid s 588FE(3).

93 Ibid s 588FE(4).

94 Ibid ss 588FDA, 588FE(6A).

95 Ibid s 588FE(5). This provision states that a transaction is voidable if it is an insolvent transaction and the company became party to the transaction for the purpose of defeating, delaying or interfering with the rights of any or all of its creditors on a winding up of the company.

96 Ibid ss 588FD, 588FE(6).

97 *Commonwealth v Byrnes* (2018) 54 VR 230. The quotes in the text above were not relevant to the subsequent High Court appeal: *Carter Holt Harvey Woodproducts Australia Pty Ltd v Commonwealth* (2019) 268 CLR 524.

in the period shortly before the insolvency, which have the effect of giving that creditor a preference over other creditors, to be recovered.[98]

Typically, an unfair preference occurs when an insolvent company repays a debt to a creditor prior to the commencement of the winding up. For example, assume that a family member has lent money to the company and the company is having difficulties paying its debts. The director considers whether to put the company into voluntary administration but, upon finding out that the family member would only receive a fraction of the debt in a voluntary administration, directs the company to repay the debt in full. If the company is subsequently wound up during the relevant clawback period, the payment to the family member may be an unfair preference. The courts have noted that the provision is directed against *unfair* preferences; therefore, the court should look at the 'ultimate effect' of the 'entire transaction' before determining whether it has involved an unfair preference within the meaning of s 588FA.[99] This includes where the company arranges for a third party to repay a debt that the third party owes to the company's creditor.[100]

The general course of dealings between the company and the creditor has to be considered, so that one transaction that is part of a series of transactions forming an integral part of a continuing business relationship is not considered in isolation (s 588FA(3)).[101] This is often referred to as a 'running account defence',[102] although the legislation phrases it as an 'exemption' rather than a 'defence'. A running account describes an ongoing relationship between a creditor and the company where goods are supplied on a predetermined schedule, often on credit. As described by the High Court in *Bryant v Badenoch Integrated Logging Pty Ltd*:

> The "running account principle" recognises that a creditor who continues to supply a company on a running account in circumstances of suspected or potential insolvency enables the company to continue to trade to the likely benefit of all creditors. The prescription of periods within which *all* transactions in a continuing business relationship are deemed to be a "single transaction" and, accordingly, may be netted off against each other to determine any unfair preference serves this purpose.[103]

In *Airservices Australia v Ferrier* ('*Airservices*'),[104] the majority of the High Court considered that the purpose of a payment under a running account provided the context to determine whether or not the payment has the 'ultimate effect' of giving an unfair preference:

> if the purpose of the payment is to induce the creditor to provide further goods or services as well as to discharge an existing indebtedness, the payment will not

98 *Commonwealth v Byrnes* (2018) 54 VR 230, 245 [59], 246–7 [68].
99 *VR Dye & Co v Peninsula Hotels Pty Ltd (in liq)* [1999] 3 VR 201.
100 *Re Emanuel (No 14) Pty Ltd (in liq)* (1997) 24 ACSR 292.
101 *Airservices Australia v Ferrier* (1996) 185 CLR 483.
102 See, eg, *Clifton v CSR Building Products Pty Ltd* [2011] SASC 103, [64].
103 *Bryant v Badenoch Integrated Logging Pty Ltd* (2023) 275 CLR 463 [70].
104 *Airservices Australia v Ferrier* (1996) 185 CLR 483.

> be a preference unless the payment exceeds the value of the goods or services acquired. In such a case a court ... looks to the ultimate effect of the transaction. ... If at the end of a series of dealings, the creditor has supplied goods to a greater value than the payments made to it during that period, the general body of creditors are not disadvantaged by the transaction – they may even be better off. The supplying creditor, therefore, has received no preference. Consequently a debtor does not prefer a creditor merely because it makes irregular payments under an express or tacit arrangement with the creditor that, while the debtor makes payments, the creditor will continue to supply goods.[105]

The continuous business relationship test under s 588FA(3)(a) recognises that the company's indebtedness to the creditor will increase and decrease from time to time as a result of the transactions between them. This is treated as a single transaction if the 'net outcome, if any, in favour of the creditor from that single transaction is the amount of the preference'.[106] In previous editions of this book, we noted that, in the past, the alleged preference has been calculated by reference to the 'peak indebtedness rule', first articulated by Barwick CJ in *Rees v Bank of New South Wales*.[107] In 2023, this approach was rejected by the High Court in *Bryant v Badenoch Integrated Logging Pty Ltd*, which held that the 'so-called' peak indebtedness rule does not form part of s 588FA(3).[108] Instead, a liquidator should look at all transactions that have occurred within the statutory period to determine whether there has been a decrease in the company's indebtedness that can be argued to be an unfair preference, particularly where the purpose of the payment was to induce a continued commercial relationship between the parties.

An unfair preference will be set aside under s 588FF if it is an insolvent transaction and a voidable transaction. In this circumstance, the recipient will be required to disgorge the benefit received in favour of the liquidator who will use the money or property recovered to enlarge the pool to be distributed among the general body of creditors.[109]

16.25.15 Uncommercial transactions

An uncommercial transaction involves the company selling or giving away assets or incurring liabilities without receiving adequate consideration. The aim of these transactions may be to put assets out of the reach of creditors. The provisions in the *Corporations Act* are aimed at preventing the company disposing of its assets in a manner that cannot be explained by normal commercial practice, and act as a deterrent against company controllers transferring its assets for less than fair value. To use a simple example, assume that a company owns a recent model Maserati sports car and sells it to the

105 Ibid 503.

106 M Murray and J Harris, *Keay's Insolvency: Personal and Corporate Law and Practice* (Lawbook, 11th ed, 2022) [5.195].

107 *Rees v Bank of New South Wales* (1964) 111 CLR 210. Under this approach, a liquidator could choose a date within the statutory period to prove that from that date there was an unfair preference given by the company.

108 *Bryant v Badenoch Integrated Logging Pty Ltd* (2023) 275 CLR 463.

109 See generally A Poulton, 'Fruitful Unfair Preference Actions—What's a Liquidator to Do?' (2012) 20(3) *Insolvency Law Journal* 195.

daughter of a director for $10,000 during the clawback period. This would likely constitute an uncommercial transaction.

Pursuant to s 588FB(1), a transaction is an uncommercial transaction if it may be expected that a reasonable person in the company's circumstances would not have entered into the transaction, having regard to:

(a) the benefits (if any) to the company of entering into the transaction; and
(b) the detriment to the company of entering into the transaction; and
(c) the respective benefits to other parties to the transaction of entering into it; and
(d) any other relevant matter

In *Capital Finance Australia Ltd v Tolcher*,[110] Gordon J summarised the relevant principles pertaining to s 588FB as follows:

(1) as the express words of s 588FB make clear, it is an objective standard to determine if a transaction is uncommercial;
(2) four criteria are to be considered—the benefits enjoyed by the company (s 588FB(1)(a)), the detriment to the company (s 588FB(1)(b)), the respective benefits others received (s 588FB(1)(c)), and any other relevant matters (s 588FB(1)(d));
(3) the objective criteria [as stipulated in ss 588FB(1)(a)–(d) set out above] are not considered in some vacuum but by reference to 'the company's circumstances' which must include the state of knowledge of those who were the directing mind of the company, such as its controlling director or directors; and
(4) for a transaction to be 'uncommercial' it must result in 'the recipient receiving a gift or obtaining a bargain of such magnitude that it [cannot] be explained by normal commercial practice or where 'the consideration ... lacks a "commercial quality"'.[111]

For example, in *Great Investments Ltd v Warner*,[112] $6 million in convertible bonds was transferred from the company to a director as part payment for his own personal debts. The company was insolvent at the time, the transactions could not be explained by 'normal commercial practice', and the company derived no benefit from the transaction.[113]

An uncommercial transaction does not have to involve a transaction between the company and one of its creditors; it may be entered into by the company and any other person.[114] Examples are where the recipient receives a gift or the company disposes of property at less than its market value.[115] Courts will scrutinise transactions at undervalue carefully, particularly if the purchaser is a related corporate entity or a related person.[116]

110 *Capital Finance Australia v Tolcher* (2007) 164 FCR 83, 109 [129].
111 Citing, inter alia, Explanatory Memorandum, Corporate Law Reform Bill 1992 (Cth) [1044].
112 *Great Investments Ltd v Warner* (2016) 243 FCR 516.
113 Ibid [133]–[139].
114 See, eg, *Featherstone v Ashala Model Agency Pty Ltd (in liq)* [2018] 3 Qd R 147, 167 [76].
115 Andrew Keay, 'Liquidators' Avoidance of Uncommercial Transactions' (1996) 70 *Australian Law Journal* 390, 398.
116 *Welcome Homes Real Estate Pty Ltd v Ziade Investments Pty Ltd (in liq)* [2007] NSWCA 167; *Old Kiama Wharf Co Pty Ltd (in liq) v Betohuwisa Investments Pty Ltd* (2011) 85 ACSR 87.

An uncommercial transaction will be set aside under s 588FF if it is an insolvent transaction and a voidable transaction. Uncommercial transactions are illustrated by *Super Art Australia Pty Ltd v Foden*[117] ('*Super Art*') at Section 16.25.55 below. In this case, a loan agreement and a mortgage debenture agreement (the mortgage) were found to be uncommercial transactions because there was no benefit to the company, as no funds had been advanced by the creditor and the transactions converted a pre-existing liability from an unsecured to a secured debt thereby disadvantaging other creditors.

16.25.20 Insolvent transactions

Before a transaction may be declared void as an unfair preference or uncommercial transaction, it must be an insolvent transaction. An 'insolvent transaction' is defined in s 588FC as an unfair preference or uncommercial transaction and:

(a) the transaction is entered into (or effected) at a time when the company is insolvent; or

(b) the company becomes insolvent because of entering into (or effecting) the transaction.

As discussed in Chapter 15 (at Section 15.10), the court may make various presumptions about insolvency under s 588E, including where the company was insolvent at any time during the previous 12 months, or where the company failed to keep adequate financial records. These presumptions may be rebutted by proof to the contrary.[118]

16.25.25 Unfair loans

Pursuant to s 588FD, a loan is unfair where the interest or charges on the loan were or have become (because of a variation) extortionate. The factors to be considered when deciding if a loan is extortionate are set out in s 588FD(2):

- the risk to which the lender was exposed
- the value of any security in respect of the loan
- the term of the loan
- the schedule for payments of interest and charges and for repayments of principal
- the amount of the loan
- any other relevant matter.

As noted in Table 16.1, there is no relation-back period that applies to unfair loans, so any loan, no matter when it was given, may be challenged. Further, it is not necessary for the liquidator to prove that the loan was an insolvent transaction—that the company was insolvent at the time the loan was given or it became insolvent as a consequence of the loan—in order for the loan to be declared void. The court will scrutinise the loan carefully where the interest rates are high.[119] However, in *Re Essendon Apartment Developments*

117 *Super Art Australia v Foden* [2014] FCA 1168.

118 For an example where the presumptions in s 588E were rebutted, see *Hussain v CSR Building Products Ltd* (2016) 246 FCR 62, 76–88 [57]–[139] (Edelman J).

119 *Hall v Ledge Finance Ltd* [2005] NSWSC 645.

Pty Ltd (in liq) (No 2),[120] loans that carried interest rates of 60 per cent and 70 per cent per annum were held not to be unfair loans because the lender assumed a high level of risk—a second mortgage over an undeveloped property—and no evidence had been led to prove the interest rate was extortionate.

16.25.30 Unreasonable director-related transactions

Section 588FDA regulates unreasonable payments made to directors and their associates. The provision targets certain transactions—such as payments, disposition of property, or an issue of securities—made by the company to a director or a close associate of a director or for the benefit of the director or close associate. The term 'close associate' is defined in s 9 to mean a relative of the director or their spouse. 'Relative' is also defined in s 9 to mean a person's spouse, parent or remoter lineal ancestor, child or remoter issue, or brother or sister.

The provision is clearly directed at bonuses given to directors prior to liquidation. However, it has a wider operation because it applies to 'unreasonable transactions'. Nettle JA stated in *Vasudevan (as joint and several liquidator of Wulguru Retail Investments Pty Ltd) (in liq) v Becon Constructions (Australia) Pty Ltd* that:

> Section 588FDA is self-evidently an anti-avoidance provision aimed at preventing errant directors from stripping benefits out of companies to their own advantage.[121]

Nettle JA concluded that 'benefit' in s 588FDA includes both direct and indirect benefits.[122]

The reasonableness of the transaction is to be assessed by the factors set out in s 588FDA(1)(c). It will be unreasonable if a reasonable person in the company's circumstances would not have entered into the transaction, having regard to:

- **(a)** the benefits (if any) to the company of entering into the transaction; and
- **(b)** the detriment to the company of entering into the transaction; and
- **(c)** the respective benefits to other parties to the transaction of entering into it; and
- **(d)** any other relevant matter.

The test of unreasonableness in s 588FDA(1)(c) is objective: it is 'what a reasonable person in the company's circumstances may be expected not to do'.[123] Further, the 'company's circumstances' 'encompass all relevant matters, starting with its status as a company and what flows from that; its controllers, shareholders, business and other activities; and the facts and circumstances of, and surrounding, the transaction'.[124] Gleeson J reviewed the authorities on s 588FDA in *Smith (in his capacity as liquidator of Action Paintball Games Pty Ltd) (in liq) v Starke (No 2).*[125]

---

120 *Re Essendon Apartment Developments Pty Ltd (in liq) (No 2)* [2013] VSC 210.
121 (2014) 41 VR 445, 451 [19].
122 Ibid.
123 *Weaver v Harburn* (2014) 103 ACSR 416, 428 [91] (McLure J).
124 Ibid 428–9 [91] (McLure J).
125 *Smith (in his capacity as liquidator of Action Paintball Games Pty Ltd) (in liq) v Starke (No 2)* (2015) 109 ACSR 145.

Her Honour discerned the following principles:

> **(a)** Impropriety or breach of director's duty is not necessary to establish an unreasonable director-related transaction ...
> **(b)** The inquiry under s 588FDA(1)(c) is concerned with the reasonableness of the company's conduct, objectively assessed ...
> **(c)** The inquiry under s 588FDA(1)(c) is conducted by reference to the company's circumstances, encompassing all relevant matters ...
> **(d)** Normal commercial practice is a relevant but not determinative matter in conducting the s 588FDA(1)(c) inquiry ...
> **(e)** A transaction of derivative benefit only can still be for the benefit of the company ...[126]

Note the findings of Davies J in *Super Art Australia Pty Ltd v Foden*[127] below at Section 16.25.55. As discussed above at Section 16.25.15, the loan and the mortgage were uncommercial transactions because the company derived no benefit from the transaction and the conversion from an unsecured to a secured debt disadvantaged creditors. The fact that Foden was a director at the time of the transaction also meant that the transactions were unreasonable director-related transactions under s 588FDA. In the Maserati example given above at Section 16.25.15, the daughter who receives the car is a close associate of the director because she is the child of a director (s 9). The transfer of the Maserati appears to be unreasonable and made for the benefit of the daughter rather than the company.

16.25.35 Creditor-defeating dispositions

Section 588FE(6B) and related sections address the situation where directors of a company that is in financial trouble cause the company's assets to be transferred to a second, unrelated company that is controlled by the same people, with the result that the assets are now beyond the reach of the first company's creditors. This practice is known colloquially as 'phoenixing', because it is intended that the business will 'rise from the ashes' of the first company, using the assets that are now under the control of the second company.[128] Instead of 'phoenixing', s 588FDB labels this a 'creditor-defeating disposition'.

A creditor-defeating disposition occurs when the consideration paid for a disposition of company property is less than either the market value of the property or the best price that was reasonably obtainable (whichever is the lesser amount) and the disposition either prevents the property from being available for the benefit of the company's creditors or it hinders or significantly delays the process of making the property so available (s 588FDB(1)).

This type of transaction is voidable under s 588FE(6B) if it occurs during the relevant period (see Table 16.1) and the company was insolvent at the time, or became insolvent

126 Ibid [104]–[110], cited by the New South Wales Court of Appeal in *Crowe-Maxwell v Frost* (2016) 91 NSWLR 414, 427 [70].

127 *Super Art Australia v Foden* [2014] FCA 1168.

128 In ancient Egyptian and Greek mythology, the phoenix was a bird that, at the end of its long life, would build a nest, set it on fire and be consumed by the flames. A new bird would then rise from the ashes of the fire. Fans of the *Dr Who* television series will be familiar with this phenomenon. See also Section 11.25.

because of the transaction, or the company went into external administration because of the transaction less than 12 months after it occurred.

Uniquely, s 588FGAA gives ASIC the power, under certain conditions, to make orders against a person who has received property or money as the result of a creditor-defeating transaction. On the face of it, this might be interpreted as an attempt to confer judicial power on a Commonwealth agency. The curiously worded sub-s (4) appears to be aimed at addressing this, stating that ASIC cannot make an order if it has reason to believe that 'if it were a court', s 588FG (discussed below at Section 16.25.50) would prevent it from making an order. Further, s 588FGAE allows a court to set aside an order made by ASIC under s 588FGAA.

Finally, ss 588GAA–GAC impose duties on company officers to prevent creditor-defeating dispositions (discussed in Chapter 11 at Section 11.25.20).

16.25.40 Invalid circulating security interests

Assets subject to a security interest held by a secured creditor do not form part of the pool that may be distributed to creditors by the liquidator. The term 'secured creditor' is defined and explained above in Chapter 15 at Section 15.15. A common type of security interest is a circulating security interest, formerly known as a 'floating charge', that allows a creditor to create a security interest in the company's circulating assets such as its inventory. Secured creditors are not generally affected by the liquidation process, unless the value of their security does not cover the extent of the company's debt owed to them, or if they lose the benefit of their security interest, as discussed below at Section 16.30.

When a company is compulsorily wound up, s 588FJ requires that certain circulating security interests are void against the liquidator. The provision is designed to prevent companies on the verge of insolvency securing past debts by granting a circulating security interest over their assets in favour of particular creditors or to capture property acquired by the company prior to the winding up so as to remove those assets from the control of the liquidator. The security interest is often created in favour of the company's controllers. Section 588FJ covers situations where a circulating security interest is created within the period six months before the relation-back day. In such a case, unless it is proved the company was still solvent, the charge is void as against the liquidator except insofar as it secures money already paid or a guarantee already given or goods and services already supplied to the company.[129]

16.25.45 Voidable transactions: consequences

To summarise the discussion so far: voidable transactions are unfair preferences or uncommercial transactions that amount to insolvent transactions, unfair loans, unreasonable director-related transactions, creditor-defeating dispositions, and invalid circulating security interests entered into during the applicable clawback period prior to the relation-back day.

If the transaction is voidable, the court may make various orders set out in s 588FF. These include ordering the repayment of money paid by the company, the transfer of property back to the company, the repayment of the amount of any benefit received, or

129 See the discussion of s 588FJ in *Re CBA Corporate Services (NSW) Pty Ltd v Walker and Moloney* (2013) 212 FCR 444 in proceedings to wind up the insolvent company under the *Corporations Act* s 459A.

the discharge of a debt or security. The court may also declare a transaction to be unenforceable. However, where a creditor has returned an unfair preference, because of an order under s 588FF or for any other reason, the creditor has put the company into the same position as if the transaction had not been entered into, the creditor may prove its debt in the winding up (s 588FI). In this situation, the creditor's rights or interests cannot be prejudiced by any (further) order of the court under s 588FF.

16.25.50 Transactions not voidable against certain people

Pursuant to s 588FG, the court cannot make an order about voidable transactions that prejudices any person (other than a party to the transaction) where it is proved that:

- the person received no benefit because of the transaction; or
- in relation to each benefit that the person received because of the transaction, the person received the benefit in good faith; and
- the person had no reasonable grounds for suspecting the company was insolvent at that time or would become insolvent; and
- a reasonable person in the person's circumstances would have had no such grounds for so suspecting.
- when an unfair loan or an unreasonable director-related transaction is alleged, the person has provided valuable consideration under the transaction or has changed their position in reliance on the transaction.

This so-called 'defence' under s 588FG is illustrated by the *Super Art* case below.

16.25.55 Voidable transactions: a case example

In *Super Art Australia Pty Ltd v Foden*,[130] it was alleged the relevant transactions were uncommercial transactions, insolvent transactions, unreasonable director-related transactions, unfair loans, or invalid circulating security interests. Davies J's judgment provides a useful insight into how the various voidable transactions interact.

In this case, an application was made by the liquidators of a Super Art Australia Pty Ltd ('SAA'), for orders against the defendant (Mr Foden) under s 588FF. Foden was a former director, secretary and shareholder of SAA and was also SAA's accountant before it was ordered to be wound up in insolvency. SAA ran a business that involved the importation of mass-produced artworks from China for sale at staged events and public venues throughout Australia, such as the Royal Adelaide Showgrounds and Melbourne Exhibition Centre. The liquidators alleged that, during the relation-back period, SAA made three payments to Foden totalling $429,000, referred to in the judgment respectively as payments (1), (2) and (3). Payment (1) was $215,000, payment (2) was $14,000, and payment (3) was $200,000. These payments were allegedly made for accountancy and other services provided by Foden to SAA from mid-September 2007.

The liquidators alleged that SAA (as borrower) and Foden (as lender) executed a loan agreement ('loan agreement') by which Foden agreed to lend SAA the sum of $215,000.

130 *Super Art Australia v Foden* [2014] FCA 1168 ('*Super Art*').

Further, the liquidators alleged that SAA executed a debenture agreement which charged all of the company's undertaking and all of its assets in favour of Foden to secure the repayment of the loan amounts ('the mortgage debenture agreement').

As stated by Davies J in the judgment:

> The liquidators allege that:
>
> **a.** the loan agreement, the mortgage ... and the three payments are 'uncommercial transactions' (s 588FB ...), 'insolvent transactions' (s 588FC), and/or 'unreasonable director-related transactions' (s 588FDA ...);
>
> **b.** the loan agreement is an 'unfair loan' (s 588FD ...); and
>
> **c.** the mortgage ... is a circulating security interest in property of SAA (ss 588FJ, 266 and 1504 ...).
>
> The liquidators allege that the agreements and payments are voidable as against the liquidators and seek declarations and orders under s 588FF that the agreements are void as against the liquidators and that they are entitled to recover the amounts that SAA paid to ... Foden; an order that the mortgage ... be removed as a charge from the records of SAA; and an order that ... Foden pay the liquidators the sum of $429,000 plus interest.[131]

Foden disputed the factual basis of the claims made against him by the liquidators.

In relation to the loan agreement and the mortgage, her Honour found that the transactions were uncommercial transactions. First, no benefit was obtained by the company in relation to the dealing with Foden as no loan funds were advanced pursuant to the loan agreement. Second, if the purpose was to secure the payment of the fees owed to Foden, that liability had already been incurred by SAA and the effect of the charge was to convert that liability from an unsecured debt that the company owed to Foden to a secured debt.

> If that be the case, the benefit to ... Foden was significant in that it secured an existing indebtedness to ... Foden, with no corresponding commercial benefit for SAA. In either circumstance, it may be concluded that a reasonable person in the company's circumstances would not have entered into those transactions.[132]

For the same reasons, her Honour found that the loan agreement and the mortgage were unreasonable director-related transactions as Foden was a director at the time of these transactions.[133]

Davies J also found (relying on a report provided by the liquidator) that the company was insolvent from December 2007 because, at that point, it was unable to pay its debts as and when they fell due under s 95A.[134] The report indicated that the insolvency of the company was due to a significant net cash deficiency throughout the period December

131 Ibid [4]–[5].
132 Ibid [47].
133 Ibid [59].
134 Ibid [69].

2007 to December 2008.[135] This was evidenced, for example, by the company's inability to fulfil orders that were paid in advance by customers.[136] Accordingly, the loan agreement, the mortgage, and payment (1) were all insolvent transactions. Payment (1) was also was an unfair preference, taking into account the liquidator's evidence that no return to the creditors of the company was expected.[137] However, as regards the allegation that an unfair loan had been made, her Honour found that no loan had in fact been made by Foden to SAA pursuant to the loan agreement because no funds were advanced by Foden; therefore, s 588FD was not engaged.[138]

Foden raised the defence under s 588FG (discussed above at Section 16.25.50) but her Honour found that a reasonable person in his position would have 'reason to suspect' insolvency at the relevant time because an inquiry was called for into SAA's capacity to pay its liabilities due to an earlier default in repayment of monies lent which had necessitated further borrowings. Therefore, the defence under s 588FG failed.

Finally, the mortgage was expressed to be a fixed and floating charge and was alleged to be a circulating security interest for the purpose of s 588FJ. Her Honour found as follows:

> As it was created during the six months ending on the relation back day, and it did not secure an advance paid to the company by ... Foden at or after that time, the charge is void as against the liquidators in so far as it charged the assets of the company to secure repayment of the loan to ... Foden.[139]

In the result, the liquidators were entitled to the relief that they sought with respect to the loan agreement, the mortgage, and payment (1).[140]

16.30 Distributing assets: ranking of creditors

The distinction between secured and unsecured creditors must first be considered when discussing payments to company creditors in a winding up. A secured creditor has a security interest, such as a mortgage, over some or all of the company's property that can be called on to cover the debt owed to them by the company. Secured creditors have priority over unsecured creditors regarding claims over the company's assets, in that they can enforce the terms of their security to recover payment of their claim. Therefore, in doing this they stand outside the winding up process.

The interests of secured creditors are dealt with by the *Personal Property Securities Act 2009* (Cth) ('*PPSA*'). The operation of that Act is explained in Chapter 8 at Section 8.20.15.

Building on that explanation, a secured creditor can lose the benefit of having a secured interest if they do not perfect the security (*PPSA* s 267), or they do perfect the

135 Ibid [70].
136 Ibid [65].
137 Ibid [62].
138 Ibid [75].
139 Ibid [91].
140 Ibid [92].

security by registration but this occurs within the timeframes specified in s 588FL of the *Corporations Act*. In either of these events, the secured interest vests in the company and is then available to the liquidator for purposes of the winding up.[141]

The starting premise for payment of unsecured creditors out of the funds that are available for distribution is found in s 555 of the *Corporations Act*, which states that 'all debts and claims proved in winding up rank equally', and where the funds are not sufficient to meet all claims in full, creditors must be paid proportionately.

This is a reflection of the pari passu principle, meaning 'on equal footing'. The principle is that in a winding up no creditor should receive preferential treatment in gaining access to the company's funds. Relatedly, the *Corporations Act* embodies the idea that winding up is a collective process, meaning that each unsecured creditor abandons any individual right of action against the company and has their claim determined by collective proceedings. This idea is found in s 471B (which also allows the court to grant leave for individual action). The idea of a collective process is important in deciding how to distribute the remaining assets of an insolvent company.

As Anderson explains:

> In the absence of sufficient assets to pay all creditors in full, sound and logical insolvency laws are needed to ensure an efficient and fair collection, realisation and distribution of the debtor's remaining assets. The collective distribution regime upon liquidation aims to provide this, and allows for modification of pre-insolvency rights in favour of preferred creditors.[142]

The reference to 'preferred creditors' takes us to an important point: the application of the pari passu principle is qualified by the introductory words to s 555, '[e]xcept as otherwise provided by this Act'. The main exception to s 555 is found in the next section of the Act.[143] Section 556(1) lists 14 different classes of unsecured debts and claims against the company that must be paid in priority to all other unsecured debts and claims and must be paid in the order in which they are listed in the section. Section 556 does not cover the full range of unsecured creditors; it does not, for example, include unsecured trade creditors of a company.

Before looking at the priority order of payments in s 556 it is worth noting that it can be affected by a 'debt subordination' agreement, as recognised in s 563C. A company creditor may agree that the debt (or part of the debt) owed to them will not be paid until the debt (or part of the debt) owed to another creditor is paid by the company. In other words, the first-mentioned debt is subordinated to the other debt. The purpose of such an agreement is to vary the statutory order of priority. The section recognises and permits such an arrangement provided that it does not disadvantage any other creditor who is not a party to the agreement.

141 A Duggan and D Brown, *Australian Personal Property Securities Law* (LexisNexis, 2nd ed, 2015) ch 13.

142 H Anderson, 'Theory and Reality in Insolvency Law: Some Contradictions in Australia' (2009) 27(8) *Company and Securities Law Journal* 506, 509.

143 Other exceptions can be found in ss 562, 562A (proceeds of contracts of insurance and reinsurance) and s 564 (the court can make orders in favour of certain creditors).

The pari passu principle applies *within* each of the classes listed in s 556. All debts and claims within a class of debts listed in each of the paragraphs in s 556(1) rank equally; if the funds are insufficient to meet them in full, they are to be paid proportionately (s 559).

For explanatory purposes, the 14 classes of priority or preferential payments listed in s 556 can be grouped under two headings.[144] First, there is a group of expenses and claims that relate to the process of winding up or administration. These are found in ss 556(1)(a)–(df).

For example, the first class of debts is expenses properly incurred by a liquidator, provisional liquidator or administrator (referred to as a 'relevant authority') in 'preserving, realising, or getting in property of the company, or in carrying on the company's business' (s 556(1)(a)). This class of debt does not include remuneration or fees for service payable to, or certain expenses incurred by, the relevant authority; these are referred to as 'deferred expenses' and are ranked ninth in the order of payment priority (s 556(1)(de)).

The second group of debts and claims are employee entitlements—remembering that an employee is a type of unsecured creditor. Amounts due to employees in the form of wages and superannuation entitlements, amounts due under industrial awards, and retrenchment payments are ranked eleventh, thirteenth and fourteenth, respectively, and are to be paid in that order (ss 556(1)(e), (g), (h)). There are specific limitations that apply to employees (called 'excluded employees' as defined in s 556(2)) who are directors, or spouses or relatives of directors; these limitations are dealt with in ss 556(1A)–(1C). Priority claims by these employees are limited to amounts of $1,500–$2,000, with the remainder of their claim falling into the general unsecured creditor pool to receive distribution pari passu under s 555.

A critical issue for employees of an insolvent company is the risk that there will be insufficient funds available to meet their claims. This is addressed by legislation separate to the *Corporations Act*. Under the Fair Entitlements Guarantee (FEG) scheme[145] an employee whose employment has ended due to the insolvency of their employer may apply for an advance to cover unpaid wages (up to 13 weeks), unpaid annual and long service leave, payment in lieu of notice (up to five weeks), and redundancy pay (up to four weeks per year of service). These payments are funded by the Commonwealth Government. This scheme is not available to employees who fall within the 'excluded employees' definition in s 556(2) of the *Corporations Act*. The payment of the advance may be paid to the employee directly or to the liquidator.[146] If the payment is made to the liquidator, then s 560 of the *Corporations Act* will apply.[147] This section provides that if a person has advanced money to a company for the purpose of payment of an employee's wages, unpaid leave or termination payment, then the person who has advanced the money has the same rights and priority in the winding up as a creditor of the company. In the context of the FEG scheme, this means that the Commonwealth has the same

144 When reading s 556, it is important to refer to s 556(2), which defines a number of key terms for the purposes of the section.

145 The scheme is established by the *Fair Entitlements Guarantee Act 2012* (Cth).

146 *Fair Entitlements Guarantee Act 2012* (Cth) s 28, also permitting payment to 'another person ... in accordance with a contract between the [person] and the Commonwealth'.

147 Ibid s 29.

rights and priority as the employee would have had in respect of advances paid to the liquidator. After the priority debts listed in s 556(1) have been paid, and if there are still available funds, the claims of other unsecured creditors will be met in accordance with the pari passu principle in s 555. Often, the payments made under s 556 will leave nothing available for further distribution.

After all of the creditors' claims have been met, attention turns to debt claims by members.[148] The claims of company members rank after those of creditors. In practice, this means that if a company is being wound up because of insolvency, it is unlikely that members will receive payment. The policy is reflected in s 563A, which provides, first, that claims against the company by members for debts owed to them *in their capacity as members* must be postponed until all other debts against the company are satisfied. An example of such a debt is a dividend that has been declared but not yet paid. The section applies, secondly, to 'any other claim that arises from buying, holding, selling or otherwise dealing in shares in the company'. This latter provision was added to s 563A in response to the 2007 decision of the High Court of Australia in *Sons of Gwalia Ltd v Margaretic*.[149] The Court's decision, and the subsequent legislative response, reveal some interesting points about statutory interpretation and the policies underlying insolvency legislation.

Sons of Gwalia Ltd was a gold mining company listed on the Australian Securities Exchange ('ASX').[150] On 18 August 2004, Mr Margaretic bought 20,000 fully-paid shares in Sons of Gwalia; 11 days later the company was placed in administration, leaving Margaretic (and other investors like him) with worthless shares. Margaretic argued that the company had failed to notify the ASX of its financial difficulties, as it was required to do under its continuous disclosure obligations, and that by making incorrect statements to the ASX the company engaged in misleading and deceptive conduct under statutory provisions including s 1041H of the *Corporations Act*.[151] Accordingly, Margaretic claimed compensation for the difference between what was originally paid for the shares and their current value (which was zero). Margaretic's argument was that he should be able to bring his claim as an unsecured creditor of the company, rather than as a member. At the time, s 563A did not make any reference to claims arising from 'buying, holding, selling or otherwise dealing in shares'; the postponement (or 'subordination') effect of the section applied only to debts owed to a person in their capacity as a member. The question for the Court was whether Margaretic's claim was for a debt owed to a member (in which case, the debt would be postponed to the claims of unsecured creditors), or in some other capacity.

In a majority decision (Callinan J dissenting), the Court upheld Margaretic's argument. In each of their judgments, Gleeson CJ and Hayne J held that the wording of statutory provisions governing misleading and deceptive conduct meant that they are

148 Note that these are 'debt' claims by members, not their right to participate in any surplus that remains after all debts have been paid.

149 *Sons of Gwalia Ltd v Margaretic* (2007) 231 CLR 160.

150 The company's exotic name apparently derived from the fact that one of the prospectors who originally discovered the site of the gold mine operated by the company hailed from Wales. Gwalia is an old Welsh name for Wales.

151 The continuous disclosure provisions and s 1041H are discussed in Chapter 17.

available to any person who suffers loss in relation to the provision of financial services. Accordingly, Margaretic's claim under those sections was not made in the capacity of a member, and s 563A (as it was then drafted)[152] had no application. In the Court's opinion, the mere fact that Margaretic's claim related to shareholding was not, on its own, sufficient to make this a claim in his capacity as a member.

The effect of the Court's decision was to elevate certain claims that might be made by members to the same status as claims by unsecured creditors (but not those covered by s 556). Critics of the decision argued that this had the potential to add significant cost and delay to the insolvency process because of the nature of misrepresentation actions and the large number of shareholders that could be involved in such actions.[153] Another concern was that it might be more difficult or expensive for companies to raise unsecured debt finance or to obtain credit from trade creditors.[154] Responding to these concerns, Parliament amended s 563A in 2010 to provide for the postponement of all claims in relation to buying, holding, selling or otherwise dealing in shares. This amendment reversed the effect of the decision in the *Sons of Gwalia* case.

16.35 Winding up under s 461

A court-ordered, or compulsory, winding up can come about in a number of ways: principally, via s 459A (winding up in insolvency), s 233 (winding up in response to finding of oppression, unfairly prejudicial or unfairly discriminatory conduct), and s 461. Section 459A is dealt with elsewhere in this present chapter (see Section 16.15.10); s 233 was dealt with in Chapter 14 (see Section 14.30.20). Here, we focus on compulsory winding up under s 461.

Section 461(1) of the *Corporations Act* lists eight grounds on which a court may order the winding up of a company.[155] Four of these grounds[156] are considered in Chapter 14 (at Section 14.40) in the context of remedies available to members of a company, and that discussion is not repeated here. Of the remaining four grounds, two are relevant in the context of this present chapter: s 461(1)(a) special resolution by members, and s 461(1)(h) report by ASIC.[157] We look at these in turn.

152 At the relevant time, s 563A provided: 'Payment of a debt owed by a company to a person in the person's capacity as a member of the company, whether by way of dividends, profits or otherwise, is to be postponed until all debts owed to, or claims made by, persons otherwise than as members of the company have been satisfied.'

153 For a review of the implications of the decision, see A Hargovan and J Harris, '*Sons of Gwalia Ltd v Margaretic*—The Shifting Balance of Shareholders' Interests in Insolvency: Evolution or Revolution?' (2007) 31(2) *Melbourne University Law Review* 591; C Di Lernia, 'Shareholder Rights in the Face of Corporate Bankruptcy Events' (2010) 38(2) *Australian Business Law Review* 83.

154 Corporations and Markets Advisory Committee, *Shareholder Claims Against Insolvent Companies: Implications of the Sons of Gwalia Decision* (Parliament of Australia, Report, 2008) 35–7.

155 Note that in s 461(1), sub-ss (b), (i) and (j) have been repealed.

156 Section 461(1)(e) directors acting in their own interests; s 461(1)(f) affairs of company conducted in oppressive, unfairly prejudicial or unfairly discriminatory manner; s 461(1)(g) act, omission, or resolution that is oppressive, unfairly prejudicial or unfairly discriminatory; and s 461(1)(k) just and equitable grounds.

157 Section 461(1)(c) permits the court to order a winding up if the company does not commence its business within one year of its date of incorporation, or suspends its business for a whole year. Section 461(1)(d) permits a court winding-up order if the company has no members.

Under s 461(1)(a), the court has discretion to order a winding up if the members have passed a special resolution that the company be wound up. A question arises concerning the relationship between this provision and s 491, which permits members, by special resolution, to resolve that a company be voluntarily wound up. The immediate point of difference is that s 491 does not require a court order for the special resolution to have effect; whereas, under s 461(1)(a), a court order is integral to the special resolution (it is, in effect, a resolution for a voluntary court-ordered winding up).

In *Hillig v Darkinjung Local Aboriginal Land Council*, Barrett J considered the relationship between these two sections. His Honour noted that the exercise of the Court's discretion to make an order under s 461(1)(a) is not ruled out by the fact that the members had available to them the option of passing their special resolution under s 491:

> [T]he availability to the shareholders of the alternative of initiating voluntary winding up by special resolution does not represent any reason for declining to make a winding up order. This ... is really no more than an aspect of statutory interpretation: if there had been some intention that the voluntary winding up mechanism should have primacy, s 461(1)(a) would not form part of the Act.[158]

Applications under s 461(1)(a) are rarely used.

Section 461(1)(h) relies upon ASIC's powers of investigation in pt 3 of the *ASIC Act*, which permit ASIC to investigate and report on contraventions of the *Corporations Act*, among other things. If ASIC states, in such a report, that it is of the opinion that a company cannot pay its debts and should be wound up, or that it is in the interests of the public, the members or the creditors that the company be wound up, then the court has discretion to make that order. Section 464 also gives ASIC standing to apply, as if it were the company, for a winding up order where the Commission has been, or is, investigating the affairs of that company.

16.40 Voluntary winding up

The *Corporations Act* provides in pt 5.5 that a company can be wound up voluntarily. A key difference between a compulsory and a voluntary winding up is that the latter does not require an application to the court, nor a court order. Indeed, there is relatively little opportunity for court involvement in the voluntary winding up process. Unless the court grants leave, a voluntary winding up cannot take place if an application for a winding up on the grounds of insolvency has already been filed or the court has ordered that the company be wound up in insolvency (s 490).

There are two forms of voluntary winding up: a members' voluntary winding up, and a creditors' voluntary winding up.

158 *Hillig v Darkinjung Local Aboriginal Land Council* (2006) 205 FLR 450, 459.

16.40.05 Members' voluntary winding up

A members' voluntary winding up requires a special resolution to be passed by the company's members (s 491). To address the risk that this mechanism could be abused by members seeking to jeopardise the interests of the company's creditors, there is a further requirement: in order for a members' voluntary winding up to proceed, a majority of the directors must make a declaration, based upon an inquiry into the company's affairs, that the company will be able to pay its debts in full for up to 12 months after the winding up commences (s 494(1)). This declaration of solvency must be accompanied by a statement of affairs of the company that describes the company's property, liabilities, and the estimated expenses of the winding up (s 494(2)). In the absence of this declaration, a voluntary winding up can only proceed as a creditors' voluntary winding up. Put another way, a members' voluntary winding up can only proceed if the company is solvent.

A voluntary winding up is deemed to commence on the day on which the special resolution is passed, unless the company was under administration, subject to a deed of company arrangement or a winding up of the company was already in progress (s 513B). When the special resolution is passed by the members, they must appoint a liquidator to wind up the affairs of the company and distribute the company's property (s 495(1)). The other consequences of appointing a liquidator are described earlier in this chapter.

16.40.10 Creditors' voluntary winding up

Where a voluntary winding up is being contemplated and the company is insolvent, it is the creditors' financial interests that are at stake rather than those of the members. Accordingly, when a company is insolvent, the creditors are given effective control over the voluntary winding up process. A creditors' voluntary winding up is the only means whereby an insolvent company can be voluntarily wound up. The creditors cannot commence a voluntary winding up themselves; instead, a voluntary winding up becomes a creditors' voluntary winding up where the matter is removed from the control of the members because of the company's insolvency.

A creditors' voluntary winding up can come about in one of three ways. The first situation occurs when the directors are not able to make the declaration that is required by s 494 regarding the company's ability to pay its debts. In this situation, the company must then call a meeting of the company's creditors, under s 499, to consider the appointment of a liquidator. The second situation arises when, after the commencement of a members' voluntary winding up, the liquidator forms the view that, despite the directors' declaration of solvency, the company is not able to pay its debts. In this situation, the liquidator must do one of three things (s 496(1)):

(1) apply for a court-ordered winding up under s 459P
(2) appoint an administrator under s 436B
(3) convene a creditors' meeting under s 499 which may then proceed with a creditors' voluntary winding up.

Third, it is possible for a creditors' voluntary winding up to come about as a consequence of the company moving out of voluntary administration. This process is described in ss 446A and 446AA.

16.40.15 Simplified process for creditors' voluntary winding up

There is a simplified process for a creditors' voluntary winding up of a small business (s 500A). This process only applies if the total liabilities of the company do not exceed $1 million (reg 5.5.03).

This process is available if the liquidator in a creditors' voluntary winding up believes, on reasonable grounds, that the company meets the 'eligibility criteria' specified in s 500AA. Those criteria require, amongst other things, that 'a triggering event' has occurred within the previous twenty days (s 500A(2)(a)), that company will not be able to pay its debts in full within the 12 months after the triggering event, and that the company has not undergone a restructuring or been subject to a simplified liquidation process within the previous seven years (reg 5.5.03).

Section 500AAA defines seven types of 'triggering event'.[159] The first is that the company's members have passed a resolution in favour of voluntary winding up under s 491. The other six events arise in the context of a company moving out of a voluntary administration into a creditors' voluntary winding up (as described in ss 446A, 446AA).

The simplified process means that certain requirements relating to reporting to ASIC, meetings, committees of inspection, and the appointment of reviewing liquidators do not apply (s 500AE(2)).

The liquidator must cease to follow the simplified process if the eligibility criteria are no longer met (s 500AC(1)) or the company or any of its directors has engaged in fraudulent or dishonest conduct that has had, or is likely to have, a material adverse effect on the interests of the creditors (reg 5.5.07). The process must also not be followed if at least 25 per cent in value of the creditors make such a request (s 500A(2)(a)).

16.40.20 Effect of a voluntary winding up

The commencement of a voluntary winding up has consequences for the company, shareholders, and employees. The effect on the company is that, from the passing of the special resolution, the company must cease to carry on its business except so far as is necessary to allow the liquidator to wind up that business. Necessarily, the company continues in existence as a corporate entity until it is deregistered (s 493). No action or other civil proceeding can be commenced or proceeded with against the company after the passing of the resolution (s 500(2)). The company's property is to be used to discharge its liabilities equally, and thereafter to be distributed among the members according to their rights and remedies (s 501). Once the company's affairs have been fully wound up the liquidator must prepare and present a report to a general meeting of the company (or to a meeting of creditors, in the case of a creditors' voluntary winding up). That report shows how the winding up has been conducted and the company's property has been disposed of. The report and accounts are then lodged with ASIC, which must deregister the company three months after lodgment (s 509).

The consequence for shareholders of the winding up resolution is that there are restrictions on the capacity of members to transfer their shares and on alterations to the

159 Further types can be prescribed in the *Corporations Regulations*: s 500AAA(h).

status of members (s 493A). In broad terms, consent of the liquidator will be required as a prerequisite to either a transfer of shares or alteration of status, noting that it is possible to appeal to the Court if the liquidator refuses to give consent.

Surprisingly, as regards employees, there is no clear statement about whether the special resolution that commences a voluntary winding up operates to terminate the employment of the company's employees. In *McEvoy v Incat Tasmania Pty Ltd*, Finkelstein J made the following observation:

> The publication of a compulsory winding up order amounts to a dismissal of the company's employees (*Re General Rolling Stock Co (Ltd); Chapman's* case (1866) LR 1 Eq 346; *In re Oriental Bank Corp; MacDowall's case* (1886) 32 ChD 366), though the contract of employment still remains on foot. The situation is probably different in a voluntary winding up. I say 'probably different' because the position is not settled and, in any event, there is no justification for any difference. Be that as it may, the preponderance of authority favours the view that a voluntary winding up does not disturb a contract with an employee: *Midland Counties District Bank Ltd v Attwood* [1905] 1 ChD 357; *Re Matthew Brothers (In Liq)* [1962] VR 262.[160]

16.45 Deregistration and reinstatement of companies

16.45.05 Introduction

A company comes into existence when it is registered with ASIC. At the other end of its lifespan, a company may be deregistered. A company ceases to exist on deregistration.[161] In certain circumstances, a deregistered company may be reinstated. The deregistration and reinstatement of companies are regulated by ch 5A of the *Corporations Act*.

16.45.10 Deregistration of companies

Deregistration may occur in several ways.

First, the company, a director, a member or a liquidator may make a voluntary application to ASIC for deregistration.[162] Such an application would only be granted where the stringent conditions in s 601AA(2) are satisfied. For example, the company must not be carrying on business, its assets must be worth less than $1,000; it must have no outstanding liabilities; and not be a party to any existing legal proceedings. Further, all members of the company must agree to the deregistration. After a period of two months' notice of the proposed deregistration, ASIC may deregister the company.

Second, the deregistration may be initiated by ASIC in circumstances where the company's affairs have been fully wound up.[163] In these circumstances, ASIC is also required to give two months' notice of the proposed deregistration following which ASIC may deregister the company.

160 *McEvoy v Incat Tasmania Pty Ltd* (2003) 130 FCR 503, 506 [7].
161 *Corporations Act* s 601AD(1).
162 Ibid s 601AA(1).
163 Ibid s 601AB.

Finally, ASIC has an obligation to deregister the company in certain circumstances, including when:

- the court has ordered ASIC to deregister the company following the completion of compulsory winding up[164]
- three months have elapsed since the liquidator lodged an 'end of administration return' in a voluntary winding up.[165]

Importantly, as stated above, the company ceases to exist on deregistration.[166] The trust property held by the company vests in the Commonwealth[167] and other property that was held by the company is vested in ASIC.[168]

16.45.15 Reinstatement of companies

Clearly, deregistration may jeopardise the interests of those who have had dealings with the company and those who were involved in the management of the company. Chapter 5A therefore provides a mechanism whereby a deregistered company may be reinstated.[169] The most common reason for reinstatement is to enable a deregistered company to be a party to litigation. This process has now been streamlined by s 601AG, which allows a person to recover from the insurer of the deregistered company an amount that was payable to the company under the insurance contract if the company had liability to the person and the insurance contract covered that liability immediately before deregistration. Under this provision, the person with a claim against the company—such as a tort claim for personal injuries—is entitled to recover from the deregistered company's insurer directly and it is not necessary to reinstate the company to have access to the insurance. It has been held that s 601AG creates a statutory cause of action in favour of the claimant against the insurer.[170] However, it may be necessary to reinstate the company if there is any uncertainty about the insurer's liability.[171]

ASIC may reinstate the company if it is satisfied that it should not have been deregistered.[172] In addition, the court may make an order that ASIC reinstate the registration of the company where an application has been made by a former liquidator or a person aggrieved by the deregistration.[173] The court will make an order if it is satisfied that it is just that the company's registration be reinstated.[174] It is necessary for the court

164 Ibid ss 480–1. Note that the discussion here is concerned with deregistration in the winding up context. ASIC also has wider power to deregister an otherwise functioning company that has failed to lodge required documents or pay fees; see s 601AB generally.

165 Ibid ss 509(1), 601AC(1)(c); *Corporations Act* sch 2 s 70-6.

166 *Corporations Act* s 601AD(1).

167 Ibid s 601AD(1A).

168 Ibid s 601AD(2).

169 Ibid s 601AH.

170 *Almario v Allianz Australia Workers Compensation (NSW) Insurance Ltd* (2005) 62 NSWLR 148, 152–3 [19]–[20] (Ipp JA, Hodgson JA and Hunt AJA concurring).

171 *Stone v ACN 000 337 940 Pty Ltd* (2008) 68 ACSR 242.

172 *Corporations Act* s 601AH(1).

173 Ibid s 601AH(2).

174 Ibid.

to consider the impact that restoration to the register would have on affected persons. One aspect of the inquiry into what is 'just' concerns the future stewardship of the reinstated company; for example, who will take up the roles of director and/or liquidator.[175] Further, potential prejudice to former members must be considered where distributions have been made in the course of a winding up which may be recovered by the liquidator of the reinstated company.[176]

The effect of reinstatement is that the company is taken to have continued in existence as if it had not been deregistered.[177] Therefore, a person who is director of the company immediately before the deregistration becomes a director again and any property of the company that is vested in the Commonwealth or ASIC re-vests in the company.[178] If the company was in liquidation prior to deregistration it returns to that state.[179]

16.50 Summary

The ease with which a company can be created contrasts with the complexity of bringing its legal existence to an end. Throughout this book we have seen that the company form can be adapted and utilised in many different ways. We have seen that during the life of a company many different interests can be affected—particularly shareholders and members, creditors (of different types), employees, directors and officers. Accordingly, it is not surprising that the process of bringing a company to the end of its legal existence is governed by detailed rules and processes that have the aim of ensuring that all interests are treated equitably and that all liabilities and responsibilities are discharged.

175 *Stone v ACN 000 337 940 Pty Ltd* (2008) 68 ACSR 242, 246 [23].
176 Ibid [28].
177 *Corporations Act* s 601AH(5).
178 Ibid.
179 *Stone v ACN 000 337 940 Pty Ltd* (2008) 68 ACSR 242, 247 [32].

CHAPTER

17

FINANCIAL MARKETS

17.05 Introduction

This chapter begins with a discussion of the broad concept of a market and financial markets. It then delves into the markets for shares (securities) and derivatives. Important actors in the financial markets are highlighted, such as the market operators (the Australian Securities Exchange (ASX)), intermediaries (such as stockbrokers), investors, and the largest and most powerful of corporations—listed companies. The regulation of financial markets in chs 6CA and 7 of the *Corporations Act* is examined, beginning with the definitions of financial products (securities and derivatives). The licensing and supervision of financial markets is then considered: first, the licensing of markets themselves and their supervision through a system of rules—the *Market Integrity Rules*, the *Operating Rules*, and the *Listing Rules*. These rules have evolved from private market relationships so there is a spectrum of legal design that applies.

This chapter then examines the interplay between certain listing rules and ch 6CA which requires disclosure by listed companies of material information to the market.

We then consider the regulation of market misconduct under pt 7.10 of the *Corporations Act*: first, by analysing the prohibition against insider trading; and second, the prohibition on other forms of market misconduct, such as false trading, misleading and deceptive conduct and market manipulation. Finally, this chapter considers the public and private enforcement of the aforementioned obligations.

In this chapter, the word 'securities' will generally be used to describe a category of financial products which includes shares. This terminology is explained at Section 17.15.10 below.

17.10 Terminology and context

17.10.05 The financial markets

A financial market is a broad term that describes a market where financial products are bought and sold. In common usage, a 'financial market' describes a market where many types of financial products are traded, such as currencies, bonds, and debt securities. These financial products are traded in exchanges and over-the-counter (OTC) markets. However, the focus in this chapter is upon exchange-traded products, particularly securities and derivatives. OTC markets are discussed at Section 17.20.05. Our primary focus when discussing securities is shares. The terms 'stock markets', 'capital markets' and 'equity markets' are often used to describe this type of trading in shares.

Starting with the meaning of the word 'market', Renton informs us that:

> [t]he term 'market' can be used to describe any mechanism under which buyers and sellers ... deal with each other, especially a mechanism providing access in an organised manner and subject to recognised rules.[1]

When we discuss financial markets, we sometimes consider the primary market for shares—also known as 'securities'—where there is a direct relationship between the company and the public: the companies enter into a direct relationship with investors by offering the opportunity to buy (subscribe for) their securities. When a company raises funds from the public, a primary market or new funds market is said to exist. Of course, in return for the funds, the company issues shares. The classic case is where a company makes an offering of newly issued shares. This type of offering is discussed in detail in Chapter 9.

This chapter will focus, instead, on dealing in the *secondary* market for exchange-traded financial products. The secondary market in shares arises when someone who has bought shares from the company sells them on to someone else, who then may sell them to a third person, and so on.

The ability to sell shares is important to shareholders because, if they hold onto their shares, the main return they derive is through the payment of dividends. Dividends are discussed in Chapter 8. The other way that a shareholder can derive a return on shares is to sell the shares for a higher price to a new purchaser. This means there needs to be a market for the shares where they can be sold to others who will then take their place as

1 NE Renton, *Understanding the Stock Exchange* (Information Australia, 3rd ed, 1998) [501].

shareholders in the company. Without this facility to have value returned to investors, it would be difficult for companies to raise funds.

However, it is important to note that:

> the trading of securities on a stock exchange in no way affects the physical assets of the company or other enterprise behind those securities. The market merely facilitates a change in the identity of the owners of those assets.[2]

The ability to trade shares in this manner benefits the company indirectly because intending shareholders may be more likely to purchase new shares if the company's existing shares have a track record of being readily tradeable. This means it is easier for the company to raise capital from the general public in the primary market. So, in this way, the share price has an important function in signalling the reputation of a company.

The main markets in which securities are bought and sold are stock exchanges, also known as 'securities exchanges'. In modern financial markets, the functions of a stock exchange are combined with markets for other types of financial products such as derivatives. We define a 'stock exchange' in general terms as:

> an agency, or medium, which promotes and facilitates contact between buyers and sellers of securities. In itself it is neither borrower or lender, and it does not create financial instruments.[3]

What are the functions of a stock exchange? Macey and Kanda argue that a stock exchange has four important functions:

(1) It enhances the liquidity of the secondary market in securities. 'Liquidity' in this context means that investors can promptly buy and sell securities at prices that closely reflect the future profit prospects of those securities. A stock exchange enhances this liquidity because it is a centralised producer and disseminator of information. Being centralised means increasing the speed at which information about securities is disseminated and, at the same time, decreasing the costs involved in producing and searching for the information.
(2) It provides an enhanced system for monitoring the behaviour of the companies that produce the securities. This also lowers the costs of monitoring by investors.
(3) It provides standardised rules. The standardised rules that an exchange imposes upon listed companies reduces costs for companies who want to have their securities publicly traded. Standardisation also reduces costs for investors seeking information about the listed companies—they can assume that all listed companies are governed by the same rules.
(4) It enables reputational signalling. Not only does the stock exchange enhance the flow of information about a company, but the fact that a company is listed on

2 Ibid [504].
3 PJ Drake and RL Matthews, 'The Securities Market' in R Hirst and R Wallace (eds), *The Australian Capital Market* (Cheshire, 1974) 3.

the stock exchange is a source of information about the company's reputation. In other words, a stock exchange works as a signalling device to investors about the quality of the securities listed.[4]

Some finance theorists rely on the 'efficient capital market hypothesis' to argue that financial markets should not be excessively regulated because they are characteristically efficient, meaning that the market produces the necessary quantum and type of information without intervention, particularly intervention that requires the mandatory disclosure of information. The efficient capital market hypothesis posits that all available information is factored into the price of financial products.[5] Fama's view is that it is impossible to 'beat the market' in the long term because the market price will adjust immediately to reflect the relevant information. Fama assessed how capital markets incorporate information into the price of securities. He considered three forms of efficiency depending on the information that is incorporated into the market price:

(1) weak form: past information
(2) semi-strong form: past and publicly available information
(3) strong form: all public and private information.[6]

Some studies contend that the Australian securities market is semi-strong efficient,[7] although there are countervailing views about the operation of markets that suggest that behavioural factors may undermine efficiency.[8]

17.10.10 Intermediaries

Intermediaries are the people who execute the transactions in the financial market, such as stockbrokers and futures brokers. They perform a wide range of functions in addition to their work in executing trade orders on behalf of their clients; for example, trading in securities as principals, underwriting, capital raising, and providing advice about mergers and acquisitions. In 2024, there were approximately 50 full-service broking firms involved in the ASX market.[9] These firms provide a range of trading, clearing or settlement services. In addition, a firm may provide financial advice to its clients and when undertaking this role may be regarded as a financial adviser. Financial advice is discussed in Chapter 18.

4 J Macey and H Kanda, 'The Stock Exchange as a Firm: The Emergence of Close Substitutes for the New York And Tokyo Stock Exchanges' (1989) 75(5) *Cornell Law Review* 1006, 1007.

5 For an interesting critique of the efficient capital market hypothesis, see J Fox, *The Myth of the Rational Market: A History of Risk, Reward, and Delusion on Wall Street* (Harper Collins, 2009).

6 E Fama, 'Efficient Capital Markets: A Review of Theory and Empirical Work' (1970) 25(2) *Journal of Finance* 383.

7 N Groenewold and K Chin Kang, 'The Semi-strong Efficiency of the Australian Share Market' (1993) 69(4) *Economic Record* 405.

8 D Langevoort, 'Taming the Animal Spirits of the Stock Markets: A Behavioral Approach to Securities Regulation' (2002) 97(1) *Northwestern University Law Review* 135.

9 ASX, *Find a Broker or Adviser* <https://www.asx.com.au/investors/start-investing/find-a-broker-adviser>.

17.10.15 Listed companies

In 2024, there were approximately 2,000 listed companies on the ASX market,[10] but most of the trading takes place in the shares of the top 50 companies.[11] The volume of trading in shares in the ASX market is measured by various indices. For example, the All Ordinaries index ('AORD' or 'All Ords index') is the 500 largest companies listed on the ASX by market capitalisation.[12] Another important index is the S&P/ASX 200, which is a portfolio of shares comprised of the top 100 companies plus an additional 100 stocks.[13]

Stock exchanges compete with one another for the listing of companies. Large companies may have a simultaneous listing on two or more stock exchanges; for example, Rio Tinto comprises Rio Tinto Limited and Rio Tinto plc. The two entities continue to exist as separate companies but operate under a dual listed companies structure. Rio Tinto Limited is listed on the ASX and Rio Tinto plc is listed on the London Stock Exchange. American depository shares of Rio Tinto plc are also traded on the New York Stock Exchange.

17.10.20 Investors

The protection afforded to investors under the *Corporations Act* is frequently based on whether investors can be characterised as 'retail investors'. Retail investors are differentiated from wholesale or sophisticated investors. Following the recommendations of the Wallis Report in 1997 (discussed below), the policy is that retail investors should be provided additional safeguards; whereas wholesale or sophisticated investors are assumed to have greater knowledge and financial literacy. Therefore, a wholesale investor is treated as autonomous and their investment decisions should not be second-guessed by the law. The legal tests that differentiate between retail and wholesale or sophisticated investors are discussed in Chapter 18 at Section 18.05.10.

17.10.25 ASIC

The Australian Securities and Investments Commission (ASIC) has an important monitoring role in this area to ensure integrity in the financial markets. ASIC's objects emphasise the importance of this role as stated in s 1(2) of the *Australian Securities and Investments Commission Act 2001* (Cth), which is discussed in Chapter 1 at Section 1.60.05. Given the dynamism of this area, ASIC's wide discretionary powers to provide exemptions from or modify specific provisions of the corporations' legislation also assume particular importance. These powers are discussed at Section 1.55.

17.15 Financial products

17.15.05 Introduction

It is important to identify the relevant financial product before determining what laws, and which provisions of the *Corporations Act*, apply.

10 ASX, *Company Directory* <https://www.asx.com.au/markets/trade-our-cash-market/directory>.
11 The 'top 50' is by reference to their market capitalisation.
12 ASX, *Glossary* <https://www.asx.com.au/investors/investment-tools-and-resources/glossary>.
13 Ibid.

This chapter focuses on the difference between a security and a derivative. There are different regimes that apply to different products, and different regimes that apply to different investors—the investors being retail and wholesale clients.

What is a 'financial product'?

The concept of 'financial product' is central to ch 7 div 3 of the *Corporations Act*. There are three parts to the definition of a financial product, outlined in s 762A:

(1) The first part (sub-div B) consists of a general definition of 'financial product', including explanations of the concepts of making a financial investment, managing financial risk and making non-cash payments. This is a broad, general definition, which focuses on the key functions performed by financial products.
(2) The second part (sub-div C) is a list of specific things that are to be treated as financial products within ch 7, whether or not they fall within the general definition. The list includes a regulation-making power to include further products. The list of inclusions is not a catch-all list, but provides examples of products that fall within the general definition. This list is subject to the list of excluded facilities in sub-div D (see (3) below).
(3) The third part (sub-div D) is a list of specific things that are not to be treated as financial products. A facility on this list is not a financial product, even if it falls within the general definition in sub-div B or is on the list in sub-div C. The list includes a regulation-making power to exclude products and an ASIC exemption power.

When we examine the subdivisions, we can start with sub-div B (beginning with s 763A), which identifies three key functions of a financial product:

- making a financial investment (s 763B)
- managing a financial risk (s 763C)
- making non-cash payments (s 763D).

Financial products are differentiated by their functions stipulated in sub-div B. For example, derivatives and insurance are regarded as products that manage financial risk; whereas debit cards facilitate non-cash payments. Superannuation and securities are financial investments.

Section 764A sets out a list of facilities that are taken to be financial products for the purposes of ch 7. It shows the breadth of the concept of 'financial product'. As we are interested in traded financial products, the following discussion will focus on the definitions of securities and derivatives. ASIC has the power to intervene to ban a financial product where it considers that the product is likely to result in 'significant consumer detriment'. This power is discussed at Section 17.15.25 and would apply to financial products offered to retail clients.[14]

---

14 *Corporations Act* pt 7.8A: Design and distribution requirements relating to financial products for retail clients.

17.15.10 Definition of security

In the *Corporations Act*, one has to be careful about the definition of 'security' because different products move in and out of the definition depending on the type of activity being regulated. Examples of products that may or may not be included in the definition of a security are interests under a registered managed investment scheme and options.

The general definition of 'securities' is in s 92 of the *Corporations Act* which states:

> Subject to this section, *securities* means:
>
> **(a)** debentures, stocks or bonds issued or proposed to be issued by a government; or
>
> **(b)** shares in, or debentures of, a body; or
>
> **(c)** interests in a managed investment scheme; or
>
> **(d)** units of such shares;
>
> but does not include:
>
> **(f)** a derivative (as defined in section 761D), other than an option to acquire by way of transfer a security covered by paragraph (a), (b), (c) or (d); or
>
> **(g)** an excluded security.

In this definition, 'derivative' does not include an option to acquire a security by way of issue[15] and an 'excluded security' is defined in s 9 to mean an interest in a retirement village.

The definition in s 92(5) takes the reader to the definition of 'security' which applies to most of ch 7.[16] This provision defines 'security' as:

> **(a)** a share in a body; or
>
> **(b)** a debenture of a body; or
>
> **(c)** a legal or equitable right or interest in a security covered by paragraph (a) or (b); or
>
> **(d)** an option to acquire, by way of issue, a security covered by paragraph (a), (b) or
>
> **(e)** a right (whether existing or future and whether contingent or not) to acquire, by way of issue ... under a rights issue, a security covered by paragraphs (a), (b), (c), or (d);[17]
>
> ...

15 See the combined effect of ss 761D(3)(c), 764A(1)(a) and 764A(1)(d) on the definition of 'security' in s 92.

16 This definition excludes pt 7.11, which deals with the title and transfer of securities as defined in s 92(5) but are beyond the scope of this book (eg, managed investment schemes and foreign passport products). There are other definitions of 'security' in s 92 (eg, the s 92(3) definition applies to takeovers under ch 6 and the continuous disclosure regime under ch 6CA). The s 92(4) definition (discussed in the text above) also applies to ch 6D regarding fundraising. Fundraising is discussed in Chapter 9.

17 The section goes on to list other financial products that are beyond the scope of this book.

This definition does not include options over securities, other than options[18] over *unissued securities*. Unissued securities are those issued by the company, usually during fundraising such as an Initial Public Offering (IPO)—this flows from the sub-s (d) definition of security in s 92(5). IPOs and fundraising are discussed in Chapter 9.

17.15.15 Definition of derivative

The functions or commercial nature of derivatives

The expression 'derivatives' is used to identify a wide range of financial and investment products including futures contracts of all kinds, currency and interest rate swaps, and options over securities and market indices. These products are 'derivative' in the sense that their value depends on (or is derived from) the value of other, more basic underlying variables such as commodities, interest rates, currency exchange rates, securities or indices. Derivatives can be traded either on an exchange or OTC.

A futures contract is the most common type of derivative: this is a commitment to deliver (in the case of a sold contract) or take delivery of (in the case of a bought contract) a specified weight or quantity of a standard grade of a commodity at a fixed price and for a specific delivery date or period at an agreed location. Contracts may be performed by delivering the commodity or by making a cash adjustment. This definition focuses on commodity futures. Historically, futures were developed entirely as a device to manage risk in the underlying commodities contract. These contracts were 'deliverable contracts'—a futures contract over a commodity or thing which *can* physically be delivered upon settlement; for example, fat lamb futures. Many modern derivatives concern an index or other item which cannot be 'delivered'. An example is the contract over the S&P/ASX 200 index. A contract of this kind is usually only settled by cash payment.

Derivatives are used for managing risk, as opposed to a security which may create ownership and proprietary rights. Derivatives may also be used for speculation.

Definition of derivative under the *Corporations Act*

Section 761D of the *Corporations Act* sets out the meaning of 'derivative'.[19] The definition focuses on the functions or commercial nature of derivatives rather than attempting to identify every product that would be regarded as a derivative.

The definition in s 761D adopts the concept of something which derives its value from something else and surrounds that concept with more detail.

In essence, a derivative is either:

- an 'arrangement' (see s 761B) having the features listed in s 761D(1), or
- anything declared by the regulations to be a derivative (s 761D(2)).

Subsections (3) and (4) then describe certain things which are specifically not derivatives.

18 An option gives an investor the right to buy or sell a security at a specified price at some 'future time'.
19 Derivatives, other than for the purposes of ch 8A, is beyond the scope of this book.

Things that are derivatives: ss 761D(1), (2)

Important features of the definition of 'derivatives' are as follows:

- Under the arrangement, a person must or may be required to provide consideration at some future time (s 761D(1)(a)). This ensures that options that otherwise fall within the definition are captured.
- The arrangement must provide for consideration of a particular kind or kinds (s 761D(1)(a)). This would cover contracts that provide for cash settlement or physical delivery.
- Section 761D(1)(b) states that 'future time' has to be more than a certain number of days, as prescribed by the regulations. Under reg 7.1.04, the prescribed period is three business days for a foreign exchange product and one business day in any other case.[20]
- The definition covers all arrangements where the amount of the consideration or the value of the arrangement varies by reference to something else (of any nature and whether deliverable or not), including but not limited to:
    - an asset
    - a rate, including an interest rate or exchange rate
    - an index
    - a commodity (s 761D(1)(c)).
- The regulations may declare anything to be a derivative for purposes of ch 7 (s 761D(2)).

Things that are not derivatives: s 761D(3)

Section 761D(3)(a) excludes from the definition of derivative a range of transactions that involve future delivery but would not normally be regarded as derivatives. There is a difficult dividing line in respect of contracts that provide for the future delivery of something, such as a contract for the sale of land with a three-month settlement period. Such contracts should not be considered to be derivatives. This may be contrasted with futures contracts where the market allows the parties to 'close out' their position by an offsetting arrangement (s 761D(3)(a)(iii)) and they are therefore often used for hedging or speculative purposes. Such contracts should be regarded as derivatives. There are other types of products excluded from the definition of derivative by s 761D(3), such as a contract for the future provision of services (s 761D(3)(b)).

In *Joffe v The Queen*,[21] the New South Wales Court of Appeal interpreted s 761D when discussing whether 'Contracts for Difference' (CFDs) are a financial product for the purposes of the prohibition on insider trading under s 1043A. The Court held that CFDs are derivatives, because the substance of the contract was the creation and implementation of a financial relationship that was based on the market performance of underlying instruments.[22] Where the purpose and object of a contract (as objectively ascertained from the

20 For a discussion of these provisions, see *Australian Securities and Investments Commission v Davidof* (2017) 35 ACLC 17-030.

21 *Joffe v The Queen* (2012) 82 NSWLR 510.

22 Ibid 544–5 [169]–[170].

contractual terms) was not to provide services, but rather to provide the acquirer with a contract which, by its terms, would produce a profit or a loss dependent on the movement of the underlying securities nominated in it, it was not a 'contract for the future provision of services' within the meaning of s 761D(3)(b) of the *Corporations Act.*[23]

17.15.20 Crypto-assets

In 2025, Australia is still developing an approach to the regulation of crypto-assets, such as cryptocurrency, tokens or stablecoins. The development of this policy involves questions about whether crypto-assets are financial products and/or financial services and whether market licence is required for crypto-asset exchanges and trading platforms (see Section 17.20.20 below).[24]

17.15.25 Financial product design and distribution obligations

Part 7.8A of the *Corporations Act* commenced in 2021, and these provisions advance a new object for ch 7 in s 760A(aa) to promote the provision of suitable financial products for consumers. Part 7.8A requires the issuers of financial products to make available and review their target market determinations for their products, thereby reducing the consumer detriment caused by buying products that do not match their needs. ASIC has extensive powers to regulate the obligations under pt 7.8A.[25]

17.20 Financial markets

17.20.05 The development of the Australian stock markets

Chapter 1 provides a history of corporate law. That history shows the capital markets (both generally and in Australia specifically) are interwoven with the history of corporate law. This is because the desire to raise capital was one of the primary motivations for the development of the modern corporation and, as institutions developed, financial markets were created so capital could be traded. As the financial markets evolved, specialist intermediaries emerged—such as stockbrokers who matched buyers with sellers.

The first stockbroking took place in coffee houses in Europe in the seventeenth century. Stock exchanges emerged as the need developed for physical facilities to effect trading. In the United Kingdom, the London Stock Exchange grew out of a coffee shop in 1773. Stockbroking is reputed to have begun in Australia in 1829 when Matthew Gregson

23 Ibid [20]–[21], [170]. See also *Australian Securities and Investments Commission v Web3 Ventures Pty Ltd* [2024] FCA 64 where Jackman J applied *Joffe*, finding that certain cryptocurrency products were not derivatives.

24 See generally Australian Securities and Investments Commission, *Crypto-Assets* (Information Sheet INFO225, 7 March 2024); T Humphrey and N Selvadurai, 'Both Sides of the Coin: Developing a Multi-Stage Rights Model to Classify Crypto-Assets under the Corporations Act' (2023) 33(4) *Journal of Banking and Finance Law and Practice* 176.

25 Australian Securities and Investments Commission, *Product Design and Distribution Obligations* (Regulatory Guide 274, 10 September 2024); C Chong, 'The Design and Distribution Obligations: An Effective Tool for Consumer Protection?' (2023) 40(2) *Company and Securities Law Journal* 83.

was given permission to deal in Bank of New South Wales shares and set up business as a dealer in shares. The business did not thrive. In 1835, William Barton, father of Australia's first Prime Minister, Edmund Barton, established himself as an 'agent for the transfer of shares'. The first Australian stock market was established in Sydney in 1871. The capital city stock exchanges (for example, Melbourne, Brisbane, etc) were set up between then and 1889.

By the mid-1980s, a trend began which reversed these earlier moves. A physical locus of trading became less important, and the stock exchanges began merging.

In 1987, the six capital city exchanges merged to form the Australian Stock Exchange (the ASX). Originally, the ASX was a company limited by guarantee and the six exchanges were its members. The brokers who conducted the buy and sell transactions of each of the state exchanges were members of that exchange. The formation of the ASX allowed for the operation of a single national stock exchange. Notably, only members of the ASX could transact buying and selling transactions, so a seat on the ASX had significant monopoly power and wealth. However, as a company limited by guarantee, the ASX was a non-profit organisation in that any profit was required to be applied solely towards promoting the objects of the ASX and could not be transferred directly or indirectly by way of dividend, profit or gain to its members.

In 1996, this was changed by the demutualisation of the ASX, whereby the ASX was converted from a company limited by guarantee to a company limited by shares. In October 1998, the shares of the ASX were listed on its own exchange.

This demutualisation caused consternation in some quarters because of the other important function of the ASX: its role as a regulator of the stock market. This role will be discussed in more detail below. The ASX had significant supervisory responsibilities over market participants, such as stockbrokers and listed companies, and about a quarter of its operating expenditure was devoted to supervision and regulatory compliance. This role was performed by the ASX under a co-regulatory arrangement with the ASIC. At the time, concern was expressed about the ASX regulating a market in which it also participated as a listed company. The ASX has increasingly retreated from its regulatory function since its demutualisation. Since 2010, ASIC has had the primary responsibility for regulating the stock market.

In 2006, the Australian Stock Exchange merged with the Sydney Futures Exchange and became known as the Australian Securities Exchange. In 2010, the Australian Securities Exchange launched a new structure: ASX Group, or simply ASX. ASX conducts a range of platforms, including securities and derivatives markets.

As stated above, in 2010, ASIC was given the responsibility for regulating securities markets under a system where financial market operators were required to be licensed. There are now other financial market operators as well as ASX; for example, Cboe and NSX, although the ASX market accounts for the greatest volume of exchange-traded products in Australia. Under the current regulatory arrangements, ASIC has the primary responsibility for regulating financial markets but some responsibilities are retained by the relevant market operator.

In this chapter, our focus is on exchange-traded markets. This may be differentiated from OTC markets, which are usually conducted by direct dealing between financial institutions and professional dealers. An OTC market is a decentralised market, so it lacks a central location and the market participants trade with one another directly via modes of communications such as apps or proprietary electronic trading systems. A trade can be effected between two participants in an OTC market without others being aware of the price at which the transaction was executed. In general, OTC markets may be less transparent than exchanges and are not as closely regulated.

17.20.10 Background to the regulation of financial markets in Australia

The first attempts to regulate the Australian financial markets gathered momentum because of the boom in the securities markets in the late 1960s, which saw a rise in both share-trading activity and the number of public companies that were floated, particularly in the mining industry. This is discussed in Chapter 1 at Section 1.40.20. The relevant subsequent history is also traversed in Chapter 1.

The major changes over the last 20 years have been in response to Financial System Inquiries (FSI). FSIs are established by the Commonwealth Government from time-to-time and examine the financial system as a whole. The reports of each FSI carry the name of the chair of the committee who conducts the inquiry. The first FSI was the Campbell Report in 1981,[26] followed by the Wallis Report in 1997.[27] The Wallis Report set the blueprint for the current statutory framework discussed in this chapter.

The report of the most recent FSI (the Murray Report) was handed down in 2014. The Murray Report considered that regulation of the market should have the following characteristics, which would lead to an effective financial system:

- Efficient: An efficient system allocates Australia's scarce financial and other resources for the greatest possible benefit to the economy, supporting growth, productivity and prosperity.
- Resilient: The financial system should adjust to changing circumstances while continuing to provide its core economic functions, even during severe shocks. Institutions in distress should be resolvable with minimal costs to depositors, policy holders, taxpayers, and the real economy.
- Fair: Fair treatment occurs where participants act with integrity, honesty, transparency, and non-discrimination. A market economy operates more effectively where participants enter into transactions with confidence they will be treated fairly.[28]

26 Committee of Inquiry, *Australian Financial System* (Final Report, September 1981) ('the Campbell Report').

27 Commonwealth of Australia, *Financial System Inquiry* (Final Report, March 1997) ('the Wallis Report').

28 Australian Government, *Financial System Inquiry* (Final Report, November 2014) xv ('the Murray Report').

The framework established in the Wallis Report was implemented via the *Financial Services Reform Act 2001* (Cth) and has the following characteristics:

- licensing of financial markets
- licensing and conduct of financial services providers
- financial product disclosure
- co-regulation by ASIC and financial market licensees, particularly ASX.

These characteristics are articulated in the objects of ch 7 of the *Corporations Act* at s 760A, which states that the main objects of that chapter are to promote:

> **(a)** confident and informed decision-making by consumers of financial products and services while facilitating efficiency, flexibility and innovation in the provision of those products and services; and
> **(aa)** the provision of suitable financial products to the consumers of products; and
> **(b)** fairness, honesty and professionalism by those who provide financial services; and
> **(c)** fair, orderly and transparent markets for financial products; and
> **(d)** the reduction of systemic risk and the provision of fair and effective services by clearing and settlement facilities.

The Wallis Report's vision for financial market and financial services regulation was articulated in ch 7 of the *Corporations Act*. In this chapter, we will focus upon the following two issues: one, the structure of financial markets in terms of licensing and supervision; and two, acts that constitute market misconduct, such as market manipulation, misleading or deceptive conduct, and insider trading.

The licensing, disclosure and other obligations of financial services providers is discussed in Chapter 18.

By 2017, the pressure was gathering for the government to establish a royal commission into banking misconduct in Australia and the Royal Commission into Misconduct in the Banking, Superannuation and Financial Services Industry was announced on 30 November 2017, to be conducted by former High Court judge Justice Kenneth Hayne ('the Hayne Royal Commission'). The establishment of the Hayne Royal Commission was not due to any single crisis or scandal but rather the cumulative effect of 'sustained exasperation, anger and resentment amongst the general public and finance industry whistleblowers, media and ... parliamentarians [about] systemic misconduct within the Australian financial sector, [and the] perceived disdain ... within the sector about the prevalence of such misconduct and its harmful impacts'.[29] The Commission's terms of reference required it to inquire into (inter alia):

> (a) whether any conduct by financial services entities might have amounted to misconduct and, if so, whether the question of criminal or other legal proceedings should be referred to the relevant agency

29 G Gilligan, 'The Hayne Royal Commission—Just Another Piece of Official Discourse?' (2019) 13(2-3) *Law and Financial Markets Review* 114, 115.

(b) whether any conduct, practices, behaviour or business activities by financial services entities fell below community standards and expectations
(c) ...
(d) whether any findings flowing from (a), (b) above are attributable to the particular culture and governance practices of a financial services entity
(e) the effectiveness of mechanisms for redress for consumers of financial services who suffer detriment
(f) the adequacy of existing laws and policies, internal systems, and industry self-regulation to identify, regulate and address misconduct
(g) the effectiveness and ability of regulators of financial services entities to identify and address misconduct
....[30]

The Hayne Royal Commission commenced hearings in early 2018 and the behaviour revealed by it 'flabbergasted and horrified most sections of the Australian community'.[31]

The Final Report of the Commission was handed down on 1 February 2019.[32] It made 76 recommendations that were cross-referenced to the key issues it had sought to address. These key issues were:

- simplifying laws and removing exceptions (such as grandfathering) in current legislation/ regulation
- removing conflicts of interest
- improving the implementation of, and compliance with, regulation
- improving culture, governance and remuneration practices in financial entities
- increasing financial consumer protection.[33]

As regards the general regulation of financial services and markets, Davis commented that the recommendations reflect a more interventionist philosophy than has prevailed since the early 1980s in Australia. He pointed to several themes, such as the demise of the free market policy approach of relying on disclosure, education and advice for achieving good financial consumer outcomes; the increased need for formal regulation in response to the failings of reliance on self-regulation by industry and professional associations; and a shift towards greater reliance on 'black letter law' rather than a 'principles based' approach.[34] As regards the latter, the Hayne Report stated that law-makers 'should identify

30 *Royal Commission into Misconduct in the Banking, Superannuation and Financial Services Industry* (Letters Patent, 14 December 2017).

31 G Gilligan, 'The Hayne Royal Commission—Just Another Piece of Official Discourse?' (2019) 13(2-3) *Law and Financial Markets Review* 114, 116.

32 *Royal Commission into Misconduct in the Banking, Superannuation and Financial Services Industry* (Final Report, 4 February 2019) ('the Hayne Report').

33 Ibid 43–50, as summarised by K Davis, 'The Hayne Royal Commission and Financial Sector Misbehaviour: Lasting Change or Temporary Fix?' (2019) 30(2) *Economic and Labour Relations Review* 200, 210.

34 K Davis, 'The Hayne Royal Commission and Financial Sector Misbehaviour: Lasting Change or Temporary Fix?' (2019) 30(2) *Economic and Labour Relations Review* 200, 210.

expressly what fundamental norms of behaviour are being pursued when particular and detailed rules are made about a particular subject matter'.[35]

The Hayne Report was critical of the performance of the regulators, particularly ASIC,[36] and attributed some of the blame for financial sector misconduct upon ASIC's methods of enforcement; notably, its prevalent use of enforceable undertakings and negotiated settlements rather than prosecutions and litigation. It recommended that ASIC should adopt an approach to enforcement whereby, as its starting point, a court should determine the consequences of a contravention.[37] ASIC initially adopted this recommendation,[38] which it described as 'Why not litigate?',[39] but has since resiled from this approach. Enforcement in this area is discussed below at Section 17.40ff.

17.20.15 Licensing as a regulatory strategy

Licensing is used extensively to regulate the activities undertaken in the financial markets and financial services and it is worth examining how this strategy operates. In deciding to regulate any area of activity, there is a broad choice between two approaches: regulate after the event (ex post regulation), or before the event (*ex ante* regulation). Of course, it is possible to have a combination of these, but even a combined system will be oriented to one approach.

From a lawyer's point of view, the classic forms of ex post regulation are found in tort and contract law, which provide a system whereby people who suffer loss from the activity can claim damages for that loss.

Ex ante regulation seeks to either prevent or to constrain the activity before it occurs. There are many ways in which the state might choose to regulate financial markets from an *ex ante* perspective. For example, such regulation may be based on *registration*—anyone can operate a financial market, provided that beforehand they register details about themselves. This is a way of keeping track of who is operating in an area and collecting basic information about the activity or thing. There are no onerous prerequisite standards to being registered.

Another option is a system of *certification*, in which market operators who demonstrate certain standards of competence and performance are certified by a government agency or professional body. Certification systems usually do not prevent non-certified people from practicing—it is left to consumers to decide who they want to deal with. This is similar to lawyers who are credentialed to practise in certain areas; for example, accredited specialists in criminal law.

Licensing works by controlling entry into an area of practice; for example, operating a financial market or giving financial advice. No unlicensed person can operate in the area. It is the preferred strategy where close supervision of an activity is required and it allows

35 *Royal Commission into Misconduct in the Banking, Superannuation and Financial Services Industry* (Final Report, 4 February 2019) 496.

36 This sector is also regulated by the Australian Prudential Regulation Authority (APRA).

37 *Royal Commission into Misconduct in the Banking, Superannuation and Financial Services Industry* (Final Report, 4 February 2019) Recommendation 6.2, 446.

38 Australian Securities and Investments Commission, 'ASIC Update on Implementation of Royal Commission Recommendations' (Media Release 19-035MR, 19 February 2019).

39 Australian Securities and Investments Commission, *ASIC Enforcement Update—January to June 2019* (Report No 625, 18 August 2019) 1.

for tailor-made supervision. Each licence-holder is constrained not only by the general rules that apply to all licence-holders, but by specific conditions that are inserted in each particular licence.

Licensing seeks to impose minimum standards in an area of activity, so it controls entry. It also controls continuing behaviour of the licence-holder under the ultimate threat of withdrawal of the licence. But—and this is another reason why it is a favoured regulatory strategy—it is flexible. There are many sanctions that a regulator can impose that fall short of licence cancellation: demerit points (as with drivers licences), warnings, imposition of stricter licence conditions in particular cases, and temporary licence suspension.

17.20.20 The licensing system for financial markets

Part 7.2 of the *Corporations Act* contains a system for licensing financial markets.

The plenary obligation to be licensed arises from s 791A, which prohibits a person from operating a financial market unless they have an Australian market licence. It also prohibits a person from holding out that the person operates such a market.

The definition of the term 'financial market' is found in s 767A:

> **(1)** A *financial market* is a facility through which:
>
> **(a)** offers to acquire or dispose of financial products are regularly made or accepted; or
>
> **(b)** offers or invitations are regularly made to acquire or dispose of financial products that are intended to result or may reasonably result, directly or indirectly, in:
>
> **(i)** the making of offers to acquire or dispose of financial products; or
>
> **(ii)** the acceptance of such offers.
>
> ...

The definition of 'financial market' is deliberately broad for two reasons. First, the purpose of ch 7 is to provide a single set of rules for a wide variety of financial products and financial behaviour. The definition is designed to cover 'traditional' markets, such as the share market operated by ASX. It also covers derivative markets and any market for any type of financial product; hence, the importance of the definition of 'financial product'. The second reason for the broad definition is that the licensing strategy will only work if entry into an area of activity is effectively closed off to unlicensed operators. Note that, although the *Corporations Act* prohibits a person from operating a financial market unless they hold an Australian market licence, the market itself is not constituted by the Act. Therefore, for example, while ASX is a market operator and certain participants such as brokers are regulated under the Act, 'the market in which they operate is not a creature of the Act'.[40]

ASIC's Regulatory Guide 172 states how the definitions should apply.[41] ASIC states that it is more likely to have 'strong regulatory interest in a market venue' if it has 'one or

40 *RNB Equities Pty Ltd v Credit Suisse Investment Services (Australia) Ltd* (2019) 370 ALR 88 [60].

41 Australian Securities and Investments Commission, *Financial Markets: Domestic and Overseas Operators* (Regulatory Guide 172, 2 August 2022).

more of the features' that enable some or all of the terms of the agreement referred to in s 767A to 'occur by *means of* the facility'.[42]

Licensing financial markets: criteria

The general procedure for applying for an Australian market licence is found in s 795A. Generally, ASIC will grant a licence where the criteria provided for in s 795B are met. Some of the criteria are elementary or 'bedrock' characteristics of modern securities exchanges, so it is worth considering them from that perspective.

Adequate operating rules: s 795B(1)(c)

The body corporate seeking approval to operate a financial market under s 795A must have made or adopted operating rules pursuant to s 793A (which, in turn, refers to regs 7.2.07 and 7.2.08). Section 9 defines operating rules of a financial market to mean any rules (however described), including the market's listing rules (if any), which deal with the activities or conduct of the market or the activities or conduct of persons in relation to the market.

A 'fair, orderly and transparent' market: ss 795B(1)(c) and 792A

The three words should be considered together, and no one word should be taken out of context.[43] For an application and discussion of this criterion, see *Transmarket Trading Pty Ltd v Sydney Futures Exchange Ltd.*[44] The obligations of ASX as a market operator under s 792A are discussed in *ISignthis Ltd v ASX.*[45]

Clearing and settlement arrangements: s 795B(1)(e)

Section 768A defines a 'clearing and settlement facility' as a facility that provides a regular mechanism for the parties to financial transactions to meet the obligations to each other that arise from entering into the transactions and are prescribed by regulations. Helpfully, s 768A gives two examples that may be applied to securities and derivatives markets respectively:

> Example 1: A facility that provides a regular mechanism for stockbrokers to pay for the shares they buy and to be paid for the shares they sell, and for records of those transactions to be processed to facilitate registration of the new ownership of the shares ...
>
> Example 2: A facility that provides a regular mechanism for registering trade in derivatives on a futures markets and that enables the calculation of payments that market participants owe by way of margins ...

Compensation arrangements: s 795B(1)(f)

This refers to pt 7.5 of the *Corporations Act*. Section 881A states that licensed markets through which participants provide services for retail clients (this is a defined term that is

42 Ibid [RG 172.32] (emphasis added).

43 Explanatory Memorandum, Financial Services Reform Bill 2001 (Cth) [7.38].

44 *Transmarket Trading Pty Ltd v Sydney Futures Exchange Ltd* (2010) 188 FCR 1, 24 [90]ff, cited in *Re Citigroup* [2017] NSWSC 969.

45 *Isignthis Ltd v ASX Ltd* (2020) 143 ACSR 679.

discussed at Section 18.05.10) must have a compensation regime if the participant holds money or other property on behalf of the client. The losses to be covered are those suffered by a client due to defalcation or fraudulent misuse of funds or an authority. The compensation regime must provide recourse for clients where a securities or derivative contract is not performed or if the intermediary becomes insolvent. Where the defalcation occurs due to the acts of a stockbroker who is a member of ASX, compensation may be available through the National Guarantee Fund (NGF).[46]

Unacceptable control situation: s 795B(1)(g)

The *Corporations Act* puts a limit on the voting power that any one person can have in a body corporate that has an Australian market licence (or in a holding company of the licence holder). The limit is stipulated in s 850B and is set at 20 per cent of the voting power.

If the preconditions under s 795B are fulfilled then ASIC may grant an Australian market licence, but in making that decision, ASIC must also have regard to the matters in s 798A—these matters are predominantly of a macro-economic nature.

17.20.25 Supervision of financial markets

Once an Australian market licence is granted, a supervision regime comes into effect. ASIC must supervise the financial markets (s 798F) by making and enforcing the market integrity rules (*MIRs*) (s 798G). The relevant *MIRs* bind the market operators and the market participants (s 798H). The Australian market licensee has an obligation to assist ASIC in relation to the performance of ASIC's supervisory functions (s 792D).[47]

Operation of the market by ASX

ASX is a public company limited by shares. Its main activity is operating a financial market. That activity spans a number of functions—such as trading in derivatives, clearing, and settlement—but our focus is on the transfer of securities in the equity market. This market has three sets of players:

(1) the investors who purchase and sell the securities that are traded on the market
(2) the companies that are listed on the ASX, so their securities can be quoted[48] for the purposes of trading
(3) the brokers who deal in financial products. In ASX terms, this means they are either a market participant or an affiliate of a market participant. This is achieved by making an application to ASX. Under ASX's *Operating Rules* (*ORs*), a market participant must be either a corporation or a partnership.[49] The *ORs* are discussed below.

Only market participants can carry on the business of trading in the relevant ASX market. For the purposes of a financial market, 'participant' is defined in ss 767A(4)–(5) of the *Corporations Act* to mean a person who is allowed to directly participate in the

46 *Corporations Act* pt 7.5 div 4, ss 887A–891C.

47 *Isignthis Ltd v ASX Ltd* (2020) 143 ACSR 679.

48 When the securities are 'quoted', their prices are quoted on the relevant stock exchange. The company itself is *listed* on the stock exchange but the price of its shares (its securities) is *quoted*.

49 ASX, *Operating Rules* (at 19 February 2024) rr 1000, 1500.

market under the market's operating rules and includes a recognised affiliate. This means that only a market participant can place orders directly into the ASX trading system. Other people who are involved in the market, such as fund managers or private clients, must get access to the ASX trading system via a market participant.

In the last iteration of reforms to financial market regulation following the Wallis Report, a system of co-regulation between ASIC and ASX was put in place. However, since 2010, ASIC has taken a dominant role in supervising the markets. Nevertheless, as the holder of an Australian market licence, ASX has the obligation to ensure that its markets are fair, orderly and transparent. It has additional obligations to notify ASIC (s 792B), give it information (s 792C), and assist ASIC (s 792D) if a concern arises about, for example, a breach of the operating rules or if it takes disciplinary action against a market participant (s 792B).

The regime for regulating the market is through a system of rules with some statutory underpinning. The regime is characterised by public and private regulation, often in curious combinations. When considering the regulation, it is critical to note the preference for private regulation which informs many of the public incursions; for example, by the statute.

Rules: listing, operating and market integrity: description

We stated above at Section 17.20.20 that s 9 defines 'operating rules' of a financial market to include any rules, including the market's listing rules, made by the operator of the facility that deal with the activities or conduct of the market, or the activities or conduct of persons in relation to the market. One must exercise caution when looking at the obligations under various rules referred to in the *Corporations Act* and in the financial markets. There are three sets of rules which have effect in a financial market. The following discussion predominantly uses ASX to exemplify the ambit of the relevant rules.

(1) *Market Integrity Rules (MIRs)*: these are made by ASIC, arising from ASIC's status as regulator of financial markets (s 798G). They provide a common set of rules that apply to all market operators, such as ASX, and their participants in the securities market[50] and, separately, in the futures markets.[51]
(2) *Listing Rules (LRs)*:[52] these are made by ASX and govern listed companies; namely, their admission to and continued inclusion in the market operated by ASX.
(3) *Operating Rules (ORs)*[53] (formerly known as the *Market Rules*): these are made by ASX and govern the actions of the brokers who are participants in the market. This is a narrower body of rules than the legal definition of 'operating rules' in s 9, and

50 Australian Securities and Investments Commission, *Market Integrity Rules (Securities Markets)* (2017); Australian Securities and Investments Commission, *Guidance on ASIC Market Integrity Rules for Participants of Securities Markets* (Regulatory Guide 265, 2 August 2022).

51 Australian Securities and Investments Commission, *Market Integrity Rules (Futures Markets)* (2017); Australian Securities and Investments Commission, *Guidance on ASIC Market Integrity Rules for Participants of Futures Markets* (Regulatory Guide 266, 2 August 2022).

52 ASX, *Listing Rules* (at 19 December 2016).

53 ASX, *Operating Rules* (at 19 February 2024).

this is the meaning that will be adopted when the words '*Operating Rules*' or '*ORs*' are used in this chapter. The definition in s 9 refers to both the *ORs* and the *LRs*.

Rules: listing, operating and market integrity: legal effect

The rules have differing legal effects and represent choices made by the legislature and market actors to create a spectrum of obligations ranging from clear statutory obligations to private contractual arrangements, with various hybrids in between.

In relation to the *MIRs*, the *Corporations Act* places a clear statutory obligation upon the operators of and the participants in licensed markets to comply with the *MIRs* (s 798H). By comparison, under s 793B(1) of the *Corporations Act*:

> The operating rules (other than listing rules) of a licensed market have effect as a contract under seal:
>
> **(a)** between the licensee and each participant in the market; and
>
> **(b)** between a participant and each other participant;
>
> ...

Under this contract, each of these persons agrees to observe the *ORs* to the extent they apply to the person and to engage in conduct as required by the operating rules.[54]

The legal effect of the *LRs* is essentially contractual but with some 'statutory recognition' under s 793C of the *Corporations Act*. The rules may be implied into contracts for the sale and purchase of securities and derivatives on the relevant market (see Section 18.15.15).

There may be overlaps between the rules, especially between the *MIRs* and the *ORs*. Where an inconsistency arises, the *MIRs* prevail (s 798H(3)).

Rules: listing, operating and market integrity: enforcement

The *MIRs* are enforced by ASIC, primarily through the Markets Disciplinary Panel (MDP).[55] The MDP is a peer review panel that consists of industry experts. Sitting panels of the MDP make decisions about whether infringement notices should be issued for alleged contraventions of the market integrity rules.[56] Part 7.2A of the *Corporations Act* establishes what may be described as an administrative or public scheme of enforcement, which includes enforceable undertakings (s 798K) and civil penalty proceedings (s 1317E).

The *ORs* may be enforced by ASX in internal disciplinary proceedings. In this respect, ASX acts like a domestic tribunal. The procedures are detailed in the *ASX Enforcement and Appeals Rulebook*. This is discussed below.

The *LRs* may be enforced by ASIC or by ASX; for example, by suspending trading in shares or delisting a company. The enforcement of the *LRs* gives rise to complex legal questions that are discussed below.

54 See generally *Transmarket Trading Pty Ltd v Sydney Futures Exchange Ltd* (2010) 188 FCR 1.

55 The composition of the panel and its procedures are explained in Australian Securities and Investments Commission, *Markets Disciplinary Panel* (Regulatory Guide 216, 21 January 2021).

56 Ibid [RG 216.1].

17.20.30 Content of the ASX *Operating Rules*

The *ORs* govern the relationship between brokers and ASX.[57] The ASX *ORs* deal with the conduct of a broker's business to ensure that a market participant has adequate resources and processes to comply with its obligations under the rules (OR 1000); establishing requirements as to the keeping of records (OR 6700); detailing the means of effecting transactions upon the ASX trading platform (for example, priority of orders (OR 4030); the procedures for crossing orders (OR 4060); engaging in principal trading (OR 1001)); and the timing of settlement applicable to such transactions (OR 3600).

A market participant must at all times continue to satisfy the admission requirements; comply with any condition that ASX has imposed on the market participant under the *ORs*; and comply with the rules, directions, decisions and requirements of ASX (OR 1400). A market participant is responsible for all actions and omissions of its employees (OR 6500).

ASX powers with respect to breach of the operating rules

As stated above, ASIC plays a major role in disciplining market participants by enforcing the *MIRs* through the MDP. Nevertheless, ASX retains wide powers to sanction market participants who have contravened the *ORs*. ASX's powers are exercised through the *ASX Enforcement and Appeals Rulebook*.[58] ASX may take disciplinary action against a regulated person if it considers that they have contravened the *ORs*. ASX has various powers under the *ASX Enforcement and Appeals Rulebook*; for example, to censure the market participant, impose a monetary penalty, or suspend a person's role as a regulated person of that market participant for a period.

Although there are some express statements in the *ASX Enforcement and Appeals Rulebook* that refer to procedural fairness,[59] there is some uncertainty whether ASX must afford procedural fairness to market participants when exercising its powers under the *ORs*. On balance, we suggest that it must, considering (by analogy) the case law which indicates that, prima facie, ASX is obliged to provide procedural fairness under the *LRs*.[60]

Although the *ORs* govern the relationship between brokers and ASX, this is not the only way in which the conduct of brokers is regulated. There is also a body of fiduciary law and other general legal principles that govern the relationship between brokers and their clients. This is discussed in Chapter 18.

17.20.35 The content of the ASX *Listing Rules*

In order for a stock exchange, such as ASX, to function as the provider of an efficient market for securities, companies must first seek listing on the exchange so that their

57 ASX, *Operating Rules* (at 19 February 2024).

58 ASX, *ASX Enforcement and Appeals Rulebook* (at 24 December 2015) r 2.2.

59 For example, r 3.6.5 states that '[a]n Appeal Tribunal will determine each matter on its own merits and must conduct the proceedings without bias and must observe the rules of procedural fairness': ASX, *ASX Enforcement and Appeals Rulebook* (at 24 December 2015) r 3.6.5.

60 *Hampton Hill Mining NL v ASX Ltd* [2020] WASC 86. See also *Reynolds & Co Pty Ltd v Australian Stock Exchange Ltd* (2003) 21 ACLC 608, where Campbell J considered the constitution of ASX required it to act fairly.

shares can be quoted and traded on the market. This depends on the company's decision to rely on public issuing and trading of securities as a means of raising capital, to use the facility of the stock exchange to implement this strategy, and on ASX agreeing to list the company and to quote its securities. The *LRs* are the main device by which a market operator such as ASX can regulate the conduct of listed companies on the stock exchange. ASX's discretion in relation to the operation of the *LRs* is discussed below.

The Introduction to the *LRs* states as follows:

> ASX's Listing Rules govern the admission of entities to the official list, quotation of securities, suspension of securities from quotation and removal of entities from the official list. They also govern disclosure and some aspects of a listed entity's conduct.
>
> An entity applying to be admitted to the ASX official list signs an agreement to comply with the Listing Rules, as in force from time to time. This applies even if the quotation of its securities is deferred, suspended or subject to a trading halt.[61]

An overview of the listing requirements

The principles on which the *LRs* are based are set out in the Introduction. These principles include the following:

- a company should satisfy appropriate minimum standards of quality, size and operations before it is admitted to the official list
- securities should have rights and obligations attaching to them that are fair to new and existing security holders
- timely disclosure should be made of information which may have a material effect on the price or value of an entity's securities
- an entity should disclose information about its corporate governance practices and explain any departure from generally accepted standards of good corporate governance
- certain significant transactions should require security holder approval.[62]

By way of overview, the *LRs* can be seen to perform three main roles:

(1) controlling entry into the stock market
(2) continuing requirements to maintain listing
(3) regulating the supply of information.

Controlling entry into the stock market

There are rules that set prerequisites for admission to the official list and for quotation of securities on ASX. These rules set minimum standards for the size of the company, its profit from ongoing activities or net tangible assets, the size of its total shareholding,

61 ASX, *Listing Rules* (at 19 December 2016) Introduction.
62 Ibid.

and so on. For example, in LR 1.2.4 there is a profit test that states that the entity's aggregated profit from continuing operations for the last three full financial years must have been at least $1 million. Listing Rule 1.3.1 has an assets test: at the time of admission, the entity must have net tangible assets of at least $4 million or a market capitalisation of at least $15 million. Listing Rule 1.1 Condition 8 sets tests for the dispersion of shareholders in the company that is seeking to be listed; for example, there must be at least 300 holders each having a parcel of the main class of securities with a value of at least $2,000.

Chapter 6 of the *LRs* deals with the nature of the securities that a company seeks to have quoted. Listing Rule 6.2 requires listed companies to have only one class of ordinary securities unless ASX approves additional classes. Shares in this main class are usually fully paid, although ASX can approve the creation of additional classes of partly paid shares. Listing Rules 6.8 and 6.9 prescribe that each fully paid ordinary security must have one vote—on a show of hands, each holder has one vote, and on a poll each holder has one vote per fully paid security.

Continuing requirements to maintain listing

These requirements apply for a company to maintain its listing. The requirements include rules which relate to the conduct of company meetings, the appointment and conduct of directors, and trading in the company's securities.

For example, ch 10 of the *LRs* regulates related party transactions—transactions between an entity and persons who are in a position to influence the entity. Some examples are the acquisitions by directors of the company's securities, payments to directors, and termination benefits for officers.

Chapter 17 of the *LRs* deals with trading halts, suspension of quotation of securities, and removal from the official list. For example, under LR 17.1, ASX may grant a trading halt at the request of an entity. This may occur in the lead up to a major announcement by a listed company. A trading halt can occur for up to two trading days. ASX may also suspend quotation of listed company's securities, either at the company's request (LR 17.2) or as required by ASX (LR 17.3).

Regulating supply of information

Broadly, we can distinguish between three types of corporate disclosure:

(1) Periodic disclosure: annual, half-yearly or quarterly reporting, usually via audited accounts
(2) Continuous or contemporaneous disclosure: a continuing or 'background' obligation to report events as they occur
(3) Special occasion disclosure: the obligation to disclose information during special transactions; for example, takeovers and fundraising by initial public offers.

The regime for periodic disclosure is discussed next. The continuous disclosure regime is discussed below at Section 17.20.45. The disclosure regimes that apply to takeovers and fundraising are dealt with respectively in Chapters 19 and 9.

17.20.40 Periodic disclosure

Listed companies are subject to periodic disclosure under ch 4 of the *LRs*. For example, listed companies must prepare a half-yearly report for ASX as well as their financial reporting requirements under the *Corporations Act*. Of increasing significance is the obligation of listed companies to report on their corporate governance practices. Listing Rule 4.10.3 states that an entity must include a corporate governance statement in its annual report or on its web page that discloses the extent to which the entity has followed the recommendations set by the ASX Corporate Governance Council ('the Council') during the reporting period.[63] If the entity has not followed all of the recommendations, the entity must identify those recommendations that have not been followed and 'what (if any) alternative governance practices it adopted in lieu of the recommendation during that period'.[64] This is known as a 'comply or explain', or an 'if not, why not' disclosure requirement. Examples of recommendations that are set by the Council include recognised good corporate governance practices such as ensuring that the majority of board members and the chair are independent directors, as well as the establishment of remuneration and audit committees.[65] The Council also recommends that listed companies have a diversity policy that requires the board to set measurable objectives and report on the progress in achieving them. The company should disclose the proportion of women on the board, in senior executive positions, and across the whole workforce. For S&P/ASX 300 companies, the measurable objective for achieving gender diversity is 30 per cent of each gender.[66]

The best practice recommendations set by the Council do not have any legal status, therefore a failure to comply with the recommendations has no immediate legal consequence. However, a failure to include a statement that discloses the extent to which the entity has followed the recommendations is potentially a breach of LR 4.10. The consequences of such a breach are discussed below.

More importantly, the disclosures made under LR 4.10 allow for a wider debate regarding corporate governance and diversity on corporate boards.[67] Therefore, it may be argued that the broader reputational effects of disclosure are more important than the legal consequences.[68]

17.20.45 Continuous disclosure

Listed companies are subject to a continuing obligation to disclose matters that have a material effect on the price of securities under ch 3 of the *LRs*. The concept of continuous

63 ASX Corporate Governance Council, *Corporate Governance Principles and Recommendations* (4th ed, February 2019).

64 ASX, *Listing Rules* (at 1 December 2019) LR 4.10.3.

65 For a detailed discussion of the *Corporate Governance Principles and Recommendations*, see Section 10.10.05.

66 ASX Corporate Governance Council, *Corporate Governance Principles and Recommendations* (4th ed, February 2019) Recommendation 1.5.

67 P Spender, 'Gender Quotas on Boards—Is It Time for Australia to Lean In?' (2015) 20(1) *Deakin Law Review*; P Spender, 'Gender Diversity on Boards in Australia—Waiting for the Great Leap Forward?' (2012) 27(1) *Australian Journal of Corporate Law* 22.

68 A Klettner, 'Corporate Governance Codes and Gender Diversity: Management-Based Regulation in Action' (2016) 39(2) *University of New South Wales Law Journal* 715.

disclosure incorporates two principal elements. 'Disclosure' encompasses the fundamental notion that companies should disclose information that is materially likely to affect the value of securities or influence investment decisions. 'Continuous' imports a temporal element, reflecting not only that the obligation is unremitting, but that it must be timely and must occur as and when the information comes into the possession of the entity. For example, BHP was obliged to immediately disclose to the market the collapse of a dam in San Marco in Brazil in 2015 that BHP ran as a joint venture. The collapse resulted in loss of life and severe environmental damage to several Brazilian villages.[69] Chapter 3 of the *LRs* incorporates elements of the efficient market hypothesis that is discussed above at Section 17.10.05. In order for the markets to achieve maximum efficiency, all material information must be supplied to the market.[70] It also complements the prohibitions on insider trading, which are discussed below. The policy is that all material information be made public immediately so that opportunities to trade on private information are minimised.

Listing Rule 3.1 states as follows:

> Once an entity is or becomes aware of any information concerning it that a reasonable person would expect to have a material effect on the price or value of the entity's securities, the entity must immediately tell ASX that information.[71]

This rule is qualified by LR 3.1A, which contains a number of exceptions to the continuous disclosure obligation:

> **3.1A**
>
> Listing Rule 3.1 does not apply to particular information while each of the following is satisfied in relation to the information:
>
> **3.1A.1**
>
> One or more of the following 5 situations applies:
>
> **(h)** It would be a breach of a law to disclose the information;
>
> **(i)** The information concerns an incomplete proposal or negotiation;
>
> **(j)** The information comprises matters of supposition or is insufficiently definite to warrant disclosure;
>
> **(k)** The information is generated for the internal management purposes of the entity; or
>
> **(l)** The information is a trade secret; and
>
> **3.1A.2**
>
> The information is confidential and ASX has not formed the view that the information has ceased to be confidential; and

69 *Impiombato v BHP Group Ltd (No 2)* [2020] FCA 1720 [3]–[8], upheld by the High Court in *BHP Group Ltd v Impiombato* (2022) 276 CLR 611, [45].

70 For a critique, see G North, 'Listed Company Disclosure and Financial Market Transparency: Is This a Battle Worth Fighting or Merely Policy and Regulatory Mantra?' (2014) 4 *Journal of Business Law* 484.

71 ASX, *Listing Rules* (at 5 June 2021) LR 3.1. For examples where disclosure is or is not required under LR 3.1, see ASX, *Continuous Disclosure: Listing Rules 3.1–3.1B* (Guidance Note 8, May 2024).

> **3.1A.3**
> A reasonable person would not expect the information to be disclosed.

Listing Rule 3.1 is complemented by LR 3.1B, which applies if ASX considers that there is or is likely to be a false market in an entity's securities. If ASX asks the entity to give the information to correct or prevent a false market, the entity must immediately give ASX that information.

The word 'immediately' in LR 3.1 and LR 3.1B has been interpreted by ASX to mean 'promptly and without delay', rather than 'instantaneously'.[72] ASX recognises that a period of time will necessarily elapse between the time when an entity first becomes obliged to give information to ASX and when it is able to provide the information in the form of a market announcement. Therefore, 'the question in each case is whether the entity is going about this process as quickly as it can in the circumstances (acting promptly) and not deferring, postponing or putting it off to a later time (acting without delay)'.[73]

The obligation of listed companies to give disclosure under LR 3.1 is underwritten by ch 6CA of the *Corporations Act*. Section 674 applies where a listed disclosing entity is bound by a disclosure requirement in the listing rules of a market. Section 674(2) states that the obligation:

> **(a)** applies to a listed disclosing entity; and
> **(b)** the entity has information that [the listing rule] provisions require the entity to notify to the market operator; and
> **(c)** the information is not generally available; and
> **(d)** a reasonable person would expect, if it were generally available, to have a material effect on the price or value of ED securities of the entity.

If these conditions are met, the entity must notify the market operator of that information in accordance with those provisions.

Chapter 6CA was amended in 2021.[74] Prior to the 2021 amendments, s 674 was often used by plaintiff litigants in securities class actions alleging contravention of the continuous disclosure requirements. Parliament considered that an imbalance had arisen between the benefits to the market of continuous disclosure and the costs imposed on entities and officers.[75] The 2021 amendments inserted s 674A which replicates s 674 but adds a qualifier in s 674A(2) that the entity knows, or is reckless or negligent with respect to the information.[76] The change was subject an independent review conducted in 2024. The review concluded that the changes be retained 'for the time being' and that they had had little, if any, impact on the number and types of continuous disclosure

72 ASX, *Continuous Disclosure: Listing Rules 3.1–3.1B* (Guidance Note 8, May 2024) [4.5].
73 Ibid.
74 *Treasury Laws Amendment (2021 Measures No 1) Act 2021* (Cth).
75 Explanatory Memorandum, Treasury Laws Amendment (2021 Measures No 1) Bill 2021 (Cth) [2.8].
76 See M Duffy, 'Takeovers and Public Securities: Modifications to Continuous Disclosure Requirements and the Role of Corporate Knowledge, Intent, Recklessness and Negligence in Breaches: A Discussion (2021) 38(2) *Company and Securities Law Journal* 138.

class actions.[77] The remedies for breach of ss 674 and 674A are discussed at Section 17.20.50.

Note that the term 'ED securities' is defined in s 111AD of the *Corporations Act*. ED stands for 'enhanced disclosure' securities and includes the securities of a listed company. Where a body is included in the official list of prescribed financial markets, the securities issued by that body are ED securities (s 111AE).

It is noteworthy that ss 674 and 674A do not create an independent statutory obligation for companies to give continuous disclosure. Rather, the obligation it creates is predicated upon a pre-existing obligation under LR 3.1 and its equivalents. Persons such as directors and officers may be involved in the contravention of a company's obligations in ch 6CA. This is discussed below at Section 17.20.50.

For the purposes of ss 674 and 674A, the term 'generally available' is defined in s 676. This term will be discussed in more detail below in the related insider trading provisions at Section 17.30.10. Sections 674, 674A and LR 3.1 each refer to information that has 'material effect' on price or value. This phrase is defined in s 677:

> For the purposes of sections 674 and 675, a reasonable person would be taken to expect information to have a material effect on the price or value of ED securities of a disclosing entity if the information would, or would be likely to, influence persons who commonly invest in securities in deciding whether to acquire or dispose of the ED securities.

Listing Rule 3.1 and s 674 were considered by the New South Wales Court of Appeal in *James Hardie Industries NV v Australian Securities and Investments Commission* ('*James Hardie*').[78] In that case, the appellant, James Hardie Industries NV ('JHINV'), was part of a corporate group. Another company in the group, JHI, had previously been a long-term manufacturer of asbestos products and had incurred significant liability for asbestos claims by people exposed to its products. The appellant had experienced difficulties in securing funding in the past due to its connection with JHI and the manufacture of asbestos. Various managers involved in the group devised a plan to separate the companies involved in the manufacture of asbestos from the rest of the group to, inter alia, make it easier for JHINV to secure future funding. In 2001, the appellant owned some partly-paid shares in JHI. In March 2003, the appellant's partly-paid shares in JHI were cancelled and ownership of JHI (which had since been renamed ABN 60 Pty Ltd) was transferred to a foundation, which was independent of the appellant. A deed was executed under which ABN 60 Pty Ltd indemnified the appellant against asbestos claims (the deed of indemnity). The separation of the appellant from ABN 60 Pty Ltd was completed by 14 April 2003. At this time, the appellant formed the view that

77 K Lewis, *Report of the Independent Review of the Changes to the Continuous Disclosure LawsMade by the Tresury Laws Amendment (2021 Measures No 1) Act 2021* (Australian Government, The Treasury, February 2024) 21. For an example of class action litigation pleading s 674A, see *Jowene Pty Ltd atf Biro Citer Souvenirs Pty Ltd Pension Fund v Downer EDI Ltd* [2023] FCA 924.

78 *James Hardie Industries NV v Australian Securities and Investments Commission* (2010) 81 ACSR 1. The *James Hardie* proceedings in the High Court did not discuss the company's liability for breaches of its continuous disclosure obligations: see Section 11.15.05 that discusses some of the history of the *James Hardie* litigation.

announcing the transaction would not affect the price of its shares and also would not affect any decision by persons who commonly invest whether or not to buy or sell them.

On 15 May 2003, the appellant disclosed to the market that it no longer owned shares in ABN 60 Pty Ltd. However, no reference was made in the announcement to the deed of indemnity. The complete separation arrangements—the cancellation of the partly paid shares and the deed of indemnity—were not disclosed until the release of the appellant's annual report on 30 June 2003.

The question for the Court was whether the relevant officers had breached LR 3.1 and s 674 of the *Corporations Act* by failing to disclose the complete separation arrangements.

The New South Wales Court of Appeal found that s 674 is remedial legislation that is intended to enhance the public interest and protect individual investors. It should be construed beneficially so as to give the fullest relief which the fair meaning of its language will allow.[79] The Court considered that any matter that affects a company's borrowing capacity will invariably have an effect on the company's share price. The Court found that the appellant well understood the connection between its ability to source finance at competitive levels and the confidence of investors in the market. Investor concern about the appellant's residual exposure to asbestos-related liability, arising because of its connection with ABN 60 Pty Ltd, were well known in the market and it was open to the trial judge to draw an inference that the association with ABN 60 Pty Ltd could have had a depressing effect on the appellant's shares.[80]

The effect of the separation arrangements was to completely dispose of the ongoing asbestos liabilities. Accordingly, the information about the separation arrangements was likely to have a material effect on the price or value of the appellant's securities.[81] Information about the deed of indemnity was material for the purposes of s 674 and the disclosure by the appellant on 15 May 2003 was insufficient to satisfy its statutory obligation under that provision because it omitted the material information about the deed of indemnity.[82] The Court also noted that evidence of the market's reaction to the release of information may be relevant as a cross-check as to the reasonableness of an ex ante judgment about that information.[83]

The Full Federal Court in *Grant-Taylor v Babcock & Brown Ltd (in liq)*[84] ('*Grant-Taylor*') provided further guidance on the interpretation of ss 674 and 677. The case concerned several types of information, but one was the payment of a dividend out of capital.[85] The Court considered that the information did not have the requisite 'material effect' because it was a mere technical breach when considering the circumstances of the

79 Ibid [356]. See also S Lombard and J Viven, 'Continuous Disclosure and Good Faith' (2014) 32(6) *Company and Securities Law Journal* 419.

80 *James Hardie Industries NV v Australian Securities and Investments Commission* (2010) 81 ACSR 1 [493], [497], [503], [530].

81 Ibid [539], [540], [547], [548].

82 Ibid [549].

83 Ibid [533]–[537].

84 *Grant-Taylor v Babcock & Brown Ltd (in liq)* (2016) 245 FCR 402.

85 Traditionally, in company law, dividends could only be paid out of profit, otherwise they were regarded as an impermissible reduction of capital. Up until 2010, this formulation was stated in the *Corporations Act*: see generally Section 8.30.05.

Babcock group. The information about the dividend did not have any economic significance[86] and did not need to be disclosed principally because it had no financial consequence for the value of Babcock shares.[87] The Court considered that 'material effect' in s 674(2) refers to information that is nontrivial and it may be necessary to balance the indicated probability that the event will occur with the anticipated magnitude of the event on the company's affairs.[88]

The Court in *Grant-Taylor* also considered the meaning of the term 'commonly invest in securities' in s 677 and held that it is a class term that refers to frequent and infrequent investors (for example, self-funded retirees) and sophisticated and unsophisticated investors (for example, those who have an occasional interest in investing). The Court also found that the word 'securities' in s 677 is not confined to listed securities.[89]

In some circumstances, it will be necessary for a company to make corrective statements under s 674 where a previous statement may have misled the market. This issue was discussed by the Full Federal Court in *Australian Securities and Investments Commission v Fortescue Metals Group Ltd.*[90] The Full Federal Court judgment was overturned by the High Court on different grounds in *Forrest v Australian Securities and Investments Commission.*[91]

Mr Forrest was the Chair and CEO of Fortescue Metals Group Ltd (FMG). In early 2004, FMG and Forrest entered into negotiations with three Chinese companies in relation to the construction of a mine in the Pilbara region, a port at Port Hedland and a railway which would connect the port to the mine. Between August and November 2004, FMG entered into several 'framework agreements' with the three Chinese companies to build and finance the mine, the railway, and the port. During this period, FMG provided information to ASX via letters and media releases where the framework agreements were described as 'binding agreements'.

In March 2006, ASIC commenced proceedings, alleging that FMG had (inter alia) engaged in misleading or deceptive conduct in contravention of s 1041H of the *Corporations Act* by falsely representing that the framework agreements were binding. In turn, ASIC alleged that these contraventions established that FMG had contravened its obligations under s 674 of the *Corporations Act.*

The Full Federal Court held that there was not an enforceable agreement between FMG and the three Chinese companies to build the infrastructure for the project. Therefore, FMG's announcements about the framework agreements contravened

86 (2016) 245 FCR 402, 405 [11].

87 Ibid [149], [153].

88 Ibid [96].

89 See JM Cheyne, 'Babcock & Brown's Last Hurrah: The Latest on Dividends and Continuous Disclosure' (2016) 34(7) *Company and Securities Law Journal* 543. For an interesting and accessible case that follows *Grant-Taylor* and explains the operation of the continuous disclosure regime (including ss 674 and 677), see *Australia and New Zealand Banking Group Ltd v Australian Securities and Investments Commission* (2024) 305 FCR 383.

90 *Australian Securities and Investments Commission v Fortescue Metals Group Ltd* (2011) 190 FCR 364.

91 *Forrest v Australian Securities and Investments Commission* (2012) 247 CLR 486.

s 1041H of the *Corporations Act*.[92] As FMG made misleading statements about the framework agreements, s 674 of the *Corporations Act* required it to correct them. FMG's failure to do so constituted a contravention of s 674 of the *Corporations Act*.[93]

Upon appeal, the High Court held that the statements made by FMG were not misleading and deceptive. The intended audience of the statements were investors and perhaps some wider section of the commercial or business community.[94] The target audience was not misled by the statements that the agreements were 'binding', therefore the announcements were not misleading and deceptive and ASIC's argument about the need for FMG to subsequently correct them by a s 674 disclosure was irrelevant.[95]

17.20.50 Remedies for breach of the continuous disclosure obligations

A failure to comply with s 674(2) is an offence under s 1311(1) and empowers ASIC to issue an infringement notice to the disclosing entity,[96] but since the 2021 amendments, the provision is not a civil penalty provision.[97] Conversely, s 674A does not create an offence but an alleged breach of this provision many lead to a civil penalty[98] and compensation proceedings.[99]

Private enforcement of the continuous disclosure obligation is still available in Australia via securities class actions, but it has allegedly become harder to prove because s 674A requires the plaintiff to prove that the entity knew or was reckless or negligent with respect to the information. Private enforcement and securities class actions are discussed further at Section 17.40.10 below.

A person who is involved in a listed company's contravention of s 674A(2) may also contravene the subsection and be exposed to a civil penalty (s 674A(3)).[100] However, a person does not contravene s 674A(3) if they prove they took reasonable steps to ensure that the entity complied with its obligations: s 674A(4). Directors may be liable for a breach of their duty under s 180 if they are involved in an entity's contravention of ch 6CA.[101]

---

92 *Australian Securities and Investments Commission v Fortescue Metals Group Ltd* (2011) 190 FCR 364 [177], [202], [215], [218].

93 Ibid [181], [189], [202], [215], [218].

94 *Forrest v Australian Securities and Investments Commission* (2012) 247 CLR 486 [38]. The High Court test for the intended audience was applied by Nicholas J in the Federal Court in *Australian Securities and Investments Commission v Vocation Ltd (in liq)* (2019) 371 ALR 155.

95 See C Di Lernia, 'Odyssey through a Forest? Continuous Disclosure and the Need for Practical Guidance' (2012) 40(6) *Australian Business Law Review* 424.

96 *Corporations Act* s 1317DAC.

97 It is not listed in the table in s 1317E(3).

98 It is listed in the table in s 1317E(3).

99 See s 1317HA. Previous case law on the operation of civil penalties for ch 6CA will be persuasive: see *Australian Securities and Investments Commission v Southcorp Ltd (No 2)* (2003) 130 FCR 406; *Australian Securities and Investments Commission v Chemeq Ltd* (2006) 58 ACSR 169. For a discussion of civil penalties under the *Corporations Act*, see Section 1.65.05.

100 See, eg, *Australian Securities and Investments Commission v Padbury Mining Ltd* (2016) 116 ACSR 208.

101 *Australian Securities and Investments Commission v Vocation Ltd (in liq)* (2019) 371 ALR 155; *Australian Securities and Investments Commission v GetSwift Ltd* [2021] FCA 1384; see also Chapter 11 on the duty of care, skill and diligence.

17.20.55 The legal nature of the listing relationship

In the introduction to the *LRs*, ASX reserves to itself an absolute discretion in administering the *LRs*:

> ASX has an absolute discretion concerning the admission of an entity to, or its removal from, the official list and the quotation or suspension of its securities. ... In exercising these discretions, ASX takes into account ... the principles on which the Listing Rules are based and the imperative of maintaining reputation, integrity and efficiency of the ASX market.[102]

ASX may waive compliance with a *LR* if it wishes to do so.[103]

What is the legal status of the *LRs*? As a formality, recall that the *LRs* come within the definition of 'operating rules' of a financial market under s 9, meaning:

> any rules ... including the market's listing rules (if any) that are made by the operator of the market, or contained in the operator's constitution, that deal with:
>
> **(i)** the activities or conduct of the market; or
>
> **(ii)** the activities or conduct of persons in relation to the market.

'Listing rules' of a financial market is also defined in s 9 as follows:

> *Listing rules* ... means any rules ... that are made by the operator of the market, or contained in the operator's constitution, and that deal with:
>
> **(a)** admitting entities to, or removing entities from, the market's official list, whether for the purpose of enabling financial products of those entities to be traded on the market or for other purposes; or
>
> **(b)** the activities or conduct of entities that are included on that list.

Because of their status as 'operating rules' under the *Corporations Act*, amendments to the *LRs* are subject to disallowance by ASIC. ASIC may disallow the whole or a specified part of an amendment within 28 days of the receipt of notice of the amendment.[104] As a consequence of this disallowance power, the amendments to the *LRs* are generally made public and debated for some time.

Although the amendment of the *LRs* is subject to disallowance by ASIC, the *LRs* are prescribed by a non-government body, therefore do not have the force of legislation. As ASX recognises, its regulatory power over listed companies is based on the contractual agreement that each company enters into by agreeing to be bound by and to comply with the *LRs*. The *LRs* now contain an express promise by listed companies to comply.[105] However, the *LRs* are enforceable against listed entities and their associates under ss 793C and 1101B of the *Corporations Act*. This potentially leads to an issue about the public enforcement of private rules.

102 ASX, *Listing Rules* (at 19 December 2016) Introduction.

103 ASX, *Waivers and In-Principle Advice* (Guidance Note 17, 12 November 2021).

104 *Corporations Act* s 793E.

105 ASX, *Listing Rules* (at 1 December 2019) r 18.6.

The main provision in the *Corporations Act* that regulates the listing relationship is s 793C. This section deals with both the enforcement of and compliance with the *LRs* and the *ORs* because it refers to 'operating rules' which under s 9 includes the *LRs* and *ORs*. In brief, s 793C allows the court to make an order concerning compliance with or enforcement of the rules, upon the application of ASIC, the licensee (usually ASX), or a person who is aggrieved by the non-compliance or non-enforcement of the rules.[106] Pursuant to s 793C(5), a person who holds financial products of a body corporate that are able to be traded on the market (for example, a shareholder) is taken to be a person aggrieved by the failure to comply with or enforce the provisions of the operating rules of the market.

Sections 793C and 110B (discussed below) have been described as 'enabling provisions' that are supplementary to the powers given by the *LRs* to the stock exchange itself. They are not a restraint upon ASX's power.[107]

The judicial interpretation of s 793C and the listing relationship

To understand the effect of s 793C, it is necessary to consider the cases decided under the forerunners of the current provision. As we will see, the courts have adopted a relatively hands-off approach to the interpretation of these sections. The listing contract lies at the core of the relationship, but the courts are usually unwilling to fetter the discretion of the market operator, which is usually ASX. We analyse public law initiatives to challenge ASX decisions below at Section 17.20.60.

When examining the case law and the statutory provisions regarding the *LRs*, it is important to note that the *LRs* state they are to be interpreted:

- in accordance with their spirit, intention and purpose;
- by looking beyond form to substance; and
- in a way that best promotes the principles on which they are based.[108]

One early provision was s 31 of the *Securities Industry Act 1975* (Vic). *Repco Ltd v Bartdon Pty Ltd*[109] ('*Repco*') was decided under that section. The case involved an action against three companies: a listed company and two unlisted companies that were shareholders of the listed company (one was a foreign company and the other a private company). The two shareholding companies were proposing to take effective control of the listed company because of the size of their shareholdings and the existence of shareholder voting agreements between them. The complaint was that this was in breach of certain *LRs* then in force. Repco sought an order for compliance. Repco was a bidder in a takeover and the voting agreements would effectively block the takeover.

Section 31 of the *Securities Industry Act 1975* (Vic) provided a remedy against a person 'under an *obligation* to observe, enforce or give effect to the *LRs* and if they fail to do so, then a person who is aggrieved by that failure may seek a court order'. Therefore, it was necessary for the Victorian Court of Appeal to determine the nature

106 See *Melbourne City Investments Pty Ltd v WorleyParsons Ltd (No 2)* (2014) 104 ACSR 15.
107 *Isignthis Ltd v ASX Ltd* (2020) 143 ACSR 679, [22].
108 ASX, *Listing Rules* (at 1 December 2016) r 19.2.
109 *Repco Ltd v Bartdon Pty Ltd* [1981] VR 1.

of this obligation. The Court noted that the only companies against which an order for compliance could be made were those that had an *obligation* to observe, enforce or give effect to the *LRs*. The Court assumed that the listed company was so obliged, but what about the other companies?

The Court held that such an obligation could only arise by statute or contract, and there was nothing in the statute that created such an obligation to comply. On a proper interpretation, s 31 implied a pre-existing obligation. Although listed companies *may* have been under a contractual obligation to observe the *LRs*, the Act did not contemplate that the *LRs* would impose obligations on anyone other than listed companies.

Implicit in their Honours' analysis is the doctrine of privity of contract. If the nature of the obligation to observe the *LRs* was derived from contract, then an unlisted company—for example, an unlisted subsidiary—that was not privy to the contract could not be subject to this obligation. It had no contractual relationship with the stock exchange to observe the *LRs*.

An important point that emerges from the judgment is that there was no intention in the section to give statutory effect or statutory force to the *LRs*. As the Court stated, 'they are drafted in the language of commerce rather than of law'.[110]

Another case decided under a forerunner to s 793C was *Designbuild Australia Pty Ltd v Endeavour Resources Ltd*.[111] Powell J was called upon to decide the very point left undecided by *Repco* whether the obligation under s 31 of the *Securities Industry Act 1975* (Cth) applied to listed companies. His Honour held that, unless the contract arising from the acceptance by the stock exchange of an application for listing—either expressly or by necessary implication—imposes on the applicant company a positive obligation to observe the *LRs*, the mere fact that a company is listed does not mean that it is subject to the relevant 'obligation' for the purposes of s 31. Powell J tested for the existence of a contractual relationship; his Honour looked at the documents alleged to form the contract to see what in fact had been promised. Here, none of the forms contained an express promise to observe the *LRs* and it was not necessary to imply that obligation to give business efficacy to the relationship between a listed company and the stock exchange because the threat of suspension or delisting provided a much greater impetus to observe the *LRs* than an implied term. As Powell J noted:

> the undoubted and in my view, unexaminable discretion of the Exchange ... whether with or without cause, to 'suspend' or 'delist' a company provides a far more powerful means of securing observance of the Official Listing requirements than would a mere promise to observe them.[112]

When the state-based *Securities Industry Acts* were replaced by the *Securities Industry Code* in 1980, s 42 (which replaced s 31) was amended by adding a new subsection (2) (now found in s 793C(3)), which *deems* a company to be under an obligation to comply with the *LRs* when it is listed on the stock exchange. This deemed contractual obligation was intended to overcome the effect of the *Designbuild Case*, while leaving the *Repco* decision intact.

110 *Repco Ltd v Bartdon Pty Ltd* [1981] VR 1, 11.

111 *Designbuild Australia Pty Ltd v Endeavour Resources Ltd* (1980) 5 ACLR 610 ('*Designbuild Case*').

112 Ibid 635; see P Spender, 'The Legal Relationship Between the Australian Stock Exchange and Listed Companies' (1995) 13(4) *Company and Securities Law Journal* 240.

Nevertheless, it was subsequently held in *Harman v Energy Research Group Australia Ltd*[113] ('*Harman*') that s 42 did not give the *LRs* 'statutory force', only 'statutory recognition'.

FAI Insurances Ltd v Pioneer Concrete Services Ltd (No 2) is the high point of judicial recognition of s 793C.[114] FAI was a takeover bidder that sought to set aside some share allotments made by the target company (Pioneer) on the grounds they breached the stock exchange listing requirements. The share allotment had the effect of diluting FAI's stake in Pioneer and defeating its takeover of Pioneer. FAI argued that the predecessor to s 793C allowed it to apply to the Court for an order that this breach be remedied by removal from Pioneer's share register of the names of the persons to whom Pioneer had issued the shares.

In the Court of Appeal, leave to appeal on this ground was refused, but the Court made some obiter comments on the scope of s 42. Although the comments are obiter, the Court was concerned to adopt a construction of the section that would give it some force.

Kirby P referred to the 'special statutory status' now accorded to the rules. He regarded the rules as being more than the private rules of a public body. He stated:

> Under s 31 ... it was necessary to establish, outside the section, a contractual or statutory obligation to observe the listing requirements. But section 42 ... imposes its duties more clearly. By the force of the section, it gives statutory recognition and significance to the listing requirements.[115]

Street CJ, with whom Samuels J agreed, took a slightly less expansive view of the effect of s 42, although he considered that the legislature had, by s 42, plainly indicated that the *LRs* are to be of a 'binding nature' and enforceable. The obligation to comply with them is expressly imposed by what is now s 793C(3).

Despite the expansive views of ss 42 and 793C, especially that of Kirby P, the majority took the view that the section does not allow the Court to interfere with the rights of a third party by removing their name from the share register of a company that is in breach of the *LRs*.

Subsequently, in *Bateman v Newhaven Park Stud Ltd*[116] ('*Bateman*'), the plaintiff alleged a breach of ch 10 of the *LRs* regarding related party transactions. The jurisdiction of the New South Wales Supreme Court to grant relief was questioned and the plaintiff relied (inter alia) upon s 793C.

Certain letters from ASX were in evidence that established that ASX did not require compliance with the *LRs* in the way alleged by the plaintiff. It was held by Barrett J, citing *Harman*, that the discretions reserved by ASX to itself meant that the obligation to comply with the *LRs* is, in reality, '... an obligation to comply with such of the listing requirements as the Stock Exchange in its discretion required the company to comply with'.[117] Because of ASX's waiver power and the explicit power it reserves to itself to

113 *Harman Energy Research Group Australia Ltd* [1986] WAR 123.

114 *FAI Insurances Ltd v Pioneer Concrete Services Ltd (No 2)* (1986) 10 ACLR 801.

115 Ibid 810.

116 *Bateman v Newhaven Park Stud Ltd* (2004) 49 ACSR 454.

117 Ibid 457 [12] quoting *Harman v Energy Research Group Australia Ltd* [1986] WAR 123, 129 (Brinsden J).

decide whether to require compliance with *LRs*, there will be no jurisdiction if ASX does not consider that a breach has occurred.[118]

Compare *Bateman* to *John Bridgeman Ltd v National Stock Exchange of Australia Ltd*,[119] where the market operator (NSX) suspended the securities of a listed company (JBL) from trading while NSX conducted an inquiry. JBL had not been informed of the suspension prior to an announcement and no information was provided by NSX about the actual conduct which supported the NSX concerns. Derrington J made orders for the discovery of documents, finding that NSX's refusal to provide information gave rise to a breach of the implied obligation of each party to the listing contract to enable the other party to have the benefit of the contract.

A further provision: s 1101B

Section 1101B is a general provision, found in the 'Miscellaneous' section of the *Corporations Act*. Under that section, ASIC can apply to the court for an order where there has been a contravention or there is about to be a contravention (s 1101B(1)(a)). ASX or a market licensee can apply to the court for an order where there has been a contravention (s 1101B(1)(b)). A person claiming to be aggrieved can apply where there has been a contravention and the person making the claim was aggrieved by that contravention (s 1101B(1)(d)). Subsections (2) and (3) make similar provision to ss 793C(5) and (6): that a shareholder is regarded as a person aggrieved, and will have standing under this provision. So, unlike s 793C, where ASIC is the applicant, s 1101B expressly covers threatened contraventions. On an application, the court can make an order and s 1101B(4) gives examples of the types of order it can make, such as giving directions about compliance with the *LRs*. For example, in *Oil Basins Ltd v Bass Strait Oil Co*,[120] Gordon J accepted an undertaking given by the listed company to ASX to remedy the breach. A declaration of contravention sufficiently addressed the need for deterrence and the undertaking dealt with the breach in a manner that was 'pragmatic, effective and equitable'.[121]

17.20.60 Challenging ASX decisions: a public law paradigm?

To what extent does the 'statutory underpinning' of the *LRs* through ss 674, 674A, 793C and 1101B (together with the requirements for ASIC approval and disallowance of their amendment) mean that the *LRs* are quasi-legislative rather than purely private contractual arrangements?

The starting point is the idea that the stock market should be regarded as entirely self-regulatory; a private organisation made up of brokers involved in the market and listed companies whose securities are quoted. As discussed above, the courts have favoured this interpretation.

118 Ibid [13].

119 *John Bridgeman Ltd v National Stock Exchange of Australia Ltd* (2019) 139 ACSR 244.

120 *Oil Basins Ltd v Bass Strait Oil Co* (2012) 91 ACSR 700.

121 Ibid [125]. See also *Australian Securities and Investments Commission v CFS Private Wealth Pty Ltd* (2018) 129 ACSR 171 where a restraining order was issued.

It is clear that ASX's decisions cannot be reviewed under the *Administrative Decisions (Judicial Review) Act 1977* (Cth) (*'AD(JR) Act'*). In *Chapmans Ltd v Australian Stock Exchange Ltd,*[122] Beaumont J held that the ASX *LRs* could not be characterised as 'being authorised or required by an enactment [and] given force or effect to by the enactment or by a principle of law applicable to the enactment'.[123] It followed that ASX's decision was not made under an enactment and was not capable of review under the *AD(JR) Act*.

There is a further question as to whether review of ASX's decisions is available at common law by use of the prerogative writs. In *New Zealand Stock Exchange v Listed Companies Association Inc,*[124] the New Zealand Court of Appeal rejected a submission that the Stock Exchange had public law responsibilities to avoid acting arbitrarily in suspending or delisting a listed company, holding that the relationship between a listed company and the Exchange was merely contractual and involved no exercise of statutory power. This case may be distinguished by the absence of any New Zealand equivalent of ss 793C and 1101B.

In contrast, in *R v Panel on Takeovers and Mergers; Ex parte Datafin*[125] (*'Datafin'*), the English Court of Appeal held that a decision made by a body is judicially reviewable, even where that body is not formed under legislative authority, if that body is performing a public duty or a function having a public element in circumstances that, but for the existence of that body, the area concerned would have been likely to have been regulated by a public body exercising statutory power.

In *Datafin,* the Court was asked to quash a decision of the UK Takeovers Panel and to order the Panel to reconsider the complaint. The Panel is not a governmental agency; it is comprised of participants in the markets but is recognised in legislation. The Court began by noting that judicial review is not available where an organisation derives its powers entirely from the consent of its members. The Court held, however, that the Panel was not such a body because it performed public duties under a self-regulatory regime at the behest of the government. In other words, it was used by the government as a central feature of the regulation of financial markets. Further, the Panel's role was underpinned by statute.

These, among other factors, led the Court to conclude that the Panel exercised a public function that gave the Court power to review its decisions. The Court emphasised that, in deciding whether judicial review is available, the nature of a body can be considered, not just the source of its power.

The issues raised by the *Datafin* case were considered by the High Court in *NEAT Domestic Trading Pty Ltd v AWB Ltd.*[126] In that case, NEAT, a trader in wheat, applied to the Wheat Authority ('the Authority') for consent for the bulk export of wheat. The Authority was obliged under the relevant legislation to consult with AWBI (a company

122 *Chapmans Ltd v Australian Stock Exchange Ltd* (1994) 51 FCR 501.
123 Ibid 511 quoting *General Newspapers Pty Ltd v Telstra Corporation* (1993) 45 FCR 164, 172; see also *Gold and Resources Development NL v Australian Stock Exchange Ltd* (1998) 30 ACSR 105.
124 *New Zealand Stock Exchange v Listed Companies Association Inc* [1984] 1 NZLR 699.
125 *R v Panel on Takeovers and Mergers; Ex parte Datafin* [1987] QB 815.
126 *NEAT Domestic Trading Pty Ltd v AWB Ltd* (2003) 216 CLR 277.

limited by shares). AWBI refused approval to each application, hence the Authority was obliged to withhold consent. NEAT applied for review under the *AD(JR) Act* of the refusal of AWBI to give its approval. Although the High Court did not decline to follow *Datafin*, the majority[127] held that public law remedies did not lie against AWBI because, inter alia, the private character of AWBI meant it was entitled to pursue the objective of maximising returns. Further, it was impossible for AWBI to have public law obligations at the same time as pursuing its private interests.[128]

Subsequently, the Victorian Court of Appeal in *Mickovski v Financial Ombudsman Service Ltd*[129] ('*Mickovski*') considered the functions of the predecessor to the Australian Financial Complaints Authority (AFCA) which is an external dispute resolution (EDR) scheme funded by its members, who are, inter alia, financial services providers.[130] Section 912A(1)(g) of the *Corporations Act* requires that an entity holding a financial services licence that services retail clients must have an EDR procedure approved by ASIC. ASIC had approved AFCA as such an organisation. The question was whether AFCA's decisions are subject to the *Datafin* principle on the basis that there is a public interest in having a mechanism for private dispute resolution of financial claims.

The Court commented that the *Datafin* principle is appealing because of the trend towards privatisation of governmental functions and the need for the availability of judicial review for a wider range of public and administrative functions.[131] However, it held that Australian courts should avoid making a decision about the application of the principle in *Datafin* unless and until it is necessary to do so.[132] Presumably, this comment was signalling that the High Court should rule on the issue. Further, the Court held that:

> it is doubtful that the principle has any application in relation to contractually based decisions and, even if it does, we [consider] ... that the public interest evident in having a mechanism for private dispute resolution ... of the kind mandated by s 912A is insufficient to sustain the conclusion that [AFCA] was exercising a public duty or a function involving a public element in circumstances where [AFCA's] jurisdiction was consensually invoked by the parties to a complaint.[133]

However, the Court confirmed that AFCA's decisions may be 'reviewable as a matter of contract'[134] Recent case law demonstrates there may be some development of the law in this area to further explore the public–private divide.[135] For example, in *Isignthis Ltd*

127 Gleeson CJ, McHugh, Hayne and Callinan JJ, with Kirby J dissenting.

128 *NEAT Domestic Trading Pty Ltd v AWB Ltd* (2003) 216 CLR 277 [49]–[51].

129 *Mickovski v Financial Ombudsman Service Ltd* (2012) 36 VR 456.

130 For the background, see I Ramsay and M Webster, 'Court Review of the Decisions of the Australian Financial Complaints Authority and Its Predecessors' (2019) 8(1) *Journal of Civil Litigation and Practice* 6, 6.

131 *Mickovski v Financial Ombudsman Service Ltd* (2012) 36 VR 456, 466 [31].

132 Ibid 466 [32].

133 Ibid.

134 Ibid 467 [37].

135 See *Australia Capital Financial Management Pty Ltd v Australian Financial Complaint Authority* (2022) 164 ACSR 215; *BFJ Capital Pty Ltd v Financial Ombudsman Service Ltd* [2019] VSC 71; E Kyrou, 'Judicial

v ASX Ltd, Davies J found that the court can review ASX suspension power under LR 18.8 for 'legal error'.[136] The *LR* was described as 'part of the armoury of administrative action available to ASX in aid of its statutory responsibilities under s 792A'.[137]

17.25 Market misconduct

17.25.05 Overview

Shapiro has argued that securities markets have certain features that make them susceptible to improper conduct, as follows.[138]

Secrecy: Companies and investment analysts want to keep information to themselves and away from the market because they believe it gives them a competitive advantage. A significant rationale for profit-making in this area is the attempt to beat the market; for example, by acquiring shares in a takeover target. If we subscribe to the efficient capital market hypothesis,[139] we would say that this objective is, at most, transitory.

Expertise: Financial products are complex and increasingly diverse. There is more pressure upon investors to understand financial products, which is discussed in Chapter 18. Investors need to rely on experts and experts, in turn, tend to specialise.[140]

Discretion: Investors rely upon experts and grant the experts considerable discretion in making decisions about their investments; for example, when to buy and sell, and what constitutes a good or bad risk.

Intermediaries: Investors rarely have direct relationships with each other.[141] Moreover, the intermediaries have their own professional communities which are close knit.

Probabilistic outcomes: There are no sure outcomes in the market. All decisions are based on the probability of desired outcomes, but not their certainty. Blue chip shares may be more certain than high risk ventures, but outcomes cannot be identified precisely. Consequently, investing in the financial markets is often compared to gambling.

Due to these reasons, the content, nature, timing and spread of information can be easily manipulated in the financial markets and investors can buy and sell using inadequate, incomplete, false or no information about financial products, issuers, or intermediaries. Further, information is disseminated formally and informally through a diversity of methods.

Consequently, regulating improper market conduct requires a variety of responses to encompass these market characteristics.

Review of Decisions of Non-governmental Bodies Exercising Governmental Powers: Is *Datafin* Part of Australian Law?' (2012) 86(1) *Australian Law Journal* 20; I Ramsay and M Webster, 'Court Review of the Decisions of the Australian Financial Complaints Authority and Its Predecessors' (2019) 8(1) *Journal of Civil Litigation and Practice* 6.

136 *Isignthis Ltd v ASX Ltd* (2020) 143 ACSR 679 [39].

137 Ibid [21].

138 S Shapiro, *Wayward Capitalists: Targets of the Securities and Exchange Commission* (Yale University Press, 1984).

139 See the discussion above at Section 17.10.05.

140 See, eg, *Wingecarribee Shire Council v Lehman Brothers Ltd (in liq)* (2012) 301 ALR 1.

141 See the discussion at Section 18.15.05 regarding the anonymity required by the ASX trading platform.

The *Corporations Act* divides its regulation of improper market conduct into two parts. Part 7.10 div 2 deals with prohibited conduct other than insider trading, such as generalised forms of market manipulation. Part 7.10 div 3 deals with insider trading. These provisions apply to all market participants, not just special categories of participants such as licence-holders, brokers or directors. Part 7.10 is generally directed to ensuring the timely release of information to the market and preventing the release of distorted information to the market.

First, we look at div 3 on insider trading (ss 1042A–45A) and then examine div 2 (ss 1040A–41K) on general market misconduct.

17.30 Insider trading

Insider trading involves a person making improper use of price sensitive information about financial products to trade in those financial products when the information is not generally available. Considerable debate and controversy surround insider trading. In *R v Firns*, Mason P described how the differing viewpoints had been embodied into the text of the legislation:

> The legislative history suggests that parliament left the courts with a scheme embodying the ambiguous embrace of the market fairness/'equal access' and market efficiency theories.[142]

The market efficiency theories were advanced by scholars who relied on economic analysis, including the efficient capital market hypothesis, to argue that in an efficient market inside information is already impacted into the price of the shares.[143] This analysis relies upon the strong form of the efficient capital market hypothesis, which posits that the price of securities includes all information both public and private.[144] On this analysis, insider trading promotes the flow of information to the market because it brings information to the market more quickly because the insider is incentivised to trade on the information as soon as possible. Carlton and Fischel contended that complete disclosure may be deleterious for a firm because it may lead to excessive revelation and is costly to produce. Insider trading allows for intermediate disclosure by trading on inside information.[145]

Manne argued that insider trading is the reward for entrepreneurial effort. He considered that the scheme for remuneration of corporate managers is insufficient even if they are paid a percentage of company profits because this remuneration is ex post facto. Insider trading provides an effective incentive for managers to work hard and allows them to be properly rewarded.[146] In reply, Schotland argued that Manne's

142 *R v Firns* (2001) 51 NSWLR 548, 557 [45].

143 See, eg, H Manne, 'In Defence of Insider Trading' (1966) 43(6) *Harvard Business Review* 113.

144 See Section 17.10.05.

145 D Carlton and D Fischel, 'The Regulation of Insider Trading' (1983) 35(5) *Stanford Law Review* 857.

146 H Manne, *Insider Trading and the Stock Market* (Free Press, 1966); H Manne, 'In Defence of Insider Trading' (1966) 43(6) *Harvard Business Review* 113; H Manne, 'Insider Trading: Hayek, Virtual Markets, and the Dog that Did Not Bark' (2005) 31(1) *Journal of Corporation Law* 167.

argument works too well, and can lead to short-term risk effects and the discounting of incremental projects.[147]

The market efficiency arguments have not been influential in the development of the Australian law of insider trading.[148] Arguments based on fairness, equal access and market confidence have been far more prominent. A variety of reports have worked on the premise that insider trading is damaging to markets because it is unfair to those who do not possess the inside information and ultimately may undermine confidence in those markets. On this argument, if we allow insider trading to go unchecked, investors will desert the market because of the perceived informational advantages of insiders. In other words, failure to prohibit insider trading will lead to 'capital flight'. In 1989, the Griffiths Committee report concluded that the basis for regulating insider trading was the need to guarantee investor confidence in the integrity of the securities markets.[149] The Griffiths Committee endorsed the principles adopted in the earlier report of the Campbell Committee, where it was stated that:

> The object of restrictions on insider trading is to ensure that the securities market operates freely and fairly, with all participants having equal access to relevant information. Investor confidence, and thus the ability of the market to mobilise savings, depends importantly on the prevention of the improper use of confidential information.[150]

The Explanatory Memorandum that accompanied the Corporations Amendment Bill 1991 (which was the genesis of the present provisions) explained that the legislation arose out of the Griffiths Committee report.[151] Although market efficiency was taken into account by the legislators, ultimately the prohibition is based on the demands of market integrity and investor fairness. This is a common judicial refrain that can be observed in the cases.[152]

17.30.05 The basic prohibition

The regulation of insider trading is found in pt 7.10 div 3. The basic prohibition is in sub-div B, commencing with s 1043A but many of the terms in the prohibition are explained in sub-div A, particularly the definitions in s 1042A.[153]

147 R Schotland, 'Unsafe at Any Price: A Reply to Manne, *Insider Trading and The Stock Market*' (1967) 53(7) *Virginia Law Review* 1425.

148 G North, 'A Re-examination of the Manne Efficiency Theory and the Insider Trading and Company Disclosure Efficiency Rationales' (2011) 25(2) *Australian Journal of Corporate Law* 209.

149 Committee on Legal and Constitutional Affairs, Parliament of Australia, *Fair Shares for All: Insider Trading in Australia* (Australian Government, 1989) [5.3.9] ('the Griffiths Committee').

150 Ibid [3.3.6] quoting from The Australian Financial System Inquiry, *Final Report of the Committee of Inquiry* (Australian Government, 1981) 382 ('the Campbell Committee').

151 Explanatory Memorandum, Corporations Legislation Amendment Bill 1991 (Cth) [35], [307].

152 See, eg, the comments of the Victorian Court of Appeal in *Kamay v The Queen* (2015) 47 VR 475, 490, [48]–[50]; cf J Overland, 'How Important is Market Integrity? Revisiting the Reasons why we Prohibit Insider Trading (2022) 38(1) *Australian Journal of Corporate Law* 132.

153 See G North, 'The Australian Insider Trading Regime: Workable or Hopelessly Complex?' (2009) 27(5) *Company and Securities Law Journal* 310.

The basic prohibition is as follows:

(1) Insiders must not apply for, acquire, or dispose of financial products, or enter into agreements to do the same upon the basis of inside information (s 1043A(1)(c)).
(2) An insider is prohibited from procuring another person to act in this way in relation to financial products (s 1043A(1)(d)).
(3) The communication of inside information to another person (ie tipping is also proscribed in certain circumstances) (s 1043A(2)).

17.30.10 Insider trading: prerequisites to the prohibition

Certain words and terms that are used in the prohibition in s 1043A are defined elsewhere as highlighted below. Section 1043A states (in summary): a person ('the insider') possesses inside information (about Division 3 financial products) and the insider knows or ought reasonably to know that it is inside information.

'Person'

Who is a 'person' for the purpose of the prohibition under s 1043A? The general meaning of 'person' is defined in s 2C of the *Acts Interpretation Act 1901* (Cth), which provides:

> (a) expressions used to denote persons generally (such as 'person', 'party', 'someone', 'anyone', 'no-one', 'one', 'another', and 'whoever'), include a body politic or corporate as well as an individual.

The courts originally read down the predecessors to s 1043A, so that only natural people could engage in insider trading. The present drafting is designed to overcome this narrow construction; therefore, companies can engage in insider trading.[154] In *Exicom Pty Ltd v Futuris Corporation Ltd*,[155] Young J observed that a company cannot be an insider in relation to its own securities. This alleviates certain practical problems; for example, if a company undertakes a share buy-back, it might be engaging in insider trading.

'possesses'

In order to prove a breach of the prohibition, it is not necessary to show a causal connection between possession of the information and the decision to trade.[156]

'Division 3 financial products'

'Division 3 financial products' is referred to in the definition of 'inside information' in s 1042A and in the prohibition in ss 1043A(1)(c) and (1)(d). The term is defined in s 1042A to mean:

> **(a)** securities; or
> **(b)** derivatives; or
> **(c)** interests in a managed investment scheme; or

154 For an example where a company engaged in insider trading, see *Australian Securities and Investments Commission v Hochtief Aktiengesellschaft* (2016) 117 ACSR 589. See generally J Overland, *Corporate Liability for Insider Trading* (Routledge, 2019).

155 *Exicom Ltd v Futuris Corporation Ltd* (1995) 13 ACLC 1758.

156 *R v Farris* (2015) 107 ACSR 26, 68–9 [173].

> **(d)** debentures ... issued by a government; or
> **(e)** superannuation products, other than those prescribed by regulations ...
> **(f)** any other financial products that are able to be traded on a financial market.

Note that the definition focuses upon financial products that are able to be traded. The specific products that are nominated in this definition—securities and derivatives—are separately defined in the *Corporations Act*.[157] The New South Wales Court of Appeal in *Joffe v The Queen*[158] held that contracts for difference (CFD) arrangements were Division 3 financial products. The Court examined the general definition of derivatives in s 761D and then scrutinised the mechanics of the CFD product. The Court found it was a contract that would produce a profit or loss dependent on the movement of underlying securities nominated in it. It was not a contract for future services or a credit facility; therefore, was not excluded under s 761D and was a Division 3 financial product in the nature of a derivative.

'Knowledge'

Corporations can have knowledge if an officer is in possession of the information (s 1042G). This is discussed in more detail below.

'Inside information'

The term 'inside information' is defined in s 1042A as information that is not generally available, and a reasonable person would expect to have a material effect on the price or value of financial products. The word 'information' is separately defined in s 1042A in broad terms: matters of supposition, matters that are insufficiently definite to warrant being made known to the public, and matters that relate to the intentions, or likely intentions, of a person. The ambit of the meaning of 'information' is intentionally wide and includes both hard or verifiable information and soft information such as rumours and suppositions.[159]

Importantly, 'information' for the purposes of the prohibition includes false information. In *Mansfield v The Queen*,[160] Malcolm Day was the managing director of AdultShop .com (A), a listed public company. Day made statements to Mansfield that A's profit would rise from \$3 million to \$11 million and its turnover would go up from approximately \$30 million to \$111 million. Day also made a statement to Mr Kizon that 'Packer had bought 4.9% of A'. Both these statements were false. Mr Packer in fact had held 1.5 per cent but had sold it prior to the statements. Mansfield and Kizon both bought or procured the purchase of shares in A. They argued that false statements did not amount to 'information' for the purposes of the definition in s 1042A.

157 For definitions of these terms, see ss 92, 761D. This is discussed at Sections 17.15.10 and 17.15.15.

158 *Joffe v The Queen* (2012) 82 NSWLR 510.

159 *Commissioner for Corporate Affairs v Green* [1978] VR 505; *Australian Securities and Investments Commission v Citigroup Global Markets Australia Pty Ltd (No 4)* (2007) 160 FCR 35; see J Overland, 'What is Inside "Information"? Clarifying the Ambit of Insider Trading Laws' (2013) 31(3) *Company and Securities Law Journal* 189.

160 *Mansfield v The Queen* (2012) 247 CLR 86.

The High Court held that 'information' includes false information. The Court adopted a purposive approach when settling on this interpretation:

> If ... Mr Day's motive for saying what he did to Mr Mansfield and Mr Kizon was 'pumping the stock of AdultShop', the market would not operate freely or fairly if the appellants acted upon what Mr Day said and invested in AdultShop shares. Prohibiting those who received false information from Mr Day that was material to the price or value of AdultShop shares from trading in those shares allows the market to operate freely and fairly. It matters not whether what Mr Day said was true or was information actually derived from the company. The operation of the market would be adversely affected by trading that was founded on information not generally available which, if generally available, would reasonably be expected materially to affect the price or value of the securities.[161]

A further example of the width of the definition of 'information' under these provisions is demonstrated by *Australian Securities and Investments Commission v Citigroup Global Markets Australia Pty Ltd (No 4)* ('*Citigroup*').[162] ASIC brought civil penalty proceedings against a merchant banking group, Citigroup, for insider trading. Toll Holdings was planning a takeover bid for Patrick Corporation. Toll had retained the services of the investment banking division of Citigroup to give it advice about the takeover. The day before Toll announced its takeover bid, an employee of Citigroup who worked in the share trading division of the firm, Manchee, purchased over 1 million Patrick shares. They had no knowledge of Citigroup's connection to Toll or of the impending takeover bid. Someone in the investment banking division noticed the purchases and spoke to the head of the share trading division, saying words to the effect of 'We may have a problem with that'. The head of share trading then instructed Manchee (in a discussion referred to in the judgment as the 'cigarette on the pavement' conversation) to stop buying Patrick shares (but said nothing about the takeover or Citigroup's role). Manchee went back to his office and began selling Patrick shares. ASIC alleged that this sale activity constituted insider trading because Manchee possessed inside information when he traded; namely, a supposition that he allegedly made when told to stop buying Patrick shares that Citigroup was advising someone in relation to a takeover of Patrick.[163] Citigroup argued that even if Manchee had made this supposition, it had not been made on the basis of any information communicated to him—it was just an 'uncommunicated thought process'. Jacobson J held that an uncommunicated supposition of this type could amount to 'information' for the purposes of the section, but in this case Manchee had not in fact made the supposition.

Jacobson J also stated that information can 'be acquired by means of a hint or a veiled suggestion from which the receiver can impute other knowledge':[164] see the discussion below about the knowledge test at Section 17.30.15.

---

161 Ibid 99 [47].

162 *Australian Securities and Investments Commission v Citigroup Global Markets Australia Pty Ltd (No 4)* (2007) 160 FCR 35, also discussed in Section 10.20.15 regarding ASIC's argument that Manchee was an 'officer'.

163 It would normally be illogical to sell shares in a potential takeover target, but making a profit or deriving a benefit from the transaction is not part of the insider trading prohibition, although it may be relevant to sentencing: see *Kamay v The Queen* (2015) 47 VR 475.

164 *Australian Securities and Investments Commission v Citigroup Global Markets Australia Pty Ltd (No 4)* (2007) 160 FCR 35, 105 [534], citing *Commissioner for Corporate Affairs v Green* [1978] VR 505, 511.

Is the information 'generally available'?

The definition of 'inside information' in s 1042A requires that the information be 'not generally available'. The term 'generally available' is defined backwards in s 1042C; that is, the section defines what *is* generally available and everything else is not available.

> [I]nformation is *generally available* if:
>
> **(a)** it consists of readily observable matter; or
>
> **(b)** both of the following subparagraphs apply:
>
> **(i)** it has been made known in a manner that would, or would be likely to, bring it to the attention of persons who commonly invest in Division 3 financial products ...; and
>
> **(ii)** ... a reasonable period for it to be disseminated among such persons has elapsed; or
>
> **(c)** it consists of deductions, conclusions or inferences made or drawn from [(a) or (b)(i)].
>
> ...

The 'readily observable matter' element in s 1042C(1)(a) was interpreted in *R v Firns* ('*Firns*').[165] Carpenter was a mining company listed on the ASX market. It had a subsidiary company that operated in Papua New Guinea (PNG) with a mining exploration licence. The PNG Government had introduced regulations that significantly reduced the value of that exploration licence. The subsidiary company challenged the validity of those regulations in court proceedings. One Friday in July 1995, judgment was handed down in an open court in PNG declaring the regulations to be invalid.

The general manager of Carpenter was in court and immediately telephoned the chairman of the board of directors in Australia. He, in turn, called his fellow directors. One of them telephoned Mr Firns (his son). Firns received the news of the court decision about half an hour after it was handed down. He immediately called a broker and purchased 400,000 Carpenter shares in his wife's name, plus another similar parcel in his friend's name. ASX was not told of the PNG court judgment until the following Monday.

Firns was convicted of insider trading. On appeal to the New South Wales Court of Criminal Appeal, the issue was whether the information about the court decision was 'generally available' in the sense that it consisted of 'readily observable matter'.

The Court upheld Firns' appeal by a majority. The majority held that information may be readily observable even if no one has in fact observed it. The PNG court judgment was readily observable to persons who were present in the court, and it did not matter how many people actually observed the relevant information.[166] There was no reason, on the wording of the section, to limit it to information that is readily observable by people in Australia.[167]

165 *R v Firns* (2001) 51 NSWLR 548.
166 Ibid 563–564 [76]–[77].
167 Ibid [80]–[82].

Mason P commented that, conversely, sometimes information will consist of things that are directly visible but may not be observable or at least not readily so. Examples include a message that is widely published but encrypted or a gold nugget lying in the corner of the desert.[168] In the present case, the information was available, understandable, and accessible to a significant group of the public and was readily observable.[169]

Section 1042C requires that, in order to be generally available, a reasonable period must have elapsed since the information was made known to people who commonly invest in the Division 3 financial products. This prevents hair-trigger trading by insiders.[170]

The information relevant to listed companies should of course be disseminated quickly to the market through the ASX continuous disclosure requirements. Recall the obligation of listed companies under LR 3.1 and ss 674 and 674A to immediately disclose price sensitive information.[171] The obligation sits alongside the obligation of insiders not to trade on the information until it is disclosed. The complementary nature of the obligations may be observed in the case law. For example, the reasoning used by the Court in *Firns* has been applied to cases involving alleged breaches of the continuous disclosure provisions.[172]

Material effect

The second limb of the definition of inside information under s 1042A requires that the information must be material. In other words, if the information were generally available, a reasonable person would expect it to have a material effect on the price or value of financial products. The term 'material effect' is defined in s 1042D by recourse to an objective test: a reasonable person would be taken to expect that the information would have a material effect on the price or value of the financial products if the information would be likely to influence persons who commonly acquire Division 3 financial products in deciding whether to acquire or dispose of those products. This definition takes into account market practices and recognises that material effect is multi-faceted: there are many different types of information and many different types of financial products, some of which are more volatile or sensitive to information.

Expert evidence will usually be led about the materiality of the information, but the source of the information can affect materiality because a reasonable person will consider the reliability of the information source when determining its materiality. In *R v Rivkin* ('*Rivkin*'),[173] Mr Rivkin was a flamboyant stockbroker who was selling his house. There was an interested buyer, Mr McGowan, who happened to be the CEO of Impulse

168 Ibid [73].

169 Ibid [76].

170 See, eg, *R v Evans* [1999] VSC 488.

171 See, eg, *Australian Securities and Investments Commission v Southcorp Ltd (No 2)* (2003) 130 FCR 406.

172 *James Hardie Industries NV v Australian Securities and Investments Commission* (2010) 81 ACSR 1; *Grant-Taylor v Babcock & Brown Ltd (in liq)* (2016) 245 FCR 402; *Australian Securities and Investments Commission v GetSwift Ltd* [2021] FCA 1384 [1089].

173 *R v Rivkin* (2004) 59 NSWLR 284.

Airlines. In a conversation with Rivkin, McGowan said that his payment of the purchase price was dependent on the outcome of a merger between Impulse and Qantas, which required ACCC approval, which he was confident to get very soon. The information about the merger was confidential, so McGowan said to Rivkin, 'Obviously now that you are aware of this, you cannot trade in Qantas shares'. McGowan had been advised to say this by his lawyer, so as to deflect liability for insider trading. Rivkin replied, 'Obviously a person of my standing would not contemplate such a thing'. Later that day, Rivkin directed his broker to buy 50,000 Qantas shares.

Rivkin was convicted of insider trading. McGowan was the source of the information and because, inter alia, he was CEO of Impulse, he was a reliable source of information, and this was relevant to its materiality.

17.30.15 The knowledge test

The knowledge test in s 1043A requires that the insider knew or ought reasonably to have known that the information was not generally available and that, if it were generally available, it would have a material effect on the price or value of the particular security or derivative.

Proof of knowledge used to be a major stumbling block to successful prosecutions in this area. But now courts are more likely to infer knowledge, due to the findings in *R v Hannes* ('*Hannes*').[174] In that case, the prosecution proved Mr Hannes' awareness of a takeover offer by relying on inferences and circumstantial evidence that he was:

(1) aware that his employer was retained by TNT with regard to a possible takeover offer
(2) approached a member of the advice team about the value the team was attributing to TNT's shares and it was above market value
(3) made late night visits (for example, when he was on leave) when he could have accessed the team's documents.

The New South Wales Court of Criminal Appeal in *Rivkin* stated that the Court can look at what the insider ought to have known, taking into account their experience, level of knowledge, and business expertise.[175]

The provisions of the *Corporations Act* are designed to capture the knowledge of corporations and partnerships. The question that then arises is how can a company or a partnership possess the information? Pursuant to ss 1042G–1942H, a company or partnership is taken to possess information if an officer or member possesses the information and that information came into their possession in the performance of their duties. As regards corporations under s 1042G, the relevant knowledge must be possessed by an 'officer'. This word is defined in s 9AD of the *Corporations Act*. It usually includes formal office holders such as directors but can include employees

174 *R v Hannes* (2000) 36 ACSR 72.

175 *R v Rivkin* (2004) 59 NSWLR 284; see J Overland, 'The Possession and Materiality of Information in Insider Trading Cases' (2014) 32(5) *Company and Securities Law Journal* 353.

if, for example, they participate in decisions affecting a substantial part of the business of the entity or they have the capacity to affect significantly the corporation's financial standing.

ASIC argued in *Citigroup*[176] that Citigroup as a corporate entity had the relevant inside information because it was possessed by the share trader, Mr Manchee. However, Jacobson J held that Manchee was not an officer, and did not have any involvement in decisions that affected the whole or a substantial part of the company's business, as discussed in depth at Section 10.20.15.

17.30.20 Relevant acts that breach the prohibition

The basic prohibition against insider trading in s 1043A states if an insider knows, or ought reasonably to know, that information is inside information in relation to particular financial products then the insider must not:

- trade (s 1043A(1)(c)) (this part of the prohibition is elaborated at Section 17.30.05ff)
- procure others to trade (s 1042F)
- communicate with others who are likely to trade (tipping) in those financial products (s 1043A(2)).

The prohibition against trading has been examined in the cases discussed above, so the following will focus upon procuring and tipping. 'Procuring' is encouraging another person to trade on the information. 'Tipping' means giving the person the information with the knowledge that the other person is likely to trade on the information.

Procure

This prohibition is in s 1043A(1)(d): the insider must not procure others to trade on the basis of the inside information. The operation of 'procure' under s 1043A(2) is defined by s 1042F, which includes inciting, inducing or encouraging the act or omission by another person. The usual meaning of 'procure' is to intentionally bring about a particular result or act; for example, when a director procures a company that she controls to acquire or dispose of the shares.[177] However, an insider could encourage a person to deal in securities without disclosing any material non-public information. A wink or a nudge might suffice. This is clear from the current wording of s 1042F, which is widely and inclusively drafted.

Tipping

The insider trading prohibition proscribes the direct or indirect communication of inside information in certain circumstances (s 1043A(2)). The communicator of such information will breach the prohibition if they knew or ought reasonably to have known that the other person is likely to trade upon the basis of the information. Therefore, the prohibition extends to giving the inside information to another person—'tipping' (communicating it)—if you know that the person is likely to trade on the information.

176 *Australian Securities and Investments Commission v Citigroup Global Markets Australia Pty Ltd (no 4)* (2007) 160 FCR 35.

177 *R v Farris* (2015) 107 ACSR 26.

In *Khoo v The Queen* ('*Khoo*'),[178] the appellant was an investment banker, who routinely obtained information in the course of his employment. He shared information about a proposed takeover with two of his friends, who were known traders. Both acted on the information and acquired financial products and made a profit. Khoo pleaded guilty and was sentenced to jail for nearly two years. One question on appeal was whether there was an error in the sentencing because the trial judge regarded the criminality of tipping as equivalent to trading. The appellant argued that the criminality of insider trading inevitably exceeds that of tipping. The New South Wales Court of Criminal Appeal rejected this argument and held that there is no rule that tipping is less criminal than insider trading. The approach to sentencing in insider trading cases that was adopted in *R v Glynatsis*[179]—that offenders ought to expect to go to jail—applies to tipping as well. The Court adopted a purposive interpretation that focused upon the need to ensure the integrity of the market: '[t]he attractiveness of the market as a whole is impacted by the unequal dissemination of information'.[180] *Khoo* also demonstrates the approach of courts in this area of promoting general deterrence.[181]

17.30.25 Exceptions and defences to the prohibition

There are several exceptions to the prohibition in pt 7.10 div 3 in ss 1043B–K. Most significant are the defences under ss 1043F and 1043G, which refer to 'Chinese walls' arrangements by bodies corporate and partnerships.

Chinese walls

The reference to 'Chinese walls' conveys the image of a company in which there are barriers to prevent and control the flow of information throughout the firm. The actual form that these barriers take is not prescribed and varies enormously. Some firms construct physical barriers such as security coded doors or locating different departments in different buildings. Internal codes of conduct are also commonly used.

Section 1042G deems the company as having the information of an officer of the company and this term may include employees.[182] Where a company has large number of employees, some of whom may be officers, the company might be perpetually engaging in insider trading, so a defence is provided in s 1043F. If it can be shown:

(1) that the decision to enter into the transaction was not taken by the person with the information;
(2) the company had in place arrangements to block the communication of information from the person with the knowledge to the trader; and
(3) the information was not in fact so communicated then the Chinese wall defence will be satisfied.

178 *Khoo v The Queen* (2013) 237 A Crim R 221.
179 *R v Glynatsis* (2013) 230 A Crim R 99.
180 *Khoo v The Queen* (2013) 237 A Crim R 221 [10] (Leeming JA).
181 For a further discussion of deterrence and sentencing in insider trading cases, see *Xiao v The Queen* (2018) 96 NSWLR 1; J Overland, 'Protecting Market Integrity through Sentencing? The Relevance of General Deterrence to Insider Trading' (2020) 3(3)5 *Australian Journal of Corporate Law* 344.
182 The equivalent provision for partnerships is s 1042H.

The Chinese wall defence was successfully established in *Citigroup*.[183] Jacobson J found that Citigroup had appropriate Chinese wall procedures in place. Citigroup led undisputed evidence regarding:

- the physical separation of key departments
- educational programs for employees
- policies regarding crossing the wall and conflicts of interest
- disciplinary sanctions for breaches of policies and procedures.[184]

This evidence satisfied Jacobson J that the Chinese wall defence under s 1043F was established.

17.30.30 Remedies for insider trading

ASIC's enforcement strategy overwhelmingly favours criminal proceedings to achieve a deterrent effect. In their study of insider trading cases between 1973–2013, Lei and Ramsay found that 92 per cent of actions brought by ASIC for breach of pt 7.10 div 3 were criminal proceedings.[185] However, there are other options. Section 1043A is a civil penalty provision (s 1317E).[186] There is an additional compensation remedy where an insider breaches s 1043A(1) recklessly (s 1043L) and it is available to those who issue, dispose of, or acquire the relevant financial products. Directors' duties may be relevant where the insider is a director (s 183).[187] Finally, administrative/occupational regulation remedies may be pursued by ASIC, such as a banning order under s 920A.[188]

17.35 General market misconduct

Part 7.10 div 2 of the *Corporations Act* concerns prohibited market misconduct other than insider trading.

In *Australian Securities and Investments Commission v Westpac Banking Corporation (No 2)*,[189] Beach J provided a valuable overview of the market misconduct provisions in pt 7.10 div 2. The classification is derived from the work of Avgouleas[190] and is used below to group the provisions broadly by the prohibited activity:

> The first category is *information-based manipulations* involving, for example the dissemination of false or misleading rumours or misleading or deceptive conduct by brokers or investment advisers seeking to 'talk up' securities or the like (cf ss 1041H and 1041E).

183 *Australian Securities and Investments Commission v Citigroup Global Markets Australia Pty Ltd (No 4)* (2007) 160 FCR 35 ('*Citigroup*').

184 Ibid [449]–[456].

185 Section 1311 and sch 3; see V Lei and I Ramsay, 'Insider Trading Enforcement in Australia' (2014) 8(3) *Law and Financial Markets Review* 214, 218.

186 See PF Hanrahan, 'Deterring White-collar Crime: Insights from Australia's Insider Trading Penalties Regime' (2017) 11(2–3) *Law and Financial Markets Review* 61.

187 *Australian Securities and Investments Commission v Vizard* (2005) 145 FCR 57.

188 *Cantena v Australian Securities and Investments Commission* (2011) 276 ALR 25.

189 *Australian Securities and Investments Commission v Westpac Banking Corporation (No 2)* (2018) 266 FCR 147.

190 E Avgouleas, *The Mechanics and Regulation of Market Abuse: A Legal and Economic Analysis* (Oxford University Press, 2005) 108–13.

> The second category of *manipulation is ... based on artificial transactions.* The artificial transaction could be fictitious trades (cf s 1041C) or 'wash sales', where the manipulator enters both a buy order and a sell order for the same security at the same price. In this situation, no change in beneficial ownership occurs (cf s 1041B(2) (a)). Another type of artificial transaction can be produced by the practice of 'matched orders' (cf s 104lB(2)(b)). This consists of one party placing an order whilst knowing that simultaneously another party has entered a sale order or purchase order from the other side matching the size and price of the first order.
>
> The third category of manipulation concerns *price manipulation* (cf s 1041A). ... Avgouleas distinguishes between three types of price manipulation. First, there are trade-based manipulations, where large or specifically structured and timed trades are designed to influence the price levels of that traded product. ... [S]uch manipulations may involve 'trading at the end of the day' scenarios or penny stock manipulations.
>
> [Next], there are contract-based manipulations involving structured and timed trades which are designed to move prices of a particular product in order to make a gain or reduce a loss in another contractual position [or another market]. In such a situation the trader's profit or other advantage is not intended to come directly from the manipulative trades, but rather from a favourable movement in its rights or obligations under a separate contract, instrument or investment.
>
> [Finally], there are market power manipulations, where market power is used to acquire a large part of the supply of or demand for a product in order to dictate the level of prices for that product. The practices of 'corners' and 'squeezes' are examples of such market power manipulations, perhaps to advantage a derivatives position; in that sense, one may have a hybrid of a market power manipulation with a contract-based manipulation.[191]

The discussion below will adopt Beach J's classification of the prohibited activities into information-based manipulations (Section 17.35.05), manipulations based on artificial transactions (Section 17.35.10) and price manipulation (Section 17.35.15).

The genesis of the present Australian law on market misconduct was the recommendations of the Rae Committee, which became law in the mid-1970s through the *Securities Industry Acts* and related Codes.[192] The Rae Committee was mainly concerned with market rigging—the creation of a false or artificial price for securities. The main way this is achieved is to give the market an impression of a high level of activity—other investors will be attracted to the securities and the increase in trading will drive up the price. Those who bought the securities when the price was low will sell when the market price has risen, but because the increase in price has been engineered rather than being based on fundamentals, the price will drop once the engineering stops and

191 *Australian Securities and Investments Commission v Westpac Banking Corporation (No 2)* (2018) 266 FCR 147 [1896]–[1902] (emphasis added).

192 The Rae Committee report and the background to the passage of the *Securities Industry Act 1980* (Cth) is discussed in Chapter 1 at Section 1.40.20.

the innocent investors will suffer a loss. Clearly, the market may also be manipulated by selling to force the market price down and fraudsters will then buy when the market price has dropped. Contemporary misconduct may involve more sophisticated practices but still reflect the basic idea. Modern variations often occur across markets: in *Australian Securities and Investments Commission v Nomura International plc*,[193] the intention was to manipulate the share price of a basket of shares to affect a share price index ('SPI') that would allow a better return for a futures contract. Similarly, in *Director of Public Prosecutions (Cth) v JM*,[194] the activity was designed to push up the share price so that a margin call would not be made. These examples demonstrate that manipulation can occur when there is actual trading in the financial products, although the trading does not reflect genuine supply and demand.[195] Another form of manipulation, called 'runs', occurs where market activity is generated by the dissemination of rumours that are either false or at least misleading and deceptive. The latter are also regulated under div 2 pt 7.10.

The prohibitions in div 2 pt 7.10 are independent but overlapping.[196] Because they have effect independently of each other, a person may contravene more than one provision at the same time.

17.35.05 Information-based manipulations

This manipulation usually occurs by people 'talking up' the value of financial products by false or misleading statements or conduct. Recently, there has been renewed interest in these provisions to combat 'greenwashing', which is the practice of misrepresenting the extent to which a financial product or service is environmentally friendly, sustainable or ethical.[197]

Misleading or deceptive conduct in relation to a financial product or financial service: s 1041H

Section 1041H creates liability for misleading or deceptive conduct in relation to a financial product or a financial service. This provision has been used frequently, particularly in securities class actions, and it creates civil liability only for breach, not criminal liability or a civil penalty. Similar tests are used by the courts to those used in s 18 of the *Australian Consumer Law*.[198]

A leading case is *Forrest v Australian Securities and Investments Commission*.[199] The facts of this case are discussed above at Section 17.20.45. The High Court emphasised the need

193 *Australian Securities and Investments Commission v Nomura International plc* (1998) 89 FCR 301.

194 *DPP (Cth) v JM* (2013) 250 CLR 135.

195 *North v Marra Developments Ltd* (1981) 148 CLR 42.

196 *Corporations Act* s 1041J; *DPP (Cth) v JM* (2013) 250 CLR 135.

197 ASIC, *How to Avoid Greenwashing When Offering or Promoting Sustainability-Related Products* (Information Sheet No 127, June 2022); Jonathan Chew, 'Emissions Reduction Commitments: A New Frontier of Greenwashing?' (2024) 39 *Australian Journal of Corporate Law* 249.

198 *Competition and Consumer Act 2010* (Cth) sch 2 (Australian Consumer Law).

199 *Forrest v Australian Securities and Investments Commission* (2012) 247 CLR 486. See also *Australian Securities and Investments Commission v GetSwift Ltd* [2021] FCA 1384 [2106]–[2142].

to identify the intended audience for the impugned statements and the messages conveyed to that audience. The High Court found that the intended audience in that case '[could] be sufficiently identified as investors (both present and possible future investors) and, perhaps, some wider section of the commercial or business community'.[200] The Court considered it was not necessary to identify the audience more precisely.[201] The Court found that the intended audience for the statements would not be misled by the statements that the agreements were binding.[202] The letter sent by Fortescue to ASX accurately recorded the framework agreement with the Chinese companies and conveyed what a commercial audience would regard as a binding contract.

There are some important carve-outs to the operation of this provision. It does not apply to takeovers, fundraising, or equity crowdfunding documents. Sections 670A, 728 and 738Y (applying to takeovers, prospectuses and equity crowdfunding offer documents respectively) have their own liability regimes and remedies and are therefore excluded from the general operation of s 1041H (s 1041H(3)). Further, the provision was altered during the 2021 amendments to the *Corporations Act* (discussed above at Section 17.20.45) to limit its operation with respect the continuous disclosure obligations under ch 6CA (s 1041H(4)). A listed company will not breach s 1041H(1) in relation to conduct that would contravene ch 6CA, unless the company knows or is reckless or negligent with respect to the materiality of the information under s 674A(2)(d).

False or misleading statements: s 1041E

Section 1041E prohibits runs; that is, false or misleading statements or the dissemination of information that is likely to induce others to enter the market or affect the price of securities.

The section proscribes the making of a statement or the dissemination of information that is 'false in a material particular or materially misleading' in the following circumstances:

(1) where the statement or information is likely to induce another person to buy or sell/ dispose of or apply for financial products (ss 1041E(1)(b)(i), (ii)); or
(2) where the statement or information is likely to have the effect of increasing, reducing, maintaining or stabilising the price for trading in financial products on a financial market (s 1041E(1)(b)(iii)); and
(3) when the person makes the statement knows, or ought reasonably to know, that the statement is false or does not care (s 1041E(1)(c)).

Two cases involving the predecessor to the section are *Australian Securities and Investments Commission v McLeod*[203] and *McLeod v Australian Securities and Investments Commission*.[204] The following analysis focuses upon the judgment of the Western

200 *Forrest v Australian Securities and Investments Commission* (2012) 247 CLR 486, 506 [36].
201 Ibid.
202 For a discussion of the *Forrest* case, see J Humphrey and S Corones, '*Forrest v ASIC:* A "Perfect Storm"' (2014) 88(1) *Australian Law Journal* 26.
203 *Australian Securities and Investments Commission v McLeod* (2000) 22 WAR 255.
204 *McLeod v Australian Securities and Investments Commission* (2002) 211 CLR 287.

Australian Court of Appeal. The subsequent High Court judgment relied on grounds that are not relevant for the present discussion.

Mr McLeod prepared a report for a listed company, Cambridge, on the results of an exploration undertaken by Cambridge in Western Australia for diamond mining. A statement was given to ASX and was based on diamonds sampled at 0.4 carats for each tonne of ore treated. McLeod arrived at a value of $135 per carat for the diamonds. The report said the company's profit would go up to $1374 million. Cambridge's share price rose from 88 cents to $410 in three weeks.

The Court found that statement was misleading because the sample was too small to assess whether diamonds were present in commercial quantities. The question is what would the ordinary member of the investing public have taken the statements about profit to mean? The answer is that the public would expect that profits in that sum would be generated when mining commenced—say, within the next three years—therefore, the statement was both predictive and misleading and deceptive.

Note that the directors in the *James Hardie* case discussed above at Section 17.20.45 were found to have breached both ss 1041H and 1041E by their statements to ASX that their asbestos liabilities were fully funded because the foundation was insufficiently funded to cover future claims by the sufferers of asbestos-related diseases.

17.35.10 Manipulation based on artificial transactions: false trading and market rigging: ss 1041B and 1041C

Section 1041B prohibits acts or omissions that are likely to have the effect of creating a false or misleading appearance of active trading in financial products. Section 1041C prohibits entering into a fictitious or artificial transaction or device if it results in the price of a financial products being maintained, inflated, or depressed, or fluctuations occurring in the price of financial products on a financial market. These sections are intended to prohibit 'wash sales' and 'matched orders', which are discussed above by Beach J in the extract from *Australian Securities and Investments Commission v Westpac* at Section 17.35. At the time of writing, there is no case law that interprets the current drafting of s 1041C. However, ss 1041B and 1041C replaced the former s 998 of the *Corporations Act*, which prohibited false trading and market rigging transactions, so cases decided under s 998 and its predecessors provide insights into ss 1041B and 1041C.

The leading case is *North v Marra Developments Ltd* ('*North*').[205] The directors of Marra decided it was vulnerable to a takeover because the net asset backing of its shares was higher than its share price.[206] The directors decided to issue bonus shares and make a takeover bid for another company (the target). The directors planned to swap Marra shares for shares in the target, but this offer would only be attractive to shareholders in the target if the price of Marra's shares increased. The directors spoke to North Stockbrokers ('North') and the brokers said that they (the brokers) had to 'establish the market price' of the shares; therefore, they should buy and sell to make the price attractive. The directors accordingly gave instructions to North to start creating

205 *North v Marra Developments Ltd* (1981) 148 CLR 42.

206 Takeovers are discussed in Chapter 19.

the 'proper market' (although the activity of North would in fact be creating a distorted market). After the bonus issue was announced (but before the announcement of the takeover offer), North bought quantities of Marra shares on the stock exchange for a higher price than previous sales and continued to pay that price after the takeover bid was announced. After doing this, North sent an invoice to Marra for services rendered, but Marra resisted payment, arguing that the contract was illegal as it breached the predecessor to s 1041B. North argued in reply there was no breach of s 1041B because they had placed real buying and selling orders; therefore, they could not create a false market or a false price or create a false or misleading appearance of the same.

Ultimately, Marra's defence was successful. North could not enforce the contract. In the proceedings before the High Court, note the comments of Mason J:

> It seems to me that the object of the section is to protect the market for securities against activities which will result in artificial or managed manipulation. The section seeks to ensure that the market reflects the forces of genuine supply and demand. By 'genuine supply and demand' I exclude buyers and sellers whose transactions are undertaken for the sole or primary purpose of setting or maintaining the market price.[207]

Mason J agreed with the New South Wales Court of Appeal in rejecting the suggestion that the section only strikes at fictitious or colourable transactions:

> Transactions which are real and genuine but only in the sense that they are intended to operate according to their terms ... are capable of creating quite a false or misleading impression as to the market or the price. This is because they would not have been entered into but for the object on the part of the buyer or of the seller of setting and maintaining the price.[208]

But Mason J recognised that the application of s 1041B to alleged market manipulation will not always be a straightforward exercise. He stated:

> It is not altogether easy to translate the generality of this language [of s1041B] into a specific prohibition against injurious activity whilst at the same time leaving people free to engage in legitimate commercial activity.[209]

This dilemma was manifested in *Fame Decorator Agencies Pty Ltd v Jeffries Industries Ltd* ('*Fame*').[210] This case involved Fame selling 170,000 shares in Jeffries at the close of trading on 28 April 1995. That date was the date Fame was entitled to convert preference shares into ordinary shares. Due to the conversion formula, the lower the average price of the ordinary shares, the greater the number of ordinary shares that would be allotted to Fame upon the conversion. The average market price of the shares in two months prior to 28 April was 25–50 cents. Mr O'Halloran, on behalf of Fame, gave

207 *North v Marra Developments Ltd* (1981) 148 CLR 42, 59.
208 Ibid.
209 Ibid 58.
210 *Fame Decorator Agencies Pty Ltd v Jeffries Industries Ltd* (1998) 28 ACSR 58.

instructions to sell from 35 cents down to 14 cents, with 90,000 shares sold at 13–14 cents. The shares were thinly traded and most of the trading occurred shortly before close of trading on 28 April 1995.

The question for the New South Wales Court of Appeal was whether the conduct created a false or misleading appearance with respect to the market for, or the price of, securities. Fame admitted the conduct was intended to take opportunistic advantage of a market situation, and argued it was immaterial that it accepted offers at a lower price than it might have obtained otherwise. But, nevertheless, it contended it was not misleading with respect to the market for, or price of, securities.

The Court applied *North* and confirmed that the purpose of s 1041B is to ensure the market reflects genuine supply and demand. Here, the conduct of the seller was calculated to effect sales at the lowest, rather than the highest, obtainable price and it was timed to deflect the possibility of the price being bidded up. The conduct had the purpose and effect of temporarily creating an artificial market and price.

The type of manipulation that was attempted in *Fame* was applied in much more dramatic circumstances in *Australian Securities and Investments Commission v Nomura International plc* ('*Nomura*').[211] Nomura was an investment bank that engaged in stock index arbitrage during the relevant period. Some of its brokers devised a plan to have a massive sell off of Australian securities in Nomura's portfolio in the 30 minutes prior to the close of the ASX market on 29 March 1996. Nomura attempted to lower the All Ords index so that it could yield a better price upon the settlement of a SPI futures contract, the value of which was based on All Ords price at the close of trading. There were two parcels of shares involved: the Sale Orders and the Bid Basket.

The sell off resulted in a loss of $1.5 billion but could have been significantly worse.[212]

ASIC sought declaratory and injunctive relief against Nomura, alleging several breaches of s 1041B:

- self-trades
- conduct intended and likely to create the appearance of active trading
- conduct intended to create a false appearance as to a futures price.

Sackville J in the Federal Court found that Nomura had contravened s 1041B as follows:

(1) Self-trades (s 1041B(1)): By the combined operation of the Sale Orders and the Bid Basket, Nomura contravened s 1041B(1) of the *Corporations Act* in the two cases in which it sold and purchased securities in a manner that involved no change of beneficial ownership.
(2) Conduct intended to create or likely to create the appearance of active trading (s 1041B(1)(a)): Nomura's purposes included bringing about an appearance of active trading that did not reflect the forces of general supply and demand. Nomura intended to bring about a number of self-trades in illiquid securities to create a false and misleading appearance of active trading.

211 *Australian Securities and Investments Commission v Nomura International plc* (1998) 89 FCR 310.
212 B Hills, 'The Sting that Stank', *Sydney Morning Herald* (Sydney, 12 September 1998) 40.

(3) Conduct intended to create a false appearance as to a futures price (s 1041B(1)(b)): Nomura intended to unilaterally determine the closing price on 29 March 1996 for some illiquid securities within the All Ords index. It knew and intended that this would have an impact on the closing level of the All Ords index and, consequently, the cash settlement price of SPI Contracts that would expire on 29 March 1996.

Sackville J made the declarations sought by ASIC that Nomura had contravened the relevant provisions of the *Corporations Act*.

For an example of a complex claim concerning securities index arbitrage, see *Australian Securities and Investments Commission v Whitebox Trading Pty Ltd (No 7)*[213] where Yates J found that ASIC failed to establish that the defendants were not pursing an ordinary or legitimate commercial strategy or behaviour involving trading during the pre-opening phase of the ASX market.[214]

17.35.15 Price manipulation: market manipulation: s 1041A

Section 1041A prohibits stock market manipulation. It prohibits a person from effecting or taking part in one or more transactions—regardless of whether the transactions involve financial products or not—that have or are likely to have the effect of:

- creating an artificial price for trading in financial products on a financial market which is operated in this jurisdiction (s 1041A(c); or
- maintaining the price of trading in financial products at an artificial level (whether or not that level was previously artificial) on a financial market operated in this jurisdiction (s 1041A(d)).

The leading case is the High Court judgment in *Director of Public Prosecutions (Cth) v JM* ('*JM*').[215] JM had borrowed money from a lender to buy options in a company (X Ltd) whose shares were listed on the ASX market. It was alleged that JM's daughter, T, bought shares in X Ltd at a price and in circumstances that prevented the day's closing price for the shares falling below the point at which the lender to JM would make a margin call requiring JM to provide additional collateral for the loan. The offer by the daughter to buy shares in X Ltd meant that the closing share price for the shares in X Ltd was fixed at 35 cents per share, which was above the amount necessitating a margin call.

The Director of Public Prosecutions alleged T made the purchase for the sole purpose, or at least the dominant purpose, of ensuring that the price of the shares did not fall below the price at which the lender would be entitled to make a margin call on her father's loan, and the transaction had the effect of creating an artificial price for shares or maintaining the share price at a level that was artificial.[216]

213 (2019) 137 ACSR 61.
214 Ibid [541]–[542].
215 *DPP (Cth) v JM* (2013) 250 CLR 135.
216 Ibid [35].

The question that arose for the interpretation of s 1041A was whether the alleged manipulator needed to have the power to monopolise the market. This was found by the Victorian Court of Appeal, relying on United States' authority that the manipulator needed to be able to 'corner' or 'squeeze' the market. The High Court rejected this interpretation because it was unlikely that such domination would be possible in the ASX market due to the operation of ch 6 of the *Corporations Act*. Chapter 6 creates a structured regime for the regulation of controlling interests in certain companies and is discussed in Chapter 19. The High Court stated that the takeover provisions of ch 6 proceed from the premise that a monopoly of, or dominance over, the ASX market for shares in a particular listed company can be achieved only by making a successful takeover for that company. Given the provisions of ch 6, it is unlikely that any buyer or seller can, in any practical sense, 'corner' or 'squeeze' the market for listed shares.[217]

Instead, the High Court relied upon Mason J's ratio in *North*, applying Mason J's 'genuine supply and demand' test to the facts of *JM* and finding that a contravention of the *Corporations Act* had occurred.[218] The Court elaborated on the *North* test by stating that 'the forces of 'genuine supply and demand' are those forces which are created in a market by buyers whose purpose is to acquire at the lowest available price and sellers whose purpose is to sell at the highest realisable price'.[219] The references to creating an artificial price or market in s 1041A should be construed as 'including a transaction where the on-market buyer or seller of listed shares undertook it for the sole or dominant purpose of setting or maintaining the price at a particular level'.[220]

17.35.20 Remedies for market misconduct

With the exception of s 1041H, breach of any of the provisions of pt 7.10 div 2 may lead to general criminal offences,[221] as well specific criminal offences stated in ss 1041E(2) (false or misleading statements) and 1041G (dishonest conduct). Civil penalties are also available to ASIC under ss 1041A, 1041B, 1041C and 1041D.[222] Civil action is the only available remedy for breaches of s 1041H (misleading and deceptive conduct). However, civil action may also be taken under s 1041I for loss or damage suffered by a person due to a contravention of ss 1041E–H.[223]

Section 1101B may apply because it targets conduct in breach of ch 7 or any other law relating to trading or dealing in securities, licence conditions, *ORs* or *LRs*. Any activity

---

217 Ibid [65].

218 Ibid [70]. See also *Australian Securities and Investments Commission v Soust* (2010) 183 FCR 21, where Goldberg J interpreted 'artificial price' in s 1041A consistently with 'false or misleading appearance' in s 1041B, applying Mason J's ratio in *North*.

219 *DPP (Cth) v JM* (2013) 250 CLR 135 Ibid [71].

220 Ibid.

221 *Corporations Act 2001* (Cth) s 1311, sch 3.

222 Ibid s 1317E(3).

223 See, eg, *Rural Funds Management Ltd as Responsible Entity for the Rural Funds Trust and RF Active v Bonitas Research LLC* (2020) 143 ACSR 241, where a declaration was made that ss 1041E, 1041F and 1041H had been contravened, but not s 1041D.

which contravenes ch 7.10 div 2 will often be a breach of these rules. The action is usually brought by ASIC. As discussed above, there are some standing limitations in s 1101B.

Finally, note the analogue provisions in the *Australian Securities and Investments Commission Act 2001* (Cth) ('*ASIC Act*'): ss 12DA (a 'mirror' provision to s 1041H), 12DB and 12GF, which allow for a compensation order where someone who has suffered loss or damage under s 12DA to recover the amount of loss or damage against that person, or any person involved in the contravention. Section 12DA is framed in a similar way to s 1041H but only applies to financial services. The substantive provisions in the *ASIC Act* such as ss 12CB and 12CC—unconscionable conduct in connection with financial services—may be pleaded in the alternative to the more technical elements required to prove a breach of the provisions in pt 7.10 div 2: see *Australian Securities and Investments Commission v Westpac Banking Corporation (No 2)*.[224]

17.40 Overview of enforcement

This chapter has discussed the rules that are derived from contract, such as the *LRs* and the *ORs*, and considered some hybrids such as ss 674, 674A and 793C, as well as a multitude of formal statutory rules in ch 7 of the *Corporations Act*. We discussed a wide range of provisions which give rise to criminal offences, civil penalties, banning orders, licence revocation, and general provisions which allow for civil recourse.

Compliance with and enforcement of the provisions of the *Corporations Act* is primarily the responsibility of ASIC through direct engagement with participants, followed by a graduated escalation to proceedings in court and tribunals. The sanctions applied by ASIC are said to 'supplement a broader system of private redress against corporate misconduct, including ... class actions'.[225] To emphasise the point: ASIC's regulatory function is complemented by private enforcement, particularly by class actions.

17.40.05 ASIC's approach to enforcement

ASIC's enforcement of the obligations in the *Corporations Act* has been criticised for being weak and deficient.[226] Nevertheless, many commentators argue that ASIC has been successful in removing blatantly fraudulent operators from the market.[227] There is a myriad of enforcement mechanisms available to ASIC, and the current regime ensures that regulators are armed with flexible responses for particular circumstances. This promotes responsive regulation, which is discussed in Chapter 1.

224 *Australian Securities and Investments Commission v Westpac Banking Corporation (No 2)* (2018) 266 FCR 147.

225 Commonwealth Treasury, *Review of Sanctions in Corporate Law* (March 2007) vii.

226 T Middleton, 'ASIC's Investigation and Enforcement Powers—Current Issues and Suggested Reforms' (2004) 22(8) *Company and Securities Law Journal* 503. See generally Senate Economics References Committee, Parliament of Australia, *Performance of the Australian Securities and Investments Commission* (Report, 2014).

227 See, eg, G Pearson, *Financial Services Law and Compliance in Australia* (Cambridge University Press, 2009) 497.

Although regulatory theorists contend that responsive regulation is the best way to approach regulation, ASIC does not always adopt this approach to enforcement. Ramsay and Webster examined ASIC's enforcement outcomes for the period 2011–16.[228] Their study shows that different types of misconduct give rise to different approaches; for example, ASIC generally uses criminal enforcement in the market misconduct area for breaches such as insider trading and market manipulation. However, infringement notices are commonly used for breaches of the market integrity rules and continuous disclosure contraventions. The analysis shows that while nearly 70 per cent of ASIC's enforcement outcomes are criminal outcomes, this is mainly due to the results obtained by ASIC'S small business compliance and deterrence team. Other regulatory areas (market integrity, corporate governance and financial services), which are perhaps more relevant to 'big business', had a greater focus on administrative outcomes.

After the Hayne Royal Commission criticised ASIC's enforcement strategy (as discussed above at Section 17.20.10), ASIC adopted a 'why not litigate' enforcement stance and publicly committed to a core focus on deterrence, public denunciation and punishment.[229] Two years later, ASIC set aside this approach in favour of a new 'lighter' approach called 'express investigation', which focused upon ASIC's early engagement with entities and prioritised 'co-operation'.[230] It is important to note that 'bureaucratic pressures' can affect regulatory/enforcement decisions.[231] A Senate Committee report in 2024 criticised ASIC's approach to enforcement as inconsistent, stating that ASIC was not 'pursuing enough of the 'right matters', nor is it using its full suite of enforcement tools'.[232]

ASIC does not prioritise the compensation of those who have been harmed by illegal financial activity. In order for compensation to be awarded, it is up to the injured parties to seek a private right of action. We discuss this below.

17.40.10 Private enforcement by class actions

The last few decades have seen the rise of private enforcement in Australia due to the radical development of the class action. The foundation of class actions is an opt-out representative proceeding that allows an applicant to bring a claim for themselves and on behalf of a class of people who have the same, similar, or related claims.[233] The class

228 I Ramsay and M Webster, 'ASIC Enforcement Outcomes: Trends and Analysis' (2017) 35(5) *Company and Securities Law Journal* 289.

229 Australian Securities and Investments Commission, *ASIC Enforcement Update—January to June 2019* (Report No 625, 18 August 2019) 1.

230 K Chester, 'Regulation for Recovery: When Pilots Become Enduring Practice' (Speech, AFR Business Summit 2021, 10 March 2021).

231 JC Coffee, 'Paradigms Lost: The Blurring of the Criminal and Civil Law Models—And What Can Be Done about It' (1992) 101(8) *Yale Law Journal* 1875.

232 Senate Economics References Committee, Parliament of Australia, *Australian Securities and Investments Commission Investigation and Enforcement* (Report, July 2024) xix.

233 *Federal Court of Australia Act 1976* (Cth) pt IVA; *Civil Procedure Act 2005* (NSW) pt 10; *Civil Proceedings Act 2011* (Qld) pt 13A; *Supreme Court Act 1986* (Vic) pt IVA, *Supreme Court Civil Procedure Act 1932* (Tas) pt VII; *Civil Procedure (Representative Proceedings) Act 2022* (WA). See generally S Colbran et al, *Civil Procedure: Commentary and Materials* (LexisNexis, 9th ed 2025) ch 11.

action regime operates alongside ASIC's enforcement powers, and evidence obtained by ASIC or the findings of previous proceedings conducted by ASIC may be used in securities class actions as an evidentiary base for private claims.[234] In this respect, commentators argue that the class action performs the role of the 'private attorney general'.[235] The importance of class actions has been amplified over the last 20 years because of the emergence of large professional plaintiff firms in Australia and litigation funders who finance class actions.[236]

A recent but significant development has been acceptance by Australian courts that loss in securities class actions may be proved by its effect on the market rather than establishing reliance by individual investors on the impugned conduct. For example, a failure by a listed company to disclose negative information immediately under ss 674 and 674A may mean that investors who hold onto their shares suffer a loss. Proving individual loss can be complicated, particularly in a class action, which is a group claim. This problem is ameliorated if the court considers the effect of the conduct on the market rather than the individual investor. The acceptance of market-based causation to some extent owes its genesis to US law which creates a rebuttable presumption that the market has been defrauded where misleading statements have been made (in an efficient market).[237] In other respects, some Australian judges have accepted that proof of market-based causation may be sufficient where loss is suffered in a market where misconduct has occurred.[238] The case law is divided.[239]

234 See, eg, *Australian Securities and Investments Commission v Newcrest Mining Ltd* (2014) 101 ACSR 46.

235 P Spender, 'Securities Class Actions: A View from the Land of the Great White Shareholder' (2002) 31(2) *Common Law World Review* 123. Research conducted by Morabito shows that 122 securities class actions were filed in Australia between 1992 and 2019. These claims constituted 32.2 per cent of all class actions in Australia in 2018–19, declining from 44.7 per cent in 2016–17: V Morabito, 'An Evidence-based Approach to Class Action Reform In Australia: Shareholder Class Actions in Australia: Myths v Facts' (Report, November 2019) 15–16 <https://www.casl.com.au/wp-content/uploads/2022/01/vince_morabito_report_nov19.pdf>. November 2019) 15–16.

236 Since the High Court judgment in *Campbell's Cash and Carry Pty Ltd v Fostif Pty Ltd* (2006) 229 CLR 386 and (later) the Full Federal Court judgment in *Money Max Int Pty Ltd v QBE Insurance Group Ltd* (2016) 245 FCR 191; see Australian Law Reform Commission, *Integrity, Fairness and Efficiency—An Inquiry into Class Action Proceedings and Third-Party Litigation Funders* (Report No 134, 24 January 2019); V Morabito, 'Group Costs Orders, Funding Commissions, Volume of Class Action Litigation, Reimbursement Payments and Biggest Settlements' (Report, 4 February 2025) <https://doi.org/10.2139/ssrn.5125031>.

237 *Basic v Levinson*, 485 US 224 (1988), upheld in *Halliburton Co v Erica P John Fund, Inc*, 134 S Ct 2398 (2014).

238 *Caason Investments Pty Ltd v Cao* (2015) 236 FCR 322; *Re HIH Insurance Ltd (in liq)* (2016) 335 ALR 320; see L Gamertsfelder, 'The Slow Embrace of Fraud on the Market Theory' (2016) 15(7) *Finance and Society Network* 128.

239 Note the views expressed by judges in Federal Court decisions handed down in 2019–25. In *Masters v Lombe (liquidator); Re Babcock & Brown Ltd (in liq)* [2019] FCA 1720, Foster J stated that 'there are difficulties with the market-based causation theory' at [390]. In *TPT Patrol Pty Ltd as trustee for Amies Superannuation Fund v Myer Holdings Ltd* (2019) 140 ACSR 38, Beach J accepted the theory of market-based causation and provided an extensive analysis of the case law and literature (at [1514]–[1672]). However, in both cases, the applicant (who relied on market-based causation) did not succeed because both judges found that the market price of the securities in question had not been inflated because of the respondent's breaches. In *Davis v Wilson* [2025] FCA 108, Shariff J discussed individual/direct reliance and market-based causation but found that the applicant had not established either on the facts of the case.

17.45 Summary

This chapter has discussed the regulation of securities and derivative markets in Australia. An understanding of these financial markets is critical to an understanding of company law, because these markets provide finance for companies and are a crucial part of the context of many decisions made by corporations. The next chapter will examine financial services, which is the activity undertaken by participants in the financial markets.

CHAPTER

18

FINANCIAL SERVICES

18.05 Introduction

This chapter discusses laws and arrangements that impose obligations upon intermediaries to achieve some protection of clients involved in financial product transactions. We have already encountered some intermediaries who provide financial services in Chapter 17: the brokers who participate in the ASX markets. However, intermediaries are often involved in transactions involving financial products, so the range of people who may be involved in, or who can influence, financial product transactions is much wider and clearly includes financial advisers. This chapter examines how the activities of some participants in this diverse group are regulated to achieve a measure of investor protection.

The question of regulation of financial advice and financial services has been contentious in Australia over the last two decades. Following several large financial collapses,[1] it is now recognised that the quality of financial advice in Australia is often poor, particularly for retail and other non-professional investors.

Concern about the quality of financial advice has led to a series of parliamentary inquiries, commencing with the Parliamentary Joint Committee on Corporations and Financial Services' *Inquiry into Financial Products and Services in Australia* ('the Ripoll Report')[2] in 2009, which recommended sweeping changes to the regulation of financial advice.

Prior to these recommendations, the regime[3] focused on disclosure and the duty of financial advisers to give advice that was suitable for retail investors.[4] The suitability obligation was not particularly onerous. There were also problems associated with the training of financial planners, since no minimum training was required, and financial planning was only beginning to evolve as a profession. Consequently, the industry was populated by many relatively unqualified people giving advice about complex products to those who were not in a position to judge the quality of the advice given.

1 For example, the Queensland-based Storm Financial Ltd, which collapsed during the 2008–9 global financial crisis with debts of approximately $88 million.

2 Joint Committee on Corporations and Financial Services, Parliament of Australia, *Inquiry into Financial Products and Services in Australia* (Report, 2009) ('the Ripoll Report').

3 Following the Wallis Report, which was implemented in the *Financial Services Reform Act 2001* (Cth): Commonwealth of Australia, *Financial System Inquiry* (Final Report, March 1997) ('the Wallis Report').

4 For a broader discussion about these reforms, see Section 17.20.10.

This problem was exacerbated by tied arrangements between financial institutions and within large vertically integrated financial institutions, such as the banks, that encouraged advisers to recommend certain financial products because they received a commission for that recommendation without appropriate disclosure to the customer.

Leading up to 2012, the Australian Securities and Investments Commission (ASIC) undertook several studies about the quality of financial advice. In these studies, individuals sought financial advice about retirement and the advice was reviewed by an expert panel. The 2012 study found that the majority of advice reviewed (58 per cent) was of adequate quality (meaning it satisfied the statutory criteria at that time); 39 per cent of the advice was poor; and only 3 per cent was of good quality.[5]

Following the Ripoll Report, the Future of Financial Advice (FOFA) reform was launched. This led to significant changes in the regulation of financial advisers. For example, financial advisers are now required to take into account the best interests of retail clients when providing advice and there is a ban on conflicted remuneration, such as commissions.[6] There has been significant debate about the professionalisation of the financial planning industry. For example, a report in December 2014 by the Parliamentary Joint Committee on Corporations and Financial Services found that reforms were needed to improve the qualifications, competence professional standards and ethics of financial advisers.[7] In 2017, legislation introduced compulsory education requirements for financial advisers and a code of ethics for the industry.[8]

In 2022, the *Quality of Advice Review*[9] concluded that the existing regulatory framework makes it 'hard for institutions to give their customers simple personal advice and it makes it hard and expensive for financial advisers to give their clients the advice they want at a price they are willing to pay'[10]. The Final Report recommended that the law in this area should be simplified by streamlining the required documentation and replacing the best interests duty to retail clients with a new duty to provide 'good advice'.[11] Some of recommendations in this report have been implemented,[12] but the recommendation about good advice had not been legislated at the time of writing.

As discussed above, the obligations imposed upon intermediaries are intended to protect clients in financial product transactions. Most of the protections are designed

---

5 Australian Securities and Investments Commission, *Shadow Shopping Study of Retirement Advice* (Report 279, March 2012) 6, 8 [18].

6 Part 7.7A div 4, although note the critique of D Mendoza-Jones, 'Reform of the Financial Advice Industries in Australia and the United States' (2013) 31(4) *Company and Securities Law Journal* 261. See generally Australian Securities and Investments Commission, *Conflicted and other Banned Remuneration* (Regulatory Guide 246, 21 November 2024).

7 Parliamentary Joint Committee on Corporations and Financial Services, Parliament of Australia, *Inquiry into Proposals to Lift the Professional, Ethical and Education Standards in the Financial Services Industry* (Report, 2014).

8 *Corporations Amendment (Professional Standards of Financial Advisers) Act 2017* (Cth). See Australian Securities and Investments Commission, *Professional Standards for Financial Advisers* (9 August 2023) <https://asic.gov.au/regulatory-resources/financial-services/financial-advice/professional-standards-for-financial-advisers/>.

9 Australian Government, The Treasury, *Quality of Advice Review* (Final Report, December 2022).

10 Ibid 1.

11 Ibid 6.

12 See, eg, *Treasury Laws Amendment (Delivering Better Financial Outcomes and Other Measures) Act 2024* (Cth).

for retail clients, so the next section will consider the general characteristics of retail investors followed by an examination of the legal definition of retail client under the *Corporations Act*. Thereafter, we examine the legal elements of the intermediary–client relationship via agency, contract, fiduciary and statutory provisions. The intermediary–client relationship will be exemplified by the broker–client and financial adviser–client relationships. Finally, this chapter discusses licensing obligations and product disclosure requirements imposed on intermediates under the *Corporations Act*.

18.05.05 Retail investors

What are the characteristics of retail investors? ASX conducts a regular survey of retail investors and this provides us with some information about what characterises an investor as a 'retail' investor.[13] The *ASX Australian Investor Study* published in 2023 found that 51 per cent of Australians own investments that are outside their home or superannuation.[14] The average age of current investors was 47 years and the median portfolio size for on-exchange investors was $170,000.[15] Overall, male investors outnumbered female investors (58 per cent to 42 per cent) but 2023 saw more Australian women investing outside of their primary residence and superannuation than ever before.[16]

Regarding financial advice, 26 per cent of investors in the *ASX Australian Investor Study* received advice in previous 12 months from a professional planner or adviser; 29 per cent of Australian adults plan to seek advice in the following 12 months; 34 per cent of Australian adults would use an adviser but think they are too expensive; and 9 per cent of investors currently use robo-advice or micro-investing platforms.[17]

Another important element of the regulation in this area are assumptions made by the legislature about the financial literacy of retail investors.[18] For example, some disclosures that must be made to retail investors when financial advice is given are based on an assumption that retail investors are 'responsibilised'.[19] In other words, it is assumed that the provision of information will allow retail investors to make their own appropriate and prudent investment choices.[20]

There is evidence that this assumption may not be correct. The *ANZ Survey of Adult Financial Literacy in Australia*, published in 2015, found that Australians have a strong

13 The sample size for the 2023 study was 5,519 Australian adults. The respondents were post-weighted slightly and calibrated to Australian Bureau of Statistics data on Australian population demographics: ASX, *ASX Australian Investor Study* (2023) 92.

14 Ibid 6.

15 Ibid 8.

16 Ibid 26.

17 Ibid 9.

18 For a general discussion about the literature on financial literacy, see Kirti Goyal and Satish Kumar, 'Financial Literacy: A Systematic Review and Bibliometric Analysis' (2021) 45(1) *International Journal of Consumer Studies* 80.

19 Toni Williams, 'Empowerment of Whom and for What? Financial Literacy Education and the New Regulation of Consumer Financial Services' (2007) 28 *Law & Policy* 226.

20 Implemented via the *Financial Services Reform Act 2001* (Cth) following the 1997 Wallis Report: see Dimity Kingsford-Smith, 'Regulating Risk: Individuals and the Global Financial Crisis' (2009) 32 *University of New South Wales Law Journal* 514.

awareness (86 per cent) that a high return is likely to mean that a financial product carries a higher risk.[21] Although 67 per cent of people recognised that good investments may fluctuate in value, only 50 per cent of people can recognise an investment as 'too good to be true'.[22] The survey found lower rates of financial literacy among younger people (< 35 years old) and older women (> 65 years old).[23]

The findings of the *ANZ Survey* with respect to superannuation products are significant. Although the focus of this and the previous chapter is on exchange-traded products, superannuation is the financial product that is most commonly encountered by average Australians. The *ANZ Survey* found that 68 per cent of superannuation fund members read their superannuation fund statements and 20 per cent do not read them.[24] The main reasons for not reading the superannuation statement were because members 'couldn't be bothered' or the statements are 'too difficult to understand'. Notably, 33 per cent of superannuation fund members said they found reading a superannuation statement difficult.[25]

Retail investors can be contrasted with institutional investors, such as insurance companies and superannuation funds, that have large pools of money[26] to invest on stock exchanges.[27] Institutional investors employ their own analysts and advisers to make decisions about investments. They may also influence the policies of listed companies.[28]

18.05.10 Definition of 'retail client'

The definition of 'retail client' is key to the operation of this regulatory system. Section 761G of the *Corporations Act* defines the meaning of retail and wholesale clients. The underlying rationale is that because less protection is given to wholesale clients, a person must be treated as a retail client unless the provision clearly states otherwise. Section 761G states that a financial product or financial service is provided to a person as a retail client unless one of the specific exemptions listed in that section applies. Section 761G(4) states that a financial product or service is provided to or acquired by a person as a wholesale client if they are not a retail client.

The focus of this chapter is on traded products, rather than insurance and superannuation products, so the relevant provision is s 761G(7). This section states that a financial product or a financial service is provided to a person as a retail client except in four circumstances:

21 Australia and New Zealand Banking Group, *ANZ Survey of Adult Financial Literacy in Australia* (ANZ, 2015) 3 ('*ANZ Survey*').

22 Ibid.

23 Ibid 11.

24 Ibid 72

25 Ibid 4.

26 Approximately $3.9 trillion is held by superannuation funds in the Australian market, of which $2.7 trillion are APRA-regulated funds. The latter would be classified as institutional investors: Australian Prudential Regulation Authority, *Quarterly Superannuation Statistics* (29 August 2024) <https://www.apra.gov.au/quarterly-superannuation-statistics>.

27 J Law, *A Dictionary of Finance and Banking* (Oxford University Press, 6th ed, 2018).

28 Ibid.

(1) the price or value of the financial product/financial service exceeds the prescribed amount in the regulations (currently $500,000)[29]
(2) where the financial product/financial service is provided for use in connection with a business that is not a *small* business (small business is defined in s 761G(12) as employing fewer than 100 people if the business is in manufacturing, otherwise 20 people)
(3) where an individual provides evidence that they have the following wealth:
   - net assets of at least $2.5 million (reg 7.1.28), or
   - gross income for each of the last two financial years of at least $250,000 (reg 7.1.28)
(4) the person is a professional investor.

The exceptions are intended for investors who may choose to decline the retail protections, presumably on the basis that they either have considerable experience in making investments or have the means to seek appropriate advice.[30] The term 'professional investor' is defined (narrowly) in s 9 of the *Corporations Act*.

A financial service or product is not provided to a person as a retail client if the client is a sophisticated investor (s 761GA). In this situation, the licensee must be satisfied that the client has previous experience in using financial services and investing in financial products to allow the client to assess the merits, value, risks, the client's own information needs, and adequacy of information given (s 761GA(d)). In this situation, the licensee must give a written statement to the client that the licensee is so satisfied, and the reasons and the client must sign a written acknowledgment that they are not receiving the retail client disclosures and obligations.

For valuable applications of these definitions to cohorts of investors, see *Australian Securities and Investments Commission v Cassimatis (No 8)*[31] that involved the Storm Financial litigation. Another case on this point is *Australian Securities and Investments Commission v AGM Markets Pty Ltd (in liq) (No 3)*. Here, Beach J found that the respondent had engaged in systemic unconscionable conduct while providing over-the-counter derivative products to retail investors in Australia.[32]

18.10 Regulating the intermediary–client relationship

Under the general law, the intermediary–client relationship is regulated by a combination of contract, agency and fiduciary principles. Intermediaries also have obligations under the *Corporations Act*, which are discussed below. The *Corporations Act* expressly

29 *Corporations Regulations 2001* (Cth) regs 7.1.18–7.1.22, but note that there are many different ways to assess 'price': it can be an income stream, investment-based, the price of a margin lending facility or the value of a derivative. See generally Australian Securities and Investments Commission, *Licensing: Financial Product Advisers—Conduct and Disclosure* (Regulatory Guide 175, 21 November 2024).

30 Explanatory Memorandum, Financial Services Reform Bill 2001 (Cth) [6.32].

31 *Australian Securities and Investments Commission v Cassimatis (No 8)* (2016) 336 ALR 209 [568]ff (Edelman J).

32 *Australian Securities and Investments Commission v AGM Markets Pty Ltd (in liq) (No 3)* (2020) 275 FCR 57.

preserves the operation of the general law, therefore the obligations under the general law will operate concurrently with the statutory provisions. This is illustrated below by reference to the broker–client relationship in Section 18.15 and by the financial adviser–client relationship in Section 18.20.

The relevant fiduciary duty may be one of the existing *status-based* fiduciary duties, such as broker–client,[33] or it may be a *fact-based* fiduciary duty that was recognised by the High Court in *Hospital Products Ltd v United States Surgical Corporation ('Hospital Products')*.[34] If a fiduciary duty is found, the ambit of the obligations may be the traditional, *proscriptive* obligations (no conflict, no profit) or wider and more general *prescriptive* duties. The High Court, in *Daly v Sydney Stock Exchange Ltd*,[35] made it clear that brokers owe a traditional status-based fiduciary duty to their clients. The situation is less clear in relation to other financial services, particularly financial advice. In addition, a statutory duty under pt 7.7A of the *Corporations Act* is owed by financial advisers to act in the best interests of their retail clients when giving advice.

The relevant law that is applied to a particular dispute may be shaped by how a case is pleaded when proceedings commence. As commentators have noted:

> A regulator in a regulatory action, or a plaintiff in a private action, may well rely on the most demanding standard—which is likely to be the no conflicts rule if it applies—to establish a breach, even if the statutory duties have been satisfied.[36]

This issue is discussed in more detail at Section 18.20 below and summarised at Section 18.20.15. The summary also explains the interactions between, and the remedial consequences of, the operation of the different bodies of law.

18.15 The broker–client relationship

18.15.05 Contract: the basic securities transaction

The basic or standard transaction for buying or selling securities on a stock exchange may be illustrated as follows:

Buyer (B)—Buyer's Broker (BB)—Seller's Broker (SB)—Seller (S)

Using the buyer as the reference point, the buyer places an order to buy securities with the BB. The BB enters a bid (which may be for a maximum specified price or for the best market price) into a device that is connected to the ASX trading platform. The bid price is considered by selling brokers who enter offers to sell until buy and sell orders are matched. The orders are automatically executed against bids of offers within parameters defined by the highest bid and lowest offer.

33 *Daly v Sydney Stock Exchange Ltd* (1986) 160 CLR 371 ('*Daly*'). These categories are referred to as 'nominate' categories in Chapter 13: see Section 13.10.20.

34 *Hospital Products Ltd v United States Surgical Corporation* (1984) 156 CLR 41; *Wingecarribee Shire Council v Lehman Brothers Ltd (in liq)* (2012) 301 ALR 1; see also *ABN AMRO Bank NV v Bathurst Regional Council* (2014) 224 FCR 1.

35 *Daly v Sydney Stock Exchange Ltd* (1986) 160 CLR 371.

36 A Black and P Hanrahan, *Securities and Financial Services Law* (LexisNexis Butterworths, 2021) 596.

The transactions are as follows:

(1) The buyer–seller contract that is ultimately reached between B and S. They will be unknown to each other.
(2) The ASX trading contract between the two brokers. Under the ASX *Operating Rules* (*ORs*), brokers are liable to each other as principals: the BB is liable to the SB to pay the price for the securities, while the SB is liable to deliver valid documents of title if necessary. In the usual case, of course, each broker will seek out and obtain an indemnification from their client. Brokers are made liable as principals because the identities of the clients are not revealed by the trading platform transaction; therefore, the other broker cannot know or vouch for the creditworthiness of the other client.
(3) The two broker–client contracts. Each contract is an agency relationship in which the client is principal and the broker is agent.

There are other forms of contract that involve a single broker acting for both buyer and seller: these are called 'crossings' and 'special crossings'.

Crossings

The term 'crossing' is defined in OR 7100 as a transaction in respect of which a trading participant acts on behalf of both buying and selling clients to that transaction, or on behalf of a buying or selling client on one side of the transaction and as principal on the other side.[37] For example, Broker A has an order from one client to purchase securities and an order from another client to sell the same number and type of securities. The broker is obliged (via OR 4060[38] and the ASX *Operating Rules Procedures*[39]) to give other brokers the chance to match their own buying or selling orders to those held by Broker A. The offer is notified to the market as a potential crossing. Where the offer is accepted by another broker, the transaction will be of the ordinary type described above. Where no match is made, Broker A can 'cross' one order with the other.

Special crossings

A 'special crossing' is defined in OR 7100 as a crossing effected in accordance with OR 4810 and the ASX *Operating Rules Procedures*. A single broker acts for both seller and buyer who have already come to an agreement about the terms of the sale/purchase. The transaction is not effected through the market, but is merely reported to the market. Special crossings usually involve large trades and/or large portfolios; therefore, minimum thresholds for the procedure are stipulated.

The special crossing rules reflect a recognition of the risk that a large block of shares placed on the market could distort the market. The special crossing mechanisms allow transactions in larger parcels of shares to be negotiated off the trading floor and then reported to the market.

37 ASX, *Operating Rules: Section 07* (at 25 March 2024) r 7100.
38 ASX, *Operating Rules Section 04* (at 19 February 2024) r 4060.
39 ASX, *Operating Rules Procedures* (at 25 March 2024).

The clearing and settlement of securities

The clearing and settlement of securities transactions in the ASX market currently take place in the CHESS system.[40] CHESS stands for 'Clearing House Subregister System'. CHESS calculates the net obligations of each broker who trades on the ASX platform for each trading day, instead of settling thousands of trades individually.

Net settlement takes place by novation of buy and sell contracts. A novation is an agreement discharging a contract and entering into a new one—usually on the same terms but with at least one of the parties being different. It is a method of releasing a party from the contract and introducing a new party in their place.[41] The novation occurs in CHESS by interposing several clearing and settlement agreements between the buyer and seller.

18.15.10 Contract: terms of the broker–client contract

The ORs and *Listing Rules* may either be express terms of the contract in the broker's contract note or they may be implied into the contract because they deal with practices or methods of dealing that have a recognised usage. In *Bell Group Ltd v Herald and Weekly Times Ltd*,[42] Kaye J held that 'to give business efficacy to an agency contract between a broker and their principal, there must be implied into their contract a term that the principal (i.e. client) will be bound by all articles, rules and regulations of the Stock Exchange which prescribe the manner of formation of a contract for the sale and purchase of a security'.[43]

18.15.15 Contract: implied terms: custom and usage

In *Con-Stan Industries of Australia Pty Ltd v Norwich Winterthur Insurance (Australia) Ltd*,[44] the High Court set out the criteria for implying a term based on custom and usage:

(1) whether the existence of the custom or usage, which will justify the implication of the term into the contract, is a question of fact in the particular case;
(2) there must be evidence that the custom relied on is so well-known and acquiesced in that everyone making a contract in that situation can be presumed to have imported that term into the contract;
(3) the term will not be implied where it is contrary to the express terms of the agreement;
(4) a person can be bound by custom even though they had no knowledge of it.

40 At the time of writing, ASX is piloting a clearing and settlement system based on blockchain that may eventually replace the CHESS system. However, the issue has become contentious. In August 2024, ASIC commenced proceedings against ASX alleging that it had made false or misleading representations to the public about the progress of the replacement of CHESS: see Australian Securities and Investments Commission, 'ASIC Sues ASX for Alleged Misleading Statements' (Media Release 24–177, 14 August 2024).

41 See, eg, *Olsson v Dyson* (1969) 120 CLR 365.

42 *Bell Group Ltd v Herald and Weekly Times Ltd* [1985] VR 613.

43 For an example of the operation of implied terms in the broker-client contract, see *FAI Traders Insurance Co Ltd v ANZ McCaughan Securities Ltd* (1990) 3 ACSR 279.

44 *Con-Stan Industries of Australia Pty Ltd v Norwich Winterthur Insurance (Australia) Ltd* (1986) 160 CLR 226.

18.15.20 Agency

The broker-client relationship is also based on agency principles. When a client gives instructions to a broker, the client grants actual authority to a broker, and the broker has a duty not to exceed that authority and to perform their instructions in good faith. However, a broker is personally liable for the contract and has a right to be indemnified by the client for all reasonable expenses incurred by the broker. Further, by custom and usage in the ASX securities and derivatives markets, a broker can close out their client's position in order to minimise loss associated with the client's default. The broker can exercise a power of sale, but it must be exercised carefully.[45]

18.15.25 The broker–client fiduciary duty

As stated above, a broker owes a fiduciary duty to their client as agent for the client.[46] The leading case for this proposition is *Daly v Sydney Stock Exchange Ltd*,[47] which recognised the general fiduciary duty owed by brokers to their clients. Here, Mr Daly approached a stockbroking firm to invest in the share market. The firm advised him that it was not a good time to buy shares and suggested his money be placed on deposit with the firm. The firm became insolvent and Daly lost his money. Daly made a claim on the National Guarantee Fund (this is discussed at Section 17.20.20). He alleged that the fiduciary duty was owed to him, a breach of which was a defalcation for the purposes of claiming on the fund.

The High Court stated that, generally speaking, a fiduciary duty will be owed between a stockbroker and client. As commented by Gibbs CJ:

> Normally the relation between a stockbroker and his [sic] client will be one of a fiduciary nature and [will] place on the broker an obligation to make to the client a full and accurate disclosure of the broker's own interest in the transaction.[48]

But here, Daly lent the money to the firm of brokers rather than entrusting it to them as part of a broker–client relationship. A debtor–creditor relationship arose that took the relevant arrangement outside the terms of the relevant statutory provisions. Therefore, Daly was not entitled to compensation out of the fund.[49]

18.20 The financial adviser–client relationship

As discussed above, under the general law a financial adviser–client relationship has elements of contract, agency and fiduciary law. In addition, as discussed in the next section, financial advisers owe statutory obligations to retail clients under pt 7.7A of the *Corporations Act*. The law pertaining to this area generally is summarised at Section 18.20.15.

45 *Option Investments (Australia) Pty Ltd v Martin* [1981] VR 138.
46 *Clayton Robard Management Ltd v Siu* (1988) 6 ACLC 57.
47 *Daly v Sydney Stock Exchange Ltd* (1986) 160 CLR 371.
48 Ibid 377.
49 See also *Georges v Seaborn International Pty Ltd* (2012) 206 FCR 408.

18.20.05 The statutory best interests obligation under pt 7.7A

Part 7.7A of the *Corporations Act* establishes a regime that obliges financial advisers to act in the best interests of their clients. Section 961 states that the obligation arises where personal advice is given to someone as a retail client. The primary obligation is in s 961B. This section has a checklist for satisfying the duty to act in the best interest of the client (ss 961B(2)(a)–(f)). Commentators have noted that the concept of 'best interest' in pt 7.7A is left undefined and the checklist in s 961B(2) provides a 'safe harbour' if the financial adviser can prove that the steps in s 961B(2) have been taken.[50] The Hayne Royal Commission questioned the operation of the so-called 'safe harbour', stating that they may 'amount to a tick a box exercise rather than a substantive test'.[51] However, the safe harbour construction is debatable because s 961B(2)(g) has a 'catch-all' provision, which obliges a financial adviser to take 'any other step that, at the time the advice was provided, would reasonably be regarded as being in the interests of the client, given the client's relevant circumstances'. In *Australian Securities and Investments Commission v NSG Services Pty Ltd*,[52] Moshinsky J held that s 961B must be read alongside s 961G, which states that the provider must only provide advice to the client that is *appropriate*, meaning the advice that would be given if the provider had satisfied the duty under s 961B to act in the best interests of the client.[53] Further, pursuant to s 961J, a provider must give priority to the interests of a retail client when giving advice when it knows, or ought reasonably know, that there is a conflict between the interests of the client and the provider.[54]

The Ripoll Committee intended to impose fiduciary-like duties upon financial advisers.[55] However, as noted in the *Quality of Advice Review*, the statutory provisions are not fiduciary duties.[56] Nevertheless, as foreshadowed above, when construing the obligations under these provisions, particularly s 961B, it is unclear whether they create obligations which are narrow, proscriptive 'fiduciary' duty that follows the classic rules of 'no conflict, no profit' or a wider obligation to act in the best interests of a party.[57]

In *Australian Securities and Investments Commission v Westpac Securities Administration Ltd*,[58] Allsop CJ in the Full Federal Court commented that the obligation in s 961B 'draws

50 H-W Liu et al, 'In Whose Best Interests? Regulating Financial Advisers, the Royal Commission and the Dilemma of Reform' (2020) 42(1) *Sydney Law Review* 37, 38.

51 Ibid, citing *Royal Commission into Misconduct in the Banking, Superannuation and Financial Services Industry* (Final Report, 4 February 2019) vol 1, 177.

52 *Australian Securities and Investments Commission v NSG Services Pty Ltd* (2017) 122 ACSR 47 [21].

53 This approach was approved by the Full Federal Court in *Australian Securities and Investments Commission v Westpac Securities Administration Ltd* (2019) 272 FCR 170.

54 See *Australian Securities and Investments Commission v Ultiqa Lifestyle Promotions Ltd (in liq)* (2022) 159 ACSR 195.

55 Joint Committee on Corporations and Financial Services, Parliament of Australia, *Inquiry into Financial Products and Services in Australia* (Report, 2009) [6.29].

56 Australian Government, *Quality of Advice Review* (Final Report, December 2022) 27.

57 See generally P Hanrahan, 'The Relationship Between Equitable and Statutory "best interests" Obligations in Financial Services Law' (2013) 7(1) *Journal of Equity* 46.

58 *Australian Securities and Investments Commission v Westpac Securities Administration Ltd* (2019) 272 FCR 170.

on the concepts of fiduciary loyalty commonly resting on persons in such a position'.[59] His Honour considered that the correct approach to interpretation of the provision is as follows:

> The circumstances that will lead to a conclusion that a provider of personal advice did not act in the best interests of his or her client may be drawn in part from the list of factors in s 961B(2), but the source of equitable faithfulness of the duty in s 961B(1) should also be recognised in the content of the phrase and the possible circumstances of its contravention.[60]

Conversely, Jagot J in the same case was more sceptical about the ambit of the provision and its tendency to promote the tick-a-box approach to compliance.

> To discharge the duty in s 961B(1) the provider must have as its purpose or object acting in the best interests of the client. The provider can effectively prove that their purpose or object was to act in the best interests of the client by doing each of the matters in s 961B(2), each of which is essentially procedural. As the Explanatory Memorandum explains the fact of harm is not the criterion against which performance of this duty is measured ...

The facts in *Westpac Securities* are set out at Section 18.25.05 and the Full Court found that s 961B had been breached. Westpac had been acting in its own interests and it was 'fortuitous' if the relevant outcome—a rollover of the customer's superannuation into the bank's accounts—was in the customer's best interests.[61] The High Court dismissed an appeal from this judgment, focusing on the concept of 'personal advice'.

The applications of pt 7.7A in recent case law suggest that a flexible approach will be adopted.[62] For example, in *Australian Securities and Investments Commission v Wealth & Risk Management Pty Ltd (No 2)*,[63] a cash rebate scheme was declared to breach the provision because it was non-compliant with the financial services laws and involved the targeting and exploitation of financially disadvantaged people.[64] Similarly, in *Australian Securities and Investments Commission v Ultiqa Lifestyle Promotions Ltd (in liq)*,[65] the adviser's promotion of interests in a holiday time-share scheme breached ss 961B, 961G and 961J because the client's relevant circumstances had not been identified (for example, a couple with five children who had casual jobs with no leave entitlements) and the advice was not appropriate. The provider had failed to give priority to the clients' interests under s 961J because a commission was payable to the respondent's authorised representative if the consumer acted on the advice and acquired an interest in the scheme.

---

59 Ibid [151], citing *Daly v Sydney Stock Exchange Ltd* (1986) 160 CLR 371, 377, 385 as discussed at Section 18.15.25.

60 (2019) 272 FCR 170 [151].

61 Ibid [301].

62 See also *Australian Securities and Investments Commission v Financial Circle Pty Ltd* (2018) 123 ACSR 624; *Australian Securities and Investments Commission v NSG Services Pty Ltd* (2017) 122 ACSR 47; *Australian Securities and Investments Commission v Ostrava Equities Pty Ltd* [2016] FCA 1064.

63 *Australian Securities and Investments Commission v Wealth & Risk Management Pty Ltd (No 2)* (2018) 124 ACSR 351.

64 Ibid [148].

65 *Australian Securities and Investments Commission v Ultiqa Lifestyle Promotions Ltd (in liq)* (2022) 159 ACSR 195.

18.20.10 Financial advisers: is a fiduciary duty evolving under the general law?

Over the last decade or so, some cases have recognised the presence of a fiduciary duty owed by a financial adviser to a client. Importantly, the facts of the cases cut across the categories where an obligation would be owed under the *Corporations Act* because the cases involve portfolios managed by the local councils that were in excess of the threshold set for a retail client under the *Corporations Act*. Therefore, the local councils did not fall within the narrow definition of retail client to whom the duties under pt 7.7A are owed. The cases are based on the status-based *Daly* fiduciary duty (which is discussed above), but also the fact-based fiduciary duty recognised in *Hospital Products*. The latter was refined by Finn J in *Grimaldi v Chameleon Mining NL (No 2)* as follows:

> A person will be in a fiduciary relationship with another when and in so far as that person has undertaken to perform such a function for, or has assumed such a responsibility to, another as would thereby reasonably entitle that other to expect that he or she will act in that other's interest to the exclusion of his or her own or a third party's interest.[66]

As applied to financial advisers, in the first case, *Wingecarribee Shire Council v Lehman Brothers Ltd (in liq)*[67] ('*Wingecarribee*'), Rares J of the Federal Court found that Lehman Brothers owed a fiduciary duty to the Wingecarribee Council. This was a class action case brought by three local governments (the Councils) against Grange Securities Limited (acquired by Lehman Brothers Group before the proceedings). The Councils argued a number of claims with respect to the sale of and sales advice regarding Synthetic Collaterised Debt Obligations (SCDOs).[68] These claims included breaches of fiduciary duty. Rares J described SCDOs as highly complex financial instruments, which are only to be sold to sophisticated clients who can withstand 'a total loss of capital'.[69] Therefore, they are high risk products. Rares J commented that the concept of SCDOs is 'beyond the grasp of most people'.[70]

Grange put itself forward to the Councils as a financial adviser that understood the investment requirements of local government, including relevant legislative and policy constraints. The Councils explained that they were looking for a low-risk and liquid investment and Grange told them that SCDOs were appropriate for a conservative investment strategy. Further, the Councils explained to Grange that they did not have the time or competence to monitor the products and would require Grange to perform this role if the Councils were to invest in the product. Grange confirmed that this was part of its service and expertise.

66 *Grimaldi v Chameleon Mining NL (No 2)* (2012) 200 FCR 296, 345 [177] citing *Hospital Products Ltd v United States Surgical Corporation* (1984) 156 CLR 41, 96–7; see also *Bell Group Ltd (in liq) v Westpac Banking Corporation* (No 9) (2009) 39 WAR 1.

67 *Wingecarribee Shire Council v Lehman Brothers Ltd (in liq)* (2012) 301 ALR 1.

68 L Bransgrove, 'Case Note: *Wingecarribee Shire Council v Lehman Brothers Australia Ltd (in liq)* [2012] FCA 1028' (2013) 24(1) *Journal of Banking and Finance Law and Practice* 52, 52.

69 *Wingecarribee Shire Council v Lehman Brothers Ltd (in liq)* (2012) 301 ALR 1, 97 [339].

70 Ibid [410].

Given that the Councils asked for low-risk liquid products, the SCDOs were an inappropriate recommendation and clearly did not meet their needs. While the Councils technically passed the wholesale client test under s 761G, and thus could be sold these products, they were by no means financially sophisticated and were clearly inexperienced investors as regards SCDOs. Rares J held that Grange owed fiduciary duties. He emphasised several elements of the analysis above regarding fiduciary relationships. He supported the judgment of *Daly*, demonstrating that the client's reasonable expectations and trust and confidence are important in the financial adviser–investor relationship.[71] However, he also relied on the principle in *Hospital Products* that the critical feature is that the 'fiduciary undertakes or agrees to act ... in the interests of another person'.[72] Rares J subsequently appeared to find a fact-based relationship derived from an undertaking given when Grange first negotiated the transactions for the Councils.

Rares J then reverted to the *Daly* formula by finding that the fiduciary duty was breached by Grange in failing to obtain the consent of the Councils to a benefit obtained by Grange from the transactions; namely, placement fees from issuers of the products.[73]

Wingecarribee is a landmark case for two reasons. First, the finding of a fiduciary duty owed by a financial adviser to an investor independent of any principal–agent finding was significant. Second, it was noteworthy that the obligations commenced without a formalised written agreement as to the advisory nature of the relationship. Furthermore, Rares J held that the Councils were to be defined as 'financially unsophisticated', even though they were defined under the legislation as wholesale clients.

The second relevant case is *ABN AMRO Bank NV v Bathurst Regional Council* ('*ABN AMRO*').[74] In that case, the Full Federal Court upheld the findings of the trial judge that the relevant body—the Local Government Financial Services Association (LGFSA)—owed a fiduciary duty to the applicant Council because the firm had 'led the client to believe that it would act in their best interests in advising and making recommendations about financial products'.[75] In this respect, the firm was engaged in a course of conduct over time which took it beyond being a 'mere salesman' of the financial products in question. It knew the context in which the clients functioned and knew that the clients perceived the firm as acting in the client's interests and not in the firm's sole interests. Therefore, in doing so, the firm moved beyond the role of mere salesman and acted as investment adviser and attracted to itself fiduciary duties: it undertook to act in the Council's interests rather than its own. The *ABN AMRO* case involved the rating, sale, and purchase of the structured financial product known as a 'constant proportion debt obligation' ('CPDO'). However, the operative conduct was a conflict of interest because the LGFSA was receiving a commission from the product. This fell within conduct contemplated by the traditional definition of a proscriptive fiduciary duty.

71 Ibid [733] quoting *Daly v Sydney Stock Exchange Ltd* (1986) 160 CLR 371, 384–5; *Wingecarribee Shire Council v Lehman Brothers Ltd* (2012) 301 ALR 1, 198 [739].

72 *Hospital Products Ltd v United States Surgical Corporation* (1984) 156 CLR 41, 97.

73 *Wingecarribee Shire Council v Lehman Brothers Ltd (in liq)* (2012) 301 ALR 1, 201 [746].

74 *ABN AMRO Bank NV v Bathurst Regional Council* (2014) 224 FCR 1.

75 Ibid [1023].

18.20.15 Summary of financial advisers' best interests duties under pt 7.7A and the general law

The current position under pt 7.7A and the general law can be summarised as follows:

(1) Section 961B (and s 961G as necessary[76]) imposes a statutory best interests duty upon financial advisers. This may be equivalent to a fiduciary duty at general law but is probably wider. However, s 961B follows the contours of the *Corporations Act* and will only apply to retail clients. Statutory remedies will apply if this obligation is breached. In particular, it is a civil penalty provision under s 961K and a civil action for loss or damage arises under s 961M. The duty may not be excluded by contract under s 960A.

(2) The cases so far tell us that when an undertaking is given by an adviser that goes beyond that of a 'mere salesman', and that undertaking is reasonably understood and acted upon by the client, then a fiduciary duty will arise. This may also apply to both wholesale clients (like the Councils in *Wingecarribee* and *ABN AMRO*) and retail clients.

(3) This fiduciary duty arises independently of the statute and may be excluded by contract.[77] It is probably wider than the traditional status-based categories of fiduciary relationships, such as the principal–agent relationship.

(4) The nature of this obligation may follow the contours of the 'traditional' fiduciary duty, which obliges the fiduciary not to profit or be conflicted, but it may be wider and closer to a duty of care. If a fiduciary relationship arises, equitable remedies are available, including tracing and constructive trusts.

18.25 Further obligations of advisers and dealers in financial products: licensing

In Australia, an additional method of regulation is to require people who provide financial services to be licensed by ASIC. The use of licensing as a regulatory strategy is discussed at Section 17.20.15. As mentioned in Chapter 17, the *Financial Services Reform Act 2001* (Cth) introduced a uniform licensing scheme that extended the obligation to obtain a licence to all persons providing a financial service or dealing in a financial product. The licence is called an Australian Financial Services Licence (AFSL). The category of 'licence holder' is not restricted to members of ASX (namely, stockbrokers). This is an area of activity that overlaps with, but extends well beyond, the activities undertaken in the stock market.

18.25.05 Who needs an Australian Financial Services Licence?

A person will need to hold an AFSL if they carry on a financial services business unless they are otherwise exempt (s 911A). What it means to 'carry on business' is defined in

76 Note the interpretation of this provision in *Australian Securities and Investments Commission v NSG Services Pty Ltd* (2017) 122 ACSR 47, discussed above at Section 18.20.05.

77 *Australian Securities and Investments Commission v Citigroup Global Markets Australia Pty Ltd (No 4)* (2007) 160 FCR 35.

ss 18–21 of the *Corporations Act*, plus the common law which says the activities must be conducted with 'system, repetition and continuity'.

First, one must discern the meaning of 'financial services business'. The term 'financial service' is defined in ss 766A–D. Pursuant to s 766A, a person provides a financial service if they (inter alia):

(a) provide financial product advice (s 766B); or
(b) deal in a financial product (s 766C); or
(c) make a market for a financial product (s 766D).

To determine the meaning of 'provide financial product advice' in s 766B, it is necessary to consider two primary questions:

(1) What is a 'financial product'? This is discussed in Chapter 17: it includes making a financial investment, managing a risk, making non-cash payments (s 763A);
(2) What is financial product advice? A recommendation or a statement of opinion, or a report of either of those things, will constitute financial product advice under s 766B if:
   - it is intended to influence a person in making a decision in relation to a financial product, or could reasonably be regarded as being intended to have such an influence; and
   - it is not exempted from the definition of 'financial product advice'.

Note that there are two types of advice under s 766B: personal and general advice. 'Personal advice' is financial product advice given or directed to a person (including by electronic means) in circumstances where:

(1) the provider of the advice has considered one or more of the person's objectives, financial situation and needs; or
(2) a reasonable person might expect the provider to have considered one or more of those matters (s 766B(3)).

All other financial product advice is 'general advice' (s 766B(4)).[78]

The High Court interpreted the meaning of the term 'personal advice' in s 766B in *Westpac Securities Administration Ltd v Australian Securities and Investments Commission*,[79] upholding the decision of the Full Federal Court in *Australian Securities and Investments Commission v Westpac Securities Administration Ltd (Westpac Securities)*.[80] In that case, the bank had conducted a telephone campaign where existing customers (members) who held external superannuation accounts were approached to roll over their superannuation funds into accounts held by a subsidiary of the bank (the BT Accounts). The bank

78 See RP Austin and Michael Vrisakis, 'Personal Financial Product Advice under the *Corporations Act*' (2017) 35(8) *Company and Securities Law Journal* 503; Australian Securities and Investments Commission, *Financial Product Advisers—Conduct and Disclosure* (Regulatory Guide 175, 21 November 2024) [RG 175.39]–[RG 175.50].

79 *Westpac Securities Administration Ltd v Australian Securities and Investments Commission* (2021) 270 CLR 118.

80 *Australian Securities and Investments Commission v Westpac Securities Administration Ltd* (2019) 272 FCR 170.

characterised it as a marketing campaign and the callers told customers that they were providing general advice only. Bank procedures encouraged the callers to 'close the call', which 'took the customers to the point of decision-making over the phone in the call'.[81] The Full Court held that there is no clear dichotomy between marketing and advising,[82] because the conversations contained '"helpful" recommendation[s] and proffered statements of opinion'.[83] The decision to consolidate superannuation funds was 'not a decision suitable for marketing or general advice ... [because] it requires attention to the personal circumstances of a customer and the features of the multiple funds held by the customer'.[84] Allsop CJ (with whom Jagot and O'Bryan JJ agreed) found that Westpac gave personal advice, because when the telephone conversations are considered as a whole and in their context, including importantly the 'closing' on the telephone by getting the decision made during the call, there was an implied recommendation in each call that the customer should accept the service to move accounts funds into their BT account, carrying with it an implied statement of opinion that this step would meet and fulfil the concerns and objectives the customer.[85]

Westpac made several arguments in the High Court to support their contention that the advice was not personal advice. First, it said that the telephone call began with a disclaimer that the advice was general advice only. Second, the advice was provided free of charge. Their third argument was that the Westpac callers revealed a lack of knowledge of the members' financial affairs which was inconsistent with the expectation required under s 766B(3) when it recommended acceptance of its rollover service.[86] The High Court rejected all three arguments made by Westpac. The disclaimer did not alter the character of the recommendation as advice about the member's personal situation or the expectation as to the quality of the advice that the phone call was apt to engender in the member. The 'free of charge' circumstance was, at best, neutral. Finally, it is sufficient for s 766B(3) for the expectation to arise where (on the express wording of the statute) one or more of the member's objectives is considered. It does not require comprehensive knowledge of the member's financial affairs.[87] Notably, the use of the word 'considered' in s 766B(3) does not require an active or comprehensive process of evaluation.[88]

Pursuant to s 766B(5), certain advice is exempted from the definition, such as advice given by lawyers in their professional capacity.

Returning to s 766A and the question of whether a person provides a *financial service,* one must then consider the meaning of 'deal in a financial product' in s 766A(1)(b). This term is defined in s 766C and involves two questions: what is dealing, and what is not.

81 Ibid [67] (Allsop CJ).
82 Ibid.
83 Ibid.
84 Ibid [5] (Allsop CJ).
85 Ibid.
86 *Westpac Securities Administration Ltd v Australian Securities and Investments Commission* (2021) 270 CLR 118 [7].
87 Ibid [8]–[10].
88 Ibid [17].

What is 'dealing'? (s 766C(1))

The meaning of 'dealing' is set out in s 766C(1) and covers the following conduct:

(a) applying for or acquiring a financial product;
(b) issuing a financial product;
(c) in relation to securities ... underwriting the securities ...
(d) varying a financial product;
(e) disposing of a financial product.

Note that, under s 766C(2), *arranging* for a person to engage in conduct referred to in sub-s (1) is also *dealing* in a financial product, unless the actions concerned amount to providing financial product advice.

What conduct is exempt from the definition of 'dealing'?

A person is not dealing where:

(a) they deal on their own behalf (s 766C(3));
(b) they are a government or local government authority, a public authority or instrumentality or agency of the Crown, body corporate etc and they deal in their own securities (s 766C(4));
(c) they act as a sub-underwriter (s 766C(6));
(d) they provide a crowd-funding service (as defined in s 766F).[89]

Finally, what is the meaning of 'make a market for a financial product'?

Section 766D explains this. A person makes a market if they:

- regularly state the prices at which they propose to acquire or dispose of financial products on their own behalf; and
- other persons have a reasonable expectation that they will be able to regularly effect transactions at those prices; and
- the actions of the person who states the price do not constitute operating a financial market (s 767A) because the person is making offers or accepting offers to acquire or dispose of financial products on their own behalf or on behalf of one of the parties to the transaction.

Therefore, a person who carries on a financial services business, as defined, must hold an Australian financial services licence pursuant to s 911A.[90]

89 For a discussion of crowdfunding, see Section 9.75.

90 There are many cases where the courts have made orders against unlicensed entities that are carrying out financial services businesses: see, eg, *Australian Securities and Investments Commission v Monarch FX Group Pty Ltd* (2014) 103 ACSR 453; *Australian Securities and Investments Commission v Park Trent Properties Group Pty Ltd (No 3)* [2015] NSWSC 1527; *Australian Securities and Investments Commission v Macro Realty Developments Pty Ltd* (2016) 111 ACSR 638; *Australian Securities and Investments Commission v Wealth & Risk Management Pty Ltd (No 2)* (2018) 124 ACSR 351. For a recent case involving a 'finfluencer', see *Australian Securities and Investments Commission v Scholz (No 2)* (2022) 167 ACSR 67.

18.25.10 Exemptions from the licence requirement

There is a long list of exemptions under in s 911A(2), but they include situations where:

(1) general advice is provided by a newspaper or periodical (s 911A(2)(ea) or by means of an information service (s 911A(2)(eb)) or in sound recordings, video recordings or data recordings which is generally available to the public (otherwise than only on subscription) and where the sole or principal purpose of the newspaper etc is not the provision of financial product advice (s 911A(2)(ec));

(2) the financial service is provided by a representative of a licence-holder; the representative does not need to be separately licensed (s 911A(2)(a)).

18.25.15 Meaning of 'representative'

Regarding financial services licensees, the term 'representative' is defined generally in s 9. This exemption is important because, in the securities and derivatives markets, most of the intermediary work is undertaken by representatives of licence-holders. The definition captures authorised representatives of the licensee, as well as employees or directors of the licensee and its related bodies corporate, or someone acting as an agent of the licensee.[91]

Under this regime, the activities of representatives are supervised by licensees. It is an offence for a person to act as a representative where the principal is not licensed and where the representative is not an employee or director of the licensee, an authorised representative of the licensee, or an employee of an authorised representative (s 911B).

The concept of 'authorised representative' is dealt with under s 916A. Licensees may give an authorised representative written notice of authority which authorises the person to provide specified financial services on behalf of the licensee. Licensees are required to notify ASIC of any persons authorised to be representatives (s 916F).

An important element of the licensee's supervisory responsibility is the imposition of liability upon them for all acts of their representatives in div 6 pt 7.6 (ss 917A–F). Under s 917A, the licensed person is treated as a principal in relation to conduct by the representative affecting a third person. The principal is liable for the acts of a representative in connection with the securities or investment business, whether or not the representative acts within the scope of their proper authority (s 917B). A limitation upon the liability of principals is provided for in s 917D which states that the principal is not liable if the agent's lack of authority is disclosed to the client. A principal is generally unable to contract out of a liability for the actions of a representative (s 917F(5)).

In *Casaclang v WealthSure Pty Ltd*,[92] Buchanan J in the Federal Court held that s 917B assigns responsibility to the licensee for the conduct of the representative even if the representative was on a 'frolic of his own'. The client need not have a relationship with the licensee. The client is simply a third party who could reasonably be expected to rely on the conduct of the representative (s 917A(1)(b)).[93]

---

91 These arrangements are discussed more fully in Australian Securities and Investments Commission, *Financial Product Advisers—Conduct and Disclosure* (Regulatory Guide 175, 21 November 2024).

92 *Casaclang v WealthSure Pty Ltd* (2015) 238 FCR 55.

93 See also the Full Federal Court judgment in *Young Investments Group Pty Ltd v Mann* (2012) 91 ACSR 89 [14], [47].

18.25.20 General licensee obligations under an AFSL

The holder of an AFSL must comply with the list of general obligations in s 912A. There is a broad obligation to do all things necessary to ensure that the financial services covered by the AFSL are provided efficiently, honestly and fairly. This obligation is discussed below.

The other licence obligations can be grouped under a series of categories that are set out in s 912A:

(1) Managing conflicts of interest
(2) Dispute resolution systems for retail clients (for example, the Australian Financial Complaints Authority (AFCA))
(3) Compliance: this includes compliance with licence conditions and financial services laws and having relevant compliance procedures in place. ASIC may impose conditions on the licences (s 914A) regarding, for example, the types of financial product that can be dealt with
(4) Supervision: the licence-holder must take reasonable steps to ensure that representatives comply with the financial services laws and adequately train representatives and ensure that they are competent to provide the financial services
(5) Resources: the licensee must have adequate financial, technological and human resources to properly provide the financial services
(6) Competence: the licensee must maintain the competence to provide the financial services, including providing adequate training for representatives
(7) Risk management systems.

18.25.25 Financial services to be provided 'efficiently, honestly and fairly'

As mentioned above, s 912A obliges a financial services licensee to do all things necessary to ensure that the financial services covered by the AFSL are provided 'efficiently, honestly and fairly'. The meaning of this phrase was expounded by Foster J in *Australian Securities and Investments Commission v Camelot Derivatives Pty Ltd (in liq)* ('*Camelot*')[94], who followed two earlier judgments: *Story v National Companies and Securities Commission*[95] ('*Story*') and *RJ Elrington Nominees Pty Ltd v Corporate Affairs Commission (SA)*[96] ('*Elrington*').[97]

94 *Australian Securities and Investments Commission v Camelot Derivatives Pty Ltd (in liq)* (2012) 88 ACSR 206 [69]. The *Camelot* judgment was considered by the Full Federal Court in *Australian Securities and Investments Commission v Westpac Securities Administration Ltd* (2019) 272 FCR 170 ('*Westpac Securities*') and followed, for example, by Beach J in *Australian Securities and Investments Commission v Westpac Banking Corporation (No 2)* (2018) 266 FCR 147; *Australian Securities and Investments Commission v AGM Markets Pty Ltd (in liq) (No 3)* (2020) 275 FCR 57; and Rofe J in *Australian Securities and Investments Commission v RI Advice Group Pty Ltd* (2022) 160 ACSR 204.

95 (1988) 13 NSWLR 661.

96 (1989) 1 ACSR 93.

97 (2018) 226 FCR 147 [2347].

Foster J made the following points about this obligation in *Camelot*:[98]

(a) The words 'efficiently, honestly and fairly' must be read as a compendious indication [that is, a single, composite concept[99]] meaning a person who goes about their duties efficiently having regard to the dictates of honesty and fairness, honestly having regard to the dictates of efficiency and fairness, and fairly having regard to the dictates of efficiency and honesty.[100]
(b) The words 'efficiently, honestly and fairly' connote a requirement of competence in providing advice and in complying with relevant statutory obligations. They also connote an element not just of even handedness in dealing with clients but a less readily defined concept of sound ethical values and judgment in matters relevant to a client's affairs.
(c) The word 'efficient' refers to a person who performs his duties efficiently, meaning the person is adequate in performance, produces the desired effect, is capable, competent and adequate. Inefficiency may be established by demonstrating that the performance of a licensee's functions falls short of the reasonable standard of performance by a dealer that the public is entitled to expect.[101]
(d) It is not necessary to establish dishonesty in the criminal sense. The word 'honestly' may comprehend conduct which is not criminal but which is morally wrong in the commercial sense.[102]
(e) The word 'honestly' when used in conjunction with the word 'fairly' tends to give the flavour of a person who not only is not dishonest, but also a person who is ethically sound.[103]

In *Story*,[104] the appellant was a licensed dealer and was employed as a stockbroker. He was attempting to interest a prospective buyer in shares in a mining company and faxed a study of the company to the prospective purchaser, which incorrectly asserted that 'there was another active bidder in the wings'. The transmission was sent in error to the mining company that was the subject of the study. The NCSC (the predecessor to ASIC) argued that the broker had consciously manufactured information in order to induce a client to deal in securities and revoked the broker's dealer's licence under the predecessor to s 915C. The appellant sought review of the decision in the Supreme Court of New South Wales, arguing that NCSC had made an error of law as to his fitness to hold a licence.

Young J observed that the section is designed to protect the public. In determining whether a licensee had performed the duties of a licence-holder 'efficiently, honestly and fairly' under the predecessor to s 915C, the Court had to determine whether the

98 *Australian Securities and Investments Commission v Camelot Derivatives Pty Ltd (in liq)* (2012) 88 ACSR 206, 225 [69]–[70].
99 Note, however, that Allsop CJ and O'Bryan J expressed doubt about this approach to interpretation in *Westpac Securities* at [170] and [424]. Allsop CJ noted that the phrase contains 'three discrete behavioural norms' ([170]).
100 *Story v National Companies and Securities Commission* (1988) 13 NSWLR 661, 672
101 Ibid.
102 *RJ Elrington Nominees Pty Ltd v Corporate Affairs Commission (SA)* (1989) 1 ACSR 93, 110.
103 *Story v National Companies and Securities Commission* (1988) 13 NSWLR 661, 672.
104 (1988) 13 NSWLR 661.

licence-holder's performance of his duties fell short of the reasonable standard of performance by a dealer which the public is entitled to expect.

Young J concluded that Story's conduct fell short of this standard.

The next question was whether this finding should lead to the revocation of Story's licence. Young J stated that one needs to weigh up several considerations, such as that qualified persons should be permitted to follow a profession and the need to protect the public from 'inefficient' brokers. Here, the plaintiff had favourable character references and, although it was 'somewhat near the borderline', the appellant's licence should not be revoked. To revoke the licence would be more punitive than a measure designed to protect the public.[105] The approach of Young J is consistent with the general standards applied in cases involving occupational regulation.[106]

Compare *Story* to *Elrington*,[107] where the licensee was in breach of the net tangible assets requirements of the licence and had offered the securities of an associate of the dealer without disclosing a conflict of interest. The Corporate Affairs Commission (a predecessor to ASIC) revoked its dealer's licence and the licensee appealed against it. It was held that failure to notify the breach of the net tangible assets requirement (within one day) did not justify revocation of licence. However, the conduct with respect to the conflict of interest did justify revocation because the conduct was 'morally wrong in the commercial sense'.[108] This is an objective test.

Recent examples of conduct that was found to breach s 912A include charging fees for no service[109] and a failure by the licensee to manage cybersecurity risks.[110]

18.25.30 Revocation or suspension of licences

Where a breach of a licence condition occurs, a licence-holder is required to provide a written report to ASIC within the timeframes set out in s 912D.

ASIC has the power to revoke an AFSL, either with or without a hearing. Licences may be suspended or cancelled under s 915B without a hearing in certain circumstances, such as where a person becomes insolvent under administration, is convicted of a serious fraud, or becomes incapable of managing their own affairs.

The grounds upon which ASIC may seek to revoke an AFSL after offering a hearing are set out in s 915C. They include where the application for the licence contained false or materially misleading matter; the licensee is not a fit and proper person to provide the financial services covered by the licence, where a banning order is made against a licensee;[111] and the licensee has not or will not perform its obligations efficiently, honestly

105 Ibid.

106 For example, similar approaches are applied in disciplinary proceedings taken against individual lawyers. See, eg, A Lamb and J Littrich, *Lawyers in Australia* (Federation Press, 2011) ch 11.

107 *RJ Elrington Nominees Pty Ltd v Corporate Affairs Commission (SA)* (1989) 1 ACSR 93.

108 Ibid 110.

109 *Australian Securities and Investments Commission v National Australia Bank Ltd* (2022) 164 ACSR 358.

110 *Australian Securities and Investments Commission v RI Advice Group Pty Ltd* (2022) 160 ACSR 204; see D Chaikin, 'Cybersecurity Risk Management in the Financial Services Industry: *Australian Securities and Investments Commission v RI Advice Group Pty Ltd*' (2023) 39(8) *Company and Securities Law Journal* 485.

111 For provisions that deal with ASIC's power to make a banning order, see s 920Aff.

or fairly. The hearing requirements are set out in s 915C(4), and include the right to appear, to be represented in a private hearing, and to make submissions to ASIC. Note that ASIC is a public body and has obligations of procedural fairness under administrative law. Decisions in this area are reviewable by the Administrative Review Tribunal.[112]

Many cases involving the revocation of AFSLs concern licensees or their representatives recommending speculative high-risk investments to retail clients with little or no regard for their needs and investment objectives.[113]

18.30 Disclosures required by providers of financial services under the *Corporations Act*

Chapter 7 of the *Corporations Act* establishes a regime which requires certain documents to be given to retail clients when a financial product or financial advice is provided. There are three documents that must be given to a retail client depending on the situation:

- Financial Services Guide (FSG)
- Statement of Advice (SOA)
- Product Disclosure Statement (PDS).

The FSG must be provided by a licensee (s 941A) or authorised representative (s 941B) where a financial service is provided to a retail client. The FSG must be given to the client as soon as practicable after it becomes apparent that it is likely that the financial service will be provided and, in any case, it must be given before the financial service is provided (s 941D). The giving of the information in the FSG may be satisfied by a website disclosure if the requirements of pt 7.7 div 2A are satisfied. The content of the FSG is set out in ss 942B and 942C and, inter alia, requires details about the provider, special instructions, remuneration (including commissions) and associations that create conflicts of interest.

The level of information required is that which would be reasonably required by a retail client acquiring the financial services.

An SOA must be given to retail clients where personal advice is being provided (s 946A) unless the investment is small (less than $15,000) and the advice does not relate to, for example, derivative or superannuation products (s 946AA and reg 7.7.09A).

The content of an SOA is stated in ss 947B (for a licensee) and 947C (for an authorised representative) and again this includes details about the advice, remuneration (including commissions) and information about conflicts of interest.

In addition, where the financial product is regarded as a derivative (a product to manage financial risk), there will be a further requirement to supply a PDS to a retail client.

112 *Corporations Act* pt 9.4A.

113 *Re Felden and Australian Securities and Investments Commission* (2003) 73 ALD 149; *Re Jungstedt and Australian Securities and Investments Commission* (2003) 73 ALD 105; *Australian Securities and Investments Commission v AGM Markets Pty Ltd (in liq) (No 3)* (2020) 275 FCR 57. See generally P Latimer, 'Providing Financial Services—"efficiently, honestly and fairly"' Part 1 (2006) 24 *Company and Securities Law Journal* 362; Part 2 (2020) 37 *Company and Securities Law Journal* 382; Part 3 (2022) 39 *Company and Securities Law Journal* 160; L Gamertsfelder, 'Efficiently, Honestly and Fairly: A Norm That Applies in an Infinite Variety of Circumstances' (2021) 50(2) *Australian Bar Review* 345.

The obligation to provide a PDS does not apply to securities (a financial investment product) (s 1010A). The obligation to provide a PDS is placed upon the licensee and their authorised representative where there is a recommendation to acquire the derivative and in certain issue and sale situations (ss 1012A, 1012B, 1012C).

Part 7.7 of the *Corporations Act* sets out enforcement options for the failure to comply with the disclosure obligations. Subdivision A (commencing with s 952A) creates offences and sub-div B (commencing with s 953A) establishes civil liability.[114] In addition, since 2019, civil penalties are available to enforce many of the provisions discussed above: see generally s 1317E.

18.35 Summary

This chapter has traversed various bodies of law that impose obligations upon intermediaries in the financial services sector to achieve the protection of clients involved in financial product transactions. Most, but not all, of the protections are directed at retail clients. Broadly speaking, the obligations are imposed via agency, contract, fiduciary and statutory provisions. The legal incidents of the intermediary-client relationship were exemplified by the broker–client and financial adviser–client relationships. These obligations are supplemented by a licensing strategy and product disclosure requirements.

114 For further information, see Australian Securities and Investmnets Commission, *Financial Product Advisers—Conduct and Disclosure* (Regulatory Guide 175, 21 November 2024); D Kingsford-Smith, 'Is "Due Diligence" Dead? Financial Services and Products Disclosure under the *Corporations Act*' (2004) 22(2) *Company and Securities Law Journal* 128.

CHAPTER

19

TAKEOVERS

19.05 Introduction

In this book, we have mostly depicted companies as legal actors in their own right that act through certain human agents. In this chapter, our focus changes: we now think of companies as things that may be owned and controlled. Nevertheless, the motivations of human agents remain at the forefront. Some of the law that we encountered in previous chapters will be relevant here, because it regulates the behaviour of the human protagonists; for example, the law on directors' duties (see Chapters 10 to 13). However, the law of takeovers in Australia is a special body of law. This law is set out in chs 6, 6A, 6B and 6C of the *Corporations Act,* together with a unique dispute resolution system that diverts disputes away from the courts and into an administrative body—the Takeovers Panel ('the Panel')—during the life of a takeover bid. The decision-making of the Panel is guided by policy and commerciality, rather than legal doctrine.

19.10 What is a takeover?

A takeover involves a change in the effective control of a company through the acquisition of a sufficient number of voting shares in the company. The person (usually another company) seeking control via an acquisition is called the 'bidder'. The company that the bidder is seeking to control is called the 'target' or the 'target company'.

In broad terms, someone who wants to acquire control of a company's business has two options: one, they can purchase the business *from* the company; or two, they can acquire control *of* the company and thereby acquire control of the business. The first option means that the target company itself is unchanged. What changes is the company's asset holdings. Basically, this option is a matter of contract law and property law insofar as there will be real and personal property to be conveyed; the *Corporations Act* has no specific impact on such a transaction, other than specific sections such as those regulating corporate contracting.

The second option may raise the operation of ch 6 of the *Corporations Act*; that is, it *may* involve what is legally classified as a takeover of the company.

The choice between these two options will be guided by a variety of factors such as taxation considerations (for example, stamp duty costs, tax savings from a merger of businesses); practical issues, such as whether the target company carries on only one business; or whether there are additional businesses that the buyer does not wish to acquire. The nature of business assets, the relative costs of the two options, and the buyer's existing corporate and business structure will also be factors to be taken into account. Note that, under the first option, it will be necessary for the new business owner to renegotiate any contracts that relate to the business; for example, contracts with suppliers, distributors and employees. Under the second option, the contracts can remain as they are.

However, the second option will not necessarily be classified for legal purposes as a take-over—there are different ways of acquiring control of a company.

19.10.05 Alternatives to takeovers: schemes of arrangement

A common alternative to a takeover is a scheme of arrangement.[1] Levy states that '[s]chemes of arrangement have steadily grown in importance in public company mergers & acquisitions over the last 25 years. They have replaced takeover bids as the dominant form of transaction for larger deals'.[2] This observation is borne out by the data. For example, in 2021, schemes of arrangement constituted 61 per cent of corporate control transactions. The remaining 39 per cent were takeovers.[3] Schemes of arrangement are governed by pt 5.1 of the Act, in particular s 411. They are often associated with corporate insolvency, as discussed at Section 15.35, but can also be used to effect a change of corporate control similar to a takeover by cancelling all of the shares in the target company other than those held by the bidder. Former shareholders of the target are paid cash or given shares in the bidder as compensation for cancellation of their shares.

The advantage of a scheme of arrangement is that the bidder has greater certainty about the outcome compared to a takeover bid. A disadvantage of a scheme of arrangement is that it requires court approval as well as approval of shareholders at a general meeting.[4] Section 411(17) states that a court must not approve a scheme of arrangement unless it is satisfied that the arrangement has not been proposed for the purpose of avoiding the operation of ch 6 of the *Corporations Act* or if a statement by ASIC is produced to the court stating that it has no objection to the arrangement.[5] Where an acquisition could have proceeded by a takeover bid, ASIC will consider whether there has been compliance with the policies[6] and disclosure obligations[7] set out in ch 6 in deciding whether to give a no objection statement.[8] The general requirements for court approval of a scheme of arrangement are discussed in Section 15.30.10.

A scheme of arrangement will generally only be able to bring about a change of control if it is a friendly or mutual agreement between the parties. If the target company does not want the change in control to occur—that is, if it is a hostile takeover—then the bidder will need to use the takeover provisions in ch 6 of the *Corporations Act*. This aspect

1 See generally T Damian and A Rich, *Schemes, Takeovers and Himalayan Peaks: The Use of Schemes of Arrangement to Effect Change of Control Transactions* (Ross Parsons Centre of Commercial, Corporate and Taxation Law, 4th ed, 2021); R Levy, 'The Efficient, Competitive and Informed Market Principle in Schemes of Arrangement' (2024) 40(3) *Company and Securities Law Journal* 124.

2 R Levy, 'The Efficient, Competitive and Informed Market Principle in Schemes of Arrangement' (2024) 40(3) *Company and Securities Law Journal* 124, 124.

3 Australian Government, The Treasury, *Corporate Control Transactions in Australia* (Report, April 2022) 3.

4 See generally *Corporations Act* s 411.

5 See *Re Coles Group Ltd (No 2)* (2007) 65 ACSR 494; *Foundation Healthcare Ltd* (2002) 43 ACSR 680; *ACM Gold Ltd and Mt Leyshon Gold Mines Ltd* (1992) 7 ACSR 231; Australian Securities and Investments Commission, *Schemes of Arrangement* (Regulatory Guide 60, September 2020); J Mignone, 'Is there Sufficient Protection for Shareholders in a Members' Scheme of Arrangement? An Analysis of the Eggleston Principles and s 411(17) of the *Corporations Act 2001* (Cth)' (2016) 30(3) *Australian Journal of Corporate Law* 259.

6 *Corporations Act* s 602; Australian Securities and Investments Commission, *Schemes of Arrangement* (Regulatory Guide 60, September 2020) [RG 60.22].

7 See, eg, the s 636 requirements for the bidder's statement.

8 Australian Securities and Investments Commission, *Schemes of Arrangement* (Regulatory Guide 60, September 2020) [RG 60.22].

needs to be taken into account when considering the success of a merger or acquisition. A 2022 Treasury paper compared the 'success rates' of schemes of arrangement and takeovers and concluded that the success of the former was 90 per cent; whereas it was 55 per cent for the latter.[9]

19.10.10 The concept of 'control'

To restate the definition set out above, a takeover involves the bidder company acquiring control over sufficient voting shares in the target company to give the bidder control over that company. The concept of 'control' is pivotal to this definition, but 'control' can occur in companies at different thresholds due to the nature of the shareholdings and other factors.[10] For example, 100 per cent ownership gives complete control but this is also the most expensive option, especially where share ownership of the target is widely dispersed. There are many additional advantages of full ownership; for example, tax advantages and reduction of administrative costs. At 75 per cent ownership, the bidder can pass special resolutions, which gives the bidder power to amend the company's constitution and engage in various corporate finance transactions that are discussed in Chapter 8, such as a selective reduction of capital. At 51 per cent ownership, the bidder can appoint directors and pass ordinary resolutions, which, in a public company, includes resolutions to dismiss directors.[11]

However, depending on the share structure of the company, the bidder may be able to achieve de facto control with far less than 50 per cent ownership of the shares. This is partly because voting in the general meeting is not compulsory, and partly because of the effect of the separation of ownership and control in companies with a widely dispersed ownership.[12] When considering the control of a company, indirect control can be equally as influential as direct control. For example, where Company A controls Company B (which owns 75 per cent of the shares in Company C), Company A may control Company C. Similarly, a shareholder or group of shareholders may control a company's board; for example, a shareholder with a significant stake in the company may demand representation on the board. Therefore, in order to effectively regulate control, the takeover laws regulate both direct and indirect forms of control.

During a takeover, the bidder makes an offer to acquire the shares (usually voting shares) held by the members of the target company. The takeover will occur when a bidder acquires a sufficient number of voting shares in the target company. A takeover is, in essence, the outcome of multiple share purchase contracts. It is the target company shareholders who ultimately determine the outcome–their decisions to sell or retain their shares will determine the success or failure of the takeover bid.

Takeover law is concerned exclusively with certain changes of control within a company. Takeover law is *not* concerned with what the internal change of control in the target company means for any change of control of the wider business or industry; for

9 Australian Government, The Treasury, *Corporate Control Transactions in Australia* (Report, April 2022) 3.

10 See generally J Varzaly, 'Shareholder Concentration and Control in Australia' (2023) 23(1) *Journal of Corporate Law Studies* 105.

11 *Corporations Act* s 203D.

12 See A Berle and G Means, *The Modern Corporation and Private Property* (Macmillan, 1933) 120.

example, if it leads to a substantial lessening of competition in a market (regulated by the *Competition and Consumer Act 2010* (Cth)), or involves a foreign acquisition (and is subject to the *Foreign Acquisitions and Takeovers Act 1975* (Cth)). Chapter 6 of the *Corporations Act* only operates where the change of control involves an acquisition of shares above a certain threshold. This is explained below.

19.10.15 Takeover activity in Australia

The level of takeover activity in Australia has fluctuated according to surrounding economic conditions. The peak was in 1987–88, when 287 takeover bids were notified to the corporate regulator. In the lead up to the global financial crisis in 2008, another peak occurred when 113 takeovers were conducted. This figure dropped to 47 in the following financial year of 2008–09. The data about takeovers is now presented in ASIC annual reports as 'Control transactions—schemes and bids' so the figures include schemes of arrangement as discussed above at Section 19.10.05. The number of corporate control transactions per annum is approximately 70, with 59 occurring in 2022–3.[13]

If we assume that each of these takeovers involves just two companies (bidder and target), takeovers represent only a small amount of activity in the corporate sector because there are over 3.3 million companies registered in Australia.[14] However, the money involved in takeover bids is quite significant. In the 2021–2 financial year, the value of Australian corporate control transactions was approximately $120.96 billion.[15] This figure dropped during 2022 but was estimated to be $75.6 billion in 2023.[16]

19.15 Why regulate takeovers?

Chapter 6 of the *Corporations Act* regulates takeovers by regulating the production and supply of information about the takeover offer and the response of the target company. So, like the fundraising provisions discussed in Chapter 9 and the law of financial markets examined in Chapter 17, one underlying concern is the disclosure of information. Therefore, the debates about mandatory disclosure of information that are traversed at Section 17.10.05 are equally relevant in this chapter. Indeed, takeover laws have been a major focus of the debate about mandatory disclosure.

Critics of takeover regulation begin with the premise that a takeover is a market process that allows for an efficient allocation of economic resources. Takeovers occur because the bidder believes the target company is undervalued due to poor or inefficient management by the current directors and managers, and the target company's assets can be put to more productive use if inefficient managers are replaced.

Furthermore, in an efficient market, we can assume that all company directors and managers are aware of the potential risk of an unwanted takeover bid, and realise that if they do not perform then the company will be taken over and they will lose their positions. The permanent background threat of a takeover provides an incentive

13 Australian Securities and Investments Commission, *Annual Report* (Report, 2022–2023) 232.
14 Australian Securities and Investments Commission, *Company Registration Statistics* (at March 2024).
15 Australian Securities and Investments Commission, *Annual Report* (Report, 2022–2023) 232.
16 Herbert Smith Freehills, *Australian Public M&A Report 2023* (Report, 15th ed, October 2023) 4.

for incumbent managers and directors to run the company efficiently. In other words, there is an incentive to maximise the wealth of shareholders so as to prevent them from selling their shares on the market which would send signals to potential takeover bidders. This is summed up by saying that there is a market for corporate control. The conclusion from this argument is that takeovers should be largely unregulated, because, if we impose mandatory legal rules and requirements, we are likely to impede the efficient operation of this market mechanism and deter takeover offers from being made. Therefore, certain theorists argue that the market for corporate control should be unimpeded by regulation.[17]

Proponents of takeover regulation argue that we must ensure that target company shareholders are given sufficient information about the takeover bid and the identity of the bidder, and sufficient time to digest and analyse that information before making a decision about selling shares to the takeover bidder. A further reason for regulating takeovers is to ensure all target company shareholders are treated equally; that they all receive the same offer and have the same opportunity to participate in any benefits that might flow from the takeover. Proponents of regulation also point out that the removal of inefficient company managers is not always the primary motivation for a takeover bid, and that not all takeovers can be assumed to be beneficial for society at large.[18]

These are the rationales that underlie ch 6 of the *Corporations Act* in its present form.[19] They are elaborated below at Section 19.20.10.

19.20 An overview of ch 6

19.20.05 The structure of ch 6

Before we examine the rules and concepts that govern takeover activity, we need to look at the overall structure of ch 6 of the *Corporations Act*. Chapter 6 primarily addresses takeover regulation; however, complementary provisions are situated in chs 6A, 6B and 6C. Chapter 6 is drafted in complex and detailed terms. To a considerable extent, this is a response to the complexity of takeover activity. The chapter endeavours to create a 'closed regulatory system'; it begins by prohibiting certain conduct[20] and then, because the aim is to regulate takeovers not to prohibit them, the chapter goes on to permit takeovers, provided they comply with specified procedures and processes. Chapter 6 is a

17 See, eg, BS Sharfman and MT Moore, 'Liberating the Market for Corporate Control' (2021) 18(2) *Berkeley Business Law Journal* 1; DR Fischel, 'Efficient Capital Market Theory, the Market for Corporate Control, and the Regulation of Cash Tender Offers' (1978) 57(1) *Texas Law Review* 1; H Manne, 'Mergers and the Market for Corporate Control' (1965) 73(2) *Journal of Political Economy* 110.

18 See, eg, E Armson, 'Evolution of Australian Takeover Legislation' (2013) 39(3) *Monash University Law Review* 654; V Brudney, 'Equal Treatment of Shareholders in Corporate Distributions and Reorganisations' (1983) 71(4) *Harvard Law Review* 1072. For a discussion of Australian takeover regulation in the global environment, see J Hill, 'Takeovers, Poison Pills and Protectionism in Comparative Corporate Governance' (Working Paper No 168/2010, ECGI Working Paper Series in Law, November 2010); R Thompson, 'Takeover Regulation after the "Convergence" of Corporate Law' (2002) 24(3) *Sydney Law Review* 323.

19 See generally The Centre for Independent Studies and the New Zealand Centre for Independent Studies, *Takeovers and Corporate Control: Towards a New Regulatory Environment* (Report, 1987).

20 As will be seen later, the prohibition is found in s 606.

prescriptive style of regulation[21] and it differs from other parts of the *Corporations Act*, such as the directors' duties provisions, that rely more on broad standards than detailed specification.

Chapter 6 prohibits share acquisitions above a particular threshold. It then provides for exceptions to that prohibition and specifies what must be done in order for a takeover to fall within one of those exceptions. The two main exceptions are off-market and on-market bids; these are described later in this chapter. In general terms, these exceptions prescribe certain information that must be provided by one takeover party to another and to target shareholders, impose restrictions on the amount that can be offered in a takeover bid, and require that specified time periods be observed at different stages of the bid.

The complexity of a takeover means that the legislation has been drafted to catch a wide range of activity that might otherwise escape the regulatory net. For this reason, ch 6 is sometimes described as a 'code' that governs takeover activity. It does this by the creation and application of specially designed concepts; for example, the idea of a 'relevant interest' in shares, which is explained later in this chapter. As a consequence, in order to understand the operation of ch 6, it is necessary to continually cross-check the meaning and scope of sections and subsections. We provide guidance on this throughout this chapter.

19.20.10 The policy framework of ch 6

Chapter 6 of the *Corporations Act* has a relatively narrow focus: it sets out the process by which a takeover is brought about and deals with its effects on shareholders within the target company. Essentially, it is a detailed set of procedures that seek to enforce the timely disclosure of relevant information to target company shareholders.

The philosophy that underlies the chapter is found in s 602. This section sets out various matters that ASIC is required to consider in administering the chapter. Section 602(a) emphasises the need to ensure that the acquisition of control of a company takes place in an 'efficient, competitive and informed market'. In this respect, s 602(a) recognises the importance of the market for corporate control as espoused by the critics of regulation. However, ss 602(b)–(c) reflect the view of the proponents of regulation. These subsections state that regulation of takeovers should have four aims. The target company's shareholders and directors should:

(1) know the identity of the offeror; and
(2) have a reasonable time to consider the offer; and
(3) have enough information to assess the merits of the offer; and
(4) have a reasonable and equal opportunity for all shareholders to participate in the offer.

21 Arie Freiberg states that 'prescriptive regulation tells regulatees what they need to do and how they should do it': A Freiberg, *Regulation in Australia* (Federation Press, 2017) 234, citing N Gunningham and E Bluff, *A Review of Key Characteristics that Determine the Efficacy of OHS Instruments* (Australian Safety and Compensation Council, 2008) 37.

The four aims are derived from the Eggleston Principles. The Eggleston Principles were developed by the Company Law Advisory Committee in 1969 (named after the committee's chair, Richard Eggleston)[22] and provide the 'philosophical basis of the present takeover legislation'.[23] They have been part of takeovers legislation in Australia for decades.[24] The first principle—an 'efficient, competitive and informed market'—was added to s 602 as a consequence of the Corporate Law Economic Reform Program (CLERP) reforms in the late twentieth century.[25] As a consequence, s 602 became a composite provision, encompassing arguments of both the proponents and critics of regulation.

The last of the four Eggleston Principles—reasonable and equal opportunity—requires further explanation. In a takeover, the bidder will offer more than the current market price of the target company shares—known as a 'premium' on the share price—to attract enough acceptances to gain control. But shareholders will not necessarily immediately respond to the takeover offer. Under the current system of regulation, all shareholders should at least have an equal opportunity; that is, the premium should be available to all of the target shareholders.

In particular, 'front-end loaded bids' are not permitted; that is, bids that offer a high premium for the first group of shareholders to accept the offer, and then a lesser offer for the remaining shareholders once control has been obtained. Equally, the bidder cannot increase the terms of the offer to induce late acceptances. These restrictions are expressed in various sections of ch 6 that are discussed below. Nevertheless, most of the rules are predicated upon the policy stated in s 602. This policy, together with the rules, is overseen by the Panel, which is also discussed below.[26]

19.25 Dispute resolution in takeovers

19.25.05 The Takeovers Panel

Before exploring the rules that govern takeovers, we discuss the context in which dispute resolution occurs during takeovers. The *Corporations Act* diverts disputes about takeovers away from the courts into a specialist tribunal (the Panel) during the bid period. The Panel is an administrative body that adopts peer review to consider policy and commercial factors when resolving takeover disputes.

22 Company Law Advisory Committee, *Second Interim Report* (Report, 1969).

23 Takeovers Panel, *Glossary of Key Takeover Terminology* <https://takeovers.gov.au/resources/key-concepts/terminology-glossary>.

24 See, eg, *Companies (Acquisition of Shares) Code* s 60. For critiques of the equal opportunity rule, see V Murphy 'Competition and Efficiency at the Mercy of Equality: Balancing the Equal Opportunity Principle and Maintaining a Competitive and Efficient Market' (2020) 37(5) *Company and Securities Law Journal* 341; J Mayanja, 'The Equal Opportunity Principle in Australian Takeover Law and Practice: Time for Review?' (2000) 12(1) *Australian Journal of Corporate Law* 1.

25 The *Corporate Law Economic Reform Program Act 1999* (Cth), which came into effect in 2000.

26 For a discussion of the background to the Eggleston principles and a critique of the prescriptive style of regulation in ch 6, see RP Austin, 'When (If Ever) Should Corporations Legislation Lay Down Succinct Normative Standards without Prescriptive Rules?' in R Teele Langford (ed), *Corporate Law and Governance in the 21st Century: Essays in Honour of Professor Ian Ramsay* (Federation Press, 2023) 73, 75ff.

The Panel was established in 1991.[27] Prior to the formation of the Panel, parties often resorted to complex and technical legal challenges in an effort to slow down the process of the bid, and to make it more expensive for the bidder. The Panel was intended to provide a speedy and relatively inexpensive forum for deciding issues and discourage the use of tactical litigation—the use of litigation to argue minor or technical points as a way of delaying or adding to the cost of the takeover bid—in the courts. The key power wielded by the Panel is a declaration of unacceptable circumstances in relation to a takeover, taking into account the policy stated in s 602.[28]

Presently, the Panel is well regarded by market participants. However, it initially had little authority and had only decided four cases when changes were made to its jurisdiction by the 1999 CLERP reforms,[29] which addressed the continuing concerns about tactical litigation.[30] According to the Explanatory Memorandum, the idea was:

> to allow takeover disputes to be resolved as quickly and efficiently as possible by a specialist body largely comprised of takeover experts so that the outcome of the bid can be resolved by the target shareholders on the basis of its commercial merits.[31]

The Panel is established under pt 10 of the *Australian Securities and Investments Commission Act 2001* (Cth) ('*ASIC Act*'). It comprises members with experience in the fields of business, company administration, the financial markets, law, economics and accounting.[32] When it sits to hear and determine matters, three members constitute a panel.[33] On average, the Panel hears 29 applications a year.[34] In the 2022–3 financial year, the Panel received 16 applications and conducted proceedings in approximately two-thirds of those matters[35] and made two declarations of unacceptable circumstances. It is not unusual for multiple applications to be made for one takeover bid.

The Panel is a commercial rather than a legal tribunal. Its website describes it as a 'peer review body' that 'seeks to decide disputes in a speedy manner by focusing primarily on commercial and policy issues'.[36] Therefore, the approach to dispute resolution by the Panel is that business people should review and assess the actions of other business people, applying policy and commercial considerations. The law is not

27 For an overview of the Panel's operation, see I Ramsay (ed), *The Takeovers Panel and Takeovers Regulation in Australia* (Melbourne University Publishing, 2010); for a comparative analysis of the Panel's performance, see E Armson, 'Assessing the Performance of Takeover Panels: A Comparative Study' in U Varottil and W Yee Wan (eds), *Comparative Takeover Regulation: Global and Asian Perspectives* (Cambridge University Press, 2017) 134ff.

28 *Corporations Act* s 657A.

29 *Corporate Law Economic Reform Program Act 1999* (Cth).

30 Explanatory Memorandum, Corporate Law Economic Reform Program Bill 1998 (Cth) [7.2].

31 Ibid [7.3]. For a discussion of strategic litigation in takeovers, see I Ramsay, 'Takeover Dispute Resolution in Australia and the United States—Takeovers Panel or Courts?' (2015) 33(5) *Company and Securities Law Journal* 341.

32 *ASIC Act* s 172.

33 Ibid s 184.

34 Takeovers Panel, *Annual Report* (Report, 2022–2023) 6.

35 Takeovers Panel, *Annual Report* (Report, 2018–2019) 6.

36 Takeovers Panel, *Who We Are* <https://takeovers.gov.au/about>.

irrelevant to the Panel's decision-making but is only one of several factors that the Panel must take into account.

Under s 174 of the *ASIC Act*, the Panel has the functions and powers conferred on it by the corporations legislation. Therefore, we look to the *Corporations Act* to determine the Panel's functions and powers. A clear indication of the Panel's role is in s 659AA of the *Corporations Act*, which states that the object is 'to make the Panel the main forum for resolving disputes about a takeover bid until the bid period has ended'. This is reinforced by s 659B, which states that only ASIC or some other public authority (such as the Director of Public Prosecutions (DPP)) can commence court proceedings 'in relation to' a takeover bid before the end of the bid period. The timing of the bid period is discussed below. So, while court proceedings are not eliminated, their role is greatly reduced.[37] The moratorium is expressed in wide terms–it seems to prohibit any proceedings in relation to a takeover bid, regardless of whether the proceedings are based on a breach of ch 6, or some other provision in the *Corporations Act*, or some other law altogether. This is confirmed by s 659B(4), which defines the proceedings which cannot be commenced as 'not limited to proceedings brought under this Chapter or this Act but includes proceedings under other Commonwealth and State and Territory laws (including the general law)'. However, while the Panel may have jurisdiction to consider, for example a contract, 'there would need to be a relevant nexus between the [contractual dispute and its] effect on control of a company before the Panel would become involved'.[38] Likewise, s 659B has been interpreted as not precluding the exercise of certain powers by the court during the bid period; for example, to give relief under s 1325A.[39] Section 1325A is discussed below at Section 19.65.05.

The Panel is expressly required under the *ASIC Regulations* to ensure that its proceedings are:

(a) fair and reasonable
(b) conducted with little formality
(c) conducted in a timely manner.[40]

Proceedings are conducted in private[41] and are primarily determined on written submissions and evidence.[42] However, the Panel may give notice to a person or the

37 As discussed below at Section 19.25.10, ASIC has power under s 655A of the *Corporations Act* to exempt or modify the operation of any provision of ch 6, including s 659B. In *Eastern Field Developments Ltd v Takeovers Panel* (2019) 135 ACSR 580, 590 [38], ASIC issued an instrument under s 655A(1)(b) declaring that ch 6 of the *Corporations Act* applied to a bidder as if s 659B(1) were omitted. This allowed the bidder to bring proceedings for judicial review of a Panel decision before the bid period ended (ie while the bid remained open). For a discussion of ASIC's powers of exemption and modification, including s 655A, see S Bottomley, 'The Notional Legislator: The Australian Securities and Investments Commission's Role as a Law-Maker' (2011) 39(1) *Federal Law Review* 1.

38 *Careers Australia Group Ltd 02* [2013] ATP 5, [32]–[33] citing *Pendant Software Pty Ltd v Harwood* (2006) 154 FCR 150.

39 *Metallicity Ltd v Allen* (2022) 165 ACSR 509; *Venturex Resources Ltd* (2009) 177 FCR 391, 393ff.

40 *Australian Securities and Investments Commission Regulations 2001* (Cth) regs 13, 16(2).

41 Takeovers Panel, *Procedural Rules 2020* (at 1 April 2021) r 6(2).

42 Ibid.

public at large of a decision of the Panel to conduct proceedings and may accept submissions from third parties who have expressed interest in the proceedings.[43] A sitting Panel may convene a conference[44] or otherwise conduct proceedings.[45] The Panel has significant powers during proceedings, including the powers to take evidence on oath and summon witnesses.[46] Under *ASIC Regulations* reg 16(2), the rules of evidence do not apply to Panel proceedings. However, under s 195(4) of the *ASIC Act*, the rules of procedural fairness do apply to the extent that they are not inconsistent with the Act.

A party to Panel proceedings may only be legally represented with the leave of the Panel.[47] The Panel rarely refuses leave but will do so when it considers that a conflict of interest may arise.[48] 'If a party is to be legally represented, the Panel prefers it to be by the commercial lawyers who have been advising it in the transaction that is the subject of the application.'[49] This means that commercial rather than litigation lawyers generally represent parties in proceedings before the Panel.

19.25.10 Applications to the Panel

The Panel's powers may only be exercised when proceedings have been commenced by an application. The Panel's jurisdiction or suite of powers is invoked by the application. Therefore, the role of the Panel is different to ASIC. It does not monitor takeovers and cannot intervene in a takeover of its own motion, and it does not have any role in the regular administration of the takeover laws.

There are three provisions of the *Corporations Act* which allow the Panel to exercise its powers:

(1) Section 656A: the Panel may review a decision made by ASIC under either s 655A (exemption from or modification of ch 6 in relation to a person) or s 673 (exemption from or modification of ch 6C—substantial shareholding provisions). ASIC has extensive powers to exempt parties from the operation of chs 6 and 6C or to modify the operation of those provisions in relation to particular parties. These powers are similar to the powers discussed in Chapter 9 at Section 9.65 in relation to fundraising. The Panel may review ASIC's exercise of these powers.
(2) Section 657C: application for a declaration of unacceptable circumstances.
(3) Section 657EA: application for review by the Panel of a decision under s 657C. This is an internal review by a differently constituted panel of a previous Panel's decision. It is similar to an appeal.

43 *Australian Securities and Investments Commission Regulations 2001* (Cth) reg 23.
44 Ibid regs 35–41.
45 *Australian Securities and Investments Commission Act 2001* (Cth) s 188.
46 Ibid s 192.
47 Ibid s 194.
48 *DRA Global Ltd* [2022] ATP 16 [124]–[125].
49 Takeovers Panel, *Procedural Guidelines* (at 1 April 2021) 9.3d. Rule 17(2) of the *Takeovers Panel Procedural Rules 2020* states that '[a] party that wishes to be legally represented other than by its commercial lawyers should state that and explain why when requesting consent'.

19.25.15 Declaration of unacceptable circumstances

The most common application to the Panel is an application for a declaration of unacceptable circumstances under s 657A. The first step is that there must be an application made to the Panel under s 657C. The application may be made by the bidder, the target, ASIC, or any other person whose interests are affected.[50] The statistics show that bidders make more applications than target companies but the figures from 2000–10 show that a spread of stakeholders use the Panel. During this period, applications were made in the following proportions: 37 per cent by bidders, 31 per cent by target companies, 24 per cent by shareholder/other, 6 per cent by rival bidders and 2 per cent by ASIC.[51] In 2018–19, shareholders were a significant source of applications.[52] This information substantiates the observation made by Bednall and Ngomba that ASIC 'play[s] a relatively minor role in the resolution of takeover disputes and the enforcement of [Chapter] 6'.[53]

The application must be made within two months of the circumstances having occurred or such longer period as the Panel allows.[54] The Panel has the power to dismiss the application if it is satisfied that it is frivolous or vexations (s 658A).

The Panel must decide quickly—it has one month from the date of the application in which to make the declaration, or three months after the circumstances have occurred—whichever is the later (s 657B). This period can only be extended by an application to the court by the Panel.[55] The Panel's proceedings are conducted swiftly. In 2022–3, it took an average of 29 days from the date of the application to make a decision.[56]

19.25.20 What are 'unacceptable circumstances'?

There is no definition of the term 'unacceptable circumstances' in the *Corporations Act*. However, s 657A does give some broad guidance as follows.

First, unacceptable circumstances may be found to exist even if there has not been a contravention of the *Corporations Act* (s 657A(1)). Therefore, the Panel's inquiry is not limited to contraventions of the *Corporations Act* or mere compliance with the letter of the law. Nevertheless, a contravention of chs 6–6C can be grounds for a declaration of unacceptable circumstances (s 657A(2)(c)).

Second, the Panel's inquiry is directed to the apparent effect of the circumstances on control of a company, or on the acquisition of a substantial interest in a company (s 657A(2)(a)). The term 'substantial interest' was, in the past, subject to a variety of judicial definitions. It is now defined by s 602A. The definition states that a substantial interest

---

50 *Corporations Act* s 657C(2).

51 Takeovers Panel, *The Takeovers Panel—An Update 2011* (Report, March 2011).

52 Takeovers Panel, *Annual Report* (Report, 2018–2019) 3.

53 T Bednall and V Ngomba, 'ASIC and the Takeovers Panel' (2011) 29(5) *Company and Securities Law Journal* 355.

54 *Corporations Act* s 657C(3). Extensions of time may be granted by the Panel where there has been a serious contravention of the takeovers legislation the effects of which appear to give rise to unacceptable circumstances and warrant a remedy: *The Market Herald Ltd* [2023] ATP 7; *Palmer Leisure Coolum Pty Ltd v Takeovers Panel* (2015) 245 FCR 371.

55 *Corporations Act* s 657B.

56 Takeovers Panel, *Annual Report* (Report, 2022–2023) 6.

is not limited to having a relevant interest, or a legal or equitable interest, or having a power or right in relation to the company. The term 'relevant interest' is discussed below.

Third, the circumstances are unacceptable having regard to the purposes of ch 6 as set out in s 602 (s 657A(2)(b)).

Fourth, the Panel must take into account the public interest and any relevant policy considerations (see the final sentence of s 657A(2)). So, unacceptability is not decided simply by what the bidder or the target think is unacceptable. It has a broader, public interest component.

Finally, the Panel must have regard to four particular factors that are set out in s 657A(3):

(1) The purposes of ch 6 set out in s 602: the need for an efficient, competitive and informed market and a reasonable and equal opportunity to participate in benefits of takeover. In regards to the latter factor, the Panel is explicitly directed (in the final sentence of s 657A(3)) to take into account the actions of directors. This means the Panel can examine the defensive tactics implemented by directors
(2) Other provisions of ch 6
(3) Any rules made by the Panel under s 658C
(4) Anything specified in the *ASIC Regulations*.

The Panel has issued a Guidance Note, which sets out its approach to making a declaration of unacceptable circumstances.[57] Examples of unacceptable circumstances include information deficiencies;[58] the lockout of rival bids;[59] a false market in securities the subject of a bid; uncommercial pricing of a rights issue[60] or a rights issue that does not provide genuine accessibility to its benefits for all shareholders;[61] frustrating a bid;[62] or coercive conduct by the bidder.[63]

A declaration by the Panel that there have been unacceptable circumstances may result in a party giving an undertaking to take some course of action; for example, to supply further information to the target's shareholders. The Panel may accept an undertaking from a person affected or likely to be affected[64] and undertakings often lead to a resolution of the issues before the Panel. If an undertaking is breached, the court can make orders for compliance or compensation on the application by the Panel.[65]

The Panel may make orders following a declaration of unacceptable circumstances (s 657D). The Panel has the choice whether to make an order, and what order it will make, but it must not make an order if that would unfairly prejudice any person (s 657D(1)).

57 Takeovers Panel, *Unacceptable Circumstances* (Guidance Note 1, 11 July 2018).

58 *Nex Metals Explorations Ltd 02* [2021] ATP 16; *Programmed Maintenance Services Ltd 02* (2008) 66 ACSR 242.

59 *Normandy Mining Ltd (No 3)* [2001] ATP 30.

60 *InvestorInfo Ltd* [2004] ATP 6 [38].

61 *Halom Investments Pty Ltd v MMA Offshore* (2017) 124 ACSR 342; *Data & Commerce Ltd* [2004] ATP 7.

62 *MacarthurCook Ltd* (2008) 67 ACSR 345.

63 *Realm Resources Ltd* [2018] ATP 13.

64 *Australian Securities and Investments Commission Act 2001* (Cth) s 201A.

65 Ibid ss 201A(3)–(4).

An order cannot be made unless all relevant parties have had a chance to make submissions to an inquiry conducted by the Panel in relation to the order (s 657D(1)).

The orders that can be made include orders aimed at protecting the rights or interests of any person affected, or will be or are likely to be affected, by the conduct in question, orders that seek to ensure that the takeover proceeds in a manner that complies with the legislation, and orders awarding costs (s 657D(2)). Section 657D(2) also refers to the possibility of 'remedial orders'. This term is defined in s 9 to have a wide operation, including orders restraining the exercise of voting rights, or the acquisition of securities, directing the disposal of securities, etc. However, the Panel is an administrative body and cannot exercise judicial power; therefore, the definition of 'remedial order' does not include a power to make orders for compensation.[66] Similarly, s 657D(2) states that the orders that may be made by the Panel do not include an order directing the person to comply with a requirement of chs 6, 6A, 6B or 6C.

It is a strict liability offence to contravene an order that is made by the Panel (s 657F). Furthermore, under s 657G, a court may make an order concerning compliance with an order of the Panel. Again, due to its administrative nature, the Panel cannot enforce its own orders; therefore, enforcement must occur through the courts. The administrative nature of the Panel is discussed below.

Section 657H allows ASIC to publish a report, statement or notice that states an application has been made to the Panel. This allows for some publicity of the proceedings and for the media and the market to be alerted. The Panel has an internal review procedure, similar to an internal appeal. ASIC or a party to the proceedings may apply for review of a decision of the Panel (s 657EA). This must be done within two business days of the Panel's decision being made.[67] A differently constituted Panel will conduct a de novo reconsideration of the original decision.[68]

19.25.25 Challenges to the Takeovers Panel

The Panel has a unique role and has occasionally come under challenge. The Panel's jurisdiction was considered by the High Court in *Attorney-General (Cth) v Alinta Ltd* ('*Alinta*').[69] The question for the High Court was whether s 657A(2) conferred judicial power on the Panel, in contravention of ch III of the *Australian Constitution*. The Court unanimously answered that question in the negative. The High Court drew on several considerations in upholding the appeal. One important consideration was that the Panel must consider the public interest and general policy, as specified in s 657A(2), and any other matters that it deems to be relevant under s 657A(3). Hayne J considered that the power of the Panel to make a declaration of unacceptable circumstances 'required [more] than proof of a contravention of the Act'.[70] Crennan and Keifel JJ considered that courts apply the law,

66 See also Takeovers Panel, *Remedies General* (Guidance Note 4, 30 January 2017).

67 *Corporations Regulations 2001* (Cth) reg 6.10.01.

68 See concluding paragraph to s 657EA(4); Takeovers Panel, *Reviewing Decisions* (Guidance Note 2, 27 May 2015).

69 *Attorney-General (Cth) v Alinta Ltd* (2008) 233 CLR 542.

70 Ibid 542, 561–2 [43].

not policy, and noted that the Panel's powers clearly contemplated that it would consider policy and '[p]olicy considerations are more often regarded as applying to a non-judicial process of decision-making'.[71] Moreover, the policy considerations reserved to the Panel potentially had a wide range,[72] which was similarly inconsistent with judicial power.

Further factors taken into account by the High Court were that the Panel has no power to enforce its own orders, and enforcement of the Panel's orders requires independent judicial authority—this being the courts.[73] Further, s 657D(2) expressly excludes the Panel from directing a person to comply with the provisions of chs 6–6C.[74] These aspects of the Panel's jurisdiction are discussed above at Section 19.25.20.

The reasoning in *Alinta* has been followed in subsequent cases; notably, by the Full Federal Court in *CEMEX Australia Pty Ltd v Takeovers Panel*.[75] However, the Panel's decisions remain vulnerable to applications for judicial review under s 75(v) of the *Constitution* and the *Administrative Decisions (Judicial Review) Act* 1977 (Cth).[76]

19.30 The basic prohibition: s 606

We now examine the rules that govern takeovers. As discussed above at Section 19.20.05, takeovers are subject to detailed regulation under the *Corporations Act*. The main focus of takeover regulation is ch 6, but chs 6A, 6B and 6C contain complementary provisions. As discussed above, the method adopted in ch 6 is to create a 'closed system'. It erects a wall around the conduct to be regulated by prohibiting that conduct completely. Then, since the aim is to regulate and not to prohibit, the legislation allows certain exemptions and exceptions, provided that they comply with the procedures specified in the legislation. The desired aim of this regulatory approach is close regulation of the conduct, combined with certainty in the application and interpretation of the law.

Section 606 states the basic prohibition. This section defines the type of takeover conduct to be regulated. Note that there are a number of special terms used in s 606. At this stage, we will explain the general prohibition so that the scope of the prohibition is clear. The special terms that are used in s 606 are then discussed at Section 19.30.10ff.

19.30.05 Prohibited share acquisitions

The prohibition applies to the acquisition of a relevant interest in issued voting shares in a company. The prohibition in s 606 is only concerned with the acquisition of voting shares in either a listed company or an unlisted company that has more than 50 members (s 606(1)(a)). Note that the term 'voting shares' differs from the word 'securities', which is defined by s 92(3) for the purposes of chs 6 to 6CA. Shares are a type of security for the

71 (2008) 233 CLR 542, 597 [168].

72 Ibid.

73 Ibid 598 [175].

74 Ibid 589 [173].

75 *CEMEX Australia Pty Ltd v Takeovers Panel* (2009) 177 FCR 98.

76 See *Aurora Funds Management Ltd v Australian Government Takeovers Panel* (2020) 144 ACSR 593; *Eastern Field Developments Ltd v Takeovers Panel* (2019) 135 ACSR 580; *Queensland North Australia Pty Ltd v Takeovers Panel* (2015) 106 ACSR 186.

purposes of chs 6, 6A, 6B and 6C. In this chapter, we mainly use the term 'shares' to illustrate the operation of the rules. However, the legislation frequently specifically refers to 'securities', which has a wider meaning than shares.[77]

Section 606(1)(c) specifies two types of prohibited share acquisitions. The first part of the prohibition may be called the '20 per cent rule'. This prohibits a person from acquiring a relevant interest in voting shares in a company if, as a result, the voting power of that person or anyone else will increase from 20 per cent or below to more than 20 per cent (s 606(1)(c)(i)). For example, a person holds 14 per cent of voting shares in X Ltd. They can acquire up to another 6 per cent without being in breach of the prohibition.

The second part of the prohibition can be called the 'more than 20 per cent but less than 90 per cent rule'. This prohibits a person from acquiring a relevant interest in voting shares in a company if, as a result, the voting power of that person or anyone else will increase from above 20 per cent to less than 90 per cent (s 606(1)(c)(ii)). For example, a person holds 22 per cent of voting shares in Y Ltd. Any further acquisition of shares will be in breach of the prohibition, unless one of the exceptions applies.

Section 606 does not deal with entitlements of over 90 per cent because these are regulated by the compulsory acquisition provisions in ch 6A. Chapter 6A is discussed below at Section 19.60ff.

The purpose of the s 606 prohibition is to force takeovers to be conducted only via one of the permitted exceptions. Although, pursuant to s 607, any acquisition which breaches the prohibition is still valid, it can be subject to a court order under s 1325A. Section 1325A deals with contraventions of chs 6–6C following an application made by ASIC, the target company, its members and former members, the persons from whom the shares were acquired, or a person whose interests are affected. Further, the effect of the breach may constitute unacceptable circumstances for the purposes of a declaration by the Panel under s 657A, and be subject to orders under s 657D,[78] as discussed above.

The permitted exceptions each have the overall effect of introducing time delays and documentation and information requirements to ensure informed shareholder decision-making about the acquisition, reinforcing the Eggleston Principles in s 602.

The expansive operation of the prohibition in s 606 is achieved using several special terms and concepts. We examine these now. In reading this material, keep in mind that these terms and concepts interconnect with each other, so the definition of one term will rely on other terms and concepts.

19.30.10 Acquisitions resulting in an increase in voting power

The prohibition focuses on whether a share acquisition results in an increase in voting power in the target company. Note that the acquirer of the shares and the holder of the increased voting power need not be the same person. The prohibition captures, for example, the situation where a parent company controls a number of subsidiaries each

77 See, eg, the discussion of s 617 at Section 19.45.

78 For example, an order that shares held in breach of the s 606 prohibition be divested: *Sovereign Gold Company Ltd* [2016] ATP 12; *World Oil Resources Ltd* [2013] ATP 1.

of which owns shares in a target company; a further acquisition of target company shares by a subsidiary will increase the voting power of the parent company. In other words, the prohibition attempts to capture indirect forms of takeover as well as direct takeovers. Section 610 sets out a formula for calculating a person's voting power. The definition of 'voting power' is examined below. The prohibition focuses on the acquisition of voting shares in a company. The term 'voting share' is defined in s 9.

The takeover activity regulated under ch 6 is defined by reference to a threshold of 20 per cent.[79] Share acquisitions that fall below this threshold, with one exception discussed below at Section 19.30.15, are not regulated by the *Corporations Act*. The threshold of 20 per cent reflects a judgment that, although circumstances will vary, a shareholding of that size will usually put a person on course to achieve some significant level of control in the company—either de facto control in the case of a widely-held company, or perhaps through the right to representation on the board.[80]

19.30.15 Substantial holdings

Chapter 6C deals with 'substantial shareholdings' and imposes 'stake-building' disclosure obligations. A person has a substantial holding if the total votes in which they or their associates have a relevant interest is 5 per cent or more of the total votes in the company (s 9). If a person acquires a substantial holding, or that holding moves up or down by at least 1 per cent, or they make a takeover bid for the company, then they must notify the company of their identity, and give details of their shareholding; for example, the obligations in s 671B in relation to listed companies. One purpose of these provisions is to alert the market and the company to the possibility of a potential takeover.[81] This knowledge can provide an impetus for the company's managers to perform efficiently, considering the market for corporate control. It may alert other potential takeover bidders that there is a possible competitor. Further, it may alert the target to the potential for defensive strategies before the takeover commences.[82] Defensive strategies are discussed at Section 19.55.10ff.

19.30.20 Relevant interests

'Relevant interests' is defined in ss 608 and 609. Essentially, a person has a relevant interest in a share if they are the holder of the shares, or if they have power or control over the voting rights attached to the share or over the disposal of the share (s 608(1)).

79 The 20 per cent threshold was arrived at following the recommendations of the Parliamentary Joint Committee on Corporations and Financial Services, *Report on the Mandatory Bid Rule* (Report, June 2000).

80 Note that other jurisdictions set different thresholds and requirements for a compulsory bid; eg, 30 per cent in the United Kingdom and China and 33.3 per cent in France. See generally R Hui Huang and CC Wang, 'The Mandatory Bid Rule under China's Takeover Law: A Comparative and Empirical Perspective' (2020) 53(2) *International Lawyer* 195; E-P Schuster, 'The Mandatory Bid Rule: Efficient, After All' (2013) 76(3) *Modern Law Review* 529; R Levy and N Pathak, 'The Mandatory Bid Rule—Where are we and can it be made to work?' (2002) 20(7) *Company and Securities Law Journal* 424.

81 *DRA Global Ltd* [2022] ATP 16 [40].

82 For a general discussion of the accountability provided by ch 6C, see D Chaikin, 'Should Chapter 6C of the *Corporations Act* Be the Model for Beneficial Ownership Disclosure Regulation of Private Companies?' (2018) 36(3) *Company and Securities Law Journal* 204.

The idea of power or control here is broad, covering direct and indirect control, formal or informal arrangements, sole or joint arrangements, regardless of whether the arrangements for power or control are enforceable (s 608(2)). In *TVW Enterprises Pty Ltd v Queensland Press Ltd*,[83] O'Bryan J held that 'control' in this context is established even if there is not complete or substantial control.[84] If a person has power to exercise some true or actual measure of control over either the right to vote or the right to dispose of the share, then that person has a relevant interest.[85] Hence, an agreement between one shareholder (A) and another (B) whereby B would, on A's request, execute a further agreement which would require B to offer shares for sale to A, satisfies this test. This is known as a 'put option'.

In *Nicholas v Wade*,[86] Marks J held that agreements about power or control may be inferred from facts and circumstances and that surrounding circumstances and contemporaneous agreements should be taken into account.[87]

This demonstrates that the concept of relevant interest is not the same as having a legal or beneficial ownership of shares.[88] Conversely, legal or beneficial control over shares is sufficient to establish there is a relevant interest.[89]

Relevant interests held through bodies corporate

Section 608(3) refers to situations where there is a company interposed between the target company and the real controller of the shares. This section may apply where several companies are placed in between the bidder and the target, and control is obscured. The first situation is where the voting power in the target company is exercised by another company, and that other company is, in turn, controlled by another person (which may be yet another company); that other person is deemed to have the same relevant interest in the voting shares as the company (s 608(3)(b)). For example:

$$\text{X—controls} \rightarrow \text{Company A} — 11\% \rightarrow \text{Company B} \left[\text{target}\right]$$

Applying s 608(3)(b), person X is deemed to have an 11 per cent relevant interest in Company B if Company A has control of Company B. Company A will control Company B if it has the capacity to determine the outcome of decisions about financial and operating policies.[90] This reasoning may be applied repeatedly along a chain. Therefore, if X is a company that is in turn controlled by Y, then X's deemed relevant interest in Company B can be attributed to Y, and so on.

83 *TVW Enterprises Pty Ltd v Queensland Press Ltd* [1983] 2 VR 529.
84 Following *Re Kornblums Furnishings Ltd* [1982] VR 123.
85 *TVW Enterprises Ltd v Queensland Press Ltd* [1983] 2 VR 529, 542–3. See also *The President's Club Ltd* [2012] ATP 10 [80]–[93]; *Edensor Nominees Pty Ltd v Australian Securities and Investments Commission* (2002) 120 FCR 78.
86 *Nicholas v Wade* (1982) 1 ACLC 459.
87 See also *Mount Gibson Iron Ltd* [2008] ATP 4.
88 See R Simkiss et al, *Takeovers and Reconstructions in Australia* (LexisNexis, online) [410ff] for many useful examples of the operation of relevant interests in ss 608 and 609, associates in s 12, and voting power in s 610.
89 *National Companies and Securities Commission v Brierley Investments Ltd* (1988) 14 NSWLR 273.
90 See the expanded definition of 'control' in ss 608(4)–(7).

Section 608(3)(a) is a variation on this. It states that if X is a body corporate (X Ltd) and it has over 20 per cent of the voting power in Company A, the same result follows: X's relevant interest is 11 per cent in Company B. However, s 608(3)(a) does not have repeated applications as indicated in the concluding paragraph in s 608(3).

The Panel has commented that 'the operation of the s 608(3) deeming provision is well-established and generally well-understood by market participants'.[91]

19.30.25 Accelerated relevant interests

The concept of 'relevant interest' is made even broader by s 608(8), which states that in certain situations a person is deemed to have a relevant interest in a share. ASIC comments that '[t]he provision is sometimes referred to as the 'accelerator provision' because it may cause a relevant interest to arise sooner than it otherwise would.[92] The subsection refers to the circumstance where a person has entered into an agreement with respect to issued shares; for example, an option to purchase the shares at some future date, also known as a 'call option'. If, on exercising the right under the agreement, the person would at that future time have a relevant interest in the share, then s 608(8) deems the person to have that relevant interest before the right is actually exercised. The aim of this provision is to prevent takeover bidders from disguising their control over the shares via arrangements that can be activated at short notice.

Re Adelaide Holdings Ltd[93] provides a clear example of this. The case involved two companies and the shares of a third company. The first two companies were Pan D'or Mining (Pan D'or) and Adelaide Holdings (Adelaide). Both companies owned shares in a third company, Archean Oil (Archean). Adelaide gave Pan D'or a put option to acquire Pan D'or's Archean shares—Adelaide agreed that, on receiving notice from Pan D'or, Adelaide would purchase an agreed number of Archean shares from Pan D'or at an agreed price and Pan D'or promised to sell the shares at the relevant time and agreed price. Pan D'or later gave the written notice, but Adelaide refused to comply. Adelaide's argument was that:

(1) it had subsequently entered into three other put options regarding Archean shares, and each of those option-holders had now served notice for Adelaide to buy the shares;
(2) Adelaide already held a significant percentage of shares in Archean at over 20 per cent.

Therefore, Adelaide argued that if it was to comply with the put option from Pan D'or it would be acting in breach of (what is now) s 606(1)—acquiring shares in a company while it already held between 20 per cent and 90 per cent. The Court held that, by virtue of s 608(8), Adelaide already had a relevant interest in the Pan D'or shareholding when it entered into the agreement with Pan D'or and thus it would not be increasing that relevant interest merely by actually purchasing the shares.

91 *Yowie Group Ltd 01 & 02* [2019] ATP 10;[49].
92 Australian Securities and Investments Commission, *Relevant Interests and Substantial Holding Notices* (Regulatory Guide 5, 27 March 2024) [RG 5.57].
93 *Re Adelaide Holdings Ltd* [1982] 1 NSWLR 167.

As Helsham CJ stated:

> the effect of [the section] ... is to bring back to the earliest possible point of time in some transactions affecting shares the moment at which a person will be treated as having a relevant interest in those shares.[94]

19.30.30 Circumstances not giving rise to a relevant interest

Section 609 describes situations that do not give rise to a relevant interest; for example, holders of proxy votes at a general meeting, holding and disposal of securities by financial services licensees, shares covered by buy-backs, pre-emptive rights, and certain mortgage and security arrangements. Section 609(9) states that a director of a company does not have a relevant interest in securities merely because their company has a relevant interest in those securities. Therefore, there must be some further relationship or connection between the director and the company for the relevant interest to arise.

19.30.35 Voting power

The basic prohibition in s 606 states that a person must not acquire a relevant interest in issued voting shares in a company. We now examine what is meant by 'voting power'. This is elaborated in s 610, which states that a person's voting power is calculated:

(1) by counting the number of votes in which they and their associates have a relevant interest
(2) dividing that number by the total number of votes in the company, and
(3) multiplying the answer by 100, to get a percentage.

The diagram in s 610(1) sets this out as follows:

$$\frac{\text{Person's and associates' votes}}{\text{Total votes in designated body}} \times 100$$

Here:

- 'person's and associates' votes' is the total number of votes attached to all the voting shares in the designated body (if any) that the person or an associate has a relevant interest in
- 'total votes in designated body' is the total number of votes attached to all voting shares in the designated body.

Note the following about s 610:

- the number of votes must be counted, not just the number of *voting shares*. In listed companies this will be the same because the ASX *Listing Rules* (*LRs*) require one vote per share,[95] but in an unlisted company shares may have different voting rights.
- any votes held by an associate of the person must be included in the count.[96]

94 Ibid 170. See also *Afro-West Mining Ltd v Australian Mining Investments Ltd* (1988) 14 ACLR 709.
95 For a discussion of the *Listing Rules*, see Chapter 17. See also ASX, *Listing Rules* (at 19 December 2016).
96 For a relatively accessible application of s 610 and its operation in tandem with s 606, see *Queensland North Australia Pty Ltd v Takeovers Panel* (2015) 106 ACSR 186.

These provisions regulate the situation in which two or more associated persons (which includes companies) jointly warehouse more than 20 per cent, although each person holds less than 20 per cent of the voting power. The significance of the 20 per cent figure is discussed above at Section 19.30.05. The obvious problem with this is that, by selling to those involved in such arrangements, existing shareholders in a target company may unwittingly participate in a change of control of the company. Had they known this, they may not have sold their shares at all, or may have demanded a higher price to reflect the premium for control.

Section 610(3) can be explained by way of example. Assume that X and Y are associates (this term is explained in the next section). Each holds shares in target Company B. Focusing on X: X's voting power is calculated by including the votes attached to Y's shares. Now, assume that Y sells her shares to X. On one view, X's position regarding voting power has not changed.

On another view, X's position is different: X now has a different and greater measure of control over those shares. Section 610(3) states that in the event of such a transaction, X's voting power is taken to have increased for the purposes of applying s 606, therefore triggering the takeover requirements.

19.30.40 Who is an associate?

The term 'associate' is defined in different ways in ss 11–17 of the *Corporations Act*. For present purposes, when considering that term in chs 6, 6A, 6B and 6C, s 12(1) states that the definition of an 'associate' is found in s 12. This section defines three different types of relationship that give rise to a person being defined as an 'associate'. All three are contained in s 12(2).[97] Section 15 contains a 'deeming' provision which nominally extends the definition of associate; however, the authors concur with Levy that the better view is that ss 12 and 16 exhaustively define associate for the purposes of chs 6, 6A, 6B and 6C.[98] Section 16 contains exceptions to the s 12 definition, as discussed below.

The first category (s 12(2)(a)) applies in defining who is an associate of a body corporate (for example, the takeover bidder or a holder of shares in a company). An associate of a body corporate is:

(1) any other body corporate that is controlled by the first body corporate (for example, a subsidiary company)
(2) any other body corporate that controls the first body corporate (for example, a holding company)
(3) any other body corporate that is controlled by an entity that also controls the first body corporate (for example, a sibling subsidiary company).

97 For a comprehensive application of s 12(2), see *Mount Gibson Iron Ltd* [2008] ATP 4.

98 Levy contends that ss 12 and 16 make 'significantly different provision relating to corporate groups and to acting in concert from ss 11 and 15 respectively'. He acknowledges, however, that in a few cases the courts 'have applied both ss 12 and 15, seemingly without asking whether s12(1) permits them to do so': Rodd Levy, *Takeovers Law & Strategy* (Lawbook, 6th ed, 2023) 53.

The term 'control' is defined in s 50AA as a situation where 'the first entity has the capacity to determine the outcome of decisions about the second entity's financial and operating policies'. This is intentionally very broad.

The second category (s 12(2)(b)) states that a person is an associate of another person if they have, or if they propose to, enter into a 'relevant agreement' for the purpose of controlling or influencing the composition of the board of directors of a body, or controlling or influencing the conduct of the body's affairs. Note that s 12(2)(b) refers to the *purpose* of the agreement, not its *effect*. The term 'relevant agreement' is defined in s 9. This definition is also broad: it is an agreement, arrangement, understanding (formal or informal), whether having legal force or not.[99] The term the 'body's affairs' is defined in s 53.[100] Again, this definition is very broad.

The third category (s 12(2)(c)) states that a person is an associate of another person if they are 'acting in concert' (or propose to act in concert) in relation to the affairs of a body corporate.

The term 'acting in concert' is not defined in the *Corporations Act*. In *Adsteam Building Industries Pty Ltd v Queensland Cement & Lime Co Ltd (No 4)*,[101] the Court interpreted the phrase 'acting in concert' to mean there must be a real combination between the persons—a common purpose or object. It is not the court's task to 'deem' an acting in concert where the evidence does not support this.[102]

Circumstantial evidence may be used to prove that parties are associates. It is not necessary to show communications between them for this purpose.[103]

These three s 12 definitions are subject to some exceptions that are set out in s 16(1). The list includes obvious exceptions for professional advisers, financial products dealers and others when they act in their professional capacity.

19.30.45 Collective action by investors and chs 6–6C

The prohibition in s 606, including its extended operation via ss 12 and 608, is intended to have a wide operation. This might mean that legitimate collective action by investors may be impeded. It may be desirable for investors to engage in collective action for the purpose of good corporate governance; for example, to hold the board accountable.[104] In order to promote investor engagement on corporate governance matters ASIC issued Regulatory Guide 128 to provide guidance to investors who wish to cooperate with each other in relation to their investment in listed companies.[105] Regulatory Guide 128 also identifies circumstances where acting together may lead to investors becoming associates or entering into a relevant agreement for the purposes of chs 6–6C.

99 See, eg, *Flinders Diamonds Ltd v Tiger International Resources Inc* (2003) 86 SASR 353.

100 Sections 12(2)(b) and (c) are prescribed provisions for the operation of s 53: *Corporations Regulations 2001* (Cth) reg 1.0.18.

101 *Adstream Building Industries Pty Ltd v Queensland Cement & Lime Co Ltd (No 4)* [1985] 1 Qd R 127, 132.

102 For a detailed application of ss 12(2)(b) and 12(2)(c), see *The Market Herald Ltd* [2023] ATP 7.

103 *Aurora Funds Management Ltd v Australian Government Takeovers Panel* (2020) 144 ACSR 593 [28].

104 Compare *Flinders Diamonds Ltd v Tiger International Resources Inc* (2004) 88 SASR 281, [35], [37] with *Re Resource Generation Ltd* [2015] ATP 12, [105]–[107].

105 Australian Securities and Investments Commission, *Collective Action by Investors* (Regulatory Guide 128, 23 June 2015).

19.35 Exemptions from the prohibition

There are a number of exemptions from the prohibition in s 606 that are listed in a table in s 611, with further details in s 612. The exemptions in ss 611 and 612 provide 'safe harbours' from the breach in s 606, provided there is strict compliance with their requirements. Most of the acquisitions referred to in s 611 are exempted because they are regulated elsewhere in the *Corporations Act*; for example, acquisitions via fundraising (items 12 and 13), schemes of arrangement under pt 5.1 (item 17), and buy-backs under s 257A (item 19). For the purposes of this chapter, we focus upon three exemptions: creeping acquisitions (item 9), takeovers by consent (item 7), and takeover bids (item 1).

19.35.05 Creeping acquisitions

This exemption in item 9 of s 611 applies when a person is entitled to at least 19 per cent of the voting power in a company and has been so entitled for at least six months. Under the exemption, that person can acquire not more than three per cent in additional voting power every subsequent six months. The idea is that this method of acquiring control of a company is slow enough to give everyone who is affected enough time to make an informed and unhurried decision about how to respond.[106] In many takeover situations, time is of the essence: the timing of a takeover is often prompted by fluctuations in market price of the target company's shares, or by news about impending defensive moves by the board. So, a creeping acquisition is not always an attractive option. Nevertheless, patience can be rewarded. Research indicates that creeping acquisitions are more common than many commentators believe.[107] For example, James Packer used the creeping provisions to acquire control of Crown Ltd, moving from a holding of 37 per cent in 2009 to a majority shareholding of 50 per cent in 2012 without paying a premium for control.[108]

19.35.10 Takeovers by consent

Where the shareholders in the target company (not including the acquirer or its associates) pass an ordinary resolution which approves the acquisition, then the provisions of ch 6 will not apply (item 7 of s 611).

In effect, item 7 allows target shareholders to voluntarily forego the protections of ch 6, including the equal opportunity to participate in the benefits of the takeover. Given this, the legislation seeks to ensure the voluntary waiver of these protections is an informed decision. Item 7 requires that the shareholders should be told the identity of the purchaser and how the purchase will affect that person's voting power in the company. The same applies for associates. The resolution must be passed with no votes being cast in favour of the resolution by the person proposing to make the acquisition and their associates or by the persons from whom the acquisition is to be made and their associates (item 7(a)).

106 For a discussion of the policy underpinning s 611 item 9, see *Molopo Energy Ltd 03R, 04R & 05R* [2017] ATP 12; *Sovereign Gold Company Ltd* [2016] ATP 12.

107 R da Silva Rosa et al, 'Evaluating Creeping Acquisitions' (2015) 37(1) *Sydney Law Review* 37.

108 R Levy, 'Time to Axe the 3pc Creep Rule', *The Australian Financial Review* (Sydney, 2 July 2012) 43.

The courts have voiced concerns about this exemption. In *National Companies and Securities Commission v Consolidated Gold Mining Areas NL (No 2)*,[109] Samuels J held that the section 'assumes that before they give or withhold agreement the existing shareholders will receive a proper and full disclosure of the relevant facts upon which alone their decision can be determined'.[110] This includes the identity of the acquirer, the number of shares, and the acquirer's existing holding.

Item 7 is controversial because it permits a person to acquire control without paying a premium or by only paying a premium to the vendor of the shareholding acquired. Therefore, it is 'keenly policed by ASIC'.[111] Levy comments that it is rare for this procedure to be used where a major shareholder is selling out to another person because minority shareholders will usually vote against it if there is any chance of them receiving a takeover bid.[112] Further, the notice of meeting may provoke a proper bid from a rival bidder.[113]

One potential problem with a takeover by consent is this: in the usual course of events, a person who wants to make such a takeover will already have come to some sort of agreement about the share purchase prior to the meeting at which the shareholders vote on the takeover. That agreement will be subject to the resolution of shareholders. Indeed, certain details will need to have been clarified so that the shareholders can make an informed vote. The potential problem is that the conditional agreement could give the purchaser a deemed relevant interest in the shares, meaning they would have breached the takeovers prohibition before the meeting can be held. The legislation now expressly excludes this type of conditional agreement from the relevant interest definition, thereby overcoming the problem (s 609(7)).

19.40 Takeover bids

Item 1 of s 611 introduces the main exception and the primary activity that is regulated by ch 6: takeover bids. Item 1 of s 611 contains a general exemption for share acquisitions that result from a takeover bid. The exemption is articulated as 'an acquisition that results from the acceptance of an offer under a takeover bid'. The term 'takeover bid' is discussed below at Section 19.40.05 and includes off-market and market bids (s 616). Therefore, the exemption in item 1 of s 611 applies to both types of bids and is reinforced by s 612, which states there is no exemption if the takeover bid contravenes certain stipulated sections.

19.40.05 What is a takeover bid?

A takeover bid involves the bidder making a formal offer to purchase the securities (usually shares) held by members in the target company. Section 616 states that there are two kinds of takeover bid: an off-market bid and a market bid. Section 616(2) conveniently summarises the sections that are relevant to each type of bid.

109 *National Companies and Securities Commission v Consolidated Mining Areas NL (No 2)* (1985) 1 NSWLR 622.
110 Ibid 625.
111 R Simkiss et al, *Takeovers and Reconstructions in Australia* (LexisNexis, online) [517].
112 R Levy, *Takeovers Law & Strategy* (Lawbook, 6th ed, 2023) 451.
113 *PowerTel Ltd (No 2)* [2003] ATP 27.

An off-market bid is the most common method of making a permissible takeover under ch 6. Market bids have certain limitations that make them less flexible for bidders. This is discussed below.

19.45 Off-market bids

According to s 618, only two types of offer are permitted in an off-market bid: an offer to acquire all the securities or an offer to acquire a specified proportion of the securities. As stated above, s 92(3) defines 'securities' for the purposes of chs 6–6C. Both types of offer are based on the idea that the bidder seeks to acquire some or all of a class of shares in the target company, known as the 'bid class'. The term 'bid class' is defined in s 9 as a 'class of securities to which the securities being bid for belong'. This is reinforced by s 617(1), which states that an off-market bid must relate to securities: (a) in a class of securities (the bid class); and (b) that exist or will exist as at the date set by the bidder under s 633(2).

In an off-market bid, the bidder may decide that the bid only applies to securities that are issued as at a particular date (s 617(1)(b)). That date must be set by the bidder in the bidder's statement or in a separate written notice given to the target on or before the date set by the bidder (s 633(2)). The bid may also apply to securities that come to be in the bid class during the period from the date set by the bidder under s 633(2) to the end of the offer period. If, on the date specified by the bidder under s 633(2), there are convertible notes, options or other securities which confer on the holder the right to be issued securities in the bid class, or which will convert to securities in the bid class, the bidder can elect to extend the bid to them (s 617(2)). Whether or not the bidder exercises this discretion is a matter for the bidder. As stated in *Re Skywest Ltd (No 2)*,[114] s 617(2) gives a bidder a clear right in all instances to determine the bid class. If the bidder chooses to extend the bid as permitted by s 617(2), the bidder's statement must disclose that that is the case (s 636(1)(j)). In companies that have only one class of shares, the bid class will usually comprise all of the shares in the company. If a company has different classes of shares, the bidder will focus upon whichever of those classes gives control of the company. Therefore, if a company has issued ordinary shares and preference shares, the ordinary shares would usually be the focus of an offer in a takeover bid.

Returning to s 618, the section stipulates two types of offers. The first is an offer to buy all of the shares in that class in which the offeror does not already have a relevant interest. This is commonly known as a 'full bid'. Alternatively, there is an offer to acquire a specified proportion of the shares in that class, as long as it is the same proportion for each existing holder of those shares. This is known as a 'proportional' or a 'partial' bid.

Regardless of whether it is a full bid or a partial bid, any offer in an off-market bid must treat the offerees equally. For example, s 619(1) requires that the offer to each target company shareholder must be the same—the same dollar amount for each share covered by the bid. Differences are permitted only if they relate to differences such as accrued dividend entitlements or differences in amount paid up on shares (s 619(2)).

114 *Re Skywest Ltd (No 2)* (2004) 50 ACSR 72 [55]–[57].

19.45.05 Navigating an off-market bid

The following section discusses the steps that are usually taken in an off-market bid. Most of the steps discussed below are set out in the diagram in s 632 and the table in s 633. As stated above, an off-market bid is the most common method of making a permissible takeover under ch 6.

19.45.10 Public announcement

The bidder may begin by publicly announcing an intention to make a takeover bid for the target company. The *Corporations Act* and ASIC require bidders to tread a careful path here. On the one hand, it is desirable that the market be kept informed of impending offers to promote economic efficiency and investor protection. On the other hand, there is a risk that a false market may be created where no bid actually eventuates, or where the actual bid differs markedly from what is foreshadowed in the announcement. Both situations are regulated by s 631. That provision requires that, where an announcement is made, the person has two months in which to make the takeover bid. The actual bid must be the same as the announcement or on 'terms and conditions' that are not substantially less favourable to the target shareholders (s 631(1)). Section 631(1) creates an offence for contravention of the provision.[115] Section 631(1A) states that strict liability attaches as regards the 'terms and conditions' component of the offence in s 631(1).

A further aim of s 631 is to prevent the making of false public announcements or proposals. These statements were described by the Eggleston Committee as 'bluffing offers'[116] and can arise where the person knows that no bid will be made or is reckless as to whether a bid will be made (s 631(2)(a)) or is reckless as to whether they will be able to perform their obligations relating to the bid if it is made (s 631(2)(b)). Section 631(2)(b) was interpreted by Beach J in *Australian Securities and Investments Commission v Mariner Corporation* ('*Mariner*'),[117] where the question was whether the bidder was reckless because it could not fund the bid at the time the announcement was made. It had intended to sell off the target's assets to fund the bid. His Honour concluded that the legislature intended to prevent the announcement of a takeover where a person had little, if any, intention of following through. The legislature's aim was to ensure the integrity of the market. His Honour found that the test for 'reckless' as used in s 631(2)(b) is subjective.[118] It requires an awareness of the risk and a conscious disregard or indifference to the risk.[119] The subjective awareness requires not just a risk, but a substantial risk that the bidder would not be able to perform its obligations.[120] In this case, his Honour examined the 'directors' mindset' and concluded that they were confident that funding could be obtained based on the break-up value of the target that was in excess of its

115 See *Brisbane Broncos Ltd (Nos 1 & 2)* (2002) 40 ACSR 459 for a discussion of the policy underpinning s 631(1).

116 Company Law Advisory Committee, *Disclosrue of Substantial Shareholdings and Takeovers* (Second Interim Report, February 1969) [37] ('the Eggleston Report').

117 *Australian Securities and Investments Commission v Mariner Corporation* (2015) 241 FCR 502.

118 Ibid [248]–[258].

119 Ibid [258].

120 Ibid [261].

market capitalisation. ASIC had not proved recklessness based upon the subjective test; therefore, ASIC's claim failed.[121]

Beach J also found that s 631(2)(b) did not require certain or guaranteed funding to be in place when the public proposal was made, let alone arrangements that are unconditional.[122]

Mariner may be compared with *Re Realestate.com.au Ltd* ('*Realestate*')[123] where the Panel made a declaration of unacceptable circumstances where a bidder had recklessly announced an unsustainable bid. The bid was subject to certain conditions, one of which was the completion of due diligence investigations of the target to the absolute satisfaction of the directors of the bidder. The bidder and its associated companies conducted due diligence and discovered a number of things that they considered to be adverse to their bid. Several weeks after the first announcement, the bidder issued another announcement that its bid terms would be altered by, inter alia, dropping a 10 cent cash component of the bid consideration.

The Panel made a declaration of unacceptable circumstances in relation to the original announcement. It favoured an objective test for s 631(2)(a): that a person is reckless as to a fact if they do not responsibly assess the likelihood that the fact exists.[124] The Panel found that the initial announcement was irresponsible and created a false market in the target company's shares. The announcement should not have been made until more extensive due diligence had been undertaken. Further, the bidder should not have relied upon the due diligence condition rather than analysing publicly available information.[125]

Realestate was not cited in the *Mariner* judgment and there appears to be a tension between the two cases even though they deal with two different subsections of s 631.

Recall that when the Panel makes a declaration of unacceptable circumstances it does not necessarily focus on whether there has been a contravention of the *Corporations Act*. In *SSH Medical Ltd*, the Panel made a link between ss 631 and 602(a), which requires that acquisitions of shares in companies should take place in an efficient, competitive and informed market.[126] The Court played a different role in *Mariner* because ASIC was bringing proceedings relying on, inter alia, a breach of s 631. In court proceedings, a party may rely on s 670E, which makes a person liable to pay compensation for a breach of s 631. A court also has power to order a person to proceed with a bid under s 1325B upon the application by ASIC if a breach of s 631 occurs.

If either the bidder or the target is listed, a public announcement must be made to ASX and ASIC must also be informed. A copy of the announcement must also be given to the target company.

121 Ibid [168]–[169].

122 Ibid [225]. In relation to s 631(2)(b), see Takeovers Panel, *Funding Arrangements* (Guidance Note 14, 26 November 2015); J Mosley and C Li, 'Takeovers Financing—Certain Funding' (2015) 26(3) *Journal of Banking and Finance Law and Practice* 199.

123 *Re Realestate.com.au Ltd* (2001) 37 ACSR 218.

124 Ibid [68].

125 Ibid [72]–[78].

126 *SSH Medical Ltd* [2003] ATP 32 [41].

19.45.15 The offer

Item 1 of s 633 states that the bidder must prepare a bidder's statement and an offer document. The offer document sets out the terms of the formal offer. The bidder's statement provides additional information and is discussed below. The offer may be included in the bidder's statement or issued separately.

Section 620 regulates the form and content of the offer. For example, the offer must be in writing and must specify that the offer will remain open until the end of the offer period. The term 'offer period' is defined in s 9, and discussed below. The offer must stand for a minimum of one month and cannot stand for longer than 12 months (s 624). This can be extended in certain situations, relying on s 650C, which is also discussed below.

Note there is a difference between the 'offer period' and the 'bid period'. The 'offer period' is defined in s 9 as 'the period for which offers by the bidder are open to be accepted by the target's members'; and the 'bid period' is defined in s 9 for an off-market bid as starting when the bidder's statement is given to the target and ending at the end of the offer period. Therefore, the offer period commences when the offer is given to the target shareholders; whereas, the bid period commences when the bidder's statement is given to the target company. The bid period ends one month later if no offers are made under the bid, or at the end of the offer period. Both periods are important to the timing of the bid. For example, the bid period is the timeframe in which the Panel is likely to accept applications because of the bar on court proceedings during this time under s 659B. Further, the end of the offer period is the point where the rights and obligations under ch 6A regarding compulsory acquisition are activated.

There are two things to highlight about the offer.

First, the consideration in the offer for an off-market bid can be cash, shares or other forms of security or a combination of a cash sum and securities (s 621(1)). Where the consideration involves securities issued by the bidder (or a body controlled by the bidder), the bidder is required to provide information in the bidder's statement that is equivalent to that set out in the prospectus provisions (ss 710–13).[127] This is so the target shareholders know the value the bidder is placing on the securities. The bidder may only offer cash under a market bid (s 621(2)).

Second, according to s 621(3), the consideration being offered in all bids must not be less than the highest price paid by the bidder during the four months prior to the dispatch of the offer. This provision ensures the equality of opportunity between sellers during the bid period and the pre-bid period.[128] The Panel held in *Re Email Ltd*[129] that s 621(3) does not require the bid consideration to be of the same kind as the consideration given in the four months before the bid, but it must be at least of equal value.

127 See Chapter 9 at Section 9.40.

128 See Takeovers Panel, *Minimum Bid Price* (Guidance Note 6, 6 May 2011); Australian Securitiesa nd Investments Commission, *Takeover Bids* (Regulatory Guide 9, 27 March 2024) [RG 9.151]ff.

129 *Re Email Ltd* (2000) 18 ACLC 708.

Conditions in an offer

The offer can be subject to conditions in an off-market bid (s 625(2)) but, under s 626, the bidder is restricted in the conditions it can put on the offer.

The case of *Re Goodman Fielder Ltd 01*[130] ('*Goodman Fielder*') is an example of a conditional bid. In late 2002, a New Zealand-based company called Burns Philp announced a takeover bid for an Australian food company, Goodman Fielder. The bid contained a number of conditions that may be grouped under the following five headings. Such conditions are commonly seen in takeover offers:

- regulatory conditions: all necessary regulatory approvals must be obtained on an unconditional basis (this would include any ACCC issues, foreign takeover approvals etc)
- accounting conditions: the offer required the board of the target to confirm a number of matters, including guaranteeing the accuracy of the company's accounts
- finance conditions: that each of the preconditions to the bidder's financing facilities would remain satisfied, and no events or potential events of default to the facilities would occur
- material adverse change conditions: there were no material adverse changes to the business, finance or trading position of the company
- minimum acceptance conditions: there was a minimum acceptance condition of 90 per cent.

In *Goodman Fielder*, the target company challenged these conditions as shifting the risk from the bidder to the target shareholders and amounting to unacceptable circumstances. Upon undertakings given by the bidder, the Panel declined to make the declaration sought.

Another common condition is a prescribed occurrence condition, which states that the bid will lapse if the target takes certain actions such as reducing its share capital, issuing convertible notes, disposing of the whole or a substantial part of its business or property, entering into a buy-back agreement; or other actions related to insolvency procedures, such as entering into a deed of company arrangement. The target company may engage in such a transaction as part of a defensive strategy. If the defensive strategy includes one of the transactions prescribed by the bidder this may trigger the operation of the condition—called a 'defeating condition'—that will cause the bid to lapse, as discussed below. Such an action by the target may constitute a 'frustrating action'. Defensive strategies and frustrating actions are discussed below.

Minimum and maximum acceptance conditions

The offer cannot impose maximum acceptance conditions. The bidder cannot make an offer that states that the bid will terminate, or that the consideration will reduce, once a certain voting power has been reached or a percentage of the voting power or a certain number of shares have been acquired (s 626(1)). However, it is permissible to have a

130 *Re Goodman Fielder Ltd 01* (2003) 44 ACSR 254.

minimum acceptance condition—the offer can state that the bidder must receive acceptances for at least X per cent of the shares or the offer will lapse. Minimum acceptance conditions are common in takeover bids.

These provisions, which prohibit maximum acceptance conditions but permit minimum conditions, reflect the policy underlying ch 6. As a general proposition, any offer that is conditional on the occurrence of some event will create a degree of uncertainty for the target shareholders and for the bidder. The question is who should bear the burden of that uncertainty. The aim of the legislation is (in part) to ensure that all target shareholders have an equal opportunity to participate in the benefits accruing to shareholders under the offer. As discussed above, this is expressed in s 602. Section 626 embodies this by requiring the bidder to bear the risk that the offer they make is more generous than is necessary to obtain the desired level of control (therefore no maximum conditions); but the section does not require an offeror who does not receive sufficient acceptances to obtain control to pursue the offer (otherwise the offeror pays the control premium without obtaining control). Therefore, one of the underlying assumptions in the present system is that the offeror should bear the risk.

Defeating conditions

The conditions set out above may take the form of 'defeating conditions'. This term is defined in s 9 as follows. For a takeover bid, the term means a condition that:

(1) will, in circumstances referred to in the condition, result in the rescission of, or entitle the bidder to rescind, a takeover contract; or
(2) prevents a binding takeover contract from resulting from an acceptance of the offer unless or until the condition is fulfilled.

Defeating conditions that are dependent upon the bidder's opinion, belief or other state of mind, or events within its sole control are void (s 629).[131] However, the Panel commented in *Goodman Fielder* that many takeover bids are subject to elements under the sole control of the bidder notwithstanding s 629. For example, the regulatory conditions often require the bidder to lodge and pursue an application for that approval. Accordingly, the assessment of whether s 629 has been breached must be 'pragmatic'.[132] However, when scrutinising defeating conditions, the Panel has emphasised the importance of drafting these conditions 'in a way that is objectively clear, rather than in a broad or generic way that is open to subjective interpretation and reliance by bidders'.[133] For example, the Panel considered material adverse conditions in *NGM Resources Ltd*[134] stating that 'there is a policy of certainty inherent in the requirements of ch 6 for takeover bids, as evidenced, for example, in ss 629 and 631'.[135] Therefore,

131 *DoloMatrix International Ltd* [2008] ATP 10 [18].
132 *Re Goodman Fielder Ltd 01* (2003) 44 ACSR 254, 255 (xiv).
133 A Colla, 'Takeovers and public securities: Some salutary lessons from the panel on keeping a safe distance between friends and on material adverse change conditions' (2011) 29(1) *Company and Securities Law Journal* 46, 46.
134 *NGM Resources Ltd* [2010] ATP 11.
135 Ibid [21].

'if a defeating condition is so likely to be triggered as to make the bid illusory'[136] it may be unacceptable.

An offer can subsequently be declared to be free of a defeating condition—that is, declared to be unconditional—but only under strictly defined circumstances regarding notice and timing set out in s 630. It is common for bidders to declare bids to be free of defeating conditions once the requisite level of control of the target has been reached.

Section 623 prohibits an offeror giving an offeree a benefit that is beyond what is specified in the takeover offer, known as a 'collateral benefit'. This reinforces the equality of opportunity principle in s 602 and can also deter greenmail.[137] The provision does not apply in an off-market bid where the target shareholder sells bid class securities on market (s 623(2)).[138]

19.45.20 The bidder's statement

Item 1 of s 633 states that the bidder must prepare a bidder's statement. This is a formal statement that must comply with s 636. The bidder's statement is the first major document in a takeover bid. If the bidder's statement does not set out all the terms of the offer, then the statement must be accompanied by an offer document that sets out the other terms.

Broadly speaking, Levy states that the 'basic standard of materiality in a bidder's statement is whether the information in question might reasonably affect, or tend to affect, the decision of the ordinary shareholder whether to accept the bidder's offer'.[139] This standard has been articulated in the case law, particularly *Pancontinental Mining Ltd v Goldfields Ltd* ('*Pancontinental*'),[140] as discussed below. The basic standard is supplemented by prescriptive disclosure requirements set out in s 636 of the *Corporations Act*. Section 636 prescribes the contents of the bidder's statement, including the following:

- the identity of the bidder (s 636(1)(a))
- details of the bidder's intentions regarding the continuation of the business of the target and any major changes to be made to the business of the target including any redeployment of fixed assets of the target and the future employment of the present employees of the target (s 636(1)(c))
- how the shares are to be paid for (s 636(1)(f)(i))
- the bidder's sources of finance to fund the offer (s 636(1)(f)(ii))
- if the bidder or an associate acquired shares in the bid class during the four months before the date of the bid, details of the consideration given (ss 636(1)(h)–636(1)(i)). Where the consideration given during the last four months was not cash, an expert's report must accompany the bidder's statement which states that the value was fair

136 Ibid [30].

137 For an application of s 623, see *Brisbane Markets Ltd* [2016] ATP 3. See also Chapter 8 at Section 8.50.05 for a definition of greenmail.

138 See Takeovers Panel, *Collateral Benefits* (Guidance Note 21, 14 April 2008).

139 R Levy, *Takeovers Law & Strategy* (Lawbook, 6th ed, 2023) 209–10, citing *Cultus Petroleum NL v OMV Australia Pty Ltd* (1999) 32 ACSR 1 [13]; *AAPT Ltd v Cable & Wireless Optus Ltd* (1999) 32 ACSR 63 [130].

140 *Pancontinental Mining Ltd v Goldfields Ltd* (1995) 16 ACSR 463.

and reasonable (s 636(2)). Independent experts' reports are discussed below at Section 19.45.30
- the bidder's current voting power in the target (s 636(1)(l)).

Section 636(1)(m) is a catch-all provision that requires the inclusion of any other information that is material to the decision by a holder of the securities whether to accept an offer under the bid. Levy states that this is the 'most important disclosure requirement for a bidder's statement' which 'requires very careful consideration'.[141]

The courts have taken the view that a bidder's statement is 'to be looked at as a document for lay shareholders [and that such] commercial documents must be considered sensibly and in a commercial sense'.[142] This means that even information in the public domain may have to be included in a bidder's statement because non-professional investors will not necessarily be aware of it. In *Solomon Pacific NL v Acacia Resources Ltd*,[143] McLelland CJ stated in obiter that ch 6 assumes that a bidder's statement will be a stand-alone document, accompanied only by the offer itself and the target company's statement. Otherwise, the *Corporations Act* safeguards relating to the contents of this document could be subverted by other documents not covered by the statute. In other words, there is no incorporation by reference as there is for prospectuses. Prospectuses are discussed in Chapter 9. However, note that the requirement in s 636(1)(m) to include other material information is subject to the rider that such information need not be included if it would be unreasonable to do so because it has been previously disclosed to holders of the securities. ASIC has published some guidance regarding the interaction between the bidder's statement and other publicly available information in Regulatory Guide 9 as follows:

> A bidder should also be mindful of how the information contained in the bidder's statement interacts with other public disclosures the bidder has made. For example, information previously disclosed to the market may need to be updated in the bidder's statement to ensure that target holders are sufficiently informed and are not misled. Any inconsistencies between the disclosures made in continuous disclosure notices and the bidder's statement must be clarified and explained.[144]

A good example of the issues that can be raised by a bidder's statement may be found in *Pancontinental*.[145] This case assists with the general requirements regarding the content of bidder's statements that are stipulated by s 636, in particular s 636(l)(m).

This case was an early event in a long-running takeover battle between Renison Goldfields Consolidated Ltd ('Renison') and Pancontinental Mining Ltd ('Pancon'). Renison was a mining and mineral exploration company, conducting business in

141 R Levy, *Takeovers Law & Strategy* (Lawbook, 6th ed, 2023) 231.

142 *Austen & Bulla Ltd v Shell Australia Ltd* (1992) 10 ACLC 735, 738 (Young J).

143 *Solomon Pacific NL v Acacia Resources Ltd* (1996) 19 ACSR 238.

144 Australian Securities and Investments Commission, *Takeover Bids* (Regulatory Guide 9, 27 March 2024) [RG 9.346].

145 *Pancontinental Mining Ltd v Goldfields Ltd* (1995) 16 ACSR 463.

Australia, Papua New Guinea (PNG) and elsewhere. Pancon was a mining company with particular interests in gold mining.

Renison created a new subsidiary company, Goldfields Ltd ('Goldfields'), to act as the takeover vehicle. If the takeover was successful, then the plan was for Renison's and Pancon's gold mining assets to be combined in the Goldfields company.

On 1 March 1995, Goldfields served a bidder's statement on Pancon containing an offer for all of Pancon's issued shares. The offer was a combination of cash and shares. The offer was $2.10 cash and one Goldfields share for every three shares in Pancon. According to the bidder's statement, the Goldfield shares were worth $3.30 each. Because Goldfield shares were not yet listed on ASX, this valuation became the subject of debate. The takeover bid valued Pancon shares at $1.80 each. The offer was subject to there being a minimum acceptance of 90 per cent of Pancon's shares.

It was planned that Goldfields would finance the cash part of the offer by borrowing money from Renison. If the takeover was successful, Goldfields would cause Pancon to sell its non-gold mining assets and use the proceeds to repay Renison.

On Friday 10 March 1995, Pancon applied to the Federal Court for an order that the bidder's statement did not comply with what is now s 636. Pancon raised many objections to the contents of the bidder's statement. Most of these were not accepted by the Court. Pancon was, however, successful on some points, two of which are noted below.

Pancon argued that the bidder's statement did not provide sufficient information about the risks associated with mining operations in PNG. Because Pancon had no current operations in that country, its shareholders would not necessarily be aware of those risks. The risks included those associated with underground mining (Pancon used open-cut mining), the PNG economy, and possible civil unrest in PNG. Tamberlin J agreed, stating:

> The [bidder's] statement does not satisfactorily raise the potential problems of the Papua New Guinea mining operations, even when read as a whole. ... In my opinion what is called for is a comprehensive statement raising and dealing with the political and other risks of mining and operating in Papua New Guinea making particular specific reference to the problems experienced by Renison/ Goldfields. There should be some discussion of the significance attributed by Goldfields to those risks.[146]

As noted earlier, the bidder's statement set the value of Goldfields shares at $3.30 each. This valuation was a crucial part of the offer price. Pancon argued that this figure was misleading, and that the bidder's statement did not sufficiently indicate how this figure was calculated. Tamberlin J agreed, but only in part. He held that the $3.30 figure was not misleading. But he added:

> I do think that there is a significant omission in the Statement as to how the figure is arrived at. Since the figure is of central importance to the takeover scheme, I consider that the offeree shareholders in Pancontinental would regard as material the data and methodology by which this figure was arrived at.[147]

146 Ibid 481, 482.
147 Ibid 483.

On these, plus two other points, Tamberlin J held that the bidder's statement contravened the Act. However, he held that these matters could be dealt with by providing a Supplementary Information Memorandum with the statement. He declared the statement to be valid.

Tamberlin J had some general comments about the interpretation of bidder's statements. These are paraphrased as follows:

(1) Materiality (referred to in s 636(1)(m)) is a question for the Court on a case-by-case basis.
(2) The underlying policy in preparing and reviewing these documents is stated in s 602; that is, promoting an efficient, competitive and informed market and equality of opportunity.
(3) The legislation assumes that any criticism of the commercial desirability of the offer will be dealt with in the formal reply made by the target company—this is not a role for the courts.
(4) The bidder's statement ought not include matters of speculation.
(5) 'The object is to put shareholders in possession of the information required to enable them to make an informed and critical assessment of the offer and an informed decision whether to accept it. Information is material which *could* affect the shareholders' assessment of whether the offeror is likely to improve its offer, the prospects of a competing offer, and the prospects of the shares if retained.'[148]
(6) The Court should be concerned only with breaches of the legislation which are 'real and of substance'.[149]
(7) The objective is to present a document which can be understood by members of the public and which does not confuse.[150]
(8) The bidder's statement must be read fairly as a whole and not in discrete parts or selectively.[151]

In the discussion below, we highlight certain aspects of s 636 which demonstrate the potential for complexity and disputation during a takeover. The Panel often deals with non-disclosure of material information or misleading statements by requiring supplementary statements.[152] Supplementary disclosure is discussed at Section 19.65.

Bidder's intentions

Section 636(1)(c) requires the bidder's statement to set out the particulars of the bidder's intentions regarding the continuation of the business of the target company and the

148 Ibid 467 (emphasis in original).
149 Ibid 467.
150 Ibid 467–8.
151 Ibid 468.
152 R Levy, *Takeovers Law and Strategy* (Lawbook, 6th ed, 2023) 209. See, eg, *Benjamin Hornigold Ltd 02 v Henry Morgan Ltd 02* [2019] ATP 1 where the Panel ordered that a replacement bidder's and a supplementary target's statement be issued. The replacement bidder's statement was required to ensure compliance with s 636 following a declaration of unacceptable circumstances.

future employment of company employees. What is meant by 'intention' for these purposes? Peter Little considered that the provision 'imposes no duty on a bidder to formulate an intention with respect to the matters in question, however it assumes that a bidder will have one or more of the intentions or proposals under active consideration'.[153] Little concluded that 'the focus of [this requirement] appears to be more concerned with what the [bidder] is proposing either to do or to attempt to do', and is not restricted to things which the bidder has a reasonable prospect of being able to do.[154]

Disclosure of these matters enables a comparison to be made between existing and potential value of the company under its existing management and that which might emerge through the implementation of the bidder's intention if the bid succeeds. However, Little argued that a bidder may be reluctant to reveal fully what it considers to be all of the wealth-creating opportunities arising from the takeover that are not immediately obvious to the market, as to do so might drive up the price or encourage shareholders not to part with their shares. It might also give an indication of the bidder's view of the full value of the target which may assist the target company directors when compiling their target's statement.[155] The target's statement is discussed below.

The focus of s 636(1)(c) is on formed intentions and it does not require the bidder to actively come to a conclusion. However, sometimes failure to do so may amount to unacceptable circumstances under s 657A. For example, in *Re Mildura Fruit Co-operative Co Ltd*,[156] the target was a former co-operative and the Panel held that the bidder needed to formulate and then disclose its intention regarding payments to suppliers who were also shareholders. The intention must be also be expressed clearly. In *ICAL Ltd v County Natwest Securities Australia Ltd*,[157] the Court held that a statement that the bidder intended to 'rationalise' the operations of the target company and carry out a 'strategic review' was too vague to satisfy this requirement. Similarly, in *Associated Diaries Ltd v Central Western Dairy Ltd*,[158] a statement about the 'integration of the target's operations' was found by Ryan J of the Federal Court not to comply with s 636(1)(c) because the bidder's statement failed to give sufficient particulars about how the integration would affect the deployment of assets and future employment of employees.[159]

The requirement that the bidder's statement must state its intention regarding the future employment of company employees recognises that 'shareholders would not necessarily act solely on economically rational grounds'.[160] Further, as Burchett J declared in *Gantry Acquisition Corporation v Parker & Parsley Petroleum Australia Ltd*, 'a shareholder might have a conscience about the future of faithful employees of the company'.[161]

153 P Little, *The Law of Company Takeovers* (LBC Information Services, 1997) 265.

154 Ibid 266.

155 Ibid 265.

156 *Re Mildura Fruit Co-operative Co Ltd* [2004] ATP 5. For an interesting discussion of this case, see A Ledder, 'Damned if You Do and Damned if You Don't' (2005) 23(1) *Company and Securities Law Journal* 55.

157 *ICAL Ltd v County Natwest Securities Australia Ltd* (1988) 39 NSWLR 214.

158 *Associated Dairies Ltd v Central Western Dairy Ltd* (1993) 44 FCR 335.

159 Ibid 344–6.

160 *ICAL Ltd v County Natwest Securities Australia Ltd* (1988) 39 NSWLR 214, 235 (Bryson J).

161 *Gantry Acquisition Corporation v Parker & Parsley Petroleum Australia Ltd* (1994) 51 FCR 554, 566.

Financing the bid

If the bid is to be paid by cash and the bidder is not providing the full amount of cash, then the bidder's statement must give details of any other person who is to provide the cash and details of the arrangements by which that cash will be provided (s 636(1)(f)). This would include any conditions imposed by a financier which can affect the outcome of the bid. Therefore, if a bank agrees to provide finance only if the minimum acceptance condition in the offer is satisfied, then this must be stated in the bidder's statement.

ASIC stated that the 'object of the requirement to disclose bid financing arrangements is to ensure that target security holders have sufficient information to enable them to assess the bidder's ability to pay for the securities it is offering to buy'.[162] Further, as stated by the Panel:

> A bidder is not required to disclose *all* of the terms of the arrangements under which it proposes to fund its bid. A bidder is only required to disclose the essential provisions of the arrangements in sufficient detail for an offeree to obtain a reasonable understanding of whether or not the funds are likely to be available to pay for acceptances under the bid and any terms likely to affect the interests of shareholders who retain their shares after successful completion of the bid.[163]

'The bidder's disclosures must include ... details of the relevant terms of its external funding arrangements that have the potential to restrict the availability of funds.'[164] Even if the terms of the finance are in the 'normal course of business' they may still be material under this provision.[165]

Bidder's voting power

Section 636(1)(l) requires the bidder to give full particulars of the bidder's voting power in the target company. The concept of voting power includes entitlements held by associates. A failure to include accurate information about the bidder's correct voting power can result in the award of injunctive relief to restrain the dispatch of the takeover bid.[166]

LODGING AND SERVING THE BIDDER'S STATEMENT

Lodge a copy of the bidder's statement with ASIC

The next step requires the bidder's statement and accompanying offer document (if there is separate offer document) to be lodged with ASIC (s 633 item 2). Under the previous law, the Commission had an obligation to vet the statement—this has been removed. It is now merely a lodgement process.

162 Australian Securities and Investments Commission, *Takeover Bids* (Regulatory Guide 9, 24 March 2024) [RG 9.366]. See also J Mosley and C Li, 'Takeovers Financing—Certain Funding' (2015) 26(3) *Journal of Banking and Finance Law and Practice* 199.

163 *Re Taipan Resources NL* [2001] ATP 5 [34(b)] (emphasis added). See also Takeovers Panel, *Funding arrangements* (Guidance Note 14, 26 November 2015).

164 Australian Securities and Investments Commission, *Takeover Bids* (Regulatory Guide 9, 24 March 2024) [RG 9.391].

165 *ICAL Ltd v County Natwest Securities Australia Ltd* (1988) 39 NSWLR 214, 236–7.

166 *Perseverance Corporation Ltd v Butte Mining plc* (1990) 3 ACSR 433.

Bidder's statement to target

The bidder must then send a copy of the bidder's statement and offer document to the target company (s 633 item 3). Note that the bidder's statement is first sent to the target company and is later sent to the target shareholders. This can be done on the day that the documents are lodged with ASIC, or within 21 days thereafter. The day the documents are lodged with ASIC is the date when the bid period begins, but the offer period has not started because the bidder's statement has not been sent to target shareholders.

The board of the target company may issue a 'take no action' statement to the target shareholders while they are considering the offer in detail. Such a statement is not binding upon the target's shareholders, but it will remind them that the offer must remain open for at least one month under s 624. This is to allow time for the target company to respond and for the target company's directors to make a recommendation regarding the offer.

BIDDER'S STATEMENT TO OPERATOR OF FINANCIAL MARKETS

On the same day that the bidder's statement is sent to the target company, the bidder must lodge a notice with ASIC stating that the bidder's statement and the offer document have been sent to the target. Also, on this day, the bidder must send a copy of the bidder's statement and offer document to each financial market on which the target company's securities are quoted, such as ASX (s 633 items 4 and 5).

Now that ASIC, ASX, and the target company have each been formally notified of the bid, the bidder must wait 14 days before sending copies of these documents to each of the target shareholders in the class to which the offer relates, although the directors of the target may agree that the offers and accompanying documents be sent earlier (s 633 item 6).

Bidder's statement to target shareholders

The bidder now has a period of 14 days in which it must send the bidder's statement to each of the target company shareholders (s 633 item 6). The dispatch must take no more than three days (s 633 item 6). The offer period under s 624 begins to run from the date that the first offer is made; that is, from the date that the first target shareholder receives the offer under s 633 item 6. A takeover bid is usually presented to target shareholders in the form of a document prepared by the bidder (generally in electronic form) comprising the formal terms of the offer, the bidder's statement, and a form of acceptance.

Notice that bidder's statement has been sent to the target shareholders

The bidder must then give notice to the target, the financial market (for example, ASX) and ASIC that the bidder's statement has been sent to the target's shareholders (s 633 items 7, 8 and 9 respectively).

19.45.25 The target's statement

Once the target company has received the bidder's statement and the offer document, its directors must respond by preparing a target's statement (s 633 item 10). This is the target company's formal response to the takeover bid. It is not unusual for the target to employ a number of defensive ploys before its formal response is given; for example, to challenge the bidder's statement before the Panel or to issue an upgraded profit forecast. The defensive tactics and strategies that may be employed by target directors are examined below.

The contents of the target's statement are prescribed by s 638, using language similar to that in s 710 regarding contents of a prospectus; that is, all information that shareholders and their professional advisers would reasonably require to make an informed assessment whether to accept the offer under the bid. Section 710 and prospectuses are discussed in Chapter 9.

Section 638(2) states the factors to be considered when deciding what information to include in the target statement:

(a) the nature of the bid class securities; and

...

(c) the matters that the holders of bid class securities may reasonably be expected to know; and

(d) the fact that certain matters may reasonably be expected to be known to their professional advisers; and

(e) the time available to the target to prepare the statement.

Each director of the target must include a statement that either provides a recommendation about whether the shareholders should accept or reject the offer and giving reasons for that recommendation (s 638(3)), or states that a recommendation is not made. If a recommendation is not made, then reasons why a recommendation is not made must be given (s 638(3)).

The target statement must be approved by a directors' resolution (s 639(1)). This requirement for a resolution ensures that the target's statement reflects the opinion of the board of the target company. However, within the target's statement, individual directors may make different recommendations regarding the bid. Directors' recommendations are discussed in more detail below. A target statement may only include a statement by a person if the person has given consent to the statement and that consent is stated in the target's statement (s 638(5)).[167] The target must keep the consent (s 638(6)).

The courts' approach to the target statements regarding the materiality of information is the same as for bidder's statements: see the discussion of the *Pancontinental* case above at Section 19.45.20. In particular, the target's statement is to be read as a stand-alone document.

Directors' recommendation

The directors' recommendation regarding the bid is set out in the target statement. In practice, the directors' recommendation is highly influential, particularly where the target's shareholding is widely dispersed. In this situation, shareholders may assume that the directors know more about the company than they do; therefore, the recommendation should be accepted. One Australian study found that a recommendation to reject the bidder's offer has a statistically significant negative effect on the outcome of the bid.[168]

167 *Re Mildura Fruit Co-operative Co Ltd* [2004] ATP 5, [44]–[47].

168 L Chapple and S Treepongkaruna, 'The Impact of Target Board Recommendations in Australian Takeovers' (12 January 2006) <https://papers.ssrn.com/sol3/papers.cfm?abstract_id=1031274>.

Clearly, s 638 gives target directors considerable power to influence the outcome of the bid by their recommendation. The quid pro quo is that the target directors are bound by their duties to the target company. All the duties discussed in Chapters 11 to 13 are potentially relevant, but the duty under the general law and s 181 to act in good faith in the best interests of the company and for a proper purpose is particularly salient in this setting. The operation of the law regarding the duties of directors of the target company in the context of a takeover is discussed below.

The Panel has encouraged directors to make recommendations, adding that the basis for a recommendation must be disclosed, must not be misleading, and must give shareholders sufficient information to make an informed assessment about whether to accept the offer.[169] A particular concern is where the directors state the offer 'undervalues' the company. In these circumstances, the Panel has held that s 638 requires that 'some guidance as to value be given'.[170] In this context, the target directors will often make use of independent expert reports.

19.45.30 The role of the independent expert

The purpose of an independent expert's report is to give shareholders an impartial basis on which to reach an informed decision. Expert's reports are commonly used in many documents that are generated during takeovers—the bidder's statement, the target's statement, and any report that requires a valuation; for example, of securities offered as consideration under a bid or where shares are being valued under a compulsory acquisition under pt 6A (see pt 6A.4).

Section 640 requires that the target statement be accompanied by an independent expert's report in certain defined instances; for example, where the bidder's voting power in the company is least 30 per cent (and may control the board), or where the bidder is a director of the target company, or a director of the bidder is a director of the target. The section sets out the material that must be included in the report: the expert must state whether in their opinion the takeover offer is fair and reasonable, and give reasons for that opinion. In some instances, an independent expert's report will also be required in the bidder's statement (s 636(2)). This is where the bidder has given consideration for bid class securities in the four months before the bid and that consideration was not cash or a quoted security (s 636(1)(h)(iii)). The independent expert must report on whether the consideration is fair and reasonable.

How is 'fair and reasonable' assessed? In Regulatory Guide 111, ASIC states that 'the words 'fair and reasonable' in s 640 establish two distinct criteria for an expert analysing a control transaction: (a) is the offer 'fair'; and (b) is it 'reasonable'? Here, 'fair and reasonable' is not regarded as a compound phrase.[171] An offer is 'fair' if the value of the offer

169 *Tully Sugar Ltd 01R* [2010] ATP 1, [16] ('*Tully*'). See also Takeovers Panel, *Recommendations and Undervalue Statements* (Guidance Note 22, 21 September 2010).

170 *Tully Sugar Ltd* [2009] ATP 26, [26]. Section 638, *Tully,* and Guidance Note 22 were considered by the Panel in *Spotless Group Holdings Ltd* [2017] ATP 9 and *Gulf Alumina Ltd* [2016] ATP 4.

171 Australian Securities and Investments Commission, *Content of Expert Reports* (Regulatory Guide 111, 22 October 2020) [RG 111.10].

price or consideration is 'equal to or greater than the value of the securities [that are] the subject of the offer'.[172] Further:

> An offer is 'reasonable' if it is fair. It might also be 'reasonable' if, despite being 'not fair', the expert believes that there are sufficient reasons for security holders to accept the offer in the absence of any higher bid before the close of the offer.[173]

ASIC gives the example where the bidder offers a price that is 'not fair' because the target is in financial distress.

> This is because the fair value of the target securities should be determined on the basis of a knowledgeable and willing, but not anxious, seller that is able to consider alternative options to the bid (e.g. an orderly realisation of the target's assets). Such an offer may nonetheless be 'reasonable' if the alternative methods of remedying the financial distress are likely to be less attractive to security holders than a successful offer.[174]

The assurance of the expert's independence is governed by s 648A. This provision applies to experts' reports in both bidder's and target's statements. The expert must not be an associate of the target or bidder (s 648A(2)). Section 12 applies to determine who is an associate for the purposes of chs 6–6C. The expert's report must indicate the details of any relationship between the expert and the target or bidder (as the case may be) and any financial interest that could affect the expert's ability to give an unbiased opinion, and any fee or payment that the expert will or has received in connection with the report (s 648A(3)).

In the past, there was a tendency for companies to shop around for experts and s 648A(1) now deals with this by stating that, where the bidder or target obtains two or more reports, all reports must accompany the bidder's statement or the target's statement.

The independence of an expert may be compromised by the manner in which a report is prepared. For example, in *Phosphate Co-operative Co of Australia Ltd v Shears (No 3)*,[175] the expert's report was found to be unreliable and the views it provided were not independent because the expert had presented draft copies of its report to the company and because pressure had been exerted by or on behalf of the company. These two factors had affected the contents of the report significantly.[176]

Lodging and serving the target's statement

SENDING THE TARGET'S STATEMENT TO THE BIDDER

The target must send the target's statement (and any accompanying report) to the bidder (s 633 item 11). This can be done at any time from when the target company receives the

172 Ibid [RG 111.11].
173 Ibid [RG 111.12].
174 Ibid [RG 111.15].
175 *Phosphate Co-operative Co of Australia Ltd v Shears (No 3)* [1989] VR 665.
176 See also Australian Securities and Investments Commission, *Independence of Experts* (Regulatory Guide 112, 30 March 2011).

bidder's statement to the day which is 15 days after the target is notified that its shareholders have been sent the bidder's statement.

NOTICE THAT TARGET'S STATEMENT HAS BEEN SENT TO THE BIDDER

On the same day that the target's statement is sent to the bidder, the target company must lodge a copy of its statement with ASIC, and send a copy to each financial market (for example, ASX) on which the target company's shares are quoted (s 633 items 13 and 14).

SENDING THE TARGET'S STATEMENT TO THE TARGET SHAREHOLDERS

Finally, the target company sends a copy of the target's statement to each of the target shareholders (s 633 item 12). This can be done at any time from the day on which it is sent to the bidder and up to 15 days after the target receives notice from the bidder that the bidder's statement has been sent to the shareholders.

Completion of the steps in an off-market bid

At the end of the process, two sets of documents have been produced: a bidder's statement (plus an offer) and a target's statement (possibly with an independent expert's report). Those documents are now in the hands of the bidder, the target company, the target company shareholders, ASIC, and the relevant financial market.

The target company shareholders will now consider the offer, the recommendation (if any) of their directors, and make a decision about whether to accept the offer by selling their shares to the bidder. Each shareholder must individually accept the offer. Under the takeover, a contract is formed by the acceptance of the offer made during the takeover bid. Therefore, the success or failure of a takeover will be the result of the aggregation of the individual decisions of the target shareholders about whether or not to accept the offer contained in the bid.

19.45.35 Variation and withdrawal of offer in off-market bids

During the period of the bid, the bidder can vary or withdraw the offer, subject to restrictions. For example, a variation to an offer may be necessary to persuade the target company's directors to change an unfavourable recommendation, to defeat a rival bidder, or to encourage further acceptances.

Variations are covered primarily by ss 650A–F. The procedures required by ss 650B, 650C and 650D are mandatory and exclusive,[177] and failure to comply with the methods nominated in those provisions will mean, subject to any remedial court order, that the bid lapses and there will be no extant offers.[178]

The permitted variations are those which increase the consideration being offered (or which substitute cash consideration for non-cash), those which extend the period for

177 Section 650A. See also *Allegiance Mining NL* [2008] ATP 3; *Pinnacle VRB Ltd v Reliable Power Inc* (2001) 39 ACSR 8 [9].

178 *Primelife Corporation Ltd v Aevum Ltd* (2005) 53 ACSR 283 [8].

which the offer remains open, or which free a bid from a defeating condition. As a summary, these types of variations all work to benefit target shareholders.

The variation is achieved by lodging a notice of the variation with ASIC and giving a copy to the target company and all offerees under the bid, including those who have already accepted. Where the variation involves a change of consideration in an off-market bid, ss 650B and 651A will apply. Section 650B states that a bidder may vary the offer to improve the consideration and the section provides an exclusive list of ways this can be achieved—again, it must improve the position of the offerees. The section also sets out the rights of persons who have already accepted (s 650B(2)). Section 651A is a deemed variation. If the price paid by the bidder during the bid period is greater than the cash consideration specified in the bid offer—for example, in the market—the offer is automatically varied so the cash consideration becomes that higher amount and shareholders who have already accepted are entitled to the increase.

19.45.40 Extensions of offer period in off-market bids

In accordance with s 650C, a bidder making an off-market bid may extend the offer period at any time before the end of the offer period. Note, however, that the *Corporations Act* allows for an automatic extension of the offer period for another 14 days if, during the last seven days of the offer period, either there is a change in consideration being offered (which, as discussed above, must be a change that improves the consideration), or the bidder's voting power in the target company increases to more than 50 per cent (s 624(2)). Events of this type indicate that the takeover bid is likely to succeed; therefore, the policy is that extra time is warranted.

As regards withdrawals of unaccepted offers, the bidder cannot withdraw the offer unless ASIC gives approval (s 652B). ASIC may consent to a withdrawal if it is clear to ASIC and to market participants that proceeding with a bid is futile; for example, because a defeating condition has been triggered.

19.50 Market bids

Market bids are the other main exception to s 606. The principal difference between an off-market bid and a market bid is that market bids are only available for securities that are quoted on a financial market (s 617(3)). An off-market bid can cover both quoted and other securities. Therefore, a market bid is only possible where the target company is listed on the ASX or another relevant financial market; that is, it is a listed public company. Financial markets are discussed generally in Chapter 17. Of course, a listed public company can be the target of an off-market bid, but only listed public companies can be the target of a market bid.

The steps of a market bid are set out in the diagram in s 634 and the table in s 635. To summarise:

(1) The first step is the preparation of a bidder's statement (the same considerations about form and content apply as in s 636, which is discussed above in relation to off-market bids).

(2) The bid is then announced to the financial market by a broker acting for the bidder. This is different to the requirement for an off-market bid which requires the offer to be put by the bidder. For a market bid, on the same day, the bidder's statement is given to the relevant financial market (such as ASX), the target company, and ASIC.
(3) There is then a 14-day 'cooling off' period. No acceptances can be given during this period. During that time, the bidder sends the bidder's statement to each of the target shareholders and the target company prepares and sends the target's statement to the financial market, the bidder, ASIC, and each target shareholder.
(4) At the end of the 14 days, the bidder must then make offers for the securities. Acceptances may start.

One key difference between a market bid and an off-market bid is the offer. There are more limitations on the terms of the offer for a market bid as discussed below. The rules that apply to financial markets also play a major role in the bid. These rules are discussed in Chapter 17.

19.50.05 The offer in a market bid

Only quoted shares can be the subject of a market bid. Also, the offer must be for all shares in the specified class of shares (s 618(3)). There can be no partial bids in a market offer. Furthermore, a market bid must be unconditional (s 625(1)).

The offer must be for a cash consideration only (s 621(2)). As with an offer under an off-market bid, the cash price being offered will be constrained by any purchases or purchase agreements regarding the target shares which the offeror has made in the four months prior to the announcement. In that event, the cash price being offered must be at least the highest price paid by the offeror during that period (s 621(3)).

Under s 617(3), the market bid must cover securities in the bid class that exist at any time in the offer period. This may be contrasted with an off-market bid where ss 617(1) and (2) allow the bidder to decide whether the bid will extend to securities that come into existence during the offer period. This is discussed above at Section 19.45.

19.50.10 Variation and withdrawal of the offer in a market bid

A market bid is vulnerable to the possibility that the market price of the shares will vary from the consideration that is being offered in the announcement. Indeed, the target company may well take steps to achieve that result in order to defeat the takeover, although the directors would have to be careful of the prohibitions against market manipulation. Sections 649A–C provide limited scope for the offer to be varied, either by raising the bid price or by extending the period of the bid. If the variation relates to an increase in the bid price, this cannot be done during the last five trading days of the bid.

Section 652C provides for the withdrawal of offers in a market bid in certain defined events; for example, where the target company reduces its share capital, or is wound up, or issues shares, options or convertible notes therefore diluting the bidder's stake. Under the provision, the bidder may only withdraw unaccepted offers.

19.55 Takeover defences

19.55.05 Introduction

This section will discuss defensive strategies and tactics that may be taken by the target. First, we ask a fundamental question: why do target managers (including directors) resist takeover bids? Maheswaran and Pinder have proposed two hypotheses:

- Shareholder interest: management will resist a bid if they believe that the bidder's offer is below the target's true market value. On this hypothesis, bid resistance is a bargaining tool that is used by management to increase the wealth of target shareholders by improving the terms of the takeover.
- Managerial entrenchment: management will resist bids that threaten their power, reputation or company-specific human capital. This approach is a defensive ploy used by self-interested management, which results in a decrease in the wealth of target shareholders.[179]

Of course, the Maheswaran and Pinder hypotheses create a binary that is disrupted in real-life transactions. Their study found that bid resistance increases target shareholder wealth in the post-announcement period, but bid hostility decreases the probability of bid success, increases the probability of bid revision, and has no effect on the probability of competing bidders entering the market.[180] These findings support both hypotheses. Regarding the second hypothesis, the Australian evidence reveals that the vast majority of directors and CEOs are removed after a successful acquisition.[181] This fact creates understandable incentives for target directors to resist the bid.

Nevertheless, takeover defences—and particularly the concern about the pursuit of shareholder interest versus management entrenchment—raise one of the central debates in corporate law: the separation of management from ownership of shares in the company and whether this separation should be regulated in certain situations. The more widely dispersed a company's share register becomes, the more likely it is that individual shareholders will act as passive investors rather than active members. As a corollary, the scope for unreviewed managerial discretion (and the furtherance of management entrenchment motives) increases.

According to one version of economic theory, it is too costly and time-consuming for most stakeholders to stay informed about managerial behaviour. Following this theory, shareholders are 'rationally ignorant'. The risk that managers will act in a self-serving way, rather than in the interests of the company as a whole, can be met, in part, by requiring directors to disclose any potential for, or any occurrence of, self-interested behaviour. This is one of the functions of the target's statement.

179 K Maheswaran and S Pinder, 'Australian Evidence on the Determinants and Impact of Takeover Resistance' (2005) 45(4) *Accounting & Finance* 613, 613.

180 Ibid.

181 M Bugeja, R da Silva Rosa and A Lee, 'The Impact of Director Reputation and Performance on the Turnover and Board Seats of Target Firm Directors' (2009) 36(1-2) *Journal of Business Finance & Accounting* 185.

We have also seen that liberal economic theory regards takeovers as having an efficiency function—they are a mechanism for displacing inefficient or unproductive managers. Shareholders benefit either by selling their shares at a price that is higher than the market price, or by remaining in the company with its new, more efficient, management team. So, any action by the incumbent directors to defeat a takeover is potentially counter-efficient. The three arguments set out below represent three main schools of thought about defensive activity: the passivity argument, the loyalty argument, and the auctioneering argument.

1. The passivity argument

According to one view, target directors should refrain from defensive conduct.[182] On this view, defensive measures cause detriment to the shareholders. This is because either the takeover is defeated, in which case the shareholders lose out on the benefits of the premium price in the takeover offer, or, if the defensive activity results in a higher bid being made, the detriment may be that future offers will be discouraged, thereby depressing the value of the shares. Therefore, externally imposed legal rules should limit the ability of managers to fight a takeover bid, even if their intention is to trigger a rival bid.[183]

A further argument is that most defensive actions consume the target company's resources, and create conflicts of interest for target company directors. Non-accepting shareholders will also benefit from a passive response by the target directors because first, the prospect of future bids is preserved, and second, if the takeover is successful the shareholders are rewarded with a more efficient management team. Therefore, the only valid form of defence against a takeover is efficient management.[184]

In the Australian context, the courts have not accepted the idea of passivity as a blanket policy. This is discussed below.

2. The loyalty argument

An alternative view is that directors, because of the position of trust and loyalty that they hold, have a duty to defend the target company against takeover bids where the directors are acting in good faith and in the best interests of the company. On this view, '[t]akeover bids are not so different from other major business decisions as to warrant a unique sterilization of the directors in favour of direct action by the shareholders'.[185]

Annunciation of this approach may be found in the US case of *Unocal v Mesa Petroleum Co*[186] ('*Unocal*'), which has been described as 'defining the scope of American judicial review in a takeover situation'.[187] The Delaware Supreme Court held that directors should respond to a takeover in the same way as they should respond to any other

182 See, eg, FH Easterbrook and DR Fischel, 'The Proper Role of a Target's Managements in Responding to a Tender Offer' (1981) 94(6) *Harvard Law Review* 1161.

183 Ibid 1178–80.

184 Ibid 1174.

185 M Lipton, 'Takeover Bids in the Target's Boardroom' (1979) 35(1) *Business Lawyer* 101, 104.

186 *Unocal v Mesa Petroleum Co*, 493 A 2d 946 (Del, 1985).

187 R Thompson, 'Takeover Regulation after the "Convergence" of Corporate Law' (2002) 24(3) *Sydney Law Review* 323, 329.

management decision—the normal rules of good faith, lack of self-interest, active decision-making should apply. However, because takeovers directly affect the interests of target shareholders, the Court provided specific guidance for directors when they take defensive measures.[188]

3. The auctioneering argument

A third possible stance is that action by the target company directors that facilitates competing takeover bids should be encouraged.[189] Directors should solicit bids from potential bidders. This approach would justify short-term or limited defensive tactics where the aim is to create or intensify a bidding contest. On this view, target shareholders benefit because an auction will elicit higher prices for their shares and this benefit will accrue regardless of the motivation of the target company directors; namely, self-serving or in the best interests of the shareholders.[190] A middle approach is to say that there should be no defensive tactics once the auction has begun: the directors should encourage an auction, then be passive.

THE AUSTRALIAN POSITION

Australian case law does not consistently adhere to any one of the arguments set out above. Certainly, Australian law accepts that target directors may engage in proactive behaviour when faced with takeover bids, so the passivity argument has not been adopted. In fact, in *Pine Vale Investments Ltd v McDonnell & East Ltd*[191] ('*Pine Vale*'), discussed below at Section 19.55.20, the Court expressly stated that the directors should not be reduced to inertia because of the bid. The auctioneering argument may be demonstrated by cases which accept that directors may legitimately mount a white knight defence. See the discussion of *Pine Vale* and *Howard Smith Ltd v Ampol Petroleum Ltd*[192] ('*Howard Smith*') at Section 19.55.20. However, where a defence is designed to thwart the takeover or to manipulate voting power or is motivated by self-interest—for example, for directors to maintain their positions—directors will potentially breach their duties and their actions may amount to a frustrating action and/or unacceptable circumstances leading to a declaration by the Panel. The *Pine Vale* and *Darvall v North Sydney Brick & Tile Co Ltd*[193] ('*Darvall*') cases recognise that target directors may legitimately pursue commercial interests even in the midst of a takeover bid. The loyalty argument represents the closest standard to that adopted in Australian cases, although there is no positive

188 For further details and an update on *Unocal* see R Thompson, 'The New *Unocal*' (2023) 65(3) *Arizona Law Review* 695.

189 L Bebchuk, 'The Case for Facilitating Competing Tender Offers' (1982) 95(5) *Harvard Law Review* 1028.

190 Ibid 1055; see also *Babcock & Brown Communities Group* [2008] ATP 25; *Consolidated Minerals Ltd 03* (2007) 25 ACLC 1739; A Lumsden and S Fridman, 'The Duty to Auction: Real or Imagined?' (2012) 30(8) *Company and Securities Law Journal* 493.

191 *Pine Vale Investments Ltd v McDonnell & East Ltd* (1983) 8 ACLR 199.

192 *Howard Smith Ltd v Ampol Petroleum Ltd* [1974] AC 821 (on appeal to the Privy Council from Street J (in equity)); see T Steel, 'Defensive Tactics in Company Takeovers' (1986) 4(1) *Company and Securities Law Journal* 3.

193 *Darvall v North Sydney Brick & Tile Co Ltd* (1988) 6 ACLC 154 (Hodgson J at first instance); *Darvall v North Sydney Brick & Tile Co Ltd* (1989) 16 NSWLR 260 (New South Wales Court of Appeal).

duty to defend a takeover, as opposed to the broader duty to act in the best interest of the company and for a proper purpose. There is no comparable Australian guidance to that issued by the Delaware Supreme Court in *Unocal.*

The following discussion of the types of defensive activity by the target will be followed by an examination of the relevant cases, legislative provisions, and guidance notes.

19.55.10 Types of defensive activity by the target

Here, we discuss defensive strategies and tactics.

Long-term defensive strategies are intended to prevent unwanted takeover bids before they occur. They attempt to make the company 'takeover-proof'. They may be referred to as 'anticipatory' or 'proactive' defensive moves.

Short-term defensive tactics are actions taken by the target company in the face of an actual or impending takeover bid; for example, after a public announcement has been made. They are intended to defeat or stall the bid. They may be referred to as 'responsive' or 'reactive' defensive moves.

Some of the strategies and tactics discussed below do not apply to listed companies because they are addressed by provisions in the *LRs*. Further, if the acts of the target directors are challenged by an application to the Panel, they may be found to be a frustrating action which may result in a declaration of unacceptable circumstances. The relevant *LRs* and an explanation of 'frustrating action' are provided below.

Defensive strategies usually rely on specific provisions located in the target company's constitution. This has three consequences:

(1) Any potential bidder who begins to acquire shares in the company has advance notice of the defences that are in place.
(2) The bidder, once they begin to acquire shares in the target company, is bound by those constitutional provisions because of s 140 of the *Corporations Act,* which states that the constitution has effect as a contract between the company and each member, between a member and each other member, and between the company and its directors.
(3) If the defensive provisions are inserted into the constitution after the company has been registered (that is, the company does not come into being with these things already written), the shareholders in the target company have a say in the extent to which their company becomes takeover-proof, because they can vote for or against the amendment to the company's constitution.

For example, the constitution of Fortescue Ltd requires shareholders to vote on any proportional takeover bid that the company might receive. Proportional bids are discussed above at Section 19.45. This means that any proportional takeover bid must be voted on at a general meeting of the company rather than being decided by the individual acceptances or rejections of shareholders. The practical effect of such a provision may be to give the company's major shareholder, Andrew Forrest, effective control over the outcome of a partial takeover bid.[194]

194 *Constitution,* Fortescue Ltd (at 23 November 2023) cl 13.12, sch 6.

Short-term tactical moves will usually rely on the exercise by the directors of their general powers of management. The general power of management is in s 198A(1) of the *Corporations Act* which states that 'The business of a company is to be managed by or under the direction of the directors.'

This is a replaceable rule, but it is adopted almost universally by companies.[195] The exercise of this power means that the use of particular defensive tactics may not necessarily be specifically sanctioned by the shareholders, and this has caused disquiet. However, a balance must be achieved between allowing target boards to take commercially reasonable and 'usual' actions during a takeover with the excessive reach that occurs when these powers are exercised to defeat the bid.

Long-term defensive strategies: examples

As stated above, long-term defensive strategies are intended to prevent unwanted takeover bids before they occur. They attempt to make the company 'takeover-proof'. The following examples demonstrate this.

- Convertible securities: the issue of securities that are convertible to ordinary shares in the event of a successful takeover offer, or even on the announcement of a bid. The point of this strategy is to increase the cost of mounting a successful takeover bid because the number of shares needed to obtain control increases. This strategy involves consideration of ss 617(2) and (3) and was implemented in *ICAL Ltd v McCaughan Dyson & Co Ltd (No 2)*.[196]
- Golden parachutes: service agreements with directors or senior managers that provide for generous termination payments in the event of a takeover. Section 1325C recognises these agreements insofar as directors and company secretaries are concerned–it allows for a court order where such an agreement is unfair or unconscionable having regard to the interests of the company. However, LR 10.18 prohibits termination benefits that are dependent on a change in control of a listed entity.
- Share transfer restrictions and pre-emption clauses: these clauses require that share transfers should be first offered to existing members of the company. Such clauses are not available to listed companies[197] but are common in non-listed companies.
- Sliding voting scales: provisions in a company's constitution that are designed to ensure that as a bidder accumulates more voting shares they can exert less influence over the company without the support of small shareholders. Such provisions are not permitted under the *LRs* that require one vote per share.[198]
- Shark repellents: provisions in a company's constitution that are intended to discourage a takeover or make it more difficult; for example, a clause requiring the

195 For further details about this power, see Section 7.10

196 *ICAL Ltd v McCaughan Dyson & Co Ltd (No 2)* (1987) 11 NSWLR 508. See also *Bridge Oil Pty Ltd v Parker & Parsley Petroleum (Australia) Pty Ltd* (1994) 15 ACSR 240.

197 For an explanation, see ASX, *Significant Changes to Activities* (Guidance Note 12, 28 August 2020) 3.4.

198 ASX *Listing Rules* 6.8 and 6.9 prescribe that each ordinary security must have one vote: on a show of hands, each holder has one vote and on a poll each holder has one vote per fully paid security.

approval of a partial bid by 50 per cent of shareholders voting at a general meeting. This is permitted, but regulated, by ss 648D–H, which impose a 'shelf-life' of three years (subject to renewal) on such clauses. The operation of such a clause in the Fortescue Ltd constitution is discussed above.

- Poison pills: an arrangement between a target and a third party under which a third party holds a right which becomes exercisable on a change of control of the target company; for example, a clause in a company's constitution that triggers the right of existing ordinary shareholders to take up further ordinary shares in the event of a takeover. This strategy may not be effective for listed companies because LR 7.9 requires shareholder approval for shares that are issued not on a pro-rata basis within three months of a proposed takeover bid.[199]

The main legal implication for constitution-based defences arises where the provision is inserted into the constitution after the company has been incorporated. In this situation, the general principles of corporate law relating to constitutional amendments, such as the need for special resolution and the protection of class rights and minority rights, will need to considered. These principles are discussed in Chapter 5. In particular, any amendment will have to avoid a claim that it is oppressive, unfairly prejudicial to or unfairly discriminatory against one or more members or contrary to the interests of the members as a whole. These claims are discussed in Chapter 14.

Short-term defensive tactics: examples

To repeat, these are just some examples of a wide range *tactics* that are adopted by the target company's directors in the face of an actual or impending takeover bid.

One obvious tactic is for the target company directors to criticise the bid and/or the bidder by commenting; for example, that the bid undervalues the target company shares or that the bidder is intent on asset-stripping the company. To the extent that this occurs in the target's statement under s 638,[200] then the company will need to be careful of the liability of misleading or deceptive statements in s 670A. This is discussed at Section 19.65.

REVISED PROFIT FORECAST OR DIVIDEND POLICY

Some tactics are intended to make the target company look good to existing shareholders or to rival bidders, inviting shareholders to reject the bidder's offer because the shareholders would be better off staying with the target company. The target might issue an upgraded profit forecast or announce a dividend or a revised dividend strategy. As previously discussed, problems may arise regarding misleading and deceptive statements and compliance with s 670A.

CROWN JEWELS

Another tactic involves a transaction which mobilises the company's key assets, known as the 'crown jewels' defence. This tactic is based on the idea that the company is an

199 See the analysis of LR 7.9 in *Bigshop.com.au Ltd 02* [2001] ATP 24.

200 See the discussion in Takeovers Panel, *Recommendations and Undervalue Statements* (Guidance Note 22, 21 September 2010).

attractive target for the bidder because it has some particular asset or assets that the bidder thinks it can use to greater effect—even if that means simply selling the assets off. Therefore, the target company directors may decide to either sell, purchase, redeploy, or tie up major assets. The idea may be to tie up the assets in a way that discourages the bidder from pursuing the bid or to demonstrate to the target shareholders that there is still future value in the company under its present management. For example, in *Pancontinental Mining Ltd v Goldfields Ltd*[201] (which is discussed above at Section 19.45.20), Pancon announced a $44 million joint venture with the New Zealand Government shortly after receiving the unwanted bid from Goldfields.

WHITE KNIGHT

The white knight defence involves the target company organising a rival, but friendly, bid. In this stance, the target directors recognise that the company will be taken over, but they are seeking a higher price and a takeover offer that is, in the directors' opinion, in the greater interests of the shareholders.

One potential problem in soliciting a rival bid is the risk of breaching the insider trading prohibition in s 1043A. This might occur where the target company board tries to entice the rival bidder by revealing information about the company that is not generally available and not available to the bidder. Insider trading is discussed in Chapter 17. Listing Rule 7.9 creates another impediment to this defence.[202]

LITIGATION

Litigation, often regarding technicalities in the bidder's statement, was previously used extensively as a defensive tactic. However, since the 1999 reforms to the Panel, it is less advantageous. The processes of the Panel provide fewer opportunities for purely tactical litigation.

Darvall v North Sydney Brick & Tile Co Ltd[203] ('*Darvall*') brings together several of these defensive tactics: crown jewels, white knight, and litigation tactics. In that case, Norbrik owned an area of land in the northwest of Sydney. The value of the land was shown in Norbrik's accounts as being between $1.5 and $2 million. In 1985, the directors were informed that the land was worth considerably more than this at approximately $60 million. The directors began to have discussions about the possibility of developing the land with a view to future sale. By June 1986, no decision had been made. In that month, a shareholder in the company, Mr Darvall, made an off-market bid for the company.

The bid was prompted by the fact that the last trading of the company's shares had been at a price that reflected the entire worth of the company as being only $2.5 million. Since that trading, the revaluation of the land had been announced, although not publicly. Hence, the market price of the shares was well below the company's actual worth.

201 *Pancontinental Mining Ltd v Goldfields Ltd* (1995) 16 ACSR 463.
202 Listing Rule 7.9 is discussed above at Section 19.55.10.
203 *Darvall v North Sydney Brick & Tile Co Ltd* (1988) 6 ACLC 154 (Hodgson J at first instance); *Darvall v North Sydney Brick & Tile Co Ltd* (1989) 16 NSWLR 260 (New South Wales Court of Appeal).

Norbrik's directors were of the view that the takeover would not be in the company's best interests, and they sought professional advice from Macquarie Bank on defensive tactics. The company was advised to do two things:

(1) arrange for a competing takeover bid at a higher price (white knight defence)
(2) make a firm agreement for the development of the land (crown jewels defence).

Acting on this advice, two things occurred. First, the managing director of Norbrik, Mr Lanceley, indicated that he would be making a rival takeover bid for the company. Second, the directors resolved to develop the land. This involved selling the land to a wholly owned subsidiary, Norwest, that would enter into a joint venture agreement with Chase Corporation to develop the land.

In the meantime, Norbrik took action against Darvall, challenging the validity of the bidder's statement issued by Darvall. Darvall also brought proceedings to set aside the joint venture agreement on the ground, inter alia, that it was a breach of the duty of the directors of Norbrik to act honestly and best interests of the company and that the directors had acted for an improper purpose.

A majority of the New South Wales Court of Appeal held that that decision to enter into the joint venture agreement and to develop the land (the crown jewels defence) was a decision that lay within the ordinary sphere of management and was consistent with advancing the company's interests.[204] The Court found that if the directors genuinely believed that the decision would advance the company's interests then the Court should not interfere with that decision.[205] The judgment in *Darvall* is discussed further below.

19.55.15 Frustrating action

The Panel, in its Guidance Note 12,[206] defines a frustrating action as 'an action by a target, whether taken or proposed, by reason of which:

- a bid may be withdrawn or lapse
- a potential bid is not proceeded with'.[207]

The following acts by the target might constitute a frustrating action if they breach a bid condition or allow a bid to be withdrawn:

(1) significant issuing or repurchasing of shares (or convertible securities or options)
(2) acquiring or disposing of a major asset, including making a takeover bid
(3) undertaking significant liabilities or changing the terms of its debt
(4) declaring a special or abnormally large dividend
(5) significant change to company share plans
(6) entering into joint ventures.[208]

204 *Darvall v North Sydney Brick & Tile Co Ltd* (1989) 16 NSWLR 260, 330, 340.
205 Ibid 338.
206 Takeovers Panel, *Frustrating Action* (Guidance Note 12, 1 December 2016).
207 Ibid [3].
208 Ibid.

When the Panel is asked to review an alleged frustrating action, it works from the policy premise that it is the shareholders who should decide on actions that may:

- interfere with the reasonable and equal opportunity of the shareholders to participate in a takeover proposal (s 602(c)); or
- inhibit the acquisition of control over their voting shares taking place in an efficient, competitive and informed market (s 602(a)).[209]

An action that triggers a defeating condition may be a frustrating action but whether it also amounts to unacceptable circumstances will depend on its effect on shareholders and the market considering ss 602(a), 602(c) and 657A.[210] The Panel's approach to defensive strategies is discussed further at Section 19.55.25.

19.55.20 Application of directors' duties

As mentioned above, long-term defensive strategies are often constitutionally based and can be sourced to a decision made by the general meeting of shareholders. Short-term tactics involve decisions and actions by the directors of the target company. Short-term tactics raise, to a much greater extent, the question of directors' duties and a fundamental question that lies at the heart of the law on directors' duties: to whom are the duties owed? In this part of the discussion, we focus upon the case law developed by the courts. At Section 19.55.25, we will consider the Panel's approach.

The basic duty of a director is to act in good faith in the 'best interests of the corporation'. What does this phrase mean? This is discussed at length in Chapter 12 at Section 12.10.20 and it is concluded that the interests of members is generally correlated with the interests of the company.[211] However, acting in the best interests of the company has been taken to mean, on the one hand, that the directors must act in the best interests of the members as a collective group,[212] and alternatively that the directors must have regard to the interests of present and future members, as well as the company as a commercial entity, even if this is not in the short-term best interests of the members.[213]

In many situations, the difference will not matter. However, when there is a takeover bid at a high cash price by a bidder who intends to strip the company of its assets, the interests of the shareholders as a whole may conflict with those of the company as a commercial entity. Similarly, if the directors elicit a rival bid and drive up the cost of the takeover it may be in the shareholders' interests but it may be disruptive to the company's business. Therefore, the characterisation of the body to whom the duties are owed is an important element of the reasoning in the case law that is reviewed below.[214]

209 Ibid [4]. For a discussion of the background to the policy, see E Armson, 'The Frustrating Action Policy: Shifting Power in the Takeover Context' (2003) 21(1) *Company and Securities Law Journal* 48.

210 See, eg, *Bigshop.com.au Ltd 02* [2001] ATP 24 [45].

211 *Kinsela v Russell Kinsela Pty Ltd (in liq)* (1986) 4 NSWLR 722, 730; *Ashburton Oil NL v Alpha Minerals NL* (1971) 123 CLR 614, 620; *Ngurli Ltd v McCann* (1953) 90 CLR 425, 438–40.

212 *Greenhalgh v Arderne Cinemas Ltd* [1951] Ch 286.

213 *Darvall v North Sydney Brick & Tile Co Ltd* (1988) 6 ACLC 154.

214 For a contribution to this debate, see J du Plessis, 'Directors' Duty to Act in the Best Interests of the Corporation: "Hard Cases Make Bad Law"' (2019) 34(1) *Australian Journal of Corporate Law* 3.

Bidder company directors' duties

Although the primary analysis of directors' duties will consider the duties of the target's directors, it is first worth noting that the directors of bidder companies also must comply with their directors' duties. Therefore, the directors of the bidder will need to consider whether the takeover bid is in the best interests of the bidder company, and exercise reasonable care and diligence in making their decision to launch the takeover bid. Further, the directors of the bidder must consider the extent to which they can rely on the advice of others such as lawyers, accountants, financiers and media strategists in developing the bid[215] and whether they will be protected by the business judgment rule.[216] If one of the directors has a prior interest in the target company—such as sitting on both boards or having a significant shareholding—they will need to make an appropriate disclosure of the conflict of interest, and ensure that the legislative procedures for abstaining from the decision are followed. These obligations are discussed in Chapters 11 to 13.[217]

Target company directors' duties

The major focus for directors' duties in a takeover situation concerns the duties of the directors of the target. Clearly, the general duty of directors is to act in the best interests of the company as a whole. This may be translated, in specific cases, to the statement that directors must exercise the powers that are conferred on them for a proper purpose.

We can identify three particular powers given to directors that may be relevant to short-term defensive conduct by target company directors:

- the general power of management
- the power to issue shares
- powers over the transfer of shares.

1. THE GENERAL POWER OF MANAGEMENT

As stated above, this is found in the replaceable rule in s 198A. The directors in the *Darvall* case relied on this power, as discussed above. The courts have generally adopted a 'hands off' approach to the interpretation of this power; that is, the courts will not second-guess a business decision made by directors where the directors can demonstrate there is a legitimate business or financial objective that is for the benefit of the company as a whole, and that the decision has been made in good faith and without the presence of disqualifying factors such as undisclosed conflicts of interest. The fact that the decision (as in the *Darvall* case) can also be shown to be a takeover defence is not of itself a disqualifying factor nor is it an improper purpose.

This was made clear in *Pine Vale Investments v McDonnell & East Ltd* ('*Pine Vale*').[218] Pine Vale ('PV') was a substantial shareholder of McDonnell & East Ltd ('M&E'), a Brisbane department store. PV announced a takeover bid for M&E. Soon after, the directors of

215 *Corporations Act* s 189.
216 Ibid s 180(2).
217 Ibid ss 191–5.
218 (1983) 8 ACLR 199.

M&E caused the company to agree to acquire the business of another company (a crown jewels defence). This acquisition was to be funded by a 'rights issue' of shares, which is an offer to existing shareholders to purchase further issued shares, usually on a pro rata basis.[219] The rights issue was offered at a premium price. The rights issue would, of course, dilute PV's stake in the company, and so PV applied for an injunction to prevent M&E from proceeding with the rights issue. PV argued that the purpose of the rights issue was to defeat the takeover bid. McPherson J found that there was no breach of duty by the M&E directors. His Honour considered the case of *Howard Smith Ltd v Ampol Petroleum Ltd*.[220] That case, discussed in depth previously at Section 12.10.35, concerned a white knight defence involving a share issue and the Privy Council held it was not a proper purpose for the directors to issue shares for the purpose of creating a new majority or for destroying an existing majority. But McPherson J held in *Pine Vale* that the directors had not been substantially motivated by the desire to thwart a takeover offer. He stated:

> Once it is established that action is commercially justified in the corporate interest it is difficult to understand why the directors should be reduced to inertia because of the pendency or possibility of a takeover offer.[221]

McPherson J found that no inference could be drawn that the timing of the transaction was 'destructive of a proper purpose' and that there was no 'contrivance' in the timing of the transaction. Here, the directors were at all times aware of the need to acquire new retail outlets for the company.[222] There was also no doubt that the company would benefit from raising funds by share issue rather than by loan.[223]

It is a separate question whether the general power of management can be used directly and openly to defend against a takeover bid. The Court of Appeal concluded in *Darvall* that the decision to involve the company in a joint venture is one that properly lies within the sphere of management[224] and then considered the situation where a dual purpose was operative. Clarke JA stated:

> It may be that in particular circumstances the taking of action designed to defeat a takeover offer may constitute an improper purpose ... But in my opinion the bald proposition that it is improper to take action to defeat a takeover offer is too widely stated to constitute a legal principle. ... in particular circumstances action taken for the dual purpose of advancing the interests of the company and of defeating a takeover offer may be within power.[225]

219 Rights issues are discussed at Section 9.25.35.

220 [1974] AC 821 (on appeal to the Privy Council from Street J (in equity)).

221 (1983) 8 ACLR 199, 209–10.

222 Ibid 210.

223 Ibid 211. Compare these findings to *Nex Metals Explorations Ltd* [2021] ATP 12 where the Panel made a declaration of unacceptable circumstances because the rights issue appeared to have been made by target to frustrate the bid. The Panel's approach to defensive actions is discussed below at Section 19.55.25.

224 *Darvall v North Sydney Brick & Tile Co Ltd* (1989) 16 NSWLR 260, 338.

225 Ibid 335.

Where a dual purpose is found, following the reasoning in *Howard Smith*, 'it is then necessary for the court ... to examine the substantial purpose for which it was exercised, and to reach a conclusion whether that purpose was proper or not'.[226] This is now recognised as the 'substantial purpose' test. In contrast, the Court in *Whitehouse v Carlton Hotel Pty Ltd*[227] preferred a 'but for' test, which can also be seen in the reasoning of Dixon J and the High Court in *Mills v Mills.*[228] As stated at Section 12.10.40, the following test appears to satisfy both requirements. It asks whether the improper purpose was a significant contributing cause to the exercise of the power, and, but for its presence, the power would not have been exercised. If so, then the duty will have been breached.

Applying this test, if the purpose of defeating the takeover was the substantial purpose or but for that purpose the actions would not have been taken, there will probably be a breach of the statutory (s 181) and general law directors' duties. However, the Panel would also focus upon the *effect* of the conduct in deciding whether it amounted to a frustrating action and/ or unacceptable circumstances; for example, if the directors impeded the target shareholders' opportunity to consider a lawful takeover offer. This is discussed below.

2. POWER TO ISSUE SHARES

The exercise of this power can include the issue of fresh shares to a friendly third party, which is a variation of the white knight defence. As stated above, it is accepted law in Australia that directors cannot issue shares with the purpose of manipulating voting power within a company.[229] Furthermore, a member has a personal right to challenge any such allotment in order to protect their personal right not to have their voting power diluted: *Residues Treatment & Trading Co Ltd v Southern Resources Ltd.*[230] This case is discussed in Chapter 14.

3. POWER OVER TRANSFER OF SHARES

As stated above, this power is not relevant to listed companies, because of the *Listing Rules.* As long as the directors can point to a specific power in the company's constitution, and they can show that the power was exercised in good faith and in the company's best interests, their decision will not be impeached by the courts.

19.55.25 Challenging defensive actions before the Panel

We have established that actions by target company directors can raise issues concerning the discharge of their fiduciary and statutory duties. What does this mean in a regulatory context where the Panel, rather than the courts, has the primary role in making decisions about takeover disputes?

226 *Howard Smith Ltd v Ampol Petroleum Ltd* [1974] 1 NSWLR 68, 77.

227 *Whitehouse v Carlton Hotel Ltd* (1987) 162 CLR 285.

228 *Mills v Mills* (1938) 60 CLR 150, 186.

229 *Whitehouse v Carlton Hotel Pty Ltd* (1987) 162 CLR 285; *Howard Smith Ltd v Ampol Petroleum Ltd* [1974] AC 821.

230 *Residues Treatment & Trading Co Ltd v Southern Resources Ltd (No 4)* (1988) 51 SASR 177.

The answer is found in the Panel's Guidance Note 12 *(Frustrating Action)*,[231] which is discussed above. The issue was first aired in the *Pinnacle* cases.[232] The target company directors had announced that their company was proposing to enter into two major transactions. This would trigger one of two defeating conditions in the bid that the target should not enter into any transactions out of the ordinary course of business. Therefore, it was alleged that the target's conduct could have the effect of frustrating the bid.

The bidder made an application to the Panel for a declaration of unacceptable circumstances and orders setting aside the transactions. In the result, the Panel held that the target directors should have submitted their plan of action to the target company shareholders for approval. In other words, the shareholders should have been given the choice of approving their directors' plans and thereby stop the takeover bid, or not approving the plans thereby keeping the bid alive.[233] The Panel stated that this approach was dictated, in part, by s 602(c)—the equality of opportunity principle. The Panel stated:

> while directors of a company may and should conduct the affairs of the company without reference to the shareholders in general meeting, decisions on control of the company should be made by the shareholders. These principles collide if a transaction which is otherwise within the directors' sphere is capable of defeating a bid. Under the policy of s 602, the right of shareholders to decide on control transactions prevails.[234]

Significantly, the Panel stated that its decision-making power was not based on any consideration of whether the directors were complying with, or breaching, their directors' duties, even though the parties had urged the Panel to deal with the matter 'simply by applying the law on directors' duties, or a policy which approximated to that branch of the law'.[235] As discussed above, the Panel is not a judicial body.

The Panel explained that its functions are limited to applying the principles in s 602; the Panel does not have the power to enforce the wider law on directors. The Panel stated:

> Our decision can only be based on the existence, prevention, removal and remediation of unacceptable circumstances which impact on [the] bid. Legal consequences of people's behaviour can obviously be [such] circumstances. But even assuming such consequences can be established fairly and reliably, they are only relevant in so far as they impact on the bid by creating unacceptable circumstances, or bear upon the public interest.[236]

One implication of this, spelled out in the *Pinnacle* decisions, is that the Panel looks to the *effect* of the directors' actions on the target company shareholders, not to the directors'

231 Takeovers Panel, *Frustrating Action* (Guidance Note 12, 18 July 2014).

232 See especially *Pinnacle VRB Ltd (No 5)* (2001) 39 ACSR 43 ('*Pinnacle No 5*'); *Pinnacle VRB Ltd (No 8)* (2001) 39 ACSR 55 ('*Pinnacle No 8*')

233 *Pinnacle No 8* [44].

234 *Pinnacle No 5* [28].

235 *Pinnacle No 8* [53].

236 *Pinnacle No 8* [56].

purpose in undertaking their actions.[237] If, however, the Panel finds that the directors acted to preserve their own positions or that the transactions had no obvious commercial merit, unacceptable circumstances may be found.[238] In other words, if the improper purpose of the target board is relatively obvious, or at least reasonably likely, the Panel is more likely to find that unacceptable circumstances have occurred.[239]

As mentioned above, the Panel has set out its approach to frustrating actions by target directors in Guidance Note 12.[240] Significantly, the Guidance Note states:

- The Panel does not enforce directors' duties—that is for a court.
- Undertaking a frustrating action may give rise to unacceptable circumstances regardless of whether it is consistent with, or a breach of, directors' duties and notwithstanding that there is no express requirement in the law for shareholder approval of frustrating actions.

The Panel will often require further disclosure to shareholders or require shareholder approval where there is sufficient evidence of a frustrating action by the target.[241]

19.55.30 Deal protection devices

Most defensive strategies by the target company occur in the context of a hostile takeover, but not all takeovers are hostile. Many takeovers occur after talks have taken place between the bidder and the target company.[242] The target directors may have even solicited the bid, either an original bid or as part of a white knight defence. In these circumstances, the directors of a target company will agree with the terms of a proposed takeover bid and recommend the offer to their shareholders. However, there is always the risk that the shareholders will not follow the recommendation and the takeover bid will be unsuccessful, leaving the bidder with significant wasted costs.

It is not uncommon for the takeover bidder to resort to deal protection measures or 'lock-up devices' to protect itself from that risk. One example is a 'break fee'. This is a sum of money that the target company agrees to pay to the bidder if the bid is unsuccessful. The takeover documents will specify the circumstances that trigger payment. The arrangement acts as an inducement for the bidder to make the bid in the first place. Related to break fees are other deal protection arrangements such as a 'no shop' agreement where the target agrees not to solicit a competing transaction for a certain period of time, a 'no talk' agreement where the target agrees not to negotiate with any third party or provide due diligence access and an 'asset lock up agreement' where the target grants

237 *Pinnacle No 8* [57]. For a further discussion, see T Bednall, 'Frustrating Actions' and R Levy, 'Frustrating Actions—A Commentary' in JG Hill and RP Austin (eds), *The Takeovers Panel after Ten Years* (Ross Parsons Centre of Commercial, Corporate and Taxation Law, 2011) 57, 59, 60.

238 *Pinnacle No 8* [64].

239 Ibid.

240 Takeovers Panel, *Frustrating Action* (Guidance Note 12, 18 July 2014).

241 See, eg, *Gondwana Resources Ltd 02* [2014] ATP 15; *World Oil Resources Ltd* [2013] ATP 1; *MacarthurCook Ltd* (2008) 67 ACSR 345.

242 See the discussion regarding the 'indicia of bid friendliness' in L Chapple, P Clarkson and J King, 'Private Equity Bidders: Barbarians or Best Friends?' (2011) 29(3) *Company and Securities Law Journal* 159, 164–7.

an option over key assets to a potential bidder.[243] The Panel looks closely at break fees and other deal protection devices[244] and has issued guidelines about what is, and what is not, acceptable.[245]

The Panel does not consider deal protection devices to be unacceptable per se, but they may be unacceptable if they prevent the acquisition of control taking place in an efficient, competitive and informed market, as required by s 602(a). For example, the Panel recommends a cap for break fees of 1 per cent of the bid or equity value of the target.[246]

19.60 Compulsory acquisitions and buy-outs

The issue of compulsory acquisition often arises at the conclusion of a takeover bid where the bidder has acquired a significant majority of the shares in the target company, but at the end of the offer period there is still a minority of shareholders who have not accepted the offer. The non-accepting minority shareholders may be in that position because of apathy or because they have been holding out deliberately. In this situation, two possibilities arise. In the first situation, the minority shareholders are compelled by law to sell their shares in the target company; that is, a compulsory sale, more commonly known as a compulsory acquisition, occurs. In the second situation, the bidder is required to purchase the remaining minority shares; that is referred to as a compulsory purchase or buy-out.

What are the policy issues at stake here? In simple terms, the policy choice is whether the interests of the majority bidder or the minority dissenters should be favoured.

What advantages accrue to a takeover bidder that is able to acquire the entire shareholding in the target company? The Companies and Securities Advisory Committee identified the following advantages where the target company has become part of a corporate group:

- tax advantages such as permitting tax losses to be transferred between wholly owned companies in a corporate group
- reduced administrative and reporting costs for the company
- avoiding the risk of greenmail by a dissenting minority
- eliminating possible conflicts of interest in partially owned companies.[247]

For these sorts of reasons, ch 6A contains compulsory acquisition mechanisms but imposes limitations on their operation. Before exploring ch 6A, there are other methods where shares can be compulsorily acquired; for example, via a scheme of arrangement,[248]

243 R Levy, *Takeovers Law & Strategy* (Lawbook, 6th ed, 2023) 362–3.

244 See, eg, *Virtus Health Ltd* [2022] ATP 5; *Ross Human Directions Ltd* [2010] ATP 8; *Ballarat Goldfields NL* [2002] ATP 7.

245 Takeovers Panel, *Deal Protection* (Guidance Note 7, 8 August 2023).

246 Ibid [48]ff.

247 Legal Committee of the Companies and Securities Advisory Committee, *Compulsory Acquisitions Report* (Report, January 1996). See also *Elkington v Shell Australia Ltd* (1993) 32 NSWLR 11, 13–18 (Kirby ACJ).

248 *Corporations Act* ss 411–14, particularly s 414.

a selective reduction of share capital,[249] and a provision in the company's constitution. These methods may amount to an involuntary expropriation of shares, which was the subject of the High Court's attention in *Gambotto v WCP Ltd* ('*Gambotto's Case*').[250] *Gambotto's Case* is discussed in more detail in Chapter 5 at Section 5.50.10ff. However, cases decided subsequent to *Gambotto* have held that the *Gambotto* principles do not apply to expropriation under specific regimes in the *Corporations Act*.[251] Therefore, the *Gambotto* principle has had minimal impact upon the interpretation of specific statutory compulsory acquisition schemes, such as ch 6A.

19.60.05 Compulsory acquisition of minority shares in a takeover

Under a full off-market bid, or under a market bid, the bidder can, in certain situations, compulsorily acquire the shares of those shareholders who do not accept the offer during the offer period, whether by intention or otherwise (s 661A).

In *Peninsula Gold Pty Ltd v Australian Securities Commission*, McLelland J stated that:

> [The section] reflects a clear policy ... to facilitate the acquisition by an offeror under a takeover ... of all relevant shares in the target company so that the target company would become a wholly owned subsidiary of the offeror, where there has been a sufficiently high level of informed acceptance of the offer by offerees, subject to prescribed safeguards against unfairness, no doubt in recognition of ... [the] indirect economic benefits to the community from such commercial activity.[252]

The circumstances and the procedure are set out in s 661A—in particular, s 661A(1). There are two conditions that must be met in order to actuate the compulsory acquisition provisions. First, during, or at the end of the offer period, the bidder and its associates must have a relevant interest in at least 90 per cent by number of the bid class securities. In determining the relevant interest, we must discount any relevant interest that is deemed to occur by s 608(3).

Section 608(3) is discussed above at Section 19.30.20.

Second, during or at the end of the offer period, the bidder and its associates must have acquired at least 75 per cent of the securities that the bidder offered to acquire under the bid. This means 75 per cent of the securities remaining to be acquired, not 75 per cent of the total number of securities.

The assumption behind the section is that where an offer has been highly successful, this implies that the terms of the offer are favourable and fair, and that the bidder should be allowed to achieve the benefits of total ownership. Presumably, the addition of the 75 per cent test is intended to be a further indication of the strength and fairness of the offer where the bidder has had to receive fewer acceptances in order to reach the

249 Ibid ss 256B–C.

250 *Gambotto v WCP Ltd* (1995) 182 CLR 432.

251 *Winpar Holdings Ltd v Goldfields Kalgoorlie Ltd* (2001) 40 ACSR 221; *Re Peninsula Gold Pty Ltd v Australian Securities Commission* (1996) 14 ACLC 958.

252 *Peninsula Gold Pty Ltd v Australian Securities Commission* (1996) 14 ACLC 1435, 1438–9.

90 per cent level. The second step is particularly important where the bidder starts with a high stake in the target company (such as 60 per cent) because the number of acceptances needed to achieve the 90 per cent threshold is lower than if the bidder began with a low stake (such as 19 per cent).

Where these two criteria are met, the bidder may serve a notice on the dissenting shareholders indicating its wish to acquire the outstanding shares (s 661B). The notice can be served before the offer period ends (if the thresholds have been reached). If not, it must be served within one month after the end of the offer period (s 661B(2)). The shares are to be acquired on the same terms as the original offer (s 661C) and once the notice is served it cannot be withdrawn (s 661B(2)).

Having served the notice, the bidder must acquire all the securities in the bid class in which the bidder does not already have a relevant interest (s 661A(4)).

19.60.10 Dissenting minorities

A dissenting shareholder may to seek an order in the court to prevent the compulsory acquisition from proceeding in relation to their shares (s 661E). The dissenting shareholder must generally make the application within one month of the compulsory acquisition notice being given (s 661E(1)). The court may order that the securities not be compulsorily acquired if it is satisfied that the consideration is not 'fair value' for the securities (s 661E(2)). A dissenting shareholder faces the difficult task of convincing the court that the 90 per cent or more of shareholders who have accepted the offer are mistaken in their assessment of the offer. Section 667C sets out a methodology to determine what is fair value for the securities.

19.60.15 Fair value for securities

As previously stated, s 667C provides the test for determining 'fair value' for the purposes of a compulsory acquisition. Section 667C(1) requires the valuer to, inter alia:

(1) assess the value of the company as a whole
(2) allocate the value among the classes of issued securities (taking into account the voting and distribution rights, and the relative financial risk of the classes)
(3) allocate the value of each class pro rata among the securities in that class (without taking into account any premium or discount for particular securities in that class).

Several cases have set out the principles to be adopted in applying this section.[253] The following principles may be distilled from these cases:

(1) 'Fair' in this context does not mean fair according to general notions of fairness. 'The words "fair value" are merely a statutory label whose sole content and meaning come from the application of the section itself. The result would be the same

253 Those cases include *Teh v Ramsay Centauri Pty Ltd* (2002) 20 ACLC 1623; *Capricorn Diamonds Investments v Catto* (2002) 20 ACLC 931.

if the section referred to "assessed value" or "prescribed value" or simply "value" instead of "fair value".'[254] In practice, the court values the company by reference to the valuations provided by experts retained by the parties but makes an independent assessment based on their reports.

(2) Determining 'fair value' means looking at the situation of the shareholders as a whole, not the situation of a particular class or group of shareholders.[255]

(3) The party making the application bears the onus of proof.

(4) Section 667C(1)(a) refers to valuing 'the company as a whole'. This means the overall enterprise viewed as a profit-making structure. The company as a 'productive organisational whole' must be examined, not a particular asset.[256] Further, the subsection is not concerned with the value of the company to any particular person, but to a hypothetical buyer who is solely concerned with the benefits and detriments of the enterprise. In particular, this aspect of the methodology in s 667C(1) is 'designed to avoid a premium or a discount being applied to a minority stake in a company'.[257]

(5) In determining the value of the company as a whole, the valuer should not include the 'special value' or synergy value that might accrue to the acquirer; for example, upon the acquisition of 100 per cent of the company.[258]

19.60.20 Compulsory buy-out of securities

The reverse situation concerns compulsory buy-outs (ss 662A–C). The idea is to prevent minority shareholders from being locked into a company. If the bidder and associates have a relevant interest in at least 90 per cent of the shares in the bid class at the end of the offer period, then, within one month of the end of the offer period, they must notify the remaining shareholders of this fact (s 662B).

The minority shareholder then has one month in which to give notice to the bidder requiring the purchase of their shares. The bidder is then required to acquire the shares on the terms that applied to the takeover immediately before the end of the offer period (s 662C).[259]

19.65 Liability and remedies

The provisions in ch 6B of the *Corporations Act* (ss 670A–E) impose criminal and civil liability on certain persons for misleading or deceptive statements or omissions in bidders' and targets' statements, as well as takeover offer documents, compulsory acquisition notices and reports (usually experts' reports).

254 *Teh v Ramsay Centauri Pty Ltd* (2002) 20 ACLC 1623, 1626–7.

255 *Dolby Australia Pty Ltd v Catto* (2004) 52 ACSR 204 [82].

256 *Teh v Ramsay Centauri Pty Ltd* (2002) 20 ACLC 1623, 1627.

257 *Ijack Pty Ltd v Cobb, Vealls Ltd* (2018) 131 ACSR 418, 432 [83].

258 See *Regional Publishers Pty Ltd v Elkington* (2006) 154 FCR 218, 229–30; *Winpar Holdings Ltd v Austrim Nylex Ltd* (2005) 54 ACSR 562 [11]–[37]; Australian Securities and Investments Commission, *Content of Expert Reports* (Regulatory Guide 111, 22 October 2020) [RG 111.50].

259 See generally Australian Securities and Investments Commission, *Compulsory Acquisitions and Buyouts* (Regulatory Guide 10, 27 March 2024).

In addition, the general misleading conduct provision in s 1041H may apply where 'a market participant makes a statement outside a "takeover document"'. For example, s 1041H may apply where a market participant makes a statement in a market announcement, media release, press conference, media interview, telephone conversation with a holder or in comments to a journalist or analyst.[260] Section 1041H(2)(b)(iii) prohibits a person from engaging in conduct which is or is likely to be misleading or deceptive in the making of a takeover bid or the making of an evaluation of, or of a recommendation in relation to, a bid. Subsections 1041H(1) and 1041H(2) do not apply where a statement is made in takeover documents because s 670A applies (s 1041H(3)).

Section 670A is the key provision. It is expressed as a prohibition—a person must not give such a document if it contains a misleading or deceptive statement, an omission of material required by ss 636 or 638, or if a new circumstance has arisen since the document was lodged with ASIC. A person is deemed to make a misleading statement about a future matter if they lack reasonable grounds for making the statement (s 670A(2)).

When the Panel is hearing an application that involves an allegation of a breach of s 670A, it may order the relevant party to issue a supplementary bidder's or target's statement to remedy the breach. Supplementary bidder's and target's statements are required under ss 643 and 644, respectively, where a bidder or target company becomes aware of a misleading or deceptive statement in a document, an omission from a document, or a new circumstance has arisen that would have been required to have been included in the documents. For example, in *Re Mildura Fruit Co-operative Co Ltd*,[261] the Panel accepted undertakings from both parties to issue supplementary bidder's and target's statements due to misleading and deceptive statements in the documents.[262]

Criminal liability is imposed by s 670A(3). If a person contravenes this prohibition, and the statement or omission or new circumstance is 'materially adverse' from the point of view of the shareholder to whom the document is given, then the person commits an offence (s 670A(3)). The words 'materially adverse' are not defined. They clearly imply that the true situation must be worse for the investor than was disclosed in the document.

Section 670A is a civil penalty provision (s 670A(4)) and general civil liability is imposed by s 670B. If a person suffers loss or damage as a result of a contravention of s 670A, they can recover that loss or damage from the person who is designated in the table in s 670B. This is strict liability in the sense that the designated person is liable even if they did not commit the contravention themselves. The list in s 670B includes the bidder, directors of the bidder company, the target company and directors of the target company. Their liability depends upon the type of document that contains the misstatement, omission etc.

Section 670C imposes an obligation on the persons who are referred to in the table to notify the issuer of a document (for example, a bidder's statement) as soon as practicable if they become aware during the bid period about a material misstatement or omission

260 Australian Securities and Investments Commission, *Takeovers: False and Misleading Statements* (Regulatory Guide 25, 22 August 2002) reg 25.17.

261 *Re Mildura Fruit Co-operative Co Ltd* [2004] ATP 5.

262 See generally *Nex Metals Explorations Ltd 05* [2022] ATP 12.

or new circumstance. This is not a defence to civil liability. Mere compliance with s 670C does not negate the possibility of liability under s 670B.

The defences are set out in s 670D. There are prescribed defences to both civil and criminal liability. The defences are framed in terms of knowledge, reliance, consent, and awareness:

- Knowledge: the person did not know that the statement was misleading or deceptive, or did not know that there was an omission.
- Reliance: the person placed reasonable reliance on information given to them by someone other than their employee or agent.
- Consent: the person withdrew their consent to being named in the document as the person who made the relevant statement.
- Awareness: the person was not aware of the new circumstance which has arisen since the document was lodged.

As discussed above, s 670E allows a person who suffers loss or damage after relying on a public proposal for an off-market bid or an announcement of a market bid under s 631 to recover the loss or damage from a person who contravened the section or a person who was involved in the contravention. Section 670F provides a defence to the offence in s 631(1) and liability under s 670E where a person 'could not reasonably have been expected to comply with those subsections because circumstances existed that the person did not know of and could not reasonably have been expected to know of; or after the proposal or announcement, a change in circumstances occurred that was not caused, directly or indirectly, by the person'. Furthermore, as discussed above, a court also has power to order a person to proceed with a bid under s 1325B upon an application by ASIC if a breach of s 631 occurs.

The regulation of alleged misleading statements by participants in takeovers has come under scrutiny in the last decade.[263] ASIC has developed a 'truth in takeovers' policy[264] in response to concerns about certain conduct for example 'last and final statements' by a bidder that it will not improve the consideration offered under its bid ('no increase statement') or not waive a defeating condition or not extend the time for acceptances of the offer.[265] Shareholders may also make 'intention statements'; that is, that they intend to accept or reject the offer[266] and these statements may also be announced by the bidder or target. Armson notes that it is common practice in the market for bidders to obtain acceptance statements[267] and Lloyd argues that information concerning the intentions of significant shareholders is beneficial to market participants.[268] However, if a participant

263 For an overview, see S Cobbett, 'Applying the Truth in Takeovers Policy: Why the Status Quo Is Better than a Train Wreck' (2020) 35(2) *Australian Journal of Corporate Law* 161.

264 Australian Securities and Investments Commission, *Takeovers: False and Misleading Statements* (Regulatory Guide 25, 22 August 2002) [RG 25.1].

265 Ibid [RG 25.21]–[25.34]; *Cardinal Resources Ltd 03 & 04* [2020] ATP 23.

266 See, eg, *Finders Resources Ltd* [2018] ATP 11.

267 E Armson, '"Truth in Takeovers" for Substantial Holders' (2019) 36(6) *Company and Securities Law Journal* 464, 465.

268 H Lloyd, 'Statements of Intention in Takeovers—ASIC Reconsidering the Policy Settings?' (2017) 35(6) *Company and Security Law Journal* 395, 396.

resiles from a statement there is potential misleading conduct under ss 1041H or 670A of the *Corporations* Act and/or unacceptable circumstances inviting scrutiny by the Takeovers Panel.[269]

19.65.05 Other remedies

The courts have considerable discretion in granting or refusing relief in particular circumstances. However, as discussed above, a moratorium on court proceedings is imposed by s 659B, which states that only ASIC or some other public authority (such as the DPP) can commence court proceedings 'in relation to' a takeover bid before the end of the bid period.

Injunctions

The court has a general power to issue an injunction under s 1324. Section 1324 injunctions are discussed at Section 14.45.

Remedial orders by a court

Under s 1325A, a court may make any order that it considers appropriate, including a remedial order, if:

(1) there is a contravention of chs 6–6C; or
(2) where a takeover bid involves offering securities as consideration, and the bid states or implies that those securities are to be quoted on a financial market, and either no application for quotation has been made within seven days after the bid has commenced, or no permission is granted for quotation within seven days after the bid has ended.

The concept of a 'remedial order' is defined in s 9 and discussed above at Section 19.25.20. An application for a remedial order may be made by ASIC, the company whose securities are involved in the contravention, a member of that company, a person from whom a relevant interest in the securities was acquired, and 'a person whose interests are affected by the contravention' (s 1325A(3)).

Section 1325D gives the courts the power to excuse a contravention if it is the result of inadvertence, mistake, non-awareness of a relevant fact or occurrence, or circumstances beyond the person's control.

The courts have frequently stated that simply establishing that a contravention of the *Corporations Act* has occurred is not sufficient to guarantee that the court will give the order which is sought. However, the powers given to the court under ss 1325A–D are often complementary with the powers exercisable by the Panel.[270]

269 See generally Takeovers Panel, *Shareholder Intention Statements* (Guidance Note 23, 11 December 2015).

270 For an opposing view see RP Austin, 'The Courts and the Panel' in J Hill and RP Austin (eds), *The Takeovers Panel after 10 Years* (Ross Parsons Centre of Commercial, Corporate and Taxation Law, 2011) 131, 146.

For example, in the case of *Re Venturex Resources Ltd*,[271] Venturex Resources Limited ('Venturex') made a takeover bid for CMG Gold Limited ('CMG') offering Venturex shares as consideration. Venturex's offer stated that the Venturex shares would be listed on the ASX. Venturex received acceptances for over 90 per cent of the CMG shares and intended to compulsorily acquire the remaining CMG shares. Apparently inadvertently, Venturex failed to make an application to ASX for admission to quotation of the Venturex shares offered under the takeover bid within the period prescribed by s 625(3). Venturex became aware of the failure to make the application to ASX and applied for remedial orders under s 1325A(2) to extend the period to make the application. In granting the relief sought, McKerracher J of the Federal Court held that the specific provisions of s 1325A(2) overrode the general provisions in s 659B and it was inappropriate to exercise any power under s 659B(2) to stay any application for relief before the Panel because the Panel was not able to exercise the jurisdiction conferred under s 1325A. The purpose of s 625(3) was to ensure that investors who received shares as consideration under the takeover offer were not left with unlisted securities when they were led to believe that the consideration offered to them would be listed on a financial market. Without intervention by the Court, the failure to comply with s 625(3) would mean that the offers made under the takeover bid were void. His Honour concluded that the grant of the orders would advance the objects of ch 6, particularly given the level of acceptances of the takeover bid.[272]

19.70 Summary

The law of takeovers in chs 6, 6A, 6B and 6C of the *Corporations Act* is a special body of law that regulates corporate control transactions in companies that have more than 50 members. The provisions intricately regulate direct and indirect control and implement a closed system where a bidder is subject to strict regulatory supervision once its interest in voting securities in a target company exceeds a threshold of 20 per cent. The provisions prescribe further requirements for the disclosure of information by bidders and target companies during takeover bids and regulate the conduct of company managers to promote the policy of reasonable and equal opportunity for members to participate in the bid and ensure, as far as possible, that the acquisition of control takes place in an efficient, competitive and informed market. Disputes are diverted into a specialist body—the Takeovers Panel—which further promotes and operationalises these policies.

271 *Re Venturex Resources Ltd* (2009) 177 FCR 391.

272 See also *Re Clime Capital Ltd* [2019] NSWSC 1479.

INDEX

For EU product safety concerns, contact us at Calle de José Abascal, 56–1°,
28003 Madrid, Spain or eugpsr@cambridge.org.

www.ingramcontent.com/pod-product-compliance
Ingram Content Group UK Ltd.
Pitfield, Milton Keynes, MK11 3LW, UK
UKHW052017290526
471652UK00014B/761
* 9 7 8 1 0 0 9 4 4 8 2 1 5 *